Mark D. Cole | Jörg Ukrow | Christina Etteldorf

On the Allocation of Competences between the European Union and its Member States in the Media Sector

An Analysis with particular Consideration of Measures concerning Media Pluralism

Zur Kompetenzverteilung zwischen der Europäischen Union und den Mitgliedstaaten im Mediensektor

Eine Untersuchung unter besonderer Berücksichtigung medienvielfaltsbezogener Maßnahmen

Die Deutsche Nationalbibliothek verzeichnet diese Publikation in
der Deutschen Nationalbibliografie; detaillierte bibliografische
Daten sind im Internet über http://dnb.d-nb.de abrufbar.

The Deutsche Nationalbibliothek lists this publication in the
Deutsche Nationalbibliografie; detailed bibliographic data
are available on the Internet at http://dnb.d-nb.de

ISBN   978-3-8487-8079-2 (Print)
        978-3-7489-2497-5 (ePDF)

British Library Cataloguing-in-Publication Data
A catalogue record for this book is available from the British Library.

ISBN   978-3-8487-8079-2 (Print)
        978-3-7489-2497-5 (ePDF)

Library of Congress Cataloging-in-Publication Data
Cole, Mark David | Ukrow, Jörg | Etteldorf, Christina
On the Allocation of Competences between the European Union and its Member States
in the Media Sector | An analysis with particular Consideration of Measures concerning
Media Pluralism
Zur Kompetenzverteilung zwischen der Europäischen Union und den Mitgliedstaaten
im Mediensektor | Eine Untersuchung unter besonderer Berücksichtigung medienvielfalts-
bezogener Maßnahmen
Mark D. Cole | Jörg Ukrow | Christina Etteldorf
824 pp.
Includes bibliographic references.

ISBN   978-3-8487-8079-2 (Print)
        978-3-7489-2497-5 (ePDF)

1st Edition 2021
© Mark D. Cole | Jörg Ukrow | Christina Etteldorf
Published by
Nomos Verlagsgesellschaft mbH & Co. KG
Waldseestraße 3–5 | 76530 Baden-Baden
www.nomos.de

Production of the printed version:
Nomos Verlagsgesellschaft mbH & Co. KG
Waldseestraße 3–5 | 76530 Baden-Baden

ISBN   978-3-8487-8079-2 (Print)
ISBN   978-3-7489-2497-5 (ePDF)
DOI   https://doi.org/10.5771/9783748924975

Onlineversion
Nomos eLibrary

This work is licensed under a Creative Commons Attribution
– Non Commercial – No Derivations 4.0 International License.

About this publication

This book compiles an English and German version of the study "On the Allocation of Competences between the European Union and its Member States in the Media Sector" which was prepared by the Institute of European Media Law (EMR) on behalf of the German Länder. Each language version is preceded by a Preface of Heike Raab, State Secretary, Plenipotentiary for Federal and European Affairs, for Media and Digital Affairs of the Land of Rhineland-Palatinate.

Readers can first find a summary table of contents, followed by the preface, a detailed table of contents and the study itself, each of them first in the English, then in the German language version.

The publication of the bilingual version of the study as a print and e-book was supported by the Mainzer Medieninstitut e.V. (Mainz Media Institute) which co-organizes the annual "Brüsseler Mediengespräch" together with and in the premises of the representation of the Land Rhineland-Palatinate, the venue originally foreseen for the presentation of the study to the public. The authors are very grateful for this support.

Since the study was completed, the European Commission has put forward the two proposals for a Digital Services Act and a Digital Markets Act.[1] A more detailed assessment by the EMR of the actual proposals in addition to the general analysis based on the (then) forthcoming proposals hereinafter, is available online.[2]

The "Rundfunkkommission der Länder" as initiator, the EMR as provider and the Mainzer Medieninstitut as supporting institution for the publication of the study are briefly introduced together with the authors (Cole; Ukrow; Etteldorf) at the end of the study. The authors would like to thank Sebastian Zeitzmann, research associate at EMR, who assumed the overall responsibility for the English translation of the study.

---

1 Proposal for a Regulation on a Single Market For Digital Services (Digital Services Act) and amending Directive 2000/31/EC, COM/2020/825 final, CELEX: 52020PC0825; Proposal for a Regulation on contestable and fair markets in the digital sector (Digital Markets Act), COM/2020/842 final, CELEX: 52020PC0842.

2 *Ukrow*, Die Vorschläge der EU-Kommission für einen Digital Services Act und einen Digital Markets Act, Impulse aus dem EMR; *Cole/Etteldorf/Ullrich*, Updating the Rules for Online Content Dissemination, Nomos 2021; https://www.nomos-elibrary.de/10.5771/9783748925934.

Über diese Veröffentlichung

Dieses Buch stellt eine englische und deutsche Version der Studie „Zur Kompetenzverteilung zwischen der Europäischen Union und den Mitgliedstaaten im Mediensektor" zusammen, die vom Institut für Europäisches Medienrecht (EMR) im Auftrag der deutschen Länder erstellt wurde. Jeder Sprachversion ist ein Vorwort von Heike Raab, Staatssekretärin in der Staatskanzlei Rheinland-Pfalz und Bevollmächtigte des Landes Rheinland-Pfalz beim Bund und für Europa, Medien und Digitales, vorangestellt.

Der Leser findet zunächst ein zusammenfassendes Inhaltsverzeichnis des Buches, gefolgt vom Vorwort, einem ausführlichen Inhaltsverzeichnis und der Studie selbst, jeweils zunächst in der englischen, dann in der deutschen Sprachversion.

Die Veröffentlichung der zweisprachigen Version der Studie als Print und E-Book wurde vom Mainzer Medieninstitut e.V. unterstützt, das das jährliche „Brüsseler Mediengespräch" gemeinsam mit und in den Räumen der Landesvertretung Rheinland-Pfalz, dem ursprünglich vorgesehenen Veranstaltungsort für die öffentliche Präsentation der Studie, organisiert. Die Autoren sind dem Mainzer Medieninstitut für die Unterstützung sehr dankbar.

Seit der Fertigstellung der Studie hat die Europäische Kommission die beiden Vorschläge für einen Digital Services Act und einen Digital Markets Act vorgelegt.[1] Eine detailliertere Bewertung der aktuellen Vorschläge durch die Autoren dieser Studie, zusätzlich zu der allgemeinen Analyse, die auf den (zu diesem Zeitpunkt noch) bevorstehenden Vorschlägen im Folgenden basiert, ist online verfügbar.[2]

---

1 Vorschlag für eine Verordnung über einen Binnenmarkt für digitale Dienste (Gesetz über digitale Dienste) und zur Änderung der Richtlinie 2000/31/EG, COM/2020/825 final, CELEX: 52020PC0825; Vorschlag für eine Verordnung über bestreitbare und faire Märkte im digitalen Sektor (Gesetz über digitale Märkte), COM/2020/842 final, CELEX: 52020PC0842.
2 *Ukrow*, Die Vorschläge der EU-Kommission für einen Digital Services Act und einen Digital Markets Act, Impulse aus dem EMR; *Cole/Etteldorf/Ullrich*, Updating the Rules for Online Content Dissemination, Nomos 2021; https://www.nomos-elibrary.de/10.5771/9783748925934.

Über diese Veröffentlichung

Die Rundfunkkommission der Länder als Initiator, das EMR als Ersteller und das Mainzer Medieninstitut als unterstützende Institution für die Veröffentlichung der Studie werden zusammen mit den Autoren (Cole; Ukrow; Etteldorf) am Ende der Studie kurz vorgestellt. Die Autoren bedanken sich bei Sebastian Zeitzmann, wissenschaftlicher Mitarbeiter am EMR, der die Gesamtverantwortung für die englische Übersetzung der Studie übernommen hat.

Overview of contents / Inhaltsübersicht

About this publication   5

Über diese Veröffentlichung   7

On the Allocation of Competences between the European Union and its Member States in the Media Sector

Preface   13

List of abbreviations   23

Executive summary   29

A. Introduction and background to the study   47
Mark D. Cole / Jörg Ukrow

B. Framework for the allocation of competences under EU primary law   57
Jörg Ukrow

C. On the significance and enshrinement in law of media diversity at EU level   147
Mark D. Cole / Christina Etteldorf

D. Secondary legal framework on "media law" and media pluralism   173
Mark D. Cole / Christina Etteldorf

E. Core problems of public international law regarding the regulation of the "media sector" with respect to possible tensions with EU law   265
Jörg Ukrow

F. The proposed Digital Services Act   331
Jörg Ukrow

G. Conclusion and political options for action   353
Mark D. Cole / Jörg Ukrow

List of references   365

Overview of contents / Inhaltsübersicht

Zur Kompetenzverteilung zwischen der Europäischen Union und den Mitgliedstaaten im Mediensektor

Vorwort	403
Abkürzungsverzeichnis	413
Executive Summary	419
A. Einleitung und Problemaufriss *Mark D. Cole / Jörg Ukrow*	437
B. Primärrechtlicher Rahmen zur Kompetenzabgrenzung *Jörg Ukrow*	447
C. Zur Bedeutung und rechtlichen Verankerung der Medienvielfalt auf EU-Ebene *Mark D. Cole / Christina Etteldorf*	541
D. Sekundärrechtlicher Rahmen zum „Medienrecht" und Medienpluralismus *Mark D. Cole / Christina Etteldorf*	569
E. Völkerrechtliche Kernprobleme der Regulierung des „Mediensektors" im Hinblick auf mögliche Spannungsverhältnisse mit dem Recht der EU *Jörg Ukrow*	671
F. Der vorgeschlagene Digital Services Act *Jörg Ukrow*	741
G. Gesamtergebnis und politische Handlungsoptionen *Mark D. Cole / Jörg Ukrow*	765
Literaturverzeichnis	777
Information on the contributors / Informationen zu den Mitwirkenden	815

On the Allocation of Competences between the European Union and its Member States in the Media Sector

Preface

The year 2020 was a year of setting the course of media politics in Germany and Europe with very important milestones: An up-to-date media regulation of television, radio and the press may not remain stuck in the "old world". On the contrary, the digital environment calls for new answers – for the 'online media world'. In 2020, the German federal states, the Länder, as media legislators adopted the State Media Treaty and simultaneously transposed the Audiovisual Media Services Directive with it. At the end of the very same year, the European Commission outlined in its proposals for a Digital Services Act and a Digital Markets Act the shape that central rules of a digital society could take from its own perspective.

As the coordinator of the Broadcasting Commission of the German Länder I am proud to say that the State Media Treaty entered into force on 7 November 2020. This major achievement in media politics is the result of a long process, started several years ago by the German Länder, which have the competence of regulating the media in Germany. It is one of the most important initiatives in media politics in recent years and provides answers to very relevant questions of a digitized media world. It creates a legal framework, which fosters diversity of opinion and equal opportunities in communication, especially online, increases the visibility of quality journalism and strengthens the accountability of the internet community. For the first time, major media platforms and intermediaries such as Google, Facebook, Twitter or Amazon are subjected to media-specific and pluralism-based regulation. The coronavirus pandemic illustrated the importance of these large platforms for the distribution of media information very clearly.

The discussions during the making of and the solutions found in the State Media Treaty show clearly: Rules for big platforms on how to deal with illegal content are important – after the German legislator implemented the Network Enforcement Act, now the European Commission rightly urges platforms to take more responsibility as well. However, we as media regulators are convinced that rules for dealing with illegal, harmful or otherwise problematic content alone are not enough to safeguard media pluralism and diversity of opinions. More is needed: When we refer to non-discriminatory findability of journalistic content in the State Media Treaty, we are not talking about liability or responsibility for illegal content. It is about how we promote equal opportunities for communication online and how we make quality journalism visible – not only during times of crisis. This requires a media-specific framework for the challenges of the digital platform economy.

The EU Member States agree that such media-specific and diversity-related regulation of media platforms and intermediaries is a necessity and that safeguarding media pluralism is primarily the responsibility of the Member States. The Member States explicitly confirmed and underlined this in the Council conclusions on safeguarding a free and pluralistic media system, which were adopted end of last year during the German Council Presidency. The Council conclusions therefore provide an important impulse for future and up-to-date, national as well as European legislation in a digital age. The German Länder are happy to take on this responsibility.

A coherent legal framework for the digital environment is not only necessary with regard to media regulation in its original meaning, but also in many other sectors on regional, national and European level. The media are indispensable for our democracies in Europe. It is our task and responsibility to maintain a free and functioning media system. Therefore, we need to consider the impact on the media that new rules in other sectors may have. The numerous laws of different legislators have to interact well with each other. This issue was also addressed by the Member States in the Council conclusions.

All of these are by no means trivial tasks, and they require every actor in the legislative process – whether at regional, national or European level – to address these issues. Regulating the online world is a shared responsibility. The goal of coherence and consistency raises difficult questions in this regard, in particular how regulation by the EU of a digital single market can be reconciled with the competence of the Member States in order to ensure media pluralism and take into account the specifics of the media sector.

In June 2020, the Broadcasting Commission commissioned the present study "On the Allocation of Competences between the European Union and its Member States in the Media Sector" by the Institute of European Media Law (EMR) to make a lasting contribution to the discussion. Prof. Dr. Mark D. Cole, Dr. Jörg Ukrow and Christina Etteldorf give important answers, which will be groundbreaking for the upcoming and future discussions on national and European level. Originally, the study should have been presented at the annual "Brüsseler Mediengespräch" in the representation of Rhineland-Palatinate in Brussels, combined with a discussion of representatives from politics, academia and the media sector. Unfortunately, the event could not yet take place due to the coronavirus pandemic. I deliberately say "not yet", because postponed is not abandoned. In the meantime, I recommend the podcast about the study, which was produced with our cooperation partners Mainzer Medieninstitut and Westdeutscher Rundfunk in December 2020.

On the web address www.rundfunkkommission.rlp.de you can listen to the podcast, which includes an introduction of the study by Prof. Cole and statements of representatives from politics, science and the media industry about the (at the time of recording yet to be presented) Digital Services Act Package.

With the proposals of the European Commission on the table, the study of the EMR has its first use case. I hope and wish that not only the German Länder will avail themselves of the study to evaluate the proposals of the European Commission, but the other players in this and the coming legislative processes will use it as well.

Heike Raab
State Secretary, Plenipotentiary for Federal and European Affairs, for Media and Digital Affairs of the Land of Rhineland-Palatinate,

9 February 2021

Table of contents

On the Allocation of Competences between the European Union and its Member States in the Media Sector   11

Executive summary   29

A. Introduction and background to the study   47
Mark D. Cole / Jörg Ukrow

B. Framework for the allocation of competences under EU primary law   57
Jörg Ukrow
    I. Basic principles of TEU/TFEU   57
  1. Introduction   57
  2. Member States as "Masters of the Treaties" vs. openness for and dynamics of integration in multilevel constitutionalism   59
  3. Uniformity and primacy of Union law vs. constitution-based reserved power for control of Member States   62
  4. Ultra vires action, no EU competence-competence and the principle of conferral   64
    a. The principle of conferral and its significance for media regulation   64
    b. Monitoring compliance with the principle of conferral through the requirement of democracy as interpreted by the FCC   68
  5. Media regulation and the catalog of EU competences   69
    a. Introduction   69
    b. Exclusive competences of the EU and media regulation   71
    c. Shared competences of the EU and media regulation   74
    d. In particular: Intensifying protection in the area of the digital single market   76
    e. Supporting competences of the EU and media regulation   77
    f. In particular: Media literacy in the focus of EU regulation   78
    g. Suspensory effect of EU law   81

Table of contents

    6. Media regulation and enhanced cooperation between individual EU Member States   84
    7. Media regulation and the relevance of subsequent institutional practice under primary law   86
  II. The EU value system and its protection as a means of ensuring freedom and diversity of the media in the EU Member States   87
    1. The EU's core set of shared values   87
    2. Securing media freedom and pluralism through the instruments of a value-based and militant democracy in the EU   90
  III. The competence areas of the EU with reference to media regulation – an overview   93
    1. The internal market competence of the EU   93
        a. Introduction   93
        b. The competence in relation to the freedom of establishment   95
        c. The competence in relation to the freedom to provide services   98
        d. Interim conclusion   100
    2. The EU competition regime   100
    3. The EU's cultural competence   103
  IV. Objectives of the EU and their significance as regards competences in view of media regulation   108
    1. Media regulation-related goals of the EU   108
    2. The flexibility clause of Art. 352 TFEU to reach EU objectives and its significance for media regulation   109
  V. The exercise of competence rules and its limitations   111
    1. Introduction   111
    2. Respect for the national identity of the Member States   112
    3. The principle of sincere cooperation   114
    4. The principle of subsidiarity   117
    5. The principle of proportionality   126
    6. The significance of limitations to the exercise of competences in the practice of media regulatory – status and perspectives for development   132
  VI. The relevance of fundamental rights   134
    1. Media-related protection of fundamental rights, the requirement of respect under Article 11(2) CFR and the question of competence   134

Table of contents

2. Protection of fundamental rights in an area of friction between review by the CJEU and national constitutional courts	138
VII. Media regulation and the principle of democracy in the EU	141
VIII. Conclusions for the competence for media regulation	144

C. On the significance and enshrinement in law of media diversity at EU level 147

Mark D. Cole / Christina Etteldorf

I. Introduction	147
II. Art. 10 ECHR and the case law of the ECtHR	148
III. Art. 11(2) CFR and CJEU jurisprudence	153
IV. Aspects of primary law	159
1. Fundamental freedoms	159
2. The EU competition regime	165
a. Control of market power and abuse of power	166
b. State aid law	168
V. Reference to the objective in secondary law and other texts	172

D. Secondary legal framework on "media law" and media pluralism ... 173

Mark D. Cole / Christina Etteldorf

I. Overview	173
II. Links in existing secondary law	175
1. E-Commerce-Directive	175
2. AVMS Directive	180
a. Historical analysis in the context of safeguarding diversity	180
b. AVMSD reform 2018	186
c. The relevance of Art. 4(1) AVMSD	190
d. Specific provisions	195
e. Interim conclusion	220
3. DSM Copyright Directive	221
4. Merger Regulation	225
5. European Electronic Communications Code	228
6. Platform-to-Business Regulation	236
a. Scope and objective	236
b. The transparency requirements	237
c. The relationship to other rules by Member States	239
d. The relationship with Directive (EU) 2019/2161	242

Table of contents

    III. Current projects for legislative acts and initiatives with a media law context   244
    1. Proposal for a regulation on preventing the dissemination of terrorist content online   244
    2. Overview of the proposed Digital Services Act   248
    3. Media and Audiovisual Action Plan and European Democracy Action Plan   250
    IV. Links at the level of EU support and coordination actions   253
    1. Code of conduct on countering illegal hate speech online   254
    2. Tackling illegal content online   257
    3. Code of Practice on Disinformation   259
    V. Conclusions and deductions on the regulatory competence for media pluralism   263

E. Core problems of public international law regarding the regulation of the "media sector" with respect to possible tensions with EU law   265
Jörg Ukrow
    I. Introduction   265
    II. Addressees of regulation   266
    1. Introduction   266
    2. Public international law framework for addressing foreign providers   267
        a. Addressing foreign providers from the perspective of the imperative of interpreting national and EU law in a manner open to public international law   267
        b. Public international law limitations on a state's power to legislate and enforce with respect to foreign providers   272
        c. The "genuine link" doctrine and action against foreign providers on the basis of the MStV and JMStV   274
        d. Links and limitations of a state's jurisdiction to prescribe and jurisdiction to enforce under public international law   279
    3. The cross-border application of German media regulation – Relevant elements of the MStV and JMStV and their interpretation   281
    4. The possibility of reaching foreign providers under the MStV and the JMStV from the perspective of EU law – an initial consideration   284
        a. Introduction   284

	b.	The possibility of reaching foreign providers under the MStV and the JMStV from the perspective of primary EU law	286
	c.	The possibility of reaching foreign providers under the MStV and the JMStV from the perspective of the AVMSD	287
	d.	The possibility of reaching foreign providers under the MStV and the JMStV from the perspective of the ECD	290
III.	Binding effect of fundamental rights in the case of enforcement measures against foreign providers		294
1.	Binding effect of European fundamental rights protection		294
	a.	Introduction	294
	b.	Extraterritorial validity of application of the ECHR and the International Covenant on Civil and Political Rights in their significance for media regulation	295
	c.	The scope of Member States' compliance with the CFR in the context of media regulation measures	297
2.	Binding effect of fundamental rights protection under German Basic Law – Extraterritorial validity of fundamental rights protection		299
	a.	Introduction	299
	b.	The FCC's judgment on the extraterritorial application of fundamental rights of 19 May 2020	303
	c.	Extraterritorial validity also of the freedom of broadcasting for foreign legal persons	304
	d.	Interim conclusion	307
IV.	Obligation to regulate the media as an expression of State obligations to protect		308
1.	Introduction		308
2.	Obligations to protect in FCC case law		308
3.	European references of the doctrine of the obligation to protect based on fundamental rights		314
	a.	Doctrine of the obligation to protect and the ECHR	314
	b.	Doctrine of the obligation to protect in light of EU law	314
	c.	Obligations to protect in the network of regulatory systems	316
V.	Substantive law aspects		317
1.	The scope of certain national legal acts		318
	a.	Country of origin principle and NetzDG	318
	b.	Country of origin principle and MStV	321
2.	Other substantive considerations		323

Table of contents

	a.	NetzDG and questions of liability	323
	b.	Excursus: frictions with similar regulations in other states	325
	c.	Copyright free use under § 24 UrhG and exhaustive harmonization	327

F. The proposed Digital Services Act ... 331
Jörg Ukrow
    I. Starting point of the discussion and plans ... 331
    II. Consideration of the results of the study in the design of the new legislative act ... 337
  1. Transparency ... 337
  2. On the criterion of illegality of the content ... 341
  3. Media regulation for information society services and new media actors by means of self-, co- and cooperative regulation ... 342
  4. Regulation of EU-foreign media content providers ... 347
  5. Reform of liability regulation with regard to service providers ... 349
  6. Options for organizational structures for improved enforcement of media-related public interests ... 350

G. Conclusion and political options for action ... 353
Mark D. Cole / Jörg Ukrow
    I. Content-related aspects ... 353
    II. Procedural aspects ... 359

List of references ... 365

Zur Kompetenzverteilung zwischen der Europäischen Union und den Mitgliedstaaten im Mediensektor ... *401*

List of abbreviations

ACT	Association of Commercial Television in Europe
AfP	Zeitschrift für das gesamte Medienrecht / Archiv für Presserecht (journal)
AG	Advocate General
AöR	Archiv des öffentlichen Rechts (journal)
API	Application programming interfaces
Art.	Article
AVMSD	Audiovisual Media Services Directive
BayVBl.	Bayerische Verwaltungsblätter (journal)
BEREC	Body of European Regulators for Electronic Communications
BFH	Bundesfinanzhof (German Federal Fiscal Court)
BFHE	Sammlung der Entscheidungen des Bundesfinanzhofs (collection of decisions of the German Federal Fiscal Court)
BGBl.	Bundesgesetzblatt (German Federal Law Gazette)
BGHZ	Entscheidungen des Bundesgerichtshofs in Zivilsachen (decisions of the German Federal Court of Justice in civil cases)
BND	Bundesnachrichtendienst (German Federal Intelligence Service)
BT-Drs.	Bundestags-Drucksache (publication of the German Bundestag)
BVerfGE	Entscheidungen des Bundesverfassungsgerichts (decisions of the German Federal Constitutional Court)
BVerfGG	Bundesverfassungsgerichtsgesetz (Act on the German Federal Constitutional Court)
BVerfGK	Sammlung der Kammerentscheidungen des Bundesverfassungsgerichts (collection of Chamber Decisions of the German Federal Constitutional Court)
BVerfSchG	Bundesverfassungsschutzgesetz (act on the German domestic intelligence service)
BVerwG	Bundesverwaltungsgericht (Federal Administrative Court)
BVerwGE	Entscheidungen des Bundesverwaltungsgerichts (Decisions of the Federal Administrative Court)
ca.	circa

List of abbreviations

CDE	Cahiers de droit européen (journal)
cf.	confer
CFR	Charter of Fundamental Rights of the European Union
CJEU	Court of Justice of the European Union
CMLRev.	Common Market Law Review (journal)
CoE	Council of Europe
CPD	Code of Practice on Disinformation
DB	Der Betrieb (journal)
DG	Directorate-General (EU Commission)
diff. op.	different opinion
Doc.	Document
DÖV	Die Öffentliche Verwaltung (journal)
DSA	Digital Services Act
DSM-Directive	Directive on copyright and related rights in the Digital Single Market and amending Directives 96/9/EC and 2001/29/EC
DVBl.	Deutsches Verwaltungsblatt (journal)
e.g.	for example
EAO	European Audiovisual Observatory
EBU	European Broadcasting Union
EC	European Community
ECB	European Central Bank
ECD	e-Commerce-Directive
ECHR	European Convention on Human Rights
ECPMF	European Centre for Press and Media Freedom
ECtHR	European Court of Human Rights
EDPD	European Data Protection Days
eds.	editor(s)
EEA	European Economic Area
EEC	European Economic Community
EECC	European Electronic Communications Code
EPG	Electronic program guide(s)
ERGA	European Regulators Group for Audiovisual Media Services
ESCB	European System of Central Banks
et al.	and others
et seq.	and the following
etc.	et cetera
EU	European Union
EuGRZ	Europäische GRUNDRECHTE-Zeitschrift (journal)
EUMR	EU Merger Regulation (EC) 139/2004

EuR	Europarecht (journal)
EuZw	Europäische Zeitschrift für Wirtschaftsrecht (journal)
EWS	Europäisches Wirtschafts- und Steuerrecht (journal)
FAZ	Frankfurter Allgemeine Zeitung (newspaper)
FCC	German Federal Constitutional Court
fn.	footnote
FSK	Freiwillige Selbstkontrolle der Filmwirtschaft (Voluntary Self-Regulation Body of the Film Industry in Germany)
GATS	General Agreement on Trade in Services
GCEU	General Court of the European Union
GDPR	General Data Protection Regulation
GLJ	German Law Journal
GlüStV	Staatsvertrag zum Glücksspielwesen in Deutschland (State Treaty on Games of Chance in Germany)
GRUR Int	Gewerblicher Rechtsschutz und Urheberrecht Internationaler Teil (journal)
HRLR	Human Rights Law Review
i.e.	that means
ibid.	in the same place
ICCPR	International Covenant on Civil and Political Rights
ICESCR	International Covenant on Economic, Social and Cultural Rights
ICJ	International Court of Justice
id.	the same
incl.	inclusive / including
IntVG	Integrationsverantwortungsgesetz (German Responsibility for Integration Act)
JILP	New York University Journal of Internal Law and Politics
JMStV	Jugendmedienschutz-Staatsvertrag (German Interstate Treaty on the protection of minors)
JURA	Juristische Ausbildung (journal)
JuS	Juristische Schulung (journal)
JZ	JuristenZeitung (journal)
K&R	Kommunikation und Recht (journal)
KEK	Kommission zur Ermittlung der Konzentration im Medienbereich (German Commission for Determining Concentration in the Media Sector)
KJ	Kritische Justiz (journal)
KJM	Kommission für Jugendmedienschutz (German Commission for the Protection of Minors in the Media)
KKZ	Kommunal-Kassen-Zeitschrift (journal)

List of abbreviations

MMR	Zeitschrift für IT-Recht und Recht der Digitalisierung (journal)
MPEPIL	Max Planck Encyclopedia of Public International Law
MStV	Medienstaatsvertrag (German State Media Treaty)
NetzDG	Netzwerkdurchsetzungsgesetz (German Network Enforcement Act)
NJW	Neue Juristische Wochenschrift (journal)
No.	Number
NVwZ	Neue Zeitschrift für Verwaltungsrecht (journal)
OJ	Official Journal of the European Union
OLG	Oberlandesgericht (Higher Regional Court (Germany))
ÖZöRV	Österreichische Zeitung für öffentliches Recht und Völkerrecht (journal)
p.	page
P2B	Platform-to-Business
para.	paragraph(s)
PCIJ	Permanent Court of International Justice
PSPP	Public Sector Purchase Programme
RBStV	Rundfunkbeitragsstaatsvertrag (German State Treaty of the Länder on Public Broadcasting fee)
RdDI	Rivista di Diritto Industriale (journal)
RdJB	Recht der Jugend und des Bildungswesens (journal)
rec.	recital(s)
Ref.	Reference
RStV	Rundfunkstaatsvertrag (State Broadcasting Treaty)
SAR	Self-Assessment Reports
SME	Small and medium enterprises
TEC	Treaty establishing the European Community
TERREG	Regulation on preventing the dissemination of terrorist content online
TEU	Treaty on European Union
TFEU	Treaty on the Functioning of the European Union
ThürVwZVG	Thüringer Verwaltungszustellungs- und Vollstreckungsgesetz (Thuringia Administrative Service and Enforcement Act)
TKG	Telekommunikationsgesetz (German Telecommunications Act)
TMG	Telemediengesetz (German Telemedia Act)
TwF	Television without Frontiers (directive)
UFITA	Archiv für Medienrecht und Medienwissenschaft (journal)

UN/UNO	United Nations Organization
UrhG	Urheberrechtsgesetz (German Act on Copyright and Related Rights)
VCLT	Vienna Convention on the Law of Treaties
Vol.	Volume
VSP(s)	video-sharing platform(s)
VVDStRL	Veröffentlichungen der Vereinigung der Deutschen Staatsrechtslehrer (publication)
VwVfG	Verwaltungsverfahrensgesetz (German Administrative Procedures Act)
VwVGBbg	Verwaltungsvollstreckungsgesetz für das Land Brandenburg (Brandenburg Administrative Enforcement Act)
VwZG	Verwaltungszustellungsgesetz des Bundes (German federal act on service in administrative procedure)
VwZVG	Bayrisches Verwaltungszustellungs- und Vollstreckungsgesetz (Bavarian service in administrative procedure and administrative enforcement act)
WTO	World Trade Organization
ZAK	Kommission für Zulassung und Aufsicht (Commission for approval and supervision in Germany)
ZaöRV	Zeitschrift für ausländisches öffentliches Recht und Völkerrecht (journal)
ZEuS	Zeitschrift für Europarechtliche Studien (journal)
ZfWG	Zeitschrift für Wett- und Glücksspielrecht (journal)
ZSR	Zeitschrift für Schweizerisches Recht (journal)
ZUM	Zeitschrift für Urheber- und Medienrecht (journal)

Executive summary

Introduction

1. The "digital decade" of Europe proposed by EU Commission President *von der Leyen* in her first State of the Union Address on 16 September 2020 can build on EU rules such as the Audiovisual Media Services Directive (AVMSD) amended in 2018 and the so-called DSM Directive on Copyright and Related Rights in the Digital Single Market from 2019, which also aimed to make the EU "fit for the digital age". Already this regulatory fitness program of the EU raised concerns about potential collisions of the future development of the EU legal framework with the regulatory framework for the media on Member State level. The new "digital decade" will pose new challenges for media regulation in the EU at the interface of Union and Member State competences. The different effects of digitization for media regulation, concerning the prevention of disinformation to the digitalization of the relevant infrastructure, have become even more apparent during the Corona pandemic. A comprehensive success of the European digital initiative can only be guaranteed if the responsibilities and competences of the Member States are strictly adhered to. For the Member State Germany this means the Länder according to the fundamental decision of the German constitution for a federal state structure. This applies not least in view of the aim of safeguarding media pluralism, which is laid down in both the European and national fundamental rights systems: the limitations of the EU's harmonization and coordination competences do not only exist with regard to traditional media concentration law, but also with regard to safeguarding pluralism in view of the digital and global challenges for the media ecosystem.

Legal Framework for the Allocation of Competences on Primary Law Level

2. Even in the course of the repeated, in some instances fundamental changes to the founding Treaties of the European Union, the EU Member States remain the "Masters of the Treaties" which includes the aspects concerning the regulation of the media contained therein. The European multilevel constitutionalism is characterized by a synthesis: the openness of each of the constitutional systems of the Member

Executive summary

  States for a European integration – however, with a limited dimension and a continuing limitation to the level of integration, which includes a digital single media market – and a constitution of the EU, which in turn is not oriented towards an unrestricted integration perspective, but – irrespective of possibilities for a dynamic interpretation of the integration goal – is bound to the purpose of an ever closer Union below unitary federal statehood of the EU.

3. At the intersection of the perspective of integration under Union law and the fundamental principles of the German constitution, which are barred from any revision and in light of the significance of the regulatory framework for the media as basis of the democratic and federal understanding of the constitution in the Basic Law, there are both reservations and absolute limits set by German constitutional law towards the EU regulating the media in the EU and its Member States in a way that is directed towards their democratic function. Similar reservations also exist in constitutional systems of other EU Member States.

4. The extent of the EU's integration program as defined in the Treaties with regard to the possibilities of media regulation is especially important in the event of a conflict between Member States' provisions ensuring media pluralism and any possible positive integration via steps towards an own EU pluralism legislation and/or negative integration by setting limits to the Member States' frameworks for the protection of media pluralism by referring to EU internal market and competition law. In this respect, ensuring pluralism continues to be subject to a collision of national law and European law.

5. This collision is resolved by the principle of primacy of EU law, the scope of which is, however, disputed between European and Member State constitutional jurisdictions. The Federal Constitutional Court (*Bundesverfassungsgericht*, FCC) claims in this respect reservations of control with regard to the EU protection of fundamental rights, the exercise of competence by the EU ("ultra vires (beyond powers) control") and the constitutional identity of the German Basic Law. All these reservations may also become significant in the further development of EU media regulation.

6. The EU – unlike a state – has no competence to create its own competences ('competence-competence'). Rather, according to the principle of conferral it may only act within the limits of the competences which the Member States have assigned to it in the Treaties – Treaty on European Union (TEU) and Treaty on the Functioning of the European Union (TFEU) – to achieve the objectives laid down therein. However, neither the TEU nor the TFEU provide a negative list of ar-

Executive summary

eas that are comprehensively excluded from EU law. There is no cultural exception in the Treaties in general, nor a media-related exception in particular. The principle of conferral does not per se impede EU media regulation from the outset. However, the more the EU regulates the media in a way that is relevant for the goal of pluralism, the greater – as a minimum requirement – the EU's burden of proof is to show a continued respect of the clauses of the Treaties that are designed to protect Member State regulatory discretion.

7. The existing division of competences under EU law also applies to matters relating to digitization: digital transformation does not create additional EU competences. Conversely, however, existing legal bases creating competence are not limited to dealing with issues that were known at the time the founding Treaties were adopted. The interpretation of primary EU law is always an interpretation in time and with openness towards new challenges. However, such openness to an interpretation oriented towards digitization finds its limits in the actual wording of the legal bases.

8. The jurisprudence developed by the FCC regarding the possibility of control based on the principle of democracy is of equal importance with regard to the transfer of federal or Länder competences. The basic structure of the German constitutional system, which is barred from any revision and cannot be amended in any context, including the EU law dimension, can be regarded to include the element of federal division of the power to regulate the media. This is to be explained with a view of the constitutional history according to which a "never again" of totalitarian rule was to be achieved. An opening of the German constitutional state for a full harmonization of media regulation by the EU would therefore be an extremely risky process from a legal perspective, not last with regard to the democratic relevance of 'media federalism' in Germany.

9. With regard to the exclusive, shared and supporting competences assigned to the EU under primary law since the Treaty of Lisbon, the media are not mentioned as such in the relevant catalogs of competences. From a legal comparative perspective, this alone speaks in favor of a restrictive understanding of the Treaties concerning the possible granting of media-related regulatory competences to the EU, which would be connected with the function of the media as cultural factor and guarantor of diversity. However, effects of internal market-related EU measures, which are directed in a general manner at all types of market participants, on the more specific question of media regulation can be observed. Such effects exist in all areas of EU competence.

Executive summary

There is no absolute suspensory effect of EU law with regard to Member State rules aiming at other objectives, even in the area of exclusive EU competences such as the determination of competition rules under Art. 3(1)(b) TFEU.

10. The EU's supporting competences, where the EU has no original regulatory competence aiming at legal harmonization, include those in the field of culture, including the media in their cultural dimension and educational policy. Media literacy is at the intersection of these competence titles. It is a soft but important component of a system of media regulation which can meet digital challenges in a democratic and socially acceptable manner. The compatibility of an increasing policy of informal regulation of the EU concerning media literacy with the requirement of "fully respecting the responsibility of the Member States for the content of teaching and the organization of education systems and their cultural and linguistic diversity" expressly recognized in Art. 165(1) TFEU is questionable.

11. The division of competences in the EU Treaties does not prevent enhanced cooperation between individual Member States in the field of media policy. Provided that this cooperation does not relate to the economic dimension of media regulation but to the cultural and diversity dimension of media regulation, there is no need to comply with the primary law requirements for enhanced cooperation. However, it is then a matter of cooperation between these Member States within the scope of their reserved competence, which is possible under EU law, but not governed by it.

12. By granting the EU, within the primary law concept of an integrated community, a competence to review the legal frameworks of the Member States – which encompasses the aspects of freedom and pluralism of the media – a certain conflict arises between the supposed restrictive understanding of the Treaties with regard to a positive media order on EU level and the reviewing authority of the Union bodies. The imperative to shield the Member States' media regulation from intervention by EU law, as it can be deduced not least from an overall view of the rules and limits on the exercise of competences in the EU Treaties, argues in favor of a very restricted approach to the exercise of reviewing authority in this area by the EU.

13. The cross-border activities of traditional audiovisual media undertakings such as broadcasters as well as new media actors such as media intermediaries are to be classified as services within the meaning of Art. 56 TFEU. A permanent establishment of a media undertaking in another EU Member State is a branch within the meaning of Art. 49 et

Executive summary

seq. TFEU. As media regulators, the Länder are obliged to ensure that this category of regulation is in conformity with the EU fundamental freedoms. Media law provisions of the German Länder which are intended to guarantee diversity of opinions and pluralism of the media are restrictions of the fundamental freedoms which are justified by overriding reasons of general interest, as long as the measures comply with the prohibition of discrimination and the principle of proportionality.

14. The EU's internal market competences do not entitle the EU to harmonize legislation in the area of media pluralism. The competence title of freedom of establishment must be interpreted narrowly, because only such an interpretation corresponds to the character of a Union consisting of Member States whose national identity must be preserved. In particular, a possible regulatory approach which would reduce the level of freedom of undertakings in the internal market would not be compatible with the internal market concept laid down in Art. 26 TFEU, which is geared at achieving progress towards free cross-border development. A further argument against resorting to regulatory competences in relation to the freedom to provide services is that this fundamental freedom is regularly only indirectly affected by national rules in the area of ensuring pluralism.

15. Competition law and the law relating to the safeguarding of pluralism are two distinct areas. However, market dominance and dominance over public opinion forming are not unrelated phenomena. In particular, competition law is in principle capable of achieving the objective of diversity of offer as a side-effect. EU primary law is not limited in its approach to a television-centered exercise of supervision authority concerning competition. It is rather open to a dynamic understanding, especially concerning the definition of the relevant market and of whether a dominant position is reached. The latter aspect also enables a supervisory response that takes account of intermediaries as such as well as network effects of the digital platform economy. Moreover, the consideration of democratic, fundamental rights and cultural principles and requirements in the context of competition policy is required in the same way and is, for example, according to Art. 167(4) TFEU, at the intersection between the protection of cultural competence of the Member States and the duty of supervision by the Commission in applying the competition rules. This means that when applying competition law, that course of action must be chosen which is most suitable for respecting and supporting the actions of Member States directed at media pluralism.

Executive summary

16. With regard to the cultural dimension of the media, the derogation in Art. 107(3)(d) TFEU on rules governing state aid is of particular importance. The so-called Amsterdam "Protocol on the system of public broadcasting in the Member States" reflects this imperative of an interpretation of Union law which preserves the Member States' margin for maneuver. This protocol openly addresses the tension that can arise between the democratic, social and cultural dimension of the media and their economic relevance – a tension that is not limited to public service broadcasting as a media (sub)category. While the former argues for a regulatory competence of the Member States, the potential internal market dimension of cross-border media activities is obvious with regard to the economic relevance.

17. The restriction for the EU to provide a positive regulatory framework for the media is affirmed for the "audiovisual sector" by the culture clause of Art. 167 TFEU. In particular, the so-called horizontal clause in paragraph 4 of this Article with the obligation to take cultural aspects into account gives rise to a whole set of requirements which are conducive to and promote diversity and which the EU must take into account in its legislative work and in monitoring the compliance of Member States' activities with EU law. Art. 167 TFEU does not preclude harmonizing media regulation on the part of the EU if it could be developed on a legal basis from the catalog of its exclusive or shared competences. However, it sets out the condition that the EU must take cultural aspects into account in any activity, which regularly amounts to a balancing of cultural and other regulatory goals (e.g. economic aspects in EU competition law). Furthermore, it follows from the system of the TFEU that cultural aspects, in particular those which ensure pluralism, cannot be the focus of rules in EU legislative acts.

18. In addition to the principle of conferral and the catalog of EU competences, substantive legal protection mechanisms such as rules and limits on the exercise of competences under the EU constitutional system should additionally ensure that the conferred powers existing at EU level are exercised in a way that does not encroach on the competences of the Member States. These rules include the requirement to respect the national identity of the Member States (Art. 4(2) TEU), the principle of sincere or loyal cooperation (Art. 4(3) TEU), the principle of subsidiarity (Art. 5(1) sentence 2 and (3) TEU) and the principle of proportionality (Art. 5(1) sentence 2 and (4) TEU).

19. The principle of subsidiarity has so far impacted the EU's use of its competences in particular in a preventive manner; no successful proceedings before the Court of Justice of the European Union (CJEU)

based on a violation of this principle have been concluded. Moreover, subsidiarity complaints and actions, given the interplay between the national and European division of competences for the Federal Republic of Germany as a Member State, have an organizational deficit insofar as the exercise of the legislative competences of the Länder is carried out without sufficient coordination between the federal body in charge, the Bundesrat, and the individual Länder parliaments with the goal of safeguarding the legislative competences of the Länder against the EU's overreaching intervention with regard to the subsidiarity principle.

20. The principle of proportionality as a limit to the exercise of powers is also likely to become more important than it has been so far with regard to the division of powers of the EU and its Member States in media regulation matters. This is due to the decision of the FCC of 5 May 2020 on the European Central Bank's government bond purchase program, irrespective of the justified scholarly criticism of this decision, which will impact at least the relationship between the EU and Germany. With this decision, the FCC has for the first time, in a way that reaches beyond the specific case and defines a scrutiny standard, stated that an EU institution acted beyond its powers (ultra vires).

21. This decision of the FCC argues for a restraint of legislative action by the EU in areas which are particularly sensitive to fundamental rights from the perspective of the constitutional framing of communication freedoms in the Member States. For example, a full harmonization of the area of media pluralism in the digital media ecosystem would strongly raise questions about exceeding the ultra vires-limits in the relationship between the CJEU and the FCC. Such an extension of the scope of application of EU media regulation *ratione personae* and/or *ratione materiae* disregarding Member State competences would further endanger the interaction between the EU and the Member States which is based on an approach of cooperation and could further strain the relationship between the CJEU and the FCC.

22. The approach of a multi-level system EU in which "democracy" and "pluralism" as addressed as values in Art. 2 TEU are based on a division across the levels, clearly speaks against a "supplementary competence" of the EU to regulate media pluralism in an overarching manner across all levels of the European integration community with the supposed goal of safeguarding democracy as a value. Such a regulation across all levels is also inconceivable in the context of the regulation of the election procedure for the European Parliament under Art. 223 TFEU.

Executive summary

23. The increasing significance of a growing "democracy community" does not imply any competence on the part of the EU for regulating media as a pre-legal prerequisite for a further deepening of this democratic bond either. The EU constitution is not designed to derive powers under integration law from integration policy objectives. To the extent the Union may deal with the prevention of disinformation campaigns, for example, then this has to happen from the perspective of the internal market: there should be no barriers to the free movement of goods and services as a result of differing approaches by the Member States concerning the prevention of such campaigns. However, this does not justify an own approach to a regulation by the Union to safeguard pluralism overall.

On the importance and legal sources of media pluralism at EU level

24. The fundamental rights of media freedom and pluralism enshrined in the Charter of Fundamental Rights of the EU (CFR) and the European Convention on Human Rights (ECHR) imply that, although it is not one of the EU's original competences, safeguarding freedom and pluralism in the media has a special role to play also at the level of EU measures. The EU is obliged to respect fundamental rights in all its actions, just like the Member States. This does not lead to the creation of a competence for media regulation, but on the contrary to a need to respect diversity, whereby the EU must choose in its actions that alternative which best enables media pluralism and correspondingly any regulation by the Member States which is necessary to attain that objective.

25. On the one hand, this applies firstly from a negative rights perspective: the EU must not interfere in an unjustified (specifically: disproportionate) way with fundamental rights protected by the CFR and the ECHR, which means that the impact of any EU action, whether legislative or executive, on the (broadly understood) freedom of the media must be considered and, where appropriate, be balanced with other legitimate interests – whether recognized by the Union as public interest objectives or the need to protect rights and freedoms of others. This also applies to measures relating to completely different areas of regulation, such as the economic sector or consumer protection. On the other hand, the positive dimension of fundamental rights in the CFR and the ECHR requires those who are bound by fundamental rights to make every effort to ensure that the conditions for the effective exercise of fundamental rights are met. These preconditions of freedom include not least the pluralism of the media. Irrespective of the extent to

Executive summary

which one wants to see this as an active duty to take action to establish, if necessary by a regulatory approach, an appropriate level of protection, which would only be addressed to Member States, because of the way the competences have been divided and how this is laid down in CFR and TFEU, it can be maintained that freedom of expression and freedom of the media and the principles and rights derived from them can justify interferences with other rights and freedoms under EU primary law.

26. Safeguarding media pluralism has always been a key issue in this context. In its case-law, the European Court of Human Rights (ECtHR) has repeatedly emphasized that media can only successfully exercise its essential role in democratic systems as "public watchdog", if the principle of pluralism is guaranteed. In that context the ECtHR addresses the Convention States as guarantors of this principle. Referring to the explicit inclusion of the obligation to respect media pluralism in Art. 11(2) CFR, the CJEU also underlines the importance of this guiding principle at EU level, referring not only to the CFR, but the ECHR and case law of the ECtHR, too. The CJEU stresses that media pluralism is undeniably an objective of general interest, the importance of which cannot be overemphasized in a democratic and pluralistic society. Pursuing this objective is therefore also capable of justifying interferences with freedom of the media and freedom of expression itself, any other fundamental rights and, last but not least, the fundamental freedoms guaranteed at EU level.

27. The significance and scope of this conclusion for the regulation of the media sector become clear when considering the fundamental freedoms guaranteed in the TFEU and the relevant case law of the CJEU in a media-related context. Especially as the rights to free movement of goods, services and establishment, the fundamental freedoms protect comprehensively the internal market and EU undertakings operating in this market in the cross-border provision of their offers by way of prohibiting restrictions and discrimination. The media, in their role as economic operators in the EU, are therefore in principle free to distribute their content, whether in digital or analogue form, in tangible or intangible form, beyond the borders of the Member State in which they are established. In doing so, they are entitled not to be treated differently from other providers or to be hindered or restricted in any other way. However, this freedom is not guaranteed without restrictions. In addition to explicit limitations to the individual fundamental freedoms, restrictions can be justified by the pursuit of recognized gen-

eral interest objectives, which, according to the settled case law of the CJEU, include the upholding of media pluralism.

28. Not only because of the rules concerning the division of competences, but also in light of recognizing a related concept of a cultural policy which may be characterized by different national (constitutional) traditions with regard to media regulation, the CJEU grants the Member States a wide margin of discretion in the fulfilment of this objective. Acknowledging that considerations of a moral or cultural nature may differ from one Member State to another, it is for the Member States to decide how to determine an adequate level of protection for the achievement of their cultural policy objectives, including media pluralism objectives, taking into account national specificities. This discretion also extends to the type of instruments they implement to achieve this level of protection. This freedom of defining and structuring the approach, which is recognized for all fundamental freedoms, is limited above all by the general principle of proportionality. Thus, fundamental freedoms and rights do not prevent the Member States from taking account of deficits in the area of media pluralism in regulatory terms, even if this affects undertakings based in other EU Member States.

29. This result of placing the safeguarding of pluralism at Member State level is also supported and underlined, as already mentioned above, by other aspects of primary law, in particular in the framework of EU competition law. Although this is clearly driven by the economic objective of establishing and protecting a free and fair internal market and leaves little room for taking into account non-economic aspects, the competition rules can indirectly contribute to media pluralism, as they keep markets open and competitive, counteract concentration, limit state influence and prevent market abuse. However, there is no explicit legal provision at EU level, nor is it recognized in the practice of monitoring, to exert an influence in the area of ensuring media pluralism besides the field of state aid control. Evaluations of measures from a cultural, in particular media pluralism perspective outside of economic market considerations – such as, for example, taking into account the emergence of predominant power over opinions – are therefore not possible at EU level.

30. Rather, opening clauses and exceptions allowing for Member States' cultural policy are provided for both in the context of monitoring market power and abuse and in the context of state aid control carried out by the European Commission when assessing EU relevant mergers, practices and state aids. For example, media concentration law is deliberately excluded from the scope of economic concentration law, as il-

Executive summary

lustrated by Art. 21(4) of the EU Merger Regulation, which authorizes Member States to adopt specific rules to safeguard legitimate interests, namely to ensure media pluralism besides the applicable EU competition provisions. This can result in Member State authorities, even in cases for which the Commission has exclusive competence to assess a merger because of its relevance for the EU market, being able to prohibit such a merger for reasons of ensuring pluralism in the "opinion market", irrespective of the Commission's previous clearance from a market power perspective. The state aid rules also provide for exceptions in which state funding of (media) undertakings is exceptionally permitted, provided that a cultural focus is set and cultural policy is conceptualized at national level. Thus, although EU competition law is deliberately not a suitable instrument for ensuring pluralism, it does not contradict the efforts of Member States to achieve this goal.

Framework for "media law" and media pluralism at secondary law level

31. Due to the described lack of competence to adopt legislative acts in this area, secondary law in the field of safeguarding pluralism which directly pursues this objective cannot exist. Corresponding attempts at EU (and formerly European Community) level were therefore quickly dismissed. However, due to the twofold nature of media as an economic and cultural asset and the convergence of the media and their distribution channels, there is nevertheless a framework of media law at EU secondary law level, within which numerous points of reference for pluralism can be found. These impact the shaping of media regulation by the Member States in different ways.

32. One category of such references concerns the establishment of explicit margins of maneuver for Member States with regard to national cultural policy, in particular the safeguarding of media pluralism, in the Union's secondary law relating to economic affairs. On the one hand, such exceptions can be found in the rulesets that are relevant to the distribution of media content: the European Electronic Communications Code (EECC), which provides for telecommunications rules, and the Directive on electronic commerce (e-Commerce Directive, ECD), which provides a partially harmonized legal framework including liability exemptions for information society services and thus in particular for intermediaries involved in the online distribution of media content, do not affect the ability of Member States to take measures to promote cultural and linguistic diversity. In addition, the EECC allows Member States to provide for so-called 'must carry' obligations in na-

tional law, i.e. to oblige network operators to transmit certain radio and television channels and related complementary services, thus extending the already existing derogation for diversity measures to this area coordinated by the EECC. The AVMSD, the heart of European "media law", also contains a derogation option for Member States to adopt stricter rules, which relates to the areas coordinated by the AVMSD and which, moreover, has hardly changed in substance over the years despite the development steps of the AVMSD.

33. Another category of references, however, concerns the EU's efforts, particularly in recent times, which contain elements of preserving pluralism and which can be found in secondary law which is not based on a competently for cultural policy. In particular, the reforms of the AVMSD and the new Directive on Copyright in the Digital Single Market (DSM Directive) have established rules which provide for a certain degree of protection of pluralism, or at least contain references to it, which is also underlined by indications of this kind in the relevant recitals. While the new copyright rules on the protection of press publications concerning online use and on the use of protected content by certain online content-sharing service providers take such diversity considerations into account, but essentially aim at the appropriate financing of (also) media offerings and thus decisively at economic factors, the new rules of the AVMSD on the promotion of European works, on the prominence of content of general interest, on media literacy and on the establishment of independent regulatory bodies assign greater weight to cultural aspects. However, in this respect too, broad discretionary powers of Member States are maintained and emphasized.

34. This aforementioned category also includes the recently introduced Platform-to-Business (P2B) Regulation, which due to its legal nature is more intrusive than Directives in terms of its impact on the Member States' legal systems. The Regulation imposes transparency obligations on online intermediary services and search engines with regard to ranking systems vis-à-vis undertakings, which potentially include media undertakings whose content is found through these gatekeepers. Although the Regulation is based on the internal market competence and aims to respond to or prevent an unequal balance of power in the digital economy, and therefore represents an economic-oriented piece of legislation, the P2B Regulation provides for important means of making the conditions for findability of content transparent also from the perspective of ensuring diversity. However, the P2B Regulation does not have a suspensory effect on the media legislation of the Mem-

Executive summary

ber States even when this regulates comparable transparency obligations for certain platform providers based on the need to guarantee pluralism.

35. The fact that more media-related initiatives such as the combating of hate speech and disinformation, which are particularly relevant in the context of the fundamental right of freedom of expression, are being shifted to the level of coordination and support measures based on self-regulation mechanisms, shows that the EU also respects the sovereignty of the Member States with regard to media regulation. This corresponds to the limitation of the EU's competence for supporting measures in such a way that support measures must not prejudge the Member State's exercise of regulatory discretion. With regard to future measures announced by the EU concerning the media sector in particular, such as those envisaged in the Media and Audiovisual Action Plan and the European Democracy Action Plan, it will be essential that stronger regulatory steps at Union level continue to be carried out with due attention to the division of competences, such as, for example, when it comes to the responsibility of Member States to actually implement possible common standards. In view of the announcements made in connection with these initiatives, in particular the intention to support competitiveness and diversity in the audiovisual sector through, inter alia, the use of EU funding instruments, as well as to strengthen efforts in the area of disinformation, hate speech and media literacy, these are at the intersection with media pluralism at national level. The inclusion of democratic, cultural and also diversity policy aspects in regulation has recently become a trend that can be observed to a greater extent than before at the level of legally binding secondary law and at the (tertiary EU law) level of implementing provisions, but also in the case of legally non-binding initiatives. This increases the tension with national rules which were adopted with the aim of ensuring pluralism.

Key problems of public international law in the regulation of the "media sector" with regard to possible conflicts with EU law

36. When considering possible tensions between the regulatory levels of the EU and its Member States, the question of responsibility for the execution of legislation plays a particularly important role. This applies especially to the decision on who is to carry out enforcement against providers in a specific case. In the national context of the Federal Republic of Germany, the state media authorities – on the basis of a teleological and historical interpretation of the relevant international

Executive summary

treaties – are authorized to take enforcement measures against foreign providers for violation of substantive provisions of the State Media Treaty (*Medienstaatsvertrag*, MStV) and the Interstate Treaty on the protection of minors (*Jugendmedienschutzstaatsvertrag*, JMStV). This empowerment is confirmed by an interpretation of these interstate treaties in conformity with EU law, in which the meaning of the provisions of the AVMSD and ECD is interpreted in the light of the Member States' competence to ensure pluralism, including in relation to situations involving providers based in other EU Member States. The European Commission's critical remarks, in particular on the rules concerning media intermediaries in the MStV as a reaction to the notification by Germany, are therefore erroneous.

37. In enforcement, a tiered regulation can differentiate according to whether offers originate in or outside a given Member State. However, refraining from enforcement attempts against foreign providers, where there are only limited alternative efforts by the other Member State in containing potential risks, would provoke the constitutional question of whether the absence of enforcement is reconcilable with the principle of equality. Such a regulation of foreign providers is determined by the fundamental rights framework of the Basic Law with regard to the media (in particular broadcasting) freedom under Art. 5(1) sentence 2, seen through the lens of the decision of the FCC of 19 May 2020 concerning the German intelligence service, at least if the provider is either a natural person or (in the broader interpretation of the FCC) a legal person with its registered office in the EU.

38. The FCC doctrine of duties to protect leads to an advance protection of fundamental rights when it comes to minimizing risks in the course of modern technological and societal developments as it was formulated by the Court. Where state duties to protect exist, these basically entail the duty to prevent, stop and sanction violations of rights, whereby legislative as well as judicial and administrative measures may be required, while maintaining a wide scope for implementation by the individual states. In this context, the increased margin for maneuver of state authorities in matters of international relations must also be taken into account with regard to the protective dimension of fundamental rights: if the exercise of the protective dimension of a fundamental right inevitably affects the legal systems of other states, the power of state authority to decide how to act is greater than when regulating legal relations with a domestic focus. In line with the so-called 'Solange-jurisprudence' of the FCC, it can be argued that the duties to protect

Executive summary

under the Basic Law need not result in action as long as a comparable level of protection exists due to the activities of other states.

39. Although there is no comparable understanding of duties of protection in the framework of the TEU and TFEU based on the CFR as is in the domestic constitutional situation, it is also not apparent that the Treaties establish limits by EU law to such an understanding. Both in the recognition of a prerogative of the Member States to assess the "how" of measures to eliminate infringements of the fundamental freedoms caused by private parties and in defining the limits of the scope of this assessment, the interpretation of fundamental freedoms shows a considerable similarity to that of the FCC on duties to protect.

40. Territorial sovereignty and the principle of non-intervention in the internal affairs of a state set limits to the legislative and executive powers in cross-border cases under public international law. The *Lotus* decision of the Permanent Court of International Justice is of continued relevance for the determination of these limits. As public international law is characterized by a territorial understanding of the state, sovereignty is exercised in principle on the national territory. On the territory of another state, public international law therefore in principle prohibits the state from enforcing its legal system. An exception in this respect requires a rule in international treaty law or recognition by customary international law. This is also important in distinguishing between *jurisdiction to prescribe* and *jurisdiction to enforce*.

41. Based on the principle of territorial jurisdiction, the territoriality principle and the effects doctrine associated with it are recognized as connecting factors to establish jurisdiction. In addition, nationality (active personality principle) and the protection of certain state interests (passive personality and protection principle) are applied to establish such a connection (genuine link). The MStV takes appropriate account of this distinction under public international law. Furthermore, an effect in Germany is particularly given if an offer specifically or exclusively deals with the political, economic, social, scientific or cultural situation in Germany in the present or past. In particular, there is a genuine link with regard to the constitutional identity of the Federal Republic of Germany and the significance of the experience with National Socialism for the German legal system, which shapes identity in an exemplary manner, in the event of violations of Art. 4(1) sentence 1 nos. 1, 2, 3, 4 and 7 JMStV. Even if it is a non-domestic, foreign provider that exercises influence on the process of attracting attention for specific content by means of aggregation, selection and presentation, in particular as regards search engines, e.g. by encouraging a prioritized use of

Executive summary

that offer in response to search queries from Germany, it creates a *genuine link* according to the interpretation of jurisdiction under public international law.

42. Apart from procedural problems regarding the treatment of foreign providers in the enforcement of media law rules, several recent legal provisions have been criticized by some as raising substantive concerns about their compatibility with European law, in particular the country of origin principle. With regard to both the MStV and the Netzwerkdurchsetzungsgesetz (Network Enforcement Act, NetzDG) – although there are indeed questions regarding the aspect of an independent supervision of the rules in the latter law – it is shown that the tension with EU law does not lead to an actual violation of it. This also applies to further changes, for example in copyright law. However, these areas of tension show that there should be an explicit recognition at EU level – beyond existing approaches – that, if the country of origin principle is retained in principle, national rules and enforcement measures can also be based on the market location principle under certain conditions.

The proposed Digital Services Act

43. In December 2020, the European Commission has presented a legislative proposal (Digital Services Act) which "will upgrade our liability and safety rules for digital platforms, services and products, and complete our Digital Single Market". Various options regarding the scope of this new framework are discussed, including, in addition to considerations directly related to the ECD, rules to safeguard democratic procedures in the EU and its Member States and to deal with network effects of the digital platform economy. With regard to the latter, ex ante measures based on competition law will also be considered. In the light of the results of this study, particular attention should be paid to improving information and transparency requirements, clarifying the understanding of "illegal content" and how it can be distinguished from content previously considered merely as "harmful", clarifying the extent to which self-regulatory approaches are sufficient and where co-regulation should be used as a minimum, strengthening the effective enforcement of public interest considerations, including when dealing with content from non-EU third countries, updating the rules on liability of providers and organizational aspects to improve enforcement in a cross-border context.

44. Based on the results of this study, in the further political process of negotiating new or amended EU legal acts, as well as in the case of sup-

plementary initiatives by the Member States, in addition to working towards a clear recognition of the delimitation of competences, early and intensive participation at EU level by the German Länder responsible for this sector should be actively sought with the aim of proposals that better consider and coordinate measures at both EU and Member State levels.

A. Introduction and background to the study

Mark D. Cole / Jörg Ukrow

In her first State of the Union address to the plenary session of the European Parliament on 16 September 2020, the President of the European Commission, Ursula von der Leyen, stated that:[1]

"*We must make this Europe's Digital Decade.*"

Irrespective of the symbolic political significance associated with this appeal – a level of significance that in the past was not associated with exclusively positive effects in terms of integration policy and law[2] – this warning also expresses the fundamental importance that digitization has for the objectives of the process of European integration. This digital dimension also shapes the further development of the European framework for the media. However, the effects of digital disruption of traditional business and communication processes that can be observed in the media ecosystem are not simultaneously linked to a logic of digital transformation of constitutional structures and guidelines for the media constitution of and in the EU. Digital waves of change are thus breaking on the quay walls of the EU's competence restrictions.

In her State of the Union address, the President of the Commission said next:

"*We need a common plan for digital Europe with clearly defined goals for 2030, such as for connectivity, skills and digital public services.*"

As this study shows, the "common ground" of the plan for a digital Europe cannot only be an organizational common ground of the Council and the Commission, the two institutions that have traditionally taken a special position in the promotion of the integration of Europe. Rather, the proposed plan requires an architectural design in which not only the EU and

---

[1] State of the Union Address by President von der Leyen at the European Parliament Plenary, 16.09.2020, https://ec.europa.eu/commission/presscorner/detail/en/speech_20_1655.
[2] Cf. on the failure of a gesture-political enrichment of the European Treaties with the European Constitutional Treaty e.g. *Häberle*, Nationalflaggen: Bürgerdemokratische Identitätselemente und Internationale Erkennungssymbole, p. 39.

its institutions but also the Member States will continue to play a decisive role. A digital Europe can only emerge from a respect for the different competences in the European multi-level system.

Incidentally, none of the areas identified as relevant to the plan are congruent with the media sector, namely the press, broadcasting and new media, although the latter were only able to develop in the process of digitization of the media ecosystem itself. But none of these areas is up to date even without touching on a media regulation that takes into account convergence phenomena at the interface of infrastructure and content as well as the interaction of regulation and the promotion of competence to achieve objectives such as the protection of human dignity, the protection of minors and consumer protection. These interfaces also raise questions about the allocation of Union and Member State competences.

Finally, the President of the Commission points out that the EU and its Member States share the same values in their commitment to digital policy. The corresponding "clear principles" are identified by von der Leyen as

> "the right to privacy and connectivity, freedom of speech, free flow of data and cybersecurity".

The references of these principles to a digital media order for the EU are evident.

Even if the thematic areas of "data" and "infrastructure", which receive special attention in the President's speech, also show similar references to the digital media ecosystem, the object of investigation of the present study refers to a problem which, in connection with the "digital decade" approach, is also relevant to the third area highlighted in the speech: "technology – and in particular artificial intelligence". This is because the topic of "algorithm regulation" highlights in a particular way problems that may arise from a competence and fundamental rights perspective in the further development of media regulation by the EU and its Member States in a regulatory environment that has been and will continue to be increasingly shaped by the megatrends of digitization and globalization:

> "We want a set of rules that puts people at the centre. Algorithms must not be a black box and there must be clear rules if something goes wrong. The Commission will propose a law to this effect next year.
> This includes control over our personal data which still have far too rarely today. Every time an App or website asks us to create a new digital identity or to easily log on via a big platform, we have no idea what happens to our data in reality.
> That is why the Commission will soon propose a secure European e-identity.

One that we trust and that any citizen can use anywhere in Europe to do anything from paying your taxes to renting a bicycle. A technology where we can control ourselves what data and how data is used."

To this regard, the President of the Commission stresses:

"None of this is an end in itself – it is about Europe's digital sovereignty, on a small and large scale."

With the objective of European sovereignty, von der Leyen takes up a topos that was first introduced into the integration law finality discussion by President Macron and which was subsequently referred to in the Franco-German "Agreement on Franco-German Cooperation and Integration"[3], hence made binding under international treaty law for the first time. This "sovereignty" perspective raises not inconsiderable legal problems with regard to the correlation between the EU and the Member States in the integration order.[4] These problems must also be kept in mind if the EU and Member States want to take the European path into the digital age together, including a media-regulatory room in the digital house Europe.

Now that the work of the previous "Juncker Commission" on the digital single market has been completed, the establishment of a legal framework for the "digital society" at the level of the European Union (EU) still remains a clear focus of the Commission's work, according to the State of the Union Address.[5] In addition to the strategies and work plans published to date by the Commission, for example on data strategy[6] or possible regu-

---

3 Gesetz zu dem Vertrag vom 22. Januar 2019 zwischen der Bundesrepublik Deutschland und der Französischen Republik über die deutsch-französische Zusammenarbeit und Integration of 15.11.2019 (Law on the Treaty of 22 January 2019 between the Federal Republic of Germany and the French Republic on Franco-German Cooperation and Integration of 15.11.2019), BGBl. 2019 II, p. 898 et seq.
4 Cf. *Ukrow* in: ZEuS 2019, 3, 21 et seq.
5 Cf. Commission Work Programme 2020, A Union that strives for more, of 29.01.2020, COM(2020) 37 final, https://ec.europa.eu/info/sites/info/files/cwp-2020_en.pdf.
6 Communication from the Commission to the European Parliament, the Council, the European Economic and Social Committee and the Committee of the Regions, A European strategy for data, of 29.02.2020, COM(2020) 66 final, https://eur-lex.europa.eu/legal-content/EN/TXT/?qid=1606205225168&uri=CELEX%3A52020DC0066. In the meanwhile, the European Commission has presented a Proposal for a Data Governance Act, https://eur-lex.europa.eu/legal-content/EN/TXT/?uri=CELEX%3A52020PC0767.

latory steps regarding the use of artificial intelligence systems[7], particularly the legislative proposals of 15 December 2020 for a "Digital Services Act"[8] and a "Digital Markets Act"[9] and thus the link to the e-Commerce Directive (ECD)[10] is of central importance for the – no longer clearly definable – "media market". With this package the Commission intends to propose clear rules that define the responsibilities of digital services, ensure a modern system of cooperation in the monitoring of and enforcement against platforms, and propose ex-ante rules for major online platforms to ensure the competitiveness of the European market. And it is precisely here – as in the regulation of audiovisual media services and the reform of the corresponding Directive 2018[11], which is still in the process of transposition in the Member States[12] – that potential conflicts arise between the two levels

---

7 European Commission, White Paper On Artificial Intelligence – A European approach to excellence and trust, of 19.02.2020, COM(2020) 65 final, https://ec.europa.eu/info/sites/info/files/commission-white-paper-artificial-intelligence-feb2020_en.pdf.
8 https://eur-lex.europa.eu/legal-content/EN/TXT/?uri=CELEX%3A52020PC0825&qid=1614595537069. For a first discussion see *Ukrow*, Die Vorschläge der EU-Kommission für einen Digital Services Act und einen Digital Markets Act, and in detail *Cole/Etteldorf/Ullrich*, Updating the Rules for Online Content Dissemination.
9 https://eur-lex.europa.eu/legal-content/en/TXT/?uri=COM%3A2020%3A842%3AFIN.
10 Directive 2000/31/EC of the European Parliament and of the Council of 8 June 2000 on certain legal aspects of information society services, in particular electronic commerce, in the Internal Market ('Directive on electronic commerce'), OJ L 178 of 17.07.2000, p. 1–16, https://eur-lex.europa.eu/legal-content/EN/TXT/?uri=CELEX%3A32000L0031&qid=1606205584504.
11 Directive (EU) 2018/1808 of the European Parliament and of the Council of 14 November 2018 amending Directive 2010/13/EU on the coordination of certain provisions laid down by law, regulation or administrative action in Member States concerning the provision of audiovisual media services (Audiovisual Media Services Directive) in view of changing market realities, OJ L 303 of 28.11.2018, p. 69–92, https://eur-lex.europa.eu/legal-content/EN/TXT/?uri=CELEX%3A32018L1808&qid=1606206126950.
12 The transposition period ended on 19 September 2020, until which only four Member States had notified transposition. In the meanwhile Germany, Austria, Bulgaria, Denmark. Finland, France, Hungary, Latvia, Lithuania, Malta, the Netherlands, Portugal, and Sweden have adopted a final transposition and Luxembourg and Spain a partial one in national law. In the other Member States legislative projects are ongoing. Cf. the overviews by the Commission (https://eur-lex.europa.eu/legal-content/EN/NIM/?uri=CELEX:32018L1808&qid=1599556794041) and in the European Audiovisual Observatory database (https://www.obs.coe.int/en/web/observatoire/avmsd-tracking).

of the EU and the Member States with regard to the allocation of competences for regulating these areas.

In the EU's multi-level system, the division of competences is not always clear, and in federal states such as the Federal Republic of Germany this is reinforced by further subdivision. This is particularly true with regard to media law, which regulates the "media" sector, because here it is not possible to allocate competences referring to only a single legal basis. Thus, it is an old insight that media have a "cultural" component, but that they are also – and in some contexts primarily – economic in nature and thus, in the EU context, internal market-related. This already existing tension between Member States' cultural competence and EU regulation of the internal market aspects takes on a further dimension when it comes to restrictions imposed on service providers in this sector. Thus, in addition to the protection of freedom of expression, the primary objective of any media regulation is to ensure a diversity of opinions and the media that is specific to the respective Member State or its regional subdivision. The competence for such restrictive rules must lie at the Member State level and both the Court of Justice of the European Union (CJEU) and, in a comparable manner, the European Court of Human Rights (ECtHR) therefore recognize the Member States' margin of appreciation and scope for design when deciding on measures to ensure diversity which at the same time have a restrictive character with regard to fundamental freedoms and/or fundamental rights.

The apparently undisputed recognition of regulatory competence reserved for Member States in this area, on the other hand, is often confronted in practice with the actual or alleged limit of regulatory power, insofar as it radiates into areas regulated by Union law. Especially recently, there have been several cases that illustrate this conflict. For instance, after the notification of the German State Media Treaty (*Medienstaatsvertrag*, MStV)[13] the Commission in its reaction gave clear indications that it takes

---

13 Staatsvertrag zur Modernisierung der Medienordnung in Deutschland (State Treaty on the Modernization of the Media Order in Germany), cf. Beschlussfassung der Konferenz der Regierungschefinnen und Regierungschefs der Länder (Resolution of the Conference of the Heads of Government of the Länder) of 5 December 2019, available at https://www.rlp.de/fileadmin/rlp-stk/pdf-Dateien/Medienpolitik/ModStV_MStV_und_JMStV_2019-12-05_MPK.pdf. The MStV came into force on 7 November 2020, cf. the Rundfunkkommission (Broadcasting Corporation) press release of 06.11.2020, available at https://www.rlp.de/de/aktuelles/einzelansicht/news/News/detail/medienstaatsvertrag-tritt-am-7-november-2020-inkraft-1/.

a different view of the Member States' scope for action in regulating online players based on the provisions of the e-Commerce Directive against the background of the fundamental freedom dimension and the inclusion of the country of origin principle.[14] In particular, the Commission expressed "certain doubts" as to "whether some of the measures contained in the notified draft could disproportionately restrict the free movement of information society services protected in the internal market", referring to its efforts (also) in the context of the at that time planned Digital Services Act to promote media diversity and media pluralism in the online environment. Furthermore, a provision in the Interstate Broadcasting Treaty that was expressly introduced to safeguard media diversity in the regional area – § 7(11) RStV as a provision that was taken over in § 8(11) MStV in substantive terms, even if not editorially identical in content – has been attacked for an alleged infringement of the freedom to provide services with the case being decided by the CJEU in February 2021.[15]

On the other hand, in addition to the MStV, which has since been signed and ratified by the state parliaments, there are further regulatory approaches in German law – such as the Federal Network Enforcement Act (NetzDG)[16], which is currently undergoing an amendment procedure[17] – as well as in the law of other Member States, the details of which could

---

14 European Commission, Notifizierung 2020/26/D, C(2020) 2823 final of 27.04.2020, https://dokumente.landtag.rlp.de/landtag/vorlagen/6754-V-17.pdf (available in German only, hereinafter own translations). *Jörg Wojahn*, representative of the European Commission in Germany, is even quoted as follows in the accompanying press release: "[…] The Commission has already announced its intention to propose a legislative package for digital services by the end of this year […]. This will clarify the responsibilities of major online platforms across the internal market, also with a view to promoting *the objective of media diversity* […]" (own translation, emphasis by authors).

15 CJEU, case C-555/19, *Fussl Modestraße Mayr*, judgment of 03.02.2021, see also the opinion of Advocate General *Szpunar* of 15.10.2020. See on the judgment *Ory* in: NJW 2021, 736, 736 et seq.; *Ukrow*, Sicherung regionaler Vielfalt – Außer Mode?. Cf. on the matter also *Cole* in: AfP 2021, 1, 1 et seq., and in detail *id.*, Zum Gestaltungsspielraum der EU-Mitgliedstaaten bei Einschränkungen der Dienstleistungsfreiheit.

16 Netzwerkdurchsetzungsgesetz (Network Enforcement Act) of 1 September 2017 (BGBl. I, p. 3352), as amended by Art. 274 of the Regulation of 19 June 2020 (BGBl. I, p. 1328), https://www.gesetze-im-internet.de/netzdg/BJNR335210017.html.

17 There are currently two draft laws that address the NetzDG with various changes; cf. Deutscher Bundestag, Entwurf eines Gesetzes zur Änderung des Netzwerkdurchsetzungsgesetzes (Draft law to amend the Network Enforcement Act), Printed paper 19/18792 of 27.04.2020, https://dip21.bundestag.de/dip21/btd/19/187/19

possibly trigger questions on the part of the EU regarding the allocation of competences. The same applies to other measures planned by the EU itself, such as the proposal for a regulation on preventing the dissemination of terrorist content online (TERREG)[18], which is still in the legislative process, and in particular the proposed Digital Services Act.

Against this background, it is necessary to comprehensively present in a study the status quo of the distribution of competences in the area of media regulation with special consideration of the regulatory goal of media diversity. Due to the existing regulatory instruments at EU level, the study focuses mainly on the area of audiovisual media. The press, especially in the online sector, as well as film, are only included in the study at relevant points. Following this general clarification, it is also necessary to show which options for action exist for the Member States in the future design of the media and "online sector" and how these, in this respect, can react to EU proposals.

Although there is existing scientific work on the question of securing media diversity and deducible questions of competence, it is based on the early case-law of the CJEU – and this in turn on that of the ECtHR – and requires updating and contextualization with regard to new rulesets and developments of recent years. In addition, findings can be derived – based on a detailed analysis – for the currently pending legislative processes at the EU level as to how these are to be shaped in view of the results found, how the Federal Republic of Germany as an EU Member State is to be involved in shaping them and, in particular, where the limits of EU regulatory activity must lie.

18792.pdf, and Entwurf eines Gesetzes zur Bekämpfung des Rechtsextremismus und der Hasskriminalität (Draft law to combat right-wing extremism and hate crime), Printed paper 19/17741 of 10.03.2020, https://dip21.bundestag.de/dip21/btd/19/177/1917741.pdf. With regard to the latter amendment, the Office of the Federal President (Bundespräsidialamt) has, according to available information, suspended the signing procedure due to data protection concerns; cf. https://www.sueddeutsche.de/politik/hate-speech-gesetz-das-koennt-ihr-besser-1.5059141. On the application of the NetzDG to date, cf. the Federal Government's report on the evaluation of the Gesetz zur Verbesserung der Rechtsdurchsetzung in sozialen Netzwerken (law to improve law enforcement in social networks) and *Eifert*, Evaluation des NetzDG, both available at https://www.bmjv.de/SharedDocs/Artikel/DE/2020/090920_Evaluierungsbericht_NetzDG.html.

18 Proposal for a Regulation of the European Parliament and of the Council on preventing the dissemination of terrorist content online, COM(2018) 640 final of 12.09.2018, https://eur-lex.europa.eu/legal-content/EN/TXT/?uri=CELEX%3A52018PC0640&qid=1606214807269.

Given the examples mentioned, it is not surprising that the issue of media pluralism has recently gained in importance again. This is also a consequence of the threats to existing structures on the media market, which are perceived as increasingly intense. In this context, options are also being discussed that go beyond mere regulation, such as active support models for providers of editorially responsible media content[19]. But even in this respect, there are intensive links to EU law, so that an overall view, detached from individual procedures or situations, is appropriate.

The aim of the study is to identify the existing area of competence of the Member States. To this end, the primary legal framework for the division of competences between the EU and the Member States is comprehensively analyzed in a first chapter B. In particular, this chapter shows, in view of the recent case law of the Federal Constitutional Court, the limits that the principle of conferral sets for EU action. In addition, the EU's system of values in its significance for the media sector, the individual relevant competence titles from primary law and the influence of the EU's aims are presented in detail. The chapter concludes with an examination of the restrictions on the exercise of competences for the EU and the significance of fundamental rights. The following Chapter C. analyzes the way the general public interest objective of media diversity is legally enshrined at EU level. For this purpose, the fundamental rights basis in European Convention on Human Rights (ECHR)and Charter of Fundamental Rights of the EU (CFR) as well as primary law aspects are addressed. The reference in and the influence of secondary law will be analyzed separately for each legislative act in Chapter D. In addition to the Audiovisual Media Services Directive (AVMSD), which was amended in 2018, the European Electronic Communications Code (EECC), which is also still in the process of being transposed in the Member States, and the Platform-to-Business (P2B) Regulation, which has recently become applicable, will be examined in this context. Current legislative projects and initiatives of the EU as well as non-legally binding measures are also included in the analysis.

Chapter E. then deals with core problems under public international law that arise in regulating the "media sector" due to the tension between national and EU law. The focus is to explain, using the example of the approach of the MStV and the Interstate Treaty on the protection of minors

---

19 In the meanwhile, the European Commission has presented its Communication on Europe's Media in the Digital Decade: An Action Plan to Support Recovery and Transformation (Media and Audiovisual Action Plan), COM/2020/784 final, https://eur-lex.europa.eu/legal-content/EN/TXT/?uri=CELEX%3A52020DC0784.

(Jugendmedienschutzstaatsvertrag, JMStV), which public international and European legal framework conditions have to be adhered to when dealing with the question of the addressees of a national regulation – i.e. in particular the question of a cross-border application of German media law rules – as well as the enforcement of the law against foreign providers. The fundamental rights dimension comprises not only the question of fundamental rights adherence in enforcement measures but also the issue of a duty to protect and the corresponding call for action by the state. The difficulties involved in the practical implementation of such measures will be pointed out with regard to the different legal levels, developing a respective solution. Concluding, this chapter deals with examples of disputed (with regard to the European legal requirements) substantive law aspects of specific rules that have an impact on German media law. Due to its significance for the currently ongoing legislative process for future regulation in the form of the EU Digital Services Act, certain aspects of the Commission proposal are addressed and classified in the light of the results of the study. Finally, Chapter G. provides some guidance on policy options for action based on the results of the study. The study is preceded by a detailed Executive Summary.

The scientific direction and overall editing of the study was assumed by *Mark D. Cole* and *Jörg Ukrow*. The individual chapters were edited by the authors as follows: Chapters B, E and F by *Jörg Ukrow*, Chapters C and D by *Mark D. Cole* and *Christina Etteldorf*, the framing chapters A and G by *Mark D. Cole* and *Jörg Ukrow*. The authors would like to thank *Jan Henrich* for preparatory work in individual sections and *Sebastian Zeitzmann* who assumed the overall responsibility for the English translation of the study.

B. Framework for the allocation of competences under EU primary law

Jörg Ukrow

I. Basic principles of TEU/TFEU

1. Introduction

Since the late 1990 s, initiatives and demands for a European law on media concentration have been circulating repeatedly in the European Commission[20] and the European Parliament[21].[22] In the founding act of EU media law, the EEC Television Directive, the topic was addressed for the first time under secondary law – in the form of a warning notice with an incidental claim to regulatory countermeasures at the European level in the event of failure of the Member States to take precautionary measures:[23]

> *"Whereas it is essential for the Member States to ensure the prevention of any acts which may prove detrimental to freedom of movement and trade in television programmes or which may promote the creation of dominant positions which would lead to restrictions on pluralism and freedom of televised information and of the information sector as a whole."*

---

20 Already in Commission communication COM (90) 78 of 21.02.1990, the importance of pluralism for the functioning of the democratic community in the European Union (then the European Communities) is emphasized.
21 Cf. European Parliament, Resolution of 15 February 1990 on concentration in the media, OJ C 68 of 19.03.1990, p. 137; European Parliament, Resolution of 16 September 1992 on media concentration and diversity of opinions, OJ C 284 of 02.11.1992, p. 44; European Parliament, Resolution of 20 January 1994 on the Commission Green Paper 'Pluralism and media concentration in the internal market', OJ C 44 of 14.02.1994, p. 177.
22 Cf. *Jungheim*, Medienordnung und Wettbewerbsrecht im Zeitalter der Digitalisierung und Globalisierung, p. 356 et seq.; *Schwartz*, Rundfunk, EG-Kompetenzen und ihre Ausübung, p. 15.
23 Rec. 16 Council Directive 89/552/EEC of 3 October 1989 on the coordination of certain provisions laid down by Law, Regulation or Administrative Action in Member States concerning the pursuit of television broadcasting activities, OJ L 298 of 17.10.1989, p. 23–30, https://eur-lex.europa.eu/legal-content/EN/TXT/?uri=celex:31989L0552.

The German states in particular have repeatedly denied the competence of the EU to issue a media concentration directive. Thus the Bundesrat already unanimously decided in its statement on the Commission's Green Paper on pluralism and media concentration in the internal market[24] on 7 May 1993[25]:

> *"1. [...] Even after the entry into force of the Maastricht Treaty, the EC would not have the competence to adopt the measures proposed in the Green Paper.*
> *2. Also under the Maastricht Treaty, the competence to set media-specific laws remains with the Member States; in the Federal Republic of Germany, it is the responsibility of the Länder. This distribution of competence must not be circumvented by the Community using its competence for economic policy regulations to intervene in the media sector in a targeted manner.*
> *Ensuring diversity of opinion in broadcasting is of fundamental importance for the free and comprehensive formation of public opinion. It is thus the very essence of democracy in the Federal Republic of Germany.*
> *This role as a medium and factor in the formation of public opinion is fulfilled by broadcasting exclusively at Member State level, since democratic opinion-making currently takes place at this level only.*
> *3. In a Europe with different social structures and different national broadcasting systems, pluralism can therefore only be defined in relation to the Member States. This reinforces the reservations about Community regulations aimed at safeguarding diversity of opinion, because these would interfere with the core area of the social functions of broadcasting in the Member States. The principle of subsidiarity enshrined in Article 3 b of the Maastricht Treaty would also stand in the way of Community action, since the objective of preventing a concentration of power of opinion through normative measures in order to ensure diversity of information and opinion can be achieved to a sufficient extent by the Member States themselves.[...]"*

---

24 European Commission, Green Paper on Pluralism and media concentration in the internal market – an assessment of the need for Community action, COM (92) 480 final of 23 December 1992. On this e.g. *Hain* in: AfP 2007, 527, 531; *Holznagel*, Vielfaltskonzepte in Europa, p. 96; *Paal*, Medienvielfalt und Wettbewerbsrecht, p. 177.
25 Cf. Deutscher Bundesrat, Resolution Printed paper 77/93(B) of 7 May 1993, http://dipbt.bundestag.de/extrakt/ba/WP12/1576/157601.html (own translation).

B. Framework for the allocation of competences under EU primary law

As will be shown below, this determination of position[26] is of continuing importance despite the deepening of the European integration process under primary law since 1993 through the Treaties of Maastricht[27], Amsterdam[28], Nice[29], and Lisbon[30]. Limits to an EU harmonization and coordination competence exist however not only with respect to classic media concentration law, but also from the perspective of safeguarding pluralism with respect to digital and global challenges of the media ecosystem.

2. Member States as "Masters of the Treaties" vs. openness for and dynamics of integration in multilevel constitutionalism

Even in the course of the repeated, sometimes fundamental changes to the founding Treaties of the European Union (EU), which emerged from the former European Economic Community (EEC) and European Community (EC), through the aforementioned Treaties, the Member States of the EU remain "Masters of the Treaties", so as to take up an – albeit controversial – linguistic image, which is found not least in the judicature of the Federal Constitutional Court.[31] Each Member State has the enduring quality of a sovereign state. However, under the conditions of digitization, Europeanization, and globalization, the concept of sovereignty does not stand in the way of a development in which formerly autonomous decision-making powers are limited, interdependent, and interrelated for the benefit of European integration and the common good that can only be effectively

---

26 It was not necessary to take a position on the draft directive "Media Ownership in the Internal Market" because this so-called Monti-plan was not promoted further by the Commission; on the genesis and content of this draft *Ress/Bröhmer*, Europäische Gemeinschaft und Medienvielfalt; *van Loon* in: EAI, Fernsehen und Medienkonzentration, p. 68 et seq.
27 Cf. OJ C 224 of 31.08.1992, p. 1 et seq.
28 Cf. OJ C 340 of 10.11.1997, p. 1 et seq.
29 Cf. OJ C 80 of 10.03.2001, p. 1 et seq.
30 Cf. OJ C 306 of 17.12.2007, p. 1 et seq.; most recent consolidated version OJ C 326 of 26.10.2012, p. 1 et seq.
31 BVerfGE 75, 223 (242); 89, 155 (190, 199); 123, 267 (370 et seq.); FCC, Judgment of the Second Senate of 5 May 2020, 2 BvR 859/15, para. 111; in the literature e.g. *Cremer* in: Calliess/Ruffert, Art. 48 TEU, para. 19; *Huber* in: VVDStRL 2001, 194, 222; *Kaufmann* in: Der Staat 1997, 521, 532; diff. op. *Everling*, Sind die Mitgliedstaaten der Europäischen Gemeinschaft noch Herren der Verträge?, p. 173 et seq.; *Franzius* in: Pechstein et al., Frankfurter Kommentar, Art. 48 TEU, para. 87 et seq.

achieved through cross-border cooperation.[32] In constitutional concordance, the Member States of the EU assume that there is no autonomous basis for the validity of EU law, which is of fundamental importance with regard to the competence order of the European constitutional order. Thus, the validity of Union law cannot be derived directly from the citizens of the Union or the EU itself, but is dependent in the Member States, both in the starting point and in the scope of its development, on an explicit order to apply the law in the respective Member State.[33] This European multilevel constitutionalism is thus characterized by a synthesis between the respective openness of the Member States' constitutional systems for a delimited and continuously delimitable program of European integration and a constitution of the EU[34] which for its part is not oriented toward an unrestricted integration perspective, but rather – regardless of dynamic options of interpretation – is bound to the purpose of an ever closer union below the qualitative level of unitary EU federalism. The diversity of Member State statehood remains untouched under the current EU Treaties framework[35] and the Member States' constitutional systems, which provide the Treaties with the possibility of regulation on Member State level.

---

32 In some cases, Member States' constitutional systems permit participation in European integration only on condition that the Member State retains sovereignty and its quality as a state; cf. on this with respect to Germany Art. 23(1) sentence 1, 3 in conjunction with Art. 79(3) GG; law-comparing *Kirchhof*, Die rechtliche Struktur der Europäischen Union als Staatenverbund, p. 899 fn. 16.

33 Cf. *Huber* in: VVDStRL 2001, 194, 214 et seq.; *Puttler* in: EuR 2004, 669, 671; *Schwarze*, Die Entstehung einer europäischen Verfassungsordnung, p. 25 et seq.; 109 et seq.; 287 et seq.; 339 et seq.; 389 et seq.

34 On this "constitutional" quality of the founding Treaties of the EU – regardless of the failure of a Constitutional Treaty – from the perspective of the CJEU cf. CJEU, case 294/83, *Parti écologiste "Les Verts" / European Parliament*, para. 23; opinion 1/91, Reports of cases 1991 I-6079 para. 21 (in each case "constitutional charter"); CJEU, joined cases C-402/05 P and C-415/05 P, *Yassin Abdullah Kadi and Al Barakaat International Foundation / Council of the European Union and Commission of the European Communities*, para. 285 ("constitutional principles of the EC Treaty"). In literature, cf. e.g. *Bieber/Kotzur* in: Bieber/Epiney/Haag/Kotzur, p. 100 et seq.; *Giegerich*, Europäische Verfassung und deutsche Verfassung im transnationalen Konstitutionalisierungsprozeß: Wechselseitige Rezeption, konstitutionelle Evolution und föderale Verflechtung, p. 149 et seq.

35 On the federal development trend in the constitutionalization of the EU cf. *Giegerich*, Europäische Verfassung und deutsche Verfassung im transnationalen Konstitutionalisierungsprozeß: Wechselseitige Rezeption, konstitutionelle Evolution und föderale Verflechtung, p. 230 et seq., 251 et seq.

B. Framework for the allocation of competences under EU primary law

Most of the Member States' constitutional systems provide their institutions with more or less strict guidelines as to the conditions under which they may require their State to take further steps toward integration. In Germany, these requirements can be found in Art. 23(1) sentence 1 of the Basic Law: Accordingly, to realize a united Europe, the Federal Republic of Germany participates in the development of the European Union, "that is committed to democratic, social and federal principles, to the rule of law and to the principle of subsidiarity and that guarantees a level of protection of basic rights essentially comparable to that afforded by this Basic Law". Part of this protection of basic rights is also the safeguarding of a free and diversity-oriented communication, as it is provided for in Art. 5 of the Basic Law. However, whether a positive imperative for an EU level media order is constitutionally prescribed in order to deepening Germany's integration readiness remains doubtful, since media federalism reflects the federal principles that the Basic Law's integration program is obliged to uphold. Furthermore, according to Art. 23(1) sentence 3 of the Basic Law, its Art. 79(2) and (3) applies with regards to the establishment of the European Union as well as to amendments to its Treaty foundations and comparable regulations which amend or supplement the content of the Basic Law or enable such amendments or supplements. According to Art. 79(3) of the Basic Law, an amendment to the Basic Law which affects the division of the Federation into Länder or the principles laid down in Arts. 1 and 20 of the Basic Law is inadmissible. At the interface of the integration perspective under Union law and fundamental norms of the Basic Law that are resistant to constitutional revision, and in view of the significance of the media order for the constitutional democratic and federal understanding in the Basic Law, this too speaks in favor of a reservation of at least German constitutional law over a final positive order of the media in the EU and its Member States by the EU. A similar reservation is likely to exist in other Member States' constitutional systems.

As long as and to the extent that control over the finality of the integration program lies with the Member States according to their constitutional law,[36] which – as will be shown in the following – is also recognized to some extent by the legal system of the EU itself, the Member States can only agree to a European integration program that develops along predictable

---

36 In a number of Member States, this understanding requires explicit constitutional amendments before the State can agree to a substantial enlargement or deepening of European integration; cf. *Gundel* in: EuR 1998, 371, 378 et seq.; *Huber* in: VVD-StRL 2001, 194, 215 et seq.; *Kirchhof*, Die rechtliche Struktur der Europäischen Union als Staatenverbund, p. 898 fn. 15; *Puttler* in: EuR 2004, 669, 672.

lines. This also applies to the media-regulatory aspects of the integration program. In Germany, the Federal Constitutional Court refers to this requirement with the term "determinability": Accordingly, sovereign rights may only be conferred for the implementation of a sufficiently determinable integration program.[37] This integration program must also be sufficiently defined with regard to a deepening of media regulation – regardless of the the need for adaptability for dynamic change, which both media regulation and the European integration program have in common.

3. Uniformity and primacy of Union law vs. constitution-based reserved power for control of Member States

The scope of the EU integration program defined by primary law with regard to the possibilities of media regulation is important not least in the case of a collision of member state safeguards as regards diversity on the one hand and possible positive integration via the EU's own diversity law and/or negative integration via the setting of barriers to the safeguarding of diversity in the Member States through the internal market and competition law of the EU on the other. In this respect, safeguards for diversity can as well be subject to a collision of national law and European law.

In its judicature, the CJEU early on – depending on the point of view – identified or constructed the principle of the primacy of Community, now Union law as one of the pillars of the Community legal order as a sui generis legal order. According to this principle, all primary and secondary law of the EU claims precedence over the law of the Member State, regardless of its rank, and thus also over national constitutional law, including the protection of fundamental rights.[38] In contrast to the constitutions of some Member States and the envisaged European Constitutional Treaty[39], the German Basic Law – in the same manner as the European Treaties

---

37 Cf. BVerfGE 89, 155 (184 et seq., 187) (Maastricht); cf. also Supreme Court of Denmark, judgment of 06.04.1998 (Maastricht), cipher 9.2, German translation in EuGRZ 1999, 49, 50.
38 Cf. e.g. CJEU, case 6/64, *Costa / E.N.E.L.*, para. 8 et seq.; CJEU, case 11/70, *Internationale Handelsgesellschaft mbH / Einfuhr- und Vorratsstelle für Getreide und Futtermittel*, para. 3; CJEU, case 106/77, *Amministrazione delle Finanze dello Stato / Simmenthal SpA*, para. 17 et seq. (settled case law).
39 Whose Art. I-6 read: "The Constitution and law adopted by the institutions of the Union in exercising competences conferred on it shall have primacy over the law of the Member States."

B. Framework for the allocation of competences under EU primary law

TEU[40] and TFEU[41] under the Lisbon Treaty – does not contain an explicit conflict-of-law rule for conflicts between German law, in particular German constitutional law, and European law. The Federal Constitutional Court, however, also recognizes the primacy of European law in its judicature – but only in principle and with different justification.[42] In view of the prominent constitutional significance of the protection of diversity in the German constitutional system, it is therefore not completely excluded from the outset that questions of primacy may arise with regard to the protection of diversity – just as is the case with other EU Member States whose recognition of primacy with regard to Union law is restricted by constitutional boundaries –, even if the potential cause of conflict and its resolution may differ from Member State to Member State.[43]

From the point of view of the FCC, the primacy of application under European law has also always been based on a constitutional authorization, now enshrined in Art. 23(1) of the Basic Law, so that it can only extend to European sovereignty exercised in Germany, including the control of media regulatory activities of the Länder, to the extent that the Federal Republic has agreed to it in the Treaty and was constitutionally permitted to do so. The FCC sees three reservations of control in this regard:

a) with regard to the EU protection of fundamental rights: In this respect, from Karlsruhe's perspective, the constitutional court's potential for control is subject to self-restriction only as long as and to the extent that a protection of fundamental rights generally comparable to the German standard is guaranteed at the EU level;

---

40 Consolidated version of the Treaty on European Union (TEU), OJ C 326 of 26.10.2012, p. 13–390, https://eur-lex.europa.eu/legal-content/EN/TXT/?uri=celex%3A12012M%2FTXT.
41 Consolidated version of the Treaty on the Functioning of the European Union (TFEU), OJ C 326 of 26.10.2012, p. 47–390, https://eur-lex.europa.eu/legal-content/EN/TXT/?uri=celex%3A12012E%2FTXT.
42 The FCC – unlike the CJEU – does not derive this precedence from the legal nature of the Community as an autonomous legal system, but bases it on the German order for the application of law. Cf. BVerfGE 73, 339 (374 et seq.); objecting *Pernice* in: VVDStRL 2001, 148, 183 et seq. In addition, in the view of the FCC, primacy is limited by the restrictions of the enabling provision of the Basic Law, and therefore does not apply where the fundamental structural principles of the Basic Law and the core of Art. 79(3) of the Basic Law, which cannot be subject to constitutional revision, are at issue. Cf. on the whole *Puttler* in: EuR 2004, 669, 684.
43 Cf. *Puttler* in: EuR 2004, 669, 684.

b) with regard to the EU exercise of competence ("ultra vires control"): Until the judgment of the FCC in the matter of government bond purchases by the European Central Bank (ECB) of 5 May 2020[44] there were apparently insurmountable obstacles to an exception to the primacy of application of Union law in its application and interpretation by the jurisdiction of the EU: in formal terms, the FCC made a referral to the CJEU and in material terms, an obvious transgression of competences, which as a result leads to a structural shift of competences in the relationship between the EU and the Member States, preconditions for the determination of an "outbreaking legal act" of the EU;

c) with regard to the constitutional identity of the German Basic Law, which in Germany is expressed in the so-called eternity clause of Art. 79(3) of the Basic Law and protects core areas of democracy and the rule of law, including the concept of human dignity in the fundamental rights system.[45]

4. Ultra vires action, no EU competence-competence and the principle of conferral

a. The principle of conferral and its significance for media regulation

In contrast to a State, the EU has no competence-competence. Therefore, the Union is also unable to create a legislative, administrative-executive or judicial competence to regulate media in general and media diversity in particular. Rather, in accordance with the "principle of conferral" enshrined in Art. 5(1) sentence 1, (2) TEU, the EU may only act within the limits of the competences that the Member States have conferred on it in the Treaties – TEU and TFEU – to achieve the objectives laid down therein.[46] All competences not conferred upon the Union in the Treaties remain with the Member States under Art. 4(1), 5(2) sentence 2 TEU. These primary law provisions confirm incidentally that prior to the beginning of the European integration process, all powers were originally held by the Member States. The respective provisions thus also confirm the principle

---

44 FCC, Judgment of the Second Senate of 5 May 2020, 2 BvR 859/15, para. 1–237, http://www.bverfg.de/e/rs20200505_2bvr085915.html.
45 Cf. *Calliess* in: NVwZ 2019, 684, 689 et seq.
46 Cf. on this recently also *Nielsen*, Die Medienvielfalt als Aspekt der Wertesicherung der EU, p. 35 et seq.

B. Framework for the allocation of competences under EU primary law

of the Member States' "universal competence" for sovereign action – regardless of the respective national division of powers in federally constituted Member States or States with local self-government.

This fundamental division of competences according to the principle of conferral affects the relationship between the EU and the Member States, but is obviously also important for the scope of the EU institutions' options for action. The actions of the EU and its institutions must remain within the limits of its powers: Thus, according to Art. 3(6) TEU, the EU shall pursue its objectives by appropriate means commensurate with the competences which are conferred upon it in the Treaties. According to Art. 13(2) sentence 1 TEU, each EU institution in turn shall act within the limits of the powers conferred on it in the Treaties, and in conformity with the procedures, conditions and objectives set out in them. If one of these two basic provisions is infringed, there may be the possibility of an action for annulment before the CJEU.

According to the principle of conferral, for every legal act of the EU – i.e. also for non-binding legal acts – not only an explicit competence but also the correct legal basis must be sought.[47] The search for the right legal basis is of utmost importance as the choice of the correct legal basis can determine, among other things, the voting procedure in the Council of the EU – unanimity with the "veto option" of each Member State or majority – as well as the exact form of the institutional balance with regards to the respective legal act. To this extent, problems of vertical conflicts of jurisdiction (between Member States and the EU) can mix with questions of horizontal conflicts of jurisdiction (between the EU institutions involved in the legislative process).[48]

However, neither the TEU nor the TFEU contain a negative catalog of areas comprehensively excluded from EU law. In the European Treaties, there is neither an *exception culturelle*, i.e. a cultural exception in general, nor a media-related exception in particular. As well, a provision for the media regulation comparable with Art. 4(2) TEU is also missing: According to this provision, "national security remains the sole responsibility of each Member State".[49] When interpreted systematically, this does not apply to media regulation in a corresponding manner. Thus, the principle of con-

---

47 Cf. e.g. *Breier* in: EuR 1995, 47, 47 et seq.; *Ruffert* in: Jura 1994, 635, 635 et seq.
48 Cf. *Calliess* in: Berliner Online-Beiträge zum Europarecht 25 (2005), p. 3; *Nettesheim* in: EuR 1993, 243, 243 et seq.
49 With regard to Art. 4(2) TEU, the CJEU has recently – in connection with data protection law – reaffirmed – in reference to earlier case law – that although it is up to the Member States of the EU to define their essential security interests and

ferral does not per se impede EU media regulation from the outset. However, the more the EU regulates the media in a way that is relevant to the regulation of diversity, the greater the burden on the EU in terms of safeguarding the clauses of the European Treaties, which are designed to protect Member State regulatory leeway.

From the perspective of European law, the question of who decides whether EU institutions have remained within the framework of the integration program as provided for in primary law or acted ultra vires when adopting a Union act must be decided by the CJEU with ultimate binding effect in order to ensure the primacy and uniformity of the Union legal order. However, this understanding of European law has never been fully recognized, at least not by the FCC. The imperative of consideration for Member States' "Mastery" of the Treaties, which in the view of the constitutional judges in Karlsruhe had been assigned under the Basic Law, is indeed unanimously accepted by both European law and the constitutional courts in so far as they classify EU action ultra vires as unlawful. Nonetheless, the respective boundaries of the integration program and the question of who is allowed to define them conclusively are the subject of ongoing and recently intensified debate, not least in the wake of the FCC's decision on the ECB's government bonds purchase program. Even before that deci-

---

to take measures to ensure their internal and external security, the mere fact that a national measure has been taken to protect national security cannot render Union law inapplicable and exempt the Member States from the need to respect that law. As a result, the CJEU adopts a narrow interpretation of Art. 4(2) TEU in this regard, while protecting as much as possible acts of secondary law against application of Art. 4(2) TEU with the objective of limiting their applicability (cf. CJEU, case C-623/17, judgment of 06.10.2020, *Privacy International*, ECLI:EU:C:2020:790, para. 44 et seq.). The CJEU acknowledges that the importance of the objective of maintaining national security enshrined in Art. 4(2) TEU goes beyond the importance of other objectives also recognized in EU data protection law in order to justify exceptions to data protection obligations, such as the fight against crime in general, including serious crime, and the protection of public security. Subject to compliance with the other requirements laid down in Art. 52(1) of the CFR, the objective of safeguarding national security is therefore capable of justifying measures which involve more serious encroachments on fundamental rights than those which could be justified by those other objectives. However, in order to comply with the requirement of proportionality, according to which the exceptions and limitations to the protection of personal data must remain within the limits of what is strictly necessary, national legislation which constitutes an interference with the fundamental rights enshrined in Arts. 7 and 8 of the Charter would have to satisfy the requirements of transparency and proportionality (cf. ibid., para. 74 et seq.).

B. Framework for the allocation of competences under EU primary law

sion, the FCC has emphasized that due to its constitutional mandate it was obliged to reserve a final and binding power of review in particular exceptional cases.[50] In the event of an an intensification of EU media regulation towards the direction of fully harmonized digital safeguarding of diversity, it cannot be ruled out that such a power of review may also take on a media-related orientation or even be extended to that regard, after the specific question of whether the funding instruments for European works and independent productions provided for in the then EEC Television Directive are still covered by the internal market competence of the EU lost much of their significance in terms of integration law after the FCC ruling of 22 March 1995[51].

In this context, however, it must be taken into account from the outset that the division of competences under EU law is fixed in a way that is resistant to digitization: Digital transformation does not create additional EU competence titles. On the other hand, existing competence titles are not limited to exclusively dealing with just those issues that were known at the time the founding Treaties were adopted. The standards of originalism or historical-traditional textualism[52] are unknown to the interpretation methodology of EU law. Such an understanding of originary interpretation of the EU's competences can be reconciled with a historical, but not with a teleological interpretation. The interpretation of primary EU law is always an interpretation in present time and open to new challenges. This openness to interpretation with regard to digitization has its limits, however – comparable to the interpretation of EU law that is open to public international law and the interpretation of national law in conformity with European and constitutional law – in the wording of the competence provisions.

---

50 Cf. BVerfGE 73, 339 (370) (Solange II); 75, 223 (234) (Kloppenburg).
51 Cf. BVerfGE 92, 203 (242 et seq.); on this *Bethge*, Deutsche Bundesstaatlichkeit und Europäische Union. Bemerkungen über die Entscheidung des Bundesverfassungsgerichts zur EG-Fernsehrichtlinie, p. 55 et seq.; *Deringer* in: ZUM 1995, 316, 316 et seq.; *Gerkrath* in: RTDE 1995, 539, 539 et seq.; *Kresse/Heinze* in: ZUM 1995, 394, 394 et seq.; *Martín y Pérez de Nanclares* in: Revista de Instituciones Europeas 1995, 887, 887 et seq.; *Müller-Terpitz*, Ein Karlsruher "Orakel" zum Bundesstaat im europäischen Staatenverbund, p. 568 et seq.; *Trautwein* in: ZUM 1995, 614, 614 et seq.; *Winkelmann* in: DöV 1996, 1, 1 et seq.
52 Cf. on this with regard to the Supreme Court's modes of interpretation of the US Constitution *Dregger*, Die Verfassungsinterpretation am US-Supreme Court, p. 40 et seq.; *Riecken*, Verfassungsgerichtsbarkeit in der Demokratie, p. 98 et seq.

b. Monitoring compliance with the principle of conferral through the requirement of democracy as interpreted by the FCC

The possibility of transferring sovereign rights to the EU, as provided for in Art. 23 of the Basic Law, may mean that not only tasks at the parliamentary level of the Federation but also those of the Länder are transferred to the supranational bodies of the EU. As a result, certain tasks can no longer be carried out by the members of the Länder parliaments, be it in the enactment of autonomous Länder legislation on media regulation or in the ratification of media-related state treaties. In such cases of transfer of legislative authority, state power no longer emanates from the people, or at least only to a limited extent.

This problem of democratic theory as to the Basic Law's openness to European integration was first taken account of by the FCC in its Maastricht decision by recognizing a power to constitutional complaint based on the violation of the principle of democracy on the occasion of legal acts transferring sovereignty to the EU. The FCC considers that the principle of democracy did not prevent the Federal Republic from being part of an international community. The only prerequisite for this was legitimacy and influence by the population also at the supranational level (within the "*Staatenverbund*" EU).[53] The FCC also points to the relationship between the Arts. 23(1) sentence 3 and 79(3) of the Basic Law: The possibility of openness towards European integration as enshrined in the Basic Law was tied to the core of its Art. 79(3), which cannot be subject of constitutional revision. This Article identified the limits of the authorization to participate in the development of the European Union. Thus, according to the Court's considerations, a discrepancy between Art. 38 and Art. 23 of the Basic Law was avoided.[54]

This judicature developed by the FCC with a view to the transfer of federal competences is equally important with regard to the transfer of competences of the Länder. The core of the German constitutional system, which is resistant to any revision and cannot be amended even in the EU law context, may as well include the element of a federal suspension in media regulation – not least in view of the constitutional-historical dimension of "never again" totalitarian rule. An opening of the German constitutional state to a full harmonization of media regulation by the EU, such as is the case in particular when abandoning the previous regulation by direc-

---

53 Cf. BVerfGE 89, 155 (184).
54 Cf. BVerfGE 89, 155 (179).

tives with the ability to take into account particularities of the Member States, would therefore – also in view of the democratic relevance of media federalism – be a process with considerable potential risks under constitutional law, notably with regard to the FCC.

Its reference to the connection between Arts. 23, 38 and 79(3) of the Basic Law is, moreover, accompanied by a special reference by the FCC to the requirement that the EU has no competence-competence and that it complies with the principle of conferral.[55] In this context, the FCC emphasizes that Union legal acts that are not covered by the Consent Act do not have any binding domestic effect and are therefore not applicable.[56] Accordingly, the Federal Constitutional Court was to examine whether legal acts of the European institutions and bodies remain within the limits of the powers granted to them or break out of them.[57] In addition, the Maastricht ruling reserves the right of the FCC to review Union institutions' actions in order to determine whether they are in accordance with the Consent Act.

5. Media regulation and the catalog of EU competences

a. Introduction

A formal protective mechanism to safeguard the principle of conferral and to ward off trends towards an EU competence-competence, introduced with the Treaty of Lisbon, is the categorization and classification of the competences of the European Union into exclusive and shared competences as well as competences for supporting, coordinating or supplementing measures.[58]

In its "Laeken Declaration", the European Council had explicitly mandated the Convention on the Future of the European Union (the "European Convention") to develop a better division and definition of compe-

---

55 Cf. BVerfGE 89, 155 (181).
56 Cf. BVerfGE 89, 155 (195).
57 Cf. BVerfGE 58, 1 (30 et seq.); 75, 223 (235, 242); 89, 155 (188); as well as *Moench/Ruttloff* in: Rengeling/Middeke/Gellermann, § 36 para. 28 et seq., 46 et seq.
58 Cf. BVerfGE 123, 267 (382) with reference to *Rossi*, Die Kompetenzverteilung zwischen der Europäischen Gemeinschaft und ihren Mitgliedstaaten, in: Scholz, Europa als Union des Rechts – Eine notwendige Zwischenbilanz im Prozeß der Vertiefung und Erweiterung, 1999, p. 196, 201; cf. furthermore e.g. also *Folz* in: Gamper et al., p. 641 et seq.; *Nettesheim* in: von Bogdandy/Bast, p. 415 et seq.

tences in the European Union.⁵⁹ In this context, it should also be examined how to prevent a "creeping expansion of the competence of the Union" and its "encroachment on the exclusive areas of competence of the Member States and [...] regions".⁶⁰ At the same time, the Convention should also take into account the need for the EU to be able to react to fresh challenges and developments and to explore new policy areas.⁶¹ These megatrends undoubtedly include digitization – also in its effects on the media ecosystem.

Even though the Constitutional Treaty developed as a result of the European Convention failed, the Treaty of Lisbon now follows on from these reflections on competences and explicitly clarifies the division of competences between the EU and its Member States.⁶² These competences are divided into three main categories:

- exclusive competences;
- shared competences and
- supporting competences.

The media are not explicitly mentioned as such in either these competence catalogs of the EU or elsewhere in the European Treaties.⁶³ Only the CFR breaks through this restraint under European law with regard to the allocation of competences in favor of the EU for the media and their regulation. This is remarkable not least since constitutions of EU Member States with a federal structure are familiar with media regulation that is also based on competence,⁶⁴ or – as in Germany – it has been clarified in a way that is also familiar to the European constitutional legislature that it is not the

---

59 Laeken Declaration on the Future of the European Union, Annex I to the Presidency Conclusions, European Council (Laeken), 14 and 15 December 2001, SN 300/1/01 REV 1, p. 21.
60 Laeken Declaration, p. 22; on the criticism of a gradual expansion of the EU's competences see e.g. BVerfGE 89, 155 (210); *Rupp* in: JZ 2003, 18, 18 et seq.
61 Laeken Declaration, p. 22; on the whole cf. *Puttler* in: EuR 2004, 669, 686.
62 Cf. on this also recently *Nielsen*, Die Medienvielfalt als Aspekt der Wertesicherung der EU, p. 39 et seq.
63 Cf. on this also *Nielsen*, Die Medienvielfalt als Aspekt der Wertesicherung der EU, p. 47 et seq.
64 Under the Austrian constitutional system, the enactment of regulations in the field of broadcasting (both in terms of content and technology) falls within the competence of the federal government. This results on the one hand from Art. 10(1) No. 9 B-VG "Postal and Telecommunications Services", on the other hand from Art. I of the Federal Constitutional Law on Safeguarding of the Independence of Broadcasting (of 10 July 1974, StF: BGBl. No. 396/1974 (NR: GP XIII AB 1265, p. 111. BR: p. 334.)), according to which more detailed provisions for

B. Framework for the allocation of competences under EU primary law

central state level but the subordinate units of the federal state that are competent for media regulation. This in itself suggests – without prejudice to any obligations to protect fundamental rights – that the European Treaties should be cautious in granting the EU media-related regulatory powers. However, it does not necessarily exclude the recourse of EU competences also to the field of media regulation as will be described in the following.

The transparency conveyed by the categorization of competences is, admittedly, limited not least by the fact that unwritten competences continue to exist[65], that the "parallel" competences claimed by both the Member States and the European Union are not clearly assigned to one competence category, and that the so-called open method of coordination is not at all referred to. "However, these derogations from the systematising fundamental approach do not affect the principle of conferral, and their nature and extent also does not call the objective of clear delimitation of competences into question."[66]

b. Exclusive competences of the EU and media regulation

According to Art. 2(1) TFEU, when the Treaties confer on the Union exclusive competence in a specific area, only the Union may legislate and adopt legally binding acts, the Member States being able to do so themselves only if so empowered by the Union or for the implementation of Union acts. It is true that the catalog of exclusive competences laid down in Art. 3 TFEU does not contain an explicit reference to media. However, a relevance of this catalog for media regulation is not excluded from the outset insofar as the EU has

- according to Art. 3(1)(a) TFEU exclusive competence in the area of customs union pursuant to Art. 31 et seq. TFEU,

---

broadcasting and its organisation are to be laid down by federal law. The Federal Constitutional Law on Safeguarding of the Independence of Broadcasting aims at declaring broadcasting a public task, which is to be fulfilled in compliance with the principles of objectivity, impartiality and diversity of opinion.

65 Cf. e.g. *Nettesheim* in: von Bogdandy/Bast, p. 415, 433 et seq.; *Rossi* in: Calliess/Ruffert, Art. 352 TFEU, para. 52; *Weber* in: Blanke/Mangiameli, Art. 5 TEU, para. 28; *Dony*, Droit de l'Union européenne, para. 120 et seq.
66 FCC, Judgment of the Second Senate of 30 June 2009, 2 BvE 2/08 and others (Lisbon), para. 303.

- according to Art. 3(1)(b) TFEU exclusive competence in the area of the establishing of the competition rules necessary for the functioning of the internal market pursuant to Part Three, Title VII, Chapter 1 of the TFEU,
- according to Art. 3(1)(c) TFEU exclusive competence in the area of monetary policy for the Member States whose currency is the euro,[67]
- according to Art. 3(1)(e) TFEU exclusive competence in the area of common commercial policy pursuant to Art. 207 TFEU and
- according to Art. 3(2) TFEU exclusive competence for the conclusion of an international agreement in terms of Art. 216 TFEU, when its conclusion is provided for in a legislative act of the Union or is necessary to

---

67 § 14(1) of the Bundesbank Act provides, that "[w]ithout prejudice to Article 128 (1) of the [TFEU], the Deutsche Bundesbank shall have the sole right to issue banknotes in the area in which this Act is law" and that banknotes denominated in euro shall be "the sole unrestricted legal tender". The State Treaty of the Länder on Public Broadcasting Fees (RBStV) stipulates in § 2(1) that the owner of each dwelling has to pay a broadcasting fee. § 9(2) RBStV authorizes the regional broadcasting to establish, by means of a regulation, the procedures for payment of the radio and television licence fee. In turn, the statutes issued on this basis stipulate that the party liable for the contribution can pay the broadcasting contributions in a cashless manner only. In the preliminary ruling proceedings currently before the CJEU against this background, the questions are now whether the exclusive competence under Art. 3(1)(c) TFEU covers monetary law and the definition of the legal tender status of the single currency, what effects the legal tender status of euro banknotes has and whether and, if so, within which limits the Member States whose currency is the euro may adopt national legislation restricting the use of euro banknotes.
In his Opinion, Advocate General *Pitruzzella* expresses doubts as to whether the exclusion without exception of the payment of the broadcasting fee in cash can be justified in the light of the importance of the exclusive competence under Art. 3(1)(c) TFEU for monetary powers. *Pitruzzella* considers that limits on payments in euro banknotes for reasons of public interest are compatible with the concept of legal tender status of euro banknotes as established in EU monetary law only if they do not lead *de jure* or *de facto* to the complete withdrawal of euro banknotes, if they are adopted for reasons of public interest and if other legal means exist for the settlement of monetary debts. They must also be capable of achieving the public interest objective pursued and must not go beyond what is necessary to achieve that objective. The Advocate General doubts the latter, if the function of social integration, which cash fulfills for vulnerable persons e.g. elderly fellow citizens, should not have been adequately considered when abolishing the cashless payment option; cf. Opinion of Advocate General *Pitruzzella* of 29.09.2020, CJEU, joined cases C-422/19 (*Dietrich / Hessischer Rundfunk*) and C-423/19 (*Häring / Hessischer Rundfunk*), ECLI:EU:C:2020:756, para. 162 et seq.

B. Framework for the allocation of competences under EU primary law

enable the Union to exercise its internal competence, or in so far as its conclusion may affect common rules or alter their scope.[68]

The importance of the EU's exclusive trade competence and its potentially restrictive scope as to Member States' regulatory competences, even in areas such as education or culture, was again emphasized by the CJEU in a judgment of 6 October 2020 in connection with a Hungarian education policy measure that is controversial beyond questions of the EU Treaties' provisions on competences, particularly in terms of fundamental rights and the EU's fundamental values. The CJEU emphasized there that it has jurisdiction to hear and determine actions alleging violations of WTO law. In this context, the CJEU reiterated that an international agreement entered into by the Union was an integral part of EU law – such as the agreement establishing the WTO, of which the GATS is a part. Next, with regard to the relationship between the exclusive competence of the EU in the field of the common commercial policy and the broad competence of the Member States in the field of education, the CJEU clarified that the commitments entered into under the GATS, including those relating to the liberalisation of trade in private educational services, fall within the EU's exclusive competence of common commercial policy.[69]

There is little to argue against the assessment that the CJEU is unlikely to deviate from this attribution, which in the case of a collision would amount to an unrestricted precedence of trade policy obligations, when attributing exclusive trade competence of the EU and Member State competences in the field of culture, including aspects of media related to culture and diversity. This makes it all the more important to limit the EU's trade policy negotiation mandates in a way that preserves culture and diversity. Accordingly, the Member States take account of the risk potential of the EU's exclusive competence for the common commercial policy by regularly excluding audiovisual services from the negotiating mandate given to the EU by the Council of the EU.[70]

The resulting exclusion of audiovisual services from the scope of free trade rules protects the cultural sovereignty of the Member States. How-

---

68 Cf. on this *Calliess* in: id./Ruffert, Art. 3 TFEU, para. 5 et seq., 14 et seq.; *Klamert* in: Kellerbauer/id./Tomkin, Art. 3 TFEU, para. 16 et seq.; *Pelka* in: Schwarze, Art. 3 TFEU, para. 7 et seq., 14 et seq.; *Streinz/Mögele* in: Streinz, Art. 3 TFEU, para. 4 et seq., 11 et seq.
69 Cf. CJEU, case C-66/18, *Commission / Hungary*, para. 68 et seq.
70 Cf. on this also in context of Brexit: *Cole/Ukrow/Etteldorf*, Research for CULT Committee – Audiovisual Sector and Brexit: the Regulatory Environment, p. 14 et seq.

ever, this extensive protection comes with a not inconsiderable shortcoming: The comprehensive removal of the cultural sector from the trade agreements, as demanded by organized culture and achieved by broadcast and telemedia engaged in journalism, is at the same time associated with risks as regards the promotion of a culture of democratic discussion in the age of globalization on the one hand, and the strengthening of populist tendencies and new digital forms of opinion manipulation on the other.[71]

c. Shared competences of the EU and media regulation

According to Art. 2 (2) sentence 1 TFEU, when the Treaties confer on the Union a competence shared with the Member States in a specific area, the Union and the Member States may legislate and adopt legally binding acts in that area. Sentence 2 stipulates that Member States shall exercise their competence to the extent that the Union has not exercised its competence. Sentence three finally provides for Member States' ability to again exercise their competence to the extent that the Union has decided to cease exercising its competence.

According to Art. 4 (1) TFEU, the Union shall share competence with the Member States where the Treaties confer on it a competence which does not relate to the areas referred to in Arts. 3 and 6 TFEU. Neither of these contain such a specific provision on media-related competence. It is true that the catalog of shared competences regulated in Art. 4 (2) to (4) TFEU does not contain any explicit reference to media either. However, a relevance of the catalog of main areas of shared competence regulated in Art. 4 (2) TFEU for media regulation cannot be excluded from the outset as the EU has

- according to Art. 4(2)(a) TFEU a shared competence in the area of the internal market pursuant to Art. 26(2) in conjunction with Art. 114 TFEU,
- according to Art. 4(2)(f) TFEU a shared competence in the area of consumer protection pursuant to Art. 169 TFEU and

---

[71] Cf. on the whole *Ukrow*, Ceterum censeo: CETA prohibendam esse? Audiovisuelle Medien im europäisch-kanadischen Freihandelssystem, p. 2 et seq.

B. Framework for the allocation of competences under EU primary law

- according to Art. 4(2)(j) TFEU a shared competence as regards the area of freedom, security and justice pursuant to Art. 67 et seq. TFEU.[72]

The internal market competence of the EU is particularly important in its previous legislation on media. According to Art. 26(1) TFEU, the Union shall adopt measures with the aim of establishing or ensuring the functioning of the internal market, in accordance with the relevant provisions of the Treaties. To this effect, according to its definition in Art. 26(2) TFEU, the internal market shall comprise an area without internal frontiers in which the free movement of goods, persons, services and capital is ensured in accordance with the provisions of the Treaties. Both the AVMSD[73] and the ECD[74] are based on EU competence provisions with regard to the free movement of services and the freedom of establishment as part of the internal market. In this respect, they complied with the established case law of the CJEU.

In view of the digitization of the media and the development of new business and communication models of a media nature, the shared competence of the EU in the areas of research and technological development pursuant to Art. 179 et seq. TFEU regulated in Art. 4(3) TFEU[75] can also be significant for media regulation. However, in the field of research and technological development, the Union's competence extends only to the adoption of measures, in particular to the preparation and implementation of programmes, without the exercise of that competence preventing the Member States from exercising theirs.

---

72 Cf. on this *Calliess* in: id./Ruffert, Art. 4 TFEU, para. 4 et seq., 14, 18; *Klamert* in: Kellerbauer/id./Tomkin, Art. 4 TFEU, para. 3, 8, 12; *Pelka* in: Schwarze, Art. 4 TFEU, para. 6, 11, 15.
73 Both Directive 2010/13/EU and amending Directive (EU) 2018/1808 are "[h]aving regard to the Treaty on the Functioning of the European Union, and in particular Article 53(1) and Article 62 thereof". On the details of the regulatory content and objectives, see chapter D.II.2.
74 Directive 2000/31/EC is "[h]aving regard to the Treaty establishing the European Community, and in particular Articles 47(2) (today: Art. 53(1) TFEU), 55 (today: Art. 62 TFEU) and 95 (today: Art. 114 TFEU) thereof". On the details of the regulatory content and objectives, see chapter D.II.1.
75 Cf. on this *Calliess* in: id./Ruffert, Art. 4 TFEU, para. 20; *Klamert* in: Kellerbauer/id./Tomkin, Art. 4 TFEU, para. 15; *Pelka* in: Schwarze, Art. 4 TFEU, para. 17; *Dony*, Droit de l'Union européenne, para. 136.

d. In particular: Intensifying protection in the area of the digital single market

A Member State may only deviate from secondary law adopted in the context of legal harmonisation in the internal market within the framework of Art. 114(4) to (10) TFEU, providing for an even more intensified protection on domestic level: This clause allows Member States to maintain or introduce stricter national provisions for the protection of important legal interests in the sense of a "unilateral national action"[76] despite the fact that legislation has been harmonized at Union level. The following requirements must be met:

- The maintenance of existing stricter national provisions must be justified by major needs referred to in Art. 36 TFEU or relating to the protection of the environment or the working environment (Art. 114(4) TFEU).
- When introducing stricter national provisions, new scientific evidence relating to the protection of the environment or the working environment must be available and the emergence of a problem specific to the Member State concerned after the adoption of the harmonization measure must be demonstrated (Art. 114(5) TFEU).
- The national provisions must be notified to the Commission and approved by it in accordance with the procedure laid down in Art. 114(6) TFEU. The Commission has to take a decision within six months of the notification, after having verified whether or not the national provision are a means of arbitrary discrimination or a disguised restriction on trade between Member States and whether or not they shall constitute an obstacle to the functioning of the internal market. In the absence of a decision by the Commission within six months, the national provision shall be deemed to have been approved. Before approval, a Member State is not entitled to apply the stricter national provision ("suspensory effect").[77]

The adoption of new national legislation following harmonization, as has been done in the field of the development of a (digital) media and commu-

---

[76] Cf. on this *Herrnfeld* in: Schwarze, Art. 114 TFEU, para. 87 et seq.; *Korte* in: Calliess/Ruffert, Art. 114 TFEU, para. 68 et seq.; *Terhechte* in: Pechstein et al., Frankfurter Kommentar, Art. 114 TFEU, para. 80 et seq.; *Kellerbauer* in: id./Klamert/Tomkin, Art. 114 TFEU, para. 48 et seq.; *Dony*, Droit de l'Union européenne, para. 723 et seq.

[77] Cf. CJEU, case C-41/93, *France / Commission*, para. 30.

B. Framework for the allocation of competences under EU primary law

nications internal market, especially by the AVMSD and the ECD, is therefore subject to particularly strict conditions, as such legislation on Member State level would increase the risk to the functioning of the internal market. Naturally, the Union institutions could not take account of national legislation when drawing up the harmonization measure. In this case, the requirements set out in Art. 36 TFEU in particular cannot be invoked. Only reasons of protection of the environment or the working environment are permissible.[78]

That these protective intensification clauses have or will have practical relevance in the field of media regulation at present or in the future is not apparent, at least with regard to the adoption of new legislation in the field of European coordination of communications and media law of the Member States. This may, however, be different for the maintenance of existing Member State provisions, especially if they – e.g. in the defense against media attacks on a free democratic discourse, such as those which can occur, for example, through disinformation and fake news – are aimed towards the protection of "public morality, public policy and public security" within the meaning of Art. 36 sentence 1 TFEU, functioning as components of a "well-fortified democracy 4.0"[79]. Moreover, from a systematic and teleological point of view, it is worth noting that if the sovereignty of the Member States is protected in areas such as the protection of the working environment or environmental protection or in (other) areas addressed by Art. 36 TFEU, which in non-economic terms are significantly less relevant than culture and the media, this must be possible *a fortiori* for the cultural and media sector.

e. Supporting competences of the EU and media regulation

Finally, according to Art. 6 sentence 1 TFEU, the Union shall have competence to carry out actions to support, coordinate or supplement the actions of the Member States. The EU's action in this area of competence can therefore only be supplementary and requires prior action by the Member States. Moreover, without prejudice to the obligation of loyalty which ap-

---

[78] Cf. CJEU, case C-512/99, *Germany / Commission*, para. 40 et seq.; case C-3/00, *Denmark / Commission*, para. 57 et seq. See in particular GCEU, joined cases T-366/03 and T-235/04, *Land Oberösterreich and Republic of Austria / Commission*; CJEU, joined cases C-439/05 P and C-454/05 P, *Land Oberösterreich and Republic of Austria / Commission*.
[79] Cf. on this *Ukrow* in: ZEuS 2021, p. 65, 65 et seq.

plies in this type of competence also, EU action does not constitute a barrier to national action. These measures with a European objective can also be taken, in accordance with Art. 6 sentence 2 (c) TFEU, in the field of "culture" and, under letter (e) of the provision, in the field of "education [and] vocational training". Linked to this provision on competence are Art. 165 (relating to education only and not also to vocational training) and Art. 167 TFEU (relating to culture).[80]

For an understanding of these competences, Art. 2(5) TFEU is also of relevance: This Article, in its first sentence, emphasizes in the first place that in those areas where, under the conditions laid down in the Treaties, the Union shall have competence to carry out actions to support, coordinate or supplement the actions of the Member States, it does so without thereby superseding Member States' competence in these areas. The Article's second sentence specifies that "[l]egally binding acts of the Union adopted on the basis of the provisions of the Treaties relating to these areas shall not entail harmonisation of Member States' laws or regulations".[81] This applies not least to the educational and cultural sectors. It would therefore be inadmissible to harmonize EU law explicitly on the basis of media freedom and diversity regulation rather than on the basis of the internal market, competition, taxation or any other EU competence title that explicitly permits legal harmonization.

f. In particular: Media literacy in the focus of EU regulation

Even for non-binding EU acts, the provisions on competence of the EU and their respective boundaries must be respected. This is also true with regard to the EU's ongoing efforts to strengthen media literacy.

Already the *Recommendation 2006/952/EC of the European Parliament and of the Council of 20 December 2006 on the protection of minors and human dignity and on the right of reply in relation to the competitiveness of the European audiovisual and on-line information services industry* included a number of possible measures to promote media literacy, such as e.g. continuing ed-

---

80 Cf. on this *Calliess* in: id./Ruffert, Art. 6 TFEU, para. 7, 9; *Klamert* in: Kellerbauer/id./Tomkin, Art. 6 TFEU, para. 6, 8; *Pelka* in: Schwarze, Art. 6 TFEU, para. 8, 10.
81 Cf. on this *Calliess* in: id./Ruffert, Art. 2 TFEU, para. 19 et seq.; *Häde* in: Pechstein et al., Frankfurter Kommentar, Art. 2 TFEU, para. 49 et seq.; *Pelka* in: Schwarze, Art. 2 TFEU, para. 22 et seq.; *Klamert* in: Kellerbauer/id./Tomkin, Art. 2 TFEU, para. 15; *Dony*, Droit de l'Union européenne, para. 139.

ucation of teachers and trainers, specific Internet training aimed at children from a very early age, including sessions open to parents, or the organization of national campaigns aimed at citizens, involving all communications media, to provide information on using the Internet responsibly.

In the 2010 Audiovisual Media Services Directive[82], media literacy was addressed for the first time in the legally binding audiovisual law of the EU. Art. 33 sentence 1 of this Directive provided for a regular report by the European Commission on the application of this Directive every three years, whereby the Commission if necessary, make[s] further proposals to adapt it to developments in the field of audiovisual media services, in particular in the light of recent technological developments, the competitiveness of the sector *and levels of media literacy in all Member States (emphasis by authors)*.

Thus, the Directive also directly addressed the connection between the teaching of media literacy and the effective safeguarding of protected interests such as the protection of minors from harmful media and media consumer protection.

In the recitals to the Directive, the EU further considered the understanding of media literacy and its meaning in the media context. Recital 47 read as follows:

> 'Media literacy' refers to skills, knowledge and understanding that allow consumers to use media effectively and safely. Media-literate people are able to exercise informed choices, understand the nature of content and services and take advantage of the full range of opportunities offered by new communications technologies. They are better able to protect themselves and their families from harmful or offensive material. Therefore the development of media literacy in all sections of society should be promoted and its progress followed closely.

Even if this initiative appeared to be welcome in a protection-oriented manner, it must not be overlooked that a certain definitional approach to the approximation of the regulation of media literacy in the Member

---

82 Directive 2010/13/EU of the European Parliament and of the Council of 10 March 2010 on the coordination of certain provisions laid down by law, regulation or administrative action in Member States concerning the provision of audiovisual media services (Audiovisual Media Services Directive), OJ L 95 of 15.04.2010, p. 1–24.
For details on the history of the directive and the new rules for the promotion of media literacy in the context of the 2018 reform cf. below, chapters D.II.2.a and D.II.2.d(3).

States was thereby achieved – a harmonization that is excluded by primary law in both the educational and cultural sectors as areas of supporting competence of the EU.

This process of gradually dissolving the purely supportive competence has been intensified by the 2018 reform of the AVMSD, an approach which is doubtful in terms of EU legal competences.[83] This is because its Art. 33 a, for the first time, enshrines a legally binding obligation of the Member States to take measures themselves to develop media literacy – combined with a competence of the Commission to issue guidelines regarding the scope of the Member States' reporting obligation to the Commission:

> (1) Member States shall promote and take measures for the development of media literacy skills.
> (2) By 19 December 2022 and every three years thereafter, Member States shall report to the Commission on the implementation of paragraph 1.
> (3) The Commission shall, after consulting the Contact Committee, issue guidelines regarding the scope of such reports.

To explain these obligations, recital 59 of the amending directive is significant. It reads:

> 'Media literacy' refers to skills, knowledge and understanding that allow citizens to use media effectively and safely. In order to enable citizens to access information and to use, critically assess and create media content responsibly and safely, citizens need to possess advanced media literacy skills. Media literacy should not be limited to learning about tools and technologies, but should aim to equip citizens with the critical thinking skills required to exercise judgment, analyse complex realities and recognise the difference between opinion and fact. It is therefore necessary that both media service providers and video-sharing platforms providers, in cooperation with all relevant stakeholders, promote the development of media literacy in all sections of society, for citizens of all ages, and for all media and that progress in that regard is followed closely.

Member States' obligation to promote under Art. 33a(1) of the Directive thus takes on a more concrete form, which is problematic in view of the mere supporting competence.

---

83 For the content of the regulation cf. chapter D.II.2.d(3).

B. Framework for the allocation of competences under EU primary law

The path towards an increasing shift from mere EU support to the shaping of media literacy at the intersection of the EU's cultural and educational competences is continued in the conclusions on "media literacy in an ever-changing world" adopted by the Council of the EU on 25 May 2020.[84] In concrete terms, these read:

> The Council of the European Union ... invites Member States ... in due compliance with the principle of subsidiarity, to
> ...
> • support the establishment and development of media literacy networks (national, regional, local, thematic) in order to bring together relevant stakeholders and enable them to cooperate and develop sustainable and long-term viable media literacy projects and initiatives;
> • develop a lifelong-learning approach to media literacy for all ages and provide support in that context for pilot and research projects, in order to create or develop and assess new methodologies, actions and content adapted to the specific needs of targeted groups;
> ...
> • improve existing training models, and if necessary design new ones, for the development of digital skills within the European cultural and creative industries in order to foster the effective use of innovative technologies and keep pace with technological progress.

The compatibility of such a media competence-related policy of informal regulation with the imperative of "fully respecting the responsibility of the Member States for the content of teaching and the organisation of education systems", which is expressly recognised in Art. 165(1)(1) TFEU, seems increasingly doubtful.

g. Suspensory effect of EU law

Closely related to the question of the primacy of EU law is the question of whether EU law triggers a suspensory effect with regard to Member States' abilities to regulate.

As far as the exclusive competences of the EU are concerned, this question is clarified by the Treaty of Lisbon, as described above: The Member States are excluded from legislation in areas of exclusive EU compe-

---

84 Council conclusions on media literacy in an ever-changing world, 2020/C 193/06, ST/8274/2020/INIT, OJ C 193 of 09.06.2020, p. 23–28.

tence – unless there is an explicit recourse for Member State action by way of re-delegation under Art. 2(1) TFEU. The exclusion of Member States from regulation leads to a "general suspensory effect", without prejudice to the possibility of re-delegation[85]; Member State regulations that are adopted in violation of this requirement are inapplicable for this reason alone. The EU does not (yet) have to have adopted secondary law (suspensory effect *ex ante*). If the EU has in turn enacted secondary law, this does not have to have direct effect to supersede conflicting national law (suspensory effect *ex post*). Thus, in areas of exclusive competence, the adoption of measures is "entirely and definitively" the sole responsibility of the EU – regardless of whether the Union takes concrete action or not.[86] However, this suspensory effect of EU law does not preclude the adoption by the Member States of parallel or supplementary regulations having the same addressees as the EU law in question and which may also use comparable instruments (e.g. transparency and disclosure obligations or prohibitions of discrimination), but having different objectives (in particular to ensure diversity), at least if the Member State regulation does not materially conflict with the EU regulation (e.g. on the basis of the EU's exclusive competence under Art. 3(1)(b) TFEU for competition law) or hampers its practical effect.

There is no comparable explicit regulation on suspensory effects in the area of shared competences of the EU. Measures adopted under this type of EU competence do not have a suspensory effect in the sense of a "stop signal" for the regulatory competence of the Member States. However, the principle of loyalty laid down in Art. 4(3) TEU results in an obligation on the Member States not to infringe Union measures and not to impair their *effet utile*, i.e. their useful effect.[87]

In the case of shared competences, the question of a possible suspensory effect, especially in connection with EU law based on directives, arises in two respects: both with regard to transposed EU law based on directives and – in the sense of a suspending pre-effect – with regard to law based on directives yet to be transposed.

---

85 Cf. *Streinz* in: id., Art. 2 TFEU, para. 5; *Klamert* in: Kellerbauer/id./Tomkin, Art. 2 TFEU, para. 5.
86 Cf. *Obwexer*, EU-rechtliche Determinierung mitgliedstaatlicher Kompetenzen, p. 1, 6.
87 Cf. *Calliess* in: id./Ruffert, Art. 2 TFEU, para. 22; *Eilmansberger/Jaeger* in: Mayer/Stöger, Art. 2 TFEU, para. 49; *Obwexer*, EU-rechtliche Determinierung mitgliedstaatlicher Kompetenzen, p. 1 (9).

B. Framework for the allocation of competences under EU primary law

With regard to national legal provisions adapted on the basis of a directive such as, for example, the relevant provisions of the State Treaty on the Modernization of the Media Order in Germany based on the amended AVMSD, this means that such provisions are no longer at the unlimited disposal of the national legislature. They may no longer be modified contrary to the specifications laid down in the directive.

However, a directive may produce legal effects even before the expiry of its transposition period and before transposition into national law of the Member States. From the date of publication of a directive pursuant to Art. 297(1) TFEU, the EU Treaty principle of loyalty prohibits the adoption in the Member States of acts which are liable to seriously compromise the result pursued by the directive.[88] Such a risk may also arise when the national telecommunications legislature disregards the scope for taking media diversity issues into account in domestic telecommunications legislation, as expressly provided for in the EECC, by deleting an obligation to take account of broadcasting interests under national telecommunications legislation when this law is amended.

However, there is no such advance effect as long as the "advance-effective" EU legal act is not published in the Official Journal of the EU. Mere intentions of the EU to introduce legislation cannot therefore have any advance effect. Consequently, the regulatory considerations in Austria with regard to the fight against hate and illegal content on the Internet – based on the German NetzDG – which were notified to the EU Commission on 1–2 September 2020,[89] do not raise any serious concerns, at least not from the perspective of the relationship between EU and Member State media regulation from the point of view of competence rules – irrespective of the considerations at that time for a Digital Services Act and a European Action Plan for Democracy and irrespective of the question of the compati-

---

88 Cf. *Streinz*, Europarecht, para. 514; *Thiele*, Europarecht, p. 114.
89 These are the drafts of (a) a Federal Act establishing civil legal and civil procedural measures to combat hate on the Internet (Combating Hate on the Internet Act [Hass-im-Netz-Bekämpfungs-Gesetz – HiNBG]) (https://ec.europa.eu/growth/tools-databases/tris/de/search/?trisaction=search.detail&year=2020&num=547), (b) a Federal Act establishing penal and media policy measures to combat hate on the Internet (https://ec.europa.eu/growth/tools-databases/tris/de/search/?trisaction=search.detail&year=2020&num=548) and (c) a Federal Act on measures to protect users on communication platforms (Communication Platforms Act [Kommunikationsplattformen-Gesetz – KoPl-G]) (https://ec.europa.eu/growth/tools-databases/tris/de/search/?trisaction=search.detail&year=2020&num=544).

bility of the planned regulations with the EU ECD. In this case, there is no unlawful intention to regulate.[90]

6. Media regulation and enhanced cooperation between individual EU Member States

Economic aspects of media regulation aiming at the creation of a digital internal market may also be the subject of enhanced cooperation under the European Treaties – although even in such enhanced cooperation, the cultural horizontal clause of Art. 167(4) TFEU would have to be observed, as would the obligation to respect fundamental rights, including the freedoms of communication and the imperative under Art. 11(2) CFR to respect the freedom and pluralism of the media.

The first prerequisite for establishing enhanced cooperation is the existence of an appropriate legal basis for the Union in the relevant policy area. According to Art. 20(1)(1) TEU, this may not fall within any policy area in which the EU has exclusive competence. However, as shown above[91], this is not the case with regard to the internal market competence – also with regard to the creation of a digital single market – as provided for in the unambiguous regulation in Art. 4(2)(a) TFEU.

According to Art. 20(1)(2) TEU, the aim of enhanced cooperation must be to further the objectives of the Union, protect its interests and reinforce its integration process. Enhanced cooperation in the area of regulation of media platforms and media intermediaries, with special consideration to their importance for ensuring diversity in the digital age, would promote this objective with a view to safeguarding pluralism from cross-border threats, as would the possible introduction of a digital tax, which would focus on this group of addressees of modern media regulation.[92]

---

[90] Cf. in detail below on the ECD (chapter D.II.1), on the Digital Services Act (chapters D.III.2 and F.) and on the European Democracy Action Plan (chapter D.III.3).

[91] Cf. on this supra, chapter B.I.5.

[92] Cf. on this, albeit after a number of Member States going ahead on their own (on this *Ukrow*, Österreich und Spanien wollen Digitalsteuer einführen, https://rsw.beck.de/cms/?toc=ZD.ARC.201902&docid=413844; *Ukrow*, Österreich: Ministerrat beschließt Digitalsteuerpaket, https://rsw.beck.de/cms/?toc=MMR.ARC.201904&docid=416999), the Conclusions of the Special meeting of the European Council of 17 to 21 July 2020 (https://www.consilium.europa.eu/media/45109/210720-euco-final-conclusions-en.pdf), which provide for the European Commission to submit a proposal for a "digital levy" in the first half of 2021

B. Framework for the allocation of competences under EU primary law

Art. 20(1)(2) sentence 2 TEU and Art. 328 TFEU require for the establishment of enhanced cooperation that it must be open to all other Member States if they fulfil the conditions of participation.

According to Art. 20(3) sentence 1 TEU, at least nine Member States must be involved in an enhanced cooperation.

However, pursuant to Art. 20(2) sentence 1 TEU, enhanced cooperation is only admissible as *ultima ratio* when the Council of the EU has established that the objectives of such cooperation cannot be attained within a reasonable period by the Union as a whole. The Member States have a wide margin of maneuver in this respect; the review of the "reasonable period" itself has only limited justiciability.[93] However, it is requested that at least one attempt to reach agreement on a concrete legislative project involving all Member States must have been made.[94]

However, enhanced cooperation does not affect the bilateral or multilateral regulatory approach under public international law with respect to a positive order in the media landscape. This is because it does not follow from the enshrinement in primary EU law of the preconditions and mechanisms of enhanced cooperation that other forms of such cooperation are prohibited within the scope of application of the European treaties..[95]

In line with this openness to alternative forms of enhanced cooperation, Art. 9 of the Franco-German Treaty of Aachen stipulates that the two states recognize the crucial role that culture and the media play in strengthening Franco-German friendship. France and Germany are therefore determined to create a common space of freedom and opportunity for their peoples, as well as a common cultural and media space. With such a space, a contribution could be made to the development of a European (partial) public sphere, which, according to the FCC's perspective on its democratic legitimacy, is indispensable for the further development of the EU. The uncertainties of the digital communication space emphasized by the FCC also affect not least the continuing legitimacy of the European target perspective of an ever closer union. Counteracting this, for example through a common Franco-German media space, represents a cultural contribution

---

so that it can be introduced "at the latest by 1 January 2023"; cf. ibid., para. A29 and para. 147. On this also chapter B.I.5.g.
93 *Ruffert* in: Calliess/id., Art. 20 TEU, para. 19; *Pechstein* in: Streinz, Art. 20 TEU, para. 13.
94 *Bribosia* in: CDE 2000, 57, 97; *Pechstein* in: Streinz, Art. 20 TEU, para. 13; *Ullrich* in: RdDI 2013, 325, 332; diff. op. *Blanke* in: id./Mangiameli, Art. 20 TEU, para. 38.
95 Cf. *Ukrow* in: ZEuS 2019, 3, 29 with further references.

to the self-assertion of a value-based Europe. The regulatory competence of the two states under the terms of Art. 9 of the Treaty could encompass not only a Franco-German digital platform for audiovisual content and information offerings, but also an ARTE radio station, a Franco-German search engine or a Franco-German Facebook, TikTok or WhatsApp counterpart.[96]

7. Media regulation and the relevance of subsequent institutional practice under primary law

The CJEU's methods of interpretation are widely viewed[97] as differing from the traditional methods of interpretation under public international law, in particular in that the CJEU does not attach any original relevance for the interpretation of Union law to the subsequent practice of the institutions, to which Art. 31(3)(b) of the Vienna Convention on the Law of Treaties (VCLT)[98] attaches considerable importance as a source of legal knowledge ("the Vienna Convention").

However, an examination of the CJEU's case law with regard to the interpretative relevance of subsequent institutional practice produces a "disparate picture".[99] Irrespective of this, subsequent practice may be of fundamental significance for an essential aspect of the functioning of Union law – namely the acceptance of a legal system with only limited means of coercion over the Member States.[100] Indeed, the acceptance by the Member States of EU media regulation aimed at deepening digital integration alone, however important it may be, cannot suffice as a basis of legitimacy in the EU as a union of law, one component of which is the preservation of the division of competences in the European Treaties.[101] Conversely, however, this acceptance inhibits the risk of judicial control over the observance of the integration program, at least in an interstate context. How-

---

96 Cf. *Ukrow* in: ZEuS 2019, 3, 49 et seq.
97 Cf. *Streinz*, Die Interpretationsmethoden des Europäischen Gerichtshofs zum Vorantreiben der Integration, 27, 32.
98 Vienna Convention on the Law of Treaties of 23.05.1969, BGBl. 1985 II, p. 927.
99 Cf. *Ukrow*, Richterliche Rechtsfortbildung durch den EuGH, p. 118 et seq.
100 *Streinz*, Die Interpretationsmethoden des Europäischen Gerichtshofs zum Vorantreiben der Integration, 27, 32, with reference to i.a. *Borchardt*, Richterrecht durch den Gerichtshof der Europäischen Gemeinschaften, in: Gedächtnisschrift für Eberhard Grabitz, 1995, p. 29, 39 et seq.
101 Cf. *Cornils*, Der gemeinschaftsrechtliche Staatshaftungsanspruch, p. 327 et seq.; *Dänzer-Vanotti*, Der Europäische Gerichtshof zwischen Rechtsprechung und Rechtsetzung, 205, 209 et seq.

B. Framework for the allocation of competences under EU primary law

ever, this does not affect the monitoring of media regulation for observance of the integration program by private entities – whether incidentally with respect to sovereign acts regulating an individual act that are based on acts of EU media regulation or with respect to adequate preservation of democratic principles as a limit to the Basic Law's openness to integration.

II. The EU value system and its protection as a means of ensuring freedom and diversity of the media in the EU Member States

1. The EU's core set of shared values

In view of digitization, Europeanization and globalization[102], the value-based elements of the European integration program play a prominent role in the EU's integration and value system[103]. These values are explicitly enshrined in Art. 2 TEU.[104]

Art. 2 TEU regulates that "[t]he Union is founded on the values of respect for human dignity, freedom, democracy, equality, the rule of law and respect for human rights, including the rights of persons belonging to minorities. These values are common to the Member States in a society in which pluralism, non-discrimination, tolerance, justice, solidarity and equality between women and men prevail". In particular, the link in Art. 2 TEU to respect for human dignity and the principle of pluralism clearly demonstrates the relevance of the EU's fundamental values in terms of media law, especially also in relation to diversity. The diversity of the media is also protected by the union's value system.[105]

In dealing with current developments in individual EU Member States that are attempting to undermine the independence of the judiciary and

---

102 Cf. *Ruffert*, Die Globalisierung als Herausforderung an das Öffentliche Recht; *Schwarze*, Globalisierung und Entstaatlichung des Rechts.
103 Cf. *Calliess* in: Berliner Online-Beiträge zum Europarecht, 1(2004).
104 Cf. on this also the recent judicature of the CJEU, case C-216/18 PPU, *Minister for Justice and Equality (Deficiencies in the system of justice)*, para. 48 and 63; CJEU, case C-619/18, *Commission / Poland*, para. 58.
105 Cf. also *Nielsen*, Die Medienvielfalt als Aspekt der Wertesicherung der EU, p. 109 et seq., 175 et seq.; *Ukrow/Cole*, Aktive Sicherung lokaler und regionaler Medienvielfalt, p. 55 et seq.

the media,[106] special[107] importance is attached to fundamental values, which also play a role in determining the supervisory mechanisms[108] of the European Treaties[109], such as the organizational structure of the supervisory bodies.

The core set of shared values in Art. 2 TEU commits the EU itself in all its internal and external actions. However, the legal content of the provision is not limited to this. Even if, according to its wording, this provision primarily addresses the EU itself, these fundamental values are also of EU law significance with respect to the legal systems of the Member States, as is already apparent from the second sentence of the provision.[110] At the same time, this set of values does not give the EU the power to adopt legislation. Art. 2 TEU does not constitute a "super-competence" that could ultimately undermine the principle of conferral.

However, as objects of protection for a militant democracy, the values of Art. 2 TEU also shape the German constitutional value system, even though the Basic Law lacks a comparable explicit catalog.[111] This can lead to a dialogical understanding of value orientation – as a result relativizing possible conflict situations with regard to parallel guard rails of regulatory activity – which can be promoted not least in the exchange between the

---

106 Cf. on this e.g. *Möllers/Schneider*, Demokratiesicherung in der Europäischen Union, p. 53 et seq., 68 et seq.
107 Cf. on this *Ukrow* in: vorgänge 55 (2016) # 216, 47, 55 et seq.; *id.* in: vorgänge 56 (2017) # 220, 69, 75 et seq.
108 Vera Jourová, Vice President of the current European Commission, is the Commissioner responsible for "Values and Transparency"; cf. https://ec.europa.eu/commission/commissioners/2019-2024/jourova_en.
109 Cf. Communication form the European Commission der Europäischen Kommission, "A new EU Framework to strengthen the Rule of Law", COM (2014) 158 final.
110 In the context of the EU, the provision is of operational relevance not only in accession procedures under Art. 49 TEU, but also in the suspension of Member State rights, including voting rights, as provided for in Art. 7 TEU. Cf. on concrete cases of application *Ukrow*, Jenseits der Grenze, p. 5.
111 On the core set of values in the Basic Law cf. from the judicature of the FCC with fundamental significance BVerfGE 7, 198 (205 et seq.); 25, 256 (263); 33, 1 (12) as well as recently e.g. BVerfGE 148, 267 (280 et seq., 283 et seq.); in the literature e.g. *Detjen*, Die Werteordnung des Grundgesetzes, 2009; *Reese*, Die Verfassung des Grundgesetzes. Rahmen- und Werteordnung im Lichte der Gefährdungen durch Macht und Moral; *von Danwitz*, Wert und Werte des Grundgesetzes, FAZ of 22.01.2019.

B. Framework for the allocation of competences under EU primary law

FCC and the constitutional courts of the EU Member States and the CJEU.[112] However, with regards to the relationship between the constitutional courts and the CJEU in its role as the European constitutional court, this approach of a value-oriented multilevel dialog of constitutional courts is at current heavily troubled, as a consequence of the FCC's decision on the ECB's government bond purchase program[113]. This decision fatally opened the political floodgates with regard to a risk to the unity of the EU as a union of law[114], since a Member State's constitutional court not only calls into question the primacy of Union law,[115] but also deprives instruments such as the preliminary ruling, which is designed for cooperation, of its practical effectiveness.

---

112 Recent topics of the corresponding expert discussions have included the "role of constitutional courts in advancing the protection of fundamental rights" (https://www.bundesverfassungsgericht.de/SharedDocs/Pressemitteilungen/EN/2017/bvg17-111.html), "dialogue between national constitutional courts and European courts" as well as "fundamental rights in the digital age" (https://www.bundesverfassungsgericht.de/SharedDocs/Pressemitteilungen/EN/2018/bvg18-055.html), "multi-level cooperation of European courts (*Europäischer Gerichtsverbund*)" (https://www.bundesverfassungsgericht.de/SharedDocs/Pressemitteilungen/EN/2019/bvg19-018.html), "impact of the decisions of the European Court of Human Rights and the European Court of Justice on the German legal system and on the work of the Federal Constitutional Court" (https://www.bundesverfassungsgericht.de/SharedDocs/Pressemitteilungen/EN/2019/bvg19-034.html) and "protection of fundamental rights in relation to private actors [as well as] data protection in the cooperation of European constitutional courts" (https://www.bundesverfassungsgericht.de/SharedDocs/Pressemitteilungen/EN/2019/bvg19-045.html).
113 FCC, Judgment of the Second Senate of 5 May 2020, 2 BvR 859/15.
114 Cf. the communication of the CJEU referring to the uniform application of Union law (Press release following the judgment of the German Constitutional Court of 5 May 2020; https://curia.europa.eu/jcms/upload/docs/application/pdf/2020-05/cp200058en.pdf) and the statement by the President of the European Commission (https://ec.europa.eu/commission/presscorner/detail/en/statement_20_846).
115 Corresponding problems already existed in the past; cf. *Mangold*, Der Widerspenstigen Zähmung, Legal Tribune Online of 13.05.2020 (https://www.lto.de/recht/hintergruende/h/bverfg-ezb-urteil-provokation-eugh-eu-vertragsverletzungsverfahren/).

2. Securing media freedom and pluralism through the instruments of a value-based and militant democracy in the EU

Both the Basic Law and the EU Treaty, as well as the ECHR,[116] take not only substantive legal but also procedural precautions to defend the value-based decision for a free and democratic basic order – which presupposes the freedom and pluralism of the media and protects them from threats – against efforts made to undermine it.[117] In the constitutional order of the Basic Law, this procedural effectuation of said value-based decision is expressed in particular in Art. 9(2) of the Basic Law with the possibility of banning unconstitutional associations as a "manifestation of a pluralist and at the same time militant constitutional democracy"[118], Art. 18 of the Basic Law with rules on the forfeiture of fundamental rights,[119] Art. 20(4) of the Basic Law with a subsidiary right of resistance of all Germans against anyone who undertakes to eliminate the free democratic order of the Basic Law, as a form of decentralized control of the militancy of democracy,[120] Art. 21(2) of the Basic Law, with its openness (subject to narrow substantive and formal conditions)[121] to a ban on unconstitutional

---

116 On the value-oriented integration and identity function of the ECtHR cf. *Keller/Kühne* in: ZaöRV 76 2016, 245, 299.
117 These constitutional safeguard mechanisms are, moreover, supplemented by the provisions of criminal law for the protection of the state and its free democratic order; cf. on this *Becker* in: Bucerius Law Journal 2012, 113, 114 et seq.
118 FCC, Order of the First Senate of 13 July 2018, 1 BvR 1474/12, para. 101.
119 For the course of the proceedings before the FCC cf. §§ 36 to 41 BVerfGG; on the low practical relevance cf. *Schnelle*, Freiheitsmissbrauch und Grundrechtsverwirkung, p. 94 et seq.
120 Cf. on this *Nowrot*, Jenseits eines abwehrrechtlichen Ausnahmecharakters – Zur multidimensionalen Rechtswirkung des Widerstandsrechts nach Art. 20 Abs. 4 GG, p. 21.
121 In the view of the FCC in its decision in the NPD party-ban proceedings, the party ban under Art. 21(2) of the Basic Law represents "the sharpest weapon, albeit a double-edged one, a democratic state under the rule of law has against an organised enemy" (FCC, Judgment of the Second Senate of 17 January 2017, 2 BvB 1/13, para. 405). It is intended "to counter risks emanating from the existence of a political party with a fundamentally anti-constitutional tendency and from the typical ways in which it can exercise influence as an association" (ibid., para. 514). In its view, the concept of the free democratic basic order within the meaning of Art. 21(2) of the Basic Law in this context covers only "those central fundamental principles which are absolutely indispensable for the free constitutional state" – human dignity (Art. 1(1) Basic Law), the principle of democracy with the possibility of equal participation by all citizens in the process of forming the political will as well as accountability to the people for the exercise of

B. Framework for the allocation of competences under EU primary law

parties, Art. 21(3) of the Basic Law with the possibility, introduced as a result of the FCC's NPD decision, of excluding from state funding parties whose objectives or the behavior of their supporters are aimed at undermining or abolishing the free democratic basic order or endangering the existence of the Federal Republic of Germany, and Art. 73(1) No. 10 (b) of the Basic Law, which contains provisions on the cooperation between the Federation and the Länder in the area of the protection of the constitution[122].

In the TEU, this value-based decision finds procedural recognition in particular in Art. 7 with the possibility, at least theoretically[123], of suspend-

---

state authority (Art. 20(1) and (2) Basic Law), the principle that organs of the state be bound by the law – rooted in the principle of the rule of law – (Art. 20(3) Basic Law) and independent courts' oversight in that regard, as well as the reservation for the use of physical force for the organs of the state which are bound by the law and subject to judicial oversight; on these requirements cf. ibid., para. 535 et seq.

In order to prohibit a political party, it is not sufficient that its aims are directed against the free democratic basic order. Instead, the party must "seek" to undermine or abolish the free democratic basic order. The notion of "seeking" requires active behaviour in that respect. The prohibition of a political party does not constitute a prohibition of views or ideology. In order to prohibit a political party, it is necessary that a party's actions amount to a fight against the free democratic basic order. It requires systematic action of the political party that amounts to a qualified preparation for undermining or abolishing the free democratic basic order or aims at endangering the existence of the Federal Republic of Germany. It is not necessary that this results in a specific risk to the goods protected under Art. 21(2) GG. Yet it requires specific and weighty indications which suggest that it is at least possible that the political party's actions directed against the free democratic basic order of the Federal Republic of Germany or against its existence could be successful (ibid., headnote 6; cf. ibid., para. 570 et seq.).

122 Cf. Gesetz über die Zusammenarbeit des Bundes und der Länder in Angelegenheiten des Verfassungsschutzes und über das Bundesamt für Verfassungsschutz (Bundesverfassungsschutzgesetz – BVerfSchG) (Law on Cooperation between the Federal Government and the Länder in Matters Relating to the Protection of the Constitution and on the Federal Office for the Protection of the Constitution, Federal Constitutional Protection Act) of 20 December 1990 (BGBl. I, p. 2954, 2970), last amended by Art. 2 of the Law of 30 June 2017 (BGBl. I, p. 2097); *Cremer* in: Isensee/Kirchhof, vol. VII, § 278.

123 On the weaknesses of the Art. 7 TEU procedure cf. e.g. *Möllers/Schneider*, Demokratiesicherung in der Europäischen Union, p. 45 et seq., 120 et seq.; *Yamato/Stephan* in: DöV 2014, 58, 58 et seq.

ing Member State rights,[124] and in the ECHR in Art. 17 with the prohibition of the abuse of fundamental rights[125]. According to its factual and procedural design, Art. 7 TEU can be invoked in exceptional circumstances only. The political nature and special procedure of this particularly controversial and difficult-to-apply Article set an extremely high threshold for its application.[126]

By granting the EU a supervisory competence that also encompasses the freedom and diversity of the media with regard to the legal order of the Member States, a certain conflict arises with the restraint of the European Treaties in relation to a positive media order of the EU and its institutions. However, this supervisory competence is structurally parallel to the EU's respective supervisory competence – also with regard to the media regulations of the Member States – on the basis of the fundamental freedoms of the internal market and the EU's competition regime. The imperative of protecting the media regulation of the Member States from Union law, as can be derived not least from an overall view of the rules and limits on the exercise of competences in the European Treaties, speaks in favor of a restrained exercise of EU supervision. It is true that this does not affect the prerogative of the competent EU institutions to assess the existence of the factual prerequisites of Art. 7 TEU. Coordination as to the content of media diversity law in the Member States by way of not only procedural but also substantive harmonization of the constituent elements of Art. 7 TEU in conjunction with Art. 2 TEU – including harmonization of the requirements arising from the pluralism requirement of the TEU's set of values – could hardly be reconciled with the division of competences as laid down in the European Treaties and the imperative of mutual consideration between the TEU and its Member States anchored therein.

---

124 Cf. e.g. European Commission, Communication from the Commission to the Council and the European Parliament on Article 7 of the Treaty on European Union – Respect for and promotion of the values on which the Union is based, COM(2003) 606 final; *Schmitt von Sydow* in: Revue du droit de l'union européenne 2001, 285, 288 et seq.
125 Cf. *Cannie/Voorhoof* in: Netherlands Quarterly of Human Rights 2011–1, 54, 56 et seq.; *Struth*, Hassrede und Freiheit der Meinungsäußerung, p. 206 et seq.
126 Cf. *Vīķe-Freiberga et al.* (High-Level Group on Media Freedom and Pluralism), Report on a free and pluralistic media to sustain European democracy, p. 21.

B. Framework for the allocation of competences under EU primary law

III. The competence areas of the EU with reference to media regulation – an overview

1. *The internal market competence of the EU*

a. Introduction

According to Art. 26(2) TFEU, "the internal market shall comprise an area without internal frontiers in which the free movement of goods, persons, services and capital is ensured in accordance with the provisions of the Treaties".

In principle, there are two basic forms of effect of Union law to be distinguished which either promote an ever closer union of the European peoples (paragraph 1 of the Preamble to the TFEU) with regard to the EU's internal market objective also, or inhibit a contrary development: (1.) restrictions of the Member States' freedom of action related to the freedom dimensions of the internal market by conflicting Union law (passive-limiting integration) and (2.) active intervention of Union law by means of replacing and supplementing national rules (active-formative integration) – including EU activities below decisionmaking level, in particular financial support measures.[127]

In particular, the CJEU's jurisprudence, which is oriented toward dynamic interpretation of Union law, has promoted passive-limiting internal market integration. The case law of the CJEU points in the direction of a uniform doctrine regarding the fundamental freedoms of the internal market,[128] which, within the framework of the so-called negative integration of the EU, are directed towards the removal of all restrictions on the exer-

---

127 Cf. *Ukrow/Ress* in: Grabitz/Hilf/Nettesheim, Art. 167 TFEU, para. 22 with further references; *Garben* in: Kellerbauer/Klamert/Tomkin, Art. 167 TFEU, para. 6; cf. in general *Klamert/Lewis* in: Kellerbauer/Klamert/Tomkin, Art. 26 TFEU, para. 1.
128 Cf. on this *Classen* in: EWS 1995, 97, 97 et seq.; *Ehlers* in: id., p. 177 et seq., 184; *Frenz*, Handbuch Europarecht vol. 1, para. 447; *Hirsch* in: ZEuS 1999, 503, 507 et seq.; *Kingreen*, Die Struktur der Grundfreiheiten des Europäischen Gemeinschaftsrechts, p. 44 et seq.; *Klamert/Lewis* in: Kellerbauer/Klamert/Tomkin, Art. 26 TFEU, para. 11; *Mojzesowicz*, Möglichkeiten und Grenzen einer einheitlichen Dogmatik der Grundfreiheiten, p. 133 et seq.; *Mühl*, Diskriminierung und Beschränkung. Grundansätze einer einheitlichen Dogmatik der wirtschaftlichen Grundfreiheiten des EG-Vertrages, p. 30 et seq., 198 et seq.; *Plötscher*, Der Begriff der Diskriminierung im Europäischen Gemeinschaftsrecht; *Schleper* in: Göttinger Online-Beiträge zum Europarecht, No. 16 (2004), 1, 1 et seq.; *Streinz*, Konvergenz der Grundfreiheiten, 199, 206 et seq.

cise of the fundamental freedoms. This covers not only direct or indirect discrimination, but also other measures, even if they apply without distinction to national providers of services and to those of other Member States, if they are likely to prohibit or otherwise impede the exercise of a service or establishment.[129]

Regulations that are based on the EU's various internal market competences in the exercise of active-formative integration have in common that they are ultimately determined. They must contribute to the establishment or functioning of the internal market. This is because, according to Art. 26(1) TFEU, the EU "shall adopt measures with the aim of establishing or ensuring the functioning of the internal market, in accordance with the relevant provisions of the Treaties". Pursuant to Art. 26(3) TFEU, it is the Council, acting on a proposal from the Commission, who "shall determine the guidelines and conditions necessary to ensure balanced progress in all the sectors concerned".

This progressive dimension of the internal market – notwithstanding the changes that in the meantime have been made to the treaty provisions with regard to the definition of the internal market and the harmonization of laws governing the internal market – indicates the continuing relevance of the legal barriers placed by the CJEU on EU legislation based on the internal market clause in its fundamental ruling on the ban on tobacco advertising of 5 October 2000. Accordingly, a legal act based on Art. 114 TFEU must actually have the purpose of improving the conditions for the establishment and functioning of the internal market.

> *"If a mere finding of disparities between national rules and of the abstract risk of obstacles to the exercise of fundamental freedoms or of distortions of competition liable to result therefrom were sufficient to justify the choice of Article 100 a* [TEC, now: Art. 114 TFEU] *as a legal basis, judicial review of compliance with the the proper legal basis might be rendered nugatory."*[130]

Although, according to the CJEU, the European legislature may act on the basis of the internal market harmonization clause to prevent the emergence of future obstacles to trade resulting from multifarious development of national laws, their emergence must be "likely and the measure in question must be designed to prevent them."[131]

---

129 Cf. CJEU, case C-76/90, *Manfred Säger / Dennemeyer & Co. Ltd*.
130 CJEU, case C-376/98, *Germany / Parliament and Council*, para. 84.
131 CJEU, case C-376/98, *Germany / Parliament and Council*, para. 86.

B. Framework for the allocation of competences under EU primary law

This suggests that the internal market competence is to be exercised to remove obstacles and not to enact even greater obstacles to the exercise of fundamental freedoms[132] – without prejudice to the continuing competence of the Member States to provide for at least temporary restrictions to the fundamental freedoms in the non-harmonized area for reasons as laid down in the respective treaty exception clauses to the fundamental freedoms or for reasons of overriding public interest. This rules out measures whose goal is not at least some degree of deregulation as well. Such deregulatory measures can in principle also be of harmonizing nature, but not every measue of harmonization necessarily also removes obstacles to the internal market.[133]

b. The competence in relation to the freedom of establishment

According to Art. 49(1) TFEU and within the framework of the provisions on the freedom of establishment, restrictions on the freedom of establishment of nationals of a Member State in the territory of another Member State shall be prohibited.[134] Such prohibition shall also apply to restrictions on the setting-up of agencies, branches or subsidiaries by nationals of any Member State established in the territory of any Member State.

Art. 49(2) TFEU provides that freedom of establishment shall include the right to take up and pursue activities as self-employed persons and to set up and manage undertakings, in particular undertakings or firms within the meaning of Art. 54(2) TFEU, under the conditions laid down for its own nationals by the law of the country where such establishment is effected, subject to the provisions of the Treaty provisions relating to capital.

In order to attain freedom of establishment as regards a particular activity, Art. 50(1) TFEU confers on the European Parliament and the Council the competence, acting in accordance with the ordinary legislative procedure and after consulting the Economic and Social Committee, to act by means of directives. Such activity may also involve audiovisual production and distribution, including aggregation, selection and presentation of audiovisual offerings.

---

132 Cf. CJEU, case C-233/94, *Germany / Parliament and Council*, para. 15, 19.
133 Cf. *Ress/Bröhmer*, Europäische Gemeinschaft und Medienvielfalt, p. 40.
134 On the question of possible impairments of fundamental freedoms by the Member States' exercise of competences cf. chapter C.IV.1.

The European Parliament, the Council and the Commission shall carry out the duties devolving upon them under Art. 49 and 50(1) TFEU, in line with Art. 50(2)(a) TFEU, in particular by according, as a general rule, priority treatment to activities where freedom of establishment makes a particularly valuable contribution to the development of production and trade. In view of the importance of digitization for all existing and emerging business models, the fact that activities related to the creation of the digital single market should be given priority does not require any special explanation.

Pursuant to Art. 50(2)(f) TFEU, the EU legislature also effects the progressive abolition of restrictions on freedom of establishment in every branch of activity under consideration, both as regards the conditions for setting up agencies, branches or subsidiaries in the territory of a Member State and as regards the subsidiaries in the territory of a Member State and as regards the conditions governing the entry of personnel belonging to the main establishment into managerial or supervisory posts in such agencies, branches or subsidiaries. This clause is of considerable importance, not least in view of the strategic expansion plans of the large U.S. Internet giants, many of which are also increasingly relevant in the process of safeguarding media freedom and diversity, if they develop their diversity-relevant business activities in EU Member States from a subsidiary based in another EU Member State, such as Ireland.

Art. 50(2)(g) TFEU provides that European Parliament and Council shall coordinate "to the necessary extent" the "safeguards" which are required by Member States of undertakings or firms within the meaning of Art. 54(2) TFEU for the protection of the interests of their members "and others", with a view to making such safeguards equivalent throughout the Union. Whether these "others" can also refer to the democratic public as such seems against the background of the individual-personal link mentioned in the provision highly doubtful. But also the position as a "third party" within the meaning of Art. 50(2)(g) TFEU of the individual user of media offerings produced, aggregated, selected, presented or disseminated by an undertaking – even taking into account a sovereign duty to protect media freedom and diversity which also determines legislation – appears more than questionable, especially since these duties to protect do not have an inherent dimension that gives rise to individual claims.

Art. 50(1) TFEU grants in principle a competence to abolish national non-discriminatory restrictions on the freedom of establishment or to replace them by a common provision of Union law, and this even if the Member State regulations are justified by overriding requirements in the

B. Framework for the allocation of competences under EU primary law

general interest and thus comply with Union law.[135] Such common rules facilitate the establishment in other Member States, since it is then in principle no longer necessary to deal with a multitude of regulations for the protection of the public interest.[136] This applies not only to safeguards with respect to familiar challenges, but also to new challenges that are just developing. This is because the concept of protection in relation to general interest does not necessarily have to be repressive, but can also be prophylactic-preventive in nature.

For the specification of the Union's competence to harmonize laws in the area of freedom of establishment, the question therefore arises whether the EU may regulate all aspects that in any way facilitate economic activity outside the own state. *De facto*, this would be tantamount to recognizing an all-encompassing economic competence of the EU, as in the age of comprehensive standardization, hardly any circumstances are conceivable in the area of economic activity in the broadest sense that are not regulated in some way by law. Harmonization under Union law would always be in conformity with Union law simply because of the resulting unification of law, as long as the rules and limits on the exercise of competence in Art. 4 and 5 TEU[137] are observed. The assertion of such a harmonization competence would be practically the same as a competence-competence rejected – as has been shown[138] – under Union and constitutional law.[139]

It is in line with the principle of conferral that also in connection with the realization of the freedom of establishment the authorization under Art. 50(1) TFEU is not infinite but clearly limited and – in contrast to the competence of the Member States – requires legitimation and justification.[140] An establishment-related coordination and harmonization competence does not therefore exist already in the case of every conceivable contact of different Member State legal systems with, or effect of their differences on the exercise of the freedom of establishment.

---

135 Cf. *Lenz* in: EuGRZ 1993, 57, 60 et seq.; *Ress/Bröhmer*, Europäische Gemeinschaft und Medienvielfalt, p. 34.
136 Cf. *Liehr*, Die Niederlassungsfreiheit zum Zwecke der Rundfunkveranstaltung und ihre Auswirkungen auf die deutsche Rundfunkordnung, p. 249 et seq.
137 Cf. on this chapter B.V.
138 Cf. on this chapter B.V.
139 Cf. *Ress/Bröhmer*, Europäische Gemeinschaft und Medienvielfalt, p. 34.
140 Cf. *Jarass*, Die Kompetenzen der Europäischen Gemeinschaft und die Folgen für die Mitgliedstaaten, p. 6.; *Ress/Bröhmer*, Europäische Gemeinschaft und Medienvielfalt, p. 36.

Mere differences in national legislation – as e.g. in the case of licensing or concession systems in different professions – are not in themselves a reason for regulation on the part of the EU. Neither a single regime (uniform regulations) nor substantively aligned (coordinated) rules are necessary for the establishment or functioning of the internal market. In particular, if Member State regulations *de facto* discriminate against EU third-country nationals, there may be a need for regulation, but not already when the conditions for the provision of services or establishment in the Member States differ. Since safeguarding media diversity and establishing media pluralism are not internal market objectives as such, these objectives may not be made a regulatory means by way of an alleged de facto obstacle to establishment or service provision.[141]

c. The competence in relation to the freedom to provide services

Freedom to provide services, which is enshrined in Art. 56 et seq. TFEU, relates, according to Art. 57 TFEU, to services that are normally provided for remuneration, in so far as they are not subject to the other overriding fundamental freedoms.[142] Media services are also covered by this competence title: Although media are (also) cultural goods, their (also) economic aspects mean that, unless they are goods, they are also economic services within the meaning of the definition in Art. 57 TFEU.[143]

In addition to the active freedom to provide services – the freedom of the service provider to provide his service in another Member State under the same conditions as a service provider established there – the competence title regulating the freedom to provide services also covers the passive freedom to provide services[144], i.e. the right of the recipient to receive a service in another Member State from a service provider established

---

141 Cf. *Ress/Ukrow*, Die Niederlassungsfreiheit von Apothekern, p. 42 et seq.
142 On the scope of application of the freedom to provide services and the question of possible impairments of fundamental freedoms by the Member States' exercise of competences cf. chapter C.IV.1.
143 This classification also includes – as does the audiovisual sector within the meaning of Art. 167(2), fourth indent, TFEU (on this *Calliess/Korte*, Dienstleistungsrecht in der EU, § 5, para. 88), and in continuous contrast to the AVMSD amended in 2018 – radio broadcasts of both a linear and non-linear nature. Critical on the AVMSD's continued blindness to radio broadcasting *Ukrow*, Zum Anwendungsbereich einer novellierten AVMD-Richtlinie, p. 3.
144 Cf. on this *Randelzhofer/Forthoff* in: Grabitz/Hilf/Nettesheim, Art. 49/50 TFEU, para. 1, 51; *Dony*, Droit de l'Union européenne, para. 680.

B. Framework for the allocation of competences under EU primary law

there. In addition, the competence title also includes the so-called freedom to provide services by correspondence, where it is neither the provider nor the recipient of a service, but the service itself that crosses the border.[145] This type of freedom to provide services is of particular importance in connection with cross-border media offerings.[146] This also applies to services provided by media intermediaries such as media agencies: The regulation of services relating to the aggregation, selection or presentation of media content, whether of a journalistic or commercial-communicative nature, is also covered by the competence title of the regulation of the freedom to provide services.

However, there is little to suggest that the competence title as regards freedom to provide services could be used to regulate media diversity in the EU. Not least the approach to the area of audiovisual services in the practice of applying the possibilities opened up by primary law to regulate the freedom to provide services to date suggests against such a competence title.

Accordingly, in Art. 2(2)(g) of Directive 2006/123/EC on services in the internal market[147], the EU excluded "audiovisual services, including cinematographic services, whatever their mode of production, distribution and transmission, and radio broadcasting" from the scope of this directive.[148] The reason for this exception was not least the concern about a possible circumvention of the specific secondary law for audiovisual media in the EU[149] – and thus, incidentally, also the concern about a disregard of Member State competences and responsibilities for ensuring media diversity.

Moreover, there is no conceivable parallel between media diversity regulation by means of an EU directive and the AVMSD. This is because that directive continues – as was the case with the EEC Television Directive[150] – to focus on regulating certain minimum requirements for cross-border audiovisual offerings, in particular comparable requirements for the protection of minors, the protection of human dignity and commercial com-

---

145 Cf. e.g. *Calliess/Korte*, Dienstleistungsrecht in der EU, § 3, para. 25 et seq.
146 Cf. already CJEU, case 155/73, *Giuseppe Sacchi*, para. 6.
147 Directive 2006/123/EC of the European Parliament and of the Council of 12 December 2006 on services in the internal market, OJ L 376 of 27.12.2006, p. 36–68.
148 According to sentence 2 of rec. 24 of that directive, "[f]urthermore, this Directive should not apply to aids granted by Member States in the audiovisual sector which are covered by Community rules on competition".
149 Cf. *Calliess/Korte*, Dienstleistungsrecht in der EU, § 5, para. 86.
150 Cf. on this *Ress/Bröhmer*, Europäische Gemeinschaft und Medienvielfalt, p. 42.

munications (specifically advertising, sponsorship and teleshopping), on which depended the validity of both the principles of free cross-border retransmission of audiovisual offerings and of country of origin control – i.e. the freedom of the service to be offered in the country of origin and received in a third country – but also the freedom of the service from multiple controls itself. Requirements on the pluralism (internal and external pluralism) of radio and television broadcasters or of providers of telemedia such as video-sharing services would, however, have nothing to do with the transferability (marketability) of these audiovisual offerings.

However, something different could apply in the case of a must-be-found or findability regulation in the online area as a new form of digital diversity protection, as it is now provided for in the MStV. This is because such regulation can at least indirectly restrict the free reception of audiovisual services.

d. Interim conclusion

It is difficult to derive from the EU's internal market competences an authorization for the EU to harmonize the law in the area of media diversity protection. The competence title of freedom of establishment must be interpreted narrowly, as only this corresponds to the character of a Union of Member States whose national identity must be preserved. In particular, any regulatory approach that would reduce the degree of entrepreneurial freedom in the internal market would hardly be compatible with the internal market concept of Art. 26 TFEU, aimed at progress towards cross-border free development. Furthermore, against the use of regulatory competences in relation to the freedom to provide services can be argued that it is likely to be only indirectly affected by national regulations in the area of safeguarding diversity.[151]

2. *The EU competition regime*

Competition law focuses on market power, diversity protection law on power over opinions.[152] They are therefore two separate matters in which

---

151 Cf. *Ress/Bröhmer*, Europäische Gemeinschaft und Medienvielfalt, p. 43.
152 Cf. on the considerations beyond the references to competence rules that are in focus here in detail chapter C.IV.2. and on merger control chapter D.II.4.

B. Framework for the allocation of competences under EU primary law

the respective control of power is also carried out with different instruments. However, control of market and opinion power are not phenomena without any points of contact. Rather, antitrust law under competition law goes hand in hand with the law of securing diversity of opinion. In particular, the competition regime is generally suitable for achieving the goal of a diverse offering as a side effect, so to speak.[153]

In the area of competition policy, the EU not merely has a shared competence – as is the case with the internal market regime – but rather an exclusive one, as set out in detail in Art. 101 et seq. TFEU – in the form of the control of a ban on cartels (i.e. the prohibition of concerted practices by colluding in an anti-competitive manner, antitrust), the abuse of a dominant market position, merger and State aid.[154] With a view to ensuring diversity in the media sector, this is of recognizable relevance to the market organization of the media.

However, the practical significance of these supervisory instruments is put into perspective by the fact that most media markets are still essentially national in scope and strongly defined by national borders – even if a high proportion of the media in some Member States are foreign-owned.

Primary Union law does not a priori preclude an exercise of supervisory competence in which ownership concentration is considered not only with regard to specific media (sub)genres, such as press, radio and television, but also across different media and with regard to distribution channels. In this respect, Union law in its the starting point is not limited to a television-centric perception of control, in which media-relevant related markets are considered for purposes of illustration at best, but is open to a dynamic understanding not least of market definition as well as of a dominant position. The latter also enables a reaction in supervisory practice that takes into account network effects of the digital platform economy.

Intermediary digital platforms, such as search engines, news aggregators, social networks and app stores,[155] can also be subject to supervision of the media sector, without EU competition law being in conflict with this from the outset. However, their ever-increasing relevance for effectively safeguarding the freedom and diversity of the media is not an aspect that is

---

153 Cf. *Cole*, Europarechtliche Rahmenbedingungen für die Pluralismussicherung im Rundfunk, p. 93, 104 et seq.; *Jungheim*, Medienordnung und Wettbewerbsrecht im Zeitalter der Digitalisierung und Globalisierung, p. 249 et seq.
154 Cf. on this *Ukrow* in: UFITA 2019, 279, 279 et seq.
155 Cf. on these possible addressees of the competition regime *Vike-Freiberga et al.* (High-Level Group on Media Freedom and Pluralism), Report on a free and pluralistic media to sustain European democracy, p. 27.

allowed beyond doubt to (co-)shape the perception of competition rules under Union law.

Given its particular significance for the free formation of individual and public opinion, as well as for social cohesion in Member States and their cultural state characteristics, the media sector, to the extent that concentration tendencies are at issue, cannot indeed be measured exclusively against the standards of the general rules on antitrust and merger control. After all, as actors bound by fundamental rights and values, the EU institutions[156] are also required to take into account the effects of their actions on democracy, fundamental rights and culture. However, the consideration of fundamental rights as well as democratic and cultural principles and requirements is equally imperative in the context of competition policy and, for example, expressly required under Art. 167(4) TFEU at the interface of the protection of cultural opportunities for action and the duty of supervision under competition law.[157]

Competition can in fact promote pluralism, but it does not necessarily do so, as it can also lead to a greater uniformity and homogenization of the content on offer. In shaping competition policy, the Commission is required also against this background to pay attention to market concentration not only from the point of view of competition, but as well from that of pluralism. Media consumption should therefore be taken into account in the question of which facts the Commission subjects to scrutiny as well.[158]

With regard to the cultural dimension of the media, the exemption under State aid rules, provided for in Art. 107(3)(d) TFEU, is of particular importance: According to this provision, "aid to promote culture and heritage conservation" may be considered "to be compatible with the internal market" "where such aid does not affect trading conditions and competition in the Union to an extent that is contrary to the common interest".

The so-called Amsterdam "Protocol on the system of public broadcasting in the Member States", "considering that the system of public broadcasting in the Member States is directly related to the democratic, social and cultural needs of each society and to the need to preserve media pluralism" takes up this imperative of an interpretation of Union law that preserves the Member States' room for maneuver by providing, as "interpreta-

---

156 Cf. on this below, chapter B.VI.1.
157 Cf. *Ress/Bröhmer*, Europäische Gemeinschaft und Medienvielfalt, p. 45.
158 Cf. *Vike-Freiberga et al.* (High-Level Group on Media Freedom and Pluralism), Report on a free and pluralistic media to sustain European democracy, p. 27.

B. Framework for the allocation of competences under EU primary law

tive provisions" annexed to the TEU and the TFEU, that the provisions of these Treaties "shall be without prejudice to the competence of Member States to provide for the funding of public service broadcasting insofar as such funding is granted to broadcasting organisations for the fulfilment of the public service remit as conferred, defined and organised by each Member State, and insofar as such funding does not affect trading conditions and competition in the Community to an extent which would be contrary to the common interest, while the realisation of the remit of that public service shall be taken into account".[159]

The Amsterdam Protocol openly addresses the tension that can exist between the democratic, social and cultural dimensions of the media and their economic relevance – a tension that, incidentally, is not limited to public service broadcasting as a media (sub)genre. While the former dimensions argue for a regulatory competence of the Member States, the potential internal market dimension of cross-border media engagement is obvious with regard to the latter.

3. The EU's cultural competence

The EU's reluctance to exercise positive regulatory competence over the media is reinforced in relation to the "audiovisual sector" by the culture Article of the TFEU. Art. 167 TFEU gives the EU a mandate to promote culture at the European level while respecting the Member States' "cultural" right of self-determination. In this context, Art. 167(1) to (3) TFEU both enables and limits the EU's active cultural policy.

Paragraph 1 states that the Union "shall contribute to the flowering of the cultures of the Member States, while respecting their national and regional diversity and at the same time bringing the common cultural heritage to the fore". According to Art. 167(2), fourth indent, TFEU, "[a]ction by the Union shall be aimed at encouraging cooperation between Member States and, if necessary, supporting and supplementing their action in the following areas: [...] artistic and literary creation, including in the audiovisual sector".[160] Media are hereby recognized under primary law as at least

---

159 In detail on this also *Ukrow/Cole*, Aktive Sicherung lokaler und regionaler Medienvielfalt, p. 72 et seq.
160 This area of creative activity covers video and film as well as the entire broadcasting sector – thus, in deviation from the scope of the AVMSD, also radio broadcasting – and the areas of on-demand audiovisual media services and audiovisual commercial communication. Cf. also *Blanke* in: Calliess/Ruffert, Art. 167 TFEU,

also a cultural phenomenon – a dimension that continues to exist at least on an equal footing with the economic significance of media, notwithstanding the increasing importance of this sector for value creation in the internal market of the EU as well as globally.

The cautious formulations of "contributing" and "encouraging" already indicate that the EU's cultural policy is not intended to counteract, standardize or replace the respective policies of the Member States, but (merely) to assume a role as the guardian of European cultural creation[161].[162] The activities of the EU in the field of culture are therefore secondary to those of the Member States, as can also be seen from an overall view with further rules enshrined in both the TEU and the TFEU. The General Court of the European Union (GCEU) has also emphasized this subsidiarity in a ruling of 10 May 2016.[163] However, it also follows from the mutual obligation of loyalty between the EU and its Member States that the latter must support the former in the performance of its tasks under Art. 167(1) and (2) TFEU, although a resulting, separate obligation to provide financing is not assumed.[164]

Art. 167(4) TFEU establishes a rule for EU action outside the areas of cultural policy referred to in paragraphs 1 to 3, according to which "[t]he Union shall take cultural aspects into account in its action under other provisions of the Treaties, in particular in order to respect and to promote the diversity of its cultures". This provision is commonly referred to as a 'cultural horizontal clause' or 'cultural compatibility clause' but does not, however, describe a cultural reserve.[165] The EU system of competences, for example in the sense of an *"exception culturelle"*, is not affected by the pro-

---

para. 12; *Ukrow/Ress* in: Grabitz/Hilf/Nettesheim, Art. 167 TFEU, para. 128 et seq.; *Vedder* in: id./Heintschel von Heinegg, Art. 167 TFEU, para. 7; *Moussis*, Access to the European Union, p. 272 et seq.

161 Cf. on this also the preamble to the TEU, which states that the EU acts "drawing inspiration from the cultural, religious and humanist inheritance of Europe, from which have developed the universal values of the inviolable and inalienable rights of the human person, freedom, democracy, equality and the rule of law".

162 *Blanke* in: Calliess/Ruffert, Art. 167 TFEU, para. 1; *Garben* in: Kellerbauer/Klamert/Tomkin, Art. 167 TFEU, para. 2 et seq.; *Vedder* in: id./Heintschel von Heinegg, Art. 167 TFEU, para. 6.

163 Cf. GCEU, case T-529/13, *Izsák and Dabis / European Commission*, para. 96.

164 Cf. in detail *Hochbaum* in: BayVBl. 1997, 680, 681.

165 Cf. e.g. *Ukrow/Ress* in: Grabitz/Hilf/Nettesheim, Art. 167 TFEU, para. 148 et seq. with further references; *Garben* in: Kellerbauer/Klamert/Tomkin, Art. 167 TFEU, para. 5.

B. Framework for the allocation of competences under EU primary law

vision, i.e. it neither constitutes an independent legal basis of competences for the EU nor does it affect existing competences.[166] The obligation to take into account cultural aspects gives rise to a whole range of diversity-friendly and diversity-promoting requirements, which the EU must take into account in its legislation as well as in its supervision of the conformity of Member State conduct with EU law. In this context, the effects of the horizontal clause on media, telecommunications, state aid and other competition law in the EU are also worthy of attention in terms of active safeguarding of diversity.[167]

Art. 167(5) TFEU then determines the instruments and procedures available to the EU in order to contribute to the achievement of the objectives mentioned above. Only recommendations adopted by the Council on a proposal from the Commission and incentive measures adopted by the European Parliament and the Council acting in accordance with the ordinary legislative procedure and after consulting the Committee of the Regions, however excluding any harmonization of the laws and regulations of the Member States[168], shall be eligible in this context. The latter negative clause within the framework of the prohibition of harmonization prohibits the EU from recourse to the general competence titles for the harmonization of laws according to Art. 114, 115 TFEU as well as special such provisions.[169] Thus, this provision does not represent a general prohibition of harmonization for measures with effects on the cultural sector of life, but rather a prohibition of harmonizing cultural measures, which is already not applicable to competence titles outside of Art. 167 TFEU and therefore has no effects on such harmonization efforts by the EU that focus on other regulatory areas.

It follows from this system in Art. 167 TFEU that the EU, provided that it can rely on a legal basis from its catalog of competences, can also act (in a regulatory manner) beyond the limits of the obligations under Art. 167 TFEU, in particular the prohibition of harmonization in Art. 167(5) TFEU – which applies only to primarily culture-oriented measures – and beyond

---

166 *Lenski*, Öffentliches Kulturrecht, p. 142.
167 Cf. e.g. *Ukrow/Ress* in: Grabitz/Hilf/Nettesheim, Art. 167 TFEU, para. 163 et seq. with further references.
168 The significance of this exclusion was also emphasized by the General Court of the European Union in its judgment of 10.05.2016; cf. GCEU, case T-529/13, *Izsák and Dabis / European Commission*, para. 101 et seq.
169 *Blanke* in: Calliess/Ruffert, Art. 167 TFEU, para. 19; similar *Niedobitek* in: Streinz, Art. 167 TFEU, para. 55; cf. *Craufurd Smith* in: Craig/de Búrca, 869, 883, 886 et seq.

Jörg Ukrow

mere incentive measures[170].[171] However, the prerequisite arising from the cultural horizontal clause is that in this context, the EU must take cultural aspects into account, which regularly amounts to a consideration between cultural and other regulatory interests (e.g. economic aspects in EU competition law[172]).[173] Moreover, it follows from the systematics of the TFEU that cultural aspects may not be the focus of a Union law-based regulation.[174]

However, what is to be understood by cultural aspects within the meaning of Art. 167 TFEU is not conclusively clarified, as EU law does not contain a definition in this regard.[175] In any case, the contours of the terminology must be drawn in accordance with Union law and must not be given

---

170 There is no common understanding of what is meant by incentive measures within the meaning of Art. 167(5) TFEU. In part (cf. *Blanke* in: Calliess/Ruffert, Art. 167 TFEU, para. 18), this is understood to mean only actual and administrative measures of the EU, both financial and non-material, but in part (*Ukrow/Ress* in: Grabitz/Hilf/Nettesheim, Art. 167 TFEU, para. 176) recourse to measures of a general regulatory nature without legally binding force is also considered permissible. Cf. further *Craufurd Smith* in: Craig/de Búrca, 869, 888 et seq.
171 *Lenski*, Öffentliches Kulturrecht, p. 142.
172 A special form of the horizontal effect derived from Art. 167 TFEU can be found in particular in Art. 107(3)(d) TFEU, which allows the European Commission to permit Member State cultural aid under certain circumstances.
173 Cf. on this also the judgment of the GCEU in case T-391/17, *Romania / European Commission*, which dealt with the question whether a European Citizens' Initiative notified to the Commission for registration with the aim of improving the protection of national and linguistic minorities and strengthening cultural and linguistic diversity in the Union was already outside the scope of competence for the adoption of legal acts by the EU and should therefore already be classified as unlawful and not be registered. Since the Commission at the registration stage excludes only initiatives aimed at legislative proposals manifestly outside the scope of competence, the question of the scope of use of the competences is not addressed in detail. However, in the context of Art. 167(5) TFEU, the General Court points out (para. 56, 61 et seq.) that legislative proposals intended to complement the Union's action in its areas of competence in order to ensure the preservation of the values listed in Art. 2 TEU and the rich cultural and linguistic diversity referred to in Art. 3(3)(4) TEU are not excluded from the outset, given that the Commission has to take into account the values and objectives of the Union in every legislative proposal and can thus also, in principle, make them the subject of a specific proposal, as long as this does not manifestly violate the values of the Union itself.
174 Settled case law of the CJEU, cf. for instance case C-155/91, *Commission of the European Communities / Council of the European Communities*.
175 Cf. also *Ukrow/Ress* in: Grabitz/Hilf/Nettesheim, Art. 167 TFEU, para. 150; *Garben* in: Kellerbauer/Klamert/Tomkin, Art. 167 TFEU, para. 4 et seq.

their imprint by the various conceptions of the Member States, as the latter would otherwise have it in their hands themselves to define the scope of the EU's duty of consideration contained in Art. 167 TFEU.[176] Incidentally, however, the various definitional approaches differ in particular with regard to their respective scope.[177] Regardless of whether, in the sense of a broad understanding, one understands it to mean "the combined spiritual, material, intellectual and emotional characteristics of a society or social group", which, "[i]n addition to literature and the arts, [...] encompasses life-style, fundamental human rights, values, traditions and beliefs"[178], or whether one only understands certain areas of intellectual and creative human activity, which undisputedly include art, literature and music, but also the audiovisual sector, as a systematic interpretation of Art. 167 TFEU shows,[179] can in the present case be left aside against the background that the media serve at least as a forum for the activities that are already protected within the framework of the narrow understanding of the definition and thus not only transport culture, but themselves establish cultural products, not least in the form of journalistic-editorial contributions. Specifically for audiovisual media, this creative-artistic function is also explicitly recognized as such in Art. 167(2), fourth indent, TFEU. But even beyond that, the concept of culture or the "cultural aspects" enshrined in Art. 167 TFEU will also have to be attributed to activities of authors as well as – even if only content-related – activities of the media, their carriers, employees and products, and likewise the media-specific aspects of the protection of pluralism (with regard to the diversity of information and opinion) and the diversity of the media.[180]

---

176 *Roider*, Perspektiven einer Europäischen Rundfunkordnung, p. 57; cf. *Craufurd Smith* in: Craig/de Búrca, 869, 874 et seq.
177 Cf. on this and the following *Roider*, Perspektiven einer Europäischen Rundfunkordnung, p. 58; *Craufurd Smith* in: Craig/de Búrca, 869, 874 et seq.
178 Opinion on the Communication from the Commission on a fresh boost for culture in the European Community, 88/C 175/15, OJ C 175 of 04.07.1988, p. 40.
179 On a systematic interpretation of the TFEU, the areas of education and science, by contrast, are exempt in view of their regulation outside Art. 167 TFEU.
180 Same as here *Schwarz* in: AfP 1993, 409, 417 with further references.

Jörg Ukrow

IV. Objectives of the EU and their significance as regards competences in view of media regulation

1. Media regulation-related goals of the EU

Art. 3 TEU establishes objectives of the Union to be achieved through integration – in the sense of a target-oriented system of action and not solely 'for the sake of integration' itself.[181] Art. 3(3)(4) TEU contains in this context the objective that the Union shall respect its rich cultural and linguistic diversity, and shall ensure that Europe's cultural heritage is safeguarded and enhanced. The objective is therefore not to create a uniform European culture or 'Euroculture', but to preserve existing cultural diversity, whose strengths lie precisely in the diversity that has grown historically.[182] The cultural heritage is composed of the national cultures of the Member States, which in turn can also include individual regional and local aspects, although a European identity as a conglomerate of these cultures also appears alongside it.[183] Against this background, measures at domestic level that are necessary to protect national and regional languages and cultures are endorsed at European level, because this ultimately contributes to cultural diversity – one of the fundamental European values.[184]

For the media, this is significant insofar as they are seen as playing a key role in protecting local cultures (whether at the state or regional level) and thus also in protecting Europe's cultural diversity.[185]

It should be noted that Art. 3(3)(4) TEU, as is the case with Art. 2 TEU, strictly does not create an autonomous legal basis in terms of competence. In this respect, the objectives laid down in Art. 3 TEU are, from the perspective of competence, generally neutral or supplementary: They do not

---

181 *Ruffert* in: Calliess/id., Art. 3 TEU, para. 3; generally on the target-orientation also *Müller-Graf* in: Pechstein et al., Art. 3 TEU, para. 1; *Heintschel von Heinegg* in: Vedder/id., Art. 3 TEU, para. 3; *Pechstein* in: Streinz, Art. 3 TEU, para. 2; *Klamert* in: Kellerbauer/id./Tomkin, Art. 3 TEU, para. 3 et seq.; *Sommermann* in: Blanke/Mangiameli, Art. 3 TEU, para. 1 et seq., and *Dony*, Droit de l'Union européenne, para. 54.
182 *Von Danwitz* in: NJW 2005, 529, 531.
183 *Neumann*, Das Recht der Filmförderung in Deutschland, p. 43, with further references.
184 Same as here *Vike-Freiberga et al.* (High-Level Group on Media Freedom and Pluralism), Report on a free and pluralistic media to sustain European democracy, p. 45.
185 *Vike-Freiberga et al.* (High-Level Group on Media Freedom and Pluralism), Report on a free and pluralistic media to sustain European democracy, p. 13.

B. Framework for the allocation of competences under EU primary law

create an original regulatory competence for the EU and its institutions in the sense of options for positive integration through legal acts based solely on Art. 3 TEU, but at the same time they also do not inhibit the exercise of competence titles of the EU that exist elsewhere, but rather give this exercise a aim and direction.

2. The flexibility clause of Art. 352 TFEU to reach EU objectives and its significance for media regulation

However, this neutrality of the EU's catalog of objectives as regards the EU's competences is affected by the so-called "dispositive powers" according to Art. 352 TFEU: If action by the Union should prove necessary, within the framework of the policies defined in the Treaties, which comprise culture including the media sector, to attain one of the objectives set out in the Treaties, and the Treaties have not provided the necessary powers, the Council, acting on a proposal from the Commission and after obtaining the consent of the European Parliament, shall adopt the appropriate measures.

To speak of a "flexibility clause" in this context seems misguided because the use of this opening clause as regards competences is linked to high hurdles:

- According to Art. 352(2) TFEU, the Commission shall draw national Parliaments' attention to proposals based on this Article by using the procedure for monitoring the subsidiarity principle referred to in Art. 5(3) TEU.
- Measures based on Art. 352 shall, according to its paragraph 3, not entail harmonisation of Member States' laws or regulations in cases where the Treaties exclude such harmonisation – which is the case with media-related regulation with an orientation towards culture or safeguarding of diversity pursuant to Art. 167(5) TFEU.
- Finally, a unanimous decision is required in the Council itself.

The CJEU has clarified that Art. 352 TFEU, "being an integral part of an institutional system based on the principle of conferred powers, cannot serve as a basis for widening the scope of Community powers beyond the general framework created by the provisions of the Treaty as a whole and, in particular, by those that define the tasks and the activities of the Community. [...] [Art. 352 TFEU] cannot be used as a basis for the adoption of provisions whose effect would, in substance, be to amend the Treaty without following the procedure which it provides for that purpose".[186]

This case law is also referred to in Declaration 42 of the Intergovernmental Conference on the Treaty of Lisbon[187]:

> *"The Conference underlines that, in accordance with the settled case law of the Court of Justice of the European Union, Article 352 of the Treaty on the Functioning of the European Union, being an integral part of an institutional system based on the principle of conferred powers, cannot serve as a basis for widening the scope of Union powers beyond the general framework created by the provisions of the Treaties as a whole and, in particular, by those that define the tasks and the activities of the Union. In any event, this Article cannot be used as a basis for the adoption of provisions whose effect would, in substance, be to amend the Treaties without following the procedure which they provide for that purpose."*

The FCC ruled in its Lisbon judgment that the formal approval of the Bundestag and the Bundesrat by law is required for Germany's representative in the Council to approve an act to be adopted on the basis of Art. 352 TFEU.[188] With regard to a legal act affecting media regulation, the approval of the state parliaments may also be required.[189]

---

186 CJEU, opinion 2/94 of 28.03.1996, *Accession by the Community to the European Convention for the Protection of Human Rights and Fundamental Freedoms*, Reports of Cases 1996 I-01759, para. 30.
187 OJ C 326 of 26.10.2012, p. 353.
188 FCC, Judgment of the Second Senate of 30 June 2009, 2 BvE 2/08, para. 417: "In so far as the flexibility clause under Article 352 TFEU is used, this always requires a law within the meaning of Article 23.1 second sentence of the Basic Law." This was stipulated in Art. 8 of the Act on the Exercise by the Bundestag and by the Bundesrat of their Responsibility for Integration in Matters concerning the European Union (Responsibility for Integration Act) (Gesetz über die Wahrnehmung der Integrationsverantwortung des Bundestages und des Bundesrates in Angelegenheiten der Europäischen Union (Integrationsverantwortungsgesetz – IntVG)) of 22 September 2009.
189 The Polish Cooperation Act also provides specific safeguards with respect to Art. 352 TFEU, which the Polish Constitutional Court considered necessary in its Lisbon judgment (judgment of 24.11.2010 (K 32/09, English version in "Selected Rulings of the Polish Constitutional Tribunal Concerning the Law of the European Union (2003–2014)", *Biuro Trybunału Konstytucyjnego*, Warsaw, 2014, p. 237 (available at http://trybunal.gov.pl/uploads/media/SiM_LI_EN_calosc.pdf). In contrast, the Czech and French constitutional courts have interpreted the flexibility clause as already being covered by the ratification of the European treaties. Other Member States, such as Austria, Denmark, Sweden, Finland, or Spain, have provisions that do not specifically refer to Art. 352

B. Framework for the allocation of competences under EU primary law

V. The exercise of competence rules and its limitations

1. Introduction

In addition to the principle of conferral and the catalog of competences for the EU, safeguard mechanisms under substantive law, namely rules and limits on the exercise of competences, should ensure that the individual competences existing at the European level are exercised in a manner that preserves the competences of the Member States. These rules include the imperative to respect the national identity of the Member States (Art. 4(2) TEU), the principle of sincere cooperation (Art. 4(3) TEU), the principle of subsidiarity (Art. 5(1) sentence 2, (3) TEU), and the principle of proportionality (Art. 5(1) sentence 2, (4) TEU). These principles were confirmed by the Treaty of Lisbon and had their content specified in some cases.

The tension that may exist between the objective enshrined in Art. 3(3) sentence 1 TEU, i.e. to establish a single European market for the benefit of EU citizens and undertakings based in the EU, and the requirements to respect the national identity of the Member States (Art. 4(2) TEU) and the richness of cultural diversity (Art. 3(3) TEU), may unfold in particular in connection with EU rules on safeguarding media diversity. Ultimately, resolving this tension is regularly a judicial task. This is because the rules and limitations on the exercise of competence outlined below are all justiciable.

In accordance with the wording of the Treaties, the CJEU has jurisdiction to make a comprehensive assessment of complaints concerning any breach of these principles. In this context, the core issues are the action for annulment pursuant to Art. 263 TFEU and the plea of illegality (collateral review) pursuant to Art. 277 TFEU. It is also possible to incidentally review the matter in the context of a preliminary ruling procedure as provided for in Art. 267 TFEU. This makes ex post control possible, even against overly "integration-friendly" legislative activities of the EU institutions in the area of media regulation.

Therefore, the question of the degree to which the relationship between the CJEU and the constitutional jurisdiction of the Member States develops in a cooperative or confrontational manner with regard to the understanding of the rules and limitations on the exercise of competences is of

---

TFEU but rather generally authorize their national parliaments to require their ministers to discuss their positions before Council meetings. Cf. on the whole *Kiiver* in: German Law Journal 2009, 1287, 1295 et seq.

direct relevance to the question of competences itself. However, the jurisprudence of the CJEU to date is not very encouraging with regard to the success of action against legal acts based on an infringement of the rules and limitations on the exercise of competences. This carries the risk of judicial conflicts that may escalate into conflicts over the question of the continued legality of the EU as a community of law and over the willingness to adhere to the concept of an ever closer union.

2. Respect for the national identity of the Member States

According to Art. 4(2) sentence 1 TEU, the Union shall respect the equality of Member States before the Treaties as well as their national identities, inherent in their fundamental structures, political and constitutional, inclusive of regional and local self-government. In this context, national identity basically includes a set of considerations and values that shape the self-perception and character of a state or a people and that can originate from different areas, such as language and culture.[190] In addition, the identity-building relevance of the region and the local context for people is also recognized in the EU Treaties.[191] Preserving regional and local concerns and diversity alongside national differences is repeatedly emphasized.[192] Also for this reason, they must be included in the assessment of Member State measures as to their compatibility with Union law.

In this context, the concept of national identity should be understood as an opening clause for Member State constitutional law, so that this must be taken into account when interpreting Art. 4(2) TEU.[193] This can also be-

---

190 *Puttler* in: Calliess/Ruffert, Art. 4 TEU, para. 14; *Streinz* in: id., Art. 4 TEU, para. 15; *Blanke* in: id./Mangiameli, Art. 4 TEU, para. 29 et seq., 32; *von Bogdandy/Schill* in: CMLRev. 2011, 1417, 1429. Cf. on this and the following *Cole*, Zum Gestaltungsspielraum der EU-Mitgliedstaaten bei Einschränkungen der Dienstleistungsfreiheit, p. 18 et seq.
191 Cf. on this *Menasse* in: Hipold/Steinmair/Perathoner, 27, 27 et seq.
192 Cf. for instance the third paragraph of the preamble of the CFR ("organisation of their public authorities at national, regional and local levels"), the wording of Art. 4(2) sentence 1 TEU on national identity or of Art. 167(1) TFEU, shown supra; at large on this *Ukrow/Ress* in: Grabitz/Hilf/Nettesheim, Art. 167 TFEU, para. 93 et seq. Cf. also the reference of Advocate General *Trstenjak*, CJEU, case C-324/07, *Coditel Brabant SA / Commune d'Uccle and Région de Bruxelles-Capitale*, para. 85.
193 Cf. for explanation and derivation comprehensively *von Bogdandy/Schill* in: ZaöRV 2010, 701, 701 et seq.

B. Framework for the allocation of competences under EU primary law

come relevant if, by overlapping competences, Member States' room for maneuver could apparently be superseded as a result of other objectives being pursued by the EU, such as the realization of fundamental freedoms. In particular, the regulation of media diversity may lead to different rules in the Member States, taking into account their respective national characteristics in terms of media and the needs to ensure a relevant media diversity. This question can therefore also reach the standard of national identity. Therefore, if necessary, the latter must also be consulted when determining the limits of the application of fundamental freedoms or Member State measures to restrict them[194], as well as when applying the competition regime in the state aid area when monitoring the financing of public service broadcasting.[195]

This is true even in the case of a CJEU review, as the Court has expressly recognized, although there have been few opportunities, at least so far, to rule on the meaning of the identity clause.[196] The fact that the CJEU regularly refrains from dealing with the principle of respect for the national identity of the Member States, even in cases in which Art. 4(2) TEU was expressly referred to in the proceedings, is not very conducive to promoting confidence in the role of the CJEU as a neutral court as regards the system of competences. At the same time, this reluctance may have resulted from the FCC's case law that national identity as defined in Art. 4(2) TEU does not coincide with constitutional identity, which the FCC reserves the right to preserve in the integration process.

As a special manifestation of the EU's obligation to respect, Art. 4(2) TEU is based on the concept that the constitutional identity of a Member State only in its core is an absolutely protected legal interest. Besides, in the interpretation and application of Art. 4(2) TEU, it is also important to create a practical concordance between the competence title under EU law and the limitation on the exercise of competence in the sense of a careful balance between Member State and European interests. In terms of procedural law, this is taken into account by the approach that the final determi-

---

194 Cf. on the importance of the duty to respect national identity recently also *Nielsen*, Die Medienvielfalt als Aspekt der Wertesicherung der EU, p. 63 et seq.
195 Cf. on this also *Nielsen*, Die Medienvielfalt als Aspekt der Wertesicherung der EU, p. 84 et seq.
196 Cf. however particularly CJEU, case C-208/09, *Ilonka Sayn-Wittgenstein / Landeshauptmann von Wien*, para. 83 ("In that regard, it must be accepted that [...] as an element of national identity, may be taken into consideration when a balance is struck between legitimate interests and the right of free movement of persons recognised under European Union law.").

nation of the scope and effectiveness of the reservation of identity in EU multilevel constitutionalism and its judicial application in the corresponding multilevel system of constitutional courts requires dialogical cooperation between the CJEU and the respective national constitutional court.[197]

3. The principle of sincere cooperation

A characteristic feature of the multilevel constitutionalism between the EU and its Member States is the integration of the national constitutions with the European treaties, the latter of which can also be described as constitutions in terms of their content. The basis of this multilevel constitutionalism is the sincere cooperation of EU and Member State institutions to keep the EU functioning. As a "central constitutional principle of the European Union" with the function of coordinating the European multilevel system in in a way that enables the Union to achieve its objectives,[198] the principle of sincere cooperation can have a recognizable decisive influence on the respective exercise of competences by the institutions of the EU and its Member States.

Within the EU, there is now an obligation of loyalty between the EU and its Member States, as well as between the Member States themselves, which is expressly recognized under primary law and governed by Art. 4(3) TEU: Pursuant to the principle of sincere cooperation, the Union and the Member States shall, in full mutual respect, assist each other in carrying out tasks which flow from the Treaties.[199] The imperative of Union-friendly conduct, which can be derived from this principle, therefore obliges not

---

197 Cf. *Calliess*, Written statement on the public hearing of the Committee on European Union Affairs of the German Bundestag on the subject of "Urteil des Bundesverfassungsgerichts vom 5. Mai 2020 (2 BvR 859/15) in Sachen Staatsanleihekäufe der Europäischen Zentralbank", https://www.bundestag.de/resource/blob/697584/69ec62de394a6348f992c1e092fa9f4b/callies-data.pdf, p. 6.

198 Cf. *Hatje*, Loyalität als Rechtsprinzip in der Europäischen Union, p. 105; cf. on Community loyalty as a fundamental standard in need of concretization also *Blanke* in: id./Mangiameli, Art. 4 TEU, para. 92 et seq.; *Bleckmann*, Europarecht, para. 697 et seq.; *Kahl* in: Calliess/Ruffert, Art. 4 TEU, para. 3 et seq.; *Klamert* in: Kellerbauer/id./Tomkin, Art. 4 TEU, para. 28 et seq.; *von Bogdandy*, Rechtsfortbildung mit Art. 5 EGV, 17, 19 et seq.; *id./Bast* in: EuGRZ 2001, 441, 447 / in: CMLRev. 2002, 227, 263; *Zuleeg* in: NJW 2000, 2846, 2846 et seq.

199 This obligation of loyalty in the relationship of the EU to the Member States and of the Member States to each other is supplemented by the obligation of loyalty

B. Framework for the allocation of competences under EU primary law

only the Member States vis-à-vis the EU, but also the Union institutions vis-à-vis the Member States[200] – namely in the exercise of all functions granted to them by the European Treaties and in all stages of this exercise – and thus, for example, also already in the preparation of an EU legal act.

The loyalty obligations are i.a. taken into account in the case law of the CJEU when interpreting abstract legal terms as well as when deciding on the infringement of obligations. This principle of cooperation, which is fundamental to the EU, is also expressed in mutual consideration and respect in the implementation and application of primary Union law. Unlike in the federal state, there are thus no hierarchies in multilevel constitutionalism with regard to the relationship between European and national law, between the CJEU and national constitutional courts. National and European courts work together in a division of labor in the light of the principle of sincere cooperation; to this extent, it is not a matter of competition, but of cooperation and dialogue. The preliminary ruling procedure provided for in Art. 267 TFEU offers the appropriate procedural instruments for this dialogical approach.[201]

The principle of sincere cooperation is considered to be of paramount importance for the cooperation between the sovereign actors of the Member States and the European constitutional bodies. However, its vagueness raises concerns about the threat of arbitrariness in the application of the law and puts the focus on the concretization of the obligations of loyalty. To date, a respective interpretation has been largely lacking on the EU side – beyond references to administrative organization law –, at least insofar as it concerns questions of the EU's obligations arising from the principle. Recent efforts to contour the principle of sincere cooperation as an embodiment of the overall legal order and its concretization as the application of law in the specific area of sovereign relations and in the specific situation of "difficult" legal situations[202] have proven to be of only limited practicability.

---

of the EU institutions to each other according to Art. 13(2) sentence 2 TEU, which is, however, not relevant for this study.
200 Cf. *Ress* in: DÖV 1992, p. 944, 947 et seq.
201 Cf. *Calliess*, Written statement on the public hearing of the Committee on European Union Affairs of the German Bundestag on the subject of "Urteil des Bundesverfassungsgerichts vom 5. Mai 2020, 2 BvR 859/15, in Sachen Staatsanleihekäufe der Europäischen Zentralbank", https://www.bundestag.de/resource/blob/697584/69ec62de394a6348f992c1e092fa9f4b/callies-data.pdf, p. 8.
202 Cf. *Benrath*, Die Konkretisierung von Loyalitätspflichten, p. 129 et seq.

In terms of content, the principle of sincere cooperation is not only aimed at prohibiting Member States from engaging in conduct that would impair the functioning of the EU as a community based on the rule of law. For its part, the EU is also prevented by the principle from exercising existing competences in a way that conflicts with the primary competence of the Member States to shape their internal cultural and democratic order, including its media diversity-related manifestations and conditions.

It is clear from the case law of the CJEU that the obligation of mutual consideration associated with the principle prohibits the Member States from taking steps that would jeopardize the legitimate interests and concerns of the EU. In positive terms, the principle aims to ensure that Member States not only respect but also promote the "effet utile" of Union law when implementing and applying it. In its case law to date, the CJEU has used the principle in particular to develop concrete requirements for the transposition and implementation of provisions of directives by the Member States on the basis of the principle. In particular, requirements for proper and effective administrative enforcement, the imperatives of publicity and implementation through binding provisions with external effect, and obligations to prevent and sanction infringements of EU provisions are the result of a so-called rule of efficiency as the central core of the loyalty requirement.[203]

Moreover, it is recognized that the principle of sincere cooperation cannot be used to correct, modify or override Union rules. The obligation of mutual loyalty rather builds on existing regulations and intensifies or makes them more effective, but without giving them a new substance.[204] Even if the relatively vague principle of loyalty under Union law may give the CJEU a wide scope for concretization, no legal consequences may be derived from Art. 4(3) TEU that undermine fundamental objectives or structural principles of the European Treaties or the constitutions of the Member States or the European Union.[205] In particular, no obligation to tolerate regulation of media diversity under European law, e.g. to avert threats to the democratic process in the EU itself or in individual Member States, can be derived from this principle.

For the area of indirect administrative implementation of Union law by the Member States, the principle of sincere cooperation is effective in par-

---

203 Cf. CJEU, case C-349/93, *Commission / Italy*; CJEU, case C-348/93, *Commission / Italy*; CJEU, case C-24/95, *Land Rheinland-Pfalz / Alcan Deutschland GmbH*.
204 Cf. *Nettesheim*, Die Erteilung des mitgliedstaatlichen Einvernehmens nach Art. 4 Abs. 2 UAbs. 1 der FFH-Richtlinie, p. 30 et seq.
205 Cf. *Jennert* in: NVwZ 2003, 937, 939 with further references.

B. Framework for the allocation of competences under EU primary law

ticular to the point that the fundamental "administrative autonomy"[206] or "institutional and procedural autonomy"[207] is not affected by this principle. This does not preclude EU law requirements for a supervisory structure for a coordinated area such as the AVMSD. It does, however, argue for a cautious understanding of the application and interpretation of these requirements in the context of the monitoring of compliance with EU law by the European Commission and the CJEU, taking into account the constitutional traditions of the Member States.

4. The principle of subsidiarity

The principle of subsidiarity, which was originally a theological and sociopolitical principle, was increasingly applied in the context of the relationship between vertically organized levels of government in states and, in the process of deepening European integration, found an explicit constitutional embodiment in the EU's founding treaties.[208] Since the Maastricht Treaty, it has been enshrined in primary law – which, in a legal comparison with other federal or decentralized organizational units for the exercise of sovereign power, is remarkable, but by no means solitary.[209] Since the Treaty of Amsterdam, the Treaty provisions on the subsidiarity principle have additionally been supplemented by a Protocol on the application of the principles of subsidiarity and proportionality.[210] However, while this Protocol in the version of the Treaty of Amsterdam not only outlined the subsidiarity principle in procedural terms by means of extensive obligations to consult, report and provide justification, but also specified it in substantive terms, the Protocol (No. 2) on the Application of the Principles of Subsidiarity and Proportionality, which has been in force since the

---

206 Cf. *Schwarze* in: NVwZ 2000, 241, 244.
207 Cf. *Rodriguez Iglesias* in: EuGRZ 1997, 289, 289 et seq.
208 Cf. *Oesch*, Das Subsidiaritätsprinzip im EU-Recht und die nationalen Parlamente, 301, 301 et seq.; *Foster*, EU Law, p. 87; *Weber* in: Blanke/Mangiameli, Art. 5 TEU, para. 8.
209 Cf. Art. 118 of the Italian Constitution, according to which "[a]dministrative functions are attributed to the Municipalities, unless they are attributed to the provinces, metropolitan cities and regions or to the State, pursuant to the principles of subsidiarity, differentiation and proportionality, to ensure their uniform implementation".
210 Consolidated version (2016) of TEU and TFEU – Protocol (No 2) on the Application of the Principles of Subsidiarity and Proportionality, OJ C 202 of 07.06.2016, p. 206–209.

Treaty of Lisbon, largely omits substantive guidelines on the application of the principle of subsidiarity.[211]

Art. 5(3) TEU contains the substantive requirements which must be fulfilled in order for a planned EU measure to be compatible with the principle of subsidiarity. In this context, the substance of the principle, now enshrined in the aforementioned provision, appears to be largely undisputed. It establishes a prerogative of competence of the smaller unit vis-à-vis the larger one according to its capability. As a consequence, the principle of subsidiarity obliges a larger entity willing to act, such as the EU, to justify the necessity and added value of taking action. At the same time, however, the principle – even in the form it has taken in EU primary law – is notable for its persistent vagueness in terms of content and openness to interpretation.

According to Art. 5(3) TEU, the union principle of subsidiarity applies when the EU "act[s]". This means, in principle, any action by an institution or body of the Union. The subsidiarity test complements the requirements arising from the relevant competence provision for the EU.[212] The only legal acts excluded from this additional requirement of control are, according to Art. 5(3) TEU, those which are adopted under an exclusive competence of the Union[213] – an exception which, with regard to media regulation on the part of the EU, is of no significant importance insofar as it concerns regulation which does not exceed the jurisdiction of the EU, but which may become important should media regulation for the EU be coordinated with third countries under public international law. Against this background, the exceptions for the audiovisual sector, which can be found throughout the negotiating mandates for trade and investment agreements, also gain particular weight from a subsidiarity perspective.

Art. 5(3) TEU addresses two substantive criteria that must be met cumulatively for the EU to be able to exercise either shared competences under Art. 4 TFEU or competences to carry out actions to support, coordinate or supplement under Arts. 5 and 6 TFEU as well as for the EU to act within

---

211 Cf. *Oesch*, Das Subsidiaritätsprinzip im EU-Recht und die nationalen Parlamente, 301, 303; *Foster*, EU Law, p. 88; *Weber* in: Blanke/Mangiameli, Art. 5 TEU, para. 10 et seq.
212 Cf. *Bast/von Bogdandy* in: Grabitz/Hilf/Nettesheim Art. 5 TEU, para. 50 et seq.; *Weber* in: Blanke/Mangiameli, Art. 5 TEU, para. 7; cf. *Dony*, Droit de l'Union européenne, para. 144.
213 Cf. on this chapter B.I.2.

B. Framework for the allocation of competences under EU primary law

the framework of the Common Foreign and Security Policy (CFSP),[214] which can become relevant not least with a view to media-related reactions to behavior by third states that is contrary to public international law and at the same time has a direct disinformation effect in a particular way or promotes such disinformation.

- First, the EU – in this respect complementing the competence-related substance of the principle of proportionality – shall act only if and in so far as the objectives of the envisaged action cannot be sufficiently achieved by the Member States. With regard to the objectives, it must be demonstrated in accordance with this necessity or negative criterion that there is a regulatory deficit that cannot be satisfactorily remedied by the factual and financial resources available to the Member States. The control relates to both the "whether" and the "how" of the action; the necessity of the Union measure must relate to all the envisaged regulatory elements of a legal act.[215] To this end, provided that the planned regulation claims Union-wide validity, an overall assessment of the situation in the EU as a whole and in all Member States respectively must be carried out.[216] The Treaty of Lisbon explicitly codified the previous practice, according to which not only the central, but also the regional and local level is to be taken into account for the assessment of the regulatory capacities of the Member States – a further example of recognition under primary law of the Europe of the regions and the federal diversity of state organization law in the Member States, which the EU is equally obliged to safeguard as it is with regards to the – also – media-related conditions of its continued existence.
- Second, the principle of subsidiarity, in the sense of an efficiency or added value criterion, requires as a positive criterion that the regulatory objectives can be better achieved at Union level by reason of the scale or effects of the envisaged measures. According to Art. 5 of the Subsidiarity Protocol, qualitative and, as far as possible, quantitative criteria are to be taken into account in this context. This involves an evaluation

---

[214] In the context of CFSP, however, the principle of subsidiarity is not subject to judicial review by the CJEU (cf. Art. 24(1) TEU in conjunction with Art. 275 TFEU); on this *Oesch*, Das Subsidiaritätsprinzip im EU-Recht und die nationalen Parlamente, 301, 304.

[215] Cf. *Oesch*, Das Subsidiaritätsprinzip im EU-Recht und die nationalen Parlamente, 301, 305; *Klamert* in: Kellerbauer/id./Tomkin, Art. 5 TEU, para. 23.

[216] Cf. *Bast/von Bogdandy* in: Grabitz/Hilf/Nettesheim, Art. 5 TEU, para. 54; *Klamert* in: Kellerbauer/id./Tomkin, Art. 5 TEU, para. 28; *Dony*, Droit de l'Union européenne, para. 145.

of the Union's problem-solving capacity or assessment of the effectiveness of the planned measure in comparison with the financial impact and administrative burden on affected authorities, economic operators and citizens.[217] An evaluative comparison between the additional integration gain and the Member States' loss of competence is required. As a result, EU powers are not to be exercised in full where the additional gain in integration is small, the encroachment on the competences of the Member States is considerable, or where the advantages of the gain in integration do not noticeably outweigh the disadvantages of the loss of Member State competence.[218]

The vagueness and openness of these criteria make it difficult, already at the outset, to reliably verify that the principle is being upheld. This diffuse picture of the control program is reinforced by the fact that both the negative and the positive criteria require that predictive decisions be taken:[219] It is focused on the future, to decide and demonstrate that Union action is necessary and implies European added value.[220]

In view of this understanding of the principle of subsidiarity as a competence oriented rule of reasoning[221] there is a strong case for a competence-based presumption in favor of preserving Member State abilities to regulate – also in the area of media regulation.[222] However, the case law of the CJEU to date speaks against a special suspensory effect conveyed by the principle of subsidiarity with regard to further Union access to subjects of regulation.[223] The methodological approach of the CJEU has so far not

---

217 Cf. *Bast/von Bogdandy* in: Grabitz/Hilf/Nettesheim, Art. 5 TEU, para. 57; *Klamert* in: Kellerbauer/id./Tomkin, Art. 5 TEU, para. 29.
218 Cf. *Calliess* in: id./Ruffert, Art. 5 TEU, para. 41.
219 Cf. *Lienbacher* in: Schwarze, Art. 5 TEU, para. 26.
220 Cf. *Oesch*, Das Subsidiaritätsprinzip im EU-Recht und die nationalen Parlamente, 301, 305.
221 Cf. *Oesch*, Das Subsidiaritätsprinzip im EU-Recht und die nationalen Parlamente, 301, 305.
222 Cf. on this recently also *Nielsen*, Die Medienvielfalt als Aspekt der Wertesicherung der EU, p. 60 et seq., as well as in general *Klamert* in: Kellerbauer/id./Tomkin, Art. 5 TEU, para. 24 with further references.
223 The CJEU has so far been very restrained both quantitatively with regard to any reference to the principle of subsidiarity and dogmatically with regard to the concrete content of the examination in individual cases. In its rulings on Art. 5 TEC, the Court has for the most part dispensed with a concrete subsidiarity test (cf. e.g. CJEU, case C-84/94, *United Kingdom of Great Britain and Northern Ireland / Council of the European Union*, para. 46 et seq.; CJEU, case C-233/94, *Germany / Parliament and Council*, para. 22 et seq.).

B. Framework for the allocation of competences under EU primary law

been consistent at all; as a rule, the Court examines the two substantive criteria under Art. 5(3) TEU together in a generalized and unstructured manner and does not distinguish between the necessity and the added value of action at Union level. In its judicial practice to date, it has never found an infringement of the principle and, remarkably, has regularly examined the added value criterion as a positive criterion aimed at regulation by the EU prior to the negative criterion of the necessity of action.[224] Accordingly, only evident infringements of the principle of subsidiarity, in which the Union institutions do not even provide a plausible justification for a regulation, appear to be contestable with any likelihood of success.[225]

The Subsidiarity Protocol contains specific procedural requirements for compliance with the principle of subsidiarity in EU legislative procedures. This takes account of the fact that the effectiveness of the principle of subsidiarity depends crucially on how the Union institutions implement the substantive requirements of Art. 5(3) TEU in day-to-day practice. Compliance with these requirements demands – in clear parallelism to the protection of fundamental rights by means of procedures – the protection of competences by means of procedures through appropriate procedural and organizational safeguards.

Art. 2 of the Subsidiarity Protocol requires the Commission to widely hold consultations before proposing a formal legislative act. This ensures that interested parties – both regulators and regulated stakeholders – can comment on any subsidiarity-critical aspects of planned media regulation at an early stage. Failure to hold such a hearing is likely to constitute a substantial procedural irregularity, which may result in the invalidity of the subsequent act.

Art. 5 of the Subsidiarity Protocol further obliges the Commission to justify draft legislative acts in detail with regard to compliance with the principle of subsidiarity. Proposals for new legal acts now regularly contain detailed statements on the compatibility of planned measures with the principle. Impact assessments are carried out as part of important initiatives and legislative projects, in which subsidiarity is also analyzed in detail.[226]

---

224 Cf. on Art. 5(3) TEU CJEU, case C-508/13, *Estonia / Parliament and Council*, para. 44 et seq.
225 Cf. *Bickenbach* in: EuR 2013, 523, 523 et seq.; *Klamert* in: Kellerbauer/id./Tomkin, Art. 5 TEU, para. 24 with further references.
226 Cf. for instance recently in the context of the proposed Digital Services Act the "legal basis and subsidiarity check" within the impact assessments on ex post

The new centerpiece of the procedural safeguarding of the principle of subsidiarity is the formalized dialogue between the Union legislature and the national parliaments. Whether this opportunity for dialogue has helped to increase the practical relevance of the principle of subsidiarity is open to controversial debate. It also seems reasonable to assess that the procedural safeguarding of the importance of this principle through the subsidiarity early warning mechanism by means of a subsidiarity complaint and the possibility of a subsidiarity action under Protocol (No. 2) through Art. 12(b) TEU and Art. 4 et seq. of the Subsidiarity Protocol, as introduced by the Treaty of Lisbon, has not changed anything worth mentioning either.

Art. 12 TEU addresses the participation of national parliaments in the EU legislative process. In this context, Art. 12(b) TEU substantiates the provisions of Art. 5(3) TEU with regard to the principle of subsidiarity. Accordingly, national parliaments actively contribute to the good functioning of the Union by ensuring that the principle of subsidiarity is respected in accordance with the procedure laid down in the Subsidiarity Protocol. It is an instrument of preventive control, in the form of a parliamentary-initiated early warning system, aiming towards safeguarding this restriction on the exercise of competences.[227]

The starting point of a possible subsidiarity complaint is Art. 4 of the Subsidiarity Protocol: It obliges the Union institutions to send draft legislative acts to national parliaments. They or the chambers of one of these parliaments may, in accordance with Art. 6 of the Subsidiarity Protocol, state within eight weeks in a reasoned opinion why they consider that the draft in question does not comply with the principle of subsidiarity.[228] In this context, it is up to the respective national parliaments to consult re-

---

(Ref. Ares(2020)2877686 – 04/06/2020, p. 4) and ex ante (Ref. Ares(2020)2877647 – 04/06/2020, p. 3) regulation.

227 Cf. *Oesch*, Das Subsidiaritätsprinzip im EU-Recht und die nationalen Parlamente, 301, 308; *Weber* in: Blanke/Mangiameli, Art. 5 TEU, para. 10; *Dony*, Droit de l'Union européenne, para. 147.

228 According to § 11(1) of the Act on the Exercise by the Bundestag and by the Bundesrat of their Responsibility for Integration in Matters concerning the European Union (Responsibility for Integration Act) (Gesetz über die Wahrnehmung der Integrationsverantwortung des Bundestages und des Bundesrates in Angelegenheiten der Europäischen Union (Integrationsverantwortungsgesetz – IntVG)) of 22 September 2009 (BGBl. I, p. 3022); amended by Art. 1 of the Act of 1 December 2009 (BGBl. I, p. 3822) the Bundestag and the Bundesrat, in their Rules of Procedure, may stipulate how a decision on the delivery of a reasoned opinion in accordance with Art. 6 of the Protocol on the ap-

gional parliaments with legislative powers, if necessary. With regard to media regulation, such legislative powers of the German state parliaments are evident according to the constitutional order of the Basic Law. According to Art. 7(1) of the Subsidiarity Protocol, the Union institutions are required to "take account of" the reasoned opinions in the further course of the legislative procedure. This "obligation to take account of" is accompanied by the obligation to deal with the objections in a well-founded manner; in contrast, there is, however, no obligation to actually incorporate the opinions into the proposal. Where reasoned opinions represent at least one third[229] of all the votes allocated to the national Parliaments, the draft must be "reviewed". The outcome of this "review obligation" is also open; the national parliaments retain no right of veto. The Commission can therefore either adhere to, amend or withdraw a media regulatory proposal against which reasoned opinions have been submitted with regard to the principle of subsidiarity.[230]

However, under the ordinary legislative procedure, where the number of reasones opinions submitted reaches at least a simple majority of the total number of votes allocated to the national parliaments, further procedural steps must be taken into account – in addition to the review obligation: If it chooses to maintain the proposal, the Commission will have, in a reasoned opinion, to justify vis-à-vis the Union legislature, i.e. Parliament and

---

plication of the principles of subsidiarity and proportionality is to be obtained. The President of the Bundestag or the President of the Bundesrat, in accordance with paragraph 2, shall transmit the reasoned opinion to the Presidents of the competent institutions of the European Union and shall inform the Federal Government accordingly. However, there is no such provision in the Rules of Procedure of the Bundesrat. This also means that the link between state parliamentary policy-forming and decision-making on the one side and the reprimanding opinion of the Bundesrat on the other is not regulated.

229 The threshold is at least a quarter of the votes in cases of drafts submitted on the basis of Art. 76 TFEU on the area of freedom, security and justice.

230 The national parliaments therefore have no possibility of imposing a legally binding obligation on the Commission to amend a legislative proposal. If the national parliaments do not succeed with their subsidiarity complaints, the best they can do is to influence the voting behavior of their government representative in the Council. Various Member States provide for corresponding procedures domestically; the approval of a legislative proposal by the government representative is made dependent on the approval by its own parliament (so-called ad referendum vote); on this *Huber* in: Streinz, Art. 12 TEU, para. 43. Thus, the early warning mechanism complements the existing channels of influencing one's own government. Cf. *Oesch*, Das Subsidiaritätsprinzip im EU-Recht und die nationalen Parlamente, 301, 309.

Council, why it considers that the proposal complies with the principle of subsidiarity and at the same time notify the reasoned opinions of the national parliaments for further consideration. Before concluding the first reading, the Union legislature shall consider whether the legislative proposal is compatible with the principle of subsidiarity, taking particular account of the reasons expressed and shared by the majority of national Parliaments as well as the reasoned opinion of the Commission. Subsequently, if, by a majority of 55 % of the members of the Council or a majority of the votes cast in the European Parliament, the Union legislature is of the opinion that the proposal is not compatible with the principle of subsidiarity, the legislative proposal shall not be given further consideration.

Art. 8 of the Subsidiarity Protocol opens the possibility for Member States and – according to the respective national legal order – national parliaments incl. their chambers to bring an action on grounds of infringement of the principle of subsidiarity.[231] This is a special form of the action for annulment under Art. 263 TFEU (to which Art. 8 of the Subsidiarity Protocol expressly refers). The subsidiarity action is also subject to the usual admissibility requirements of Art. 263 TFEU. Accordingly, the time limit for bringing an action is two months from the publication of the act in the Official Journal of the EU pursuant to Art. 263(6) TFEU.

Art. 8 of the Subsidiarity Protocol has constitutive significance only insofar as the decision on the initiation of legal action is also a matter for the parliaments or parliamentary chambers in the domestic context. Consequently, various Member States – including Germany – have set the quorums for bringing an action (significantly) below the simple majority. In this respect, the subsidiarity action has the function of a minority right,

---

231 According to § 12(1) of the Act on the Exercise by the Bundestag and by the Bundesrat of their Responsibility for Integration in Matters concerning the European Union (Responsibility for Integration Act) (Gesetz über die Wahrnehmung der Integrationsverantwortung des Bundestages und des Bundesrates in Angelegenheiten der Europäischen Union (Integrationsverantwortungsgesetz – IntVG)) the Bundestag is required, at the request of one quarter of its members, to bring an action under Art. 8 of the Subsidiarity Protocol. At the request of one quarter of the Members of the Bundestag who do not support the bringing of the action, their view shall be made clear in the application. According to § 12(2), in its Rules of Procedure, the Bundesrat may stipulate how a decision on the bringing of an action within the meaning of paragraph 1 is to be obtained. However, a corresponding regulation has not yet been issued. If a motion is tabled in the Bundestag or the Bundesrat for the bringing of an action under paragraph 1 or paragraph 2, the other institution may deliver an opinion, according to § 12(5).

B. Framework for the allocation of competences under EU primary law

since there is a realistic possibility for opposition forces also to bring an action.

If a parliament or a chamber brings a subsidiarity action, the government shall immediately submit the action to the CJEU. However, the conduct of the proceedings shall then be incumbent upon the plaintiff parliament or chamber. The right to file a subsidiarity action exists, moreover, independently of a prior subsidiarity complaint by national parliaments.

However, subsidiarity complaints and actions as instruments for implementing the principle of subsidiarity are associated with problems, not least when it comes to safeguarding the media regulation competence of the German federal states. For one thing, it is unclear to what extent the legal basis chosen for the legislative act must be reviewed in an examination limited solely to subsidiarity. This question arises in a subsidiarity action because Art. 8 Protocol (No. 2) expressly limits judicial review to the principle of subsidiarity.[232] The FCC drew attention to this in its decision of 30 June 2009 on the Treaty of Lisbon and emphasized that it would also depend on "whether the standing of the national parliaments and of the Committee of the Regions to bring an action will be extended to the question, which precedes the monitoring of the principle of subsidiarity, of whether the European Union has competence for the specific lawmaking project".[233] The Bundesrat assumes in its established decision-making practice that the subsidiarity complaint pursuant to Art. 12(b) TEU also covers the question of the competence of the EU.[234]

Furthermore, the FCC has already drawn attention in its Lisbon decision to the fact that the effectiveness of the early warning mechanism introduced by the Lisbon Treaty for monitoring compliance with the principle of subsidiarity depends on "the extent to which the national parliaments will be able to make organisational arrangements that place them in

---

232 Cf. *Oesch*, Das Subsidiaritätsprinzip im EU-Recht und die nationalen Parlamente, 301, 305; also allowing for an examination of infringements of the principle of conferral of powers *Weber* in: Blanke/Mangiameli, Art. 5 TEU, para. 11.
233 BVerfGE 123, 267 (383 et seq.) with reference to Wuermeling, Kalamität Kompetenz: Zur Abgrenzung der Zuständigkeiten in dem Verfassungsentwurf des EU-Konvents, EuR 2004, p. 216 (225); *von Danwitz*, Der Mehrwert gemeinsamen Handelns, Frankfurter Allgemeine Zeitung of 23.10.2008, p. 8.
234 Cf. on this e.g. the opinions of the Bundesrat of 9 November 2007, BR-Printed paper 390/07 (resolution), cipher 5; of 26 March 2010, BR-Printed paper 43/10 (resolution), cipher 2; and of 16 December 2011, BR-Printed paper 646/11 (resolution), cipher 2.

a position to make appropriate use of the mechanism within the short period of eight weeks".[235]

5. The principle of proportionality

The principle of proportionality is a general principle of Union law codified in Art. 5(1) sentence 2, (4) TEU, which – as the FCC rightly pointed out in its ECB decision – has its roots in common law in particular,[236] but also and especially in German law – there, however, not with regard to the clarification of questions of competence in multi-level systems, but particularly in the area of the protection of fundamental rights and administrative law.[237] From these roots, the principle of proportionality – as the FCC points out – has found its way into all European (partial) legal orders via the case law of the European Court of Human Rights[238] and the CJEU.[239]

Not only in Germany,[240] but also in other EU Member States such as France, Austria, Poland, Sweden, Spain and Hungary,[241] the assessment of whether the principle of proportionality has been met is carried out in the sections on monitoring the suitability, necessity and appropriateness of a sovereign measure. The Italian Constitutional Court takes a similar ap-

---

235 BVerfGE 123, 267 (383) with reference to *Mellein*, Subsidiaritätskontrolle durch nationale Parlamente, 2007, p. 269 et seq.
236 The BVerfG (2 BvR 859/15) refers to "*Blackstone*, Commentaries on the Laws of England, 4th ed. 1899, p. 115; *Klatt/Meister*, Der Staat 2012, p. 159 (160 et seq.); *Saurer*, Der Staat 2012, p. 3 (4); *Peters* in: Festschrift für Daniel Thürer, Drei Versionen der Verhältnismäßigkeit im Völkerrecht, 2015, p. 589 et seq.; *Tridimas* in: Schütze/id., Oxford Principles of European Union Law, 2018, p. 243.
237 The case law and literature cited by the FCC in this respect (BVerfGE 3, 383 <399>; *Lerche*, Übermaß und Verfassungsrecht – zur Bindung des Gesetzgebers an die Grundsätze der Verhältnismäßigkeit und der Erforderlichkeit, 1961 <Nachdruck 1999>, p. 19 et seq.) also does not point in the direction of a significance of the principle of proportionality as regards making use of competences.
238 Cf. *von Danwitz* in: EWS 2003, 394, 400.
239 Cf. *Tuori* in: von Bogdandy/Grabenwarter/Huber, vol. VI, § 98, para. 84; cf. also Emiliou, The principle of proportionality in European Law, p. 169; *Craig* in: New Zealand Law Review 2010, 265, 267.
240 Cf. BVerfGE 16, 147 (181); 16, 194 (201 et seq.); 30, 292 (316 et seq.); 45, 187 (245); 63, 88 (115); 67, 157 (173); 68, 193 (218); 81, 156 (188 et seq.); 83, 1 (19); 90, 145 (172 et seq.); 91, 207 (221 et seq.); 95, 173 (183); 96, 10 (21); 101, 331 (347); 120, 274 (321 et seq.); 141, 220 (265, para. 93).
241 Cf. law-comparing FCC, Judgment of the Second Senate of 5 May 2020, 2 BvR 859/15, para. 125.

B. Framework for the allocation of competences under EU primary law

proach and adds to its review the criterion of rationality, which is based on a balanced observance of constitutional values.[242]

The CJEU has recognized the principle of proportionality as an unwritten element of Union law even before it was expressly enshrined in the European Treaties,[243] requiring in this respect "that acts of the EU institutions be appropriate for attaining the legitimate objectives pursued by the legislation at issue and do not exceed the limits of what is appropriate and necessary in order to achieve those objectives".[244] In the doctrine of the principle – (also in this respect) i.a. in contrast to its understanding in the FCC's case law –, the coherence criterion is of particular importance, in particular in CJEU case law on gambling[245]: Accordingly, a measure is suitable within the meaning of the principle of proportionality if it actually meets the objective of achieving the desired goal in a coherent and systematic manner.[246] In this context, the CJEU often limits itself to checking whether the measure in question does not appear to be manifestly unsuitable for achieving the objective pursued.[247] In the context of the assessment of the necessity of a measure, the CJEU examines – (also) in this re-

---

242 Cf. FCC, Judgment of the Second Senate of 5 May 2020, 2 BvR 859/15, para. 125, referring to *Bifulco/Paris* in: v. Bogdandy/Grabenwarter/Huber, vol. VI, § 100, para. 49 et seq.
243 Cf. *Nußberger* in: NVwZ-Beilage 2013, 36, 39; *Trstenjak/Beysen* in: EuR 2012, 265, 265; *Hofmann* in: Barnard/Peers, p. 198, 205; *Weber* in: Blanke/Mangiameli, Art. 5 TEU, para. 12; *Dony*, Droit de l'Union européenne, para. 151.
244 CJEU, joined cases C-293/12 and C-594/12, *Digital Rights Ireland Ltd v Minister for Communications, Marine and Natural Resources and Others and Kärntner Landesregierung and Others*, para. 46; cf. already CJEU, case 8/55, *Fédération Charbonnière de Belgique / High Authority of the European Coal and Steel Community*; cf. also CJEU, case C-491/01, *The Queen / Secretary of State for Health, ex parte British American Tobacco (Investments) Ltd and Imperial Tobacco Ltd.*, para. 122; CJEU, case C-343/09, *Afton Chemical Limited / Secretary of State for Transport*, para. 45; CJEU, case C-283/11, *Sky Österreich GmbH / Österreichischer Rundfunk*, para. 50; CJEU, case C-101/12, *Herbert Schaible / Land Baden-Württemberg*, para. 29.
Recently, the CJEU has occasionally tended to examine the criteria of appropriateness and necessity together (cf. CJEU, case C-58/08, *Vodafone and Others*, para. 53 et seq.; CJEU, case C-176/09, *Luxembourg / Parliament and Council*, para. 63; CJEU, case C-569/18, *Caseificio Cirigliana and Others*, para. 43; cf. *Pache* in: Pechstein et al., Art. 5 TEU, para. 140; *Klamert* in: Kellerbauer/id./Tomkin, Art. 5 TEU, para. 36.
245 Cf. *Ukrow* in: ZfWG 2019, 223, 232.
246 Cf. CJEU, case C-64/08, *Engelmann*, para. 35; CJEU, case C-137/09, *Josemans*, para. 70; CJEU, case C-28/09, *Commission / Austria*, para. 126.
247 Cf. FCC, Judgment of the Second Senate of 5 May 2020, 2 BvR 859/15, para. 126 with extensive references to the case law of the CJEU; *Bast* in: Grabitz/Hilf/

spect in accordance with procedures familiar from German constitutional law doctrine – whether the objective cannot be achieved equally effectively by other measures that impair the asset to be protected to a lesser extent.[248] In contrast, the examination of the appropriateness of a measure – i.e. proportionality in the narrower sense – plays at best a subordinate role in the case law of the CJEU.[249]

The FCC used the proportionality principle in its decision on the ECB's bond policy to find ultra vires action by an EU institution for the first time.[250] It considers the ECB's PSPP decisions to be disproportionate within the meaning of Art. 5(1) sentence 2, (4) TEU.[251] This decision has provoked justified criticism from EU lawyers.[252] Not least, it is unconvincing in its dogmatic approach. This is because the FCC fails to recognize that

Nettesheim, Art. 5 TEU, para. 73; *Klamert* in: Kellerbauer/id./Tomkin, Art. 5 TEU, para. 39; *Weber* in: Blanke/Mangiameli, Art. 5 TEU, para. 12.

248 Cf. also in this respect FCC, Judgment of the Second Senate of 5 May 2020, 2 BvR 859/15, para. 126 with further extensive references to the case law of the CJEU.

249 Cf. also in this respect FCC, Judgment of the Second Senate of 5 May 2020, 2 BvR 859/15, para. 126 with further extensive references to the case law of the CJEU; *Calliess* in: id./Ruffert, Art. 5 TEU, para. 44; *von Danwitz* in: EWS 2003, 393, 395; *Lecheler* in: Merten/Papier, vol. VI/1, § 158, para. 31; *Pache* in: Pechstein et al., Art. 5 TEU, para. 149; *Trstenjak/Beysen* in: EuR 2012, p. 265, 269 et seq.; *Klamert* in: Kellerbauer/id./Tomkin, Art. 5 TEU, para. 36; *Weber* in: Blanke/Mangiameli, Art. 5 TEU, para. 12; cf. also *Emiliou*, The principle of proportionality in European Law, p. 134.

250 Contrary to what has been widely portrayed, the FCC did not qualify "the PSPP" as such as an ultra vires act. Rather, the court makes the "conclusive" assessment of the program "in its specific form" dependent on a "proportionality assessment by the Governing Council of the ECB, which must be substantiated with comprehensible reasons". In the FCC's view, ultra vires was merely the alleged failure to conduct such an examination, which is said to have led to a "lack of balancing and lack of stating the reasons informing such balancing". Cf. FCC, Judgment of the Second Senate of 5 May 2020, 2 BvR 859/15, para. 177 et seq.; *Guber* in: ZEuS 2020, 625.

251 FCC, Judgment of the Second Senate of 5 May 2020, 2 BvR 859/15, para. 177.

252 Cf. *Giegerich*, Mit der Axt an die Wurzel der Union des Rechts; *Ludwigs*, The consequences of the judgement of 5 May 2020 of the Second Senate of the German Constitutional Court (BVerfG), Committee on Legal Affairs Committee on Constitutional Affairs, Public Hearing, 14 July 2020 (https://www.europarl.europa.eu/cmsdata/210045/AFCO%20JURI%20Hearing%2014%20July%20-%20Prof%20Ludwigs.pdf); *Mayer*, Das PSPP-Urteil des BVerfG vom 5. Mai 2020. Thesen und Stellungnahme zur öffentlichen Anhörung, Deutscher Bundestag, Ausschuss für die Angelegenheiten der Europäischen Union, 25. Mai 2020 (https://www.bundestag.de/resource/blob/697586/cd

B. Framework for the allocation of competences under EU primary law

the treaty-based rule on the delimitation of competences between the EU and its Member States differs fundamentally in content and function from the principle of proportionality, as it has been established by the FCC in decades of settled case law as a fixed component and minimum of any fundamental rights review.[253]

In its *Kalkar II* decision of 22 May 1990, the FCC itself emphasized that, apart from the duty to act in a federal-friendly manner – a duty corresponding to the duty of sincere cooperation in the relationship between the EU and the Member States – there were no constitutional principles "from which limits could be derived for the exercise of competences in the federal-state relationship, which is determined by statehood and the common good. Restrictions on state intervention in the legal sphere of the individual derived from the principle of the rule of law are not applicable in the federal-state relationship as regards the rules on competences. This applies in particular to the principle of proportionality; it has a function of defending the individual sphere of rights and freedoms. The associated thinking in the categories of free space and encroachment cannot be applied specifically to the state's substantive competence, which is determined by a competitive relationship between the federal government and the state, nor to delimitations of competence in general."[254]

---

f8025132586d197288f57569776bff/mayer-data.pdf); *Rath*, Ein egozentrischer deutscher Kompromiss, 05.05.2020 (https://www.lto.de/recht/hintergruende/h/bverfg-ezb-eugh-pspp-entscheidung-kommentar-konflikt-polen-ungarn/); *Thiele*, Das BVerfG und die Büchse der ultra-vires-Pandora, 05.05.2020 (https://verfassungsblog.de/vb-vom-blatt-das-bverfg-und-die-buechse-der-ultra-vires-pandora/); *Wegener*, Verschroben verhoben!, 05.05.2020 (https://verfassungsblog.de/verschroben-verhoben/).

253 Cf. *Guber* in: ZEuS 2020, 625.

254 Own translation ("…aus denen Schranken für die Kompetenzausübung in dem von Staatlichkeit und Gemeinwohlorientierung bestimmten Bund-Länder-Verhältnis gewonnen werden könnten. Aus dem Rechtsstaatsprinzip abgeleitete Schranken für Einwirkungen des Staates in den Rechtskreis des Einzelnen sind im kompetenzrechtlichen Bund-Länder-Verhältnis nicht anwendbar. Dies gilt insbesondere für den Grundsatz der Verhältnismäßigkeit; ihm kommt eine die individuelle Rechts- und Freiheitssphäre verteidigende Funktion zu. Das damit verbundene Denken in den Kategorien von Freiraum und Eingriff kann weder speziell auf die von einem Konkurrenzverhältnis zwischen Bund und Land bestimmte Sachkompetenz des Landes noch allgemein auf Kompetenzabgrenzungen übertragen werden", BVerfGE 81, 310 (338) with reference to BVerfGE 79, 311 (341)).

In a budgetary law case, the FCC also ruled that the defense against a disturbance of the macroeconomic balance and a limitation of borrowing do not oppose each other like an encroachment on fundamental rights and an area of

There was no reason to abandon this constitutional preconception on the occasion of the ECB decision. An effort to parallelize constitutional and Union law conceptions of the meaning of the principle of proportionality would also have argued in favor of a fundamental rights-centered understanding of the principle at the outset, as this also shapes the case law of the CJEU. Particularly in its decision in the preliminary ruling proceedings initiated by the FCC on the ECB's bond policy, however, the CJEU also recognized the importance of the principle in terms of competences.

In this decision, the CJEU – following up on an initial decision interpreting issues at the interface of monetary and economic policy[255] – emphasized that it follows from Arts. 119(2) and 127(1) TFEU in conjunction with Art. 5(4) TEU that a bond purchase program constituting part of monetary policy can only be validly adopted and implemented if the measures it covers are proportionate in view of the objectives of that policy. According to settled case law of the CJEU, the principle of proportionality requires "that acts of the EU institutions be appropriate for attaining the legitimate objectives pursued by the legislation at issue and do not go beyond what is necessary in order to achieve those objectives".[256] As regards judicial review of compliance with those conditions, the CJEU held that, since the European System of Central Banks (ESCB) is required, when it prepares and implements an open market operations programme of the kind provided for in Decision 2015/774[257], to make choices of a technical nature and to undertake complex forecasts and assessments, it must be allowed, in that context, a broad discretion.[258]

In view of the information before the Court, it did not appear "that the ESCB's economic analysis — according to which the PSPP was appropriate, in the monetary and financial conditions of the euro area, for con-

---

rights or freedom affected by this encroachment. Therefore, it could also not be understood from Art. 115(1) sentence 2 of the Basic Law that credit financing of consumptive expenditures may only take place subject to the principle of proportionality. This decision also argues against a significance of the principle of proportionality where it exceeds the limits of the fundamental rights review in the direction of a regulation limiting the exercise of competences in multi-level relationships.

255 CJEU, case C-62/14, *Peter Gauweiler and Others / Deutscher Bundestag*, para. 66 et seq.
256 CJEU, case C-62/14, *Peter Gauweiler and Others / Deutscher Bundestag*, para. 67.
257 Decision (EU) 2015/774 of the European Central Bank of 4 March 2015 on a secondary markets public sector asset purchase programme (ECB/2015/10), OJ L 121 of 14.05.2015, p. 20–24.
258 CJEU, case C-493/17, *Heinrich Weiss and Others*, para. 73.

B. Framework for the allocation of competences under EU primary law

tributing to achieving the objective of maintaining price stability — is vitiated by a manifest error of assessment".[259]

In view of the foreseeable effects of the PSPP and given that it did not appear that the ESCB's objective could have been achieved by any other type of monetary policy measure entailing more limited action on the part of the ESCB, the Court held that, in its underlying principle, the PSPP did not manifestly go beyond what is necessary to achieve that objective.[260] The fact that that reasoned analysis is disputed did not, in itself, suffice to establish a manifest error of assessment on the part of the ESCB, since, given that questions of monetary policy are usually of a controversial nature and in view of the ESCB's broad discretion, nothing more could be required of the ESCB apart from that it use its economic expertise and the necessary technical means at its disposal to carry out that analysis with all care and accuracy.[261] Finally, having regard to the information in the documents before the Court and to the broad discretion enjoyed by the ESCB, it was not apparent that a government-bonds purchase programme of either more limited volume or shorter duration would have been able to bring about – as effectively and rapidly as the PSPP – changes in inflation comparable to those sought by the ESCB, for the purpose of achieving the primary objective of monetary policy laid down by the authors of the Treaties.[262]

Lastly, according to the CJEU, "the ESCB weighed up the various interests involved so as effectively to prevent disadvantages which are manifestly disproportionate to the PSPP's objective from arising on implementation of the programme".[263]

This decision, which relates to the interplay of monetary and economic policy competences, cannot be easily applied to the interplay between the EU's internal market competence and the Member States' media and, in particular, diversity regulation competence. There is, however, much to suggest that, not least, a sufficient explanation of the process of consideration in the course of further legislation to create a digital single market, as well as the complex forecasts and assessments, which are also required in the case of preventive legislation to safeguard diversity with a view to threats to the diversity objective by new media players, such as media intermediaries in particular, are likely to limit from the outset the chances of

---

259   CJEU, case C-493/17, *Heinrich Weiss and Others*, para. 78.
260   CJEU, case C-493/17, *Heinrich Weiss and Others*, para. 81.
261   CJEU, case C-493/17, *Heinrich Weiss and Others*, para. 91.
262   CJEU, case C-493/17, *Heinrich Weiss and Others*, para. 92.
263   CJEU, case C-493/17, *Heinrich Weiss and Others*, para. 93.

success of proceedings based on a violation of the principle of proportionality. This would be true at least if the preventive safeguarding of diversity were not the main purpose of regulation on the part of the EU, but an accompanying purpose in the effort to make fundamental freedoms more effective for the new media players.

In terms of regulatory policy, however, in order to avoid deepening of the line of conflict between the CJEU and the FCC, originating in the ECB bond policy, on the interpretation of ultra vires limits in light of the principle of proportionality, this argues for restraint in European lawmaking in areas that are particularly sensitive to fundamental rights from the perspective of the constitutional doctrines of communications freedoms in the Member States. In particular, full harmonization of the law of diversity in the digital media ecosystem would provoke questions about overstepping the ultra vires boundaries in the relationship between the CJEU and the FCC. Such an insensitive extension of the scope of application of European "media regulation" *ratione personae* and/or *ratione materiae* would equally endanger the cooperation between the EU and its Member States and potentially further strain the relationship between the CJEU and the FCC.

6. The significance of limitations to the exercise of competences in the practice of media regulatory – status and perspectives for development

In the practice of media regulation to date, neither the principle of proportionality nor the principle of subsidiarity have played a role easily recognizable from the outside and have, to that extent, been of accordingly little relevance. In the recitals of the amended AVMSD, there is only a rudimentary reference to the principle of proportionality, which, moreover, is not based on competence but on fundamental rights, in connection with the so-called quota regulations.[264] With regard to the principle of subsidiarity, there is not even any recital specifically related to this principle.

---

264 After rec. 37 of the amended AVMSD first emphasizes that broadcasters currently invested more in European audiovisual works than providers of on-demand audiovisual media services, it concludes: "Therefore, if a targeted Member State chooses to impose a financial obligation on a broadcaster that is under the jurisdiction of another Member State, the direct contributions to the production and acquisition of rights in European works, in particular co-productions, made by that broadcaster, should be taken into account, *with due consideration for the principle of proportionality*" (own emphasis).

B. Framework for the allocation of competences under EU primary law

However, this does not mean that the principle of subsidiarity is without practical relevance: In its legislative proposals, including those with more or less intensive reference to media regulation, the European Commission regularly addresses the issue of compatibility with the principle of subsidiarity, thus enabling third-party regulators, but also the interested public, to raise critical objections as to the compatibility of the proposed regulation with the principle of subsidiarity. It is reasonable to assume that this procedural opening towards a subsidiarity-related burden of justification also takes into account the procedural effects of the principle of subsidiarity, in particular the early warning system.

In recent years, national parliaments have occasionally made use of the possibility to criticize insufficient compliance with the principle of subsidiarity in EU legislative proposals.[265] However, the state parliaments, which are ultimately responsible for media regulation in Germany, do not have the ability to reprimand. So far, they have not been able to make an institutional mark as "guardians" of the principle of subsidiarity.

However, as far as appears, the early warning mechanism has never led to the Commission subsequently amending a legislative proposal in a substantial way, even beyond the field of media regulation, although the views of the institutions and other actors, including national parliaments, on compliance with the principle of subsidiarity sometimes diverge strongly. The Commission's adherence to its own proposals can probably be explained to some extent by the fact that the quorums for triggering the special review requirement were reached only exceptionally in very few legislative proposals. In order for national parliaments to achieve the necessary clout, careful coordination and consultation would be required not only in the domestic sphere of cooperative parliamentary federalism, but also in transnational European parliamentary networking. A joint approach is essentially the prerequisite for the early warning mechanism to be used effectively. The Conference of Parliamentary Committees for Union Affairs of Parliaments of the European Union (COSAC) could be used as a "clearing house" for this purpose.

In addition, Art. 4a(2)(2) AVMSD now provides that "[i]n cooperation with the Member States, the Commission shall facilitate the development

---

265 Cf. on this and the following the Commission's annual reports on the application of the principles of subsidiarity and proportionality, most recently for 2019, COM(2020) 272 final, https://ec.europa.eu/info/sites/info/files/com-2020-272-en.pdf.

of Union codes of conduct, where appropriate, in accordance with the principles of subsidiarity and proportionality".[266]

The importance of both principles in the further development of the regulatory framework for media governance in the EU cannot be underestimated. This is because the reference in the Directive to EU codes of conduct is adressed in Art. 4a(1) and (2) of the Directive, providing for regulation by means of co- and self-regulation: According to Art. 4a(1) sentence 1, "Member States shall encourage the use of co-regulation and the fostering of self-regulation through codes of conduct adopted at national level in the fields coordinated by this Directive to the extent permitted by their legal systems".[267] Additionally, according to Art. 4a(2) sentence 1, "Member States and the Commission may foster self-regulation through Union codes of conduct drawn up by media service providers, video-sharing platform service providers or organisations representing them, in cooperation, as necessary, with other sectors such as industry, trade, professional and consumer associations or organisations".[268]

VI. The relevance of fundamental rights

1. Media-related protection of fundamental rights, the requirement of respect under Article 11(2) CFR and the question of competence

Freedom and pluralism of the media are not solely of fundamental importance for a functioning democracy at the level of the Member States of the EU. Without such protection of the media, an integration process committed to the fundamental values of Art. 2 TEU cannot be set in motion. Questions of media regulation thus touch on the foundation of the European Union – the "universal values of the inviolable and inalienable rights of

---

266 In detail on the AVMSD see chapter D.II.2.
267 According to Art. 4a(1) sentence 2 AVMSD, "[t]hose codes shall (a) be such that they are broadly accepted by the main stakeholders in the Member States concerned; (b) clearly and unambiguously set out their objectives; (c) provide for regular, transparent and independent monitoring and evaluation of the achievement of the objectives aimed at; and (d) provide for effective enforcement including effective and proportionate sanctions".
268 According to Art. 4a(2) sentence 2 AVMSD, "[t]hose codes shall be such that they are broadly accepted by the main stakeholders at Union level and shall comply with points (b) to (d) of paragraph 1". According to sentence 3, "[t]he Union codes of conduct shall be without prejudice to the national codes of conduct".

B. Framework for the allocation of competences under EU primary law

the human person, freedom, democracy, equality and the rule of law" as embodied in the preamble to the TEU.[269]

It is also against this background that freedom and pluralism of the media have always played a prominent role in the development of the EU's protection of fundamental rights. They are a central part of the rights, freedoms and principles enshrined in the ECHR as well as in the CFR and are deeply rooted in the constitutional traditions of the Member States. "They [...] therefore form a normative corpus that has already had, and will potentially have, a role in the interpretation and application of European law"[270] – not least in shaping the digital transformation of (not only) the media ecosystem in a way that safeguards and promotes freedom and at the same time is compatible with democracy and socially acceptable.

In view of the focus of the study, the following does not deal in depth with the scope of the protection of fundamental rights, but with its significance from the perspective of competences. Nevertheless, a brief recourse to the media-related relationship between European and national fundamental rights protection is already at this point significant in terms of competences.[271]

The CFR contains civil, political, economic, social and Union citizenship rights. According to the first sentence of Art. 52(3) CFR, the rights guaranteed therein may not be inferior in meaning and scope to those guaranteed in the ECHR. This protection of the ECHR is to be understood as a minimum standard; the Charter can therefore offer more extensive protection, as is confirmed in its Art. 52(3) sentence 2. This is relevant also with regard to the protection of media fundamental rights.

According to Art. 10(1) sentence 1 ECHR, everyone has the right to freedom of expression. According to the second sentence, this right shall include freedom to hold opinions and to receive and impart information and ideas without interference by public authority and regardless of frontiers. Under the third sentence of Art. 10(1) ECHR, this Article shall not prevent States from requiring the licensing of broadcasting, television or cinema enterprises.

The exercise of these freedoms, according to Art. 10(2) ECHR, "carries with it duties and responsibilities [and hence] may be subject to such for-

---

269 Cf. on this context *Vike-Freiberga et al.* (High-Level Group on Media Freedom and Pluralism), Report on a free and pluralistic media to sustain European democracy, p. 20.
270 *Brogi/Gori*, European Commission Soft and Hard Law Instruments for Media Pluralism and Media Freedom, p. 67.
271 Cf. furthermore also below, chapters C.II and C.III.

malities, conditions, restrictions or penalties as are prescribed by law and are necessary in a democratic society, in the interests of national security, territorial integrity or public safety, for the prevention of disorder or crime, for the protection of health or morals, for the protection of the reputation or rights of others, for preventing the disclosure of information received in confidence, or for maintaining the authority and impartiality of the judiciary".

The scope of protection of Art. 11 CFR goes further than the protection under Art. 10 ECHR. While Art. 11(1) sentence 1 CFR is identical in wording to Art. 10(1) sentence 1 ECHR and Art. 11(1) sentence 2 CFR is identical in wording to Art. 10(1) sentence 2 ECHR, Art. 11(2) CFR furthermore stipulates that "[t]he freedom and pluralism of the media shall be respected".

The term "media", already from its wording, goes beyond the classical terms of radio and television used in Art. 10(1) sentence 3 ECHR and also encompasses more than just this traditional broadcasting and the press. Even if Art. 10 ECHR is to be understood dynamically according to settled case law of the Strasbourg Human Rights Court, it is noteworthy that Art. 11(2) CFR already from its wording takes a broader personal scope of application of the fundamental right in question into consideration. Already on a semantic interpretation, this personal scope of application includes not only classic categories of media, but all – including future, i.e. not known at the time of the drafting and adoption of the Charter – transmission media for communication directed at the general public. This special openness to future and development[272] must also be taken into account in the further development of the regulation of communication beyond individual communication, i.e. also as regards regulation that relates to social networks and media intermediaries. Since the possibility of exercising fundamental rights in the digital space must also be protected by the state, there is an obligation in this respect also to protect against disruptions of a free mass-communicative discourse to the detriment of democratic freedom and participation through technical or other instruments such as network effects. The necessity of openness as regards the protection of fundamental rights against new threats, as emphasized by the FCC in its "III. Weg" decision, is therefore also important with regard to the protection of fundamental rights in Europe.

It is also evident that a decentralisation of media regulation can contribute to the pluralism of the media. In this respect, measures to safeguard

---

272 Cf. *Frenz*, Handbuch Europarecht, para. 1747.

B. Framework for the allocation of competences under EU primary law

regional and local diversity are not least also suitable for supporting the objective of Art. 11(2) CFR.

Under the Treaty of Lisbon, the CFR has acquired the status of primary law via Art. 6(1) TEU. According to Art. 51(1) sentence 1 CFR, the provisions of the Charter are addressed to the institutions, bodies, offices and agencies of the Union; they also apply to the Member States, insofar as they act within the scope of application of Union law, e.g. when implementing and enforcing Union law.[273]

Whether fundamental rights beyond their defensive function also imply the transfer of obligations to protect onto the sovereign is disputed and is open to differentiated consideration depending on the fundamental right in question. The "obligation to respect" of Art. 11(2) CFR speaks against a merely defensive quality of the pluralism dimension of that fundamental right. The CJEU has already affirmed – though not yet in relation to Art. 11(2) CFR – a function of objective law for certain fundamental rights.[274] In all cases in which an obligation to protect is to be affirmed, the public authority must intervene in the event of violations of fundamental rights, for example by private third parties, or even prevent them (by law), which would mean that the European legislature would have an obligation to act – however not beyond the EU's existing areas of competence. This is because neither the European recognition of media freedom as a fundamental right nor the obligation to respect the pluralism of the media gives rise to any additional competence title or even a regulatory primacy on the part of the EU. This follows from Art. 51(2) CFR: Accordingly, "[t]he Charter does not extend the field of application of Union law beyond the powers of the Union or establish any new power or task for the Union, or modify powers and tasks as defined in the Treaties".

---

273 Cf. CJEU, case 12/86, *Meryem Demirel / Stadt Schwäbisch Gmünd*, para. 28; CJEU, case 5/88, *Hubert Wachauf / Bundesamt für Ernährung und Forstwirtschaft*, para. 17 et seq.
274 Cf. CJEU, case C-288/89, *Stichting Collectieve Antennevoorziening Gouda and others / Commissariaat voor de Media*, para. 22; CJEU, case C-368/95, *Vereinigte Familiapress Zeitungsverlags- und vertriebs GmbH / Heinrich Bauer Verlag*, para. 18. Cf. on this also chapter C.IV.1. in the context of the permissible restriction of fundamental freedoms in the area of diversity protection.

2. *Protection of fundamental rights in an area of friction between review by the CJEU and national constitutional courts*

Questions of fundamental rights protection have long shaped the relationship and assignment of EU law and national constitutional law. In the development of the relevant FCC case law, remarkable shifts of emphasis can be observed, which have continued into recent times.

The starting point for this jurisprudence on the conflict between European law and constitutional law was the so-called *Solange I* decision of the FCC. Therein, the FCC first emphasized that national law and supranational law were two independent and coexisting legal spheres.[275] More explosive – and at the time already open to legal criticism – was its suggestion that European protection of fundamental rights did not meet the requirements of such protection in Germany. Building on this (mis)judgment, the FCC concluded:

> "*As long as the integration process has not progressed so far that Community law receives a catalogue of fundamental rights decided on by a parliament and of settled validity, which is adequate in comparison with the catalogue of fundamental rights contained in the Basic Law, a reference by a court of the Federal Republic of Germany to the Federal Constitutional Court in judicial review proceedings, following the obtaining of a ruling of the European Court under Article 177 of the Treaty, is admissible and necessary if the German court regards the rule of Community law which is relevant to its decision as inapplicable in the interpretation given by the European Court, because and in so far as it conflicts withone of the fundamental rights of the Basic Law.*"[276]

With its *Solange II* decision, the FCC – also in the light of the CJEU's case law on fundamental rights that had been handed down in the meantime – initiated a departure from this course of confrontation under conflict of laws. Therein, the Karlsruhe judges emphasized:

> "*As long as the European Communities, in particular European Court case law, generally ensure effective protection of fundamental rights as against the sovereign powers of the Communities which is to be regarded as substantially similar to the protection of fundamental rights required unconditionally by the Constitution, and in so far as they generally safeguard the essential*

---

275 Cf. BVerfGE 37, 271 (278).
276 BVerfGE 37, 271 (285), translation available at https://law.utexas.edu/transnational/foreign-law-translations/german/case.php?id=588.

B. Framework for the allocation of competences under EU primary law

> *content of fundamental rights, the Federal Constitutional Court will no longer exercise its jurisdiction to decide on the applicability of secondary Community legislation cited as the legal basis for any acts of German courts or authorities within the sovereign jurisdiction of the Federal Republic of Germany, and it will no longer review such legislation by the standard of the fundamental rights contained in the Basic Law; references to the Court under Article 100 (1) Basic Law for those purpose are therefore inadmissible."*[277]

With the FCC in this decision reserving its power of judicial review in theory but withdrawing it considerably in practice, the Karlsruhe Court continued to adhere to this case law in subsequent years. In particular, in its *Banana Market Regulation* decision, it considered the protection of fundamental rights at the European level as sufficient and emphasized that, even after its *Maastricht* decision[278], it would exercise its power of judicial review only under certain conditions. Therefore, references to the FCC were inadmissible if their justification did not show that the development of European law and the case law of the CJEU had fallen below the required standard of fundamental rights protection after the *Solange II* decision.[279] It would therefore be necessary to explain why a provision of secondary Community law in detail did not generally guarantee the protection of fundamental rights imperative in each case.[280]

More recently, however, the FCC has distanced itself from this case law designed towards cooperation with the CJEU, not only in its ECB decision in 2020, but already earlier in relation to fundamental rights.

As early as 2016,[281] for the first time, it added elements to its fundamental rights review of the preservation of constitutional identity by reserving the right to review the protection of human dignity in light of the German Basic Law not only in the event of a general drop in standards – in line with the *Solange II* approach – but also in individual cases. The reason for this widening of the extent of jurisdiction was that Art. 1 of the Basic Law is referred to in Art. 79(3) of the Basic Law – with the consequence that human dignity is as well part of the constitutional identity of the Basic Law and to that extent subject to identity review. While the decision, which in

---

277 BVerfGE 73, 339 (387), translation available at https://law.utexas.edu/transnational/foreign-law-translations/german/case.php?id=572.
278 Cf. on this supra, chapter B.V.4.
279 BVerfGE 102, 147 (165).
280 BVerfGE 102, 147 (164).
281 BVerfGE 140, 317 (333 et seq.).

terms of content was about the compatibility of an extradition (apparently) mandatory under European law with the principle of guilt, was welcomed by some commentators as a call to the CJEU to take the protection of fundamental rights more seriously, it was classified by others as a "Solange IIa" or "Solange III" decision[282]; there was talk of an almost detonated "identity review bomb"[283]. It is evident that this decision already was not necessarily fully compatible with the CJEU case law on the role of national protection of fundamental rights in the multi-level system of fundamental rights.

The latter issue is made particularly virulent by the Order of the First Senate of 6 November 2019. Already the first headnote shows its fundamental significance in connecting to the "Solange" terminology:

"To the extent that fundamental rights of the Basic Law are inapplicable due to the precedence of EU law, the Federal Constitutional Court reviews the domestic application of EU law by German authorities on the basis of EU fundamental rights. By applying this standard of review, the Federal Constitutional Court fulfils its responsibility with regard to European integration under Article 23(1) of the Basic Law.

Regarding the application of legal provisions that are fully harmonised under EU law, the relevant standard of review does not derive from the fundamental rights of the Basic Law, but solely from EU fundamental rights; this follows from the precedence of application of EU law. This precedence of application is subject, inter alia, to the reservation that the fundamental right in question be given sufficiently effective protection through the EU fundamental rights that are applicable instead."[284]

This decision is also noteworthy in the context of the present study because it originates from a situation related to media regulation and in this context emphasizes the dimension of fundamental rights beyond their classic understanding as defensive rights against the state.

Just like the fundamental rights of the Basic Law, those of the Charter, in view of the FCC, are not limited to protecting citizens vis-à-vis the state, but also afford protection in disputes between private actors, as the court

---

282 Cf. on the debate e.g. *Bilz*, JuWissBlog, 15.03.2016, with further references.
283 "Identitätskontrollbombe", *Steinbeis*, Verfassungsblog, 26.01.2016.
284 FCC, Order of the First Senate of 6 November 2019, 1 BvR 276/17, Headnotes 1 and 2; cf. also ibid., para. 47, 50, 53.

B. Framework for the allocation of competences under EU primary law

emphasizes with reference particularly to the extensive case law of the CJEU.[285]

> *"Where affected persons request that search engine operators refrain from referencing and displaying links to certain online contents in the list of search results, the necessary balancing must take into account not only the right of personality of affected persons (Articles 7 and 8 of the Charter), but must also consider, in the context of search engine operators' freedom to conduct a business (Article 16 of the Charter), the fundamental rights of the respective content provider as well as Internet users' interest in obtaining information. Insofar as a prohibition of the display of certain search results is ordered on the basis of an examination of the specific contents of an online publication, and the content provider is thus deprived of an important platform for disseminating these contents that would otherwise be available to it, this also constitutes a restriction of the content provider's freedom of expression."*[286]

VII. Media regulation and the principle of democracy in the EU

According to Art. 2 sentence 1 TEU, "democracy" is also part of the value system of the EU, on which "[t]he Union is founded". At the same time, the relationship between democracy and "pluralism" is pointed out in Art. 2 sentence 2 TEU – there, however, not with regard to the EU, but with regard to Member States and society. This disconnection between democracy and pluralism in addressing the respective value in the multi-level system of the EU already argues against an "annex competence" of the EU, based on the importance of media pluralism for democracy, to regulate pluralism across all levels of the European integration system, aiming towards preserving the value of democracy. Such cross-level regulation is also out of the question on the occasion of the regulation of the election procedure to the European Parliament pursuant to Art. 223 TFEU.

---

285 FCC, Order of the First Senate of 6 November 2019, 1 BvR 276/17, headnote 4 und para. 96 with reference to CJEU, case C-275/06, *Promusicae / Telefónica de España SAU*, para. 65 et seq.; CJEU, case C-580/13, *Coty Germany GmbH / Stadtsparkasse Magdeburg*, para. 33 et seq.; CJEU, case C-516/17, *Spiegel Online GmbH / Volker Beck*, para. 51 et seq.; on this also *Streinz/Michl* in: EuZW 2011, 384, 385 et seq.; *Frantziou* in: HRLR 2014, 761, 771; *Fabbrini* in: de Vries/Bernitz/Weatherill, p. 261, 275 et seq.; *Lock* in: Kellerbauer/Klamert/Tomkin, Art. 8 CFR, para. 5.
286 FCC, Order of the First Senate of 6 November 2019, 1 BvR 276/17, Headnote 5 and para. 114 et seq.

It is obvious that diversity of opinion and of the media are indispensable for maintaining a democratic order. The FCC emphasizes in a manner that is also applicable beyond the German constitutional order that

> *"Democracy, if it is not to remain merely a formal principle of attribution, depends on the existence of certain pre-legal preconditions, such as ongoing free debate between social forces, interests and ideas that encounter each other, in which political objectives too are clarified and change, and out of which public opinion pre-shapes political will."*[287]

That among these conditions is "that the citizen entitled to vote be able to communicate in his own language with the bodies exercising sovereign power to which he is subject"[288] cannot be disputed. However, a democratic European integration system does not presuppose that this communication has to take place only in a single common language. Linguistic diversity is not an obstacle to democratic cohesion, as has already been shown by countries with several official languages, such as Switzerland, and by countries that are increasingly moving away from the dominance of one language, such as the USA. A reduction of linguistic diversity is therefore not appropriate for the creation of transnational pluralism and would, moreover, be in obvious contradiction to imperatives of public international law with regard to cultural diversity, such as the protection and preservation of minority languages.

Insofar as the FCC emphasized in its *Maastricht* decision that the pre-legal prerequisites also include that

> *"both the decision-making process amongst those institutions which implement sovereign power and the political objectives in each case should be clear and comprehensible to all"*,[289]

one may at least speak of a clear facilitation of pre-legal prerequisites of a democratic shape of the EU when looking at the reform steps of constitutional nature that have taken place since the Maastricht Treaty, such as the reduction of different legislative procedures, the consolidation of cross-border partisan cooperation and the increasing transparency of the political objectives of the Commission and the European Parliament.

---

287 BVerfGE 89, 155 (185) (partly own translation).
288 BVerfGE 89, 155 (185) (own translation).
289 BVerfGE 89, 155 (185); translation available at https://iow.eui.eu/wp-content/uploads/sites/18/2013/04/06-Von-Bogdandy-German-Federal-Constitutional-Court.pdf, p. 18.

B. Framework for the allocation of competences under EU primary law

The European integration system is therefore increasingly also a democratic system – not only a group of democratic states designed for the dynamic development of the EU, but also, in the course of deepening European integration, increasingly a group of these states together with an EU that itself becomes a vehicle for the exercise of democratic rule. In its *Maastricht* decision of 12 October 1993, the FCC already emphasized that

> "[a]s the functions and powers of the Community are extended, the need will increase for representation of the peoples of the individual States by a European Parliament that exceeds the democratic legitimation and influence secured via the national parliaments, and which will form the basis for democratic support for the policies of the European Union."[290]

With the citizenship of the Union established by the Treaty of Maastricht, a lasting legal bond was created between the citizens of the individual Member States which, although it did not have an intensity comparable to common citizenship of a state, nevertheless did lend a legally binding expression to that level of existential community which already exists. The FCC then emphasizes that:

> "The influence which derives from the citizens of the Community may develop into democratic legitimation of European institutions, to the extent that the [...] conditions for such legitimation are fulfilled by the peoples of the European Union."[291]

In the almost three decades since the Maastricht Treaty, to which the FCC's 1993 decision referred, such actual conditions have increasingly developed within the institutional framework of the European Union, not only as a legal instrument for action, but they have also become established in social reality. Not least the climate and Corona crises, but also populist attacks on value-based democratic cooperation are proving to be catalysts of a transnational formation of opinion in order to shape democratic processes of response to the threats.

However, this expanding democratic system does not give rise to any competence on the part of the EU to promote the regulatory prerequisites for a further deepening of the democratic system. Admittedly, this deepen-

---

[290] BVerfGE 89, 155 (184); translation available at https://iow.eui.eu/wp-content/uploads/sites/18/2013/04/06-Von-Bogdandy-German-Federal-Constitutional-Court.pdf, p. 18.

[291] BVerfGE 89, 155 (184 et seq.); translation available at https://iow.eui.eu/wp-content/uploads/sites/18/2013/04/06-Von-Bogdandy-German-Federal-Constitutional-Court.pdf, p. 18.

ing requires a more intensive engagement of the media in the Member States in communicating democratic decision-making processes and their outcomes in relation to the EU's integration program. This is because a European public sphere as a driving force and amplifier for strengthening the EU as a bearer of genuine, democratically legitimized sovereignty also requires openness and transparency supported by the media with regard to the way in which, on the one hand, the Member States internally and between each other and, on the other hand, the EU institutions internally and between each other deal with the competences available to the EU from the European Treaties. However, the constitutional structure of the EU is not designed to enable the Union to draw competences under integration law from integration policy desiderata.

Accordingly, the EU's potential for harmonizing media regulation, which, if anything, can be derived from the principle of democracy, exists in essence to the extent that democratic desiderata, such as the defense against disinformation campaigns from the perspective of the internal market in order to avoid obstacles to the free movement of goods and services, are accompanied by different concepts of well-fortified democracy in a primarily business-oriented regulation.

VIII. Conclusions for the competence for media regulation

The principle of conferral also applies to media regulation by the EU. It is not possible to make conclusive statements about the EU's scope for action in media regulation, since the competence rules of the European Treaties are open to a dynamic understanding that addresses digital challenges.

The European Treaties, in their competence rules providing for regulatory options for the EU, do not contain any exceptions for the media; the EU's "functional" competences, not least in the area of creating a (also digital) single market and a competition regime (in the future also aimed at Europe's digital sovereignty), do not extend to the cultural and diversity-securing function of media, but they do extend to all areas of their economically significant activities.

Neither does the EU have any comprehensive authority to regulate the media. There is no explicit reference to media regulation in the EU competence catalogs; the medias' cultural and educational dimension is only open to regulation by the EU below the level of legal harmonization, supporting the actions of the Member States.

In particular, the inclusion of pluralism in the EU's value system under Art. 2 TEU does not give rise to any regulatory competence on the part of

B. Framework for the allocation of competences under EU primary law

the EU in this regard. The EU's value system provides guidelines for the exercise of the EU's competences provided for elsewhere in the Treaties. Due to the principle of conferral, the imperative of pluralism cannot be considered as a legal basis for genuine regulation of media diversity, not even in the form of an annex competence.

The influence of EU law on media regulation in the Member States to date – and to be expected in the future within the framework of the European Digital Decade proclaimed by Commission President von der Leyen –, whether in the way of active-positive integration through EU legal acts with reference to the media and not least to media diversity, or in the way of negative integration through the review of media regulation in the Member States against the standards of primary EU law (not least fundamental freedoms and competition law), cannot be regarded either as *ultra vires* in principle or even generally, nor as generally permissible. The question of whether an act of media regulation by the EU is outside the EU's integration program remains, at the outset, a question of case-by-case consideration.

However, an overall view of the structural principles of the European Treaties with their rules and restrictions on the exercise of competences, in particular the principles of subsidiarity and proportionality, argues for a continuing primacy at least of culture- and diversity-related media regulation on the part of the Member States. Ultimately, two guidelines for the EU's media regulation in this regard correspond to this: As little interference in Member States' regulatory competence through negative integration as possible, as little harmonization and positive integration as necessary.

C. On the significance and enshrinement in law of media diversity at EU level

Mark D. Cole / Christina Etteldorf

I. Introduction

> *"The concept of pluralism can be defined both in terms of its function and in terms of its objective: it is a legal concept whose purpose is to limit in certain cases the scope of the principle of freedom of expression with a view to guaranteeing diversity of information for the public."*

It is with these words that in 1992, the European Commission attempted in its Green paper on Pluralism and media concentration in the internal market[292] to establish a definition of pluralism in the media and thus a starting point for what is needed to protect and preserve media diversity. Less than two years later, the Council of Europe defined media pluralism in much more concrete and media-related terms, referring to internal and external pluralistic structures of the media themselves as either

> *"internal in nature, with a wide range of social, political and cultural values, opinions, information and interests finding expression within one media organization, or external in nature, through a number of such organizations, each expressing a particular point of view".*[293]

Over the decades since, new definitional approaches have been sought repeatedly at both the scientific and political levels.[294] However, there is still no uniform and supranationally valid definition of what is to be understood by media pluralism. In fact, against the background of the necessity

---

[292] European Commission, Green Paper on Pluralism and media concentration in the internal market – an assessment of the need for Community action, COM (92) 480 final of 23 December 1992, p. 18.
[293] Council of Europe's Committee of Experts on Media Concentrations and Pluralism (1994), 'The Activity Report of the Committee of Experts on Media Concentrations and Pluralism', submitted to the 4th European Ministerial Conference on Mass Media Policy, Prague, 7–8 December 1994.
[294] Cf. in detail on the development of the term *Costache*, De-Regulation of European Media Policy 2000–2014, p. 15 et seq.

of conceptual openness, which must not permit a definitional narrowing and is therefore immanent to media pluralism, there can be no such definition at all. Rather, it also depends on the starting point from which the observation is made. This can, for example, be just as much a media concentration law perspective as an information law one, which asks what significance media pluralism has for the acquisition of information by citizens and thus for the democratic process of developing an informed opinion and mustering a political will.

As outlined in the previous chapter against the background of competence rules, safeguarding media diversity – even though it is not one of the EU's genuine competences – finds such diverse links in Union law also, for example within the EU's value system. Against the background of this study's focus more significant are, however, media diversity's roots in the substantive content of fundamental rights at the level of the ECHR and the CFR as well as in primary law, especially within the EU competition regime and its fundamental freedoms. As will be shown below, safeguarding media diversity in this context is not a direct starting point for legislative measures, but rather a value or objective of general public interest which the EU and its Member States must take into account and uphold in other regulatory areas and which can therefore have justifying or restrictive effects. This chapter will only provide an overview of the enshrinement in secondary law. An in-depth look at the framework of media law at the level of EU secondary law, with a particular focus on aspects of safeguarding diversity, will be taken in the following chapter.

II. Art. 10 ECHR and the case law of the ECtHR

Art. 10 ECHR guarantees that everyone has the right to freedom of expression, including the freedom to hold opinions and to receive and impart information. Freedom of expression, opinion and information constitute rights that are also of crucial importance against the backdrop of media pluralism, since safeguarding and preserving diversity must fulfill their functions with a view to the democratic process of developing an informed opinion and mustering a political will. The accession of the EU to the ECHR has been on the European agenda for half a century, but has not yet taken place, probably also due to the complexity of the accession of a supranational organization with an autonomous legal order to a human

C. On the significance and enshrinement in law of media diversity at EU level

rights protection system under public international law.[295] However, the 27 Member States of the EU are bound by the ECHR and remain so in principle even when sovereign rights are transferred to supranational bodies.[296] Moreover, the EU applies its own fundamental rights protection vis-à-vis the ECHR, guaranteed through the CFR, even more widely than many legal orders of EU Member States do[297], in that Art. 52(3) CFR provides that, to the extent that the CFR contains rights equivalent to those guaranteed by the ECHR, they shall have the same meaning and scope as given to them in the said Convention. This provision does not preclude Union law from providing more extensive protection.

Based on the ECtHR's broad understanding of the term as already mentioned in Section B.VI.1., Art. 10(1) ECHR also protects the mass media dissemination of information, in particular the freedom of public and private broadcasters to broadcast[298], whereby advertising[299] is also part of the protected communication process. In this context, the scope of protection extends to the communication process on the Internet also.[300] Just as little as the distribution channel does the professionalism of media offerings play a role for the application of the scope of protection. In a more recent decision, the ECtHR argues that, for example, so-called citizen journalism (such as e.g. in the form of offerings and channels by users on video-sharing platforms (VSP) like YouTube) can also be an important additional means of exercising freedom of expression and to receive and impart information and ideas, especially against the background that and when political information is ignored by the traditional media.[301]

Broadly defined is also the notion of interference, which covers both preventive measures and repressive prohibitions and sanctions, ranging from the prevention or impediment of the reception/accessibility of media services or individual contents to mere flagging.[302] In this context, the intensity of the interference, i.e., the severity of the impairment of the fundamental right due to the interference, is weighted only at the level of justifi-

---

295 Cf. on this in detail *Obwexer* in: EuR 2012, 115, 115 et seq.
296 *Ress*, Menschenrechte, Gemeinschaftsrechte und Verfassungsrecht, p. 920 et seq.
297 Cf. on this *Krämer* in: Stern/Sachs, Art. 52 CFR, para. 65; *Lock* in: Kellerbauer/Klamert/Tomkin, Art. 52 CFR, para. 25.
298 ECtHR, No. 50084/06, *RTBF / Belgium*, para. 5, 94.
299 ECtHR, No. 33629/06, *Vajnai / Hungary*; No. 15450/89, *Casado Coca / Spain*.
300 ECtHR, No. 36769/08, *Ashby Donald u.a. / France*, para. 34.
301 Cf. ECtHR, No. 48226/10 and 14027/11, *Cengiz and others / Turkey*.
302 Cf. for instance ECtHR, No. 26935/05 and 13353/05, *Hachette Filipacchi Presse Automobile and Dupuy and Société de Conception de Presse et d'Edition and Ponson / France*.

cation, because the ECHR does not guarantee freedom of expression and of the media without restriction, but accepts that freedom of expression also entails a certain responsibility and therefore permits restrictions based on higher-ranking legal interests. The ECtHR grants the Convention States a margin of discretion, within which, however, they must establish an appropriate balance between the restriction of freedom of expression and the legitimate objective pursued.[303]

Media diversity[304] has always been of particular importance in the context of Art. 10 ECHR. Even though this does not follow directly from the text of the Convention, it does so from the established case law of the ECtHR. It has repeatedly emphasized the fundamental role of freedom of expression for a democratic society, especially insofar as it serves to disseminate information and ideas of general interest, which the public has a right to receive.[305] The media act here in their function as "public watchdog"[306] and make an important contribution to the public debate – as mediator of information and forum for public discourse. Such an effort, the ECtHR emphasizes, could only be successful if it was based on the principle of pluralism, of which the state is the guarantor.[307] In this context, the Court even goes so far as to observe that there could be no democracy without pluralism[308], democracy being characterized by the protection of cultural or intellectual heritage as well as artistic, literary and socio-economic ideas

---

303 ECtHR, No. 39954/08, *Axel Springer AG / Germany*.
304 Recommendation No. R (94) 13 of the Committee of Ministers to member states on measures to promote media transparency (1994); Recommendation No. R (99) 1 of the Committee of Ministers to member states on measures to promote media pluralism (1999); Recommendation Rec (2003) 9 of the Committee of Ministers to member states on measures to promote the democratic and social contribution of digital broadcasting (2003); Recommendation CM/Rec(2007)2 of the Committee of Ministers to member states on media pluralism and diversity of media content (2007); Recommendation CM/Rec(2012)1 of the Committee of Ministers to member states on public service media governance (2012). For an overview of the Council of Europe's recommendations in the area of media and the information society, see also Recommendations and declarations of the Committee of Ministers of the Council of Europe in the field of media and information society, 2016, https://rm.coe.int/1680645b44.
305 ECtHR, No. 13585/88, *Observer and Guardian / United Kingdom*; No. 17207/90, *Informationsverein Lentia and others / Austria*.
306 Cf. for a concretization of the role as public watchdog e.g. ECtHR, No. 21980/93, *Bladet Tromsø / Norway*.
307 ECtHR, No. 17207/90, *Informationsverein Lentia and others / Austria*, para. 38.
308 ECtHR, No. 13936/02, *Manole and others / Moldova*, para. 95.

C. On the significance and enshrinement in law of media diversity at EU level

and concepts.[309] Not least because of this outstanding importance, the ECtHR does not assign a purely defensive dimension to Art. 10(1) ECHR with regard to securing media pluralism, but considers the state to be – in the last instance – the guarantor of the principle of pluralism.[310] However, the question of whether the ECHR states from this are subject to an obligation to create equivalent diversity in European communication spaces, or merely to the obligation to protect and promote media diversity, has not yet been conclusively clarified.[311] The ECtHR's understanding in this respect is at least that if pluralism leads to tensions, the state's action must not be directed against pluralism, but rather must ensure that the groups involved tolerate each other.[312] Moreover, a purely defensive conception is not compatible with the Convention in general, especially against the background of its Art. 1, according to which states shall secure the rights and freedoms under the Convention. In the audiovisual sector, pluralism must be guaranteed at least in an effective way by providing an appropriate framework – in legal and administrative terms.[313]

Irrespective of whether and to what extent positive obligations to act on the part of the Convention States are to be derived from Art. 10(1) ECHR, the enshrinement of the obligation to protect media pluralism in the ECHR and its classification as an objective of general interest is significant with regard to the justification of the interference with fundamental freedoms.[314] Interference with fundamental rights, such as freedom of the media itself or freedom of property under Art. 1 of the First Additional Protocol to the ECHR, for instance, can be justified by diversity safeguarding measures adopted by the Convention States, since fundamental rights in turn are subject to restrictions in order to realize public interest objectives, provided that these are necessary (i.e. proportionate) in a democratic society.

---

309 ECtHR, No. 44158/98, *Gorzelik and others / Poland*, para. 92.
310 ECtHR, No. 17207/90, *Informationsverein Lentia and others / Austria*, para. 38; No. 24699/94, *VgT Verein gegen Tierfabriken / Switzerland*, para. 73.
311 Cf. for instance *Gersdorf* in: AöR 1994, 400, 414; *Daiber* in: Meyer-Ladewig/Nettesheim/von Raumer, Art. 11, para. 60.
312 ECtHR, No. 74651/01, *Association of Citizens Radko & Paunkovski / Former Yugoslav Republic of Macedonia*; cf. on this and the following also *Ukrow/Cole*, Aktive Sicherung lokaler und regionaler Medienvielfalt, p. 83 et seq.
313 ECtHR, No. 48876/08, *Animal Defenders International / United Kingdom*, para. 134. On this supra, chapter B.VI.1.
314 Cf. ECtHR, No. 38433/09, *Centro Europa 7 S.R.L. and di Stefano / Italy*, para. 214 et seq.

Consequently, the aforementioned comments on the aspects of safeguarding diversity to be derived from Art. 10(1) ECHR also apply in parallel with the broad understanding of the scope of protection. The ECtHR does particularly emphasize the importance of diversity in certain media sectors, especially in the audiovisual sector because of its traditionally more pervasive ("very widely") effect than, for example, the press.[315] However, the imperative to maintain pluralism in the sense of a threat-oriented interpretation of fundamental rights protection applies wherever a medium acquires significance for the transmission of information. Thus, the ECtHR also emphasizes the particular significance of the Internet for the democratic process of developing an informed opinion and mustering a political will[316] – which is not least important for the distribution channels of traditional media –, without diminishing the important role of traditional media alongside new players such as social media or other platforms. Rather, the ECtHR seems to assume that an interplay of different means of reception constitutes pluralism. This may lead to a situation where, in the event of a (sufficiently serious) uneven shift of influence on the formation of public opinion, specific countermeasures would have to be taken by the Convention States.[317]

However, the ECtHR does not specify how the Convention States are to design measures to safeguard diversity – apart from general statements on the necessity of measures in a democratic society or the weighting of differing interests protected by fundamental rights. Within the framework of its jurisdiction, however, it increasingly refers to recommendations of the Council of Europe, in particular the Recommendation of the Committee of Ministers to member states on media pluralism and diversity of media

---

315 ECtHR, No. 37374/05, *Társaság a Szabadságjogokért / Hungary*, para. 26; No. 17207/90, *Informationsverein Lentia and others / Austria*, para. 38; No. 24699/94, *VgT Verein gegen Tierfabriken / Switzerland*, para. 73.
316 ECtHR, No. 3002/03 and 23676/03, *Times Newspapers Ltd (No. 1 and 2) / United Kingdom*, para. 27.
317 This option was considered by the ECtHR in its judgment of 22.04.2013 (No. 48876/08, *Animal Defenders International / United Kingdom*, para. 119: "*Notwithstanding therefore the significant development of the internet and social media in recent years, there is no evidence of a sufficiently serious shift in the respective influences of the new and of the broadcast media in the respondent State to undermine the need for special measures for the latter*"), but was ultimately rejected in light of the circumstances of the digital transformation in the media landscape at that time.

content[318], which equally affirms that pluralistic expression should be protected and actively promoted.[319] The Council of Europe itself bases its recommendations for Member States' options for action on Art. 10 ECHR and the resulting obligations imposed on its Member States. In particular, they are to adapt the existing regulatory framework, especially with regard to media ownership, and take all necessary regulatory and financial measures to ensure media transparency and structural pluralism as well as diversity. In this context, the Council of Europe's sector-specific recommendations also contain more concrete proposals for measures to safeguard diversity based on an analysis of potential threats, such as the introduction of transparency obligations or must-carry/must-offer rules. However, due to the non-binding nature of such recommendations, whether and how they are "implemented" is in any case left to the Member States.[320]

III. Art. 11(2) CFR and CJEU jurisprudence

At EU level, the counterpart to Art. 10(1) ECHR is found in Art. 11(1) CFR, according to which everyone has the right to freedom of expression, which shall include freedom to receive and impart information and ideas without interference by public authority and regardless of frontiers. As under the ECHR, the scope of protection (in conjunction with Art. 11(2), which also explicitly addresses freedom of the media) covers traditional media such as the press, radio and film, as well as any other form of mass communication that already exists or will come into existence in the future, provided that it is addressed to the general public.[321] Art. 11 CFR was introduced into the Charter in close accordance with Art. 10 ECHR or, as far as the degree of protection is concerned, in direct incorporation. Only the specific limitations of Art. 10(2) ECHR were not explicitly reproduced,

---

318 Recommendation CM/Rec(2007)2 of the Committee of Ministers to member states on media pluralism and diversity of media content, adopted on 31 January 2007, available at https://search.coe.int/cm/Pages/result_details.aspx?ObjectId=09000016805d6be3.
319 ECtHR, No. 48876/08, *Animal Defenders International / United Kingdom*,, para. 135.
320 Cf. on this *Tichy* in: ZaöRV 2016, p. 415, 415 et seq.
321 *Von Coelln* in: Stern/Sachs, Art. 11 CFR, para. 30; *Lock* in: Kellerbauer/Klamert/Tomkin, Art. 11 CFR, para. 3.

as the CFR contains an autonomous and horizontally applicable limitation provision in its Art. 52(1).[322]

In contrast to a very comprehensive jurisprudence of the ECtHR, the CJEU's jurisprudence on communication freedoms is less developed. This is also due to the fact that media regulation, and thus also restrictions on communications freedoms, are the responsibility of the Member States due to the limited powers of the EU in this respect and therefore play a lesser role in, e.g., preliminary ruling procedures.[323] In this context, however, it should be noted that, in line with the growing importance of invoking the CFR in the case law of the CJEU and in the requests for referral of the Member States as a whole[324], the emphasis on Art. 11 CFR has also increased[325], even though the decisions in question were mainly based on the relevant secondary law and Art. 11 CFR was regularly used only to emphasize the importance of the rights and freedoms laid down therein. However, the case law of the ECtHR on Art. 10 ECHR and thus the previous remarks can be referred to with regard to Art. 11(1) CFR, which results both from the corresponding explanations of the preamble to Art. 11 CFR[326] and from the equivalence clause of Art. 52(3) CFR and, moreover, also corresponds to CJEU practice, following the interpretation of the ECtHR.[327]

The fundamental right under Art. 11(1) CFR is also subject to potential restrictions. According to the uniform limitation rule of Art. 52(1) CFR, however, any limitation on the exercise of the rights and freedoms recognised by the Charter must be provided for by law and respect the essence

---

322 *Cornils* in: Sedelmeier/Burkhardt, § 1, para. 88; *von Coelln* in: Stern/Sachs, Art. 11 CFR, para. 7 et seq.
323 *Cornils* in: Sedelmeier/Burkhardt, § 1, para. 1, 46, 86.
324 In 2018, the CJEU referred to the CFR in 356 cases (up from 27 in 2010). When national courts address requests for preliminary rulings to the CJEU, they increasingly refer to the CFR (84 times in 2018 compared to 19 times in 2010). European Commission, 2018 report on the application of the EU Charter of Fundamental Rights, https://op.europa.eu/de/publication-detail/-/publication/784b02a4-a1f2-11e9-9d01-01aa75ed71a1/language-en, p. 15.
325 In 29 judgments, Art. 11 CFR was referred to by the CJEU (although not always in a way relevant to the decision), 8 of which date from 2019, 3 already from 2020. Source: CJEU case law database, http://curia.europa.eu/juris/recherche.jsf?language=en.
326 Explanations relating to the Charter of Fundamental Rights, OJ C 303 of 14.12.2007, p. 17–35, available at http://eur-lex.europa.eu/legal-content/EN/TXT/HTML/?uri=CELEX:32007X1214(01)&from=EN.
327 Cf. CJEU, case C-368/95, *Vereinigte Familiapress Zeitungsverlags- und vertriebs GmbH / Heinrich Bauer Verlag*.

C. On the significance and enshrinement in law of media diversity at EU level

of those rights and freedoms. Subject to the principle of proportionality, limitations may be made only if they are necessary and genuinely meet objectives of general interest recognised by the Union or the need to protect the rights and freedoms of others.

Yet, against the background of questions concerning the establishment of diversity safeguarding measures under competence rules, Art. 11(2) CFR is more interesting, as it stipulates that the freedom of the media *and their pluralism* shall be respected. Due to the weaker wording compared to the draft version[328], the question of whether and to what extent this should result in objective legal obligations for safeguarding diversity on the part of the EU or its Member States, for example in the sense of preventive concentration control[329], has still not been conclusively clarified.[330] While a positive regulatory mandate to the Union legislature must already be ruled out for competence reasons, diversity protection thus remains a competence of the Member States alone[331], and the interpretation of Art. 11(2) CFR in the sense of a serving fundamental right such as Art. 5(1) sentence 2 Basic Law is likely to go too far[332], the regulation cannot be denied a certain objective legal component.[333] An interpretation in this sense is also consistent with the considerations regarding the enshrinement of freedom of the media and pluralism in Art. 10 ECHR, the meaning of which the rules of the CFR, in accordance with its Art. 53, must not fall short of. According to the CFR's explanations[334], to which – in line with the preamble to the CFR – due regard has to be taken by the the courts of the Union and

---

328 The first draft version still contained the wording "shall be guaranteed". Cf. on this also *Schmittmann/Luedtke* in: AfP 2000, 533, 534.
329 *Stock*, AfP 2001, 289, 301.
330 Cf. on this in detail and with further references *Ukrow/Cole*, Aktive Sicherung lokaler und regionaler Medienvielfalt, p. 87 et seq.; as well as *Institut für Europäisches Medienrecht*, Nizza, die Grundrechte-Charta und ihre Bedeutung für die Medien in Europa; cf. further *Lock* in: Kellerbauer/Klamert/Tomkin, Art. 11 CFR, para. 17.
331 Cf. supra, chapter B.VI.1. Same as here *Ukrow/Cole*, Aktive Sicherung lokaler und regionaler Medienvielfalt, p. 89 et seq.; *Valcke*, Challenges of Regulating Media Pluralism in the European Union, p. 27; *Craufurd Smith*, Culture and European Union Law, p. 626 et seq.
332 Same as here *von Coelln* in: Stern/Sachs, Art. 11 CFR, para. 40 fn. 108 with further references; *Streinz* in: id., Art. 11 CFR, para. 17.
333 Same as here *von Coelln* in: Stern/Sachs, Art. 11 CFR, para. 40; *Thiele* in: Pechstein et al., Art. 11 CFR, para. 17.
334 Explanations relating to the Charter of Fundamental Rights, OJ C 303 of 14.12.2007, p. 17–35, https://eur-lex.europa.eu/legal-content/de/ALL/?uri=CELEX%3A32007X1214%2801%29.

the Member States when interpreting the Charter, Art. 11(2) is based in particular on CJEU case-law regarding television[335], on the Protocol on the system of public broadcasting in the Member States[336] – which states that "the system of public broadcasting in the Member States is directly related to the democratic, social and cultural needs of each society and to the need to preserve media pluralism" –, and on the Television Broadcasting Directive 89/552/EEC (in force when the Charter was drafted), in particular its recital 17, which in turn emphasizes that "it is essential for the Member States to ensure the prevention of any acts which may prove detrimental to freedom of movement and trade in television programmes or which may promote the creation of dominant positions which would lead to restrictions on pluralism and freedom of televised information and of the information sector as a whole".

However, Art. 11(2) CFR has to date only in a few decisions been explicitly[337] referred to by the CJEU (with regard to the media pluralism to be respected under this provision).[338] While the CJEU in the *Sky Italia* case did not address in detail the question referred for a preliminary ruling on a national competition law provision based on Art. 11(2) CFR due to the incompleteness of the reference decision on the legal and factual basis for assessment, it particularly emphasized the significance of Art. 11(2) in its recent *Vivendi* ruling, which concerned an Italian threshold rule on shareholdings in media undertakings and electronic communications undertakings. Citing its previous case law, the CJEU emphasized the importance of media pluralism and the resulting possibilities for restricting fundamental freedoms as follows:

> "*The Court has held that the safeguarding of the freedoms protected under Article 11 of the Charter of Fundamental Rights, which in paragraph 2*

---

335 Particularly in CJEU, case C-288/89, *Stichting Collectieve Antennevoorziening Gouda and others / Commissariaat voor de Media*.
336 Protocol (No 29) on the system of public broadcasting in the Member States, OJ C 326 of 26.10.2012, p. 312–312.
337 The CJEU also refers more frequently to the importance of media pluralism without resorting to Art. 11(2) CFR in this context, cf. for instance CJEU, case C-250/06, *United Pan-Europe Communications Belgium SA and Others / Belgian State*, para. 41; CJEU, case C-336/07, *Kabel Deutschland Vertrieb und Service GmbH & Co. KG / Niedersächsische Landesmedienanstalt für privaten Rundfunk*, para. 37.
338 CJEU, case C-283/11, *Sky Österreich GmbH / Österreichischer Rundfunk*; CJEU, case C-234/12, *Sky Italia srl / Autorità per le Garanzie nelle Comunicazioni*; CJEU, case C-719/18, *Vivendi SA / Autorità per le Garanzie nelle Comunicazioni*; CJEU, case C-87/19, *TV Play Baltic AS / Lietuvos radijo ir televizijos komisija*.

C. On the significance and enshrinement in law of media diversity at EU level

thereof refers to the freedom and pluralism of the media, unquestionably constitutes a legitimate aim in the general interest, the importance of which in a democratic and pluralistic society must be stressed in particular, capable of justifying a restriction on freedom of establishment [...].
Protocol No 29 on the system of public broadcasting in the Member States, annexed to the EU and FEU Treaties, also refers to media pluralism, stating that 'the system of public broadcasting in the Member States is directly related to the democratic, social and cultural needs of each society and to the need to preserve media pluralism'."[339]

This fundamental significance of pluralism could justify interference with fundamental freedoms (for more details see section C.IV.1.) by Member States' rules.

In the *TV Play Baltic AS* case, the CJEU fleshed this out with regard to the freedom to provide services against the maintenance of a pluralistic broadcasting system, referring to Art. 11 CFR and Art. 10 ECHR. The enormous importance of pluralism for the democratic system had, however, already been established by the CJEU in its judgment *Sky Österreich*, which dealt with the broadcasting of major events, and in particular with the compatibility of Art. 15 AVMSD with higher-ranking law. Art. 15 AVMSD or rather its national transposition, which grants television broadcasters access to events of high interest to the public in which third parties hold exclusive rights, was challenged at the time by a private television broadcaster as the exclusive rights holder vis-à-vis a public broadcaster as the beneficiary of the regulation. The CJEU held that the pursuit of the objective of safeguarding pluralism, derived from Art. 11(2) CFR, can also justify interference with other fundamental rights, as in this case with the right to freedom to conduct a business under Art. 16 CFR. More interestingly, the CJEU also attributed to Art. 15 AVMSD itself the objective of counteracting the increasingly exclusive marketing of events of high interest to the public, thereby safeguarding society's fundamental right to information (Art. 11(1) CFR) and promoting the pluralism protected by Art. 11(2) CFR through the diversity of news production and programming. Therefore, the CJEU concluded, against the background of Art. 11(2) CFR, the EU legislature was entitled to adopt "rules such as those laid down in Article 15 of Directive 2010/13/EU, which limit the freedom to conduct a business, and to give priority, in the necessary bal-

---

[339] CJEU, case C-719/18, *Vivendi SA / Autorità per le Garanzie nelle Comunicazioni*, para. 57, 58.

ancing of the rights and interests at issue, to public access to information over contractual freedom"[340].

It can be deduced from this that both the Member States and the Union legislature cannot invoke Art. 11(2) CFR in the sense of a competence title, but that they can make use of the provision with regard to the pursuit of public interest objectives as a justification for interference with other fundamental freedoms and rights. However, this also means that Art. 11(2) CFR, due to the distribution of competences in interaction with Art. 51(1) CFR, prohibits Union action which runs counter to the objective of securing media pluralism in the Member States.[341]

There is one more aspect that can be concluded from the enshrinement of media pluralism at the level of fundamental rights within the EU: at least comparable to the "interplay" between the Council of Europe's action, the ECtHR's jurisprudence and the legal basis of Art. 10 ECHR outlined in the previous section, the existence of Art. 11 at EU level equally gives the Commission more freedom to include provisions on media pluralism in its recommendations and guidelines, although these then regularly leave the details of safeguarding freedom and pluralism in the media to the Member States.[342] It is discussed whether it also follows that the EU institutions in principle have the power, if they deem it necessary, to set out rules requiring Member States to take appropriate measures to safeguard media diversity.[343] Thus, the Commission considers not only Union legislation in the area relevant to media law as "application of the CFR" and thus of relevance to fundamental rights, but also recommendations in the area relevant to media (such as the Recommendation on measures to effectively tackle illegal content online[344]), communications (such as the com-

---

340 CJEU, case C-283/11, *Sky Österreich GmbH / Österreichischer Rundfunk*, para. 66. In his Opinion of 15.10.2020 in CJEU, case C-555/19, *Fussl Modestraße Mayr*, para. 63, Advocate General *Szpunar* emphasizes the broad discretionary power of the national legislature in introducing measures to safeguard pluralism, including in the regional and local media sector. The CJEU in its judgment of 03.02.2021 has followed a more narrow approach, cf. *Ukrow*, Sicherung regionaler Vielfalt – Außer Mode?.
341 *Cole*, Zum Gestaltungsspielraum der EU-Mitgliedstaaten bei Einschränkungen der Dienstleistungsfreiheit, p. 20.
342 *Costache*, De-Regulation of European Media Policy (2000–2014), p. 26.
343 So e.g. *EU Network of independent experts on fundamental rights*, Report on the situation of fundamental rights in the European Union in 2003, p. 73.
344 Commission Recommendation (EU) 2018/334 of 1 March 2018 on measures to effectively tackle illegal content online, C/2018/1177, OJ L 63 of 06.03.2018, p. 50–61.

C. On the significance and enshrinement in law of media diversity at EU level

munication "Tackling online disinformation: a European Approach"[345]), action plans and accompanying initiatives, funding initiatives (such as the MEDIA program), and the funding of projects (also oriented toward pluralistic goals) such as the European Centre for Press and Media Freedom (ECPMF)[346] and the Media Pluralism Monitor of the Centre for Media Pluralism and Media Freedom[347].[348] In any case, however, it could not be deduced from this consideration that the EU institutions could also instruct the Member States as to which concrete measures are to be taken to safeguard media diversity.

IV. Aspects of primary law

In addition to the connections in the EU competence framework, in particular within the cultural horizontal clause of Art. 167 TFEU, and in the EU's value system, which have already been described in detail in Chapter B, there are also media-relevant links within the substantive primary law of the EU. In particular, this applies to the fundamental freedoms as individual rights enshrined in primary law, as well as to the competition regime's references to safeguarding diversity in the media. Although both areas are significantly geared towards protecting and guaranteeing a free and fair internal market in the EU, which concerns the media as participants in economic dealings and commerce, they also contain exceptions and limits with regard to the consideration of, as well, cultural aspects. These will be presented hereafter, as far as relevant for the present study.

1. Fundamental freedoms

In the media sector, the freedom of establishment and the freedom to provide services are particularly relevant, and media undertakings can invoke

---

345 Communication from the Commission to the European Parliament, the Council, the European Economic And Social Committee and the Committee Of The Regions, Tackling online disinformation: a European Approach (COM/2018/236 final of 26.04.2018).
346 For further information cf. https://www.ecpmf.eu/about/.
347 For further information cf. https://cmpf.eui.eu/media-pluralism-monitor/.
348 European Commission, 2018 report on the application of the EU Charter of Fundamental Rights.

them within the EU.³⁴⁹ Whereas the freedom of establishment under Art. 49 et seq. TFEU refers to the right to take up and pursue an activity as a self-employed person or to establish and manage undertakings in another Member State in accordance with the conditions laid down by the law of that state, the freedom to provide services refers to the provision of services by persons that are regularly self-employed, in the course of economic activity, as listed by way of example in Art. 57 TFEU.³⁵⁰ Both fundamental freedoms require economic activity with a cross-border dimension, whereby these characteristics are to be interpreted broadly.³⁵¹ The free movement of goods (Art. 34–36 TFEU), on the other hand, protects the right to market, acquire, offer, put on display or sale, keep, prepare, transport, sell, dispose of for valuable consideration or free of charge, import or use goods.³⁵² For the media sector, the free movement of goods in contrast to the freedom to provide services is of importance particularly when it comes to the dissemination and distribution of tangible products, especially, for instance, in case of restrictions on import and export of press³⁵³ or film products³⁵⁴, or when the area of advertising within the media is affected at large (possibly reflexively).³⁵⁵ The distinction from the freedom to provide services, which the CJEU draws according to the focal point of the overall transaction, is of significance primarily for the justification in the context of the distinction between product-related and distribution-related requirements of CJEU case law³⁵⁶, the detailed discussion of which is not relevant in the context of the present study.

---

349 Cf. on this chapter in detail and with special reference to and analysis of the relevant case law of the CJEU: *Cole*, Zum Gestaltungsspielraum der EU-Mitgliedstaaten bei Einschränkungen der Dienstleistungsfreiheit.
350 *Randelzhofer/Forsthoff* in: Grabitz/Hilf/Nettesheim, Art. 49, 50 TFEU, para. 80; *Tomkin* in: Kellerbauer/Klamert/id., Art. 49 TFEU, para. 19.
351 CJEU, case 36/74, *B.N.O. Walrave, L.J.N. Koch / Association Union cycliste internationale and Others*, para. 4; CJEU, case 196/87, *Udo Steymann / Staatssecretaris van Justitie*, para. 9.
352 CJEU, case C-293/94, *Brandsma*, para. 6.
353 On this *Müssle/Schmittmann* in: AfP 2002, 145, 145 et seq.
354 Cf. CJEU, joined cases 60/84 and 61/84, *Cinéthèque SA and others / Fédération nationale des cinémas français*.
355 On the significance of the free movement of goods for the media cf. for instance *Cole* in: Fink/id./Keber, Europäisches Medienrecht, chapter 2, para. 32 et seq.
356 This is particularly relevant in the field of advertising. On the area of advertising outside of media-relevant aspects cf. for instance *Kingreen* in: Calliess/Ruffert, Art. 34–36, para. 179 et seq. With regard to the distribution of goods cf. also CJEU, case C-244/06, *Dynamic Medien Vertriebs GmbH / Avides Media AG*.

C. On the significance and enshrinement in law of media diversity at EU level

According to Art. 57 TFEU, the freedom to provide services, which is enshrined in Art. 56 et seq. TFEU, refers to services that are normally provided for remuneration, insofar as they are not subject to the other fundamental freedoms, to which the freedom to provide services is subsidiary. Although the media are (also) cultural assets, as the CJEU has recognized, the Court classifies them as services – both vis-à-vis recipients and potentially vis-à-vis advertisers in the media – within the meaning of the TFEU due to their (also) economic nature.[357] But also the distributors, intermediaries who play a role in the web of content distribution and marketing, whether in the digital or analog domain, and relevant third parties can invoke this fundamental freedom.[358] Therefore, the freedom to provide services will be the focus of the present analysis – however, due to the CJEU's uniform doctrine on limitations, the observations also apply to the freedom of establishment[359] and the free movement of goods.

The freedom to provide services comprises an absolute prohibition of discrimination, i.e., the prohibition of treating domestic and foreign providers differently, and a relative prohibition of restrictions[360], i.e., the general prohibition of measures that prevent, hinder or make less attractive the exercise of this freedom. The freedom to provide services is therefore closely linked to one of the most important objectives of the Union (Art. 3(2), (3) TEU), which is to establish a competitive internal market free of frontiers, and it is also reflected in the country of origin principle, which is enshrined in many acts of secondary law (also relevant in the media sector), such as the AVMSD and the ECD (see Chapter D. for more details). The country of origin principle means that a Member State applies

---

357 Fundamental: CJEU, case 155/73, *Giuseppe Sacchi*. Cf. on the freedom to provide services against the background of the references to media law at the EU level also *Böttcher/Castendyk* in: Castendyk/Dommering/Scheuer, p. 85 et seq.
358 For cable networks cf. e.g. CJEU, case 352/85, *Bond van Adverteerders and others / The Netherlands State*, para. 14; on Google for instance CJEU, case C-482/18, *Google Ireland Limited / Nemzeti Adó- és Vámhivatal Kiemelt Adó- és Vámigazgatósága*.
359 The considerations outlined in the area of justification of interference with the freedom to provide services also apply to the freedom of establishment. In particular, aspects of safeguarding media diversity would also have to be taken into account here in the same approach. Cf. on this *Cole* in: Fink/id./Keber, chapter 2, para. 29 et seq.; in more detail *Dörr*, Das Zulassungsregime im Hörfunk: Spannungsverhältnis zwischen europarechtlicher Niederlassungsfreiheit und nationaler Pluralismussicherung, 71, 71 et seq.
360 Established case law since CJEU, case C-33/74, *Van Binsbergen / Bedrijfsvereniging voor de Metaalnijverheid*.

its regulatory framework only to providers under its jurisdiction and otherwise ensures the free movement of services to providers under the jurisdiction of another EU Member State.[361] This does not mean, however, that the freedom to provide services, by virtue of its binding effect, imperatively obliges the EU or the Member States to enshrine the country of origin principle in their legislation, i.e. preventing them from resorting to the lex loci solutionis, or a market location principle, or from linking aspects of the country of origin and lex loci solutionis principles.[362] Rather, the freedom to provide services only stipulates the removal of barriers to market entry – irrespective of any specific requirements as to how this equivalence for service providers is to be established by the EU or its Member States.[363]

However, restrictions on the movement of services – in the sense of a broadly understood concept applied by the CJEU[364] – by the Member States can be justified. In addition to the limitations expressly provided for in the TFEU, this is primarily the case where the respective measure pursues a legitimate general interest objective and equally complies with the principle of proportionality, i.e. it is necessary and appropriate, in particular it does not go beyond what is necessary to achieve this objective.[365] It is precisely here that the Member States have the scope to act within the framework of their cultural policies.

Even before the entry into force of the CFR, which explicitly enshrined the importance of pluralism in its Art. 11(2), the CJEU had recognized media diversity as an essential feature of freedom of expression, drawing on Art. 10 ECHR, and in this context had not only fundamentally established that the maintenance of a pluralistic broadcasting system is related to the freedom of expression guaranteed by Art. 10 ECHR, but also that a cultural policy pursuing this objective may constitute an overriding reason in the general interest justifying restrictions on the movement of services.[366] In

---

361 In detail on the country of origin principle: *Cole*, The Country of Origin Principle, 113, 113 et seq.
362 In detail and further on this question: *Waldheim*, Dienstleistungsfreiheit und Herkunftslandprinzip; *Albath/Giesel* in: EuZW 2006, 38, 39 et seq.; *Hörnle* in: International and Comparative Law Quarterly 1–2005, 89, 89 et seq.
363 Cf. on this e.g. CJEU, case C-55/94, *Reinhard Gebhard / Consiglio dell'Ordine degli Avvocati e Procuratori di Milano*.
364 CJEU, case C-76/90, *Manfred Säger / Dennemeyer & Co. Ltd.*, para. 12.
365 CJEU, case C-19/92, *Dieter Kraus / Land Baden-Württemberg*, para. 32; CJEU, case C-272/94, *Criminal proceedings against Michel Guiot and Climatec SA*, para. 11.
366 CJEU, case C-353/89, *Commission / Netherlands*, para. 30; CJEU, case C-288/89, *Stichting Collectieve Antennevoorziening Gouda and others / Commissariaat voor de Media*, para. 23.

C. On the significance and enshrinement in law of media diversity at EU level

this context, the CJEU also recognizes the Member States' objective of seeking to protect different social, cultural, religious and spiritual needs[367], which also allows for different regulatory approaches by the Member States[368].

Particularly noteworthy in this context is the CJEU decision *Dynamic Medien*, which addressed the question of whether and to what extent national rules that make the distribution of image storage media (DVDs, videos) by mail order dependent on them being labelled as having been examined as to the availability to young persons by national bodies are compatible with fundamental freedoms (in that case the free movement of goods). In the underlying legal dispute, *Dynamic Medien Vertriebs GmbH* demanded an injunction against the sale of Japanese animated films imported from the United Kingdom, which – although they had already been tested in the UK as regards their suitability for young persons and provided with a corresponding label (15+) – had not undergone the testing procedure provided for under the German Law on the protection of young persons (as regards i.a. harmful media) with the participation of the Voluntary Self-Regulation Body of the Film Industry (FSK).[369] Hence, at the heart of the decision was a national regulation to protect children from media harmful for their development – like safeguarding diversity, a matter with a cultural policy focus. The CJEU stated here that the Member States must be allowed broad discretion, as views on the degree to be granted when it comes to the protection of minors (even if there is agreement amongst Member States that a certain adequate degree of protection must be ensured) may differ from one Member State to another depending on considerations of a moral or cultural nature in particular. In the absence of harmonization at Union level of the protection of young persons from harmful media, it is for the Member States to decide, at their discretion, to which degree they wish to ensure the protection of the interest at issue, al-

---

367   CJEU, case C-288/89, *Stichting Collectieve Antennevoorziening Gouda and others / Commissariaat voor de Media*, para. 31.
368   On this CJEU, case C-244/06, *Dynamic Medien Vertriebs GmbH / Avides Media AG*, para. 49. So already CJEU, case C-124/97, *Markku Juhani Läärä and Others / Finland*, para. 36; CJEU, case C-36/02, *Omega Spielhallen- und Automatenaufstellungs GmbH / Oberbürgermeisterin der Bundesstadt Bonn*, para. 38. Most recently, in his opinion of 15 October 2020 in CJEU, case C-555/19, *Fussl Modestraße Mayr*, Advocate General *Szpunar* emphasized that the difference in national regulatory approaches does not lead to an incompatibility of the stricter regulation with EU law, para. 70.
369   CJEU, case C-244/06, *Dynamic Medien Vertriebs GmbH / Avides Media AG*, para. 44, 45, 49.

though they must do so in compliance with the principles of EU law. These considerations cannot only be transferred to the area of diversity safeguarding measures, but show that the CJEU respects cultural policy priorities at the national level and regards them as justification for different rules and does not attempt to place uniform assessment standards before discretionary considerations of the Member States via internal market connections.

This case law has been developed by the Court already before in numerous rulings.[370] In the pursuit of objectives of public interest – which also include the protection of linguistic diversity as well as access to local information[371] – the Member States have a degree of freedom, which is all the greater where the restrictive measure does not aim towards regulation of economic nature, such as trade or services, but instead focuses on cultural policy objectives. In these cases, the CJEU's power of review, which the Court undisputedly possesses in particular with regard to compliance with the principle of proportionality, is also limited[372]. The Court's scope of assessment is whether the restriction does not completely and permanently preclude the practical effectiveness of the fundamental freedom[373] and whether it actually meets the aim of achieving the objective in a coherent and systematic manner[374]. In this context, market effects of the restrictive measure play a role, the investigation and assessment of which, however, the CJEU places with the national courts.[375] Incidentally, this also and especially applies to restrictions on the free movement of goods: In the *Familiapress* case, which concerned the prohibition of selling magazines that allow participation in promotional contests, the CJEU fundamentally held that the maintenance of media diversity may constitute an overriding re-

---

370 CJEU, case C-148/91, *Vereniging Veronica Omroep Organisatie / Commissariaat voor de Media*, para. 9; CJEU, case C-23/93, *TV10 SA / Commissariaat voor de Media*, para. 18; CJEU, case C-368/95, *Vereinigte Familiapress Zeitungsverlags- und vertriebs GmbH / Heinrich Bauer Verlag*, para. 19.
371 CJEU, case C-250/06, *United Pan-Europe Communications Belgium SA and Others / Belgian State*, para. 43.
372 In detail and on the scope of the Member States' discretionary powers cf. *Cole*, Zum Gestaltungsspielraum der EU-Mitgliedstaaten bei Einschränkungen der Dienstleistungsfreiheit, p. 26 et seq.
373 CJEU, case C-250/06, *United Pan-Europe Communications Belgium SA and Others / Belgian State*, para. 45.
374 CJEU, case C-137/09, *Josemans*, para. 70 with further references; equally e.g. recently in CJEU, case C-235/17, *European Commission / Hungary*, para. 61.
375 CJEU, case C-368/95, *Vereinigte Familiapress Zeitungsverlags- und vertriebs GmbH / Heinrich Bauer Verlag*, para. 29.

C. On the significance and enshrinement in law of media diversity at EU level

quirement that also justifies a restriction on the free movement of goods. This diversity contributed to the preservation of the right to freedom of expression, which is protected by Art. 10 ECHR and fundamental freedoms and was one of the fundamental rights protected by the Community legal order.[376] In this context, it is up to the Member States to determine how they will strive to achieve this diversity goal, giving them a wide margin of discretion. Similar restrictions on the freedom to provide services can be far-reaching, as Advocate General *Szpunar* recently stated in his opinion in the *Fussl Modestraße Mayr* case.[377]

Thus, the regulatory competence of the Member States in the area of safeguarding pluralism is also taken into account at the level of fundamental freedoms.

2. The EU competition regime

The primary objective of the EU competition regime is to enable the proper functioning of the internal market as a crucial factor in the well-being of the European economy and society. The competition regime is therefore initially purely economic and sector-neutral, which has its basis in competence rules also (on this point, see already chapter B.III.2.). It therefore also affects the media in their capacity as participants in economic transactions, in the context of which they compete with other undertakings on many different levels – whether for the attention and purchasing power of recipients or potential advertising or business customers. Against the background of safeguarding diversity, however, it is all the more important that fair conditions prevail on the "media market", that market power does not become opinion power, and that smaller undertakings (i.e., for example, local, regional, industry-specific or other information which society in the internal market as a whole does not have an interest in receiving) are enabled to enter the market. Although the competition regime leaves little

---

376 CJEU, case C-368/95, *Vereinigte Familiapress Zeitungsverlags- und vertriebs GmbH / Heinrich Bauer Verlag*, para. 18. Cf. also CJEU, case C-244/06, *Dynamic Medien Vertriebs GmbH / Avides Media AG*.
377 CJEU, case C-555/19, *Fussl Modestraße Mayr*, opinion of 15 October 2020. Cf. in particular para. 53, 69 et seq., 63, 67. The assessment of fundamental rights also takes place within a broad scope of discretion, para. 83. The national court's review of whether there might be less restrictive measures must be limited to measures that could actually be taken by the national legislature; purely theoretical measures must be disregarded, para. 74.

room for taking non-economic aspects into account, it is therefore nevertheless generally acknowledged that it indirectly also contributes to safeguarding media diversity, as it keeps markets open and competitive by counteracting concentration developments, limiting state influence and preventing market abuse.[378]

a. Control of market power and abuse of power

With the instruments of market power control (prohibition of cartels under Art. 101 TFEU, prohibition of abuse of a dominant market position under Art. 102 TFEU and merger control under the Merger Regulation[379]), the European Commission can to a certain extent exert (a limiting) influence on the market power of undertakings if they occupy or would occupy a dominant position on a given market. In the area of media, however, influencing the market also regularly means potentially influencing the power of undertakings, linked to their market power, to influence opinion.

Without going into the details of market power and abuse control, reference here shall only be made to the fact that a number of antitrust decisions have already been issued in relation to undertakings in the media sector and its environment.[380] In this context, especially in the media sector, the definition and delimitation of the relevant market is essential and characterized by several peculiarities.

On the one hand, the media operate in a two-sided market consisting of the recipient market and the advertising market, in which they each compete with one another for attention and advertising revenues. Both markets are also important in terms of ensuring diversity of opinion, since diversity only exists where content reaches an audience and the ability to (re)finance content also directly determines the existence of media providers.

On the other hand, the media sector is characterized by the (increasing) convergence of media, which is leading to a blurring of the boundaries between different forms of transmission, forms of offering and of providers and has resulted in a considerable influence of gatekeepers such as search

---

378 Cf. on this *Valcke*, Challenges of Regulating Media Pluralism in the EU, p. 27, with further references.
379 On this see D.II.4.
380 Cf. on this in detail *Cole/Hans* in: Cappello, Medieneigentum – Marktrealitäten und Regulierungsmaßnahmen, p. 20 et seq.; *Bania*, The Role of Media Pluralism in the Enforcement of EU Competition Law.

C. On the significance and enshrinement in law of media diversity at EU level

engines and other platforms. In its decision-making practice, however, the Commission makes a decisive distinction between the markets for free TV, pay TV, other markets and the purchase of broadcasting rights, and separates the online and offline markets.[381] This assessment of the market already shows the economically oriented approach of the Commission, in which only economic assessment criteria are taken into account, but not cultural policy aspects.

Accordingly, market-driven is also the investigation of the abusive nature of a conduct, which is considered in all conduct of an undertaking that may affect the structure of a market where competition is already weakened precisely because of the presence of an undertaking, and which impedes the maintenance or development of existing competition through measures that deviate from the means of normal product and service competition on the basis of performance.[382] This can be illustrated, for example, by the Commission's investigations and decisions on Google search, in which the importance of the search engine, also for the searchability of media content (and thus the recipient's horizon), has so far played no role, but only economic aspects of the placement of advertisements or the preference for undertaking-owned services.[383] It is about products and services that are judged according to objective and economic criteria and therefore leave no room for considering the quality of certain products or services compared to other similar products and services (read: content), which would be relevant in the field of safeguarding diversity.

Safeguarding diversity can therefore only have knee-jerk concern in the area of antitrust measures at EU level, which rather aim at establishing fair conditions with regard to economic aspects and in particular do not aim at the existence of a diverse offering. In particular, the Commission is not seeking to exert a controlling influence on the basis of imbalances that

---

381 Cf. for instance the more recent decisions on *Walt Disney / Century Fox* (M.8785) of 06.11.2018, in which the Commission maintains the separation between digital distribution forms of films and physical distribution, cf. para. 50, https://ec.europa.eu/competition/mergers/cases/decisions/m8785_2197_3.pdf; as well as in the Sky / Fox (M.8354) case of 07.04.2017 on the distinction between the production of television content on behalf of and the licensing of broadcasting rights for pre-produced television content, cf. para. 62, https://ec.europa.eu/competition/mergers/cases/decisions/m8354_920_8.pdf.
382 CJEU, case 85/76, *Hoffmann-La Roche / Commission*; Commission Decision of 14 December 1985 relating to a proceeding under Article 86 of the EEC Treaty (IV/30.698 – ECS/AKZO), OJ L 374 of 31.12.1985, p. 1–27.
383 Cf. on this e.g. cases No. 39740 (Google Search (Shopping)) and No. 40411 (Google Search (AdSense)).

may have been identified in the area of diversity of opinion and information.[384] Therefore, while market power and abuse control at the EU level is not a suitable instrument for safeguarding pluralism in this context, it also does not run counter to corresponding efforts by Member States.

b. State aid law

State aid is generally prohibited in the EU under Art. 107(1) TFEU, as it favors certain undertakings, economic sectors or industries over competitors and thus (may) distort free competition in the European internal market to the extent that it affects trade between Member States as a result. The economic orientation of EU state aid law is already obvious from the wording of the provision. Although this does not fall within the competences of the EU, discussions at both national and European level on the system of dual broadcasting and the associated financing of public broadcasting by means of license fee, for example in Germany,[385] but also in other countries,[386] have, however, illustrated the particular relevance of state aid law also for the media and cultural policies of the Member States.

On the one hand, state aid law contains a fundamental prohibition of state influence (albeit in economic/financial terms) on the media, which is also suitable for strengthening pluralism by preventing individual undertakings from gaining a stronger position on the market (of opinions) through state support or at least taking into account the subliminal risk that exists in this regard. On the other hand, however, state aid law also contains exceptions to this fundamental prohibition in the area of cultural policy, which allow Member States to align their media regulations with national characteristics and thus equally underline the regulatory sovereignty of the Member States, although a review by the Commission

---

384 Cf. on this, but also on possibly unexploited potentials for taking into account also pluralism-relevant aspects within the framework of the EU competition regime *Bania*, The Role of Media Pluralism in the Enforcement of EU Competition Law.
385 Cf. as to that e.g. Commission Decision 2006/513/EC of 9 November 2005 on the State Aid which the Federal Republic of Germany has implemented for the introduction of digital terrestrial television (DVB-T) in Berlin-Brandenburg, OJ L 200 of 22.07.2006, p. 14–34.
386 State funding measures relating to broadcasting and monitored by the European Commission can also be found in the legal systems of other EU Member States such as Austria, Finland, Sweden, the Czech Republic, Estonia, Cyprus, Latvia, Lithuania, Malta, Poland, Slovenia, Slovakia, Bulgaria, and Romania.

C. On the significance and enshrinement in law of media diversity at EU level

when certain limits are exceeded is ensured by the requirement of notification[387]. The focus of this study will be on the latter aspect.[388]

State aid, which, based on a broad understanding of the term in the media sector, may take the form of subsidies or grants for media undertakings, tax relief for the production of content or advertising measures, sales subsidies for the press, etc., may be considered compatible with the internal market and thus permitted in general (Art. 107(2) TFEU) or, after an investigation by the European Commission[389], in individual cases (Art. 107(3) TFEU). In the opinion of the European Commission[390], Art. 106(2) TFEU also conceives a derogation from the prohibition of state aid. Against the background of measures for safeguarding diversity at the Member State level, Art. 106(2), 107(3)(d) (and, if applicable, (c)) TFEU are particularly relevant in this context. Against the background of the current Corona pandemic, which has had a severe and probably lasting impact on the media sector and may thus also have a multiplier effect, attention should also be drawn to Art. 107(2)(b), which allows aid to make good the damage caused by natural disasters.[391]

---

387 The European Commission must be notified of any intended introduction or alteration of aid (Art. 108(3) TFEU) and may initiate proceedings under Art. 108(2) TFEU if it has doubts about the compatibility of the project with the internal market. However, this only applies in the case of the factual existence of aid, which is based in particular on the existence of certain thresholds against the background of the possibility of influencing trade within the EU.
388 For a consideration in detail with respect to regional and local media cf. *Ukrow/ Cole*, Aktive Sicherung lokaler und regionaler Medienvielfalt, p. 65 et seq.; see also *Martini* in: EuZW 2015, 821, 821 et seq.
389 According to the apparently prevailing opinion, the EU Commission has discretionary powers with regard to compatibility with the internal market within the framework of Art. 107(3) TFEU, in contrast to (2); cf. in detail *Cremer* in: Calliess/Ruffert, Art. 107 TFEU, para. 31, 38 et seq.
390 In the Commission's view, Art. 106(2) TFEU is designed as a derogation; cf. Communication from the Commission on the application of State aid rules to public service broadcasting, OJ C 257 of 27.10.2009, p. 1–14, https://eur-lex.europa.eu/legal-content/EN/TXT/?uri=celex:52009XC1027(01), para. 37.
391 Cf. on this as to media support opportunities against the backdrop of the pandemic *Ukrow*, Schutz der Medienvielfalt und medienbezogene Solidaritätspflichten in Corona-Zeiten.
Many Member States have already taken support measures for the media sector against the pandemic background. Denmark's "COVID-19 compensation plan", which provides for aid to the media sector (print, electronic media, broadcasting, etc.) amounting to the equivalent of around EUR 32 million, has already gone through the notification procedure, in which the Commission accepted rescue aid under Art. 107(2)(b) TFEU. While the Commission focused primarily

For undertakings entrusted with the operation of services of general economic interest, Art. 106(2) TFEU provides Member States with a possibility of derogation which, in particular, also allows for the state financing of public service broadcasting. Accordingly, state aid is possible for such undertakings entrusted with the operation of services of general economic interest. As early as in its *Altmark* ruling of 2003, the CJEU set out specific parameters in this regard that must be observed in the context of the financing of public service broadcasting against the background of its social role and task.[392] These have been further developed over the years in the Commission's case practice – also in proceedings against Germany[393] – and have now been laid down in a Commission communication.[394]

At the Union level, it is assumed that despite the function of public broadcasting being in the general interest, state funding cannot be possible without restrictions. Although the importance of public service broadcasting for the promotion of cultural diversity and the possibility for Member States to take diversity-enhancing measures is emphasized[395], the Commission calls above all for independent control, transparency and measures against overcompensation with regard to the establishment of financing systems. In contrast, the reason for funding, i.e. in the case of public service broadcasting the definition of the public service remit, is subject to only limited review, leaving the Member States room for maneuver in setting cultural priorities, which may be shaped by national peculiarities. In designing the models, it requires consideration of the competitive relationship with commercial broadcasters and print media, which could potentially be negatively affected by state funding of public broadcasting with

---

on economic factors in this context, the Danish government emphasized in the proceedings in particular the need for state funding against the background of the importance of cultural diversity as an essential value in a democratic society, which demands the existence of private media as a balance in addition to publicly funded media.

392 CJEU, case C-280/00, *Altmark Trans GmbH und Regierungspräsidium Magdeburg / Nahverkehrsgesellschaft Altmark GmbH.*
393 European Commission decision of 24 April 2007, K(2007) 1761 FINAL, available at https://ec.europa.eu/competition/state_aid/cases/198395/198395_678609_35_1.pdf.
394 In particular through the Communication from the Commission on the application of State aid rules to public service broadcasting, OJ C 257 of 27.10.2009, p. 1–14, as well as through case-by-case decisions (see list at http://ec.europa.eu/competition/sectors/media/decisions_psb.pdf).
395 Communication from the Commission on the application of State aid rules to public service broadcasting, OJ C 257 of 27.10.2009, p. 1–14, para. 13.

C. On the significance and enshrinement in law of media diversity at EU level

regard to the development of new business models. Since these providers also enrich the cultural and political debate and increase the choice of content, their protection must also be considered.[396] This shows that – in contrast to the market control mentioned in the previous chapter – under state aid law not only the Member States are free to exercise their competence to regulate cultural policy, but that the Commission also includes certain aspects that safeguard diversity in its respective investigation.

In the area of commercial media, too, there are – against the background of safeguarding diversity – opportunities for the Member States for support[397], in particular under Art. 107(3)(d) TFEU, which permits aid to promote culture and heritage conservation where such aid does not affect trading conditions and competition in the Union to an extent that is contrary to the common interest. The definition of culture is made in parallel with Art. 167 TFEU and thus also covers, in particular, the promotion of artistic and literary creation, including journalistic and editorial activity, especially in the audiovisual sector.[398] In past investigations, the Commission has sometimes reviewed media subsidies under Art. 107(3)(d) TFEU, with a restrictive interpretation leading to the fact that the content and nature of the "product" is what matters in the review, but not the medium or its mode of dissemination per se.[399] The measure of support must have a cultural focus. Conditions and limits (in particular transparency requirements and cap limits) specifically for the film industry and other audiovisual works are provided in a corresponding Commission Communication.[400] In this framework, the promotion of audiovisual production is also and precisely understood as a suitable means of promoting the diversity

---

396 Communication from the Commission on the application of State aid rules to public service broadcasting, OJ C 257 of 27.10.2009, p. 1–14, para. 16.
397 For the area of funding opportunities for private broadcasting and, in particular, the investigation of the compatibility of state-initiated funding with European state aid rules cf. *Cole/Oster*, Zur Frage der Beteiligung privater Rundfunkveranstalter in Deutschland an einer staatlich veranlassten Finanzierung, p. 26 et seq.
398 On this in detail and leading further: *Ress/Ukrow* in: Grabitz/Hilf/Nettesheim, Art. 167 TFEU, para. 128 et seq.
399 Decision of 1 August 2016, C(2016) 4865 final, State aid SA.45512 (2016/N). The case concerned the promotion of print and digital media in minority languages.
400 Communication from the Commission on State aid for films and other audiovisual works, OJ C 332 of 15.11.2013, p. 1–11, https://eur-lex.europa.eu/legal-content/EN/LSU/?uri=CELEX:52013XC1115(01), as amended by the Communication from the Commission amending the Communications from the Commission on EU Guidelines for the application of State aid rules in relation to the rapid deployment of broadband networks, on Guidelines on regional State aid

and richness of European culture.[401] In this context, it is even emphasized that the goal of cultural diversity justifies the special nature of national aid for film and television and that these precisely contribute decisively to the shaping of the European audiovisual market.

V. Reference to the objective in secondary law and other texts

Due to a lack of legislative powers, there can be no secondary law in the area of safeguarding diversity that directly pursues this objective.[402] Nevertheless, there is a certain framework of media law at the EU level within which links can be found with regard to safeguarding pluralism. These various legal acts and, beyond them, legally non-binding but nevertheless relevant measures as well as current EU initiatives are presented comprehensively in Section D. below.

---

for 2014–2020, on State aid for films and other audiovisual works, on Guidelines on State aid to promote risk finance investments and on Guidelines on State aid to airports and airlines, 2014/C 198/02, OJ C 198, 27.06.2014, p. 30–34, https://eur-lex.europa.eu/legal-content/EN/TXT/?uri=CELEX:52014XC0627(02).
401 Communication from the Commission on State aid for films and other audiovisual works, OJ C 332 of 15.11.2013, p. 1–11, as amended by the Communication from the Commission 2014/C 198/02, OJ C 198, 27.06.2014, p. 30–34, para. 4.
402 Cf. supra, chapter B.

D. Secondary legal framework on "media law" and media pluralism

Mark D. Cole / Christina Etteldorf

I. Overview

In 1996, the European Commission presented an internal draft for a directive on media diversity[403], which was withdrawn after opposition even before it was introduced into the legislative process at the Commission level. This was primarily due to doubts relating to competences, since the very title of the directive would not have justified an invocation of the internal market competence and the content could not have been based on any existing legal basis.[404] A subsequent draft for a directive on media ownership in the internal market[405] was not primarily aimed at securing media diversity, but was intended to achieve this goal indirectly by making the internal market a reality, although the invocation of internal market-related competences was also strongly questioned.[406] The draft was also eventually withdrawn due to opposition from Member States.[407] Moreover, numerous attempts by the European Parliament, especially in the 1990s and the first decade of the 21st century, to persuade the European Commission to take concrete measures to safeguard media diversity have also been unsuccessful.[408] Taking into account the competence of the Member States in

---

403 Unpublished. Cf. on this and the following in detail *Ress/Bröhmer*, Europäische Gemeinschaft und Medienvielfalt; *Cole*, Europarechtliche Rahmenbedingungen für die Pluralismussicherung im Rundfunk, p. 93, 94 et seq.
404 *Paal*, Medienvielfalt und Wettbewerbsrecht, p. 178.
405 Unpublished. Cf. on this and the following in detail *Ress/Bröhmer*, Europäische Gemeinschaft und Medienvielfalt. Further notes on the content of the draft *van Loon* in: Media Law & Policy 2001, 11, 17 et seq.; *Westphal* in: European Business Law Review 2002, 459, p. 465 et seq.
406 Cf. *Ress/Bröhmer*, Europäische Gemeinschaft und Medienvielfalt; *van Loon* in: Media Law & Policy 2001, 11, 17 et seq.; *Westphal* in: European Business Law Review 2002, 459, p. 465 et seq; see also *Paal*, Medienvielfalt und Wettbewerbsrecht, p. 179, with further references.
407 *Frey* in: ZUM 1998, 985, 985.
408 On this: *Valcke*, Challenges of Regulating Media Pluralism in the European Union, p. 26.

this area, there is to date no secondary law of the European Union which directly regulates media diversity.[409] Media law as a whole – also in the sense of a broad concept of a horizontal issue – is not and could not be fully harmonized within the framework of the distribution of competencies at EU level.

However, there are a number of acts of secondary law that either directly address the media or at least have a relevant impact on the media themselves or their distribution channels and thus serve as components of a "European media law", which, however, essentially only makes specifications for implementation but does not aim for full harmonization. First and foremost in this context is the AVMSD, which – as the only one of the legislative acts to be presented below – focuses on the regulation of (in this case audiovisual) media in the sense of content regulation and can therefore be seen as the centerpiece of "European media law". However, against the backdrop of the modern media landscape, in which the boundaries between content providers and platforms are becoming increasingly blurred, intermediaries are acting as gatekeepers for information gathering from a user perspective and for visibility from a media provider perspective on the one hand, but are also competing with traditional media undertakings on the other, the e-Commerce Directive (ECD) is also becoming increasingly importan. As a horizontal legal instrument that in particular provides liability privileges for information society services, it also plays a central role with regard to the dissemination of media content. Since it has not been amended since its adoption in 2000, the strongest need for action in this respect is recognized at the EU level, after numerous relevant acts of secondary law have been amended or newly adopted on the initiative of the last Commission.[410] This also includes rules of copyright law, telecommunications law and consumer protection law, in particular to the extent that they contain special provisions or exceptions for the media. In addition, the concretizations of competition law through secondary law also play an

---

409 Cf. on the pros and cons of shifting the safeguarding of pluralism to the EU level also *Gounalakis/Zagouras* in: ZUM 2006, 716, 716 et seq., who, for understandable reasons, argue in favor of an (at that time) EC safeguarding of pluralism without, however, in this context going into the problem of competences in more detail, but instead justify it in favor of the EC on the basis of differences in national regulations (724 et seq.); objecting in turn with convincing arguments *Hain* in: AfP 2007, 527, 532 et seq.; generally at a glance *Cole*, Europarechtliche Rahmenbedingungen für die Pluralismussicherung im Rundfunk, p. 93 et seq.
410 Cf. on this at a glance *Cole/Etteldorf/Ullrich*, Cross-border Dissemination of Online Content, p. 91 et seq.

D. Secondary legal framework on "media law" and media pluralism

important role, with the Merger Regulation being the most relevant here due to its connection with safeguarding diversity.

These legal bases under secondary law will be considered in this chapter and examined with regard to the connection with the Member States' competence for safeguarding media diversity. This section is supplemented by a look at planned legal acts at EU level, which shed light on emerging trends and possibly also conflicts. The chapter concludes with an overview of current EU measures in the form of coordination and support measures, which are worth examining especially in light of the fact that these can be precursors to legislative measures or are chosen as instruments in areas in which the EU has no genuine regulatory competence. The chapter thus considers and summarizes in the conclusions which implications are to be drawn from the secondary law foundations for the (competence to) safeguarding media diversity and the adoption of corresponding regulation.

II. Links in existing secondary law

1. E-Commerce-Directive

The aim of the e-Commerce Directive (ECD)[411] was to provide a coherent framework for Internet commerce. The core of the directive is therefore also the elimination of legal uncertainties for cross-border online services and the guarantee of the free movement of information society services between the Member States.[412] This is in line with the objective as laid down in Art. 1 ECD: The Directive seeks to contribute to the proper functioning of the internal market by ensuring the free movement of information society services between the Member States and, to this end, by approximating certain national rules applicable to information society services. To ensure this, the ECD establishes the country of origin principle as well as the principle excluding prior authorisation for information society services on a

---

411 Directive 2000/31/EC of the European Parliament and of the Council of 8 June 2000 on certain legal aspects of information society services, in particular electronic commerce, in the Internal Market ('Directive on electronic commerce'), OJ L 178 of 17.07.2000, p. 1–16, https://eur-lex.europa.eu/legal-content/EN/ALL/?uri=celex%3A32000L0031.
412 In detail on the ECD as well as on the question of whether it still meets the realities of the digital age in relation to the media sector cf. *Cole/Etteldorf/Ullrich*, Cross-border Dissemination of Online Content. On the historical development cf. *Valcke/Dommering* in: Castendyk/Dommering/Scheuer, p. 1083.

binding basis and sets out requirements with which such services must comply.[413] These include information requirements (including in relation to commercial communications), provisions on the handling of electronic contracts, extrajudicial dispute resolution, court actions, and on cooperation. In contrast, the ECD does not contain concrete requirements for the supervision of the services covered by it, but leaves the task of ensuring the enforcement of the ECD entirely to the Member States (Art. 20 ECD). The minimum harmonization approach pursued within the framework of the ECD is already documented in its recital 10, which states that, in accordance with the principle of proportionality, the measures provided for in the directive were strictly limited to the minimum needed to achieve the objective of the proper functioning of the internal market for information society services – from the perspective of the time.[414]

The centerpiece of the ECD is the horizontally applicable tiered liability system set forth in Art. 12 to 15. In the form of a categorization of different providers into caching, access, and hosting providers, it privileges these (without having to go into detail here on the individual provisions and their interpretation by the CJEU[415]). However, the precondition for exemption from liability for illegal content available via the service is that they are merely passive providers of services for the distribution of third-party content and have no knowledge of the illegality of the content in question. Moreover, no active monitoring obligations may be imposed on these providers. For media regulation, these provisions are relevant on the one hand because media undertakings regularly have a presence on such platforms themselves, i.e., the information society services act as distributors, and on the other hand because media undertakings in certain cases compete with the platforms for the same or similar recipient and advertising market (although and to the extent that the platforms provide third-party, for example user-generated, content and are not themselves content creators, because they then fall under a different category of responsibility anyway) or compete on the platforms with other content providers.

While, e.g., the liability privileges in Art. 12 to 15 ECD must be observed by the Member States when implementing rules that affect the

---

413 On the differences as to the country of origin principle in the ECD compared to the AVMSD (or TwF Directive) *Cole*, The Country of Origin Principle, 113, 113 et seq.
414 Cf. in detail on the ECD e.g. *Büllesbach et al.*, Concise European IT Law, Part II; *Valcke/Dommering* in: Castendyk/Dommering/Scheuer, p. 1083 et seq.
415 In detail *Cole/Etteldorf/Ullrich*, Cross-border Dissemination of Online Content, p. 169 et seq.

question of liability for content that can be accessed via platforms, this does not apply if a regulation – for example within the framework of media regulation in the Member States – also affects providers that fall within the scope of the ECD. The broad definition of information society services in the Information Procedures Directive[416] results in many services that did not exist at the time the ECD was adopted nevertheless being covered by it. This also applies, and especially against the backdrop of the digital transformation and the blurring of the boundaries between media providers and intermediaries, to forms of offerings that play an important role in the dissemination of information as information society services, such as VSP or search engines. Calls for the creation of a new category of platform providers for content (distribution) in the ECD or another piece of legislation, which were already made during the last revision of the AVMSD[417] and then again during the discussions on the reform of the ECD or prior to the legislative proposal for the Digital Services Act[418] have not yet been taken up. For the time being, the traditional internal market orientation of the ECD applies, which does not differentiate according to the type of intermediary – apart from the distinction within the categories in the case of liability privileges.

With regard to the assignment of competence for safeguarding media pluralism to the Member State level, the ECD therefore refers to media pluralism as an objective of general public interest in such a way that, despite the broad scope of the Directive, existing rules – or such to be created in the future – of the Member States – and of the Union – with this objective remain unaffected.[419] Art. 1(6) ECD states in this regard:

---

416 Directive 98/34/EC of the European Parliament and of the Council of 22 June 1998 aying [sic] down a procedure for the provision of information in the field of technical standards and regulations and of rules on Information Society services, OJ L 204 of 21.07.1998, p. 37–48, repealed by Directive (EU) 2015/1535 of the European Parliament and of the Council of 9 September 2015 laying down a procedure for the provision of information in the field of technical regulations and of rules on Information Society services, OJ L 241 of 17.09.2015, p. 1–15. Cf. also the consolidated text of Directive 98/34/EC, available at https://eur-lex.europa.eu/legal-content/EN/TXT/?uri=CELEX%3A01998L0034-20151007.
417 Cf. *Bárd/Bayer/Carrera*, A comparative analysis of media freedom and pluralism in the EU Member States, p. 75, who want to address separately such services that consist in the transmission or distribution of information provided by another person.
418 Cf. on this *ERGA*, Position Paper on the Digital Services Act, which advocates the introduction of a new category in the form of online content platforms.
419 See also *Valcke*, Challenges of Regulating Media Pluralism in the EU, p. 27, with reference to Art. 8(1), 9(4) and 18(1) of the Framework Directive and its rec. 5, 6

> *This Directive does not affect measures taken at Community or national level, in the respect of Community law, in order to promote cultural and linguistic diversity and to ensure the defence of pluralism.*

This is to be emphasized first of all insofar as Art. 1(6) ECD also speaks of *Community* (from the point of view of that time; today therefore "the European Union") measures that serve to promote cultural diversity. However, this must not be misunderstood to mean that it was a legal basis for rules on safeguarding diversity. First, Union action requires a legal basis under primary law, as has been considered in detail above. This is precisely what is lacking with regard to rules on safeguarding diversity. Second, primary law explicitly limits Union action in the cultural sphere to funding opportunities, as can be seen from the cultural clause of Art. 167 TFEU. Accordingly, the ECD provision refers to measures aimed, e.g., at promoting cooperation between Member States and, where appropriate, supplementary measures in the cultural segment, such as preserving cultural heritage. This is confirmed by the related recital 63, which defines the exception of Art. 1(6) ECD in more detail and in this context only addresses measures of the Member States and in particular recognizes the diversity of cultural objectives:

> *The adoption of this Directive will not prevent the Member States from taking into account the various social, societal and cultural implications which are inherent in the advent of the information society; in particular it should not hinder measures which Member States might adopt in conformity with Community law to achieve social, cultural and democratic goals taking into account their linguistic diversity, national and regional specificities as well as their cultural heritage, and to ensure and maintain public access to the widest possible range of information society services; in any case, the development of the information society is to ensure that Community citizens can have access to the cultural European heritage provided in the digital environment.*

Member State rules on safeguarding diversity are thus unaffected by the ECD, if only for systematic reasons of competence.[420] This equally refers both to rules already in place at the time and to any regulation issued in

---

and 31. See on this for the comparable area of network regulation especially under D.II.5.

420 Cf. on this *Paal*, Intermediäre: Regulierung und Vielfaltssicherung, p. 38, who, however, does not rely on Art. 1(6) in the sense of an derogation, but sees measures for safeguarding diversity in publishing as already not covered by the coor-

the future. However, the Member States are limited by the fact that the measures taken must be in line with Community (today: Union) law, in particular with general legal principles such as fundamental rights.[421]

In addition to this exception, there is – again comparable to a procedure also known from the AVMSD – also another option to deviate from the country of origin principle enshrined in the Directive, which is relevant in connection with the regulation of the media. While this principle, as just mentioned, normally prevents Member States from restricting the free movement of information society services from another Member State for reasons falling within the coordinated field, there is a possibility to derogate from it for the protection of overriding important legal interests: According to Art. 3(4) ECD, Member States may deviate from this principle in individual cases if this is necessary for reasons of protection of minors or the fight against any incitement to hatred on grounds of race, sex, religion or nationality. The authority to deviate is also subject to the condition of appropriateness and the existence of interference with or serious danger to the above-mentioned protected interests. In addition, a procedure explained in Art. 4(b), 5 and 6 must be followed – unless urgent cases are involved – which provides for the involvement of the Member State of establishment of the respective provider and the European Commission.

Both aspects, the exception as well as the power to deviate, document that the ECD has not led to a standardization in the sense that Member States' action to protect general interests such as media pluralism or the fight against certain crimes is excluded. This takes account of the fact – apart from the abstract problem that Union action must be fully covered by the respective legal basis and must not make action by the Member States in these reserved areas impossible – that the Member States are in a better position to assess certain contexts, such as in this case the necessary measures to safeguard pluralism.

---

dinated area of the Directive according to Art. 3(2) in conjunction with Art. 2(h) ECD. These provisions require Member States not to impede cross-border access to services for reasons that fall within the coordinated scope of the Directive. However, the coordinated field does not refer to every regulation on information society services, but only for certain aspects of their activity. The Union also has no legislative competence in other areas.

421 Cf. on this in detail under D.II.2.c. *Liesching* (Das Herkunftslandprinzip nach E-Commerce- und AVMSD, p. 78 et seq.) does not go into more detail on Art. 1(6) against the background of the question examined there limited solely on the country of origin principle (and thus not in the focus of aspects of safeguarding diversity) and merely refers to the Commission's comments in the notification procedure for the MStV in connection with the country of origin principle.

2. AVMS Directive

a. Historical analysis in the context of safeguarding diversity

As a predecessor to the AVMSD, the Television without Frontiers Directive (TwF Directive)[422] was created in 1989 with the aim of establishing rules for the cross-border transmission of television broadcasts that would ensure the transition from national markets to a common market for the production and distribution of programs and that would guarantee fair conditions of competition, without prejudice to television's function of safeguarding the general interest.[423] This objective was pursued with the approach of minimum harmonization[424] on the underlying country of origin principle[425] as the core element of regulation.

In substantive terms, the key points of the TwF Directive were quota regulations for the promotion of European works – regulations that the German states felt were outside the EU competences[426] –, the regulation of advertising and sponsorship, provisions on the protection of minors and on content inciting hatred, and the right of reply. In total and as regards its scope, the Directive should regulate only the "minimum rules needed" to enable the free movement of broadcasts, but should not interfere with the competence of the Member States with regard to organization, financing or program content.[427] In particular, autonomous cultural developments in the Member States and the preservation of cultural diversity in the Community should not be affected by the Directive.[428] Safeguarding diversity played less of a role as an independent regulatory goal than as a side

---

422 Council Directive 89/552/EEC of 3 October 1989 on the coordination of certain provisions laid down by Law, Regulation or Administrative Action in Member States concerning the pursuit of television broadcasting activities, OJ L 298 of 17.10.1989, p. 23–30, https://eur-lex.europa.eu/legal-content/EN/TXT/?uri=celex:31989L0552.
423 Rec. 3 TwF Directive.
424 Directive 89/552/EEC already contains the wording that this directive regulates "the minimum rules needed to guarantee freedom of transmission in broadcasting".
425 Cf. on this *Cole*, The Country of Origin Principle, 113, 113 et seq.
426 Cf. BVerfGE 92, 203 (205 et seq.).
427 Cf. rec. 13 TwF Directive.
428 Cf. rec. 13 TwF Directive. Cf. on the history of the TwF and AVMS Directives against the background of an economic approach also *Broughton Micova*, The Audiovisual Media Services Directive: Balancing liberalisation and protection (DRAFT).

D. Secondary legal framework on "media law" and media pluralism

effect therein: By preventing actions that could interfere with the free flow of broadcasts or encourage the emergence of dominant positions, potential threats to pluralism and freedom of information could also be countered.[429] Ensuring this, however, remained a task for the Member States. This is documented in particular by three factors that could be identified in the TwF Directive:

(1.) the deliberately chosen approach of minimum harmonization, documented by the recitals to the Directive,
(2.) granting in part wide latitude even within harmonized rules – e.g. in the sense of setting targets through the Directive, but leaving the way to do so to the Member States –[430], and
(3.) the introduction of a general power of derogation in Art. 3(1) TwF Directive.

The latter allows Member States to lay down stricter or more detailed provisions for television broadcasters under their jurisdiction in the areas covered by the Directive, for example to allow for an active policy in favor of a particular language or for other "certain circumstances"[431], including the pursuit of cultural objectives.[432]

In contrast, it is not possible to identify a distinct cultural policy focus in the individual regulatory areas of the TwF Directive. Rather, they served to protect other legally protected interests, in particular consumer protection (e.g. advertisement labeling and sponsoring), youth protection (e.g. advertising that impairs development) and the internal market (e.g. country of origin principle). This also applies to the rules for the promotion of (independent) European works, which at first glance appear to be measures for the protection of cultural diversity and the preservation of European film culture, but in fact – as the recitals (especially 20, 23) demonstrate – were in particular aimed at favoring the formation of markets for television productions in the Member States, the promotion of new

---

429 Cf. on this rec. 16 TwF Directive.
430 For example, with regard to the promotion of independent European works, Art. 5 sentence 1 TwF Directive formulated – as one of the core concerns in establishing the Directive – that Member States should ensure "where practicable and by appropriate means" that broadcasters reserve "at least" ten percent of their broadcasting time for independent works.
431 Rec. 25, 26 TwF Directive.
432 See on this in detail below in chapter D.II.2.c. Cf. on the wording of Art. 3 TwF Directive also *Dommering/Scheuer/Adler* in: Castendyk/Dommering/Scheuer, p. 857 et seq.

sources for television productions as well as of small and medium-sized enterprises in the television industry and the creation of employment opportunities, i.e. aimed at industry, fairness of trade and competition.[433] This strengthening of the European film and TV industry occurred not least because of the influence of major U.S. content providers, whose channels penetrated the European market.[434] The background for the special emphasis on economic motives for the regulation in this context was probably also the lack of a competence basis for creating a regulation that focused on cultural policy. The wording of the Directive, which left it to the Member States to assess whether appropriate measures should be taken, was therefore accordingly cautious.

This line was also maintained in the reform of the Directive, which took place once every decade in the following period.[435] In an effort to adapt the provisions of the TwF Directive to a new advertising environment and technological developments in television broadcasting, Directive 97/36/EC[436] introduced important innovations in the areas of teleshopping and the broadcasting of major events, and deepened the provisions of the law on the protection of minors from harmful content. From the procedural point of view, the provisions on jurisdiction were concretized in the form of the criteria for determining jurisdiction and the Contact Committee was established. However, the basic concept of minimum harmonization was retained, in particular also with the reaffirmation that the concept of basic harmonization chosen by the TwF Directive was still necessary, but also sufficient, to ensure the free reception of television broadcasts in the Community.[437] Accordingly, the objectives in the form of protection of the right to information (e.g. broadcasting of major events), improved

---

433 Accordingly, in its 1986 proposal for a directive, the Commission also already emphasized that "the vulnerability of European cultural industries is not due to lack of creative talent, but to fragmented production and distribution systems", OJ C 179 of 17.07.1986, p. 4–10, 6.
434 *Broghton Micova*, The Audiovisual Media Services Directive: Balancing liberalisation and protection (DRAFT), p. 4 et seq.
435 In detail on the genesis of the TwF Directive *Weinand*, Implementing the Audiovisual Media Services Directive, p. 70 et seq.
436 Directive 97/36/EC of the European Parliament and of the Council of 30 June 1997 amending Council Directive 89/552/EEC on the coordination of certain provisions laid down by law, regulation or administrative action in Member States concerning the pursuit of television broadcasting activities, OJ L 202 of 30.07.1997, p. 60–70, https://eur-lex.europa.eu/legal-content/EN/TXT/?uri=CELEX:31997L0036.
437 Rec. 44 Directive 97/36/EC.

D. Secondary legal framework on "media law" and media pluralism

competitiveness of the programme industry (e.g. revision of the provisions and exceptions for the promotion of European works), consumer protection (e.g. regulation of teleshopping) and protection of minors (e.g. prohibition of content that seriously impairs development) were also at the forefront of the reform. In this context, cultural aspects were only taken into account in activities based on other provisions, as the obligation under the cultural horizontal clause already required at that time.[438]

While the power to derogate under Art. 3(1) of the TwF Directive remained essentially untouched by the reform, the recitals now specified the other "certain circumstances" in which Member States were to be able to adopt stricter provisions. Recital 44 listed for this purpose, in particular and among other things, the protection of the public interest in terms of television's role as a provider of information, education, culture and entertainment, the need to safeguard pluralism in the information industry and the media, and the protection of competition with a view to avoiding the abuse of dominant positions. Although such Member State rules must be compatible with Community law, the safeguarding of pluralism in the (audiovisual) media is thus clearly seen here as being within the competence and interests of the Member States, even in areas in which the European legislature has already documented its regulatory intent and competence for legal and economic aspects relating to services by harmonizing precisely those rules in the Directive.

This line was continued with the next reform. Ten years after the previous revision of the Directive, Directive 2007/65/EC[439] aimed to respond once again to new technical circumstances, in particular against the background of the growing importance of the Internet, and to adapt the legal framework to the convergence of the media. To this end, provisions were introduced for on-demand services as part of a tiered regulatory approach that, while separating linear and non-linear offerings, recognized the television-like nature of audiovisual on-demand offerings on the Internet and therefore introduced similar obligations in certain areas. There was a renewed concretization of the provisions on jurisdiction, information re-

---

438 So explicitly rec. 25 with reference to Art. 128(4) TEC (Amsterdam consolidated version), OJ C 340 of 10.11.1997, p. 173–306 (now Art. 167 TFEU).
439 Directive 2007/65/EC of the European Parliament and of the Council of 11 December 2007 amending Council Directive 89/552/EEC on the coordination of certain provisions laid down by law, regulation or administrative action in Member States concerning the pursuit of television broadcasting activities, OJ L 332 of 18.12.2007, p. 27–45, https://eur-lex.europa.eu/legal-content/EN/TXT/?uri=celex%3A32007L0065.

quirements for providers were introduced or revised, the right to short news reports was established, and adjustments were made in the area of commercial communications, in particular with regard to product placement. In the context of Art. 3, approaches of self-regulation and co-regulation were also introduced into the Directive for the first time by stipulating that the Member States promote such regulations in the coordinated field – but only to the extent permitted under national law. However, the concretization and scope of the use of such regulatory instruments was left to the Member States – in line with a minimum harmonization approach.

While aspects of safeguarding diversity in the media played a greater role in the general considerations for Directive 2007/65/EC than in the predecessor directives[440], safeguarding pluralism is not taken up as a direct objective in the text of the Directive – in line with the lack of a legal basis in terms of competence. In its 2003 Green Paper on services of general interest, the Commission also explicitly emphasized that "[A]t present, secondary Community legislation does not contain any provisions directly aiming to safeguard the pluralism of the media"[441]. However, individual innovations were framed in the context of media pluralism. Thus, the clarification of competence rules was placed under the point of view that in order to "enhance media pluralism throughout the European Union", only one Member State should have jurisdiction over an audiovisual media service provider and that "pluralism of information should be a fundamental principle of the European Union"[442]; the introduction of the right to short news reports was justified by the absolute essentiality to promote pluralism through the diversity of news production and programming across the EU[443]; the obligation to promote European works on the part of on-demand audiovisual media service providers was underpinned at least by the fact that the providers thereby (also) contribute actively to the promotion of cultural diversity[444].

However, this greater emphasis on media diversity was not accompanied by a reorientation of the Directive to the effect that safeguarding diversity would have become an objective of the EU, pursued with concrete

---

440 Cf. rec. 1, 3, 4, 5, 8, which refer to the general direction of the EU's regulatory policy in the audiovisual area, understanding diversity of opinion and the media as a cornerstone in this context.
441 Green paper on services of general interest, COM/2003/0270 final, https://eur-lex.europa.eu/legal-content/EN/TXT/?uri=celex:52003DC0270, para. 74.
442 Rec. 28 Directive 2007/65/EC.
443 Rec. 38 Directive 2007/65/EC.
444 Rec. 48 Directive 2007/65/EC.

D. Secondary legal framework on "media law" and media pluralism

rules at the level of secondary law. Rather, the stronger inclusion of diversity considerations was probably also due to corresponding statements in the EU Commission's communication on the future of European regulatory audiovisual policy, which immediately preceded the reform.[445] However, it is pointed out therein that the protection of pluralism in the media is primarily the responsibility of the Member States, but that some Community legal acts nevertheless contribute more or less indirectly to the protection of media pluralism, such as in competition law and certain provisions of the TwF Directive (esp. as regards the promotion of European works). Accordingly, the 2007 reform also emphasizes that the Member States are free to choose the appropriate instruments according to their legal traditions and established structures when transposing the Directive, whereby the instruments chosen should contribute to the promotion of media pluralism.[446]

In 2010, a codification of the Directive took place, which brought together in one text all the adaptations set out in the amending Directives up to that point and re-promulgated the act as the Audiovisual Media Services Directive. This was not coupled with a change in content. In particular, the recitals of Directive 2007/65/EC dealing with aspects of safeguarding diversity have also been incorporated verbatim and in full into Directive 2010/13/EU, i.e. their continued validity has been recognized.[447] A change in audiovisual policy and the previous line of locating safeguarding diversity at Member State level – albeit as an important principle at EU level – had therefore not taken place.

---

[445] Communication from the Commission of 15 December 2003 on the future of European regulatory audiovisual policy, COM(2003) 784 final, https://eur-lex.europa.eu/legal-content/EN/TXT/?uri=CELEX%3A52013D-C0784&qid=1614597375820.
[446] Rec. 65 Directive 2007/65/EC.
[447] Comparing Directive 2007/65/EC with (Directive 2010/13/EU): 1(4), 3(5), 4(6), 5(7), 8(12), 28(34), 38(48) and 65(94).

b. AVMSD reform 2018

With a comprehensive reform[448], the AVMSD, initiated by a Commission proposal in May 2016[449], was revised in 2018 and significantly expanded in terms of scope to adapt it – once again – to the realities of a rapidly evolving media landscape. The requirements of the Directive were to be transposed by the Member States by 19 September 2020, with only Germany and Denmark having adopted a final transposition and Austria a partial one in national law by the end of the transposition period. In other Member States, however, legislative projects have already been initiated.[450]

The reform was triggered in 2013 by the Green Paper on media convergence, in which the Commission in particular raised the question of the timeliness of existing regulation and the impact of media convergence on media diversity.[451] With regard to aspects of safeguarding diversity against the backdrop of the changing media landscape, the Commission emphasized, among other things, that the AVMSD and competition rules contribute to the preservation of media pluralism both at EU and Member

---

448 For an overview of the developments in the trilogue procedure, cf. the synopsis by EMR, available at https://emr-sb.de/synopsis-avms/. A comparison of the versions of the Directive before and after the changes made by the directive adopted in 2018 can also be found there, as well as a (non-official) consolidated version of the AVMSD.

449 Proposal for a Directive of the European Parliament and of the Council amending Directive 2010/13/EU on the coordination of certain provisions laid down by law, regulation or administrative action in Member States concerning the provision of audiovisual media services in view of changing market realities, COM(2016) 287 final, 25.5.2016, https://eur-lex.europa.eu/legal-content/EN/TXT/?uri=celex:52016PC0287. An initial assessment of the proposed amendment can be found at *Weinand*, Implementing the Audiovisual Media Services Directive, p. 719 et seq.; *Burggraf/Gerlach/Wiesner* in: Media Perspektiven 10/2018, 496, 496 et seq.; as well as *Cole/Etteldorf*, Von Fernsehen ohne Grenzen zu Video-Sharing-Plattformen, Hate Speech und Overlays – die Anpassung der EU-Richtlinie über audiovisuelle Mediendienste an das digitale Zeitalter.

450 Cf. on this the overviews in the databases of the Commission (https://eur-lex.europa.eu/legal-content/EN/NIM/?uri=CELEX:32018L1808&qid=1599556794041) and the European Audiovisual Observatory (https://www.obs.coe.int/en/web/observatoire/home/-/asset_publisher/9iKCxBYgiO6S/content/which-eu-countries-have-transposed-the-avmsd-into-national-legislation-?_101_INSTANCE_9iKCxBYgiO6S_viewMode=view/).

451 European Commission, Green Paper Preparing for a Fully Converged Audiovisual World: Growth, Creation and Values, COM(2013) 231 final, 24.4.2013, https://eur-lex.europa.eu/legal-content/EN/TXT/?uri=CELEX%3A52013DC0231&qid=1614597256678.

D. Secondary legal framework on "media law" and media pluralism

State level. In this context, the Commission explained in a footnote that the AVMSD supports media pluralism (only) by allowing audiovisual media services to freely circulate within the single market, based on the country of origin principle and e.g. through Art. 14, which in turn, together with the specific rules on the promotion of European works, supports media pluralism.[452] Also in a different context dealing with the values underlying the regulation of audiovisual media services, the Commission emphasizes in the Green Paper that the promotion of media pluralism and cultural diversity should be seen in the context of Art. 167(4) TFEU and that these regulatory objectives were not paramount for the purposes of the AVMSD.[453] Potential threats to the diversity of opinion and the media were identified in the Green Paper in particular with regard to the filtering and highlighting of content by gatekeepers such as search engines and other intermediary platforms, since these – although they can also strengthen the citizen's ability to obtain information – can influence the spectrum of accessible media offerings without the users' knowledge. Further considerations were made on the general legal framework, commercial communication, protection of minors, accessibility of audiovisual content for persons with disabilities, and other complementary aspects.

These considerations are reflected in the amending Directive (EU) 2018/1808, which was adopted later.[454] One of the significant changes is the (renewed) expansion of the scope of the AVMSD, to include the newly introduced category of video-sharing platforms (VSP). These are covered by the new version of the Directive for the first time – provided they were not previously already providers of non-linear services with own editorial responsibility and therefore subject to the AVMSD since the 2007 revision – and are thus held more accountable, in particular with regard to the protection of the general public from certain illegal content, commercial communication and the protection of minors. The rules for non-linear audiovisual media services were also adjusted again, aligning them even further (but not completely) with the provisions for television providers. These

---

452 European Commission, Green Paper Preparing for a Fully Converged Audiovisual World: Growth, Creation and Values, COM(2013) 231 final, 24.4.2013, p. 13, fn. 63.
453 European Commission, Green Paper Preparing for a Fully Converged Audiovisual World: Growth, Creation and Values, COM(2013) 231 final, 24.4.2013, p. 10, fn. 50.
454 For an overview on the reform cf. also *Cole/Etteldorf*, Von Fernsehen ohne Grenzen zu Video-Sharing-Plattformen, Hate Speech und Overlays – die Anpassung der EU-Richtlinie über audiovisuelle Mediendienste an das digitale Zeitalter.

changes were made in consideration of the fact that newer players in the audiovisual market, in particular streaming providers such as Netflix (in the VoD area) and video distribution/access platforms such as YouTube (in the VSP area), compete with providers of traditional services such as television for the attention of the same recipients and advertisers and should therefore be subject to at least approximately similar regulation.

Other amendments include a minimal concretization to clarify responsibility criteria with regard to the country of origin principle[455], the requirements for the protection of minors[456] and hate speech,[457] the modernization of the obligation to promotion of European works[458], the tightening of qualitative and liberalization of quantitative advertising rules[459], the so-called signal integrity[460] as well as the obligation of the Member States to contribute to the promotion of media literacy. In addition, institutional and formal arrangements were made, which in turn may have significant implications for the overall shape of media regulation in the future: so-called codes of conduct (including European codes of conduct) are emphasized as new forms of regulation in the context of the overall strengthening of self-regulation and co-regulation, and there is a commitment to greater cooperation among regulators.[461]

With regard to aspects of safeguarding diversity as an objective in general, the reform has not brought any significant changes. Although recital 53 (in the context of the fulfillment of tasks by the national regulatory authorities) speaks, among other things, of media pluralism and cultural diversity as "objectives", the implementation of this objective is ultimately also confirmed by recital 61 insofar as it is to be located at the level of the Member States: These are to respect the freedom of expression and information and

---

455 Cf. in detail *Cole*, The AVMSD Jurisdiction Criteria concerning Audiovisual Media Service Providers after the 2018 Reform.
456 On this *Ukrow*, Por-No Go im audiovisuellen Binnenmarkt?.
457 On this *Cole/Etteldorf* in: Medienhandbuch Österreich, 56, 60 et seq.
458 On this *Cole*, Guiding Principles in establishing the Guidelines for Implementation of Article 13 (6) AVMSD; also *Etteldorf* in: UFITA 2019, 498, 506 et seq. with regard to the implementation of promotion obligations in national law.
459 On this *Etteldorf*, Zwischen Fernsehen ohne Grenzen und Werbung ohne Grenzen.
460 On this *Cole*, Die Neuregelung des Artikel 7b Richtlinie 2010/13/EU (AVMD-RL).
461 A detailed overview of the changes can be found at *Weinand*, UFITA 2018, 260, 260 et seq.; further *Jäger*, ZUM 62(2019)6, 477, 477 et seq. On the institutional and formal reforms cf. in detail *Cole/Etteldorf/Ullrich*, Cross-border Dissemination of Online Content, 101 et seq., 152 et seq.

D. Secondary legal framework on "media law" and media pluralism

media pluralism, as well as cultural and linguistic diversity, in accordance with the Unesco Convention on the Protection and Promotion of the Diversity of Cultural Expressions[462] in any measure taken under the Directive.

With regard to certain rules in particular, however, the idea of (also) safeguarding media diversity plays a greater role in the context of the recent reform of the AVMSD. Areas in the context of which the safeguarding of pluralism is particularly emphasized are the obligation (now enshrined for the first time at EU level in the audiovisual field) to establish independent regulatory bodies[463], the ability of creating national rules to appropriately ensure prominence of content of general interest[464], transparency requirements regarding ownership structures[465], and the (amended obligation to) promote European works, which are described in detail in chapter D.II.2.d.

It should be noted in general and with regard to safeguarding media diversity that despite the fact that the scope of application and harmonization of the AVMSD has been constantly expanded over time, full harmonization at this level is far from being achieved and the TwF Directive's approach of minimum harmonization is being continued in certain areas. This is expressed not only in general and further by the character of the AVMSD as a directive[466], but also by the explicit power of the Member States, provided for in Art. 4(1), to deviate from the rules. Also the CJEU only recently emphasized in its *Vivendi* decision as follows:

---

462   UNESCO, 2005 Convention for the Protection and Promotion of the Diversity of Cultural Expressions, https://en.unesco.org/creativity/sites/creativity/files/passeport-convention2005-web2.pdf.
463   Cf. rec. 54 and 55 as well as the remarks in the ex post REFIT evaluation prior to the reform, Commission staff working document SWD/2016/0170 final – 2016/0151 (COD), https://eur-lex.europa.eu/legal-content/EN/TXT/?qid=1596711526774&uri=CELEX:52016SC0170, in the context of which the existence of independent regulatory bodies at the national level was assessed as a prerequisite for the protection of media diversity.
464   Cf. on this rec. 25 Directive (EU) 2018/1808.
465   Cf. rec. 16 Directive (EU) 2018/1808.
466   By choosing the instrument of a directive, which according to Art. 288(3) TFEU leaves the choice of form and methods of transposition to the national authorities, the Union legislature has at the same time taken into account the horizontal cultural policy clause in Art. 167 TFEU with its effect of protecting the sovereignty of the Member States in terms of media policy in a manner related to the type of legal act. Cf. on this *Ukrow/Ress* in: Grabitz/Hilf/Nettesheim, Art. 167 TFEU, para. 148 et seq.

"[...] both the Framework Directive and the Audiovisual Media Services Directive effect a non-exhaustive harmonisation of national rules in their respective fields, leaving the Member States with a margin of discretion to adopt decisions at national level. In particular, in accordance with Article 1(3) of the Framework Directive, the Member States remain competent to pursue general interest objectives, in particular relating to content regulation and audiovisual policy, having due regard for EU law."[467]

c. The relevance of Art. 4(1) AVMSD

Art. 4(1) AVMSD regulates the Member States' power of derogation, which relates to the regulatory fields coordinated by the Directive. This can therefore also lead to stricter rules in national law with regard to the harmonized regulations of the AVMSD, but these may then only be applied to providers under their own jurisdiction and – in line with the country of origin principle – not to services received from other EU countries. Thus, this regulation is one of the key elements of the discretion left to the Member States in the regulation of audiovisual media services or the key element for determining Member State powers when it comes to areas which are already (partially) harmonized by the Directive. However, Art. 4(1) AVMSD does not apply in cases where Member States' regulations refer to or have an effect on services covered by the Directive but do not concern the field coordinated by the AVMSD, even if they have cross-border effects[468]. In this respect, there is room for maneuver for the Member States anyway.

The power to derogate already existed in the original TwF Directive. While the prohibition of circumvention (Art. 4(2) AVMSD) and the procedure of recourse to providers under other jurisdiction (Art. 4(4) and (5) AVMSD) were established only over time, namely with Directives 1997/36/EC[469] and 2007/65/EC, and amended by Directive (EU)

---

467 CJEU, case C-719/18, *Vivendi SA / Autorità per le Garanzie nelle Comunicazioni*, para. 47.
468 On this in particular CJEU, joined cases C-244/10 and C-245/10, *Mesopotamia Broadcast A/S METV and Roj TV A/S / Bundesrepublik Deutschland*, para. 37. On this in detail Cole in: R.D.T.I. 47/2012, 50, 50 et seq.
469 Thus, in particular, settled case law of the CJEU to that date (e.g. cases 33/74, *Van Binsbergen / Bedrijfsvereniging voor de Metaalnijverheid*, and C-23/93, *TV10 SA / Commissariaat voor de Media*) has found its way into the Directive, according to which a Member State retains the right to take action against a broadcaster

D. Secondary legal framework on "media law" and media pluralism

2018/1808, para. 1 has changed little since its creation, as can be seen from the following synopsis.

89/552/EEC	97/36/EC	2007/65/EC	(EU) 2018/1808
Member States shall remain free to require television broadcasters under their jurisdiction to lay down more detailed or stricter rules in the areas covered by this Directive.	Member States shall remain free to require television broadcasters under their jurisdiction to **comply with** more detailed or stricter rules in the areas covered by this Directive.	Member States shall remain free to require **media service providers** under their jurisdiction to comply with more detailed or stricter rules in the **fields coordinated** by this Directive **provided that such rules are in compliance with Community law.**	Member States shall remain free to require media service providers under their jurisdiction to comply with more detailed or stricter rules in the fields coordinated by this Directive, provided that such rules are in compliance with **Union** law.

The general necessity of this rule and its substance in the form of the ability to derogate from the harmonized fields of the Directive has never been questioned. For example was merely clarified that the rules adopted by the Member States must comply with Community or Union law – a requirement which, as shown in the previous chapters, already results from general principles of Union law anyway and thus has only declaratory effect. In the context of imposing stricter obligations on audiovisual media service providers, consideration should be given in particular to fundamental freedoms, fundamental rights and general principles of Union law, in particular the freedom to provide services (Art. 56 et seq. TFEU), the freedom of the media (Art. 11 CFR) and the general principle of equal treatment.[470]

---

which establishes itself in another Member State but whose activities are wholly or mainly directed towards the territory of the first Member State, if the broadcaster has established itself with the intention of evading the rules which would be applicable to it if it were established in the territory of the first Member State.

470 Cf. on this in particular CJEU, case C-234/12, *Sky Italia srl / Autorità per le Garanzie nelle Comunicazioni*, para. 15 et seq.

The definition of the objective of "general interest" does not follow from the Directive itself. However, certain objectives which the EU legislature in particular included and includes under this term can be inferred rom the recitals. These include, e.g., goals that are geared to language criteria[471] or serve the realization of language policy goals[472] (which in turn are intrinsically linked to cultural measures[473]), consumer protection, protection of minors, and cultural policy.[474] However, the lists there are by no means exhaustive. Rather, with Art. 4(1), the EU legislature takes up the long-established case law of the CJEU, developed over decades, on the definition of the general interest.[475] Accordingly, in its case law on Art. 4 AVMSD (or Art. 3 TwF Directive)[476], the CJEU does not initially examine the existence of an objective of general interest in order to justify the applicability of Art. 4(1) AVMSD, but shifts this examination to the level of the assessment of the violation of Union law, in particular of fundamental freedoms, in the context of which it is equally a matter of pursuing overriding reasons of general interest.[477] Therefore, reference can be made here to the explanations on the determination of an objective of general interest in the light of the justification of restrictions of fundamental rights and freedoms in chapters C.II, C.III and C.IV.1, which in particular conceive safeguarding diversity as such an objective, which, as explained there, is based on an approach of the ECtHR that again goes back a long way. It follows that, irrespective of whether a measure taken by a Member State falls within the fields covered by the Directive, Member States remain in

---

[471] Rec. 26 Directive 89/552/EEC.
[472] Rec. 44 Directive 1997/36/EC.
[473] So expressly CJEU, C-222/07, *Unión de Televisiones Comerciales Asociadas (UTECA) / Administración General del Estado*, para. 33.
[474] Rec. 32 Directive 2007/65/EC.
[475] So expressly with reference to the case law on Art. 43 and 49 TEC rec. 32 Directive 2007/65/EC.
[476] In particular CJEU, case C-6/98, *Arbeitsgemeinschaft Deutscher Rundfunkanstalten (ARD) / Pro Sieben Media AG*; CJEU, case C-500/06, *Corporación Dermoestética SA / To Me Group Advertising Media*; CJEU, case C-222/07, *Unión de Televisiones Comerciales Asociadas (UTECA) / Administración General del Estado*; CJEU, case C-234/12, *Sky Italia srl / Autorità per le Garanzie nelle Comunicazioni*; CJEU, case C-314/14, *Sanoma Media Finland Oy – Nelonen Media / Viestintävirasto*.
[477] Cf. on this e.g. CJEU, case C-6/98, *Arbeitsgemeinschaft Deutscher Rundfunkanstalten (ARD) / Pro Sieben Media AG*; CJEU, case C-500/06, *Corporación Dermoestética SA / To Me Group Advertising Media*, para. 31 et seq.

D. Secondary legal framework on "media law" and media pluralism

principle competent to adopt such a measure, provided that they comply with Union law.[478]

As far as the definition of the "fields coordinated by this Directive" is concerned, to which Art. 4(1) AVMSD alone applies, while in other areas Member States' rules with regard to the services covered by the Directive are "only" to be measured against higher-ranking law such as fundamental rights and freedoms, the case law of the CJEU must also be referred to. In its *de Agostini* decision[479] the CJEU clarified in this context firstly that the coordinated fields can only relate to those services which fall within the scope of the Directive (at that time only television programs) and secondly that the coordination by the Directive must also have reached a certain degree in order to influence the scope of the Member States' regulatory leeway, and in particular that partial coordination is not sufficient for this purpose.[480] In this context, the CJEU assumed only such partial coordination even in the area of advertising, for which the then version of the Directive contained a number of principles of both a quantitative and qualitative nature[481]. The decision dates back to 1997 and therefore still refers to the TwF Directive as it stood at that time, so one could question the continued validity of these principles. However, the decision related to the area of advertising, which was similarly extensively regulated then as now. Furthermore, even more recent decisions on Directive 2010/13/EU still make reference to the de Agostini decision and the comments made there on the coordinated field, emphasizing the non-exhaustive nature of the Directive.[482]

---

478 CJEU, case C-222/07, *Unión de Televisiones Comerciales Asociadas (UTECA) / Administración General del Estado*, para. 19, 20; as well as CJEU, joined cases C-244/10 and C-245/10, *Mesopotamia Broadcast A/S METV and Roj TV A/S / Bundesrepublik Deutschland*, para. 34.
479 CJEU, joined cases C-34/95, C-35/95 and C-36/95, *Konsumentombudsmannen (KO) / De Agostini (Svenska) Förlag AB and TV-Shop i Sverige AB*.
480 CJEU, joined cases C-34/95, C-35/95 and C-36/95, *Konsumentombudsmannen (KO) / De Agostini (Svenska) Förlag AB and TV-Shop i Sverige AB*, para. 26 and 32. On this in detail the annotations of *Novak* in: DB 1997, 2589, 2589 et seq.; *Lange* in: EWS 1998, 189, 190; *Heermann* in: GRUR Int 1999, 579, 588 et seq., *Stuyck* in: CMLRev. 1997, 1445, 1466 et seq.
481 Provisions on the manner of broadcasting, the use of certain advertising techniques and broadcasting time, content requirements (human dignity, discrimination, cigarettes and tobacco products, medicines and medical treatment, alcoholic beverages), and the protection of minors.
482 Cf. for instance CJEU, joined cases C-244/10 and C-245/10, *Mesopotamia Broadcast A/S METV und Roj TV A/S / Bundesrepublik Deutschland*, para. 32, 36 et seq. With reference to the fields of public order, morality and safety; C-622/17, *Baltic*

Moreover, the following conclusion can be drawn from the provision of Art. 4(1) AVMSD: if already the only set of regulations at EU level that directly addresses the media sector in regulatory terms provides Member States with leeway and explicitly allows them to adopt stricter provisions in the field coordinated by the EU for domestic providers[483], in particular in the cultural policy area of safeguarding media diversity, then corresponding possibilities must not be blocked in principle with regard to other (coordinated) sectors that are affected by measures to safeguard diversity. In particular, the power of derogation deliberately created by Art. 4(1) AVMSD against the background of cultural policy and constitutional considerations in the various Member States cannot be completely undermined by other sectoral provisions at the level of EU secondary law. This applies in particular against the background that the use of the derogation power by enacting stricter rules is often not very attractive for reasons of competition policy and law: On the one hand, it is important for the individual Member States not to lose or reduce their attractiveness as a location for media undertakings due to economic interests (tax revenues) and also cultural policy interests (diverse media landscape), and on the other hand, not to impair the competitiveness of domestic media undertakings in competition with foreign undertakings.[484] A fortiori, therefore, if the objective of Art. 4(1) AVMSD to give the Member States the opportunity to create their own framework conditions for media policy in certain fields, can no longer or less sensibly be achieved, this objective must not be further hindered or even restricted by the fact that harmonization is taking place in other areas, which regularly affects the media sector only as a reflex.

Media Alliance Ltd / Lietuvos radijo ir televizijos komisija, para. 73 et seq., however, against the background of Art. 3(1) AVMSD with reference to the pursuit of objectives in the public interest.

483 *Liesching* (Das Herkunftslandprinzip nach E-Commerce- und AVMD-Richtlinie, p. 40) comes to the conclusion with regard to the adoption of national rules also for foreign providers with regard to general media law regulation (outside of specifically diversity-securing regulatory objectives) that the transmitting state principle according to Art. 3 AVMSD in the coordinated field in principle does not permit national abstract-general rules with regard to providers of audiovisual media services with an establishment in another Member State, insofar as these rules in their application mean impediments to the further dissemination of their services. This does not apply if the rules serve a purpose other than the fields and objectives harmonized by the Directive. These include measures to safeguard media pluralism, which is the focus of this study.

484 Cf. on this etwa *Harrison/Woods*, Jurisdiction, forum shopping and the 'race to the bottom', 173, 174 et seq.; *Vlassis* in: Politique européenne 2017/2, 102, 102 et seq.

d. Specific provisions

Although, as described in detail above, the AVMSD is still not aimed at creating rules with cultural policy implications, but rather at enabling the free movement of audiovisual media services in the European internal market and removing obstacles in this regard, there are also links to safeguarding diversity by the Member States, either by actively promoting certain media content through them or their regulatory frameworks, or by reacting restrictively to certain negative developments or dangers (also in the light of pluralism). In the following, we will therefore look at those rules that are related to safeguarding diversity in the media, in order to draw conclusions for the delimitation of competences between the Union and the Member States from the way they are structured in terms of the exercise of competences.

(1) Promotion of European works

Already under the TwF Directive, television broadcasters were obliged to reserve the majority of their broadcasting time, which did not consist of news, sports reports, game shows or advertising and teletext services, for the transmission of European works. 10 % of broadcasting time or, alternatively, at the choice of the Member State, 10 % of the budget should be reserved for European works by independent producers. Broadcasters must report on compliance with this quota requirement. However, these rules – then as now – do not apply to television broadcasts aimed at a local audience that are not connected to a national television network, thus privileging these providers to that extent by exempting them from broadcasting and reporting requirements.[485] It is true that the quota regulations have been critically evaluated both from a perspective of legal competence and against the background of the entrepreneurial freedom of media providers and their organization, not only in the FCC's ruling on the TwF Directive (there at least in connection with the federal government's observance of federal states' rights in the legislative process in the Council as an expres-

---

485 In detail on the exception for local providers: *Ukrow/Cole*, Förderung lokaler und regionaler Medienvielfalt, p. 91 et seq.

sion of the obligation to act in a way that is friendly to the federal states),[486] but also in the literature.[487] Notwithstanding the question, which has not yet been conclusively clarified or discussed by either the CJEU or the FCC, as to whether the EU's service-related competence title provides a sufficient legal basis for audiovisual quota regulations, these quotas do, however, prove to be an important means of promoting cultural aspects and have been described by the Commission in its regular reports to the European Parliament and the Council as very successful, based on information from the Member States, at least with regard to the regulations in the AVMSD and the respective national transposition.[488] As indirect addressees of a binding European quota regulation, media providers are initially burdened by this, so that it could be inferred that the main objective cannot be safeguarding media diversity. However, it is not only the film production landscape that benefits from the quota obligation or the greater variety of offerings from the viewer's perspective. Rather, the resulting effect of also promoting the production of national works and European co-productions leads to the situation, also advantageous for media providers, that a greater range of program material is available on the market, from which they can profit (for the providers of linear and non-linear services, as the case may be, also reciprocally[489]).

---

486 Cf. BVerfGE 92, 203 (238 et seq.). Cf. on this *Bethge*, Deutsche Bundesstaatlichkeit und Europäische Union. Bemerkungen über die Entscheidung des Bundesverfassungsgerichts zur EG-Fernsehrichtlinie, p. 55 et seq.; *Holtz-Bacha*, Medienpolitik für Europa, p. 127 et seq.; *Deringer* in: ZUM 1995, 316, 316 et seq.; *Gerkrath* in: RTDE 1995, 539, 539 et seq.; *Kresse/Heinze* in: ZUM 1995, 394, 394 et seq.; *Martín y Pérez de Nanclares* in: Revista de Instituciones Europeas 1995, 887, 887 et seq.; *Müller-Terpitz*, Ein Karlsruher "Orakel" zum Bundesstaat im europäischen Staatenverbund, p. 568 et seq.; *Trautwein* in: ZUM 1995, 614, 614 et seq.; *Winkelmann* in: DöV 1996, 1, 1 et seq.
487 Cf. for the area of television: *Broughton Micova*, Content quotas: what and whom are they protecting; *Middleton* in: Denver Journal of International Law and Policy 31/2020, 607, 614 et seq.
488 Cf. for instance Report from the Commission to the European Parliament, the Council, the European Economic and Social Committee and the Committee of the Regions, First Report on the Application of Articles 13, 16 and 17 of Directive 2010/13/EU for the period 2009–2010 Promotion of European works in EU scheduled and on-demand audiovisual media services, COM/2012/0522 final, https://eur-lex.europa.eu/legal-content/EN/TXT/?uri=celex%3A52012DC0522.
489 Cf. for instance recently the securing by Netflix of the U.S. broadcasting rights for the series "Babylon Berlin," which was co-produced by ARD, among others. Cf. on this furthermore also *Etteldorf* in: UFITA 2019, 498, 506 et seq.

D. Secondary legal framework on "media law" and media pluralism

As mentioned at the beginning of the historical observation, however, the main focus of the introduction of this rule was not the establishment of cultural policy guidelines, but was primarily motivated by aspects of an economic nature, which was (and continues to be) in particular a consequence of the lack of a legal competence for setting cultural policy priorities at the Union level. Attractive markets for television productions should be favored at the European level – through a step-by-step approach – as far as the general conditions[490] in the respective Member States allow. This gradual introduction of rules, which, however, was to leave the choice of appropriate means to the Member States, in particular did not contain any concrete and strictly prescriptive regulations, in this context demonstrates the cautious approach – at least in comparison to original regulatory considerations[491]. The 1997 reform, which further harmonized national legislation promoting European works, maintained this economic focus – strengthening and improving the competitiveness of the program industry in Europe (recitals 26, 28 Directive 1997/36/EC).

The 2007 reform, whose most significant amendment was the inclusion of non-linear audiovisual media services in the scope of the Directive, also partially changed the approach to the promotion of European works. Although the harmonization of the regulatory framework between linear and non-linear services for some regulatory areas was based on the consideration that, due to the similarity of these services to television and a similar audience and advertising market, a level playing field should consequently apply (recital 7), and therefore the original (mainly economic) efforts to introduce existing rules should also continue to apply, the introduction of promotion obligations for European works of on-demand audiovisual media services was (also) justified by the consideration that these providers "should, where practicable, promote the production and distribution of European works and thus contribute actively to the promotion of cultural diversity"[492]. However, as with the origin rule for linear providers, the specific implementation of this objective was largely left to the Member States ("shall ensure [...] where practicable and by appropriate means"). Unlike the quota requirement for linear services ("majority proportion of their transmission time"), the provision regarding non-linear services was more open, with the Directive listing examples of possible re-

---

490 Exemptions for Member States were already provided for at that time, in particular for Member States with a low audiovisual production capacity or a restricted language area, cf. rec. 22 Directive 89/552/EEC.
491 Cf. on this BVerfGE 92, 203 (243 et seq.).
492 Rec. 48 Directive 2007/65/EC.

quirements for achieving this promotion by such providers (imposition of financial contribution obligations or obligations to ensure prominence).[493] The regulations issued on this basis in the individual Member States, if they exist at all, are therefore very diffuse and regularly distinguish between models of quotas, prominence, investment obligations and indicators.[494]

The latest 2018 amending directive further aligned the rules for linear and non-linear providers. Accordingly, on-demand audiovisual media service providers are now also subject to a fixed quota obligation as a direct result of rules at EU level (Art. 13 AVMSD). However, in contrast to television broadcasters (50% – since "majority proportion of transmission time"), these providers must make available in their catalogs only a minimum of 30% of European works. In addition, providers should ensure appropriate prominence of European works in their catalogs. However, this obligation – equally with other financial contribution obligations that Member States may impose on linear and non-linear service providers – does not apply to media service providers with low turnover or low audience. Member States may also refrain from applying the rule to providers with regard to specific offerings if this would be impracticable or unjustified given the nature or theme of the audiovisual media services. Besides, during the deliberations on this Directive, the German states maintained, by means of a corresponding opinion of the Bundesrat, that it is the Member States alone that decide on the form of the promotion of European works.[495]

For the concrete calculation of the share of European works and for the definition of low audience and low turnover, the Commission, according to Art. 13(7) AVMSD, shall issue guidelines.[496] This codifies a practice according to which the Commission already in the past wanted to provide instructions through the provision of corresponding guidance within the framework of the Contact Committee in order to achieve a largely uni-

---

493 On implementation processes at the time at large: *Apa et al.* in: Nikoltchev, Videoabrufdienste und die Förderung europäischer Werke.
494 Cf. on this comprehensively *EAI*, Mapping of national rules for the promotion of European works in Europe; as well as *VVA et al.*, study on the Promotion of European Works in Audiovisual Media Services, SMART 2016/0061.
495 Cf. https://www.bundesrat.de/SharedDocs/drucksachen/2016/0201-0300/288-2-16.pdf?__blob=publicationFile&v=5, cipher 20.
496 Cf. on this in detail *Cole*, Guiding Principles in establishing the Guidelines for Implementation of Article 13 (6) AVMSD.

D. Secondary legal framework on "media law" and media pluralism

form approach in the Member States when calculating the quotas.[497] The Commission published these guidelines in July 2020.[498] The guidelines are not legally binding on the Member States and do not preclude the application of special rules in the Member States, provided that they comply with Union law. However, they are an expression of the Commission's interpretation of the requirements of the AVMSD and can – and it is to be expected will – therefore be used by the Commission for future evaluation processes of Member States' implementation.[499] Due to this effect, too, it should ideally have been assumed that the Commission's guidelines were already available at a time when the Member States could still take them into account in their transposition. This is even more true for further guidelines that the Commission was entitled to issue to define the "essential functionality" criterion for defining video-sharing platforms and also published in parallel in July 2020 (on this see chapter D.II.2.d(5)). Since the guidelines regarding the promotion obligation were also only announced just before the end of the transposition period, it will be necessary to observe which Member States have taken them into account at all in greater detail when drafting the legal basis, or how the Commission will deal with non-inclusion of the guidelines at least in the application practice by the supervisory authorities. The approach taken in the MStV of authorizing the state media authorities in its § 77 sentence 3 to regulate details of the implementation of the quota regulations for providers of television-like telemedia by means of joint statutes is in this respect not only un-

---

[497] Cf. *Cole*, Guiding Principles in establishing the Guidelines for Implementation of Article 13 (6) AVMSD, with further references; cf. also Report from the Commission to the European Parliament, the Council, the European Economic and Social Committee and the Committee of the Regions, First Report on the Application of Articles 13, 16 and 17 of Directive 2010/13/EU for the period 2009–2010 Promotion of European works in EU scheduled and on-demand audiovisual media services, COM/2012/0522 final.

[498] Communication from the Commission Guidelines pursuant to Article 13(7) of the Audiovisual Media Services Directive on the calculation of the share of European works in on-demand catalogues and on the definition of low audience and low turnover, OJ C 223 of 07.07.2020, p. 10–16, https://eur-lex.europa.eu/legal-content/EN/TXT/?uri=uriserv:OJ.C_.2020.223.01.0010.01.ENG&toc=OJ:C:2020:223:TOC.

[499] Cf. on this European Commission – Questions and answers, Guidelines on the revised Audiovisual Media Services Directive, 02.07.2020, available at https://ec.europa.eu/commission/presscorner/detail/en/QANDA_20_1208; in detail also *Cole*, Guiding Principles in establishing the Guidelines for Implementation of Article 13 (6) AVMSD.

objectionable under European law, but also a welcome form of integrating the guidelines into the implementing legislation.

In addition to the quota obligation itself, there is a comprehensive evaluation obligation for the transposition of the various promotion measures provided for in Art. 13 AVMSD. To this end, the Member States must first report to the Commission on the application of the national rules, and the Commission in turn must report to the European Parliament and the Council from this and from an independent evaluation of the application of these rules by the Member States. In this context, it should take into account the market and technological developments, as well as "the goal of cultural diversity" (Art. 13(5) AVMSD). On the one hand, this wording makes it clear that, irrespective of the emphasis on the economic objective – also due to the otherwise questionable legal basis – at the time of the introduction of the funding obligation, the promotion to safeguard (European, i.e. the Member States' own) cultural diversity has always existed as an objective in the background. In this context, Art. 13(5) AVMSD merely emphasizes that special attention should be paid to the extent to which the rule and the measures taken on its basis contribute to cultural diversity and its safeguarding (by guaranteeing production and distribution through broadcasting). Neither the directive nor the more technically oriented guidelines, which refer to calculation parameters for the catalog share of 30 % and the services to be excluded from the promotion obligations, call into question the sovereignty of the Member States to define the cultural policy aspect of the regulation. Overall, the Union provision is thus within the scope of competence and is in particular covered by Art. 167 TFEU, as it concerns the support (development) of cultures in the Union, which does not interfere with the cultural policy of the Member States and is also based on the competitiveness of the European audiovisual market.[500]

This only supplementary support dimension is also evident in the Commission's formulation of the guidelines. According to them, "it is thus important to find a right balance between the objectives of preserving a necessary innovation space for smaller audiovisual players and that of promoting cultural diversity through adequate financing for European works *under Member States' cultural policies*".[501] Nevertheless, care must also be taken in the future to ensure that the Commission is not able to curtail the re-

---

500 So *Harrison/Woods*, Television Quotas: protecting European Culture?.
501 Communication from the Commission Guidelines pursuant to Article 13(7) of the Audiovisual Media Services Directive on the calculation of the share of European works in on-demand catalogues and on the definition of low audience and low turnover, OJ C 223 of 07.07.2020, p. 10–16, at III.1.

D. Secondary legal framework on "media law" and media pluralism

serve of competences of the Member States, even in the transposition of directives, through only vague or narrowly conferral of the right to define the details by means of (again: legally non-binding) guidelines. In fact – and in case of doubt also in a sensible way – such guidelines will have a harmonizing effect for partial areas regardless of their legally non-binding nature, because de facto Member States will only disregard the guidelines in case of a need for deviation that is necessary and justifiable from their point of view.

A further leeway at the national level already lies in the broad definition (given at the EU level) of European works, which according to Art. 1(1)(n) AVMSD are to be understood as works originating in Member States and such originating in European third States[502] party to the European Convention on Transfrontier Television of the Council of Europe, as well as works co-produced within the framework of agreements related to the audiovisual sector concluded between the Union and third countries[503] and fulfilling the conditions defined in each of those agreements. This broad understanding of the term recognizes the possibility for Member States to clarify this definition in compliance with Union law and taking into account the objectives of the AVMSD for media service providers under their jurisdiction.[504] The latter means in particular that Member States can incorporate their own cultural considerations into this type of support for national providers, in particular responding to national peculiarities when they concretize the term. For example, in France – a Member State

---

502 In particular, safeguards are needed for EEA States if they are to benefit from such rules. On the impact of Brexit in this context cf. *Cole/Etteldorf/Ukrow*, Audiovisual Sector and Brexit: the Regulatory Environment. As a signatory to the Convention on Transfrontier Television, productions from the United Kingdom will continue to count as European works, but there will be no reporting obligation to the Commission. Following a consultation process, the government announced its intention to review the existing quota rules in UK law and (for the time being) came out against the introduction of a levy requirement. Cf. on this Department for Digital, Culture, Media & Sport, Consultation outcome Audiovisual Media Services, Government response to public consultations on the government's implementation proposals, 30.5.2019, https://www.gov.uk/government/consultations/audiovisual-media-services/outcome/audiovisual-media-services-government-response-to-public-consultations-on-the-governments-implementation-proposals.
503 Cf. e.g. the CoE Convention on Cinematographic Co-Production (1992, revised in 2017), which provides a comprehensive legal framework and standards for multilateral co-productions and bilateral co-productions between parties that have not concluded a bilateral treaty.
504 Cf. rec. 32 Directive 2010/13/EU.

that not only has a strong film industry, but in whose tradition French film plays a special role – media service providers are obliged to serve a large part of their broadcasting and delivery obligations with French-language works, while in the Netherlands the Dutch- or Frisian-language program is shaped by public service broadcasting quotas.[505]

Accordingly, the Member States are also free to impose investment obligations on media service providers under their jurisdiction, for example in order to safeguarding diversity. This was already the case under the previous regulation, as it was left to the Member States to decide how the funding obligation was to be structured in detail.[506] Through the explicit inclusion in the AVMSD, it has also been clarified since 2018 that the imposition of such investment or levy obligations is also possible vis-à-vis providers who target viewers in a Member State territory with their offerings, but are not under its jurisdiction as they are established in another Member State. In this respect, Art. 13(2) AVMSD merely requires that the relevant rules be proportionate and non-discriminatory.

(2) Prominence of general interest content

Art. 7a AVMSD, which was newly inserted in 2018, also addresses aspects of safeguarding diversity, but on the basis of a different approach. It clarifies that the Directive is without prejudice to the possibility for Member

---

505 On this law-comparing *Etteldorf*, UFITA 2019, 498, 507 et seq.
506 Cf. on this, for example, the German regulation in § 152 of the Law on the funding of film production (Filmförderungsgesetz, FFG), which – or its approval by the European Commission – was challenged by both Apple and Netflix before the GCEU because, according to the plaintiff undertakings, it was not compatible with the country of origin principle enshrined in the AVMSD and the freedom to provide services and freedom of establishment, as well as the prohibition of discrimination, since it also imposed a levy obligation on undertakings not established in Germany depending on profits generated there. Both actions by Apple (case T-101/17, *Apple Distribution International / European Commission*) and Netflix (case T-818/16, *Netflix International BV and Netflix, Inc. / European Commission*) have been dismissed by the GCEU as already inadmissible due to a lack of proof of "individual concern" by the plaintiff undertakings. Among other things, the undertakings had failed to show that their services had been materially interfered with and individually concerned by the changes in the FFG. This could have been done, e.g., by filing national levy orders or such. A direct action before the GCEU requires a regulatory act which does not entail implementing measures, which was not the case here. The appeal to the CJEU initially filed by Apple against this (case C-633/18 P) was subsequently withdrawn.

D. Secondary legal framework on "media law" and media pluralism

States to impose obligations on service providers to ensure the appropriate prominence of content that is necessary and proportionate according to specified general interest objectives. Consequently, the issue at hand is not the presence of diverse content, as in the context of the quota regulations for European works just described, or the possibility of receiving certain content of general interest, as in the context of the must-carry obligations under telecommunications law, which will be described below[507], but rather the visibility of such content which has a particular value for society. The focus here is on the recipient's perspective, in other words, on the quality and variety of information presented to the user.

Against the background of the significance of information quality and diversity for the process of free democratic policy-forming and decision-making, however, these are also directly related to media diversity and the diversity of available sources from which users can obtain information respectively. A plural media landscape cannot fulfill its democratic function where the content is not perceived at all – a risk that exists above all on such platforms used by users (also) for information purposes, which make third-party content available collectively and therefore act as gatekeepers for media content, and is related to potentially risk-increasing phenomena such as disinformation[508] – this has become particularly illustrative against the background of the Covid19 pandemic[509] – and filter bubbles and echo chambers[510]. The effects of the latter two phenomena, insofar as they are algorithmically driven[511], on the pluralism of information, opinion, and

---

507 Cf. on this chapter D.II.5.
508 The relationship between media diversity on the one hand and disinformation on the other has not yet been conclusively studied scientifically. The existence of a risk potential in the absence of pluralism is likely, however, because in these cases there could be a lack of a strong and lively public discourse that confronts disinformation with rational argumentation and opposing views. Cf. on this *Bayer* in: Was ist Desinformation?, p. 46.
509 Cf. by way of example Joint Communication to the European Parliament, the European Council, the Council, the European Economic and Social Committee and the Committee of the Regions, Tackling COVID-19 disinformation – Getting the facts right, 10.06.2020, JOIN(2020) 8 final, https://eur-lex.europa.eu/legal-content/EN/TXT/HTML/?uri=CELEX:52020JC0008.
510 On the conceptual and actual distinction between the two phenomena cf. *Stark/Magin/Jürgens*, Maßlos überschätzt. Ein Überblick über theoretische Annahmen und empirische Befunde zu Filterblasen und Echokammern (Preprint), with further references.
511 A distinction must be made between this and the user-controlled personalization of content (through the targeted selection, liking, following or indication of in-

media have been the subject of much discussion in recent times.[512] Although a connection between algorithm-driven personalization of content and the emergence of filter bubbles or echo chambers as well as their effects on pluralism of opinion have not yet been conclusively empirically investigated and/or proven, and in particular more recent studies relativize the actual negative effects in practice on large platforms, risk potentials cannot be dismissed out of hand.[513] The algorithmic steering and personalization of content can lead to the fact that, on the one hand, "extraneous" considerations in the form of economic interests of the providers are relevant for the selection of the content to be displayed and that these selection criteria are often not at all or not sufficiently transparent and controllable for the users, who therefore do not know why they see what and, above all, what they do not see. On the other hand, this type of steering also harbors the danger that media align their content with the dictates of algorithms in order to be seen (also for refinancing reasons), i.e., high-quality, plural content of general interest is no longer in the foreground.[514] The FCC formulated this in another context in such a way that "[s]uch ser-

terests), which can also lead to users enveloping themselves in an "information cocoon" (cf. on this *Sunstein*, Infotopia: How Many Minds Produce Knowledge), but which is precisely an expression of democracy-based freedom of opinion and information through volitional action and can thus equally be an opportunity for pluralism.

512 Cf. on this also *Cole/Etteldorf* in: Cappello, Media pluralism and competition issues, p. 21 et seq.

513 Cf. for an overview and analysis of the state of research to date, instead of many, for instance *Stark/Magin/Jürgens*, Maßlos überschätzt. Ein Überblick über theoretische Annahmen und empirische Befunde zu Filterblasen und Echokammern (Preprint), which, while finding that the actual scope of filter bubbles and echo chambers is widely overestimated, nevertheless conclude that there is no question that algorithmic personalization influences individual and collective opinion formation. For an English-language overview and analysis of the state of research to date, see also *Zuiderveen Borgesius et al.* in: Internet Policy Review 1/2016, which come to a similar conclusion and refer to the further development possibilities of algorithmic technologies with regard to the risk potential. Leading further also *Helberger et al.*, Implications of AI-driven tools in the media for freedom of expression, *Haim/Graefe/Brosius* in: Digital Journalism 3/2018, 330, 330 et seq.; *Nechushtai/Lewis* in: Computers in Human Behavior 2019, 298, 298 et seq.

514 EPRA refers to this danger as a "feedback loop", cf. Media plurality in the age of algorithms – New challenges to monitor pluralism and diversity, Background document 51st EPRA Meeting, https://www.epra.org/attachments/51st-epra-meeting-media-plurality-in-the-age-of-algorithms-new-challenges-to-monitor-pluralism-and-diversity-background-document.

vices do not aim to reflect diverse opinions; rather, they are tailored to one-sided interests or the rationale of a business model that aims to maximise the time users spend on a website, thus increasing the advertising value of the platform for its clients".[515] Factors influencing the extent of these risk potentials are, in addition to the transparency of algorithmic systems and, directly related to this, the media literacy of users, also the visibility and discoverability of quality content.

The new provision of Art. 7a AVMSD is also interesting in the context of the present study because it underscores the existing distribution of competences in safeguarding media pluralism. On the one hand, recital 25, which is part of the provision, identifies media pluralism and cultural diversity in particular as objectives of general interest. In this context, it is emphasized that the Directive "is without prejudice to the ability of Member States" to impose obligations on service providers to ensure prominence. Neither are Member States obliged to do so, nor does the rule specify how such obligations are to be designed if the Member State decides to introduce them – unlike the new provision on signal and content integrity in Art. 7b, which, due to its defining and more concrete wording as well as the corresponding explanations from the recitals, provides the Member States with a certain characterization in the transposition also from the perspective of consumer protection law[516]. It is merely stated in a declaratory manner that the obligations are only to be introduced taking into account the principle of proportionality and must therefore be compatible with Union law.

Although in the run-up to the reform proposal there were calls from some Member States and many regulatory authorities for a rule on the discoverability of content, this option was rejected by the Commission on the grounds that, on the one hand, no consensus could be found on the scope and limits of such a rule and, on the other hand, the AVMSD was not the right regulatory framework for this due to its scope, which is limited to audiovisual media services (and now VSP) and does not cover the platform area in particular.[517] The Commission's proposal therefore did not initially include any substantive regulation on the appropriate prominence of pub-

---

515 FCC, 1 BvR 1675/16, and others, para. 79.
516 On this in detail *Cole*, Die Neuregelung des Artikel 7b Richtlinie 2010/13/EU (AVMD-RL).
517 Cf. Commission staff working document SW(2016) 168 final, impact assessment accompanying the Proposal for a Directive of the European Parliament and of the Council amending Directive 2010/13/EU on the coordination of certain provisions laid down by law, regulation or administrative action in Member States

lic value content. Only a recital[518] was to clarify that this can be an important instrument, but that it remains in the hands of the Member States to decide on it. Due to the importance for users, Art. 7 a in the draft – which, in contrast to the final version, still contained an exemplary enumeration of objectives of general interest in the norm text itself and not merely in the recitals – was included in the trilogue negotiations at the suggestion of the Parliament.[519] "In order to safeguard media pluralism and diversity, Member States shall have the right to take measures to ensure the appropriate prominence of audiovisual media services of general interests" – so the justification given by the European Parliament's Committee on Culture and Education for the corresponding initiative.[520] Even if the final wording of the rule is very brief and gives the Member States extensive discretion as to 'whether' but also 'how' to impose an obligation, it is interesting for this very reason: although it is recognized that not only the diversity of offerings but also the diversity of choice for the user is highly relevant, this issue is clearly located in the area of Member States' competence.

Art. 7 a therefore serves as a regulation that takes into account the consideration of (media) pluralism as a value also at EU level, without interfering with the structure of competences in the area of culture. The imperative of an appropriate balance of interests in the implementation of the re-

---

concerning the provision of audiovisual media services in view of changing market realities, https://ec.europa.eu/digital-single-market/en/news/impact-assessment-accompanying-proposal-updated-audiovisual-media-services-directive.

518 Rec. 38, as in the Commission's proposal, read: "This Directive is without prejudice to the ability of Member States to impose obligations to ensure discoverability and accessibility of content of general interest under defined general interest objectives such as media pluralism, freedom of speech and cultural diversity. Such obligations should only be imposed where they are necessary to meet general interest objectives clearly defined by Member States in conformity with Union law. In this respect, Member States should in particular examine the need for regulatory intervention against the results of the outcome of market forces. Where Member States decide to impose discoverability rules, they should only impose proportionate obligations on undertakings, in the interest of legitimate public policy considerations".

519 Cf. EMR, AVMD-Synopse 2018, available at https://emr-sb.de/synopsis-avms/.

520 European Parliament, Committee on Culture and Education, Draft Report on the proposal for a directive of the European Parliament and of the Council amending Directive 2010/13/EU on the coordination of certain provisions laid down by law, regulation or administrative action in Member States concerning the provision of audiovisual media services in view of changing market realities, 05.09.2016, https://www.europarl.europa.eu/RegData/commissions/cult/projet_rapport/2016/587655/CULT_PR(2016)587655_EN.pdf, p. 82.

spective provision applies – which is familiar in constitutional categories as the imperative of establishing practical concordance[521] – which is already opposed to an interpretation of the scope for implementation exclusively prescribed by the Union legislature because the respective balance of interests prescribed by Union law is predetermined by different constitutional traditions of the Member States in the field of basic rights. Ultimately, even without such a rule, the competence of the Member States to regulate prominence obligations would remain unaffected; however, from the perspective of the legislature, the inclusion of such a rule is supported by the fact that it serves as a reminder of the importance such measures can have for effectively safeguarding media pluralism and diversity of access to offerings. Member States are thus invited, so to speak, to consider intensively the introduction of corresponding obligations in order to achieve this goal. These are closely related to the actual regulation of the media, so that their location outside the infrastructure-related regulatory texts, namely the EECC (see below in chapter D.II.5), is understandable.

(3) Promotion of media literacy

Another area that is related to media pluralism in the context of previously described considerations of discoverability of content[522] disinformation, algorithmically controlled selection of content, and similar phenomena is also the promotion of media literacy. With the 2018 reform, this has for the first time explicitly found its way into the substantive regulations of the Directive. According to Art. 33a AVMSD, Member States shall promote and take measures for the development of media literacy skills. ERGA shall also exchange experience and best practices in the area of media literacy (Art. 30b(3)(b)).

Media literacy refers to the skills, knowledge and understanding necessary for consumers to use media effectively and safely.[523] However, a legal definition of this term, which is understood very broadly in the EU con-

---

521 Cf. e.g. BVerfGE 41, 29 (51); 77, 240 (255); 81, 298 (308); 83, 130 (143).
522 Cf. on this also *Devaux et al.*, Study on media literacy and online empowerment issues raised by algorithm-driven media services, SMART 2017/0081, https://ec.europa.eu/digital-single-market/en/news/study-media-literacy-and-online-empowerment-issues-raised-algorithm-driven-media-services-smart.
523 Cf. rec. 47 Directive 2010/13/EU.

text[524], is lacking, as are concrete rules on what the promotion of media literacy should look like. Thus, the Member States are not given any requirements for implementation. Solely recital 59 puts the regulation in the context that only the necessary literacy in the use of media will enable citizens to access information and to use, critically assess and create media content responsibly and safely. Citizens should be equipped with the critical thinking skills required to exercise judgment, analyse complex realities and recognise the difference between opinion and fact.

While the phenomenon of disinformation is thus also covered by this consideration, literacy in dealing with (especially digital) media is generally required in order to be able to navigate the digital information environment, in particular to access a variety of sources. Media literacy thus contributes indirectly to media pluralism and media diversity by reducing the digital divide on the user side, facilitating informed decision-making, and enabling the detection and combating of false or misleading information as well as harmful and illegal online content, thus promoting the provision of reliable or legal and non-harmful content.[525] As already considered above in the discussion of rules for ensuring prominence of specific content, the mere existence of a pluralistic media landscape is not purposeful if it is not perceived or cannot be perceived (completely or correctly) by users due to a lack of media literacy.[526] The implementation of methods from behavioral science towards users of, for example, social networks is discussed as a possible approach to counteract cognitive bias and promote plural media consumption.[527]

The cautiousness at EU level in regulating this matter ("promote", "take measures", each referring to the Member States) is due on the one hand to

---

524 The Council of the European Union includes among them "all the technical, cognitive, social, civic and creative capacities that allow us to access and have a critical understanding of and interact with both traditional and new forms of media", Developing media literacy and critical thinking through education and training – Council conclusions (30 May 2016), p. 6, http://data.consilium.europa.eu/doc/document/ST-9641-2016-INIT/en/pdf.

525 Recommendation CM/Rec(2018)1[1] of the Committee of Ministers to member States on media pluralism and transparency of media ownership, https://search.coe.int/cm/Pages/result_details.aspx?ObjectId=0900001680790e13, para. 10.

526 Cf. also *Cole/Etteldorf* in: Cappello, Media pluralism and competition issues, p. 21 et seq.

527 Cf. on this and on further proposals e.g. *Hoorens/Lupiáñez-Villanueva*, Study on media literacy and online empowerment issues raised by algorithm-driven media services (SMART 2017/0081).

D. Secondary legal framework on "media law" and media pluralism

the fact that the approaches to the promotion of media literacy in the Member States to date differ greatly, both in terms of scope and in terms of their nature and basis. In many Member States, the relevant promoters are civil society bodies that do not act on the basis of a statutory mandate.[528] Therefore, the general – but vaguely formulated – obligation to promote in Art. 33 a is supplemented by a reporting obligation on the part of the Member States. The Commission is to receive a regular overview of which approaches are being developed in the Member States, and through the reporting obligation – which takes place every three years – there is a certain pressure to take appropriate measures that can be used to prove implementation by the Member States. This is considered to be so important that, in order to ensure a comparable type of reporting under Art. 33a(3) AVMSD, the Commission must also publish guidelines defining the "scope" of such reports. In addition, there is a corresponding obligation of ERGA according to Art. 30b(3)(b) AVMSD to find a common basis at supranational level in the form of best practices.

On the other hand, (digital) education is an area that is clearly rooted in the cultural policies of the Member States, so that they have and must have a large degree of freedom to act and shape their own policies, and the EU may not intervene in a regulatory capacity via the AVMSD. However, initial recommendations for the Member States have already been developed at EU level in this context. The May 2020 Council of the EU conclusions on media literacy in an ever-changing world[529] not only ask Member States to engage in specific media literacy-related activities, also in light of experiences with the Corona crisis, but also, i.a., to (1.) continue to explore opportunities for promoting and strengthening professional journalism as a viable element of the global digital media environment and (2.) to improve existing training models for the development of digital competences in the European cultural and creative industries – and, if necessary, to design new models for this purpose – in order to promote the effective use of innovative technologies and to keep pace with technological progress.[530]

---

528 *EAI*, Mapping of media literacy practices and actions in EU-28.
529 Council conclusions on media literacy in an ever-changing world, 8274/20, of 26.05.2020, https://www.consilium.europa.eu/media/44117/st08274-en20.pdf; cf. on this *Ukrow*, MMR aktuell 11/2020.
530 A similar form of inducement for measures of promotion aimed at strengthening professional journalism and thus the creative landscape in the EU can be seen in the Commission's declaration of intent to use a Media and Audiovisual Action Plan to support the media and audiovisual sector in its digital transfor-

(4) Establishment of independent regulatory bodies

Also with regard to media regulation, the basic distribution of competences applies with regard to the design of the administration or administrative procedures. Since (also) the application of EU law is carried out by national administrations, its exact definition is left to regulation by Member States' law. Insofar as a subject matter requires a specific form of the institution or authority responsible for implementation, this may also be specified by the respective EU legal act. This applies, for example, to the guarantee of the independence and functioning of authorities for monitoring compliance with data protection rules already under the validity of the Data Protection Directive[531] and even more so since the revision in the form of a Regulation ((EU) 2016/679)[532].[533]

As far as supervisory bodies or authorities, which monitor media undertakings' compliance with the provisions of media law, are concerned – including the national transposition of the AVMSD – there was a lack of requirements in the Directive for a long time, also because the Member States rejected harmonization through EU requirements. This was due to the existence of such requirements for the form of supervision on national level, closely linked to traditional understandings of media freedom in the domestic context – e.g., in Germany through internal control in the case of public broadcasting or state media authorities established independent from the state in the case of private broadcasting. In the 2007 revision of the TwF Directive on the AVMSD, the existence of independent regulatory authorities at the national level was also merely presupposed by Art. 23 b

---

mation through the use of EU funding instruments. On this in more detail below in chapter D.III.3.

531 Directive 95/46/EC of the European Parliament and of the Council of 24 October 1995 on the protection of individuals with regard to the processing of personal data and on the free movement of such data, OJ L 281 of 23.11.1995, p. 31–50.

532 Regulation (EU) 2016/679 of the European Parliament and of the Council of 27 April 2016 on the protection of natural persons with regard to the processing of personal data and on the free movement of such data, and repealing Directive 95/46/EC (General Data Protection Regulation), OJ L 119 of 04.05.2016, p. 1–88.

533 Art. 51 et seq. GDPR, which in particular contain requirements to ensure the independence of supervisory authorities at the Member States level. Cf. on this e.g. CJEU, joined cases C-465/00, C-138/01 and C-139/01, Österreichischer Rundfunk and Others; CJEU, case C-288/12, *European Commission / Hungary*, para. 47; leading further also *Cole/Etteldorf/Ullrich*, Cross-border dissemination of Online Content, p. 134 et seq.

D. Secondary legal framework on "media law" and media pluralism

(which was renumbered to Art. 30 by codification in Directive 2010/13/EU)[534], without any specifications being made in this regard.[535] On the contrary, the original draft with more detailed requirements was explicitly rejected and the last version only mentioned in general terms the existence of these independent regulatory bodies[536], while recital 94 (of the codified Directive 2010/13/EU) reiterates the responsibility for the effective transposition of the Directive as a duty of the Member States which in this context are free "to choose the appropriate instruments according to their legal traditions and established structures, and, *in particular*, the form of their competent independent regulatory bodies" (emphasis added by the authors).

This only changed with the 2018 revision.[537] In the meantime, the Commission had commissioned several studies on the independence and effec-

---

534 Art. 30 Directive 2010/13/EU read: "Member States shall take appropriate measures to provide each other and the Commission with the information necessary for the application of this Directive, in particular Articles 2, 3 and 4, in particular through their competent independent regulatory bodies".
The corresponding recitals read: "(94) In accordance with the duties imposed on Member States by the Treaty on the Functioning of the European Union, they are responsible for the effective implementation of this Directive. They are free to choose the appropriate instruments according to their legal traditions and established structures, and, in particular, the form of their competent independent regulatory bodies, in order to be able to carry out their work in implementing this Directive impartially and transparently. More specifically, the instruments chosen by Member States should contribute to the promotion of media pluralism.
(95) Close cooperation between competent regulatory bodies of the Member States and the Commission is necessary to ensure the correct application of this Directive. Similarly close cooperation between Member States and between their regulatory bodies is particularly important with regard to the impact which broadcasters established in one Member State might have on another Member State. Where licensing procedures are provided for in national law and if more than one Member State is concerned, it is desirable that contacts between the respective bodies take place before such licences are granted. This cooperation should cover all fields coordinated by this Directive.".
535 Cf. *ERGA* Report on the independence of NRAs; at large also *Schulz/Valcke/Irion*, The Independence of the Media and Its Regulatory Agencies, therein in particular *Valcke/Voorhoof/Lievens*, Independent media regulators: Condition sine qua non for freedom of expression?.
536 On this *Dörr* in: Dörr/Kreile/Cole, para. B 101; *Furnémont*, Independence of audiovisual media regulatory authorities and cooperation between them: time for the EU lawmaker to fill the gaps.
537 On this *Dörr* in HK-MStV, B4, para. 101 et seq.; *Gundel* in: ZUM 2019, 131, 136 et seq.

tiveness of the national institutions responsible for media supervision (or compliance with the requirements from the AVMSD).[538] Probably also the recognition of the very different approaches in the Member States, which were not always able to ensure a sufficient guarantee of the independence of the regulatory bodies, enabled a compromise to be reached between the legislative bodies Parliament and Council[539], which led to an explicit stipulation in the substantive part of the Directive. Since then, Art. 33(1) AVMSD has required Member States to designate one or more national regulatory authorities or bodies and to ensure that they are legally separate from government bodies and functionally independent of their respective governments and other public or private bodies, although this does not preclude the possibility of establishing "convergent regulatory bodies" with competence for multiple sectors.[540] Further details on the necessary competences and resources, the definition of the requirements related to the regulatory bodies in a clear legal basis, as well as requirements for the creation of rules on the appointment or dismissal of functionaries can be found in the following paragraphs.

This represents a clear departure from the previous cautious formulation of requirements and a level of detail comparable to that of data protection law. However, care has been taken to ensure that the fundamental authority for "official", i.e. by authorities, supervision remains within the

---

538 *Cole et al.*, AVMS-RADAR (SMART 2013/0083); INDIREG (SMART 2009/0001).
539 The Commission's proposal, which provided for the establishment of the characteristic of independence, was thus adopted by the Parliament. However, the Council initially deleted the feature in its General Approach of 24 May 2017 (https://eur-lex.europa.eu/legal-content/EN/TXT/PDF/?uri=CON-SIL:ST_9691_2017_INIT&from=EN) and instead included the following wording in the recitals: "Member States should ensure that their national regulatory authorities are legally distinct from the government. However, this should not preclude Member States from exercising supervision in accordance with their national constitutional law. Regulatory authorities or bodies of the Member States should be considered to have achieved the requisite degree of independence if those regulatory authorities or bodies, including those that are constituted as public authorities or bodies, are functionally and effectively independent of their respective governments and of any other public or private body. [...]". Cf. on the development of the rule in the trilogue the EMR synopsis, available at https://emr-sb.de/synopsis-avms/.
540 This now also standardizes requirements for the independence of supervision from politics, which are already known from the area of infrastructure regulators for telecommunications (cf. on this in chapter D.II.5.), energy and railroads and, as already mentioned at the beginning, data protection authorities. Cf. on this also *Gundel* in: ZUM 2019, 131, 136.

D. Secondary legal framework on "media law" and media pluralism

scope of competence of the Member States' administrative (procedural) law. In particular, constitutional particularities should be able to be included by Member States for this purpose, as recital 53 explicitly states. The AVMSD does not aim to standardize the "structure of authorities" in the new version either; rather, it sets minimum requirements that must be met in order to be able to adequately demonstrate the independent status of such a regulatory body.

The independence of supervision of the audiovisual sector is seen as central to achieving the objectives of the Directive when it is transposed, while preserving the independence of the media from the state – and thus also of their supervision – as stipulated by constitutional law. In this context, Art. 30(2) lists as objectives "in particular media pluralism, cultural and linguistic diversity, consumer protection, freedom from barriers and discrimination, the smooth functioning of the internal market and the promotion of fair competition". In an earlier opinion, ERGA described the regulatory responsibilities of the competent bodies somewhat differently, using the examples of audience protection, including the protection of minors, freedom of expression, diversity, pluralism and other areas such as media ownership.[541] It is noteworthy that since the revision of Art. 30 AVMSD, media pluralism as well as cultural and linguistic diversity have been explicitly included among the objectives of the Directive in connection with the need for independence of regulatory authorities. Also recital 54 stresses that the services covered by the Directive have as one purpose "to serve the interests of individuals and shape public opinion", and in order to inform "individuals and society as completely as possible and with the highest level of variety", an independence from any state interference and "influence by national regulatory authorities or bodies [...] beyond the mere implementation of law" must be ensured.

In other EU legal acts, such target provisions and explanations of what is necessarily involved in achieving the target are also already found with the first version in the substantive part, often as an opening provision. Thus, the ECD is intended to contribute to the proper functioning of the internal market and the GDPR is intended to protect the fundamental rights and freedoms of natural persons and in particular their right to the protection of personal data on the one hand and the free movement of data on the other. No such declaration was found in the substantive part of

---

541 ERGA statement on the independence of NRAs in the audiovisual sector, ERGA (2014)3, https://erga-online.eu/wp-content/uploads/2016/10/State_indep_nra_1014.pdf.

the AVMSD prior to 2018. In recital 7 of Directive 1997/36/EC, to "create the legal framework for the free movement of services" was stated as an objective of the Directive; in recital 67 of Directive 2007/65/EC, this was supplemented by the addition of "whilst ensuring at the same time a high level of protection of objectives of general interest, in particular the protection of minors and human dignity as well as promoting the rights of persons with disabilities". With the extension by Directive (EU) 2018/1808, additional objectives of general interest are now explicitly referred to and not only mentioned in the recitals. This also includes regulatory objectives that in themselves could not support (at least harmonizing) EU action. Rather, the purpose of the reference is to designate an overall goal that will be realized through transposition by the Member States. Nor can the objective of an EU regulatory framework be equated with the exercise of a corresponding competence, because, as in primary law, a distinction must be made between objectives (there: of the Union) and competences. The legal basis for the adoption of a legal act in each case will be found in the introductory part preceding the recitals. It could not be based on a provision of primary law under pluralism protection for the AVMSD, as there is no such provision. As mentioned above, Art. 30(2) refers to the establishment of independent regulatory bodies by the Member States and thus to an area which is incumbent on the Member States in terms of its design and is guided only by general guarantees or requirements under EU law.

(5) Regulation of video-sharing platforms

As already mentioned before, one of the main innovations of Directive (EU) 2018/1808 is that since then, VSP are also covered by AVMSD. VSP services are defined as services the principal purpose of which or of a dissociable section thereof or an essential functionality of the service is devoted to providing programmes, user-generated videos, or both, to the general public, for which the video-sharing platform provider does not have direct (editorial) responsibility, in order to inform, entertain or educate, by means of electronic communications networks. The organization of the broadcasts or videos must be determined by the VSP provider, which includes the use of algorithms or other automated means. Accordingly, the definition is very broad.

The AVMSD does not provide for a general exception, such as Art. 17(6) of the new DSM Copyright Directive (on this see chapter D.II.3.) for smaller providers with regard to responsibilities for the use of protected content. However, there is room for nuance in assessing the appropriateness of

D. Secondary legal framework on "media law" and media pluralism

measures to be taken. Thus, not only offerings such as YouTube are clearly covered by the definition of VSP, but also smaller platforms as well as, under certain circumstances, social networks[542] or – insofar as these do not already fall under the definition of a non-linear service due to editorial responsibility – stand-alone parts of online newspapers featuring audiovisual programmes or user-generated videos,[543] where those "parts can be considered dissociable from their main activity". The interpretation of the criterion "essential functionality" of the service will be decisive for the future assessment of ambiguous cases.[544] This means that services that are not already clearly identifiable as VSP can also be categorized as such if the main function of the service is to offer and share (also user-generated) videos. Even though, as mentioned, social networks were not the primary target of the regulation, this definition was intended to maintain an openness to development since greater use of video distribution functions also seemed likely on previously more text-based platforms.

In order to achieve some consistency in the transposition and application of the Directive's provisions, recital 5 of the Directive allows the Commission to issue guidelines on the meaning of essential function. Unlike the guidelines described above with regard to the provision on the promotion of European works, which constitute an obligation and are formulated in the substantive part as a duty of the Commission, it has discretion with regard to the VSP-related guidelines. However, although here the possibility is mentioned only in the recitals, the legal nature equally is the same as with the other guidelines and the text is not legally binding. The Commission has already exercised its guideline authority and presented guidelines on the practical application of the essential functionality criterion in July 2020[545]. Therein, the Commission considers the relationship of audiovisual content to other economic activities of the service, its qualitative and quantitative importance, how and whether audiovisual content is monetized, and whether tools are in place to increase the visibility or attractiveness of specifically audiovisual content in the service.

---

542 Cf. rec. 5 Directive (EU) 2018/1808.
543 Cf. rec. 3 Directive (EU) 2018/1808.
544 In detail on this *Kogler* in: K&R 2018, 537, 537 et seq.
545 Communication from the Commission Guidelines on the practical application of the essential functionality criterion of the definition of a 'video-sharing platform service' under the Audiovisual Media Services Directive, 2020/C 223/02, OJ C 223 of 07.07.2020, p. 3–9, https://eur-lex.europa.eu/legal-content/EN/TXT/?uri=uriserv:OJ.C_.2020.223.01.0003.01.ENG&toc=OJ:C:2020:223:TOC.

In addition to the definition and a separate regulation on jurisdiction[546] in Art. 28 a AVMSD, the applicability of certain substantive regulations to VSP is found in Art. 28 b.

With regard to audiovisual commercial communication, VSP are subject to the same rules regarding in particular surreptitious advertising, subliminal techniques, tobacco products and alcoholic beverages as other (audiovisual) media service providers have been up to now (Art. 28b(2) in conjunction with Art. 9(1) AVMSD). Only the consequence of the applicability of the rules for the provider is different from the linear and non-linear services covered so far, because the question of the economic advantage for the platform providers is also relevant when deciding on their liability. Towards the users, the platforms (only) have to urge compliance with the provisions on commercial communication by means of suitable measures, whereas they themselves have to ensure compliance if they market, sell or compile the commercial communication themselves.

In addition, Art. 28 b establishes a set of obligations that VSP providers must comply with in order to protect minors and the general public from certain (developmentally harmful, punishable or inciting) content, and the Directive requires Member States to take appropriate measures leading to this result. However, the Directive already refers to concrete measures such as the adaptation of general terms and conditions, the establishment of categorization options for uploaders and of age verification tools as well as reporting and complaint systems, which Member States may provide for by way of example as obligations for the providers under their jurisdiction covered by the provision, whereby the (legal) determination of measures must be made by the Member States, but a selection of measures is reserved to them ("shall ensure", Art. 28 b (1) – (3) AVMSD). In order to implement the requirements, the Member States shall in particular use instruments of co-regulation pursuant to Art. 4a(1) AVMSD. In addition, Mem-

---

546 According to Art. 28a(1), a VSP provider is in principle under the jurisdiction of the Member State in which it is established. However, under (2), a VSP provider shall also be deemed to be established in the territory of a Member State for the purposes of the Directive if either a parent undertaking or a subsidiary undertaking of that provider is established in the territory of that Member State, or the provider is part of a group and another undertaking of that group is established on the territory of that Member State. This provision is noteworthy as it represents a departure from the country of origin principle, as an establishment of the provider itself is no longer mandatory for establishing competence, but a connection (also going beyond the jurisdiction criteria subsidiary to establishment applicable to media service providers) suffices.

D. Secondary legal framework on "media law" and media pluralism

ber States and also the Commission may promote self-regulation with the help of so-called Union codes of conduct pursuant to Art. 4a(2).

The list of obligations for VSP is, however, subject to a condition of expediency and the requirement that the obligations imposed on them by the Member States be aligned with the size of the platform, which in this respect may protect smaller or niche-specific offerings from excessive requirements. The AVMSD clarifies that "appropriate" measures must be taken, which can work both in favor of and against providers, in the sense that the requirements must not be disproportionate, but must also have an effective impact in view of the goals to be achieved. According to Art. 28b(5) AVMSD, the assessment of the appropriateness of the measures taken is the responsibility of Member States' regulatory bodies, which accordingly must be brought into a co-regulation system with decisive effect.

This therefore not only introduces a new category of providers into the AVMSD, but also a new type of transposition requirement for Member States and an increased emphasis on the instrument of self- and co-regulation. In principle, systems of co- and self-regulation have already been established in many Member States, in particular for the area of media regulation.[547] However, the specific regulation of VSP is new and will therefore, in addition to the providers covered by the rules for the first time, also pose new challenges to the regulatory bodies in terms of implementation, precisely because they are tasked with regularly assessing the appropriateness of the measures even within a co-regulatory solution.[548] In order to promote consistent application and implementation of these rules in the EU, in particular as the the rules will only be applied by a few Member States on large VSP providers, as there is only a very small number of such providers dominating the market in Europe (and also globally) as a whole, ERGA has already launched a working group to this effect. This focuses on studying and coordinating the implementation of the provisions of Art. 28 b.[549]

Although the rules on VSP in the Directive provide the Member States with a relatively detailed catalog of actions, they remain competent for the concrete design. In addition, the objective of the provision in Art. 28 b

---

547 *Cappello*, Selbst- und Ko-Regulierung in der neuen AVMD-Richtlinie.
548 Cf. on challenges and opportunities also *Kukliš*, Video-Sharing platforms in AVMSD – a new kind of content regulation (draft); as well as *id.* in: mediaLAWS 02/2020, 95, 95 et seq.
549 Cf. on this the Terms of Reference of the „Implementation of the revised AVMS Directive" working group, http://erga-online.eu/wp-content/uploads/2019/03/ERGA-2019-SG-3-ToR_adopted.pdf.

AVMSD is in particular the protection of consumers and minors, but not measures to promote diversity, for which it would have to be examined more closely with regard to competence whether the scope for action is not too restricted. Irrespective of this, however, the provision of Art. 28 b also needs to be clarified in some key elements. In addition to the definition of "editorial responsibility" or the "dissociable" part of a service, this primarily concerns the question of when content is illegal in the sense of the AVMSD, i.e. in particular incites hatred or is detrimental to development and therefore requires a response by the provider. Even if – similar to the concrete assessment of content relevant to the protection of minors[550] – differences between Member States may persist in this respect, taking into account national peculiarities or constitutional traditions, in practice there will be a concentration of the significant application of this rule in one (or a few) Member States.[551] This is due to the fact that the branches of the big VSP providers[552] are to a large extent concentrated in one Member State, as the jurisdiction for them can be clearly determined according to Art. 28a(1) AVMSD.[553] This makes the Irish regulator, as the competent supervisor, keeper of a very decisive role in monitoring the measures taken by providers and, where appropriate, in developing guidelines and best practices. For example, the Irish legislature in its first draft law appears to intend to leave to the competent Irish regulator the specific design, func-

---

550 See on this CJEU, case C-244/06, *Dynamic Medien Vertriebs GmbH / Avides Media AG*.
551 Same as here *Barata*, Regulating content moderation in Europe beyond the AVMSD.
552 Against the background of Brexit, the question of the design of cooperation mechanisms by and with Member State regulatory bodies outside the EU will also become interesting. The Plum Report (*Chan/Wood/Adshead*, Understanding video-sharing platforms under UK jurisdiction) identifies (with overlap to the Irish regulator's assessment, cf. next fn. 557) several major providers as falling under UK jurisdiction, including Twitch.tv, Vimeo, Imgur, TikTok, Snapchat, LiveLeak, and two major adult content providers.
553 In its submission to a Government Public Consultation on the Regulation of Harmful Content and the Implementation of the Revised Audiovisual Media Services Directive (BAI, Submission to the Department of Communications, Climate Action & Environment Public Consultation on the Regulation of Harmful Content on Online Platforms and the Implementation of the Revised Audiovisual Media Service Directive, http://www.bai.ie/en/download/134036/), the Irish Broadcasting Authority listed in particular YouTube, TikTok, Vimeo, DailyMotion and Twitch as VSP subject to its competence, as well as Facebook, Twitter, Instagram, Snapchat, LinkedIn and Reddit as (social network) services with an essential functionality of offering audiovisual content.

D. Secondary legal framework on "media law" and media pluralism

tionality and standards to be observed of the complaints system to be established by VSP.⁵⁵⁴

In order to address the situation described above, where the majority of regulatory bodies themselves cannot take action due to the jurisdiction of another Member State, even though the content distributed via the VSP is accessible in all Member States – to a much greater extent and with easier access – the regulatory bodies within ERGA work on forms of cooperation, for example to provide for expedited notifications of problematic content and response procedures.⁵⁵⁵ As far as the Member States' regulatory sovereignty for aspects of media law is concerned, it can additionally be pointed out that in the provision of Art. 28b(6) AVMSD – corresponding to Art. 4(1) AVMSD (which applies to audiovisual media services only and thus not to VSP) – the Member States are free to provide for more detailed or stricter measures for providers under their own jurisdiction. In this form of "reverse discrimination", they are only limited by other requirements of Union law, in particular Art. 12 to 15 ECD or Art. 25 Directive 2011/93/EU.⁵⁵⁶. More extensive measures remain possible – similar to those applicable to information society services under Art. 1(6) ECD. Only (limited) partial coordination has taken place with regard to VSP, which does not block (stricter) Member States' rules for VSP against the background of safeguarding diversity or other general interest objectives.

---

554 Cf. General Scheme Online Safety Media Regulation Bill 2019 (https://www.dccae.gov.ie/en-ie/communications/legislation/Pages/General-Scheme-Online-Safety-Media-Regulation.aspx), explaining also *Barata*, Regulating content moderation in Europe beyond the AVMSD.
555 Cf. on this the announced ERGA work programs for 2020 (https://erga-online.eu/wp-content/uploads/2020/01/ERGA_2019_WorkProgramme-2020.pdf) and 2021 (https://erga-online.eu/wp-content/uploads/2020/08/ERGA_WorkProgramme2021.pdf) as well as the Terms of reference for the newly created Subgroup 1 – Enforcement (Subgroup 1 – 2020 Terms of Reference, https://erga-online.eu/wp-content/uploads/2020/03/ERGA_SG1_2020_ToR_Adopted_2-03-2020.pdf).
556 Directive 2011/93/EU of the European Parliament and of the Council of 13 December 2011 on combating the sexual abuse and sexual exploitation of children and child pornography, and replacing Council Framework Decision 2004/68/JHA, OJ L 335 of 17.12.2011, p. 1–14, https://eur-lex.europa.eu/legal-content/EN/TXT/?uri=celex%3A32011L0093.

e. Interim conclusion

The consideration of the AVMSD in particular against the background of diversity-securing links has documented a certain change in the EU's audiovisual regulatory policy. Whereas under the TwF Directive the focus of regulation was still clearly on economic policy objectives and ensuring a free internal market, the character of the AVMSD has changed to some extent in the course of the reforms. Although the freedom to provide services remains the main focus and the core principles have been retained in the form of the minimum harmonization approach, the power to derogate and the country of origin principle, new links have also been added that relate to cultural policy aspects. This is also in line with the European Commission's 2003 Communication on the future of European regulatory audiovisual policy[557], in which it emphasized that regulatory policy in this sector must continue to safeguard certain general interests such as cultural diversity, the right to information, media pluralism, the protection of minors and consumers, as well as promote awareness and media literacy among the general public.

At the same time, however, the Communication stated, with reference to the Commission's Green Paper on services of general interest[558] that the protection of pluralism in the media clearly falls within the competence of the Member States.[559] This position is repeatedly emphasized by the Commission in all relevant activities.[560] Nevertheless, some EU legal acts contribute at least indirectly to preserving media pluralism. A regulatory policy understood in this way[561] does not contradict the distribution of competences if a legal basis is to be found with regard to the primary objectives and care is taken in particular not to limit the possibility of Member

---

557 Communication from the Commission of 15 December 2003 on the future of European regulatory audiovisual policy, COM(2003) 784 final.
558 Commission of the European Communities, Green Paper on services of general interest, 21.05.2003, COM(2003) 270 final.
559 As here also rec. 16, 25, 53, 61 Directive (EU) 2018/1808.
560 Cf. e.g. most recently with regard to the preparation of the DSA in the context of the Digitalkonferenz on the occasion of the German Council Presidency, the remarks of *Anthony Whelan*, Digital Policy Adviser, Cabinet von der Leyen, VoD available at https://eu2020-medienkonferenz.de/en/session-1-en/.
561 There are also repeatedly attempts, in particular by the EU Parliament and the Commission, to open up the field of safeguarding pluralism to the EU as an area of active regulation under EU law; cf. on this and on the various (non-legally binding) initiatives of the Parliament and the Commission in detail *Komorek*, Media Pluralism and European Law, chapter 2.2.

D. Secondary legal framework on "media law" and media pluralism

States' rules (which are then aimed at establishing and safeguarding pluralism).

3. DSM Copyright Directive

Another focus of the last Commission's Digital Single Market Strategy was the copyright reform at EU level. First of all, the so-called Online SatCab Directive[562] was introduced, which ensures the cross-border availability of content by means of corresponding rules, without having to resort to instruments such as geo-blocking due to a lack of license clarifications, because a separate act requiring a license takes place when content is received or retransmitted in a Member State other than one's own. Most importantly, Directives 96/6/EC[563] and 2001/29/EC (the Copyright Directive)[564] have been adapted by the adoption of an entirely new Directive containing provisions designed to modernize copyright law: the Copyright in the Digital Single Market Directive (DSM Directive)[565] was intended to update copyright so that it can still be effective in the "digital age". This should, in turn, promote cultural diversity in Europe and the availability of content over the Internet by also establishing clearer rules for all Internet stakeholders with regard to copyright-triggered obligations.[566]

---

562 Directive (EU) 2019/789 of the European Parliament and of the Council of 17 April 2019 laying down rules on the exercise of copyright and related rights applicable to certain online transmissions of broadcasting organisations and retransmissions of television and radio programmes, and amending Council Directive 93/83/EEC, OJ L 130 of 17.05.2019, p. 82–91, https://eur-lex.europa.eu/legal-content/EN/TXT/?uri=CELEX%3A32019L0789&qid=1612877506288.
563 Directive 96/9/EC of the European Parliament and of the Council of 11 March 1996 on the legal protection of databases, OJ L 77 of 27.03.1996, p. 20–28, https://eur-lex.europa.eu/legal-content/EN/ALL/?uri=CELEX%3A31996L0009.
564 Directive 2001/29/EC of the European Parliament and of the Council of 22 May 2001 on the harmonisation of certain aspects of copyright and related rights in the information society, OJ L 167 of 22.06.2001, p. 10–19, https://eur-lex.europa.eu/legal-content/EN/ALL/?uri=CELEX%3A32001L0029.
565 Directive (EU) 2019/790 of the European Parliament and of the Council of 17 April 2019 on copyright and related rights in the Digital Single Market and amending Directives 96/9/EC and 2001/29/EC, OJ L 130 of 17.05.2019, p. 92–125, https://eur-lex.europa.eu/legal-content/EN/TXT/?uri=CELEX%3A32019L0790.
566 Cf. on this the press release of the EU Commission of 14 September 2016, https://ec.europa.eu/commission/presscorner/detail/en/IP_16_3010.

The DSM Directive contains rules on copyright contract law, text and data mining, neighboring rights for publishers of press publications, but also rules on the use of protected content by online services. In addition to the existing rules on copyright protection, the exploitation of protected works and copyright limitations, which are of course of outstanding importance in the media context, both in terms of the financing of offerings and in reporting, the latter two innovations are of particular interest in the context of this study.

In this context, it should first be generally noted that European copyright law leaves the Member States room for maneuver, in particular where aspects of safeguarding freedom of the media and freedom of information are concerned. For example, Member States may choose from a catalog of possible limitations and exceptions to the author's exclusive reproduction and distribution right (Art. 2 Copyright Directive) when it comes to reproductions by the press, reporting of current events, or use of the work by way of quotation for the purpose of criticism or review (Art. 5(3) (c) and (d) Copyright Directive) as well as other contexts. The same applies to exceptions and limitations to the other exclusive rights set forth in the Copyright Directive. In this context, it is also clear that the harmonization of copyright as a contribution to the better functioning of the internal market, in particular cross-border trade in copyrighted works, remains limited in order to allow Member States' traditions and differences to persist. Although there should be general agreement that copyright law must not prevent the reporting of current events and thus the informative contribution to the process of formation of public opinion, there is no harmonization in this respect; differences in the Member States are respected in that the selection of the exceptions is left to the Member States.[567]

In the context of measures to safeguard diversity, however, the aforementioned new rules on neighboring rights for publishers of press publications and the new rules for online services are more relevant, as they are related to the goal of safeguarding pluralism.

Art. 15 DSM Directive provides that the Member States shall establish a neighboring right for publishers of press publications which secures them an appropriate share of the revenues generated by the online use of their press publications by providers of information society services. According

---

567 However, the catalog of exceptions, from which Member States may implement those they deem necessary, is exhaustively set out in the Copyright Directive (now as amended by the DSM Directive). This was recently underlined by the CJEU, cf. CJEU, case C-476/17, *Pelham GmbH and Others / Ralf Hütter and Florian Schneider-Esleben*.

D. Secondary legal framework on "media law" and media pluralism

to its wording, the regulation even goes so far that in the future only mere acts of hyperlinking or the "use of individual words or very short extracts of a press publication" will be possible without a license, thus ensuring very far-reaching protection of this media content. In this context, the definition of an information society service is congruent with that of the ECD, so that a large number of providers can also be covered here. However, the reason for the establishment of the regulation were primarily news aggregators, media monitoring services, general news services and feeds, which compile press content and present it in excerpts using the original texts. The regulation aims to protect investments (and thus also recognizes the importance of investments in journalistic work), which indirectly also secures the financing of these media offerings, and thus also indirectly contains a regulation that safeguards diversity with regard to the preservation of externally pluralistic structures.[568] This is remarkable not only because a regulation is being created directly at EU level (and not, as hitherto, through the opening up of Member States' scope for action) which relates explicitly and exclusively to the protection of media undertakings[569], but also because it actively ensures that such media offerings should continue to have a prospect of refinancing. Recital 54 even explicitly states that the purpose of the new regulation is to ensure diversity: "A free and pluralist press is essential to ensure quality journalism and citizens' access to information". Recital 55 goes on to state that "[t]he organisational and financial contribution of publishers in producing press publications needs to be recognised and further encouraged to ensure the sustainability of the publishing industry and thereby foster the availability of reliable information".

Although economic policy objectives certainly played a role in the creation of the regulation – the press is, after all, also a service and labor market – cultural policy considerations at least also played a role, which the EU apparently wanted to see harmonized at EU level due to the cross-border activity of the information society services in question. The room for maneuver left to the Member States in this context is comparatively small. Despite the purpose of ensuring diversity, it should not go unmentioned at this point that the new regulation could also pose a threat to media diversity in the online sector. The norm addressees, such as news aggregators, could refrain from distributing content due to risk considerations or limit their aggregation out to cost considerations to those services that make

---

568 Cf. on this also *Cole/Etteldorf* in: Cappello, Media pluralism and competition issues, p. 21 et seq.
569 In particular, only journalistic publications are to be covered, cf. rec. 56.

223

their content freely available or agree to licensing terms favorable to the intermediaries. In this case, the selection of content would not depend on factors such as quality, topicality, or personalization by algorithms, but on economic factors, which would run counter to the desire for pluralism, in particular on the part of recipients.

The provision of Art. 17 also provides links in the area of safeguarding diversity. It refers to service providers whose activity is "online content-sharing services". The DSM Directive defines these in Art. 2(6) as providers of an information society service of which the main or one of the main purposes is to store and give the public access to a large amount of copyright-protected works or other protected subject matter uploaded by its users, which it organises and promotes for profit-making purposes. In this context, recital 61 generally acknowledges that such services "enable diversity and ease of access to content" but nevertheless present challenges in the form of mass unauthorized use of copyrighted works without appropriate compensation to authors. Therefore, Art. 17 first clarifies that online content-sharing service providers perform an act of communication to the public in copyright terms when they give the public access to copyright-protected works, and then regulates that the providers are also responsible for copyright infringements (committed by their users) unless they provide evidence to the contrary, which is linked to the fulfillment of certain criteria.

This rule, which was intensively discussed during and in the run-up to the reform under the catchword of "upload filters"[570], is associated with increased obligations for the providers addressed, such as VSP, which must, for example, clarify the licensing of content before it is made available and must have systems in place (the concrete design of which is left to the transposition in the Member States, which is why the discussions about the rule and its adequate transposition continue[571]), that must enable the claiming, reporting and identification of copyrighted material in case of doubt. The DSM Directive therefore deviates significantly in this respect

---

570 Cf. on this *Henrich*, Nach der Abstimmung ist (fast) vor der Umsetzung.
571 Cf. on this in particular the issue of Zeitschrift für Urheber- und Medienrecht (ZUM 2020, issue 10) dedicated to the discussion draft of the German Federal Ministry of Justice and Consumer Protection on the DSM Directive, which comments on the draft transposition in particular with regard to Art. 17 with contributions by various authors; on the German transposition proposal of Art. 17 in detail also *Husovec/Quintais* in: Kluwer Copyright Blog of 26.08.2020.

D. Secondary legal framework on "media law" and media pluralism

from the principles on limited responsibility established within the ECD.[572] This provision is also primarily aimed at protecting the authors' (also economic) interests in the refinancing of their creative work, but unlike Art. 15, the protected addressees here do not only include media undertakings or journalistic publications.

Although it is therefore reflexively also about the (financial) preservation of a variety of diverse offerings, the two-sidedness of this regulation against the background of safeguarding pluralism is made clear by the wording in recital 61, which points out that online services are both an opportunity and a challenge for safeguarding a relevant diversity. The risks for the diversity of (also media) offerings in the online area, which results from the legal manifestation of filtering obligations or the practical establishment by providers due to risk considerations, was already discussed during the reform under the aforementioned catchword "upload filters". Without having to go into this discussion here, this new regulation clearly shows that rules in EU law that are not directly related to pluralism can and should also have (supporting) effects on the diversity of offerings, but also on the plurality of providers themselves by ensuring economic compensation for the investment in copyright-protected works – for example by media undertakings, but not only. This does not encroach on the area of competence of the Member States for safeguarding pluralism in the media sector; rather, one of the reasons for including both rules in harmonizing EU law is the recognition that the factual situation regarding the most relevant online providers covered by both rules argued for a supranational solution, and not one in the Member States only, for reasons of effectiveness.

4. Merger Regulation

EU competition law – as is also the view of the European Commission in the media context[573] – also has at least an indirect effect in securing diversi-

---

572 Cf. *Kuczerawy*, EU Proposal for a Directive on Copyright in the Digital Single Market: Compatibility of Art. 13 with the EU Intermediary Liability Regime, 205, 205 et seq.; see also: *Cole/Etteldorf/Ullrich*, Cross-border Dissemination of Online Content, p. 139 et seq.
573 Communication from the Commission of 15 December 2003 on the future of European regulatory audiovisual policy, COM(2003) 784 final.

ty.⁵⁷⁴ Among other things, it prohibits mergers (including of media undertakings) that could lead to an impediment to cross-border competition if dominant market positions are achieved.⁵⁷⁵ This means that mergers can already be prohibited in view of the market power situation, which can already ensure diversity in the case of undertakings in the media sector or with an influence on it. In addition, merger control law, which has otherwise a fully harmonizing approach at EU level due to its regulatory nature and the clear definition of competences, recognizes that other, non-market power related tests and reasons for prohibition may also exist. Art. 21(4) Merger Regulation (ECMR)⁵⁷⁶ allows the Member States to prohibit mergers which should actually be cleared from a competition law perspective if they appear problematic for other legitimate interests of the Member States. The rule explicitly mentions "plurality of the media" as one such legitimate interest. In order to protect it, Member States enjoy a power of derogation, despite the actual EU competence for concentrations of Union-wide significance, which are decided exclusively on the basis of EU law and by the Commission. This means that the competent authorities in the Member States have the specific option of prohibiting mergers in order to protect media diversity, even if these mergers have been classified by the Commission as unobjectionable from a competition law perspective.⁵⁷⁷ However, they cannot subsequently approve such mergers that have been prohibited by the Commission, for example with the argument of increasing the diversity of supply.⁵⁷⁸

The rules on media concentration law vary widely in the Member States and, above all, to varying degrees.⁵⁷⁹ Many continue to limit themselves to

---

574 In detail on this *Cole*, Europarechtliche Rahmenbedingungen für die Pluralismussicherung im Rundfunk, p. 93, 102 et seq.
575 On this in detail supra, in chapter C.IV.2 on primary law.
576 Council Regulation (EC) No 139/2004 of 20 January 2004 on the control of concentrations between undertakings (the EC Merger Regulation), OJ L 24 of 29.01.2004, p. 1–22, https://eur-lex.europa.eu/legal-content/EN/TXT/?uri=CELEX %3A32004R0139&qid=1612892936591.
577 Cf. on this, e.g., the *Fox / Sky* case, which the Commission found to raise no competition concerns, but which the competent regulatory authority in the United Kingdom found to be contrary to the public interest against the background of media pluralistic concerns, Commission decision: M.8354 FOX / SKY, https://ec.europa.eu/competition/elojade/isef/case_details.cfm?proc_code=2_M_8354, Ofcom: https://www.gov.uk/government/collections/proposed-merger-between-twenty-first-century-fox-inc-and-sky-plc.
578 On this and the following *Cole/Hans* in: Cappello, Medieneigentum – Marktrealitäten und Regulierungsmaßnahmen, p. 27.
579 Cf. *European Institute for Media*, The Information of the Citizen in the EU.

D. Secondary legal framework on "media law" and media pluralism

monitoring concentration in the broadcasting sector; some also provide for the review of cross-media links.[580] But even if media concentration is limited by the establishment of rules on diversity, this does not automatically mean the creation of media pluralism. Rather, the implementation of further rules beyond competition law in the sense of e.g. support instruments is often required.[581]

In any event, the ECMR and thus the Commission's exclusive competence relate solely to the assessment of the effects of proposed mergers on competition in the various affected markets within the EEA. The assessment does not include those factors that would be relevant for the evaluation of a dominant power of opinion and thus provide information on whether a merger would have a negative impact on a pluralistic media landscape.[582] The purpose and legal framework for assessing competition and media plurality are very different. Competition rules broadly focus on whether consumers would face higher prices or lower innovation as a result of a transaction. An assessment of media plurality typically addresses the question of whether the number, scope, and diversity of individuals or undertakings controlling media undertakings are sufficiently plural. The Commission does recognize this difference and that this can lead to different assessments of mergers also.[583]

Media concentration law is therefore an area that is deliberately excluded from the law on economic concentration. Art. 21(4) ECMR is a significant confirmation that even in subject matters which are clearly within the competence of the EU, such as competition law, the regulatory sovereignty of the Member States is respected – in this case through the application in practice to merger projects – and made operational in the relevant acts of secondary law through a special provision.

---

580 *Cole/Hans* in: Cappello, Medieneigentum – Marktrealitäten und Regulierungsmaßnahmen, p. 125 et seq.
581 *Cole/Hans* in: Cappello, Medieneigentum – Marktrealitäten und Regulierungsmaßnahmen, p. 127.
582 Cf. on this, but also on possibly unexploited potentials for taking into account also pluralism-relevant aspects within the framework of the EU competition regime *Bania*, The Role of Media Pluralism in the Enforcement of EU Competition Law.
583 Same as here the EU Commission in connection with the case of the merger of Fox and Sky, cf. press release of 7 April 2017, https://ec.europa.eu/commission/presscorner/detail/en/IP_17_902.

5. European Electronic Communications Code

The EECC[584] entered into force on 21 December 2018 and in particular both amended and consolidated Directives 2002/19/EC (Access Directive)[585], 2002/20/EC (Authorisation Directive), 2002/21/EC (Framework Directive) and 2002/22/EC (Universal Service Directive)[586] into a comprehensive regulatory framework for telecommunications services. The EECC regulates electronic communications networks and services, i.e., transmission paths and technically oriented services, but contains provisions that are highly relevant in the context of ensuring pluralism in the media sector.

According to Art. 61(2)(d) EECC (formerly Art. 5(1)(b) Access Directive), the regulatory authorities of the Member States may order undertakings with significant market power to provide digital radio and television broadcasting services and related complementary services, access to application programming interfaces (APIs) and electronic programme guides (EPGs) on reasonable and non-discriminatory terms. In addition, pursuant to Art. 114(1) EECC (formerly Art. 31 Universal Service Directive), the Member States may continue to provide for so-called 'must carry' obligations in national law, i.e., to oblige network operators to transmit certain radio and television broadcast channels and related complementary services. This addresses in particular operators of cable television networks, IP-TV, satellite broadcasting networks and terrestrial broadcasting networks, as well as possibly operators of other networks if they are used (now or in the future) by a significant number of end-users as their main means of receiving radio and television broadcasts. The imposition of obligations is subject to the condition that they are necessary for an (explicitly defined) objective of general interest and that they are proportionate and transparent. Such objectives include in particular safeguarding media diversity. Ac-

---

584 Directive (EU) 2018/1972 of the European Parliament and of the Council of 11 December 2018 establishing the European Electronic Communications Code (Recast), OJ L 321 of 17.12.2018, p. 36–214, https://eur-lex.europa.eu/legal-content/EN/TXT/?uri=celex:32018L1972.

585 Directive 2002/19/EC of the European Parliament and of the Council of 7 March 2002 on access to, and interconnection of, electronic communications networks and associated facilities (Access Directive), OJ L 108 of 24.04.2002, p. 7–20, https://eur-lex.europa.eu/legal-content/EN/ALL/?uri=CELEX%3A32002L0019.

586 Directive 2002/22/EC of the European Parliament and of the Council of 7 March 2002 on universal service and users' rights relating to electronic communications networks and services (Universal Service Directive), OJ L 108 of 24.04.2002, p. 51–77, https://eur-lex.europa.eu/legal-content/EN/TXT/?uri=celex:32002L0022.

D. Secondary legal framework on "media law" and media pluralism

cordingly, the rules were also introduced against the background of the need for Member States, in the light of their cultural sovereignty, to be able to ensure that certain programs and, above all, the information conveyed therein, are accessible to a wide audience.[587] In this context, it is important to note that, due to the high degree of harmonization of the regulations, the authorization for this must already be laid down in EU law, which, however, leaves the Member States free to introduce such 'must carry' obligations and also as regards their design only specifies the purpose and the framework conditions to be fulfilled, due to the relevance of the interference to fundamental rights. As will be considered in more detail below, this leaves the room for maneuver with the Member States. On the one hand, the concept of ensuring access for the "general public" to important content is close to the concept of a basic service, as laid down in German law, e.g., for telecommunications services as an infrastructure facility in Art. 87f(1) Basic Law.[588] On the other hand, this idea also originates from the establishment of public service providers or offerings whose state-initiated funding leads to a special status and a kind of "claim to access" for the citizens funding the service. In Germany, this is laid down in the basic service mandate, also confirmed by the Federal Constitutional Court, according to which public broadcasting has a comprehensive mandate not only in terms of content, but also in terms of accessibility, which in turn justifies its funding basis.[589]

According to Art. 1(2) EECC, its objectives (like those of the predecessor directives) are, on the one hand, to implement an internal market in electronic communications networks and services that results in the deployment and take-up of very high capacity networks, sustainable competition, interoperability of electronic communications services, accessibility, security of networks and services and end-user benefits. The second is to ensure the provision throughout the Union of good quality, affordable, publicly available services through effective competition and choice, to deal with circumstances in which the needs of end-users, including those with disabilities in order to access the services on an equal basis with others, are not satisfactorily met by the market and to lay down the necessary end-user rights. It is therefore a question of the internal market, competition, consumer protection and also network infrastructure within the EU. The men-

---

587 Cf. on this *Arino et al.* in: EAI, Haben oder nicht haben. Must-Carry-Regeln.
588 Same as here *Assion*, Must Carry: Übertragungspflichten auf digitalen Rundfunkplattformen, p. 207.
589 On this *Ukrow/Cole*, Aktive Sicherung lokaler und regionaler Medienvielfalt, p. 98.

tion of "choice" in the objectives (Art. 1(2)(b)) is not to be understood as a cultural policy orientation with regard to content services carried via the networks, but rather means the existence of a large number of (competing) offerings of communications networks within the EU from the consumers' point of view. This is also clarified by recital 7, which states that the EECC does not cover the content of services delivered over electronic communications networks using electronic communications services, such as broadcasting content, financial services and certain information society services. In addition, recital 7 makes it unambiguously clear however, that the EECC is without prejudice to measures taken at Union or national level in respect of such services, in order to promote cultural and linguistic diversity and to ensure the defence of media pluralism. With regard to the increasing technical convergence of "infrastructure", recital 7 recognizes that the services carried over it from a regulatory perspective remain separate from it, although this does not prevent the "taking into account of the links existing between them, in particular in order to guarantee media pluralism, cultural diversity and consumer protection". However, the EECC places this possibility of achieving cultural policy goals such as pluralism of the media and securing cultural diversity also via "technical" regulation essentially at the level of the Member States[590]. With regard to national regulators, recital 7 explicitly requires that "competent authorities should contribute to ensuring the implementation of policies aiming to promote those objectives".

As already mentioned above, this also applies explicitly to access rules and the so-called 'must carry' rules. Art. 61 and 114 EECC generally only open the possibility on EU level to introduce them by the Member States. They can, in particular with regard to the latter, decide whether 'must carry' obligations are to be introduced at all, and if so, which providers or which offerings (public broadcasting, private broadcasting etc.) are to be covered by them, whether, by whom and to what extent compensation and/or payments are to be made for the transmission, how many providers or offerings should benefit from 'must carry' obligations, and other general conditions. Most Member States[591] have made use of this option in vari-

---

[590] Cf. rec. 115: "Those objectives should include the promotion of cultural and linguistic diversity and media pluralism, as defined by Member States in accordance with Union law".

[591] Only Cyprus, Estonia, Spain, Italy (except for local offerings), and Luxembourg have no 'must carry' obligations; rules on discoverability in electronic program guides are in place in about half of the EU Member States so far. Cf. European Institute of Media, study to support Impact Assessment of AVMSD, p. 80.

D. Secondary legal framework on "media law" and media pluralism

ous forms, but in doing so, they have generally based the main rule on the wording of the (previously applicable) directives,[592] so that the specific application is carried out by the regulatory authorities or bodies.

The EECC, which was to be transposed by 21 December 2020, supplements the existing rules, to which the implementation in the Member States until now is still oriented, not insignificantly, as can be seen from the following extracts of a synoptic overview:

Access Directive	EECC
Recital (10) Competition rules alone may not be sufficient to ensure cultural diversity and media pluralism in the area of digital television. […]	Recital (159) Competition rules alone may not **always** be sufficient to ensure cultural diversity and media pluralism in the area of digital television. […]
Universal Service Directive	EECC
Art. 31 (1) Member States may impose reasonable "must carry" obligations, for the transmission of specified radio and television broadcast channels and services, on undertakings under their jurisdiction providing electronic communications networks used for the distribution of radio or television broadcasts to the public where a significant number of end-users of such networks use them as their principal means to receive radio and television broadcasts.	**Art. 114** (1) Member States may impose reasonable 'must carry' obligations for the transmission of specified radio and television broadcast channels and **related complementary** services, **in particular accessibility services to enable appropriate access for end-users with disabilities and data supporting connected television services and EPGs,** on undertakings under their jurisdiction providing electronic communications networks **and services** used for the distribution of radio or television broadcast **channels** to the public, where a significant number of end-users of such networks **and services** use them as

---

592 *EAI*, Must-Carry: Renaissance oder Reformation?; on this comprehensively with regard to Art. 31 Universal Service Directive also EAI, Access to TV platforms: must-carry rules, and access to free-DTT.

Such obligations shall only be imposed where they are necessary to meet clearly defined general interest objectives and shall be proportionate and transparent. The obligations shall be subject to periodical review. (2) Neither paragraph 1 of this Article nor Article 3(2) of Directive 2002/19/EC (Access Directive) shall prejudice the ability of Member States to determine appropriate remuneration, if any, in respect of measures taken in accordance with this Article while ensuring that, in similar circumstances, there is no discrimination in the treatment of undertakings providing electronic communications networks. Where remuneration is provided for, Member States shall ensure that it is applied in a proportionate and transparent manner.	their principal means to receive radio and television broadcast **channels**. Such obligations shall **be imposed only** where they are necessary to meet general interest objectives **as clearly defined by each Member State** and shall be proportionate and transparent. (2) **By 21 December 2019 and every five years thereafter, Member States shall review the obligations referred to in the paragraph 1, except where Member States have carried out such a review within the previous four years.** (3) Neither paragraph 1 of this Article nor **Article 59(2)** shall prejudice the ability of Member States to determine appropriate remuneration, if any, in respect of measures taken in accordance with this Article while ensuring that, in similar circumstances, there is no discrimination in the treatment of **providers of** electronic communications networks **and services**. Where remuneration is provided for, **Member States shall ensure that the obligation to remunerate is clearly set out in national law, including, where relevant, the criteria for calculating such remuneration.** Member States shall **also** ensure that it is applied in a proportionate and transparent manner.

Further and additional clarifications can also be found in the recitals to the new Directive, which also go beyond the text of the previous recitals to the Universal Service Directive. For example, recital 308 clarifies that 'must

D. Secondary legal framework on "media law" and media pluralism

carry' obligations must relate to certain specified radio and television broadcast channels and complementary services thereto. It is even more strongly emphasized that the regulations for this must be transparent, proportionate and "clearly defined" and leave sufficient development opportunities for network operators to invest in their infrastructures. Under recital 309, the review period for such 'must carry' obligations is now specifically set at five-year periods in order to review to a specified extent whether market developments have rendered the obligations of network operators, which according to the following recital now also explicitly include "IP-TV", superfluous. It is also important to clarify that, "[i]n light of the growing provision and reception of connected television services and the continued importance of EPGs for end-user choice the transmission of programme-related data necessary to support connected television and EPG functionalities can be included in 'must carry' obligations" (recital 310).

While the Member States (and thus also the national regulatory authorities) continue to remain free as to "whether" to introduce must carry rules under the EECC, the Directive as part of the reform provides certain specifications as to "how" to do so. In particular, the objective of general interests, which is regularly the safeguarding of diversity when establishing 'must carry' obligations, must be explicitly enshrined in law. Where previously only a "periodical" review was required, the EECC now requires one every five years. The expansion of 'must carry' rules to include "complementary services" is also new. Such complementary services may include program-related services specifically designed to improve accessibility for end-users with disabilities (e.g., teletext, subtitles for deaf or hearing-impaired end-users, audio description, spoken subtitles, and sign language interpretation) and may include, where necessary, access to related source data; they may also include program-related connected television services.[593] Program-related data means such data as is necessary to support functions of connected television services and electronic program guides, and regularly includes information about program content and the method of access.[594] However, the clarifications, some of which also take up rulings of the CJEU[595], leave intact the principle that, despite the high degree of har-

---

[593] On the term cf. also the European Parliament resolution of 4 July 2013 on connected TV, (2012/2300(INI)), https://www.europarl.europa.eu/sides/getDoc.do?pubRef=-//EP//TEXT+TA+P7-TA-2013-0329+0+DOC+XML+V0//EN.
[594] Cf. on this rec. 153 and 310 EECC.
[595] Cf. CJEU, case C-250/06, *United Pan-Europe Communications Belgium SA and Others / Belgian State*, para. 31; CJEU, case C-353/89, *Commission / Netherlands*, para. 25.

monization in the area of electronic communications networks and services and also despite technological developments which, in principle, permit more diversity of offerings in terms of technical possibilities, complementary measures for safeguarding diversity must continue to be taken by the Member States and only by them. This recognizes that the assessments to be made to decide on the need for such 'must carry' obligations can only be made at the level of and by the Member States or national regulatory authorities.

This far-reaching recognition of the Member States' room for maneuver also does not affect the result of an earlier CJEU ruling, according to which 'must carry' obligations can lead to all program slot allocations being predetermined in the (analog) cable network without infringement of the proportionality requirement under EU law.[596] Admittedly, the question of analog cable coverage is hardly relevant any more, and the new EECC makes it clear that 'must carry' obligations in this respect are to be provided for only in exceptional cases. It remains the realization, however, that despite the interference with the freedom to provide services and fundamental rights of network operators, Member States have extensive possibilities for control. Excessive demands on network operators shall be prevented by the precise requirements as to which conditions have to be met in the context of 'must carry' obligations. But the purpose, emphasized by the CJEU, "to preserve the pluralist and cultural range of programmes available on television distribution networks and to ensure that all television viewers have access to pluralism and to a wide range of programmes"[597], remains relevant when it comes to other types of obligations imposed on network operators for the purpose of safeguarding pluralism. However, the Member States must specifically express this objective[598] in the legal regulation. In addition, as mentioned above, the rules must be proportionate and transparent, which in turn means, as in the previous sections, an examination of the national rules against Union law and the fundamental principles laid down therein, as specifically stated in Art. 61,

---

596 CJEU, case C-336/07, *Kabel Deutschland Vertrieb und Service GmbH & Co. KG / Niedersächsische Landesmedienanstalt für privaten Rundfunk*; cf. on this also Cole in: HK-MStV, § 51 b, para. 22 et seq., on the judgment in particular 27 et seq.
597 CJEU, case C-250/06, *United Pan-Europe Communications Belgium SA and Others / Belgian State*, para. 40.
598 The mere formulation of declarations of principle and general policy objectives in the recitals of the national regulation cannot be regarded as sufficient in this respect, cf. CJEU, case C-250/06, *United Pan-Europe Communications Belgium SA and Others / Belgian* State, para. 46.

D. Secondary legal framework on "media law" and media pluralism

114 EECC. In this respect, too, the CJEU leaves to the Member States, in this case to the competent courts, the assessment whether the criteria have been observed in the individual case.[599] The Member States therefore also have a wide scope for action in the context of infrastructure regulation in the light of their cultural policies.

Of particular relevance, however, is Art. 1(3)(b) EECC. It already clarifies at the beginning of the Directive with regard to its scope that measures taken at Union or national level, in accordance with Union law, to pursue general interest objectives remain unaffected by the EECC. The list of examples explicitly mentions "content regulation and audiovisual policy" in addition to data protection as one such objective. As noted above, the related recital 7 clarifies that this does not require a strict separation of rules on technical network-related areas and those that are content-related. However, the two areas must be distinguished from each other, and the competence for regulation must be located with the Member States in the case of content regulation, in particular when it is carried out with a view to safeguarding pluralism. This provision thus corresponds to the exemption as set forth in Art. 1(6) ECD (cf. chapter D.II.1.) and, in this respect, also against the background of telecommunications law, leaves the Member States room for (additional) regulations on safeguarding diversity which may affect providers covered by the EECC. However, in this respect, the EECC requires the Member States to regulate the two areas differently and not to include content-related rules in the law on the transposition of the EECC.

With view to national implementation in Germany also, this means that a deletion without replacement of existing broadcasting-related consideration requirements in the TKG does not appear to be readily compatible with the implementation obligation with regard to Art. 1(3) EECC. At the very least, an amendment to the TKG aimed at such a deletion without replacement would, not only for reasons of constitutional law, trigger an at least considerable effort to explain the compatibility of the amendment with higher-ranking law, i.e. also EU law – especially since even in the case of acts transposing EU directives, there is an obligation to respect the imperative of media pluralism enshrined in Art. 11(2) CFR.

---

599 However, the review must, in case of doubt, be carried out by national courts and not by the CJEU; cf. CJEU, case C-336/07, *Kabel Deutschland Vertrieb und Service GmbH & Co. KG / Niedersächsische Landesmedienanstalt für privaten Rundfunk*.

6. Platform-to-Business Regulation

As already mentioned in connection with the new rules for prominence of content in the general interest in the AVMSD (chapter D.II.2.d(2)), ensuring the visibility of media content is a significant element of safeguarding diversity. This idea of the "visibility" of content or information is not only found in secondary law with a media law orientation, but is also laid out in a legal act that has only recently become applicable, which refers to competition-oriented aspects of the economic sector of (certain) online service providers. The P2B Regulation[600], directly applicable in all Member States since 12 July 2020, must also be considered in more detail in the overall context of this study.

a. Scope and objective

This legislation was created with the aim of providing greater transparency, fairness and effective remedies in the area of online intermediation services. They are defined in the Regulation (Art. 2(2)) as information society services that allow business users, on the basis of contractual relationships, to offer goods or services to consumers with a view to facilitating the initiating of direct transactions between those business users and consumers, irrespective of where those transactions are ultimately concluded. Hence, the Regulation is about services that stand as intermediaries and thus, in many cases, gatekeepers (in particular with regard to SMEs) between sellers of goods or services and consumers. As a significant part of online commerce takes place with the involvement of such intermediaries, it is important from the perspective of the EU legislature that undertakings have confidence in these services and that they ensure transparency towards them. The Directive also separately addresses online search engines, which are understood to be a digital service that allows users to input queries in order to perform searches of, in principle, all websites, or all websites in a particular language, on the basis of a query on any subject in the form of a keyword, voice request, phrase or other input, and returns results in any format in which information related to the requested content can be

---

600 Regulation (EU) 2019/1150 of the European Parliament and of the Council of 20 June 2019 on promoting fairness and transparency for business users of online intermediation services, OJ L 186, 11.07.2019, p. 57–79; https://eur-lex.europa.eu/legal-content/EN/ALL/?uri=CELEX%3A32019R1150.

D. Secondary legal framework on "media law" and media pluralism

found. Search engines also regularly serve as a link and gatekeeper between undertakings and consumers.

By specifically addressing search engines, the Regulation responds to well-founded concerns that they are not neutral in how they display and arrange their search results.[601] The Regulation focuses on the proper functioning of the internal market and responds to an (also potentially) unequal power structure in the digital economy and aims to prevent negative effects of this power structure respectively. Thus, there are parallels to the situation concerning the relationships between recipients, media intermediaries and content providers. The P2B Regulation does not refer to the general interest of safeguarding pluralism, which neither lies in its objective nor could be a link as regards competence, but the parallelism of the links means that the Regulation in its practical application can have at least an indirect effect on safeguarding diversity.

b. The transparency requirements

Art. 5 P2B Regulation stipulates that providers of online intermediation services and online search engines must make the main parameters that determine the order or weighting of the presentation or listing ("ranking") of their services comprehensible by means of explanations in plain and intelligible language in the GTCs or on the website of their own service. Essentially, this is about describing the algorithms that (co-)determine the display and thus also the discoverability. Online intermediation services are directly required by the Regulation itself to set up complaint systems for business users in order to ensure that the Regulation's requirements on complaints by business users are implemented in practice. This obligation does not apply directly to online search engines. However, Member States are required to ensure adequate and effective enforcement of the Regulation in relation to all providers covered by it (Art. 15). In addition, a concrete form of monitoring of the impact of the Regulation by the Commission is laid down (Art. 16). The development of codes of conduct is called for (Art. 17), which are to ensure the "proper application" of the Regulation, whereby the wording "contribute to the proper application" makes

---

601 As stated by the EU project CHORUS in its study from 2010: *Boujemaa et al.*, Cross-disciplinary Challenges and Recommendations regarding the Future of Multimedia Search Engines. Cf. furthermore also *Meckel*, Vielfalt im digitalen Medienensemble, p. 12 et seq.

it clear that they are meant as an instrument of substantiating co-regulation and should not lead to a pure self-regulation of the sector.

Since the definition of "business users"[602] or "users with a corporate website"[603], which are to be protected by the Regulation and the specified transparency obligations, potentially also includes media undertakings with their online offerings, (also) they are being given an important tool to strengthen their position vis-à-vis gatekeepers such as online search engines and social media[604] which play an important role in the online distribution and discoverability of their content.[605] In particular, (also) they may benefit from requiring intermediaries and search engines to disclose more detailed information about how their services work. Although the obligation arising from the Regulation does not entail disclosure of the detailed mode of operation or the algorithms themselves, it does entail a publicly available and constantly updated explanation of the significance and weighting assigned to individual parameters and whether the ranking is influenced by the payment of a fee (not only in the form of monetary payments).

In order to implement these requirements, the EU Commission – similar to the new provisions of the AVMSD – according to Art. 5(7) shall issue guidelines with regard to the most important content of the Regulation, the application of the rule on "ranking". These are currently still drafted.[606] Even if the concrete ramifications of the Regulation, as they will also result from the guidelines, are not yet foreseeable in detail (also) for the media sector, it is nevertheless a rule that is related to the undistorted perceptibility of relevant services (also: the offering of content) and therefore its impact should also be pursued from a diversity-safeguarding perspective. The transparency requirements could also improve the review of the

---

602 As per Art. 2(1) P2B Regulation, any private individual acting in a commercial or professional capacity who, or any legal person which, through online intermediation services offers goods or services to consumers for purposes relating to its trade, business, craft or profession.
603 As per Art. 2(7) P2B Regulation, any natural or legal person which uses an online interface, meaning any software, including a website or a part thereof and applications, including mobile applications, to offer goods or services to consumers for purposes relating to its trade, business, craft or profession.
604 Cf. on this rec. 11 P2B Regulation.
605 On the possibilities of safeguarding diversity through search engines cf. *Nolte* in: ZUM 2017, 552, 552 et seq.
606 On the current status cf. https://ec.europa.eu/digital-single-market/en/news/ranking-transparency-guidelines-framework-eu-regulation-platform-business-relations-explainer.

D. Secondary legal framework on "media law" and media pluralism

functioning of this sector in general, so that as a consequence, future regulatory proposals could be developed, if necessary, on the basis of research results found in this way.

c. The relationship to other rules by Member States

In light of the focus of this study, the P2B Regulation should also be examined for another reason: as a regulation, it is directly applicable law in all Member States. Its scope and the outlined obligations for service providers, which as shown can reflexively also have diversity-promoting effects in the media sector, leads to the question of whether the Regulation has a suspensory effect or otherwise limits Member States' regulatory approaches with regard to providers already covered by the Regulation and transparency requirements for them. It must be emphasized that, unlike the, e.g., AVMSD, the Regulation neither contains any explicit power to derogate from the coordinated field in favor of stricter regulations nor, as does the ECD, an additional power of restriction for the Member States for reasons such as the protection of minors. Art. 1(4) P2B Regulation merely refers to certain unaffected Member State rules from the respective national civil law. Regulations are binding in their entirety and not, like directives, merely as to the result to be achieved, so that transposing acts by Member States are unnecessary and even prohibited where they would conceal the direct applicability of the regulation.[607] This also includes a prohibition of repetition developed early on by the CJEU, according to which a merely repetitive presentation of the subject matter of a regulation in Member States' law is prohibited as this would create uncertainty about the author and legal nature of a legal act and jeopardize the simultaneous and uniform application of EU law.[608] This is different in the case of regulations that contain implementing provisions addressed to the Member States or are deliberately limited in their geographical scope[609] or, by means of often so-called "opening clauses", allow Member States room for maneuver with regard to certain rules of the regulation despite its character as such. However, the provisions of the P2B Regulation that are relevant here are not such types of rules.

---

607 *Ruffert* in: Calliess/id., Art. 288 TFEU, para. 19, with further references.
608 Cf. for instance CJEU, case 39/72, *Commission / Italy*, para. 17.
609 Cf. on this *Nettesheim* in Grabitz/Hilf/id., Art. 288 TFEU, para. 99 et seq.

However, the prohibition of Member States' rules in the area of a regulation only applies to the extent that a regulatory area – such as safeguarding diversity – is covered by it. The P2B Regulation addresses "potential frictions in the online platform economy" from a competition law and consumer protection law perspective (recitals 2 and 3) and therefore does not distinguish between specific undertakings that are to benefit from transparency, i.e. it is sector-neutral. However, this does not address the issue that there may be factors specific to certain sectors that make it particularly relevant for undertakings in that sector to learn more about how the service operates through a transparent presentation of ranking systems. Equally, the regulation does not address the general interest in displaying certain content according to certain criteria. In addition to the media sector and the dissemination of information there, where aspects of safeguarding diversity also play an important role in the perception of the end-user, examples of this include the pharmaceutical sector with regard to health protection or the political sector with regard to equal opportunities for political parties against the background of the principle of democracy. The distinction of requirements regarding the presentation of ranking factors between online intermediation services and search engine operators made in the Regulation also does not imply any consideration of sector-specific features, but is connected with the different relationships between the undertakings within the scope of protection of the Regulation and the service providers for these two categories, in particular the factor that search engines do not have a direct contractual relationship with the undertakings (or their websites) displayed in the context of search results.

General interests that require special protection of certain undertakings or the involvement of the public in the disclosure of information are thus not covered by the Regulation. It remains within the scope of the general competition-related considerations, as is also repeatedly apparent from the recitals. As a horizontally applicable legal instrument that aims to protect competition from unfair practices, distortions and unequal treatment in all sectors of the economy, the Regulation is not designed to take into account other sector-specific interests.[610]

In the online consultation process on the development of the guidelines on the transparency obligation, the Commission points out that one of the aims of the guidelines should be to also provide sector-specific guidance on

---

610 Cf. rec. 51, which explicitly states only the competition objective: "...ensure a fair, predictable, sustainable and trusted online business environment within the internal market".

D. Secondary legal framework on "media law" and media pluralism

the application of the transparency obligation where necessary.[611] However, there is no indication yet for which sectors such specific guidance might be provided or which aspects it might cover. However, the relevance of transparency requirements for such providers for media sector undertakings is also demonstrated by primarily stakeholders from this sector taking part in the survey, outlining media policy aspects.[612] According to the Commission's announcement, the guidelines should have been published by 12 July 2020, but they are still missing.

However, the Commission in its guideline authority is in any case bound by the requirements from the Regulation and cannot go beyond what is covered by it. Powers to issue guidelines are granted where more general rules need to be clarified and the underlying context is dynamically evolving. This also applies to the highly technical and digital area, as is the case here with the authorization under Art. 5(7) P2B Regulation. However, clarification should not be done simply because it seems reasonable. Rather, the Commission must remain within the scope of the competence and thus the regulatory context (here: of the Regulation), otherwise this would indirectly lead to a de facto transfer of powers to the Commission in the administrative network, although it does not have[613] or should not have such competence.[614] This also applies to the pursuit of cultural policy objectives with regard to transparency requirements for providers of certain online intermediation services or search engines, which may also not result from the guidelines due to the competence of the Member States and the limited content of the Regulation. Although the Commission has stated that it recognizes potential legal overlaps between the P2B Regu-

---

611 "Provide sector specific guidance, if and where appropriate."; cf. Targeted online survey on the ranking transparency guidelines in the framework of the EU regulation on platform-to-business relations, https://ec.europa.eu/digital-single-market/en/news/targeted-online-survey-ranking-transparency-guidelines-framework-eu-regulation-platform.
612 Cf. the opinions of e.g. the EBU or ACT, available at https://ec.europa.eu/digital-single-market/en/news/ranking-transparency-guidelines-framework-eu-regulation-platform-business-relations-explainer.
613 On the criticism regarding the granting of competence through guideline authority cf. *Lecheler* in: DVBl. 2008, 873, 873 et seq.; *Weiß* in: EWS 2010, 257, 257 et seq.
614 Cf. on this with further references *Ruffert* in Calliess/id., Art. 288 TFEU, para. 102, who also refers to the danger of a shift resulting from the fact that guidelines can have a high steering effect, but in contrast have only a weak enshrinement under primary law.

lation and Member States' media legislation[615] insofar as the latter imposes transparency requirements, this observation has no basis in the Regulation, which does not have the objective of safeguarding media diversity. Therefore, neither the Regulation nor, a fortiori, the legally non-binding guidelines yet to be issued impose a limit on the Member States' scope for action to achieve this general interest objective. Thus, the provisions of the P2B Regulation also do not conflict with Member States' regulations e.g. for promoting fairness and transparency among new media players such as media intermediaries and media agencies[616], as long as these are not aimed at economic consumer protection and cross-border marketability of online services, but rather at safeguarding media diversity under the conditions of digitization and globalization and tackling new threats to diversity through business models geared toward aggregation, selection and presentation of media content.

d. The relationship with Directive (EU) 2019/2161

A brief consideration of Directive (EU) 2019/2161[617], which entered into force only a few months after the P2B Regulation, also proves that Member States retain scope for regulating media pluralism as an objective of general interest. The Directive contains various requirements for the enforcement and modernization of the Union's consumer protection legislation. In contrast to the P2B Regulation, it does not refer to the relationship between undertakings and the platforms covered by the act (online intermediation services and search engines), but to the relationship between final consumers and the platforms. In this context, too, the ranking or a highlighted placement of commercial offers in the results of a search query by providers of online search functions play a significant role, as these can have a considerable impact on the (purchasing) decision of consumers.[618]

---

615 Cf. on this the comments of the Commission in the notification procedure, European Commission, Notifizierung 2020/26/D, C(2020) 2823 final of 27.04.2020, p. 9.
616 Cf. *Ukrow/Cole*, Zur Transparenz von Mediaagenturen, p. 52 et seq.
617 Directive (EU) 2019/2161 of the European Parliament and of the Council of 27 November 2019 amending Council Directive 93/13/EEC and Directives 98/6/EC, 2005/29/EC and 2011/83/EU of the European Parliament and of the Council as regards the better enforcement and modernisation of Union consumer protection rules, OJ L 328 of 18.12.2019, p. 7–28, https://eur-lex.europa.eu/legal-content/EN/TXT/?uri=CELEX%3A32019L2161&qid=1614597549259.
618 Cf. rec. 18 Directive (EU) 2019/2161.

D. Secondary legal framework on "media law" and media pluralism

As a result of an amendment to the Consumer Rights Directive 2011/83/EU, providers of online marketplaces[619] are subject to more far-reaching information requirements in their relationship with consumers (Art. 6 a): before a consumer is bound by a distance contract, or any corresponding offer, on an online marketplace, the provider of the online marketplace shall provide the consumer in a clear, comprehensible and recognizable manner about, i.a., general information on the main parameters determining ranking of offers presented to the consumer as a result of the search query on the online marketplace and the relative importance of those parameters as opposed to other parameters. This information must be made available in a specific section of the online interface that is directly and easily accessible from the page where the offers are presented. In parallel, a corresponding provision is incorporated into the Unfair Commercial Practices Directive[620], which defines such information as material and thus classifies its withholding as a misleading omission. However, the latter provision is expressly not intended to apply to online search engines within the meaning of the P2B Regulation, to which the Unfair Commercial Practices Directive otherwise applies. The purpose of this is not to construct an exception for them, but to avoid duplication of already existing obligations. This is clarified in recital 21, according to which the transparency requirements are to be ensured by the Directive also vis-à-vis consumers, in a comparable manner to the P2B Regulation. However, since with regard to search engines there is already a comprehensive obligation from the Regulation to provide publicly accessible information on the parameters, repetition is unnecessary in this respect.

The Directive thus ensures that consumers do not just reflexively benefit from increased transparency of ranking systems between undertakings and intermediaries introduced by the P2B Regulation, but that explicit guarantees also apply to the consumer. In this context, in addition to the provisions of the Directive, the Member States are not prevented from imposing

---

619 Defined as "a service using software, including a website, part of a website or an application, operated by or on behalf of a trader which allows consumers to conclude distance contracts with other traders or consumers", Art. 2(1) no. 17 Directive 2011/83/EU as amended by Directive (EU) 2019/2161.
620 Directive 2005/29/EC of the European Parliament and of the Council of 11 May 2005 concerning unfair business-to-consumer commercial practices in the internal market and amending Council Directive 84/450/EEC, Directives 97/7/EC, 98/27/EC and 2002/65/EC of the European Parliament and of the Council and Regulation (EC) No 2006/2004 of the European Parliament and of the Council ('Unfair Commercial Practices Directive'), OJ L 149 of 11.06.2005, p. 22–39, https://eur-lex.europa.eu/legal-content/EN/TXT/?uri=celex:32005L0029.

additional information requirements on providers of online marketplaces on grounds of consumer protection (Art. 6a(2)). This makes two things clear: From an EU law perspective already, transparency requirements for online service providers are possible for different purposes, so far regulated in EU law from a competition law (P2B Regulation) and consumer protection law (Directive (EU) 2019/2161) perspective. In addition, it is recognized that even if certain minimum requirements exist (here: from the Regulation), it is possible to go beyond them or to set more specific requirements to achieve the other objective. If, for example, there is a particular need for consumer protection, the transparency requirements can be specially designed. Equally, it remains possible for Member States to impose more far-reaching transparency requirements from yet another angle, the consideration of which falls within their competence. Accordingly, safeguarding media pluralism can justify such requirements for certain intermediaries that (also) play a significant role in the distribution of media content, and the corresponding possibility for action is not blocked by the P2B Regulation.

III. Current projects for legislative acts and initiatives with a media law context

1. Proposal for a regulation on preventing the dissemination of terrorist content online

In the fall of 2018, the European Commission presented a draft Regulation of the European Parliament and of the Council on preventing the dissemination of terrorist content on the Internet (TERREG)[621]. It intends to increase the effectiveness of current measures to detect, identify and remove terrorist content on online platforms. However, the proposal had not reached agreement in the trilogue process by the time the previous Commission's mandate expired.[622] On 17 April 2019, the European Parlia-

---

621 Proposal for a Regulation of the European Parliament and of the Council on preventing the dissemination of terrorist content online. A contribution from the European Commission to the Leaders' meeting in Salzburg on 19–20 September 2018, COM/2018/640 final, https://eur-lex.europa.eu/legal-content/EN/TXT/?uri=COM%3A2018%3A640%3AFIN.
622 On the state of the proceedings cf. https://eur-lex.europa.eu/legal-content/EN/HIS/?uri=COM:2018:640:FIN.

ment[623] had considered the proposal at first reading, adding a number of amendments, thereby allowing it to be referred again following the election of a new Parliament and the constitution of a new Commission. However, the General Approach of the Council is still pending, so that it is not foreseeable whether such a Regulation will actually enter into force in the near future and how it will relate to any newly adopted legal acts concerning the providers covered by the proposed Regulation.

TERREG, according to the Commission's proposal and – with regard to this point – in principle also approved by the Parliament, pursues an approach that is also found in the German Network Enforcement Act (NetzDG)[624]. The proposed rules primarily target hosting service providers within the meaning of Art. 14 ECD that offer their services within the EU, regardless of their place of establishment or size (in particular, no thresholds or exemptions for SMEs are foreseen).[625] In this context, however, the draft does not refer to the corresponding provision of the ECD, but itself defines "hosting service provider" in Art. 2(1) as a provider of information society services consisting in the storage of information provided by and at the request of the content provider and in making the information stored available to third parties. The definition thus circumscribes the hosting provider as somewhat passive by linking it to the function as order fulfiller, but does not (like the ECD) presuppose exclusive passivity as mandatory. Rather, providers defined in this way could at least also perform active acts in the provision of content. Under TERREG, the content provider is also the active part, as the "user who has provided information that is stored on his behalf by a hosting service provider". In particular, these may also include media undertakings that (also) distribute their offerings via hosting services. However, the focus of TERREG regulation is not directly on content providers, but on hosting service providers.

With respect to hosting service providers, the TERREG draft contains rules on duties of care to be applied by them in order to prevent the dissemination of terrorist content through their services and, if necessary, to

---

623 European Parliament legislative resolution of 17 April 2019 on the proposal for a regulation of the European Parliament and of the Council on preventing the dissemination of terrorist content online (COM(2018)0640 – C8-0405/2018 – 2018/0331(COD)), https://eur-lex.europa.eu/legal-content/EN/TXT/?uri=EP:P8_TA(2019)0421.
624 Network Enforcement Act (Netzwerkdurchsetzungsgesetz) of 1 September 2017 (BGBl. I, p. 3352), as amended by Article 274 of the Regulation of 19 June 2020 (BGBl. I, p. 1328).
625 Point 3.2. in the impact assessment of the draft.

ensure the prompt removal of such content. In addition, a number of measures are listed to be implemented by Member States to identify terrorist content, enable its rapid removal by hosting service providers, and facilitate cooperation with the competent authorities of other Member States, hosting service providers and, where appropriate, the competent Union bodies. For this purpose, Art. 4 of the draft TERREG provides in particular that the competent national authority is authorized to issue decisions requiring hosting service providers to remove or block terrorist content within one hour. In addition, providers must also take proactive measures to automatically detect and remove terrorist material in certain circumstances or at the instruction of the authority – although recital 5 of the draft emphasizes that the provisions of the ECD, in particular Art. 14, are to remain unaffected. In addition, the establishment of complaint mechanisms, transparency obligations and cooperation mechanisms are envisaged.

Thus, TERREG would not only create detailed regulation related to the online sector, but would also affect the media sector as producers of the distributed content, since when content is removed, freedom of expression or media freedom is also potentially at risk. This risk is addressed in recital 7 of the draft, which states that competent authorities and hosting service providers should only take strictly targeted measures which are necessary, appropriate and proportionate within a democratic society, taking into account the particular importance accorded to the freedom of expression and information, which constitutes one of the essential foundations of a pluralist, democratic society, and is one of the values on which the Union is founded. Hosting service providers are seen as playing a central role in this regard because they facilitate public debate and access to information.[626] Freedom and pluralism of opinion and media are therefore not the direct subject of regulation in the draft TERREG, which is primarily intended to protect public security. However, due to the (potential) impact on these, the limiting function of these goods protected by fundamental rights must also be taken into account in a possible application of TERREG, as the latter itself recognizes in the form of certain safeguard mechanisms. These include, in particular, notification requirements by hosting service providers vis-à-vis authorities and information requirements vis-à-vis content providers when content is blocked or removed, as well as the establish-

---

[626] Cf. on the question of the extent to which the "general public" objective of a content is or can be a link to a media regulation that then takes effect *Cole* in: UFITA 2018, 436, 436 et seq., on TERREG p. 452.

D. Secondary legal framework on "media law" and media pluralism

ment of complaint mechanisms for content providers and the limitation of automated procedures in connection with the review of content.

Similar to the P2B Regulation, however, the scope for maneuver that would be left to the Member States within the regulatory scope of TER-REG is limited – both in terms of the obligations of the providers and the safeguard mechanisms. This is a result not only of the character of TER-REG as a regulation, but also of the design and wording of the individual rules themselves. They rely on appropriate and effective measures by hosting providers to achieve their goals, so that these are largely predetermined and it would be less important to adequately ensure that Member States "implement" these requirements. Due to the character of the Regulation as secondary law of the EU, the level would be on a par with the ECD, so that proactive obligations of the providers, when introduced, would either have to be coordinated with the liability privileges of the ECD, or the Regulation would – also due to its adoption subsequent to the ECD – mean a departure from the rules therein. However, the issue of the relationship would thus be clarified at EU level, whereby the question would then arise as to whether any liability privileges at Member State level could continue to exist in transposition of the ECD or would rather be superseded by higher-ranking Regulation law, directly binding due to the character of this legal act. However, depending on how the process of discussion on the TERREG draft develops, it should be observed that leeway or possibilities for exceptions for the Member States must be explicitly provided for, in particular in the area of safeguard mechanisms to ensure media freedom when removing or blocking content, in order to comply with the distribution of competences in this respect as well. In particular, it would be important to clarify how TERREG would relate to legislative acts at the national level[627] that also provide for procedures to delete certain illegal content, but not limited to terrorist content, in order to protect public safety and order.

---

627 Similar regulations already exist at the level of the Member States, such as the NetzDG in Germany or in France the *Loi visant à lutter contre les contenus haineux sur internet*, Loi n° 2020–766 (http://www.assemblee-nationale.fr/dyn/15/dossiers/lutte_contre_haine_internet), which, however, was declared partially unconstitutional by the French Constitutional Council (decision number 2020–801 DC of 18 June 2020). Nevertheless, many Member States continue to follow the approach, as illustrated, e.g., by the Austrian draft federal law on actions to protect users on communications platforms (https://ec.europa.eu/growth/tools-databases/tris/de/search/?trisaction=search.detail&year=2020&num=544#:~:text=Das%20Bundesgesetz%20%C3%BCber%20Ma%C3%9Fnahmen%20zum,mit%20bestimmten%20rechtswidrigen%20Inhalten%20vor.).

2. Overview of the proposed Digital Services Act

Already when taking up her duties, the new Commission President *Ursula von der Leyen* in her political guidelines announced her intention to make Europe fit for the digital age, under the title "A Union that strives for more". This included the announcement of a new digital services act to regulate liability and security on digital platforms. This intention became more concrete in the Commission's 2020 Work Program[628], in which a legislative proposal for the 4th quarter of 2020 was announced. The proposal was presented by the Commission on 15 December 2020.[629] In its announcement "Shaping Europe's Digital Future", the Commission places the planned actions in the area of digital services in an overall context that also affects content distribution and thus the media sector: It was essential that the rules governing digital services across the EU be strengthened and modernized by clarifying the roles and responsibilities of online platforms, in particular combating the distribution of illegal content online as effectively as offline.[630] The reform measures, now titled the "Digital Services Act package", comprise two main pillars:

First, to propose clear rules that define the responsibilities of digital services to address the risks faced by their users and protect their rights. To this end, a modern system of cooperation in monitoring platforms should in particular also be ensured, thus guaranteeing effective enforcement of

---

628 Communication from the Commission to the European Parliament, the Council, the European Economic and Social Committee and the Committee of the Regions, Commission Work Programme 2020: A Union that strives for more, COM(2020) 37 final, of 28 January 2020, p. 5, adapted against the Corona pandemic background by Communication from the Commission to the European Parliament, the Council, the European Economic and Social Committee and the Committee of the Regions, Adjusted Commission Work Programme 2020, COM(2020) 440 final, vom 27. Mai 2020, available at https://ec.europa.eu/info/p ublications/2020-commission-work-programme-key-documents. With regard to the act on digital services, however, the adjustment of the work program did not result in any changes; cf. p. 2 of the Adjusted Work Programme.
629 https://eur-lex.europa.eu/legal-content/EN/TXT/?uri=CELEX %3A52020PC0825&qid=1614597643982.
630 Communication from the Commission to the European Parliament, the Council, the European Economic and Social Committee and the Committee of the Regions, Shaping Europe's digital future, COM(2020) 67 final, 19 February 2020, https://ec.europa.eu/info/publications/communication-shaping-europes-digital-future, p. 13.

D. Secondary legal framework on "media law" and media pluralism

the new obligations. In its impact assessment[631] on this complex, the Commission identifies in particular the dissemination of illegal content such as child pornography, but also hate speech and copyright infringing material on digital platforms, as well as the use of platforms for targeted disinformation campaigns and propaganda, and the lack of protection of particularly vulnerable Internet users, such as children in particular, as threats in the digital environment that will be addressed under the Digital Services Act package. In addition, the Commission points to information asymmetries between platforms, their users and authorities, as well as the insufficiently effective supervision of platforms. The measures deemed necessary[632], in particular a review of the liability rules of the ECD, are based by the Commission on the legal basis of Art. 114 TFEU. In view of the fundamentally cross-border nature of many digital services and the related risks and opportunities, the adaptation of the rules would have to take place at EU level, as the objectives could not be effectively achieved by any Member State alone.

Second, to propose ex ante rules for large online platforms that act as gatekeepers and can therefore impose requirements on their users equally as they do on competitors. The initiative is intended to ensure that platforms compete fairly so that new entrants and competitors can challenge them in a fair competition. The aim should be that consumers have the widest possible choice and that the internal market remains open to innovation.[633] Risk potentials are seen in existing dominant market positions – also based on considerable power over a large amount of data – of a few platforms, which make it considerably more difficult for smaller platforms to access the market due to closed platform systems and network effects.[634]

---

631 European Commission, Combined evaluation roadmap/inception impact assessment on Digital Services Act package: deepening the Internal Market and clarifying responsibilities for digital services, Ref. Ares(2020)2877686 – 04/06/2020, https://ec.europa.eu/info/law/better-regulation/have-your-say/initiatives/12417-Digital-Services-Act-deepening-the-Internal-Market-and-clarifying-responsibilities-for-digital-services.
632 See on this in detail in chapter F.I.
633 Cf. the announcement of the European Commission, available at https://ec.europa.eu/digital-single-market/en/digital-services-act-package.
634 European Commission, inception impact assessment, Digital Services Act package: Ex ante regulatory instrument for large online platforms with significant network effects acting as gate-keepers in the European Union's internal market, Ref. Ares(2020)2877647 – 04/06/2020, https://ec.europa.eu/info/law/better-regulation/have-your-say/initiatives/12418-Digital-Services-Act-package-ex-ante-regulatory-instrument-of-very-large-online-platforms-acting-as-gatekeepers.

Ex-ante measures[635], which the Commission intends to take in this area, should be based on Art. 114 TFEU. In this context, too, it is pointed out that individual approaches in the Member States do not promise success against the background of the cross-border nature of gatekeeper platforms and their offerings, and could even lead to the contradictory result that it would become even more difficult for startup platforms and smaller undertakings to access the market and compete with existing providers.

In both areas, the Commission had launched a public consultation process that ran until 8 September 2020, the results of which have in the meantime been presented[636]. The impact of the components of the Digital Services Act package on media regulation could be far-reaching. Therefore, based on the interim results of the study, important key points to be considered in the further discussion of the legislative proposals are elaborated below in chapter F.II.

3. Media and Audiovisual Action Plan and European Democracy Action Plan

In its communication "Shaping Europe's Digital Future"[637], the Commission had also announced two further actions for the fourth quarter of 2020, presented on 3 December 2020, that are relevant in the present context, in addition to the specification of the Digital Services Act just mentioned.

First, a Media and Audiovisual Action Plan[638] will help support the digital transformation and competitiveness of the audiovisual and media sector, promote access to quality content and media pluralism. In response to

---

635 See on this in detail in chapter F.I.
636 See on this https://ec.europa.eu/digital-single-market/en/news/summary-report-open-public-consultation-digital-services-act-package.
637 Communication from the Commission to the European Parliament, the Council, the European Economic and Social Committee and the Committee of the Regions, Shaping Europe's digital future, COM(2020) 67 final, 19 February 2020, p. 13 et seq.
638 Communication from the Commission to the European Parliament, the Council, the European Economic and Social Committee and the Committee of the Regions, Europe's Media in the Digital Decade: An Action Plan to Support Recovery and Transformation (Media and Audiovisual Action Plan), COM/2020/784 final.

D. Secondary legal framework on "media law" and media pluralism

a question from the European Parliament[639] the Commissioner responsible, *Thierry Breton*, said that against the backdrop of ongoing convergence, the Commission saw the need for a holistic approach to the media sector, encompassing the legal framework and financial support instruments. In this context, the Commission would seek to present an action plan on the competitiveness and pluralistic diversity of the audiovisual sector and the media. In particular, the Commission intended to focus on the implementation of the AVMSD and smart use of EU financial programs and instruments to support the media and audiovisual sector in the digital transformation. This would be supplemented by the proposed Digital Services Act in relation to combating certain types of illegal content.[640]

Second, a European Democracy Action Plan[641], put forward in December 2020, aims to improve the resilience of democratic societies in the EU, support media pluralism, and counter the dangers of external intervention in European elections. With its Action Plan on Human Rights and Democracy 2020–2024, which continues its predecessor plan for 2015–2019, the EU reaffirms its determination to promote and protect these values worldwide, taking into account political change and new technologies. As key objectives, the Commission emphasizes strengthening EU leadership on human rights and streamlining its decision-making; intensifying partnerships with governments, undertakings and social partners; addressing accountability deficits and preventing the erosion of the rule of law, and identifying areas where new technologies can help strengthen human rights.[642] The legal basis is the affirmation in the TEU that EU external action is guided by the principles which have inspired its own creation, development and enlargement, and which it seeks to advance in the wider world: democracy, the rule of law, the universality and indivisibility of hu-

---

639 Parliamentary question by Petra Kammerevert of 18 December 2019, P-004472/2019, https://www.europarl.europa.eu/doceo/document/P-9-2019-004472_EN.html.
640 Answer to parliamentary question P-004472/2019, Thierry Breton, 14 February 2020, https://www.europarl.europa.eu/doceo/document/P-9-2019-004472-ASW_EN.html.
641 Communication from the Commission to the European Parliament, the Council, the European Economic and Social Committee and the Committee of the Regions, On the European democracy action plan, COM/2020/790 final, https://eur-lex.europa.eu/legal-content/EN/TXT/?uri=CELEX:52020DC0790.
642 Roadmap EU Action Plan on Human Rights and Democracy 2020–2024, Ref. Ares(2020)440026 – 23/01/2020, https://ec.europa.eu/info/law/better-regulation/have-your-say/initiatives/12122-EU-Action-Plan-on-Human-Rights-and-Democracy-2020-2024.

man rights and fundamental freedoms, respect for human dignity, the principles of equality and solidarity, and respect for the principles of the United Nations Charter and public international law. The Action Plan is, however, only intended to complement the policies of the Member States.[643] In a media law context, however, it is interesting to note that the EU's leadership role is also to be strengthened, among other things, where it is a matter of protecting fundamental and human rights with regard to disinformation and the intimidation of and threats to journalists and independent media.[644] Specifically, this shall involve supporting legislative initiatives in the areas of access to information, right to privacy and protection of personal data in line with European and international standards and the effective implementation of these rules; promoting independent media, quality and investigative journalism (including at the local level); and stepping up efforts to combat disinformation, incitement, extremist and terrorist content, including the promotion of online media literacy and digital competence.

Both initiatives operate in an area that is generally reserved for the policies of the Member States. Accordingly, the wording at EU level ("promote", "support", "intensify efforts", etc.) is cautious and located within the competence for support, coordination and supplementary actions in the sense of Art. 6 TFEU. Accordingly, in its Rule of Law Report 2020, the Commission deliberately addresses the areas of media freedom and media diversity only in an observational manner.[645] A restrictive effect on actions at Member State level, in particular in the area of safeguarding media diversity, cannot be derived from this. However, related actions taken by the EU in the areas addressed here, such as combating disinformation and hate speech, show that the concrete initiatives resulting from the Action Plan are not limited to mere support actions, but can, e.g., also take the form of

---

643 Roadmap EU Action Plan on Human Rights and Democracy 2020–2024, Ref. Ares(2020)440026 – 23/01/2020, p. 1.
644 Joint Communication to the European Parliament and the Council, EU Action Plan on Human Rights and Democracy 2020–2024, JOIN(2020) 5 final, 25 March 2020, https://eur-lex.europa.eu/legal-content/EN/TXT/?uri=CELEX%3A52020JC0005&qid=1614597685493.
645 Communication from the Commission to the European Parliament, the Council, the European Economic and Social Committee and the Committee of the Regions, COM(2020) 580 final. The Commission acknowledges in particular the existence of high standards of media freedom and diversity in the Member States, but expresses concerns about the independence and adequate funding (and thus effective performance of duties) of media authorities in some Member States, as well as the existence of threats to journalists.

D. Secondary legal framework on "media law" and media pluralism

a coordination of self-regulation, in the context of which the Commission is endowed with monitoring powers. In the area of combating disinformation, e.g., which is currently largely characterized by the voluntary commitment of platforms to the Code of Practice against Disinformation (on this see chapter D.IV.3) it is to be expected that the Commission will adopt stronger regulatory instruments, for example in the form of co-regulatory mechanisms – a demand that has already been expressed by many parties.[646] This applies not least in areas where existing regulatory means are deemed inadequate.[647]

IV. Links at the level of EU support and coordination actions

The area of supporting, coordinating and supplementary actions at EU level comprises various instruments taken by the European Commission either in the context of exercising its powers under Art. 6 in conjunction with Art. 2(5) TFEU, if the EU does not have a competence to adopt binding legal acts, or to prepare legal acts (subsequently in the form of binding acts) for which it is responsible, for instance under shared competence (Art. 4 TFEU).[648] These (coordinating or preparatory) actions include, i.a., the preparation of "roadmaps" indicating how the Commission intends to address an issue in the future, the establishment of working groups composed of experts and stakeholders, and, finally, the preparation and issuance of recommendations adopted by the legislative bodies as non-binding instruments.

---

646 Cf. e.g. the opinions of ERGA or ACT: ERGA Position Paper on the Digital Services Act, https://erga-online.eu/wp-content/uploads/2020/06/ERGA_SG1_DSA_Position-Paper_adopted.pdf, p. 9; ACT, Feedback on Roadmap on European Democracy Action Plan, 10 August 2020, https://ec.europa.eu/info/law/better-regulation/have-your-say/initiatives/12506-European-Democracy-Action-Plan/F541816, p. 2.
647 Cf. on the code of practice on disinformation, e.g., the study by *VVA*, Assessment on the implementation of the code of practice on disinformation; as well as *ERGA*, Report on disinformation.
648 Under Art. 6, the EU is responsible to carry out actions to support, coordinate or supplement the actions of the Member States, which may also affect the area of culture, without the EU having a competence in this context that would replace the competence of the Member States (Art. 2(5) TFEU), cf. on this supra, chapter B.I.5.e.

Recently, the EU has been active in this area, particularly with regard to the media sector. In addition to the area of protection of minors[649], which has already long been considered in parallel with early regulatory approaches for the online sector, this now relates to combating disinformation as well as hate speech and other illegal content on digital platforms. These two areas will be outlined below, as they offer important links that are also relevant for diversity-safeguarding instruments. This applies both in thematic terms and with regard to specifications for technical regulatory instruments, at least for the area of disinformation. Furthermore, this (preparatory) work provides indications of what future EU regulatory approaches in the platform area might look like. Finally, experience related to self-regulatory mechanisms can also be derived from it.

1. Code of conduct on countering illegal hate speech online

In May 2016, the Commission agreed with Facebook, Microsoft, Twitter, and Google (YouTube) on a "Code of conduct on countering illegal hate speech online" which aims to prevent and combat the spread of illegal hate speech online, help users report illegal hate speech on these platforms, and improve civil society support and coordination with national authorities.[650] In the meantime, Instagram, Snapchat, Dailymotion, Google+, Tik-Tok, and Jeuxvideo.com have also joined this Code, so that almost all[651]

---

649 Cf. on this Recommendation of the European Parliament and of the Council of 20 December 2006 on the protection of minors and human dignity and on the right of reply in relation to the competitiveness of the European audiovisual and on-line information services industry, OJ L 378 of 27.12.2006, p. 72–77; Council Recommendation of 24 September 1998 on the development of the competitiveness of the European audiovisual and information services industry by promoting national frameworks aimed at achieving a comparable and effective level of protection of minors and human dignity, OJ L 270 of 07.10.1998, p. 48–55, in detail und leading further on this *Lievens*, Protecting Children in the Digital Era: The Use of Alternative Regulatory Instruments.
650 Available at https://ec.europa.eu/info/policies/justice-and-fundamental-rights/combatting-discrimination/racism-and-xenophobia/eu-code-conduct-countering-illegal-hate-speech-online_en.
651 In its Assessment of the Code of conduct on hate speech online, State of Play, Progress on combating hate speech online through the EU Code of conduct 2016–2019, the Commission states that this means that 96% of the EU market share of online platforms that may be affected by the illegal content covered are subject to the Code. This did not yet take into account the entry of TikTok (2020) and thus a platform that has recently gained significant market share,

relevant major market players in the EU have thus signed up to it. The Code of conduct builds on the 2008 Council Framework Decision on combating certain forms and expressions of racism and xenophobia by means of criminal law[652] and transfers the principles set out there to the new context of digital offerings. In this context, however, the focus is less on calls for effective criminal law protection against such content directed at states, but rather on the inclusion of service providers through whose offerings users distribute and consume such content.

The Code of conduct primarily addresses the problem that while robust systems exist at the national level to enforce criminal sanctions against individual perpetrators of hate speech, these systems need to be effectively complemented in the online sphere by measures taken by e.g. intermediaries and social networks. Signatories therefore commit to providing clear and effective procedures for reviewing reports of illegal hate speech on their services so that they can remove or block such content. According to the Code of conduct, a review of potentially illegal content should – at least in a majority of cases – take place within 24 hours of a report of such content. In addition, signatories commit to establishing rules or community guidelines that clarify that promoting incitement to violence and hatred is prohibited on these platforms. Other important points concern the announcement made by the signatories to improve the existing information requirements in practical application and to be more transparent to society in general, including by better providing notices to users and labeling content. The Commission evaluates the implementation of the Code "rules" by the signatories on a regular basis.

In its 2016–2019 assessment[653], the Commission concludes that the Code of conduct has helped make progress, in particular in the rapid review and removal of hate speech (on average, 72 % of reported content was removed in 2019 across all providers, compared to 28 % in 2016; 89 % of reported content was reviewed within 24 hours in 2019, compared to 40 % in 2016). The Code had strengthened trust and cooperation between IT

---

https://ec.europa.eu/info/sites/info/files/aid_development_cooperation_fundamental_rights/assessment_of_the_code_of_conduct_on_hate_speech_on_line_-_state_of_play__0.pdf.

652 Council Framework Decision 2008/913/JHA of 28 November 2008 on combating certain forms and expressions of racism and xenophobia by means of criminal law, OJ L 328 of 06.12.2008, p. 55–58, https://eur-lex.europa.eu/legal-content/EN/TXT/?uri=CELEX%3A32008F0913.

653 Assessment of the Code of conduct on hate speech online, State of Play, Progress on combating hate speech online through the EU Code of conduct 2016–2019.

undertakings, civil society organizations and Member States' authorities in the form of a structured process of mutual learning and knowledge sharing. However, the Commission believes that platforms need to further improve their feedback to users reporting content and provide more transparency overall.

Despite this fundamentally positive assessment of the impact of the Code of conduct by the Commission, it should be emphasized that it is not binding and that the signatories have only committed themselves voluntarily. Withdrawal from this agreement is possible unilaterally at any time. As such, it differs decisively from a legally binding regulation as in the German Network Enforcement Act[654] despite its in many respects similar approach. The Code of conduct also does neither contain any mechanisms for enforcing the law nor any sanctions[655]. This also applies to the data provided by participating providers, which form the basis for the Commission's evaluation reports. In this context, it is not clear what data must be made available and access to the data can be unilaterally restricted at any time.

The Code of conduct assumes that the parties involved are committed to freedom of expression, and it emphasizes the particular significance of protecting this fundamental right, but apart from information requirements vis-à-vis users, there are no explicit safeguard mechanisms for the (unjustified) blocking or deletion of content. This can be problematic, especially because of the very broad definition of illegal hate speech in the Code. In addition, concerns similar to those expressed about the German Network Enforcement Act[656], are raised about the Code, according to which in particular there was a lack of procedural guarantees, the risk of overblocking was increased, and the assessment of the illegality of content was left to the platforms' own responsibility.[657] However, the Code does not in itself have a suspensory effect on or limit measures taken by the Member States against illegal content, whether in the form of binding laws or comparable approaches to voluntary commitment in the form of soft

---

654 Cf. on this in detail chapter E.V.1.a.
655 The publication of the assessments by the Commission could at most be understood as a kind of "moral sanction".
656 Cf. on this in detail chapter E.V.1.a.
657 For critical evaluation cf. in particular *Bukovská*, The European Commission's Code of Conduct for Countering Illegal Hate Speech Online.

D. Secondary legal framework on "media law" and media pluralism

law. However, the evaluations and potentially best practices[658] resulting from the platforms' collaboration can be harnessed in the political process.

2. Tackling illegal content online

In the context of tackling illegal content online, it is also important to take into account the respective Communication published by the Commission in 2017[659], which subsequently led to Commission Recommendation (EU) 2018/334[660].

The initial Communication established a set of guidelines and principles for online platforms (in particular hosting services as defined in Art. 14 ECD) aimed at facilitating and intensifying the implementation of best practices to prevent, detect, remove and block access to illegal content. Accordingly, the aim is to ensure the effective removal of illegal content, increased transparency and the protection of fundamental rights also in the online sector. Furthermore, platforms should be given more legal certainty about their liability if they take proactive measures to detect, remove or block access to illegal content ("good samaritan measures").[661] The Communication calls for online platforms to systematically strengthen their cooperation with competent authorities in Member States, while the latter should ensure that courts are able to respond effectively to illegal content online, and facilitate greater (cross-border) cooperation between authorities. In this regard, online platforms and law enforcement or other

---

[658] Cf. on this also the inclusion of and the work of the High Level Group on combating racism, xenophobia and other forms of intolerance, on this https://ec.europa.eu/newsroom/just/item-detail.cfm?item_id=51025.

[659] Communication from the Commission to the European Parliament, the Council, the European Economic and Social Committee and the Committee of the Regions, Tackling Illegal Content Online, Towards an enhanced responsibility of online platforms, COM(2017) 555 final, of 28 September 2017, https://eur-lex.europa.eu/legal-content/EN/TXT/?uri=CELEX%3A52017D-C0555&qid=1613064172613.

[660] Commission Recommendation (EU) 2018/334 of 1 March 2018 on measures to effectively tackle illegal content online, C/2018/1177, OJ L 63 of 06.03.2018, p. 50–61, https://eur-lex.europa.eu/legal-content/EN/ALL/?uri=CELEX%3A32018H0334.

[661] The Commission's position here is that proactive measures taken by these online platforms to detect and remove illegal content they host – including the use of automated tools and resources to ensure that previously removed content is not re-uploaded – do not in and of themselves result in a loss of immunity from liability.

competent authorities should designate effective contact points in the EU and, where appropriate, establish digital interfaces to facilitate their interaction. In addition, the Commission promotes transparency, close cooperation between online platforms and so-called trusted flaggers, and the establishment of easily accessible and user-friendly mechanisms that allow users to report content deemed illegal. It also aims to promote the application of automatic filters against content re-uploads and procedures for counter-notifications.

The subsequent recommendation on tackling illegal content online, which takes up the descriptive approach from the prior Communication in a somewhat streamlined manner by translating it into the form of (more) concrete (but still legally non-binding) rules, is particularly interesting with regard to two aspects: firstly, the first section contains a list of definitions that are closely aligned with existing EU directives – such as the definition of "hosting service provider". "Illegal content" is defined here as "any information which is not in compliance with Union law or the law of a Member State concerned". On the other hand, the Recommendation focuses on cooperation between hosting service providers and Member States (e.g., regarding designated points of contact for matters relating to illegal content online and the provision of fast-track procedures to process notices submitted by competent authorities), (other) trusted flaggers (e.g. providing fast-track procedures to process notices submitted by certified experts, publishing clear and objective conditions for designating such specially highlighted internet referral units), and with other hosting service providers (e.g. by sharing experience, technological solutions and best practices).

The two documents contain – without being legally binding – a wide range of possible regulatory and technical measures for tackling illegal content online. Therefore, they are taken up in connection with legislative projects such as the proposals for TERREG or the Digital Services Act.[662]

---

662 Cf. e.g. Deutscher Bundestag, Kurzinformation Follow-up zur Empfehlung der Europäischen Kommission für wirksame Maßnahmen im Umgang mit illegalen Online-Inhalten, https://www.bundestag.de/resource/blob/571506/df067279aaaa 45b3e95efae57f5194f2/PE-6-125-18-pdf-data.pdf; *Hoffmann/Gasparotti*, Liability for illegal content online, p. 23 et seq.; *Chapuis-Doppler/Delhomme* in: European papers 5(2020)1, 411, 426.

D. Secondary legal framework on "media law" and media pluralism

3. Code of Practice on Disinformation

At the EU level, measures to combat online disinformation took concrete shape, also in response to a European Parliament resolution, in the establishment of a High Level Group on Fake News and Online Disinformation in 2018. Following an investigation, it provided its assessment in a report[663], on the basis of which the Commission in turn drafted its Communication on tackling online disinformation[664] and published it in April 2018.[665] Therein, the Commission argues that economic, technological, political and ideological circumstances were the cause of the spread of disinformation. This included, e.g., the rise of platforms in the media sector, which in turn influenced the "more traditional" media in that they (have to) look for new ways to monetize their content, as well as the creation of new or the manipulation of existing technologies in the area of social networks that enable or at least facilitate the spread of disinformation. Against this background, the Commission concluded that the fight against disinformation could and would only be successful in the long term if it was accompanied by a clear political will to strengthen collective resilience and support democratic efforts and European values. In addition, on 5 December 2018, the Commission and the High Representative for Foreign Affairs and Security Policy presented an Action Plan against Disinformation[666], proposing concrete actions to tackling disinformation, including setting up an early warning system, facilitating the exchange of data between Member States, and providing additional funding for media literacy projects.

The measures proposed under the Action Plan also include closer monitoring of the implementation of a self-regulatory instrument that had been established just a few weeks earlier, and an increase in the resources re-

---

663 *De Cock Buning et al.*, Report of the independent High level Group on fake news and online disinformation.
664 Communication from the Commission to the European Parliament, the Council, the European Economic and Social Committee and the Committee of the Regions, Tackling online disinformation: a European Approach, COM/2018/236 final, https://eur-lex.europa.eu/legal-content/EN/TXT/?uri=CELEX%3A52018DC0236.
665 On the whole process cf. in detail *Ukrow/Etteldorf*, Fake News als Rechtsproblem.
666 Joint Communication to the European Parliament, the European Council, the Council, the European Economic and Social Committee and the Committee of the Regions, Action Plan against Disinformation, JOIN(2018) 36 final, of 05.12.2018, https://eur-lex.europa.eu/legal-content/EN/TXT/?uri=CELEX%3A52018JC0036&qid=1613115235976.

quired for this purpose: the need for action seen by the Commission in the area of disinformation resulted in September 2018 in a Code of Practice on Disinformation (CPD)[667], which representatives of online platforms, leading social networks, and the advertising and platform industry agreed on with the Commission.[668] The CPD – while explicitly referring to the liability privileges under the ECD, which remain unaffected by this – sets out a wide range of (self-)obligations, ranging from transparency in political advertising to blocking fake accounts and demonetarizing the spreaders of disinformation. It includes commitments regarding the review of ad placements, political and topic-related advertising, the integrity of services, and the empowerment of consumers and the research community. With regard to monitoring effectiveness, the signatories undertake to publish an annual report on the actions they have taken in connection with combating disinformation. The Code also contains an appendix listing best practices that signatories commit to apply in order to implement the Code's provisions. In the area of advertising policy, stakeholders profess an effort to counter disinformation by applying "follow-the-money" approaches[669] and preventing disseminators of disinformation from benefiting financially. In the area of political advertising, online platforms are developing solutions to increase the transparency of such advertising and allow consumers to understand why they are seeing a particular ad. The platforms further announce plans to develop tools to enable civil society to better understand the online political advertising ecosystem. Platforms further want to try to protect the integrity of the services by applying policies that limit abuse of their service by inauthentic users or accounts, such as policies that limit the creation of fake profiles.[670] Finally, to put consumers and researchers in a better position, platforms announce they will provide users with information, tools, and support to empower consumers online. This is to include complaint and reporting systems.

---

667 Code of Practice on Disinformation, available at https://ec.europa.eu/digital-single-market/en/news/code-practice-disinformation.
668 Incl. Facebook, Twitter, Mozilla, Google, Microsoft and TikTok, cf. https://ec.europa.eu/digital-single-market/en/news/roadmaps-implement-code-practice-disinformation.
669 The "follow the money" approach generally aims to cut revenues from infringements. The Commission has committed to such an approach in its Communication on a Digital Single Market Strategy, which aims to reduce the revenue streams that monetize IPR infringement.
670 E.g. YouTube Policy on impersonation, https://support.google.com/youtube/answer/2801947?hl=en-GB.

D. Secondary legal framework on "media law" and media pluralism

From the best practices listed, it can be seen that the initiatives in the area of disinformation focus primarily on the areas of (misleading) advertising and election and political advertising. That disinformation can pose considerable dangers in other areas as well, however, was demonstrated by developments in the Corona pandemic. The abundance of circulating misinformation, which has led to considerable uncertainty in society, has prompted the Commission (together with the High Representative for Foreign Affairs and Security Policy) to also publish a specific communication on tackling disinformation in the context of COVID-19.[671] Therein, measures from the previous initiatives are taken up and specified once again, with a particular focus on transparency, cooperation and communication as a means of tackling (corona) disinformation. This could also play a role in the context of the proposed Digital Services Act.[672] On the other hand, the pandemic has also shown that platforms are quite capable, both actually and technically, of taking actions to tackle misinformation.[673] Certain conclusions can be drawn from this about the influence that these providers can exert.

Disinformation also plays a role in the context of safeguarding diversity, as the aforementioned Covid communication from the Commission points out: free and pluralistic media are central to tackling disinformation and providing fact-based information to citizens.[674] Even though disinformation can also be observed in countries with a pluralistically structured media landscape, disinformation without such plurality may have a particularly dangerous effect on the freedom of information and the formation

---

671 Joint Communication to the European Parliament, the European Council, the Council, the European Economic and Social Committee and the Committee of the Regions, Tackling COVID-19 disinformation – Getting the facts right, JOIN(2020) 8 final, of 10.06.2020, https://eur-lex.europa.eu/legal-content/EN/TXT/?uri=CELEX%3A52020JC0008&qid=1613118073016.
672 Cf. on this e.g. Draft report with recommendations to the Commission on Digital Services Act: Improving the functioning of the Single Market (2020/2018(INL)) of 24.04.2020, no. 11 et seq., in which in particular the problem of disinformation on Covid-19 in the field of transparency regulations is addressed.
673 E.g., the search engine service Google listed information from the World Health Organization above all other search results and in a visually separated manner for search queries related to Corona or disease symptoms. Videos from specialist institutions were also visibly listed on the YouTube homepage.
674 Joint Communication to the European Parliament, the European Council, the Council, the European Economic and Social Committee and the Committee of the Regions, Tackling COVID-19 disinformation – Getting the facts right, JOIN(2020) 8 final, of 10.06.2020, p. 13.

of opinion and thus intensify the related risks. Such disinformation undermines trust in political institutions and in digital and traditional media. It damages the democratic process because citizens can no longer make informed decisions.[675]

Although the CPD, like the code of conduct on hate speech, is nonbinding, it is more detailed and contains stronger wording and more specific requirements. However, again, there are no enforcement mechanisms or sanctions. A degree of monitoring is done at least externally through the reports. Both compliance with the CPD rules and the provision of the relevant data by undertakings to allow third parties to verify the activities are nevertheless currently merely voluntary and cannot be required by any authority or sanctioned in the event of non-availability or non-compliance. The resulting assessment problems were outlined by the association of Member States' regulatory bodies, the ERGA as provided for in the AVMSD, which was asked by the Commission to act as an advisory body to support the monitoring of the effectiveness of the implementation of the CPD rules, in its Report of the activities carried out to assist the European Commission in the intermediate monitoring of the Code of practice on disinformation as follows: "The platforms were not in a position to meet a request to provide access to the overall database of advertising, even on a limited basis, during the monitoring period. This was a significant constraint on the monitoring process and emerging conclusions"[676]. Also in its final report for 2019, ERGA concludes that more transparency was needed, in particular by providing more detailed data to assess the effectiveness of activities, and therefore suggests that platforms should provide datasets, data monitoring tools, and country-specific information that enables independent monitoring by national regulators. In addition, it is also pointed out in this context that many activities provided for in the CPD are very general in their wording, which would lead to very different implementation by the signatories. While the current self-regulatory model had proven to be an important and necessary first step, more effective action needed to be taken against disinformation on the Internet, for example by establishing a co-regulatory approach.[677] The Commission also picked up on these points in its final evaluation in 2020, although it did

---

675 *Ukrow* in: Cappello (ed.) media pluralism and competition issues, p. 10.
676 *ERGA*, Report of the activities carried out to assist the European Commission in the intermediate monitoring of the Code of Practice on Disinformation, 2019, p. 3, übersetzt aus dem Englischen.
677 *ERGA*, Report on Disinformation, 2020.

D. Secondary legal framework on "media law" and media pluralism

not address specific future actions to respond to the shortcomings found.[678]

The Commission's activities with regard to disinformation fit in with the projects in the area of the European Democracy Action Plan outlined in chapter D.III.3.

V. Conclusions and deductions on the regulatory competence for media pluralism

Two things follow from current and developing EU secondary law, as well as from other EU actions and initiatives at the level of both coordination and support:

First, there are no rules or initiatives at this level that directly address the issue of safeguarding media pluralism or that set out guidelines with this goal in mind (alone), which would already be impossible for competence reasons. Rather, secondary law respects the regulatory power of the Member States in the area of media and diversity protection law by containing cultural policy exceptions that leave the Member States a broad scope for constitutional considerations, or by not including cultural policy aspects in the respective coordinated field. This applies both to legal acts that directly address the media, as shown by the exceptions in the AVMSD in the area of audiovisual media services and VSP, and to such secondary law that has a business-oriented and thus not media- and culture-related objective, as shown, e.g., by the possibility under the EECC to enact must-carry provisions or the ECMR with regard to options under media concentration law. The fact that more media-related projects, such as tackling hate speech and disinformation, which are relevant in particular in the context of freedom of expression protected by fundamental rights, are being shifted to the level of coordination and support action based on self-regulatory mechanisms shows that the EU respects this area of Member State sovereignty. This corresponds to the limitation of the EU's support competence to the effect that support action must not prejudice the Member States' exercise of regulatory leeway.

---

678 Assessment of the Code of Practice on Disinformation – Achievements and areas for further improvement, SWD(2020) 180 final, of 10.09.2020, https://ec.europa.eu/transparency/regdoc/rep/10102/2020/EN/SWD-2020-180-F1-EN-MAIN-PART-1.PDF.

Secondly, there are nevertheless links for safeguarding diversity in secondary law outside of the scope of discretion and exceptions for the Member States. In particular, this applies to the AVMSD, for example, in the context of the rules on the promotion of European works or the promotion of media literacy, although these are at least also justified by economic considerations. The P2B Regulation also contains elements that are likely to be relevant to safeguarding pluralism when it comes to discoverability of content and quality journalism. In particular, however, developments in the context of this Regulation indicate that media-related aspects will also play a role in a regulatory framework based on competition law, possibly through specifications in the Commission's guidelines. This approach of increasingly incorporating cultural policy aspects into regulation is a trend that has recently become more apparent at the level of secondary law and in sub-legislative initiatives than before. This creates a risk that the tension in relation to national regulations enacted with the aim of safeguarding diversity could intensify in the future.

E. Core problems of public international law regarding the regulation of the "media sector" with respect to possible tensions with EU law

Jörg Ukrow[679]

I. Introduction

In the age of digitization and globalization, media regulation is not exclusively a regulatory system in the area of conflict between regulatory options and requirements under Member States' and EU law. Member States' and the EU's regulatory efforts must also comply with the (in particular human rights) standards set for the respective actors by international treaties. In terms of content, these standards can originate in treaties under public international law with a claim of universal validity – such as the International Covenants on Human Rights[680] –, with a claim of regional validity – such as the ECHR – or with a regional starting point but a global opening in terms of the possibility of participation – as in the case of the Council of Europe's Cybercrime Convention[681]. In the context of this study, however, questions of competences arise first and foremost: under what conditions may the EU or its Member States include in their regulation media actors who cannot be assigned to the EU's legal sphere qua affiliation, as established, e.g., by the nationality or domicile of an actor?

The worldwide expansion of transmission and dissemination possibilities for media establishes global impact risks of the behavior of media content providers as well as of infrastructure actors who influence the aggregation, selection, presentation and perceptibility of media content. Such risks

---

679 The following Chapter E ties in with earlier considerations in an unpublished expert opinion as well as the study by *Ukrow/Cole*, Aktive Sicherung lokaler und regionaler Medienvielfalt – Rechtliche Möglichkeiten und Grenzen der Förderung inhaltlicher Qualität in Presse-, Rundfunk- und Online-Angeboten.
680 Cf. Art. 19 and 20 International Covenant on Civil and Political Rights of 19 December 1966 (BGBl. 1973 II, p. 1553); Art. 15 International Covenant on Economic, Social and Cultural Rights of 19 December 1966 (BGBl. 1973 II, p. 1569).
681 Convention on Cybercrime of 23.11.2001, SEV-no. 185, entry into force in Germany on 01.07.2009 (BGBl. 2008 II, p. 1242); on this *Fink* in: ZaöRV 2014, 505, 506 et seq.

arise in a particular way in a situation in which concentration tendencies can be observed both among receivers for audiovisual media content and among media intermediaries, be they search engines or social networks – in the latter case in particular as a result of the network effects of digital platform economies.[682] As the international media market is increasingly characterized by an oligopoly of globally operating, structurally connected corporations, the question arises for both the EU and its Member States as to how to design media regulation in conformity with public international law, which also wants to include such transnationally operating players with globally oriented business models in regulation.

II. Addressees of regulation

1. Introduction

When considering the personal scope of regulation of the "media sector", in addition to the limits imposed by EU law on access to persons and undertakings not resident or domiciled in the regulating EU Member State on the basis of the principle of country-of-origin control, the limits imposed by public international law on regulation *ratione personae* must also be taken into account.[683]

In connection with the question of whether media regulation by Member States or the EU may also have access to (EU) foreign providers, the question also arises as to the extent to which such regulatory acts of a legislative, executive or judicial nature, depending on the legal personality of

---

682 Cf. on this e.g. *KEK*, Sicherung der Meinungsvielfalt im digitalen Zeitalter, p. 429 et seq.; *Lobigs/Neuberger*, Meinungsmacht im Internet und die Digitalstrategien von Medienunternehmen, p. 34 et seq.; *Neuberger/Lobigs*, Die Bedeutung des Internets im Rahmen der Vielfaltssicherung, p. 27 et seq.

683 The question of whether the German regulatory authorities (i.e., the body acting on behalf of the competent state media authorities in accordance with the provisions of the MStV and the JMStV) are competent to also take action against foreign providers for infringement of the substantive provisions of the MStV and/or the JMStV must be answered by interpretation of the MStV and the JMStV in accordance with the classical methods of semantic, systematic, teleological and historical interpretation (cf. on this e.g. *Larenz/Canaris*, Methodenlehre der Rechtswissenschaft, p. 133 et seq.; *Lodzig*, Grundriss einer verantwortlichen Interpretationstheorie des Rechts, p. 25 et seq.; *Potacs*, Rechtstheorie, p. 153 et seq.). The result reached thereby must then be tested against the standards of an interpretation in conformity with European and public international law.

E. Core problems of public international law

the provider, are also bound by fundamental rights – whether of the Basic Law, in particular the constitutional freedom of broadcasting of Art. 5(1) sentence 2 Basic Law, or of the European fundamental rights regime.[684]

2. Public international law framework for addressing foreign providers

a. Addressing foreign providers from the perspective of the imperative of interpreting national and EU law in a manner open to public international law

The Basic Law has programmatically committed German state authority to international cooperation (Art. 24) and to European integration (Art. 23). It has given the general rules of public international law precedence over ordinary statutory law (Art. 25 sentence 2) and, through Art. 59(2), has placed international treaty law within the system of separation of powers. It has also opened the possibility of integration into systems of mutual collective security (Art. 24(2)), mandated the peaceful settlement of interstate disputes through arbitration (Art. 24(3)), and declared the disturbance of the peace, in particular war of aggression, unconstitutional (Art. 26).

With this set of norms, the German constitution aims, also according to its preamble, to integrate the Federal Republic of Germany as a peaceful and equal member of an international legal order, committed to peace, into the community of states. All this is an expression of the fact that the Basic Law is open to public international law, which promotes the exercise of state sovereignty through international treaty law and international cooperation as well as the incorporation of the general rules of public international law. It is therefore to be interpreted as far as possible in such a way that a conflict with obligations of the Federal Republic of Germany under public international law does not arise.[685]

The Basic Law, however, has not gone the furthest in opening up to public international law commitments. International treaty law is not to be treated directly, i.e. without an approving act under Art. 59(2) Basic Law, as applicable law and – like international customary law (cf. Art. 25

---

[684] The question of the competence of the EU and/or its Member States to take regulatory actions, dealt with in this chapter, must be clearly distinguished from the question of a possible obligation to take action, which could follow not least from state obligations to protect. This obligation dimension of the question of action against foreign providers is discussed in chapter E.IV.

[685] BVerfGE 63, 343 (370); 111, 307 (317 et seq.).

Basic Law) – is not endowed with the status of constitutional law. The Basic Law is clearly based on the classical notion that the relationship between public international law and national law is one between two different legal spheres and that the nature of this relationship from the perspective of national law can only be determined by national law itself. This is shown by the existence and wording of Art. 25 and 59(2) Basic Law. Openness to public international law unfolds its effect only within the framework of the democratic and constitutional system of the Basic Law.[686]

The Basic Law does neither order the subjection of the German legal order to the international one nor the unconditional primacy of public international law over constitutional law. It does, however, seek to "increase respect for international organisations that preserve peace and freedom, and for public international law, without giving up the final responsibility for respect for human dignity and for the observance of fundamental rights by German state authority". This corresponds to a "duty to respect public international law, a duty that arises from the fact that the Basic Law is open to public international law".[687]

However, not only the German constitutional legal order, but also the legal order of the EU as a *sui generis* entity[688] is characterized by an openness to public international law.[689] Since this system of integration has its starting point, as well as its further development under primary law, in a series of founding acts under public international law, a certain openness to public international law is inherent in the EU from its very roots. In the TEU, this openness to public international law is confirmed not least in Art. 3(5) sentence 2 and Art. 21(1). In the TFEU, openness to public international law is reinforced by its Art. 216(2).

- According to Art. 3(5) sentence 2 TEU, the EU "shall contribute [...] to the strict observance and the development of international law, including respect for the principles of the United Nations Charter"".
- According to Art. 21(1) TEU, the EU's action on the international scene shall be guided by "the principles which have inspired its own creation, development and enlargement, and which it seeks to advance in the

---

[686] BVerfGE 111, 307 (318).
[687] BVerfGE 112, 1 (25 et seq.).
[688] Cf. on this BVerfGE 22, 293 (296).
[689] Cf. on this also *Schriewer*, Zur Theorie der internationalen Offenheit und der Völkerrechtsfreundlichkeit einer Rechtsordnung und ihrer Erprobung am Beispiel der EU-Rechtsordnung, p. 127 et seq.

E. Core problems of public international law

wider world", including "respect for the principles of the United Nations Charter and international law".
- According to Art. 216(2) TFEU, "[a]greements concluded by the Union are binding upon the institutions of the Union and on its Member States".

The "openness of the state"[690] and the "openness to international law" of the Basic Law, i.e. the opening of the German legal order to public international law, can be derived not least from the preamble and Art. 23 to 26 of the Basic Law. In this respect, particular significance is attached to Art. 25, which reads:

"The general rules of international law shall be an integral part of federal law. They shall take precedence over the laws and directly create rights and duties for the inhabitants of the federal territory."

Art. 25 sentence 1 Basic Law issues a general command to apply the law. This provision has the consequence that "the general rules of international law find their way into the German legal order without a transformation law, i.e. directly, and take precedence over German domestic law".[691] The "general rules of international law" within the meaning of Art. 25 Basic Law include customary international law, including *ius cogens*, as well as the recognized general principles of law within the meaning of Art. 38(1) (c) ICJ Statute.[692]

These general rules of public international law also include the principle of the sovereign equality of states, described in the following, which today has found an enshrinement in international treaties (and an interpretation in the Friendly Relations Declaration[693]), in particular in Art. 2 No. 1

---

690 Cf. on this e.g. *di Fabio*, Das Recht offener Staaten; *Fassbender*, Der offene Bundesstaat; *Giegerich*, Der „offene Verfassungsstaat" des Grundgesetzes nach 60 Jahren; *Häberle*, Der kooperative Verfassungsstaat, 141, 141 et seq.; *Hobe*, Der offene Verfassungsstaat zwischen Souveränität und Interdependenz; *Schorkopf*, Grundgesetz und Überstaatlichkeit; *Sommermann*, Offene Staatlichkeit: Deutschland, 3, 3 et seq.; *Vogel*, Die Verfassungsentscheidung des Grundgesetzes für die internationale Zusammenarbeit, p. 42.
691 BVerfGE 6, 309 (363).
692 Cf. e.g. *Talmon* in: JZ 2013, 12, 13.
693 UN Declaration on Principles of International Law concerning Friendly Relations and Cooperation among States of 24.10.1970, International Legal Materials, 9 (1970), p. 1292 (also available at http://www.un-documents.net/a25r2625.htm).

UN Charter.⁶⁹⁴ The traditionally cited contents of the principle of sovereign equality are that no state should be subject to international legal obligations against its will and that no state is to be judged by the courts of other states (*par in parem non habet iudicium*).⁶⁹⁵ The territorial and personal sovereignty of states⁶⁹⁶ are direct manifestations of their sovereignty, the prohibition of intervention serves to protect sovereignty by prohibiting other states from interfering in their internal affairs.⁶⁹⁷

The obligation to strictly comply with public international law pursuant to Art. 3(5) sentence 2 TEU also includes the preservation of limitations of jurisdiction under customary international law – in this case of the EU. This also follows from CJEU case law, according to which the EU must exercise its regulatory powers, in particular also its legislative powers, in compliance with public international law, including the rules of customary international law.⁶⁹⁸ However, this limitation applies not only to legislative but also to executive action of the EU, which may also be significant, for example, with regard to obligations under international law to protect cultural diversity, such as those arising from the UNESCO Convention in this regard.⁶⁹⁹

It is indisputable that enforcement measures taken by state media authorities on the basis of the MStV and/or the JMStV constitute sovereign acts from a public international law perspective, just as, for example, the EU Commission's competition supervision. For the corresponding qualification, it is not relevant whether the action in question has a coercive character.⁷⁰⁰ Independent of such a coercive character is also the qualification of the measure with regard to the question of an infringement of the territorial sovereignty of a state. For a possible infringement of this territorial sovereignty by acts of a state or the EU on foreign territory or by measures

---

694 Cf. on this e.g. *Dombrowski*, Extraterritoriale Strafrechtsanwendung im Internet, p. 5; *Epping* in: Ipsen, § 5, para. 254 et seq.; *Kau* in: *Graf Vitzthum/Proelß*, Dritter Abschnitt, para. 87 et seq.
695 Cf. *Baker*, The Doctrine of Legal Equality of States, 1, 11 et seq.; *Kokott* in: ZaöRV 2004, 517, 519.
696 Cf. on this e.g. *Bertele*, Souveränität und Verfahrensrecht, p. 65 et seq.
697 Cf. e.g. *Stein/Buttlar/Kotzur*, Völkerrecht, p. 194 et seq.
698 Cf. CJEU, case C-162/96, *Racke / Hauptzollamt Mainz*, para. 45 et seq.
699 On 18 December 2006, the EU ratified the UNESCO Convention on the Protection and Promotion of the Diversity of Cultural Expressions, which was also ratified in Germany. One of the main reasons for the EU's involvement is that the areas covered by the Convention relate in part to EU and in part to Member State competences. Cf. on this *Klamert* in: ZöR 2009, 217, 217 et seq.
700 Cf. also BVerfGE 63, 343 (372).

E. Core problems of public international law

with extraterritorial effect cannot legally cease to exist by the fact that a coercive character of the act or measure is eliminated by the consent of the private party concerned. This is because imperatives of public international law, such as respect for territorial sovereignty, are not at the disposition of private parties.[701]

However, immanent limitations on the scope of Art. 25 Basic Law and Art. 3(5) sentence 2 TEU also arise from public international law itself with regard to the requirement of respect for the territorial sovereignty of a third state.[702] Insofar as public international law sets limits on the validity or application of customary international law, this also limits its domestic application. In this respect, the FCC has held that a general rule of public international law becomes part of federal law only "with its respective scope under international law".[703] As will be shown in detail below, the applicable public international law does not (any longer) contain any principle that national or EU administrative law, be it media law such as the law on the protection of minors from harmful media or media consumer protection law of Member States, be it competition supervision law of the EU, may not also be applied to foreign-related content.[704]

In this respect, it is also significant from a constitutional and EU law perspective that public international law also recognizes the jurisdiction of the state or community of states on whose territory the impact of conduct carried out in a third state occurs. This objective territoriality principle, which has clear parallels to the effects doctrine in antitrust law,[705] will also be examined below in terms of its significance for extraterritorially effective German media regulation.

---

701 Cf. *Dombrowski*, Extraterritoriale Strafrechtsanwendung im Internet, p. 10 et seq.; *Geck* in: Strupp/Schlochauer p. 795 et seq.; *Germann*, Gefahrenabwehr und Strafverfolgung im Internet, p. 642; *Okresek* in: ÖZöRV 1985, 325, 339 et seq.; *Schmidt*, Die Rechtmäßigkeit staatlicher Gefahrenabwehrmaßnahmen im Internet, p. 264; *Valerius*, Ermittlungen der Strafverfolgungsbehörden in den Kommunikationsdiensten des Internet, p. 147.
702 Cf. BVerfGE 15, 25 (34 et seq.); 23, 288 (317); 94, 315 (328); 95, 96 (129); 96, 68 (86); 112, 1 (25, 27 et seq.) as well as e.g. *Talmon* in: JZ 2013, 12, 12.
703 BVerfGE 46, 342 (403) (own translation). Cf. also BVerfGE 18, 441 (448); 23, 288 (316 et seq.).
704 Cf. on this e.g. *Schmidt*, Die Rechtmäßigkeit staatlicher Gefahrenabwehrmaßnahmen, p. 257.
705 Cf. *Fox* in: JILP 2009/2010, 159, 160, 167, 174; *Staker* in: Evans, International Law, p. 309 (316 et seq.); *Oxman* in: MPEPIL, 546, 550; *Uerpmann-Wittzack* in: GLJ 2010, 1245, 1254.

b. Public international law limitations on a state's power to legislate and enforce with respect to foreign providers

An important component of state sovereignty in the sense of public international law[706] is the control, understood as territorial sovereignty, over all sovereign powers exercised on the territory of the state. The own territory literally remains the fundamental element of a state. The division and legal order of the world under public international law is to date based on territoriality.[707] However, this territorial sovereignty is accompanied by a responsibility recognized under customary international law, prohibiting a state from allowing its territory to be used to cause harm on the territory of another state.[708] From this, at least in individual cases, a duty of the state to extraterritorially respect and protect human rights is derived in public international law doctrine.[709] This indicates a changing concept of sovereignty in public international law, which is not limited to a negative defensive side, but also understands sovereignty as responsibility. Understood in this way, sovereignty requires the assumption of duties for the protection of central common goods, even where it is a matter of defending against violations of protected goods by private parties.[710]

---

706 Sovereignty in the sense of public international law is the state's legal capacity to act internally and externally, which is not derived from or dependent on anyone and is only limited in certain respects by restrictions arising from the basic order of public international law (minimum requirements for minimal human rights protection, prohibition of slavery, etc.), but is otherwise unrestricted. Sovereignty includes in particular the right and legal power to freely choose and shape the political, economic and social order, as well as the free choice and implementation – and responsibility – of one's own solutions to all factual problems arising for the political community and, finally, the free choice and exercise – or, if necessary, restriction – of contacts with other states and international and supranational organizations; cf. on the concept of sovereignty under public international law e.g. *von Arnauld*, Völkerrecht, para. 89 et seq., 312 et seq.
707 The territorial competences of the state are expressed in its territorial sovereignty, i.e. the (regulatory) authority in the territory, and in its territorial sovereignty, i.e. the (dispositive) authority over the territory. In state practice, the two can diverge when it comes to the exercise of sovereignty on foreign territory; cf. *Gornig/Horn*, Territoriale Souveränität und Gebietshoheit, p. 21 et seq., 35 et seq.
708 Cf. Trail Smelter Case (U.S. / Canada), in: Reports of International Arbitral Awards, 16 April 1938 and 11 March 1941, 1905 (1941), https://legal.un.org/riaa/cases/vol_III/1905-1982.pdf.
709 Cf. *de Schutter et al.* in: Human Rights Quarterly 2012, 1084, 1169, 1095 et seq.
710 Cf. *Seibert-Fohr* in: ZaöRV 2013, 37, 59 et seq.

With regard to protected interests such as human dignity and the protection of minors, the prohibition of intervention under public international law has proved to be similarly open to development and increasingly characterized by a shift, still in the process of development, from a classic, purely state-centered dogmatics of defense to a dogmatics of responsibility. This prohibition of interference by states in the internal affairs of other states is one of the principles constituting the international legal order. Although it is not explicitly enshrined in the UN Charter,[711] it is indisputably recognized – also beyond regional codifications – as a provision of customary international law.

For the understanding of this provision, the so-called *Friendly Relations Declaration* of the UN is of particular significance. It goes back to the *Declaration on the Inadmissibility of Intervention in the Domestic Affairs of States and on their Independence and Sovereignty* of 21.12.1965.[712] Accordingly, the principle implies the duty not to interfere, in accordance with the Charter, in matters which are within the internal competence of a State:

> *"No State or group of States has the right to intervene, directly or indirectly, for any reason whatever, in the internal or external affairs of any other State. Consequently, armed intervention and all other forms of interference or attempted threats against the personality of the State or against its political, economic and cultural elements, are in violation of international law.*
> *No State may use or encourage the use of economic political or any other type of measures to coerce another State in order to obtain from it the subordination of the exercise of its sovereign rights and to secure from it advantages of any kind. [...]*
> *Every State has an inalienable right to choose its political, economic, social and cultural systems, without interference in any form by another State.*
> *Nothing in the foregoing paragraphs shall be construed as reflecting the relevant provisions of the Charter relating to the maintenance of international peace and security."*[713]

The object of protection of the prohibition of intervention is the internal affairs of a state. This includes all those matters which have not been removed from the exclusive competence of the state by agreements under public international law. In principle, it can be assumed that the constitu-

---

[711] Which, in Art. 2 No. 7, merely regulates the prohibition of intervention on the part of the UN in the affairs of its members.
[712] Cf. *Seibert-Fohr* in: ZaöRV 2013, 37, 59 et seq.
[713] Annex 2625 (XXV), adopted on 24 October 1970, p. 123, https://treaties.un.org/doc/source/docs/A_RES_2625-Eng.pdf.

tional order, the political, economic, social and cultural system of a state are part of its internal affairs. However, these internal affairs also include administrative access by sovereign authority to the nationals and citizens of a third country. However, the scope of internal affairs is decreasing more and more, as increasing internationalization has subjected numerous issues to regulation under public international law. This applies in particular to the area of human rights, which has also become an international issue in terms of the protection of human dignity and the protection of minors from harmful media, at least in some areas.[714]

However, the prohibition of intervention does not only set limitations to the legislative and executive powers of a state or a community of states with regard to foreign providers. It can also be activated with a view to protecting domestic citizens from foreign influence through Internet offerings. This duty to refrain from harmful interference, which is derived from the prohibition of intervention, found a particularly striking expression in the 2011 Council of Europe Ministerial Declaration on Internet governance principles.[715]

c. The "genuine link" doctrine and action against foreign providers on the basis of the MStV and JMStV

The concept of jurisdiction of states under public international law describes the power of the state to comprehensively regulate the legal and living conditions of natural and legal persons. In accordance with the principle of sovereign equality of states enshrined in Art. 2(1) of the UN Charter and as a result of the prohibition of intervention, the jurisdiction of one state finds its boundaries in the jurisdiction of other states. The main feature of this approach is that a state may (in principle only) exercise territorial sovereignty over its territory and personal sovereignty over its citizens. An extension of this jurisdiction requires a regulation under international treaty law or recognition in customary international law. In this context, the exercise of such jurisdiction beyond territorial and personnel

---

714 Cf. for instance *Ukrow* in: RdJB 2017, 278, 278 et seq.
715 The 3. principle of this declaration indicates that states, in the exercise of their sovereignty rights, should "refrain from any action that would directly or indirectly harm persons or entities outside of their territorial jurisdiction". Cf. CoE, Declaration by the Committee of Ministers on Internet governance principles, at the 1121st meeting of the Ministers' Deputies on 21.09.2011.

sovereignty requires a so-called genuine link.[716] Under public international law, a state may only regulate matters to which it has a sufficiently close connection after balancing its interests against the sovereignty interests of other states[717]. This is not least an expression of the prohibition of arbitrary action: a state may only regulate matters with a foreign connection if this is not done arbitrarily.[718]

Based on the principle of territorial sovereignty, the territoriality principle and the associated effects doctrine are recognized as linking elements in the sense of the genuine link criterion. In addition, nationality (principle of active personality) and the protection of certain state interests (principle of passive personality and protection principle) are accepted as such links under public international law.[719]

According to the principle of territoriality, states have jurisdiction over property and persons located on their own territory.[720] However, this territorial jurisdiction includes not only acts that take place on the territory of the state, but also, according to the effects doctrine – which is recognized as a further development of the principle of territoriality – such acts whose success is realized on the territory of the state. This doctrine complements the objective principle of territoriality insofar as the territorial sovereignty of states also suggests a potential for regulation of all influences on the territory of the state.[721]

However, an unrestricted application of the effects doctrine would lead to undesirable results from a public international law perspective when it comes to the question of whether a state may take sovereign measures against the provider of Internet content that can be accessed on its territory. This is because such an approach would lead to potentially universal conflicts of jurisdiction, since content on the Internet can regularly be per-

---

716 Cf. on this e.g. *Ziegenhain*, Exterritoriale Rechtsanwendung und die Bedeutung des Genuine link Erfordernisses, p. 47 with further references.
717 Cf. *Ziegenhain*, Exterritoriale Rechtsanwendung und die Bedeutung des Genuine link Erfordernisses, p. 47 et seq.
718 Cf. *Dombrowski*, Extraterritoriale Strafrechtsanwendung im Internet, p. 53.
719 Cf. *Tietje/Bering/Zuber*, Völker- und europarechtliche Zulässigkeit extraterritorialer Anknüpfung einer Finanztransaktionssteuer, p. 9.
720 Cf. *Hobe*, Einführung in das Völkerrecht, p. 99; *Stein/von Buttlar/Kotzur*, Völkerrecht, para. 611 et seq.
721 Cf. *Burmester*, Grundlagen internationaler Regelungskumulation und -kollision unter besonderer Berücksichtigung des Steuerrechts, p. 95 et seq., 104 et seq.; *Hobe*, Einführung in das Völkerrecht, p. 99; *Stein/von Buttlar/Kotzur*, Völkerrecht, para. 613; *Tietje/Bering/Zuber*, Völker- und europarechtliche Zulässigkeit extraterritorialer Anknüpfung einer Finanztransaktionssteuer, p. 9.

ceived from almost any state in the world. Without limiting the effects doctrine, an offer on the Internet would have to comply with the legal orders of over 200 states in order to guarantee legal certainty for the provider. This would recognizably exceed the possibilities of an ordinary online provider in the long term. Such unworkable and inappropriate outcomes are recognizably not desired under public international law.[722]

A design of a German language offering can at least be classified as being directed at Germany if no elements are added which indicate that the offering was only intended to address the public in a German-speaking third country.[723]

Moreover, a targeted provision for retrievability in or an impact on Germany is given in particular if an offer specifically focuses on or exclusively deals with the political, economic, social, scientific or cultural situation of Germany in the present or in the past. In particular, there is a genuine link with regard to the reference to the constitutional identity of the Federal Republic of Germany and the counter-image identity-shaping significance of National Socialism for the German legal order in the case of infringements of § 4(1) sentence 1 nos. 1, 2, 3, 4 and 7 JMStV. This is because it is in these provisions that the "counter-image identity-shaping significance of National Socialism for the Basic Law"[724] finds its counterpart in the law on the protection of minors from harmful media. The inhuman and arbitrary tyranny of National Socialism was and is of essential importance for the shaping of the constitutional order, so that the Basic Law can virtually be regarded as a counter-draft to the totalitarianism of the National Socialist regime.[725] Those provisions of the JMStV that declare offerings to be inadmissible in order to distance from the tyranny of National Socialism have such a strong connection to Germany's constitutional identity in view of

---

722 Incidentally, the ICJ already recognized this in the pre-digital era in the *Barcelona Traction* Case (ICJ Reports 1970, p. 3, para. 70, 101) and, in the case of competing links, balanced them against each other and based the justification of a state's competence on the narrower link. Cf. on this e.g. also *Dombrowski*, Extraterritoriale Strafrechtsanwendung im Internet, p. 60 et seq.
723 A respective orientation towards a third country is e.g. if the prices for the perception of an offer are exclusively given in Swiss Francs; cf. OLG München, judgment of 08.10.2009, 29 U 2636/09.
724 BVerfGE 124, 300 (327 et seq.); FCC, Judgment of the Second Senate of 17 January 2017, 2 BvB 1/13, para. 591, 596 (own translation).
725 BVerfGE 124, 300 (328); FCC, Judgment of the Second Senate of 17 January 2017, 2 BvB 1/13, para. 596.

this counter-image identity-shaping significance that a genuine link can be assumed.[726]

A foreign provider also aims to make his offer available in Germany when he has his own offer included in a platform of a provider who is based in Germany and/or makes his offer available exclusively or at least also in Germany. It thus endeavors to make his offering relevant to the process of individual and public opinion-forming in Germany, which is sufficient to justify a genuine link. The same also applies to a foreign provider who aims to ensure that his offering is given priority in search queries in Germany. If the offering of a foreign provider is advertised in Germany in general or by means of an individualized approach to residents of Germany, this indicates, irrespective of the language of the offering itself, that it is intended to have a conscious and deliberate impact at least in Germany as well. Commercial communication taking place in Germany for a foreign offer thus also establishes a genuine link to this offer. Finally, membership in a recognized institution of voluntary self-regulation also establishes a genuine link to the German system of regulated self-regulation and, via this, to the Federal Republic of Germany.

The MStV operates in this context of public international law when it states in § 1(8) sentence 1 that it applies to media intermediaries, media platforms and user interfaces, insofar as they are intended for use in Germany, and in this context regulates in sentence 2 that this is the case if they are aimed in the overall picture, in particular through the language used, the content or marketing activities, at users in Germany or or if they aim to refinance a substantial part of their refinancing in Germany. The same applies to the JMStV in the version of the State Treaty on the Modernization of the Media Order in Germany, if this now regulates in § 2(1) sentence 2 that the rules of this State Treaty also apply to providers who do not have their registered office in Germany according to the provisions of

---

726 This link may be doubtful in view of the opening of the Völkerstrafgesetzbuch (International Criminal Code) for a large number of the offenses addressed in Section 4(1) sentence 1 no. 4 JMStV to third countries in addition to Germany, since in this respect the objective of limiting the effects doctrine related to the genuine link could be jeopardized. However, not least the genesis of international criminal law in roots of Nazi injustice as well as the continuing special editorial treatment of Germany via the Enemy States Clause of the UN Charter show Germany's special responsibility, which finds an expedient counterpart in the authority under public international law to take defensive action also against foreign threats to the free democratic basic order and the anti-Nazi heritage according to the principle of "no freedom for the enemies of freedom". Cf. on this also *Ukrow*, Wehrhafte Demokratie 4.0.

the Telemediengesetz and the MStV, insofar as the offerings are intended for use in Germany and in compliance with the requirements of Art. 3 and 4 AVMSD, as well as Art. 3 ECD. When to assume this intention for use in Germany, is regulated by § 2(1) sentence 3 JMStV, as amended by the Modernization Treaty, in parallel to § 1(8) sentence 2 MStV.

The principle of active personality, which is linked to the personal sovereignty of a state, grants a state comprehensive sovereignty over the rights and obligations of its nationals, irrespective of whether they are in Germany or abroad.[727] The principle of active personality also covers commercial audiovisual activities of any kind – from broadcasting and offering telemedia to the selection, aggregation and presentation of content. Consequently, the principle of (active) personality also offers an approach for taking enforcement measures against foreign providers due to a violation of the MStV or the JMStV, insofar as these providers are own nationals residing abroad.

In contrast to the principle of active personality, the principle of passive personality is not based on a state's sovereignty over its own nationals, but on the state's interest in preventing or prosecuting acts against its own nationals. Although it cannot (yet) be assumed that this principle has found recognition in customary international law, state practice at least indicates toleration in the case of certain offenses.[728] Moreover, the principle of protection, which is related to the principle of passive personality, allows for an extraterritorial link in cases that endanger state interests of particular significance.[729]

---

[727] Cf. *Burmester*, Grundlagen internationaler Regelungskumulation und -kollision unter besonderer Berücksichtigung des Steuerrechts, p. 103 et seq.; *Crawford*, Brownlie's Principles of Public International Law, p. 459 et seq.; *Kment*, Grenzüberschreitendes Verwaltungshandeln, p. 114 et seq.; *Stein/von Buttlar/Kotzur*, Völkerrecht, para. 617; *Tietje/Bering/Zuber*, Völker- und europarechtliche Zulässigkeit extraterritorialer Anknüpfung einer Finanztransaktionssteuer, p. 9.

[728] Cf. *Burmester*, Grundlagen internationaler Regelungskumulation und -kollision unter besonderer Berücksichtigung des Steuerrechts, p. 107 et seq.; *Stein/von Buttlar/Kotzur*, Völkerrecht, para. 620 et seq.; *Tietje/Bering/Zuber*, Völker- und europarechtliche Zulässigkeit extraterritorialer Anknüpfung einer Finanztransaktionssteuer, p. 9 et seq.

[729] Cf. *Burmester*, Grundlagen internationaler Regelungskumulation und -kollision unter besonderer Berücksichtigung des Steuerrechts, p. 98 et seq.; *Dahm/Delbrück/Wolfrum*, Völkerrecht, vol. I/1, p. 321; *Kment*, Grenzüberschreitendes Verwaltungshandeln, p. 123 et seq.; *Stein/von Buttlar/Kotzur*, Völkerrecht, para. 622; *Tietje/Bering/Zuber*, Völker- und europarechtliche Zulässigkeit extraterritorialer Anknüpfung einer Finanztransaktionssteuer, p. 10.

d. Links and limitations of a state's jurisdiction to prescribe and jurisdiction to enforce under public international law

As a result of the so-called *Lotus* jurisprudence, the established distinction between the jurisdiction to prescribe, jurisdiction to enforce and jurisdiction to adjudicate has developed in public international law[730] with regard to the authority of jurisdiction of a state or other subject of public international law, such as the EU. This distinction is indispensable for a precise understanding of jurisdiction problems.

In order to assess the admissibility of extraterritorial factual links under public international law, a distinction must first be made between the *territorial scope* and the *substantive scope* of a provision.[731] The territorial scope determines in which territorial area a provision claims validity. In the case of a provision under administrative law, the territorial scope thus regulates the area in which the provision binds authorities and courts in their administrative or judicial activities. The substantive scope, on the other hand, determines the circumstances to which a provision applies. This may also include situations outside the territory of the state whose authority has taken sovereign action on the basis of a provision of administrative law. Public international law does not per se prevent a distinction between territorial and substantive scope.[732]

In line with the observations of the League of Nations' Permanent Court of International Justice (PCIJ) in its 1927 *Lotus* decision[733], which re-

---

730 Cf. on this e.g., Brownlie's Principles of Public International Law, p. 456; *Epping/Gloria* in: Ipsen, Völkerrecht, § 23, para. 86; *Schweisfurth*, Völkerrecht, chapter 9, para. 177.
731 Cf. *Epping/Gloria* in: Ipsen, Völkerrecht, § 23, para. 87; *Tietje/Bering/Zuber*, Völker- und europarechtliche Zulässigkeit extraterritorialer Anknüpfung einer Finanztransaktionssteuer, p. 6.
732 Cf. on this e.g. *Koch*, Die grenzüberschreitende Wirkung von nationalen Genehmigungen für umweltbeeinträchtigende industrielle Anlagen, p. 32 et seq.; *Linke*, Europäisches Internationales Verwaltungsrecht, p. 28 et seq.; *Ohler* in: DVBl. 2007, 1083, 1088.
733 "Not the first and foremost restriction imposed by international law upon a State is that – failing the existence of a permissive rule to the contrary – it may not exercise its power in any form in the territory of another State. In this sense jurisdiction is certainly territorial; it cannot be exercised by a State outside its territory except by virtue of a permissive rule derived from international custom or convention. It does not, however, follow that international law prohibits a State from exercising jurisdiction in its own territory, in respect of any case which relates to acts which have taken place abroad, and in which it cannot rely on some permissive rule of international law. Such a view would only be tenable if inter-

flect the state of public international law dogmatics, the territorial scope of the exercise of jurisdiction is, as a rule, limited to a state's own territory. At the same time, however, it follows from the ruling that states are free to factually link to events abroad.[734] The imperative of respecting foreign sovereign rights is therefore not already interfered with by the sovereign regulation of a state A if a state B permits the performance of an act taking place on its territory, but state A prohibits such an act under administrative law, irrespective of where it takes place, and its sovereign authority declares this administrative law to be applicable also in the case of facts relating to third states and sanctions precisely this conduct due to its impact on its own territory.[735]

According to the *Lotus* decision, states are largely free to decide how far they wish to extend the substantive scope of their legal order. In this respect, legislative power is not exclusive under public international law, but always competing.[736] In contrast, due to the limited territorial sovereignty, the enforcement power is subject to far-reaching restrictions insofar as the enforcement of legal provisions outside the territory of the enforcing state authority is concerned.[737] However, the cautious attitude of the judiciary with regard to questions of administrative conduct by regulatory authorities with extraterritorial effect and the only rudimentary normative material on such conduct extending beyond national borders available under in-

---

  national law contained a general prohibition to States to extend the application of their laws and the jurisdiction of their courts to persons, property and acts outside their territory, and if, as an exception to this general prohibition, it allowed States to do so in certain specific cases. But this is certainly not the case under international law as it stands at present. Far from laying down a general prohibition to the effect that States may not extend the application of their laws and the jurisdiction of their courts to persons, property and acts outside their territory, it leaves them in this respect a wide measure of discretion which is only limited in certain cases by prohibitive rules; as regards other cases, every State remains free to adopt the principles which it regards as best and most suitable". The Case of the S.S. Lotus, Judgment No. 9, P.C.I.J., Series A, No. 10 (1927), 18 et seq.

734 Cf. *Tietje/Bering/Zuber*, Völker- und europarechtliche Zulässigkeit extraterritorialer Anknüpfung einer Finanztransaktionssteuer, p. 7.
735 So in the approach *Dombrowski*, Extraterritoriale Strafrechtsanwendung im Internet, p. 51.
736 *Dahm/Delbrück/Wolfrum*, Völkerrecht, vol. I/1, p. 319.
737 Cf. *Dahm/Delbrück/Wolfrum*, Völkerrecht, vol. I/1, p. 318 et seq.; *Tietje/Bering/Zuber*, Völker- und europarechtliche Zulässigkeit extraterritorialer Anknüpfung einer Finanztransaktionssteuer, p. 7.

ternational treaty law to date does not per se stand in the way of the permissibility of such conduct under public international law.

According to all this, public international law does not require that the territorial scope of national regulations must end at the national border. In contrast, it is generally illegal under public international law for a German authority to exercise sovereignty independently on foreign territory, because in this case the subject of public international law, Germany, regularly interferes with the sovereignty of the third country concerned.[738]

This classification is also significant in the distinction between jurisdiction to prescribe and jurisdiction to enforce. While the substantive scope of the MStV and JMStV, towards which the jurisdiction to prescribe is directed, can also be opened up beyond the Federal Republic of Germany, the territorial scope of the two State Treaties, towards which the jurisdiction to enforce is directed, is limited to the territory of the sixteen states of the Federal Republic of Germany. Jurisdiction to enforce outside the Federal Republic would only be opened up if, on the one hand, this were provided for domestically and, on the other hand, this domestic regulation were secured under international treaty law.

3. *The cross-border application of German media regulation – Relevant elements of the MStV and JMStV and their interpretation*

The JMStV itself does not contain the terms "foreign country", "foreigner" or comparable terminology at any point. In this respect, when interpreted semantically, it appears at first glance to be neutral with regard to the question of whether the state media authorities or the KJM can access foreign providers. However, § 2(1) sentence 2 JMStV, in the version created by Art. 3 No. 2(a) of the State Treaty on the Modernization of the Media Order in Germany, expressly states that the rules of the JMStV also apply to providers who do not have their registered office in Germany according to the provisions of the Telemediengesetz and the MStV, insofar as the offerings are intended for use in Germany and in compliance with the requirements of Art. 3 and 4 AVMSD, as well as Art. 3 ECD. This argues semantically for the cross-border openness of the JMStV.

---

738 Cf. also *Bertele*, Souveränität und Verfahrensrecht, p. 78 et seq., 89, 93; *Dombrowski*, Extraterritoriale Strafrechtsanwendung im Internet, p. 52; *Ziegenhain*, Exterritoriale Rechtsanwendung und die Bedeutung des Genuine-link-Erfordernisses, p. 2 et seq.

For the MStV, conversely, the wording of § 106(1) sentence 2 of the MStV already indicates an opening towards cross-border application of its provisions: for nationwide offerings, where the broadcaster or provider is based abroad, the state media authority which first dealt with the matter has power to issue supervisory decisions. In this respect, it is irrelevant who initiated a referral; action on own initiative ex officio is also possible.

This semantic result, which can also not be relativized by the title of the State Treaty on the Modernization of the Media Order "in Germany", which links the MStV and the JMStV, is confirmed by teleological considerations: e.g., the purpose of the JMStV according to its § 1 is "consistent protection of children and adolescents against content in electronic information and communication media which impairs or harms their development or education, and for the protection against content in electronic information and communication media which violates human dignity or other legal goods protected under the German Criminal Code". This purpose is also not explicitly territorially contained. § 1, according to its wording, neither takes into account only children and young people who are resident in or nationals of Germany, nor does it refer exclusively to offers in electronic information and communication media that can be attributed to the Federal Republic via a criterion such as the provider's registered office. Rather, the purpose of § 1 JMStV is formulated in a twofold territorially open manner in relation to the addressees – both with regard to the beneficiaries or protected persons and with regard to the perpetrators.

Historical aspects also reinforce the result of openness toward regulation with cross-border impact. The official explanatory memorandum to the JMStV[739] does not explicitly consider the question of whether the KJM is competent to deal with offerings that are distributed from abroad and can be received in Germany. However, it contains a passage on § 13 JMStV that is of considerable importance with regard to the answer to this question:

> *"§ 13 concerns the scope of the rules on procedure as well as enforcement for providers other than public broadcasters. §§ 14 – 21 and 24(4) sentence 6 shall therefore apply only to cross-border offerings. In this context, cross-border offerings include offerings that are distributed or made accessible nationwide as well as offerings that are only distributed or made accessible in the*

---

739 Available only in German at https://www.kjm-online.de/fileadmin/user_upload/ Rechtsgrundlagen/Gesetze_Staatsvertraege/JMStV_Genese/ Amtliche_Begru__ndung_zum_JMStV.pdf (all excerpts here: own translation).

E. Core problems of public international law

territory of several federal states. All offerings on the Internet are cross-border anyway."

The last sentence is significant in several respects for the present contexts:

- First, the legislature takes note that "all offerings on the Internet" are cross-border. In this regard, "all" clearly means not only such offerings that originate in Germany.
- Secondly, for Internet offerings, the legislature assumes – as evidenced by the label "anyway" – an obvious competence of the KJM via the factual linking criterion "cross-border".
- Thirdly, the legislature refrains from differentiating regarding the competence of the KJM depending on whether an Internet offering originates in Germany or a third country. Such a differentiation would have been obvious, however, in view of the potentially global problem, recognized by the legislature, of content that is questionable under the law on the protection of minors from harmful media, if the legislature had intended to limit the competence of the KJM from the outset exclusively to matters that have only domestic links.

Such a differentiation to limit the competence of the KJM with regard to the recognition of the international impact possibilities on the Internet would only have been unnecessary if already, for reasons of public international law, the competence of the KJM for cases in which the violation of the substantive provisions of the JMStV originates abroad is out of the question.

For the question of whether the legislature also has foreign offerings in view, the official explanatory memorandum of § 5(3) JMStV is also significant. It reads:

"As an alternative for broadcasting and telemedia, the JMStV provides that due to the time of distribution or making available, the provider can assume that children or young people do not perceive these offerings. This provision, adopted from previous law, also applies to telemedia. Here, too, it has emerged that, with appropriate software, the cross-time zone offering can be blocked for individual time zones and thus designed differently over the course of a day. However, this is only one option for a provider, which otherwise leaves it free to make other arrangements, by technical or other means [...]."

Such a passage on the treatment of cross-time zone offerings would be superfluous if the legislature had assumed that only domestic offerings could be the subject of any regulatory access based on the JMStV at all.

Accordingly, the state media authorities are authorized to take enforcement measures against foreign providers for violating substantive provisions of the MStV and/or the JMStV, based on a semantic, teleological and historical interpretation of the MStV and JMStV.

4. *The possibility of reaching foreign providers under the MStV and the JMStV from the perspective of EU law – an initial consideration*

a. Introduction

The question of the relationship between national media law and EU law is no longer about the problem of whether Art. 5(1) sentence 2 Basic Law has a suspensory effect on provisions of secondary EU law.[740] This question has been clarified in principle, at the latest since the FCC's decision on the then EEC's TwF Directive[741], in the direction of a recognition by the FCC of the EU's regulatory competence with regard to audiovisual media from an internal market perspective. Rather, the question is whether EU law imposes a priori limitations on an approach that basically recognizes regulatory competences of domestic authorities vis-à-vis (EU) foreign providers.

The goal of the Federal Republic of Germany to promote world peace as an equal partner in a united Europe, as enshrined in the Preamble and Art. 23 Basic Law, is constitutionally bound, as the FCC emphasized in its decision on the Treaty of Lisbon[742]; the constitution, however, is itself open to Europe and, beyond that, also oriented toward international cooperation.[743] This leads to the conclusion that the Basic Law does not assume a mere coexistence of national, European and international legal systems,[744] but in particular also requires an intertwining and inclusion of the European common good in the interpretation and application of funda-

---

740 Skeptical in this respect early on e.g. *Ossenbühl*, Rundfunk zwischen nationalem Verfassungsrecht und europäischem Gemeinschaftsrecht, p. 58 et seq.
741 BVerfGE 92, 203.
742 BVerfGE 123, 267 (345 et seq.); critical to the decision with regard to the integration limits shown, e.g. *Ukrow* in: ZEuS 2009, 717, 720 ff.
743 On the choice for an openness of statehood cf. *Vogel*, Die Verfassungsentscheidung des Grundgesetzes für eine internationale Zusammenarbeit; as well as e.g. *Kment*, Grenzüberschreitendes Verwaltungshandeln, p. 165 et seq.
744 Cf. im Ansatz *Kirchhof* in: JZ 1989, 453, 454.

E. Core problems of public international law

mental rights, i.e. a specific interpretation of fundamental rights based on European law.[745]

Conversely, the above-mentioned rules and limitations on the exercise of competences, as well as the horizontal cultural and media policy clause of Art. 167(4) TFEU and the EU's obligation to respect media pluralism, call for an application and interpretation of EU law that is directed toward upholding EU Member States' instruments to safeguarding diversity.

This is also recognized in principle by the European Commission in its communication of 27 April 2020 to the Federal Republic of Germany as part of the notification procedure on the State Treaty on the Modernization of the Media Order in Germany.[746]

In the notification details, the German authorities justified the draft measure and the requirements imposed on online service providers of media content (so-called "gatekeepers") with the need to safeguard media pluralism on the Internet.[747] They point to the fundamental changes in the media landscape, in particular the increasing importance of certain online services ("gatekeepers") for the discoverability of media offerings and reaching them. The goal of the draft treaty was to preserve pluralism and promote diversity. To this, the European Commission responded with "general comments"[748]:

> *"Media pluralism is a fundamental value of the European Union, as enshrined in Article 11(2) [CFR]. In this respect, the Commission recognizes and shares the objective of initiatives to promote media pluralism. At the Union level, the Commission promotes this pluralism by, among other things, funding the Media Pluralism Monitor, which is currently studying the impact of digitization on media pluralism across the EU.*
>
> *The Commission is also committed to preserving and promoting media diversity and media pluralism in the online environment. In this context, the*

---

745 Cf. on this BVerfGE 73, 339 (386). Cf. on this *Ress* in: VVDStRL 1990, 56, 81; *Streinz*, Bundesverfassungsgerichtlicher Grundrechtsschutz und Europäisches Gemeinschaftsrecht, p. 260 et seq.
746 In this context, Art. 1 §§ 1, 2, 18, 19, 22, 74, 78 to 96, 117(1) sentence 2 no. 2, 16, 21 to 44 (as provisions of the MStV) and Art. 2 of the draft State Treaty on the Modernization of the Media Order in Germany (as a repeal of the Interstate Broadcasting Treaty) were notified in accordance with Directive (EU) 2015/1535.
747 In addition, the German authorities describe the notified draft as a partial transposition of Directive (EU) 2018/1808 of 14 November 2018 amending the AVMSD.
748 European Commission, Notifizierung 2020/26/D, C(2020) 2823 final of 27.04.2020, p. 2 (own translation).

> *Commission has announced its intention to regulate the responsibility of online platforms with regard to content at EU level in the announced "Digital Services Act". It shall also be examined whether the role of online platforms as online 'gatekeepers' should lead to new ex ante rules at EU level.*
>
> *However, having examined the notified draft and taking into account the responses of the German authorities to the Commission services' request for additional information, the Commission has certain concerns as to whether some of the measures contained in the notified draft may disproportionately restrict the free movement of information society services protected in the internal market."*

As will be shown below, however, the recognition of Member States' initiatives to promote media pluralism does not sufficiently take into account the at least primary, if not exclusive, legislative competence of the Member States to respond to new threats to media diversity.

b. The possibility of reaching foreign providers under the MStV and the JMStV from the perspective of primary EU law

From the Basic Law's commitment to European integration, an approach could be derived in view of the attribution of conduct of the Member States' authorities responsible for safeguarding audiovisual protection of human dignity and the protection of minors from harmful media that German enforcement authorities are per se prevented from taking enforcement measures against EU foreign providers in the sense of a comprehensive obligation to respect the conduct of third EU countries. In such a view, European integration would result in a limitation of the options for action by Member State administrative authorities in EU-internal cross-border cases.

Such a view would take full account of the principle of home country control, one of the fundamental principles shaping the internal market concept of the TFEU. At the same time, the risk of conflicting administrative decisions in the EU judicial area would be sustainably curbed – but possibly at the price of insufficient preservation of protected interests.

However, such a restrictive view would at the same time fail to recognize that the home country control system applies only as a principle. E.g., the CJEU has expressly ruled in the area of regulation of gambling and games of chance that a Member State does not have to recognize the validity of gambling licenses issued by other Member States, but may make the offering of gambling products or services on its territory dependent on the possession of a license issued by its own authorities.⁷⁴⁹ What applies in view of an initial situation of active state action by an EU third state – in this case the granting of a license – must apply a fortiori in the event that a third state has not at all dealt with the conduct of a person attributable to it yet. Informal toleration of certain private conduct by an EU third state cannot therefore have a general and comprehensive suspensory effect with regard to own sovereign actions.⁷⁵⁰ A Member State on whose territory a service is used that infringes in particular that state's protection of minors, human dignity or diversity-safeguarding provisions is therefore entitled to control and take actions against the service – but with regard to the country of origin principle as an exception to this only if there is a justification for restricting the freedom to provide services and this has been applied proportionately.⁷⁵¹

This approach is easily transferable in the area of protection of minors from harmful media, of human dignity and safeguarding pluralism, also through e.g. findability regulation, in view of enforcement measures against providers outside the area of EU integration. This is already because the freedom to provide services – unlike the freedom of capital and payment⁷⁵² – does not have an *erga omnes* effect. Accordingly, providers from outside the EU cannot invoke a possible violation of the freedom to provide services due to supervisory measures relating to the protection of minors, human dignity or safeguarding diversity.

c. The possibility of reaching foreign providers under the MStV and the JMStV from the perspective of the AVMSD

The fact that foreign EU providers can also be the subject of Member States' legislative acts transposing the AVMSD already follows directly

---

749 Cf. e.g. CJEU, joined cases C-316/07, C-358/07 to C-360/07, C-409/07 and C-410/07, *Stoß*, para. 108 et seq.
750 There is also in any case the possibility of a complaint to the Commission, which may initiate infringement proceedings against the other Member State; under certain circumstances, the initiative for such proceedings may even be taken by the Member State affected by this failure to act.
751 Cf. on this also supra, chapter C.IV.1.
752 On the *erga omnes* effect of the freedom of capital and payments as a deviation from the dogmatics of the other fundamental freedoms cf. e.g. *Ukrow/Ress* in: Grabitz/Hilf/Nettesheim, Art. 63 TFEU (forthcoming).

from the continuing openness of this Directive to departure from the principle of home country control.

This is also confirmed in principle by the European Commission in its communication of 27 April 2020 to Germany as part of the notification procedure for the State Treaty on the Modernization of the Media Order in Germany. The concerns expressed by the Commission do not relate to the "whether" of this legislative regulatory possibility of reach, but to the "how" of its transposition, in particular with regard to (a) the so-called derogation procedure pursuant to Art. 3(2) of the amended AVMSD and (b) the so-called anti-circumvention procedure pursuant to its Art. 4. The Commission expresses "doubts in particular as to the compatibility of §§ 104[753] and 52 of the draft MStV with the amended AVMSD and thus with the applicable internal market rules"[754].

Insofar as the Commission complains in that regard that the principle of free reception and free retransmission was only partially implemented, this does not affect the question of the possibility of reaching foreign providers. However, it can still be pointed out on this occasion that the freedom of reception – in contrast to the Commission's view – did not require any State Treaty or other simple law regulation in addition to the regulation of the permissibility of retransmission, as this freedom is already directly enshrined in Art. 5(1) Basic Law as a fundamental right applicable to all. It is also to be found – confirming this constitutional starting point, but without having any genuine constitutive effect in terms of the freedom – in a number of state media laws. It is a further expression of a lack of sensitivity to the coexistence of State Treaty provisions and such of autonomous state media law when the Commission also criticizes that "the national transposition laws must allow retransmission or reception not only nationwide, but also in part of the German territory". This is because such retransmission regulations relating to offerings that cannot be received nationwide can be found in the individual states' media laws, which are as suitable for the transposition of the requirements of the AVMSD as the MStV and JMStV.

That the German states, by explicitly referring to Art. 3 AVMSD in § 104(1) sentence 2 MStV and to Art. 4(3) AVMSD in § 104(4) MStV, "do not ensure the necessary clarity and accessibility of the rules applicable at national level in order to guarantee legal certainty in the application of the

---

753 Now: § 103 MStV.
754 European Commission, Notifizierung 2020/26/D, C(2020) 2823 final of 27.04.2020, p. 6.

E. Core problems of public international law

Directive" is an accusation made by the Commission which is not confirmed beyond doubt by the case law to date on the transposition requirements in relation to EU directives.[755]

Even insofar as the Commission expresses doubts as to the compatibility of the procedure for refusal of a license in connection with circumvention facts, as regulated in § 52(2) MStV, with Art. 4 of the amended AVMSD, these doubts do not affect the possibility of access by a Member State to foreign providers. Under the regulatory model of § 52(2) MStV, the country of establishment would refuse to grant a license to a provider who has established itself in the territory of a Member State in order to circumvent the regulations of the country of destination, without activating the procedure under Art. 4 of the amended AVMSD. Whether this mechanism would be compatible with EU law in light of the requirements of the freedom of establishment and the free movement of services even if the provider is not from a third country outside the CoE's Television Convention is rightly doubted by the Commission. Therefore, it is understandable to some degree that the Commission asked Germany to "clarify that § 52 does not apply to providers established in Germany if their programs are directed in whole or in part at the population of another Member State". However, this request is excessive, at least to the extent that the licensing requirement set forth in § 51(1) MStV may also apply to providers established in Germany, in conformity with EU law, if their programs are directed in whole or in part at the population of another Member State.

The level of legislative regulation must be distinguished from regulation by enforcement. The fact that the state media authorities are not generally prevented by Union law from also reaching foreign providers due to a violation of the requirements of the MStV and JMStV results from the system of exceptions to the principles of control by the broadcasting state and free retransmission regulated in the AVMSD. As already explained, these principles do not apply without restriction. Rather, in certain, albeit very narrowly defined, exceptional cases (for example, for reasons of protection of minors and human dignity), another Member State may suspend the (further) distribution of audiovisual media services on its territory, subject to compliance with the procedure regulated in the AVMSD.

This means that foreign providers can be made the subject of enforcement measures under the system of the AVMSD, which essentially sup-

---

755 It is undisputed that a literal adoption of the requirements of the AVMSD, as can be found e.g. in § 1(3) sentence 2 MStV, fulfills the implementation requirement beyond doubt.

ports the interpretation found above of a possibility of reaching to foreign providers in the interest of safeguarding the protective purposes of the MStV and the JMStV.

d. The possibility of reaching foreign providers under the MStV and the JMStV from the perspective of the ECD

With respect to the applicability of the ECD, the Commission, in its notification of 27 April 2020, considers at the outset that based on the information made available to it

> "Directive 2000/31/EC ('Directive on electronic commerce') which constitutes the horizontal framework for information society services, applies to the relevant provisions of the notified draft".

In contrast, the German authorities argued in the notification procedure that the notified draft fell under Article 1(6) of the ECD, according to which

> "[t]his Directive does not affect measures taken at Community or national level, in the respect of Community law, in order to promote cultural and linguistic diversity and to ensure the defence of pluralism".

In this respect, the Commission considered that:

> "In order to invoke such a provision, the measures must actually and objectively serve to protect media pluralism and be proportionate to the objectives of the measure. In similar, relevant cases, the [CJEU] has recalled the conditions that Member States must meet when taking measures to safeguard pluralism that could constitute a restriction on the freedom to provide services. In addition, under Article 1(6), even where the [ECD] does not affect Member States' measures to promote pluralism, Member States must comply with wider EU law, including the provisions of the [ECD], when adopting such measures.
> Therefore, Article 1(6) does not exclude the provisions of the Directive (as opposed to Article 1(5)), but rather emphasizes the importance that the EU attaches to the protection of pluralism as a factor that Member States may take into account when regulating the provision of information society services (cf. recital 63 of the Directive)."

This line of argumentation of the Commission is not convincing:

It is true that Member States' measures based on Art. 1(6) ECD must actually and objectively serve to protect media pluralism. The Commission

E. Core problems of public international law

fails, however, to demonstrate that the MStV regulations criticized by it do not actually and objectively serve to protect media pluralism – and in view of the threats to diversity of opinion, which provided the impetus for the corresponding regulation on the part of the states, this cannot even be demonstrated.

Similarly, the Commission has not demonstrated that the measures taken in the MStV are disproportionate to the objectives of the measure. Moreover, this disproportionality cannot be demonstrated either. In particular, the measures taken are suitable for the protection of media pluralism and necessary for the timely prevention of undesirable developments, to which the FCC refers in its settled case law on prevention of risks to diversity.

The Commission fundamentally fails to recognize the prerogative as granted to Member States by the CJEU to assess and evaluate measures that restrict fundamental freedoms and are justified by overriding considerations of general interest, such as safeguarding media pluralism.[756] Its review program exceeds the limits of the supervisory competence on the part of the EU institutions recognized in the case law:

- It is true that the CJEU considers a restriction of a fundamental freedom to be justified by an overriding reason in the general interest only if the principle of proportionality is observed: the measures taken by the Member States must therefore be suitable for ensuring that the objective pursued is achieve[757] and must not go beyond what is necessary to achieve that objective.
- In this context, a national provision in terms of a Union law coherence criterion is only suitable to ensure the realization of the cited objective if it actually meets the requirement to achieve this in a coherent and systematic manner. There is no sufficient evidence that the regulation of the MStV does not satisfy this coherence criterion.
- It is equally not apparent that the restriction of fundamental freedoms associated with regulation by the MStV is being applied in a discriminatory manner.

---

756 Cf. on this and the following supra chapter C.IV.1; in detail also *Cole*, Zum Gestaltungsspielraum der EU-Mitgliedstaaten bei Einschränkungen der Dienstleistungsfreiheit, p. 27 et seq.
757 As regards suitability, the CJEU limits itself to an evidence control as to whether a measure is ex ante obviously unsuitable to achieve the intended objective; cf. *Cole*, Zum Gestaltungsspielraum der EU-Mitgliedstaaten bei Einschränkungen der Dienstleistungsfreiheit, p. 30 et seq.

- A Member State must provide, in addition to the (written or unwritten) justifications for a restriction of a fundamental freedom that it may invoke, appropriate evidence or an inquiry into the appropriateness and proportionality of the restrictive measure it has adopted, as well as precise information in support of its claim. With this objective verifiability as well as the legal certainty of the limitations of the unwritten exception clauses, there is also a procedural effectuation of the protection of the fundamental freedom with regard to the imperative considerations of the general interest.[758] In the event of a dispute, however, the states can easily satisfy this requirement as well, in view of the large number of expert opinions on media and constitutional law that have triggered and substantiated their readjustments to German media law through the MStV.
- In the event of a dispute, the CJEU carries out its own review of restrictions of a fundamental freedom by a Member State measured against the principle of proportionality – but only in the sense of a plausibility test with regard to the suitability and necessity of the restrictions for achieving the objective.[759] The regulations of the MStV examined in the notification procedure can recognizably be subjected to this plausibility test, without the lack of plausibility being verifiable.

The Commission's review program in the notification procedure exceeds this already ambitious program according to CJEU case law by substituting its own assessments of suitability and necessity for those of a Member State. This is no longer covered by the Commission's supervisory competence with regard to unwritten justifications.

Moreover, the Commission erodes the meaning of Art. 1(6) ECD when it acknowledges the non-affection content of this provision, but at the same time emphasizes the continued binding nature of this very Directive. The fact that certain subject matters are excluded from its scope in Art. 1(5) ECD and that the protection of pluralism is not covered by it, is, when interpreted systematically, teleologically and historically, not to be understood in the sense of a deliberate inclusion of measures for the protection of pluralism in the scope of the Directive, but is an expression of

---

758 Cf. on this Ukrow/Ress in: Grabitz/Hilf/Nettesheim, Das Recht der EU, Art. 63 TFEU, para. 228 (forthcoming).
759 Cf. on this *Ukrow/Ress* in: Grabitz/Hilf/Nettesheim, Das Recht der EU, Art. 63 TFEU, para. 229 (forthcoming). Cf. on this also *Cole*, Zum Gestaltungsspielraum der EU-Mitgliedstaaten bei Einschränkungen der Dienstleistungsfreiheit, p. 30 et seq.

E. Core problems of public international law

the principle that the EU, at least in case of doubt, lacks competence for regulations whose main purpose is the protection of pluralism. The fact that the protection of pluralism is not explicitly referred to in recital 63 ECD mentioned by the Commission speaks in favor of this interpretation, which is aimed at recognizing and preserving the regulatory competence of Member States to safeguard pluralism.

In this context, there is also much to suggest that the new services covered by the MStV, insofar as the application of the ECD to them is not already denied via its Art. 1(6), are not easily subject to the provisions of the Directive as "information society services": this is because, unlike the broadcasting services covered by Annex I of Directive (EU) 2015/1535[760], they cannot be readily excluded from the category of services provided "at the individual request of a recipient" covered by the ECD on the basis of the situation of use. In terms of their importance for the process of formation of individual and public opinion, however, they are increasingly comparable with these broadcasting services in functional terms. Moreover, they are clearly more important for this process, which is subject to the regulatory competence of the Member States, than traditional telemedia, to which the Commission refers. This is already evident from the qualifying characteristics listed in the MStV for the definition of services beyond the mere characteristic as telemedia. However, the general approach of a narrow interpretation of exceptions to obligations under primary or secondary law suggests that, in the absence of an explicit amendment of Directive (EU) 2015/1535, the Commission will assume in the course of its supervisory activities that the services newly covered by the MStV are covered by this Directive.

Also in the context of ECD, regulation qua enforcement must be separated from the level of legislative regulation. Even when reaching foreign providers, the restrictions on liability triggered by the ECD, transposed into German national law by the Telemedia Act (TMG)[761], must be ob-

---

760 Directive (EU) 2015/1535 of the European Parliament and of the Council of 9 September 2015 laying down a procedure for the provision of information in the field of technical regulations and of rules on Information Society services, OJ L 241 of 17.09.2015, p. 1–15, available at https://eur-lex.europa.eu/legal-content/EN/TXT/HTML/?uri=CELEX:32015L1535&from=DE.
761 Telemedia Act (Telemediengesetz) of 26 February 2007 (BGBl. I, p. 179), as last amended by Art. 11 of the Act of 11 July 2019 (BGBl. I, p. 1066).

served. In particular, foreign access and host providers[762] are generally not liable for data transmitted or stored by users, but can only be held liable from a certain degree of involvement. For access providers, this is, e.g., an actual initiation of the transmission or a modifying intervention in the information to be transmitted. A host provider is liable for data stored by users only if it has knowledge of an illegal activity and does not take immediate action to remove the data or block access to it.

However, the liability rules explicitly allow EU Member States to enable their courts and administrative authorities to require the service provider to stop or prevent the infringement. Therefore, the ECD does not have a general suspensory effect on any enforcement measures taken by the state media authorities against foreign providers on the basis of the MStV or JMStV.

III. Binding effect of fundamental rights in the case of enforcement measures against foreign providers

1. Binding effect of European fundamental rights protection

a. Introduction

The obligation of public authorities to respect fundamental rights on the basis of European and public international law is undoubted in cases where they act within German territory and the sovereignty has domestic effects. What validity European and international fundamental and human rights have, in contrast, for the actions of German public authorities extraterritorially, requires an in-depth discussion.

Not only the FCC has developed principles of extraterritorial application of the Basic Law's fundamental rights in its case law. The ECtHR has also shed light on the extraterritorial application of the ECHR in a number of decisions. Finally, questions of extraterritorial validity may also arise in view of the fundamental rights enshrined in the CFR and in the International Covenant on Civil and Political Rights (ICCPR)[763].

---

762 These are service providers that either provide users with access to the Internet (so-called access providers) or enable them to use the content of the Internet by providing storage space (so-called host providers); cf. *die medienanstalten/Institut für Europäisches Medienrecht*, Europäische Medien- und Netzpolitik, p. 61.

763 Cf. for Germany Gesetz zu dem Internationalen Pakt vom 19. Dezember 1966 über bürgerliche und politische Rechte, BGBl. no. 60 of 20.11.1973, p. 1533.

E. Core problems of public international law

This extraterritorial application is important in the present context in view of enforcement measures directed against foreign providers, in particular due to the protection of freedom of broadcasting and media in Art. 10 ECHR, Art. 11 CFR and (if the provision is understood in a way that assumes its practical relevance to a greater extent than suggested by the wording, the limits and the system of control) Art. 19(2) ICCPR.

A distinction must be made between this extraterritorial application of fundamental rights standards under European and public international law and the question of the extent to which a Member State's media regulation is bound by CFR.

b. Extraterritorial validity of application of the ECHR and the International Covenant on Civil and Political Rights in their significance for media regulation

According to Art. 1 ECHR, Contracting Parties shall secure to everyone within their jurisdiction the rights and freedoms defined in the Convention.[764] With regard to the question of an extraterritorial effect of the ECHR, the case law of the ECtHR[765] follows the guidelines of general public international law on the jurisdiction of states[766]: the Court emphasizes that Art. 1 ECHR limits the application of the Convention territorially. According to the ECtHR, extraterritorial action establishes the jurisdiction of a state in a manner that opens the applicability of the ECHR if the state (1.) exercises all or some of the sovereign powers normally exercised by the government of the territory on the basis of effective territorial control as a consequence of an occupation by war or on the basis of the invitation or the express or tacit consent of the government of the territory or (2.) exercises sovereignty extraterritorially on the basis of other links recognized by international treaty law or customary international law – as is the case, e.g., with the diplomatic or consular corps of a State. A more far-reaching liability was not intended by the ECHR. It was not the purpose of Art. 1 ECHR

---

764 The authentic English and French versions of the ECHR use the terms "jurisdiction" and "juridiction" respectively, for sovereignty. These terms are amenable to a highly different German semantic conceptual understanding.
765 Cf. ECtHR, No. 11755/85, *Stocké / Germany*, para. 166; No. 12747/87, *Drozd and Janousek / France and Spain*, para. 91; No. 40/1993/435/514, *Loizidou / Turkey*, para. 62; No. 25781/94, *Cyprus / Turkey*, para. 77; No. 20652/92, *Dijavit An / Cyprus*, para. 18–23.
766 Cf. on this supra, chapter B.VI.

to subject to the protection of the Convention everyone whose rights guaranteed by it were affected by an extraterritorial act of the Contracting Parties. Such an interpretation would place the question of whether a person was subject to the jurisdiction of states on an equal footing with the question of whether a person's rights guaranteed by the Convention had been violated.[767]

According to the ECtHR, extraterritorial action must therefore establish a situation in which the state authorities control persons or property in such a way that the extraterritorial exercise of sovereignty is comparable to the domestic one. This can be achieved through effective territorial control or the consent of the government of the territory concerned. Accordingly, the Court focuses on the forms of regular exercise of state authority. Since the Contracting Party must actually be in a position to ensure that the Convention rights are respected, the jurisdiction to enforce is decisive. Normally, a state is not in a position to guarantee the rights and freedoms of the Convention even to its own citizens residing abroad, since it has only the limited means of diplomatic protection at its disposal due to a lack of executive power.[768]

According to its Art. 2(1), the protection of the ICCPR extends to all individuals within the territory of a State Party and subject to its jurisdiction. The monitoring body responsible under the Covenant, the Human Rights Committee, assumes extraterritorial protection under the Covenant in this context.[769] In 1981 already, the Committee stated in view of Art. 2(1) ICESCR[770] which is identical in text in this respect, that for the necessary establishment of authority, it is not the place of the state action that is relevant, but whether a human rights violation results from the relationship between the state and the individual.[771] The Committee reaffirmed this approach in 2004 in its General Comment No. 31, focusing solely on

---

767 Cf. ECtHR, No. 52207/99, *Bankovic and others / Belgium and others*, para. 66, 71, 73, printed in: ILM 2002, 517–531.
768 Cf. *Fischer-Lescano/Kreck*, Piraterie und Menschenrechte, p. 6 et seq.; *Krieger* in: ZaöRV 2002, 669, 672.
769 On this and the following *Fischer-Lescano/Kreck*, Piraterie und Menschenrechte, p. 12.
770 International Covenant on Economic, Social and Cultural Rights (ICESCR). For its wording cf. http://www.ohchr.org/EN/ProfessionalInterest/Pages/CESCR.aspx; a German version is available at http://www.sozialpakt.info/.
771 Human Rights Committee, *Delia Saldias de Lopez / Uruguay*, Communication No. 52/1979, U.N. Doc. CCPR/C/OP/1 (29.07.1981), §§ 12.1.-12.3.; equally Human Rights Committee, Communication No. 106/1981: Uruguay, UN Doc. CCPR/C/18/D/ 106/1981 (31.03.1983), § 5.

E. Core problems of public international law

whether the person within the power or effective control of the State, regardless of the location of the event.[772]

According to the categorical classification of the ECtHR, a foreign provider who is affected by the exercise of German sovereignty in such a way that it is accessed from the perspective of diversity or minor media protection law due to a violation of the substantive provisions of the MStV or the JMStV can rely on Convention rights insofar as the relevant administrative acts of the competent state media authorities are concerned. If, in contrast, the provider's state of residence were to take enforcement measures on the basis of relevant agreements under public international law between Germany and that state, the ECHR could not be invoked before the courts of the state of residence, at least if that state is not itself an EU Member State and/or a party to the ECHR.

c. The scope of Member States' compliance with the CFR in the context of media regulation measures

According to Art. 51(1), sentence 1, clause 2 CFR, the Member States are bound by the Charter "only when they are implementing Union law". In this context, EU law is primary as well as secondary law, such as the AVMSD and the ECD. Union law also includes legislation adopted on authorization in secondary law, i.e. so-called tertiary law – such as the Commission's guidelines on the application of individual provisions of the AVMSD referred to in that Directive.

The "implementation" of EU law is, on the one hand, undoubtedly concerned with the administrative enforcement of EU law that is directly applicable – such as, in particular, parts of primary law and secondary law in the form of regulations – and with the interpretation and application of EU and implementation law by national courts.[773]

---

772 Human Rights Committee, General Comment No. 31: Nature of the General Legal Obligation Imposed on States Parties to the Covenant, UN Doc. CCPR/C/21/Rev.1/ Add.13 (26.05.2004), § 10: "States Parties are required by article 2, para. 1, to respect and to ensure the Covenant rights to all persons who may be within their territory and to all persons subject to their jurisdiction. This means that a State Party must respect and ensure the rights laid down in the Covenant to anyone within the power or effective control of that State Party, even if not situated within the territory of the State Party.".
773 Cf. *Jarass* in: NVwZ 2012, 457, 459 et seq.; *Tamblé*, Der Anwendungsbereich der EU-Grundrechtecharta (GRC) gem. Art. 51 I 1 GRC, p. 15.

It remains controversial whether the Member States are also bound by the Charter fundamental rights in cases where they exploit leeway granted under EU law – for example, when transposing directives. In that regard, this is about the parts of national transposition law that are not mandatory under EU law, which are also referred to as not determined under EU law.[774] There are strong arguments in favor of an interpretation that the obligation of the Member States is (also) far-reaching in this area, but not infinite: there is no binding effect at least where the national rule does not make use of any leeway granted by the Union and the issue is thus outside the scope of EU law. Such a leeway granted unionally is one granted to transpose directives equally as the leeway granted to restrict fundamental freedoms. That the Union has competence in an area of law is not sufficient in view of "implementation" if it has not yet exercised the competence.[775] There is therefore no link to the CFR in particular with regard to the regulations on user interfaces and intermediaries in the MStV, even if the EU may have competence in this area to harmonize the law in relation to the digital single market.

However, CJEU case law points to a more far-reaching superseding effect of European over national fundamental rights protection, even if the Court seems to take a different path in its 2013 *Melloni* ruling: there, the CJEU had left national courts free to measure national implementation law also against domestic fundamental rights "provided that the level of protection provided for by the Charter, as interpreted by the Court, and the primacy, unity and effectiveness of EU law are not thereby compromised".[776] It must be doubted whether this decision implies a restriction of the application order, as found in the preceding CJEU judgment in the *Åkerberg Fransson* case in 2013. There, the CJEU had ruled that the Member States' obligation to the Charter extended to "all situations governed by European Union law" and thus to all regulations that fell within the "scope of European Union law".[777] In view of the shown requirements, it is not easily possible to speak of a true cooperative relationship as regards

---

774 Cf. *Kingreen* in Calliess/Ruffert, Art. 51 CFR, para. 10; *Tamblé*, Der Anwendungsbereich der EU-Grundrechtecharta (GRC) gem. Art. 51 I 1 GRC, p. 16.
775 Cf. *Jarass* in: NVwZ 2012, 457, 460; *Tamblé*, Der Anwendungsbereich der EU-Grundrechtecharta (GRC) gem. Art. 51 I 1 GRC, p. 20.
776 CJEU, case C-399/11, *Melloni / Ministerio Fiscal*, para. 60.
777 CJEU, case C-617/10, *Åklagaren / Åkerberg Fransson*, para. 19; cf. on this *Gstrein/Zeitzmann*, in: ZEuS 2013, 239, 239 et seq.

fundamental rights protection.⁷⁷⁸ However, the FCC clearly opposed the expansion of the scope in its *Antiterrordatei* ruling.⁷⁷⁹

2. *Binding effect of fundamental rights protection under German Basic Law – Extraterritorial validity of fundamental rights protection*

a. Introduction

If state media authorities take action against foreign providers, the question arises as to the extent to which these providers may rely on fundamental rights, in particular the freedom of broadcasting under Art. 5(1) sentence 2 Basic Law, against corresponding enforcement measures.

The traditional scope of fundamental rights in the run-up to globalization and Europeanization was the domestic sphere in the relations of German state authority to Germans and to foreigners living in Germany, although for the latter the scope was limited to the "everyone" fundamental rights. However, the scope of fundamental rights in Germany, which is particularly dependent on foreign relations, can no longer be exhaustively defined by a domestic focus.⁷⁸⁰

In the "post-national age" of the "fragmentation" of statehood⁷⁸¹, state authority (also of Germany) is embedded into a complex political, economic, cultural, civil-societal as well as individual-related network of international relations. This also legally connects national (constitutional) law in particular with international and European (not least EU) law, as well as, i.a., international administrative⁷⁸² and international criminal

---

778 Critical e.g. *Tamblé*, Der Anwendungsbereich der EU-Grundrechtecharta (GRC) gem. Art. 51 I 1 GRC, p. 22 et seq.
779 FCC, 1 BvR 1215/07, NJW 2013, 1499, para. 88–91 – *Antiterrordatei*.
780 Cf. on the leveling of status differences between nationals and foreigners by international and European law *Gundel* in: Isensee/Kirchhof, vol. IX, § 198, para. 11 et seq.
781 *Giegerich*, Internationale Standards – aus völkerrechtlicher Perspektive, 101, 176.
782 Cf. on this e.g. *Breining-Kaufmann in*: ZSR 2006, 5, 5 et seq.; *Glaser*, Internationale Verwaltungsbeziehungen; *Kingsbury/Donaldson* in: MPEPIL, para. 4 et seq.; *Kingsbury et al.* in: Law & Contemporary Problems 2005/3–4, 1, 1 et seq.; *Kment*, Grenzüberschreitendes Verwaltungshandeln; *Ohler*, Die Kollisionsordnung des Allgemeinen Verwaltungsrechts; *Tietje*, Internationalisiertes Verwaltungshandeln; *id.*, Die Internationalität des Verwaltungsstaates; *id.*, Die Exekutive. Verwaltungshandeln im Kontext von Globalisierung und Internationalisierung, 53, 53 et seq.

law[783] and, based on these areas of law, with foreign law. Domestic state authority thus comes into contact with foreign legal subjects and their legal sphere in many ways. This multiple European and international connection and integration results in German state authority having effects not only domestically but also abroad, i.e. extraterritorially.[784]

Against this background, fundamental rights have generally binding effect on German state authority, in particular in the exercise of sovereign power, even "insofar as the effects of its activities occur abroad".[785]

However, the fact that Art. 1(3) Basic Law provides for a comprehensive binding effect of fundamental rights on legislature, executive authority and jurisdiction does not yet result in a conclusive determination of the territorial scope of fundamental rights.

> "The Basic Law does not content itself with defining the internal order of the German state but also determines the essential features of the German state's relationship to the community of states. In this respect, the Basic Law assumes that a delimitation between states and legal systems is necessary, and that co-ordination between states and legal systems is also necessary. On the one hand, the scope of competence and responsibility of organs of the German state must be taken into account when determining the scope of application of the fundamental rights.[786] On the other hand, constitutional law must be co-ordinated with international law. International law, however, does not, in principle, preclude the validity of fundamental rights in matters that bear on relations with foreign countries. The territorial scope of the fundamental rights, however, must be drawn from the Basic Law itself, taking into account Article 25 of the Basic Law."[787]

Moreover, "by its very nature, a fundamental right may presuppose a specific relationship to the order of life within the constitution's area of application, so that unrestricted enforcement in circumstances wholly or predominantly related to foreign countries would miss the point of fundamental rights protection."[788]

---

783 Cf. on this e.g. *Ambos/Rackow/Miller*, Internationales Strafrecht; *Gless*, Internationales Strafrecht; *Safferling*, Internationales Strafrecht.
784 Cf. *Stern*, Das Staatsrecht der Bundesrepublik Deutschland, vol. III/1, p. 1224 et seq.
785 BVerfGE 6, 290 (295) (own translation); 57, 1 (23). Cf. on this also *Hofmann*, Grundrechte und grenzüberschreitende Sachverhalte, p. 31 et seq.
786 Cf. on this BVerfGE 66, 39 (57 et seq.); 92, 26 (47).
787 BVerfGE 100, 313 (362 et seq.).
788 BVerfGE 31, 58 (77).

E. Core problems of public international law

In the case of the Basic Law's freedom of broadcasting, at the latest in the age of (also information-related) globalization, it is not apparent that a complete waiver of the fundamental rights obligation in matters with a foreign connection would represent an appropriate balancing of the fundamental rights position and the protection of sovereignty.

That the impact of domestic acts of sovereignty on foreign territory predominantly raises problems of international[789] does not exclude constitutional relevance of the issue with regard to the binding effect of fundamental rights. In this context, Art. 1(2) Basic Law could be seen as a first relevant constitutional link. The commitment there to "inviolable and inalienable human rights as the basis of every community, of peace and of justice in the world" does not, however, provide a universal guarantee of German fundamental rights for all natural and legal persons, without there being a link from the perspective of the Basic Law or a "genuine link" from the perspective of public international law. A universal claim to validity of German fundamental rights would recognizably overstretch Germany's competence under public international law. Such an imperial claim to fundamental rights[790] in the sense of a fundamental rights octroi would clearly contradict the openness of the Basic Law to public international law and the fundamental respect for foreign legal orders[791].[792] The boundaries of the permissible exercise of German sovereignty under public international law by virtue of competence therefore also mark the outermost boundary of the possible scope of fundamental rights.[793]

On the basis of this delimitation, which is open to public international law and respects the sovereign equality of legal orders, three approaches to defining the scope of fundamental rights in view of situations with a foreign connection are generally conceivable:

- The most restrictive delimitation with regard to the application of fundamental rights outside purely internal circumstances, but at the same time the one that most strongly emphasizes sovereign equality, would

---

[789] Cf. on this *Beitzke* in: Strupp/Schlochauer p. 504 et seq.; *Geck* in: Strupp/Schlochauer p. 55; *Schlochauer*, Die extraterritoriale Wirkung von Hoheitsakten nach dem öffentlichen Recht der Bundesrepublik Deutschland und nach internationalem Recht.

[790] Cf. on this *Isensee* in: VVDStRL 1974, 49, 63.

[791] Cf. on this BVerfGE 18, 112 (120 et seq.).

[792] Cf. also *Schröder*, Zur Wirkkraft der Grundrechte bei Sachverhalten mit grenzüberschreitenden Elementen, 137, 141; *Stern*, Das Staatsrecht der Bundesrepublik Deutschland, vol. III/1, p. 1228.

[793] Cf. *Isensee* in: id./Kirchhof, § 190, para. 33 et seq., 58.

be to generally restrict the validity of fundamental rights in the sense of the territoriality principle to the territory of the German state.[794] In an age of open statehood, however, this strict alignment with territorial sovereignty is no longer convincing.[795]

- Conversely, it would be the most far-reaching delimitation with regard to the application of fundamental rights outside of purely internal circumstances, but at the same time also the most burdensome for sovereign equality, if one were to assume the validity of fundamental rights in the sense of the principle of effects everywhere where Germany exercises state power or where this has effects.[796]
- An approach that mediates between these two poles, albeit with stronger links to the principle of effects, is in the sense of a principle of status generally based on the *status passivus* of the holder of the fundamental right, who must be subject either to Germany's territorial or to its personal sovereignty.[797]

Such a mediating approach in the sense of a moderately understood binding effect of fundamental rights deserves approval in principle. For "an unrestricted enforcement [of the binding effect of fundamental rights] in wholly or predominantly foreign-related circumstances would miss the point of fundamental rights protection". It must be determined "in each case by interpreting the relevant constitutional norm whether, based on its wording, meaning and purpose, it claims validity for every conceivable application of sovereign authority within the Federal Republic or whether it permits or requires a differentiation in the case of situations with a more or less intensive foreign connection".[798]

Following the latter approach ensures that the binding effect of fundamental rights under Art. 1(3) Basic Law is also territorially sufficiently effective. Not only is all state authority bound, but all German state authori-

---

[794] Cf. on this e.g. *Heintzen*, Auswärtige Beziehungen privater Verbände, p. 100 et seq., 123 et seq.; *Oppermann*, Transnationale Ausstrahlungen deutscher Grundrechte?, 521, 523, 526.
[795] Cf. on this also *Schröder*, Zur Wirkkraft der Grundrechte bei Sachverhalten mit grenzüberschreitenden Elementen, 137, 140 et seq.
[796] Cf. on this e.g. *Stern*, Das Staatsrecht der Bundesrepublik Deutschland, vol. III/1, p. 1230.
[797] Cf. on this e.g. *Heintzen*, Auswärtige Beziehungen privater Verbände, p. 127 et seq.; *Isensee* in: VVDStRL 1974, 49, 61 et seq.
[798] BVerfGE 31, 58 (77) (own translation).

E. Core problems of public international law

ty is generally bound wherever it acts or has an impact.[799] Accordingly, anyone who is subject to German state authority enjoys the protection of fundamental rights. Who in contrast is not exposed to it, cannot be considered as a holder of fundamental rights.[800] This means that, in principle, foreign providers facing enforcement measures by the state media authorities on the basis of the MStV or JMStV can also invoke the protection of fundamental rights under the Basic Law.[801]

b. The FCC's judgment on the extraterritorial application of fundamental rights of 19 May 2020

In its so-called BND judgment of 19 May 2020, the FCC emphasized that the binding of German state authority to fundamental rights under Art. 1(3) Basic Law was not limited to German territory. However, the protection of individual fundamental rights could differ at home and abroad. In any case, the protection of Art. 10(1) and Art. 5(1) sentence 2 Basic Law as rights of defense against a telecommunications surveillance also extended to foreigners abroad. In the view of the FCC, Art. 1(3) Basic Law "provides that German state authority is comprehensively bound by the fundamental rights of the Basic Law. No restrictive requirements that make the binding effect of fundamental rights dependent on a territorial connection with Germany or on the exercise of specific sovereign powers can be inferred from the provision." This applied in any case to fundamental rights as rights of defense against surveillance measures such as those at issue here.[802]

In the FCC's view, fundamental rights bind state authority "comprehensively and universally by the fundamental rights, irrespective of the specific functions, the types of action or the respective object of the exercise of state functions. State authority must be understood broadly, covering not only orders and prohibitions or measures based on sovereign powers. Fundamental rights are binding in relation to any decision that can claim to be made on behalf of all citizens at the relevant level of decision-making with-

---

799 Cf. on this also *Stern*, Das Staatsrecht der Bundesrepublik Deutschland, vol. III/1, p. 1230.
800 Cf. *Rüfner* in: *Isensee/Kirchhof*, vol. IX, § 196, para. 34 et seq.
801 On the particularities of the extraterritorial effect of fundamental rights in the case of cross-border broadcasting cf. *Stern*, Das Staatsrecht der Bundesrepublik Deutschland, vol. III/1, p. 1233 with further references.
802 FCC, Judgment of the First Senate of 19 May 2020, 1 BvR 2835/17, para. 88.

in the state. This includes both sovereign and non-sovereign measures, statements and actions. Thus, any action of state organs or organisations constitutes an exercise of state authority that is bound by fundamental rights within the meaning of Art. 1(3) [Basic Law] because such actions are performed in the exercise of their mandate to serve the common good." Notwithstanding the state media authorities' own fundamental rights, this also includes sovereign acts taken by them in application of the MStV or JMStV.[803]

In this context, the binding effect of fundamental rights on German state authority is also abroad not limited to a mere objective law obligation. Rather, it corresponds with a fundamental right entitlement of those who are identified as protected fundamental rights holders by the respective fundamental rights guarantees: "[t]he Basic Law does not provide for fundamental rights that bind the state vis-à-vis individual fundamental rights holders without also providing the individual with a corresponding subjective right. It is a key part of fundamental rights protection under the Basic Law that fundamental rights are rights of the individual".[804]

As the FCC points out, the binding effect of fundamental rights on German state authority, even when acting vis-à-vis foreigners abroad, also corresponds to the integration of the Federal Republic into the international community of states.[805]

c. Extraterritorial validity also of the freedom of broadcasting for foreign legal persons

However, the BND judgment does not provide an answer to the question of whether foreign providers, be they broadcasters, telemedia providers or intermediaries, can rely on the fundamental right of freedom of broadcasting *ratione personae* against enforcement measures based on the MStV or JMStV. In this respect, a distinction must be made between foreign providers who are natural persons and providers in the form of legal persons (also) in view of freedom of broadcasting which may be impaired by such enforcement measures.

---

803 FCC, Judgment of the First Senate of 19 May 2020, 1 BvR 2835/17, para. 91.
804 FCC, Judgment of the First Senate of 19 May 2020, 1 BvR 2835/17, para. 92.
805 FCC, Judgment of the First Senate of 19 May 2020, 1 BvR 2835/17, para. 93 et seq.

E. Core problems of public international law

The freedom of broadcasting under Art. 5(1) sentence 2 Basic Law is conceived as an "everyone" fundamental right. Consequently, not only Germans but also third-country nationals can invoke this freedom. Against this background, it is initially clear that foreign providers in the form of natural persons affected by enforcement measures of the state media authorities on the basis of the JMStV can invoke Art. 5(1) sentence 2 Basic Law on the grounds of an alleged violation of fundamental rights.

The legal situation is more difficult where foreign legal persons act as providers. In this respect, as a starting point, Art. 19(3) Basic Law deserves consideration. Accordingly, "basic rights shall also apply to domestic legal persons to the extent that the nature of such rights permits".

It is evident that the freedom of broadcasting under Art. 5(1) sentence 2 Basic Law is, by its very nature, also applicable from the outset to legal persons – regardless of whether domestic or foreign. This is confirmed by a large number of judgments in which domestic undertakings, as legal persons under private law, have successfully invoked a violation of this fundamental right.[806]

However, the FCC has ruled until recently that foreign legal persons cannot invoke substantive fundamental rights such as freedom of broadcasting – unlike procedural fundamental rights such as Art. 101(1) sentence 2 and Art. 103(1) Basic Law[807]. In justifying its decision, the FCC referred to the wording and meaning of Art. 19(3) Basic Law, which prohibited a respective expansive interpretation.[808]

In a judgment of 19 July 2011, the FCC had to deal for the first time with the more specific question of whether foreign legal persons that have their registered office in the EU can be holders of substantive fundamental rights under the Basic Law. This question was prior controversial in the literature.[809]

---

806 BVerfGE 95, 220 (234).
807 Cf. BVerfGE 12, 6 (8); 18, 441 (447); 21, 362 (373); 64, 1 (11).
808 Cf. BVerfGE 21, 207 (208 et seq.); 23, 229 (236); 100, 313 (364). In other decisions, the FCC has expressly left the fundamental rights entitlement of foreign legal persons in doubt (cf. in general BVerfGE 12, 6 (8); 34, 338 (340); 64, 1 (11) as well as BVerfGE 18, 441 (447) in view of Art. 14(1) Basic Law.
809 Cf. in favor *Drathen*, Deutschengrundrechte im Lichte des Gemeinschaftsrechts; *Dreier* in: id., Art. 19(3) GG, para. 20 et seq., 83 et seq.; *Kotzur* in: DÖV 2001, 192, 195 et seq.; disapproving *Bethge*, Die Grundrechtsberechtigung juristischer Personen nach Art. 19 Abs. 3 Grundgesetz, p. 46 et seq.; *Quaritsch* in: Isensee/Kirchhof, vol. V, § 120, para. 36 et seq.; *Weinzierl*, Europäisierung des deutschen Grundrechtsschutzes?.

According to the wording of Art. 19(3) Basic Law, fundamental rights apply only "to domestic legal persons". Due to the restriction to domestic legal persons, an extension of application cannot be justified on the basis of the wording of Art. 19(3) Basic Law. It would exceed the boundaries of wording if one wanted to interpret in conformity with EU law by understanding the characteristic "domestic" as "German including European" legal persons.[810] Also, while EU third countries are no longer "classic" foreign countries, they are not "domestic" in the sense of territorial sovereignty either.[811]

However, Art. 19(3) Basic Law was also not based on the express intention of the constitutional legislature to permanently exclude the invocation of fundamental rights also by legal persons from EU Member States. The EU has meanwhile developed into a highly integrated "Staatenverbund"[812] in which Germany participates in accordance with Art. 23(1) Basic Law. The extension of the application of Art. 19(3) Basic Law reflects this development.[813] An extension of the application of fundamental rights protection to legal persons from the EU corresponds to the treaty obligations assumed by Germany through TEU and TFEU, as expressed in particular in the European fundamental freedoms and – subsidiarily – the general prohibition of discrimination in Art. 18 TFEU. "The fundamental freedoms and the general ban on discrimination prohibit the unequal treatment of domestic and foreign enterprises from the European Union in the sphere of application of Union law, and in this regard override the limitation of protection of fundamental rights to domestic legal persons provided for in Article 19.3 of the Basic Law."[814]

As a result of the extension of the application of Art. 19(3) Basic Law, legal persons with a registered office in another EU state are treated equally to domestic legal persons. Conversely, however, this also means that the same constitutional provisions (including the limitations on freedom of broadcasting under Art. 5(2) Basic Law) can be invoked against EU foreigners as against domestic legal persons.[815]

---

810 BVerfGE 129, 78 (96).
811 Cf. BVerfGE 123, 267 (402 et seq.).
812 BVerfGE 123, 267 (348).
813 Cf. BVerfGE 129, 78 (96 et seq.).
814 BVerfGE 129, 78 (97).
815 Cf. BVerfGE 129, 78 (97 et seq.). The control of EU law assigned to the FCC with regard to the preservation of constitutional identity, compliance with the competences conferred according to the principle of conferral, and the guarantee of a level of protection essentially equivalent to that of German fundamental

E. Core problems of public international law

One could, at the outset, consider making this dogmatic derivation of the extension of the application of Art. 19(3) Basic Law, particularly via the prohibition of discrimination in Art. 18 TFEU, fruitful not only in view of the scope of protection of fundamental rights and their limits, but also in view of an obligation to protect derived from fundamental rights, in such a way that the corresponding obligation exists not only vis-à-vis domestic natural and legal persons, but also vis-à-vis foreign natural and legal persons. However, such a dogmatic approach would fail to recognize that the prohibition of discrimination only applies within the scope of the TFEU. In particular the fundamental freedoms of the TFEU do not generally give rise to any obligation to protect private third parties.

d. Interim conclusion

Based on a teleological and historical interpretation of the JMStV, the state media authorities are authorized to take enforcement measures against foreign providers for violating substantive provisions of the JMStV. This authority is confirmed to some degree by an interpretation of the JMStV in conformity with EU law, at least in the case of situations involving providers with their registered office in an EU Member State. An interpretation of the JMStV in conformity with public international law does not per se preclude such an authority: this is because the applicable public international law does not (any longer) contain a principle that national administrative law may not also be applied to foreign-related content.

Insofar as the state media authorities take action against foreign providers, they are bound by the fundamental rights provisions of the Basic Law with regard to the freedom of broadcasting in Art. 5(1) sentence 2 at least if the provider is either a natural person or a legal person based in the EU.

---

rights protection is maintained. The constitutional identity (cf. BVerfGE 123, 267 (354, 398 et seq.); 126, 286 (302 et seq.) is obviously not affected by the extension of the application of Art. 19(3) Basic Law; cf. BVerfGE 129, 78 (100).

IV. Obligation to regulate the media as an expression of State obligations to protect

1. Introduction

According to by now prevailing constitutional doctrine, the fundamental rights of the Basic Law are not only rights of defense against disproportionate state interference in the freedom they guarantee. Rather, the state is also categorically obligated to legal regulations that protect the fundamental rights of its citizens. A state fulfills this obligation to protect not only by providing performance, but also by taking measures to avert threats to fundamental rights posed by third parties.[816]

The starting point of this constitutional dogmatic approach is that threats to the legal interests protected by fundamental rights do not only emanate from the state, but can also be triggered by nature (in particular in the form of natural disasters or other extraordinary emergencies, especially epidemic situations), but also by third parties, be they individuals or legal persons. The constitutional approach to dealing with such threats is a balance between the lack of third-party effect of fundamental rights on the one hand and the state's monopoly on the use of force on the other. The former leads to the risk of impairment of fundamental rights in the absence of a respective obligation on the part of private parties, while the latter sets limits to the self-protection of those entitled to fundamental rights.[817]

Against this background, the dogmatics of the obligation to protect ties in with the understanding of fundamental rights as an objective value system, whereby the state is transformed from an opponent to a guarantor of fundamental rights.[818]

2. Obligations to protect in FCC case law

The FCC has developed the dual function of fundamental rights as rights of defense and protection particularly in view of the fundamental right to

---

816 Cf. *Würtenberger*, Schranken der Forschungsfreiheit und staatliche Schutzpflichten, p. 12.
817 Cf. on this also *Moritz,* Staatliche Schutzpflichten gegenüber pflegebedürftigen Menschen, p. 95 et seq.
818 Cf. BVerfGE 39, 1 (41 et seq.).

E. Core problems of public international law

life and physical integrity.[819] However, it also has dogmatic significance in view of other fundamental rights. With regard to the protection of minors from harmful media, however, the state's obligation to protect physical integrity is already evident. With regard to the goal of safeguarding diversity, the state's, in the guise of the Länder, positive obligation to order and the obligation to protect run parallel under constitutional law.

The obligations to protect are directed in particular, but not exclusively, to the legislature. The obligation to protect may also include risk prevention related to threats to fundamental rights.[820] The constitutional obligation to protect may require the exercise of sovereign authority in such a way that the danger of violations of fundamental rights also remains contained; whether, when and with what content such exercise is constitutionally required depends on the nature, proximity and extent of possible dangers, the nature and rank of the constitutionally protected legal interest and the regulatory safeguards already in place.[821] In view of the preservation of media pluralism, this dynamic understanding of obligations to protect is of particular significance, not least in view of the role of media intermediaries in the digital media ecosystem.

If the legislature has made a decision the basis of which is decisively called into question by new developments that were not yet foreseeable at the time the law was enacted, then, according to the FCC's case law, it may be required by the constitution to review whether the original decision is to be upheld even under the changed circumstances.[822] This obligation to evaluate, monitor and, if necessary, make improvements is recognized in principle, also in view of changed media usage behavior with regard to the previous television-centered State Treaty law to ensure diversity in the media sector, by cipher 5 of the protocol declaration of all states to the State Treaty on the Modernization of the Media Order in Germany[823]. It applies in the same way in cases in which the enforcement of existing legislation

---

819 Cf. BVerfGE 39, 1 (42); 46, 160 (164); 56, 54 (78); 90, 145 (195); 115, 320 (346); 121, 317 (356).
820 Cf. BVerfGE 49, 89 (140 et seq.); 52, 214 (220); 53, 30 (57).
821 Cf. with respect to the legislative dimension of obligations to protect BVerfGE 56, 54 (78).
822 Cf. BVerfGE 49, 89 (143 et seq.); 56, 54 (79).
823 With an introductory reference to the fact that the federal states agree "that the adaptation of the legal framework to the digital transformation is not completed with the present State Treaty", they declare that they "work on further reform proposals" on, i.a., media concentration law, whereby they consider on this in the protocol declaration: "[t]he federal states are committed to a sustainable media concentration law. This must be able to effectively counteract the actual

serving the protection of interests based on fundamental rights is carried out on the basis of an enforcement concept, the effectiveness of which is decisively called into question as a result of new developments not yet foreseeable at the time the concept was drafted.

In settled case law, the FCC[824] emphasizes that the state bodies were primarily and in own responsibility in charge for decisions on how the obligation to protect derived from the respective fundamental right was to be fulfilled; they decided which measures were appropriate and imperative in order to ensure effective protection. This corresponds to a limitation of the FCC's constitutional review to whether the state bodies can be found to have evidently violated the basic decisions embodied in the fundamental rights.[825]

> *"This limitation of constitutional review appears imperative because it is regularly a highly complex question how a positive state obligation to protect and act, which is only derived by way of constitutional interpretation from the basic decisions embodied in fundamental rights, is to be realized by active legislative measures. Various solutions are possible depending on the assessment of the actual circumstances, the specific objectives and their priority, and the suitability of the conceivable ways and means. According to the principle of separation of powers and the democratic principle, the decision, which often requires compromises, belongs to the responsibility of the legislature, which is directly legitimized by the people, and can generally be reviewed by the [FCC] only to a limited extent, unless legal interests of the highest importance are at stake. These considerations are more important when the question is not only whether the legislature has violated an obligation to protect that can be derived from fundamental rights, but when also the further question is controversial whether it has committed this violation by failing to remedy the situation. The [FCC] can only find a violation of the Constitution of this kind if it is evident that an originally lawful regulation has become unconstitutional due to a change in circumstances in the meantime, and if the legislature has nevertheless continued to remain inactive or has taken obviously erroneous remedial measures."*[826]

---

threats to diversity of opinion. In the last few years, the media markets have experienced an opening that has brought other media genres besides television, the possible consequences of cross-media mergers and also those on upstream and downstream markets increasingly into focus. A reformed media concentration law must therefore take all media-relevant markets into view." (own translation).
824 BVerfGE 39, 1 (44); 46, 160 (164).
825 Cf. BVerfGE 4, 7 (18); 27, 253 (283); 33, 303 (333); 36, 321 (330 et seq.).
826 BVerfGE 56, 54 (81) (own translation, emphasis in the original).

This restriction of judicial review in the FCC's *Fluglärm* decision, which is based on legislative manifestations of the obligation to protect fundamental rights, also applies accordingly in view of the exercise of fundamental rights obligations to protect by other organs of state authority.

Accordingly, fundamental rights obligations to protect do not in principle give rise to any concrete obligations to act on the part of the sovereign authority. "The Constitution specifies protection as an objective, but not its detailed form. Courts are precluded from substituting their own assessment of how the obligation to protect should be expediently discharged for that of the relevant acting institution. This reduction in the density of judicial control follows in particular from the principle of separation of powers. The doctrine of the obligation to protect – as a further performance dimension of fundamental rights – in any case means an extension of judicial review of legislative or executive actions and omissions. If the courts were to substitute their assessment of the appropriateness of a protective measure for that of the authority acting in each case, the review of legality by the courts provided for in the Basic Law would become a comprehensive review of appropriateness incompatible with the principle of separation of powers and, as a result, the judiciary would have ultimate decision-making authority."[827]

In fulfilling the obligations to protect under fundamental rights, not only the legislature[828] but all state authorities therefore have a broad scope for assessment, evaluation and design. This broad scope for decision exists in particular when the obligations to protect are related to the foreign policy sphere.[829]

In deciding how the state fulfills its obligation to protect within its broad discretion, several factors must be considered. The objective need for protection of fundamental rights, as well as the subjective need for protection of the individual fundamental rights holder, depend on the sensitivity of the protected interest concerned, on the type, scope and intensity of the (potential and actual) encroachment, as well as on the possibility of legitimate and reasonable remedial action by the fundamental rights holder

---

827 VG Köln, judgment of 27.05.2015, 3 K 5625/14, para. 58, 60 (own translation).
828 Cf. on this BVerfGE 46, 160 (164).
829 VG Köln, judgment of 27.05.2015, 3 K 5625/14, para. 71, 73 with reference to FCC, 2 BvR 1720/03, BVerfGK 14, 192; *von Arnauld*, Freiheit und Regulierung in der Cyberwelt: Transnationaler Schutz der Privatsphäre aus Sicht des Völkerrechts, 27, 28.

himself. The obligation of the state is subject to what is factually[830] and constitutionally possible.

However, the broad scope for assessment, evaluation and design is undercut if it is obvious that the protective measures taken are completely inadequate or unsuitable. In this regard, the scope for design is limited in narrowly defined exceptional cases by the prohibition of undercutting.[831] The state may not secure the fundamental rights of its citizens below the required degree.[832] The FCC can only find a breach of such an obligation to protect in this respect if protective measures are either not taken at all, if the regulations and measures taken are obviously unsuitable or completely inadequate to achieve the required objective of protection, or if they fall considerably short of that objective.[833]

These requirements also apply with regard to obligations to protect under the law on the protection of minors from harmful media: indeed, the protection of minors is expressly defined as a state task in the Constitutions of the State of Baden-Württemberg (Art. 13), the Free State of Bavaria (Art. 126(3)), the Free Hanseatic City of Bremen (Art. 25(1), (2)), the State of Mecklenburg-Western Pomerania (Art. 14(3)), the State of North Rhine-Westphalia (Art. 6(2)), Rhineland-Palatinate (Art. 25(2) sentence 1), Saarland (Art. 25 sentence 1), the Free State of Saxony (Art. 9 (2)), the State of Saxony-Anhalt (Art. 24(4)), and the State of Schleswig-Holstein (Art. 6a) only.[834] However, the constitutional dimension of the protection of minors is not limited exclusively to its quality as a protective purpose justifying restrictions on fundamental rights, also outside these particularities of state constitutional law. Rather, the protection of minors in the Federal Republic of Germany as a whole is a legal asset with constitutional status.[835] Accordingly, it is equivalent to fundamental rights and the other legal rights with constitutional rank – with the exception of human dignity, which is superior to all of them.[836]

---

830 Cf. on this also *Moritz*, Staatliche Schutzpflichten gegenüber pflegebedürftigen Menschen, p. 120.
831 Cf. BVerfGE 88, 203 (251 et seq.); 98, 265 (356).
832 Cf. on this also *Moritz*, Staatliche Schutzpflichten gegenüber pflegebedürftigen Menschen, p. 115.
833 Cf. BVerfGE 56, 54 (80); 77, 170 (215); 92, 26 (46); 125, 39 (78 et seq.) as well as on this e.g. *Würtenberger*, Schranken der Forschungsfreiheit und staatliche Schutzpflichten, p. 12 et seq.
834 Cf. *Ukrow*, Jugendschutzrecht, para. 12.
835 Cf. BVerfGE 30, 336 (347 et seq.); 47, 109 (117); 77, 345 (356); 83, 130 (139 et seq.); BVerwGE 39, 197 (208); 77, 75 (82); 91, 223 (224 et seq.).
836 Cf. *Ukrow*, Jugendschutzrecht, para. 12.

E. Core problems of public international law

The right of children and adolescents to "become a person"[837] is guaranteed by the right to free development of personality in Art. 2(1) Basic Law and the guarantee of human dignity in Art. 1(1) Basic Law.[838] This right to "become a person" beyond its defensive side also has a content of objective law.[839] Accordingly, the state is assigned the task of protecting this right of minors or creating the conditions for it to be realized. Influences that could lead to considerable undesirable developments that are difficult or impossible to correct must be kept away from minors by the state.[840] It must "ensure, as far as possible, the external conditions for the spiritual and mental development of children and adolescents in accordance with the Basic Law's conception of human being".[841]

The question of whether the state has an obligation to protect minors with regard to the effective protection of minors from harmful media has not yet been addressed by the highest courts. A corresponding extension of the doctrine of the obligation to protect to minors requires a separate dogmatic justification. Only where a comparison of the position of minors in situations of audiovisual confrontation with content harmful to them or their development with the constellations from the previous case law on the obligation to protect results in a comparable need for protection, does an extension seem constitutionally required. It is not evident that the federal states would not comply with such an obligation to protect, assuming its existence, via legislative measures under the requirements of the JMStV as amended by Art. 3 of the State Treaty on the Modernization of the Media Order in Germany. In addition, at the latest since the media supervisory authority began intervening directly against foreign providers, it is not apparent that there is a violation of the duty to protect at the level of enforcement which, based on the dogmatic approach of the FCC, amounts to a violation of fundamental rights.

---

837 Cf. *Ditzen* in: NJW 1989, 2519, 2519 ("Right to become human"); *Engels* in: AöR 1997, 212, 219 et seq., 226 et seq.
838 Cf. on this e.g. also *Nikles* in: id./Roll/Spürck/Erdemir/Gutknecht, Teil I, para. 5.
839 Cf. also *Langenfeld* in: MMR 2003, 303, 305.
840 Cf. BVerfGE 30, 336 (347 et seq.); BVerwGE 77, 75 (82); *Dörr/Cole*, Jugendschutz in den elektronischen Medien, p. 20; *Engels* in: AöR 1997, 212, 219 et seq., 226 et seq.; *Isensee/Axer*, Jugendschutz im Fernsehen, p. 69.
841 *BVerwG* NJW 1987, 1429 (1430) (own translation); *Schulz* in: MMR 1998, 182, 183; *Ukrow*, Jugendschutzrecht, para. 13.

3. European references of the doctrine of the obligation to protect based on fundamental rights

a. Doctrine of the obligation to protect and the ECHR

With regard to the ECHR, the fundamental existence of obligations to protect ("*positive obligations*" / "*obligations positives*") – derived from obligations to act – can be established by interpreting a number of judgments.[842] At the same time, however, there is (also) on the basis of the ECHR a leeway for implementation by the states in the exercise of such obligations, so that it is not necessarily a legal regulation that has to follow; also duties to investigate or information requirements come into consideration.[843] However, obligations to act may also give rise to obligations to protect in relations between private parties.[844]

b. Doctrine of the obligation to protect in light of EU law

Within the framework of EU law there is not yet any doctrine of the obligation to protect on the basis of the CFR that is comparable to the situation under constitutional law.[845] Such an approach to obligation to protect would, however, in the current state of integration, in any case collide with Art. 51(2) CFR, according to which the Charter "does not extend the field of application of Union law beyond the powers of the Union or establish any new power or task for the Union, or modify powers and tasks as defined in the Treaties".

However, it is also not evident that TEU or TFEU impose limitations under EU law on the constitutional doctrine of the obligation to protect. One argument against this is that it is now recognized that the prohibitions of fundamental freedoms apply not only to direct state conduct, but

---

842 Cf. in particular ECtHR, No. 23144/93, *Özgür Gundem / Turkey*, para. 42 as well as e.g. *Dröge*, Positive Verpflichtungen der Staaten in der Europäischen Menschenrechtskonvention, p. 1 et seq., 71 et seq., 179 et seq.; *Jaeckel*, Schutzpflichten im deutschen und europäischen Recht, p. 128 et seq.; *Klatt* in: ZaöRV 2011, 691, 692 et seq.; *Koenen*, Wirtschaft und Menschenrechte, p. 58; *Ress* in: ZaöRV 2004, 621, 628.
843 Cf. *Koenen*, Wirtschaft und Menschenrechte, p. 59 et seq.
844 Cf. *Koenen*, Wirtschaft und Menschenrechte, p. 66 et seq.
845 Cf. *Jarass*, Charta der Grundrechte der Europäischen Union, Art. 51, para. 39; *Kingreen* in: Calliess/Ruffert Art. 51 CFR, para. 25 et seq.

also to private conduct attributable to a Member State. In this respect, the considerations of the CJEU in *Commission / France* from 1997[846], which relate to the scope of the free movement of goods, also deserve consideration *mutatis mutandis* for the delimitation of the scope of the other fundamental freedoms. The fundamental freedoms thus not only prohibit measures that are attributable to a Member State and themselves create restrictions on trade between Member States, but "also appl[y] where a Member State abstains from adopting the measures required in order to deal with obstacles to the free movement of goods (or other fundamental freedoms; author's addition) which are not caused by the State".[847] Indeed, fundamental freedoms may be interfered with, equally to an act by a Member State, by a Member State's inaction or failure to take sufficient measures to remove obstacles to a fundamental freedom created, in particular, by acts of private persons on its territory that are directed against the activity protected by the fundamental freedom.[848] Thus, Art. 34 and 63 TFEU "require[...] the Member States not merely themselves to abstain from adopting measures or engaging in conduct liable to constitute an obstacle to trade (or other obstacles to a fundamental freedom, author's addition), but also, when read with [Art. 5 TEC, now: Art. 4(3) TEU], to take all necessary and appropriate measures to ensure that that fundamental freedom(s) [are] respected on their territory".[849]

The measures taken by a Member State in the event of interference by private parties with a fundamental freedom of the TFEU must be sufficient – taking into account the frequency and seriousness of such interference – to guarantee that fundamental freedom by "preventing and effectively dissuading the perpetrators of the offences in question from committing and repeating them".[850] The Member State concerned must, "unless it can show that action on its part would have consequences for public order with which it could not cope by using the means at its disposal, [...] adopt all appropriate measures to guarantee the full scope and effect of [Union]

---

846 CJEU, case C-265/95, *Commission / France*.
847 CJEU, case C-265/95, *Commission / France*, para. 30; cf. also *Pache* in: Schulze/Zuleeg/Kadelbach, § 10, para. 214.
848 Cf. on the approach of the CJEU in its trade in goods jurisprudence CJEU, case C-265/95, *Commission / France*, para. 31.
849 CJEU, case C-265/95, *Commission / France*, para. 32.
850 CJEU, case C-265/95, *Commission / France*, para. 52; zur gebotenen Abschreckung cf. furthermore *Meier*, Anmerkung, EuZW 1998, 87, 87.

law so as to ensure its proper implementation in the interests of all economic operators".[851]

In this context, the Member States have considerable discretion as to which measures are most appropriate in a given situation to eliminate interference with fundamental freedoms by private parties. Accordingly, the EU institutions are not competent to substitute themselves for the Member States and to prescribe to them which measures to adopt and actually apply in order to ensure the fundamental freedoms from, into and through their territory.[852] This prerogative of evaluation recognized in the relationship between the Member States and the EU level shows recognizable structural parallels to the prerogative of evaluation of state bodies in relation to a domestic judicial supervisory authority such as the FCC with regard to the question of how an obligation to protect is satisfied.

However, the CJEU has competence to examine, taking into account the aforementioned discretion in the cases submitted to it, whether the Member State concerned has taken appropriate measures to ensure the fundamental freedoms. In view of the Member State's prerogative of evaluation, a breach of the obligation to protect fundamental freedoms can only be assumed if the interference with the fundamental freedom proves to be so serious that the conduct of the Member State no longer appears acceptable, even taking into account the prerogative of evaluation to which it is entitled.[853] The parallelism of this limit to said prerogative with the prohibition of undercutting in the FCC's case law is also evident.

c. Obligations to protect in the network of regulatory systems

Based on the FCC's Solange jurisprudence[854], it can also be argued that the obligations to protect under the Basic Law do not have to be exercised as long as and to the extent that a roughly comparable level of protection exists through the activities of third countries. Such an approach, based on cooperation between regulatory authorities in the interest of the protection of human dignity and of minors from harmful media, takes into account the openness to integration and to public international law of the

---

851 CJEU, case C-265/95, *Commission / France*, para. 56.
852 CJEU, case C-265/95, *Commission / France*, para. 33 et seq.
853 Cf. CJEU, case C-112/00, *Schmidberger / Austria*, para. 80 et seq.; cf. also *Jeck/Langner*, Die Europäische Dimension des Sports, p. 25 et seq.; *Lengauer*, Drittwirkung von Grundfreiheiten, p. 218 et seq., 227 et seq.
854 Cf. on this in detail already supra, chapter B.VI.2.

E. Core problems of public international law

Basic Law. It adds an executive facet to the existing justice-oriented process of reciprocal reception of Member State, European and international fundamental rights guarantees with a view to the protective aspects, and at the same time relieves the regulatory authorities of unnecessary duplication of work. However, such a comparable level of protection based on obligations under public international law is lacking in view of the protection of human dignity and, to a large extent, also of minors from harmful media. In particular, the constitutional obligations to protect extend beyond mere protection against child pornography, which is now recognized under international treaty law.

V. Substantive law aspects

In terms of substantive law, some regulations in current German legal acts that are relevant to the media sector take on shapes that not only raise questions – which do not need to be discussed further in the present context – about the coherence of regulation at the domestic level, but also do not appear to rule out a certain potential for conflict with the European legal framework, to say the least. In particular, the Network Enforcement Act (NetzDG) has triggered controversial debates about its legal conformity since its inception – not only with regard to questions of its (primarily formal) constitutionality,[855] which will not be discussed in detail here,[856]

---

855 Critical of the legislative competence of the Bund e.g. *Feldmann* in: K&R 2017, 292, 294; *Gersdorf* in: MMR 2017, 439, 441; *Hain/Ferreau/Brings-Wiesen* in: K&R 2017, 433, 434; *Kalscheuer/Hornung* NVwZ 2017, 1721, 1721 et seq.; *Müller-Franken* in: AfP 2018, 1, 2 et seq.; *Nolte* in: ZUM 2017, 552, 561; diff. op. e.g. *Bautze* in: KJ 2019, 203, 208; *Peifer* in: AfP 2018, 14, 21 et seq. Incidentally, the FCC considers constitutional complaints directly directed against provisions of the NetzDG to be inadmissible (cf. Order of 23.04.2019 – 1 BvR 2314/18, para. 6 et seq.), as there is no exhaustion of the specialized courts' legal remedies if no action is taken against the enforcement act (such as blocking or deletion of content by the network providers), in which case the constitutionality of the rules of the NetzDG can also be reviewed incidentally.
856 The constitutionality of the amendment to the NetzDG by the Act to Combat Right-Wing Extremism and Hate Crime (BT-Drs. 19/17741 and 19/20163) is also controversial. In the wake of, i.a., an expert opinion by the Scientific Service of the German Bundestag (available at https://cdn.netzpolitik.org/wp-upload/2020/09/WD-10-030-20-Gesetz-Hasskriminalitaet.pdf), according to media reports (https://netzpolitik.org/2020/gutachten-zum-netzdg-gesetz-gegen-hasskriminalitaet-verfassungswidrig/#vorschaltbanner), the Federal President is hesitating to sign the amendment passed by the Bundestag and Bundesrat because of con-

but also with regard to its compatibility with EU law, which is doubted in parts of the literature.⁸⁵⁷

1. The scope of certain national legal acts

a. Country of origin principle and NetzDG

Pursuant to Art. 3(1) ECD, the state in which a service provider is established must ensure that its offering complies with domestic provisions. According to Art. 3(2) ECD, Member States may not restrict the freedom to provide information society services from another Member State for reasons falling within the so-called "coordinated field". This country of origin principle, already described above, is intended to ensure the smooth movement of services in the internal market for this sector. This means that Member States may not, in principle, impose regulations on providers from other EU States that differ from those of their country of origin. The newly introduced Art. 28a(1), (5) AVMSD reiterates this principle for VSP, which may include social networks.⁸⁵⁸

The scope of the NetzDG, which came into force in Germany in 2017, applies to telemedia service providers who operate platforms on the Internet with the intention of making a profit, which are intended for users to share any content with other users or make it accessible to the public (social networks), and thus generally also covers service providers established in (EU) countries outside Germany. The regulations define the scope of the law in accordance with the objective of more effectively combating hate crime as well as other punishable content, specified in the law, on social networks platforms in order to avert the related threats to peaceful coexistence and to a free, open and democratic society.⁸⁵⁹ The NetzDG is thus in tension with the country of origin principle, insofar as it lays down

---

stitutional concerns. Cf. also tagesschau.de, Verfassungsrechtliche Bedenken – Scheitert das Anti-Hass-Gesetz?, https://www.tagesschau.de/investigativ/ndr-wdr/hasskriminalitaet-gesetz-101.html.
857 So e.g. *Spindler* in: ZUM 2017, 473, 473 et seq.; *Hoeren*, Netzwerkdurchsetzungsgesetz europarechtswidrig.
858 *Nölscher* in: ZUM 2020, 301, 306. Cf. on this in detail and with further references supra, chapter D.II.2.d(5).
859 Cf. on this the explanatory memorandum to the then draft law of the CDU/CSU and SPD parliamentary groups of the German Bundestag, BT-Drs. 18/12356 of 16.05.2017, p. 18.

E. Core problems of public international law

stricter rules than the respective (EU) country of origin of a network within the meaning of the law and with a certain significance in Germany, as regards the scope of the catalog of obligations for the deletion of illegal content, the administrative offenses that are subject to fines, or the requirement of domestic authorised agents.[860]

However, Art. 3(4) ECD provides exceptions to the country of origin principle. Thus, according to Art. 3(4)(a) ECD, Member States may, by way of derogation from the country of origin principle, take measures if they are necessary for the protection of public policy, in particular the prevention, investigation, detection and prosecution of criminal offences, including the protection of minors and the fight against any incitement to hatred on grounds of race, sex, religion or nationality, and violations of human dignity concerning individual persons, and concern a particular information society service which prejudices one of these objectives or at least poses a serious and grave risk to them. In this context, the measure must be proportionate to the objective pursued.

In particular the characteristics of a "given information society service"[861] as well as the appropriateness[862] are seen as worthy of discussion in the context of the NetzDG. What is meant by a "given [...] service" affected is that the exception set forth in Art. 3(3) ECD does not represent a derogation. Thus, it is at least questionable whether the abstract-general obligations of the NetzDG, for example with regard to reporting obligations affecting an entire group of information society services, can fall within this exception.[863] The appropriateness of the regulation is also viewed very critically by individual authors with regard to the blanket rule on response times and presumed negative impacts on freedom of expression on the Internet.[864]

In part, this fundamental problem of compatibility with the country of origin principle is addressed in the current draft of a law amending the Network Enforcement Act (NetzDGÄndG-E)[865] with regard to VSP. The explanation to the NetzDGÄndG-E emphasizes that Art. 28a(5) AVMSD

---

860 *Hoeren*, Netzwerkdurchsetzungsgesetz europarechtswidrig.
861 In more detail on this *Nölscher* in: ZUM 2020, 301, 307.
862 Critical on this *Hoeren*, Netzwerkdurchsetzungsgesetz europarechtswidrig.
863 *Nölscher* concludes that much speaks in favor of an extensive interpretation of the exception, ZUM 2020, 301, 310; critical with regard to the reference to a "given [...] service" *Spindler* in: ZUM 2017, 473, 476.
864 *Hoeren*, Netzwerkdurchsetzungsgesetz europarechtswidrig.
865 Deutscher Bundestag, Entwurf eines Gesetzes zur Änderung des Netzwerkdurchsetzungsgesetzes. BT-Drs. 19/18792 of 27.04.2020.

referred to the application of the ECD for providers of VSP services. For such services that are not located or deemed to be located in Germany, the NetzDG should therefore generally not apply. However, the authority responsible under § 4 NetzDG (the Federal Office of Justice) is to be able to determine the general applicability of the NetzDG and its scope with regard to the obligations under §§ 2, 3 and 3 b (of the then amended) NetzDG on a case-by-case basis (for providers specified then), subject to the requirements of § 3(5) TMG. This is intended to take account of the country of origin principle enshrined in the ECD, on which the AVMSD is also based.[866]

Although the legality under EU law of the law in its current version is not clear and there are in particular constitutional concerns about a supervisory function of an authority that is not independent of the state, such as the Federal Office of Justice, within the scope of the amended AVMSD[867], the question nevertheless arises as to how adequate fundamental rights protection is to be achieved at all in the context of a very restrictive interpretation of the country of origin principle in light of greatly changed communications.[868] Risk situations are addressed differently in the Member States, and regulatory approaches follow different frameworks and balancing of interests. With the definition of certain standards for VSP within the framework of Art. 28 b AVMSD, the European legislature has addressed this issue in part. Other initiatives both at EU level[869] and in other Member States[870] show that digital mass phenomena such as social networks, which have become an integral part of communication in democratic societies, have a special responsibility for which also a regulatory framework must be found. A clearer regulation on how, while maintaining the country of origin principle for certain enforcement issues, a market location principle or elements of such can also be applied is to be made at EU level.

---

866 So the Scientific Service of the German Bundestag, WD 10 – 3000 – 023/20, available at https://www.bundestag.de/resource/blob/691846/cb11c99d9a39b6e73151549e22d76b73/WD-10-023-20-pdf-data.pdf.
867 Cf. on the requirement of independent regulatory bodies under the 2018 AVMSD reform in detail supra, chapter D.II.2.d(4).
868 On this also *Cole/Etteldorf/Ullrich*, Cross-border Dissemination of Online Content, p. 221 et seq.
869 Cf. in detail supra, chapter D.III.1.
870 E.g. France with the *Loi visant à lutter contre les contenus haineux sur internet*, Loi n° 2020-766.

b. Country of origin principle and MStV

In the notification procedure[871], the European Commission commented on the draft State Treaty on the Modernization of the Media Order in Germany, as repeatedly described above. It concludes therein that the MStV is in principle compatible with EU law, but expresses concerns about possible conflicts with the ECD.

The notification procedure under the Directive laying down a procedure for the provision of information in the field of technical regulations and of rules on Information Society services (Directive (EU) 2015/1535) provides for various ways for the Commission to respond to notified rules, including the submission of comments (Art. 5(2)) and the delivery of a detailed opinion (Art. 6(2)). The submission of a detailed opinion may trigger an extension of the so-called standstill period. In contrast, comments made as in the present case do not hinder the national legislative procedure. However, according to Art. 5(2) they must be observed as far as possible in the further procedure.[872]

From a substantive law perspective, the Commission is critical in particular of the provision in § 1(8) MStV on the territorial scope for media intermediaries, media platforms and user interfaces in its current form due to a possible infringement of the ECD. In principle, § 1(7) MStV provides that the State Treaty applies only to providers of telemedia if they are established in Germany in accordance with the provisions of the TMG. In deviation from this, § 1(8) MStV stipulates that the State Treaty nevertheless applies to media intermediaries, media platforms and user interfaces, insofar as they are intended for use in Germany. This is assumed to be the case "if they are aimed at users in [...] Germany, in particular through the language used, the content or marketing activities offered, or if they aim to refinance a substantial part of such in [...] Germany" (§ 1(8) sentence 2 MStV). In this context, the aforementioned categories of services constitute information society services; the substantive obligations also relate to the taking up or pursuit of activities within the scope of the ECD. For example, additional obligations are imposed on the services under the trans-

---

871 European Commission, Notifizierung 2020/26/D, C(2020) 2823 final of 27.04.2020.
872 In details on the significance and course of the information procedure *Cole* in: HK-MStV, § 61, para. 1 et seq., v.a. 4 et seq.

parency and nondiscrimination rules applicable to them.⁸⁷³ The explanation to the MStV⁸⁷⁴ considers the following in this regard:

> *"For these special telemedia, the so-called market location principle is thus enshrined in deviation from the general rule of (7). The enshrinement of the market location principle is also necessary in the absence of corresponding European rules and due to the lack of regulatory competence of the European Union in order to ensure media pluralism as well as communicative equality of opportunity in Germany."*

The federal states also invoke Art. 1(6) ECD. It provides that the Directive does not affect measures taken at Community or national level, in the respect of Community law, in order to promote cultural and linguistic diversity and to ensure the defence of pluralism. In this regard, the Commission considers that measures must actually and objectively serve to protect media pluralism and must be proportionate to the objectives of the measure. In addition, Member States would have to comply with other EU law when adopting such measures, which includes the provisions of the ECD.⁸⁷⁵

However, these concerns on the part of the Commission did not lead to a detailed opinion This result of the notification procedure by means of mere comments does not have any blocking or binding effect with regard to a possible subsequent review of conformity with EU law by the Commission by way of initiation of infringement proceedings before the CJEU.⁸⁷⁶ However, it is apparent from the reasoning that the concerns were not considered sufficient to justify a broader response to the draft. This is in line with the conclusion, as detailed above, that the Commission's line of reasoning is not convincing insofar as a possible infringement of the ECD is implied.⁸⁷⁷

---

873 The Commission assumes this in particular for the notification obligation in § 79 MStV as well as the transparency of systems for the selection and organization of content in §§ 85 and 93 MStV.
874 Begründung zum Staatsvertrag zur Modernisierung der Medienordnung in Deutschland, on § 1, available at https://www.rlp.de/index.php?id=32764.
875 Cf. on the background of deviation possibilities already the explanations on the ECD in chapter D.II.1. and on the requirements under fundamental freedoms in chapter C.IV.1.
876 See also *Holznagel*, Stellungnahme zur schriftlichen Anhörung des Ausschusses für Kultur und Medien des Landtags Nordrhein-Westfalen, 17/2858, available at https://www.landtag.nrw.de/portal/WWW/dokumentenarchiv/Dokument/MMS T17-2858.pdf.
877 See above chapter E.II.4.d.

E. Core problems of public international law

2. Other substantive considerations

a. NetzDG and questions of liability

Another potential tension in media sector regulation issues relates to ECD liability rules. In this respect, too, some argue that the NetzDG leads to an inadmissible deviation from the ECD's liability privilege (Art. 14(1)(b) for hosting services).[878]

Art. 14 ECD regulates the liabilities of information society services consisting in the storage of information entered by a user. This also includes social networks mentioned in § 1 NetzDG. According to Art. 14 ECD, such service providers are not liable for the information stored at the request of a user, provided they do not have actual knowledge of illegal activity or information and, as regards claims for damages, are not aware of facts or circumstances from which the illegal activity or information is apparent. However, the providers upon obtaining such knowledge or awareness, must act expeditiously to remove or to disable access to the information.[879]

In this context, the rigid deadlines for removing or blocking illegal content pursuant to § 3 NetzDG could contradict the characteristic of "immediacy".[880] As a legal concept of Union law, this criterion is subject to interpretation by the CJEU, which is guided by the relevant recitals.[881] Recitals 10 (relating to the general objective of the ECD) and 46 (relating to the liability privileges) explain that the graduated responsibility and the need to immediately react to illegal content that has come to light are intended to safeguard a high level of legal protection on the one hand and freedom of expression on the other.

The organizational obligations of § 3 NetzDG for providers of social networks provide for a procedure for dealing with complaints, according to which it must be ensured that notice is taken of the complaint without delay and that it is examined whether the content reported in the complaint is illegal. Accordingly, obviously illegal content is to be removed or blocked within 24 hours of receipt of the complaint, § 3(2) no. 2 NetzDG. Other illegal content must be removed or blocked without delay, as a rule within seven days of receipt of the complaint, in accordance with § 3(2)

---

878 *Spindler* in: ZUM 2017, 473, 479 et seq.; *Wimmers/Heymann* in: AfP 2017, 93, 95.
879 In detail on the meaning of Art. 14 ECD and its interpretation by the CJEU *Cole/Etteldorf/Ullrich*, Cross-border Dissemination of Online Content, p. 183 et seq.
880 *Liesching* in Spindler/Schmitz, § 1 NetzDG, para. 20.
881 *Cole/Etteldorf/Ullrich*, Cross-border Dissemination of Online Content, p. 188 et seq.; *Nölscher* in: ZUM 2020, 301 (302).

no. 3 NetzDG. With regard to the expiration of the time limit, the NetzDG therefore already links to the receipt of the complaint and thus possibly even before the knowledge of the illegality provided for by the ECD, which presupposes an evaluation of the complaint – if the possible illegality was only indicated in this way. Partly, it is assumed in that regard that Art. 14 ECD authorizes the Member States to develop an effective procedure. Member States' regulations on the time period between receipt and notification of complaints, as explicitly set out in the NetzDG, are therefore in conformity with European law.[882] However, the processing time from receipt of the complaint is criticized by some. This could result in regulatory liability of the service provider in the form of fines under § 4(1) no. 3 NetzDG if a complaint has been received but no concrete knowledge of the illegality has yet been reached. Since Art. 14 ECD is linked to awareness, this could be a limitation of regulatory liability for the preceding period.

Also, the short deadline for reaction of service providers in the case of "apparently illegal content" is seen as stricter than the European requirement.[883] However, it is countered that the 24-hour processing period for such content where illegality is immediately apparent is appropriately long and thus the conflicting objectives of the ECD are thereby reconciled and protection of the conflicting legal interests is made possible when using modern communication channels. Thus, the issue of the early start of the deadline was also to be brought in line with EU law by means of an interpretation within the context of the sanction order in conformity with European law. It is argued that the NetzDG speeded up the processing of complaints, but did not eliminate the liability set out in the ECD.[884]

The tension between such regulations concerning the liability of service providers such as social networks is thus at least considered resolvable in the literature.

---

882 *Nölscher* in: ZUM 2020, 301, 302. Not discussing the questions of constitutionality or conformity with European law, but outlining and assessing the NetzDG also against a background of European law cf. in particular *Eifert et al.*, Evaluation des NetzDG.
883 *Spindler* in: ZUM 2017, 473, 479.
884 In this direction argues *Nölscher* in: ZUM 2020, 301, 304. Cf. on the state of discussion in particular *Eifert et al.*, Evaluation des NetzDG, p. 9, with further references. *Eifert et al.* point out in particular that the question of a possible deviation from Art. 14 ECD also strongly depends on the requirements to be placed on the complaint under the NetzDG.

b. Excursus: frictions with similar regulations in other states

A comparable potential for conflict between competing interests is evident not only in the NetzDG, but also in regulatory approaches with a comparable thrust in other states.[885]

In a decision dated 18 June 2020, the French Constitutional Council[886] classified as unconstitutional certain passages of Law No. 2020–766 of 24 June 2020, subsequently promulgated, on tackling hate content on the Internet[887]. The envisaged Art. 1(I) of the Law, which has clear parallels with the NetzDG, was one of them. The law authorizes administrative authorities to require hosts or publishers of an online communications service to remove certain terrorist or child pornography content. In case of non-compliance with this obligation, the application of a penalty of one year of imprisonment and a fine of 250,000 euros is foreseen. The Constitutional Council based its decision on the fact that the determination of the unlawfulness of the content in question was not based on its manifest character, but was entirely subject to the assessment of the administration. In addition, there would be insufficient legal protection against removal orders.[888]

The Constitutional Council further declared unconstitutional Art. 1(II) of the Law, which was intended to oblige certain operators of online platforms, under threat of criminal sanctions, to remove or make inaccessible within 24 hours obviously illegal content because of its hateful or sexual nature. The commitment would not have been subject to prior judicial intervention or other conditions. It was therefore up to the operator to check all content reported to him, even if it was on a large scale, in order to avoid the risk of criminal sanctions. Moreover, the obligation of the operators of online platforms to comply with the request for deletion or blocking within 24 hours was particularly short in view of the difficulties in assessing the obvious illegality of the reported content and the risk of numerous, possibly unfounded reports.

In an overall view, the Constitutional Council concludes that, given the difficulties in assessing the obvious illegality of the reported content, the penalty imposed as of the first infringement, and the lack of a concrete rea-

---

885 In addition to the states briefly examined here, Austria's regulatory approach can be cited as another example, cf. on this supra, chapter B.I.5.g and fn. 93.
886 Decision n° 2020–801 DC of 18.06.2020, available in French at: https://www.conseil-constitutionnel.fr/decision/2020/2020801DC.htm.
887 *Loi visant à lutter contre les contenus haineux sur internet*, Loi n° 2020–766.
888 *Ukrow*, Frankreich: Verfassungsgericht zum „französischen NetzDG", MMR Aktuell, issue 14/2020 of 25.08.2020.

son for exemption from liability, the contested provisions of the Law could encourage operators of online platforms to delete or block the content reported to them, regardless of whether it is actually obviously illegal or not.[889] In the view of the Constitutional Council, this provision therefore interfered with the pursuit of freedom of expression and communication in a manner that was not appropriate, necessary and proportionate to the objective pursued.

Similar legislative projects are also to be considered outside the EU, although in the example presented here due to its design the tension and difficult balancing of freedom of expression and effective protection of legal interests becomes even clearer. In a fast-track procedure without stakeholder consultation, the Turkish Parliament passed a law on social media control on 29 July 2020[890], the regulations of which came into force on 1 October 2020. According to its explanation, the purpose of the law is to combat hate speech and harassment on the Internet. According to the law, during the creation of which supposed references to the NetzDG were pointed out, all social networks with more than two million daily users must appoint a local representative in Turkey. These local representatives are required to respond to government requests to block or remove content.[891] If there is a court order and "personality rights" or "privacy" are violated, they must remove the content within 48 hours. Networks in infringement of this may be subject to advertising bans and fines. Judges can also order Internet providers to reduce the bandwidth of social networks by up to 90 percent, which would effectively block access to these sites. The law also contains provisions that require social networks to store users' data locally. Providers may be required to forward this data to Turkish authorities.[892]

This law has been criticized in particular for initiating possible blocking and monitoring by government agencies, and there are fears of a chilling effect on the exercise of communication freedoms by Turkish social media users. In recent years, traditional print and broadcast media in Turkey had

---

889 For an assessment of the risks of the NetzDG for so-called over-blocking cf. *Eifert et al.*, Evaluation des NetzDG, p. 51 et seq.
890 İnternet Ortamında Yapılan Yayınların Düzenlenmesi ve Bu Yayınlar Yoluyla İşlenen Suçlarla Mücadele Edilmesi Hakkında Kanun, Kanun No. 7253, Kabul Tarihi: 29/7/2020, available in Turkish language at https://www.resmigazete.gov.tr/eskiler/2020/07/20200731-1.htm.
891 Cf. on previous regulatory approaches in Turkey regarding content available online *Keser* in: Cappello, Medienrechtsdurchsetzung ohne Grenzen, p. 91, 100 et seq.
892 *Ukrow*, Türkei: Gesetz zur Kontrolle sozialer Medien verabschiedet, MMR Aktuell, issue 15/2020 of 09.09.2020.

E. Core problems of public international law

already come under increasing state pressure.[893] As a result, social media and smaller online news portals are used more often for independent news.[894] The extent to which the law will stand up to judicial review remains to be seen.

c. Copyright free use under § 24 UrhG and exhaustive harmonization

A further example of potential tensions between media sector regulation and EU law emerged in 2019 in the area of copyright. There, the question arose as to the extent to which certain legal figures recognized in national law fall within exhaustively harmonized areas of the European legal framework on copyright.

In its "Sampling Judgment" of 29 July 2019[895], the CJEU had ruled that § 24 of the German Copyright Act (UrhG) is contrary to EU law. The rule permitted the exploitation and publication of another work by an independent work created in free use of that other work.[896] The legal concept of free use was established in German copyright law with the objective – quasi like a general clause limiting the subject matter of protection – of reconciling the exclusive rights and interests of authors to only decide themselves on the use of their work with the cultural interests of the general public.[897] The Court assumed, however, that the effectiveness of the harmonization of copyright and related rights brought about by the Copyright Directive 2001/29/EC, as well as the objective of legal certainty pursued by it, would be jeopardized if, notwithstanding the express intention of the EU legislature, every Member State was allowed to provide for dero-

---

893 Cf. *Keser* in: Cappello, Medienrechtsdurchsetzung ohne Grenzen, p. 91 et seq.
894 See also netzpolitik.org, Türkisches Internet-Gesetz – Die bislang schlimmste Kopie des deutschen Netzwerkdurchsetzungsgesetzes (05.08.2020), available at https://netzpolitik.org/2020/tuerkisches-internet-gesetz-die-bislang-schlimmste-kopie-des-deutschen-netzwerkdurchsetzungsgesetzes/#vorschaltbanner.
895 CJEU, case C-476/17, *Pelham GmbH and Others / Ralf Hütter and Florian Schneider-Esleben*.
896 Cf. on the judgment *Frenz* in: DVBl. 2019, 1471, 1471 et seq.; *Hieber* in: ZUM 2019, 738, 738 et seq., in particular 747 et seq. with regard to § 24 UrhG. Addressing the right to edit against the backdrop of the CJEU (case C-476/17) and BGH (Az. I ZR 115/16) rulings also *Döhl* in: UFITA 2020, 236, 236 et seq.
897 *Schulze* in: Dreier/id., § 24 UrhG, para. 1.

gations from the author's exclusive rights under Art. 2 to 4 of the Directive, outside the exceptions and limitations provided for in its Art. 5.[898]

§ 24 UrhG, which in its practical application goes beyond the use of works for the purpose of caricatures, parodies or pastiches, which are listed in EU law but not implemented in the German system of limitations[899], was thus understood by the CJEU as a statutory limitation not provided for in the exhaustive catalog of Art. 5 Copyright Directive. From the German view, however, free use was previously close to the right to edit (systematically based on § 23 UrhG), which, in contrast to the catalog of limitations of EU copyright law, has not yet undergone comprehensive harmonization.[900] Thus, a legal copyright figure existing solely at Member State level could have existed in the system of minimum and maximum harmonization of the EU legal framework.[901] In the meantime, the German legislature has conceded the dual function of § 24 UrhG, according to which it limits the scope of protection for existing works on the one hand, but also acts as a limitation to copyright on the other. With the insertion of the limitation of the scope of protection in the area of § 23 UrhG as well as the future explicit inclusion of the exceptions mentioned in Art. 5 Copyright Directive in the German catalog of exceptions, this double function is to be solved.[902]

The aforementioned problem is interesting in particular with regard to the planned German rules on the liability of upload platforms under the draft Copyright Service Provider Act (UrhDaG-E)[903], which provides for statutory permission for non-commercial petty uses. Criticism has already been voiced against this as well, claiming that the fuly harmonizing char-

---

[898] CJEU, case C-476/17, *Pelham GmbH and Others / Ralf Hütter and Florian Schneider-Esleben*, para. 66.
[899] The draft of a second law for the adaptation of copyright law to the requirements of the digital single market, as of 24 June 2020, provides for an explicit regulation of the limitations for caricatures, parodies and pastiches in § 51 a UrhG-E, available at https://www.bmjv.de/SharedDocs/Gesetzgebungsverfahren/Dokumente/DiskE_II_Anpassung%20Urheberrecht_digitaler_Binnenmarkt.pdf?__blob=publicationFile&v=2.
[900] *Schulze* in: Dreier/id., § 24 UrhG, para. 1.
[901] On this see also Summaries of EU Legislation, European Union directives, available at https://eur-lex.europa.eu/legal-content/EN/TXT/HTML/?uri=LEGISSUM:l14527&from=DE.
[902] Explanation to the draft of a second law for the adaptation of copyright law to the requirements of the digital single market, as of 24 June 2020, p. 44.
[903] Draft of a second law for the adaptation of copyright law to the requirements of the digital single market.

E. Core problems of public international law

acter of EU copyright law would prevent such a solution.⁹⁰⁴ The Federal Ministry of Justice, however, believes that Art. 17 DSM Directive establishes a new type of liability system that goes beyond the existing EU copyright law. Therefore, it was lawful to formulate new legal permissions in this limited area of the use of works on upload platforms.⁹⁰⁵

---

904 Cf. e.g., Bertelsmann's opinion as part of the public consultation on the transposition of the EU directives in copyright law (DSM Directive and Online SatCab Directive), available at https://www.bmjv.de/SharedDocs/Gesetzgebungsverfahren/Stellungnahmen/2019/Downloads/090619_Stellungnahme_Bertelsmann_EU-Richtlinien_Urheberrecht.pdf?__blob=publicationFile&v=2.
905 FAQ on the discussion draft for the transposition of the copyright directives (EU) 789/2019 ("Online-SatCab-Directive") and (EU) 790/2019 ("DSM-Directive"), 24.06.2020, p. 3, available at https://www.bmjv.de/SharedDocs/Gesetzgebungsverfahren/Dokumente/DiskE_II_Anpassung%20Urheberrecht_digitaler_Binnenmarkt_FAQ.pdf?__blob=publicationFile&v=1.

F. The proposed Digital Services Act

Jörg Ukrow

I. Starting point of the discussion and plans

Commission President *von der Leyen* had already announced the introduction of a "Digital Services Act" in her "agenda for Europe" published on the occasion of her 2019 appointment procedure under the title "A Union that strives for more". On this Act, the "Political Guidelines for the next European Commission 2019–2024" presented by the Commission President-designate stated:[906]

> "A new Digital Services Act will upgrade our liability and safety rules for digital platforms, services and products, and complete our Digital Single Market."

With this approach, von der Leyen was able to build on preliminary work done by DG Connect. This had, as the core of a "Digital Services Act" – not least in view of the fundamental change in the digital economy and its products since the ECD came into force in 2000 –, already envisaged the closing of regulatory gaps, the harmonization of various areas of law, regulations on hate speech and political disinformation at EU level, greater scope for innovative digital business models, and an "update" of the liability of platforms, specifically in order to be able to regulate Internet giants such as Google, YouTube or Amazon in a more targeted and comprehensive manner.

The Commision, in its communication "Shaping Europe's digital future" of 19 February 2020, announced as "key actions" for the goal of a fair and competitive economy i.a.:[907]

> "The Commission will further explore, in the context of the Digital Services Act package, ex ante rules to ensure that markets characterised by large platforms with significant network effects acting as gate-keepers, remain fair and

---

[906] *Von der Leyen*, A Union that strives for more. My agenda for Europe, 2019, p. 13 (available at https://ec.europa.eu/info/sites/info/files/political-guidelines-next-commission_en.pdf).
[907] COM(2020) 67 final, p. 10.

contestable for innovators, businesses, and new market entrants. (Q4 2020)."

In view of the goal of an open, democratic and sustainable society, the Commission announced in the communication as "key actions", among others:[908]

> "New and revised rules to deepen the Internal Market for Digital Services, by increasing and harmonising the responsibilities of online platforms and information service providers and reinforce the oversight over platforms' content policies in the EU. (Q4 2020, as part of the Digital Services Act package).
>
> [...]
>
> Media and audiovisual Action Plan to support digital transformation and competitiveness of the audiovisual and media sector, to stimulate access to quality content and media pluralism (Q4 2020)
>
> European Democracy Action Plan to improve the resilience of our democratic systems, support media pluralism and address the threats of external intervention in European elections (Q4 2020)".

In a combined evaluation roadmap and impact assessment, the Commission first presented three ex-post regulatory options related to the ECD "update":[909]

- In option 1, a limited legal instrument would regulate online platforms' procedural obligations and essentially make binding the horizontal provisions of the 2018 Commission Recommendation on measures to effectively tackle illegal content online[910] (legally non-binding under Art. 288(5) TFEU). Regulation would build on the scope of the ECD, focusing on services established in the EU. In this context, the responsibilities of online platforms with regard to sales of illegal products and services and dissemination of illegal content and other illegal activities of their users would be laid out. Under this option, proportionate obligations such as effective notice-and-action mechanisms to report illegal content or goods, as well as effective redress obligations such as counter notice procedures and transparency obligations, would be put

---

908 COM(2020) 67 final, p. 12.
909 European Commission, Combined evaluation roadmap/inception impact assessment – Ares(2020)2877686, p. 4 et seq., available at https://ec.europa.eu/info/law/better-regulation/have-your-say/initiatives/12417-Digital-Services-Act-deepening-the-Internal-Market-and-clarifying-responsibilities-for-digital-services.
910 C(2018) 1177 final of 1.3.2018.

F. The proposed Digital Services Act

in place. However, the liability rules of the ECD for platforms or other online intermediaries would neither be clarified nor updated.

- Option 2 as established by the Commission provides for a more comprehensive legal intervention, updating and modernising the rules of the ECD, while preserving its main principles. This option would clarify and upgrade the liability and safety rules for digital services and remove disincentives for their voluntary actions to address illegal content, goods or services they intermediate, in particular in what concerns online platform services. Definitions of what is illegal online would be based on other legal acts at EU and national level. In this option, the Commission envisages harmonizing a set of specific, binding and proportionate obligations and defining the different responsibilities in particular for online platform services.[911] In addition to a basic set of generally applicable obligations, the Commission believes that further asymmetric obligations may be needed depending on the type, size, and/or risk a digital service presents.

Obligations could include:

   o harmonised obligations to maintain "notice-and-action" systems covering all types of illegal goods, content, and services, as well as "know your customer" schemes for commercial users of marketplaces;
   o rules ensuring effective cooperation of digital service providers with the relevant authorities and "trusted flaggers" (e.g. the IN-HOPE hotlines for a swifter removal of child sexual abuse material) and reporting, as appropriate;
   o risk assessments could be required from online platforms for issues related to exploitation of their services to disseminate some categories of harmful, but not illegal, content, such as disinformation;
   o more effective redress and protection against unjustified removal for legitimate content and goods online;
   o a set of transparency and reporting obligations related to these processes.

   This option would also explore transparency, reporting and independent audit obligations to ensure accountability with regards to algorithmic systems for (automated) content moderation and rec-

---

[911] Particular attention is drawn to ensuring consistency with the new rules of the AVMSD, in particular with regard to VSP. Cf. European Commission, Combined evaluation roadmap/inception impact assessment – Ares(2020)2877686, p. 5, fn. 8.

ommender systems, as well as online advertising and commercial communications, including political advertising and micro-targeting aspects, beyond personal data protection rights and obligations. Such measures would, in the Commission's view, enable effective oversight of online platforms and would support the efforts to tackle online disinformation.

This option would also explore extending coverage of such measures to all services directed towards the European single market, including when established outside the Union, with a view to identifying the most effective means of enforcement.

The regulatory instrument envisaged under this option would also establish dissuasive and proportionate sanctions for systematic failure to comply with the harmonised responsibilities or the respect of fundamental rights.

- The Commission's option 3, which complements options 1 and 2, would aim to reinforce the updated set of rules as per options 1 or 2, creating an effective system of regulatory oversight, enforcement and cooperation across Member States, supported at EU level. Based on the country-of-origin principle, it would allow Member States' authorities to deal with illegal content, goods or services online, including swift and effective cooperation procedures for cross-border issues in the regulation and oversight over digital services. Public authorities' capabilities for supervising digital services would be strengthened including through appropriate powers for effective and dissuasive sanctions for systemic failure of services established in their jurisdiction to comply with the relevant obligations, potentially supported at EU level. Options for effective judicial redress would also be explored.

For all the options, coherence with sector-specific regulation – e.g. DSM Directive, the revised AVMSD, the TERREG proposal – as well as the EU's international obligations will be ensured.[912]

At the same time, the Commission presented ideas for an ex ante regulatory instrument of very large online platforms with significant network effects acting as gatekeepers in the EU's internal market, as the second pillar

---

912 European Commission, Combined evaluation roadmap/inception impact assessment – Ares(2020)2877686, p. 6.

F. *The proposed Digital Services Act*

of the planned regulation.[913] These considerations include (at a minimum) the following options[914]:

- (1) revision of the horizontal framework set in the P2B Regulation[915]. In this context, further horizontal rules could be established for all online intermediation services that are currently falling within the scope of this regulation. This could cover prescriptive rules on different specific practices that are currently addressed by transparency obligations in the P2B Regulation as well as on new, emerging practices (e.g. certain forms of "self-preferencing", data access policies and unfair contractual provisions). A revised P2B Regulation could also reinforce the existing oversight, enforcement and transparency requirements. This revision would build on new or emerging issues identified in ongoing fact-findings, as well as on the information, to the extent already available, gathered from the transparency provisions introduced by the P2B Regulation (e.g. on data access transparency; on the effectiveness of the dispute resolution mechanisms). This revision of the P2B Regulation would not seek to review the current provisions of the Regulation, but relate to certain targeted horizontally applicable additional provisions in view of the specific issues identified;
- (2) adoption of a horizontal framework empowering regulators to collect information from large online platforms acting as gatekeepers. Under this option further horizontal rules could be envisaged with a purpose to enable collection of information from large online platforms acting as gatekeepers by a dedicated regulatory body at the EU level to gain, e.g., further insights into their business practices and their impact on these platforms' users and consumers. These rules would not only envisage further transparency (option 1), but would in view of the Commission enable targeted collection of information by a dedicated regulatory body at EU level. While these horizontal rules would enable information gathering, they would not imply any power to impose substantive behavioural and/or structural remedies on the large online

---

913 European Commission, inception impact assessment, Digital Services Act package: Ex ante regulatory instrument for large online platforms with significant network effects acting as gate-keepers in the European Union's internal market, Ref. Ares(2020)2877647.
914 European Commission, inception impact assessment, Digital Services Act package: Ex ante regulatory instrument for large online platforms with significant network effects acting as gate-keepers in the European Union's internal market, Ref. Ares(2020)2877647, p. 3 et seq.
915 Cf. on this chapter D.II.6.

platforms that would fall within the scope of such rules. According to the Commission, this would not exclude, however, enforcement powers in order to address the risk of refusal to provide the requested data by the large online platforms acting as gatekeepers;
- (3) adoption of a new and flexible ex ante regulatory framework for large online platforms acting as gatekeepers. This option would provide a new ex ante regulatory framework, which would apply to large online platforms that benefit from significant network effects and act as gatekeepers supervised and enforced through an enabled regulatory function at EU level. The new framework would complement the horizontally applicable provisions of P2B Regulation, which would continue to apply to all online intermediation services. The more limited subset of large online platforms subject to the additional ex ante framework would be identified on the basis of a set of clear criteria, such as significant network effects, the size of the user base and/or an ability to leverage data across markets. This option would include two sub-options:
  o prohibition or restriction of certain unfair trading practices by large online platforms acting as gatekeepers ("blacklisted" practices). Such a set of clearly defined and predetermined obligations and prohibited practices would aim at ensuring open and fair trading online, especially when these practices are potentially market-distorting or entrenching economic power of the large online platforms. This option explores both principles-based prohibitions that apply regardless of the sector in which the online platforms concerned intermediate (e.g. a horizontal prohibition of intra-platform "self-preferencing"), as well as more issue-specific substantive rules on emerging problems associated only with certain actors, e.g. relating to operating systems, algorithmic transparency, or issues relating to online advertising services;
  o adoption of tailor-made remedies on a case-by-case basis where necessary and justified. Examples of such remedies that would be adopted and enforced by a competent regulatory body (which, in view of the Commission, would in principle act at the EU level) could include platform-specific non-personal data access obligations, specific requirements regarding personal data portability, or interoperability requirements. The Commission believes that in this regard, the experience gained from targeted regulation of telecommunications services (despite existing differences) could serve as an inspiration, given the similarities deriving from network control and network effects. This second pillar of an ex ante

F. The proposed Digital Services Act

regulatory framework would address the diversity and fast evolution of specific phenomena in the online platform economy.

In the Commission's view, the various policy options are not mutually exclusive, so that they could be considered as regulatory options not only as alternatives but also cumulatively.[916]

II. Consideration of the results of the study in the design of the new legislative act

1. Transparency

As the FCC emphasized in its *Rundfunkbeitrag* ruling, the digitization of the media and "in particular the focus on Internet networks and platforms, including social media", fosters concentration and monopolization tendencies among "content providers, disseminators and intermediaries".[917] In this way, the FCC itself significantly expands the range of media actors relevant to a positive broadcasting system beyond the traditional addressees, the broadcasters. This extension does not have any direct significance under EU law. However, in view of a level playing field at the interface of fundamental freedom and competition law regulation on the part of the EU, ongoing Member State prerogatives and ultimate responsibility for respecting the principle of pluralism in media systems, this inventory is also not irrelevant in terms of EU law. In view of the dual nature of media content as both a cultural and an economic good, this also applies to the FCC's reference in this decision to "the danger that content can be deliberately tailored to users' interests and preferences, also by means of algorithms, which leads to the reinforcement of the same range of opinions".[918] Such services did not aim to reflect diverse opinions; rather, they were tailored to one-sided interests or the rationale of a business model that aims to maximise the time users spend on a website, thus increasing

---

916 In the meanwhile, the European Commission has presented its legislative proposals on 15 December 2020, https://eur-lex.europa.eu/legal-content/EN/TXT/?uri=CELEX%3A52020PC0825&qid=1614597643982, https://eur-lex.europa.eu/legal-content/en/TXT/?uri=COM%3A2020%3A842%3AFIN. For a first discussion see *Ukrow*, Die Vorschläge der EU-Kommission für einen Digital Services Act und einen Digital Markets Act, and in detail *Cole/Etteldorf/Ullrich*, Updating the Rules for Online Content Dissemination.
917 FCC, Judgment of the First Senate of 18 July 2018, 1 BvR 1675/16, para. 79.
918 FCC, Judgment of the First Senate of 18 July 2018, 1 BvR 1675/16, para. 79.

the advertising value of the platform for its clients. In that respect, results shown by search engines were also pre-filtered, they were in part financed through advertising, and in part depended on the number of clicks. In this respect, algorithmic processes are also recognizably important in the media industry ecosystem.

To make the framework conditions of such algorithm-based aggregation, selection and recommendation processes transparent is a legislative reaction that is at least reasonable in the line of this expansion of the scope to the economic dimension of media-related business models, if not imperative in the interest of the coherence of fundamental freedom restrictions associated with transparency obligations.[919]

Disclosure requirements imposed by EU law from an economic perspective with regard to algorithm-based aggregation, selection and recommendation processes can make a significant contribution to counteracting new uncertainties regarding the credibility of sources and evaluations. They relieve the individual user in processing and assessing the information provided by the mass media that, in the FCC's view[920], they must take on now that conventional filters of professional selection have lost importance due to the digitization of the media.[921]

Already the current EU media law provides links that can be activated in view of threats posed by insufficient transparency of the actions of new players relevant to (constitutional) media law, such as providers of media platforms, user interfaces, media intermediaries and voice assistants. This is because the State Broadcasting Treaty already lays down transparency obligations, at least also for private media players. In this respect, attention should be paid in particular to information requirements for the identification of media players and regulations on the law of commercial communication. However, in their current formulation, the obligations in question are not suitable for triggering supervisory measures vis-à-vis the aforementioned new media players directly aimed at creating transparency in their actions: a general transparency requirement for all participants in the media value chain, including new players, cannot be inferred from the current body of media law, already with regard to the limits imposed on an expanding interpretation of secondary EU law by the principle of conferral. Such a feasible transparency obligation cannot be derived from consti-

---

[919] Cf. on the importance of transparency also *O'Neil*, Angriff der Algorithmen, p. 288 et seq.; *Schallbruch*, Schwacher Staat im Netz, p. 22; *Ukrow*, Algorithmen, APIs und Aufsicht, p. 8 et seq.
[920] FCC, Judgment of the First Senate of 18 July 2018, 1 BvR 1675/16, para. 80.
[921] Cf. *Ukrow*, Algorithmen, APIs und Aufsicht, p. 9.

tutional considerations[922] either: EU constitutional law, too, at most imposes a duty of transparency, but does not specify its details. However, an analogous extension of the corresponding facts would be possible in view of the same regulatory objective.[923]

When a digital service receives a notice from a user requesting the removal or blocking of access to illegal online content (e.g., illegal incitement to violence, hatred, or discrimination on any protected grounds such as race, ethnicity, gender, or sexual orientation; child sexual abuse material; terrorist propaganda; defamation; content that infringes intellectual property rights; infringements of consumer law), it is consistent with the concept of transparency that the user be informed of any measures taken as a result of that notice.

Transparency requirements of this kind are a familiar phenomenon in the EU's internal market; there are no overriding objections under EU law to extending the transparency requirements beyond the existing information requirements to include the processing of notifications of illegal online content. On a superficial view, they can indeed hardly be classified as imperative for the realization of the internal market within the meaning of Art. 26(1) TFEU (and thus, e.g., by using the legal basis of Art. 114 TFEU). In any case, the information requirements related to the processing of communications would share this categorization with the information required under Art. 5 of the amended AVMSD. Even more so than in the case of information requirements within the meaning of Art. 5 AVMSD, however, such requirements relating to the handling of illegal online content could be considered to support the system of decentralized control of the application of EU law.

Regarding the information requirements under Art. 5 of the amended AVMSD, the recital 15 of Directive (EU) 2018/1808 considers:

> *"Transparency of media ownership is directly linked to the freedom of expression, a cornerstone of democratic systems. Information concerning the ownership structure of media service providers, where such ownership results in the control of, or the exercise of a significant influence over, the content of the services provided, allows users to make an informed judgement about such content. Member States should be able to determine whether and to what extent information about the ownership structure of a media service provider should be accessible to users, provided that the essence of the funda-*

---

922 Cf. on this e.g. *Bröhmer*, Transparenz als Verfassungsprinzip.
923 Cf. in detail *Ukrow/Cole*, Zur Transparenz von Mediaagenturen, p. 46 et seq.

Jörg Ukrow

> *mental rights and freedoms concerned is respected and that such measures are necessary and proportionate."*

Information requirements relating to the processing of notifications of illegal online content would of course also have to respect the freedom of the media pursuant to Art. 11(2) CFR and would also have to be proportionate in their formulation.

Moreover, transparency aspects could also be made fruitful in terms of legal harmonization in connection with the functioning of recommendation systems beyond the existing requirements of the P2B Regulation, also in view of other media intermediaries. This is because the discoverable information about how the recommendation systems work on the various platforms is currently very different. In some cases, there are already regulations in this regard, such as § 93 MStV,[924] but in the vast majority of Member States they have not yet been established. In view of the dual nature of broadcasting and comparable telemedia as cultural and economic assets, the possibility of discriminating against offerings has direct relevance to the internal market and competition. In this respect, links for regulation on the part of the EU are essentially recognizable. However, at present it is not foreseeable that discrimination occurs on the basis of criteria that are incompatible with the EU's integration program. A prioritization of discoverability, e.g., by language of the offering, remains a permissible criterion of differentiation, at least by intermediaries of private provenance, notwithstanding efforts to promote a European public sphere.

Incidentally, there are also deficits in transparency, in need of correction, which call into question the *effet utile* of the existing information requirements, not least when it comes to identifying those responsible for illegal online content. In this respect, registrars often refer to actual or perceived limitations that are or appear to be set by the General Data Protection Regulation. In addition, registrars in Germany, among other countries, are not yet required to verify the data provided. Fake names and addresses are the result of this sanctionless misconduct, which can render

---

[924] § 93 MStV stipulates that providers of media intermediaries must keep the following information easily perceptible, immediately accessible and constantly available to ensure diversity of opinion: (1.) The criteria that determine the access of a content to a media intermediary and the whereabouts; (2.) the central criteria of an aggregation, selection and presentation of content and their weighting including information about the functioning of the algorithms used in understandable language. Providers of media intermediaries who have a thematic specialisation are obliged to make this specialisation perceptible by designing their offer.

empty the protection objectives of the information requirements under the AVMSD and ECD. A readjustment in the design of the regime for information requirements, as a result of which regulators can reliably identify the content provider, could close this gap of an effective supervisory possibility for compliance with EU law by the respective responsible parties.

2. On the criterion of illegality of the content

In the effort to adequately protect minors from harmful behavior such as cybergrooming or bullying, or developmentally harmful content within the framework of the Digital Services Act, the distinction between illegal and harmful content, the definition of which differs in part at European and national level, is already proving problematic. Whereas the European Commission apparently understands "illegal content" to mean content related to criminal law, in Germany, e.g., "illegal content" refers to content that contradicts a prohibitory norm – such a norm, however, does not necessarily have to be sanctioned by criminal law, but can also be prosecuted in the form of administrative (offence) proceedings.[925]

The very important area of protection against developmentally harmful offerings thus risks falling into a gray area of lower protection intensity under EU law. This is because often exemption regulations recognized by the EU only cover criminal proceedings and thus not the area of administrative (offence) proceedings necessary for the effective protection of minors from harmful media. This makes enforcement of the regulations considerably more difficult, in particular in the online sector. At least a clarifying adjustment of the understanding of the term "illegal" in the sense of including administrative prohibitions would in this respect be helpful in view of the continuing intended protection perspective with regard to (not least underage) users of information society services in the design of the proposed Digital Services Act.

---

925 Providers transmitting or making accessible content suited to impair the development of children or adolescents into self-responsible and socially competent personalities are required by § 5 JMStV to use technical or temporal instruments to ensure that children or adolescents do not normally see or hear such content. Absence of such an instrument makes the offering illegal according to German understanding, as it contradicts a prohibition norm of the JMStV. Under EU law, by contrast, the offering would merely be harmful, since the infringement is not subject to criminal sanctions.

3. Media regulation for information society services and new media actors by means of self-, co- and cooperative regulation

According to Art. 4a(1) sentence 1 of the amended AVMSD, "Member States shall encourage the use of co-regulation and the fostering of self-regulation through codes of conduct adopted at national level in the fields coordinated by this Directive to the extent permitted by their legal systems".

In view of the fact that the fundamental structural principles of the AVMSD and the ECD, which already include the principle of cross-border freedom of provision and the principle of home country control as well as transparency obligations with regard to provider-related information requirements, should be as similar as possible, the regulatory concepts of the two sets of rules should also be parallelized. This would also take into account the principles of subsidiarity and proportionality in terms of regulation.[926] In addition, the considerations in the Commission's Communication "Better regulation for better results – An EU agenda" would be facilitated. In this Communication, the Commission emphasized that it would consider legislative as well as non-legislative options consistent with the principles for better self- and co-regulation when assessing approaches to better regulation. Building on these considerations, it also makes sense, in line with convergence in the media sector, to use the proposed Digital Services Act to aim for the greatest possible convergence of fundamental structural principles not only for information society services, but also for new media players such as media intermediaries.

In view of the system of self-regulation and co-regulation in Art. 4a of the amended AVMSD, recitals 12 to 14 therein considered:

> *"A number of codes of conduct set up in the fields coordinated by Directive 2010/13/EU have proved to be well designed, in line with the Principles for Better Self- and Co-regulation. The existence of a legislative backstop was considered an important success factor in promoting compliance with a self- or co-regulatory code. It is equally important that such codes establish specific targets and objectives allowing for the regular, transparent and independent monitoring and evaluation of the objectives aimed at by the codes of conduct. The codes of conduct should also provide for effective enforcement. These principles should be followed by the self- and co-regulatory codes adopted in the fields coordinated by Directive 2010/13/EU.*

---

926 Cf. on the connection between self-regulation and co-regulation on these principles as rules for the exercise of competence Art. 4a(2)(2) AVMSD.

F. The proposed Digital Services Act

Experience has shown that both self- and co-regulatory instruments, implemented in accordance with the different legal traditions of the Member States, can play an important role in delivering a high level of consumer protection. Measures aimed at achieving general public interest objectives in the emerging audiovisual media services sector are more effective if they are taken with the active support of the service providers themselves.

Self-regulation constitutes a type of voluntary initiative which enables economic operators, social partners, non-governmental organisations and associations to adopt common guidelines amongst themselves and for themselves. They are responsible for developing, monitoring and enforcing compliance with those guidelines. Member States should, in accordance with their different legal traditions, recognise the role which effective self-regulation can play as a complement to the legislative, judicial and administrative mechanisms in place and its useful contribution to the achievement of the objectives of Directive 2010/13/EU. However, while self-regulation might be a complementary method of implementing certain provisions of Directive 2010/13/EU, it should not constitute a substitute for the obligations of the national legislator. Co-regulation provides, in its minimal form, a legal link between self-regulation and the national legislator in accordance with the legal traditions of the Member States. In co-regulation, the regulatory role is shared between stakeholders and the government or the national regulatory authorities or bodies. The role of the relevant public authorities includes recognition of the co-regulatory scheme, auditing of its processes and funding of the scheme. Co-regulation should allow for the possibility of state intervention in the event of its objectives not being met. Without prejudice to the formal obligations of the Member States regarding transposition, Directive 2010/13/EU encourages the use of self- and co-regulation. This should neither oblige Member States to set up self- or co-regulation regimes, or both, nor disrupt or jeopardise current co-regulation initiatives which are already in place in Member States and which are functioning effectively."

These considerations, in particular also in terms of definition as well as on the opportunities of these regulatory instruments for effectively achieving protected interests such as consumer protection and on requirements for the design of the instruments, could also be made fruitful *mutatis mutandis* in an amendment and supplement to the ECD within the framework of the proposed Digital Services Act.[927]

---

[927] With regard to information society services and media intermediaries, the codes would also have to – in line with Art. 4a(1) sentence 2 of the amended AVMSD – "(a) be such that they are broadly accepted by the main stakeholders in the

Measures to achieve the public interest objectives of the proposed Digital Services Act, in particular in the area of new media players, are also likely to prove more effective if taken with the active support of the providers concerned themselves. However, self-regulation, although it could be a complementary method for implementing certain rules of an amended and supplemented ECD, should not fully replace the obligation of Member States to implement not least also regulation (at least indirectly safeguarding media pluralism) on discoverability issues through this regulation by of the EU. In a system of regulated self-regulation, which is also referred to as a system of co-regulation, it is in line with the above to continue to provide for government intervention in the event that the objectives of regulation via self-regulation alone do not promise to be achieved.

In co-regulation, as also emphasized in the recent amendment to the AVMSD,[928] stakeholders and state authorities or national regulators share the regulatory function. The responsibilities of the relevant public authorities include recognizing and funding the co-regulation program, as well as reviewing its procedures. Co-regulation should continue to provide for government intervention in the event that its objectives are not met.

In addition to the positive experience already gained with the approach of regulated self-regulation in the protection of minors in the media, which is recognized as a constitutionally protected right in the same way as the safeguarding of diversity, the limits that are generally imposed on exclusively traditional sovereign regulation under the conditions of digitization and globalization speak in favor of including this concept in the structure of the proposed Digital Services Act[929]:[930]

- Such a traditional concept of regulation can meet the interests of the objects of control only to a very limited extent (in particular through lobbying during the legislative process) and may therefore promote less a will to cooperate than rather a will to resist by exhausting the possibilities for legal action under the rule of law.

> Member States concerned; (b) clearly and unambiguously set out their objectives; (c) provide for regular, transparent and independent monitoring and evaluation of the achievement of the objectives aimed at; and (d) provide for effective enforcement including effective and proportionate sanctions".

928 Cf. rec. 14 Directive (EU) 2018/1808.
929 Cf. on this in an approach also *Russ-Mohl*, Die informierte Gesellschaft und ihre Feinde: Warum die Digitalisierung unsere Demokratie gefährdet, p. 269 et seq.
930 Cf. on the following in an approach *Schulz/Held*, Regulierte Selbstregulierung als Form modernen Regierens, p. A-8; *Ukrow*, Die Selbstkontrolle im Medienbereich in Europa, p. 10 et seq.

F. *The proposed Digital Services Act*

- There is an increasing knowledge deficit (not only) on the part of the controlling public authority (whether EU or state); even research results are only available to a limited extent as a resource for the development of a prophylactic approach to avert threats to diversity; moreover, such research is particularly dependent on the willingness of researched media actors to cooperate.
- In modern information and communication societies, meta-data on the extraction, processing and personalized preparation of information have developed into an important "scarce resource" under oligopolistic or even monopolistic control; these meta-data are therefore likely to become an increasingly decisive "control resource" over which the EU and its Member States do not have privileged access – even if there is no knowledge deficit in the specific case – as is the case with the resource "power", but where they are confronted with new power holders.
- Globalization no longer merely increases the possibilities of so-called "forum shopping" to avoid national regulations, as was the case at the beginning of the classifications of new regulatory systems under legal dogma; in the meantime, globalization has rather led to the fact that the national legal space of all EU states is dominated as a territorial link of democratic sovereignty in view of the offering of media platforms, user interfaces, voice assistants and media intermediaries by actors whose business policy is determined under corporate law outside the EU.
- Own initiative, innovation and a sense of responsibility cannot be enforced by law.
- Moreover, traditional sovereign-imperative control is typically selective, not process-oriented, as would be appropriate for control of complex regulatory tasks, including not least control of the influence of algorithm-based systems on the formation of individual and public opinion.[931]

In view of any potential elements of the Digital Services Act relating to the democratic process, it is particularly worth noting with regard to approaches to self-regulation that independent fact-checking – beyond the relevance of content under criminal law – could still prove to be an effective way of identifying false reports and inhibiting the impact of disinfor-

---

931 Cf. *Ukrow*, Algorithmen, APIs und Aufsicht, p. 16 et seq.

mation campaigns based on them.[932] In addition, the engagement of individual media intermediaries, such as Google and Facebook, should be mentioned, which highlight validated information and make it constantly available in the news feed, e.g. on the topic of COVID-19.

While this proves to be a signal for a strengthening of self-regulation, there are, on the other hand, also contrary experiences: for example, the Self-Assessment Reports (SAR) of the platforms under the European Union's Action Plan against Disinformation include information on the implementation of the Code of Practice against Disinformation commitments.[933] One of the biggest criticisms of the SAR is that the data and information contained refer only to the European level and are not broken down to the individual Member States. Thus, the SAR were insufficient to perform a meaningful and valid analysis of compliance with the commitments.

Moreover, in the sense of a cooperative regulatory approach, projects that rely on deeper cooperation between law enforcement authorities, media regulators and media players – in particular in the reporting of illegal online content in a broad sense – can also help to consistently tackle the dissemination of illegal content online[934], which could become one of the purposes of the Digital Services Act.

---

932 Studies conducted to date present mixed results with regard to the concrete effectiveness of fact-checkers (especially in the area of political information). In this context, the factor that recipients in the digital environment can actively select or avoid the information corrected by fact checkers is also and primarily relevant. However, the contribution of fact-checking to tackling disinformation campaigns cannot be dismissed out of hand, at least on the whole. Cf. for an overview of studies and for a classification in particular *Hameleers/van der Meer* in: Communication Research 2019–2, 227, 227 et seq.; as well as *Barrera Rodriguez/Guriev/Henry/Zhuravskaya* in: Journal of Public Economics 2020, 104, 104 et seq.
933 On this in detail already supra, chapter D.IV.3.
934 In this regard, the projects of the Landesmedienzentrum Baden-Württemberg (https://www.lmz-bw.de/landesmedienzentrum/programme/respektbw/), the Bayerischen Landeszentrale für neue Medien (https://www.blm.de/konsequent-gegen-hass.cfm), the Landesanstalt für Medien NRW (https://www.medienanstalt-nrw.de/themen/hass/verfolgen-statt-nur-loeschen-rechtsdurchsetzung-im-netz.html) as well as the Landeszentrale für Medien und Kommunikation Rheinland-Pfalz (https://medienanstalt-rlp.de/medienregulierung/aufsicht/verfolgen-und-loeschen/) can be cited as examples – without chronological order of emergence.

4. Regulation of EU-foreign media content providers

In the course of their supervisory activities, EU regulators are increasingly identifying illegal content originating in third countries but targeted at the regulator's respective Member State market. This applies not least to the German state media authorities.

In the case of EU-foreign offerings, the media authorities currently apply a procedure similar to that for EU offerings under Art. 3 AVMSD or Art. 3 ECD. Even if such a procedure is not required by law, the first step is to consult the national regulatory authority in the country of origin on the matter.

The competent authorities in the country of origin are informed of the offering and the infringements identified and requested to take measures. This applies to the countries of origin of both content and host providers. If the country of origin declines to intervene, if the response proves to be unreasonably long or inadequate in view of the protected legal interest, the provider's own measures are taken after consultation with the provider.[935]

Against this background, the objective of the proposed Digital Services Act could also be to demand or promote Member State precautions to ensure that undertakings from third countries, by being assigned to the jurisdiction of a Member State, do not benefit too easily from the country of origin principle of the EU internal market and the liability privilege of the ECD, the validity of which in the EU internal market is linked to compliance with certain minimum standards for the protection of public interests. Such minimum standards are lacking in relation to service providers based outside the EU. To avoid uncoordinated regulatory action against undertakings from non-EU countries, it would also appear to be expedient to lay down EU requirements for sustainable and effective agreements on action against undertakings from non-EU countries between the national regulatory authorities within the framework of their respective European groups (above all ERGA and BEREC).

Since there are currently no clear regulations under EU law with regard to content from non-EU countries, Member States' regulatory authorities

---

935 In the case of an offering from Israel targeted at the German market, the competent ministry declined to intervene itself and declared its agreement with measures taken by German media regulators. After hearing and issuing a decision, an adjustment of the offering was achieved due to the cooperation of the provider (https://www.medienanstalt-nrw.de/presse/pressemitteilungen/pressemitteilungen-2020/2020/april/coin-master-an-deutschen-jugendschutz-angepasst.html).

are dependent on the cooperation of the country of origin and the provider in these proceedings. Otherwise, the only option is to access domestic third parties such as telecommunications or payment service providers to mitigate the risk.

The planned new State Treaty on Games of Chance[936] takes account of this shortcoming with regard to the achievement of the protection objectives defined in § 1 GlüStV in supervisory practice by means of a corresponding responsibility regime. § 9 of the State Treaty soon to be signed stipulates:

> „(1) *Gaming supervisory has the task of supervising compliance with the public-law provisions enacted by or pursuant to the present State Treaty, and of preventing illegal gaming and advertising for illegal gaming. The authority responsible for all Federal States or in the respective Federal State can issue the necessary orders in individual cases. It may take the following actions without prejudice to other measures provided for in this State Treaty and other legal provisions, in particular*
>
> *1. request at any time information and submission of any and all documents, data and evidence needed for the inspections as referred to in sentence 1, and to enter any commercial premises and plots where public gaming is being organised or brokered for purposes of such inspections during normal business and work hours,*
>
> *2. place requirements on the organisation, performance and brokerage of public games of chance and advertising for public games of chance, as well as on the development and implementation of the social concept,*
>
> *3. ban the organisation, performance and brokerage of illicit games of chance as well as any associated advertising,*
>
> *4. prohibit the parties involved in payment transactions, in particular the credit and financial service institutions, upon prior notification of illegal gaming offers, from participating in payments for illegal gaming and in payments from illegal gaming without requiring prior mobilisation of the organiser or broker of public games of chance by the gaming supervisory authority; […] and*
>
> *5. after prior notification of illegal gaming offers, take measures to block these offers against responsible service providers as per §§ 8 to 10 of the Telemedia Act, in particular connectivity providers and registrars, provided that measures against an organiser or broker of this game of chance cannot be car-*

---

936 The draft version of the State Treaty notified to the European Commission can be accessed via https://ec.europa.eu/growth/tools-databases/tris/en/index.cfm/search/?trisaction=search.detail&year=2020&num=304&mLang=.

F. *The proposed Digital Services Act*

ried out or are not promising; these measures can also be taken if the illegal gaming offer is inextricably linked to other content. [...]"

There are no convincing reasons why not least the regulations on IP and payment blocking should not serve as a model for the further development of the AVMSD and the ECD in the interest of the proposed Digital Services Act's objectives of human dignity, minor and consumer protection, while preserving the substantive and procedural significance of fundamental rights protection under EU law.

5. Reform of liability regulation with regard to service providers

The categorization of provider types made in the ECD no longer reflects the current state of digitization.[937] The categorization of services emerged at a time when their number operating on the market was much more limited and they were clearly delineated. In the meantime, many hybrid forms have emerged, which can be classified differently depending on the business line of their undertaking. Equally, the business models of service providers have become much more complex, which makes it difficult to classify them clearly, even when looking at the main focus.

Practical experience also shows that many service providers act, e.g., as both host and content providers, i.e. they manage third-party content and at the same time make their own content available on their platform. From the media regulators' pespective, however, it is difficult to classify what type of content is involved in a specific case, as the services are either not clearly labeled or are not necessarily clearly classifiable as specific services.

This multiple character of platforms is also reflected in the EU legal acts that have emerged over the last few years: each of these develops its own definitions of services and assigns new responsibilities (e.g. AVMSD – VSP; Copyright Directive – service providers for sharing online content; P2B Regulation – online intermediation services and online search engines; TERREG draft – addresses hosting service providers, but in a new way, as active obligations are imposed on them)[938].

In addition to the definition of service, the service liability regime also appears increasingly deficient – although not in its starting point: in the

---

937 In detail *Cole/Etteldorf/Ullrich*, Cross-border Dissemination of Online-Content, p. 91 et seq.
938 Cf. on this in detail supra, chapter D.

349

case of illegal online content, the ECD has so far suggested priority action against the provider or editor responsible for the inadmissible or harmful content. This rationale also seems worth preserving in the development of the Digital Services Act for reasons of proportionality. Therefore, obligations for traditional service providers as well as for new media players such as media intermediaries, media platforms and user interfaces should essentially be limited to obligations to cooperate. These actors should fulfill their overall responsibility for a free and legally compliant Internet by enabling independent regulators to take action against content providers when necessary. Specifically, this requires granting media supervisory authorities the right to information.

However, according to the experience gained since the ECD came into force, this alone is often not sufficient to safeguard general interests, which are also protected by the fundamental rights and values of the EU. In view of such undesirable developments, it is obvious to also provide for a binding co-responsibility of the platforms in case of a lack of enforcement possibilities against the editor in charge of a media content.

A future liability regime should allow for recourse against the service provider by the media regulator whenever the former is unwilling or unable to provide information about the identity of the infringing user. This principle is not unknown to the European legal structure; in this respect, the Digital Services Act could tie in with regulatory models in EU law.

In this context, it is worth considering basing the extent of a service provider's liability on the degree of anonymization it allows for its users: the more a service relies on the anonymity of its users, the sooner it seems responsible to make it liable for content that it did not create itself or adopt as its own.

The basis for possible liability could be the last identifiable person or organization. In this case, the service provider only benefits from the liability privilege if it acts purely as a host of content of verified participants. If it allows anonymization on its platform, it cannot invoke the liability privilege and is liable for possible violations of legal rights. Anonymization on platforms would therefore remain possible under the condition that the service provider can be called upon to combat infringements.

6. Options for organizational structures for improved enforcement of media-related public interests

The cooperation of regulatory authorities and institutions in the Member States active in the field of and related to media regulation is of fundamental significance for sustainable law enforcement on the Net. At least if it is possible to intensify cooperation between the various competent institutions in the area of media, telecommunications, data protection, and competition supervision in their respective European associations of organizations (namely ERGA, BEREC, and EDPD) and to design them in a manner appropriate to their tasks, the establishment of a uniform regulatory authority operating throughout the EU would appear to be problematic under primary law – not least in view of the formative power of the principle of subsidiarity under organizational law. Experience with ERGA and BEREC suggests that a decentralized structure in the media sector or in areas related to the media is best suited to protecting fundamental European values in their respective national manifestations while ensuring adequate safeguards for freedom of expression and information.

In this context, the principle of the independence from the state of media supervision, as laid down in Art. 30 AVMSD, must also be upheld for newer media in the online sector as well as for new media players such as media agencies and media intermediaries, insofar as it is not their economic activities but rather their diversity-related activities that are at issue, and thus freedom of opinion must be protected. Supervision of processes relevant to diversity, which is also the case with the aggregation, selection and presentation of media content in new digital form, by an authority, and be it one of the EU, which does not act in social feedback but in a state or supranational manner, is not compatible with the democratic understanding of a media landscape independent of the state and influences of Union institutions, as is stipulated for the EU by the fact that it is bound by fundamental rights.

Even to the extent that Art. 30 AVMSD requires that regulatory bodies be provided with financial and personnel resources that enable them to pursue a regulatory concept that is as holistic as possible, this organizational concept also serves as a model for the regulation of new media players relevant to diversity. This requires, not least, the involvement of expertise in the areas of the platform economy and artificial intelligence, in particular also with a view to algorithmic aspects of findability regulation.

There is also a need for improved legally binding bases for effective cross-border service and enforcement of notices and decisions by media regulatory authorities. The underlying procedures must be clearer and simpler than those in European and international acts and agreements limited to civil and commercial disputes (e.g. Regulation (EC) No 1393/2007 on the service in the Member States of judicial and extrajudicial documents in civil or commercial matters; Brussels Convention on jurisdiction and the enforcement of judgments in civil and commercial matters). Media regulators also need mutual legal assistance capabilities in order to achieve more efficient law enforcement in certain international circumstances.

G. Conclusion and political options for action

Mark D. Cole / Jörg Ukrow

I. Content-related aspects

The presence of a tension between the level of the EU and that of its Member States in the exercise of competences is not a new phenomenon. It is inherent in a system in which the EU, as a supranational organization, has been given certain regulatory powers by the Member States in accordance with the principle of conferral, but at the same time these allocations of powers are neither clear in themselves, nor do they automatically identify areas of competence in which the EU Member States retain the unrestricted possibility of exercising their powers. The Member States as "Masters of the Treaties" are the only responsible entities to authorize the EU on the basis of the public international law treaties which created the EU (originally as a purely "European Economic Community") and clarified its functional modalities. However, these Treaties, as interpreted by the CJEU, provide the basis for a dynamic understanding of the EU's competences, which deprives the principle of conferral of much of the power that it is supposed to place on the Member States' position. It is precisely in the area of media regulation, which – due to the complexity of the regulatory elements involved – cannot be attached to a single legal basis alone, for which the tension is particularly intense. Indeed, media regulation always concerns the cultural and social foundations of the Member States as well as the functioning of democratic societies and is particularly influenced by Member State traditions and differences. Against this background, the present study clarifies fundamental questions of a European and specific media law nature regarding the distribution of competences between the EU and the Member States, especially with regard to measures that are intended to ensure media pluralism.

The concrete division of competences between the EU and the Member States is defined in EU law on the basis of three different types: exclusive competences of the EU, competences shared between the EU and its Member States, and merely supporting or supplementary options for action on the part of the EU. There is no negative catalog explicitly listing specific areas that are completely unaffected by EU law – neither a cultural nor a media-related exception to the EU's competences exists. In addition, the allocation of actual competences between the EU and its Member States is also structured by the Treaties in a highly complex manner that makes it prone to disputes: for example, in the case of shared competences, on the one hand the Member States may only act to the extent that the EU has not yet taken final action, but the EU must be able to justify its actions based on a need to use the competence at EU level in lieu of the Member State level. In accordance with the principle of subsidiarity, action must be limited to what is necessary to provide added value at EU level. Beyond that, the EU must also respect the principle of proportionality and may only act to the extent necessary to achieve the desired objective above Member States' approaches. On the other hand, even where competences are shared, for example concerning rules to improve the functioning of the internal market, the question arises in specific aspects of media regulation as to whether the respective rule is actually based on economic considerations and thus falls under the competence of the internal market or whether aspects which ensure media pluralism are possibly even in the focus of the rules and thereby reach into an area that is reserved for the Member States. Safeguarding pluralism is actually the key objective of media law altogether.

This particular tension can also lead to conflicts. The application of the principle of subsidiarity, which is still not very well developed in practice, at least as a subject for review by the CJEU with regard to the monitoring of EU legal actions, is a reason for national constitutional courts to issue critical opinions on the scope and manner in which the EU institutions exercise their competences in some areas. For example, the FCC has recently clarified that action by the Union outside its field of competence – i.e. ultra vires – and the accompanying consequence that a legal act is not being needs not be observed in the national context, is not a purely theoretical assumption. Taking account of the national identity of the Member States and of the principle of sincere or loyal cooperation, which applies not only in relations between the Member States and the EU but also vice versa, requires the EU to exercise its powers, in particular for the establishment of an internal market and the adoption of competition rules necessary for its operation, in such a way as to preserve to the extent possible the Member States' room for maneuver and their margin of appreciation.

For media regulation, this means that even the seemingly obvious shift of rules to the supranational level, in particular with regard to online services which by their very nature have a cross-border distribution and reception, is only possible insofar as the undisputed primary competence of the Member States to establish rules ensuring media pluralism remains unaf-

G. Conclusion and political options for action

fected. Irrespective of the recognition of the objective of pluralism in the EU's system of values and the important supporting measures the EU adopts to this end, culture and diversity related media regulation remains within the priority of the Member States. This is particularly important with a view to preserving local and regional diversity as a starting point for a continued experience of democratic participation in a world characterized by digitization and globalization. The particular importance which the FCC attaches to a positive media order by the Länder (in the sense of an explicit legislative framework) for safeguarding the democratic and federal foundations of the constitutional order of the Basic Law, illustrates the continuing relevance of the Member States' prerogative in safeguarding and promoting pluralism especially for the Federal Republic of Germany. Safeguarding media pluralism in a federally distributed system is at the heart of the national identity of this Member State, which the EU must respect in accordance with Art. 4(2) TEU.

The question of whether EU legal acts and other measures with an impact on media regulation are permissible, can only ever be answered on a case-by-case basis because there is no clear sectoral exception for the media sector as a potential object of EU rules. Especially the EU's internal market competence, which is aimed at facilitating cross-border trade, can be just as relevant for the actions of media undertakings as the EU competition law monitoring. In cases of doubt, however, the EU must exercise restraint with regard to harmonizing or even unifying regulatory approaches aimed at opening up markets and safeguarding competition, if disproportionate negative effects on the regulatory powers of the Member States directed at the objective of ensuring pluralism can occur, particularly in view of national specificities. This applies not only to EU legislation, but also where the Commission has a supervisory role with regard to compliance with EU law by the Member States and by media undertakings in the Member States. Such a monitoring role also exists in the enforcement of Member States' rules that safeguard media pluralism (and other rules that remain entirely in the Member State competence) and with regard to the coordinated practices of undertakings directed towards ensuring pluralism. The EU and its institutions must take into account this duty to consider the Member State sphere also when responding to the challenges identified by Commission President *von der Leyen* in order to make the EU fit for the digital age and when proposing future legislative acts.

This result on the division of competences is further supported – and not at all qualified – by the emphasis placed on recognizing the objective of media pluralism in the EU legal system. Beyond the importance of media pluralism as a legitimate aim when restricting fundamental freedoms, which has been emphasized by the ECtHR with regard to the ECHR, the CJEU has for decades been referring to this objective with the same understanding in its own case law. This jurisprudence of the Strasbourg Court is also repeatedly referred to by the EU's legislative bodies. Beyond this "Convention approach", media pluralism is even explicitly mentioned as a parameter to be observed both in the EU's system of values according to Art. 2 TEU and in Art. 11(2) CFR.

This does not mean that the EU institutions themselves are addressed in order to take legislative action to safeguard media pluralism – neither Art. 2 TEU nor the CFR establish new EU competences. In fact, the Charter explicitly stipulates this. That explicit restriction reaffirms the principle of conferral and underlines the obligation to take account of the exercise of Member State competences in order to safeguard aspects of diversity of opinion and the media in a way that is relevant to the Member State concerned, including in enforcement measures by the Union institutions. Since the Member States of the EU as parties to the ECHR must meet the obligation to guarantee or protect the special role of the media as developed by the ECtHR and in addition the EU, for its part, must take the utmost account of the requirements of the ECHR, even without being a signatory to the ECHR, the protection of freedom of expression and media pluralism must be considered by the EU as an objective in the general interest. This also means that it cannot restrict action by the Member States when they restrict fundamental freedoms on the basis of this legitimate aim. The differences in considerations of a democratic, ethical, social, communicative or cultural nature between the Member States justify that they decide themselves which is the appropriate level of protection and the instruments to best achieve their general interest objectives in this respect. This includes that they can exercise them in such a way, as long as limitations imposed by EU law in particular by means of the principle of proportionality are respected, that they affect undertakings established in other Member States.

Irrespective of the finding that the EU does not only have any legislative competence with regard to rules aimed at safeguarding media pluralism in a targeted way, but that it must additionally take account of the Member State's competence for this field when applying the EU legal framework, there is nonetheless a range of harmonizing secondary law relating to the internal market that is relevant for media pluralism aspects. The economic dimension of the media and other offers which are important for the formation of public opinion, which in the audiovisual sector are mostly considered to be services in the meaning of the TFEU, but may also (as in the case of user interfaces of receivers) involve a variety of relevant forms of

G. Conclusion and political options for action

goods, allows EU action as long as it respects the limits of primary law. For this reason, the relevant legal acts contain, to varying degrees, explicit exceptions to their scope of application, for which then only Member State law applies, or references to reserved competences of the Member States, which are to remain unaffected by the relevant EU legislative act. These include, for example, the EECC and the ECD, which explicitly refer to the continued competence of Member States to ensure pluralism. The AVMSD, which already achieves a high degree of harmonization in some areas of content-related rules, continues to allow for room for maneuver in transposition of the Directive and even for Member States to deviate from the country of origin principle so that national enforcement against providers established in other EU countries is also possible under certain conditions.

However, it should be pointed out that, despite the lack of competence for rules directly aimed at protecting pluralism, there are increasingly at least indirect effects arising from acts which are not aimed at this goal directly. This applies in particular for two recent legislative acts which address the role and obligations of online platforms in a new way (namely the DSM-Directive and P2B-Regulation). These approaches include transparency requirements and thereby an instrument that is known from measures securing pluralism. Irrespective, they do not trigger a suspensory effect for measures at Member State level either, which go beyond this level of action but are taken with a different objective, such as transparency obligations to disclose information for the purpose of monitoring media pluralism.

In addition to binding legislative acts, supplementary, legally non-binding EU measures, such as recommendations or resolutions, should also be taken into account, especially as they may be a preliminary stage to subsequent binding secondary law. Such non-binding acts currently exist, for example, concerning illegal content or disinformation. Due to the non-binding nature of recommendations and other communications, there may be less emphasis in practice on existing Member State reserved competences by these, because the potential conflict does not seem so pertinent. However, the division of competences in the EU legal order also applies to such non-binding legal acts. If, following such preparatory work, binding legal acts are developed at a later stage, failure to take Member State competences into account at an early stage can become problematic, which is why it is recommended – as is also emphasized below – that the Member States, in the case of Germany in the area of media regulation the Länder, develop a comprehensive regulatory early warning system and take an early position on such measures presented by the Commission in a way that preserves competences or at least protects them from further infringement. Currently, this monitoring and presence recommendation refers for example to the Media and Audiovisual Action Plan or the European Democracy Action Plan. These are intended to defend or find an agreement on common standards based on core European values, which in terms of strengthening the EU as a union of values seems reasonable, especially in view of the new threats to this foundation of values both within the EU and from outside. However, any implementing measures must also ensure that they do not undermine national approaches to ensuring pluralism in the media or Member State reserved competences for the execution of the laws.

In addition, law enforcement which ensures that Member States' legitimate interests are protected and which can also take account of particular national characteristics in specific cases, is best carried out at Member State level and in accordance with national procedural rules, which must, however, comply with the principles of non-discrimination and effectiveness. In Germany, this essentially concerns the state media authorities, which, irrespective of agreement on common standards and certain rules on jurisdiction at EU level, can in principle also take action against foreign providers not based in one of the EU Member States in the event of a breach of substantive legal requirements, for example under the MStV. Such action necessitates that the limits of jurisdictional power under customary international law are observed. Although it is appropriate to differentiate the enforcement of the law according to the degree of the possibility of access, foreign providers cannot be permanently ignored when it comes to law enforcement in cases where no enforcement measures which achieve a comparable level of protection are taken abroad. However, the obligation to respect fundamental rights in enforcement also applies if, and in particular if, the provider concerned has its registered office in another EU Member State. There is a need to ensure equal treatment in the application of measures restricting fundamental rights, as well as compliance with EU law requirements in order to derogate from the otherwise applicable principle of a control by the country of origin.

Although limitations imposed by public international law on a jurisdiction approach as described above which extends even to "foreign" providers result from the requirement to respect state sovereignty, it is in principle possible to enforce such a limitation against these providers if a genuine link exists between a provider and the domestic territory – for example, by services which focus on or exclusively deal with the political, economic or social situation in a state, in this case namely the Federal Republic of Germany. Although, in the case of secondary law based on the country of origin principle as regards jurisdictional sovereignty, any en-

G. Conclusion and political options for action

forcement by other states faces a tension with this principle, so that enforcement is only possible under certain circumstances, it is however already not excluded in the legal acts relevant to the present. Nevertheless, it would be welcomed if – for example in new horizontally applicable provisions in Union law – it were to be explicitly clarified that, under certain circumstances, enforcement of the law according to common standards may be based on the market location principle despite the continued application of the country of origin principle.

II. Procedural aspects

The substantive analysis thus clearly shows that the allocation of competences between the EU and the Member States is non-negotiable and follows, in principle, clear rules. Not least in light of deficits in attempting a clear-cut delimitation of competences between the EU and its Member States at the substantive level, procedural aspects are of particular importance in resolving resulting tensions in the division of competences. In this respect, too, resolving the tensions in the area of shared competences and also with a view to safeguarding the primary competence of the Member States to regulate media pluralism proves to be no easy task.

The mechanisms existing in the run-up to a legislative act, such as the complaint procedure for disregarding the principle of subsidiarity, are used only very cautiously because they can be understood as being confrontational in nature. This applies all the more to possible reactions to legal acts that have already entered into force, such as actions for annulment by a Member State before the CJEU, which are very rare in practice – in contrast to infringement proceedings by the European Commission against Member States. In terms of content, the question also arises for Member States as to whether they will oppose an initiative for reasons of competence law, because they regard it to be exceeding the limits of the EU's competences, in case they subscribe to an actual necessity for such an approach, its objective and the meaningfulness of the legislative initiative by the EU. However, such considerations which only focus on the content of specific initiatives threaten to undermine the EU's competence restrictions – and this without certainty that the EU's exercise of competences will continue to be fulfilling also the media regulatory policy of each Member State in a satisfactory manner.

However, from the Commission's perspective, the question of taking account of competences presents itself in a different light: the Commission is obliged under the Treaties to initiate legislative procedures with presenting proposals whenever it sees a need for such action. Furthermore, as the "Guardian of the Treaties", the Commission is obliged to investigate any Member State behavior which it considers to be an infringement of EU law and, where appropriate, to initiate infringement proceedings before the CJEU if it identifies unjustified obstacles to the free movement of services.

In view of the European Commission's dynamic approach to integration, which is geared towards an ever closer Union by means of harmonization of the laws, it is obvious that, particularly in view of the global challenges of digitization, the Commission emphasizes the need for the EU to take action to meet these challenges. It should be noted that this need is not only affirmed if previous action by the Member States had proven to be insufficient. Accordingly, a certain tendency can be observed for the EU to make proposals for action at Union level – based on the principle of precaution – even before Member States have approached an issue with a regulatory dimension. The efforts to achieve digital sovereignty for Europe might encourage consideration of relying more strongly than in the past on the instrument of Regulations – and thus of accepting a benefit in terms of speed of reaction due to the lack of a transposition requirement at the price of a loss of the opportunity to take account of special characteristics in the Member States when transposing EU Directives. Such an increased use of Regulations could be further stimulated by positive experiences with the effectiveness of the GDPR also vis-à-vis non-EU based entities.

This implies that in the future, even more important than in the past, there will be a differing view on the competence division between the EU institutions Commission and Parliament focused towards integration and the Member States. This likely will include the organizational form as well as the institutional set-up and can therefore lead to increased tensions even in clearly assigned competence areas such as the safeguarding of pluralism.

For this reason, it is also particularly important that Member States – in the case of federal states with a corresponding distribution of responsibilities, the individual federal states such as the Länder – involve themselves in the political (negotiation) process at EU level at an early stage and in a comprehensive manner. This applies not only (and only when) concrete proposals for binding legislative acts are made, but also to supplementary initiatives and generally in the run-up to the discussion on possible priorities being set. This way of "showing presence" should help to demonstrate on EU level specific features of national approaches through participation in various fora and in order to promote appropriate consideration of such approaches. In addition to formal and informal participation through exchanges in the legislative process, this may include scientific activities or activities aimed towards the general public. In the actual legislative process, it is recommended to identify, in cooperation with other EU Member States, points of tension in the exercise of Member State competences which are caused by EU rules and proposals and to take a joint position at an early stage in cooperation with other Member States which share similar backgrounds, in particular with regard to the protection of media pluralism, or which, for different reasons, have the same concerns on the same issues with regard to a too far-reaching harmonization trend.

Specifically in the area of media regulation, this means for the German Länder that they should further develop and strengthen the pathways already taken to make their interests known "in Brussels" and reflect the full consideration of EU measures affecting the media and the online sector by an appropriately broadly based response to these measures. For the current discussion on the Digital Services Act, this means that a position should be worked out not only with regard to the expected content-related legal proposal, but also – insofar as there are points of contact with media regulation – for the further component of the (also new, ex ante) competition law instruments for reacting to the platform economy, which is one of the important elements from an EU perspective. This may also involve showing how comparable instruments on different levels can nevertheless coexist in different ways because they have different objectives, as is the case with transparency obligations.

On the one hand, it is a matter of actively participating in proposals on how certain rules at the level of EU law can best be updated. Such issues include clarifying the notion of illegal content compared to harmful content and whether the latter should be introduced as a separate category, to be further defined, or specifying responsibilities alongside liability of service providers. On the other hand, from the perspective of the Member States, it is important to work towards a functioning interaction between the EU and the national level. This includes, for example, the establishment of new or more concrete forms of cooperation between competent authorities or bodies, both in terms of their scope of responsibilities and, in particular, in cross-border cooperation regarding enforcement.

However, this also includes examining whether existing regulatory models can be transferred to the area relevant for the present context and proposing them accordingly at Union level: an example of this could be that even when the GDPR was established as a directly applicable Regulation, the competence of the Member States was respected, inter alia, by including clauses that reserved the creation of rules concerning e.g. data processing for journalistic purposes for the Member States level (Art. 85

GDPR). Such opening clauses, which can be considered not only for Regulations but also with regard to the scope which defines the transposition requirement of a Directive, or an explicit recognition of "reserved" competences of the Member States, are promising ways of linking the two systems, which promise better interaction in the multi-level framework between Members States and the EU. Such recognition and respecting of Member State characteristics not only at the enforcement level allows the constitutional traditions and specific characteristics of the Member States to be taken into account when adopting more far-reaching rules. This applies even in the case of Regulations – in actual fact, as far as there is a link to EU competition law, new instruments in this area are likely to be proposed as Regulations – but even more so in the case of Directives (e.g. where horizontal rules for platforms are introduced but additional Member State rules or basic rules to be further detailed by Member States, e.g. in relation to "media platforms", are explicitly provided for).

This endeavor to take account of the Member States' competence to regulate media pluralism also requires institutional safeguards. Thus, for example, it is particularly important that any legally non-binding agreement on standards of pluralism and democracy does not have to lead to uniformity in enforcement or – without prejudice to the control over compliance with the EU's values under Art. 7 TEU – to a transfer of monitoring tasks to the level of the EU. As long as the Member States ensure effective enforcement by authorities or bodies set up on national level, where appropriate within the framework of the requirements of EU secondary law, by means of appropriate authorization and equipment, common standards can be enforced by different actors cooperating in a defined way. Not least, the organizational law dimension of the subsidiarity principle in the area of EU media regulation also argues in favor of the Member State regulatory bodies being equipped in line with their functions and needs. Indeed, without such resources, the thresholds set by the subsidiarity principle for EU activities instead of Member State action will be lower because it can be argued that there would then be a lack of visibility of impact of the regulatory framework for the media in a digital environment.

Understood in this way, the tension can at least be defused by ensuring that the achievement of the objectives through EU action does not lead to a permanent erosion of Member State competences. In view of the fact that the case law of the CJEU still tends to be in favor of integration – which in individual cases results in a narrowing of the Member States' room for maneuver by too far-reaching substantive review of a specific disputed measure of a Member State – it is particularly important to attempt to achieve a balance already when legislative acts are created and not only

G. Conclusion and political options for action

when they are later reviewed or implementing measures are checked by the Court. In relevant proceedings, which are sometimes restricted by the CJEU in its review to the fundamental freedoms perspective without sufficiently considering the effect on the Member State's competence to safeguard pluralism, a clear positioning of the Länder should nevertheless be achieved. Insofar as such a position can also be defined at European level while maintaining the (German) constitutional allocation of competences between the Federal and the Länder level in accordance with Art. 23 of the Basic Law, this will further promote the protection of the objective of ensuring pluralism in terms of the competent level.

List of references

Albath, L.; Giesel, M.: Das Herkunftslandprinzip in der Dienstleistungsrichtlinie – eine Kodifizierung der Rechtsprechung, in: Europäische Zeitschrift für Wirtschaftsrecht, 2, 2006, p. 38–42.
cited as: *Albath/Giesel* in: EuZW 2006, 38, p.

Ambos, K.; Rackow, P.; Miller, D.: Internationales Strafrecht: Strafanwendungsrecht, Völkerstrafrecht, Europäisches Strafrecht, Munich 2006.
cited as: *Ambos/Rackow/Miller*, Internationales Strafrecht.

Assion, S.: Must Carry: Übertragungspflichten auf digitalen Rundfunkplattformen, Hamburg 2015.
cited as: *Assion*, Must Carry: Übertragungspflichten auf digitalen Rundfunkplattformen.

Barata, J.: New EU Proposal on the Prevention of Terrorist Content Online – An Important Mutation of the E-Commerce Intermediaries' Regime, white paper, http://cyberlaw.stanford.edu/publications/new-eu-proposal-prevention-terrorist-content-online-important-mutation-e-commerce.
cited as: *Barata*, New EU Proposal on the Prevention of Terrorist Content Online – – An Important Mutation of the E-Commerce Intermediaries' Regime.

id.: Regulating content moderation in Europe beyond the AVMSD, 25.2.2020, https://blogs.lse.ac.uk/medialse/2020/02/25/regulating-content-moderation-in-europe-beyond-the-avmsd/.
cited as: *Barata*, Regulating content moderation in Europe beyond the AVMSD.

Bárd, P.; Bayer, J.; Carrera, S: A comparative analysis of media freedom and pluralism in the EU Member States, study for the LIBE Committee, 2016, https://www.statewatch.org/media/documents/news/2016/oct/ep-study-media-freedom-in-EU.pdf.
cited as: *Bárd/Bayer/Carrera*, A comparative analysis of media freedom and pluralism in the EU Member States.

Barrera Rodriguez, O.; Guriev, S.; Henry, E.; Zhuravskaya, E.: Facts, Alternative Facts, and Fact Checking in Times of Post-Truth Politics, in: Journal of Public Economics 182(2020), p. 104–123, https://doi.org/10.1016/j.jpubeco.2019.104123.
cited as: *Barrera Rodriguez/Guriev/Henry/Zhuravskaya* in: Journal of Public Economics 2020, 104, p.

Baker, J.P.: The Doctrine of Legal. Equality of States, in: The British Year Book of International Law 1923–24, 4th edition, London 1923, p. 1–21.
cited as: *Baker*, The Doctrine of Legal Equality of States, 1, p.

Bania, K.: The Role of Media Pluralism in the Enforcement of EU Competition Law, Paris/New York 2019.
cited as: *Bania*, The Role of Media Pluralism in the Enforcement of EU Competition Law.

List of references

Bauer, H.: Die Bundestreue, Tübingen 1992.
cited as: *Bauer*, Die Bundestreue.

Bautze, K.: Verantwortung im Netz – Anmerkungen zum Netzwerkdurchsetzungsgesetz, in: KJ 02/2019, p. 203–212.
cited as: *Bautze* in: KJ 2019, 203, p.

Becker, C.: Freiheitliche Ordnung, wehrhafte Demokratie und Staatsschutzstrafrecht, in: Bucerius Law Journal, 2013, p. 113–118.
cited as: *Becker* in: Bucerius Law Journal 2012, 113, p.

Becker, T.: Warum scheitert die Regulierung des Glücksspielmarktes?, in: ZfWG 06/2015, p. 410–419.
cited as: *Becker* in: ZfWG 2015, 410, p.

Benrath, D.: Die Konkretisierung von Loyalitätspflichten. Strukturen und Werkzeuge der Konkretisierung von Verfahrensregelungen in der EU durch den Grundsatz der loyalen Zusammenarbeit, Tübingen 2019.
cited as: *Benrath*, Die Konkretisierung von Loyalitätspflichten.

Bertele, J.: Souveränität und Verfahrensrecht. Eine Untersuchung der aus dem Völkerrecht ableitbaren Grenzen staatlicher extraterritorialer Jurisdiktion im Verfahrensrecht, Tübingen 1998.
cited as: *Bertele*, Souveränität und Verfahrensrecht.

Bethge, H.: Deutsche Bundesstaatlichkeit und Europäische Union. Bemerkungen über die Entscheidung des Bundesverfassungsgerichts zur EG-Fernsehrichtlinie, in: Wendt/Höfling/Kapern (ed.) Staat – Wirtschaft – Steuern: Festschrift für Karl Heinrich Friauf zum 65. Geburtstag, Heidelberg 1996.
cited as: *Bethge*, Deutsche Bundesstaatlichkeit und Europäische Union. Bemerkungen über die Entscheidung des Bundesverfassungsgerichts zur EG-Fernsehrichtlinie.

id.: Die Grundrechtsberechtigung juristischer Personen nach Art. 19 Abs. 3 Grundgesetz, Passau 1985.
cited as: *Bethge*, Die Grundrechtsberechtigung juristischer Personen nach Art. 19 Abs. 3 Grundgesetz.

Bickenbach, C.: Das Subsidiaritätsprinzip in Art. 5 EUV und seine Kontrolle, in: EuR, Vol. 48 (2013), Issue 5, p. 523 – 548.
cited as: *Bickenbach* in EuR 2013, 523, p.

Bieber, R.; Epiney, A.; Haag M.; Kotzur, M. (ed.): Die Europäische Union. Europarecht und Politik, 13th edition, Baden-Baden 2019.
cited as: *author* in: Bieber/Epiney/Haag/Kotzur.

Bilz, C.: Konfrontation statt Kooperation? „Solange III" und die Melloni-Entscheidung des EuGH, in: JuWissBlog, 15.03.2016 (available at https://www.juwiss.de/26-2016/, last assessed 08.01.2021).
cited as: *Bilz*, JuWissBlog, 15.03.2016.

Blanke, H.-J.; Mangiameli, S. (ed.): The Treaty on European Union (TEU). A Commentary, Heidelberg i.a. 2013.
cited as: *author* in: Blanke/Mangiameli.

Bleckmann, A.: Europarecht: das Recht der Europäischen Union und der Europäischen Gemeinschaften, 5th edition, Cologne 1990.
cited as: *Bleckmann*, Europarecht.

Boujemaa, H. u.a.: Cross-disciplinary Challenges and Recommendations regarding the Future of Multimedia Search Engines, Publications Office of the European Union, Luxembourg 2009.
cited as: *Boujemaa u.a.*, Cross-disciplinary Challenges and Recommendations regarding the Future of Multimedia Search Engines.

Breier, S.: Der Streit um die richtige Rechtsgrundlage in der Rechtsprechung des Europäischen Gerichtshofes, in: EuR 1995, p. 47–53.
cite cited as d: *Breier* in: EuR 1995, 47, p.

Breining-Kaufmann, C.: Internationales Verwaltungsrecht, in: ZSR 125 (2006), p. 5–73.
cited as: *Breining-Kaufmann* in: ZSR 2006, 5, p.

Bribosia, H.: Différenciation et avant-gardes au sein de l'Union Européenne, in: CDE 2000, p. 57–115.
cited as: *Bribosia* in: CDE 2000, 57, p.

Broadcasting Authority of Ireland: Submission to the Department of Communications, Climate Action & Environment Public Consultation on the Regulation of Harmful Content on Online Platforms and the Implementation of the Revised Audiovisual Media Service Directive, 2019, http://www.bai.ie/en/download/134036/.
cited as: *BAI*, Submission to the Department of Communications, Climate Action & Environment Public Consultation on the Regulation of Harmful Content on Online Platforms and the Implementation of the Revised Audiovisual Media Service Directive.

Bröhmer, J.: Transparenz als Verfassungsprinzip: Grundgesetz und Europäische Union, Tübingen 2004.
cited as: *Bröhmer*, Transparenz als Verfassungprinzip.

Brogi, E.; Gori, P.: European Commission Soft and Hard Law Instruments for Media Pluralism and Media Freedom, in: European Union Competencies in Respect of Media Pluralism and Media Freedom, RSCAS Policy Papers No. 01. Robert Schuman Centre for Advanced Studies, Centre for Media Pluralism and Media Freedom, 2013.
cited as: *Brogi/Gori*, European Commission Soft and Hard Law Instruments for Media Pluralism and Media Freedom.

Broughton Micova, S.: The Audiovisual Media Services Directive: Balancing liberalisation and protection (DRAFT), in: Handbook on EU Media Law and Policy, Elda Brogi and Pier Luigi Parcu (ed.), Cheltenham 2020 (not yet published), https://papers.ssrn.com/sol3/papers.cfm?abstract_id=3586149.
cited as: *Broughton Micova*, The Audiovisual Media Services Directive: Balancing liberalisation and protection (DRAFT).

List of references

id.: Content Quotas: What and Whom Are They Protecting?, in: Donders/Pauwels/Loisen (ed.), Private Television in Western Europe, Brussels i.a., 2013, p. 245–259.
cited as: *Broughton Micova*, Content Quotas: What and Whom Are They Protecting.

Büllesbach, A.; Gijrath, S.; Prins, C.; Poullet, Y. (ed.): Concise European IT Law, 2nd edition, Alphen aan den Rijn 2010.
cited as: *Büllesbach u.a.*, Concise European IT Law.

Bukovská, B.: The European Commission's Code of Conduct for Countering Illegal Hate Speech Online – An analysis of freedom of expression implications, 2019, https://www.ivir.nl/publicaties/download/Bukovska.pdf.
cited as: *Bukovská*, The European Commission's Code of Conduct for Countering Illegal Hate Speech Online.

Bumke, U.: Die öffentliche Aufgabe der Landesmedienanstalten: Verfassungs- und organisationsrechtliche Überlegungen zur Rechtsstellung einer verselbständigten Verwaltungseinheit, Munich 1995.
cited as: *Bumke*, Die öffentliche Aufgabe der Landesmedienanstalten.

Burggraf, J.; Gerlach, C.; Wiesne, J.: Europäische Medienregulierung im Spannungsfeld zwischen EU- und mitgliedstaatlicher Kompetenz, in: Media Perspektiven 10/2018, p. 496–510.
cited as: *Burggraf/Gerlach/Wiesner* in: Media Perspektiven 10/2018, 496, p.

Burmester, G.: Grundlagen internationaler Regelungskumulation und -kollision unter besonderer Berücksichtigung des Steuerrechts, Baden-Baden 1993.
cited as: *Burmester*, Grundlagen internationaler Regelungskumulation und -kollision unter besonderer Berücksichtigung des Steuerrechts.

Calliess, C.: 70 Jahre Grundgesetz und europäische Integration: „Take back control" oder „Mehr Demokratie wagen"?, in: Neue Zeitschrift für Verwaltungsrecht (NVwZ) 2019, p. 684–692.
cited as: *Calliess* in: NVwZ 2019, 684, p.

id.: Die Binnenmarktkompetenz der EG und das Subsidiaritätsprinzip, in: Berliner Online-Beiträge zum Europarecht, No. 25, 2005, https://www.jura.fu-berlin.de/forschung/europarecht/bob/berliner_online_beitraege/Paper25-Calliess/Paper25--Die-Binnenmarktkompetenz-der-EG-und-das-Subsidiaritaetsprinzip.pdf.
cited as: *Calliess* in: Berliner Online-Beiträge zum Europarecht 25(2005).

id.: Die Werte in der Europäischen Union – Der europäische Staaten- und Verfassungsverbund als Werteverbund -, Berliner Online-Beiträge zum Europarecht, No. 1, 2004, https://www.jura.fu-berlin.de/forschung/europarecht/bob/berliner_online_beitraege/Paper01-Calliess/Paper01--Globalisierung-der-Wirtschaft-und-Internationalisierung-des-Staates.pdf.
cited as: *Calliess* in: Berliner Online-Beiträge zum Europarecht 1(2004).

Calliess, C.; Korte, S.: Dienstleistungsrecht in der EU, Munich 2011.
cited as: *Calliess/Korte*, Dienstleistungsrecht in der EU.

Calliess, C.; Ruffert, M.: EUV/AEUV, Das Verfassungsrecht der Europäischen Union mit Europäischer Grundrechtecharta, Kommentar, 5th edition, Munich 2016.
cited as: *author* in: Calliess/Ruffert.

Cannie, H.; Voorhoof, D.: The Abuse Clause and Freedom of Expression in the European Human Rights Convention: An Added Value for Democracy and Human Rights Protection? In: Netherlands Quarterly of Human Rights, Vol. 29, 2011, p. 54–83.
cited as: *Cannie/Voorhoof* in: Netherlands Quarterly of Human Rights, 2011-1, 54, p.

Cappello, M. (ed.): Media pluralism and competition issues, IRIS Spezial 2020-1, European Audiovisual Observatory, Strasbourg 2020.
cited as: *author* in: Cappello, Media pluralism and competition issues.

id. (ed.): Medienrechtsdurchsetzung ohne Grenzen, IRIS Spezial, European Audiovisual Observatory, Strasbourg 2018, https://rm.coe.int/medienrechtsdurchsetzung-ohne-grenzen/1680907efd.
cited as: *author* in: Cappello, Medienrechtsdurchsetzung ohne Grenzen.

id. (ed.): Medieneigentum – Marktrealitäten und Regulierungsmaßnahmen, IRIS Spezial 2016-2, European Audiovisual Observatory, Strasbourg 2016.
cited as: *author* in: Cappello, Medieneigentum – Marktrealitäten und Regulierungsmaßnahmen.

Castendyk, O.; Dommering, E.; Scheuer, A. (ed.): European Media Law, Berlin, Amsterdam und Saarbrücken 2008.
cited as: *author* in: Castendyk/Dommering/Scheuer.

Chan, Y. S.; Wood, S.; Adshead, S.: Understanding video-sharing platforms under UK jurisdiction, A report for the Department for Digital, Culture, Media & Sport December 2019, https://assets.publishing.service.gov.uk/government/uploads/system/uploads/attachment_data/file/865313/Understanding_VSPs_under_UK_jurisdiction.pdf.
cited as: *Chan/Wood/Adshead*, Understanding video-sharing platforms under UK jurisdiction.

Chapuis-Doppler, A.; Delhomme, V.: Regulating Composite Platform Economy Services: The State-of-play After Airbnb Ireland, in: European papers, Vol. 5, 2020, No. 1, p. 411–428, http://www.europeanpapers.eu/en/system/files/pdf_version/EP_EF_2020_I_018_Augustin_Chapuis_Doppler_Vincent_Delhomme_0.pdf.
cited as: *Chapuis-Doppler/Delhomme* in: European papers 5(2020)1, 411, p.

Classen, D.: Auf dem Weg zu einer einheitlichen Dogmatik der EG-Grundfreiheiten?, in: Europäisches Wirtschafts- und Steuerrecht, 1995, p. 97–106.
cited as: *Classen* in: EWS, 1995, 97, p.

Cole, M.D.: Zum Gestaltungsspielraum der EU-Mitgliedstaaten bei Einschränkungen der Dienstleistungsfreiheit – Eine Untersuchung am Beispiel einer Regelung bezüglich der Medienvielfalt in Deutschland, in: AfP 2021, S. 1–7.
cited as: *Cole* in: AfP 2021, 1, p.

List of references

id.: Zum Gestaltungsspielraum der EU-Mitgliedstaaten bei Einschränkungen der Dienstleistungsfreiheit – Eine Untersuchung am Beispiel einer Regelung bezüglich der Medienvielfalt in Deutschland, 2020, https://emr-sb.de/wp-content/uploads/2020/06/Zum-Gestaltungsspielraum-der-EU-Mitgliedstaaten-bei-Einschr%c3%a4nkungen-der-Dienstleistungsfreiheit.pdf.
cited as: *Cole*, Zum Gestaltungsspielraum der EU-Mitgliedstaaten bei Einschränkungen der Dienstleistungsfreiheit.

id.: Guiding Principles in establishing the Guidelines for Implementation of Article 13 (6) AVMSD – Criteria for exempting certain providers from obligations concerning European Works, 2019, https://emr-sb.de/wp-content/uploads/2019/05/Study-AVMSD-guidelines-Art-13.pdf.
cited as: *Cole*, Guiding Principles in establishing the Guidelines for Implementation of Article 13 (6) AVMSD.

id.: Das Zielpublikum „Öffentlichkeit" als Anknüpfungspunkt für (Medien-) Regulierung, in: UFITA 82(2018)2, p. 436–458.
cited as: *Cole* in: UFITA 2018, 436, p.

id.: Note d'observations, "Roj TV" entre ordre public et principe du pays d'origine, in: Revue du Droit des Technologies de l'Information, No. 47, 2012, p. 50–61.
cited as: *Cole* in: R.D.T.I. 2012, 50, p.

id.: The Country of Origin Principle. From State Sovereignty under Public International Law to Inclusion in the Audiovisual Media Services Directive of the European Union, in: Meng/Ress/Stein (ed.), Europäische Integration und Globalisierung – Festschrift zum 60-jährigen Bestehen des Europa-Instituts, Baden-Baden 2011, p. 113–130.
cited as: *Cole*, The Country of Origin Principle, 113, p.

id.: Europarechtliche Rahmenbedingungen für die Pluralismussicherung im Rundfunk, in: BLM-Symposion Medienrecht, Freiheitssicherung durch Regulierng: Fördert oder gefährdet die Wettbewerbsaufsicht publizistische Vielfalt im Rundfunk?, Munich 2009, p. 93–129.
cited as: *Cole*, Europarechtliche Rahmenbedingungen für die Pluralismussicherung im Rundfunk.

Cole, M.D.; Etteldorf, C.: Von Fernsehen ohne Grenzen zu Video-Sharing-Plattformen, Hate Speech und Overlays – die Anpassung der EU-Richtlinie über audiovisuelle Mediendienste an das digitale Zeitalter, in: Medienhandbuch Österreich 2019, Vienna 2019, p. 56–65.
cited as: *Cole/Etteldorf* in: Medienhandbuch Österreich 2019, 56, p.

Cole, M.D.; Etteldorf, C.; Ullrich, C.: Cross-Border Dissemination of Online Content – Current and Possible Future Regulation of the Online Environment with a Focus on the EU E-Commerce Directive, in: Schriftenreihe Medienforschung der Landesanstalt für Medien NRW, Vol. 81, 2020, https://doi.org/10.5771/9783748906438.
cited as: *Cole/Etteldorf/Ullrich*, Cross-Border Dissemination of Online Content.

List of references

Cole, M.D.; Etteldorf, C.; Ullrich, C.: Updating the Rules for Online Content Dissemination – Legislative Options of the European Union and the Digital Services Act Proposal, in: Schriftenreihe Medienforschung der Landesanstalt für Medien NRW, 2021 (forthcoming).
cited as: *Cole/Etteldorf/Ullrich*, Updating the Rules for Online Content Dissemination.

Cole, M.D.; Iacino, G.; Matzneller, P.; Metzdorf, J.; Schweda, S.: AVMS-RADAR: AudioVisual Media Services – Regulatory Authorities' Independence and Efficiency Review, Update on recent changes and developments in Member States and Candidate Countries that are relevant for the analysis of independence and efficient functioning of audiovisual media services regulatory bodies (SMART 2013/0083), study prepared for the Commission DG CNECT by the EMR and the University of Luxembourg, https://op.europa.eu/de/publication-detail/-/publication/b6e4a837-8775-11e5-b8b7-01aa75ed71a1/language-de.
cited as: *Cole i.a.*, AVMS-RADAR (SMART 2013/0083).

Cole, M.D.; Oster, J.: Zur Frage der Beteiligung privater Rundfunkveranstalter in Deutschland an einer staatlich veranlassten Finanzierung, Rechtsgutachten im Auftrag der ProSiebenSat1 Media p. E, 2016, https://www.prosiebensat1.com/uploads/2017/07/03/P7S1_RundfunkfinanzierungBeitrag_Gutachten.pdf.
cited as: *Cole/Oster*, Rundfunkfinanzierung und private Veranstalter.

Cole, M.D.; Ukrow, J.; Etteldorf, C.: Research for CULT Committee – Audiovisual Sector and Brexit: the Regulatory Environment, European Parliament, Policy Department for Structural and Cohesion Policies, Brussels 2018.
cited as: *Cole/Ukrow/Etteldorf*, Research for CULT Committee – Audiovisual Sector and Brexit: the Regulatory Environment.

Cornils, M.: Der gemeinschaftsrechtliche Staatshaftungsanspruch: Rechtsnatur und Legitimität eines richterrechtlichen Haftungsinstituts, Baden-Baden 1995.
cited as: *Cornils*, Der gemeinschaftsrechtliche Staatshaftungsanspruch.

Costache, M.: De-regulation of european media policy (2000–2014) The debate on media governance and media pluralism in the EU, Barcelona 2014.
cited as: *Costache*, De-regulation of european media policy (2000–2014).

Craig, P.: Proportionality, Rationality and Review, in New Zealand Law Review 2010, p. 265–301.
cited as: *Craig* in: New Zealand Law Review 2010, 265, p.

Craufurd Smith, R.: The Evolution of Cultural Policy in the European Union, in: Craig, P./de Búrca, G. (ed.), The Evolution of EU Law, 2nd edition, Oxford 2011, p. 869–895.
cited as: *Craufurd Smith*, in: Craig/de Búrca, 869, p.

id.: Culture and European Union Law, in Yearbook of European Law, Vol. 24, Issue 1, 2005, p. 626–633.
cited as: *Craufurd Smith*, Culture and European Law, 626, p.

Crawford, J.: Brownlie's Principles of Public International Law, 8th edition, Oxford 2012.
cited as: *Crawford*, Brownlie's Principles of Public International Law.

List of references

Dänzer-Vanotti, W.: Der Europäische Gerichtshof zwischen Rechtsprechung und Rechtsetzung, in: Due/Lutter/Schwarze (ed.), Festschrift für Ulrich Everling, Vol. I, Baden-Baden 1995, p. 205–221.
cited as: *Dänzer-Vanotti*, Der Europäische Gerichtshof zwischen Rechtsprechung und Rechtsetzung, 205, p.

Dahm, G.; Delbrück, J.; Wolfrum, R.: Völkerrecht, Vol. I/1, 2nd edition, Berlin 1989.
cited as: *Dahm/Delbrück/Wolfrum*, Völkerrecht, Vol. I/1.

de Cock Buning, M. i.a.: Report of the independent High level Group on fake news and online disinformation, A multi-dimensional approach to disinformation, 30.4.2018, https://op.europa.eu/en/publication-detail/-/publication/6ef4d-f8b-4cea-11e8-be1d-01aa75ed71a1.
cited as: *de Cock Buning i.a.*, Report of the independent High Level Group on fake news and online disinformation.

de Schutter, O.; Eide, A.; Khalfan, A.; Orellana, M.; Salomon, M.; Seiderman, I.: Commentary to the Maastricht Principles on Extraterritorial Obligations of States in the Area of Economic, Social and Cultural Rights, in: Human Rights Quarterly, 34 (2012), p. 1084–1169.
cited as: *de Schutter i.a.* in: Human Rights Quarterly 2012, 1084, p.

de Vries, S.; Bernitz, U.; Weatherill, S. (ed.): The EU Charter of Fundamental Rights as a Binding Instrument, Oxford 2015.
cited as: *author* in: de Vries/Bernitz/Weatherill.

Deringer, A.: Pyrrhussieg der Länder, in: ZUM 1995, p. 316–318.
cited as: *Deringer* in: ZUM 1995, 316, p.

Detjen, J.: Die Werteordnung des Grundgesetzes, Wiesbaden 2013.
cited as: *Detjen*, Die Werteordnung des Grundgesetzes.

di Fabio, U.: Das Recht offener Staaten, Tübingen 1998.
cited as: *di Fabio*, Das Recht offener Staaten.

id.: Grundrechtsgeltung in digitalen Systemen, Munich 2016.
cited as: *di Fabio*, Grundrechtsgeltung in digitalen Systemen.

die medienanstalten; Institut für Europäisches Medienrecht (ed.): Europäische Medien- und Netzpolitik, 2nd edition, Leipzig 2016.
cited as: *die medienanstalten/Institut für Europäisches Medienrecht*, Europäische Medien- und Netzpolitik.

Ditzen, C.: Das Menschwerdungsgrundrecht des Kindes, in: NJW 1989, p. 2519–2520.
cited as: *Ditzen* in NJW 1989, 2519, p.

Döhl, F.: Systemwechsel – Vom Gebot des Verblassens zum Gebot der Interaktion. Kunstspezifische Betrachtung des Bearbeitungsrechts nach den Urteilen von EuGH (C-476/17) und BGH (I ZR 115/16) in Sachen Metall auf Metall, in: UFITA 84(2020)1), p. 236–283.
cited as: *Döhl* in: UFITA 2020, 236, p.

Dörr, D.: Das Zulassungsregime im Hörfunk: Spannungsverhältnis zwischen europarechtlicher Niederlassungsfreiheit und nationaler Pluralismussicherung, in: Becker/Gebrande (ed.), Der Rundfunkstaatsvertrag als föderales Instrument der Regulierung und Gestaltung des Rundfunks, Symposion für Wolf-Dieter Ring zum 60. Geburtstag, UFITA-Schriftenreihe, Vol. 215, Baden-Baden 2004, p. 71–89.
cited as: *Dörr*, Das Zulassungsregime im Hörfunk: Spannungsverhältnis zwischen europarechtlicher Niederlassungsfreiheit und nationaler Pluralismussicherung, 71, p.

Dörr, D.; Kreile, J.; Cole, M.D.: Medienrecht, 3rd, fully reworked edition, Frankfurt 2021, forthcoming.
cited as: *author* in: Dörr/Kreile/Cole.

Dörr, D.; Cole, M.D.: Jugendschutz in den elektronischen Medien – Bestandsaufnahme und Reformabsichten, Munich 2001.
cited as: *Dörr/Cole*, Jugendschutz in den elektronischen Medien.

Dombrowski, N.: Extraterritoriale Strafrechtsanwendung im Internet, Berlin 2014.
cited as: *Dombrowski*, Extraterritoriale Strafrechtsanwendung im Internet.

Donders, K.; Pauwels, C.; Loisen, J (ed.): The Palgrave Handbook of European Media Policy, London 2014.
cited as: *author* in: Donders/Pauwels/Loisen.

Dony, M.: Droit de l'Union européenne, 5th edition, Brussels 2014.
cited as: *Dony*, Droit de l'Union européenne.

Drathen, K.: Deutschengrundrechte im Lichte des Gemeinschaftsrechts. Grundrechtsgewährleistungen für natürliche und juristische Personen der EU-Mitgliedstaaten im Bereich der Bürgerrechte und des Art. 19 Abs. 3 GG, Bonn 1994.
cited as: *Drathen*, Deutschengrundrechte im Lichte des Gemeinschaftsrechts.

Dregger, S.: Die Verfassungsinterpretation am US-Supreme Court, Baden-Baden 2019.
cited as: *Dregger*, Die Verfassungsinterpretation am US-Supreme Court.

Dreier, H. (ed.): Grundgesetz Kommentar, Tübingen 2004.
cited as: *author* in: Dreier.

Dreier, T.; Schulze, G. (ed.): Urheberrechtsgesetz: UrhG, Verwertungsgesellschaftengesetz, Kunsturhebergesetz, Kommentar, 6th edition, Munich 2018.
cited as: *author* in: Dreier/Schulze.

Dröge, C.: Positive Verpflichtungen der Staaten in der Europäischen Menschenrechtskonvention, Berlin 2003.
cited as: *Dröge*, Positive Verpflichtungen der Staaten in der Europäischen Menschenrechtskonvention.

Ehlers, D. (ed.): Europäische Grundrechte und Grundfreiheiten, 4th edition, Berlin/Boston 2014.
cited as: *author* in: Ehlers.

List of references

Eifert, M. i.a.: Rechtsgutachten zur Evaluation des NetzDG im Auftrag des BMJV, 2020, https://www.bmjv.de/SharedDocs/Downloads/DE/News/PM/090920_Juristisches_Gutachten_Netz.pdf;jsessionid=F638B8E91234E5E5E9C7CCEBD48EF337.1_cid324?__blob=publicationFile&v=3.
cited as: *Eifert i.a.*, Evaluation des NetzDG.

Emilio, N.: The Principle of Proportionality in European Law: A Comparative Study, London 1997.
cited as: *Emilio*, The Principle of Proportionality in European Law.

Etteldorf, C.: Das Recht der Filmförderung im europäischen Vergleich, in: UFITA 83(2019)2, p. 498–519.
cited as: *Etteldorf* in: UFITA 2019, 498, p.

id.: Zwischen Fernsehen ohne Grenzen und Werbung ohne Grenzen – Kommerzielle Kommunikation nun lieber liberal?, in: EMR Impuls, 2018, https://emr-sb.de/wp-content/uploads/2017/10/EMR-Impuls_AVMD-Trilog_Kommerzielle-Kommunikation.pdf.
cited as: *Etteldorf*, Zwischen Fernsehen ohne Grenzen und Werbung ohne Grenzen.

Engels, S.: Kinder- und Jugendschutz in der Verfassung, in: AöR 1997, p. 212–247.
cited as: *Engels* in: AöR 1997, 212, p.

ERGA: Position Paper on the Digital Services Act, 2020, https://erga-online.eu/wp-content/uploads/2020/06/ERGA_SG1_DSA_Position-Paper_adopted.pdf.
cited as: *ERGA*, Position Paper on the Digital Services Act.

id.: Report on disinformation: Assessment of the implementation of the Code of Practice, 2020, https://erga-online.eu/wp-content/uploads/2020/05/ERGA-2019-report-published-2020-LQ.pdf.
cited as: *ERGA*, Report on disinformation, 2020.

id: Report of the activities carried out to assist the European Commission in the intermediate monitoring of the Code of practice on disinformation, 2019, https://erga-online.eu/wp-content/uploads/2019/06/ERGA-2019-06_Report-intermediate-monitoring-Code-of-Practice-on-disinformation.pdf.
Zitiert: *ERGA*, Report of the activities carried out to assist the European Commission in the intermediate monitoring of the Code of practice on disinformation, 2019.

EU network of independent experts on fundamental rights: Report on the situation of fundamental rights in the European Union in 2003, CFR-CDF.repSI.2003, January 2004.
cited as: *EU network of independent experts on fundamental rights*, Report on the situation of fundamental rights in the European Union in 2003.

European Audiovisual Observatory (ed.): Mapping of national rules for the promotion of European works in Europe, Strasbourg 2019, https://rm.coe.int/european-works-mapping/16809333a5.
cited as: *EAI*, Mapping of national rules for the promotion of European works in Europe.

id. (ed.): Mapping of media literacy practices and actions in EU-28, Bericht im Auftrag der Europäischen Kommisison, SMART 2016/008, Strasbourg 2016, https://ec.europa.eu/digital-single-market/en/news/reporting-media-literacy-europe.
cited as: *EAI*, Mapping of media literacy practices and actions in EU-28.

id. (ed.): Access to TV platforms: must-carry rules, and access to free-DTT European, Audiovisual Observatory for the European Commission – DG COMM, Strasbourg 2015, https://rm.coe.int/16807835e4.
cited as: *author* in: EAI, Access to TV platforms: must-carry rules, and access to free-DTT.

id. (ed.): Must-Carry: Renaissance oder Reformation?, IRIS plus 2012–5, Strasbourg 2013, https://rm.coe.int/1680783db3.
cited as: *author* in: EAI, Must-Carry: Renaissance oder Reformation?.

id. (ed.): Haben oder nicht haben. Must-Carry-Regeln, IRIS Spezial 2005–2, Strasbourg 2005, https://rm.coe.int/168078349 a.
cited as: *author* in: EAI, Haben oder nicht haben. Must-Carry-Regeln.

id. (ed.): Fernsehen und Medienkonzentration – Regulierungsmodelle auf nationaler und europäischer Ebene, IRIS Spezial 2001, Strasbourg 2001.
cited as: *author* in: EAI, Fernsehen und Medienkonzentration.

European Institute for the Media: The Information of the Citizen in the EU: Obligations for the Media and the Institutions Concerning the Citizen's Right to Be Fully and Objectively Informed, Studie im Auftrag des europäischen Parlaments, 2005, https://www.europarl.europa.eu/thinktank/ga/document.html?reference=IPOL-JOIN_ET%282004%29358896.
cited as: *European Institute for the Media*, The Information of the Citizen in the EU.

Evans, M.: International Law 4th edition, Oxford 2014.
cited as: *author* in: Evans, International Law.

Everling, U.: Sind die Mitgliedstaaten der Europäischen Gemeinschaft noch Herren der Verträge? Zum Verhältnis von Europäischem Gemeinschaftsrecht und Völkerrecht, in: Bernhardt/Geck/Jaenicke (ed.), Völkerrecht als Rechtsordnung – Internationale Gerichtsbarkeit – Menschenrechte, Festschrift für Hermann Mosler, Berlin 1983, p. 173 et seq.
cited as: *Everling*, Sind die Mitgliedstaaten der Europäischen Gemeinschaft noch Herren der Verträge?.

Fassbender, B.: Der offene Bundesstaat, Tübingen 2007.
cited as: *Fassbender*, Der offene Bundesstaat.

Feldmann, T.: Zum Referentenentwurf eines NetzDG: Eine kritische Betrachtung, in: K&R 5/2017, p. 292–297.
cited as: *Feldmann* in: K&R 2017, 292, p.

Fink, U.: Medienregulierung im Europarat, in: ZaöRV 74 (2014), p. 505–520.
cited as: *Fink* in: ZaöRV 2014, 505.

Fink, U.; Cole, M.D.; Keber, T.: Europäisches und Internationales Medienrecht, Heidelberg 2008.
cited as: *author* in: Fink/Cole/Keber, Europäisches Medienrecht.

List of references

Fischer-Lescano, A.; Kreck, L.: Piraterie und Menschenrechte: Rechtsfragen der Bekämpfung der Piraterie im Rahmen der europäischen Operation Atalanta, Bremen 2009.
cited as: *Fischer-Lescano/Kreck*, Piraterie und Menschenrechte.

Foster, N.: Foster on EU Law, 7th edition, Oxford 2019.
cited as: *Foster*, EU Law.

Frantziou, E.: Further Developments in the Right to be Forgotten: The European Court of Justice's Judgment in Case C-131/12, Google Spain, SL, Google Inc v Agencia Espanola de Proteccion de Datos, in: HLRL 2014, Vol. 14, Issue 4, p. 761–777.
cited as: *Frantziou* in: HLRL 2014, 761, p.

Frenz, W.: Handbuch Europarecht Band 1: Europäische Grundfreiheiten, 2nd edition, Heidelberg 2012.
cited as: *Frenz*, Handbuch Europarecht Vol. 1.

id.: Anm. zu EuGH, Urt. v. 29.07.2019 — C-476/17 — Sampling, in: DVBL 22/2019, p. 1471–1473.
cited as: *Frenz* in: DVBl. 2019, 1471, p.

Frey, D.: Die europäische Fusionskontrolle und die Medienvielfalt, Zeitschrift für Urheber- und Medienrecht (ZUM) 1998, p. 985–1001.
cited as: *Frey* in: ZUM 1998, 985, p.

Furnémont, J.-F.: Independence of audiovisual media regulatory authorities and cooperation between them: time for the EU lawmaker to fill the gaps, Opinion on the EC proposal for amending the AVMS Directive and the EP CULT Committee draft report, 2016, https://www.die-medienanstalten.de/fileadmin/user_upload/die_medienanstalten/Ueber_uns/Positionen/Europa/Studie_zur_Unabhaengigkeit_der_Regulierungsbehoerden_im_Auftrag_des_Bueros_der_ERGA-Vorsitzenden_2.pdf.
cited as: *Furnémont*, Independence of audiovisual media regulatory authorities and cooperation between them: time for the EU lawmaker to fill the gaps.

Fox, E.M.: Modernization of Effects Doctrine: From Hands-Off to Hands-Linked, in: New York University Journal of Internal Law and Politics (JILP) 42(2009/2010), p. 159–174.
cited as: *Fox* in: JILP 2009/2010, 159, p.

Gamper, A. u.a. (ed.): Föderale Kompetenzverteilung in Europa, Baden-Baden 2016.
cited as: *author* in: Gamper i.a.

Gerkrath, J.: L'arrêt du Bundesverfassungsgericht du 22 mars 1995 sur la directive « télévision sans frontières ». Les difficultés de la répartition des compétences entre trois niveaux de législation, in: RTDE 1995, p. 539–559.
cited as: *Gerkrath* in: RTDE 1995, 539, p.

Germann, M.: Gefahrenabwehr und Strafverfolgung im Internet, Berlin 2000.
cited as: *Germann*, Gefahrenabwehr und Strafverfolgung im Internet.

Gersdorf, H.: Hate Speech in sozialen Netzwerken, in: MMR 07/2017, p. 439–446.
cited as: *Gersdorf* in: MMR 2017, 439, p.

id.: Funktionen der Gemeinschaftsgrundrechte im Lichte des Solange II-Beschlusses des Bundesverfassungsgerichts, in: AöR 1994, p. 400–426.
cited as: *Gersdorf* in: AöR 1994, 400, p.

Giegerich, T.: Mit der Axt an die Wurzel der Union des Rechts – Vier Fragen an das Bundesverfassungsgericht zum 70. Europa-Tag, 2020, http://jean-monnet-saar.eu /?page_id=2642.
cited as: *Giegerich*, Mit der Axt an die Wurzel der Union des Rechts.

id.: Internationale Standards – aus völkerrechtlicher Perspektive, in: Paulus u.a. (ed.), Internationales, nationales und privates Recht: Hybridisierung der Rechtsordnungen – Immunität, Heidelberg i.a. 2014, p. 101–186.
cited as: *Giegerich*, Internationale Standards – aus völkerrechtlicher Perspektive, 101, p.

id.: Europäische Verfassung und deutsche Verfassung im transnationalen Konstitutionalisierungsprozeß: Wechselseitige Rezeption, konstitutionelle Evolution und föderale Verflechtung, Heidelberg 2012.
cited as: *Giegerich*, Europäische Verfassung und deutsche Verfassung im transnationalen Konstitutionalisierungsprozeß: Wechselseitige Rezeption, konstitutionelle Evolution und föderale Verflechtung.

id. (ed.): Der „offene Verfassungsstaat" des Grundgesetzes nach 60 Jahren, Berlin 2010.
cited as: *Giegerich*, Der „offene Verfassungsstaat" des Grundgesetzes nach 60 Jahren.

Glaser, M.A.: Internationale Verwaltungsbeziehungen, Tübingen 2010.
cited as: *Glaser*, Internationale Verwaltungsbeziehungen.

Gless, S.: Internationales Strafrecht. Grundriss für Studium und Praxis. 2nd edition, München 2015.
cited as: *Gless*, Internationales Strafrecht.

Gornig, G.H.; Horn, H.-D. (ed.), Territoriale Souveränität und Gebietshoheit, Berlin 2016.
cited as: *Gornig/Horn*, Territoriale Souveränität und Gebietshoheit.

Gounalakis, G.; Zagouras, G.: Plädoyer für ein europäisches Medienkonzentrationsrecht, in: ZUM 2006, p. 716–725.
cited as: *Gounalakis/Zagouras* in: ZUM 2006, 716, p.

Grabitz, E.; Hilf, M.; Nettesheim, M.: Das Recht der Europäischen Union: EUV/AEUV, Kommentar, 70. edition, Munich 2020.
cited as: *author* in: Grabitz/Hilf/Nettesheim.

Graf Vitzthum, W.; Proelß, A. (ed.): Völkerrecht, 7th edition, Berlin 2016.
cited as: *author* in: Graf Vitzthum/Proelß.

Gstrein, O.; Zeitzmann, S.: Die „Åkerberg Fransson"-Entscheidung des EuGH – „Ne bis in idem" als Wegbereiter für einen effektiven Grundrechtsschutz in der EU?, in: ZEuS 2013, p. 239–260.
cited as: *Gstrein/Zeitzmann*, in: ZEuS 2013, 239, p.

Guber, T.: Discours de la méthode: Ist das PSPP-Urteil des BVerfG noch „nachvollziehbar"?, in: ZEuS 2020, p. 625–641.
cited as: *Guber* in: ZEuS 2020, 625, p.

List of references

Gundel, J.: Die Fortentwicklung der europäischen Medienregulierung: Zur Neufassung der AVMD-Richtlinie, in: ZUM 2019, p. 131–139.
cited as: *Gundel* in: ZUM 2019, 131, p.

id.: Die Kontrolle der europäischen Integration durch den französischen Verfassungsrat: zugleich Besprechung der Entscheidung des Conseil constitutionnel vom 31.12.1997 zur Verfassungsmäßigkeit des Vertrags von Amsterdam, in Europarecht (EuR) 1998, p. 371–385.
cited as: *Gundel* in: EuR 1998, 371, p.

Häberle, P.: Häberle, Nationalflaggen: Bürgerdemokratische Identitätselemente und Internationale Erkennungssymbole, Berlin 2008.
cited as: *Häberle*, Nationalflaggen: Bürgerdemokratische Identitätselemente und Internationale Erkennungssymbole.

id.: Der kooperative Verfassungsstaat, in: Kaalbach/Krawietz (ed.), Recht und Gesellschaft. Festschrift für Helmut Schelsky, Berlin 1978, p. 141–177.
cited as: *Häberle*, Der kooperative Verfassungsstaat, 141, p.

Hain, K.-E.: Sicherung des publizistischen Pluralismus auf europäischer Ebene?, in: AfP 2007, p. 527–534.
cited as: *Hain* in: AfP 2007, 527, p.

Hain, K.-E.; Ferreau, F.; Brings-Wiesen, T.: Regulierung sozialer Netzwerke revisited, in: K&R 07–08/2017, p. 433–438.
cited as: *Hain/Ferreau/Brings-Wiesen* in: K&R 07–08/2017, 433, p.

Haim, M.; Graefe, A.; Brosius, H.-B.: Burst of the Filter Bubble? Effects of personalization on the diversity of Google News, in: Digital Journalism, Vol. 6, Issue 3, 2018, p. 330–343, https://doi.org/10.1080/21670811.2017.1338145.
cited as: *Haim/Graefe/Brosius* in: Digital Journalism 3/2018, 330, p.

Hameleers, M.; van der Meer, T.G.: Misinformation and Polarization in a High-Choice Media Environment: How Effective Are Political Fact-Checkers?, in: Communication Research 47(2019)2, p. 227–250, https://doi.org/10.1177%2F0093650218819671.
cited as: *Hameleers/van der Meer* in: Communication Research 2019–2, 227, p.

Hans-Bredow-Institut für Medienforschung: Indicators for independence and efficient functioning of audiovisual media services regulatory bodies for the purpose of enforcing the rules in the AVMS Directive – INDIREG – study prepared for the European Commission, SMART 2009/0001, 2011, https://ec.europa.eu/digital-single-market/en/news/study-indicators-independence-and-efficient-functioning-audiovisual-media-services-regulatory-0.
cited as: INDIREG (SMART 2009/0001), Studie des HBI im Auftrag der Europäischen Kommisison.

Harrison, J.; Woods, L.: Jurisdiction, forum shopping and the 'race to the bottom', in: Harrison/Woods, European Broadcasting Law and Policy, Cambridge 2007, p. 173–193.
cited as: *Harrison/Woods*, Jurisdiction, forum shopping and the 'race to the bottom', 173, p.

id.: Television Quotas: Protecting European Culture?, in: Entertainment Law Review, 12(1), 5–14, 2001.
cited as: *Harrison/Woods*, Television Quotas: Protecting European Culture?.

Harstein, R; Ring, W.-D.; Kreile, J.; Dörr, D.; Stettner, R.; Cole, M.D.; Wagner, E. (ed.): Medienstaatsvertrag, Jugendmedienschutz-Staatsvertrag, Handkommentar (HK-MStV), Munich, last update of August 2020.
cited as: *author* in: HK-MStV.

Hatje, A.: Loyalität als Rechtsprinzip in der Europäischen Union, Baden-Baden 2001.
cited as: *Hatje*, Loyalität als Rechtsprinzip in der Europäischen Union.

Heermann, P.W.: Artikel 30 EGV im Lichte der "Keck"-Rechtsprechung: Anerkennung sonstiger Verkaufsmodalitäten und Einführung eines einheitlichen Rechtfertigungstatbestands?, in: GRUR Int. 7/1998, p. 579–594.
cited as: *Heermann* in: GRUR Int. 1998. 579, p.

Heintzen, M.: Auswärtige Beziehungen privater Verbände. Eine staatsrechtliche, insbesondere grundrechtskollisionsrechtliche Untersuchung, Berlin 1988.
cited as: *Heintzen*, Auswärtige Beziehungen privater Verbände.

Helberger, N.; Eskens, S.; van Drunen, M.; Bastian, M.; Moeller, J.: Implications of AI-driven tools in the media for freedom of expression, in: Artificial Intelligence – Intelligent Politics Challenges and opportunities for media and democracy Background Paper, Ministerial Conference, Cyprus 2020, https://rm.coe.int/cyprus-2020-ai-and-freedom-of-expression/168097fa82.
cited as: *Helberger i.a.*, Implications of AI-driven tools in the media for freedom of expression.

Hieber, T.: »Metall auf Metall« – doch ein Ende ohne Schrecken? – Anmerkung zu EuGH, Urteil vom 29.7.2019 – C-476/17 – Pelham u. a./Hütter u. a., in: ZUM 10/2019, p. 738–750.
cited as: *Hieber* in: ZUM 2019, 738, p.

Hirsch, G.: Die aktuelle Rechtsprechung des EuGH zur Warenverkehrsfreiheit in: ZEuS 1999, p. 503–511.
cited as: *Hirsch* in: ZEuS 1999, 503, p.

Hobe, S.: Einführung in das Völkerrecht, 10th edition, Tübingen 2014.
cited as: *Hobe*, Einführung in das Völkerrecht.

id.: Der offene Verfassungsstaat zwischen Souveränität und Interdependenz, Berlin 1998.
cited as: *Hobe*, Der offene Verfassungsstaat zwischen Souveränität und Interdependenz.

Hochbaum, I.: Der Begriff der Kultur im Maastrichter und Amsterdamer Vertrag, in: BayVBl. 1997, p. 641–654.
cited as: *Hochbaum* in: BayVBl. 1997, 641, p.

Hök, G.-S.: Vollstreckung öffentlicher-rechtlicher Forderungen im Ausland, in: Juristisches Internet Journal, http://www.eurojurislawjournal.net/RA/Hoek-Dr/Beitraege-d/Vollstr-Ausl-3-11-98.htm.
cited as: *Hök*, Vollstreckung öffentlicher-rechtlicher Forderungen im Ausland.

List of references

Hoeren, T.: Netzwerkdurchsetzungsgesetz europarechtswidrig, beck-blog f. 30.3.2017, available at https://community.beck.de/2017/03/30/netzwerkdurchsetzungsgesetz-europarechtswidrig.
cited as: *Hoeren*, Netzwerkdurchsetzungsgesetz europarechtswidrig.

Hörnle, J.: International and Comparative Law Quarterly, Vol. 54, Issue 1, 2005, p. 89–126.
cited as: *Hörnle* in: International and Comparative Law Quarterly 1–2005, 89, p.

Hofmann, H.C.H.: General principles of EU law and EU administrative law, in: Barnard, C./Peers, p. 198 et seq., European Union Law, 2nd edition, Oxford 2017.
cited as: *Hofmann*, in: Barnard/Peers. S. 198, p.

Hofmann, R.: Grundrechte und grenzüberschreitende Sachverhalte, Berlin 1993.
cited as: *Hofmann*, Grundrechte und grenzüberschreitende Sachverhalte.

Hoffmann, A.; Gasparotti, A.: Liability for illegal content online Weaknesses of the EU legal framework and possible plans of the EU Commission to address them in a "Digital Services Act", March 2020, https://www.cep.eu/fileadmin/user_upload/cep.eu/Studien/cepStudie_Haftung_fuer_illegale_Online-Inhalte/cepStudy_Liability_for_illegal_content_online.pdf.
cited as: *Hoffmann/Gasparotti*, Liability for illegal content online.

Holtz-Bacha, C.: Medienpolitik für Europa, Berlin 2006.
cited as: *Holtz-Bacha*, Medienpolitik für Europa.

Holznagel, B.: Vielfaltskonzepte in Europa, in: Kohl (ed.), Vielfalt im Rundfunk. Interdisziplinäre und internationale Annäherungen, Konstanz 1997, p. 94–104.
cited as: *Holznagel*, Vielfaltskonzepte in Europa.

Hoorens, S.; Lupiáñez-Villanueva, F. (ed.): Study on media literacy and online empowerment issues raised by algorithm-driven media services, Studie im Auftrag der Europäischen Kommission (DG CNECT), SMART 2017/0081, Brussels 2019.
cited as: *Hoorens/Lupiáñez-Villanueva*, Study on media literacy and online empowerment issues raised by algorithm-driven media services (SMART 2017/0081).

Huber, P.: Europäisches und nationales Verfassungsrecht, in: VVDStRL 60 (2001), p. 194–245.
cited as: *Huber* in: VVDStRL 2001, 194, p.

Husovec, M.; Quitais, J.P.: Article 17 of the Copyright Directive: Why the German implementation proposal is compatible with EU law – Part 1, in: Kluwers Copyright Blog from 26. August 2020, http://copyrightblog.kluweriplaw.com/2020/08/26/article-17-of-the-copyright-directive-why-the-german-implementation-proposal-is-compatible-with-eu-law-part-1/.
cited as: *Husovec/Quintais* in: Kluwer Copyright Blog f. 26.8.2020.

Institut für Europäisches Medienrecht (ed.): Nizza, die Grundrechte-Charta und ihre Bedeutung für die Medien in Europa, Baden-Baden 2001.
cited as: *Institut für Europäisches Medienrecht (ed.)*, Nizza, die Grundrechte-Charta und ihre Bedeutung für die Medien in Europa.

List of references

Ipsen, K. (ed.): Völkerrecht, 6th edition, Munich 2014.
cited as: *author* in: Ipsen.

Isensee, J.: Die staatsrechtliche Stellung der Ausländer in der Bundesrepublik Deutschland, in: VVDStRL 32 (1974), p. 49–106.
cited as: *Isensee* in: VVDStRL 2001, 49, p.

Isensee, J.; Axer, P.: Jugendschutz im Fernsehen. Verfassungsrechtliche Vorgaben für staatsvertragliche Beschränkungen der Ausstrahlung indexbetroffener Sendungen, Munich 1998.
cited as: *Isensee/Axer*, Jugendschutz im Fernsehen.

Isensee, J.; Kirchhof, G. (ed.) Handbuch des Staatsrechts der Bundesrepublik Deutschland, Band IV: Aufgaben des Staates, 3rd edition, Heidelberg 2006.
cited as: *author* in: Isensee/Kirchhof, Vol. IV.

id.: Handbuch des Staatsrechts der Bundesrepublik Deutschland, Vol. V: Rechtsquellen, Organisation, Finanzen, 3rd edition, Heidelberg 2007.
cited as: *author* in: Isensee/Kirchhof, Vol. V.

id.: Handbuch des Staatsrechts der Bundesrepublik Deutschland, Vol. IX: Allgemeine Grundrechtslehren, 3rd edition, Heidelberg 2011.
cited as: *author* in: Isensee/Kirchhof, Vol. IX.

id.: Handbuch des Staatsrechts der Bundesrepublik Deutschland, Vol. XII: Normativität und Schutz der Verfassung, 3rd edition, Heidelberg 2014.
cited as: *author* in: Isensee/Kirchhof, Vol XII.

Jarass, H.D.: Charta der Grundrechte der Europäischen Union, 3rd edition, Munich 2016.
cited as: *Jarass*, Charta der Grundrechte der Europäischen Union.

id.: Die Bindung der Mitgliedstaaten an die EU-Grundrechte, in: NVwZ 2012, p. 457–461.
cited as: *Jarass* in: NVwZ 2012, 457, p.

id.: Die Kompetenzen der Europäischen Gemeinschaft und die Folgen für die Mitgliedstaaten, Bonn 1997.
cited as: *Jarass*, Die Kompetenzen der Europäischen Gemeinschaft und die Folgen für die Mitgliedstaaten.

Jaeckel, L.: Schutzpflichten im deutschen und europäischen Recht. Eine Untersuchung der deutschen Grundrechte, der Menschenrechte und Grundfreiheiten der EMRK sowie der Grundrechte und Grundfreiheiten der Europäischen Gemeinschaft, Baden-Baden 2001.
cited as: *Jaeckel*, Schutzpflichten im deutschen und europäischen Recht.

Jäger, M.: Die Novellierung der AVMD-RL – Anwendungsbereich und Werberegulierung – eine erneut vertane Chance?, in: ZUM 63 (2019) 6, p. 477–489.
cited as: *Jäger*, ZUM (2019)6, 477, p.

Jeck, T; Langner, B.: cepStudie. Die Europäische Dimension des Sports, Freiburg 2010.
cited as: *Jeck/Langner*, Die Europäische Dimension des Sports.

Jennert, C.: Die zukünftige Kompetenzabgrenzung zwischen der Europäischen Union und den Mitgliedstaaten, in: NVwZ 2003 Issue 8, p. 936–942.
cited as: *Jennert* in: NVwZ 2003, 936, p.

Jungheim, S.: Medienordnung und Wettbewerbsrecht im Zeitalter der Digitalisierung und Globalisierung, Tübingen 2012.
cited as: *Jungheim*, Medienordnung und Wettbewerbsrecht im Zeitalter der Digitalisierung und Globalisierung.

Kalscheuer, F.; Hornung, C.: Das Netzwerkdurchsetzungsgesetz – Einverfassungswidriger Schnellschuss, in: NVwZ 23/2017, p. 1721–1724.
cited as: *Kalscheuer/Hornung* in: NVwZ 2017, 1721, p.

Kaufmann, M.: Permanente Verfassungsgebung und verfassungsrechtliche Selbstbindung im europäischen Staatenverbund, in: Der Staat 1997, Vol. 36, No. 4, p. 521–546.
cited as: *Kaufmann*, Der Staat 1997, 521, p.

Keller, H.; Kühne, D.: Zur Verfassungsgerichtsbarkeit des Europäischen Gerichtshofs für Menschenrechte in: Zeitschrift für ausländisches öffentliches Recht und Völkerrecht, 2016, p. 246–305.
cited as: *Keller/Kühne* in: ZaöRV 2016, 246, p.

Kellerbauer, M.; Klamert, M.; Tomkin, J. (ed.): The EU Treaties and the Charter of Fundamental Rights: A Commentary, Oxford 2019.
cited as: *author* in: Kellerbauer/Klamert/Tomkin.

Kiiver, P.: German Participation in EU Decision-Making after the Lisbon Case: A Comparative View on Domestic Parliamentary Clearance Procedures, in: German Law Journal, Vol. 10, Heft 8, 2009, p. 1287–1296.
cited as: *Kiiver* in: German Law Journal, 2009, 1287, p.

Kingreen, T.: Die Struktur der Grundfreiheiten des Europäischen Gemeinschaftsrechts, Berlin 1999.
cited as: *Kingreen*, Die Struktur der Grundfreiheiten des Europäischen Gemeinschaftsrechts.

Kingsbury, C.; Donaldson, M.: Global Administrative Law, in: Wolfrum (ed.), The Max Planck Encyclopedia of Public International Law (MPEPIL), Oxford 2012, www.mpepil.com.
cited as: *Kingsbury/Donaldson* in: MPEPIL, para.

Kingsbury, B.; Krisch, N.; Stewart, R.B.; Wiener, J.B.: Global Governance as Administration — National and Transnational Approaches to Global Administrative Law, in: Law & Contemporary Problems 68(2005)3&4, p. 1–13.
cited as: *Kingsbury u.a.* in: Law & Contemporary Problems 2005/3–4, 1, p.

Kirchhof, P.: Die rechtliche Struktur der Europäischen Union als Staatenverbund, in: von Bogdandy (ed.), Europäisches Verfassungsrecht, Dordrecht/Heidelberg i.a. 2003, p. 893–928.
cited as: *Kirchhof*, Die rechtliche Struktur der Europäischen Union als Staatenverbund.

id.: Nach vierzig Jahren: Gegenwartsfragen an das Grundgesetz, in: JZ 10 (1989), p. 453–465.
cited as: *Kirchhof* in: JZ 1989, 453, p.

List of references

Klamert, M.: Rechtsprobleme gemischter Abkommen am Beispiel der UNESCO Konvention zum Schutz und der Förderung der Diversität kultureller Ausdrucksformen, in: ZöR 64 (2009), p. 217–235.
cited as: *Klamert* in: ZöR 2009, 217, p.

Klatt, M.: Positive Obligations under the European Convention on Human Rights, in: ZaöRV 71 (2011), p. 691–718.
cited as: *Klatt* in: ZaöRV 2011, 691, p.

Kment, M.: Grenzüberschreitendes Verwaltungshandeln, Tübingen 2010.
cited as: *Kment*, Grenzüberschreitendes Verwaltungshandeln.

Koch, S.: Die grenzüberschreitende Wirkung von nationalen Genehmigungen für umweltbeeinträchtigende industrielle Anlagen, Frankfurt/Main 2010.
cited as: *Koch*, Die grenzüberschreitende Wirkung von nationalen Genehmigungen für umweltbeeinträchtigende industrielle Anlagen.

Koenen, T.: Wirtschaft und Menschenrechte. Staatliche Schutzpflichten auf der Basis regionaler und internationaler Menschenrechtsverträge, Berlin 2012.
cited as: *Koenen*, Wirtschaft und Menschenrechte.

Kogler, M.R.: Hauptzweck und wesentliche Funktionalität der Bereitstellung audiovisueller Inhalte, in: K&R 2018, Issue 9, p. 537–543.
cited as: *Kogler* in: K&R 2018, 537, p.

Kokott, J.: Souveräne Gleichheit und Demokratie im Völkerrecht, ZaöRV 64 (2004), p. 517–533.
cited as: *Kokott* in: ZaöRV 2004, 517, p.

Kommission zur Ermittlung der Konzentration im Medienbereich: Sicherung der Meinungsvielfalt im digitalen Zeitalter, Bericht der Kommission zur Ermittlung der Konzentration im Medienbereich (KEK) über die Entwicklung der Konzentration und über Maßnahmen zur Sicherung der Meinungsvielfalt im privaten Rundfunk, in: Schriftenreihe der Landesmedienanstalten Vol. 52, 2018.
cited as: *KEK*, Sicherung der Meinungsvielfalt im digitalen Zeitalter.

Komorek, E. Media Pluralism and European Law, Alphen aan den Rijn 2013.
cited as: *Komorek*, Media Pluralism and European Law.

Kotzur, M.: Der Begriff der inländischen juristischen Personen nach Art. 19 Abs. 3 GG im Kontext der EU, in: DÖV 2001, Issue 5, p. 192–198.
cited as: *Kotzur* in DÖV 2001, 192, p.

Kresse, H.; Heinze, M.: Der Rundfunk: Das »jedenfalls auch kulturelle Phänomen«. Ein Pyrrhus-Sieg der Länder? – Eine Kurzanalyse des Urteils des BVerfG zur EU-Fernsehrichtlinie, in: ZUM 1995, p. 394–396.
cited as: *Kress/Heinze* in: ZUM 1995, 394, p.

Krieger, H.: Die Verantwortlichkeit Deutschlands nach der EMRK für seine Streitkräfte im Auslandseinsatz, in: ZaöRV 62 (2002), p. 669–703.
cited as: *Krieger* in: ZaöRV 2002, 669, p.

List of references

Kuczerawy, A.: EU Proposal for a Directive on Copyright in the Digital Single Market: Compatibility of Article 13 with the EU Intermediary Liability Regime, in: Petkova/Ojanen (ed.), Fundamental Rights Protection Online: The Future Regulation of Intermediaries, Cheltenham 2020, p. 205–219.
cited as: *Kuczerawy*, EU Proposal for a Directive on Copyright in the Digital Single Market: Compatibility of Art. 13 with the EU Intermediary Liability Regime, 205, p.

Kukliš, L.: Video-Sharing platforms in AVMSD – a new kind of content regulation (draft), in: Research Handbook on EU Media Law and Policy, Cheltenham 2021 (not yet published).
cited as: *Kukliš*, Video-Sharing platforms in AVMSD – a new kind of content regulation (draft).

id.: Media regulation at a distance: video-sharing platforms in AVMS Directive and the future of content regulation, in: mediaLAWS 02/2020, p. 95–110.
cited as: *Kukliš* in: mediaLAWS 02/2020, 95, p.

Landesanstalt für Medien NRW (ed.): Was ist Desinformation? Betrachtungen aus sechs wissenschaftlichen Perspektiven, Düsseldorf 2020, https://www.medienanstalt-nrw.de/fileadmin/user_upload/NeueWebsite_0120/Themen/Desinformation/WasIstDesinformation_Paper_LFMNRW.pdf.
cited as: *author* in: Was ist Desinformation?.

Lange, W.K.: Sponsoring und Europarecht, in: EWS 6/1998, p. 189–195.
cited as: *Lange* in: EWS 1998, 189, p.

Langenfeld, C.: Die Neuordnung des Jugendschutzes im Internet, in: MMR 2003, Issue 5, p. 303–309.
cited as: *Langenfeld* in: MMR 2003, 303, p.

Larenz, K.; Canaris, C.-W.: Methodenlehre der Rechtswissenschaft, 3rd edition, Berlin/Heidelberg 1995.
cited as: *Larenz/Canaris*, Methodenlehre der Rechtswissenschaft.

Lecheler, H.: Ungereimtheiten bei den Handlungsformen des Gemeinschaftsrechts – dargestellt anhand der Einordnung von „Leitlinien", in: DVBl. 2008, p. 873–880.
cited as: *Lecheler* in: DVBl. 2008, 873, p.

Lengauer, A.-M.: Drittwirkung von Grundfreiheiten: Ein Modell. Bausteine der Systematik, Berlin 2011.
cited as: *Lengauer*, Drittwirkung von Grundfreiheiten.

Lenski, S.C.: Öffentliches Kulturrecht, Tübingen 2013.
cited as: *Lenski*, Öffentliches Kulturrecht.

Lenz, C.: Immanente Grenzen des Gemeinschaftsrechts, in: Europäische Grundrechte-Zeitschrift, 1993, p. 57–65.
cited as: *Lenz* in: EuGRZ, 1993, 57, p.

Liehr, J.: Die Niederlassungsfreiheit zum Zwecke der Rundfunkveranstaltung und ihre Auswirkungen auf die deutsche Rundfunkordnung, Munich 1995.
cited as: *Liehr*, Die Niederlassungsfreiheit zum Zwecke der Rundfunkveranstaltung und ihre Auswirkungen auf die deutsche Rundfunkordnung.

Liesching, M.: Das Herkunftslandprinzip nach E-Commerce- und AVMD-Richtlinie. Anwendbarkeit von NetzDG, JuSchG, MStV und JMStV auf Soziale Netzwerke mit Sitz in anderen EU Mitgliedstaaten, Munich 2020.
cited as: *Liesching*, Das Herkunftslandprinzip nach E-Commerce- und AVMD-Richtlinie.

Lievens, E.: Protecting Children in the Digital Era: The Use of Alternative Regulatory Instruments, in: International Studies in Human Rights, Vol. 105, 2010.
cited as: *Lievens*, Protecting Children in the Digital Era: The Use of Alternative Regulatory Instruments.

Linke, C.E.: Europäisches Internationales Verwaltungsrecht, Frankfurt/Main 2001.
cited as: *Linke*, Europäisches Internationales Verwaltungsrecht.

Lodzig, B.: Grundriss einer verantwortlichen Interpretationstheorie des Rechts, Göttingen 2015.
cited as: *Lodzig*, Grundriss einer verantwortlichen Interpretationstheorie.

Mangold, A.: Der Widerspenstigen Zähmung, 13.05.2020, https://www.lto.de/recht/hintergruende/h/bverfg-ezb-urteil-provokation-eugh-eu-vertragsverletzungsverfahren/.
cited as: *Mangold*, Der Widerspenstigen Zähmung.

Martín y Pérez de Nanclares, J. Las competencias de los länder y el derecho derivado ante el Tribunal Constitucional Alemán (comentario a la sentencia del Tribunal Constitucional Alemán Bundesverfassungsgericht) de 22 de marzo de 1995, in: Revista de Instituciones Europeas, Vol. 22, Issue 3, 1995, p. 887–909.
cited as: *Martín y Pérez de Nanclares* in: Revista de Instituciones Europeas 1995, 887, p.

Martini, M.: Die Presseförderung im Fadenkreuz des Unionsrechts, in: EuZW 2015, p. 821–831.
cited as: *Martini* in: EuZW 2015, 821, p.

Maunz, T.; Dürig, G.: Grundgesetz, Kommentar, 90th edition, Munich 2020.
cited as: *author* in Maunz/Dürig.

Mayer, H.; Stöger, K. (ed.): Kommentar zu EUV und AEUV, Vienna 2016.
cited as: *author* in: Mayer/Stöger.

Meckel, M. Vielfalt im digitalen Medienensemble. Gutachten im Auftrag von ICOMP, St. Gallen 2012.
cited as: *Meckel*, Vielfalt im digitalen Medienensemble.

Menasse, R.: Kurze Geschichte der Europäischen Zukunft, in: Hilpold/Steinmair/Perathoner (ed.), Europa der Regionen, Berlin 2016, p. 27–37.
cited as: *Menasse* in: Hilpold/Steinmair/Perathoner, 27, p.

Merten, D.; Papier, H. J. (ed.): Handbuch der Grundrechte in Deutschland und Europa, Vol. VI/1: europäische Grundrechte, Munich 2010.
cited as: *author* in: Merten/Papier, Vol. VI/1.

Meyer-Ladewig, J.; Nettesheim, M.; von Raumer, S. (ed.): EMRK. Europäische Menschenrechtskonvention, Handkommentar, 4th edition, Baden-Baden 2017.
cited as: *author* in: Meyer-Ladewig/Nettesheim/von Raumer.

List of references

Middleton, J.: The Effectiveness of Audiovisual Regulation Inside the European Union: The Television without Frontiers Directive and Cultural Protectionism Denver Journal of International Law and Policy 31/2020, p. 607–628.
cited as: *Middleton* in: Denver Journal of International Law and Policy 31/2020, 607, p.

Mojzesowicz, K.: Möglichkeiten und Grenzen einer einheitlichen Dogmatik der Grundfreiheit, Baden-Baden 2001.
cited as: *Mojzesowicz*, Möglichkeiten und Grenzen einer einheitlichen Dogmatik der Grundfreiheit.

Möllers, C.; Schneider, L.: Demokratiesicherung in der Europäischen Union, Studie zu einem Dilemma, Tübingen 2018.
cited as: *Möllers/Schneider*, Demokratiesicherung in der Europäischen Union.

Moritz, S.: Staatliche Schutzpflichten gegenüber pflegebedürftigen Menschen, Baden-Baden 2013.
cited as: *Moritz*, Staatliche Schutzpflichten gegenüber pflegebedürftigen Menschen.

Moussis, N.: Access to the European Union: Law, Economics, Policies, 22nd edition, Cambridge 2016.
cited as: *Moussis*, Access to the European Union.

Mühl, A.: Diskriminierung und Beschränkung. Grundansätze einer einheitlichen Dogmatik der wirtschaftlichen Grundfreiheiten des EG-Vertrages, Schriften zum Europäischen Recht, Vol. 104, Berlin 2004.
cited as: *Mühl*, Diskriminierung und Beschränkung. Grundansätze einer einheitlichen Dogmatik der wirtschaftlichen Grundfreiheiten des EG-Vertrages.

Müller-Franken, S.: Netzwerkdurchsetzungsgesetz: Selbstbehauptung des Rechts oder erster Schritt in die selbstregulierte Vorzensur? – Verfassungsrechtliche Fragen, in: AfP 01/2018, p. 1–14.
cited as: *Müller-Franken* in: AfP 2018, 1, p.

Müller-Terpitz, R. Ein Karlsruher "Orakel" zum Bundesstaat im europäischen Staatenverbund, in: Menzel (ed.), Verfassungsrechtsprechung. Hundert Entscheidungen des Bundesverfassungsgerichts in Retrospektive, Tübingen 2000, p. 568–574.
cited as: *Müller-Terpitz*, Ein Karlsruher "Orakel" zum Bundesstaat im europäischen Staatenverbund.

Müssle, I.; Schmittmann, M.: Der Gemeinsame Markt und die Presse – Let's go Europe?, in: AfP 2002, p. 145–148.
cited as: *Müssle/Schmittmann* in: AfP 2002, 145, p.

Nechushtai, E.; Lewis, S. C.: What Kind of News Gatekeepers Do We Want Machines to Be? Filter Bubbles, Fragmentation, and the Normative Dimensions of Algorithmic Recommendations, in: Computers in Human Behavior, January 2019: p. 298–307, https://doi.org/10.1016/j.chb.2018.07.043.
cited as: *Nechushtai/Lewis* in: Computers in Human Behavior 2019, 298, p.

List of references

Neuberger, C.; Lobigs, F.: Meinungsmacht im Internet und die Digitalstrategien von Medienunternehmen: neue Machtverhältnisse trotz expandierender Internet-Geschäfte der traditionellen Massenmedien-Konzerne: Gutachten für die Kommission zur Ermittlung der Konzentration im Medienbereich (KEK), Leipzig 2018.
  cited as: *Neuberger/Lobigs*, Meinungsmacht im Internet und die Digitalstrategien von Medienunternehmen.

id.: Die Bedeutung des Internets im Rahmen der Vielfaltssicherung: Gutachten im Auftrag der Kommission zur Ermittlung der Konzentration im Medienbereich (KEK), Berlin 2010.
  cited as: *Neuberger/Lobigs*, Die Bedeutung des Internets im Rahmen der Vielfaltssicherung.

Neumann, T.: Das Recht der Filmförderung in Deutschland, Konstanz 2016.
  cited as: *Neumann*, Das Recht der Filmförderung in Deutschland.

Nettesheim, M.: Die Erteilung des mitgliedstaatlichen Einvernehmens nach Art. 4 Abs. 2 UAbs. 1 der FFH-Richtlinie – Vorgaben des Gemeinschaftsrechts und des Grundgesetzes, Tübingen 2007, http://www.fuesser.de/fileadmin/dateien/service/aktuelles/Einvernehmenserteilung/Gutachten_Einvernehmen_FFH.pdf.
  cited as: *Nettesheim*, Die Erteilung des mitgliedstaatlichen Einvernehmens nach Art. 4 Abs. 2 UAbs. 1 der FFH-Richtlinie.

id.: Horizontale Kompetenzkonflikte in der EG, in: EuR 1993, p. 243–260.
  cited as: *Nettesheim* in: EuR 1993, 243, p.

Nielsen, J.: Die Medienvielfalt als Aspekt der Wertesicherung der EU, Berlin 2019.
  cited as: *Nielsen*, Die Medienvielfalt als Aspekt der Wertesicherung der EU.

Nölscher, P.: Das Netzwerkdurchsetzungsgesetz und seine Vereinbarkeit mit dem Unionsrecht, in: ZUM 2020, p. 301–311.
  cited as: *Nölscher* in: ZUM 2020, 301, p.

Nikles, B.W.; Roll, S.; Spürck, D.; Erdemir, M.; Gutknecht, S. (ed.): Jugendschutzrecht. Kommentar zum Jugendschutzgesetz (JuSchG) und zum Jugendmedienschutz-Staatsvertrag (JMStV) mit auszugsweiser Kommentierung des Strafgesetzbuchs, 3rd edition, Munich 2011.
  cited as: *author* in Nikles/Roll/Spürck/Erdemir/Gutknecht.

Nikoltchev, S. (ed.): Videoabrufdienste und die Förderung europäischer Werke, IRIS Spezial, European Audiovisual Observatory, Strasbourg 2013.
  cited as: *author* in: Nikoltchev, Videoabrufdienste und die Förderung europäischer Werke.

Nolte, G.: Hate-Speech, Fake-News, das »Netzwerkdurchsetzungsgesetz« und Vielfaltsicherung durch Suchmaschinen, ZUM 07/2017, p. 552–564.
  cited as: *Nolte* in: ZUM 2017, 552, p.

Novak, M.: Ungleichbehandlung von ausländischen Produkten oder Dienstleistungen – Einheitliche Rechtfertigtatbestände im EG-Vertrag, in: DB 1997, p. 2589–2593.
  cited as: *Novak* in: DB 1997, 2589, p.

List of references

Nowrot, K.: Jenseits eines abwehrrechtlichen Ausnahmecharakters. Zur multidimensionalen Rechtswirkung des Widerstandsrechts nach Art. 20 Abs. 4 GG, in: Knops/Körner/Novrot (ed.), Rechtswissenschaftliche Beiträge der Hamburger Sozialökonomie, Issue 5, 2016.
cited as: *Nowrot*, Jenseits eines abwehrrechtlichen Ausnahmecharakters – Zur multidimensionalen Rechtswirkung des Widerstandsrechts nach Art. 20 Abs. 4 GG.

Nußberger, A.: Das Verhältnismäßigkeitsprinzip als Strukturprinzip richterlichen Entscheidens in Europa, in: NVwZ 2013, enclosure 1, 60 Jahre BVerwG, Festheft, p. 36–44.
cited as: *Nußberger* in: NVwZ-Beilage 2013, 36, p.

O'Neil, C.: Angriff der Algorithmen: Wie sie Wahlen manipulieren, Berufschancen zerstören und unsere Gesundheit gefährden, Munich 2017.
cited as: *O'Neil*, Angriff der Algorithmen.

Obwexer, W.: EU-rechtliche Determinierung mitgliedstaatlicher Kompetenzen, in: id. i.a. (ed.), EU-Mitgliedschaft und Südtirols Autonomie. Die Auswirkungen der EU-Mitgliedschaft auf die Autonomie des Landes Südtirol am Beispiel ausgewählter Gesetzgebungs- und Verwaltungskompetenzen, Vienna 2015.
cited as: *Obwexer*, EU-rechtliche Determinierung mitgliedstaatlicher Kompetenzen.

id.: Der Beitritt der EU zur EMRK: Rechstgrundlagen, Rechtsfragen und Rechtsfolgen, in: EuR, Vol. 47 (2012), Issue 2, p. 115–148.
cited as: *Obwexer* in: EuR 2012, 115, p.

Oesch, M.: Das Subsidiaritätsprinzip im EU-Recht und die nationalen Parlamente, in: Epiney/Diezig (ed.), Schweizerisches Jahrbuch für Europarecht 2012/2013, p. 301–315.
cited as: *Oesch*, Das Subsidiaritätsprinzip im EU-Recht und die nationalen Parlamente, 301, p.

Ohler, C.: Die Entwicklung eines Internationalen Verwaltungsrechts als Aufgabe der Rechtswissenschaft, in: DVBl. 122 (2007), p. 1083–1090.
cited as: *Ohler* in: DVBl. 2007, 1083, p.

id.: Die Kollisionsordnung des Allgemeinen Verwaltungsrechts – Strukturen des deutschen Internationalen Verwaltungsrechts, Tübingen 2005.
cited as: *Ohler*, Die Kollisionsordnung des Allgemeinen Verwaltungsrechts.

Okresek, W.: Hoheitsakte auf fremdem Staatsgebiet. Eine Betrachtung anhand praktischer Fälle, in: ÖZöRV 35 (1985), p. 325–344.
cited as: *Okresek* in: ÖZöRV 1985, 325, p.

Oppermann, T.: Transnationale Ausstrahlungen deutscher Grundrechte? Erörtert am Beispiel des transnationalen Umweltschutzes, in: Kroneck/Oppermann (ed.), Im Dienste Deutschlands und des Rechtes: Festschrift für Wilhelm G. Grewe zum 70. Geburtstag am 16. Oktober 1981, Baden-Baden 1981, p. 521–538.
cited as: *Oppermann*, Transnationale Ausstrahlung deutscher Grundrechte?, 521, p.

Ory, S.: Medienpolitik mit prozessualen Mitteln: Regionale TV-Werbung in bundesweiten Programmen vor dem EuGH, in: NJW 2021, p. 736–740.
cited as: *Ory* in: NJW 2021, 736, p.

Ossenbühl, F: Rundfunk zwischen nationalem Verfassungsrecht und europäischem Gemeinschaftsrecht, Frankfurt/M. 1986.
cited as: *Ossenbühl*, Rundfunk zwischen nationalem Verfassungsrecht und europäischem Gemeinschaftsrecht.

Oxman, B.H.: Jurisdiction of States, in: Wolfrum (ed.), The Max Planck Encyclopedia of Public International Law (MPEPIL), Oxford 2012, p. 546–557.
cited as: *Oxman* in: MPEPIL, 546, p.

Paal, B.: Intermediäre: Regulierung und Vielfaltssicherung, Rechtsgutachten im Auftrag der Landesanstalt für Medien Nordrhein-Westfalen, March 2018, https://www.medienanstalt-nrw.de/fileadmin/user_upload/lfm-nrw/Foerderung/Forschung/Dateien_Forschung/Paal_Intermediaere_Regulierung-und-Vielfaltssicherung_Gutachten-2018.pdf.
cited as: *Paal*, Intermediäre: Regulierung und Vielfaltssicherung.

id.: Medienvielfalt und Wettbewerbsrecht, Tübingen 2010.
cited as: *Paal*, Medienvielfalt und Wettbewerbsrecht.

Pechstein, M.; Nowak, C.; Häde, U. (ed.): Frankfurter Kommentar zu EUV, GRC und AEUV, Tübingen 2017.
cited as: *author* in: Pechstein et al., Frankfurter Kommentar.

Peifer, K.-N.: Netzwerkdurchsetzungsgesetz: Selbstbehauptung des Rechts oder erster Schritt in die selbstregulierte Vorzensur? – Zivilrechtliche Aspekte, in: AfP 01/2018, p. 14–23.
cited as: *Peifer* in: AfP 01/2018, 14, p.

Pernice, I.: Europäisches und nationales Verfassungsrecht, in: VVDStRL 60 (2001), p. 148–193.
cited as: *Pernice* in: VVDStRL 2001, 148, p.

Plötscher, S.: Der Begriff der Diskriminierung im Europäischen Gemeinschaftsrecht, Berlin 2003.
cited as: *Plötscher*, Der Begriff der Diskriminierung im Europäischen Gemeinschaftsrecht.

Potacs, M.: Rechtstheorie, Vienna 2015.
cited as: *Potacs*, Rechtstheorie.

Puttler, A.: Sind die Mitgliedstaaten noch "Herren" der EU? – Stellung und Einfluss der Mitgliedstaaten nach dem Entwurf des Verfassungsvertrages der Regierungskonferenz, in: Europarecht (EuR) 2004, p. 669–691.
cited as: *Puttler* in: EuR 2004, 669, p.

Reese, B.: Die Verfassung des Grundgesetzes. Rahmen- und Werteordnung im Lichte der Gefährdungen durch Macht und Moral, Berlin 2013.
cited as: *Reese*, Die Verfassung des Grundgesetzes. Rahmen- und Werteordnung im Lichte der Gefährdungen durch Macht und Moral.

Ress, G.: Supranationaler Menschenrechtsschutz und der Wandel der Staatlichkeit, in: ZaöRV 64 (2004), p. 621–639.
cited as: *Ress* in: ZaöRV 2004, 621, p.

id.: Staatszwecke im Verfassungsstaat — nach 40 Jahren Grundgesetz, in: VVD-StRL 48 (1990), p. 56–118.
 cited as: *Ress* in: VVDStRL 1990, 56, p.

id.: Menschenrechte, europäisches Gemeinschaftsrecht und nationales Verfassungsrecht, in: Haller/Kopetzki/Novak/Paulson/Raschauer/Ress/Wiederin (ed.), Staat und Recht: Festschrift für Günther Winkler, Vienna 1997, p. 897–932.
 cited as: *Ress*, Menschenrechte, europäisches Gemeinschaftsrecht und nationales Verfassungsrecht, 897, p.

id.: Die neue Kulturkompetenz der EG, in: DÖV 1992, p. 944–955.
 cited as: *Ress* in: DÖV 1992, 944, p.

Ress, G.; Bröhmer, J.: Europäische Gemeinschaft und Medienvielfalt. Die Kompetenzen der Europäischen Gemeinschaft zur Sicherung des Pluralismus im Medienbereich, Saarbrücken 1998.
 cited as: *Ress/Bröhmer*, Europäische Gemeinschaft und Medienvielfalt.

Ress, G.; Ukrow, J.: Die Niederlassungsfreiheit von Apothekern in Europa, Stuttgart 1991.
 cited as: *Ress/Ukrow*, Die Niederlassungsfreiheit von Apothekern.

Rengeling, H.-W.; Middeke, A.; Gellermann, M. (ed.): Handbuch des Rechtsschutzes in der Europäischen Union, 3rd edition, Munich 2014.
 Zitiert: *author* in: Rengeling/Middeke/Gellermann.

Riecken, J.: Verfassungsgerichtsbarkeit in der Demokratie. Grenzen verfassungsgerichtlicher Kontrolle unter besonderer Berücksichtigung von John Hart Elys prozeduraler Theorie der Repräsentationsverstärkung, Berlin 2003.
 cited as: *Riecken*, Verfassungsgerichtsbarkeit in der Demokratie.

Rodriguez Iglesias, G. C.: Zu den Grenzen der verfahrensrechtlichen Autonomie der Mitgliedstaaten bei der Anwendung des Gemeinschaftsrechts, EuGRZ 1997, p. 289–295.
 cited as: *Rodriguez Iglesias* in: EuGRZ 1997, 289, p.

Roider, C.: Perspektiven einer Europäischen Rundfunkordnung, Berlin 2001.
 cited as: *Roider*, Perspektiven einer Europäischen Rundfunkordnung.

Ruffert, M.: Die Globalisierung als Herausforderung an das Öffentliche Recht, Stuttgart i.a. 2004.
 cited as: *Ruffert*, Die Globalisierung als Herausforderung an das Öffentliche Recht.

id.: Kontinuität oder Kehrtwende im Streit um die gemeinschaftsrechtlichen Umweltschutzkompetenzen?, in: Jura 1994, p. 635–643.
 cited as; *Ruffert* in: Jura 1994, 635, p.

Rupp, H.H.: Anmerkungen zu einer Europäischen Verfassung, in: JuristenZeitung Vol. 58, No. 1, p. 18–22.
 cited as: *Rupp* in: JZ 2003, 18, p.

Russ-Mohl, S.: Die informierte Gesellschaft und ihre Feinde: Warum die Digitalisierung unsere Demokratie gefährdet, Cologne 2017.
 cited as: *Russ-Mohl*, Die informierte Gesellschaft und ihre Feinde: Warum die Digitalisierung unsere Demokratie gefährdet.

List of references

Safferling, C.: Internationales Strafrecht: Strafanwendungsrecht – Völkerstrafrecht – Europäisches Strafrecht, Berlin/Heidelberg 2011.
cited as: *Safferling*, Internationales Strafrecht.

Schallbruch, M.: Schwacher Staat im Netz: Wie die Digitalisierung den Staat in Frage stellt, Berlin 2018.
cited as: *Schallbruch*, Schwacher Staat im Netz.

Schmidt, S.: Die Rechtmäßigkeit staatlicher Gefahrenabwehrmaßnahmen im Internet unter besonderer Berücksichtigung des Europäischen Gemeinschaftsrechts, Frankfurt/M. i.a. 2006.
cited as: *Schmidt*, Die Rechtmäßigkeit staatlicher Gefahrenabwehrmaßnahmen im Internet unter besonderer Berücksichtigung des Europäischen Gemeinschaftsrechts.

Schmitt von Sydow, H.: Liberté, démocratie, droits fondamentaux et État de droit: analyse de l'article 7 du traité UE in: Revue du droit de l'union européenne, 2001, p. 285–328.
cited as: *Schmitt von Sydow* in: Revue du droit de l'union européenne 2001, 285, p.

Schmittmann, M.; Luedtke, A.: Die Medienfreiheiten in der Europäischen Grundrechtecharta, in: AfP 2000, p. 533–534.
cited as: *Schmittmann/Luedtke* in: AfP 2000, 533, p.

Stelkens, P.; Bonk, H.J.; Sachs, M. (ed.): Verwaltungsverfahrensgesetz, 8th edition, Munich 2014.
cited as: *author* in: Stelkens/Bonk/Sachs.

Schnelle, E.: Freiheitsmissbrauch und Grundrechtsverwirkung, Versuch einer Neubestimmung von Artikel 18 GG, Berlin 2014.
cited as: *Schnelle*, Freiheitsmissbrauch und Grundrechtsverwirkung.

Schleper, N.: Auf dem Weg zu einer einheitlichen Dogmatik der Grundfreiheiten?, in: Institut für Völkerrecht der Universität Göttingen, Abteilung Europarecht – Göttinger Online-Beiträge zum Europarecht, No. 16 (2004), https://www.jura.fu-berlin.de/forschung/europarecht/bob/berliner_online_beitraege/Paper16-Schleper/Paper16---Auf-dem-Weg-zu-einer-einheitlichen-Dogmatik-der-Grundfreiheiten.pdf.
cited as: *Schleper* in: Göttinger Online-Beiträge zum Europarecht, No. 16 (2004).

Schlochauer, H.J.: Die extraterritoriale Wirkung von Hoheitsakten nach dem öffentlichen Recht der Bundesrepublik Deutschland und nach internationalem Recht, Frankfurt 1962.
cited as: *Schlochauer*, Die extraterritoriale Wirkung von Hoheitsakten nach dem öffentlichen Recht der Bundesrepublik Deutschland und nach internationalem Recht.

Schorkopf, F.: Grundgesetz und Überstaatlichkeit, Tübingen 2007.
cited as: *Schorkopf*, Grundgesetz und Überstaatlichkeit.

Schriewert, B.: Zur Theorie der internationalen Offenheit und der Völkerrechtsfreundlichkeit einer Rechtsordnung und ihrer Erprobung am Beispiel der EU-Rechtsordnung, Berlin 2017.
cited as: *Schriewert*, Zur Theorie der internationalen Offenheit und der Völkerrechtsfreundlichkeit einer Rechtsordnung und ihrer Erprobung am Beispiel der EU-Rechtsordnung.

Schröder, M.: Zur Wirkkraft der Grundrechte bei Sachverhalten mit grenzüberschreitenden Elementen, in: Münch (ed.), Staatsrecht – Völkerrecht – Europarecht, Festschrift für Hans-Jürgen Schlochauer zum 75. Geburtstag am 28. März 1981, Frankfurt 1981, p. 137–150.
cited as: *Schröder*, Zur Wirkkraft der Grundrechte bei Sachverhalten mit grenzüberschreitenden Elementen, 137, p.

Schulz, W.: Jugendschutz bei Tele- und Mediendiensten, in: MMR 1998, Issue 4, p. 182–187.
cited as: *Schulz* in MMR 1998, 182, p.

Schulz, W.; Held, T.: Regulierte Selbstregulierung als Form modernen Regierens, Bericht im Auftrag des Bundesbeauftragten für Angelegenheiten der Kultur und der Medien, May 2002, https://www.hans-bredow-institut.de/uploads/media/Publikationen/cms/media/a80e5e6dbc2427639ca0f437fe76d3c4c95634ac.pdf.
cited as: *Schulz/Held*, Regulierte Selbstregulierung als Form modernen Regierens.

Schulz, W.; Valcke, P.; Irion, K.: The Independence of the Media and Its Regulatory Agencies – shedding new light on formal and actual independence against the national context, Chicago 2013.
cited as: *author* in: Schulz/Valcke/Irion, The Independence of the Media and Its Regulatory Agencies.

Schulze, R.; Zuleeg, M.; Kadelbach, S. (ed.): Europarecht. Handbuch für die deutsche Rechtspraxis, 3rd edition, Munich 2015.
cited as: *author* in Schulze/Zuleeg/Kadelbach.

Schwartz, I.E.: Rundfunk, EG-Kompetenzen und ihre Ausübung, in: Stern (ed.), Eine Rundfunkordnung für Europa – Chancen und Risiken; Vortragsveranstaltung vom 18. und 19. Mai 1990, Munich 1990.
cited as: *Schwartz*, Rundfunk, EG-Kompetenzen und ihre Ausübung.

Schwarz, T.: Subsidiarität und EG-Kompetenzen, in: Zeitschrift für Meiden- und Kommunikationsrecht, 1993, p. 409–417.
cited as: *Schwarz* in: AfP, 1993, 409, p.

Schwarze, J. (ed.): Globalisierung und Entstaatlichung des Rechts, Tübingen 2008.
cited as: *Schwarze*, Globalisierung und Entstaatlichung des Rechts.

Schwarze, J.: Europäische Rahmenbedingungen für die Verwaltungsgerichtsbarkeit, in: NVwZ 2000 Issue 3, p. 241–251.
cited as: *Schwarze* in: NVwZ 2000, 241, p.

Schwarze, J. (ed.): Die Entstehung einer europäischen Verfassungsordnung. Das Ineinandergreifen von nationalem und europäischem Verfassungsrecht, Baden-Baden 2000.
cited as: *Schwarze*, Die Entstehung einer europäischen Verfassungsordnung.

Schweisfurth, T.: Völkerrecht, Tübingen 2006.
cited as: *Schweisfurth*, Völkerrecht.

Sedelmeier, K.; Burkhardt, E. (ed.): Löffler (founder), Kommentar zum Presserecht, 6th edition, Munich 2015.
cited as: *author* in: Sedelmeier/Burkhardt.

Seibert-Fohr, A.: Die völkerrechtliche Verantwortung des Staats für das Handeln von Privaten: Bedarf nach Neuorientierung?, in: ZaöRV 73 (2013), p. 37–60.
cited as: *Seibert-Fohr* in: ZaöRV 2013, 37, p.

Sommermann, K.-P.: Offene Staatlichkeit: Deutschland, in: von Bogdandy/Cruz Villalón/Huber (ed.), Handbuch Ius Publicum Europaeum, Vol. II: Offene Staatlichkeit – Wissenschaft vom Verfassungsrecht, Heidelberg 2008, p. 3–35.
cited as: *Sommermann*, Offene Staatlichkeit: Deutschland, 3, p.

Spindler, G.: Der Regierungsentwurf zum Netzwerkdurchsetzungsgesetz – europarechtswidrig?, in: ZUM 2017, p. 473–506.
cited as: *Spindler* in: ZUM 2017, 473, p.

Spindler, G.; Schmitz, P. (ed.): Telemediengesetz: TMG mit Netzwerkdurchsetzungsgesetz (NetzDG), Kommentar, 2nd edition, Munich 2018.
cited as: *author* in: Spindler/Schmitz.

Stark, B.; Margin, M.; Jürgens, P.: Maßlos überschätzt. Ein Überblick über theoretische Annahmen und empirische Befunde zu Filterblasen und Echokammern (Preprint), erscheint in: Eisenegger/Blum/Ettinger/Prinzing (ed.), Digitaler Strukturwandel der Öffentlichkeit: Historische Verortung, Modelle und Konsequenzen, 2020, auch abrufbar als Preprint unter http://melanie-magin.net/wp-content/uploads/2019/11/Stark_Magin_Juergens_2019_Preprint.pdf.
cited as: *Stark/Margin/Jürgens*, Maßlos überschätzt. Ein Überblick über theoretische Annahmen und empirische Befunde zu Filterblasen und Echokammern (Preprint).

Stein, T.; von Buttlar, C.; Kotzur, M.: Völkerrecht, 14th edition, Munich 2017.
cited as: *Stein/von Buttlar/Kotzur*, Völkerrecht.

Steinbeis, M.: Europarechtsbruch als Verfassungspflicht: Karlsruhe zündet die Identitätskontrollbombe, in: Verfassungsblog, 26.01.2016 (available at https://verfassungsblog.de/europarechtsbruch-als-verfassungspflicht-karlsruhe-zuendet-die-identitaetskontroll-bombe/, last assessed 08.01.2021).
cited as: *Steinbeis*, Verfassungsblog, 26.01.2016.

Stern, K.: Das Staatsrecht der Bundesrepublik Deutschland, Vol. III/1, Munich 1988.
cited as: *Stern*, Das Staatsrecht der Bundesrepublik Deutschland, Vol. III/1.

Stern, K.; Sachs, M. (ed.): Europäische Grundrechte-Charta: GRCh, Munich 2016.
cited as: *author* in: Stern/Sachs.

Streinz, R.: Europarecht, 11th edition, Heidelberg 2019.
cited as: *Streinz*, Europarecht.

id. (ed.): EUV/AEUV, Vertrag über die Europäische Union, Vertrag über die Arbeitsweise der Europäischen Union, Charta der Grundrechte der Europäischen Union, commentary, 3rd edition, Munich 2018.
cited as: *author* in: Streinz.

id.: Die Interpretationsmethoden des Europäischen Gerichtshofs zum Vorantreiben der Integration, in: Rill (ed.), Die Dynamik der europäischen Institutionen, Munich 2011, p. 27–40.
cited as: *Streinz,* Die Interpretationsmethoden des Europäischen Gerichtshofs zum Vorantreiben der Integration, 27, p.

id.: Konvergenz der Grundfreiheiten. Aufgabe der Differenzierungen des EG-Vertrags und der Unterscheidung zwischen unterschiedlichen und unterschiedslosen Maßnahmen? Zu Tendenzen der Rechtsprechung des EuGH, in: Arndt/Knemeyer/Kugelmann (ed.), Völkerrecht und deutsches Recht: Festschrift für Walter Rudolf zum 70. Geburtstag, Munich 2001, p. 199–221.
cited as: *Streinz,* Konvergenz der Grundfreiheiten, 199, p.

id.: Bundesverfassungsgerichtlicher Grundrechtsschutz und Europäisches Gemeinschaftsrecht, Baden-Baden 1989.
cited as: *Streinz,* Bundesverfassungsgerichtlicher Grundrechtsschutz und Europäisches Gemeinschaftsrecht.

Streinz, R.; Michl, W.: Die Drittwirkung des europäischen Datenschutzgrundrechts (Art. 8 GRCh) im deutschen Privatrecht, in: EuZW 2011, p. 384–388.
cited as: *Streinz/Michl* in EuZW 2011, 384, p.

Strupp, K.; Schlochauer, H.-J. (ed.): Wörterbuch des Völkerrechts, Vol. I, Berlin 1960.
cited as: *author* in: Strupp/Schlochauer, p.

Struth, A.: Hassrede und Freiheit der Meinungsäußerung: Der Schutzbereich der Meinungsäußerungsfreiheit in Fällen demokratiefeindlicher Äußerungen nach der Europäischen Menschenrechtskonvention, dem Grundgesetz und der Charta der Grundrechte der Europäischen Union, Berlin 2019.
cited as: *Struth,* Hassrede und Freiheit der Meinungsäußerung.

Stuyck, J.: Joined Cases C-34/95, C-35/95 and C-36/95, Konsumentombudsmannen (KO) v. De Agostini (Svenska) Förlag AB and Konsumentombudsmannen (KO) v. TV-Shop i Sverige AB, Judgment of 9 July 1997, in: CMLRev. 6/1997, p. 1445–1468.
cited as: *Stuyck* in: CMLRev. 1997, 1445, p.

Sunstein, C. R.: Infotopia: How Many Minds Produce Knowledge, Oxford 2006.
cited as: *Sunstein,* Infotopia: How Many Minds Produce Knowledge.

Talmon, S.: Die Grenzen der Anwendung des Völkerrechts im deutschen Recht, JZ 68 (2013), p. 12–21.
cited as: *Talmon* in: JZ 2013, 12, p.

Tamblé, P.: Der Anwendungsbereich der EU-Grundrechtecharta (GRC) gem. Art. 51 I 1 GRC – Grundlagen und aktuelle Entwicklungen, Halle 2014.
cited as: *Tamblé,* Der Anwendungsbereich der EU-Grundrechtecharta (GRC) gem. Art. 51 I 1 GRC.

Tichy, H.: Recommendations des Europarats, in: ZaöRV 76 (2016), p. 415–424.
cited as: *Tichy* in: ZaöRV 2016, 415, p.

List of references

Tietje, C.: Die Exekutive. Verwaltungshandeln im Kontext von Globalisierung und Internationalisierung, in: Delbrück/Einsele (ed.), Wandel des Staates im Kontext europäischer und internationaler Integration, Baden-Baden 2006, p. 53–70.
cited as: *Tietje*, Die Exekutive. Verwaltungshandeln im Kontext von Globalisierung und Internationalisierung, 53, p.

id.: Die Internationalität des Verwaltungsstaates – Vom internationalen Verwaltungsrecht des Lorenz von Stein zum heutigen internationalisierten Verwaltungshandeln, in: Quellen zur Verwaltungsgeschichte No. 16, Kiel 2001.
cited as: *Tietje*, Die Internationalität des Verwaltungsstaates.

id.: Internationalisiertes Verwaltungshandeln, in: Veröffentlichungen des Walther-Schücking-Instituts für Internationales Recht an der Universität Kiel (VIIR), Vol. 136, Berlin 2001.
cited as: *Tietje*, Internationalisiertes Verwaltungshandeln.

Tietje, C.; Bering, J.; Zuber, T.: Völker- und europarechtliche Zulässigkeit extraterritorialer Anknüpfung einer Finanztransaktionssteuer, Halle 2014.
cited as: *Tietje/Bering/Zuber*, Völker- und europarechtliche Zulässigkeit extraterritorialer Anknüpfung einer Finanztransaktionssteuer.

Thiele, A.: Europarecht, 15th edition, Vienna 2018.
cited as: *Thiele*, Europarecht.

Trautwein, T.: Das BVerfG, der EuGH und das Fernsehen – Anmerkungen zum Urteil des BVerfG zur EG-Fernsehrichtlinie, in: ZUM 1995, p. 614–617.
cited as: *Trautwein* in: ZUM 1995, 614, p.

Trstenjak, V; Beysen, E.: Das Prinzip der Verhältnismäßigkeit in der Unionsrechtsordnung, in: EuR 2012, p. 265–284.
cited as: *Trstenjak/Beysen* in: EuR 2012, 265, p.

Uerpmann-Wittzack, R.: Principles of International Internet Law, in: German Law Journal (GLJ) 11(2010)11, p. 1245–1263.
cited as: *Uerpmann-Wittzack* in: GLJ 2010, 1245, p.

Ukrow, J.: Wehrhafte Demokratie 4.0 – Grundwerte, Grundrechte und Social Media-Exzesse, in: ZEuS 2021, p. 65–98.
cited as: *Ukrow* in: ZEuS 2021, 65, p.

id.: Das aktuelle Stichwort: Sicherung regionaler Vielfalt – Außer Mode? Anmerkungen aus Anlass des Urteils des Europäischen Gerichtshofs vom 3. Februar 2021, Rs. C-555/19, Fussl Modestraße Mayr GmbH ./. SevenOne Media GmbH, ProSiebenSat.1 TV Deutschland GmbH, ProSiebenSat.1 Media SE, https://emr-sb.de/wp-content/uploads/2021/02/EMR_Aktuelles-Stichwort-zum-EuGH-Urteil-in-Sachen-Fussl-Modestrasse-Mayr.pdf.
cited as: *Ukrow*, Sicherung regionaler Vielfalt – Außer Mode?.

id.: Die Vorschläge der EU-Kommission für einen Digital Services Act und einen Digital Markets Act. Darstellung von und erste Überlegungen zu zentralen Bausteinen für eine digitale Grundordnung der EU, in: Impulse aus dem EMR, 2021, https://emr-sb.de/wp-content/uploads/2021/01/Impulse-aus-dem-EMR_DMA-und-DSA.pdf.
cited as: *Ukrow*, Die Vorschläge der EU-Kommission für einen Digital Services Act und einen Digital Markets Act.

List of references

id.: Schutz der Medienvielfalt und medienbezogene Solidaritätspflichten in Corona-Zeiten. Eine europa- und verfassungsrechtliche Betrachtung, in: Impulse aus dem EMR, 2020, https://emr-sb.de/wp-content/uploads/2020/03/EMR-Impulse-Vielfalt-Corona-200330.pdf.
cited as: *Ukrow*, Schutz der Medienvielfalt und medienbezogene Solidaritätspflichten in Corona-Zeiten.

id.: Élysée 2.0 im Lichte des Europarechts – Der Vertrag von Aachen und die „immer engere Union", in: Zeitschrift für Europarechtliche Studien 2019, p. 3–59.
cited as: *Ukrow*, Élysée 2.0 im Lichte des Europarechts, ZEuS 2019, 3, p.

id.: Online-Glücksspiel in der Regulierung – Kohärenz im Werden?, in: ZfWG 2019, p. 223–234.
cited as: *Ukrow* in: ZfWG 2019, 223, p.

id.: Algorithmen, APIs und Aufsicht. Überlegungen zur organisations- und verfahrensrechtlichen Effektuierung einer positiven Ordnung der Vielfaltssicherung im digitalen Raum, in: Impulse aus dem EMR, 2019, https://emr-sb.de/impulse-aus-dem-emr-algorithmen-apis-und-aufsicht/.
cited as: *Ukrow*, Algorithmen, APIs und Aufsicht.

id.: Indexierung des Rundfunkbeitrags und Stabilität der deutschen Rundfunkfinanzierung. Ansätze einer europarechtlichen Risikoanalyse, UFITA 83(2019)1, p. 279–330.
cited as: *Ukrow* in: UFITA 2019, 279, p.

id.: Wer ist gegen Europa? Analyse der Wahlen nach dem Brexit-Referendum, vorgänge 56 (2017) H. 220, p. 69.
cited as: *Ukrow*, Wer ist gegen Europa? vorgänge 56 (2017) H. 220, p. 69

id.: Zum Anwendungsbereich einer novellierten AVMD-Richtlinie. Impulse für das anstehende AVMD-Trilog-Verfahren, 2017, https://emr-sb.de/wp-content/uploads/2017/09/EMR-AVMD-Impulse-1708-01-Anwendungsbereich.pdf.
cited as: *Ukrow*, Zum Anwendungsbereich einer novellierten AVMD-Richtlinie.

id.: Por-No Go im audiovisuellen Binnenmarkt? Jugendmedienschutz im Level-Playing-Field und die geplante Abkehr vom absoluten Pornographieverbot im Fernsehen, in: EMR Impuls, 2017, https://emr-sb.de/wp-content/uploads/2017/10/EMR-AVMD-Impulse-1710-01-Jugendschutz.pdf.
cited as: *Ukrow*, Por-No Go im audiovisuellen Binnenmarkt?.

id.: Internationaler und europäischer Jugendmedienschutz – Bestandsaufnahme, Entwicklungstendenzen und Herausforderungen in: Recht der Jugend und des Bildungswesens (RdJB) 65(2017)3, p. 278–296.
cited as: *Ukrow* in: RdJB 2017, 278, p.

id.: Wächst Europa an seinen rechtspopulistischen Feinden? Europäische wehrhafte Demokratie und Schutz der Grundwerte in der EU, in: vorgänge 55 (2016) H. 216, p. 47.
cited as: *Ukrow* in: vorgänge 55 (2016) 216, 47, p.

id.: Ceterum censeo: CETA prohibendam esse? Audiovisuelle Medien im europäisch-kanadischen Freihandelssystem, in: EMR – Das aktuelle Stichwort, 2016, https://emr-sb.de/wp-content/uploads/2017/01/20170109_EMR_Das-aktuelle-Stichwort_CETA.pdf.
cited as: *Ukrow*, Ceterum censeo: CETA prohibendam esse? Audiovisuelle Medien im europäisch-kanadischen Freihandelssystem.

id.: Deutschland auf dem Weg vom Motor zum Bremser der europäischen Integration? Kritische Anmerkungen zum „Lissabon"-Urteil des Bundesverfassungsgerichts vom 30. Juni 2009, in: ZEuS 2009, p. 717–729.
cited as: *Ukrow* in: ZEuS 2009, 717, p.

id.: Jugendschutzrecht, Munich 2004.
cited as: *Ukrow*, Jugendschutzrecht.

id.: Die Selbstkontrolle im Medienbereich in Europa, Munich/Berlin 2000.
cited as: *Ukrow*, Die Selbstkontrolle im Medienbereich in Europa.

id.: Richterliche Rechtsfortbildung durch den EuGH. Dargestellt am Beispiel der Erweiterung des Rechtsschutzes des Marktbürgers im Bereich des vorläufigen Rechtsschutzes und der Staatshaftung, Baden-Baden 1995.
cited as: *Ukrow*, Richterliche Rechtsfortbildung durch den EuGH.

Ukrow, J.; Cole, M. D.: Aktive Sicherung lokaler und regionaler Medienvielfalt – Rechtliche Möglichkeiten und Grenzen der Förderung inhaltlicher Qualität in Presse-, Rundfunk- und Online-Angeboten, TLM Schriftenreihe Vol. 25, 2019.
cited as: *Ukrow/Cole*, Aktive Sicherung lokaler und regionaler Medienvielfalt.

id.: Zur Transparenz von Mediaagenturen – Eine rechtswissenschaftliche Untersuchung, Gutachten im Auftrag der Friedrich-Ebert-Stiftung, 2017 available at https://library.fes.de/pdf-files/akademie/13233.pdf.
cited as: *Ukrow/Cole*, Zur Transparenz von Mediaagenturen.

Ukrow, J.; Etteldorf, C.: Fake News" als Rechtsproblem, in Ory/Cole/Ukrow (ed.), EMR/Script, Band 5, https://emr-sb.de/wp-content/uploads/2018/04/EMR-SCRIPT-Band-5_Fake-News-als-Rechtsproblem.pdf.
cited as: *Ukrow/Etteldorf*, Fake News als Rechtsproblem.

Ullrich, H.: Enhanced Cooperation in the Area of Unitary Patent Protection and European Integration, in: RdDI 2013, p. 325–351.
cited as: *Ullrich* in: RdDI 2013, 325, p.

Valcke, P.: Challenges of Regulating Media Pluralism in the European Union: the Potential of Risk-Based Regulation, Quaderns del CAC 38 Vol. XV (1), June 2012.
cited as: *Valcke*, Challenges of Regulating Media Pluralism in the European Union.

Valdani, Vicari and Associates (VVA): Assessment on the implementation of the code of practice on disinformation, Studie im Auftrag der Europäischen Kommission, SMART 2019/0041, 2020, https://ec.europa.eu/digital-single-market/en/news/study-assessment-implementation-code-practice-disinformation.
cited as: *VVA*, Assessment on the implementation of the code of practice on disinformation.

List of references

VVA, KEA, attentional: Study on the Promotion of European Works in Audiovisual Media Services, SMART 2016/0061, study prepared for the European Commission DG Communications Networks, Content & Technology, 2020, https://ec.curopa.eu/digital-single-market/en/news/study-promotion-european-works-1.
cited as: *VVA i.a.*, study on the Promotion of European Works in Audiovisual Media Services, SMART 2016/0061.

Valerius, B.: Ermittlungen der Strafverfolgungsbehörden in den Kommunikationsdiensten des Internet. Hoheitliche Recherchen in einem grenzüberschreitenden Medium, Berlin 2004.
cited as: *Valerius*, Ermittlungen der Strafverfolgungsbehörden in den Kommunikationsdiensten des Internet. Hoheitliche Recherchen in einem grenzüberschreitenden Medium.

van Loon, A.: Freedom versus access rights in a European context, in: Media Law & Policy 2001–1, p. 12–31.
cited as: *van Loon* in: Media Law & Policy 2001, 12, p.

Vedder, C.; Heintschel von Heinegg, W. (ed.): Europäisches Unionsrecht, EUV, AEUV, GRCh, EAGV, Kommentar, 2nd edition, Baden-Baden 2018.
cited as: *author* in: Vedder/Heintschel von Heinegg.

Vike-Freiberga, V.; Däubler-Gmelin, H.; Hammersley, B.; Maduro, L.: High-Level Group on Media Freedom and Pluralism, Report on a free and pluralistic media to sustain European democracy, 2013, https://ec.europa.eu/digital-single-market/sites/digital-agenda/files/HLG%20Final%20Report.pdf.
cited as: *Vike-Freiberga u.a.* (High-Level Group on Media Freedom and Pluralism), Report on a free and pluralistic media to sustain European democracy.

Visionary Analytics, SQW Limited, Ramboll Management Consulting: Survey and data gathering to support the Impact Assessment of a possible new legislative proposal concerning Directive 2010/13/EU (AVMSD) and in particular the provisions on media freedom, public interest and access for disabled people, study prepared for the European Commission DG Communications Networks, Content & Technology, SMART 2015/0048, 2016, https://www.visionary.lt/wp-content/uploads/2016/05/AVMSD.pdf.
cited as: *Visionary Analytics et al.*, Study to support Impact Assessment of AVMSD.

Vlassis, A.: The review of the Audiovisual Media Services Directive. Many political voices for one digital Europe?, in: Politique européenne 2017/2 (No. 56), p. 102–123.
cited as: *Vlassis* in: Politique européenne 2017/2, 102, p.

Vogel, K.: Die Verfassungsentscheidung des Grundgesetzes für eine internationale Zusammenarbeit, Tübingen 1964.
cited as: *Vogel*, Die Verfassungsentscheidung des Grundgesetzes für eine internationale Zusammenarbeit.

von Arnauld, A.: Völkerrecht, 3rd edition, Heidelberg 2016.
cited as: *von Arnauld*, Völkerrecht.

id.: Freiheit und Regulierung in der Cyberwelt: Transnationaler Schutz der Privatsphäre aus Sicht des Völkerrechts, Heidelberg 2016, p. 27–30.
cited as: *von Arnauld*, Freiheit und Regulierung in der Cyberwelt: Transnationaler Schutz der Privatsphäre aus Sicht des Völkerrechts, 27, p.

von Bogdandy, A.: Rechtsfortbildung mit Artikel 5 EG-Vertrag. Zur Zulässigkeit gemeinschaftsrechtlicher Innovationen nach EG-Vertrag und Grundgesetz, in: Randelzhofer u.a. (ed.), Gedächtnisschrift für Eberhard Grabitz, Munich 1995, p. 17–28.
cited as: *von Bogdandy*, Rechtsfortbildung mit Artikel 5 EG-Vertrag, p.

von Bogdandy, A.; Grabenwarter, C.; Huber, P.M. (ed.): Ius Publicum Europaeum, Vol. VI: Verfassungsgerichtsbarkeit in Europa: Institutionen, Munich 2016.
cited as: *author* in: von Bogdandy/Grabenwarter/Huber, Vol. VI.

von Bogdandy, A.; Bast, J.: Die vertikale Kompetenzordnung der Europäischen Union, in: EuGRZ 2001, p. 441–458.
also available in English: The European Union's vertical order of competences: The current law and proposals for its reform, in: 39 CMLRev. (2002), p. 227–268.
cited as: *von Bogdandy/Bast* in: EuGRZ 2001, 441, S / CMLRev. 2002, 227, p.

id. (ed.): Europäisches Verfassungsrecht, Berlin 2009.
cited as: *author* in: von Bogdandy/Bast.

von Bogdandy, A.; Schill, S.: Die Achtung der nationalen Identität unter dem reformierten Unionsvertrag Zur unionsrechtlichen Rolle nationalen Verfassungsrechts und zur Überwindung des absoluten Vorrangs, in: ZaöRV 70 (2010), p. 701–734.
cited as: *von Bogdandy/Schill* in: ZaöRV 2010, 701, p.

id..: Overcoming Absolute Primacy: Respect for National identity under the Lisbon Law, in: CMLRev. 48 (2011), p. 1417–1454.
cited as: *von Bogdandy/Schill* in: CMLRev. 2011, 1417, p.

von Danwitz, T.: Wert und Werte des Grundgesetzes, FAZ f. 22.01.2019, https://www.faz.net/aktuell/politik/die-gegenwart/thomas-von-danwitz-wert-und-werte-des-grundgesetzes-15998825.html?printPagedArticle=true#pageIndex_3.
cited as: *von Danwitz*, Wert und Werte des Grundgesetzes, FAZ f. 22.01.2019.

id.: Die Kultur in der Verfassungsordnung der Europäischen Union, in: Neue Juristische Wochenschrift 2005, p. 529–536.
cited as: *von Danwitz* in: NJW 2005, 529, p.

id.: Der Grundsatz der Verhältnismäßigkeit im Gemeinschaftsrecht, in: EWS 2003, p. 393–402.
cited as: *von Danwitz* in: EWS 2003, 393, p.

Waldheim, S.J.: Dienstleistungsfreiheit und Herkunftslandprinzip: prinzipielle Möglichkeiten und primärrechtliche Grenzen der Liberalisierung eines integrierten europäischen Binnenmarktes für Dienstleistungen, Göttingen 2008.
cited as: *Waldheim*, Dienstleistungsfreiheit und Herkunftslandprinzip.

List of references

Weinand, J.: Implementing the EU Audiovisual Media Services Directive. Selected issues in the regulation of AVMS by national media authorities of France, Germany and the UK, Baden-Baden 2018.
cited as: *Weinand*, Implementing the EU Audiovisual Media Services Directiv.

id.: The revised Audiovisual Media Services Directive 2018 – has the EU learnt the right lessons from the past?, in: UFITA 82(2018)1, p.260 – 293.
cited as: *Weinand*, UFITA 2018, 260, p.

Weinzierl, R.: Europäisierung des deutschen Grundrechtsschutzes? Der personelle Geltungsbereich des Art. 19 Abs. 3 GG und der Deutschengrundrechte im Lichte des europarechtlichen Diskriminierungsverbotes und Effektivitätsgebotes, Regensburg 2006.
cited as: *Weinzierl*, Europäisierung des deutschen Grundrechtsschutzes?.

Weiß, W.: Das Leitlinien(un)wesen der Kommission verletzt den Vertrag von Lissabon, in: EWS 2010, Issue 7, p. 257–260.
cited as: *Weiß* in: EWS 2010, 257, p.

Westphal, D.: Media Pluralism and European Regulation, in: European Business Law Review, Vol. 13, Issue 5 (2002), p. 459–487.
cited as: *Westphal* in: European Business Law Review, 2002, 459, p.

Winkelmann, I.: Die Bundesregierung als Sachwalter von Länderrechten – zugleich Anmerkung zum EG-Fernsehrichtlinienurteil des Bundesverfassungsgerichts, in: DöV 1996, p. 1–11.
cited as: *Winkelmann* in: DöV 1996, 1, p.

Würtenberger, T.: Schranken der Forschungsfreiheit und staatliche Schutzpflichten, 2013, https://www.ethikrat.org/fileadmin/PDF-Dateien/Veranstaltungen/anhoerung-25-04-2013-wuertenberger.pdf.
cited as: *Würtenberger*, Schranken der Forschungsfreiheit und staatliche Schutzpflichten.

Yamato, R.; Stephan J.: Eine Politik der Nichteinmischung – Die Folgen des zahnlosen Art. 7 EUV für das Wertefundament der EU am Beispiel Ungarns in: Die öffentliche Verwaltung 2014, p. 58–66.
cited as: *Yamato/Stephan* in: DöV 2014, 58, p.

Ziegenhain, H.-J.: xterritoriale Rechtsanwendung und die Bedeutung des Genuine-link-Erfordernisses, Munich 1992.
cited as: *Ziegenhain*, Exterritoriale Rechtsanwendung und die Bedeutung des Genuine-link-Erfordernisses.

Zuiderveen Borgesius, F. J.; Trilling, D.; Möller, J.; Bodó, B.; de Vreese, C. H.:Should we worry about filter bubbles?, in: Internet Policy Review, 5th edition, Issue 1, 2016, https://doi.org/10.14763/2016.1.401.
cited as: *Zuiderveen Borgesius u.a.* in: Internet Policy Review 1/2016.

Zuleeg, M.: Die föderativen Grundsätze der Europäischen Union, in: NJW 2000, p. 2846–2851.
cited as: *Zuleeg* in: NJW 2000, 2846, p.

Zur Kompetenzverteilung zwischen der Europäischen
Union und den Mitgliedstaaten im Mediensektor

Vorwort

Das Jahr 2020 war medienpolitisch ein Jahr der Weichenstellungen in Deutschland und in Europa: Eine zeitgemäße Medienregulierung des Fernsehens, des Radios und der Zeitungen darf nicht in der „alten Welt" stehen bleiben. Es braucht vielmehr gerade auch Antworten für das digitale Umfeld – für die Medienwelt online. In Deutschland haben die Länder als Mediengesetzgeber im Jahr 2020 den Medienstaatsvertrag vorgelegt und zugleich die Richtlinie über audiovisuelle Mediendienste umgesetzt. Auch die Europäische Kommission hat Ende des Jahres mit ihren Vorschlägen für einen Digital Services Act und einen Digital Market Act skizziert, wie aus ihrer Sicht zentrale Regeln in einer digitalen Gesellschaft aussehen könnten.

Als Koordinatorin der Rundfunkkommission der deutschen Länder bin ich stolz, dass der Medienstaatsvertrag am 7. November 2020 in Kraft getreten ist. Dieser medienpolitische Meilenstein ist das Ergebnis eines mehrjährigen Prozesses der 16 Bundesländer, welche die Kompetenz zur Medienregulierung in Deutschland haben. Er ist eines der wichtigsten medienpolitischen Vorhaben der letzten Jahre und gibt Antworten auf zentrale Fragen einer digitalisierten Medienwelt. Mit ihm schaffen wir rechtliche Rahmenbedingungen, die Meinungsvielfalt und kommunikative Chancengleichheit gerade auch im Netz fördern, Qualitätsjournalismus sichtbar machen und die Eigenverantwortung der Netzcommunity stärken. Erstmals werden auch die großen Online-Medienplattformen und -intermediäre, wie Google, Facebook, Twitter oder Amazon einer medienspezifischen und vielfaltsbezogenen Regulierung unterliegen. Welche Bedeutung gerade diese großen Plattformen bei der Verbreitung medialer Informationen haben, hat sich auch gerade während der Corona-Pandemie gezeigt.

Die Debatten rund um den Medienstaatsvertrag und die mit ihm gefundenen Lösungen zeigen dabei ganz deutlich: Regeln zum Umgang der großen Plattformen mit illegalen Inhalten sind wichtig – nach dem deutschen Gesetzgeber mit dem Netzwerkdurchsetzungsgesetz möchte nun zu Recht auch die Europäische Kommission mit dem Digital Services Act die Plattformen hier stärker in die Verantwortung nehmen. Allein reichen nach unserer Überzeugung Regeln zum Umgang mit illegalen, schädlichen oder anderweitig problematischen Inhalten aber nicht aus, um Medien- und Meinungsvielfalt zu sichern. Hier braucht es mehr: Wenn wir im Medienstaatsvertrag über die diskriminierungsfreie Auffindbarkeit journalistischer

Vorwort

Angebote sprechen, geht es nicht um die Haftung oder Verantwortung für illegale Inhalte. Es geht darum, wie wir online kommunikative Chancengleichheit fördern und wie wir Qualitätsjournalismus sichtbar machen. Hierzu bedarf es medienspezifischer Regeln für die Herausforderungen der digitalen Plattformökonomie.

Die Mitgliedstaaten der Europäischen Union sind sich einig, dass eine solche medienspezifische und vielfaltsbezogene Regulierung von Medienplattformen und -intermediären notwendig ist und dass die Sicherung des Medienpluralismus dabei in erster Linie in die Zuständigkeit der Mitgliedstaaten fällt. Dies haben sie in den Schlussfolgerungen des Rates zur Sicherung eines freien und pluralistischen Mediensystems, die unter deutscher Ratspräsidentschaft in der zweiten Jahreshälfte 2020 verabschiedet wurden, noch einmal ausdrücklich bekräftigt. Die Ratsschlussfolgerungen geben damit einen wichtigen Impuls für eine zukünftige und zeitgemäße, nationale sowie europäische Gesetzgebung in einem digitalen Zeitalter. Die deutschen Länder stellen sich dieser Verantwortung gerne.

Ein kohärenter Rechtsrahmen für das digitale Umfeld ist aber nicht nur im Rahmen der originären Medienregulierung notwendig, sondern auch in vielen anderen Bereichen auf regionaler, nationaler und europäischer Ebene. Medien sind unabdingbar für die Demokratien in Europa. Es ist unsere Aufgabe und Verpflichtung, ein freies und funktionierendes Mediensystem zu erhalten. Deshalb gilt es immer auch einen Blick darauf zu richten, welche Auswirkungen Regeln in anderen Bereichen auf die Medien haben. Die zahlreichen Gesetze unterschiedlicher Gesetzgeber müssen zusammenspielen. Auch dieses Anliegen haben die Mitgliedstaaten in den Ratsschussfolgerungen betont.

Dies alles sind keine trivialen Aufgaben und sie bedingen, dass sich jeder Akteur im Gesetzgebungsprozess – ob auf regionaler, nationaler oder europäischer Ebene -mit diesen Fragen auseinandersetzen muss. Die Regulierung der „Online-Welt" ist eine gemeinsame Verantwortung. Das Ziel von Kohärenz und Konsistenz wirft dabei schwierige Fragen auf, insbesondere wie europäische Regulierung eines digitalen Binnenmarkts mit der Kompetenz der Mitgliedstaaten in Einklang gebracht werden kann, um den Medienpluralismus und die Besonderheiten des Mediensektors sicherzustellen.

Um in dieser Diskussion einen langfristigen Beitrag zu leisten, hat die Rundfunkkommission im Juni 2020 die vorliegende Studie „Zur Kompetenzverteilung zwischen der Europäischen Union und den Mitgliedstaaten im Mediensektor" beim Institut für Europäisches Medienrecht (EMR) in Auftrag gegeben. Prof. Dr. Mark D. Cole, Dr. Jörg Ukrow und Christina Etteldorf geben darin wichtige Antworten, die für die kommenden Diskus-

Vorwort

sionen auf nationaler und europäischer Ebene wegweisend sein werden. Die Studie hätte ursprünglich im Rahmen des jährlich stattfindenden Brüsseler Mediengesprächs in der Landesvertretung Rheinland-Pfalz in Brüssel vorgestellt werden sollen, verknüpft mit einer Diskussion von Vertreterinnen und Vertretern aus Politik, Wissenschaft und Medienbranche. Aufgrund der anhaltenden Corona-Pandemie konnte diese Veranstaltung jedoch bislang leider nicht stattfinden. Ich sage bewusst „bislang", denn es gilt das Motto "aufgeschoben ist nicht aufgehoben". Für die Zwischenzeit empfehle ich Ihnen den mit unseren Kooperationspartnern, dem Mainzer Medieninstitut und dem Westdeutschen Rundfunk, im Dezember 2020 aufgenommenen Podcast zur Studie.

Sie können sich unter www.rundfunkkommission.rlp.de den spannenden Podcast mit einer Einführung in die Studie von Prof. Dr. Mark D. Cole und Statements aus Politik, Wissenschaft und der Medienbranche zu dem (zum Zeitpunkt der Aufnahme noch angekündigten) Digital Services Package anhören.

Mit den nun vorliegenden Vorschlägen für einen Digital Services Act und einen Digital Market Act hat die Studie nun auch bereits ihren ersten Anwendungsfall. Ich hoffe und wünsche mir, dass nicht nur wir Länder als Auftraggeber der Studie diese bei der Bewertung der aktuellen Vorschläge und zukünftigen Vorhaben heranziehen, sondern auch die übrigen Akteure dieses und der kommenden Gesetzgebungsverfahren.

Heike Raab,
Staatssekretärin in der Staatskanzlei Rheinland-Pfalz und Bevollmächtigte des Landes Rheinland-Pfalz beim Bund und für Europa, Medien und Digitales,

9. Februar 2021

Inhaltsverzeichnis

On the Allocation of Competences between the European Union and its Member States in the Media Sector   11

Executive Summary   419

A. Einleitung und Problemaufriss   437
Mark D. Cole / Jörg Ukrow

B. Primärrechtlicher Rahmen zur Kompetenzabgrenzung   447
Jörg Ukrow
    I. Grundprinzipien des EUV/AEUV   447
      1. Einleitung   447
      2. Die Mitgliedstaaten als „Herren" der Verträge vs. Integrationsoffenheit und -dynamik im Verfassungsverbund   449
      3. Einheitlichkeit und Vorrang des Unionsrechts vs. verfassungsgerichtliche Kontrollreserve von Mitgliedstaaten   452
      4. Ultra vires-Handeln, fehlende Kompetenz-Kompetenz der EU und das Prinzip der begrenzten Ermächtigung   455
        a. Das Prinzip begrenzter Ermächtigung und seine Bedeutung für die Medienregulierung   455
        b. Die Kontrolle der Einhaltung des Prinzips der begrenzten Ermächtigung durch das Demokratiegebot in der Auslegung des BVerfG   458
      5. Medienregulierung und der Zuständigkeitskatalog der EU   460
        a. Einführung   460
        b. Ausschließliche Zuständigkeiten der EU und Medienregulierung   462
        c. Geteilte Zuständigkeiten der EU und Medienregulierung   465
        d. Insbesondere: Schutzintensivierung im Bereich des digitalen Binnenmarktes   467
        e. Unterstützende Zuständigkeiten der EU und Medienregulierung   469

f. Insbesondere: Medienkompetenz im Blickfeld der EU-Regulierung 470
g. Sperrwirkung des EU-Rechts 473
6. Medienregulierung und verstärkte Zusammenarbeit zwischen einzelnen Mitgliedstaaten der EU 476
7. Medienregulierung und die primärrechtliche Bedeutung nachfolgender Organpraxis 478
II. Die Werteordnung der EU und ihr Schutz als Hebel der Sicherung von Freiheit und Vielfalt der Medien in den Mitgliedstaaten der EU 479
1. Das Wertefundament der EU 479
2. Die Sicherung von Freiheit und Pluralität der Medien über die Instrumente wertebasierter wehrhafter Demokratie der EU 482
III. Die Kompetenztitel der EU mit Bezug zur Medienregulierung – ein Überblick 485
1. Die Binnenmarktkompetenz der EU 485
   a. Einleitung 485
   b. Die Kompetenz in Bezug auf die Niederlassungsfreiheit 487
   c. Die Kompetenz in Bezug auf die Dienstleistungsfreiheit 490
   d. Zwischenfazit 492
2. Die Wettbewerbsordnung der EU 493
3. Die Kulturkompetenz der EU 496
IV. Die Ziele der EU und ihre kompetenzielle Bedeutung mit Blick auf Medienregulierung 501
1. Medienregulierungsbezogene Ziele der EU 501
2. Die zieleorientierte Abrundungskompetenz des Art. 352 AEUV und ihre Bedeutung für die Medienregulierung . . 502
V. Kompetenzausübungsregeln und -schranken 504
1. Einleitung 504
2. Die Achtung der nationalen Identität der Mitgliedstaaten 505
3. Der Grundsatz der loyalen Zusammenarbeit 508
4. Das Subsidiaritätsprinzip 511
5. Der Grundsatz der Verhältnismäßigkeit 520
6. Die Bedeutung der Kompetenzausübungsschranken in der medienregulatorischen Praxis – Stand und Entwicklungsperspektive 527
VI. Die Bedeutung der Grundrechte 529
1. Der medienbezogene Grundrechtsschutz, das Achtungsgebot des Art. 11 Abs. 2 Grundrechtecharta und die Kompetenzfrage 529

2. Grundrechtsschutz im Spannungsfeld von Kontrolle durch
EuGH und nationaler Verfassungsgerichtsbarkeit   532
VII. Medienregulierung und das Demokratieprinzip in der EU   536
VIII. Schlussfolgerungen für die Kompetenz zur Medienregulierung   539

C. Zur Bedeutung und rechtlichen Verankerung der Medienvielfalt
auf EU-Ebene   541
Mark D. Cole / Christina Etteldorf
I. Allgemeines   541
II. Art. 10 EMRK und Rechtsprechung des EGMR   542
III. Art. 11 Abs. 2 GRC und Rechtsprechung des EuGH   547
IV. Primärrechtliche Aspekte   554
1. Grundfreiheiten   554
2. EU-Wettbewerbsordnung   560
   a. Marktmachtkontrolle und Missbrauchsaufsicht   561
   b. Beihilferecht   563
V. Verankerung des Ziels in Sekundärrechtsakten und weiteren Texten   568

D. Sekundärrechtlicher Rahmen zum „Medienrecht" und
Medienpluralismus   569
Mark D. Cole / Christina Etteldorf
I. Überblick   569
II. Anknüpfungspunkte im bestehenden Sekundärrecht   571
1. E-Commerce-Richtlinie   571
2. AVMD-Richtlinie   577
   a. Historische Betrachtung im Kontext von Vielfaltssicherung   577
   b. AVMD-Reform 2018   583
   c. Bedeutung von Art. 4 Abs. 1 AVMD-Richtlinie   587
   d. Einzelne Bestimmungen   593
   e. Zwischenfazit   620
3. DSM-Urheberrechtsrichtlinie   621
4. Fusionskontroll-Verordnung   626
5. Kodex für die elektronische Kommunikation   629
6. Platform-to-Business-Verordnung   638
   a. Geltungsbereich und Zielsetzung   638
   b. Die Transparenzvorgaben   640

Inhaltsverzeichnis

	c. Das Verhältnis zu weiteren mitgliedstaatlichen Regelungen	641
	d. Das Verhältnis zur Richtlinie (EU) 2019/2161	645
III.	Aktuelle Vorhaben zu Rechtsakten und Initiativen mit medienrechtlichem Kontext	647
1.	Vorschlag für eine Verordnung zur Verhinderung der Verbreitung terroristischer Online-Inhalte	647
2.	Überblick zum vorgeschlagenen Digital Services Act	651
3.	Media and Audiovisual Action Plan und European Democracy Action Plan	654
IV.	Anknüpfungspunkte auf Ebene von EU-Unterstützungs- und Koordinierungsmaßnahmen	657
1.	Verhaltenskodex zur Bekämpfung illegaler Hassreden im Internet	658
2.	Bekämpfung illegaler Online-Inhalte	661
3.	Desinformations-Verhaltenskodex	663
V.	Schlussfolgerungen und Ableitungen zur Medienpluralismus-Regelungskompetenz	668

E. Völkerrechtliche Kernprobleme der Regulierung des „Mediensektors" im Hinblick auf mögliche Spannungsverhältnisse mit dem Recht der EU   671

Jörg Ukrow

    I. Einführung   671
   II. Adressaten der Regulierung   672
     1. Einleitung   672
     2. Völkerrechtliche Rahmenbedingungen einer Adressierung ausländischer Anbieter   673
       a. Die Adressierung ausländischer Anbieter unter dem Blickwinkel des Gebots völkerrechtsfreundlicher Auslegung nationalen Rechts wie des Rechts der EU   673
       b. Völkerrechtliche Schranken der Rechtsetzungsgewalt und Vollzugsgewalt eines Staates mit Bezug auf ausländische Anbieter   678
       c. Die „genuine link" Doktrin und das Vorgehen gegen ausländische Anbieter auf der Grundlage von MStV und JMStV   681
       d. Völkerrechtliche Anknüpfungspunkte und Schranken der Rechtsetzungsgewalt und Vollzugsgewalt eines Staates (jurisdiction to prescribe und jurisdiction to enforce)   686

3. Die grenzüberschreitende Anwendung deutscher
   Medienregulierung – Staatsvertragliche Ausgangspunkte in
   MStV und JMStV und ihre Interpretation 689
4. Die Zugriffsmöglichkeit auf ausländische Anbieter nach dem
   MStV und dem JMStV unter dem Blickwinkel des Rechts der
   EU – eine erste Betrachtung 692
   a. Einleitung 692
   b. Die Zugriffsmöglichkeit auf ausländische Anbieter nach
      dem MStV und JMStV unter dem Blickwinkel des primären Unionsrechts 694
   c. Die Zugriffsmöglichkeit auf ausländische Anbieter nach
      dem MStV und JMStV unter dem Blickwinkel der
      AVMD-Richtlinie 696
   d. Die Zugriffsmöglichkeit auf ausländische Anbieter nach
      dem MStV und JMStV unter dem Blickwinkel der ECRL 698
III. Grundrechtsbindung bei Vollzugsmaßnahmen gegen ausländische Anbieter 703
1. Bindung an den europäischen Grundrechtsschutz 703
   a. Einleitung 703
   b. Die extraterritoriale Geltung der EMRK und des Internationalen Pakts über bürgerliche und politische Rechte in
      ihrer Bedeutung für die Medienregulierung 704
   c. Die Reichweite der Bindung der Mitgliedstaaten an die
      Grundrechtecharta der EU bei Maßnahmen der Medienregulierung 706
2. Bindung an den grundgesetzlichen Grundrechtsschutz –
   Extraterritoriale Geltung des Grundrechtsschutzes 708
   a. Einleitung 708
   b. Die Entscheidung des BVerfG zur extraterritorialen Geltung von Grundrechten vom 19. Mai 2020 712
   c. Extraterritoriale Geltung auch der Rundfunkfreiheit für
      ausländische juristische Personen 714
   d. Zwischenfazit 717
IV. Pflicht zur Medienregulierung als Ausdruck hoheitlicher
    Schutzpflichten 717
1. Einleitung 717
2. Schutzpflichten in der Rechtsprechung des
   Bundesverfassungsgerichts 718
3. Europäische Bezüge der grundrechtlich fundierten
   Schutzpflichtdogmatik 723
   a. Schutzpflichten-Dogmatik und EMRK 723

　　　　b. Schutzpflichten-Dogmatik im Lichte des EU-Rechts　　724
　　　　c. Schutzpflichten im Verbund der Regulierungssysteme　　726
　　V. Materiell-rechtliche Aspekte　　727
　　1. Anwendungsbereich bestimmter nationaler Rechtsakte　　728
　　　　a. Herkunftslandprinzip und NetzDG　　728
　　　　b. Herkunftslandprinzip und MStV　　731
　　2. Weitere materiell-rechtliche Erwägungen　　733
　　　　a. NetzDG und Fragen der Verantwortlichkeit　　733
　　　　b. Exkurs: Konfliktlagen bei ähnlichen Regelungen in
　　　　　　anderen Staaten　　736
　　　　c. Die urheberrechtliche freie Benutzung nach § 24 UrhG
　　　　　　und die abschließende Harmonisierung　　738

F. Der vorgeschlagene Digital Services Act　　741
Jörg Ukrow
　　I. Ausgangspunkt der Diskussion und Pläne　　741
　　II. Berücksichtigung der Untersuchungsergebnisse bei der
　　　　Ausgestaltung des neuen Rechtsaktes　　747
　　1. Transparenz　　747
　　2. Zum Kriterium der Illegalität des Inhaltes　　752
　　3. Medienregulierung für Dienste der Informationsgesellschaft
　　　　und neue Medienakteure mittels Selbst-, Ko- und
　　　　kooperativer Regulierung　　753
　　4. Regulierung nicht der EU zugehöriger Anbieter von
　　　　Medieninhalten　　758
　　5. Reform der Verantwortlichkeitsregulierung in Bezug auf
　　　　Service-Provider　　761
　　6. Organisationsrechtliche Optionen für eine verbesserte
　　　　Durchsetzung von medienbezogenen Gemeinwohlinteressen　　763

G. Gesamtergebnis und politische Handlungsoptionen　　765
Mark D. Cole / Jörg Ukrow
　　I. Inhaltliche Aspekte　　765
　　II. Verfahrensaspekte　　771

Literaturverzeichnis　　777

Abkürzungsverzeichnis

a.A.	andere Ansicht / andere Auffassung
aaO	am angegebenen Ort
abgedr.	abgedruckt
ABl.	Amtsblatt
Abs.	Absatz
ACT	Association of Commercial Television in Europe
AEUV	Vertrag über die Arbeitsweise der Europäischen Union
AfP	Zeitschrift für das gesamte Medienrecht / Archiv für Presserecht
AöR	Archiv des öffentlichen Rechts (Zeitschrift)
API	Anwendungsprogramm-Schnittstellen
Appl.	Individualbeschwerde
Art.	Artikel
Aufl.	Auflage
AVMD-Richtlinie	Richtlinie über audiovisuelle Mediendienste
BayVBl.	Bayerische Verwaltungsblätter (Zeitschrift)
Bd.	Band
BFH	Bundesfinanzhof
BFHE	Sammlung der Entscheidungen des Bundesfinanzhofs
BGBl.	Bundesgesetzblatt
BGHZ	Entscheidungen des Bundesgerichtshofs in Zivilsachen
BND	Bundesnachrichtendienst
Buchst.	Buchstabe
bspw.	beispielsweise
BT-Drs.	Bundestags-Drucksache
BVerfG	Bundesverfassungsgericht
BVerfGE	Entscheidungen des Bundesverfassungsgerichts
BVerfGG	Bundesverfassungsgerichtsgesetz
BVerfGK	Sammlung der Kammerentscheidungen des Bundesverfassungsgerichts
BVerfSchG	Bundesverfassungsschutzgesetz
BVerwG	Bundesverwaltungsgericht
BVerwGE	Entscheidungen des Bundesverwaltungsgerichts
BvR	Aktenzeichen einer Verfassungsbeschwerde zum Bundesverfassungsgericht

bzw.	beziehungsweise
C	EU Mitteilungen und Bekanntmachungen
ca.	circa
CMLRev.	Common Law Review (Zeitschrift)
COM	Communication / Mitteilung der EU-Kommission
COSAC	Konferenz der Europa-Ausschüsse der Parlamente
CPD	Code of Practice on Disinformation
ders.	derselbe
d.h.	das heißt
DG	Directorate-General / Generaldirektion (EU-Kommission)
Doc.	Document / Dokument
DÖV	Die Öffentliche Verwaltung (Zeitschrift)
DSA	Digital Services Act
DSM-Richtlinie	Richtlinie über das Urheberrecht und die verwandten Schutzrechte im digitalen Binnenmarkt u
DVBl.	Deutsches Verwaltungsblatt
EAI	Europäische Audiovisuelle Informationsstelle
EBU	European Broadcasting Union
ECPMF	Europäisches Zentrum für Presse- und Medienfreiheit
ECRL	e-Commerce-Richtlinie
EDSA	Europäischer Datenschutzausschuss
EEKK	Europäischer Kodex für die elektronische Kommunikation
EG	Europäische Gemeinschaft
EGMR	Europäischer Gerichtshof für Menschenrechte
EGV	Vertrag über die Europäische Gemeinschaft
EMRK	Europäische Menschenrechtskonvention
ERGA	European Regulators Group for Audiovisual Media Services
ESZB	Europäisches System der Zentralbanken
etc.	et cetera
EU	Europäische Union
EU ABl.	Amtsblatt der Europäischen Union
EuG	Gericht der Europäischen Union
EuGH	Gerichtshof der Europäischen Union
EuGRZ	Europäische GRUNDRECHTE-Zeitschrift
EuR	Europarecht (Zeitschrift)
EUV	Vertrag über die Europäische Union
EuGVVO	Verordnung über die gerichtliche Zuständigkeit und die Anerkennung und Vollstreckung von Entscheidungen in Zivil- und Handelssachen
EuGVÜ	Europäisches Gerichtsstands- und Vollstreckungsübereinkommen

EuVTVO	Verordnung zur Einführung eines Europäischen Vollstreckungstitels für unbestrittene Forderungen
EuZW	Europäische Zeitschrift für Wirtschaftsrecht
Erwgr.	Erwägungsgrund/Erwägungsgründe
EPG	Elektronische Programmführer
EWG	Europäische Wirtschaftsgemeinschaft
EWS	Europäisches Wirtschafts- und Steuerrecht (Zeitschrift)
EZB	Europäische Zentralbank
FAZ	Frankfurter Allgemeine Zeitung
f.	folgende
ff.	fortfolgende
FKVO	Fusionskontrollverordnung
Fn.	Fußnote
FS	Festschrift
FSK	Freiwillige Selbstkontrolle der Filmwirtschaft
GA	Generalanwalt
GASP	Gemeinsame Außen- und Sicherheitspolitik
gem.	gemäß
GEREK	Gremium Europäischer Regulierungsstellen für elektronische Kommunikation
GG	Grundgesetz
ggf.	gegebenenfalls
GLJ	German Law Journal
GlüStV	Staatsvertrag zum Glücksspielwesen in Deutschland
GRC	Grundrechte Charta
GRUR Int	Gewerblicher Rechtsschutz und Urheberrecht Internationaler Teil
GVK	Gremienvorsitzendenkonferenz
Hrsg.	Herausgeber
HRLR	Human Rights Law Review
HZÜ	Haager Übereinkommen über die Zustellung gerichtlicher und außergerichtlicher Schriftstücke im Ausland in Zivil- oder Handelssachen
ICJ	International Court of Justice
i.d.R.	in der Regel
i.e.	id est / das heißt
IGH	Internationaler Gerichtshof
IPBR	Internationaler Pakt über bürgerliche und politische Rechte
i.S.	im Sinne
i.S.d.	im Sinne der/des
i.S.v.	im Sinne von

Abkürzungsverzeichnis

i.V.m.	in Verbindung mit
i.w.S.	im weiteren Sinne
IntVG	Integrationsverantwortungsgesetz
JILP	New York University Journal of Internal Law and Politics
JMStV	Jugendmedienschutz-Staatsvertrag
JuS	Juristische Schulung (Zeitschrift)
JZ	JuristenZeitung
KEK	Kommission zur Ermittlung der Konzentration im Medienbereich
KJ	Kritische Justiz (Zeitschrift)
KJM	Kommission für Jugendmedienschutz
KKZ	Kommunal-Kassen-Zeitschrift
KMU	Kleine und Mittelständische Unternehmen
K&R	Kommunikation und Recht (Zeitschrift)
LZG NRW	Landeszustellungsgesetz Nordrhein-Westfahlen
MMR	Zeitschrift für IT-Recht und Recht der Digitalisierung
MPEPIL	Max Planck Encyclopedia of Public International Law
MStV	Medienstaatsvertrag
m.w.N.	mit weiteren Nachweisen
NetzDG	Netzwerkdurchsetzungsgesetz
NJW	Neue Juristische Wochenschrift
No.	Number / Nummer
Nr(n).	Nummer(n)
NVwZ	Neue Zeitschrift für Verwaltungsrecht
OLG	Oberlandesgericht
ÖZöRV	Österreichische Zeitung für öffentliches Recht und Völkerrecht.
PSPP	Public Sector Purchase Programme
P2B	Platform-to-Business
Ref.	Reference
RL	Richtlinie
Rn.	Randnummer(n)
Rs.	Rechtssache
rsp.	respektive
S.	Seite
s.	siehe
SAR	Self-Assessment Reports
Slg.	Sammlung der Rechtsprechung des Gerichtshofes und des Gerichts Erster Instanz
st. Rspr.	ständige Rechtsprechung
StIGH	Ständiger Internationaler Gerichtshof

sog.	sogenannte / sogenanntes
TERREG	Verordnung zur Verhinderung der Verbreitung terroristischer Online-Inhalte
ThürVwZVG	Thüringer Verwaltungszustellungs- und Vollstreckungsgesetz
TK	Telekommunikation
TKG	Telekommunikationsgesetz
TMG	Telemediengesetz
TwF	Television without Frontiers (Richtlinie)
u.	und
u.a.	und andere / unter anderem
Unterabs.	Unterabsatz
UN/UNO	Vereinte Nationen
UrhG	Urheberrechtsgesetz
u.U.	unter Umständen
v.	von/vom
verb. Rs.	verbundene Rechtssachen
Verf.	Verfassung
VGH	Verwaltungsgerichtshof
vgl.	vergleiche
VSP(s)	Video-Sharing-Plattform(en)
VVDStRL	Veröffentlichungen der Vereinigung der Deutschen Staatsrechtslehrer
VwVfG	Verwaltungsverfahrensgesetz
VwVGBbg	Verwaltungsvollstreckungsgesetz für das Land Brandenburg
VwZG	Verwaltungszustellungsgesetz des Bundes
VwZVG	Bayrisches Verwaltungszustellungs- und Vollstreckungsgesetz
WVRK	Wiener Vertragsrechtskonvention
ZAK	Kommission für Zulassung und Aufsicht
ZaöRV	Zeitschrift für ausländisches öffentliches Recht und Völkerrecht
z.B.	zum Beispiel
z.T.	zum Teil
ZEuS	Zeitschrift für Europarechtliche Studien
ZfWG	Zeitschrift für Wett- und Glücksspielrecht
ZSR	Zeitschrift für Schweizerisches Recht
ZUM	Zeitschrift für Urheber- und Medienrecht

Executive Summary

Einleitung

1. Die von EU-Kommissionspräsidentin von der Leyen in ihrer ersten Rede zur Lage der Union am 16. September 2020 vorgeschlagene „digitale Dekade" Europas kann an Regelwerke der EU wie die 2018 novellierte Richtlinie über audiovisuelle Mediendienste und die sog. DSM-Richtlinie über das Urheberrecht und die verwandten Schutzrechte im digitalen Binnenmarkt aus 2019 anknüpfen, die bereits das Ziel hatten die EU „fit für das digitale Zeitalter" zu machen. Schon bislang war dieses regulatorische Fitness-Programm der EU mit möglichen Kollisionen der Fortentwicklung der EU-Rechtsordnung mit der mitgliedstaatlichen Medienordnung verbunden. Die neue „digitale Dekade" wird die Medienregulierung in der EU an der Schnittstelle von unionalen und mitgliedstaatlichen Regulierungskompetenzen vor neue Herausforderungen stellen. Die unterschiedlichen Bedeutungsebenen der Digitalisierung für die Medienregulierung, von der Abwehr von Desinformationen bis zur Digitalisierung von medienrelevanter Infrastruktur, ist in der Corona-Pandemie nochmals deutlicher geworden. Ein umfassender Erfolg des europäischen Digital-Projekts erscheint nur bei strikter Wahrung fortdauernder Verantwortlichkeiten und Zuständigkeiten der Mitgliedstaaten, in Deutschland nach der grundgesetzlichen Grundentscheidung für einen föderalen Staatsaufbau der Länder, gewährleistet. Dies gilt nicht zuletzt auch mit Blick auf das in der europäischen wie nationalen Grundrechtsordnung vorgegebene Ziel einer medialen Vielfaltssicherung: Denn Grenzen einer Harmonisierungs- und Koordinierungskompetenz der EU bestehen nicht nur in Bezug auf das klassische Medienkonzentrationsrecht, sondern auch in der Perspektive der Pluralismussicherung mit Blick auf digitale und globale Herausforderungen des Medien-Ökosystems.

Primärrechtlicher Rahmen zur Kompetenzabgrenzung

2. Auch im Zuge der wiederholten, teilweise grundlegenden Änderungen der Gründungsverträge der Europäischen Union bleiben die Mitgliedstaaten der EU „Herren" der Verträge – auch in ihrem medienregulatorischen Gehalt. Der europäische Verfassungsverbund zeichnet sich durch eine Synthese zwischen jeweiliger Offenheit der mitglied-

staatlichen Verfassungsordnungen für ein abgegrenztes und fortdauernd abgrenzbares Programm europäischer Integration – auch im Sinne eines digitalen Medien-Binnenmarktes – und einer Verfassung der EU aus, die ihrerseits nicht auf eine schrankenlose Integrationsperspektive ausgerichtet ist, sondern – ungeachtet dynamischer Auslegungsmöglichkeiten – an den Zweck einer immer engeren Union unterhalb unitarischer Bundesstaatlichkeit der EU gebunden ist.

3. An der Schnittstelle von unionsrechtlicher Integrationsperspektive und verfassungsrevisionsfesten Grundnormen des deutschen Grundgesetzes mit Blick auf die Bedeutung der Medienordnung für das demokratische und föderative Verfassungsverständnis des Grundgesetzes bestehen Vorbehalte und absolute Grenzen des deutschen Verfassungsrechts gegenüber einer auf die demokratische Funktion der Medien gerichteten Ordnung der Medien in der EU und ihren Mitgliedstaaten durch die EU. Vergleichbare Vorbehalte bestehen auch in Verfassungsordnungen anderer EU-Mitgliedstaaten.

4. Der Reichweite des vertraglich definierten Integrationsprogramms der EU in Bezug auf Möglichkeiten der Medienregulierung kommt Bedeutung nicht zuletzt auch für den Fall der Kollision von mitgliedstaatlicher Vielfaltssicherung und etwaiger positiver Integration über Schritte zu einem eigenen Vielfaltsrecht der EU und/oder negativer Integration über Schrankensetzungen für die Vielfaltssicherung der Mitgliedstaaten durch das Binnenmarkt- und das Wettbewerbsrecht der EU zu. Insoweit kann sich auch Vielfaltssicherung fortdauernd im Feld einer Kollision von nationalem Recht und Europarecht bewegen.

5. Zur Auflösung dieser Kollision dient der europarechtliche Anwendungsvorrang, dessen Reichweite allerdings seinerseits zwischen europäischer und mitgliedstaatlicher Verfassungsgerichtsbarkeit strittig ist. Das Bundesverfassungsgericht (BVerfG) macht insoweit Kontrollvorbehalte hinsichtlich des europäischen Grundrechtsschutzes, der europäischen Kompetenzausübung („ultra-vires-Kontrolle") und der Verfassungsidentität des deutschen Grundgesetzes geltend. Alle diese Vorbehalte können auch bei einer Weiterentwicklung der Medienregulierung der EU bedeutsam werden.

6. Die EU verfügt – im Unterschied zu einem Staat – über keine Kompetenz-Kompetenz. Vielmehr darf sie nach dem Grundsatz der begrenzten Einzelermächtigung nur innerhalb der Grenzen der Zuständigkeiten tätig werden, die die Mitgliedstaaten ihr in den Verträgen – EUV und AEUV – zur Verwirklichung der darin niedergelegten Ziele übertragen haben. Weder EUV noch AEUV enthalten allerdings einen Negativkatalog von umfassend vom EU-Recht ausgenommenen Berei-

chen. Es gibt in den europäischen Verträgen weder eine *exception culturelle* im Allgemeinen noch eine auf Medien bezogene Bereichsausnahme im Besonderen. Das Prinzip begrenzter Ermächtigung enthält nicht per se eine Medienregulierung der EU schon im Ansatz hemmende Wirkung. Je stärker Medienregulierung der EU allerdings in einer für die Vielfaltsregulierung relevanten Weise erfolgt, um so höher sind zumindest die Darlegungslasten der EU in Bezug auf die Wahrung der Klauseln der europäischen Verträge, die auf Schonung mitgliedstaatlicher Regulierungsspielräume ausgerichtet sind.

7. Die Kompetenzordnung des EU-Rechts gilt auch in Bezug auf Sachverhalte der Digitalisierung: Digitale Wandlungen schaffen nicht zusätzliche Kompetenztitel der EU. Umgekehrt sind vorhandene Kompetenztitel aber auch nicht auf die Bewältigung von Problemlagen hin begrenzt, die zum Zeitpunkt der Verabschiedung der Gründungsverträge bekannt waren. Die Auslegung des primären EU-Rechts ist stets eine Auslegung in der Zeit und mit Offenheit für neue Herausforderungen. Eine solche digitalisierungsorientierte Auslegungsoffenheit findet ihre Grenzen aber im Wortlaut der Kompetenznormen.

8. Die vom BVerfG mit Blick auf die Übertragung von Kompetenzen des Bundes entwickelte Judikatur zur Kontrollmöglichkeit am Maßstab des Demokratiegebots ist mit Blick auf die Übertragung von Kompetenzen des Bundes oder der Länder in gleicher Weise bedeutsam. Zum revisionsfesten, einer Abänderung auch in europarechtlichen Zusammenhängen entzogenen Grundstruktur der deutschen Verfassungsordnung dürfte – nicht zuletzt auch mit Blick auf die verfassungshistorische Dimension des „Nie wieder" totalitärer Herrschaft – das Element der föderalen Brechung von Medienregulierung zählen. Eine Öffnung des deutschen Verfassungsstaates für eine Vollharmonisierung der Medienregulierung durch die EU wäre daher – auch im Blick auf die demokratische Relevanz des Medienföderalismus – ein mit erheblichem juristischem Risikopotential verbundener Vorgang.

9. Bei den primär-unionsrechtlich seit dem Vertrag von Lissabon der EU zugeordneten ausschließlichen, geteilten und unterstützenden Zuständigkeiten finden die Medien in den betreffenden Zuständigkeitskatalogen keine Erwähnung. Schon dies spricht bei rechtsvergleichender Betrachtung für eine Zurückhaltung der europäischen Verträge bei der Einräumung medienbezogener Regulierungskompetenzen der EU, die an die Medien als Kulturfaktor und Vielfaltsgarant anknüpfen. Allerdings sind Auswirkungen binnenmarktbezogener Maßnahmen der EU, die allgemein an Marktteilnehmer jeder Art gerichtet sind, auf die Medienregulierung zu beobachten. Solche Auswirkungen bestehen im Be-

reich sämtlicher Zuständigkeitsformen der EU. Eine absolute Sperrwirkung des EU-Rechts in Bezug auf mitgliedstaatliche Regelungen mit anderer Zielsetzung besteht dabei selbst im Bereich ausschließlicher Zuständigkeiten der EU wie z.B. bei der Festlegung der Wettbewerbsregeln nach Art. 3 Abs. 1 Buchst. b) AEUV nicht.

10. Zu den unterstützenden Zuständigkeiten der EU, in denen die EU keine originäre, auf Rechtsharmonisierung zielende Regelungskompetenz besitzt, zählen auch solche im Bereich der Kultur, einschließlich der Medien in ihrer kulturellen Funktionalität, und der allgemeinen Bildung. Medienkompetenz bewegt sich an der Schnittstelle dieser Zuständigkeitstitel. Sie ist ein weicher, aber wichtiger Bestandteil eines digitale Herausforderungen demokratie- und gesellschaftsverträglich bewältigenden Systems der Medienregulierung. Die Vereinbarkeit einer zunehmend beobachtbaren medienkompetenzbezogenen Politik informeller Regelsetzung der EU mit dem in Art. 165 Abs. 1 Unterabs. 1 AEUV ausdrücklich anerkannten Gebot einer „strikte(n) Beachtung der Verantwortung der Mitgliedstaaten für die Lehrinhalte und die Gestaltung des Bildungssystems" ist fraglich.

11. Die Kompetenzordnung der EU-Verträge steht einer verstärkten Zusammenarbeit zwischen einzelnen Mitgliedstaaten im Medienbereich nicht entgegen. Sofern sich diese Zusammenarbeit nicht auf die ökonomische, sondern auf die kulturelle und vielfaltssichernde Dimension von Medienregulierung bezieht, bedarf es nicht der Einhaltung der primärrechtlichen Vorgaben an die verstärkte Zusammenarbeit. Es handelt sich dann aber um eine Zusammenarbeit zwischen diesen Mitgliedstaaten im Rahmen der ihnen verbleibenden Zuständigkeit, die vom EU-Recht ermöglicht, nicht aber durch dieses gesteuert wird.

12. Indem der EU im Rahmen des primärrechtlichen Konzepts einer Integrationsgemeinschaft auch eine die Freiheit und Vielfalt der Medien umfassende Prüfkompetenz in Bezug auf die Rechtsordnung der Mitgliedstaaten eingeräumt wird, kommt es zu einem gewissen Konflikt zur Zurückhaltung der europäischen Verträge in Bezug auf eine positive Medienordnung der EU und der Zuständigkeit ihrer Organe. Das Gebot einer Schonung der Medienregulierung der Mitgliedstaaten vor unionsrechtlichem Zugriff, wie es sich nicht zuletzt aus einer Gesamtschau der Kompetenzausübungsregelungen und -schranken der europäischen Verträge ableiten lässt, spricht für eine zurückhaltende Ausübung der Kontrollmöglichkeiten durch die EU.

13. Die grenzüberschreitenden Tätigkeiten traditioneller audiovisueller Medienunternehmen wie z.B. Rundfunkveranstalter wie auch neuer Medienakteure wie z.B. Medienintermediäre sind als Dienstleistung

Executive Summary

i.S. der Art. 56 AEUV einzustufen. Bei einer dauerhaften Ansiedlung eines Medienunternehmens in einem anderen EU-Mitgliedstaat handelt es sich um eine Niederlassung i.S. der Art. 49 ff. AEUV. Die Länder sind als Medienregulierer verpflichtet, die Regulierung grundfreiheitenkonform zu gestalten. Medienrechtliche Vorgaben der deutschen Länder, die Meinungs- und Medienvielfalt gewährleisten sollen, sind durch zwingende Gründe des Allgemeininteresses gerechtfertigte Beschränkungen der Grundfreiheiten, soweit die Maßnahmen den Vorgaben des Diskriminierungsverbotes und der Verhältnismäßigkeit genügen.

14. Aus den Binnenmarktkompetenzen der EU ist eine Ermächtigung der EU zur Rechtsharmonisierung im Bereich der Medienvielfaltssicherung nicht ableitbar. Der Kompetenztitel der Niederlassungsfreiheit ist eng auszulegen, weil nur dies dem Charakter einer Union aus Mitgliedstaaten, deren nationale Identität zu wahren ist, entspricht. Insbesondere ein etwaiger Regulierungsansatz, der den Bestand an unternehmerischer Freiheit im Binnenmarkt reduzieren würde, wäre mit dem auf Fortschritt in Richtung auf grenzüberschreitende freie Entfaltung ausgerichteten Binnenmarktkonzept des Art. 26 AEUV nicht in Einklang zu bringen. Gegen die Heranziehung der Regulierungskompetenzen in Bezug auf die Dienstleistungsfreiheit spricht darüber hinaus, dass diese Grundfreiheit durch nationalstaatliche Regelungen im Bereich der Vielfaltssicherung regelmäßig nur mittelbar betroffen ist.

15. Beim Wettbewerbsrecht und dem Recht der Vielfaltssicherung handelt es sich zwar um zwei getrennte Sachbereiche. Markt- und Meinungsmachtkontrolle sind indessen keine Phänomene ohne Berührungspunkte. Insbesondere ist die Wettbewerbsordnung grundsätzlich geeignet, das Ziel eines vielfältigen Angebots als Nebeneffekt zu erreichen. Das primäre Unionsrecht ist dabei in seinem Ausgangspunkt nicht auf eine fernsehzentrierte Wahrnehmung der Wettbewerbsaufsicht beschränkt, sondern steht einem dynamischen Verständnis nicht zuletzt der Marktdefinition wie auch einer marktbeherrschenden Stellung offen. Letzteres ermöglicht auch eine Reaktion in der Aufsichtspraxis, die Intermediäre ebenso wie Netzwerkeffekte der digitalen Plattformökonomie in den Blick nimmt. Im Übrigen ist die Berücksichtigung demokratischer, grundrechtlicher und kultureller Grundsätze und Anforderungen im Rahmen der Wettbewerbspolitik in gleicher Weise und z.B. nach Art. 167 Abs. 4 AEUV an der Schnittstelle von Schonung kultureller Handlungsmöglichkeiten und wettbewerbsrechtlicher Aufsichtspflicht ausdrücklich geboten. Das bedeutet, dass bei der Anwendung des Wettbewerbsrechts diejenige Handlungsalter-

native zu wählen ist, die am meisten geeignet ist, die Medienvielfaltssicherung durch die Mitgliedstaaten zu unterstützen.

16. In Bezug auf die kulturelle Dimension der Medien kommt der beihilfeaufsichtsrechtlichen Ausnahmebestimmung in Art. 107 Abs. 3 Buchst. d) AEUV besondere Bedeutung zu. Das sog. Amsterdamer „Protokoll zum öffentlich-rechtlichen Rundfunk in den Mitgliedstaaten" greift dieses Gebot einer Handlungsspielräume der Mitgliedstaaten wahrenden Auslegung des Unionsrechts auf. In diesem Protokoll wird offen das Spannungsverhältnis angesprochen, das zwischen der demokratischen, sozialen und kulturellen Dimension der Medien und deren ökonomischer Relevanz bestehen kann – ein Spanungsverhältnis, das im Übrigen nicht auf den öffentlich-rechtlichen Rundfunk als Medien(teil)gattung begrenzt ist. Während erstere für eine Regelungskompetenz der Mitgliedstaaten streitet, ist mit Blick auf letztere die potentielle Binnenmarkt-Dimension grenzüberschreitenden Medienengagements offenkundig.

17. Die Zurückhaltung der EU in Bezug auf eine positive Ordnungskompetenz für die Medien seitens der EU wird in Bezug auf den „audiovisuellen Bereich" durch den Kultur-Artikel 167 des AEUV bekräftigt. Namentlich folgt aus der in Absatz 4 dieses Artikels verankerten sog. Querschnittsklausel mit der Pflicht zur Berücksichtigung kultureller Aspekte eine ganze Reihe von vielfaltschonenden und -fördernden Anforderungen, denen die EU bei ihrer Rechtsetzung wie bei der Aufsicht über die Unionsrechtskonformität mitgliedstaatlichen Verhaltens Rechnung tragen muss. Art. 167 AEUV sperrt zwar nicht eine rechtsharmonisierende Medienregulierung der EU, die auf eine Rechtsgrundlage aus dem Katalog ihrer ausschließlichen und geteilten Zuständigkeiten gestützt ist. Voraussetzung ist jedoch, dass sie dabei kulturelle Aspekte berücksichtigen muss, was regelmäßig auf eine Güterabwägung zwischen kulturellen und anderen Regulierungsinteressen (so z.B. wirtschaftlichen Gesichtspunkten im unionsrechtlichen Wettbewerbsrecht) hinausläuft. Zudem folgt aus der Systematik des AEUV, dass kulturelle, insbesondere vielfaltssichernde Aspekte nicht Mittelpunkt einer unionsrechtlichen Regelung sein dürfen.

18. Jenseits der vertraglichen Verankerung des Prinzips der begrenzten Ermächtigung und des Zuständigkeitskataloges für die EU sollen auch materiell-rechtliche Schutzmechanismen wie Kompetenzausübungsregeln und -schranken nach der Verfassungsordnung der EU gewährleisten, dass die auf europäischer Ebene bestehenden Einzelermächtigungen in einer die mitgliedstaatlichen Zuständigkeiten schonenden Weise wahrgenommen werden. Zu diesen Regeln zählen das Gebot, die

Executive Summary

nationale Identität der Mitgliedstaaten zu achten (Art. 4 Abs. 2 EUV), der Grundsatz der loyalen Zusammenarbeit (Art. 4 Abs. 3 EUV), der Grundsatz der Subsidiarität (Art. 5 Abs. 1 Satz 2 und Abs. 3 EUV) und der Grundsatz der Verhältnismäßigkeit (Art. 5 Abs. 1 Satz 2 und Abs. 4 EUV).

19. Der Grundsatz der Subsidiarität entfaltet seine die Kompetenzausübung der EU steuernde Kraft bislang insbesondere präventiv; erfolgreich auf eine Verletzung dieses Grundsatzes gestützte Verfahren vor dem EuGH sind bislang nicht bekannt. Subsidiaritätsrüge und -klage weisen im Übrigen im Zusammenspiel zwischen nationaler und europäischer Kompetenzordnung für den Mitgliedstaat Bundesrepublik Deutschland insoweit ein organisationsrechtliches Defizit auf, als die Wahrnehmung der Wahrung von Gesetzgebungskompetenzen der Länder gegenüber am Maßstab des Subsidiaritätsprinzip überschießendem Zugriff der EU ohne eine hinreichende Rückkopplung des Bundesorgans Bundesrat mit den einzelnen Landesparlamenten erfolgt.

20. Dem Verhältnismäßigkeitsgrundsatz als Kompetenzausübungsschranke dürfte auch mit Blick auf die Abschichtung von Kompetenzbereichen der EU und ihrer Mitgliedstaaten bei der Medienregulierung im Ergebnis der Entscheidung des BVerfG vom 5. Mai 2020 zur Anleihepolitik der EZB ungeachtet der berechtigten fachlichen Kritik an dieser Entscheidung stärker als bislang Bedeutung zumindest im Verhältnis der EU- und deutscher Regulierungsebene Bedeutung zukommen. Denn mit dieser Entscheidung hat das BVerfG erstmalig in einer, was den entwickelten Prüfkatalog betrifft, über den Einzelfall hinaus bedeutsamen Weise ein ultra-vires-Handeln eines EU-Organs festgestellt.

21. Die genannte Entscheidung des BVerfG spricht für eine Zurückhaltung der europäischen Rechtsetzung in Bereichen, die in besonderer Weise grundrechtssensibel aus Sicht der verfassungsrechtlichen Dogmatik von Kommunikationsfreiheiten in den Mitgliedstaaten sind. So würde eine Vollharmonisierung des Rechts der Vielfaltssicherung im digitalen Medien-Ökosystem deutliche Fragen nach einer Überschreitung der *ultra-vires*-Grenzen im Verhältnis EuGH – BVerfG aufwerfen. Eine solche Ausdehnung des Anwendungsbereichs europarechtlicher Medienregulierung *ratione personae* und/oder *ratione materiae* ohne Rücksichtnahme auf die mitgliedstaatliche Kompetenz würde das auf Kooperation angelegte Zusammenspiel zwischen EU und Mitgliedstaaten ebenso zusätzlich gefährden wie sie das Verhältnis zwischen EuGH und BVerfG weiter belasten könnte.

22. Schon die Brechung des Konnexes zwischen „Demokratie" und „Pluralismus" in der Adressierung des jeweiligen in Art. 2 EUV verankerten

Executive Summary

Wertes im Mehr-Ebenen-System EU spricht gegen eine auf die Bedeutung des Medienpluralismus für die Demokratie gestützte „Annexkompetenz" der EU zur übergreifenden, alle Ebenen des europäischen Integrationsverbundes erfassenden Pluralismusregulierung zu Zwecken der Wahrung des Wertes Demokratie. Eine solche ebenen-übergreifende Regulierung kommt auch aus Anlass der Regulierung des Wahlverfahrens zum Europäischen Parlament nach Art. 223 AEUV nicht in Betracht.

23. Auch aus dem im Wachsen begriffenen Demokratieverbund folgt keine Kompetenz der EU zur regulatorischen Förderung der medialen vor-rechtlichen Voraussetzungen einer weiteren Vertiefung des Demokratieverbunds. Denn die Verfassung der EU ist nicht darauf ausgerichtet, aus integrationspolitischen Zielen integrationsrechtliche Befugnisse ableiten zu können. Soweit sich die Union etwa mit der Abwehr von Desinformationskampagnen beschäftigen kann, dann aus der Perspektive des Binnenmarktes: es sollen durch unterschiedliche Herangehensweisen der Mitgliedsstaaten bei der Abwehr solcher Angriffe keine Hemmnisse für den freien Verkehr von Waren und Dienstleistungen entstehen. Eine eigenständige Regelung der Union zur Vielfaltssicherung ist damit nicht zu begründen.

Zur Bedeutung und rechtlichen Verankerung der Medienvielfalt auf EU-Ebene

24. Die grundrechtliche Verankerung von Medienfreiheit und Medienvielfalt in der Grundrechtecharta der EU (GRC) sowie der Europäischen Menschenrechtskonvention (EMRK) hat zur Folge, dass – wenngleich sie nicht zu den originären Kompetenzen der EU gehört – die Sicherung von Freiheit und Pluralismus in den Medien eine besondere Rolle auch auf Ebene von Maßnahmen der Union einnimmt, die – wie die Mitgliedstaaten – bei all ihren Handlungen an die Grundrechte gebunden ist. Das führt nicht zur Kompetenzbegründung für eine Medienregulierung, sondern im Gegenteil zum Gebot der zur Beachtung der Vielfalt, indem die EU bei Maßnahmen diejenige Alternative wählen muss, die Medienvielfalt und die dafür gegebenenfalls notwendige mitgliedstaatliche Regulierung am besten ermöglicht.

25. Das gilt einerseits zunächst aus rein abwehrrechtlicher Perspektive: Die EU darf nicht in ungerechtfertigter (vor allem unverhältnismäßiger) Weise in die durch die GRC und die EMRK geschützten Grundrechte eingreifen, was dazu führt, dass die Auswirkungen jedweder Maßnahmen der EU, ob legislativer oder exekutiver Natur, auf die (umfassend zu verstehende) Freiheit der Medien mit zu berücksichti-

Executive Summary

gen und ggf. mit anderen schutzwürdigen Belangen – seien es von der Union anerkannt, dem Gemeinwohl dienende Zielsetzungen, oder Erfordernisse des Schutzes der Rechte und Freiheiten anderer – abzuwägen sind, auch wenn sich die Maßnahmen auf völlig andere Regelungsbereiche wie zum Beispiel den Wirtschafts- oder Verbraucherschutzsektor beziehen. Zum anderen folgt aus der Grundrechtsdogmatik in GRC und EMRK aber auch eine schutzrechtliche Komponente, die von den Grundrechtsverpflichteten verlangt, sich für die Voraussetzungen einer effektiven Möglichkeit der Grundrechtsausübung wahrend einzusetzen. Zu diesen Voraussetzungen der Freiheit zählt nicht zuletzt auch die Vielfalt der Medien. Unabhängig davon, inwieweit man darin eine aktive Handlungspflicht zur, wenn nötig regulatorischen, Herstellung eines angemessenen Schutzniveaus sehen will, die aufgrund des vorhandenen Kompetenzgerüstes und dessen Absicherung in GRC und AEUV allerdings nur die Mitgliedstaaten treffen könnte, folgt daraus, dass die aus der Meinungs- bzw. Medienfreiheit ableitbaren Rechte und Prinzipien dazu führen, dass Eingriffe in andere Rechte und Freiheiten aus dem Primärrecht der Union gerechtfertigt werden können.

26. Die Sicherung von medialer Vielfalt nimmt in diesem Kontext seit jeher eine hervorgehobene Rolle ein. Der EGMR hat in seiner Rechtsprechung immer wieder betont, dass die Medien ihre im demokratischen System bedeutende Rolle als „public watchdog" nur dann erfolgreich ausüben können, wenn das Prinzip der Pluralität gewährleistet ist, wobei der Gerichtshof die Konventionsstaaten als Garanten dieses Prinzips begreift. Anknüpfend an die ausdrückliche Verankerung der Pflicht zur Achtung der Pluralität der Medien in Art. 11 Abs. 2 GRC unterstreicht auch der Europäische Gerichtshof (EuGH) auf EU-Ebene die Bedeutung dieses Leitprinzips unter Bezugnahme auf die GRC, die EMRK und die Rechtsprechung des EGMR. Er hebt hervor, dass der Pluralismus der Medien unbestreitbar ein im Allgemeininteresse liegendes Ziel darstellt, dessen Bedeutung in einer demokratischen und pluralistischen Gesellschaft nicht genug betont werden kann, und dass daher die Verfolgung dieses Ziels auch geeignet ist, eine Beeinträchtigung der Medien- und Meinungsfreiheit selbst, anderer Grundrechte sowie nicht zuletzt auch der auf EU-Ebene gewährleisteten Grundfreiheiten zu rechtfertigen.

27. Bedeutung und Tragweite dieser Aussage für die Regulierung des Mediensektors werden deutlich, wenn man die grundfreiheitlichen Garantien im AEUV und die hierzu ergangene Rechtsprechung des EuGH im medialen Kontext betrachtet. Vor allem in Form der Waren-

verkehrs-, Dienstleistungs- und Niederlassungsfreiheit schützen die Grundfreiheiten den Binnenmarkt und die darin agierenden EU-Unternehmen umfassend bei der grenzüberschreitenden Erbringung ihrer Leistungen in Form von Beschränkungs- und Diskriminierungsverboten. Medien, in ihrer Rolle als Teilnehmer am Wirtschaftsverkehr in der EU, sind daher grundsätzlich frei, ihre Inhalte, digital oder analog, in verkörperter Form oder unkörperlich, über die Grenzen ihres Niederlassungsstaates hinaus zu verbreiten. Sie haben dabei das Recht, nicht unterschiedlich zu anderen Anbieter behandelt oder in sonstiger Weise behindert oder eingeschränkt zu werden. Diese Freiheit wird allerdings nicht schrankenlos gewährleistet. Neben ausdrücklichen Schranken der einzelnen Grundfreiheiten können Beschränkungen durch die Verfolgung anerkannter Ziele des Allgemeinwohlinteresses gerechtfertigt werden, wozu nach ständiger Rechtsprechung des EuGH auch die Aufrechterhaltung von Medienpluralismus gehört.

28. Nicht nur aus kompetenzrechtlichen Gründen, sondern auch vor dem Hintergrund der Anerkennung eines damit zusammenhängenden Konzepts einer Kulturpolitik, die von unterschiedlichen nationalen (Verfassungs-)Traditionen in Bezug auf die Medienordnung geprägt sein kann, räumt der EuGH den Mitgliedstaaten bei der Ausfüllung dieser Zielsetzung einen breiten Ermessensspielraum ein. In Anerkennung, dass Erwägungen moralischer oder kultureller Natur von Mitgliedstaat zu Mitgliedstaat verschieden sein können, obliegt es den Mitgliedstaaten, darüber zu entscheiden, wie sie ein angemessenes Schutzniveau für die Erreichung ihrer kultur-, einschließlich medienvielfaltspolitischen Ziele unter Berücksichtigung nationaler Besonderheiten bestimmen und mit welchen Instrumenten sie dieses Schutzniveau erreichen wollen. Grenze dieser in der einheitlichen Dogmatik der Grundfreiheiten anerkannten Definitions- und Gestaltungsfreiheit ist dabei vor allem der allgemeine Verhältnismäßigkeitsgrundsatz. Grundfreiheiten und Grundrechte hindern die Mitgliedstaaten also nicht, vorgefundenen Defiziten im Bereich medialer Vielfalt auch regulatorisch Rechnung zu tragen, selbst wenn dadurch Unternehmen mit Sitz in anderen Mitgliedstaaten der EU betroffen werden.

29. Getragen und unterstrichen wird dieses Ergebnis der Verortung der Vielfaltssicherung auf mitgliedstaatlicher Ebene im Übrigen, wie bereits dargestellt, auch auf der weiteren primärrechtlichen Ebene, insbesondere im Rahmen der EU-Wettbewerbsordnung. Obwohl das EU-Wettbewerbsrecht aufgrund seiner eindeutig wirtschaftspolitischen Zielsetzung der Etablierung und des Schutzes eines freien und fairen Binnenmarkts wenig Spielraum für die Berücksichtigung nichtwirt-

schaftsbezogener Aspekte lässt, kann die Wettbewerbsordnung indirekt auch zur medialen Vielfaltssicherung beitragen, da sie die Märkte offen und kompetitiv hält, Konzentrationsentwicklungen entgegenwirkt, staatliche Einflussnahme begrenzt und Marktmissbrauch verhindert. Allerdings ist auf EU-Ebene eine steuernde Einflussnahme im Bereich der Vielfaltssicherung jenseits der Beihilfenaufsicht weder explizit gesetzlich vorgesehen noch für die Praxis der Wettbewerbsaufsicht anerkannt. Bewertungen von Maßnahmen aus kultur-, namentlich medienvielfaltsrechtlichem Blickwinkel außerhalb wirtschaftlicher Markterwägungen – wie zum Beispiel die Berücksichtigung des Entstehens vorherrschender Meinungsmacht – sind insoweit auf EU-Ebene nicht möglich.

30. Vielmehr sind sowohl im Rahmen der Marktmachtkontrolle und der Missbrauchsaufsicht als auch im Rahmen der Beihilfeaufsicht durch die Europäische Kommission im Bereich der Bewertung unionsrelevanter Zusammenschlüsse, Verhaltensweisen und staatlicher Beihilfen Öffnungsklauseln und Ausnahmen für die mitgliedstaatliche Kulturpolitik vorgesehen. So ist das Medienkonzentrationsrecht bewusst aus dem Wirtschaftskonzentrationsrecht ausgeklammert, was Art. 21 Abs. 4 der EU-Fusionskontrollverordnung verdeutlicht, der den Mitgliedstaaten zur Wahrung berechtigter Interessen an der Herstellung der Medienvielfalt erlaubt, Sonderregeln zu treffen, die im Ergebnis dazu führen können, dass mitgliedstaatliche Behörden selbst bei ausschließlicher Zuständigkeit der Kommission für einen Zusammenschluss von unionsweiter Bedeutung die Möglichkeit erhalten, diesen Zusammenschluss aus vorgefundenen Gründen der Vielfaltsgewichtung auf dem „Meinungsmarkt" unabhängig von der Unbedenklichkeitseinstufung durch die Kommission zu untersagen. Auch das Beihilferecht stellt Ausnahmen, in denen die staatliche Unterstützung von (Medien-)Unternehmen ausnahmsweise erlaubt ist, unter die Bedingung einer kulturellen Schwerpunktsetzung und einer auf nationaler Ebene konzeptualisierten Kulturpolitik. Demnach ist das EU-Wettbewerbsrecht zwar bewusst kein geeignetes Instrument zur Pluralismussicherung, steht dabei aber entsprechenden mitgliedstaatlichen Bestrebungen nicht entgegen.

Sekundärrechtlicher Rahmen zum „Medienrecht" und zum Medienpluralismus

31. Aufgrund mangelnder Rechtsetzungskompetenzen kann es im Bereich der Vielfaltssicherung zwar kein Sekundärrecht geben, das unmittelbar diese Zielsetzung verfolgt. Entsprechende Anläufe auf Ebene der EU

Executive Summary

bzw. vormals der EG wurden daher auch jeweils schnell verworfen. Allerdings gibt es dennoch – auch bedingt durch den Doppelcharakter der Medien als Wirtschafts- und Kulturgut gleichermaßen und die Konvergenz der Medien und deren Verbreitungswege – einen gewissen medienrechtlichen Rahmen auf EU-Sekundärrechtsebene, innerhalb dessen sich auch zahlreiche Anknüpfungspunkte für den Pluralismus finden, die sich aber unterschiedlich auf die Ausgestaltung der Medienordnung durch die Mitgliedstaaten auswirken.

32. Eine Gruppe von Anknüpfungspunkten betrifft dabei die Festlegung von expliziten mitgliedstaatlichen Gestaltungsspielräumen in Bezug auf die nationale Kulturpolitik, insbesondere die Sicherung von Medienpluralismus, in der wirtschaftsbezogenen Sekundärrechtsetzung der Union. Solche Ausnahmemöglichkeiten finden sich einerseits in Regelungswerken, die für die Distribution von medialen Inhalten relevant sind: Der Europäische Kodex für die elektronische Kommunikation (EEKK), der telekommunikationsrechtliche Regelungen enthält, sowie die Richtlinie über den elektronischen Geschäftsverkehr (e-Commerce-Richtlinie, ECRL), die einen teilharmonisierten Rechtsrahmen inklusive von Haftungsprivilegien für Dienste der Informationsgesellschaft und damit insbesondere für Intermediäre bei der Online-Verbreitung von medialen Inhalten stellt, lassen die Möglichkeit der Mitgliedstaaten unberührt, Maßnahmen zu ergreifen, die der Förderung der kulturellen und sprachlichen Vielfalt dienen. Darüber hinaus können die Mitgliedstaaten nach dem EEKK im nationalen Recht sog. Must-Carry-Pflichten vorsehen, also Netzbetreiber zur Übertragung von bestimmten Hörfunk- und Fernsehkanälen und damit verbundenen ergänzenden Diensten verpflichten, was die ohnehin bestehende Ausnahmebefugnis für Vielfaltssicherungsmaßnahmen auch auf diesen von der Richtlinie koordinierten Bereich erweitert. Auch die Richtlinie über audiovisuelle Mediendienste (AVMD-RL) als Herzstück europäischer „Medienregulierung" enthält eine Abweichungsbefugnis zum Erlass strengerer Regeln, die sich auf die von der Richtlinie koordinierten Bereiche bezieht und die sich trotz der Weiterentwicklung der Richtlinie im Übrigen über die Jahre hinweg kaum inhaltlich verändert hat.

33. Eine andere Gruppe von Anknüpfungspunkten betrifft allerdings Bestrebungen der Union mit vielfaltssichernden Bezügen, die vor allem in jüngster Zeit zu beobachten sind und in der Sekundärrechtssetzung ihren Niederschlag finden, ohne sich dabei kompetenziell auf eine kulturelle Schwerpunktsetzung zu stützen. Insbesondere die Reformen der AVMD-Richtlinie und durch die neue Richtlinie über das Urhe-

Executive Summary

berrecht im Digitalen Binnenmarkt (DSM-Richtlinie) haben Vorschriften etabliert, die einen gewissen vielfaltssichernden Charakter oder mindestens Bezug haben, der auch durch entsprechende Anhaltspunkte in den Erwägungsgründen unterstrichen wird. Während die neuen urheberrechtlichen Vorschriften zum Leistungsschutzrecht für Presseverlage und zum Schutz von Werken auf bestimmten Online-Plattformen solche Vielfaltsgesichtspunkte mitberücksichtigen, dabei aber im Wesentlichen auf die angemessene Finanzierung von (auch) medialen Angeboten und damit maßgeblich auf wirtschaftliche Faktoren abzielen, ist den neuen Regeln der AVMD-Richtlinie zur Förderung europäischer Werke, zur Herausstellung von Inhalten von allgemeinem Interesse, zur Medienkompetenzförderung und zur Einrichtung unabhängiger Regulierungsstellen eine stärkere Gewichtung von kulturellen Faktoren zuzusprechen. Allerdings werden auch insoweit weite mitgliedstaatliche Gestaltungs- und Ermessensspielräume erhalten und betont.

34. Zu dieser Gruppe zählt auch die erst vor kurzem anwendbar gewordene Platform-to-Business-(P2B-)Verordnung, die aufgrund ihrer Rechtsnatur stärker in den mitgliedstaatlichen Bereich eingreift als Richtlinien. Die Verordnung legt Online-Vermittlungsdiensten und -Suchmaschinen Transparenzpflichten in Bezug auf Rankingsysteme gegenüber Unternehmen auf, zu denen potentiell auch Medienunternehmen gehören können, deren Inhalte über diese Gatekeeper aufgefunden werden. Obwohl die Verordnung auf die Binnenmarktkompetenz gestützt ist und sie auf ein ungleiches Machtgefüge in der digitalen Wirtschaft reagieren bzw. dem vorbeugen will, entsteht ein wirtschaftlich intendiertes, aber auch im Blick auf Vielfaltsgesichtspunkte bedeutendes Mittel zur Transparenz der Bedingungen für die Auffindbarkeit von Inhalten. Eine Sperrwirkung für die mitgliedstaatliche Medienrechtssetzung, soweit diese unmittelbar aus Gründen der Vielfaltsgewährleistung vergleichbare Offenlegungspflichten für bestimmte Plattformanbieter regelt, wird aber durch die P2B-Verordnung nicht erreicht.

35. Dass stärker medienbezogene, weil insbesondere im Kontext der grundrechtlich geschützten Meinungsfreiheit relevante Vorhaben wie die Bekämpfung von Hassrede und Desinformation auf die Ebene von Koordinierungs- und Unterstützungsmaßnahmen auf Grundlage von Selbstregulierungsmechanismen verlagert werden, zeigt, dass die EU den mitgliedstaatlichen Hoheitsbereich der Medienregulierung auch in diesem Zusammenhang beachtet. Dies entspricht der Begrenzung einer Unterstützungskompetenz der EU dahingehend, dass über Maßnahmen zur Unterstützung keine Vorprägung mitgliedstaatlicher

Executive Summary

Wahrnehmung von Regulierungsspielräumen erfolgen darf. Im Rahmen zukünftiger, von der EU angekündigter Maßnahmen, die den Mediensektor im Besonderen betreffen, etwa des *Media and Audiovisual Action Plan* und des *European Democracy Action Plan*, wird es wichtig sein, dass stärker auf Unionsebene regulierende Schritte weiterhin unter Berücksichtigung der Kompetenzverteilung erfolgen, was etwa die mitgliedstaatliche Durchführungskompetenz etwaiger gemeinsamer Standards betrifft. Aufgrund der Ankündigung innerhalb dieser Initiativen insbesondere die Wettbewerbsfähigkeit und pluralistische Vielfalt im audiovisuellen Sektor durch unter anderem den Einsatz von EU-Finanzierungsinstrumenten unterstützen zu wollen, sowie die Bemühungen im Bereich von Desinformation, Hassrede und Medienkompetenz verstärken zu wollen, sind dabei Schnittpunkte zur medialen Vielfaltssicherung auf nationaler Ebene gegeben. Die Einbeziehung demokratie-, kultur- und auch vielfaltspolitischer Gesichtspunkte in die Regulierung, ist eine in jüngerer Vergangenheit stärker als bislang auf Ebene rechtlich verbindlichen Sekundärrechts wie auf (tertiärer unionsrechtlicher) Ebene von Ausführungsbestimmungen, aber auch bei rechtlich unverbindlichen Initiativen zu beobachtende Tendenz. Diese vergrößert das Spannungsverhältnis zu nationalen Regelungen, die mit dem Ziel der Vielfaltssicherung erlassen wurden.

Völkerrechtliche Kernprobleme der Regulierung des „Mediensektors" im Hinblick auf mögliche Spannungsverhältnisse mit dem Recht der EU

36. Bei der Betrachtung möglicher Spannungsverhältnisse zwischen den Regulierungsebenen von EU und Mitgliedstaaten spielt insbesondere auch die Frage der Durchführungszuständigkeit eine wichtige Rolle. Dies gilt insbesondere bei der Entscheidung darüber, wer im konkreten Fall die Rechtsdurchsetzung gegenüber Anbietern vorzunehmen hat. Im nationalen Kontext der Bundesrepublik Deutschland sind die Landesmedienanstalten unter Zugrundelegung einer teleologischen und historischen Auslegung der betreffenden Staatsverträge zu Vollzugsmaßnahmen gegen ausländische Anbieter wegen Verletzung materiell-rechtlicher Vorgaben des MStV und des JMStV befugt. Diese Befugnis wird durch eine europarechtskonforme Auslegung dieser Staatsverträge, bei der die Auslegung der Regelungen der AVMD- und der e-Commerce-Richtlinie unter Berücksichtigung der Verantwortlichkeit der Mitgliedstaaten für die Pluralismussicherung erfolgt, auch in Bezug auf Sachverhalte, bei denen es sich um Anbieter handelt, die ihren Sitz in einem Mitgliedstaat der EU haben, im Ansatz bestätigt. Die kri-

tischen Anmerkungen der Europäischen Kommission namentlich zur Medienintermediäre-Regulierung des MStV im Notifizierungsverfahren gehen insoweit fehl.

37. Eine abgestufte Regulierung kann im Vollzug zwar danach differenzieren, ob Angebote ihren Ursprung im In- oder im Ausland haben. Ein dauerhafter Verzicht auf Regulierung gegenüber ausländischen Anbietern könnte allerdings, je weniger alternative Bemühungen um eine Eingrenzung von Schutzgefährdungen aus dem Ausland nachhaltig erfolgreich sind, die verfassungsrechtliche Frage provozieren, ob der Verzicht noch mit den Vorgaben des Gleichheitsgrundsatzes in Deckung zu bringen ist. Bei der Regulierung ausländischer Anbieter besteht im Übrigen, auch im Lichte der BND-Entscheidung des BVerfG vom 19. Mai 2020, eine Bindung an die grundrechtlichen Vorgaben des Grundgesetzes im Hinblick auf die Rundfunkfreiheit des Art. 5 Abs. 1 Satz 2 GG zumindest dann, wenn es sich bei dem Anbieter entweder um eine natürliche Person oder (in der erweiterten Auslegung des BVerfG) um eine juristische Person mit Sitz in der EU handelt.

38. Die Schutzpflichtenlehre des BVerfG führt zu einem vorverlagerten Grundrechtsschutz, wenn es um die „Minimierung von Risiken im Gefolge moderner technologischer und zivilisatorischer Entwicklung geht". Sofern staatliche Schutzpflichten existieren, folgt aus diesen grundsätzlich die Pflicht, Rechtsverletzungen zu verhindern, zu unterbinden und zu sanktionieren, wobei – unter Wahrung eines weiten Umsetzungsspielraums der Staaten – legislative wie auch judikative und administrative Maßnahmen geboten sein können. Dabei gilt es auch in Bezug auf die schutzrechtliche Dimension der Grundrechte bei Sachverhalten mit Auslandsbezug den gesteigerten Gestaltungsspielraum staatlicher Gewalt zu beachten: Berührt die Wahrnehmung der schutzrechtlichen Dimension eines Grundrechts zwangsläufig die Rechtsordnungen anderer Staaten, ist die Gestaltungsbefugnis staatlicher Gewalt größer als bei der Regelung von Rechtsbeziehungen mit inländischem Schwerpunkt. In Anlehnung an die Solange-Judikatur des BVerfG kann die These vertreten werden, dass die Schutzpflichten des Grundgesetzes solange nicht wahrgenommen werden müssen, solange ein im Ansatz vergleichbares Schutzniveau durch die Tätigkeit von Drittstaaten besteht.

39. Zwar findet sich im Rahmen von EUV und AEUV noch keine der verfassungsrechtlichen Situation vergleichbare Schutzpflichten-Dogmatik auf der Grundlage der GRC. Allerdings ist auch nicht ersichtlich, dass EUV oder AEUV der aufgezeigten Schutzpflichten-Dogmatik europarechtliche Schranken setzen. Sowohl bei der Anerkennung einer Ein-

Executive Summary

schätzungsprärogative der Mitgliedstaaten zum „wie" der Maßnahmen, um Beeinträchtigungen der Grundfreiheiten von privater Seite zu beseitigen, wie bei der Definition der Grenzen des betreffenden Einschätzungsspielraums weist die grundfreiheitliche Dogmatik eine erhebliche Nähe zur Schutzpflichten-Dogmatik des BVerfG auf.

40. Die territoriale Souveränität und das Interventionsverbot setzen der Rechtsetzungs- und Vollzugsgewalt bei grenzüberschreitendem Bezug völkerrechtliche Schranken. Für die Bestimmung dieser Schranken ist die *Lotus*-Entscheidung des StIGH von fortdauernder Bedeutung. Da das Völkerrecht von einem territorialen Staatsverständnis geprägt ist, wird Hoheitsgewalt grundsätzlich über das Staatsgebiet ausgeübt. Auf dem Gebiet eines anderen Staates verbietet das Völkerrecht dem Staat daher grundsätzlich die Durchsetzung seiner Rechtsordnung. Eine diesbezügliche Ausnahme bedarf einer völkervertragsrechtlichen Regelung oder einer Anerkennung im Völkergewohnheitsrecht. Diese Abschichtung ist auch bedeutsam bei der Unterscheidung von *jurisdiction to prescribe* und *jurisdiction to enforce*.

41. Ausgehend vom Grundsatz der Gebietshoheit sind zunächst das Territorialitäts- sowie das damit verbundene Auswirkungsprinzip als Anknüpfungstatbestände für eine Jurisdiktionsgewalt anerkannt. Darüber hinaus werden die Staatszugehörigkeit (aktives Personalitätsprinzip) und der Schutz bestimmter staatlicher Interessen (passives Personalitäts- und Schutzprinzip) für eine solche Anknüpfung (*genuine link*) verwendet. Die Regulierung des MStV trägt dieser völkerrechtlichen Grenzziehung angemessen Rechnung. Eine Auswirkung auf Deutschland ist im Übrigen insbesondere gegeben, wenn sich ein Angebot konkret im Schwerpunkt oder ausschließlich mit der politischen, wirtschaftlichen, gesellschaftlichen, wissenschaftlichen oder kulturellen Situation Deutschlands in Gegenwart oder Vergangenheit befasst. Insbesondere liegt ein *genuine link* mit Blick auf den Bezug zur Verfassungsidentität der Bundesrepublik Deutschland und die gegenbildlich identitätsprägende Bedeutung des Nationalsozialismus für die deutsche Rechtsordnung bei Verstößen gegen § 4 Abs. 1 Satz 1 Nrn. 1, 2, 3, 4 und 7 JMStV vor. Auch wer als ausländischer Anbieter auf den Prozess der Schaffung von Aufmerksamkeit für Inhalte mittels Aggregation, Selektion und Präsentation, namentlich bei Suchmaschinen, Einfluss ausübt, insbesondere indem er z.B. auf eine vorrangige Berücksichtigung seines Angebots bei Suchanfragen in Deutschland hinwirkt, schafft einen *genuine link* i.S. der völkerrechtlichen Jurisdiktionsdogmatik.

Executive Summary

42. Neben prozeduralen Problemlagen bezüglich der Behandlung ausländischer Anbieter beim Vollzug medienrechtlicher Bestimmungen werden teilweise bezüglich einiger neuerer gesetzlicher und staatsvertraglicher Vorschriften materielle Bedenken hinsichtlich der Vereinbarkeit mit europarechtlichen Vorgaben, insbesondere dem Herkunftslandprinzip, vorgebracht. Sowohl bezüglich des MStV als auch im Ergebnis – wenngleich dort mit noch offenen Fragen, soweit es um die Frage einer staatsfernen Aufsicht geht – bezüglich des NetzDG wird aufgezeigt, dass das Spannungsverhältnis mit dem Recht der EU in diesen Fällen nicht zu einem Verstoß führt. Dies gilt auch für weitere Änderungen etwa im Urheberrecht. Jedoch zeigen diese Spannungsfelder, dass auf Ebene der EU – über die bisherigen Ansätze hinaus – eine explizite Anerkennung erfolgen sollte, dass bei grundsätzlicher Beibehaltung des Herkunftslandprinzips innerstaatliche Regelungen und Vollzugsmaßnahmen auch unter bestimmten Voraussetzungen am Marktortprinzip ausgerichtet werden können.

Der vorgeschlagene Digital Services Act

43. Im Dezember 2020 hat die Europäische Kommission ihren Legislativvorschlag für einen *Digital Services Act* vorgelegt, um „über digitale Dienste [...] bessere Haftungs- und Sicherheitsvorschriften für digitale Plattformen, Dienste und Produkte" zu schaffen. Dabei werden verschiedene Optionen, was den Regelungsumfang betrifft, diskutiert, zu denen neben unmittelbar auf die ECRL bezogenen Überlegungen auch Regelungen zur Sicherung des demokratischen Prozesses in der EU und ihren Mitgliedstaaten und die Bewältigung von Netzwerkeffekten der digitalen Plattformökonomie zählen. In Bezug auf letztere werden auch ex ante-Maßnahmen erwogen, die wettbewerbsrechtlich gestützt sind. Im Blick auf die Ergebnisse der Studie verdienen namentlich die Verbesserung von Informations- und Transparenzanforderungen, die Klarstellung des Verständnisses, was unter „illegale Inhalte" fallen soll und deren Abgrenzung zu bislang als nur schädlich eingestuften Inhalten, die Klärung, inwieweit Selbstregulierungsansätze ausreichen und wo mindestens Koregulierung einzusetzen ist, eine stärker an der effektiven Durchsetzung von Erwägungen des Gemeinwohls auch im Umgang mit Inhalten aus Nicht-EU-Drittstaaten, die Aktualisierung der Verantwortlichkeitsregeln für Anbieter und organisationsrechtliche Aspekte zur verbesserten Rechtsdurchsetzung im grenzüberschreitenden Kontext besondere Beachtung.
44. Auf Basis der Ergebnisse der Studie ist im weiteren politischen Prozess der Verhandlung neuer oder geänderter Rechtsakte der EU ebenso wie

Executive Summary

bei ergänzenden Initiativen durch die Mitgliedstaaten neben einer Hinwirkung auf eine klare Anerkennung der Kompetenzabgrenzung aktiv mit Vorschlägen einer besseren Rücksichtnahme und Abstimmung von Maßnahmen auf beiden Ebenen eine frühzeitige und intensive Beteiligung auf der Ebene der EU durch die insoweit zuständigen Länder anzustreben.

A. Einleitung und Problemaufriss

Mark D. Cole / Jörg Ukrow

Die Präsidentin der Europäischen Kommission, Ursula von der Leyen, hat in ihrer ersten Rede zur Lage der Union bei der Plenartagung des Europäischen Parlaments am 16. September 2020 erklärt:[1]

„Das kommende Jahrzehnt muss Europas „Digital Decade" sein."

Unabhängig von der symbolpolitischen Bedeutung, die mit diesem Appell verbunden ist – eine Bedeutungsebene, die in der Vergangenheit integrationspolitisch wie -rechtlich nicht nur mit positiven Effekten verbunden war[2] –, kommt in dieser Mahnung zugleich die grundlegende Bedeutung zum Ausdruck, die der Digitalisierung auch im Blick auf die Ziele des europäischen Integrationsprozesses zukommt. Diese digitale Dimension prägt auch die Fortentwicklung der europäischen Medienordnung. Mit den im Medien-Ökosystem beobachtbaren Prozessen digitaler Disruption traditioneller Geschäfts- wie Kommunikationsprozesse ist indessen nicht zugleich auch eine Logik der digitalen Transformation von Verfassungsstrukturen und -leitlinien für die Medienverfassung der und in der EU verbunden. Digitale Wellen des Wandels brechen sich insofern an den Kaimauern der Kompetenzbeschränkungen der EU.

In ihrer Rede zur Lage der Union führte die Kommissionspräsidentin sodann aus:

„Wir brauchen einen gemeinsamen Plan für das digitale Europa mit klar definierten Zielen bis 2030 für Bereiche wie Konnektivität, digitale Kompetenzen und öffentliche Verwaltung."

Die „Gemeinsamkeit" des Plans für das digitale Europa kann – wie in der Studie aufgezeigt wird – nicht nur eine organisatorische Gemeinsamkeit

---

[1] Präsidentin von der Leyens Rede zur Lage der Union bei der Plenartagung des Europäischen Parlaments, 16.9.2020, https://ec.europa.eu/commission/presscorner/detail/de/speech_20_1655.
[2] Vgl. zum Scheitern einer symbolpolitischen Anreicherung der europäischen Verträge mit dem Europäischen Verfassungsvertrag z.B. *Häberle*, Nationalflaggen: Bürgerdemokratische Identitätselemente und Internationale Erkennungssymbole, S. 39.

der traditionell die Integration Europas in besonderer Weise fördernden Organe Rat und Kommission sein. Der angeregte Plan bedarf vielmehr einer architektonischen Strukturierung, an der neben der EU mit ihren Organen fortdauernd auch die Mitgliedstaaten maßgeblichen Anteil haben. Ein digitales Europa kann nur aus einem Respekt vor den unterschiedlichen Befähigungen im europäischen Mehr-Ebenen-System erwachsen.

Keiner der als planrelevant aufgezeigten Bereiche ist im Übrigen deckungsgleich mit dem Bereich der Medien, namentlich Presse, Rundfunk und neue Medien, wobei sich letztere allerdings erst im Prozess der Digitalisierung auch des Medien-Ökosystems entwickeln konnten. Aber keiner dieser Bereiche ist auch ohne Berührungspunkte zu einer Medienregulierung auf der Höhe der Zeit, die Konvergenzphänomene an der Schnittstelle von Infrastruktur und Inhalte ebenso in den Blick nimmt wie das Zusammenspiel von Regulierung und Kompetenzförderung zur Erreichung von Schutzzielen wie dem Schutz der Menschenwürde, dem Jugendschutz und dem Verbraucherschutz. Auch an diesen Schnittstellen stellen sich jeweils Fragen der Zuordnung unionaler und mitgliedstaatlicher Kompetenzen.

Schließlich verweist die Kommissionspräsidentin auf die Wertegebundenheit hin, die EU wie Mitgliedstaten auch in ihrem digitalpolitischen Engagement gemeinsam ist. Als die entsprechenden „klaren Prinzipien" identifiziert von der Leyen

„das Recht auf Privatsphäre und Zugang, freie Meinungsäußerung, freier Datenfluss und Cybersicherheit"

Die Bezüge dieser Prinzipien zu einer digitalen Medienordnung für die EU sind evident.

Auch wenn die Themenfelder „Daten" und „Infrastruktur", die in der Rede besondere Beachtung finden, in gleicher Weise Bezüge auch zum digitalen Medien-Ökosystem aufweisen, bezieht sich der Untersuchungsgegenstand der vorliegenden Studie auf eine Problematik, die im Zusammenhang mit dem "digitale Dekade"-Ansatz auch für das dort als drittes in der Rede hervorgehobenes Themenfeld relevant ist: „Technologie – und hier insbesondere die künstliche Intelligenz". Denn das Thema „Algorithmen-Regulierung" zeigt in besonderer Weise Problemlagen auf, die sich aus kompetenz- wie grundrechtlicher Perspektive insgesamt bei der Weiterentwicklung der Medienregulierung durch die EU wie durch ihre Mitgliedstaaten in einem Regelungsumfeld stellen können, das durch die Megatrends der Digitalisierung und Globalisierung zunehmend geprägt wurde und weiter wird.:

A. Einleitung und Problemaufriss

> „*Wir in Europa wollen ein Regelwerk, das den Menschen in den Mittelpunkt stellt.*
> *Algorithmen dürfen keine Black Box sein und es muss klare Regeln geben für den Fall, dass etwas schiefgeht.*
> *Die Kommission wird im nächsten Jahr ein entsprechendes Gesetz vorschlagen.*
> *Dazu gehört auch die Kontrolle über unsere persönlichen Daten, die wir heute viel zu selten haben.*
> *Jedes Mal, wenn eine Website uns aufgefordert, eine neue digitale Identität zu erstellen oder uns bequem über eine große Plattform anzumelden, haben wir in Wirklichkeit keine Ahnung, was mit unseren Daten geschieht.*
> *Aus diesem Grund wird die Kommission demnächst eine sichere europäische digitale Identität vorschlagen.*
> *Eine, der wir vertrauen und die Bürgerinnen und Bürger überall in Europa nutzen können, um alles zu tun, vom Steuern zahlen bis hin zum Fahrrad mieten.*
> *Eine Technologie, bei der wir selbst kontrollieren können, welche Daten ausgetauscht und wie sie verwendet werden.* "

Die Kommissionspräsidentin betont dabei:

> „*All das ist kein Selbstzweck – es geht um Europas digitale Souveränität, im Kleinen wie im Großen.* "

Mit der Zielsetzung der Souveränität Europas greift von der Leyen einen Topos auf, der erstmalig von Präsident *Macron* in die integrationsrechtliche Finalitätsdiskussion eingeführt wurde und der anschließend im deutsch-französischen „Vertrag über die deutsch-französische Zusammenarbeit und Integration"[3] aufgegriffen und erstmalig mit völkervertragsrechtlicher Bindungskraft versehen wurde. Diese „Souveränitäts"-Perspektive wirft im Blick auf die Zuordnung von EU und Mitgliedstaaten im Integrationsverbund nicht unerhebliche Rechtsprobleme auf.[4] Auch diese Probleme gilt es im Blick zu behalten, wenn EU und Mitgliedstaaten gemeinsam den europäischen Weg ins Digitalzeitalter auch mit einem medienregulatorischen Zimmer im digitalen Haus Europa gehen wollen.

Nach Abschluss der Arbeiten der letzten „Juncker-Kommission" im Bereich des Digitalen Binnenmarktes bleibt mithin nach der Rede zur Lage

---

3 Gesetz zu dem Vertrag vom 22. Januar 2019 zwischen der Bundesrepublik Deutschland und der Französischen Republik über die deutsch-französische Zusammenarbeit und Integration v. 15. November 2019, BGBl. 2019 II S. 898 ff.
4 Vgl. *Ukrow* in: ZEuS 2019, 3, 21 f.

der Union die Etablierung eines Rechtsrahmens für die „digitale Gesellschaft" auf Ebene der Europäischen Union (EU) erkennbar ein Schwerpunkt der Arbeit der Kommission.[5] Neben den bislang von der Kommission veröffentlichten Strategien und Arbeitsplänen etwa zur Datenstrategie[6] oder möglichen Regulierungsschritten bezüglich des Einsatzes künstlicher Intelligenz-Systeme[7], ist für den „Medienmarkt" – der so schon nicht mehr eindeutig zu fassen ist – insbesondere der Legislativvorschläge vom 15.12.2020 zur Schaffung eines *Digital Services Act*[8] bzw. eines *Digital Markets Act*[9] und damit die Anknüpfung an die E-Commerce-Richtlinie (ECRL)[10] von zentraler Bedeutung. Mit diesem Paket will die Kommission klare Regeln vorschlagen, die die Verantwortlichkeiten der digitalen Dienste festlegen, ein modernes System der Zusammenarbeit bei der Überwachung von und der Rechtsdurchsetzung gegenüber Plattformen gewährleisten sowie ex-ante-Regeln für große Online-Plattformen vorschlagen, die die Wettbewerbsfähigkeit des europäischen Marktes sicherstellen. Und genau hier – so wie in Ansätzen auch schon bei der Regulierung audiovisuel-

---

5 Vgl. hierzu Arbeitsprogramm der Kommission für 2020, Eine Union, die mehr erreichen will, v. 29.1.2020, COM(2020) 37 final, https://ec.europa.eu/info/sites/info/files/cwp-2020_de.pdf.
6 Mitteilung der Europäischen Kommission an das Europäische Parlament, den Rat, den Wirtschafts- und Sozialausschuss und den Ausschuss der Regionen, Eine europäische Datenstrategie, v. 29.2.2020, COM(2020) 66 final, https://eur-lex.europa.eu/legal-content/DE/TXT/?qid=1593073685620&uri=CELEX%3A52020DC0066. Zwischenzeitlich hat die Kommission ihren Vorschlag für ein Daten-Governance-Gesetz vorgelegt, https://eur-lex.europa.eu/legal-content/de/TXT/?uri=CELEX%3A5 2020PC0767.
7 Europäische Kommission, Weißbuch zur Künstlichen Intelligenz – ein europäisches Konzept für Exzellenz und Vertrauen, v. 29.2.2020, COM(2020) 66 final, https://ec.europa.eu/info/sites/info/files/commission-white-paper-artificial-intellige nce-feb2020_de.pdf.
8 https://eur-lex.europa.eu/legal-content/DE/TXT/?uri=CELEX%3A52020PC0825&qi d=1614595537069. Einen ersten Überblick dazu bei *Ukrow*, Die Vorschläge der EU-Kommission für einen Digital Services Act und einen Digital Markets Act, und detaillierte Analyse bei *Cole/Etteldorf/Ullrich*, Updating the Rules for Online Content Dissemination.
9 https://eur-lex.europa.eu/legal-content/DE/TXT/?uri=COM%3A2020%3A842%3AFI N.
10 Richtlinie 2000/31/EG des Europäischen Parlaments und des Rates vom 8. Juni 2000 über bestimmte rechtliche Aspekte der Dienste der Informationsgesellschaft, insbesondere des elektronischen Geschäftsverkehrs, im Binnenmarkt ("Richtlinie über den elektronischen Geschäftsverkehr"), EU ABl. L 178, 17.7.2000, S. 1–16, https://eur-lex.europa.eu/legal-content/DE/ALL/?uri=celex%3A32000L0031.

ler Mediendienste und der Reform der entsprechenden Richtlinie 2018[11], die sich noch im Umsetzungsprozess in den Mitgliedstaaten befindet[12] – kommt es zu möglichen Konflikten zwischen den beiden Ebenen EU und Mitgliedstaaten bezüglich der Kompetenzzuteilung zur Regelung dieser Bereiche.

Im Mehrebenensystem der EU sind Kompetenzabgrenzungen nicht immer eindeutig, was in Föderalstaaten wie der Bundesrepublik Deutschland durch eine weitere Untergliederung verstärkt wird. Dies gilt gerade für das Medienrecht, das den „Medien"-Sektor reguliert, weil hier nicht nur die Zuordnung zu einer einzigen Rechtsmaterie möglich ist. So ist es eine alte Erkenntnis, dass Medien eine „kulturelle" Komponente haben, aber eben auch – und in manchen Zusammenhängen vorrangig – ökonomischer Natur sind und damit im EU-Kontext binnenmarktbezogen. Dieses schon damit bestehende Spannungsverhältnis zwischen mitgliedstaatlicher Kulturkompetenz und EU-Regulierung der Binnenmarktbezüge erhält eine weitere Dimension, wenn es um Beschränkungen geht, die dienstleistenden Unternehmen in diesem Sektor auferlegt werden. So gehört neben dem Schutz der Meinungsfreiheit die Sicherstellung einer auf den jeweiligen Mitgliedstaat bzw. seine regionale Untergliederung bezogenen Meinungs- und Medienvielfalt zum vornehmlichen Ziel jeder Medienregulierung. Die Kompetenz für solchermaßen beschränkende Regelungen muss auf

---

11 Richtlinie (EU) 2018/1808 des Europäischen Parlaments und des Rates vom 14. November 2018 zur Änderung der Richtlinie 2010/13/EU zur Koordinierung bestimmter Rechts- und Verwaltungsvorschriften der Mitgliedstaaten über die Bereitstellung audiovisueller Mediendienste (Richtlinie über audiovisuelle Mediendienste) im Hinblick auf sich verändernde Marktgegebenheiten, EU ABl. L 303, 28.11.2018, S. 69–92, https://eur-lex.europa.eu/legal-content/DE/TXT/?uri=celex:32 018L1808.

12 Die Umsetzungsfrist endete am 19. September 2020; bislang haben neben Deutschland Österreich, Bulgarien, Dänemark, Finnland, Frankreich, Ungarn, Lettland, Litauen, Malta, die Niederlande, Portugal und Schweden eine finale Umsetzung sowie Luxemburg und Spanien eine teilweise Umsetzung im nationalen Recht verabschiedet. In den anderen Mitgliedstaaten laufen die Gesetzesvorhaben noch. Vgl. hierzu die Übersichten in den Datenbank der Kommission (https://eur-lex.europa.eu/legal-content/DE/NIM/?uri=CELEX:32018L1808&qid=1 599556794041) und der Europäischen Audiovisuellen Informationsstelle (https://www.obs.coe.int/en/web/observatoire/home/-/asset_publisher/9iKCxBYgiO6S/content/which-eu-countries-have-transposed-the-avmsd-into-national-legislation-?inheritRedirect=false&redirect=https%3A%2F%2Fwww.obs.coe.int%2Fen%2Fweb%2Fobservatoire%2Fhome%3Fp_p_id%3D101_INSTANCE_9iKCxBYgiO6S%26p_p_lifecycle%3D0%26p_p_state%3Dnormal%26p_p_mode%3Dview%26p_p_col_id%3Dcolumn-1%26p_p_col_count%3D3).

mitgliedstaatlicher Ebene liegen und sowohl der Gerichtshof der Europäischen Union (EuGH) als auch in vergleichbarer Weise der Europäische Gerichtshof für Menschenrechte (EGMR) anerkennen daher einen Beurteilungs- bzw. Gestaltungsspielraum der Mitgliedstaaten bei der Entscheidung über vielfaltssichernde Maßnahmen, die zugleich einen beschränkenden Charakter bezüglich Grundfreiheiten und/oder Grundrechten haben.

Die scheinbar unbestrittene Anerkennung mitgliedstaatlich vorbehaltener Regelungskompetenz in diesem Bereich ist in der Praxis hingegen häufig mit der tatsächlichen oder behaupteten Grenze der Regelungsbefugnis konfrontiert, soweit sie in durch Unionsrecht geregelte Bereiche ausstrahlt. Gerade in letzter Zeit gab es einige Fälle, die illustrativ für diesen Konflikt sind. So hat die Kommission nach der Notifizierung des Medienstaatsvertrags[13] in ihrer Reaktion darauf deutliche Hinweise darauf gegeben, dass sie eine andere Sichtweise auf den mitgliedstaatlichen Handlungsspielraum bei der Regulierung von Online-Akteuren aufgrund der Vorschriften der E-Commerce-Richtlinie vor dem Hintergrund der grundfreiheitlichen Dimension und Verankerung des Herkunftslandprinzips vertritt.[14] Die Kommission äußerte insbesondere „gewisse Bedenken" hinsichtlich der Frage, „ob einige der im notifizierten Entwurf enthaltenen Maßnahmen den im Binnenmarkt geschützten freien Verkehr von Diensten der Informationsgesellschaft in unverhältnismäßiger Weise beschränken könnten" und verwies dabei auf ihre Bestrebung (auch) im Rahmen des damals im Planungsstadium befindlichen *Digital Services Act*, die Medienvielfalt und den Medienpluralismus im Online-Umfeld fördern zu wollen. Des Weiteren wird eine ausdrücklich zur Sicherung der Medienvielfalt im regionalen

---

13 Staatsvertrag zur Modernisierung der Medienordnung in Deutschland, vgl. Beschlussfassung der Konferenz der Regierungschefinnen und Regierungschefs der Länder vom 5. Dezember 2019, abrufbar unter https://www.rlp.de/fileadmin/rlp-stk/pdf-Dateien/Medienpolitik/ModStV_MStV_und_JMStV_2019-12-05_MPK.pdf. Der Medienstaatsvertrag ist am 7. November 2020 in Kraft getreten, vgl. hierzu die Pressemitteilung der Rundfunkkommission vom 6.11.2020, abrufbar unter https://www.rlp.de/de/aktuelles/einzelansicht/news/News/detail/medienstaatsvertrag-tritt-am-7-november-2020-in-kraft-1/.

14 Europäische Kommission, Notifizierung 2020/26/D, Mitteilung v. 27.4.2020, C(2020) 2823 final, https://dokumente.landtag.rlp.de/landtag/vorlagen/6754-V-17.pdf. *Jörg Wojahn*, Vertreter der EU-Kommission in Deutschland, wird in der dazugehörigen Pressemitteilung sogar wie folgt zitiert: „[…] Die Kommission hat bereits angekündigt, bis Ende dieses Jahres ein Gesetzespaket für digitale Dienste vorzuschlagen […]. Hiermit werden die Verantwortlichkeiten großer Online-Plattformen im gesamten Binnenmarkt geklärt, auch mit Blick auf *das Ziel, die Medienvielfalt* zu fördern […]" (Hervorhebung durch Verfasser).

A. Einleitung und Problemaufriss

Bereich eingeführte Regelung im Rundfunkstaatsvertrag – § 7 Abs. 11 RStV als eine Vorschrift, die materiell, wenn auch nicht redaktionell inhaltsgleich in § 8 Abs. 11 MStV übernommen wurde – wegen eines vermeintlichen Verstoßes gegen die Dienstleistungsfreiheit angegriffen und vom EuGH mit Urteil aus dem Februar 2021 entschieden wurde.[15]

Auf der anderen Seite gibt es neben dem zwischenzeitlich unterzeichneten und durch die Länderparlamente ratifizierten Medienstaatsvertrag weitere Regulierungsansätze im deutschen Recht – wie etwas das Netzwerkdurchsetzungsgesetz des Bundes (NetzDG)[16], das aktuell ein Änderungsverfahren[17] durchläuft – ebenso wie im Recht anderer Mitgliedstaaten, deren Ausgestaltungen möglicherweise Fragen auf Seiten der EU hinsichtlich kompetenzieller Zuordnung auslösen könnten. Gleiches gilt für weitere geplante Maßnahmen der EU selbst, etwa der bereits vorgelegte Vorschlag für eine Verordnung zur Verhinderung der Verbreitung terroristischer Online-Inhalte (TERREG)[18], die noch im Legislativprozess ist, sowie insbesondere der vorgeschlagene *Digital Services Act*.

---

15 EuGH, Rs. C-555/19, *Fussl Modestraße Mayr*, Urteil vom 03.02.2021, s. auch die Schlussanträge von Generalanwalt *Szpunar* vom 15.10.2020. S. zum Urteil *Ory* in: NJW 2021, 736, 736 ff.; *Ukrow*, Sicherung regionaler Vielfalt – Außer Mode?. Vgl. ferner *Cole* in: AfP 2021, 1, 1 ff., und im Detail *ders.*, Zum Gestaltungsspielraum der EU-Mitgliedstaaten bei Einschränkungen der Dienstleistungsfreiheit.
16 Netzwerkdurchsetzungsgesetz vom 1. September 2017 (BGBl. I S. 3352), das durch Artikel 274 der Verordnung vom 19. Juni 2020 (BGBl. I S. 1328) geändert worden ist, https://www.gesetze-im-internet.de/netzdg/BJNR335210017.html.
17 Aktuell liegen zwei Gesetzesentwürfe vor, die das NetzDG mit verschiedenen Änderungen adressieren; vgl. Deutscher Bundestag, Entwurf eines Gesetzes zur Änderung des Netzwerkdurchsetzungsgesetzes, Drucksache 19/18792 v. 27.4.2020, https://dip21.bundestag.de/dip21/btd/19/187/1918792.pdf, sowie Entwurf eines Gesetzes zur Bekämpfung des Rechtsextremismus und der Hasskriminalität, Drucksache 19/17741 v. 10.3.2020, https://dip21.bundestag.de/dip21/btd/19/177/1 917741.pdf. In Bezug auf letztere Novelle hat das Bundespräsidialamt nach vorliegenden Informationen das Ausfertigungsverfahren wegen datenschutzrechtlicher Bedenken ausgesetzt; vgl. https://www.sueddeutsche.de/politik/hate-speech-gesetz-das-koennt-ihr-besser-1.5059141. Zur bisherigen Anwendung des NetzDG vgl. den Bericht der Bundesregierung zur Evaluierung des Gesetzes zur Verbesserung der Rechtsdurchsetzung in sozialen Netzwerken sowie *Eifert*, Evaluation des NetzDG, beides abrufbar unter https://www.bmjv.de/SharedDocs/Artikel/DE/2020/09 0920_Evaluierungsbericht_NetzDG.html.
18 Vorschlag für eine Verordnung des Europäischen Parlaments und des Rates zur Verhinderung der Verbreitung terroristischer Online-Inhalte, COM(2018) 640 final v. 12.9.2018, https://eur-lex.europa.eu/legal-content/de/TXT/?uri=celex:52018P C0640.

Vor diesem Hintergrund ist es notwendig, in einer Studie umfassend den Status quo der Kompetenzverteilung im Medienregulierungsbereich unter besonderer Berücksichtigung des Regulierungsziels Medienvielfalt darzustellen. Dabei konzentriert sich die Studie im Wesentlichen aufgrund der vorhandenen Regelungsinstrumente auf EU-Ebene auf den Bereich der audiovisuellen Medien. Die Presse, insbesondere im Online-Bereich, sowie der Film, wird lediglich an relevanten Stellen in die Betrachtung miteinbezogen. Nach dieser Grundsatzklärung ist weiterhin aufzuzeigen, welche Handlungsoptionen bei der zukünftigen Ausgestaltung des Medien- und „Online-Sektors" für die Mitgliedstaaten bestehen und wie insoweit auf Vorschläge in der EU reagiert werden kann.

Zwar gibt es wissenschaftliche Vorarbeiten zur Frage der Medienvielfaltssicherung und ableitbarer Kompetenzfragen, aber diese basieren auf der frühen Rechtsprechung des EuGH – sowie diese wiederum auf derjenigen des EGMR – und bedürfen einer Aktualisierung und Kontextualisierung im Hinblick auf neue Regelungstexte und Entwicklungen der letzten Jahre. Zudem lassen sich – basierend auf einer fundierten Untersuchung – für die aktuell anstehenden Legislativprozesse auf der Ebene der EU Erkenntnisse ableiten, wie diese mit Blick auf die gefundenen Ergebnisse auszugestalten, durch den Mitgliedstaat Bundesrepublik Deutschland mitzugestalten sind und insbesondere wo Grenzen der EU-Regulierungstätigkeit liegen müssen.

Es überrascht angesichts der genannten Beispiele nicht, dass die Frage des Medienpluralismus in letzter Zeit wieder an Bedeutung zugenommen hat. Dies ist auch eine Folge der als zunehmend intensiv empfundenen Gefährdungen bestehender Strukturen auf dem Medienmarkt. Dabei werden auch Optionen diskutiert, die über eine Regelung hinaus etwa aktive Förderungsmodelle für Anbieter redaktionell verantworteter Medieninhalte vorsehen[19]. Doch auch insoweit bestehen intensive Berührungspunkte mit dem Recht der EU, so dass eine Gesamtbetrachtung losgelöst von einzelnen Verfahren oder Sachlagen angezeigt ist.

Ziel der Studie ist es, den bestehenden Kompetenzbereich der Mitgliedstaaten herauszuarbeiten. Dazu wird in einem ersten Kapitel B. der primärrechtliche Rahmen zur Kompetenzabgrenzung zwischen der EU und den Mitgliedstaaten umfassend analysiert. Insbesondere wird dort im Blick auf

---

19 Zwischenzeitlich hat die Europäische Kommission ihre Kommunikation zu Europas Medien in der digitalen Dekade: Ein Aktionsplan zur Unterstützung der Erholung und des Wandels (*Media and Audiovisual Action Plan*) vorgelegt, COM/ 2020/784 final, https://eur-lex.europa.eu/legal-content/DE/TXT/?uri=CELEX%3A5 2020DC0784.

die jüngere Rechtsprechung des BVerfG aufgezeigt, welche Grenzen das Prinzip der begrenzten Ermächtigung dem Handeln der EU setzt. Zudem werden die Werteordnung der EU in ihrer Bedeutung für den Mediensektor, die einzelnen einschlägigen Kompetenztitel aus dem Primärrecht sowie der Einfluss der Zielsetzung der EU ausführlich dargestellt. Das Kapitel schließt mit einer Betrachtung der Kompetenzausübungsschranken für die EU und die Bedeutung der Grundrechte. Im folgenden Kapitel C. wird die rechtliche Verankerung des Allgemeinwohlziels Medienvielfalt auf EU-Ebene untersucht. Dazu werden die grundrechtliche Basis in EMRK und GRC ebenso wie primärrechtliche Aspekte abgehandelt. Die Bezugnahme in und der Einfluss von Sekundärrechtsakten wird in diesem Zusammenhang dann im Kapitel D. für jeden Rechtsakt gesondert analysiert, wobei neben der 2018 geänderten AVMD-Richtlinie insbesondere der ebenfalls noch im Umsetzungsprozess befindliche Europäische Kodex für die elektronische Kommunikation (EEKK) sowie die jüngst anwendbar gewordene P2B-Verordnung beleuchtet werden. Auch aktuelle Rechtsetzungsvorhaben und Initiativen der EU ebenso wie nicht rechtlich bindende Maßnahmen werden einbezogen.

Im Kapitel E. geht es dann um völkerrechtliche Kernprobleme, die sich bei der Regulierung des „Mediensektors" aufgrund des Spannungsverhältnisses zwischen nationalem und dem Recht der EU stellen. Der Schwerpunkt liegt darin, am Beispiel der Herangehensweise des MStV und JMStV zu erläutern, welche völker- und europarechtlichen Rahmenbedingungen zu beachten sind bei der Frage der Adressaten einer nationalen Regulierung – also insbesondere der Frage einer grenzüberschreitenden Anwendung der deutschen Medienregulierung – ebenso wie der Rechtsdurchsetzung gegenüber ausländischen Anbietern. Die grundrechtliche Dimension umfasst dabei neben der Frage der Grundrechtsbindung bei Vollzugsmaßnahmen auch die Frage einer Schutzpflicht und damit einhergehenden Handlungsaufforderung an den Staat. Die Problemlagen in der praktischen Durchführung solcher Maßnahmen werden bezüglich der unterschiedlichen Rechtsebenen aufgezeigt und einer Lösung zugeführt. Abschließend wird in diesem Kapitel exemplarisch auf im Blick auf die europarechtlichen Vorgaben strittige materiellrechtliche Aspekte einzelner Regelungen mit medienrechtlicher Auswirkung in Deutschland eingegangen. Aufgrund der Bedeutung für den gerade anlaufenden Legislativprozess zur zukünftigen Regulierung in Form des *Digital Services Act* der EU werden einzelne Punkte des Kommissionsvorschlags angesprochen und im Blick auf die Ergebnisse der Studie eingeordnet. Abschließend gibt es im Kapitel G. einige Hinweise zu politischen Handlungsoptionen, die sich aus den Ergebnissen der Studie ergeben. Der Studie vorangestellt ist eine ausführliche Executive Summary.

Die wissenschaftliche Leitung und Gesamtredaktion der Studie wurden von Mark D. Cole und Jörg Ukrow übernommen. Die Bearbeitung der einzelnen Kapitel erfolgte durch die Autoren folgendermaßen: Kapitel B, E und F von *Jörg Ukrow*, Kapitel C und D von *Mark D. Cole* und *Christina Etteldorf*, die einrahmenden Kapitel A und G von *Mark D. Cole* und *Jörg Ukrow*. Die Autoren danken *Jan Henrich* für Vorarbeiten in einzelnen Abschnitten.

B. Primärrechtlicher Rahmen zur Kompetenzabgrenzung

Jörg Ukrow

I. Grundprinzipien des EUV/AEUV

1. Einleitung

Schon seit Ende der 1990er Jahre kursieren bei Europäischer Kommission[20] und Europäischem Parlament[21] immer wieder Initiativen zu und Forderungen nach einem europäischem Medienkonzentrationsrecht.[22] In der Gründungsakte des EU-Medienrechts, der EWG-Fernsehrichtlinie, wurde das Thema erstmalig sekundärrechtlich adressiert – in Form eines Warnhinweises mit inzidentem Anspruch auf regulatorisches Gegensteuern auf europäischer Ebene bei Vorsorgeversagen der Mitgliedstaaten:[23]

> *„Es ist unerläßlich, daß die Mitgliedstaaten dafür Sorge tragen, daß Handlungen unterbleiben, die den freien Fluß von Fernsehsendungen beeinträchtigen bzw. die Entstehung beherrschender Stellungen begünstigen könnten, welche zu Beschränkungen des Pluralismus und der Freiheit der Fernsehinformation sowie der Information in ihrer Gesamtheit führen würden."*

---

20 Schon in der Mitteilung der Kommission (KOM(90)78 vom 21.12.1990) wird nachdrücklich auf die Bedeutung des Pluralismus für das Funktionieren des demokratischen Gemeinwesens in der Europäischen Union hingewiesen.

21 Vgl. Europäisches Parlament, Entschließung vom 15. Februar 1990 zur Konzentration im Medienbereich (ABl. C 68 vom 19.03.1990, S. 137), Entschließung vom 16. September 1992 zur Medienkonzentration und Meinungsvielfalt (ABl. C 284 vom 02.11.1992, S. 44), Entschließung vom 20. Januar 1994 zum Grünbuch der Kommission „Pluralismus und Medienkonzentration im Binnenmarkt" (ABl. C 44 vom 14.02.1994, S. 177).

22 Vgl. *Jungheim*, Medienordnung und Wettbewerbsrecht im Zeitalter der Digitalisierung und Globalisierung, S. 356 ff.; *Schwartz*, Rundfunk, EG-Kompetenzen und ihre Ausübung, S. 15.

23 16. Erwägungsgrund der Richtlinie 89/552/EWG des Rates vom 3. Oktober 1989 zur Koordinierung bestimmter Rechts- und Verwaltungsvorschriften der Mitgliedstaaten über die Ausübung der Fernsehtätigkeit, EG ABl. L 298, 17.10.1989, S. 23–30, https://eur-lex.europa.eu/legal-content/DE/TXT/?uri=celex:31989L0552.

Insbesondere die deutschen Länder haben immer wieder die Kompetenz der EU zum Erlass einer Medienkonzentrationsrichtlinie bestritten. So hat der Bundesrat bereits in seiner Stellungnahme zum Grünbuch der Kommission über Pluralismus und Medienkonzentration im Binnenmarkt[24] am 7. Mai 1993[25] einstimmig beschlossen:

„1. [...] Auch nach Inkrafttreten des Maastrichter Vertrages würden der EG Kompetenzen zum Erlaß der im Grünbuch vorgeschlagenen Maßnahmen nicht zustehen.
2. Die Kompetenz, medienspezifisches Recht zu setzen, liegt auch nach dem Maastrichter Vertrag bei den Mitgliedstaaten; in der Bundesrepublik Deutschland bei den Ländern. Diese Kompetenzverteilung darf nicht dadurch umgangen werden, daß die Gemeinschaft ihre Kompetenz für wirtschaftspolitische Regelungen zu gezielten Eingriffen in den Medienbereich benutzt.
Die Sicherung der Meinungsvielfalt im Rundfunk ist von grundlegender Bedeutung für die freie und umfassende öffentliche Meinungsbildung. Sie ist damit schlechthin konstituierend für die Demokratie in der Bundesrepublik Deutschland.
Diese Funktion als Medium und Faktor der öffentlichen Meinungsbildung erfüllt der Rundfunk ausschließlich auf der Ebene der Mitgliedstaaten, weil die demokratische Willensbildung derzeit nur auf dieser Ebene stattfindet.
3. Pluralismus kann in einem Europa mit unterschiedlichen gesellschaftlichen Strukturen und unterschiedlichen nationalen Rundfunkordnungen deshalb nur auf die Mitgliedstaaten bezogen definiert werden. Dies verstärkt die Bedenken gegen Regelungen der Gemeinschaft zur Sicherung der Meinungsvielfalt, weil diese in den Kernbereich der gesellschaftlichen Funktionen des Rundfunks in den Mitgliedstaaten eingreifen würden. Auch das in Artikel 3 b des Vertrages von Maastricht verankerte Subsidiaritätsprinzip würde einem Tätigwerden der Gemeinschaft entgegenstehen, denn das Ziel, durch normative Maßnahmen eine Konzentration von Meinungsmacht zu verhindern, um auf diese Weise Informations- und Meinungsvielfalt zu ge-

---

24 Europäische Kommission, Grünbuch Pluralism and media concentration in the internal market – an assessment of the need for Community action, COM (92) 480 final vom 23. Dezember 1992. Hierzu z.B. *Hain* in: AfP 2007, 527, 531; *Holznagel*, Vielfaltskonzepte in Europa, S. 96; *Paal*, Medienvielfalt und Wettbewerbsrecht, S. 177.
25 Vgl. Deutscher Bundesrat, Beschlussdrucksache 77/93(B) vom 7. Mai 1993, http://dipbt.bundestag.de/extrakt/ba/WP12/1576/157601.html.

B. Primärrechtlicher Rahmen zur Kompetenzabgrenzung

währleisten, kann in ausreichendem Maße von den Mitgliedstaaten selbst erreicht werden. [...]"

Diese Positionsbestimmung[26] ist, wie im Folgenden aufgezeigt wird, ungeachtet der seit 1993 erfolgten primärrechtlichen Vertiefung des europäischen Integrationsprozesses durch die Verträge von Maastricht,[27] Amsterdam,[28] Nizza[29] und Lissabon[30] von fortdauernder Bedeutung. Grenzen einer Harmonisierungs- und Koordinierungskompetenz der EU bestehen aber nicht nur in Bezug auf das klassisches Medienkonzentrationsrecht, sondern auch in der Perspektive der Pluralismussicherung mit Blick auf digitale und globale Herausforderungen des Medien-Ökosystems.

2. Die Mitgliedstaaten als „Herren" der Verträge vs. Integrationsoffenheit und -dynamik im Verfassungsverbund

Auch im Zuge der wiederholten, z.T. grundlegenden Änderungen der Gründungsverträge der Europäischen Union (EU), die aus der vormaligen Europäischen Wirtschaftsgemeinschaft (EWG) und Europäischen Gemeinschaft (EG) hervorgegangen ist, durch die vorgenannten Vertragswerke bleiben die Mitgliedstaaten der EU, um ein – allerdings strittiges – Sprachbild aufzugreifen, das sich nicht zuletzt in der Judikatur des Bundesverfassungsgerichts findet, „Herren" der Verträge.[31] Sie besitzen nicht nur fortdauernd jeweils die Qualität eines souveränen Staates, wobei der Souveränitätsbegriff allerdings unter den Bedingungen von Digitalisierung, Europäisierung und Globalisierung einer Entwicklung nicht entgegensteht, in

---

26 Zu dem Entwurf einer Richtlinie „Medieneigentum im Binnenmarkt" bedurfte es keiner Positionierung, weil dieser Monti-Plan kommissionsseitig nicht weiter befördert wurde; zur Genese und zum Inhalt dieses Entwurfs *Ress/Bröhmer*, Europäische Gemeinschaft und Medienvielfalt; *van Loon* in: EAI (Hrsg.) Fernsehen und Medienkonzentration, S. 68 f.
27 Vgl. ABl. EG Nr. C 224 v. 31. August 1992, S. 1 ff.
28 Vgl. ABl. EG Nr. C 340 v. 10. November 1997, S. 1 ff.
29 Vgl. ABl. EG Nr. C 80 v. 10. März 2001, S. 1 ff.
30 Vgl. ABl. EU Nr. C 306 v. 17. Dezember 2007, S. 1 ff.; jüngste konsolidierte Fassung ABl. EU Nr. C 326 v. 26. Oktober 2012, S. 1 ff.
31 BVerfGE 75, 223 (242); 89, 155 (190, 199); 123, 267 (370 f.); BVerfG, Urteil des Zweiten Senats vom 05. Mai 2020, 2 BvR 859/15, Rn. 111; im Schrifttum z. B. *Cremer* in: Calliess/Ruffert, Art. 48 EUV, Rn. 19; *Huber* in: VVDStRL 2001, 194, 222; *Kaufmann* in: Der Staat 1997, 521, 532; a. A. *Everling*, Sind die Mitgliedstaaten der Europäischen Gemeinschaft noch Herren der Verträge?, S. 173 ff.; *Franzius* in: Pechstein u.a., Frankfurter Kommentar, Art. 48 EUV, Rn. 87 ff.

deren Folge vormals autonome Entscheidungsbefugnisse zum Wohle der europäischen Integration wie zum Wohl von nur noch grenzüberschreitend effektiv erreichbaren Gemeinwohlinteressen beschränkt, voneinander abhängig und auf einander bezogen sind.[32] Im verfassungsrechtlichen Gleichklang gehen die Mitgliedstaaten der EU, was mit Blick auf die kompetenzielle Ordnung des europäischen Verfassungsverbundes von fundamentaler Bedeutung ist, davon aus, dass es keinen autonomen Geltungsgrund für das Recht der EU gibt, seine Geltung mithin nicht unmittelbar von den Bürgern der Union oder EU selbst ableitbar ist, sondern dass die Geltung des EU-Rechts in den Mitgliedstaaten im Ausgangspunkt wie in der Reichweite seiner Entwicklungsfähigkeit von einem originären Rechtsanwendungsbefehl im jeweiligen Mitgliedstaat abhängig ist.[33] Dieser europäische Verfassungsverbund zeichnet sich mithin durch eine Synthese zwischen jeweiliger Offenheit der mitgliedstaatlichen Verfassungsordnungen für ein abgegrenztes und fortdauernd abgrenzbares Programm europäischer Integration und einer Verfassung der EU[34] aus, die ihrerseits nicht auf eine schrankenlose Integrationsperspektive ausgerichtet ist, sondern – ungeachtet dynamischer Auslegungsmöglichkeiten – an den Zweck einer immer engeren Union unterhalb unitarischer Bundesstaatlichkeit der EU gebunden ist. Die Vielfalt mitgliedstaatlicher Staatlichkeit bleibt beim derzeitigen Stand der europäischen Verträge[35] wie der ihnen zu innerstaatli-

---

32 Teilweise erlauben mitgliedstaatliche Verfassungsordnungen die Beteiligung an der europäischen Integration nur unter der Voraussetzung, dass der Mitgliedstaat Souveränität und Staatsqualität behält; vgl. hierzu für Deutschland Art. 23 Abs. 1 Satz 1, 3 i.V.m. Art. 79 Abs. 3 GG; rechtsvergleichend *Kirchhof*, Die rechtliche Struktur der Europäischen Union als Staatenverbund, S. 899 Fn. 16.

33 Vgl. *Huber* in: VVDStRL 2001, 194, 214 f.; *Puttler* in: EuR 2004, 669, 671; *Schwarze*, Die Entstehung einer europäischen Verfassungsordnung, S. 25 ff; 109 ff; 287 ff; 339 ff; 389 ff.

34 Zu dieser „Verfassungs"-Qualität der Gründungsverträge der EU – ungeachtet des Scheiterns eines Verfassungsvertrages – aus Sicht des EuGH vgl. EuGH, Rs. 294/83, *„Les Verts"/Europäisches Parlament*, Rn. 23; Gutachten 1/91, Slg. 1991 I-6079 Rn. 21 (jeweils „Verfassungsurkunde"); Rs. C-402/05 P und C-415/05 P, *Yassin Abdullah Kadi und Al Barakaat International Foundation / Rat der Europäischen Union und Kommission der Europäischen Gemeinschaften*, Rn. 285 („Verfassungsgrundsätze des EG-Vertrag"). Aus der Literatur vgl. z.B. *Bieber/Kotzur*, in: Bieber/Epiney/Haag/Kotzur, S. 100 ff.; *Giegerich*, Europäische Verfassung und deutsche Verfassung im transnationalen Konstitutionalisierungsprozeß: Wechselseitige Rezeption, konstitutionelle Evolution und föderale Verflechtung, S. 149 ff.

35 Zur föderalen Entwicklungstendenz der Konstitutionalisierung der EU vgl. *Giegerich*, Europäische Verfassung und deutsche Verfassung im transnationalen Konsti-

B. Primärrechtlicher Rahmen zur Kompetenzabgrenzung

cher Regulierungsmöglichkeit verhelfenden mitgliedstaatlichen Verfassungsordnungen unangetastet.

Die meisten Verfassungsordnungen der Mitgliedstaaten machen ihren Organen mehr oder weniger strikte Vorgaben, unter welchen Bedingungen sie ihren Staat zu weiteren Integrationsschritten verpflichten dürfen. In Deutschland finden sich diese Vorgaben in Art. 23 Abs. 1 Satz 1 GG: Danach wirkt die Bundesrepublik zur Verwirklichung eines vereinten Europas bei der Entwicklung der Europäischen Union mit, „die demokratischen, rechtsstaatlichen, sozialen und föderativen Grundsätzen und dem Grundsatz der Subsidiarität verpflichtet ist und einen diesem Grundgesetz im wesentlichen vergleichbaren Grundrechtsschutz gewährleistet". Zu diesem Grundrechtsschutz zählt auch der Schutz einer freiheitlichen und auf Vielfaltssicherung ausgerichteten Kommunikationsverfassung, wie sie in Art. 5 GG gewährleistet ist. Ob auch ein positives Medien-Ordnungsgebot auf Ebene der EU für die Vertiefung der Integrationsbereitschaft Deutschlands verfassungsrechtlich vorgegeben ist, erscheint indessen fraglich, da sich gerade auch im Medienföderalismus die föderativen Grundsätze spiegeln, auf deren Beibehaltung das Integrationsprogramm des Grundgesetzes verpflichtet ist. Für die Begründung der Europäischen Union sowie für Änderungen ihrer vertraglichen Grundlagen und vergleichbare Regelungen, durch die dieses Grundgesetz seinem Inhalt nach geändert oder ergänzt wird oder solche Änderungen oder Ergänzungen ermöglicht werden, gilt zudem nach Art. 23 Abs. 1 Satz 3 GG dessen Artikel 79 Abs. 2 und 3. Da nach Art. 79 Abs. 3 GG eine Änderung des Grundgesetzes, durch welche die Gliederung des Bundes in Länder oder die in den Artikeln 1 und 20 GG niedergelegten Grundsätze berührt werden, unzulässig ist, spricht auch dies an der Schnittstelle von unionsrechtlicher Integrationsperspektive und verfassungsrevisionsfesten Grundnormen des Grundgesetzes mit Blick auf die Bedeutung der Medienordnung für das demokratische und föderative Verfassungsverständnis des Grundgesetzes für eine Reserve zumindest des deutschen Verfassungsrechts gegenüber einer abschließenden positiven Ordnung der Medien in der EU und ihren Mitgliedstaaten durch die EU. In dritten mitgliedstaatlichen Verfassungsordnungen dürfte ein vergleichbarer Vorbehalt bestehen.

---

tutionalisierungsprozeß: Wechselseitige Rezeption, konstitutionelle Evolution und föderale Verflechtung, S. 230 ff., 251 ff.

Solange und soweit die Herrschaft über die Finalität des Integrationsprogramms qua Verfassungsrecht bei den Mitgliedstaaten liegt,[36] was – wie im Folgenden aufgezeigt wird – im Ansatz auch durch die Rechtsordnung der EU selbst anerkannt wird, können die Mitgliedstaaten nur einem europäischen Integrationsprogramm zustimmen, das sich in vorhersehbaren Bahnen entwickelt. Dies gilt auch in Bezug auf medienregulatorische Gleise des Integrationsprogramms. In Deutschland beschreibt das Bundesverfassungsgericht diese Anforderung mit dem Begriff der „Bestimmbarkeit": Hoheitsrechte dürfen danach nur zur Umsetzung eines hinreichend bestimmbar festgelegten Integrationsprogramms übertragen werden.[37] Auch in Bezug auf eine Vertiefung der Medienregulierung muss dieses Integrationsprogramm hinreichend bestimmt sein – ungeachtet der Medienregulierung wie europäischem Integrationsprogramm gemeinsamen Facette des Erfordernisses der Adaptionskraft für dynamischen Wandel.

3. Einheitlichkeit und Vorrang des Unionsrechts vs. verfassungsgerichtliche Kontrollreserve von Mitgliedstaaten

Der Reichweite des primärrechtlich definierten Integrationsprogramms der EU in Bezug auf Möglichkeiten der Medienregulierung kommt Bedeutung nicht zuletzt auch für den Fall der Kollision von mitgliedstaatlicher Vielfaltssicherung und etwaiger positiver Integration über eigenes Vielfaltsrecht der EU und/oder negativer Integration über Schrankensetzungen für die Vielfaltssicherung der Mitgliedstaaten durch das Binnenmarkt- und das Wettbewerbsrecht der EU zu. Insoweit kann sich auch Vielfaltssicherung im Feld einer Kollision von nationalem Recht und Europarecht bewegen.

Der Europäische Gerichtshof (EuGH) hat in seiner Judikatur schon früh als einen Grundpfeiler der Gemeinschaftsrechtsordnung als Rechtsordnung sui generis den Grundsatz des Vorrangs des Gemeinschafts-, nun-

---

36 In einer Reihe von Mitgliedstaaten bedarf es im Zuge dieses Verständnisses ausdrücklicher Verfassungsänderungen, bevor der Staat einer wesentlichen Erweiterung oder Vertiefung der europäischen Integration zustimmen darf; vgl. *Gundel* in: EuR 1998, 371, 378 f.; *Huber* in: VVDStRL 2001, 194, 215 f.; *Kirchhof*, Die rechtliche Struktur der Europäischen Union als Staatenverbund, S. 898 Fn. 15; *Puttler* in: EuR 2004, 669, 672.
37 Vgl. BVerfGE 89, 155 (184 ff, 187) (Maastricht); vgl. auch Dänischer Oberster Gerichtshof, Urteil vom 6,4.1998 (Maastricht), Ziffer 9.2, deutsche Übersetzung in EuGRZ 1999, 49, 50.

B. Primärrechtlicher Rahmen zur Kompetenzabgrenzung

mehr Unionsrechts – je nach Betrachtungsweise – identifiziert bzw. konstruiert, nach dem jedwedes primäres und sekundäres Recht der EU Vorrang vor mitgliedstaatlichem Recht unabhängig von dessen Rang beansprucht, mithin auch Vorrang vor nationalem Verfassungs- einschließlich Recht des Grundrechtsschutzes.[38] Im Unterschied zu den Verfassungen einiger Mitgliedstaaten und zum geplanten Europäischen Verfassungsvertrag[39] enthält das deutsche Grundgesetz zwar – ebenso wie im Übrigen die europäischen Verträge EUV[40] und AEUV[41] nach dem Vertrag von Lissabon – keine ausdrückliche Kollisionsnorm für Konflikte zwischen deutschem Recht, insbesondere deutschem Verfassungsrecht, und Europarecht. Das Bundesverfassungsgericht erkennt in seiner Judikatur allerdings einen Vorrang des Europarechts gleichfalls an – allerdings nur grundsätzlich und mit anderer Begründung.[42] Es ist mit Blick auf die herausgehobene verfassungsrechtliche Bedeutung des Vielfaltsschutzes in der deutschen Verfassungsordnung daher nicht schon vom Ansatz her völlig ausgeschlossen, dass sich auch mit Blick auf Vielfaltssicherung Vorrangfragefragestellungen stellen können – ebenso wie bei dritten Mitgliedstaaten der EU, deren Vorranganerkennung in Bezug auf das Unionsrecht durch verfassungsrechtliche Grenzen eingehegt ist –, mag auch die potentielle Kollisionsursache wie auch deren Auflösung von Mitgliedstaat zu Mitgliedstaat unterschiedlich sein.[43]

---

38 Vgl. z.B. EuGH, Rs. 6/64, *Costa / ENEL*, Rn. 8 ff.; Rs.11/70, *Internationale Handelsgesellschaft mbH / Einfuhr- und Vorratsstelle für Getreide und Futtermittel*, Rn. 3; Rs. 106/77, *Staatliche Finanzverwaltung / S.p.A. Simmenthal*, Rn. 17 ff. (st. Rspr.).
39 Dessen Art. I-6 lautete: „Die Verfassung und das von den Organen der Union in Ausübung der der Union übertragenen Zuständigkeiten gesetzte Recht haben Vorrang vor dem Recht der Mitgliedstaaten".
40 Konsolidierte Fassung des Vertrags über die Europäische Union (EUV), EU ABl. C 326, 26.10.2012, S. 13–390, https://eur-lex.europa.eu/legal-content/DE/TXT/?uri=celex%3A12012M%2FTXT.
41 Konsolidierte Fassung des Vertrags über die Arbeitsweise der Europäischen Union (AEUV), EU ABl. C 326, 26.10.2012, S. 47–390, https://eur-lex.europa.eu/legal-content/DE/TXT/?uri=celex%3A12012E%2FTXT.
42 Das BVerfG leitet diesen Vorrang – anders als der EuGH – nicht aus der Rechtsnatur der Gemeinschaft als autonomer Rechtsordnung ab, sondern stützt ihn auf den deutschen Rechtsanwendungsbefehl. Vgl. BVerfGE 73, 339 (374 f.); dagegen *Pernice* in: VVDStRL 2001, 148, 183 ff. Zudem ist der Vorrang aus Sicht des BVerfG durch die Grenzen der Ermächtigungsnorm des GG beschränkt, greift mithin dort nicht, wo die grundlegenden Strukturprinzipien des Grundgesetzes und der verfassungsrevisionsfeste Kern des Art. 79 Abs. 3 GG in Rede stehen. Vgl. zum Ganzen *Puttler* in: EuR 2004, 669, 684.
43 Vgl. *Puttler* in: EuR 2004, 669, 684.

Aus Sicht des BVerfG beruht auch der europarechtliche Anwendungsvorrang seit jeher auf einer, nunmehr in Art. 23 Abs. 1 GG verankerten verfassungsrechtlichen Ermächtigung, so dass er für in Deutschland ausgeübte europäische Hoheitsgewalt, einschließlich der Kontrolle medienregulatorischer Tätigkeiten der Länder, nur so weit reichen kann, wie die Bundesrepublik ihr im Vertrag zugestimmt hat und verfassungsrechtlich zustimmen durfte. Diesbezüglich bestehen aus Sicht des BVerfG drei Kontrollvorbehalte:

a) hinsichtlich des europäischen Grundrechtsschutzes: Insoweit unterliegt das verfassungsgerichtliche Kontrollpotential aus Karlsruher Perspektive nur solange und insoweit einer Selbstbeschränkung, als auf europäischer Ebene ein dem deutschen Standard generell vergleichbarer Grundrechtsschutz gewährleistet wird;
b) hinsichtlich der europäischen Kompetenzausübung („Ultra-Vires-Kontrolle"). Hier bestanden bis zur Entscheidung des BVerfG in Sachen Staatsanleihekäufe der Europäischen Zentralbank (EZB) vom 5. Mai 2020[44] scheinbar unüberwindbare Hürden einer Durchbrechung des Anwendungsvorrangs des Unionsrechts in seiner Anwendung und Auslegung durch die Gerichtsbarkeit der EU, als das BVerfG in formeller Hinsicht eine Vorlage an den EuGH und in materieller Hinsicht eine offensichtliche Kompetenzüberschreitung, die im Ergebnis zu einer strukturellen Kompetenzverschiebung im Verhältnis zwischen EU und Mitgliedstaaten führt, zu Voraussetzungen der Feststellung eines „ausbrechenden Rechtsakts" der EU machte;
c) hinsichtlich der Verfassungsidentität des deutschen Grundgesetzes, die in Deutschland in der sog. Ewigkeitsklausel des Art. 79 Abs. 3 GG zum Ausdruck kommt und Kernbereiche von Demokratie und Rechtsstaatlichkeit einschließlich des Menschenwürdegehalts der Grundrechte schützt.[45]

---

44 BVerfG, Urteil des Zweiten Senats vom 05. Mai 2020, 2 BvR 859/15, Rn. 1–237, http://www.bverfg.de/e/rs20200505_2bvr085915.html.
45 Vgl. *Calliess* in: NVwZ 2019, 684, 689 ff.

B. Primärrechtlicher Rahmen zur Kompetenzabgrenzung

4. Ultra vires-Handeln, fehlende Kompetenz-Kompetenz der EU und das Prinzip der begrenzten Ermächtigung

a. Das Prinzip begrenzter Ermächtigung und seine Bedeutung für die Medienregulierung

Die EU verfügt – im Unterschied zu einem Staat – über keine Kompetenz-Kompetenz. Sie ist mithin auch nicht imstande, sich selbst eine legislative, administrativ-exekutive oder judikative Regulierungskompetenz in Bezug auf Medien im Allgemeinen und Medienvielfalt im Besonderen zu schaffen. Vielmehr darf die EU nach dem in Art. 5 Abs. 1 Satz 1, Absatz 2 EUV verankerten „Grundsatz der begrenzten Einzelermächtigung" nur innerhalb der Grenzen der Zuständigkeiten tätig werden, die die Mitgliedstaaten ihr in den Verträgen – EUV und AEUV – zur Verwirklichung der darin niedergelegten Ziele übertragen haben.[46] Alle der Union nicht in den Verträgen übertragenen Zuständigkeiten verbleiben nach Art. 4 Abs. 1, Artikel 5 Abs. 2 Satz 2 EUV bei den Mitgliedstaaten. Diese primärrechtlichen Regelungen bestätigen inzident, dass vor Beginn des europäischen Integrationsprozesses ursprünglich alle Befugnisse bei den Mitgliedstaaten lagen und damit den Grundsatz der „Allzuständigkeit" der Mitgliedstaaten für hoheitliches Handeln – ungeachtet der jeweiligen innerstaatlichen Kompetenzabgrenzung in föderal verfassten Mitgliedstaaten bzw. Staaten mit kommunaler Selbstverwaltung.

Diese grundlegende Kompetenzabgrenzung nach dem Prinzip der begrenzten Einzelermächtigung betrifft das Verhältnis der EU zu den Mitgliedstaaten, ist aber offenkundig auch für die Reichweite der Handlungsmöglichkeiten der EU-Organe bedeutsam. Das Handeln der EU und ihrer Organe muss in den Grenzen ihrer Befugnisse bleiben: So verfolgt die EU nach Art. 3 Abs. 6 EUV ihre Ziele mit geeigneten Mitteln nur entsprechend den Zuständigkeiten, die ihr in den Verträgen übertragen sind. Jedes Organ der EU handelt gemäß Art. 13 Abs. 2 Satz 1 EUV wiederum nur nach Maßgabe der ihm in den Verträgen zugewiesenen Befugnisse nach den Verfahren, Bedingungen und Zielen, die in den Verträgen festgelegt sind. Wird eine dieser beiden Grundnormen verletzt, besteht u.U. die Möglichkeit einer Nichtigkeitsklage beim EuGH.

Nach dem Prinzip begrenzter Ermächtigung ist für jeden Rechtsakt der EU – d.h. auch für nicht verbindliche Rechtsakte – nicht nur eine aus-

---

46 Vgl. hierzu jüngst auch *Nielsen*, Die Medienvielfalt als Aspekt der Wertesicherung der EU, S. 35 ff.

drückliche, sondern auch die richtige Kompetenzgrundlage zu suchen.[47] Die Suche nach der korrekten Kompetenzgrundlage ist fortdauernd bedeutsam, weil die Wahl der richtigen Kompetenzgrundlage unter anderem auch über den Abstimmungsmodus im Rat der EU – Einstimmigkeit mit „Vetomöglichkeit" eines jeden Mitgliedstaats oder Mehrheit – wie auch über die konkrete Ausformung des institutionellen Gleichgewichts beim jeweiligen Rechtsakt bestimmen kann. Insoweit können sich Probleme vertikaler Kompetenzkonflikte (zwischen Mitgliedstaaten und EU) mit Fragen horizontaler Kompetenzkonflikte (zwischen den am Rechtsetzungsverfahren beteiligten EU-Organen) vermengen kann.[48]

Weder EUV noch AEUV enthalten allerdings einen Negativkatalog von umfassend vom EU-Recht ausgenommenen Bereichen. Es gibt in den europäischen Verträgen weder eine *exception culturelle*, d.h. eine kulturelle Bereichsausnahme im Allgemeinen, noch eine auf Medien bezogene Bereichsausnahme im Besonderen. Zudem fehlt auch eine Art. 4 Abs. 2 EUV vergleichbare Regelung für die Medienregulierung: Nach dieser Bestimmung fällt „die nationale Sicherheit weiterhin in die alleinige Verantwortung der einzelnen Mitgliedstaaten".[49] Dies gilt für die Medienregulierung bei systematischer Auslegung nicht in entsprechender Weise. Das Prinzip

---

47 Vgl. z.B. *Breier* in: EuR 1995, 47, 47 ff.; *Ruffert* in: Jura 1994, 635, 635 ff.
48 Vgl. *Calliess* in: Berliner Online-Beiträge zum Europarecht 25 (2005), S. 3; *Nettesheim* in: EuR 1993, 243, 243 ff.
49 In Bezug auf Art. 4 Abs. 2 EUV hat der EuGH jüngst – in Anknüpfung an frühere Judikatur – in datenschutzrechtlichem Zusammenhang erneut bestätigt, dass es zwar Sache der Mitgliedstaaten der EU ist, ihre wesentlichen Sicherheitsinteressen zu definieren und Maßnahmen zur Gewährleistung ihrer inneren und äußeren Sicherheit zu ergreifen, dass aber die bloße Tatsache, dass eine nationale Maßnahme zum Schutz der nationalen Sicherheit getroffen wurde, nicht die Unanwendbarkeit des Unionsrechts zur Folge haben und die Mitgliedstaaten von der erforderlichen Beachtung dieses Rechts befreien kann. Im Ergebnis folgt der EuGH dabei einer engen Auslegung des Art. 4 Abs. 2 EUV unter möglichst umfassender Schonung von Akten des Sekundärrechts, gegen deren Anwendbarkeit Art. 4 Abs. 2 EUV geltend gemacht wird (vgl. EuGH, Urt. v. 6. 10. 2020, Rs. C-623/17, Privacy International, ECLI:EU:C:2020:790 Rn. 44 ff.). Zwar anerkennt der EuGH, dass die Bedeutung des in Art. 4 Abs. 2 EUV verankerten Ziels der Wahrung der nationalen Sicherheit über die Bedeutung anderer auch im Datenschutzrecht der EU zur Rechtfertigung von Ausnahmen zu datenschutzrechtlichen Verpflichtungen anerkannten Zielen wie der Bekämpfung der Kriminalität im Allgemeinen, auch der schweren Kriminalität, und des Schutzes der öffentlichen Sicherheit hinausgeht. Vorbehaltlich der Einhaltung der anderen in Art. 52 Abs. 1 der GRC festgelegten Anforderungen sei das Ziel der Wahrung der nationalen Sicherheit daher geeignet, Maßnahmen zu rechtfertigen, die schwerwiegendere Eingriffe in die Grundrechte beinhalteten als diejenigen, die durch diese anderen

B. Primärrechtlicher Rahmen zur Kompetenzabgrenzung

begrenzter Ermächtigung enthält mithin nicht per se eine Medienregulierung der EU schon im Ansatz hemmende Wirkung. Je stärker Medienregulierung der EU allerdings in einer für die Vielfaltsregulierung relevanten Weise erfolgt, um so höher sind zumindest die Darlegungslasten der EU in Bezug auf die Wahrung der Klauseln der europäischen Verträge, die auf Schonung mitgliedstaatlicher Regulierungsspielräume ausgerichtet sind.

Die Frage, wer darüber entscheidet, ob sich Organe der EU beim Erlass eines Unionsaktes noch im Rahmen des primärrechtlich vorstrukturierten Integrationsprogramms gehalten oder *ultra vires* gehandelt haben, muss aus europarechtlicher Perspektive letztverbindlich durch den EuGH entschieden werden, um Vorrang wie Einheitlichkeit der Unionsrechtsordnung sicherzustellen. Dieses europarechtliche Verständnis war indessen zumindest beim BVerfG seit jeher nie uneingeschränkt anerkannt. Dem Gebot der Rücksichtnahme auf die „Herrschaft" über die Verträge, wie sie aus Sicht der Karlsruher Verfassungsrichter grundgesetzlich aufgegeben war, tragen zwar europarechtliches wie verfassungsgerichtliches Verständnis insoweit einmütig Rechnung, als sie ein Handeln der EU *ultra-vires* als rechtswidrig einordnen. Indessen herrscht über die jeweiligen Grenzziehungen des Integrationsprogramms wie über die Frage, wer die Grenzen abschließend definieren darf, nicht zuletzt im Zuge der Entscheidung des BVerfG zum EZB-Programm zum Ankauf von Staatsanleihen fortdauernder und neuerlich intensivierter Streit. Schon vor seiner EZB-Entscheidung betonte das BVerfG, dass es wegen seiner verfassungsrechtlichen Aufgabenstellung dazu verpflichtet sei, sich für besondere Ausnahmefälle eine letztverbindliche Prüfungsbefugnis vorzubehalten.[50] Es kann nicht ausgeschlossen werden, dass eine solche Prüfungsbefugnis bei einer Verdichtung der Medienregulierung der EU in Richtung auf vollharmonisierte digitale Vielfaltssicherung auch eine medienbezogene Ausrichtung oder gar Ausdehnung erfährt, nachdem die spezifische Frage, ob die in der damaligen EWG-Fernsehrichtlinie geregelten Förderinstrumente für europäische Werke und unabhängige Produktionen noch von der Binnenmarktkompe-

---

Ziele gerechtfertigt werden könnten. Um jedoch dem Erfordernis der Verhältnismäßigkeit zu genügen, wonach sich die Ausnahmen und Einschränkungen des Schutzes personenbezogener Daten im Rahmen des unbedingt Notwendigen halten müssen, müssten nationale Rechtsvorschriften, die einen Eingriff in die in den Artikeln 7 und 8 der Charta verankerten Grundrechte darstellen, den Anforderungen der Transparenz und der Verhältnismäßigkeit genügen (vgl. ibidem, Rn. 74 ff.).

50 Vgl. BVerfGE 73, 339 (370) (Solange II); 75, 223 (234) (Kloppenburg).

tenz der EU erfasst sind, nach dem Urteil des BVerfG vom 22. März 1995[51] ihre integrationsrechtliche Bedeutung weithin eingebüßt hat.

Allerdings ist in diesem Zusammenhang von Beginn an zu berücksichtigen, dass die Kompetenzordnung des EU-Rechts digitalisierungsfest fest: Digitale Wandlungen schaffen nicht zusätzliche Kompetenztitel der EU. Umgekehrt sind vorhandene Kompetenztitel aber auch nicht auf die Bewältigung von Problemlagen hin begrenzt, die zum Zeitpunkt der Verabschiedung der Gründungsverträge bekannt waren. Vorgaben des *originalism* bzw. des historisch-traditionalen *Textualismus*[52] sind der Interpretationsmethodik des EU-Rechts fremd. Ein solches Verständnis versteinerter Auslegung der Ermächtigungen der EU lässt sich zwar mit einer historischen, nicht aber mit einer telelogischen Auslegung in Deckung bringen. Die Auslegung des primären EU-Rechts ist stets eine Auslegung in der Zeit und mit Offenheit für neue Herausforderungen. Eine solche digitalisierungsorientierte Auslegungsoffenheit findet ihre Grenzen aber – vergleichbar der völkerrechtsfreundlichen Auslegung des EU-Rechts und der Europa- und verfassungskonformen Auslegung nationalen Rechts – im Wortlaut der Kompetenznormen.

b. Die Kontrolle der Einhaltung des Prinzips der begrenzten Ermächtigung durch das Demokratiegebot in der Auslegung des BVerfG

Durch die Möglichkeit, Hoheitsrechte auf die EU zu übertragen, wie sie Art. 23 GG vorsieht, werden u.U. nicht nur Aufgaben der parlamentarischen Ebene des Bundes, sondern auch solche der Länder auf die supranationalen Organe der EU übertragen, so dass bestimmte Aufgaben in der Folge nicht mehr von den Abgeordneten des Landesparlamente, sei es beim Erlass autonomen Landesrechts der Medienregulierung, sei es anläss-

---

51 Vgl. BVerfGE 92, 203 (242 ff.); hierzu *Bethge*, Deutsche Bundesstaatlichkeit und Europäische Union. Bemerkungen über die Entscheidung des Bundesverfassungsgerichts zur EG-Fernsehrichtlinie, S. 55 ff.; *Deringer* in: ZUM 1995, 316, 316 ff.; *Gerkrath* in: RTDE 1995, 539, 539 ff.; *Kresse/Heinze* in: ZUM 1995, 394, 394 ff.; *Martín y Pérez de Nanclares* in: Revista de Instituciones Europeas 1995, 887, 887 ff.; *Müller-Terpitz*, Ein Karlsruher "Orakel" zum Bundesstaat im europäischen Staatenverbund, S. 568 ff.; *Trautwein* in: ZUM 1995, 614, 614 ff.; *Winkelmann* in: DöV 1996, 1, 1 ff.
52 Vgl. hierzu für Linien der Auslegung der US-Verfassung im Supreme Court *Dregger*, Die Verfassungsinterpretation am US-Supreme Court, S. 40 ff.; *Riecken*, Verfassungsgerichtsbarkeit in der Demokratie, S. 98 f.

B. Primärrechtlicher Rahmen zur Kompetenzabgrenzung

lich der Ratifikation von medienbezogenen Staatsverträgen wahrgenommen werden können. Die Staatsgewalt geht in solchen Fällen der Übertragung von legislativer Gestaltungsmacht nicht mehr oder zumindest nur noch eingeschränkt vom Volke aus.

Diesem demokratietheoretischen Problem der Integrationsoffenheit des Grundgesetzes hat das BVerfG erstmals in seiner Maastricht-Entscheidung durch die Anerkennung einer auf die Verletzung des Demokratieprinzips gestützten Verfassungsbeschwerdebefugnis anlässlich von Rechtsakten der Übertragung von Hoheitsgewalt auf die EU Rechnung getragen. Das BVerfG führt dazu aus, dass die Bundesrepublik durch das Demokratieprinzip zwar nicht daran gehindert werde Teil einer zwischenstaatlichen Gemeinschaft zu sein. Voraussetzung dafür sei lediglich die Legitimation und Einflussnahme durch die Bevölkerung auch auf supranationaler Ebene (innerhalb des Staatenverbundes).[53] Zudem weist das BVerfG auf das Verhältnis von Art. 23 Abs. 1 Satz 3 GG zu Art. 79 Abs. 3 GG hin: Die grundgesetzliche Öffnungsmöglichkeit für eine europäische Integration sei an den verfassungsrevisionsfesten Kern des Art. 79 Abs. 3 GG gebunden, welcher die Grenzen der Ermächtigung für das Mitwirken bei der Entwicklung der Europäischen Union aufzeige. So werde eine Diskrepanz zwischen Art. 38 GG und Art. 23 GG nach Ausführungen des Gerichts vermieden.[54]

Diese vom BVerfG mit Blick auf die Übertragung von Kompetenzen des Bundes entwickelte Judikatur ist mit Blick auf die Übertragung von Kompetenzen der Länder in gleicher Weise bedeutsam. Zum revisionsfesten, einer Abänderung auch in europarechtlichen Zusammenhängen entzogenen Grundstruktur der deutschen Verfassungsordnung dürfte – nicht zuletzt auch mit Blick auf die verfassungshistorische Dimension des „Nie wieder" totalitärer Herrschaft – das Element der föderalen Brechung von Medienregulierung zählen. Eine Öffnung des deutschen Verfassungsstaates für eine Vollharmonisierung der Medienregulierung durch die EU, wie sie namentlich bei Abkehr von der bisherigen Richtlinienregulierung mit Fähigkeit zur Berücksichtigung mitgliedstaatlicher Besonderheiten gegeben ist, wäre daher – auch im Blick auf die demokratische Relevanz des Medienföderalismus – ein mit erheblichem verfassungsrechtlichem, insbesondere verfassungsgerichtliche Risikopotential verbundener Vorgang.

Mit seinem Hinweis auf den Konnex zwischen Art. 23, 38 und 79 Abs. 3 GG geht im Übrigen ein besonderer Hinweis des BVerfG auf das Erforder-

---

53 Vgl. BVerfGE 89, 155 (184).
54 Vgl. BVerfGE 89, 155 (179).

nis einher, dass die EU keine Kompetenz-Kompetenz besitzt sowie das Prinzip der begrenzten Einzelermächtigung einhält.[55] In diesem Zusammenhang betont das BVerfG, dass Rechtsakte der Union, welche nicht vom Zustimmungsgesetz gedeckt sind, keine innerstaatliche Verbindlichkeit besitzen und deshalb nicht anzuwenden sind.[56] Dementsprechend prüfe das Bundesverfassungsgericht, ob Rechtsakte der europäischen Einrichtungen und Organe sich in den Grenzen der ihnen eingeräumten Hoheitsrechte halten oder aus ihnen ausbrechen.[57] (vgl.).Darüber hinaus hält es sich im Maastricht-Urteil die Befugnis vor, Handlungen der Unionsorgane daraufhin zu überprüfen, ob sie sich im Einklang mit dem Zustimmungsgesetz befinden.

5. Medienregulierung und der Zuständigkeitskatalog der EU

a. Einführung

Ein formaler Schutzmechanismus zur Sicherung des Prinzips der begrenzten Ermächtigung und zur Abwehr von Entwicklungstendenzen in Richtung auf eine Kompetenz-Kompetenz der EU ist die erstmalig im Vertrag von Lissabon vorgenommene Kategorisierung und Klassifizierung der Zuständigkeiten der Europäischen Union in ausschließliche und geteilte Zuständigkeiten sowie Zuständigkeiten für Unterstützungs-, Koordinierungs- oder Ergänzungsmaßnahmen.[58]

Der Europäische Rat hatte in seiner „Erklärung von Lacken" den Verfassungskonvent ausdrücklich mandatiert, eine bessere Aufteilung und Festlegung der Zuständigkeiten in der Europäischen Union zu entwickeln.[59] Dabei sollte zugleich geprüft werden, wie eine „schleichende Ausuferung der

---

55 Vgl. BVerfGE 89, 155 (181).
56 Vgl. BVerfGE 89, 155 (195).
57 Vgl. BVerfGE 58, 1 (30 f.); 75, 223 (235, 242); 89, 155 (188); sowie *Moench/Ruttloff* in: Rengeling/Middeke/Gellermann (Hrsg.), § 36 Rn. 28 f., 46 ff.
58 Vgl. BVerfGE 123, 267 (382) unter Bezugnahme auf *Rossi*, Die Kompetenzverteilung zwischen der Europäischen Gemeinschaft und ihren Mitgliedstaaten, in: Scholz, Europa als Union des Rechts -- Eine notwendige Zwischenbilanz im Prozeß der Vertiefung und Erweiterung, 1999, S. 196, 201; vgl. im Übrigen z.B. auch *Folz* in: Gamper u.a. (Hrsg.), S. 641 ff.; *Nettesheim* in: von Bogdandy/Bast (Hrsg.), S. 415 ff.
59 Erklärung von Laeken zur Zukunft der Europäischen Union, Anlage I zu den Schlussfolgerungen des Vorsitzes, Europäischer Rat (Laeken), 14. und 15. Dezember 2001, SN 300/1/01 REV 1, S. 21.

B. Primärrechtlicher Rahmen zur Kompetenzabgrenzung

Zuständigkeiten der Union" und ihr „Vordringen in die Bereiche der ausschließlichen Zuständigkeit der Mitgliedstaaten und [...] der Regionen" verhindert werden könnte.[60] Zugleich sollte der Konvent in seine Überlegungen aber auch einbeziehen, dass die EU auf neue Herausforderungen und Entwicklungen reagieren und sich neue Politikbereiche erschließen können müsse.[61] Zu diesen Megatrends zählt zweifelsohne auch die Digitalisierung – auch in ihren Auswirkungen auf das Medien-Ökosystem.

Selbst wenn der im Ergebnis des Verfassungskonvents entwickelte Verfassungsvertrag scheiterte, knüpft nunmehr der Vertrag von Lissabon an diese kompetenziellen Überlegungen an und erläutert ausdrücklich die Aufteilung der Zuständigkeiten zwischen der EU und ihren Mitgliedstaaten.[62] Diese Zuständigkeiten sind in drei Hauptkategorien unterteilt:

- ausschließliche Zuständigkeiten;
- geteilte Zuständigkeiten und
- unterstützende Zuständigkeiten.

Die Medien finden weder in diesen Zuständigkeitskatalogen der EU noch an anderer Stelle der europäischen Verträge als solche eine ausdrückliche Erwähnung.[63] Nur in der Grundrechte-Charta der EU findet sich eine Durchbrechung dieser europarechtlichen Zurückhaltung in Bezug auf Zuständigkeitszuordnungen zu Gunsten der EU für die Medien bzw. deren Regulierung. Dies ist auch deshalb bemerkenswert, weil Verfassungen von Mitgliedstaaten der EU, die föderal strukturiert sind, eine auch zuständigkeitsbezogene Medienregulierung vertraut ist[64] bzw. – wie in Deutschland – in einer auch dem europäischen Verfassungsgesetzgeber vertrauten Wei-

---

60 Erklärung von Lacken, aaO (Fn. 63), S. 22; zur Kritik an einer allmählichen Kompetenzerweiterung der EU z.B. BVerfGE 89, 155 (210); *Rupp* in: JZ 2003, 18, 18 f.
61 Erklärung von Lacken, aaO (Fn. 63), S. 22; zum Ganzen vgl. *Puttler* in: EuR 2004, 669, 686.
62 Vgl. hierzu jüngst auch *Nielsen*, Die Medienvielfalt als Aspekt der Wertesicherung der EU, S. 39 ff.
63 Vgl. hierzu auch *Nielsen*, Die Medienvielfalt als Aspekt der Wertesicherung der EU, S. 47 f.
64 Der Erlass von Regelungen im Bereich des Rundfunks (und zwar sowohl in inhaltlicher als auch in technischer Hinsicht) fällt nach der österreichischen Verfassungsordnung in die Kompetenz des Bundes. Dies ergibt sich zum einen aus Art. 10 Abs. 1 Ziff. 9 B-VG "Post- und Fernmeldewesen", zum anderen aus Art. I des Bundesverfassungsgesetzes über die Sicherung der Unabhängigkeit des Rundfunks (vom 10. Juli 1974, StF: BGBl. Nr. 396/1974 (NR: GP XIII AB 1265 S. 111. BR: S. 334.)), wonach "...nähere Bestimmungen für den Rundfunk und seine Organisation bundesgesetzlich festzulegen" sind. Das Bundesverfassungsgesetz über die Sicherung der Unabhängigkeit des Rundfunks zielt darauf ab, den Rundfunk

se geklärt ist, dass nicht die zentrale staatliche Ebene, sondern die Gliedeinheiten des Bundesstaates für die Medienregulierung kompetent sind. Schon dies spricht – unbeschadet von etwaigen grundrechtsbezogenen Schutzpflichten – für eine Zurückhaltung der europäischen Verträge bei der Einräumung medienbezogener Regelungskompetenzen der EU. Allerdings schließt es die im Folgenden darzustellenden Zugriffe von EU-Zuständigkeiten auch auf das Feld der Medienregulierung nicht aus.

Die durch die Kategorisierung der Zuständigkeiten vermittelte Transparenz wird zwar im Übrigen nicht zuletzt dadurch eingeschränkt, dass auch weiterhin ungeschriebene Kompetenzen gibt[65] und dass die sowohl von den Mitgliedstaaten als auch von der Europäischen Union beanspruchten "parallelen" Zuständigkeiten im Vertrag von Lissabon nicht eindeutig einer Kategorie zugeordnet werden und die sogenannte Methode der offenen Koordinierung unerwähnt bleibt. „Diese Abweichungen von dem systematisierenden Grundansatz berühren jedoch das Prinzip der begrenzten Einzelermächtigung nicht und stellen nach Art und Umfang auch nicht das Ziel klarer Kompetenzabgrenzung in Frage".[66]

b. Ausschließliche Zuständigkeiten der EU und Medienregulierung

Übertragen die Verträge der EU für einen bestimmten Bereich eine ausschließliche Zuständigkeit, so kann nach Art. 2 Abs. 1 AEUV nur die Union gesetzgeberisch tätig werden und verbindliche Rechtsakte erlassen; die Mitgliedstaaten dürfen in einem solchen Fall nur tätig werden, wenn sie von der Union hierzu ermächtigt werden, oder um Rechtsakte der Union durchzuführen. Zwar weist der in Art. 3 AEUV geregelte Katalog ausschließlicher Zuständigkeiten keine ausdrückliche Bezugnahme zu Medien auf. Allerdings ist eine Relevanz dieses Katalogs auch für die Medienregulierung insoweit nicht von vornherein ausgeschlossen, als die EU

- nach Art. 3 Abs. 1 Buchst. a) AEUV die ausschließliche Zuständigkeit im Bereich der Zollunion gemäß Art. 31 f. AEUV,

---

zur "öffentlichen Aufgabe zu erklären", die unter Wahrung der Prinzipien der Objektivität, der Unparteilichkeit und der Meinungsvielfalt zu erfüllen ist.
65 Vgl. z.B. *Nettesheim* in: von Bogdandy/Bast (Hrsg.), S. 415, 433 ff.; *Rossi* in: Calliess/Ruffert Art. 352 AEUV, Rn. 52; *Weber* in: Blanke/Mangiameli, Art. 5 EUV, Rn. 28; *Dony*, Droit de l'Union européenne, Rn. 120 ff.
66 BVerfGE 123, 267 (382 f.).

B. Primärrechtlicher Rahmen zur Kompetenzabgrenzung

- nach Art. 3 Abs. 1 Buchst. b) AEUV die ausschließliche Zuständigkeit im Bereich der Festlegung der für das Funktionieren des Binnenmarkts erforderlichen Wettbewerbsregeln gemäß Kapitel 1 von Titel VII des Dritten Teils des AEUV,
- nach Art. 3 Abs. 1 Buchst. c) AEUV die ausschließliche Zuständigkeit im Bereich der Währungspolitik für die Mitgliedstaaten, deren Währung der Euro ist,[67]

---

[67] § 14 Abs. 1 des Gesetzes über die Deutsche Bundesbank regelt, dass die Deutsche Bundesbank „unbeschadet des Artikels 128 Absatz 1 [AEUV] das ausschließliche Recht (hat), Banknoten im Geltungsbereich dieses Gesetzes auszugeben" und dass auf Euro lautende Banknoten „das einzige unbeschränkte gesetzliche Zahlungsmittel" sind. Der Rundfunkbeitragsstaatsvertrag (RBStV) sieht in § 2 Abs. 1 vor, dass für jede Wohnung deren Inhaber einen Rundfunkbeitrag zu entrichten hat. § 9 Abs. 2 RBStV ermächtigt die Landesrundfunkanstalten die Einzelheiten des Verfahrens zur Leistung des Rundfunkbeitrags durch Satzung zu regeln. Die auf dieser Grundlage erlassenen Satzungen sehen wiederum vor, dass der Beitragsschuldner die Rundfunkbeiträge nur bargeldlos entrichten kann. In dem EuGH vor diesem Hintergrund aktuell vorliegenden Vorabentscheidungsverfahren geht es nunmehr um die Fragen, ob die ausschließliche Zuständigkeit nach Art. 3 Abs. 1 Buchst. c) AEUV das Währungsrecht und die Festlegung der der einheitlichen Währung zukommenden Eigenschaft eines gesetzlichen Zahlungsmittels umfasst, welche Auswirkungen die Eigenschaft eines gesetzlichen Zahlungsmittels, die Euro-Banknoten zukommt, hat und ob und ggf. innerhalb welcher Grenzen in diesem Rahmen die Mitgliedstaaten, deren Währung der Euro ist, nationale Rechtsvorschriften erlassen dürfen, die die Verwendung von Euro-Banknoten beschränken.
In seinen Schlussanträgen lässt Generalanwalt *Pitruzella* im Ergebnis Zweifel erkennen, ob der ausnahmslose Ausschluss der Entrichtung des Rundfunkbeitrages mittels Bargeld im Lichte der Bedeutung der ausschließlichen Zuständigkeit nach Art. 3 Abs. 1 Buchst. c) AEUV für währungsrechtliche Befugnisse rechtfertigbar ist. Denn Begrenzungen für Zahlungen in Euro-Banknoten aus Gründen des öffentlichen Interesses sind seines Erachtens nur dann mit dem im Währungsrecht der EU geschaffenen Begriff der Eigenschaft eines gesetzlichen Zahlungsmittels, die Euro-Banknoten zukommt, vereinbar, wenn sie nicht *de iure* oder *de facto* zur vollständigen Abschaffung der Euro-Banknoten führen, wenn sie aus Gründen des öffentlichen Interesses beschlossen werden und wenn andere rechtliche Mittel für die Begleichung von Geldschulden bestehen. Sie müssen zudem geeignet sein, das verfolgte Ziel des öffentlichen Interesses zu erreichen, und dürfen nicht über das hinausgehen, was zur Erreichung dieses Zieles erforderlich ist. Letzteres bezweifelt der Generalanwalt, sofern bei der Abschaffung der bargeldlosen Zahlungsmöglichkeit die Funktion sozialer Eingliederung, die Bargeld für schutzbedürftige Personen wie z.B. ältere Mitbürger/innen erfüllt, nicht angemessen berücksichtigt worden sein sollte; vgl. Schlussanträge des Generalanwalts vom 29.09.2020, verb. Rs. C-422/19 (Dietrich/HR) und C-423/19 (Häring/HR), ECLI:EU:C:2020:756, Rn. 162 ff.

- nach Art. 3 Abs. 1 Buchst. e) AEUV die ausschließliche Zuständigkeit im Bereich der gemeinsamen Handelspolitik gemäß Art. 207 AEUV und
- nach Art. 3 Abs. 2 AEUV die ausschließliche Zuständigkeit für den Abschluss internationaler Übereinkünfte i.S. des Art. 216 AEUV hat, wenn der Abschluss einer solchen Übereinkunft in einem Gesetzgebungsakt der EU vorgesehen ist, wenn er notwendig ist, damit sie ihre interne Zuständigkeit ausüben kann, oder soweit er gemeinsame Regeln beeinträchtigen oder deren Tragweite verändern könnte.[68]

Die Bedeutung und potentiell mitgliedstaatliche Regelungskompetenzen selbst in Bereichen wie der Bildung oder der Kultur begrenzende einschränkende Tragweite der ausschließlichen Handelskompetenz der EU hat der EuGH in einem Urteil vom 6. Oktober 2020 nochmals im Zusammenhang mit einer – jenseits kompetenzrechtlicher Fragen insbesondere grundrechtlich und in Bezug auf das Wertefundament der EU umstrittenen bildungspolitischen Maßnahme Ungarns hervorgehoben. Der EuGH betonte dort, dass er für die Verhandlung und Entscheidung über Beschwerden zuständig ist, in denen Verstöße gegen das WTO-Recht behauptet werden. In diesem Zusammenhang wies der EuGH nochmals darauf hin, dass jede internationale Vereinbarung, der die EU beitrete, ein integraler Bestandteil des EU-Rechts sei – wie z.B. das Abkommen zur Gründung der WTO, zu dem auch das GATS gehört. Sodann stellte der EuGH hinsichtlich der Beziehung zwischen der ausschließlichen Zuständigkeit der EU im Bereich der gemeinsamen Handelspolitik und der breiten Zuständigkeit der Mitgliedstaaten im Bereich der Bildung klar, dass die im Rahmen des GATS eingegangenen Verpflichtungen, einschließlich der Verpflichtungen im Zusammenhang mit der Liberalisierung des Handels mit privaten Bildungsdiensten, unter die gemeinsame Handelspolitik fallen.[69]

Wenig spricht gegen die Einschätzung, dass der EuGH von dieser Zuordnung, die im Kollisionsfall auf einen uneingeschränkten Vorrang handelspolitischer Verpflichtungen hinauslaufen, bei der Zuordnung von ausschließlicher Handelskompetenz der EU und mitgliedstaatlichen Zuständigkeiten im Bereich der Kultur einschließlich der kultur- und vielfaltsbezogenen Aspekte von Medien kaum abweichen dürfte. Umso wichtiger ist

---

68 Vgl. hierzu *Calliess* in: ders./Ruffert, Art. 3 AEUV, Rn. 5 ff., 14 ff.; *Klamert* in: Kellerbauer/ders./Tomkin, Art. 3 AEUV, Rn. 16 ff.; *Pelka* in: Schwarze, Art. 3 AEUV, Rn. 7 ff., 14 ff.; *Streinz/Mögele* in: Streinz, Art. 3 AEUV, Rn. 4 ff., 11 ff.
69 Vgl. EuGH, Rs. C-66/18, *Kommission/Ungarn*, Rn. 68 ff.

eine kultur- und vielfaltsschonende Begrenzung handelspolitischer Verhandlungsmandate der EU. Dem Risikopotential der ausschließlichen Zuständigkeit der EU für die gemeinsame Handelspolitik tragen die Mitgliedstaaten dementsprechend durch eine regelmäßige Herausnahme audiovisueller Dienstleistungen aus dem seitens des Rates der EU erteilten Verhandlungsmandats für die EU Rechnung.[70]

Die damit im Ergebnis verbundene Herausnahme audiovisueller Dienstleistungen aus dem Anwendungsbereich der Freihandelsregeln schützt die kulturelle Souveränität der Mitgliedstaaten. Dieser weitreichende Schutz ist allerdings mit einem nicht unerheblichen Manko versehen: Denn mit der seitens der organisierten Kultur geforderten und für den Bereich nicht zuletzt von Rundfunk und publizistisch wirksamen Telemedien erreichten umfassenden Herausnahme des Kultur-Sektors aus den Handelsabkommen sind zugleich Risiken mit Blick auf die Förderung demokratischer Diskussionskultur im Zeitalter von Globalisierung einerseits, Erstarken von populistischen Tendenzen und neuen digitalen Formen der Meinungsmanipulation andererseits verbunden.[71]

c. Geteilte Zuständigkeiten der EU und Medienregulierung

Übertragen die Verträge der EU für einen bestimmten Bereich eine mit den Mitgliedstaaten geteilte Zuständigkeit, so können die Union und die Mitgliedstaaten nach Art. 2 Abs. 2 Satz 1 EUV in diesem Bereich gesetzgeberisch tätig werden und verbindliche Rechtsakte erlassen. Die Mitgliedstaaten nehmen ihre Zuständigkeit nach Satz 2 der Regelung wahr, sofern und soweit die EU ihre Zuständigkeit nicht ausgeübt hat. Die Mitgliedstaaten nehmen ihre mit der EU geteilte Zuständigkeit nach Art. 2 Abs. 2 Satz 3 EUV zudem erneut wahr, sofern und soweit die Union entschieden hat, ihre Zuständigkeit nicht mehr auszuüben.

Die EU teilt ihre Zuständigkeit gemäß Art. 4 Abs. 1 AEUV mit den Mitgliedstaaten, wenn ihr die Verträge außerhalb der in den Art. 3 und 6 AEUV genannten Bereiche eine Zuständigkeit übertragen. Weder in Art. 3 noch in Art. 6 AEUV ist eine solche spezifisch auf Medien bezogene Zuständigkeitsregelung zu finden. Zwar weist auch der in Art. 4 Abs. 2 bis 4

---

[70] Vgl. hierzu auch im Kontext des Brexit: *Cole/Ukrow/Etteldorf*, Research for CULT Committee – Audiovisual Sector and Brexit: the Regulatory Environment, S. 14 ff.
[71] Vgl. zum Ganzen *Ukrow*, Ceterum censeo: CETA prohibendam esse? Audiovisuelle Medien im europäisch-kanadischen Freihandelssystem, S. 2 ff.

AEUV geregelte Katalog geteilter Zuständigkeiten keine ausdrückliche Bezugnahme zu Medien auf. Allerdings ist eine Relevanz des Katalogs in Art. 4 Abs. 2 AEUV geregelter Hauptbereiche geteilter Zuständigkeiten auch für die Medienregulierung insoweit nicht von vornherein ausgeschlossen, als die EU

- nach Art. 4 Abs. 2 Buchst. a) AEUV eine geteilte Zuständigkeit im Bereich des Binnenmarktes gemäß Art. 26 Abs. 2 i.V.m. Art. 114 AEUV,
- nach Art. 4 Abs. 2 Buchst. f) AEUV die geteilte Zuständigkeit im Bereich des Verbraucherschutzes gemäß Art. 169 AEUV und
- nach Art. 4 Abs. 2 Buchst. j) AEUV die geteilte Zuständigkeit im Bereich des Raumes der Freiheit, der Sicherheit und des Rechts gemäß Art. 67 ff. AEUV

hat.[72]

Besonders der „Binnenmarkt"-Zuständigkeit der EU kommt in deren bisheriger Rechtsetzung in Bezug auf Medien besonderes Gewicht zu. Die EU erlässt nach Art. 26 Abs. 1 AEUV die erforderlichen Maßnahmen, um nach Maßgabe der einschlägigen Bestimmungen der Verträge den Binnenmarkt zu verwirklichen beziehungsweise dessen Funktionieren zu gewährleisten. Dabei umfasst der Binnenmarkt nach dessen Definition in Art. 26 Abs. 2 AEUV „einen Raum ohne Binnengrenzen, in dem der freie Verkehr von Waren, Personen, Dienstleistungen und Kapital gemäß den Bestimmungen der Verträge gewährleistet ist". Sowohl die AVMD-Richtlinie[73] als auch die E-Commerce-Richtlinie (ECRL)[74] sind auf Kompetenznormen der EU in Bezug auf den freien Dienstleistungsverkehr und die Niederlassungsfreiheit als Teil des Binnenmarktes gestützt. Sie folgten insoweit gefestigter Judikatur des EuGH.

Mit Blick auf die Digitalisierung der Medien wie auch mit Blick auf die Entwicklung neuer Geschäfts- und Kommunikationsmodelle medialer Art

---

72 Vgl. hierzu *Calliess* in: ders./Ruffert, Art. 4 AEUV, Rn. 4 ff., 14, 18; *Klamert* in: Kellerbauer/ders./Tomkin, Art. 4 AEUV, Rn. 3, 8, 12; *Pelka* in: Schwarze, Art. 4 AEUV, Rn. 6, 11, 15.
73 Die Richtlinie 2010/13/EU wie die Änderungsrichtlinie 2018/1808/EU sind „gestützt auf den Vertrag über die Arbeitsweise der Europäischen Union, insbesondere auf Artikel 53 Absatz 1 und Artikel 62". Eingehend zum Regelungsgehalt und zur Zielsetzung Abschnitt D.II.2.
74 Die Richtlinie 2000/31/EG ist „gestützt auf den Vertrag zur Gründung der Europäischen Gemeinschaft, insbesondere auf Artikel 47 Absatz 2 (nunmehr: Art. 53 Abs. 1 AEUV) und die Artikel 55 (nunmehr: Art. 62 AEUV) und 95 (nunmehr: Art. 114 AEUV)". Eingehend zum Regelungsgehalt und zur Zielsetzung Abschnitt D.II.1.

kann zudem auch die in Art. 4 Abs. 3 AEUV geregelte geteilte Zuständigkeit der EU für die Bereiche Forschung und technologische Entwicklung nach Art. 179 ff. AEUV[75] auch für die Medienregulierung bedeutsam sein. In den Bereichen Forschung und technologische Entwicklung erstreckt sich die Zuständigkeit der Union allerdings nur darauf, Maßnahmen zu treffen, insbesondere Programme zu erstellen und durchzuführen, ohne dass die Ausübung dieser Zuständigkeit die Mitgliedstaaten hindert, ihre Zuständigkeit auszuüben.

d. Insbesondere: Schutzintensivierung im Bereich des digitalen Binnenmarktes

Von den – im Rahmen der Rechtsharmonisierung im Binnenmarkt erlassenen – sekundär-unionsrechtlichen Vorgaben kann ein Mitgliedstaat nur im Rahmen der Schutzintensivierungsklausel nach Art 114 Abs. 4 bis 10 AEUV abweichen: Diese Klausel eröffnet den Mitgliedstaaten die Möglichkeit, i.S. eines „nationalen Alleingangs"[76] trotz erfolgter Rechtsangleichung auf Unionsebene zum Schutze wichtiger Rechtsgüter strengere nationale Bestimmungen beizubehalten bzw. neu einzuführen. Dazu müssen folgende Voraussetzungen vorliegen:

- Die Beibehaltung bestehender strengerer nationaler Bestimmungen muss durch wichtige Erfordernisse i.S.d. Art 36 AEUV oder in Bezug auf den Schutz der Arbeitsumwelt oder den Umweltschutz gerechtfertigt sein (Art. 114 Abs. 4 AEUV).
- Bei der Neueinführung strengerer nationaler Bestimmungen müssen neue wissenschaftliche Erkenntnisse bezüglich des Schutzes der Umwelt oder der Arbeitsumwelt vorliegen und die Entstehung eines spezifischen Problems für den betroffenen Mitgliedstaat nach Erlass der Rechtsangleichungsmaßnahme nachgewiesen werden (Art 114 Abs. 5 AEUV).

---

75 Vgl. hierzu *Calliess* in: ders./Ruffert, Art. 4 AEUV, Rn. 20; *Klamert* in: Kellerbauer/ders./Tomkin, Art. 4 AEUV, Rn. 15; *Pelka*, in: Schwarze, Art. 4 AEUV, Rn. 17; *Dony*, Droit de l'Union européenne, Rn. 136.
76 Vgl. hierzu *Herrnfeld* in: Schwarze, Art. 114 AEUV, Rn. 87 ff.; *Korte* in: Calliess/Ruffert, Art. 114 AEUV, Rn. 68 ff.; *Terhechte* in: Pechstein u.a., Frankfurter Kommentar, Art. 114 AEUV, Rn. 80 ff.; *Kellerbauer* in: ders./Klamert/Tomkin, Art. 114 AEUV, Rn. 48 ff.; *Dony*, Droit de l'Union européenne, Rn. 723 ff.

- Die nationalen Bestimmungen müssen der Kommission mitgeteilt und von dieser im Verfahren gemäß Art 114 Abs. 6 AEUV gebilligt werden. Die Kommission hat binnen sechs Monaten nach der Mitteilung zu entscheiden, nachdem sie geprüft hat, ob die nationale Bestimmung den zwischenstaatlichen Handel diskriminiert und beschränkt und ob sie das Funktionieren des Binnenmarktes behindert. Hat die Kommission nach sechs Monaten noch nicht entschieden, gilt die nationale Bestimmung als gebilligt. Vor der Billigung ist ein Mitgliedstaat nicht befugt, die strengere nationale Bestimmung anzuwenden („Sperrwirkung").[77]

Der Erlass neuer einzelstaatlicher Rechtsvorschriften nach erfolgter Rechtsangleichung, wie sie im Bereich der Entwicklung eines (digitalen) Medien- und Kommunikationsbinnenmarktes insbesondere durch die AVMD- und die E-Commerce-Richtlinie erfolgt ist, unterliegt mithin besonders strengen Voraussetzungen, da dadurch das Funktionieren des Binnenmarktes stärker gefährdet würde. Die Unionsorgane konnten die einzelstaatliche Regelung naturgemäß bei der Ausarbeitung der Rechtsangleichungsmaßnahme nicht berücksichtigen. In diesem Fall können insbesondere die in Art 36 AEUV genannten Erfordernisse nicht herangezogen werden. Zulässig sind allein Gründe des Schutzes der Umwelt oder der Arbeitsumwelt.[78]

Dass diese Schutzintensivierungsklauseln im Bereich der Medienregulierung aktuell oder zukünftig praktische Relevanz hat oder erfahren wird, ist zwar zumindest in Bezug auf den Erlass neuer Rechtsvorschriften im Bereich der europarechtlichen Koordinierung von Kommunikations- und Medienrecht der Mitgliedstaaten nicht erkennbar. Für die Beibehaltung bestehender mitgliedstaatlicher Vorschriften mag dies indessen anders sein, insbesondere wenn sie – z.B. in der Abwehr von medialen Angriffen auf einen freien demokratischen Diskurs, wie sie z.B. durch Desinformation und Fake News erfolgen können – als Bestandteile einer „wehrhaften Demokratie 4.0"[79] auf den Schutz der „öffentlichen Sittlichkeit, Ordnung und Sicherheit" i.S. des Art. 36 Satz 1 AEUV ausgerichtet sind. Im Übrigen verdient bei systematischer und teleologischer Betrachtung Beachtung, dass wenn in Bereichen wie dem Schutz der Arbeitsumwelt oder den Um-

---

77 Vgl. EuGH, C-41/93, *Frankreich / Kommission*, Rn. 30.
78 Vgl. EuGH, C-512/99, *Deutschland / Kommission*, Rn. 40 f.; C-3/00, *Dänemark / Kommission*, Rn. 57 ff. Siehe insbesondere EuG, T-366/03 u T-235/04, *Land Oberösterreich und Republik Österreich / Kommission*; EuGH, C-439/05 P u Rs C-454/05 P, *Land Oberösterreich und Republik Österreich/Kommission*.
79 Vgl. hierzu *Ukrow* in: ZEuS 2021, S. 65, 65 ff.

weltschutz oder in (sonstigen) Bereichen, die Art. 36 AEUV adressiert, die deutlich weniger als die Kultur und die Medien außerökonomisch relevant sind, Souveränität der Mitgliedstaaten geschützt wird, dies erst recht für den Kultur- und Medienbereich möglich sein muss.

e. Unterstützende Zuständigkeiten der EU und Medienregulierung

Schließlich ist die EU nach Art. 6 Satz 1 AEUV für die Durchführung von Maßnahmen zur Unterstützung, Koordinierung oder Ergänzung der Maßnahmen der Mitgliedstaaten zuständig. In diesem Zuständigkeitsbereich darf die EU mithin nur ergänzend tätig werden; ihr Handeln setzt also ein vorangegangenes Handeln der Mitgliedstaaten voraus. Das Handeln der EU begründet zudem, unbeschadet der auch in diesem Zuständigkeitsbereich geltenden Loyalitätspflicht, keine Sperrwirkung für nationales Handeln. Diese Maßnahmen mit europäischer Zielsetzung können nach Art. 6 Satz 2 Buchst. c) AEUV auch im Bereich „Kultur" und nach Buchst. e) dieser Regelung auch im Bereich „allgemeine und berufliche Bildung" getroffen werden. An diese Zuständigkeitsregelung knüpfen der (auf die allgemeine, nicht berufliche Bildung bezogene) Artikel 165 AEUV wie der (Kultur-) Artikel 167 AEUV an.[80]

Für das Verständnis dieser Zuständigkeiten ist auch Art. 2 Abs. 5 AEUV bedeutsam: Dieser betont in Satz 1 zunächst, dass in den Bereichen, in denen die Union nach Maßgabe der Verträge dafür zuständig ist, Maßnahmen zur Unterstützung, Koordinierung oder Ergänzung der Maßnahmen der Mitgliedstaaten durchzuführen, dies nicht zur Folge hat, dass die Zuständigkeit der Union für diese Bereiche an die Stelle der Zuständigkeit der Mitgliedstaaten tritt. In Satz 2 wird ferner präzisiert, dass „die verbindlichen Rechtsakte der Union, die aufgrund der diese Bereiche betreffenden Bestimmungen der Verträge erlassen werden, keine Harmonisierung der Rechtsvorschriften der Mitgliedstaaten beinhalten (dürfen)".[81] Dies gilt nicht zuletzt auch für den Bildungs- und den Kulturbereich. Eine nicht auf den Binnenmarkt-, Wettbewerbs-, Steuer- oder einen sonstigen, ausdrück-

---

80 Vgl. hierzu *Calliess* in: ders./Ruffert, Art. 6 AEUV, Rn. 7, 9; *Klamert* in: Kellerbauer/ders./Tomkin, Art. 6 AEUV, Rn. 6, 8; *Pelka* in: Schwarze, Art. 6 AEUV, Rn. 8, 10.
81 Vgl. hierzu *Calliess* in: ders./Ruffert, Art. 2 AEUV, Rn. 19 ff.; *Häde*, in: Pechstein u.a., Frankfurter Kommentar, Art. 2 AEUV, Rn. 49 ff.; *Pelka* in: Schwarze, Art. 2 AEUV, Rn. 22 ff.; *Klamert* in: Kellerbauer/ders./Tomkin, Art. 2 AEUV, Rn. 15; *Dony*, Droit de l'Union européenne, Rn. 139.

lich Rechtsharmonisierung ermöglichenden Kompetenztitel der EU, sondern stattdessen ausdrücklich auf den Aspekt Medienfreiheits- und Vielfaltsregulierung gestützte Rechtsharmonisierung der EU wäre mithin unzulässig.

f. Insbesondere: Medienkompetenz im Blickfeld der EU-Regulierung

Auch für nicht verbindliche Rechtsakte der EU sind die Zuständigkeitsregelungen der EU und deren jeweilige Grenzziehungen zu beachten. Dies betrifft auch die fortdauernden Bemühungen der EU um eine Stärkung der sog. media literacy.

Schon die Empfehlung des Europäischen Parlaments und des Rates vom 20. Dezember 2006 über den Schutz Minderjähriger und den Schutz der Menschenwürde und über das Recht auf Gegendarstellung im Zusammenhang mit der Wettbewerbsfähigkeit des europäischen Industriezweiges der audiovisuellen Dienste und Online-Informationsdienste enthielt eine Reihe möglicher Maßnahmen zur Förderung der Medienkompetenz, wie z. B. eine ständige Fortbildung von Lehrern und Ausbildern, spezifische Internetschulungen schon für sehr kleine Kinder, auch unter Einbeziehung der Eltern, oder die Organisation nationaler, an die Bürger gerichteter Informationskampagnen in allen Kommunikationsmedien, um Informationen über eine verantwortungsvolle Nutzung des Internets bereitzustellen.

Bereits in der Richtlinie über audiovisuelle Mediendienste aus dem Jahr 2010[82], wurde Medienkompetenz erstmalig im rechtsverbindlichen audiovisuellen Recht der EU angesprochen. Art. 33 Satz 1 dieser Richtlinie sah einen regelmäßigen Bericht der Europäischen Kommission im dreijährigen Turnus über die Anwendung dieser Richtlinie vor, wobei die Kommission

> erforderlichenfalls Vorschläge zu ihrer Anpassung an die Entwicklungen im Bereich der audiovisuellen Mediendienste, und zwar insbeson-

---

82 Richtlinie 2010/13/EU des Europäischen Parlaments und des Rates vom 10. März 2010 zur Koordinierung bestimmter Rechts- und Verwaltungsvorschriften der Mitgliedstaaten über die Bereitstellung audiovisueller Mediendienste (Richtlinie über audiovisuelle Mediendienste) EU ABl. L 95, 15.4.2010, S. 1–24.
Eingehend zur Historie der Richtlinie und der neuen Regel zur Medienkompetenzförderung im Rahmen der Reform 2018 vgl. unten, Abschnitte D.II.2.a und D.II.2.d(3).

B. Primärrechtlicher Rahmen zur Kompetenzabgrenzung

dere im Lichte neuerer technologischer Entwicklungen, der Wettbewerbsfähigkeit dieses Sektors *und des Niveaus der Medienkompetenz in allen Mitgliedstaaten* (machte). *(Hervorhebung der Verf.).*

Damit wurde auch in der Richtlinie unmittelbar der Zusammenhang zwischen der Vermittlung von Medienkompetenz und der effektiven Sicherung von Schutzgütern wie dem Jugendmedienschutz und dem Medienverbraucherschutz angesprochen.

In den Erwgr. zu der Richtlinie fanden sich weitere Ausführungen zum Verständnis von Medienkompetenz und ihrer Bedeutung im medialen Kontext seitens der EU. Der 47. Erwgr. lautete:

Die „Medienkompetenz" bezieht sich auf die notwendigen Fähigkeiten und Kenntnisse sowie das nötige Verständnis für eine wirksame und sichere Nutzung der Medien durch die Verbraucher. Medienkompetente Menschen sind in der Lage, fundierte Entscheidungen zu treffen, das Wesen von Inhalt und Dienstleistungen zu verstehen und das gesamte Spektrum der durch die neuen Kommunikationstechnologien gebotenen Möglichkeiten zu nutzen. Sie sind in der Lage, sich und ihre Familien besser vor schädlichen oder anstößigen Inhalten zu schützen. Daher sollte die Entwicklung der Medienkompetenz in allen Gesellschaftsschichten gefördert werden, und die dabei erzielten Fortschritte sollten genau beobachtet werden.

Auch wenn diese Initiative schutzorientiert begrüßenswert erschien, darf nicht verkannt werden, dass damit ein gewisser definitorischer Ansatz für die Angleichung der Regulierung von Medienkompetenz in den Mitgliedstaaten erfolgte – eine Harmonisierung, die im Bildungs- wie im Kulturbereich als Bereichen unterstützender Zuständigkeiten der EU gerade primärrechtlich ausgeschlossen ist.

Dieser Weg einer allmählichen Auflösung der rein unterstützenden Zuständigkeit findet in der Novelle der AVMD-Richtlinie 2018 eine kompetenzrechtlich bedenkliche Vertiefung.[83] Denn dort wird in Art. 33 a erstmalig eine rechtsverbindliche Verpflichtung der Mitgliedsstaaten verankert, selbst Maßnahmen zur Entwicklung von Medienkompetenz zu ergreifen – verbunden mit einer Leitlinienkompetenz der Kommission in Bezug auf den Umfang der Berichtspflicht der Mitgliedstaaten an die Kommission:

---

83 Zu inhaltlichen Aspekten der Regelung vgl. Abschnitt D.II.2.d(3).

(1) Die Mitgliedstaaten fördern die Entwicklung von Medienkompetenz und ergreifen entsprechende Maßnahmen.
(2) Bis zum 19. Dezember 2022 und anschließend alle drei Jahre berichten die Mitgliedstaaten der Kommission über die Durchführung des Absatzes 1.
(3) Die Kommission gibt nach Konsultation des Kontaktausschusses Leitlinien zum Umfang solcher Berichte heraus.

Zur Erläuterung dieser Verpflichtungen ist der 59. Erwgr. der Änderungsrichtlinie bedeutsam. Dieser lautet:

„Medienkompetenz" bezieht sich auf die Fähigkeiten, Kenntnisse und das Verständnis, die es Bürgern ermöglichen, Medien wirksam und sicher zu nutzen. Damit die Bürger auf verantwortungsvolle und sichere Weise auf Informationen zugreifen und Medieninhalte verwenden, kritisch beurteilen und erstellen können, müssen sie über fortgeschrittene Medienkompetenzen verfügen. Medienkompetenz sollte sich nicht darauf beschränken, Wissen über Tools und Technologien zu erwerben, sondern das Ziel verfolgen, Bürgern Fähigkeiten des kritischen Denkens zu vermitteln, die notwendig sind, um Bewertungen vorzunehmen, komplexe Realitäten zu analysieren und zwischen Meinungen und Tatsachen zu unterscheiden. Daher müssen sowohl Mediendiensteanbieter als auch Video-Sharing-Plattform-Anbieter in Zusammenarbeit mit allen relevanten Akteuren die Entwicklung von Medienkompetenz in allen Bereichen der Gesellschaft, bei Bürgern aller Altersgruppen und in Bezug auf alle Medien fördern und der hierbei erzielte Fortschritt muss aufmerksam verfolgt werden.

Die Förderpflicht nach Art. 33a Abs. 1 der Richtlinie erfährt damit eine im Hinblick auf die bloße Unterstützungskompetenz ihrerseits problematische Konkretisierung.

Der Weg zu einer zunehmenden Verschiebung von der Unterstützung zur Gestaltung von Medienkompetenz seitens der EU an der Schnittstelle der Kultur- und Bildungskompetenzen der EU findet in den Schlussfolgerungen zur „Medienkompetenz in einer sich ständig wandelnden Welt" seine Fortsetzung, die der Rat der Europäischen Union am 25. Mai 2020 angenommen hat.[84]

---

84 Schlussfolgerungen des Rates zur Medienkompetenz in einer sich ständig wandelnden Welt 2020/C 193/06, ST/8274/2020/INIT, EU ABl. C 193, 9.6.2020, S. 23–28.

B. Primärrechtlicher Rahmen zur Kompetenzabgrenzung

Konkret heißt es in diesen:

Der Rat der Europäischen Union ersucht die Mitgliedsstaaten ... unter Wahrung des Subsidiaritätsprinzips

...

• die Einrichtung und die Weiterentwicklung von (nationalen, regionalen, lokalen, thematischen) Medienkompetenznetzwerken zu unterstützen, um die einschlägigen Akteure zusammenzubringen und sie in die Lage zu versetzen, zusammenzuarbeiten und nachhaltige und langfristig tragfähige Projekte und Initiativen im Bereich Medienkompetenz zu entwickeln;

• ein Konzept für lebenslanges Lernen im Bereich Medienkompetenz für alle Altersgruppen zu entwickeln und in diesem Zusammenhang Pilot- und Forschungsprojekte zu unterstützen, um neue Methoden, Maßnahmen und Inhalte zu schaffen, weiterzuentwickeln und zu bewerten, die auf die spezifischen Bedürfnisse der Zielgruppen zugeschnitten sind;

...

• bestehende Ausbildungsmodelle für die Entwicklung digitaler Kompetenzen in der europäischen Kultur- und Kreativwirtschaft zu verbessern und erforderlichenfalls neue Modelle hierfür zu entwerfen, um die wirksame Nutzung innovativer Technologien zu fördern und mit dem technologischen Fortschritt Schritt zu halten.

Die Vereinbarkeit einer solchen medienkompetenzbezogenen Politik informeller Regelsetzung mit dem in Art. 165 Abs. 1 Unterabs. 1 AEUV ausdrücklich anerkannten Gebot einer „strikte(n) Beachtung der Verantwortung der Mitgliedstaaten für die Lehrinhalte und die Gestaltung des Bildungssystems" erscheint zunehmend fraglich.

g. Sperrwirkung des EU-Rechts

Eng mit der Frage des Anwendungsvorrangs des EU-Rechts verknüpft ist die Frage, ob EU-Recht eine Sperrwirkung in Bezug auf mitgliedstaatliche Regulierungsmöglichkeiten auslöst.

In Bezug auf die ausschließlichen Zuständigkeiten der EU ist diese Frage, wie dargestellt, durch den Vertrag von Lissabon geklärt: Die Mitgliedstaaten sind in den Bereichen ausschließlicher Zuständigkeit der EU von der Rechtsetzung ausgeschlossen – sofern es keine ausdrückliche Öffnung für ein mitgliedstaatliches Tätigwerden im Wege der Rückdelegation nach Art. 2 Abs. 1 AEUV gibt. Der Ausschluss der Mitgliedstaaten von der Regulierung führt unbeschadet der Möglichkeit zur Rückdelegation zu einer „generellen Sperrwirkung";[85] mitgliedstaatliche Regelungen, die in Verletzung dieser Vorgabe beschlossen werden, sind schon aus diesem Grund unanwendbar. Die EU muss (noch) keine Sekundärrechtsakte erlassen haben (Sperrwirkung *ex ante*). Hat die EU Sekundärrechtsakte erlassen, müssen diese nicht unmittelbare Wirkung entfalten, um kollidierendes nationales Recht zu verdrängen (Sperrwirkung *ex post*). Mithin obliegt in den Bereichen ausschließlicher Zuständigkeit der Erlass von Maßnahmen „vollkommen und endgültig" allein der EU – unabhängig davon, ob diese konkret tätig wird oder nicht.[86] Diese Sperrwirkung des EU-Rechts steht allerdings dem Erlass von parallelen bzw. ergänzenden Regelungen der Mitgliedstaaten, die den gleichen Adressatenkreis wie das betreffende EU-Recht haben und sich ggf. auch vergleichbarer Instrumentarien (z.B. Transparenz- und Offenlegungspflichten oder Diskriminierungsverbote) wie das EU-Recht bedienen, allerdings eine unterschiedliche Zielsetzung (namentlich vielfaltssichernder Art) aufweisen, zumindest dann nicht entgegen, wenn die mitgliedstaatliche Regelung materiell nicht mit der (z.B. auf der Grundlage der ausschließlichen Zuständigkeit der EU nach Art. 3 Abs. 1 Buchst. b) AEUV für das Wettbewerbsrecht erlassenen) Regelung der EU kollidiert bzw. deren praktische Wirksamkeit hemmt.

An einer vergleichbaren ausdrücklichen Regelung zur Sperrwirkung fehlt es im Bereich der geteilten Zuständigkeiten der EU. Im Rahmen dieser Zuständigkeit der Union erlassene Maßnahmen entfalten keine Sperrwirkung i.S. eines Stoppsignals für die Regulierungskompetenz der Mitgliedstaaten. Allerdings resultiert aus dem Loyalitätsgebot nach Art 4 Abs. 3 EUV eine Pflicht der Mitgliedstaaten, nicht gegen Maßnahmen der Union zu verstoßen und deren *effet utile*, d.h. deren nützliche Wirkung, nicht zu beeinträchtigen.[87]

Bei geteilten Zuständigkeiten stellt sich die Frage einer etwaigen Sperrwirkung insbesondere im Zusammenhang mit Richtlinienrecht der EU in doppelter Hinsicht – sowohl mit Blick auf umgesetztes Richtlinienrecht als auch – i.S. einer sperrenden Vorwirkung – mit Blick auf noch umzusetzendes Richtlinienrecht.

---

85 Vgl. *Streinz* in: ders., Art. 2 AEUV, Rn. 5; *Klamert* in: Kellerbauer/ders./Tomkin, Art. 2 AEUV, Rn. 5.
86 Vgl. *Obwexer*, EU-rechtliche Determinierung mitgliedstaatlicher Kompetenzen, S. 1, 6.
87 Vgl. *Calliess* in: ders./Ruffert, Art. 2 AEUV, Rn. 22; *Eilmansberger/Jaeger* in: Mayer/Stöger, Art. 2 AEUV, Rn. 49; *Obwexer*, EU-rechtliche Determinierung mitgliedstaatlicher Kompetenzen, S. 1 (9).

B. Primärrechtlicher Rahmen zur Kompetenzabgrenzung

In Bezug auf die aufgrund einer Richtlinie wie z.B. der novellierten AVMD-Richtlinie angepassten nationalen Rechtsvorschriften wie im Beispielsfall die betreffenden Regelungen des Modernisierungsstaatsvertrages der Länder bedeutet das, dass diese nicht mehr zur unbeschränkten Disposition des nationalen Gesetzgebers stehen. Sie dürfen nicht mehr entgegen den Richtlinienvorgaben abgeändert werden.

Eine Richtlinie kann indessen bereits vor Ablauf ihrer Umsetzungsfrist und vor Umsetzung in mitgliedstaatliches Recht Rechtswirkungen entfalten. Ab dem Zeitpunkt der Bekanntgabe einer Richtlinie gemäß Art. 297 Abs. 1 AEUV verbietet es der Grundsatz der Vertragstreue, dass in den Mitgliedstaaten Handlungen vorgenommen werden, die geeignet sind, das durch die Richtlinie vorgegebene Ziel ernstlich zu gefährden.[88] Eine solche Gefährdung kann auch darin bestehen, dass ein richtlinienrechtlich anerkannter Spielraum für die Berücksichtigung von medialen Vielfaltsbelangen im mitgliedstaatlichen Telekommunikationsrecht, wie er sich ausdrücklich im EEKK findet, durch den nationalen TK-Gesetzgeber dadurch missachtet wird, dass eine im nationalen TK-Recht bislang vorhandene Rücksichtnahmepflicht auf Rundfunkbelange anlässlich einer Novelle dieses Rechts gestrichen wird.

An einer solchen Vorwirkung fehlt es allerdings zumindest so lange, bis der „vorwirkende" Rechtsakt der EU im Amtsblatt der EU veröffentlicht wurde. Bloße Regulierungsabsichten der EU vermögen mithin keine Vorwirkung zu entfalten. Mithin begegnen auch die, inhaltlich am deutschen NetzDG orientierten Regelungsüberlegungen in Österreich in Bezug auf die Bekämpfung von Hass und illegalen Inhalten im Netz, die der EU-Kommission am 1. und 2. September 2020 notifiziert wurden,[89] zumindest unter kompetenzrechtlichem Blickwinkel des Verhältnisses zwischen EU- und mitgliedstaatlicher Medienregulierung – ungeachtet der damaligen Überlegungen für einen *Digital Services Act* und einen *European Action*

---

[88] Vgl. *Streinz*, Europarecht, Rn. 514; *Thiele*, Europarecht, S. 114.
[89] Es handelt sich um die Entwürfe (a) eines Bundesgesetzes, mit dem zivilrechtliche und zivilprozessuale Maßnahmen zur Bekämpfung von Hass im Netz getroffen werden (Hass-im-Netz-Bekämpfungs-Gesetz) (https://ec.europa.eu/growth/tools-d atabases/tris/de/search/?trisaction=search.detail&year=2020&num=547), (b) eines Bundesgesetz, mit dem straf- und medienrechtliche Maßnahmen zur Bekämpfung von Hass im Netz getroffen werden (https://ec.europa.eu/growth/tools-datab ases/tris/de/search/?trisaction=search.detail&year=2020&num=548) und (c) eines Bundesgesetzes über Maßnahmen zum Schutz der Nutzer auf Kommunikationsplattformen (Kommunikationsplattformen-Gesetz – KoPl-G) (https://ec.europa.eu /growth/tools-databases/tris/de/search/?trisaction=search.detail&year=2020&num= 544).

Plan for Democracy und unbeschadet der Frage der Vereinbarkeit der vorgesehenen Regelungen mit der ECRL der EU – keinen durchgreifenden Bedenken, es handelt sich um keine rechtswidrige Regulierungsabsicht.[90]

6. Medienregulierung und verstärkte Zusammenarbeit zwischen einzelnen Mitgliedstaaten der EU

Auch ökonomische Aspekte der Medienregulierung in Richtung auf die Schaffung eines digitalen Binnenmarktes sind im Übrigen möglicher Gegenstand verstärkter Zusammenarbeit nach den europäischen Verträgen – wobei auch bei einer solchen verstärkten Zusammenarbeit die kulturelle Querschnittsklausel des Art. 167 Abs. 4 AEUV ebenso zu beachten wäre wie die Bindung an die Grundrechte einschließlich der Kommunikationsfreiheiten und des Gebotes nach Art. 11 Abs. 2 GRC, die Freiheit der Medien und ihre Pluralität zu achten.

Erste Voraussetzung für die Einrichtung einer Verstärkten Zusammenarbeit ist das Vorliegen einer geeigneten Kompetenzgrundlage der Union in dem entsprechenden Politikbereich. Dieser darf nach Art. 20 Abs. 1 UAbs. 1 AEUV in kein Sachgebiet fallen, auf dem die EU die ausschließliche Kompetenz hat. Dies ist allerdings bei der Binnenmarkt-Kompetenz – auch in Bezug auf die Schaffung eines digitalen Binnenmarktes – wie aufgezeigt[91] nach der klaren Regelung in Art. 4 Abs. 2 Buchst. a) EUV nicht der Fall.

Ziel der Verstärkten Zusammenarbeit muss es nach Art. 20 Abs. 1 UAbs. 2 EUV sein, die Ziele der Union zu fördern, ihre Interessen zu schützen und ihren Integrationsprozess zu stärken. Eine verstärkte Zusammenarbeit im Bereich der Regelung von Medienplattformen und Medienintermediären unter besonderer Berücksichtigung ihrer Bedeutung für die Vielfaltssicherung im digitalen Zeitalter würde diese Zielsetzung mit Blick auf die Sicherung von Pluralismus vor grenzüberschreitenden Gefährdungen ebenso befördern wie es ggf. auch die Einführung einer Digitalsteuer, die u.a. diesen Adressatenkreis moderner Medienregulierung in den Blick nimmt, könnte.[92]

---

90 Vgl. eingehend unten zur ECRL (Abschnitt D.II.1), zum *Digital Services Act* (Abschnitt D.III.2 und Kapitel F.) und zum *European Democracy Action Plan* (Abschnitt D.III.3).
91 Vgl. hierzu oben, Abschnitt B.I.5.
92 Vgl. hierzu allerdings nach einer Reihe nationaler mitgliedstaatlicher Alleingänge (dazu *Ukrow*, Österreich und Spanien wollen Digitalsteuer einführen, https://rsw.

B. Primärrechtlicher Rahmen zur Kompetenzabgrenzung

Art. 20 Abs. 1 UAbs. 2 S. 2 EUV und Art. 328 AEUV setzen für die Begründung einer Verstärkten Zusammenarbeit voraus, dass diese allen übrigen Mitgliedstaaten offenstehen muss, wenn sie die Teilnahmevoraussetzungen erfüllen.

An einer Verstärkten Zusammenarbeit müssen gemäß Art. 20 Abs. 3 S. 1 EUV mindestens neun Mitgliedstaaten beteiligt sein.

Die Verstärkte Zusammenarbeit ist gemäß Art. 20 Abs. 2 S. 1 EUV allerdings nur als *ultima ratio* zulässig, wenn der Rat feststellt, dass die mit der Zusammenarbeit angestrebten Ziele von der Union in ihrer Gesamtheit nicht innerhalb eines vertretbaren Zeitraums verwirklicht werden können. Hierbei wird den Mitgliedstaaten ein weiter Spielraum zugestanden; auch die Überprüfung des „vertretbaren Zeitraums" ist nur beschränkt justiziabel.[93] Es wird jedoch gefordert, dass wenigstens ein Versuch einer Einigung über ein konkretes Gesetzgebungsvorhaben unter Beteiligung aller Mitgliedstaaten unternommen worden sein muss.[94]

Von der verstärkten Zusammenarbeit unberührt bleibt allerdings der bi- oder multilaterale Regulierungsabsatz völkerrechtlicher Art in Bezug auf eine positive Ordnung der Medienlandschaft. Denn aus der primärunionsrechtlichen Verankerung von Voraussetzungen und Mechanismen einer verstärkten Zusammenarbeit folgt nicht, dass im Anwendungsbereich der europäischen Verträge andere Formen einer verstärkten Zusammenarbeit verboten sind.[95]

Dieser Offenheit für alternative Formen verstärkter Zusammenarbeit folgend erkennen nach Art. 9 des Vertrages von Aachen Deutschland und Frankreich die entscheidende Rolle an, die die Kultur und die Medien für die Stärkung der deutsch-französischen Freundschaft spielen. Daher sind sie entschlossen, für ihre Völker einen gemeinsamen Raum der Freiheit und der Chancen sowie einen gemeinsamen Kultur- und Medienraum zu

---

beck.de/cms/?toc=ZD.ARC.201902&docid=413844; *Ukrow*, Österreich: Ministerrat beschließt Digitalsteuerpaket, https://rsw.beck.de/cms/?toc=MMR.ARC.201904&docid=416999) die Schlussfolgerungen der Außerordentlichen Tagung des Europäischen Rates vom 17. bis 21. Juli 2020 (https://www.consilium.europa.eu/media/45136/210720-euco-final-conclusions-de.pdf), in denen vorgesehen ist, dass die Europäische Kommission im ersten Halbjahr 2021 einen Vorschlag für eine „Digitalabgabe" vorlegt, damit diese „spätestens zum 1. Januar 2023" eingeführt werden kann; vgl. ibidem, Rn. A29 und Rn. 147. Dazu auch Abschnitt B.I.5.g.

93 *Ruffert* in: Calliess/ders., Art. 20 EUV, Rn. 19; *Pechstein* in: Streinz, Art. 20 EUV, Rn. 13.
94 *Bribosia* in: CDE 2000, 57, 97; *Pechstein* in: Streinz, Art. 20 EUV, Rn. 13; *Ullrich* in: RdDI 2013, 325, 332; a. A. *Blanke* in: ders./Mangiameli, Art. 20 EUV, Rn. 38.
95 Vgl. *Ukrow* in: ZEuS 2019, 3, 29 m.w.N.

schaffen. Mit einem solchen Raum könnte ein Beitrag zur Entwicklung einer europäischen (Teil-) Öffentlichkeit geschaffen werden, die für die Weiterentwicklung der EU aus Sicht des BVerfG zu deren demokratischer Legitimationsfähigkeit unverzichtbar ist. Die vom BVerfG betonten Unsicherheiten des digitalen Kommunikationsraums berühren nicht zuletzt auch die fortdauernde Legitimität der europäischen Zielperspektive einer immer engeren Union. Dem auch durch einen gemeinsamen deutsch-französischen Medienraum entgegenzuwirken, stellt einen kulturellen Beitrag zur Selbstbehauptung eines wertegebundenen Europas dar. Die Regelungskompetenz der Länder in Ausformung des Art. 9 des Vertrages könnte neben einer deutsch-französischen digitalen Plattform für audiovisuelle Inhalte und Informationsangebote auch ein Hörfunk-ARTE, eine deutsch-französische Suchmaschine sowie ein deutsch-französisches Facebook-, TikTok- oder WhatsApp-Pendant umfassen.[96]

7. Medienregulierung und die primärrechtliche Bedeutung nachfolgender Organpraxis

Nach verbreiteter Auffassung[97] unterscheiden sich die Auslegungsmethoden des EuGH insbesondere insoweit von den traditionellen völkerrechtlichen Interpretationsmethoden, als der EuGH der nachfolgenden Organpraxis, der in Art. 31 Abs. 3 Buchst. b) der Wiener Vertragsrechtskonvention (WVRK)[98] eine erhebliche Bedeutung als Rechtserkenntnisquelle beigemessen wird, für die Auslegung des Unionsrechts keine originäre Relevanz beimisst.

Indessen vermittelt eine Untersuchung der Rechtsprechung des EuGH im Hinblick auf die Auslegungsrelevanz späterer Praxis ein „disparates Bild".[99] Losgelöst davon kann die nachfolgende Praxis von grundlegender Bedeutung für einen wesentlichen Aspekt der Funktionsweise des Unionsrechts sein – „nämlich die Akzeptanz einer nur beschränkt über Zwangsmittel gegenüber den Mitgliedstaaten verfügenden Rechtsordnung".[100]

---

96 Vgl. *Ukrow* in: ZEuS 2019, 3, 49 f.
97 Vgl. *Streinz*, Die Interpretationsmethoden des Europäischen Gerichtshofs zum Vorantreiben der Integration, 27, 32.
98 Wiener Übereinkommen über das Recht der Verträge vom 23.5. 1969, BGBl. 1985 II 927.
99 Vgl. *Ukrow*, Richterliche Rechtsfortbildung durch den EuGH, S. 118 ff.
100 *Streinz*, Die Interpretationsmethoden des Europäischen Gerichtshofs zum Vorantreiben der Integration, 27, 32, unter Bezugnahme u.a. auf *Borchardt*, Richter-

B. Primärrechtlicher Rahmen zur Kompetenzabgrenzung

Zwar kann die mitgliedstaatliche Akzeptanz einer auf Vertiefung der digitalen Integration gerichteten Medienregulierung der EU, so wichtig sie auch ist, allein in der EU als einer Union des Rechts, zu deren Bestandteil auch die Wahrung der Kompetenzordnung der europäischen Verfassungsurkunde zählt, als Legitimationsgrundlage nicht genügen.[101] Indessen hemmt diese Akzeptanz umgekehrt das Risiko einer gerichtlichen Kontrolle der Wahrung des Integrationsprogramms zumindest im zwischenstaatlichen Kontext. Eine Kontrolle der Medienregulierung auf Wahrung des Integrationsprogramms durch Private – sei es inzident im Blick auf Hoheitsakte zur Regelung eines Einzelaktes, die auf Akte der EU-Medienregulierung gestützt sind, sei es im Hinblick auf die hinreichende Wahrung demokratischer Gestaltungssubstanz als Grenze der Integrationsoffenheit des Grundgesetzes – bleibt hiervon allerdings unberührt.

II. Die Werteordnung der EU und ihr Schutz als Hebel der Sicherung von Freiheit und Vielfalt der Medien in den Mitgliedstaaten der EU

1. Das Wertefundament der EU

Den wertebezogenen Elementen des europäischen Integrationsprogramms kommt im Blick auf Digitalisierung, Europäisierung und Globalisierung[102] im Integrations- und Werteverbund der EU[103] eine herausgehobene Rolle zu. In Art. 2 EUV erfahren diese Werte eine ausdrückliche Verankerung.[104]

Art. 2 EUV regelt, dass „(d)ie Werte, auf die sich die Union gründet, ... die Achtung der Menschenwürde, Freiheit, Demokratie, Gleichheit, Rechtsstaatlichkeit und die Wahrung der Menschenrechte einschließlich der Rechte der Personen, die Minderheiten angehören (sind). Diese Werte sind allen Mitgliedstaaten in einer Gesellschaft gemeinsam, die sich durch

---

recht durch den Gerichtshof der Europäischen Gemeinschaften, in: Gedächtnisschrift für Eberhard Grabitz, 1995, S. 29, 39 ff.

101 Vgl. *Cornils*: Der gemeinschaftsrechtliche Staatshaftungsanspruch, S. 327 ff.; *Dänzer-Vanotti*, Der Europäische Gerichtshof zwischen Rechtsprechung und Rechtsetzung, 205, 209 ff.
102 Vgl. *Ruffert*, Die Globalisierung als Herausforderung an das Öffentliche Recht; *Schwarze*, Globalisierung und Entstaatlichung des Rechts.
103 Vgl. *Calliess* in: Berliner Online-Beiträge zum Europarecht, 1(2004).
104 Vgl. hierzu auch die jüngere Judikatur des EuGH, Rs. C-216/18 PPU, *Minister for Justice and Equality (Défaillances du système judiciaire)*, Rn. 48 und 63; C-619/18, *Kommission / Polen*, Rn. 58.

Pluralismus, Nichtdiskriminierung, Toleranz, Gerechtigkeit, Solidarität und die Gleichheit von Frauen und Männern auszeichnet". Insbesondere die Anknüpfung des Art. 2 EUV an die Wahrung der Menschenwürde und an das Pluralismusgebot zeigt die medienrechtliche, namentlich auch vielfaltsbezogene Relevanz der Grundwerte der EU deutlich auf. Auch die Medienvielfalt ist Schutzgut der unionalen Werteordnung.[105]

Den Grundwerten kommt in der Auseinandersetzung mit Entwicklungstendenzen in einzelnen Mitgliedstaaten der EU, die die Unabhängigkeit von Justiz und Medien zu unterhöhlen bemüht sind,[106] besondere,[107] auch die Aufsichtsmechanismen der europäischen Verträge[108] wie die Organisationsstruktur der Aufsichtsinstanzen[109] mitbestimmende Bedeutung zu.

Das Wertefundament des Art. 2 EUV bindet die EU selbst bei jedem Handeln nach innen wie nach außen. Damit ist der rechtliche Gehalt der Norm allerdings nicht erschöpft. Auch wenn sich diese Norm nach ihrem Wortlaut primär an die EU selbst richtet, kommt, wie bereits aus Satz 2 der Norm ersichtlich ist, diesen Grundwerten unionsrechtliche Bedeutung auch in Bezug auf die Rechtsordnungen der Mitgliedstaten zu.[110] Umgekehrt erwächst aus diesem Wertekatalog nicht zugleich auch eine rechtsetzende Regulierungskompetenz der EU. Über Art. 2 EUV wird keine „Super-Kompetenz" konstituiert, die das Prinzip der begrenzten Einzelermächtigung im Ergebnis aushebeln könnte.

Die Werte des Art. 2 EUV prägen allerdings, auch wenn es im Grundgesetz an einem vergleichbaren ausdrücklichen Katalog fehlt, auch die deutsche verfassungsrechtliche Werteordnung als Schutzobjekte wehrhafter

---

105 Vgl. auch *Nielsen*, Die Medienvielfalt als Aspekt der Wertesicherung der EU, 2019, S. 109 ff., 175 ff; *Ukrow/Cole*, Aktive Sicherung lokaler und regionaler Medienvielfalt, S. 55 ff.
106 Vgl. hierzu z.B. *Möllers/Schneider*, Demokratiesicherung in der Europäischen Union, S. 53 ff., 68 ff.
107 Vgl. hierzu *Ukrow* in: vorgänge 55 (2016) # 216, 47, 55 ff.; *ders.* in: vorgänge 56 (2017) 220, 69, 75 ff.
108 Vgl. Mitteilung der Europäischen Kommission, „Ein neuer EU-Rahmen zur Stärkung des Rechtsstaatsprinzips", COM (2014) 158 final.
109 Die Vize-Präsidentin der aktuellen Europäischen Kommission *Vera Jourová* ist als Kommissarin zuständig für „Werte und Transparenz"; vgl. https://ec.europa.eu/commission/commissioners/2019-2024/jourova_en.
110 Operationelle Bedeutung kommt der Norm im Kontext der EU nicht nur in Beitrittsverfahren nach Art. 49 EUV, sondern auch bei der Aussetzung mitgliedstaatlicher Rechte, einschließlich Stimmrechte, nach Art. 7 EUV zu. Vgl. zu konkreten Anwendungsfällen *Ukrow*, Jenseits der Grenze, S. 5.

B. Primärrechtlicher Rahmen zur Kompetenzabgrenzung

Demokratie.[111] Insoweit kann es zu einem – etwaige kompetenzielle Konfliktsituationen mit Blick auf gleichlaufende Leitplanken regulatorischer Betätigung im Ergebnis relativierenden – dialogischen Verständnis der Werteorientierung kommen, das nicht zuletzt im Austausch zwischen dem BVerfG und den Verfassungsgerichten der Mitgliedstaaten der EU sowie dem EuGH befördert werden kann.[112] Allerdings wird dieser dialogische Ansatz eines werteorientierten Verfassungsgerichtsverbundes im Verhältnis zwischen diesen Verfassungsgerichten und dem EuGH als europäischem Verfassungsgericht aktuell durch die Entscheidung des BVerfG zur EZB-Anleihepolitik[113] massiv belastet. Diese Entscheidung stellt sich als fataler Dammbruch mit Blick auf die Einheit der EU als Union des Rechts[114] dar, da damit durch ein mitgliedstaatliches Verfassungsgericht nicht nur der Vorrang des Unionsrechts in Frage gestellt wird,[115] sondern ein Instru-

---

111 Zur Werteordnung des Grundgesetzes vgl. aus der Judikatur des BVerfG grundlegend BVerfGE 7, 198 (205 f.); 25, 256 (263); 33, 1 (12) sowie aus jüngster Zeit z.B. BVerfGE 148, 267 (280 f., 283 f.); aus der Literatur z.B. *Detjen*, Die Werteordnung des Grundgesetzes, 2009; *Reese*, Die Verfassung des Grundgesetzes. Rahmen- und Werteordnung im Lichte der Gefährdungen durch Macht und Moral; *von Danwitz*, Wert und Werte des Grundgesetzes, FAZ v. 22.01.2019.
112 Themen der entsprechenden Gespräche waren in jüngerer Zeit u.a. „die Rolle der Verfassungsgerichte bei der Fortentwicklung des Grundrechtsschutzes" (https://www.bundesverfassungsgericht.de/SharedDocs/Pressemitteilungen/DE/2017/bvg17-111.html), der „Dialog zwischen nationalen Verfassungsgerichten und Europäischen Gerichten" sowie „die Grundrechte im digitalen Zeitalter" (https://www.bundesverfassungsgericht.de/SharedDocs/Pressemitteilungen/DE/2018/bvg18-055.html), „der Europäische Gerichtsverbund" (https://www.bundesverfassungsgericht.de/SharedDocs/Pressemitteilungen/DE/2019/bvg19-018.html), „die Auswirkungen der Rechtsprechung des Europäischen Gerichtshofs für Menschenrechte und des Europäischen Gerichtshofs auf das deutsche Rechtssystem und die Arbeit des Bundesverfassungsgerichts" (https://www.bundesverfassungsgericht.de/SharedDocs/Pressemitteilungen/DE/2019/bvg19-034.html) und „(der) Grundrechtsschutz im Verhältnis zu Privaten und (der) Datenschutz im europäischen Verfassungsgerichtsverbund" (https://www.bundesverfassungsgericht.de/SharedDocs/Pressemitteilungen/DE/2019/bvg19-045.html).
113 BVerfG, Urteil des Zweiten Senats vom 05. Mai 2020, 2 BvR 859/15.
114 Vgl. die auf die einheitliche Anwendung des Unionsrechts rekurrierende Mitteilung des EuGH (Pressemitteilung im Nachgang zum Urteil des deutschen Bundesverfassungsgerichts vom 5. Mai 2020; https://curia.europa.eu/jcms/upload/docs/application/pdf/2020-05/cp200058de.pdf) wie die Erklärung der Präsidentin der Europäischen Kommission (https://ec.europa.eu/commission/presscorner/detail/de/statement_20_846).
115 Entsprechende Problemlagen gab es schon früher; vgl. *Mangold*, Der Widerspenstigen Zähmung, Legal Tribune Online v. 13.05.2020 (https://www.lto.de/re

mentarium wie das Vorabentscheidungsersuchen, das auf Kooperation angelegt ist, seiner praktischen Wirksamkeit beraubt wird.

2. Die Sicherung von Freiheit und Pluralität der Medien über die Instrumente wertebasierter wehrhafter Demokratie der EU

Grundgesetz wie EU-Vertrag, aber auch die EMRK,[116] treffen im Übrigen nicht nur materiell-rechtliche, sondern zudem auch prozedurale Vorkehrungen zur Verteidigung der zentralen Wertentscheidungen für eine freiheitlich-demokratische, nicht zuletzt auch die Freiheit und Pluralität der Medien voraussetzende und diese vor Gefährdungen absichernde Grundordnung gegen Bestrebungen zu deren Aus- und Unterhöhlung.[117] In der grundgesetzlichen Ordnung kommt diese prozedurale Effektuierung der Werte-Entscheidungen insbesondere in Art. 9 Abs. 2 GG mit der Möglichkeit des Verbots verfassungswidriger Vereinigungen „als Ausdruck einer pluralistischen, aber zugleich wehrhaften verfassungsstaatlichen Demokratie",[118] Art. 18 GG mit Regelungen zur Verwirkung von Grundrechten,[119] Art. 20 Abs. 4 GG mit einem subsidiären Widerstandsrecht aller Deutschen gegen jeden, der es unternimmt, die freiheitlich-demokratische Ordnung des Grundgesetzes zu beseitigen, als Form dezentraler Kontrolle der Wehrhaftigkeit der Demokratie,[120] Art. 21 Abs. 2 GG mit der (an enge inhaltliche wie formale Voraussetzungen geknüpften)[121] Offenheit des Grundge-

---

cht/hintergruende/h/bverfg-ezb-urteil-provokation-eugh-eu-vertragsverletzungsverfahren/).

116 Zur werteorientierten Integrations- und Identitätsfunktion des EGMR vgl. *Keller/Kühne* in: ZaöRV 76 2016, 245, 299.

117 Diese verfassungsrechtlichen Schutzmechanismen werden im Übrigen durch die strafrechtlichen Regelungen zum Schutz des Staates und seiner freiheitlich-demokratischen Ordnung ergänzt; vgl. hierzu *Becker* in: Bucerius Law Journal 2012, 113, 114 ff.

118 BVerfG, Beschluss des Ersten Senats vom 13. Juli 2018, 1 BvR 1474/12, Rn. 101.

119 Zum Ablauf des Verfahrens vor dem BVerfG vgl. §§ 36 bis 41 BVerfGG; zur geringen praktischen Relevanz vgl. *Schnelle*, Freiheitsmissbrauch und Grundrechtsverwirkung, S. 94 f.

120 Vgl. hierzu *Nowrot*, Jenseits eines abwehrrechtlichen Ausnahmecharakters – Zur multidimensionalen Rechtswirkung des Widerstandsrechts nach Art. 20 Abs. 4 GG, S. 21.

121 Das Parteiverbot nach Art. 21 Abs. 2 GG stellt aus Sicht des BVerfG in seiner Entscheidung im NPD-Verbotsverfahren „die schärfste und überdies zweischneidige Waffe des demokratischen Rechtsstaats gegen seine organisierten Feinde" dar (BVerfG, Urteil des Zweiten Senats vom 17. Januar 2017, 2 BvB 1/13,

B. Primärrechtlicher Rahmen zur Kompetenzabgrenzung

setzes für ein Verbot verfassungswidriger Parteien, Art. 21 Abs. 3 GG mit der im Ergebnis der NPD-Entscheidung des BVerfG eingeführten Möglichkeit, Parteien, die nach ihren Zielen oder dem Verhalten ihrer Anhänger darauf ausgerichtet sind, die freiheitliche demokratische Grundordnung zu beeinträchtigen oder zu beseitigen oder den Bestand der Bundesrepublik Deutschland zu gefährden, von staatlicher Finanzierung auszuschließen, und Art. 73 Abs. 1 Nr. 10 Buchst. b) GG mit Regelungen zur Zusammenarbeit des Bundes und der Länder im Bereich des Verfassungsschutzes[122] zum Ausdruck.

Rn. 405). Es soll den Risiken begegnen, die von der Existenz einer Partei mit verfassungsfeindlicher Grundtendenz und ihren typischen verbandsmäßigen Wirkungsmöglichkeiten ausgehen (ebenda, Rn. 514). Der Begriff der freiheitlichen demokratischen Grundordnung im Sinne von Art. 21 Abs. 2 GG umfasst aus seiner Sicht dabei nur jene zentralen „Grundprinzipien, die für den freiheitlichen Verfassungsstaat schlechthin unentbehrlich" sind – die Würde des Menschen (Art. 1 Abs. 1 GG), das Demokratieprinzip mit der Möglichkeit gleichberechtigter Teilnahme aller Bürgerinnen und Bürger am Prozess der politischen Willensbildung und der Rückbindung der Ausübung der Staatsgewalt an das Volk (Art. 20 Abs. 1 und 2 GG), die im Rechtsstaatsprinzip wurzelnde Rechtsbindung der öffentlichen Gewalt (Art. 20 Abs. 3 GG) und die Kontrolle dieser Bindung durch unabhängige Gerichte sowie der Vorbehalt für die Anwendung physischer Gewalt zu Gunsten der gebundenen und gerichtlicher Kontrolle unterliegenden staatlichen Organe; zu diesen Anforderungen (vgl. ebenda Rn. 535 ff.). Eine gegen die freiheitliche demokratische Grundordnung gerichtete Zielsetzung einer Partei reicht für die Anordnung eines Parteiverbots nicht aus. Vielmehr muss die Partei auf die Beeinträchtigung oder Beseitigung der freiheitlichen demokratischen Grundordnung „ausgehen". Ein solches „Ausgehen" setzt begrifflich ein aktives Handeln voraus. Das Parteiverbot ist kein Gesinnungs- oder Weltanschauungsverbot. Notwendig ist ein Überschreiten der Schwelle zur Bekämpfung der freiheitlichen demokratischen Grundordnung durch die Partei. Es muss ein planvolles Vorgehen gegeben sein, das im Sinne einer qualifizierten Vorbereitungshandlung auf die Beeinträchtigung oder Beseitigung der freiheitlichen demokratischen Grundordnung oder auf die Gefährdung des Bestandes der Bundesrepublik Deutschland gerichtet ist. Dass dadurch eine konkrete Gefahr für die durch Art. 21 Abs. 2 GG geschützten Rechtsgüter begründet wird, ist nicht erforderlich. Allerdings bedarf es konkreter Anhaltspunkte von Gewicht, die einen Erfolg des gegen die freiheitliche demokratische Grundordnung oder den Bestand der Bundesrepublik Deutschland gerichteten Handelns zumindest möglich erscheinen lassen (vgl. ebenda, Rn. 570 ff.).

122 Vgl. Gesetz über die Zusammenarbeit des Bundes und der Länder in Angelegenheiten des Verfassungsschutzes und über das Bundesamt für Verfassungsschutz (Bundesverfassungsschutzgesetz – BVerfSchG) vom 20. Dezember 1990 (BGBl. I S. 2954, 2970), das zuletzt durch Artikel 2 des Gesetzes vom 30. Juni 2017 (BGBl. I S. 2097) geändert worden ist; *Cremer* in: Isensee/Kirchhof, Band VII, § 278.

Im EUV findet diese Wertentscheidung insbesondere in Art. 7 EUV mit der danach zumindest theoretisch[123] bestehenden Möglichkeit des Entzugs von mitgliedstaatlichen Rechten,[124] in der EMRK in Art. 17 mit dem Verbot des Missbrauchs der Grundrechte[125] prozedurale Anerkennung. Auf Art. 7 EUV kann nach seiner tatbestandlichen und verfahrensmäßigen Ausformung nur unter außergewöhnlichen Umständen zurückgegriffen werden. Der politische Charakter und das spezielle Verfahren dieses besonders strittigen und schwierig anzuwendenden Artikels setzen die Schwelle für seine Anwendung äußerst hoch.[126]

Indem der EU damit eine auch die Freiheit und Vielfalt der Medien umfassende Prüfkompetenz in Bezug auf die Rechtsordnung der Mitgliedstaaten eingeräumt wird, kommt es zu einem gewissen Konflikt zur Zurückhaltung der europäischen Verträge in Bezug auf eine positive Medienordnung der EU und ihrer Organe. Allerdings steht diese Kontrollkompetenz in einer strukturellen Parallelität zur Kontrollkompetenz der EU auch in Bezug auf die mitgliedstaatlichen Medienordnungen am Maßstab der Grundfreiheiten des Binnenmarktes und der Wettbewerbsordnung der EU. Das Gebot einer Schonung der Medienregulierung der Mitgliedstaaten vor unionsrechtlichem Zugriff, wie es sich nicht zuletzt aus einer Gesamtschau der Kompetenzausübungsregelungen und -schranken der europäischen Verträge ableiten lässt, spricht für eine zurückhaltende Ausübung der Kontrollmöglichkeiten durch die EU. Zwar wird die Einschätzungsprärogative der zuständigen EU-Organe in Bezug auf das Vorliegen der tatbestandlichen Voraussetzungen des Art. 7 EUV hierdurch nicht berührt. Eine inhaltliche Koordinierung des Medienvielfaltsrechts der Mitgliedstaaten auf dem Umweg über eine nicht nur verfahrensbezogene, sondern auch materiell-rechtliche Harmonisierung der Tatbestandsmerkmale des Art. 7 EUV i.V.m. Art. 2 EUV – einschließlich einer Harmonisierung

---

123 Zu den Schwächen des Verfahrens nach Art. 7 EUV vgl. z.B. *Möllers/Schneider*, Demokratiesicherung in der Europäischen Union, S. 45 ff., 120 ff.; *Yamato/Stephan* in: DöV 2014, 58, 58 ff.

124 Vgl. z.B. Europäische Kommission, Mitteilung an den Rat und an das Europäische Parlament zu Artikel 7 des Vertrags über die Europäische Union – Wahrung und Förderung der Grundwerte der Europäischen Union, COM(2003) 606 final: *Schmitt von Sydow* in: Revue du droit de l'union européenne 2001, 285, 288 ff.

125 Vgl. *Cannie/Voorhoof* in: Netherlands Quarterly of Human Rights 2011–1, 54, 56 ff.; *Struth*, Hassrede und Freiheit der Meinungsäußerung, S. 206 ff.

126 Vgl. *Viķe-Freiberga u.a.* (Hochrangige Gruppe zur Freiheit und Vielfalt der Medien), Bericht zu freien und pluralistischen Medien als Rückhalt der europäischen Demokratie, 2013, S. 21.

B. Primärrechtlicher Rahmen zur Kompetenzabgrenzung

der Anforderungen aus dem Pluralismus-Gebot der Werteordnung der EU – wäre mit der Kompetenzordnung der europäischen Verträge und dem hierin inzident verankerten Gebot wechselseitiger Rücksichtnahme zwischen der EU und ihren Mitgliedstaaten kaum in Deckung zu bringen.

III. Die Kompetenztitel der EU mit Bezug zur Medienregulierung – ein Überblick

1. Die Binnenmarktkompetenz der EU

a. Einleitung

Der Binnenmarkt umfasst nach Art. 26 Abs. 2 AEUV „einen Raum ohne Binnengrenzen, in dem der freie Verkehr von Waren, Personen, Dienstleistungen und Kapital gemäß den Bestimmungen der Verträge gewährleistet ist".

Es lassen sich grundlegend zwei Wirkungsformen des Unionsrechts unterscheiden, die einen immer engeren Zusammenschluss der europäischen Völker (1. Absatz der Präambel des AEUV) auch in Bezug auf das Binnenmarktziel der EU befördern bzw. eine gegenläufige Entwicklung hemmen: (1.) Beschränkungen der mitgliedstaatlichen, auf die Freiheitsdimensionen des Binnenmarktes bezogenen Handlungsfreiheit durch entgegenstehendes Unionsrecht (passiv-begrenzende Integration) und (2.) aktive Einwirkungen des Unionsrechts mittels Ersetzung und Ergänzung nationaler Regelungen (aktiv-gestalterische Integration) – einschließlich Aktivitäten der EU unterhalb der Normebene, insbesondere finanzielle Förderungsmaßnahmen.[127]

Insbesondere die auf dynamische Interpretation des Unionsrechts ausgerichtete Rechtsprechung des EuGH hat die passiv-begrenzende binnenmarktbezogene Integration befördert. Die Rechtsprechung des EuGH weist in Richtung auf eine einheitliche Dogmatik der Grundfreiheiten des Binnenmarktes,[128] die im Rahmen der sog. negativen Integration der EU auf die Aufhebung aller Beschränkungen für die Ausübung der Grundfrei-

---

127 Vgl. *Ukrow/Ress* in: Grabitz/Hilf/Nettesheim, Art. 167 AEUV, Rn. 22 m.w.N.; *Garben* in: Kellerbauer/Klamert/Tomkin, Art. 167 AEUV, Rn. 6; vgl. allg. *Klamert/Lewis* in: Kellerbauer/Klamert/Tomkin, Art. 26 AEUV, Rn. 1.
128 Vgl. hierzu *Classen* in: EWS 1995, 97, 97 ff.; *Ehlers* in: ders., S. 177 ff., 184; *Frenz*, Handbuch Europarecht Bd. 1, Rn. 447; *Hirsch* in: ZEuS 1999, 503, 507 ff.; *Kingreen*, Die Struktur der Grundfreiheiten des Europäischen Gemeinschaftsrechts,

heiten gerichtet sind, was nicht nur unmittelbare oder mittelbare Diskriminierungen, sondern auch sonstige Maßnahmen erfasst, selbst wenn sie unterschiedslos für einheimische sowie Marktakteure anderer Mitgliedstaaten gelten, wenn sie geeignet sind, die Ausübung einer Dienstleistung oder eine Niederlassung zu unterbinden oder zu behindern".[129]

Regelungen, die in Ausübung aktiv-gestalterischer Integration auf die unterschiedlichen Binnenmarktkompetenzen der EU gestützt sind, haben gemeinsam, dass sie final determiniert sind. Sie müssen der Verwirklichung oder dem Funktionieren des Binnenmarktes dienen. Denn die EU erlässt nach Art. 26 Abs. 1 AEUV „die erforderlichen Maßnahmen, um nach Maßgabe der einschlägigen Bestimmungen der Verträge den Binnenmarkt zu verwirklichen beziehungsweise dessen Funktionieren zu gewährleisten". Der Rat legt nach Art. 26 Abs. 3 AEUV auf Vorschlag der Kommission „die Leitlinien und Bedingungen fest, die erforderlich sind, um in allen betroffenen Sektoren einen ausgewogenen Fortschritt zu gewährleisten".

Diese Fortschrittsdimension des Binnenmarktes spricht – ungeachtet der zwischenzeitlich in Bezug auf die Binnenmarkt-Definition wie die Binnenmarkt-Rechtsangleichung erfolgten Änderungen der vertraglichen Normen – für eine fortdauernde Relevanz der Schranken, die der EuGH in seinem grundlegenden Tabakwerbeverbotsurteil vom 5. Oktober 2000 einer auf die Binnenmarkt-Klausel gestützten Rechtsetzung der EU setzt. Danach muss ein auf Art. 114 AEUV gestützter Rechtsakt tatsächlich den Zweck haben, die Voraussetzungen für die Errichtung und das Funktionieren des Binnenmarktes zu verbessern.

„Genügten bereits die bloße Feststellung von Unterschieden zwischen den Vorschriften und die abstrakte Gefahr von Beeinträchtigungen der Grundfreiheiten oder daraus möglicherweise entstehenden Wettbewerbsverzerrungen, um die Wahl von Artikel 100 a (EGV; nunmehr: Art. 114 AEUV) als Rechtsgrundlage zu rechtfertigen, so könnte der gerichtlichen Kontrolle der Wahl der Rechtsgrundlage jede Wirksamkeit genommen werden".[130]

S. 44 ff.; *Klamert/Lewis* in: Kellerbauer/Klamert/Tomkin, Art. 26 AEUV, Rn. 11; *Mojzesowicz*, Möglichkeiten und Grenzen einer einheitlichen Dogmatik der Grundfreiheiten, S. 133 ff.; *Mühl*, Diskriminierung und Beschränkung. Grundansätze einer einheitlichen Dogmatik der wirtschaftlichen Grundfreiheiten des EG-Vertrages, S. 30 ff., 198 ff.; *Plötscher*, Der Begriff der Diskriminierung im Europäischen Gemeinschaftsrecht; *Schleper* in: Göttinger Online-Beiträge zum Europarecht, Nr. 16 (2004), 1, 1 ff.; *Streinz*, Konvergenz der Grundfreiheiten, 199, 206 ff.
129 Vgl. EuGH, Rs. C-76/90, *Manfred Säger / Dennemeyer & Co. Ltd*.
130 EuGH, Rs. C-376/98, *Deutschland/Rat und Parlament*, Rn. 84.

B. Primärrechtlicher Rahmen zur Kompetenzabgrenzung

Zwar dürfe, so der EuGH, der europäische Gesetzgeber auf Grundlage der Binnenmarkt-Rechtsangleichungs-Grundlage tätig werden, um der Entstehung neuer Hindernisse für den Handel infolge einer heterogenen Entwicklung der nationalen Rechtsvorschriften vorzubeugen, deren Entstehen müsse jedoch „wahrscheinlich sein und die fragliche Maßnahme ihre Vermeidung bezwecken".[131]

Dies spricht dafür, dass die Binnenmarkt-Kompetenz dahingehend wahrzunehmen ist, Hindernisse zu beseitigen und nicht, noch größere Hürden für die Ausübung der Grundfreiheiten zu erlassen[132] – unbeschadet der fortdauernden Kompetenz der Mitgliedstaaten, im nicht harmonisierten Bereich aus Gründen, wie sie sich in den jeweiligen vertraglichen Ausnahmeklauseln zu den Grundfreiheiten finden, oder aus Gründen zwingenden Allgemeinwohls, zumindest temporäre Beschränkungen der Grundfreiheiten vorzusehen. Das schließt Maßnahmen aus, deren Ziel nicht wenigstens auch ein gewisses Maß an Deregulierung ist. Solche Deregulierungsmaßnahmen können grundsätzlich auch Rechtsvereinheitlichungen sein, aber nicht jede Rechtsvereinheitlichung beseitigt zwangsläufig Hindernisse für den Binnenmarkt.[133]

b. Die Kompetenz in Bezug auf die Niederlassungsfreiheit

Nach Art. 49 Abs. 1 AEUV sind die Beschränkungen der freien Niederlassung von Staatsangehörigen eines Mitgliedstaats im Hoheitsgebiet eines anderen Mitgliedstaats nach Maßgabe der folgenden Bestimmungen verboten.[134] Das Gleiche gilt für Beschränkungen der Gründung von Agenturen, Zweigniederlassungen oder Tochtergesellschaften durch Angehörige eines Mitgliedstaats, die im Hoheitsgebiet eines Mitgliedstaats ansässig sind.

Vorbehaltlich des Kapitels über den Kapitalverkehr umfasst die Niederlassungsfreiheit gemäß Art. 49 Abs. 2 AEUV die Aufnahme und Ausübung selbstständiger Erwerbstätigkeiten sowie die Gründung und Leitung von Unternehmen, insbesondere von Gesellschaften i.S. des Art. 54 Abs. 2 AEUV, nach den Bestimmungen des Aufnahmestaats für seine eigenen Angehörigen.

---

131 EuGH, Rs. C-376/98, *Deutschland/Rat und Parlament*, Rn. 86.
132 Vgl. EuGH, Rs. C-233/94, *Deutschland/Europäisches Parlament*, Rn. 15, 19.
133 Vgl. *Ress/Bröhmer*, Europäische Gemeinschaft und Medienvielfalt, S. 40.
134 Zu der Frage nach möglichen Beeinträchtigungen von Grundfreiheiten durch die mitgliedstaatliche Ausübung von Kompetenzen vgl. Abschnitt C.IV.1.

Nach Art. 50 Abs. 1 AEUV erlassen das Europäische Parlament und der Rat gemäß dem ordentlichen Gesetzgebungsverfahren und nach Anhörung des Wirtschafts- und Sozialausschusses Richtlinien zur Verwirklichung der Niederlassungsfreiheit für eine bestimmte Tätigkeit. Um eine solche Tätigkeit kann es sich auch bei audiovisueller Produktion und Verbreitung, einschließlich der Aggregation, Selektion und Präsentation von audiovisuellen Angeboten handeln.

Das Europäische Parlament, der Rat und die Kommission erfüllen die Aufgaben, die ihnen durch Art. 49 und 50 Abs. 1 AEUV übertragen sind, gemäß Art. 50 Abs. 2 Buchst. a) AEUV, indem sie insbesondere im Allgemeinen diejenigen Tätigkeiten mit Vorrang behandeln, bei denen die Niederlassungsfreiheit die Entwicklung der Produktion und des Handels in besonderer Weise fördert. Das Tätigkeiten, die einen Bezug zur Herstellung des digitalen Binnenmarktes aufweisen, insoweit vorrangig behandelt werden sollten, bedarf mit Blick auf die Bedeutung der Digitalisierung für sämtliche bisherigen wie für sich neu entwickelnde Geschäftsmodelle keiner besonderen Erläuterung.

Nach Art. 50 Abs. 2 Buchst. f) AEUV haben die Rechtsetzungsorgane der EU zudem zu veranlassen, dass bei jedem in Betracht kommenden Wirtschaftszweig die Beschränkungen der Niederlassungsfreiheit in Bezug auf die Voraussetzungen für die Errichtung von Agenturen, Zweigniederlassungen und Tochtergesellschaften im Hoheitsgebiet eines Mitgliedstaats sowie für den Eintritt des Personals der Hauptniederlassung in ihre Leitungs- oder Überwachungsorgane schrittweise aufgehoben werden. Diese Klausel ist nicht zuletzt auch mit Blick auf die strategischen Ausdehnungspläne der großen US-amerikanischen Internetgiganten, denen vielfach auch eine wachsende Relevanz im Prozess der Sicherung von Medienfreiheit und -vielfalt zukommt, von erheblicher Bedeutung, wenn diese von einer Tochtergesellschaft mit Sitz in einem EU-Mitgliedstaat wie z.B. Irland aus ihre vielfaltsrelevante Geschäftstätigkeit in dritten Mitgliedstaaten der EU entfalten.

Nach Art. 50 Abs. 2 Buchst. g) AEUV haben die Rechtsetzungsorgane der EU ferner, „soweit erforderlich", die „Schutzbestimmungen" zu koordinieren, die in den Mitgliedstaaten den Gesellschaften i.S. des Art. 54 Abs. 2 AEUV im Interesse der Gesellschafter „sowie Dritter" vorgeschrieben sind, um diese Bestimmungen gleichwertig zu gestalten. Ob es sich bei diesen Dritten auch um die demokratische Öffentlichkeit als solche handeln kann, erscheint mit Blick auf den individuell-personalen Anknüpfungspunkt höchst zweifelhaft. Aber auch eine Stellung des einzelnen Nutzers von medialen Angeboten, die eine Gesellschaft produziert, aggregiert, selektiert, präsentiert oder verbreitet, als „Dritter" i.S. des Art. 50 Abs. 2

Buchst. g) AEUV erscheint – selbst unter Berücksichtigung einer die Rechtsetzung mitbestimmenden hoheitlichen Schutzpflicht für Medienfreiheit und -vielfalt – mehr als fraglich, zumal diesen Schutzpflichten keine individuelle Ansprüche begründende Dimension eigen ist.

Art. 50 Abs. 1 AEUV gewährt grundsätzlich eine Kompetenz zur Abschaffung nationaler nichtdiskriminierender Beschränkungen der Niederlassungsfreiheit bzw. deren Ersetzung durch eine einheitliche unionsrechtliche Vorschrift, und dies selbst dann, wenn die mitgliedstaatlichen Regelungen durch zwingende Erfordernisse eines Allgemeininteresses gerechtfertigt und damit unionsrechtskonform sind.[135] Durch solche Regelungen wird die Niederlassung in anderen Mitgliedstaaten erleichtert, da dann grundsätzlich keine Auseinandersetzung mit einer Vielzahl von Regelungen zum Schutz des Gemeinwohlinteresses mehr erforderlich ist.[136] Dies betrifft nicht nur die Schutzvorkehrungen mit Blick auf vertraute Herausforderungen, sondern auch neue Herausforderungen, die sich erst entwickeln. Denn die Schutzkonzeption in Bezug auf Allgemeinwohlinteressen muss nicht zwingend repressiv, sondern kann auch prophylaktisch-präventiv ausgerichtet sein.

Für die Konkretisierung der unionalen Rechtsangleichungskompetenz im Bereich der Niederlassungsfreiheit ergibt sich daher die Frage, ob die EU alles regeln darf, was in irgendeiner Weise eine wirtschaftliche Tätigkeit auch außerhalb des eigenen Staates erleichtert. Dies käme *de facto* der Anerkennung einer wirtschaftsbezogenen Allzuständigkeit der EU gleich, denn im Zeitalter der umfassenden Normierung sind im Bereich der wirtschaftlichen Betätigung im weitesten Sinne kaum Sachverhalte denkbar, die nicht in irgendeiner Weise gesetzlich geregelt sind. Die unionsrechtliche Harmonisierung wäre allein schon wegen der dadurch eintretenden Rechtsvereinheitlichung immer unionsrechtskonform, solange die Kompetenzausübungsregelungen und -schranken der Art. 4 und 5 EUV[137] Beachtung finden. Die Behauptung einer derartigen Harmonisierungskompetenz wäre von einer – wie aufgezeigt[138] – unions- wie verfassungsrechtlich abgelehnten Kompetenz-Kompetenz praktisch gleich.[139]

---

135 Vgl. *Lenz* in: EuGRZ 1993, 57, 60 f.; *Ress/Bröhmer*, Europäische Gemeinschaft und Medienvielfalt, S. 34.
136 Vgl. *Liehr*, Die Niederlassungsfreiheit zum Zwecke der Rundfunkveranstaltung und ihre Auswirkungen auf die deutsche Rundfunkordnung, S. 249 ff.
137 Vgl. hierzu Abschnitt B.V.
138 Vgl. hierzu Abschnitt B.V.
139 Vgl. *Ress/Bröhmer*, Europäische Gemeinschaft und Medienvielfalt, S. 34.

Dem Prinzip der begrenzten Ermächtigung entspricht es, dass auch im Zusammenhang mit der Verwirklichung der Niederlassungsfreiheit die Ermächtigung nach Art. 50 Abs. 1 AEUV nicht uferlos, sondern klar begrenzt ist und – im Unterschied zur Kompetenz der Mitgliedstaaten – der Legitimation und Begründung bedarf.[140] Eine niederlassungsbezogenen Koordinierungs- und Rechtsangleichungskompetenz besteht mithin nicht bereits bei jedweder denkbaren Berührung oder Auswirkung von Unterschieden mitgliedstaatlicher Rechtsordnungen auf die Wahrnehmung der Niederlassungsfreiheit.

Die bloße Verschiedenheit nationaler Rechtsvorschriften – wie z.B. bei den Konzessionssystemen in verschiedenen Berufen – ist für sich noch allein noch kein Grund für eine Regulierung seitens der EU. Für die Herstellung oder das Funktionieren des Binnenmarktes sind weder einheitliche (uniforme) noch inhaltlich angeglichene (koordinierte) Regelungen erforderlich. Insbesondere wenn mitgliedstaatliche Regelungen EU-Drittstaatsangehörige faktisch diskriminieren, kann ein anzuerkennender Regelungsbedarf bestehen, nicht jedoch schon dann, wenn die Voraussetzungen für die Erbringung von Dienstleistungen bzw. die Niederlassung in den Mitgliedstaaten unterschiedlich sind. Da die Sicherung von Medienvielfalt und die Herstellung des Medienpluralismus als solche keine Binnenmarktziele sind, dürfen diese Ziele nicht auf dem Umweg einer behaupteten faktischen Niederlassungs- oder Dienstleistungsbehinderung zum Regelungsziel gemacht werden.[141]

c. Die Kompetenz in Bezug auf die Dienstleistungsfreiheit

Die in Art. 56 ff. AEUV verankerte Dienstleistungsfreiheit bezieht sich nach Art. 57 AEUV auf Leistungen, die in der Regel gegen Entgelt erbracht werden, soweit sie nicht den übrigen vorrangigen Grundfreiheiten unterfallen.[142] Auch mediale Dienstleistungen sind von diesem Kompetenztitel erfasst: Denn Medien sind zwar (auch) Kulturgut, aufgrund ihrer (auch) wirtschaftlichen Bezüge sind diese, soweit es sich nicht um Waren handelt,

---

140 Vgl. *Jarass*, Die Kompetenzen der Europäischen Gemeinschaft und die Folgen für die Mitgliedstaaten, S. 6.; *Ress/Bröhmer*, Europäische Gemeinschaft und Medienvielfalt, S. 36.
141 Vgl. *Ress/Ukrow*, Die Niederlassungsfreiheit von Apothekern, 1991, S. 42 ff.
142 Zur Reichweite des Anwendungsbereichs der Dienstleistungsfreiheit und der Frage nach möglichen Beeinträchtigungen von Grundfreiheiten durch die mitgliedstaatliche Ausübung von Kompetenzen vgl. Abschnitt C.IV.1.

allerdings zugleich auch ökonomische Leistungen i.S. der Definition des Art. 57 AEUV.[143]

Neben der aktiven Dienstleistungsfreiheit – der Freiheit des Dienstleisters, seine Dienstleistung in einem anderen Mitgliedstaat zu den gleichen Bedingungen wie ein dort niedergelassener Dienstleister zu erbringen – wird vom Kompetenztitel zur Regulierung der Dienstleistungsfreiheit auch die passive Dienstleistungsfreiheit[144] umfasst, also das Recht des Empfängers, eine Dienstleistung in einem anderen Mitgliedstaat von einem dort niedergelassenen Dienstleister zu erhalten. Zudem umfasst der Kompetenztitel auch die sog. Korrespondenzdienstleistungsfreiheit, bei der nicht Erbringer oder Empfänger einer Dienstleistung, sondern die Leistung selbst die Grenze überschreitet.[145] Dieser Variante der Dienstleistungsfreiheit kommt im Zusammenhang mit grenzüberschreitenden medialen Angeboten besondere Bedeutung zu.[146] Dies gilt auch für Leistungen von Medienintermediären wie Mediaagenturen: Auch die Regulierung von Leistungen der Aggregation, Selektion oder Präsentation von medialem Content, sei es solcher journalistischer oder kommerziell-kommunikativer Art, ist vom Kompetenztitel der Regelung der Dienstleistungsfreiheit im Ausgangspunkt erfasst.

Wenig spricht allerdings dafür, dass der dienstleistungsrechtliche Kompetenztitel eine Medienvielfaltsregulierung der EU tragen könnte. Nicht zuletzt die Behandlung des Feldes audiovisueller Dienste in der bisherigen Praxis der Anwendung der primärrechtlich eröffneten Möglichkeiten zur Regelung der Dienstleistungsfreiheit spricht gegen einen solchen Kompetenztitel.

So hat die EU in Art. 2 Abs. 2 Buchst. g) der Richtlinie 2006/123/EG über Dienstleistungen im Binnenmarkt[147] „audiovisuelle Dienste, auch im Kino- und Filmbereich, ungeachtet der Art ihrer Herstellung, Verbreitung

---

143 Diese Einordnung umfasst – ebenso wie der audiovisuelle Bereich i.S. des Art. 167 Abs. 2 4. Spiegelstrich AEUV (hierzu *Calliess/Korte*, Dienstleistungsrecht in der EU, § 5 Rn. 88) und fortdauernd anders als die 2018 novellierte AVMD-Richtlinie – auch Hörfunkangebote linearer wie non-linearer Art. Kritisch zu der fortdauernden Hörfunk-Blindheit der AVMD-Richtlinie *Ukrow*, Zum Anwendungsbereich einer novellierten AVMD-Richtlinie, S. 3.
144 Vgl. hierzu *Randelzhofer/Forthoff* in: Grabitz/Hilf/Nettesheim, Art. 49/50 AEUV, Rn. 1, 51; *Dony*, Droit de l'Union européenne, Rn. 680.
145 Vgl. z.B. *Calliess/Korte*, Dienstleistungsrecht in der EU, 2011, § 3 Rn. 25 ff.
146 Vgl. bereits EuGH, Rs. 155/73, *Sacchi*, Rn. 6.
147 Richtlinie 2006/123/EG des Europäischen Parlaments und des Rates vom 12. Dezember 2006 über Dienstleistungen im Binnenmarkt, EU ABl. L 376, 27.12.2006, S. 36–68.

und Ausstrahlung, und Rundfunk" vom Anwendungsbereich dieser Richtlinie ausgenommen.[148] Ratio legis dieser Ausnahme war nicht zuletzt die Sorge um eine etwaige Umgehung des spezifischen Sekundärrechts für audiovisuelle Medien in der EU[149] – und damit inzident auch die Sorge um eine Missachtung mitgliedstaatlicher Kompetenzen und Verantwortlichkeiten für die mediale Vielfaltssicherung.

Eine denkbare Parallele einer Medienvielfaltsregulierung mittels EU-Richtlinie zur AVMD-Richtlinie besteht zudem nicht. Denn bei dieser geht es auch weiterhin – wie schon zuvor bei der Fernsehrichtlinie der EWG[150] – im Schwerpunkt um die Regelung bestimmter Mindestvoraussetzungen für grenzüberschreitende Angebote audiovisueller Art, namentlich vergleichbare Anforderungen an den Jugendschutz, den Schutz der Menschenwürde und die kommerzielle Kommunikation (namentlich Werbung, Sponsoring und Teleshopping), von denen die Geltung des Grundsatzes freier grenzüberschreitender Weiterverbreitung der audiovisuellen Angebote und des Prinzips der Herkunftslandskontrolle – also die Freiheit der Dienstleistung zum Angebot im Herkunftsland und zum Empfang in einem Drittstaat – und die Freiheit der Dienstleistung von Mehrfachkontrollen selbst abhing. Anforderungen an die Pluralität (Binnen- und Außenpluralität) von Rundfunk- und Fernsehveranstaltern oder von Anbietern von Telemedien wie z.B. Video-Sharing-Diensten hätten indessen nichts mit der Übertragbarkeit (Verkehrsfähigkeit) dieser audiovisuellen Angebote zu tun.

Etwas anderes könnte allerdings für den Fall einer Auffindbarkeitsregulierung im Online-Bereich als neuer Form digitaler Vielfaltssicherung, wie sie sich nunmehr im Medienstaatsvertrag findet, gelten. Denn von einer solchen Regulierung können zumindest mittelbare Beschränkungen für die freie Empfangbarkeit audiovisueller Angebote ausgehen.

d. Zwischenfazit

Aus den Binnenmarktkompetenzen der EU ist eine Ermächtigung der EU zur Rechtsharmonisierung im Bereich der Medienvielfaltssicherung nur

---

148 Nach Satz 2 des 24. Erwägungsgrundes dieser Richtlinie „sollte diese Richtlinie (ebenso wenig) für Beihilfen gelten, die von den Mitgliedstaaten im audiovisuellen Sektor gewährt werden und die unter die gemeinschaftlichen Wettbewerbsvorschriften fallen".
149 Vgl. *Calliess/Korte*, Dienstleistungsrecht in der EU, § 5 Rn. 86.
150 Vgl. hierzu *Ress/Bröhmer*, Europäische Gemeinschaft und Medienvielfalt, S. 42.

B. Primärrechtlicher Rahmen zur Kompetenzabgrenzung

schwerlich ableitbar. Der Kompetenztitel der Niederlassungsfreiheit ist eng auszulegen, weil nur dies dem Charakter einer Union aus Mitgliedstaaten, deren nationale Identität zu wahren ist, entspricht. Insbesondere ein etwaiger Regulierungsansatz, der den Bestand an unternehmerischer Freiheit im Binnenmarkt reduzieren würde, wäre mit dem auf Fortschritt in Richtung auf grenzüberschreitende freie Entfaltung ausgerichteten Binnenmarktkonzept des Art. 26 AEUV kaum in Einklang zu bringen. Gegen die Heranziehung der Regulierungskompetenzen in Bezug auf die Dienstleistungsfreiheit spricht darüber hinaus, dass sie durch nationalstaatliche Regelungen im Bereich der Vielfaltssicherung regelmäßig nur mittelbar betroffen sein dürfte.[151]

2. Die Wettbewerbsordnung der EU

Wettbewerbsrecht hat Marktmacht, Recht der Vielfaltssicherung Meinungsmacht im Blick.[152] Es handelt sich also um zwei getrennte Sachbereiche, bei denen die jeweilige Machtkontrolle entsprechend auch mit unterschiedlichen Instrumentarien erfolgt. Markt- und Meinungsmachtkontrolle sind indessen keine Phänomene ohne Berührungspunkte. Vielmehr geht das wettbewerbsrechtliche Kartellrecht Hand in Hand mit dem Recht der Meinungsvielfaltssicherung. Insbesondere ist die Wettbewerbsordnung grundsätzlich geeignet, das Ziel eines vielfältigen Angebots gleichsam als Nebeneffekt zu erreichen.[153]

Im Bereich der Wettbewerbsordnung verfügt die EU nicht nur – wie im Fall der Binnenmarktordnung – über geteilte, sondern sogar über ausschließliche, in den Art. 101 ff. AEUV im Einzelnen aufgezeigte Zuständigkeiten – namentlich in Gestalt der Kontrolle eines Kartellverbots, des Missbrauchs einer marktbeherrschenden Stellung und der Beihilfenaufsicht.[154] Dies ist mit Blick auf Vielfaltssicherung im Medienbereich von erkennbarer, die Marktordnung der Medien betreffender Relevanz.

---

151 Vgl. bereits *Ress/Bröhmer*, Europäische Gemeinschaft und Medienvielfalt, S. 43.
152 Vgl. zu den Erwägungen außerhalb der an dieser Stelle im Fokus stehenden kompetenzrechtlichen Bezugnahmen eingehend Abschnitt C.IV.2. sowie zur Fusionskontrolle D.II.4.
153 Vgl. *Cole*, Europarechtliche Rahmenbedingungen für die Pluralismussicherung im Rundfunk, 93, 104 f.; *Jungheim*, Medienordnung und Wettbewerbsrecht im Zeitalter der Digitalisierung und Globalisierung, S. 249 ff.
154 Vgl. hierzu *Ukrow* in: UFITA 2019, 279, 279 ff.

Allerdings wird die praktische Bedeutung dieser Aufsichtsinstrumente dadurch relativiert, dass die meisten Medienmärkte im Wesentlichen nach wie vor national ausgerichtet und durch nationale Grenzen stark abgegrenzt sind – auch wenn die Medien in einigen Mitgliedstaaten zu einem hohen Anteil in ausländischer Hand sind.

Das primäre Unionsrecht steht einer Wahrnehmung der Kontrollkompetenzen nicht von vornherein entgegen, bei der die Eigentumskonzentration nicht nur im Hinblick auf bestimmte Medien(teil)gattungen wie z.B. Presse, Hörfunk und Fernsehen betrachtet wird, sondern über verschiedene Medien hinweg und auch in Bezug auf die Vertriebskanäle. Insofern ist das Unionsrecht in seinem Ausgangspunkt nicht auf eine fernsehzentrierte Kontrollwahrnehmung beschränkt, bei der medienrelevante verwandte Märkte allenfalls colorandi causa in den Blick genommen werden, sondern steht einem dynamischen Verständnis nicht zuletzt der Marktdefinition wie auch einer marktbeherrschenden Stellung offen. Letzteres ermöglicht auch eine Reaktion in der Aufsichtspraxis, die Netzwerkeffekte der digitalen Plattformökonomie in den Blick nimmt.

Auch zwischengeschaltete digitale Ebenen, wie Suchmaschinen, Nachrichtenaggregatoren, soziale Netze und App-Stores[155] können bei der Überwachung des Mediensektors berücksichtigt werden, ohne dass dem das primärrechtliche wettbewerbsrechtliche Ordnungsprogramm schon im Ausgangspunkt entgegenstehen würde. Ihre ständig wachsende Relevanz für eine effektive Sicherung von Freiheit und Vielfalt der Medien ist allerdings kein Aspekt, der die Wahrnehmung der Wettbewerbsregeln unionsrechtlich zweifelsfrei (mit-) prägen darf.

Wegen seiner Besonderheiten für die freie individuelle und öffentliche Meinungs- und Bildung wie auf für den gesellschaftlichen Zusammenhalt in und die kulturstaatliche Ausprägung von Mitgliedstaaten kann der Mediensektor zwar, soweit Konzentrationstendenzen in Rede stehen, nicht ausschließlich am Maßstab des allgemeinen Rechts der Kartellverbots und der Fusionskontrolle gemessen werden. Denn auch die Organe der EU sind als grundrechts- und grundwertegebundene Akteure[156] zur Beachtung von Auswirkungen ihres Verhaltens für Demokratie, Grundrechte und Kultur gehalten. Die Berücksichtigung demokratischer, grundrechtlicher und kultureller Grundsätze und Anforderungen ist aber im Rahmen der

---

155 Vgl. zu diesen möglichen Adressaten der Wettbewerbsordnung bereits *Viķe-Freiberga u.a.* (Hochrangige Gruppe zur Freiheit und Vielfalt der Medien), Bericht zu freien und pluralistischen Medien als Rückhalt der europäischen Demokratie, 2013, S. 27.
156 Vgl. hierzu unten, Abschnitte B.VI.1.

Wettbewerbspolitik in gleicher Weise und z.B. nach Art. 167 Abs. 4 AEUV an der Schnittstelle von Schonung kultureller Handlungsmöglichkeiten und wettbewerbsrechtlicher Aufsichtspflicht ausdrücklich geboten.[157]

Wettbewerb kann zwar, muss aber nicht unbedingt den Pluralismus fördern, denn er kann auch dazu führen, dass das Inhalteangebot stärker vereinheitlicht und homogenisiert wird. Bei der Ausgestaltung der Wettbewerbspolitik ist die Kommission auch vor diesem Hintergrund gehalten, auf die Marktkonzentration nicht nur unter dem Gesichtspunkt des Wettbewerbs, sondern auch des Pluralismus achten. Auch der Medienkonsum sollte deshalb bei der Frage, welche Sachverhalte die Kommission einer Prüfung unterzieht, berücksichtigt werden.[158]

In Bezug auf die kulturelle Dimension der Medien kommt der beihilfeaufsichtsrechtlichen Ausnahmebestimmung in Art. 107 Abs. 3 Buchst. d) AEUV besondere Bedeutung zu: Danach können „Beihilfen zur Förderung der Kultur und der Erhaltung des kulturellen Erbes" als „mit dem Binnenmarkt vereinbar angesehen werden", „soweit sie die Handels- und Wettbewerbsbedingungen in der Union nicht in einem Maß beeinträchtigen, das dem gemeinsamen Interesse zuwiderläuft".

Das sog. Amsterdamer „Protokoll zum öffentlich-rechtlichen Rundfunk in den Mitgliedstaaten" greift dieses Gebot einer Handlungsspielräume der Mitgliedstaaten wahrenden Auslegung des Unionsrechts auf, indem es „in der Erwägung, dass der öffentlich-rechtliche Rundfunk in den Mitgliedstaaten unmittelbar mit den demokratischen, sozialen und kulturellen Bedürfnissen jeder Gesellschaft sowie mit dem Erfordernis verknüpft ist, den Pluralismus in den Medien zu wahren" als „auslegende Bestimmungen", die EUV wie AEUV beigefügt sind, regelt, dass die Bestimmungen dieser Verträge „nicht die Befugnis der Mitgliedstaaten (berühren), den öffentlich-rechtlichen Rundfunk zu finanzieren, sofern die Finanzierung der Rundfunkanstalten dem öffentlich-rechtlichen Auftrag, wie er von den Mitgliedstaaten den Anstalten übertragen, festgelegt und ausgestaltet wird, dient und die Handels- und Wettbewerbsbedingungen in der Union nicht in einem Ausmaß beeinträchtigt, das dem gemeinsamen Interesse zuwider-

---

157 Vgl. bereits *Ress/Bröhmer*, Europäische Gemeinschaft und Medienvielfalt, 1998, S. 45.
158 Vgl. *Vīķe-Freiberga u.a.* (Hochrangige Gruppe zur Freiheit und Vielfalt der Medien), Bericht zu freien und pluralistischen Medien als Rückhalt der europäischen Demokratie, 2013, S. 27.

läuft, wobei den Erfordernissen der Erfüllung des öffentlich-rechtlichen Auftrags Rechnung zu tragen ist".[159]

In dem Amsterdamer Protokoll wird offen das Spannungsverhältnis angesprochen, das zwischen der demokratischen, sozialen und kulturellen Dimension der Medien und deren ökonomischer Relevanz bestehen kann – ein Spanungsverhältnis, das im Übrigen nicht auf den öffentlich-rechtlichen Rundfunk als Medien(teil)gattung begrenzt ist. Während erstere für eine Regelungskompetenz der Mitgliedstaaten streitet, ist mit Blick auf letztere die potentielle Binnenmarkt-Dimension grenzüberschreitenden Medienengagements offenkundig.

3. Die Kulturkompetenz der EU

Die Zurückhaltung der EU in Bezug auf eine positive Ordnungskompetenz für die Medien seitens der EU wird in Bezug auf den „audiovisuellen Bereich" durch den Kultur-Artikel des AEUV bekräftigt. Art. 167 AEUV erteilt der EU einen Auftrag zur Kulturförderung auf europäischer Ebene unter Wahrung des „kulturellen" Selbstbestimmungsrechts der Mitgliedstaaten. Art. 167 Abs. 1 – 3 AEUV ermöglichen dabei einerseits und begrenzen anderseits die aktive Kulturpolitik der EU.

Die Union soll nach Absatz 1 „einen Beitrag zur Entfaltung der Kulturen der Mitgliedstaaten unter Wahrung ihrer nationalen und regionalen Vielfalt sowie gleichzeitiger Hervorhebung des gemeinsamen kulturellen Erbes (leisten)". Nach Art. 167 Abs. 2 4. Spiegelstrich AEUV „fördert (die EU) durch ihre Tätigkeit die Zusammenarbeit zwischen den Mitgliedstaaten und unterstützt und ergänzt erforderlichenfalls deren Tätigkeit in den Bereichen „künstlerische(n) und literarische(n) Schaffen(s), einschließlich im audiovisuellen Bereich".[160] Medien werden hiermit als zumindest auch kulturelles Phänomen primärrechtlich anerkannt – eine Dimension, die

---

159 Eingehend hierzu auch *Ukrow/Cole*, Aktive Sicherung lokaler und regionaler Medienvielfalt, S. 72 ff.
160 Dieser Bereich kreativen Schaffens umfasst sowohl den Video- und Filmbereich als auch den gesamten Rundfunk – mithin, in Abweichung vom Anwendungsbereich der AVMD-Richtlinie, auch den Hörfunk – sowie die Bereiche audiovisueller Mediendienste auf Abruf und audiovisueller kommerzieller Kommunikation. Vgl. auch *Blanke* in: Calliess/Ruffert, EUV/AEUV, Art. 167 Rn. 12; *Ukrow/Ress* in: Grabitz/Hilf/Nettesheim, Art. 167 AEUV, Rn. 128 f.; *Vedder* in: ders./Heintschel von Heinegg, Art. 167 AEUV, Rn. 7; *Moussis*, Access to the European Union, S. 272 f.

B. Primärrechtlicher Rahmen zur Kompetenzabgrenzung

zumindest gleichrangig neben der ökonomischen Bedeutung von Medien ungeachtet der zunehmenden Bedeutung dieses Sektors für Wertschöpfung im Binnenmarkt der EU wie auch global fortbesteht.

Bereits aus den zurückhaltenden Formulierungen des „Beitrag Leistens" und „Förderns" lässt sich ablesen, dass die EU im Rahmen ihrer Kulturpolitik nicht diejenige der Mitgliedstaaten konterkarieren, vereinheitlichen oder ersetzen soll, sondern (lediglich) eine Rolle als Wahrer europäischer Kulturschöpfung[161] einnimmt.[162] Die Tätigkeit der EU im Bereich Kultur ist mithin zu derjenigen der Mitgliedstaaten der EU subsidiär, wie sich auch aus einer Zusammenschau mit weiterem Normenmaterial des EUV wie auch des AEUV ergibt. Auch das Gericht der Europäischen Union (EuG) hat diese Subsidiarität in einem Urteil vom 10. Mai 2016 betont.[163] Aus der wechselseitigen Loyalitätsverpflichtung zwischen der EU und ihren Mitgliedstaaten folgt allerdings auch, dass die Mitgliedstaaten die EU bei der Wahrnehmung ihrer Aufgaben nach Art. 167 Abs. 1 und 2 AEUV unterstützen müssen, wobei eine hieraus resultierende, separate Finanzierungsverpflichtung jedoch nicht angenommen wird.[164]

Art. 167 Abs. 4 AEUV stellt eine Regelung für das Tätigwerden der EU außerhalb der in den Abs. 1 bis 3 genannten Bereiche der Kulturpolitik auf, wonach die Union bei ihrer Tätigkeit aufgrund anderer Bestimmungen der Verträge den kulturellen Aspekten Rechnung trägt, insbesondere zur Wahrung und Förderung der Vielfalt ihrer Kulturen. Diese Bestimmung wird gemeinhin als ‚kulturelle Querschnittsklausel' oder ‚Kulturverträglichkeitsklausel' bezeichnet, beschreibt jedoch nicht etwa einen Kulturvorbehalt.[165] Die Kompetenzordnung der EU etwa im Sinne einer „*exception culturelle*" wird von der Regelung gerade nicht berührt, das heißt, weder stellt sie eine eigenständige Kompetenzgrundlage für die EU dar noch beeinträchtigt sie bestehende Zuständigkeiten.[166] Aus der Pflicht zur

---

161 Vgl. hierzu auch die Präambel zum EUV in der es heißt, dass die EU „schöpfend aus dem kulturellen, religiösen und humanistischen Erbe Europas, aus dem sich die unverletzlichen und unveräußerlichen Rechte des Menschen sowie Freiheit, Demokratie, Gleichheit und Rechtsstaatlichkeit als universelle Werte entwickelt haben" agiert.
162 *Blanke* in: Calliess/Ruffert, Art. 167 Rn. 1; *Garben* in: Kellerbauer/Klamert/Tomkin, Art. 167 AEUV, Rn. 2 ff.; *Vedder* in: ders./Heintschel von Heinegg, Art. 167 AEUV, Rn. 6.
163 Vgl. EuG, Rs. T-529/13, *Izsák u. Dabis / Europäische Kommission*, Rn. 96.
164 Vgl. ausführlich: *Hochbaum* in: BayVBl. 1997, 680, 681.
165 Vgl. z.B. *Ukrow/Ress*, in: Grabitz/Hilf/Nettesheim, Art. 167 AEUV, Rn. 148 ff. m.w.N.; *Garben* in: Kellerbauer/Klamert/Tomkin, Art. 167 AEUV, Rn. 5.
166 *Lenski*, Öffentliches Kulturrecht, S. 142.

Berücksichtigung kultureller Aspekte folgen eine ganze Reihe von vielfaltschonenden und -fördernden Anforderungen, denen die EU bei ihrer Rechtssetzung wie bei der Aufsicht über die Unionsrechtskonformität mitgliedstaatlichen Verhaltens Rechnung tragen muss. Im Blick auf die aktive Vielfaltssicherung verdienen dabei nicht zuletzt auch die Einwirkungen der Querschnittsklausel auf das Medien-, das Telekommunikations- und das Beihilfe- und sonstige Wettbewerbsaufsichtsrecht der EU Beachtung.[167]

Art. 167 Abs. 5 AEUV bestimmt sodann die Handlungsinstrumente und Verfahren, die der EU zur Durchsetzung der eingangsgenannten Ziele zur Verfügung stehen. Ausschließlich vom Rat auf Vorschlag der Kommission erlassene Empfehlungen sowie Fördermaßnahmen, die das Europäische Parlament und der Rat gemäß dem ordentlichen Gesetzgebungsverfahren und nach Anhörung des Ausschusses der Regionen, jedoch unter Ausschluss jeglicher Harmonisierung der Rechts- und Verwaltungsvorschriften der Mitgliedstaaten[168] erlassen, kommen dabei in Betracht. Letztere Negativklausel im Rahmen des Harmonisierungsverbotes verbietet der EU den Rekurs auf die allgemeinen Kompetenztitel zur Rechtsangleichung gemäß Art. 114, 115 AEUV sowie spezieller Rechtsangleichungsvorschriften.[169] Somit stellt sich diese Regelung nicht als generelles Harmonisierungsverbot für Maßnahmen mit Auswirkungen auf den kulturellen Lebensbereich dar, sondern als Verbot harmonisierender Kulturmaßnahmen, das auf Kompetenztitel außerhalb von Art. 167 AEUV bereits nicht anwendbar ist und daher auf solche schwerpunktmäßig in anderen Regelungsbereichen liegenden Harmonisierungsbestrebungen der EU keine Auswirkungen hat.

Aus diesem System in Art. 167 AEUV folgt, dass die EU, sofern sie sich auf eine Rechtsgrundlage aus ihrem Kompetenzkatalog stützen kann, auch jenseits der Bindungen aus Art. 167 AEUV, insbesondere des Harmonisierungsverbotes des Art. 167 Abs. 5 AEUV, das nur für primär kulturausge-

---

167 Vgl. z.B. *Ukrow/Ress* in: Grabitz/Hilf/Nettesheim, Art. 167 AEUV, Rn. 163 ff. m.w.N.
168 Die Bedeutung dieses Ausschlusses hat mit Urteil vom 10.5.2016 auch das Gericht der Europäischen Union betont; vgl. EuG, Rs. T-529/13, *Izsák u. Dabis / Europäische Kommission*, Rn. 101 ff. –.
169 *Blanke* in: Calliess/Ruffert, Art. 167 AEUV, Rn. 19; ähnlich: *Niedobitek* in: Streinz, Art. 167 AEUV, Rn. 55; vgl. *Craufurd Smith* in: Craig/de Búrca, 869, 883, 886 ff.

B. Primärrechtlicher Rahmen zur Kompetenzabgrenzung

richtete Maßnahmen gilt, und über bloße Förderungsmaßnahmen[170] hinausgehend (regulierend) tätig werden kann.[171] Die aus der kulturellen Querschnittsklausel hervorgehende Voraussetzung ist jedoch, dass sie dabei kulturelle Aspekte berücksichtigen muss, was regelmäßig auf eine Güterabwägung zwischen kulturellen und anderen Regulierungsinteressen (so z.B. wirtschaftlichen Gesichtspunkten im unionsrechtlichen Wettbewerbsrecht[172]) hinausläuft.[173] Zudem folgt aus der Systematik des AEUV, dass kulturelle Aspekte nicht Mittelpunkt einer unionsrechtlichen Regelung sein dürfen.[174]

---

170 Was unter Fördermaßnahmen im Sinne von Art. 167 Abs. 5 zu verstehen ist, wird nicht einhellig beurteilt. Teilweise (Vgl. *Blanke* in: Calliess/Ruffert, Art. 167 AEUV, Rn. 18) werden darunter nur tatsächliche und administrative Maßnahmen der EU sowohl finanzieller als auch ideeller Art verstanden, teilweise (*Ukrow/Ress* in: Grabitz/Hilf/Nettesheim, Art. 167 AEUV, Rn. 176) wird aber auch der Rückgriff auf Maßnahmen mit allgemeinem Regelungscharakter ohne Rechtsverbindlichkeit als zulässig erachtet. Vgl. weiterhin *Craufurd Smith* in: Craig/de Búrca, 869, 888 f.
171 *Lenski*, Öffentliches Kulturrecht, S. 142.
172 Eine Sonderausprägung der aus Art. 167 AEUV abzuleitenden Querschnittswirkung findet sich insbesondere in Art. 107 Abs. 3 Buchst. d) AEUV, die es der Europäischen Kommission erlaubt, unter bestimmten Umständen mitgliedstaatliche Kulturbeihilfen zu gestatten.
173 Vgl. hierzu auch die Entscheidung des EuG in der Rs. T-391/17, *Rumänien / Europäische Kommission*, in der es um die Frage ging, ob eine bei der Kommission zur Registrierung angemeldete Europäische Bürgerinitiative mit dem Ziel, den Schutz nationaler und sprachlicher Minderheiten zu verbessern und die kulturelle und sprachliche Vielfalt in der Union zu stärken, sich bereits außerhalb des kompetenzrechtlichen Rahmens zum Erlass von Rechtsakten durch die EU bewege und schon daher als rechtswidrig einzustufen und nicht zu registrieren sei. Da die Kommission im Stadium der Registrierung nur Initiativen, die auf offenkundig außerhalb des Kompetenzrahmens liegende Rechtsaktsvorschläge zielen, auszuschließen habe, ist die Frage des Umfangs der Nutzung der Kompetenzen nicht ausführlich behandelt. Jedoch weist das Gericht im Zusammenhang mit Art. 167 Abs. 5 AEUV darauf (Rn. 56, 61 f.), dass Rechtsaktsvorschläge, die die Tätigkeit der Union in ihren Zuständigkeitsbereichen ergänzen sollen, um die Wahrung der in Art. 2 EUV aufgeführten Werte und des in Art. 3 Abs. 3 Unterabs. 4 EUV genannten Reichtums ihrer kulturellen und sprachlichen Vielfalt sicherzustellen, nicht von vornherein ausgeschlossen sind, weil die Kommission die Werte und Ziele der Union bei jedem Legislativvorschlag zu beachten hat und diese damit auch grundsätzlich zum Gegenstand in einem spezifischen Vorschlag machen kann, solange damit nicht offenkundig gegen die Werte der Union selbst verstoßen wird.
174 Ständige Rechtsprechung des EuGH, vgl. etwa Rs. C-155/91, *Kommission der Europäischen Gemeinschaften / Rat der Europäischen Gemeinschaften*.

Was indes unter kulturellen Aspekten im Sinne von Art. 167 AEUV zu verstehen ist, ist nicht abschließend geklärt, da das EU-Recht keine Definition hierzu enthält.[175] Die Konturen der Begrifflichkeit sind dabei allerdings unionsrechtlich zu zeichnen und dürfen nicht durch die verschiedenen mitgliedstaatlichen Vorstellungen ihr Gepräge erhalten, da diese es ansonsten in der Hand hätte, die Reichweite der in Art. 167 AEUV enthaltenen Rücksichtnahmepflichten der EU selbst zu definieren.[176] Im Übrigen unterscheiden sich die verschiedenen Definitionsansätze aber insbesondere bezüglich ihrer jeweiligen Reichweite.[177] Gleichgültig ob man im Sinne eines weiten Verständnisses darunter „die Gesamtheit der geistigen, materiellen, intellektuellen und emotionalen Faktoren [...], die das Wesen einer Gesellschaft oder einer gesellschaftlichen Gruppe ausmachen" versteht, die „neben den schönen Künsten und den Geisteswissenschaften die Lebensformen, die menschlichen Grundrechte, die Wertordnungen, die Traditionen und die Glaubensformen"[178] ausmachen, oder ob man lediglich gewisse Bereiche geistig-schöpferischer Betätigung des Menschen, zu denen unbestritten Kunst, Literatur und Musik, aber auch der audiovisuelle Bereich zählen, wie eine systematische Auslegung des Art. 167 AEUV zeigt,[179] kann indes vorliegend vor dem Hintergrund dahinstehen, dass die Medien mindestens ein Forum für die auch im Rahmen des engen Definitionsverständnisses geschützten Tätigkeiten dienen und damit nicht nur Kultur transportieren, sondern selbst kulturelle Erzeugnisse nicht zuletzt in Form journalistisch-redaktioneller Beiträge, begründen. Speziell für audiovisuelle Medien ist diese kreativ-künstlerische Funktion als solche auch explizit in Art. 167 Abs. 2 Spiegelstrich 4 anerkannt. Aber auch darüber hinaus wird man dem in Art. 167 AEUV verankerten Kulturbegriff bzw. den „kulturellen Aspekten" auch Tätigkeiten von Urhebern sowie – wenn auch nur inhaltebezogen – Aktivitäten der Medien, ihrer Träger, Arbeitnehmer und Erzeugnisse zuordnen müssen, genauso wie die medienspezifischen Aspek-

---

175 Vgl. auch *Ukrow/Ress* in: Grabitz/Hilf/Nettesheim, Art. 167 AEUV, Rn. 150; *Garben* in: Kellerbauer/Klamert/Tomkin, Art. 167 AEUV, Rn. 4 ff.
176 *Roider*, Perspektiven einer Europäischen Rundfunkordnung, S. 57; vgl. *Craufurd Smith* in: Craig/de Búrca, 869, 874 ff.
177 Vgl. hierzu und zum Folgenden: *Roider*, Perspektiven einer Europäischen Rundfunkordnung, S. 58; *Craufurd Smith* in: Craig/de Búrca, 869, 874 ff.
178 Stellungnahme zu der Mitteilung der Kommission über neue Impulse für die Aktion der Europäischen Gemeinschaft im kulturellen Bereich, 88/C 175/15, Amtsblatt der Europäischen Gemeinschaften, C 175, 4. Juli 1988.
179 Bildung und Wissenschaft sind bei systematischer Auslegung des AEUV mit Blick auf ihre Regelung außerhalb des Art. 167 AEUV demgegenüber nicht erfasst.

te des Schutzes des Pluralismus (in Bezug auf die Informations- und Meinungsvielfalt) und die Medienvielfalt.[180]

IV. Die Ziele der EU und ihre kompetenzielle Bedeutung mit Blick auf Medienregulierung

1. Medienregulierungsbezogene Ziele der EU

Art. 3 EUV stellt Ziele der Union auf, die durch Integration – im Sinne eines zielorientierten Handlungssystems und nicht allein ‚um der Integration' selbst willen – erreicht werden sollen.[181] Art. 3 Abs. 3 Unterabs. 3 EUV enthält dabei unter anderem die Zielsetzung, dass die Union den Reichtum ihrer kulturellen und sprachlichen Vielfalt wahrt und für den Schutz und die Entwicklung des kulturellen Erbes Europas sorgt. Zielsetzung ist es daher gerade nicht eine europäische Einheitskultur oder ‚Eurokultur' zu schaffen, sondern vorhandene kulturelle Vielfalt, deren Stärken gerade in der historisch gewachsenen Vielfalt liegen, zu erhalten.[182] Das kulturelle Erbe setzt sich aus den Nationalkulturen der Mitgliedstaaten, zu denen wiederum auch einzelne regionale und lokale Aspekte gehören können, zusammen, wobei allerdings daneben auch eine europäische Identität als Konglomerat dieser Kulturen tritt.[183] Vor diesem Hintergrund werden Maßnahmen auf nationaler Ebene, die zum Schutz nationaler und regionaler Sprachen und Kulturen erforderlich sind, auf europäische Ebene befürwortet, denn damit wird letztlich ein Beitrag zur kulturellen Vielfalt – einem der europäischen Grundwerte – geleistet.[184]

Für die Medien hat dies insoweit Bedeutung, als ihnen eine Schlüsselfunktion bei dem Schutz lokaler Kulturen (sei es auf staatlicher oder auf

---

180 So auch *Schwarz* in: AfP 1993, 409, 417 m.w.N.
181 *Ruffert* in: Calliess/ders., Art. 3 EUV, Rn. 3; grundsätzlich zur Zielorientierung auch: *Müller-Graf* in: Pechstein u.a., Art. 3 EUV, Rn. 1, *Heintschel von Heinegg* in: Vedder/ders., Art. 3 EUV, Rn. 3; *Pechstein* in: Streinz, Art. 3 EUV, Rn. 2; *Klamert* in: Kellerbauer/ders./Tomkin, Art. 3 EUV, Rn. 3 ff.; *Sommermann* in: Blanke/Mangiameli, Art. 3 EUV, Rn. 1 ff., und *Dony*, Droit de l'Union européenne, Rn. 54.
182 *Von Danwitz* in: NJW 2005, 529, 531.
183 *Neumann*, Das Recht der Filmförderung in Deutschland, S. 43, m.w.N.
184 So auch: *Vīķe-Freiberga u.a.* (Hochrangige Gruppe zur Freiheit und Vielfalt der Medien), Bericht zu freien und pluralistischen Medien als Rückhalt der europäischen Demokratie, 2013, S. 45.

regionaler Ebene) zuerkannt wird und damit auch in Bezug auf den Schutz der kulturellen Vielfalt Europas.[185]

Hinzuweisen ist darauf, dass Art. 3 Abs. 3 Unterabs. 3 EUV grundsätzlich ebenso wenig wie Art. 2 EUV eine eigenständige kompetenzrechtliche Grundlage schafft. Die Zielsetzungen des Art. 3 EUV sind insoweit grundsätzlich aus kompetenzieller Perspektive neutral bzw. komplementär: Sie schaffen keine originäre Regulierungskompetenz für die EU und ihre Organe i.S. positiver Integrationsmöglichkeiten über einzig auf Art. 3 EUV gestützte Rechtsakte, hemmen aber auch nicht die Wahrnehmung an dritter Stelle vorhandener Kompetenztitel der EU, sondern geben dieser Wahrnehmung Ziel und Richtung.

2. Die zieleorientierte Abrundungskompetenz des Art. 352 AEUV und ihre Bedeutung für die Medienregulierung

Diese kompetenzrechtliche Neutralität des Zielkatalogs der EU erfährt allerdings durch die sog. „Abrundungskompetenz" nach Art. 352 AEUV eine Durchbrechung: Erscheint ein Tätigwerden der Union im Rahmen der in den Verträgen festgelegten Politikbereiche, zu denen auch die Kultur einschließlich des Mediensektors zählt, „erforderlich, um eines der Ziele der Verträge zu verwirklichen," und sind in den Verträgen die hierfür erforderlichen Befugnisse nicht vorgesehen, so erlässt der Rat auf Vorschlag der Kommission und nach Zustimmung des Europäischen Parlaments „die geeigneten Vorschriften".

Von einer „Flexibilitätsklausel" zu sprechen erscheint in diesem Zusammenhang deshalb verfehlt, weil die Nutzung dieser kompetenzrechtlichen Öffnungsklausel an hohe Hürden gekoppelt ist:

- Die Kommission macht gemäß Art. 352 Abs. 2 AEUV die nationalen Parlamente im Rahmen des Verfahrens zur Kontrolle der Einhaltung des Subsidiaritätsprinzips nach Art. 5 Abs. 3 EUV auf die Vorschläge aufmerksam, die sich auf diesen Artikel stützen.
- Die auf diesem Artikel beruhenden Maßnahmen dürfen nach Art. 352 Abs. 3 AEUV keine Harmonisierung der Rechtsvorschriften der Mitgliedstaaten in den Fällen beinhalten, in denen die Verträge eine solche Harmonisierung ausschließen – was bei einer medienbezogenen Regu-

---

[185] *Vīķe-Freiberga u.a.* (Hochrangige Gruppe zur Freiheit und Vielfalt der Medien), Bericht zu freien und pluralistischen Medien als Rückhalt der europäischen Demokratie, 2013, S. 13.

B. Primärrechtlicher Rahmen zur Kompetenzabgrenzung

lierung mit kultureller rsp. vielfaltssichernder Ausrichtung nach Art. 167 Abs. 5 AEUV der Fall ist.
- Schließlich bedarf es im Rat selbst einer einstimmigen Beschlussfassung.

Der EuGH hat klargestellt, dass Artikel 352 AEUV „integrierender Bestandteil einer auf dem Grundsatz der begrenzten Einzelermächtigung beruhenden institutionellen Ordnung ist und daher keine Grundlage dafür bieten kann, den Bereich der Unionsbefugnisse über den allgemeinen Rahmen hinaus auszudehnen, der sich aus der Gesamtheit der Bestimmungen der Verträge und insbesondere der Bestimmungen ergibt, die die Aufgaben und Tätigkeiten der Union festlegen. [...] Artikel [352 AEUV] kann [...] nicht als Rechtsgrundlage für den Erlass von Bestimmungen dienen, die der Sache nach, gemessen an ihren Folgen, auf eine Änderung der Verträge ohne Einhaltung des hierzu in den Verträgen vorgesehenen Verfahrens hinausliefen".[186]

Auf diese Rechtsprechung wird auch in der Erklärung 42 der Regierungskonferenz zum Vertrag von Lissabon[187] hingewiesen:

„Die Konferenz unterstreicht, dass nach der ständigen Rechtsprechung des Gerichtshofs der Europäischen Union Artikel 352 des Vertrags über die Arbeitsweise der Europäischen Union integrierender Bestandteil einer auf dem Grundsatz der begrenzten Einzelermächtigung beruhenden institutionellen Ordnung ist und daher keine Grundlage dafür bieten kann, den Bereich der Unionsbefugnisse über den allgemeinen Rahmen hinaus auszudehnen, der sich aus der Gesamtheit der Bestimmungen der Verträge und insbesondere der Bestimmungen ergibt, die die Aufgaben und Tätigkeiten der Union festlegen. Dieser Artikel kann jedenfalls nicht als Rechtsgrundlage für den Erlass von Bestimmungen dienen, die der Sache nach, gemessen an ihren Folgen, auf eine Änderung der Verträge ohne Einhaltung des hierzu in den Verträgen vorgesehenen Verfahrens hinausliefen."

Das BVerfG hat in seinem Lissabon-Urteil entschieden, dass die förmliche Zustimmung des Bundestages und des Bundesrates durch Gesetz erforderlich ist, damit der Vertreter Deutschlands im Rat einen auf der Grundlage

---

186 EuGH, Gutachten 2/94 vom 28. März 1996, *Beitritt der Gemeinschaft zur Konvention zum Schutze der Menschenrechte und Grundfreiheiten*, Sammlung der Rechtsprechung 1996 I-01759, Rn. 30.
187 EU ABl. 2012 Nr. C 326/353.

von Artikel 352 AEUV zu erlassenden Rechtsakt billigen kann.[188] In Bezug auf einen die Medienregulierung berührenden Rechtsakt bedürfte es ggf. ergänzend der Zustimmung der Landesparlamente.[189]

V. Kompetenzausübungsregeln und -schranken

1. Einleitung

Jenseits der vertraglichen Verankerung des Prinzips der begrenzten Ermächtigung und des Zuständigkeitskataloges für die EU sollen auch materiell-rechtliche Schutzmechanismen, namentlich Kompetenzausübungsregeln und -schranken, gewährleisten, dass die auf europäischer Ebene bestehenden Einzelermächtigungen in einer die mitgliedstaatlichen Zuständigkeiten schonenden Weise wahrgenommen werden. Zu diesen Regeln zählen das Gebot, die nationale Identität der Mitgliedstaaten zu achten (Art. 4 Abs. 2 EUV), der Grundsatz der loyalen Zusammenarbeit (Art. 4 Abs. 3 EUV), der Grundsatz der Subsidiarität (Art. 5 Abs. 1 Satz 2 und Abs. 3 EUV) und der Grundsatz der Verhältnismäßigkeit (Art. 5 Abs. 1 Satz 2 und Abs. 4 EUV). Diese Grundsätze wurden durch den Vertrag von Lissabon bestätigt und teilweise inhaltlich präzisiert.

Das Spannungsverhältnis, das namentlich zwischen dem in Art. 3 Abs. 3 Satz 1 EUV verankerten Ziel, namentlich zu Gunsten der EU-Bürger und

---

188 BVerfG, Urteil des Zweiten Senats vom 30. Juni 2009, 2 BvE 2/08, Rn. 417: „Soweit von der Flexibilitätsklausel in Art. 352 AEUV Gebrauch gemacht werden soll, erfordert dies jeweils ein Gesetz im Sinne von Art. 23 Abs. 1 Satz 2 GG." Dies wurde in Artikel 8 des Integrationsverantwortungsgesetzes vom 22. September 2009 festgeschrieben.

189 Auch das polnische Kooperationsgesetz sieht in Bezug auf Artikel 352 AEUV spezifische Garantien vor, die das polnische Verfassungsgericht in seinem Lissabon-Urteil (Urteil vom 24. November 2010 (K 32/09, englische Fassung in „Selected Rulings of the Polish Constitutional Tribunal Concerning the Law of the European Union (2003- 2014)", *Biuro Trybunału Konstytucyjnego*, Warschau, 2014, S. 237 (abrufbar unter http://trybunal.gov.pl/uploads/media/SiM_LI_EN_calosc.pdf) für erforderlich erachtete. Im Gegensatz dazu haben das tschechische und das französische Verfassungsgericht die Flexibilitätsklausel als von der Ratifizierung der europäischen Verträge umfasst ausgelegt. Andere Mitgliedstaaten wie Dänemark, Schweden, Finnland, Österreich oder Spanien verfügen über Bestimmungen, die nicht speziell auf Artikel 352 AEUV abstellen und ihre nationalen Parlamente allgemein ermächtigen, ihre Minister vor Ratstagungen zur Erörterung ihrer Standpunkte zu verpflichten. Vgl. zum Ganzen *Kiiver* in: German Law Journal 2009, 1287, 1295 f.

B. Primärrechtlicher Rahmen zur Kompetenzabgrenzung

der in der EU ansässigen Unternehmen einen europäischen Binnenmarkt zu errichten, und den Vorgaben, die nationale Identität der Mitgliedstaaten zu achten (Art. 4 Abs. 2 EUV) und den Reichtum der kulturellen Vielfalt zu wahren (Art. 3 Abs. 3 EUV) bestehen kann, kann sich insbesondere im Zusammenhang mit Regelungen der EU zur medialen Vielfaltssicherung entfalten. Dieses Spannungsverhältnis aufzulösen, ist am Ende regelmäßig eine justizielle Aufgabe. Denn die im Folgenden dargestellten Kompetenzausübungsregeln und -schranken sind sämtlich justiziabel.

Der EuGH ist nach dem Wortlaut der Verträge befugt, Beschwerden über einen allfälligen Verstoß gegen diese Grundsätze umfassend zu beurteilen. Im Zentrum stehen dabei die Nichtigkeitsklage gemäß Art. 263 AEUV und die Inzidenzklage gemäß Art. 277 AEUV. Inzident ist auch eine Prüfung im Rahmen eines Vorabentscheidungsverfahrens gemäß Art. 267 AEUV möglich. Damit wird eine ex post-Kontrolle auch gegen allzu „integrationsfreundliche" Rechtssetzungsaktivitäten der Unionsorgane im Bereich der Medienregulierung dem Grunde nach ermöglicht.

Von daher kommt der Frage, inwieweit sich das Verhältnis zwischen EuGH und mitgliedstaatlicher Verfassungsgerichtsbarkeit in Bezug auf das Verständnis der Kompetenzausübungsregelungen und -schranken in kooperativer oder konfrontativer Atmosphäre entwickelt, unmittelbare Relevanz für die Kompetenzfrage zu. Allerdings ist die bisherige Judikatur des EuGH wenig angetan, auf einen Erfolg des Vorgehens gegen Rechtsakte zu setzen, bei dem das Vorgehen gegen den betreffenden Rechtsakt auf eine Verletzung der Kompetenzausübungsregeln und -schranken gestützt ist. Dies birgt das Risiko von Justizkonflikten in sich, die zu Konflikten über die Frage der fortdauernden Legalität der EU als einer Gemeinschaft des Rechts und über die Bereitschaft, am Konzept einer immer engeren Union festzuhalten, eskalieren können.

2. Die Achtung der nationalen Identität der Mitgliedstaaten

Nach Art. 4 Abs. 2 S. 1 EUV achtet die Union die Gleichheit der Mitgliedstaaten vor den Verträgen und ihre jeweilige nationale Identität, die in ihren grundlegenden politischen und verfassungsmäßigen Strukturen einschließlich der regionalen und lokalen Selbstverwaltung zum Ausdruck kommt. Zur nationalen Identität gehört dabei grundsätzlich ein Bestand an Ideengehalten und Werten, die das Selbstverständnis und die Eigenart dieses Staates oder Volkes prägen und die aus unterschiedlichen Bereichen stammen können wie etwa Sprache und Kultur.[190] Darüber hinaus ist auch die identitätsstiftende Bedeutung der Region und des kommunalen Kontextes für den Menschen in den Verträgen der EU anerkannt.[191] Die Wahrung regionaler und lokaler Belange und Unterschiede neben den nationalen Unterschieden wird wiederholt hervorgehoben.[192] Auch deshalb sind sie bei der Bewertung von mitgliedstaatlichen Maßnahmen auf ihre Vereinbarkeit mit Unionsrecht mit einzubeziehen.

Der Begriff der nationalen Identität sollte dabei als Öffnungsklausel für mitgliedstaatliches Verfassungsrecht verstanden werden, so dass dieses bei der Auslegung von Art. 4 Abs. 2 EUV zu rezipieren ist.[193] Dies kann auch relevant werden, wenn durch Kompetenzüberlagerungen mitgliedstaatliche Handlungsspielräume scheinbar wegen anderer von der EU zu verfolgender Ziele wie der Verwirklichung der Grundfreiheiten verdrängt werden könnten. Insbesondere die Regelung der Medienvielfalt kann zu unterschiedlichen Vorschriften in den Mitgliedstaaten führen, mit denen ihre je nationalen Besonderheiten hinsichtlich der Medien und der Bedürfnisse zur Sicherstellung einer relevanten Medienvielfalt Beachtung finden. Diese Frage kann daher auch an den Standard der nationalen Identität heranreichen, weshalb er gegebenenfalls auch bei der Bestimmung der Grenzen der Anwendung von Grundfreiheiten bzw. mitgliedstaatlicher Maßnahmen zu deren Beschränkung ebenso heranzuziehen ist[194] wie bei der Wahrnehmung der Wettbewerbsordnung im Beihilfensegment bei der der Kontrolle der Finanzierung des öffentlich-rechtlichen Rundfunks.[195]

---

190 *Puttler* in: Calliess/Ruffert, Art. 4 EUV, Rn. 14; *Streinz* in: ders., Art. 4 EUV, Rn. 15; *Blanke* in: ders./Mangiameli, Art. 4 EUV, Rn. 29 ff., 32; *von Bogdandy/Schill* in: CMLRev. 2011, 1417, 1429. Vgl. hierzu und zum Folgenden bereits *Cole*, Zum Gestaltungsspielraum der EU-Mitgliedstaaten bei Einschränkungen der Dienstleistungsfreiheit, S. 18 f.
191 Vgl. hierzu *Menasse* in: Hilpold/Steinmair/Perathoner, 27, 27 ff.
192 Vgl. etwa den dritten Absatz der Präambel der GRC, die Formulierung des Art. 4 Abs. 2 S. 1 EUV zur nationalen Identität („...Organisation ihrer staatlichen Gewalt auf nationaler, regionaler und lokaler Ebene") oder des oben dargestellten Art. 167 Abs. 1 AEUV; insgesamt dazu *Ukrow/Ress* in: Grabitz/Hilf/Nettesheim, Art. 167 AEUV, Rn. 93 f. Vgl. auch den Hinweis von *GA Trstenjak*, Rs. C-324/07, *Coditel Brabant SA / Commune d'Uccle und Région de Bruxelles-Capitale*, Rn. 85.
193 Vgl. zur Erläuterung und Herleitung umfassend *von Bogdandy/Schill* in: ZaöRV 2010, 701, 701 ff.
194 Vgl. zur Bedeutung der Pflicht zur Achtung der nationalen Identität jüngst auch *Nielsen*, Die Medienvielfalt als Aspekt der Wertesicherung der EU, S. 63 ff.
195 Vgl. hierzu auch *Nielsen*, Die Medienvielfalt als Aspekt der Wertesicherung der EU, S. 84 ff.

B. Primärrechtlicher Rahmen zur Kompetenzabgrenzung

Dies gilt auch bei einer Prüfung durch den EuGH, wie dieser ausdrücklich anerkannt hat, wenngleich es zumindest bislang wenig Gelegenheiten gab, zur Bedeutung der Identitätsklausel zu urteilen.[196] Dass der EuGH selbst in Fällen, in denen im Verfahren ausdrücklich auf Art. 4 Abs. 2 EUV abgestellt wurde, auf eine Auseinandersetzung mit dem Prinzip der Achtung der nationalen Identität der Mitgliedstaaten regelmäßig verzichtet, ist wenig geeignet, das Vertrauen in eine Rolle des EuGH als neutrales Kompetenzordnungs-Gericht zu befördern. Umgekehrt mag diese Zurückhaltung indessen in jüngerer Zeit wiederum auch Ergebnis der Rechtsprechungslinie des BVerfG sein, dass die nationale Identität i.S. des Art. 4 Abs. 2 EUV nicht mit der Verfassungsidentität, deren Wahrung im Integrationsprozess sich das BVerfG vorbehält, deckungsgleich ist.

Als besondere Ausprägung der Rücksichtnahmepflicht der EU liegt Art. 4 Abs. 2 EUV die Konzeption zugrunde, dass die mitgliedstaatliche Verfassungsidentität nur in ihrem Kern ein absolut geschütztes Rechtsgut ist, im Übrigen gilt es auch bei Auslegung und Anwendung des Art. 4 Abs. 2 EUV eine praktische Konkordanz zwischen unionsrechtlichem Kompetenztitel und Kompetenzausübungsschranke i.S. eines schonenden Ausgleichs zwischen mitgliedstaatlichen und europäischen Belangen zu schaffen. Dem trägt verfahrensrechtlich ein Ansatz Rechnung, dass die abschließende Bestimmung von Reichweite und Wirkkraft des Identitätsvorbehalts im Staaten- und Verfassungsverbund der EU und seine gerichtliche Anwendung im korrespondierenden Verfassungsgerichtsverbund eines dialogischen Zusammenwirkens zwischen dem EuGH und dem jeweiligen nationalen Verfassungsgericht bedarf.[197]

---

196 Vgl. aber insbesondere EuGH, Rs. C-208/09, *Ilonka Sayn-Wittgenstein / Landeshauptmann von Wien*, Rn. 83 („Insoweit ist einzuräumen, dass ... als Teil der nationalen Identität bei der Abwägung legitimer Belange auf der einen Seite und dem vom Unionsrecht gewährten Recht der Freizügigkeit von Personen auf der anderen berücksichtigt werden kann.").

197 Vgl. *Calliess*, Schriftliche Stellungnahme zur Öffentlichen Anhörung des Ausschusses für die Angelegenheiten der Europäischen Union des Deutschen Bundestages zum Thema „Urteil des Bundesverfassungsgerichts vom 5. Mai 2020 (2 BvR 859/15) in Sachen Staatsanleihekäufe der Europäischen Zentralbank", https://www.bundestag.de/resource/blob/697584/69ec62de394a6348f992c1e092fa9f4b/callies-data.pdf, S. 6.

3. Der Grundsatz der loyalen Zusammenarbeit

Typisch für den Staaten- und Verfassungsverbund, den die EU und ihre Mitgliedstaaten bilden, ist die Verzahnung der nationalen Verfassungen mit den europäischen Verträgen, die man mit Blick auf ihren Inhalt ebenfalls als Verfassung bezeichnen kann. Basis des Verbundes ist die loyale Zusammenarbeit europäischer und mitgliedstaatlicher Institutionen, um die EU funktionsfähig zu halten. Als „zentrales Verfassungsprinzip der Europäischen Union" mit der Funktion, „das europäische Mehrebenensystem so zu koordinieren, dass die Union ihre Ziele erreichen kann",[198] kann der Grundsatz der loyalen Zusammenarbeit erkennbar die jeweilige Kompetenzwahrnehmung durch die Organe der EU und ihrer Mitgliedstaaten prägende Wirkung entfalten.

Im Rahmen der EU besteht nunmehr eine auch ausdrücklich primärrechtlich anerkannte, in Art. 4 Abs. 3 EUV geregelte Loyalitätsverpflichtung zwischen der EU und ihren Mitgliedstaaten sowie zwischen den Mitgliedstaaten untereinander: Nach dem Grundsatz der loyalen Zusammenarbeit achten und unterstützen sich die Union und die Mitgliedstaaten gegenseitig bei der Erfüllung der Aufgaben, die sich aus den Verträgen ergeben.[199] Das Gebot des unionsfreundlichen Verhaltens, welches sich aus diesem Grundsatz ableiten lässt, verpflichtet mithin nicht nur die Mitgliedstaaten gegenüber der EU, sondern auch die Unionsorgane gegenüber den Mitgliedstaaten[200] – und zwar bei der Wahrnehmung sämtlicher Funktionen, die ihnen die europäischen Verträge einräumen und in allen Phasen dieser Wahrnehmung – und damit z.B. auch bereits bei der Vorbereitung eines Rechtsetzungsaktes der EU.

Die Loyalitätspflichten werden u.a. von der Rechtsprechung des Europäischen Gerichtshofs bei der Auslegung von unbestimmten Rechtsbegriffen sowie der Entscheidung über die Verletzung von Pflichten berücksichtigt. Dieses für die EU grundlegende Kooperationsprinzip drückt

---

198 *Hatje*, Loyalität als Rechtsprinzip in der Europäischen Union, S. 105; vgl. zur Gemeinschaftstreue als konkretisierungsbedürftiger Grundsatznorm auch *Blanke* in: ders./Mangiameli, Art. 4 EUV, Rn. 92 ff. *Bleckmann*, Europarecht, Rn. 697 ff.; *Kahl* in: Calliess/Ruffert, Art. 4 EUV, Rn. 3 ff.; *Klamert* in: Kellerbauer/ders./Tomkin, Art. 4 EUV, para. 28 f.; *von Bogdandy*, Rechtsfortbildung mit Art. 5 EGV, 17, 19 ff.; ders./Bast, in: EuGRZ 2001, 441, 447 / in: CMLRev. 2002, 227, 263S.; *Zuleeg* in: NJW 2000, 2846, 2846 f.
199 Diese Loyalitätspflicht im Verhältnis der EU zu den Mitgliedstaaten und der Mitgliedstaaten zueinander wird durch die – für diese Studie nicht relevante – Loyalitätspflicht der EU-Organe zueinander nach Art. 13 Abs. 2 Satz 2 EUV ergänzt.
200 Vgl. *Ress* in: DÖV 1992, S. 944, 947 ff.

B. Primärrechtlicher Rahmen zur Kompetenzabgrenzung

sich auch in gegenseitiger Rücksichtnahme bei der Umsetzung und Anwendung des vorrangigen Unionsrechts aus. Anders als im Bundesstaat gibt es im Staaten- und Verfassungsverbund im Verhältnis von europäischem und nationalen Recht, von EuGH und nationalen Verfassungsgerichten somit keine Hierarchien. Nationale und europäische Gerichte arbeiten im Lichte des Grundsatzes der loyalen Zusammenarbeit arbeitsteilig zusammen, insoweit geht es nicht um Konkurrenz, sondern um Kooperation und Dialog. Das Vorlageverfahren des Art. 267 AEUV bietet für diesen dialogischen Ansatz das passende verfahrensrechtliche Instrumentarium.[201]

Dem Grundsatz der loyalen Zusammenarbeit wird zwar eine herausragende Bedeutung für das Miteinander der hoheitlich agierenden Akteure mitgliedstaatlicher Staatsgewalten und europäischer Verfassungsorgane beigemessen. Seine Unbestimmtheit erregt jedoch Bedenken wegen einer drohenden Beliebigkeit der Rechtsanwendung und rückt die Konkretisierung der Loyalitätspflichten in den Fokus. Hieran fehlt es bislang im Interpretationsverbund der EU zumindest insoweit – jenseits verwaltungsorganisationsrechtlicher Hinweise – weitgehend, als es um die Fragen der sich aus dem Prinzip folgenden Pflichten der EU geht. Jüngste Bemühungen, den Grundsatz der loyalen Zusammenarbeit als Verkörperung der Gesamtrechtsordnung und seine Konkretisierung als Rechtsanwendung im spezifischen Bereich hoheitlicher Beziehungen und in der spezifischen Situation "schwieriger" Rechtslagen zu konturieren,[202] erweisen sich als für die praktische Handhabung nur begrenzt nutzbringend.

Inhaltlich zielt der Grundsatz der loyalen Zusammenarbeit nicht nur darauf ab, den Mitgliedstaaten ein Verhalten zu verbieten, durch das die Funktionsfähigkeit der EU als einer Rechtsgemeinschaft beeinträchtigt würde. Auch die EU ist ihrerseits durch den Grundsatz daran gehemmt, vorhandene Kompetenzen in einer Weise auszuüben, die mit der vorrangigen Zuständigkeit der Mitgliedstaaten für die Gestaltung der kulturellen und demokratischen Ordnung in den Mitgliedstaaten einschließlich ihrer medienvielfaltsbezogenen Ausprägungen und Voraussetzungen kollidiert.

---

201 Vgl. *Calliess*, Schriftliche Stellungnahme zur Öffentlichen Anhörung des Ausschusses für die Angelegenheiten der Europäischen Union des Deutschen Bundestages zum Thema „Urteil des Bundesverfassungsgerichts vom 5. Mai 2020, 2 BvR 859/15, in Sachen Staatsanleihekäufe der Europäischen Zentralbank", https://www.bundestag.de/resource/blob/697584/69ec62de394a6348f992c1e092fa9f4b/callies-data.pdf, S. 8.
202 Vgl. *Benrath*, Die Konkretisierung von Loyalitätspflichten, S. 129 ff.

Durch die Judikatur des EuGH geklärt ist, dass die mit dem Grundsatz verbundene Pflicht zur gegenseitigen Rücksichtnahme es den Mitgliedstaaten verbietet, Schritte zu unternehmen, durch die berechtigte Interessen und Belange der EU gefährdet würden. In positiver Hinsicht zielt der Grundsatz darauf ab, dass die Mitgliedstaaten bei der Durchführung und Anwendung des Unionsrechts dessen „*effet utile*" nicht nur respektieren, sondern auch fördern müssen. Der EuGH zieht den Grundsatz in seiner bisherigen Rechtsprechung insbesondere heran, um auf seiner der Grundlage konkrete Anforderungen an die mitgliedstaatliche Umsetzung und Durchführung von Richtlinienbestimmungen zu entwickeln. Namentlich Anforderungen an einen ordnungsgemäßen und effektiven Verwaltungsvollzug, die Gebote der Publizität und der Umsetzung durch verbindliche Normen mit Außenwirkung und Pflichten zur Bewehrung und Sanktionierung von Verstößen gegen Normen der EU sind Ergebnis eines sog. Effizienzgebots als zentralem Kern des Loyalitätsgebotes.[203]

Es ist im Übrigen anerkannt, dass sich den Grundsatz der loyalen Zusammenarbeit nicht unionsrechtliche Regelungen korrigieren, modifizieren oder überschreiben lassen. Die Pflicht zur wechselseitigen Loyalität knüpft vielmehr an bestehenden Regelungen an und intensiviert bzw. effektiviert diese, ohne ihnen aber inhaltlich eine neue Richtung zu geben.[204] Auch wenn der relativ unbestimmte Grundsatz der unionsrechtlichen Loyalität dem EuGH ein weites Maß an Konkretisierungsspielraum eröffnen mag, dürfen aus Art. 4 Abs. 3 EUV keine Rechtsfolgen abgeleitet werden, die grundlegende Ziele oder Strukturprinzipien der europäischen Verträge oder der Verfassungen der Mitgliedstaaten oder der Europäischen Union unterhöhlen.[205] Aus dem Grundsatz kann mithin insbesondere keine Pflicht zur Duldung einer europarechtlichen Regelung von medialer Vielfaltssicherung z.B. zur Abwehr von Gefährdungen für den demokratischen Prozess in der EU selbst oder in einzelnen ihrer Mitgliedstaaten abgeleitet werden.

Für den Bereich des indirekten Verwaltungsvollzugs des Unionsrechts durch die Mitgliedstaaten entfaltet der Grundsatz der loyalen Zusammenarbeit Wirkung insbesondere dahin, dass die grundsätzliche „Verwaltungs-

---

203 Vgl. EuGH, Rs. C-349/93, *Kommission/Italien*; Rs. C-348/93, *Kommission/Italien*; Rs. 24/95, *Alcan/Deutschland*.
204 Vgl. *Nettesheim*, Die Erteilung des mitgliedstaatlichen Einvernehmens nach Art. 4 Abs. 2 Uabs. 1 der FFH-Richtlinie, S. 30 f.
205 Vgl. *Jennert* in: NVwZ 2003, 937, 939 m.w.N.

autonomie"²⁰⁶ bzw. „institutionelle und Verfahrensautonomie"²⁰⁷ durch diesen Grundsatz nicht angetastet wird. Dies steht zwar unionsrechtlichen Vorgaben an eine Aufsichtsstruktur für einen koordinierten Bereich wie z.B. den der AVMD-Richtlinie nicht entgegen, spricht aber für ein zurückhaltendes, mitgliedstaatliche Verfassungstraditionen berücksichtigendes Verständnis der Anwendung und Auslegung dieser Vorgaben im Rahmen der Kontrolle der Einhaltung des Unionsrechts durch die Europäische Kommission und den EuGH.

4. Das Subsidiaritätsprinzip

Das Subsidiaritätsprinzip, bei dem es sich ursprünglich um ein theologisch-gesellschaftspolitisches Prinzip handelte, hat, nachdem es zunehmend auf das Verhältnis vertikal angeordneter staatlicher Ebenen übertragen wurde, im Prozess der Vertiefung der europäischen Integration auch eine ausdrückliche verfassungsrechtliche Verankerung in den Gründungsverträgen der EU gefunden.²⁰⁸ Beginnend mit dem Vertrag von Maastricht ist es primärrechtlich verankert – was im Rechtsvergleich mit der Situation in dritten föderal bzw. dezentral strukturierten Organisationseinheiten der Ausübung hoheitlicher Gewalt bemerkenswert, aber keineswegs solitär ist.²⁰⁹ Seit dem Vertrag von Amsterdam wird die primärrechtliche Regelung des Subsidiaritätsprinzips zudem durch ein Protokoll über die Anwendung der Grundsätze der Subsidiarität und der Verhältnismäßigkeit ergänzt.²¹⁰ Während dieses Protokoll allerdings in der Fassung des Vertrages von Amsterdam das Subsidiaritätsprinzip nicht nur verfahrensrechtlich durch umfangreiche Konsultations-, Berichts- und Begründungspflichten

---

206 Vgl. *Schwarze* in: NVwZ 2000, 241, 244.
207 Vgl. *Rodriguez Iglesias* in: EuGRZ 1997, 289, 289 ff.
208 Vgl. *Oesch*, Das Subsidiaritätsprinzip im EU-Recht und die nationalen Parlamente, 301, 301 f.; *Foster*, EU Law, S. 87; *Weber* in: Blanke/Mangiameli, Art. 5 EUV, Rn. 8.
209 Vgl. Art. 118 der italienischen Verfassung, wonach „die Verwaltungsbefugnisse ... den Gemeinden zuerkannt (sind), unbeschadet der Fälle, in denen sie den Provinzen, Großstädten mit besonderem Status, Regionen und dem Staat zugewiesen werden, um deren einheitliche Ausübung auf der Grundlage der Prinzipien der *Subsidiarität*, der Differenzierung und der Angemessenheit zu gewährleisten".
210 Konsolidierte Fassung des Vertrags über die Arbeitsweise der Europäischen Union – Protokoll (Nr. 2) über die Anwendung der Grundsätze der Subsidiarität und der Verhältnismäßigkeit, EU ABl. C 115 vom 9.5.2008, S. 206–209.

konturierte, sondern auch materiellrechtlich konkretisierte, verzichtet das seit dem Vertrag von Lissabon geltende Protokoll (Nr. 2) über die Anwendung der Grundsätze der Subsidiarität und der Verhältnismäßigkeit weitgehend auf materiell-rechtliche Leitlinien zur Anwendung des Subsidiaritätsprinzips.[211]

Art. 5 Abs. 3 EUV enthält die materiell-rechtlichen Voraussetzungen, welche erfüllt sein müssen, damit eine geplante unionale Maßnahme mit dem Subsidiaritätsprinzip vereinbar ist. Der zentrale Aussagegehalt des nunmehr in Art. 5 Abs. 3 EUV verankerten Subsidiaritätsprinzips scheint dabei weitgehend unbestritten. Es begründet eine Zuständigkeitsprärogative der kleineren Einheit gegenüber der größeren nach Maßgabe ihrer Leistungsfähigkeit. Als Folge davon verpflichtet das Subsidiaritätsprinzip eine handlungswillige größere Einheit wie die EU, die Erforderlichkeit und den Mehrwert eines Tätigwerdens zu begründen. Gleichzeitig fällt das Subsidiaritätsprinzip allerdings – auch in der Ausformung, die es im Primärrecht der EU erfahren hat – durch seine fortdauernde inhaltliche Unbestimmtheit und Wertungsoffenheit auf.

Das unionale Subsidiaritätsprinzip findet gemäß Art. 5 Abs. 3 EUV Anwendung, wenn die EU „tätig wird". Damit ist grundsätzlich jedes Handeln eines Organs oder einer Einrichtung der Union gemeint. Die Prüfung der Wahrung der Subsidiarität ergänzt die Anforderungen, welche sich aus der entsprechenden Kompetenznorm für die EU ergeben.[212] Ausgeschlossen von diesem zusätzlichen Kontrollgebot sind nach Art. 5 Abs. 3 EUV einzig Rechtsakte, welche in Ausübung einer ausschließlichen Zuständigkeit der Union ergehen[213] – eine Bereichsausnahme, die mit Blick auf eine Medienregulierung seitens der EU zwar insoweit ohne erhebliche Bedeutung ist, als es um eine den Raum der EU nicht überschreitende Regulierung geht, die indessen Bedeutung gewinnen kann, soweit Medienregulierung für die EU völkerrechtlich mit Drittstaaten koordiniert werden soll. Vor diesem Hintergrund gewinnen die in den Verhandlungsmandaten für Handels- und Investitionsabkommen durchgehend zu findenden Ausnahmen für den audiovisuellen Bereich auch unter Subsidiaritätsperspektive besonderes Gewicht.

---

211 Vgl. *Oesch*, Das Subsidiaritätsprinzip im EU-Recht und die nationalen Parlamente, 301, 303; *Foster*, EU Law, S. 88; *Weber* in: Blanke/Mangiameli, Art. 5 EUV, Rn. 10 f.
212 Vgl. *Bast/von Bogdandy*, in: Grabitz/Hilf/Nettesheim Art. 5 EUV, Rn. 50 f.; *Weber* in: Blanke/Mangiameli, Art. 5 EUV, Rn. 7; *Dony*, Droit de l'Union européenne, Rn. 144.
213 Vgl. hierzu Abschnitt B.I.2.

B. Primärrechtlicher Rahmen zur Kompetenzabgrenzung

Art. 5 Abs. 3 EUV greift zwei materiell-rechtliche Kriterien auf, die kumulativ erfüllt sein müssen, damit die EU gestützt auf geteilte Zuständigkeiten nach Art. 4 AEUV oder Zuständigkeiten im Bereich von Unterstützungs-, Koordinierungs- und Ergänzungsmaßnahmen nach Art. 5 und Art. 6 AEUV sowie im Rahmen der Gemeinsamen Außen- und Sicherheitspolitik (GASP),[214] die nicht zuletzt auch mit Blick auf medienbezogene Reaktionen auf völkerrechtswidriges Verhalten von Drittstaaten, die zugleich in besonderer Weise unmittelbar desinformierend wirken oder solche Desinformation befördern, tätig werden kann.

- Zum einen darf die EU – insoweit in Ergänzung des kompetenzrechtlichen Gehalts des Verhältnismäßigkeitsgrundsatzes – nur tätig werden, sofern und soweit die Ziele der geplanten Maßnahme von den Mitgliedstaaten nicht ausreichend verwirklicht werden können. Mit Blick auf die Ziele ist nach diesem Erforderlichkeits- bzw. Negativkriterium darzulegen, dass ein Regelungsdefizit besteht, das durch die den Mitgliedstaaten zur Verfügung stehenden tatsächlichen und finanziellen Mittel nicht zufriedenstellend behoben werden kann. Die Kontrolle bezieht sich sowohl auf das „ob" als auch auf das „wie" des Tätigwerdens; die Erforderlichkeit der unionalen Maßnahme muss sich auf alle vorgesehenen Regelungselemente eines Rechtsaktes beziehen.[215] Hierzu ist – sofern die geplante Regelung unionsweite Geltung beansprucht — eine Gesamtwürdigung der Situation in der EU insgesamt bzw. in allen Mitgliedstaaten vorzunehmen.[216] Mit dem Vertrag von Lissabon wurde die bisherige Praxis ausdrücklich kodifiziert, wonach für die Beurteilung der mitgliedstaatlichen Regulierungskapazitäten nicht nur die zentrale, sondern auch die regionale und lokale Ebene zu berücksichtigen ist – ein weiteres Beispiel primärrechtlicher Anerkennung des Europas der Regionen und der föderalen Vielfältigkeit staatsorganisationsrechtlicher Gestaltung in den Mitgliedstaaten, zu deren Wahrung die EU ebenso verpflichtet ist wie zur Wahrung der – auch – medienbezogenen Bedingungen ihres fortdauernden Bestandes.

---

214 Im Rahmen der GASP unterliegt das Subsidiaritätsprinzip allerdings keiner gerichtlichen Kontrolle durch den EuGH (vgl. Art. 24 Abs. 1 EUV i.V.m. Art. 275 AEUV); hierzu *Oesch*, Das Subsidiaritätsprinzip im EU-Recht und die nationalen Parlamente, 301, 304.
215 Vgl. *Oesch*, Das Subsidiaritätsprinzip im EU-Recht und die nationalen Parlamente, 301, 305; *Klamert* in: Kellerbauer/ders./Tomkin, Art. 5 EUV, Rn. 23.
216 Vgl. *Bast/von Bogdandy*, in: Grabitz/Hilf/Nettesheim Art. 5 EUV, Rn. 54; *Klamert* in: Kellerbauer/ders./Tomkin, Art. 5 EUV, Rn. 28; *Dony*, Droit de l'Union européenne, Rn. 145.

- Des Weiteren fordert das Subsidiaritätsprinzip i.S. eines Effizienz- bzw. Mehrwertkriteriums als Positivkriterium, dass die Regelungsziele mit Blick auf den Umfang oder die Wirkungen der geplanten Maßnahmen auf Unionsebene besser verwirklicht werden können. Nach Art. 5 des Subsidiaritäts-Protokolls sind dabei qualitative und, soweit möglich, quantitative Kriterien zu berücksichtigen. Es geht um eine Beurteilung der unionalen Problemlösungskapazität bzw. Einschätzung der Wirksamkeit der geplanten Maßnahme im Vergleich zu den finanziellen Belastungen und zum Verwaltungsaufwand für betroffene Behörden, Wirtschaftsteilnehmer und Bürger.[217] Es bedarf eines wertenden Vergleichs zwischen dem zusätzlichen Integrationsgewinn und dem mitgliedstaatlichen Kompetenzverlust. Im Ergebnis sind Befugnisse der EU nicht voll auszuüben, wo der zusätzliche Integrationsgewinn gering, der Eingriff in die Zuständigkeiten der Mitgliedstaaten beträchtlich ist oder wo die Vorteile des Integrationsgewinns die Nachteile des mitgliedstaatlichen Kompetenzverlusts nicht merklich überwiegen.[218]

Die Unbestimmtheit und Offenheit dieser Kriterien erschweren schon im Einstieg eine verlässliche Prüfung der Wahrung des Prinzips. Dieses diffuse Bild des Kontrollprogramms wird dadurch verstärkt, dass beide aufgezeigten Kriterien verlangen, Prognoseentscheidungen zu treffen:[219] Es ist auf die Zukunft ausgerichtet, zu entscheiden und darzulegen, dass ein Tätigwerden der Union erforderlich ist und einen europäischen Mehrwert bedeutet.[220]

Mit Blick auf dieses Verständnis des Subsidiaritätsprinzips als kompetenzrechtliche Argumentationslastregel[221] spricht zwar vieles für eine kompetenzielle Vermutungsregel zu Gunsten der Wahrung mitgliedstaatlicher Regulierungsmöglichkeiten – auch im Bereich der Medienregulierung.[222] Indessen spricht die bisherige Judikatur des EuGH gegen eine besondere durch das Subsidiaritätsprinzip vermittelte Sperrwirkung gegenüber weite-

---

217 Vgl. *Bast/von Bogdandy*, in: Grabitz/Hilf/Nettesheim, Art. 5 EUV, Rn. 57; *Klamert* in: Kellerbauer/ders./Tomkin, Art. 5 EUV, Rn. 29.
218 Vgl. *Calliess* in: ders./Ruffert, Art. 5 EUV, Rn. 41.
219 Vgl. *Lienbacher* in: Schwarze, Art. 5 EUV, Rn. 26.
220 Vgl. *Oesch*, Das Subsidiaritätsprinzip im EU-Recht und die nationalen Parlamente, 301, 305.
221 Vgl. *Oesch*, Das Subsidiaritätsprinzip im EU-Recht und die nationalen Parlamente, 301, 305.
222 Vgl. hierzu jüngst auch *Nielsen*, Die Medienvielfalt als Aspekt der Wertesicherung der EU, S. 60 ff. sowie *Klamert* in: Kellerbauer/ders./Tomkin, Art. 5 EUV, Rn. 24 m.w.N.

rem unionalen Zugriff auf Regelungsgegenstände.[223] Das methodische Vorgehen des EuGH präsentiert sich bislang als keineswegs konsistent; in aller Regel prüft er pauschal und unstrukturiert die beiden materiell-rechtlichen Kriterien gemäß Art. 5 Abs. 3 EUV gemeinsam und unterscheidet nicht zwischen der Erforderlichkeit und dem Mehrwert eines Tätigwerdens auf unionaler Ebene. In seiner bisherigen Entscheidungspraxis hat er einen Verstoß gegen das Prinzip nie festgestellt und bemerkenswerterweise regelmäßig das Mehrwertkriterium als positives, auf Regelung durch die EU gerichtetes Kriterium vor dem negativen Kriterium der Erforderlichkeit des Handelns geprüft.[224] Mit Aussicht auf Erfolg erscheinen danach allenfalls evidente Verstöße gegen das Subsidiaritätsprinzip angreifbar, in denen die Unionsorgane nicht einmal einen plausiblen Begründungsansatz für eine Regelung liefern.[225]

Das Subsidiaritäts-Protokoll enthält spezifische verfahrensrechtliche Vorgaben für die Einhaltung des Subsidiaritätsprinzips in unionalen Gesetzgebungsverfahren. Damit wird berücksichtigt, dass die Effektivität des Subsidiaritätsprinzips entscheidend davon abhängt, wie die Unionsorgane die materiell-rechtlichen Vorgaben von Art. 5 Abs. 3 EUV in der täglichen Praxis umsetzen. Die Einhaltung dieser Vorgaben bedarf – in deutlicher Parallelität zum Grundrechtsschutz durch Verfahren – des Kompetenzschutzes mittels Verfahren durch entsprechende prozedurale und organisatorische Absicherung.

Art. 2 des Subsidiaritäts-Protokolls verpflichtet die Kommission, umfangreiche Anhörungen durchzuführen, bevor sie einen förmlichen Gesetzgebungsakt vorschlägt. Damit wird gewährleistet, dass sich interessierte Kreise – sowohl Regulierer als auch regulierte Interessenträger – frühzeitig zu allfälligen subsidiaritätskritischen Aspekten geplanter Medienregulierung äußern können. Ein Verzicht auf eine solche Anhörung dürfte einen wesentlichen Verfahrensmangel darstellen, der die Nichtigkeit des späteren Rechtsakts zur Folge haben kann.

---

223 Der EuGH hat sich bislang sowohl in quantitativer Hinsicht in Bezug auf die Erwähnung des Subsidiaritätsprinzips als auch in dogmatischer Hinsicht, was die konkrete inhaltliche Ausgestaltung der Prüfung im Einzelfall betrifft, sehr zurückgehalten. In seinen zu Art. 5 EGV ergangenen Urteilen hat er auf eine konkrete Subsidiaritätsprüfung zumeist verzichtet (vgl. z.B. EuGH, Rs. C-84/94, *Vereinigtes Königreich Großbritannien und Nordirland / Rat der Europäischen Union*, Rn. 46 ff.; Rs. C-233/94, *Deutschland / Parlament und Rat*, Rn. 22 ff.).
224 Vgl. zu Art. 5 Abs. 3 EUV EuGH, Rs. C-508/13, *Estland/Parlament und Rat*, Rn. 44 ff.
225 Vgl. *Bickenbach* in: EuR 2013, 523, 523 ff.; *Klamert* in: Kellerbauer/ders./Tomkin, Art. 5 EUV, Rn. 24 m.w.N.

Art. 5 des Subsidiaritäts-Protokolls verpflichtet die Kommission weiter, Entwürfe von Rechtsetzungsakten im Hinblick auf die Einhaltung des Subsidiaritätsprinzips detailliert zu begründen. Vorschläge zu neuen Rechtsakten enthalten mittlerweile regelmäßig ausführliche Stellungnahmen zur Vereinbarkeit geplanter Maßnahmen mit dem Subsidiaritätsprinzip. Im Rahmen wichtiger Initiativen und Gesetzgebungsprojekte erfolgen Folgenabschätzungen (*impact assessments*), in denen auch die Subsidiarität eingehend analysiert wird.[226]

Das neue Herzstück der verfahrensmäßigen Absicherung des Subsidiaritätsprinzips stellt der formalisierte Dialog zwischen dem Unionsgesetzgeber und den nationalen Parlamenten dar. Ob diese Dialogmöglichkeit dazu beigetragen hat, die praktische Relevanz des Subsidiaritätsprinzips zu erhöhen, kann kontrovers diskutiert werden. Vertretbar erscheint auch eine Einschätzung, dass auch die verfahrensrechtliche Absicherung der Bedeutung dieses Prinzips durch den Subsidiaritäts-Frühwarnmechanismus mittels Subsidiaritätsrüge und die Möglichkeit einer Subsidiaritätsklage nach dem Protokoll Nr. 2 durch Art. 12 Buchst. b) EUV und Art. 4 ff. des Subsidiaritätsprotokolls, wie sie der Vertrag von Lissabon einführten, nichts Nennenswertes geändert hat.

Art. 12 EUV regelt die Beteiligung der nationalen Parlamente am Prozess der Rechtsetzung der EU. Art. 12 Buchst. b) EUV konkretisiert dabei die Vorgaben des Art. 5 Abs. 3 EUV in Bezug auf das Subsidiaritätsprinzip. Demnach tragen die nationalen Parlamente aktiv zur guten Arbeitsweise der Union bei, indem sie dafür sorgen, dass der Grundsatz der Subsidiarität gemäß dem im Subsidiaritäts-Protokoll vorgesehenen Verfahren beachtet wird. Dabei handelt es sich um ein Instrument präventiver Kontrolle der Wahrung dieser Kompetenzausübungsschranke in Gestalt eines parlamentarisch initiierten Frühwarnsystems.[227]

Ausgangspunkt einer möglichen Subsidiaritätsrüge ist Art. 4 des Subsidiaritäts-Protokolls: Er verpflichtet die Unionsorgane, Entwürfe für Gesetzgebungsakte den nationalen Parlamenten zukommen zu lassen. Die nationalen Parlamente oder die Kammern eines dieser Parlamente können gemäß Art. 6 des Subsidiaritäts-Protokolls binnen acht Wochen in einer be-

---

[226] Vgl. etwa jüngst im Rahmen des vorgeschlagenen *Digital Services Act* den „legal basis and subsidiarity check" innerhalb der Folgeabschätzungen zu einer ex post- (Ref. Ares(2020)2877686 – 04/06/2020, S. 4) und ex ante- (Ref. Ares(2020)2877647 – 04/06/2020, S. 3) Regulierung.

[227] Vgl. *Oesch*, Das Subsidiaritätsprinzip im EU-Recht und die nationalen Parlamente, 301, 308; *Weber* in: Blanke/Mangiameli, Art. 5 EUV, Rn. 10; *Dony*, Droit de l'Union européenne, Rn. 147.

B. Primärrechtlicher Rahmen zur Kompetenzabgrenzung

gründeten Stellungnahme darlegen, weshalb der Entwurf nicht mit dem Subsidiaritätsprinzip vereinbar ist.[228] Dabei obliegt es den jeweiligen nationalen Parlamenten, gegebenenfalls regionale Parlamente mit Gesetzgebungsbefugnissen zu konsultieren. Solche Gesetzgebungsbefugnisse der deutschen Landesparlamente sind nach der Verfassungsordnung des GG in Bezug auf die Medienregulierung evident. Gemäß Art. 7 Abs. 1 des Subsidiaritäts-Protokolls sind die Unionsorgane gehalten, die begründeten Stellungnahmen im weiteren Verlauf des Rechtsetzungsverfahrens zu „berücksichtigen". Mit dieser „Berücksichtigungspflicht" geht die Pflicht einher, sich fundiert mit den Einwänden auseinanderzusetzen; eine (kassatorische) Verpflichtung, die Stellungnahmen tatsächlich in den Vorschlag einfließen zu lassen, existiert demgegenüber nicht. Sofern die Anzahl der eingereichten Stellungnahmen mindestens einen Drittel[229] der Gesamtzahl der möglichen Stimmen erreicht, muss der Entwurf „überprüft" werden. Auch das Ergebnis dieser „Überprüfungspflicht" ist offen; ein Vetorecht steht den nationalen Parlamenten weiterhin nicht zu. Die Kommission kann mithin an einem medienregulatorischen Vorschlag, gegen den begründete Stellungnahmen mit Blick auf das Subsidiaritätsprinzip vorgetragen wurden, festzuhalten, ihn abzuändern oder zurückzuziehen.[230]

---

228 Nach § 11 Abs. 1 des Gesetzes über die Wahrnehmung der Integrationsverantwortung des Bundestages und des Bundesrates in Angelegenheiten der Europäischen Union (Integrationsverantwortungsgesetz – IntVG) vom 22. September 2009 (BGBl. Teil I S. 3022); geändert durch Art. 1 des Gesetzes vom 1. Dezember 2009 (BGBl. I S. 3822) können der Bundestag und der Bundesrat in ihren Geschäftsordnungen regeln, wie eine Entscheidung über die Abgabe einer begründeten Stellungnahme gemäß Art. 6 des Protokolls über die Anwendung der Grundsätze der Subsidiarität und der Verhältnismäßigkeit herbeizuführen ist. Der Präsident des Bundestages oder der Präsident des Bundesrates übermittelt nach Absatz 2 der Regelung die begründete Stellungnahme an die Präsidenten der zuständigen Organe der Europäischen Union und setzt die Bundesregierung darüber in Kenntnis. In der Geschäftsordnung des Bundesrates findet sich eine solche Regelung allerdings nicht. Ungeregelt ist damit auch die Verkopplung zwischen landesparlamentarischer Willensbildung und rügender Stellungnahme des Bundesrates.
229 Die Schwelle beträgt mindestens ein Viertel der Stimmen, wenn ein Entwurf auf der Grundlage des Art. 76 AEUV betreffend den Raum der Freiheit, der Sicherheit und des Rechts zur Debatte steht.
230 Die nationalen Parlamente besitzen mithin keine Möglichkeit, die Kommission rechtlich verbindlich zur Änderung eines Gesetzgebungsvorschlags zu zwingen. Sofern die nationalen Parlamente mit ihren Subsidiaritätsrügen nicht durchdringen, bleibt ihnen allenfalls die Möglichkeit, das Abstimmungsverhalten ihres Regierungsvertreters im Rat zu beeinflussen. Verschiedene Mitgliedstaaten sehen innerstaatlich entsprechende Verfahren vor; die Zustimmung zu einem Ge-

Sofern die Anzahl eingereichter Stellungnahmen mindestens die einfache Mehrheit der Gesamtzahl der den nationalen Parlamenten zugewiesenen Stimmen erreicht, sind im ordentlichen Gesetzgebungsverfahren allerdings – zusätzlich zur Überprüfungspflicht – weitere Verfahrensschritte zu berücksichtigen: Sofern die Kommission am Vorschlag festhält, muss sie den Unionsgesetzgeber, also den Rat und das Parlament, mit einer begründeten Stellungnahme über die unterschiedlichen Ansichten unterrichten. Der Unionsgesetzgeber ist sodann verpflichtet, vor Abschluss der ersten Lesung unter Berücksichtigung der Stellungnahmen der nationalen Parlamente und der Kommission zu prüfen, ob der Vorschlag mit dem Subsidiaritätsprinzip im Einklang steht. Sofern der Unionsgesetzgeber mit der Mehrheit von 55 % der Mitglieder des Rates oder einer einfachen Mehrheit des Parlaments der Ansicht ist, dass der Gesetzgebungsvorschlag das Subsidiaritätsprinzip tatsächlich verletzt, wird der Vorschlag nicht weiter geprüft.

Art. 8 des Subsidiaritäts-Protokolls eröffnet den Mitgliedstaaten sowie – entsprechend der jeweiligen innerstaatlichen Rechtsordnung – nationalen Parlamenten inkl. Kammern die Möglichkeit, Klage wegen Verstoßes gegen das Subsidiaritätsprinzip zu erheben.[231] Dabei handelt es sich um eine spezielle Ausprägung der Nichtigkeitsklage gemäß Art. 263 AEUV (auf die Art. 8 des Subsidiaritäts- Protokolls ausdrücklich verweist). Auch die Subsidiaritätsklage unterliegt den üblichen Zulässigkeitsvoraussetzungen von Art. 263 AEUV. Die Klagefrist beträgt dementsprechend nach Art. 263 Abs. 6 AEUV zwei Monate ab Veröffentlichung des Rechtsaktes im Amtsblatt der EU.

---

    setzgebungsvorschlag durch den Regierungsvertreter wird von der Zustimmung durch das eigene Parlament abhängig gemacht (sog. Stimmabgabe ad referendum); dazu *Huber* in: Streinz, Art. 12 EUV, Rn. 43. Damit ergänzt der neue Frühwarnmechanismus die vorhandenen Kanäle der Beeinflussung der eigenen Regierung. Vgl. *Oesch*, Das Subsidiaritätsprinzip im EU-Recht und die nationalen Parlamente, 301, 309.

231 Nach § 12 Abs. 1 IntVG ist der Bundestag auf Antrag eines Viertels seiner Mitglieder verpflichtet, eine Klage gemäß Art. 8 des Subsidiaritäts-Protokolls zu erheben. Auf Antrag eines Viertels seiner Mitglieder, die die Erhebung der Klage nicht stützen, ist deren Auffassung in der Klageschrift deutlich zu machen. Der Bundesrat kann nach § 12 Abs. 2 in seiner Geschäftsordnung regeln, wie ein Beschluss über die Erhebung einer Klage gemäß Absatz 1 herbeizuführen ist. Eine entsprechende Regelung ist allerdings bislang unterblieben. Wird im Bundestag oder im Bundesrat ein Antrag zur Erhebung einer Klage gemäß Absatz 1 oder gemäß Absatz 2 gestellt, so kann das andere Organ nach Absatz 5 der Regelung eine Stellungnahme abgeben.

B. Primärrechtlicher Rahmen zur Kompetenzabgrenzung

Konstitutive Bedeutung besitzt Art. 8 des Subsidiaritäts-Protokolls nur insofern, als die Entscheidung über die Klageeinleitung innerstaatlich auch den Parlamenten bzw. parlamentarischen Kammern zusteht. Konsequenterweise haben diverse Mitgliedstaaten – einschließlich Deutschland – die Quoren für eine Klageerhebung (deutlich) unter dem einfachen Mehr angesiedelt. Insoweit kommt der Subsidiaritätsklage die Funktion als Minderheitenrecht zu, da auch für oppositionelle Kräfte eine realistische Möglichkeit zur Klageerhebung besteht.

Sofern ein Parlament oder eine Kammer Subsidiaritätsklage erhebt, übermittelt die Regierung die Klage unverzüglich dem EuGH. Die Prozessführung obliegt sodann aber dem klagenden Parlament bzw. der klagenden Kammer. Das Recht, eine Subsidiaritätsklage einzureichen, besteht im Übrigen unabhängig von einer vorherigen Subsidiaritätsrüge durch nationale Parlamente.

Indessen sind Subsidiaritätsrüge wie -klage als Instrumente der Effektuierung des Subsidiaritätsprinzips nicht zuletzt auch bei der Wahrung der Medienregulierungskompetenz der deutschen Länder mit Problemen verbunden. Denn zum einen ist ungeklärt, inwieweit bei einer allein auf die Subsidiarität beschränkten Prüfung die für den Gesetzgebungsakt gewählte Rechtsgrundlage zu untersuchen ist. Diese Frage stellt sich bei einer Subsidiaritätsklage, da Art. 8 Protokoll Nr. 2 die gerichtliche Kontrolle ausdrücklich auf das Subsidiaritätsprinzip begrenzt.[232] Das BVerfG hat hierauf in seiner Entscheidung vom 30. Juni 2009 zum Vertrag von Lissabon aufmerksam gemacht und betont, dass es auch darauf ankommen werde, „ob das Klagerecht der nationalen Parlamente und des Ausschusses der Regionen auf die der Überprüfung des Subsidiaritätsgrundsatzes vorgelagerte Frage erstreckt wird, ob die Europäische Union über eine Zuständigkeit für das konkrete Rechtssetzungsvorhaben verfügt".[233] Der Bundesrat geht in ständiger Beschlusspraxis davon aus, dass die Subsidiaritätsrüge gemäß Art. 12 Buchstabe b EUV auch die Frage der Zuständigkeit der EU erfasst.[234]

---

232 Vgl. *Oesch*, Das Subsidiaritätsprinzip im EU-Recht und die nationalen Parlamente, 301, 305; *Weber* in: Blanke/Mangiameli, Art. 5 EUV, Rn. 11.
233 BVerfGE 123, 267 (383 f.) unter Bezugnahme auf Wuermeling, Kalamität Kompetenz: Zur Abgrenzung der Zuständigkeiten in dem Verfassungsentwurf des EU-Konvents, EuR 2004, S. 216 (225); *von Danwitz*, Der Mehrwert gemeinsamen Handelns, Frankfurter Allgemeine Zeitung vom 23. Oktober 2008, S. 8.
234 Vgl. hierzu z.B. die Stellungnahmen des Bundesrates vom 9. November 2007, BR-Drucksache 390/07 (Beschluss), Ziffer 5, vom 26. März 2010, BR-Drucksache

Jörg Ukrow

Des Weiteren hat das BVerfG hat in seiner Lissabon-Entscheidung bereits darauf aufmerksam gemacht, dass die Effektivität des durch den Vertrag von Lissabon eingeführten Frühwarnmechanismus zur Kontrolle der Einhaltung des Subsidiaritätsprinzips davon abhängt, „inwieweit sich die nationalen Parlamente organisatorisch darauf einrichten können, den Mechanismus innerhalb der kurzen Frist von acht Wochen sinnvoll zu nutzen".[235]

5. Der Grundsatz der Verhältnismäßigkeit

Der Grundsatz der Verhältnismäßigkeit ist ein allgemeiner, in Art. 5 Abs. 1 Satz 2 und Abs. 4 EUV kodifizierter Rechtsgrundsatz des Unionsrechts, der – worauf das BVerfG in seiner EZB-Entscheidung zutreffend hingewiesen hat – seine Wurzeln insbesondere im Common Law,[236] vor allem aber auch im deutschen Recht hat – dort allerdings nicht in Bezug auf die Klärung von Kompetenzfragen in Mehrebenensystemen, sondern namentlich im Bereich des Grundrechtsschutzes und des Verwaltungsrechts.[237] Von diesen Wurzeln her hat der Grundsatz der Verhältnismäßigkeit – wie das BVerfG aufzeigt – über die Rechtsprechung des Europäischen Gerichtshofs für Menschenrechte[238] und des EuGH Eingang in alle europäischen (Teil-) Rechtsordnungen gefunden.[239]

43/10 (Beschluss), Ziffer 2, und vom 16. Dezember 2011, BR- Drucksache 646/11 (Beschluss), Ziffer 2).
235 BVerfGE 123, 267 (383) unter Bezugnahme auf *Mellein*, Subsidiaritätskontrolle durch nationale Parlamente, 2007, S. 269 ff.
236 Das BVerfG (2 BvR 859/15) verweist auf *Blackstone*, Commentaries on the Laws of England, 4. Aufl. 1899, S. 115; *Klatt/Meister*, Der Staat 2012, S. 159 (160 f.); *Saurer*, Der Staat 2012, S. 3 (4); *Peters*, in: Festschrift für Daniel Thürer, Drei Versionen der Verhältnismäßigkeit im Völkerrecht, 2015, S. 589 f.; *Tridimas*, in: Schütze/ders., Oxford Principles of European Union Law, 2018, S. 243.
237 Auch die vom BVerfG insoweit zitierte Judikatur und Literatur (BVerfGE 3, 383 <399>; Lerche, Übermaß und Verfassungsrecht – zur Bindung des Gesetzgebers an die Grundsätze der Verhältnismäßigkeit und der Erforderlichkeit, 1961 <Nachdruck 1999>, S. 19 ff.) weist nicht in Richtung auf eine kompetenzrechtliche Bedeutung des Verhältnismäßigkeitsgrundsatzes.
238 Vgl. *von Danwitz* in: EWS 2003, 394, 400.
239 Vgl. *Tuori* in: von Bogdandy/Grabenwarter/Huber, Band VI, § 98 Rn. 84; vgl. auch Emiliou, The principle of proportionality in European Law, S. 169; *Craig* in: New Zealand Law Review 2010, 265, 267.

B. Primärrechtlicher Rahmen zur Kompetenzabgrenzung

Nicht nur in Deutschland,[240] sondern auch in dritten Mitgliedstaaten der EU wie Frankreich, Österreich, Polen, Schweden, Spanien und Ungarn[241] erfolgt die Prüfung, ob dem Grundsatz der Verhältnismäßigkeit genügt wurde, in den Abschnitten der Kontrolle der Geeignetheit, Erforderlichkeit und Angemessenheit einer hoheitlichen Maßnahme. Der italienische Verfassungsgerichtshof geht ähnlich vor und ergänzt sein Kontrollprogramm noch um das auf eine ausgewogene Beachtung der Verfassungswerte abstellende Kriterium der Rationalität.[242]

Der EuGH hat den Verhältnismäßigkeitsgrundsatz bereits vor dessen ausdrücklicher Verankerung in den europäischen Verträgen als ungeschriebenen Bestandteil des Unionsrechts anerkannt[243] und insoweit gefordert, „dass die Handlungen der Organe geeignet sind, die mit der fraglichen Regelung zulässigerweise verfolgten Ziele zu erreichen, und nicht die Grenzen dessen überschreiten, was zur Erreichung dieser Ziele geeignet und erforderlich ist".[244] In der Dogmatik des Grundsatzes kommt – (auch insoweit) u.a. abweichend von dessen Verständnis in der Judikatur des BVerfG – dem Kohärenzkriterium – insbesondere auch in seiner glücks-

---

[240] Vgl. BVerfGE 16, 147 (181); 16, 194 (201 f.); 30, 292 (316 f.); 45, 187 (245); 63, 88 (115); 67, 157 (173); 68, 193 (218); 81, 156 (188 f.); 83, 1 (19); 90, 145 (172 f.); 91, 207 (221 ff.); 95, 173 (183); 96, 10 (21); 101, 331 (347); 120, 274 (321 f.); 141, 220 (265 Rn. 93).

[241] Vgl. rechtsvergleichend BVerfG, Urteil des Zweiten Senats vom 05. Mai 2020, 2 BvR 859/15, Rn. 125.

[242] Vgl. BVerfG, Urteil des Zweiten Senats vom 05. Mai 2020 – 2 BvR 859/15 -, Rn. 125 unter Bezugnahme auf *Bifulco/Paris*, in: v. Bogdandy/Grabenwarter/Huber, Band VI, § 100 Rn. 49 f.

[243] Vgl. *Nußberger* in: NVwZ-Beilage 2013, 36, 39; *Trstenjak/Beysen* in: EuR 2012, 265, 265; *Hofmann* in: Barnard/Peers, S. 198, 205; *Weber* in: Blanke/Mangiameli, Art. 5 EUV, Rn. 12; *Dony*, Droit de l'Union européenne, Rn. 151.

[244] So schon EuGH, Rs. C-8/55, *Fédération charbonnière de Belgique / Hohe Behörde*; vgl. auch EuGH, Rs. C-491/01, *The Queen gegen Secretary of State for Health, ex parte British American Tobacco (Investments) Ltd und Imperial Tobacco Ltd.*, Rn. 122); Rs. C-343/09, Afton Chemical / Secretary of State for Transport, Rn. 45); Rs. C-283/11, *Sky Österreich / Österreichischer Rundfunk*, Rn. 50; Rs. C-101/12, *Schaible / Land Baden-Württemberg*, Rn. 29; Rs. C-293/12 u.a., *Digital Rights / Minister for Communications, Marine and Natural Resources u. a. und Kärntner Landesregierung u. a.*, Rn. 46.
In jüngerer Zeit neigt der EuGH dazu, die Kriterien der Geeignetheit und Erforderlichkeit gelegentlich gemeinsam zu prüfen (vgl. EuGH, C-58/08, Vodafone u.a., Rn. 53 f.; Rs. C-176/09, *Luxemburg / Parlament und Rat*, Rn. 63); Rs. C-569/18, *Cirigliana*, Rn. 43; vgl. auch *Pache* in: Pechstein u.a. Art. 5 EUV, Rn. 140; *Klamert* in: Kellerbauer/ders./Tomkin, Art. 5 EUV, Rn. 36.

spielrechtlichen Judikatur[245] – besondere Bedeutung zu: Eine Maßnahme ist danach dann i.S. des Grundsatzes der Verhältnismäßigkeit geeignet, wenn sie tatsächlich dem Anliegen gerecht wird, das angestrebte Ziel in kohärenter und systematischer Weise zu erreichen.[246] Dabei beschränkt sich der EuGH vielfach auf die Kontrolle, ob die betreffende Maßnahme nicht als offensichtlich ungeeignet zur Verwirklichung des angestrebten Ziels erscheint.[247] Im Rahmen der Prüfung der Erforderlichkeit einer Maßnahme kontrolliert der EuGH – (auch) insoweit in Übereinstimmung mit aus der deutschen Verfassungsrechtsdogmatik vertrauten Vorgehensweise- ob das Ziel nicht ebenso wirksam durch andere Maßnahmen erreicht werden kann, die das zu schützende Gut weniger beeinträchtigen.[248] Die Prüfung der Angemessenheit einer Maßnahme – d.h. die Verhältnismäßigkeit im engeren Sinne – spielt demgegenüber in der Judikatur des EuGH bestenfalls eine untergeordnete Rolle.[249]

Das BVerfG hat den Verhältnismäßigkeitsgrundsatz in seiner Entscheidung zur Anleihepolitik der EZB herangezogen, um erstmalig ein *ultra-vires*-Handeln eines EU-Organs festzustellen.[250] Er hält die PSPP-Beschlüsse

---

245 Vgl. *Ukrow* in: ZfWG 2019, 223, 232.
246 Vgl. EuGH, Rs. C-64/08, *Engelmann*, Rn. 35; Rs. C-137/09, *Josemans*, Rn. 70; Rs. C-28/09, *Kommission / Österreich*, Rn. 126.
247 Vgl. BVerfG, Urteil des Zweiten Senats vom 05. Mai 2020, 2 BvR 859/15, Rn. 126 mit umfangreichen Nachweisen zur Judikatur des EuGH; *Bast* in: Grabitz/Hilf/Nettesheim, Art. 5 EUV, Rn. 73; *Klamert* in: Kellerbauer/ders./Tomkin, Art. 5 EUV, Rn. 39; *Weber* in: Blanke/Mangiameli, Art. 5 EUV, Rn. 12.
248 Vgl. auch insoweit BVerfG, Urteil des Zweiten Senats vom 05. Mai 2020, 2 BvR 859/15, Rn. 126 mit weiteren umfangreichen Nachweisen zur Judikatur des EuGH.
249 Vgl. auch insoweit BVerfG, Urteil des Zweiten Senats vom 05. Mai 2020, 2 BvR 859/15, Rn. 126 mit weiteren umfangreichen Nachweisen zur Judikatur des EuGH; *Calliess* in: ders./Ruffert, Art. 5 EUV, Rn. 44; *von Danwitz* in: EWS 2003, 393, 395; *Lecheler* in: Merten/Papier, Band VI/1, § 158 Rn. 31; *Pache*, in: Pechstein u.a., Art. 5 EUV, Rn. 149; *Trstenjak/Beysen* in: EuR 2012, S. 265, 269 f.; *Klamert* in: Kellerbauer/ders./Tomkin, Art. 5 EUV, Rn. 36; *Weber* in: Blanke/Mangiameli, Art. 5 EUV, Rn. 12; vgl. auch *Emiliou*, The principle of proportionality in European Law, S. 134.
250 Anders als vielfach dargestellt hat das BVerfG nicht „das PSPP" als *Ultra-vires*-Akt qualifiziert. Vielmehr macht das Gericht die „endgültige" Beurteilung des Programms „im konkreten Fall" von einer „nachvollziehbar dargelegten Verhältnismäßigkeitsprüfung" abhängig. *Ultra vires* war nach Auffassung des BVerfG lediglich das angebliche Unterlassen einer solchen Prüfung, das zu einem „Abwägungs- und Darlegungsausfall" geführt haben soll. Vgl. BVerfG, Urteil des Zweiten Senats vom 05. Mai 2020, 2 BvR 859/15, Rn. 177 ff.; *Guber* in: ZEuS 4/2020 (erscheint demnächst).

der EZB für unverhältnismäßig im Sinne des Art. 5 Abs. 1 Satz 2 und Abs. 4 EUV.[251] Diese Entscheidung ist auf berechtigte europarechtliche Kritik gestoßen.[252] Sie vermag nicht zuletzt auch in der dogmatischen Ableitung nicht zu überzeugen. Denn das BVerfG übersieht, dass sich die vertragsrechtliche Regel zur Kompetenzabgrenzung zwischen EU und Mitgliedstaaten nach Inhalt und Funktion fundamental von jenem Grundsatz der Verhältnismäßigkeit unterscheidet, wie ihn das BVerfG in jahrzehntelanger ständiger Rechtsprechung als festen Bestandteil und Minimum jeglicher Grundrechtsprüfung etabliert hat.[253]

Das BVerfG hat in seiner *Kalkar II*-Entscheidung vom 22. Mai 1990 selbst betont, dass es neben der Pflicht zu bundesfreundlichem Verhalten – eine Pflicht, die der Pflicht zur loyalen Zusammenarbeit im Verhältnis EU – Mitgliedstaaten korrespondiert – keine Verfassungsgrundsätze gebe, „aus denen Schranken für die Kompetenzausübung in dem von Staatlichkeit und Gemeinwohlorientierung bestimmten Bund-Länder-Verhältnis gewonnen werden könnten. Aus dem Rechtsstaatsprinzip abgeleitete Schranken für Einwirkungen des Staates in den Rechtskreis des Einzelnen sind im kompetenzrechtlichen Bund-Länder-Verhältnis nicht anwendbar. Dies gilt insbesondere für den Grundsatz der Verhältnismäßigkeit; ihm kommt eine die individuelle Rechts- und Freiheitssphäre verteidigende Funktion zu. Das damit verbundene Denken in den Kategorien von Freiraum und Eingriff kann weder speziell auf die von einem Konkurrenzver-

---

251 BVerfG, Urteil des Zweiten Senats vom 05. Mai 2020, 2 BvR 859/15, Rn. 177.
252 Vgl. *Giegerich*, Mit der Axt an die Wurzel der Union des Rechts; *Ludwigs*, The consequences of the judgement of 5 May 2020 of the Second Senate of the German Constitutional Court (BVerfG), Committee on Legal Affairs Committee on Constitutional Affairs, Public Hearing, 14 July 2020 (https://www.europarl.europa.eu/cmsdata/210045/AFCO%20JURI%20Hearing%2014%20July%20-%20Prof%20Ludwigs.pdf); *Mayer*, Das PSPP-Urteil des BVerfG vom 5. Mai 2020. Thesen und Stellungnahme zur öffentlichen Anhörung, Deutscher Bundestag, Ausschuss für die Angelegenheiten der Europäischen Union, 25. Mai 2020 (https://www.bundestag.de/resource/blob/697586/cdf8025132586d197288f57569776bff/mayer-data.pdf); *Rath*, Ein egozentrischer deutscher Kompromiss, 05.05.2020 (https://www.lto.de/recht/hintergruende/h/bverfg-ezb-eugh-pspp-entscheidung-kommentar-konflikt-polen-ungarn/); *Thiele*, Das BVerfG und die Büchse der ultra-vires-Pandora, 05.05.2020 (https://verfassungsblog.de/vb-vom-blatt-das-bverfg-und-die-buechse-der-ultra-vires-pandora/); Wegener, Verschroben verhoben!, 05.05.20200 (https://verfassungsblog.de/verschroben-verhoben/).
253 Vgl. *Guber* in: ZEuS 4/2020 (erscheint demnächst).

hältnis zwischen Bund und Land bestimmte Sachkompetenz des Landes noch allgemein auf Kompetenzabgrenzungen übertragen werden".[254]

Dafür, dieses verfassungsrechtliche Vorverständnis aus Anlass der EZB-Entscheidung zu verlassen, bestand kein Anlass. Auch ein Bemühen um eine Parallelisierung von verfassungs- und unionsrechtlichem Verständnis der Bedeutung des Verhältnismäßigkeitsgrundsatzes hätte im Ausgangspunkt für ein grundrechtszentriertes Verständnis des Prinzips gesprochen. Denn dieses prägt auch die Judikatur des EuGH. Gerade in seiner Entscheidung im durch das BVerfG initiierten Vorabentscheidungsverfahren zur EZB-Anleihepolitik hat der EuGH allerdings auch eine kompetenzrechtliche Bedeutung des Prinzips anerkannt.

In dieser Entscheidung hat der EuGH – in Anknüpfung an eine erste Entscheidung zur Auslegung von Fragen an der Schnittstelle von Währungs- und Wirtschaftspolitik[255] – betont, dass aus Art. 119 Abs. 2 und Art. 127 Abs. 1 AEUV in Verbindung mit Art. 5 Abs. 4 EUV hervorgehe, dass ein zur Währungspolitik gehörendes Programm für den Ankauf von Anleihen nur in gültiger Weise beschlossen und durchgeführt werden kann, wenn die von ihm umfassten Maßnahmen in Anbetracht der Ziele dieser Politik verhältnismäßig sind. Nach ständiger Rechtsprechung des EuGH verlange der Grundsatz der Verhältnismäßigkeit, „dass die Handlungen der Unionsorgane zur Erreichung der mit einer Regelung verfolgten legitimen Ziele geeignet sind und nicht über die Grenzen dessen hinausgehen, was zur Erreichung dieser Ziele erforderlich ist"[256]. Was die gerichtliche Nachprüfung der Einhaltung dieser Voraussetzungen anbelange, sei dem Europäischen System der Zentralbanken (ESZB), da es bei der Ausarbeitung und Durchführung eines Programms für Offenmarktge-

---

254 BVerfGE 81, 310 (338) unter Bezugnahme auf BVerfGE 79, 311 (341).
In einem haushaltsrechtlichen Verfahren hat das BVerfG zudem entschieden, dass sich die Abwehr einer Störung des gesamtwirtschaftlichen Gleichgewichts und eine Begrenzung der Kreditaufnahme nicht wie ein Grundrechtseingriff und ein von diesem Eingriff betroffener Rechts- oder Freiheitsbereich gegenüberstehen. Daher könne auch Art. 115 Abs. 1 Satz 2 GG nicht entnommen werden, dass eine Kreditfinanzierung konsumtiver Ausgaben nur unter Bindung an das Verhältnismäßigkeitsprinzip erfolgen dürfe. Auch diese Entscheidung spricht gegen eine die Grenzen der Grundrechtsprüfung überschreitende Bedeutung des Verhältnismäßigkeitsgrundsatzes in Richtung auf eine Regelung zur Beschränkung von Kompetenzausübungen in Mehr-Ebenen-Verhältnissen.
255 EuGH, Rs. C-62/14, *Peter Gauweiler u. a. / Deutscher Bundestag*, Rn. 66 ff.
256 EuGH, Rs. C-62/14, *Peter Gauweiler u. a. / Deutscher Bundestag*, Rn. 67.

schäfte, wie es im Beschluss 2015/774[257] vorgesehen ist, Entscheidungen technischer Natur treffen und komplexe Prognosen und Beurteilungen vornehmen müsse, in diesem Rahmen ein weites Ermessen einzuräumen.[258]

Nach den Angaben, über die der EuGH verfügte, war es aus Sicht des EuGH „nicht ersichtlich, dass die wirtschaftliche Analyse des ESZB, der zufolge das PSPP unter den monetären und finanziellen Bedingungen des Euro-Währungsgebiets geeignet war, zur Erreichung des Ziels der Gewährleistung der Preisstabilität beizutragen, einen offensichtlichen Beurteilungsfehler aufweist".[259]

In Anbetracht der vorhersehbaren Auswirkungen des PSPP und da nicht ersichtlich sei, dass das vom ESZB verfolgte Ziel durch eine andere Art geldpolitischer Maßnahmen hätte erreicht werden können, die ein weniger weitreichendes Tätigwerden des ESZB beinhaltet hätte, sei davon auszugehen, dass das PSPP nach seinem Grundgedanken nicht offensichtlich über das zur Erreichung dieses Ziels Erforderliche hinausgehe.[260] Der Umstand, dass gegen die mit einer Begründung versehene Analyse des ESZB Einwände erhoben wurden, könne als solcher nicht genügen, um einen offensichtlichen Beurteilungsfehler des ESZB festzustellen, da vom ESZB mit Rücksicht darauf, dass geldpolitische Fragen gewöhnlich umstritten sind und es über ein weites Ermessen verfügt, nicht mehr als der Einsatz seines wirtschaftlichen Sachverstands und der ihm zur Verfügung stehenden notwendigen technischen Mittel verlangt werden könne, um diese Analyse mit aller Sorgfalt und Genauigkeit durchzuführen.[261] Schließlich erscheine es angesichts der Angaben in den dem EuGH vorliegenden Akten und des weiten Ermessens des ESZB nicht offensichtlich, dass ein Programm für den Erwerb von Staatsanleihen von geringerem Umfang oder kürzerer Dauer genauso wirkungsvoll und schnell wie das PSPP eine vergleichbare Entwicklung der Inflation hätte gewährleisten können, wie sie vom ESZB angestrebt werde, um das von den Verfassern der Verträge festgelegte vorrangige Ziel der Währungspolitik zu erreichen.[262]

---

257 Beschluss (EU) 2015/774 der Europäischen Zentralbank vom 4. März 2015 über ein Programm zum Ankauf von Wertpapieren des öffentlichen Sektors an den Sekundärmärkten (EZB/2015/10), EU ABl. L 121 vom 14.5.2015, S. 20–24.
258 EuGH, Rs. C-62/14, *Peter Gauweiler u. a. / Deutscher Bundestag*, Rn. 71 ff.
259 EuGH, Rs. C-62/14, *Peter Gauweiler u. a. / Deutscher Bundestag*, Rn. 78.
260 EuGH, Rs. C-62/14, *Peter Gauweiler u. a. / Deutscher Bundestag*, Rn. 81.
261 EuGH, Rs. C-62/14, *Peter Gauweiler u. a. / Deutscher Bundestag*, Rn. 91.
262 EuGH, Rs. C-62/14, *Peter Gauweiler u. a. / Deutscher Bundestag*, Rn. 92.

Schließlich hatte das ESZB aus Sicht des EuGH „die verschiedenen beteiligten Interessen so gegeneinander abgewogen, dass tatsächlich vermieden wird, dass sich bei der Durchführung des PSPP Nachteile ergeben, die offensichtlich außer Verhältnis zu dessen Zielen stehen".[263]

Auch wenn diese auf das Zusammenspiel währungs- und wirtschaftspolitischer Kompetenzen bezogene Entscheidung erkennbar nicht ohne Weiteres für das Zusammenspiel zwischen Binnenmarktkompetenz der EU und Medien-, namentlich Vielfaltsregulierungskompetenz der Mitgliedstaaten fruchtbar gemacht werden kann, spricht doch vieles dafür, dass nicht zuletzt eine hinreichende Darlegung des Abwägungsprozesses im Zuge weiterer Gesetzgebung zur Herstellung eines digitalen Binnenmarktes wie auch die komplexen Prognosen und Beurteilungen, derer es auch bei europarechtlicher Rechtssetzung zur Vielfaltsprophylaxe mit Blick auf Gefährdungen des Vielfaltsziels durch neue Medienakteure wie namentlich Medienintermediäre bedürfen würde, die Erfolgschancen eines auf die Verletzung des Verhältnismäßigkeitsgrundsatzes gestützten Verfahrens von vornherein begrenzen dürften. Dies gilt zumindest dann, wenn die Vielfaltsprophylaxe nicht Hauptzweck der Regulierung seitens der EU, sondern begleitender Zweck bei dem Bemühen um Effektivierung der Grundfreiheiten für die neuen Medienakteure wäre.

Regulierungspolitisch spricht dies allerdings zur Vermeidung einer Vertiefung der aus Anlass der Anleihepolitik der EZB ausgebrochenen Konfliktlinie zwischen EuGH und BVerfG zur Auslegung der *ultra-vires*-Grenzen im Lichte des Verhältnismäßigkeitsgrundsatzes für eine Zurückhaltung der europäischen Rechtsetzung in Bereichen, die in besonderer Weise grundrechtssensibel aus Sicht der verfassungsrechtlichen Dogmatik von Kommunikationsfreiheiten in den Mitgliedstaaten ist. Namentlich würde eine Vollharmonisierung des Rechts der Vielfaltssicherung im digitalen Medien-Ökosystem Fragen nach einer Überschreitung der *ultra-vires*-Grenzen im Verhältnis EuGH – BVerfG provozieren. Eine solche unsensible Ausdehnung des Anwendungsbereichs europarechtlicher „Medienregulierung" *ratione personae* und/oder *ratione materiae* würde das auf Kooperation angelegte Zusammenspiel zwischen EU und Mitgliedstaaten ebenso zusätzlich gefährden wie sie das Verhältnis zwischen EuGH und BVerfG weiter belasten könnte.

---

263 EuGH, Rs. C-62/14, *Peter Gauweiler u. a. / Deutscher Bundestag,* Rn. 93.

B. Primärrechtlicher Rahmen zur Kompetenzabgrenzung

6. Die Bedeutung der Kompetenzausübungsschranken in der medienregulatorischen Praxis – Stand und Entwicklungsperspektive

In der bisherigen medienregulatorischen Praxis haben weder das Verhältnismäßigkeits- noch das Subsidiaritätsprinzip eine nach außen ohne Weiteres erkennbare und insoweit auch herausgehobene Rolle gespielt. In den Erwgr. der novellierten AVMD-Richtlinie findet sich in Bezug auf den Verhältnismäßigkeitsgrundsatz nur eine rudimentäre, im Übrigen nicht kompetenz- sondern grundrechtlich ausgerichtete Erwähnung im Zusammenhang mit den sog. Quotenregelungen.[264] In Bezug auf das Subsidiaritätsprinzip findet sich sogar keinerlei spezifisch auf diesen Grundsatz bezogene Erwägung.

Dies bedeutet allerdings nicht, dass nicht zuletzt auch der Subsidiaritätsgrundsatz ohne praktische Relevanz wäre: Die Europäische Kommission nimmt in ihren Rechtsetzungsvorschlägen, auch denjenigen mit mehr oder weniger intensivem Bezug zur Medienregulierung, regelmäßig zur Vereinbarkeit mit dem Subsidiaritätsprinzip Stellung und ermöglicht damit dritten Regulierern, aber auch der interessierten Öffentlichkeit, kritische Einwände zur Vereinbarkeit des Regelungsvorhabens mit dem Subsidiaritätsprinzip vorzubringen. Die Vermutung ist naheliegend, dass diese prozedurale Öffnung zu einer subsidiaritätsbezogenen Begründungslast nicht zuletzt auch den verfahrensmäßigen Effektuierungen des Subsidiaritätsprinzips, insbesondere dem Frühwarnsystem, Rechnung trägt.

Nationale Parlamente haben zwar in den letzten Jahren gelegentlich von der Möglichkeit Gebrauch gemacht, die unzureichende Beachtung des Subsidiaritätsprinzips bei Rechtsetzungsvorschlägen der EU zu rügen.[265] An einer entsprechenden Rügebefähigung der für die Medienregulierung

---

[264] Nachdem im 37. Erwägungsgrund der novellierten AVMD-Richtlinie 2018/1808/EU zunächst betont wird, dass Fernsehveranstalter momentan stärker in europäische audiovisuelle Werke investieren als Anbieter von audiovisuellen Mediendiensten auf Abruf, wird hieraus gefolgert: „Falls ein Zielmitgliedstaat sich entscheidet, einem der Rechtshoheit eines anderen Mitgliedstaats unterworfenen Fernsehveranstalter eine finanzielle Verpflichtung aufzuerlegen, sollte er daher *unter gebührender Berücksichtigung des Grundsatzes der Verhältnismäßigkeit* die direkten Beiträge dieses Fernsehveranstalters zur Produktion europäischer Werke und zum Erwerb von Rechten an europäischen Werken — insbesondere Koproduktionen — berücksichtigen."

[265] Vgl. hierzu und zum Folgenden die jährlichen Berichte der Kommission über die Anwendung der Grundsätze der Subsidiarität und der Verhältnismäßigkeit, zuletzt für das Jahr 2019, COM(2020) 272 final, https://ec.europa.eu/info/sites/info/files/com-2020-272-de.pdf.

in Deutschland letztverantwortlichen Landesparlamente fehlt es indessen. Sie konnten sich bislang als „Hüter" des Subsidiaritätsprinzips nicht institutionell profilieren.

Allerdings hat, soweit ersichtlich, der Frühwarnmechanismus auch jenseits des Feldes der Medienregulierung bislang noch nie dazu geführt, dass die Kommission einen Rechtsetzungsvorschlag nachträglich in substantieller Weise abgeändert hätte, auch wenn die Auffassungen der Organe und weiterer Akteure, inklusive nationaler Parlamente, über die Einhaltung des Subsidiaritätsprinzips „zuweilen stark auseinander" gingen. Das Festhalten der Kommission an den eigenen Vorschlägen ist bis zu einem gewissen Grad wohl dadurch zu erklären, dass die Quoren für die Auslösung der speziellen Überprüfungspflicht bei keinem Gesetzgebungsvorschlag erreicht wurden. Damit die nationalen Parlamente die nötige Schlagkraft erreichen, bedürfte es sorgfältiger Koordination und Absprache nicht nur im innerstaatlichen Bereich des kooperativen Parlamentsföderalismus, sondern auch in der transnationalen europäischen parlamentarischen Vernetzung. Ein gemeinsames Vorgehen ist letztlich die Voraussetzung dafür, dass der Frühwarnmechanismus effektiv genutzt werden kann. Die Konferenz der Europa-Ausschüsse der Parlamente (COSAC) könnte hierzu als „Clearingstelle" genutzt werden.

Zudem sieht Art. 4a Abs. 2 Unterabs. 2 der AVMD-Richtlinie nunmehr vor, dass die Kommission „in Zusammenarbeit mit den Mitgliedstaaten [...] im Einklang mit den Grundsätzen der Subsidiarität und der Verhältnismäßigkeit gegebenenfalls die Erstellung von Verhaltenskodizes der Union" erleichtert.[266]

Damit kommt beiden Prinzipien in der Fortentwicklung des medienregulatorischen Rahmens für *media governance* in der EU nicht zu unterschätzende Bedeutung zu. Denn diese Richtlinien-Verweisung auf Verhaltenskodizes der EU hat das in Art. 4a Abs. 1 und 2 der Richtlinie adressierte Regulierung mittels Ko- und Selbstregulierung im Blick: Nach Art. 4a Abs. 1 Satz 1 „unterstützen [die Mitgliedstaaten] die Nutzung der Koregulierung und die Förderung der Selbstregulierung mithilfe von Verhaltenskodizes, die auf nationaler Ebene in den von dieser Richtlinie koordinierten Bereichen angenommen werden, soweit das nach ihrem jeweiligen Rechtssystem zulässig ist".[267] Die Mitgliedstaaten und die Kommission „können" gemäß Art. 4a Abs. 2 Satz 1 zudem „die Selbstregulierung durch

---

266 Eingehend zur AVMD-Richtlinie in Abschnitt D.II.2.
267 Diese Kodizes müssen nach Art. 4a Abs. 1 Satz 2 der Regelung derart gestaltet sein, dass sie (a) von den Hauptbeteiligten in den betreffenden Mitgliedstaaten

Verhaltenskodizes der Union fördern, die von Mediendiensteanbietern, Video-Sharing-Plattform-Anbietern oder Organisationen, die solche Anbieter vertreten, erforderlichenfalls in Zusammenarbeit mit anderen Sektoren wie Industrie-, Handels-, Berufs- und Verbraucherverbänden oder -organisationen aufgestellt werden".[268]

VI. *Die Bedeutung der Grundrechte*

1. *Der medienbezogene Grundrechtsschutz, das Achtungsgebot des Art. 11 Abs. 2 Grundrechtecharta und die Kompetenzfrage*

Freiheit und Pluralismus der Medien sind nicht nur für eine funktionierende Demokratie auf Ebene der Mitgliedstaaten der EU von fundamentaler Bedeutung. Ohne diese mediale Absicherung lässt sich auch ein den Grundwerten des Art. 2 EUV verpflichteter Integrationsprozess nicht ins Werk setzen. Fragen der Medienregulierung berühren mithin die Grundlage der Europäischen Union – die „unverletzlichen und unveräußerlichen Rechte des Menschen sowie Freiheit, Demokratie, Gleichheit und Rechtsstaatlichkeit als universelle Werte" i.S. der Präambel des EUV.[269]

Auch vor diesem Hintergrund haben Freiheit und Pluralität der Medien in der Entwicklung des Grundrechtsschutzes der EU stets eine prominente Rolle gespielt. Sie sind zentraler Bestandteil der in der Europäischen Menschenrechtskonvention (EMRK) wie der Charta der Grundrechte der EU (GRC) verankerten Rechte, Freiheiten und Grundsätze und in den Verfassungstraditionen der Mitgliedstaaten tief verwurzelt. „Sie bilden damit eine normative Kraft, die sich bereits auf die Auslegung und Anwendung des Europarechts ausgewirkt hat und wohl auch in Zukunft eine wichtige

---

allgemein anerkannt werden, (b) ihre Ziele klar und unmissverständlich darlegen, (c) eine regelmäßige, transparente und unabhängige Überwachung und Bewertung ihrer Zielerfüllung vorsehen und (d) eine wirksame Durchsetzung einschließlich wirksamer und verhältnismäßiger Sanktionen vorsehen.

268 Solche Kodizes müssen nach Art. 4a Abs. 2 Satz 2 der Regelung derart gestaltet sein, dass sie von den Hauptbeteiligten auf Unionsebene allgemein anerkannt werden und mit Absatz 1 Buchstaben b bis d in Einklang stehen. Die nationalen Verhaltenskodizes bleiben nach Art. 4a Abs. 2 Satz 3 der Regelung von den Verhaltenskodizes der Union unberührt.

269 Vgl. zu diesem Zusammenhang *Viķe-Freiberga u.a.* (Hochrangige Gruppe zur Freiheit und Vielfalt der Medien), Bericht zu freien und pluralistischen Medien als Rückhalt der europäischen Demokratie, 2013, S. 20.

Rolle spielen wird"[270] – nicht zuletzt auch bei einer freiheitssichernden und -fördernden und zugleich demokratie- und sozialverträglichen Gestaltung des digitalen Wandels (nicht nur) des Medien-Ökosystems.

Im Folgenden erfolgt mit Blick auf den Schwerpunkt der Studie keine vertiefte Auseinandersetzung mit der Reichweite des Grundrechtsschutzes, sondern mit dessen Bedeutung in kompetenzrechtlicher Perspektive. Dessen ungeachtet ist ein kurzer Rekurs zum medienbezogenen Verhältnis von europäischem und nationalem Grundrechtsschutz schon an dieser Stelle kompetenzrechtlich bedeutsam.[271]

Die Grundrechte Charta der EU enthält bürgerliche, politische, wirtschaftliche, soziale und Unionsbürgerrechte. Die in der Charta garantierten Rechte dürfen nach deren Art. 52 Abs. 3 Satz 1 denen der EMRK in Bedeutung und Tragweite nicht nachstehen. Dieser EMRK-Schutz ist mithin als Mindeststandard zu verstehen, die Charta kann also, was in deren Art. 52 Abs. 3 Satz 2 bekräftigt wird, einen weitergehenden Schutz bieten. Dies ist auch mit Blick auf den Medien-Grundrechtsschutz bedeutsam.

Nach Art. 10 Abs. 1 Satz 1 EMRK hat jede Person das Recht auf freie Meinungsäußerung. Dieses Recht schließt nach Satz 2 die Meinungsfreiheit und die Freiheit ein, Informationen und Ideen ohne behördliche Eingriffe und ohne Rücksicht auf Staatsgrenzen zu empfangen und weiterzugeben. Dieser Artikel hindert die Staaten nach Art. 10 Abs. 1 Satz 3 EMRK nicht, für Hörfunk-, Fernseh- oder Kinounternehmen eine Genehmigung vorzuschreiben.

Die Ausübung dieser Freiheiten ist gemäß Art. 10 Abs. 2 EMRK „mit Pflichten und Verantwortung verbunden; sie kann daher Formvorschriften, Bedingungen, Einschränkungen oder Strafdrohungen unterworfen werden, die gesetzlich vorgesehen und in einer demokratischen Gesellschaft notwendig sind für die nationale Sicherheit, die territoriale Unversehrtheit oder die öffentliche Sicherheit, zur Aufrechterhaltung der Ordnung oder zur Verhütung von Straftaten, zum Schutz der Gesundheit oder der Moral, zum Schutz des guten Rufes oder der Rechte anderer, zur Verhinderung der Verbreitung vertraulicher Informationen oder zur Wahrung der Autorität und der Unparteilichkeit der Rechtsprechung."

Der Schutzumfang des Art. 11 GRC geht über diesen Schutz nach Art. 10 EMRK hinaus. Während Art. 11 Abs. 1 Satz 1 GRC mit Art. 10 Abs. 1 S. 1 EMRK und Art. 11 Abs. 1 Satz 2 GRC mit Art. 10 Abs. 1 S. 2

---

270 *Brogi/Gori*, European Commission Soft and Hard Law Instruments for Media Pluralism and Media Freedom, S. 97 ff.
271 Vgl. im Übrigen auch unten, Abschnitt C.II und C.III.

B. Primärrechtlicher Rahmen zur Kompetenzabgrenzung

EMRK jeweils wortgleich ist, gibt Art. 11 Abs. 2 GRC zudem vor, dass „die Freiheit der Medien und ihre Pluralität ... geachtet (werden)".

Der Begriff „Medien" geht schon von seinem Wortlaut her über die in Art. 10 Abs. 1 Satz 3 EMRK benutzten klassischen Begriffe von Hörfunk und Fernsehen hinaus und umspannt auch mehr als diesen traditionellen Rundfunk und die Presse. Auch wenn Art. 10 EMRK nach ständiger Rechtsprechung der Straßburger Menschenrechtsgerichtsbarkeit dynamisch zu verstehen ist, so ist doch bemerkenswert, dass Art. 11 Abs. 2 GRC schon von seinem Wortlaut her einen breiteren personellen Anwendungsbereich der Achtungspflichten in den Blick nimmt. Dieser personelle Anwendungsbereich umfasst bereits bei semantischer Auslegung nicht nur klassische Mediengattungen, sondern alle – auch zukünftige, d.h. im Zeitpunkt der Entwicklung und Verabschiedung der Charta nicht bekannte – Übertragungsmedien für an die Allgemeinheit gerichtete Kommunikation. Dieser besonderen Zukunfts- und Entwicklungsoffenheit[272] ist auch bei der Weiterentwicklung der Regulierung von Kommunikation jenseits der Individualkommunikation, d.h. auch bei Regulierung, die sich auf soziale Netzwerke und Medienintermediäre bezieht, Rechnung zu tragen. Da die Möglichkeit der Grundrechtsausübung im digitalen Raum ebenfalls vom Staat geschützt sein muss, besteht auch an dieser Stelle eine Pflicht zum Schutz vor Störungen eines freien massenkommunikativen Diskurses zu Lasten demokratischer Freiheit und Teilhabe durch technische oder sonstige Instrumente wie z.B. Netzwerkeffekte. Die Erforderlichkeit einer Offenheit des Grundrechtsschutzes für neue Gefährdungslagen, wie sie das BVerfG in seiner III. Weg-Entscheidung betont hat, ist mithin auch für den europäische Grundrechtsschutz bedeutsam.

Es ist zudem offenkundig, dass eine föderale Brechung von Medienregulierung einen Beitrag zur Pluralität der Medien leisten kann. Insofern sind nicht zuletzt auch Maßnahmen zur Sicherung von regionaler und lokaler Vielfalt geeignet, auf eine Unterstützung des Achtungsziels des Art. 11 Abs. 2 GRC hinzuwirken.

Durch den Vertrag von Lissabon hat die Grundrechtecharta zwar über Art. 6 Abs. 1 EUV den Rang von Primärrecht erlangt. Die damit verbundenen Pflichten sind nach Art. 51 Abs. 1 Satz 1 GRC an die Organe, Einrichtungen und sonstige Stellen der Union adressiert; sie betreffen darüber hinaus die Mitgliedstaaten, sofern sie im Anwendungsbereich des Unions-

---

[272] Vgl. *Frenz*, Handbuch Europarecht, Rn. 1747.

rechts tätig werden, also etwa bei der Umsetzung und Vollziehung von Unionsrecht.[273]

Ob die Grundrechte über ihre Abwehrfunktion hinaus auch Schutzpflichten für die Hoheitsträger beinhalten, ist umstritten und ist einer differenzierenden Betrachtung je nach in Rede stehendem Grundrecht zugänglich. Die „Achtungspflicht" des Art. 11 Abs. 2 GRC spricht für eine nicht nur abwehrrechtliche Dimension der Pluralitäts-Dimension des Grundrechts. Der EuGH hat – allerdings noch nicht in Bezug auf Art. 11 Abs. 2 GRC – bei bestimmten Grundrechten bereits eine objektiv-rechtliche Funktion bejaht.[274] In allen Fällen, in denen eine Schutzpflicht zu bejahen ist, muss der Hoheitsträger bei Grundrechtsverletzungen, etwa durch private Dritte, einschreiten oder ihnen sogar (gesetzlich) vorbeugen, womit eine Handlungspflicht zu für den europäischen Gesetzgeber zu bejahen wäre – allerdings nicht über den bestehenden Kompetenzbereich der EU hinaus. Denn aus der europäischen Anerkennung der Medienfreiheit als Grundrecht wie auch aus dem Achtungsgebot in Bezug auch auf die Pluralität der Medien folgt kein zusätzlicher Kompetenztitel oder gar ein Regelungsprimat der EU. Dies ergibt sich aus Art. 51 Abs. 2 GRC: Danach „dehnt (die Charta) den Geltungsbereich des Unionsrechts nicht über die Zuständigkeiten der Union hinaus aus und begründet weder neue Zuständigkeiten noch neue Aufgaben für die Union, noch ändert sie die in den Verträgen festgelegten Zuständigkeiten und Aufgaben".

2. Grundrechtsschutz im Spannungsfeld von Kontrolle durch EuGH und nationaler Verfassungsgerichtsbarkeit

Fragen des Grundrechtsschutzes haben das Verhältnis und die Zuordnung von EU-Recht und nationalem Verfassungsrecht schon seit langem geprägt. In der diesbezüglichen Judikatur des BVerfG lassen sich auf der Zeitachse bemerkenswerte Akzentverschiebungen feststellen, die bis in die jüngste Zeit fortdauern.

---

273 Vgl. EuGH, Rs. 12/86, *Meryem Demirel / Stadt Schwäbisch Gmünd*, Rn. 28; Rs. 5/88, *Hubert Wachauf / Bundesamt für Ernährung und Forstwirtschaft*, Rn. 17ff.
274 Vgl. EuGH, Rs. C-288/89, *Stichting Collectieve Antennevoorziening Gouda und andere / Commissariaat voor de Media*, Rn. 22; EuGH, Rs. C-368/95, *Vereinigte Familiapress Zeitungsverlags- und vertriebs GmbH / Heinrich Bauer Verlag*, Rn. 18. Vgl. dazu auch Abschnitt C.IV.1. im Kontext der zulässigen Beschränkung von Grundfreiheiten im Bereich der Vielfaltssicherung.

B. Primärrechtlicher Rahmen zur Kompetenzabgrenzung

Ausgangspunkt dieser Judikatur zur Kollision von europäischem Recht und Verfassungsrecht war die sog. *Solange I*-Entscheidung des BVerfG. Dort betonte es zunächst, dass nationales Recht und supranationales Recht zwei voneinander unabhängige und nebeneinanderstehende Rechtskreise seien.[275] Brisanter – und zum damaligen Zeitpunkt bereits angreifbar – war sein Hinweis, dass der europäische Grundrechtsschutz nicht den Anforderungen des deutschen Grundrechtsschutzes entspreche. Aufbauend auf dieser (Fehl-) Einschätzung formulierte das BVerfG:

> *„Solange der Integrationsprozeß der Gemeinschaft nicht so weit fortgeschritten ist, daß das Gemeinschaftsrecht auch einen von einem Parlament beschlossenen und in Geltung stehenden formulierten Katalog von Grundrechten enthält, der dem Grundrechtskatalog des Grundgesetzes adäquat ist, ist nach Einholung der in Art. 177 des Vertrags geforderten Entscheidung des Europäischen Gerichtshofs die Vorlage eines Gerichts der Bundesrepublik Deutschland an das Bundesverfassungsgericht im Normenkontrollverfahren zulässig und geboten, wenn das Gericht die für es entscheidungserhebliche Vorschrift des Gemeinschaftsrechts in der vom Europäischen Gerichtshof gegebenen Auslegung für unanwendbar hält, weil und soweit sie mit einem der Grundrechte des Grundgesetzes kollidiert".*[276]

Mit seiner *Solange II*-Entscheidung leitete das BVerfG dann – auch im Lichte der zwischenzeitlich ergangenen grundrechtlichen Judikatur des EuGH – eine Abkehr von diesem kollisionsrechtlichen Konfrontationskurs ein. Dort betonten die Karlsruher Richter:

> *„Solange die Europäischen Gemeinschaften, insbesondere die Rechtsprechung des Gerichtshofs der Gemeinschaften einen wirksamen Schutz der Grundrechte gegenüber der Hoheitsgewalt der Gemeinschaften generell gewährleisten, der dem vom Grundgesetz als unabdingbar gebotenen Grundrechtsschutz im Wesentlichen gleichzuachten ist, zumal den Wesensgehalt der Grundrechte generell verbürgt, wird das Bundesverfassungsgericht seine Gerichtsbarkeit über die Anwendbarkeit von abgeleitetem Gemeinschaftsrecht, das als Rechtsgrundlage für ein Verhalten deutscher Gerichte oder Behörden im Hoheitsbereich der Bundesrepublik Deutschland in Anspruch genommen wird, nicht mehr ausüben und dieses Recht mithin nicht mehr am Maßstab der Grundrechte des Grundgesetzes überprüfen; entsprechende Vorlagen nach Art. 100 Abs. 1 GG sind somit unzulässig".*[277]

---

275 Vgl. BVerfGE 37, 271 (278).
276 BVerfGE 37, 271 (285).
277 BVerfGE 73, 339 (387).

An dieser Judikatur, mit der sich das BVerfG seine Prüfungszuständigkeit zwar theoretisch vorbehielt, sie aber praktisch stark zurücknahm, hat das Verfassungsgericht auch in den Folgejahren festgehalten. Es hat namentlich auch in seiner *Bananenmarkt-Verordnung*-Entscheidung den Grundrechtsschutz auf europäischer Ebene als ausreichend bezeichnet und betont, dass es auch nach seiner *Maastricht*-Entscheidung[278] seine Prüfungsbefugnis nur unter bestimmten Voraussetzungen ausübe. Deshalb seien Vorlagen beim BVerfG unzulässig, wenn ihre Begründung nicht darlege, dass die europäische Rechtsentwicklung sowie die Rechtsprechung des EuGH nach Ergehen der *Solange II*-Entscheidung unter den erforderlichen Grundrechtsstandard abgesunken ist.[279] Es bedürfe daher der Darlegung, warum eine Regelung des sekundären Gemeinschaftsrechts im Einzelnen den jeweils als unabdingbar gebotenen Grundrechtsschutz generell nicht gewährleiste.[280]

In jüngerer Zeit hat das BVerfG indessen von diesem auf Kooperation mit dem EuGH hin angelegten Judikatur nicht nur bei seiner EZB-Entscheidung 2020, sondern zuvor bereits grundrechtsbezogen Abstand genommen.

So hat es bereits 2016[281] erstmalig seine Grundrechtskontrolle um Elemente der Kontrolle der Wahrung der Verfassungsidentität angereichert, indem es sich im Hinblick auf den Schutz der Menschenwürde nicht erst – dem *Solange II*-Ansatz folgend – bei einem generellen Absinken des Standards, sondern auch im Einzelfall eine Prüfung am Maßstab des deutschen Grundgesetzes vorbehält. Seinen Grund fand diese Ausdehnung der Kontrolldichte darin, dass Art. 1 GG in Art. 79 Abs. 3 GG in Bezug genommen wird – mit der Folge, dass die Menschenwürde zugleich zur Verfassungsidentität des Grundgesetzes gehört und insoweit der Identitätskontrolle unterfällt. Während der Beschluss, bei dem es im inhaltlichen Ausgangspunkt um die Vereinbarkeit einer nach Europarecht (scheinbar) zwingenden Auslieferung mit dem Schuldprinzip ging, in Teilen seiner Kommentierung als Aufforderung an den EuGH, den Grundrechtsschutz ernster zu nehmen, begrüßt wurde, wurde er in anderen Teilen als „Solange IIa" bzw. „Solange III"-Entscheidung[282] eingestuft; von einer beinahe gezündeten „Identitätskontrollbombe"[283], war die Rede. Dass schon dieser Beschluss

---

278 Vgl. hierzu oben, Abschnitt B.V.4.
279 BVerfGE 102, 147 (165).
280 BVerfGE 102, 147 (164).
281 BVerfGE 140, 317 (333 f.).
282 Vgl. Zur Debatte etwa *Bilz*, JuWissBlog, 15.03.2016, m.w.N.
283 *Steinbeis*, Verfassungsblog, 26.01.2016.

B. Primärrechtlicher Rahmen zur Kompetenzabgrenzung

nicht ohne Weiteres mit der EuGH-Rechtsprechung zur Rolle des nationalen Grundrechtsschutzes im grundrechtlichen Mehrebenensystem vereinbar war, ist evident.

Die letztgenannte Fragestellung wird durch den Beschluss des Ersten Senats des BVerfG vom 06. November 2019 besonders virulent. Schon der erste Leitsatz zeigt in der Anknüpfung an die „Solange"-Terminologie seine grundlegende Bedeutung:

> *„Soweit die Grundrechte des Grundgesetzes durch den Anwendungsvorrang des Unionsrechts verdrängt werden, kontrolliert das Bundesverfassungsgericht dessen Anwendung durch deutsche Stellen am Maßstab der Unionsgrundrechte. Das Gericht nimmt hierdurch seine Integrationsverantwortung nach Art. 23 Abs. 1 GG wahr.*
>
> *Bei der Anwendung unionsrechtlich vollständig vereinheitlichter Regelungen sind nach dem Grundsatz des Anwendungsvorrangs des Unionsrechts in aller Regel nicht die Grundrechte des Grundgesetzes, sondern allein die Unionsgrundrechte maßgeblich. Der Anwendungsvorrang steht unter anderem unter dem Vorbehalt, dass der Schutz des jeweiligen Grundrechts durch die stattdessen zur Anwendung kommenden Grundrechte der Union hinreichend wirksam ist."*[284]

Bemerkenswert ist diese Entscheidung im Zusammenhang mit vorliegender Studie auch deshalb, weil sie einen medienregulierungsbezogenen Sachverhalt zum Ausgangspunkt hat und dabei die grundrechtliche Dimension jenseits des klassischen staatsabwehrenden Verständnisses betont.

Wie die Grundrechte des Grundgesetzes gewährleisten auch die Grundrechte der Charta aus Sicht des BVerfG nicht nur Schutz im Staat-Bürger-Verhältnis, sondern auch in privatrechtlichen Streitigkeiten, wie das Gericht unter Bezugnahme v.a. auf reichhaltige Judikatur des EuGH unterstreicht.[285]

> *„Soweit Betroffene von einem Suchmaschinenbetreiber verlangen, den Nachweis und die Verlinkung bestimmter Inhalte im Netz zu unterlassen, sind in die danach gebotene Abwägung neben den Persönlichkeitsrechten der Betrof-*

---

[284] BVerfG, Beschluss des Ersten Senats vom 06. November 2019, 1 BvR 276/17, BVerfGE 102, Leitsätze 1 und 2; vgl. auch ebenda Rn. 47, 50, 53.

[285] BVerfG, aaO (Fn. 288), Leitsatz 4 und Rn. 96 unter Bezugnahme auf EuGH, Rs. C-275/06, *Promusicae / Telefónica de España SAU*, Rn. 65 ff.; Rs. C-580/13, *Coty Germany / Stadtsparkasse Magdeburg*, Rn. 33 ff.; C-516/17, *Spiegel Online / Volker Beck*, Rn. 51 ff.; dazu auch *Streinz/Michl* in: EuZW 2011, 384, 385 ff.; *Frantziou* in: HRLR 2014, 761, 771; *Fabbrini* in: de Vries/Bernitz/Weatherill, S. 261, 275 ff.; *Lock*, in: Kellerbauer/Klamert/Tomkin, Art. 8 GRC, Rn. 5.

fenen (Art. 7 und Art. 8 GRC) im Rahmen der unternehmerischen Freiheit der Suchmaschinenbetreiber (Art. 16 GRC) die Grundrechte der jeweiligen Inhalteanbieter sowie die Informationsinteressen der Internetnutzer einzustellen. Soweit das Verbot eines Suchnachweises in Ansehung des konkreten Inhalts der Veröffentlichung ergeht und dem Inhalteanbieter damit ein wichtiges Medium zu dessen Verbreitung entzieht, das ihm anderweitig zur Verfügung stünde, liegt hierin eine Einschränkung seiner Meinungsfreiheit."[286]

VII. Medienregulierung und das Demokratieprinzip in der EU

Bestandteil der Werteordnung der EU, „auf die sich die Union gründet", ist nach Art. 2 Satz 1 EUV auch die „Demokratie". Zugleich wird in Art. 2 Satz 2 EUV der Bezug zwischen Demokratie und „Pluralismus" aufgezeigt – dort allerdings im Einstieg nicht auf die EU, sondern mitgliedstaaten- und gesellschaftsbezogen. Schon diese Brechung des Konnexes zwischen Demokratie und Pluralismus in der Adressierung des jeweiligen Wertes im Mehr-Ebenen-System EU spricht gegen eine auf die Bedeutung des Medienpluralismus für die Demokratie gestützte „Annexkompetenz" der EU zur übergreifenden, alle Ebenen des europäischen Integrationsverbundes erfassenden Pluralismusregulierung zu Zwecken der Wahrung des Wertes Demokratie. Eine solche ebenen-übergreifende Regulierung kommt auch aus Anlass der Regulierung des Wahlverfahrens zum Europäischen Parlament nach Art. 223 AEUV nicht in Betracht.

Dass Meinungs- und Medienvielfalt für die Aufrechterhaltung einer demokratischen Ordnung unverzichtbar sind, ist offenkundig. Das Bundesverfassungsgericht betont in einer auch jenseits der deutschen Verfassungsordnung zutreffenden Weise, dass

„Demokratie, soll sie nicht lediglich formales Zurechnungsprinzip bleiben, [...] vom Vorhandensein bestimmter vorrechtlicher Voraussetzungen abhängig (ist), wie einer ständigen freien Auseinandersetzung zwischen sich begegnenden sozialen Kräften, Interessen und Ideen, in der sich auch politische Ziele klären und wandeln und aus der heraus eine öffentliche Meinung den politischen Willen verformt".[287]

Dass zu diesen Voraussetzungen zählt, „dass der wahlberechtigte Bürger mit der Hoheitsgewalt, der er unterworfen ist, in seiner Sprache kommuni-

---

286 BVerfG, aaO (Fn. 288), Leitsätze 5 und 6 und Rn. 114 ff.
287 BVerfGE 89, 155 (185).

B. Primärrechtlicher Rahmen zur Kompetenzabgrenzung

zieren kann",[288] kann zwar nicht bestritten werden. Indessen setzt ein demokratischer europäischer Integrationsverbund nicht voraus, dass diese Kommunikation nur in einer einheitlichen gemeinsamen Sprache erfolgen muss. Sprachliche Vielfalt ist – wie bereits bislang Staaten mit mehreren Amtssprachen wie die Schweiz zeigten und wie sich sprachlich zunehmend von der Dominanz einer Sprache entfernende Staaten wie die USA zeigen – kein Hemmnis für demokratischen Zusammenhalt. Ein Abbau sprachlicher Vielfalt ist mithin zur Schaffung von transnationalem Pluralismus nicht geboten und würde überdies auch in erkennbarem Widerspruch zu völkerrechtlichen Geboten in Bezug auf kulturelle Vielfalt wie den Schutz und die Wahrung von Minderheitensprachen stehen.

Soweit das BVerfG in seiner Maastricht-Entscheidung betonte, dass zu den vorrechtlichen Voraussetzungen auch gehört, dass

„die Entscheidungsverfahren der Hoheitsgewalt ausübenden Organe und die jeweils verfolgten politischen Zielvorstellungen allgemein sichtbar und verstehbar sind,"[289]

wird man im Zuge der seit dem Vertrag von Maastricht erfolgten Reformschritte vertraglicher Art mit dem Abbau von unterschiedlichen Rechtsetzungsverfahren, der Verfestigung grenzüberschreitender parteilicher Zusammenarbeit und der wachsenden Transparenz der politischen Zielsetzungen von Kommission und Europäischem Parlament zumindest von einer deutlichen Förderung vorrechtlicher Voraussetzungen einer demokratischen Gestalt der EU sprechen dürfen.

Der europäische Integrationsverbund ist deshalb zunehmend auch ein Demokratieverbund – nicht nur ein auf eine dynamische Entwicklung der EU angelegter Verbund demokratischer Staaten, sondern im Zuge der Vertiefung der europäischen Integration zunehmend auch ein Verbund dieser Staaten mit einer EU, die selbst zum Träger demokratischer Herrschaftsausübung wird. Das BVerfG hat schon in seiner Maastricht-Entscheidung vom 12. Oktober 1993 betont, dass

„mit dem Ausbau der Aufgaben und Befugnisse der Gemeinschaft die Notwendigkeit (wächst), zu der über die nationalen Parlamente vermittelten demokratischen Legitimation und Einflußnahme eine Repräsentation der Staatsvölker durch ein europäisches Parlament hinzutreten zu lassen, von

---

[288] BVerfGE 89, 155 (185).
[289] BVerfGE 89, 155 (185).

der ergänzend eine demokratische Abstützung der Politik der Europäischen Union ausgeht."[290]

Mit der durch den Vertrag von Maastricht begründeten Unionsbürgerschaft werde zwischen den Staatsangehörigen der Mitgliedstaaten ein auf Dauer angelegtes rechtliches Band geknüpft, das zwar nicht eine der gemeinsamen Zugehörigkeit zu einem Staat vergleichbare Dichte besitzt, dem bestehenden Maß existentieller Gemeinsamkeit jedoch einen rechtlich verbindlichen Ausdruck verleihe. Das BVerfG hebt sodann hervor:

„Die von den Unionsbürgern ausgehende Einflußnahme kann in dem Maße in eine demokratische Legitimation der europäischen Institutionen münden, in dem bei den Völkern der Europäischen Union die Voraussetzungen hierfür erfüllt sind."[291]

Derartige tatsächliche Bedingungen haben sich, wie aufgezeigt, in den fast drei Jahrzehnten seit dem Vertrag von Maastricht, auf den sich die Entscheidung des BVerfG aus 1993 bezog, im institutionellen Rahmen der Europäischen Union zunehmend nicht nur als rechtliches Handlungsinstrumentarium entwickelt, sondern auch in der gesellschaftlichen Wirklichkeit etabliert. Nicht zuletzt die Klima- und die Corona-Krise, aber auch populistische Angriffe auf ein wertebasiertes demokratisches Miteinander erweisen sich als Katalysatoren einer transnationalen Meinungsbildung zur Prägung demokratischer Bewältigung der Gefährdungslagen.

Indessen erwächst aus diesem im Wachsen begriffenen Demokratieverbund keine Kompetenz der EU zur regulatorischen Förderung der vorrechtlichen Voraussetzungen einer weiteren Vertiefung des Demokratieverbunds. Zwar bedarf es für diese Vertiefung eines intensiveren Engagements der Medien in den Mitgliedstaaten bei der Vermittlung von demokratischen Entscheidungsabläufen und -ergebnissen in Bezug auf das Integrationsprogramm der EU. Denn eine europäische Öffentlichkeit als Resonanzboden wie Impulsgeber für eine Stärkung der EU als Träger originär demokratisch legitimierter Hoheitsgewalt bedarf auch medial gestützter Offenheit und Transparenz in Bezug auf den Umgang einerseits in wie zwischen den Mitgliedstaaten, andererseits in wie zwischen den EU-Organen mit den Kompetenzen, die der EU durch die europäischen Verträge eröffnet sind. Indessen ist die Verfassung der EU nicht darauf ausgerichtet, aus integrationspolitischen Desiderata integrationsrechtliche Befugnisse ableiten zu können.

---

290 BVerfGE 89, 155 (184).
291 BVerfGE 89, 155 (184 f.).

B. Primärrechtlicher Rahmen zur Kompetenzabgrenzung

Aus dem Demokratieprinzip allenfalls ableitbare Potentiale der EU zur rechtsharmonisierenden Medienregulierung bestehen danach im Kern insoweit, als demokratische Desiderata wie die Abwehr von Desinformationskampagnen unter Binnenmarkt-Blickwinkel zur Vermeidung von Hemmnissen für den freien Verkehr von Waren und Dienstleistungen durch unterschiedliche Konzepte wehrhafter Demokratie einer primär wirtschaftsorientierten Regulierung begleitend zugeführt werden.

VIII. Schlussfolgerungen für die Kompetenz zur Medienregulierung

Auch für die Medienregulierung seitens der EU gilt das Prinzip der begrenzten Ermächtigung. Abschließende Aussagen über den medienregulatorischen Handlungsspielraum der EU können nicht getroffen werden, da die Kompetenzregelungen der europäischen Verträge einem dynamischen, digitale Herausforderungen aufgreifenden Verständnis zugänglich sind.

Die europäischen Verträge enthalten in ihren regulatorische Handlungsoptionen für die EU eröffnenden Kompetenzregelungen keine Bereichsausnahme für die Medien; die „funktionellen" Zuständigkeiten der EU, nicht zuletzt im Bereich der Schaffung eines (auch digitalen) Binnenmarktes und einer (zukünftig auch auf digitale Souveränität Europas) ausgerichteten Wettbewerbsordnung, erstrecken sich zwar nicht auf die kulturelle und vielfaltssichernde Funktion von Medien, wohl aber auf alle Bereiche ihrer wirtschaftlich bedeutsamen Aktivitäten.

Indessen besteht auch keine umfassende Handlungskompetenz der EU zur Medienregulierung. In den Zuständigkeitskatalogen für die EU findet sich kein ausdrücklicher Hinweis auf die Regulierung von Medien; deren kultur- und bildungsbezogene Dimension ist nur mitgliedstaatliches Handeln unterstützender Regulierung der EU unterhalb der Ebene der Rechtsharmonisierung zugänglich.

Namentlich erwächst aus der Einbeziehung des Pluralismus in die Werteordnung der EU nach Art. 2 EUV keine diesbezügliche Regulierungskompetenz der EU. Die Werteordnung der EU leitet die Wahrnehmung an dritter vertraglicher Stelle eröffneter Kompetenzen der EU. Das Pluralismus-Gebot kommt als Rechtsgrundlage für eine originäre Medienvielfaltsregulierung wegen des Prinzips der begrenzten Ermächtigung nicht als kompetenzbegründend, und sei es in Form einer Annexkompetenz, in Betracht.

Die bisherigen und künftig im Rahmen der von Kommissionspräsidentin von der Leyen ausgerufenen digitalen Dekade Europas zu erwartenden Einwirkungen des Unionsrechts auf Medienregulierung der Mitgliedstaten, sei es in Gestalt aktiv-positiver Integration durch Rechtsakte der EU mit Medien- nicht zuletzt auch Medienvielfaltsbezug, sei es in Gestalt negativer Integration durch die Prüfung mitgliedstaatlicher Medienregulierung an den Maßstäben des primären Unionsrechts (nicht zuletzt Grundfreiheiten und Wettbewerbsrecht) können weder als grundsätzlich oder gar generell *ultra vires* noch als generell zulässig angesehen werden. Die Frage, ob ein Akt der Medienregulierung durch die EU sich außerhalb des Integrationsprogramms der EU bewegt, bleibt im Ausgangspunkt eine Frage der Einzelfallbetrachtung.

Allerdings spricht eine Zusammenschau der Strukturprinzipien der europäischen Verträge mit deren Kompetenzausübungsregeln und -beschränkungen, insbesondere dem Subsidiaritäts- und dem Verhältnismäßigkeitsgrundsatz, für einen fortdauernden Primat zumindest der kultur- und vielfaltsbezogenen Medienregulierung seitens der Mitgliedstaaten. Dem entsprechen im Ergebnis zwei Leitlinien für die diesbezügliche Medienregulierung der EU: So wenig Eingriff in mitgliedstaatliche Regelungskompetenz über negative Integration wie möglich, so wenig Harmonisierung und positive Integration wie nötig.

C. Zur Bedeutung und rechtlichen Verankerung der Medienvielfalt auf EU-Ebene

Mark D. Cole / Christina Etteldorf

I. Allgemeines

> „Der Begriff des Pluralismus kann sowohl nach seiner Funktion als auch nach seiner Zielsetzung definiert werden: Es handelt sich um einen Rechtsbegriff, der darauf abzielt, in bestimmten Fällen die Reichweite des Prinzips der Meinungsfreiheit einzuschränken, um die Informationsvielfalt für die Öffentlichkeit zu gewährleisten."

Mit diesen Worten versuchte die Europäische Kommission 1992 in ihrem Grünbuch zu Pluralismus und Medienkonzentration[292] eine Definition für Pluralismus in den Medien und damit einen Ausgangspunkt für das zu finden, was zum Schutz und zum Erhalt der Medienvielfalt erforderlich ist. Wesentlich konkreter und medienbezogener definierte der Europarat knapp zwei Jahre später Medienpluralismus unter Bezugnahme auf binnen- und außenpluralistische Strukturen der Medien selbst als entweder

> „interner Natur, mit einem breiten Spektrum sozialer, politischer und kultureller Werte, Meinungen, Informationen und Interessen, die innerhalb einer Medienorganisation zum Ausdruck kommen, oder externer Natur, durch eine Reihe solcher Organisationen, von denen jede einen bestimmten Standpunkt zum Ausdruck bringt."[293]

Über die Jahrzehnte hinweg wurden seitdem sowohl auf wissenschaftlicher wie politischer Ebene immer wieder neue definitorische Ansätze gesucht.[294] Eine einheitliche und supranational gültige Definition dessen, was unter Medienpluralismus zu verstehen ist, gibt es aber bis heute nicht und kann es auch vor dem Hintergrund der Notwendigkeit der Begriffsof-

---

292 aaO (Fn. 28), S. 18; Übersetzung aus dem Englischen.
293 Europarat, Activity report of the Committee of Experts on Media Concentrations and Pluralism, Beitrag zur vierten Ministerkonferenz zur Politik der Massenmedien, vom 7./8. Dezember 1994. Übersetzung aus dem Englischen.
294 Vgl. eingehend zur Entwicklung des Begriffs *Costache*, De-Regulation of European Media Policy 2000–2014, S. 15 ff.

fenheit nicht geben, die eine definitorische Verengung nicht zulassen darf und dem Medienpluralismus daher immanent ist. Vielmehr kommt es auch auf den Anknüpfungspunkt an, aus dessen Perspektive heraus die Betrachtung erfolgt. Dies kann beispielsweise genauso ein medienkonzentrationsrechtlicher Blickwinkel sein wie ein informationsrechtlicher, der danach fragt, welche Bedeutung der Medienpluralismus für die Informationsgewinnung der Bürger und damit für den demokratischen Willensbildungsprozess hat.

Wie im vorangegangenen Kapitel vor einem kompetenzrechtlichen Hintergrund dargestellt, findet die Sicherung der Medienvielfalt – wenngleich sie nicht zu den originären Kompetenzen der EU gehört – solche verschiedenen Anknüpfungspunkte auch im Unionsrecht, zum Beispiel innerhalb der Werteordnung der EU. Bedeutender vor dem Hintergrund des Schwerpunkts vorliegender Studie ist jedoch ihre Verwurzelung im materiellrechtlichen Gehalt der Grundrechte auf Ebene der EMRK und der GRC sowie dem Primärrecht, insbesondere innerhalb der europäischen Wettbewerbsordnung und der Grundfreiheiten. Wie nachfolgend darzustellen sein wird, stellt sich die Sicherung medialer Vielfalt in diesem Rahmen nicht als unmittelbarer Anknüpfungspunkt legislativer Maßnahmen dar, sondern vielmehr als ein Wert bzw. Ziel von allgemeinem öffentlichem Interesse, den es für EU und ihre Mitgliedstaaten in anderen Regelungsbereichen zu berücksichtigen und zu wahren gilt und der dementsprechend rechtfertigende oder beschränkende Wirkungen entfalten kann. Die sekundärrechtliche Verankerung soll in diesem Kapitel nur überblickhaft dargestellt werden, wonach im folgenden Kapitel eine eingehende Betrachtung des medienrechtlichen Rahmens auf EU-Sekundärrechtsebene unter besonderer Berücksichtigung von Aspekten der Vielfaltssicherung erfolgt.

II. Art. 10 EMRK und Rechtsprechung des EGMR

Art. 10 EMRK garantiert, dass jeder das Recht auf freie Meinungsäußerung hat, einschließlich der Freiheit, eine Meinung zu äußern und Informationen zu erhalten und weiterzugeben. Dominiert wird diese Regelung demnach durch die Garantie des Rechts auf freie Meinungsäußerung, das auch die Informationsfreiheit und die Freiheit der Meinungsbildung mit einschließt – Rechte, die auch vor dem Hintergrund des Medienpluralismus eine entscheidende Bedeutung haben, da die Sicherung und der Erhalt von Vielfalt ihre Funktionen mit Blick auf den demokratischen Willensbildungsprozess erfüllen müssen. Der Beitritt der EU zur EMRK steht bereits ein halbes Jahrhundert auf der europäischen Agenda, ist aber bislang wohl auch aufgrund der Komplexität des Beitritts einer supranationalen Organisation mit autonomer Rechtsordnung zu einem völkerrechtlichen Menschenrechtsschutzsystem noch nicht erfolgt.[295] Allerdings sind die 27 Mitgliedstaaten der EU an die EMRK gebunden und bleiben dies grundsätzlich auch dann, wenn Hoheitsrechte auf zwischenstaatliche Einrichtungen übertragen werden.[296] Zudem öffnet die EU ihren eigenen, durch die GRC garantierten Grundrechtsschutz für die EMRK sogar weiter als dies viele Rechtsordnungen der EU-Mitgliedstaaten tun[297], indem Art. 52 Abs. 3 GRC bestimmt, dass, soweit die GRC Rechte enthält, die den durch die EMRK garantierten Rechten entsprechen, sie die gleiche Bedeutung und Tragweite haben, wie sie ihnen in der genannten Konvention verliehen wird. Diese Bestimmung steht dem nicht entgegen, dass das Recht der Union einen weitergehenden Schutz gewährt.

Unter Zugrundlegung des weiten, bereits in Abschnitt B.VI.1. angesprochenen Begriffsverständnisses des EGMR wird von Art. 10 Abs. 1 EMRK auch die massenmediale Verbreitung von Informationen geschützt, insbesondere auch die Rundfunkfreiheit öffentlich-rechtlicher wie privater Rundfunkveranstalter[298], wobei auch die Werbung[299] Teil des geschützten Kommunikationsprozesses ist. Auch der Kommunikationsprozess im Internet ist dabei geschützt.[300] Ebenso wenig wie der Verbreitungsweg, spielt die Professionalität von medialen Angeboten für die Eröffnung des Schutzbereichs eine Rolle. In einer jüngeren Entscheidung argumentiert der EGMR, dass zum Beispiel auch der so genannte Bürgerjournalismus (beispielsweise auch in Form von Angeboten und Kanälen von Nutzern auf Video-Sharing-Plattformen (VSP) wie YouTube) ein wichtiges zusätzliches Mittel zur Ausübung der Meinungsfreiheit sein kann, Informationen und Ideen zu empfangen und weiterzugeben, insbesondere vor dem Hintergrund, dass und wenn politische Informationen von den traditionellen Medien ignoriert werden.[301]

Weit gefasst wird auch der Eingriffsbegriff, der sowohl präventive Maßnahmen als auch repressive Verbote und Sanktionen erfasst, die von der

---

295 Vgl. hierzu eingehend, *Obwexer* in: EuR 2012, 115, 115 ff.
296 *Ress*, Menschenrechte, Gemeinschaftsrechte und Verfassungsrecht, S. 920 f.
297 Vgl. hierzu *Krämer* in: Stern/Sachs, Art. 52 GRC, Rn. 65; *Lock*, in: Kellerbauer/Klamert/Tomkin, Art. 52 GRC, Rn. 25.
298 EGMR, Nr. 50084/06, *RTBF / Belgien*, Rn. 5, 94.
299 EGMR, Nr. 33629/06, *Vajnai / Ungarn*; Nr. 15450/89, *Casado Coca / Spanien*.
300 EGMR, Nr. 36769/08, *Ashby Donald u.a. / Frankreich*, Rn. 34.
301 Vgl. EGMR, Nrn. 48226/10 und 14027/11, *Cengiz u.a. / Türkei*.

Verhinderung oder Erschwerung der Rezeption/Zugänglichkeit von medialen Dienste oder einzelnen Inhalte bis hin zur bloßen Kennzeichnung reichen.[302] Eine Gewichtung der Eingriffsintensität, also der Schwere der Beeinträchtigung des Grundrechts aufgrund des Eingriffs, findet dabei erst auf der Ebene der Rechtfertigung statt, denn die die EMRK garantiert die Meinungs- und Medienfreiheit nicht uneingeschränkt, sondern akzeptiert, dass die freie Meinungsäußerung auch mit einer gewissen Verantwortung verbunden ist und lässt daher Beschränkungen aufgrund höherrangiger Rechtsgüter zu. Den Konventionsstaaten räumt der EGMR einen Ermessensspielraums ein, innerhalb dessen sie allerdings ein angemessenes Verhältnis zwischen der Einschränkung der Meinungsfreiheit und dem verfolgten berechtigten Ziel herstellen müssen.[303]

Die Medienvielfalt[304] nimmt im Rahmen von Art. 10 EMRK seit jeher eine besondere Bedeutung ein. Dies ergibt sich zwar nicht unmittelbar aus dem Konventionstext, wohl aber aus der gefestigten Rechtsprechung des EGMR. Der EGMR hat mehrfach die grundlegende Rolle der Meinungsfreiheit für eine demokratische Gesellschaft hervorgehoben, vor allem soweit sie der Verbreitung von Informationen und Ideen von allgemeinem Interesse, auf deren Empfang die Öffentlichkeit ein Recht hat, dient.[305] Die Medien agieren hier in ihrer Funktion als „Wachhund" (‚*public watchdog*')[306] und leisten einen wichtigen Beitrag zur öffentlichen Debatte – als

---

302 Vgl. etwa EGMR, Nrn. 26935/05 und 13353/05, *Hachette Filipacchi Presse Automobile und Dupuy und Société de Conception de Presse et d'Edition und Ponson / Frankreich*.
303 EGMR, Nr. 39954/08, *Axel Springer AG / Deutschland*.
304 Recommendation No. R (94) 13 of the Committee of Ministers to member states on measures to promote media transparency (1994); Recommendation No. R (99) 1 of the Committee of Ministers to member states on measures to promote media pluralism (1999); Recommendation Rec (2003) 9 of the Committee of Ministers to member states on measures to promote the democratic and social contribution of digital broadcasting (2003); Recommendation CM/Rec(2007)2 of the Committee of Ministers to member states on media pluralism and diversity of media content (2007); Recommendation CM/Rec(2012)1 of the Committee of Ministers to member states on public service media governance (2012); Für einen Überblick zu den Empfehlungen des Europarates im Bereich der Medien und der Informationsgesellschaft s.a. Recommendations and declarations of the Committee of Ministers of the Council of Europe in the field of media and information society, 2016, https://rm.coe.int/1680645b44.
305 EGMR, Nr. 13585/88, *Observer und Guardian / Vereinigtes Königreich*; Nr. 17207/90, *Informationsverein Lentia u.a. / Österreich*.
306 Vgl. für eine Konkretisierung der Rolle als public watchdog etwa EGMR, Nr. 21980/93, *Bladet Tromsø / Norwegen*.

C. Zur Bedeutung und rechtlichen Verankerung der Medienvielfalt auf EU-Ebene

Informationsmittler und Forum für den öffentlichen Diskurs. Ein solches Unterfangen könne, betont der EGMR, nur dann erfolgreich sein, wenn es auf dem Prinzip der Pluralität, dessen Garant der Staat ist, basiere.[307] Dabei geht der Gerichtshof sogar soweit, zugespitzt festzustellen, dass es ohne Pluralismus keine Demokratie gibt[308], wobei sich Demokratie wiederum durch den Schutz des kulturellen oder geistigen Erbes sowie künstlerischer, literarischer und sozioökonomischer Ideen und Konzepte auszeichne.[309] Nicht zuletzt aufgrund dieser herausragenden Bedeutung erkennt der EGMR in Bezug auf die Medienvielfaltssicherung Art. 10 Abs. 1 EMRK nicht nur eine rein abwehrrechtliche Dimension zu, sondern sieht den Staat als – in letzter Instanz – Garanten des Prinzips des Pluralismus.[310] Die Frage jedoch, ob sich daraus eine Verpflichtung der der EMRK unterworfenen Staaten zur Herstellung gleichwertiger Vielfalt in den europäischen Kommunikationsräumen ableiten lässt, oder lediglich die Pflicht, sich schützend und fördernd vor das Schutzgut der Medienvielfalt zu stellen, ist bislang nicht abschließend geklärt.[311] Das Verständnis des EGMR geht insoweit zumindest dahin, dass wenn Pluralität zu Spannungen führt, sich das Handeln des Staates nicht gegen den Pluralismus richten dürfe, sondern vielmehr sicherstellen müsse, dass sich die beteiligten Gruppen tolerieren.[312] Zudem verträgt sich eine rein abwehrrechtliche Konzeption nicht mit der Konvention im Allgemeinen, insbesondere vor dem Hintergrund des Art. 1 EMRK, nach dem die Staaten die Rechte und Freiheiten aus der Konvention zusichern sollen. Im audiovisuellen Sektor muss Pluralismus zumindest auf effektive Weise durch die Bereitstellung eines geeigneten Rahmens – in gesetzlicher und administrativer Hinsicht – garantiert werden.[313]

Unabhängig davon, ob und inwieweit man nun aus Art. 10 Abs. 1 EMRK positive Handlungspflichten der Konventionsstaaten ableiten will, hat die Verankerung der Schutzpflicht für Medienvielfaltssicherung in der

---

307 EGMR, Nr. 17207/90, *Informationsverein Lentia u.a. / Österreich*, Rn. 38.
308 EGMR, Nr. 13936/02, *Manole u.a. / Moldova*, Rn. 95.
309 EGMR, Nr. 44158/98, *Gorzelik u.a. / Polen*, Rn. 92.
310 EGMR, Nr. 17207/90, *Informationsverein Lentia u.a. / Österreich*, Rn. 38; Nr. 24699/94, *VgT Verein gegen Tierfabriken / Schweiz*, Rn. 73.
311 Vgl. etwa *Gersdorf* in: AöR 1994, 400, 414; *Daiber* in: Meyer-Ladewig/Nettesheim/von Raumer, Artikel 11, Rn. 60.
312 EGMR, Nr. 74651/01, *Association of Citizens Radko & Paunkovski / ehemalige jugoslawische Republik Mazedonien*; Vgl. hierzu und zum Folgenden auch *Ukrow/Cole*, Aktive Sicherung lokaler und regionaler Medienvielfalt, S. 83 ff.
313 EGMR, Nr. 48876/08, *Animal Defenders International / Vereinigtes Königreich*, Rn. 134. Hierzu bereits Abschnitt B.VI.1.

EMRK sowie deren Einordnung als Ziel von allgemeinem Interesse Bedeutung mit Blick auf die Rechtfertigung der Beeinträchtigung von Grundfreiheiten.[314] So können etwa Beeinträchtigungen von Grundrechten wie zum Beispiel der Medienfreiheit selbst oder der Eigentumsfreiheit des Art. 1 des 1. Zusatzprotokolls zur EMRK durch Vielfaltssicherungsmaßnahmen der Konventionsstaaten gerechtfertigt werden, da die Grundrechte ihrerseits Schranken in der Verwirklichung von Zielen von öffentlichem Interesse finden, sofern diese in einer demokratischen Gesellschaft notwendig (i.w.S. also verhältnismäßig) sind.

Konsequenterweise gelten die vorgenannten Ausführungen zu den aus Art. 10 Abs. 1 EMR abzuleitenden Aspekten der Vielfaltssicherung auch im Gleichlauf mit dem weiten Schutzbereichsverständnis. Der EGMR hebt zwar in bestimmten medialen Sektoren die Bedeutung von Vielfalt besonders hervor, was vor allem für den audiovisuellen Sektor aufgrund der diesem traditionell zukommenden Wirkung als ‚durchdringenderes' Medium gegenüber beispielsweise der Presse gilt.[315] Allerdings gilt das Gebot der Aufrechterhaltung von Pluralismus im Sinne einer gefährdungsorientierten Auslegung des Grundrechtsschutzes überall dort, wo ein Medium Bedeutung für die Informationsvermittlung erlangt. So betont der EGMR auch die besondere Bedeutung des Internets für den demokratischen Willensbildungsprozess[316] – was nicht zuletzt Bedeutung auch für die Verbreitungswege von klassischen Medien hat –, ohne dass dadurch die wichtige Rolle klassischer Medien neben neuen Playern wie sozialen Medien oder anderen Plattformen geschmälert würde. Vielmehr scheint der EGMR davon auszugehen, dass ein Zusammenspiel verschiedener Rezeptionsmöglichkeiten Pluralismus ausmacht, was dazu führen kann, dass bei einer (ausreichend ernstlichen) ungleichmäßigen Verlagerung von Einflussnahmemöglichkeiten auf die öffentliche Meinungsbildung spezielle Gegenmaßnahmen von den Konventionsstaaten zu ergreifen wären.[317]

---

314 Vgl. EGMR, Nr. 38433/09, *Centro Europa 7 S.R.L. und di Stefano /Italien*, Rn. 214 ff.

315 EGMR, Nr. 37374/05, *Társaság a Szabadságjogokért / Ungarn*, Rn. 26; Nr. 17207/90, *Informationsverein Lentia u.a. / Österreich*, Rn. 38; Nr. 24699/94, *VgT Verein gegen Tierfabriken / Schweiz*, Rn. 73.

316 EGMR, Nrn. 3002/03 und 23676/03, *Times Newspapers Ltd (Nrn. 1 und 2) / Vereinigtes Königreich*, Rn. 27.

317 Diese Möglichkeit wurde vom EGMR in seinem Urteil vom 22. April 2013 (Nr. 48876/08, *Animal Defenders International / UK*, Rn. 119) angedeutet („*Notwithstanding therefore the significant development of the internet and social media in recent years, there is no evidence of a sufficiently serious shift in the respective influences of the new and of the broadcast media in the respondent State to undermine the*

C. Zur Bedeutung und rechtlichen Verankerung der Medienvielfalt auf EU-Ebene

Wie die Konventionsstaaten vielfaltssichernde Maßnahmen allerdings auszugestalten haben, gibt der EGMR – abgesehen von allgemeinen Ausführungen zur Notwendigkeit von Maßnahmen in einer demokratischen Gesellschaft oder der Gewichtung verschiedener grundrechtlich geschützter Interessen – nicht vor. Im Rahmen seiner Rechtsprechung verweist er allerdings verstärkt auf Empfehlungen des Europarates, insbesondere die Empfehlung des Ministerkomitees zum Medienpluralismus und zur Vielfalt von Medieninhalten[318], in der ebenso bekräftigt wird, dass pluralistische Äußerungen geschützt und aktiv gefördert werden sollen.[319] Der Europarat stützt seine Empfehlungen für mitgliedstaatliche Handlungsoptionen wiederum selbst auf Art. 10 EMRK und die daraus resultierenden Pflichten der Mitgliedstaaten des Europarates. Insbesondere sollen die Mitgliedstaaten hiernach die bestehenden regulatorischen Rahmenbedingungen, vor allem im Hinblick auf das Medieneigentum, anpassen und alle erforderlichen regulatorischen und finanziellen Maßnahmen ergreifen, um Medientransparenz und Strukturpluralismus sowie Vielfalt zu gewährleisten. Dabei enthalten die bereichsspezifischen Empfehlungen des Europarates auch konkretere Vorschläge für vielfaltssichernde Maßnahmen auf Basis einer Analyse von Gefährdungspotenzialen wie zum Beispiel die Einführung von Transparenzpflichten oder Must Carry/Must Offer-Regeln. Deren ob und wie der „Umsetzung" ist aber aufgrund des unverbindlichen Charakters solcher Empfehlungen ohnehin den Mitgliedstaaten überlassen.[320]

III. Art. 11 Abs. 2 GRC und Rechtsprechung des EuGH

Auf Unionsebene findet sich das Gegenstück zu Art. 10 Abs. 1 EMRK in Art. 11 Abs. 1 GRC, wonach jede Person das Recht auf freie Meinungsäußerung hat, wobei dieses Recht auch die Freiheit erfasst, Informationen und Ideen ohne behördliche Eingriffe und ohne Rücksicht auf Staatsgren-

---

need for special measures for the latter"), im Ergebnis aber vor dem Hintergrund der damaligen Gegebenheiten des digitalen Wandels in der Medienlandschaft verneint.

318 Recommendation CM/Rec(2007)2 of the Committee of Ministers to member states on media pluralism and diversity of media content, angenommen am 31. Januar 2007, abrufbar (englisch) unter https://search.coe.int/cm/Pages/result_details.aspx?ObjectId=09000016805d6be3.
319 EGMR, aaO (Fn. 317), Rn. 135.
320 Vgl. hierzu *Tichy* in: ZaöRV 2016, S. 415, 415 ff.

zen zu empfangen und weiterzugeben. Wie im Rahmen der EMRK erfasst der Schutzbereich (i.V.m Art. 11 Abs. 2 der die Freiheit der Medien auch ausdrücklich adressiert) traditionelle Medien wie Presse, Radio und Film sowie jede andere Form der Massenkommunikation, die bereits existiert oder erst in Zukunft entstehen wird, sofern sie an die breite Öffentlichkeit gerichtet ist.[321] Art. 11 GRC wurde in enger Übereinstimmung mit Art. 10 EMRK bzw., was den Schutzumfang betrifft, in direkter Übernahme in die Charta aufgenommen. Nur die spezifischen Schranken von Art. 10 Abs. 2 EMRK wurden nicht explizit übernommen, weil die GRC eine autonome und horizontal anwendbare Schrankenregelung in Art. 52 Abs. 1 enthält.[322]

Im Gegensatz zu einer sehr umfassenden Rechtsprechung des EGMR ist die Rechtsprechung des EuGH in Bezug auf die Kommunikationsfreiheiten weniger ausgeprägt. Dies ist auch darauf zurückzuführen, dass die Medienregulierung und damit auch die Einschränkungen der Kommunikationsfreiheiten aufgrund der insoweit begrenzten Befugnisse der EU in den Zuständigkeitsbereich der Mitgliedstaaten fallen und daher etwa in Vorlageverfahren seltener eine Rolle spielen.[323] Dabei sei allerdings angemerkt, dass sich entsprechend der wachsenden Bedeutung der Berufung auf die GRC in der Rechtsprechung des EuGH und in den Vorlagegesuchen der Mitgliedstaaten insgesamt[324] auch die Betonung von Art. 11 GRC gesteigert hat[325], wenngleich sich die betreffenden Entscheidungen maßgeblich auf das einschlägige Sekundärrecht stützten und Art. 11 GRC regelmäßig lediglich zur Betonung der Bedeutung der darin niedergelegten Rechte und Freiheiten herangezogen wurde. Auf die Rechtsprechung des EGMR

---

321 *Von Coelln* in: Stern/Sachs, Art. 11 GRC, Rn. 30; *Lock*, in: Kellerbauer/Klamert/Tomkin, Art. 11 GRC, Rn. 3.
322 *Cornils* in: Sedelmeier/Burkhardt, § 1 Rn. 88; *von Coelln* in: Stern/Sachs, Art. 11 GRC, Rn. 7 ff.
323 *Cornils* in: Sedelmeier/Burkhardt, § 1 Rn. 1, 46, 86.
324 2018 verwies der Gerichtshof der Europäischen Union (EuGH) in 356 Fällen auf die Charta (gegenüber 27 im Jahr 2010). Wenn nationale Gerichte Anfragen (Ersuchen um Vorabentscheidungen) an den EuGH richten, beziehen sie sich zunehmend auf die Charta (84 Mal im Jahr 2018 gegenüber 19 Mal im Jahr 2010). Europäische Kommission, Bericht über die Anwendung der Charta der Grundrechte der Europäischen Union 2018, https://op.europa.eu/de/publication-detail/-/publication/784b02a4-a1f2-11e9-9d01-01aa75ed71a1/language-de, S. 15.
325 In 29 Urteilen fand Art. 11 GRC (wenngleich nicht immer in entscheidungserheblicher Weise) Erwähnung durch den EuGH, 8 davon stammen aus dem Jahr 2019, 3 bereits aus 2020. Quelle: Rechtsprechungsdatenbank des EuGH, http://curia.europa.eu/juris/recherche.jsf?language=de.

C. Zur Bedeutung und rechtlichen Verankerung der Medienvielfalt auf EU-Ebene

zu Art. 10 EMRK und somit auf die vorherigen Ausführungen kann allerdings in Bezug auf Art. 11 Abs. 1 GRC zurückgegriffen werden, was sich sowohl aus den entsprechenden Erläuterungen der Präambel zu Art. 11 GRC[326] als auch aus der Äquivalenzklausel des Art. 52 Abs. 3 GRC ergibt und im Übrigen auch der Praxis des EuGH entspricht, die sich an der Interpretation des EGMR orientiert.[327]

Auch das Grundrecht nach Art. 11 Abs. 1 GRC ist nicht schrankenlos zu gewährleisten. Nach der einheitlichen Schrankenregelung von Art. 52 Abs. 1 GRC muss jede Einschränkung der Ausübung der in der Charta anerkannten Rechte und Freiheiten gesetzlich vorgesehen sein und den Wesensgehalt dieser Rechte und Freiheiten achten. Unter Wahrung des Grundsatzes der Verhältnismäßigkeit dürfen Einschränkungen nur vorgenommen werden, wenn sie notwendig sind und den von der Union anerkannten dem Gemeinwohl dienenden Zielsetzungen oder den Erfordernissen des Schutzes der Rechte und Freiheiten anderer tatsächlich entsprechen.

Vor dem Hintergrund von Fragen zur kompetenzrechtlichen Verankerung von Vielfaltssicherungsmaßnahmen interessanter ist jedoch Art. 11 Abs. 2 GRC, der vorschreibt, dass die Freiheit der Medien *und ihre Pluralität geachtet* werden. Wegen der im Vergleich zur Entwurfsfassung schwächeren Formulierung[328], ist die Frage, ob und inwieweit sich daraus objektiv-rechtliche Pflichten zur Vielfaltssicherung für die EU oder ihre Mitgliedstaaten ergeben, etwa im Sinne einer vorbeugenden Konzentrationskontrolle[329], nach wie vor nicht abschließend geklärt.[330] Während ein positiver Regelungsauftrag an den Unionsgesetzgeber dabei bereits aus kompetenzrechtlichen Gründen ausscheiden muss, Vielfaltssicherung daher kom-

---

326 Erläuterungen zur Charta der Grundrechte, ABl. C 303/17, abrufbar unter http://eur-lex.europa.eu/legal-content/EN/TXT/HTML/?uri=CELEX:32007X1214(01)&from=DE.
327 Vgl. Rs. C-368/95, *Vereinigte Familiapress Zeitungsverlags- und vertriebs GmbH / Heinrich Bauer Verlag*.
328 Die Entwurfsfassung enthielt damals noch die Formulierung „werden gewährleistet". Vgl. hierzu auch *Schmittmann/Luedtke* in: AfP 2000, 533, 534.
329 *Stock*, AfP 2001, 289, 301.
330 Vgl. hierzu eingehend und m.w.N. *Ukrow/Cole*, Aktive Sicherung lokaler und regionaler Medienvielfalt, S. 87 ff.; sowie *Institut für Europäisches Medienrecht (Hrsg.)*, Nizza, die Grundrechte-Charta und ihre Bedeutung für die Medien in Europa; vgl. weiterhin *Lock*, in: Kellerbauer/Klamert/Tomkin, Art. 11 GRC, Rn. 17.

petenziell allein Aufgabe der Mitgliedstaaten bleibt[331] und auch die Auslegung von Art. 11 Abs. 2 GRC im Sinne eines dienendes Grundrecht wie Art. 5 Abs. 1 S. 2 GG zu weit gehen dürfte[332], kann der Regelung eine gewisse objektiv-rechtliche Komponente nicht abgesprochen werden.[333] Eine Auslegung in diesem Sinne deckt sich auch mit den Ausführungen zur Verankerung der Medienfreiheit und des Pluralismus in Art. 10 EMRK, hinter dessen Aussagegehalt die Regelungen der GRC gemäß Art. 53 GRC nicht zurückbleiben dürfen. Gemäß den Erläuterungen zur Charta der Grundrechte[334], die nach der Präambel zur GRC bei der Auslegung von der Union und den Mitgliedstaaten zu berücksichtigen sind, stützt sich Art. 11 Abs. 2 insbesondere auf die Rechtsprechung des Gerichtshofs bezüglich des Fernsehens[335], auf das Protokoll über den öffentlich-rechtlichen Rundfunk in den Mitgliedstaaten[336] – in dem es heißt, dass „der öffentlich-rechtliche Rundfunk in den Mitgliedstaaten unmittelbar mit den demokratischen, sozialen und kulturellen Bedürfnissen jeder Gesellschaft sowie mit dem Erfordernis verknüpft ist, den Pluralismus in den Medien zu wahren" – sowie auf die (bei Verfassen der Charta geltende) Fernsehrichtlinie, insbesondere deren Erwgr. 17, der wiederum betont, dass es unerlässlich ist, dass „die Mitgliedstaaten dafür Sorge tragen, daß Handlungen unterbleiben, die den freien Fluß von Fernsehsendungen beeinträchtigen bzw. die Entstehung beherrschender Stellungen begünstigen könnten, welche zu Beschränkungen des Pluralismus und der Freiheit der Fernsehinformation sowie der Information in ihrer Gesamtheit führen würden".

Art. 11 Abs. 2 GRC fand (im Hinblick auf die hiernach zu achtende Pluralität der Medien) bislang allerdings erst in wenigen Entscheidungen ex-

---

331 Vgl. bereits Abschnitt B.VI.1. So *auch Ukrow/Cole*, Aktive Sicherung lokaler und regionaler Medienvielfalt, S. 89 f.; *Valcke*, Challenges of Regulating Media Pluralism in the European Union, S. 27; *Craufurd Smith*, Culture and European Union Law, S. 626 ff.

332 So auch *von Coelln* in: Stern/Sachs, Art. 11 GRC, Rn. 40, Fn. 108 m.w.N; *Streinz* in: ders., Art. 11 GRC, Rn. 17.

333 So auch *von Coelln* in: Stern/Sachs, Art. 11 GRC, Rn. 40; *Thiele* in: Pechstein u.a., Art. 11 GRC, Rn. 17.

334 Erläuterungen zur Charta der Grundrechte, EU ABl. C 303, 14.12.2007, S. 17–35, https://eur-lex.europa.eu/legal-content/de/ALL/?uri=CELEX%3A32007X1214%2801%29.

335 Insbesondere in der Rs. C-288/89, *Stichting Collectieve Antennevoorziening Gouda u. a. / Commissariaat voor de Media*.

336 Protokoll (Nr. 29) über den öffentlich-rechtlichen Rundfunk in den Mitgliedstaaten, EU ABl. C 326, 26.10.2012, S. 312–312.

C. Zur Bedeutung und rechtlichen Verankerung der Medienvielfalt auf EU-Ebene

plizit[337] Erwähnung durch den EuGH.[338] Während der EuGH in der Rechtssache *Sky Italia* auf die auf Art. 11 Abs. 2 abzielende Vorlagefrage zu einer nationalen wettbewerbsrechtlichen Regelung aufgrund der Unvollständigkeit der Vorlageentscheidung zur rechtlichen und tatsächlichen Beurteilungsgrundlage nicht näher einging, hob er die Bedeutung von Art. 11 Abs. 2 GRC in seiner erst kürzlich ergangenen *Vivendi*-Entscheidung, in der es um eine italienische Schwellenwert-Regelung zu Beteiligungsverhältnissen an Medienunternehmen bzw. elektronischen Kommunikationsunternehmen ging, besonders hervor. Unter Berufung auf seine bisherige Rechtsprechung betonte der EuGH, Die Bedeutung des Medienpluralismus und die daraus resultierenden Möglichkeiten zur Einschränkung von Grundfreiheiten wie folgt:

> *„Der Gerichtshof hat entschieden, dass die Wahrung der Freiheiten, die durch Art. 11 der Grundrechtecharta, der in seinem Abs. 2 die Freiheit und den Pluralismus der Medien nennt, geschützt werden, unbestreitbar ein im Allgemeininteresse liegendes Ziel darstellt, dessen Bedeutung in einer demokratischen und pluralistischen Gesellschaft nicht genug betont werden kann. Im Protokoll Nr. 29 über den öffentlich-rechtlichen Rundfunk in den Mitgliedstaaten, das dem EU- und dem AEU-Vertrag beigefügt ist, wird ebenfalls auf den Pluralismus der Medien Bezug genommen und erklärt, dass „der öffentlich-rechtliche Rundfunk in den Mitgliedstaaten unmittelbar mit den demokratischen, sozialen und kulturellen Bedürfnissen jeder Gesellschaft sowie mit dem Erfordernis verknüpft ist, den Pluralismus in den Medien zu wahren".* "[339]

Diese grundlegende Bedeutung des Pluralismus könne einen Eingriff in die Grundfreiheiten (dazu näher in Abschnitt C.IV.1.) durch mitgliedstaatliche Regelungen rechtfertigen.

In der Sache *TV Play Baltic AS* konkretisierte der EuGH dies in Bezug auf die Dienstleistungsfreiheit gegenüber der Aufrechterhaltung eines pluralistischen Rundfunkwesens unter Bezugnahme auf Art. 11 GRC und

---

337 Auch im Übrigen verweist der EuGH häufiger auf die Bedeutung der Pluralität der Medien ohne dabei auf Art. 11 Abs. 2 GRC zurückzugreifen, vgl. etwa EuGH, Rs. C-250/06, *United Pan-Europe Communications Belgium SA u.a. / État belge*, Rn. 41; Rs. C-336/07, *Kabel Deutschland Vertrieb und Service GmbH & Co. KG / Niedersächsische Landesmedienanstalt für privaten Rundfunk*, Rn. 37.

338 EuGH, Rs. C-283/11, *Sky Österreich GmbH / Österreichischer Rundfunk*; C-234/12, *Sky Italia Srl / AGCOM*; C-719/18 *Vivendi SA / AGCOM*; C-87/19, *TV Play Baltic AS / Lietuvos radijo ir televizijos komisija*.

339 EuGH, Rs. C-719/18, aaO (Fn. 342), Rn. 58, 59.

Art. 10 EMRK. Die enorme Bedeutung des Pluralismus für das demokratische System hatte der EuGH aber bereits in seinem Urteil in der Rechtssache *Sky Österreich* statuiert, in der es um die Übertragung von Großereignissen ging, insbesondere um die Vereinbarkeit von Art. 15 AVMD-Richtlinie mit höherrangigem Recht. Art. 15 AVMD-Richtlinie bzw. dessen nationale Umsetzung, die Fernsehveranstaltern Zugang zu Ereignissen von großem öffentlichen Interesse einräumt, an denen Dritte Exklusivrechte besitzen, wurde damals von einem privaten Fernsehveranstalter als Exklusivrechteinhaber gegenüber einem öffentlich-rechtlichen Rundfunkveranstalter als Profiteur der Regelung angegriffen. Der EuGH entschied, dass die Verfolgung des aus Art. 11 Abs. 2 ableitbaren Ziels der Pluralismussicherung auch eine Beeinträchtigung anderer Grundrechte rechtfertigen könne wie in diesem Fall das Recht auf unternehmerische Freiheit nach Art. 16 GRC. Interessanter noch, schrieb der EuGH allerdings Art. 15 AVMD-Richtlinie selbst die Zielsetzung zu, der zunehmend exklusiven Vermarktung von Ereignissen von großem öffentlichen Interesse entgegenzuwirken und damit das Grundrecht auf Information der Gesellschaft (Art. 11 Abs. 1 GRC) zu wahren und den durch Art. 11 Abs. 2 der Charta geschützten Pluralismus durch die Vielfalt der Nachrichten und Programme zu fördern. Deshalb, so der EuGH im Ergebnis, stand es dem Unionsgesetzgeber vor dem Hintergrund von Art. 11 Abs. 2 GRC frei, „Bestimmungen wie die in Art. 15 der Richtlinie 2010/13 zu erlassen, die Beschränkungen der unternehmerischen Freiheit vorsehen und zugleich im Hinblick auf die erforderliche Gewichtung der betroffenen Rechte und Interessen den Zugang der Öffentlichkeit zu Informationen gegenüber der Vertragsfreiheit privilegieren"[340].

Daraus lässt sich ableiten, dass sich nicht nur die Mitgliedstaaten, sondern auch der Unionsgesetzgeber zwar nicht im Sinne eines Kompetenztitels auf Art. 11 Abs. 2 GRC berufen können, wohl aber im Hinblick auf die Verfolgung von Zielen von öffentlichem Interesse als Rechtfertigungsgrundlage für Beeinträchtigungen von anderen Grundfreiheiten und Grundrechten. Das bedeutet allerdings auch, dass Art. 11 Abs. 2 GRC aufgrund der Kompetenzverteilung im Zusammenspiel mit Art. 51 Abs. 1

---

340 EuGH, Rs. C-283/11, *Sky Österreich GmbH / Österreichischer Rundfunk*, Rn. 66. Den weiten Ermessensspielraum des nationalen Gesetzgebers bei der Einführung von Maßnahmen zur Pluralismussicherung auch im regionalen und lokalen Medienbereich betont GA Szpunar in seinen Schlussanträgen vom 15.10.2020 in der Rs. C-555/19, *Fussl Modestraße Mayr*, Rn. 63. Der EuGH hat in seinem Urteil vom 03.02.2021 einen engeren Ansatz verfolgt, vgl. dazu *Ukrow*, Sicherung regionaler Vielfalt – Außer Mode?

C. Zur Bedeutung und rechtlichen Verankerung der Medienvielfalt auf EU-Ebene

GRC ein Unionshandeln verbietet, das dem Ziel der Medienvielfaltssicherung in den Mitgliedstaaten zuwiderläuft.[341]

Aus der Verankerung des Medienpluralismus auf Grundrechtsebene innerhalb der EU lässt sich allerdings noch ein weiterer Aspekt schlussfolgern: Zumindest vergleichbar mit dem im vorangegangenen Abschnitt dargestellten „Wechselspiel" zwischen der Tätigkeit des Europarates, der Rechtsprechung des EGMR und der Grundlage des Art. 10 EMRK, gibt die Existenz von Art. 11 auf EU-Ebene der Kommission ebenso mehr Freiheit dazu, Vorschriften zum Medienpluralismus in ihren Empfehlungen und Leitlinien aufzunehmen, wenngleich diese dann regelmäßig die Einzelheiten der Sicherstellung von Freiheit und Pluralismus in den Medien den Mitgliedstaaten überlassen.[342] Diskutiert wird, ob daraus auch folgt, dass die EU-Institutionen grundsätzlich die Befugnis haben, wenn sie es für nötig halten, Regeln zu formulieren, die den Mitgliedstaaten aufgeben, angemessene Maßnahmen zur Sicherung der Medienvielfalt zu ergreifen.[343] So begreift die Kommission auch nicht nur die Gesetzgebung der Union im medienrechtlich relevanten Bereich als „Anwendung der GRC" und damit grundrechtsrelevant, sondern auch Empfehlungen im medienrelevanten Bereich (wie beispielsweise die Empfehlung für wirksame Maßnahmen im Umgang mit illegalen Online-Inhalten[344]), Mitteilungen (wie beispielsweise die Mitteilung „Bekämpfung von Desinformation im Internet: ein europäisches Konzept"[345]), Aktionspläne und begleitende Initiativen, Förderinitiativen (wie zum Beispiel das MEDIA-Programm) sowie die Finanzierung von (auch an pluralistischen Zielen ausgerichteten) Projekten wie dem Europäischen Zentrums für Presse- und Medienfreiheit (ECPMF)[346] und den Media Pluralism Monitor des Zentrums für Medienpluralismus und

---

341 *Cole*, Zum Gestaltungsspielraum der EU-Mitgliedstaaten bei Einschränkungen der Dienstleistungsfreiheit, S. 20.
342 *Costache*, De-Regulation of European Media Policy (2000–2014), S. 26.
343 So etwa *EU Network of independent experts on fundamental rights*, Report on the situation of fundamental rights in the European Union in 2003, S. 73.
344 Empfehlung (EU) 2018/334 der Kommission vom 1. März 2018 für wirksame Maßnahmen im Umgang mit illegalen Online-Inhalten, C/2018/1177, EU ABl. L 63 vom 6.3.2018, S. 50–61.
345 Mitteilung der Kommission an das Europäische Parlament, den Rat, den Europäischen Wirtschafts- und Sozialausschuss und den Ausschuss der Regionen Bekämpfung von Desinformation im Internet: ein europäisches Konzept (COM/2018/236 final vom 26.4.2018).
346 Für weitere Informationen vgl. https://www.ecpmf.eu/about/.

Medienfreiheit[347].[348] Aus dieser Erwägung ließe sich aber jedenfalls nicht ableiten, dass die EU-Institutionen den Mitgliedstaaten auch aufgeben könnten, welche Maßnahmen konkret zur Sicherung der medialen Vielfalt zu ergreifen sind.

IV. Primärrechtliche Aspekte

Neben den Anknüpfungspunkten im kompetenzrechtlichen Rahmen, insbesondere innerhalb der kulturellen Querschnittsklausel des Art. 167 AEUV, sowie in der Werteordnung der EU, die bereits im Rahmen von Kapitel B eingehend dargestellt wurden, gibt es medienrelevante Bezugspunkte auch innerhalb des materiell geprägten Primärrechts der EU. Das gilt namentlich für die Grundfreiheiten als primärrechtlich verankerte individuelle Rechte sowie für die medial vielfaltssicherungsrelevanten Bezüge der Wettbewerbsordnung. Wenngleich beide Bereiche maßgeblich auf den Schutz und die Gewährleistung eines freien und fairen Binnenmarkts in der EU ausgerichtet sind, was die Medien als Teilnehmer am Wirtschaftsverkehr betrifft, finden sich dort auch Ausnahmen und Grenzen in Bezug auf die Berücksichtigung auch kultureller Aspekte. Diese sollen, soweit es für die vorliegende Studie relevant ist, nachfolgend dargestellt werden.

1. Grundfreiheiten

Im medialen Bereich sind vor allem die Dienstleistungsfreiheit und die Niederlassungsfreiheit relevant, auf die sich Medienunternehmen innerhalb der EU berufen können.[349] Während die Niederlassungsfreiheit nach Art. 49 ff. AEUV das Recht bezeichnet, in einem anderen Mitgliedstaat gemäß den dortigen Bestimmungen eine selbständige Tätigkeit aufzunehmen und auszuüben oder Unternehmen zu gründen und zu leiten, geht es bei der Dienstleistungsfreiheit um das Angebot von regelmäßig von Selb-

---

347 Vgl. für weitere Informationen https://cmpf.eui.eu/media-pluralism-monitor/.
348 Europäische Kommission, Bericht über die Anwendung der Charta der Grundrechte der Europäischen Union 2018, aaO (Fn. 328).
349 Vgl. zu diesem Abschnitt eingehend und unter besonderer Berücksichtigung und Analyse der einschlägigen Rechtsprechung des EuGH: *Cole*, Zum Gestaltungsspielraum der EU-Mitgliedstaaten bei Einschränkungen der Dienstleistungsfreiheit.

C. Zur Bedeutung und rechtlichen Verankerung der Medienvielfalt auf EU-Ebene

ständigen im Wirtschaftsverkehr erbrachten Leistungen, wie sie beispielhaft in Art. 57 AEUV aufgezählt werden.[350] Beide Grundfreiheiten fordern eine Wirtschaftstätigkeit mit grenzüberschreitendem Bezug, wobei diese Merkmale weit auszulegen sind.[351] Die Warenverkehrsfreiheit (Art. 34–36 AEUV) schützt demgegenüber das Recht, Waren zu erwerben, anzubieten, auszustellen oder feilzuhalten, zu besitzen, herzustellen, zu befördern, zu verkaufen, entgeltlich oder unentgeltlich abzugeben, einzuführen oder zu verwenden.[352] Für den medialen Bereich hat die Warenverkehrsfreiheit in Abgrenzung zur Dienstleistungsfreiheit insbesondere dann Bedeutung, wenn es um die Verbreitung und den Vertrieb von körperlichen Produkten, insbesondere etwa Import- und Exportbeschränkungen von Presse-[353] oder Filmerzeugnissen[354], oder insgesamt (dann ggf. reflexhaft) den Bereich der Werbung innerhalb von Medien geht.[355] Die Abgrenzung zur Dienstleistungsfreiheit, die der EuGH nach dem Schwerpunkt des Gesamtvorgangs vornimmt, hat dabei vor allem bei der Rechtfertigung im Rahmen der Abgrenzung zwischen produkt- und vertriebsbezogenen Anforderungen der EuGH-Rechtsprechung Bedeutung[356], worauf im Rahmen der vorliegenden Studie nicht näher eingegangen werden muss.

Die in Art. 56 ff. AEUV verankerte Dienstleistungsfreiheit bezieht sich nach Art. 57 AEUV auf Leistungen, die in der Regel gegen Entgelt erbracht werden, soweit sie nicht den übrigen vorrangigen Grundfreiheiten unterfallen. Medien sind zwar (auch) Kulturgut, wie der EuGH anerkannt hat, aufgrund ihrer (auch) wirtschaftlichen Bezüge ordnet der Gerichtshof diese allerdings als Dienstleistung – sowohl gegenüber Rezipienten als auch potentiell gegenüber den in den Medien Werbetreibenden – im Sinne des

---

350 *Randelzhofer/Forsthoff* in: Grabitz/Hilf/Nettesheim, Art. 49, 50 AEUV, Rn. 80; *Tomkin* in: Kellerbauer/Klamert/ders., Art. 49 AEUV, Rn. 19.
351 Rs. C-36/74, *B.N.O. Walrave, L.J.N. Koch / Association Union cycliste internationale u.a.*, Rn. 4; C-196/87, *Udo Steymann / Staatssecretaris van Justitie*, Rn. 9.
352 EuGH, Rs. C-293/94, *Brandsma*, Rn. 6.
353 Hierzu *Müssle/Schmittmann* in: AfP 2002, 145, 145 ff.
354 Vgl. EuGH, Rs. 60/84 und 61/84, *Cinéthèque SA u.a. / Fédération nationale des cinémas français*.
355 Zur Bedeutung der Warenverkehrsfreiheit für die Medien vgl. etwa *Cole* in: Fink/Cole/Keber, Europäisches Medienrecht, Kapitel 2 Rn. 32 ff.
356 Das ist vor allem im Bereich der Werbung von Relevanz. Zum Bereich der Werbung außerhalb medial relevanter Aspekte vgl. etwa *Kingreen* in: Calliess/Ruffert, Art. 34–36 Rn. 179 ff. Bezüglich des Vertriebs von Waren vgl. auch EuGH, Rs. C-244/06, *Dynamic Medien Vertriebs GmbH / Avides Media AG*.

AEUV ein.³⁵⁷ Aber auch die Verbreiter, Mittler und Intermediäre, die im Geflecht der Verbreitung und Vermarktung von Inhalten eine Rolle spielen, ob im digitalen oder analogen Bereich, können sich auf diese Grundfreiheit berufen.³⁵⁸ Daher soll die Dienstleistungsfreiheit vorliegend im Fokus der Betrachtung stehen – die Ausführungen gelten aber aufgrund der einheitlichen Schrankendogmatik des EuGH auch in Bezug auf die Niederlassungsfreiheit³⁵⁹ und die Warenverkehrsfreiheit.

Die Dienstleistungsfreiheit umfasst zunächst ein absolutes Diskriminierungsverbot, also das Verbot, in- und ausländische Anbieter nicht unterschiedlich zu behandeln, sowie ein relatives Beschränkungsverbot³⁶⁰, d.h. das grundsätzliche Verbot von Maßnahmen, die die Ausübung dieser Freiheit unterbinden, behindern oder weniger attraktiv machen. Die Dienstleistungsfreiheit ist daher eng mit einer der bedeutendsten Zielsetzungen der Union verbunden (Art. 3 Abs. 2 und 3 EUV), einen wettbewerbsfähigen Binnenmarkt frei von Grenzen zu errichten, und findet ihre Ausprägung auch innerhalb des Herkunftslandprinzips, das in vielen (auch im medialen Bereich relevanten) Sekundärrechtsakten wie zum Beispiel der AVMD-Richtlinie und der ECRL (dazu eingehend Kapitel D.) verankert ist. Das Herkunftslandprinzip besagt, dass ein Mitgliedstaat seinen Regelungsrahmen nur auf unter seiner Rechtshoheit stehende Anbieter anwendet und ansonsten den freien Dienstleistungsverkehr gewährleistet für Anbieter, die der Rechtshoheit eines anderen EU-Mitgliedstaates unterfallen.³⁶¹ Das bedeutet allerdings nicht, dass die Dienstleistungsfreiheit über ihre Bindungswirkung die EU oder die Mitgliedstaaten bei ihrer Rechtssetzung zwingend zur Verankerung des Herkunftslandprinzips verpflichtet,

---

357 Grundlegend: Rs. C-155/73, *Giuseppe Sacchi*. Vgl. zur Dienstleistungsfreiheit vor dem Hintergrund der Bezüge zum Medienrecht auf EU-Ebene zudem *Böttcher/Castendyk* in: Castendyk/Dommering/Scheuer (Hrsg.) S. 85 ff.
358 Für Kabelnetze vgl. bspw. EuGH, Rs. C-352/82, *Bond van Adverteerders u.a. / Niederländischer Staat*, Rn. 14; zu Google etwa EuGH, Rs. C-482/18, *Google Ireland Limited gegen Nemzeti Adó- és Vámhivatal Kiemelt Adó- és Vámigazgatósága*.
359 Die im Bereich der Rechtfertigung von Beeinträchtigungen dargestellten Erwägungen zur Dienstleistungsfreiheit gelten auch für den Bereich der Niederlassungsfreiheit. Insbesondere wären auch hier Aspekte der Medienvielfaltssicherung in gleicher Herangehensweise zu berücksichtigen. Vgl. dazu *Cole* in: Fink/Cole/Keber, Kapitel 2, Rn. 29 f.; ausführlicher *Dörr*, Das Zulassungsregime im Hörfunk: Spannungsverhältnis zwischen europarechtlicher Niederlassungsfreiheit und nationaler Pluralismussicherung, 71, 71 ff.
360 Gefestigte Rechtsprechung seit EuGH, Rs. C-33/74, *Johannes Henricus Maria van Binsbergen / Bestuur van de Bedrijfsvereniging voor de Metaalnijverheid*.
361 Eingehend zum Herkunftslandprinzip: *Cole*, The Country of Origin Principle, 113, 113 ff.

C. Zur Bedeutung und rechtlichen Verankerung der Medienvielfalt auf EU-Ebene

also ihnen den Rückgriff auf das Marktortprinzip oder eine Verknüpfung von Aspekten des Herkunftsland- und Marktortprinzips verwehrt.[362] Die Dienstleistungsfreiheit fordert vielmehr nur, Schranken für den Marktzutritt abzubauen – unabhängig von konkreten Vorgaben dazu, wie diese Äquivalenz für Dienstleister durch die EU oder ihre Mitgliedstaaten herzustellen ist.[363]

Beschränkungen des Dienstleistungsverkehrs – im Sinne eines weit verstandenen Begriffsverständnisses, das der EuGH anlegt[364] – durch die EU oder die Mitgliedstaaten können jedoch gerechtfertigt werden. Neben den im AEUV ausdrücklich vorgesehenen Schranken ist dies vor allem dann der Fall, wenn mit der jeweiligen Maßnahme ein legitimes Ziele als Allgemeinwohlinteresse verfolgt wird und die Maßnahmen im Übrigen auch dem Verhältnismäßigkeitsprinzip entsprechen, also erforderlich und angemessen sind, insbesondere nicht über das zur Erreichung dieses Ziels erforderliche Maß hinausgehen.[365] Eben hier setzt der Spielraum der Mitgliedstaaten an, im Rahmen ihrer Kulturpolitik tätig zu werden.

Schon vor Inkrafttreten der GRC, die die Bedeutung des Pluralismus in Art. 11 Abs. 2 ausdrücklich verankerte, hat der EuGH die Medienvielfalt unter Heranziehung von Art. 10 EMRK als wesentliches Merkmal der Meinungsfreiheit anerkannt und dabei nicht nur grundlegend festgestellt, dass die Aufrechterhaltung eines pluralistischen Rundfunkwesens in einem Zusammenhang mit der durch Artikel 10 EMRK garantierten Meinungsfreiheit steht, sondern auch, dass eine Kulturpolitik, die dieses Ziel verfolgt, einen zwingenden Grund des Allgemeininteresses darstellen kann, der Beschränkungen des Dienstleistungsverkehrs rechtfertigt.[366] In diesem Zusammenhang erkennt der EuGH auch die mitgliedstaatliche Zielsetzung an, die Bedürfnisse verschiedener gesellschaftlicher, kultureller, religiöser

---

362 Eingehend und weiterführend zu dieser Frage: *Waldheim*, Dienstleistungsfreiheit und Herkunftslandprinzip; *Albath/Giesel* in: EuZW 2006, 38, 39 ff.; *Hörnle* in: International and Comparative Law Quarterly 1–2005, 89, 89 ff.
363 Vgl. hierzu z.B. EuGH, Rs. C-55/94, *Reinhard Gebhard / Consiglio dell'Ordine degli Avvocati e Procuratori di Milano*.
364 EuGH, Rs. C-76/90, *Manfred Säger / Dennemeyer & Co. Ltd.*, Rn. 12.
365 EuGH, Rs. C-19/92, *Dieter Kraus / Land Baden-Württemberg*, Rn. 32; Rs. C-272/94, *Strafverfahren gegen Michel Guiot und Climatec SA*, Rn. 11.
366 Rs. 353/89, *Kommission / Niederlande*, Rn. 30; C—288/89, *Stichting Collectieve Antennevoorziening Gouda u. a. / Commissariaat voor de Media*, Rn. 23.

und geistiger Bedürfnisse schützen zu wollen[367], was auch unterschiedliche Regelungsansätze der Mitgliedstaaten ermöglicht[368].

Hervorzuheben ist in diesem Kontext vor allem die Entscheidung des Gerichtshofs in der Rechtssache *Dynamic Medien*, in der es um die Frage ging, ob und inwieweit nationale Vorschriften, die den Vertrieb von Bildträgern (DVDs, Videos) im Versandhandel davon abhängig machen, dass sie Kennzeichnungen über die Prüfung der Jugendfreiheit durch nationale Einrichtungen tragen, mit den Grundfreiheiten (hier: der Warenverkehrsfreiheit) vereinbar sind. In dem zu Grunde liegenden Rechtsstreit verlangte die *Dynamic Medien Vertriebs GmbH* die Unterlassung des Verkaufs aus Großbritannien eingeführter, japanischer Zeichentrickfilme, die – obwohl sie in Großbritannien bereits auf ihre Jugendfreigabe getestet und mit einer entsprechenden Kennzeichnung (15+) versehen worden waren – nicht das nach deutschem Recht vorgesehene Prüfverfahren nach dem Jugendmedienschutzrecht unter Beteiligung der Freiwilligen Selbstkontrolle der Filmwirtschaft (FSK) durchlaufen hatten.[369] Im Kern der Entscheidung ging es also um nationale Regelung zum Schutz von Kindern vor entwicklungsbeeinträchtigenden Medien – wie die Vielfaltssicherung also eine Materie mit kulturpolitischem Schwerpunkt. Der EuGH stellte hier fest, dass den Mitgliedstaaten ein weites Ermessen zuzuerkennen ist, da die Auffassungen im Hinblick auf das zum Schutz von Minderjährigen zu gewährleistende Schutzniveau (auch wenn innerhalb der Mitgliedstaaten Einigkeit darüber besteht, dass ein gewisses angemessenes Schutzniveau zu gewährleisten ist) je nach Erwägungen insbesondere moralischer oder kultureller Art von Mitgliedstaat zu Mitgliedstaat verschieden sein können. In Ermangelung einer Harmonisierung auch des Jugendmedienschutzes auf Unionsebene, sei es Sache der Mitgliedstaaten, nach ihrem Ermessen darüber zu befinden, auf welchem Niveau sie den Schutz des in Frage stehenden Interesses gewährleisten wollen, wenngleich sie dies unter Wahrung der Grundsätze des Gemeinschaftsrechts tun müssen. Diese Erwägungen

---

367 Rs. C—288/89, *Stichting Collectieve Antennevoorziening Gouda u. a. / Commissariaat voor de Media*, Rn. 31.

368 Hierzu EuGH, Rs. C-244/06, *Dynamic Medien Vertriebs GmbH / Avides Media AG*, Rn. 49. So bereits Rs. C-124/97, *Markku Juhani Läärä u.a. / Finnland*, Rn. 36; Rs. C-36/02, *Omega Spielhallen- und Automatenaufstellungs GmbH / Oberbürgermeisterin der Bundesstadt Bonn*, Rn. 38. Zuletzt hat GA Szpunar in seinen Schlussanträgen vom 15. Oktober 2020 in der Rs. C-555/19, *Fussl Modestraße Mayr*, betont, dass die Unterschiedlichkeit nationaler Regelungsansätze nicht zu einer Unvereinbarkeit der strengeren Regelung mit Unionsrecht führe, Rn. 70.

369 Rs.C-244/06, aaO (Fn. 372), Rn. 44, 45, 49.

C. Zur Bedeutung und rechtlichen Verankerung der Medienvielfalt auf EU-Ebene

lassen sich nicht nur auf den Bereich von Vielfaltssicherungsmaßnahmen übertragen, sondern zeigen, dass der EuGH kulturpolitische Schwerpunktsetzungen auf nationaler Ebene achtet und als Rechtfertigung für unterschiedliche Regelungen ansieht und gerade nicht versucht, über die Binnenmarktbezüge einheitliche Bewertungsmaßstäbe vor mitgliedstaatliche Ermessenserwägungen zu stellen.

Diese Rechtsprechung hat der Gerichtshof bereits vorher in zahlreichen Entscheidungen entwickelt.[370] Bei der Verfolgung von Allgemeinwohlzielen – zu denen auch der Schutz der sprachlichen Vielfalt sowie des Zugangs zu lokalen Informationen gehören[371] – kommt den Mitgliedstaaten ein Gestaltungsspielraum zu, der sich dann umso größer darstellt, wenn es bei der beschränkenden Maßnahme oder Regelung nicht um handels(dienstleistungs-)bezogene Regulierungstendenzen geht, sondern kulturpolitische Ziele im Vordergrund stehen. In diesen Fällen ist auch die Überprüfungsbefugnis des EuGH, die der Gerichtshof unstreitig insbesondere in Bezug auf die Wahrung des Verhältnismäßigkeitsgrundsatzes besitzt, zurückgenommen[372], wobei vornehmlich geprüft wird, ob die Beschränkung nicht die praktische Wirksamkeit der Grundfreiheit vollständig und dauerhaft ausschließt[373] und tatsächlich dem Anliegen gerecht wird, die Zielsetzung in kohärenter und systematischer Weise zu erreichen[374]. In diesem Zusammenhang spielen Marktauswirkungen der beschränkenden Maßnahme eine Rolle, deren Untersuchung und Beurteilung der EuGH allerdings bei den nationalen Gerichten verortet.[375] Das gilt im Übrigen auch und gerade für Beschränkungen der Warenverkehrsfreiheit: In der Rs. *Familiapress*, in der es um das Verbot ging, Zeitschriften

---

370 EuGH, Rs. C-148/91, *Vereniging Veronica Omroep Organisatie / Commissariaat voor de Media*, Rn. 9; Rs. C-23/93, *TV10 SA / Commissariaat voor de Media*. Rn. 18; Rs. C-368/95, *Vereinigte Familiapress Zeitungsverlags- und vertriebs GmbH gegen Heinrich Bauer Verlag*, Rn. 19.
371 EuGH, Rs. C-250/06, *United Pan-Europe Communications Belgium SA u.a. / État belge*, Rn. 43.
372 Im Detail und zur Reichweite des mitgliedstaatlichen Gestaltungsspielraum s. Cole, Zum Gestaltungsspielraum der EU-Mitgliedstaaten bei Einschränkungen der Dienstleistungsfreiheit, S. 26 ff.
373 EuGH, Rs. C-250/06, *United Pan-Europe Communications Belgium SA u.a. / État belge*, Rn. 45.
374 EuGH, Rs. C-137/09, *Marc Michel Josemans / Burgemeester van Maastricht*, Rn. 70 m.w.N.; ebenso z.B. jüngst in Rs. C-235/17, *Europäische Kommission / Ungarn*, Rn. 61.
375 EuGH, Rs. C-368/95, *Vereinigte Familiapress Zeitungsverlags- und vertriebs GmbH gegen Heinrich Bauer Verlag*, Rn. 29.

zu verkaufen, die die Teilnahme an Preisausschreiben ermöglichen, hat der EuGH grundlegend festgestellt, dass die Aufrechterhaltung der Medienvielfalt ein zwingendes Erfordernis darstellen kann, das auch eine Beschränkung des freien Warenverkehrs rechtfertigt. Diese Vielfalt trage nämlich zur Wahrung des Rechts der freien Meinungsäußerung bei, das durch Artikel 10 EMRK und Grundfreiheiten geschützt ist und zu den von der Gemeinschaftsrechtsordnung geschützten Grundrechten gehöre.[376] Dabei obliegt es den Mitgliedstaaten, die dabei einen weiten Ermessensspielraum haben, wie sie die Erreichung dieses Vielfaltsziels anstreben. Entsprechende Beschränkungen der Dienstleistungsfreiheit können weitreichend sein, wie GA Szpunar jüngst in seinen Schlussanträgen in der Rs. *Fussl Modestraße Mayr* festgehalten hat.[377]

Auch auf grundfreiheitlicher Ebene wird also der Regelungskompetenz der Mitgliedstaaten im Bereich der Pluralismussicherung Rechnung getragen.

2. EU-Wettbewerbsordnung

Die vorrangige Zielsetzung der europäischen Wettbewerbsordnung liegt darin, das ordnungsgemäße Funktionieren des Binnenmarktes als entscheidenden Faktor des Wohlergehens der europäischen Wirtschaft und Gesellschaft zu ermöglichen. Die Wettbewerbsordnung ist daher zunächst rein wirtschaftsbezogen und sektorneutral, was auch kompetenzrechtlich begründet ist (dazu bereits Abschnitt B.III.2.). Sie betrifft daher auch die Medien in ihrer Eigenschaft als Teilnehmer am Wirtschaftsverkehr, in deren Rahmen sie auf vielen unterschiedlichen Ebenen in Wettbewerb zu anderen Unternehmen treten – ob um die Aufmerksamkeit und Kaufkraft von Rezipienten oder potentieller Werbe- oder Geschäftskunden. Vor dem Hintergrund der Vielfaltssicherung ist es aber umso bedeutender, dass auf dem „Medienmarkt" faire Bedingungen herrschen, Marktmacht nicht zu Meinungsmacht wird und kleineren Unternehmen (d.h. etwa lokalen, re-

---

376 Wie vor, Rn. 18. Vgl. auch Rs. C-244/06, aaO (Fn. 372).
377 Schlussanträge vom 15. Oktober 2020, Rs. C-555/19, *Fussl Modestraße Mayr*. Vgl. insbesondere Rn. 53, 69 f., 63, 67, auch die grundrechtliche Abwägung findet in einem weiten Ermessensspielraum statt, Rn. 83. Die Überprüfung durch das nationale Gericht, ob es ggf. weniger restriktive Maßnahmen geben könne, müsse sich beschränken auf Maßnahmen, „die vom nationalen Gesetzgeber tatsächlich ergriffen werden" könnten, rein theoretische Maßnahmen sind außer Acht zu lassen, Rn. 74. Das Urteil durch den EuGH in der Rs. steht noch aus.

C. Zur Bedeutung und rechtlichen Verankerung der Medienvielfalt auf EU-Ebene

gionalen, branchenspezifischen oder anderen Informationen, an deren Empfang nicht die Gesamtheit der Gesellschaft im Binnenmarkt ein Interesse hat) der Marktzutritt ermöglicht wird. Obwohl die Wettbewerbsordnung wenig Spielraum für die Berücksichtigung nichtwirtschaftsbezogener Aspekte lässt, ist daher dennoch allgemein anerkannt, dass sie indirekt auch zur medialen Vielfaltssicherung beiträgt, da sie die Märkte offen und kompetitiv hält, indem sie Konzentrationsentwicklungen entgegenwirkt, staatliche Einflussnahme begrenzt und Marktmissbrauch verhindert.[378]

a. Marktmachtkontrolle und Missbrauchsaufsicht

Mit den Instrumenten der Marktmachtkontrolle (Kartellverbot des Art. 101 AEUV, Verbot des Missbrauchs einer marktbeherrschenden Stellung des Art. 102 AEUV und Fusionskontrolle nach der Fusionskontroll-Verordnung[379]), kann die Europäische Kommission in bestimmtem Umfang (einen begrenzenden) Einfluss auf die Marktmacht von Unternehmen nehmen, wenn diese auf einem bestimmten Markt eine beherrschende Stellung einnehmen oder einnehmen würden. Im Bereich der Medien bedeutet eine Einflussnahme auf den Markt allerdings auch regelmäßig eine potentielle Einflussnahmemöglichkeit auf die Meinungsmacht von Unternehmen, die an die Marktmacht gekoppelt ist.

Ohne in diesem Rahmen im Detail auf die Einzelheiten im Bereich der Markt- und Missbrauchsaufsicht eingehen zu wollen, sei daher an dieser Stelle lediglich erwähnt, dass bereits eine Reihe von kartellrechtlichen Entscheidungen in Bezug auf Unternehmen aus dem Mediensektor und dessen Umfeld ergangen sind.[380] Dabei ist die Definition und Abgrenzung des relevanten Marktes gerade im Mediensektor essentiell und von mehreren Besonderheiten gekennzeichnet.

Zum einen bewegen sich die Medien in einem zweiseitigen Markt bestehend aus dem Rezipientenmarkt und dem Werbemarkt, in denen sie jeweils um Aufmerksamkeit und Werbeinnahmen miteinander konkurrieren. Beide Märkte sind auch vor dem Hintergrund der Sicherung von Meinungsvielfalt bedeutsam, da Vielfalt nur dort vorhanden ist, wo Inhalte ein

---

378 Vgl. dazu *Valcke*, Challenges of Regulating Media Pluralism in the EU, S. 27, m.w.N.
379 Dazu unter D.II.4.
380 Vgl. hierzu eingehend *Cole/Hans* in: Cappello (Hrsg.), Medieneigentum – Marktrealitäten und Regulierungsmaßnahmen, S. 20 ff.; *Bania*, The Role of Media Pluralism in the Enforcement of EU Competition Law.

Publikum auch erreichen und die (Re-)Finanzierbarkeit von Inhalten unmittelbar auch die Existenz von Medienanbietern bedingt.

Zum anderen ist der Mediensektor geprägt von der (zunehmenden) Konvergenz der Medien, die zu einem Verschwimmen der Grenzen zwischen verschiedenen Übertragungsformen, Angebotsformen und Anbietern führt und zu einem erheblichen Einfluss von Gatekeepern wie Suchmaschinen und anderen Plattformen geführt hat. Die Kommission trifft allerdings in ihrer Entscheidungspraxis maßgeblich eine Unterscheidung zwischen den Märkten für Free-TV, Pay-TV, sonstigen Märkten sowie den Kauf von Übertragungsrechten und trennt zwischen dem Online- und Offline-Marktes.[381] Bereits an dieser Beurteilung des Marktes zeigt sich die wirtschaftlich orientierte Betrachtungsweise der Kommission, in die lediglich wirtschaftliche Beurteilungskriterien einfließen, nicht aber kulturpolitische Aspekte.

Marktgeprägt ist entsprechend auch die Beurteilung der Missbräuchlichkeit eines Verhaltens, die in allen Verhaltensweisen eines Unternehmens gesehen wird, die die Struktur eines Marktes beeinflussen können, auf dem der Wettbewerb gerade wegen der Anwesenheit eines Unternehmens bereits geschwächt ist und die die Aufrechterhaltung oder Entwicklung des bestehenden Wettbewerbs durch Maßnahmen behindern, die von den Mitteln eines normalen Produkt- und Dienstleistungswettbewerbs auf der Grundlage der Leistungen abweichen.[382] Illustrieren lässt sich das etwa anhand der Untersuchungen und Entscheidungen der Kommission zur Google-Suche, in denen bislang die Bedeutung der Suchmaschine auch für die Auffindbarkeit von medialen Inhalten (und damit der Empfängerhorizont) keine Rolle gespielt hat, sondern lediglich wirtschaftliche Aspekte der Schaltung von Werbeanzeigen oder der Bevorzugung unternehmenseigener Dienste.[383] Es geht um Produkte und Dienstleistungen, die nach ob-

---

381 Vgl. etwa die jüngeren Entscheidungen zu *Walt Disney / Century Fox* (M.8785) vom 6.11.2018, in deren Rahmen die Kommission an der Trennung zwischen digitalen Vertriebsformen von Filmen und der physischen Distribution festhält, vgl. Rn. 50, https://ec.europa.eu/competition/mergers/cases/decisions/m8785_21 97_3.pdf; sowie im Fall Sky / Fox (M.8354) vom 7.4.2017 an der Unterscheidung von Produktion von Fernsehinhalten im Auftrag und der Lizenzierung von Übertragungsrechten für vorproduzierte Fernsehinhalte, vgl. Rn. 62, https://ec.europa.eu/competition/mergers/cases/decisions/m8354_920_8.pdf.
382 EuGH, Rs. 85/76, *Hoffmann-La Roche / Kommission*; Kommission, Entscheidung vom 14. Dezember 1985 betreffend ein Verfahren nach Artikel 86 des EWG-Vertrags (IV/30 698 – *ECS/AKZO*), EU ABl. L 374 vom 31.12.1985.
383 Vgl. hierzu etwa die Fälle Nr. 39740 (Google Search (Shopping)) und Nr. 40411 (Google Search (AdSense)).

C. Zur Bedeutung und rechtlichen Verankerung der Medienvielfalt auf EU-Ebene

jektiven und wirtschaftlichen Kriterien beurteilt werden und daher keinen Raum für die Berücksichtigung der Qualität von bestimmten Produkten oder Dienstleistungen gegenüber anderen ähnlichen Produkten und Dienstleistungen (sprich: Inhalten) lassen, was im Bereich der Vielfaltssicherung relevant wäre.

Vielfaltssicherung kann daher im Bereich kartellrechtlicher Maßnahmen auf Unionsebene, die auf die Herstellung fairer Verhältnisse im Hinblick auf ökonomische Gesichtspunkte zielen, insbesondere nicht das Vorhandensein eines vielfältigen Angebots anstreben, nur reflexhaft betroffen sein. Insbesondere ist eine steuernde Einflussnahme auf Basis von möglicherweise im Bereich der Meinungs- und Informationsvielfalt festgestellten Ungleichgewichten durch die Kommission auch nicht angestrebt.[384] Daher ist die Markt- und Missbrauchskontrolle auf EU-Ebene zwar einerseits kein geeignetes Instrument zur Pluralismussicherung, steht dabei aber andererseits aber auch nicht entsprechenden mitgliedstaatlichen Bestrebungen entgegen.

b. Beihilferecht

Staatliche Beihilfen sind in der EU gemäß Artikel 107 Abs. 1 AEUV grundsätzlich verboten, da sie bestimmte Unternehmen, Wirtschaftszweige oder Industrien gegenüber Mitbewerbern begünstigen und damit den freien Wettbewerb im europäischen Binnenmarkt verzerren (können), soweit sie aufgrund wettbewerbsverfälschender Wirkungen den Handel zwischen den Mitgliedstaaten beeinträchtigen. Die wirtschaftliche Ausrichtung auch des Beihilferechts der EU ist aus diesem Wortlaut der Bestimmung bereits offensichtlich. Wenngleich diese nicht in die Zuständigkeit der EU fällt, haben allerdings Diskussionen sowohl auf nationaler als auch auf europäischer Ebene über das System der dualen Rundfunkordnung und die damit verbundene Gebührenfinanzierung des öffentlich-rechtlichen Rundfunks

---

384 Vgl. hierzu, aber auch zu möglicherweise nicht ausgeschöpften Potentialen zur Berücksichtigung auch pluralismusrelevanter Aspekte im Rahmen der EU-Wettbewerbsordnung *Bania*, The Role of Media Pluralism in the Enforcement of EU Competition Law.

zum Beispiel in Deutschland,[385] aber auch in anderen Ländern[386] die besondere Relevanz des Beihilferechts auch für die Medien- und Kulturpolitik der Mitgliedstaaten veranschaulicht.

Einerseits enthält das Beihilferecht ein grundsätzliches Verbot staatlicher Einflussnahme (wenngleich in wirtschaftlicher/finanzieller Hinsicht) auf die Medien, das geeignet ist, auch den Pluralismus zu stärken, indem nicht einzelne Unternehmen durch staatliche Förderung auf dem Markt (der Meinungen) eine gewichtigere Position erlangen könnten bzw. mindestens dem hierzu bestehenden unterschwelligen Risiko Rechnung tragen. Andererseits enthält aber das Beihilferecht auch Ausnahmen von diesem grundsätzlichen Verbot im kulturpolitischen Bereich, die bei der Ausgestaltung ihrer Medienordnung eine Orientierung der Mitgliedstaaten an nationalen Besonderheiten ermöglichen und damit gleichermaßen die Regelungshoheit der Mitgliedstaaten unterstreichen obwohl eine Überprüfung durch die Kommission beim Überschreiten bestimmter Grenzen durch die Notifizierungspflicht[387] sichergestellt ist. Auf letzterem Aspekt soll nachfolgend vor dem Hintergrund der der Schwerpunktsetzung vorliegender Studie der Fokus liegen.[388]

Staatliche Beihilfen, die ausgehend von einem weiten Begriffsverständnis im Mediensektor etwa die Gestalt von Subventionen oder Zuschüssen für Medienunternehmen, Steuererleichterungen für die Produktion von Inhalten oder Werbemaßnahmen, Vertriebsförderungen für die Presse, etc. annehmen können, können generell (Art. 107 Abs. 2 AEUV) oder nach

---

385 Vgl. hierzu etwa die Entscheidung der Europäischen Kommission vom 9. November 2005 über die Staatliche Beihilfe, die die Bundesrepublik Deutschland zugunsten der Einführung des digitalen terrestrischen Fernsehens (DVB-T) in Berlin-Brandenburg gewährt hat, ABl. der EU L 200/14.

386 Auch im Rechtssystem anderer europäischer Staaten wie Österreich, Finnland, Schweden, Tschechien, Estland, Zypern, Lettland, Litauen, Malta, Polen, Slowenien, Slowakei, Bulgarien und Rumänien finden sich staatliche Finanzierungsmaßnahmen in Bezug auf den Rundfunk, die von der Europäischen Kommission beobachtet werden.

387 Die Europäische Kommission ist über jede beabsichtigte Einführung oder Umgestaltung von Beihilfen zu unterrichten (Art. 108 Abs. 3 AEUV) und kann bei Bedenken über die Vereinbarkeit des Vorhabens mit dem Binnenmarkt ein Verfahren nach Art. 108 Abs. 2 AEUV einleiten. Das gilt allerdings nur bei tatbestandlichem Vorliegen einer Beihilfe, die sich insbesondere am Vorliegen von bestimmten Schwellenwerten vor dem Hintergrund der Möglichkeit der Beeinflussung des Handels innerhalb der EU orientiert.

388 Für eine Betrachtung im Detail in Bezug auf regionale und lokale Medien vgl. *Ukrow/Cole*, Aktive Sicherung lokaler und regionaler Medienvielfalt, S. 65 ff.; s.a. *Martini* in: EuZW 2015, 821, 821 ff.

C. Zur Bedeutung und rechtlichen Verankerung der Medienvielfalt auf EU-Ebene

einer Bewertung durch die Europäische Kommission[389] im Einzelfall (Art. 107 Abs. 3 AEUV) als mit dem Binnenmarkt vereinbar betrachtet und damit erlaubt sein. Auch Art. 106 Abs. 2 AEUV konzipiert nach Auffassung der Europäischen Kommission[390] eine Ausnahme vom Beihilfeverbot. Vor dem Hintergrund von Maßnahmen zur Vielfaltssicherung auf mitgliedstaatlicher Ebene sind dabei vor allem die Art. 106 Abs. 2, Art. 107 Abs. 3 Buchst. d) (ggf. auch Buchst. c)) AEUV relevant. Auf Art. 107 Abs. 2 Buchst. b), der Beihilfen zur Beseitigung von Naturkatastrophenschäden erlaubt, sei zudem vor dem Hintergrund der aktuellen Corona-Pandemie hingewiesen, die den Mediensektor schwer und wahrscheinlich nachhaltig getroffen hat und sich damit auch vielfaltsgefährdend auswirken kann.[391]

Für Unternehmen, die mit Dienstleistungen von allgemeinem wirtschaftlichem Interesse betraut sind, gibt Art. 106 Abs. 2 AEUV den Mitgliedstaaten eine Ausnahmemöglichkeit, die insbesondere auch die staatliche Finanzierung des öffentlich-rechtlichen Rundfunks ermöglicht. Danach sind staatliche Beihilfe für Unternehmen möglich, die mit Dienstleistungen von allgemeinem wirtschaftlichem Interesse betraut sind. Bereits in seinem Altmark-Urteil von 2003 hatte der EuGH hierzu konkrete Parameter aufgestellt, die im Rahmen der Finanzierung des öffentlich-rechtlichen Rundfunks vor dem Hintergrund seiner gesellschaftlichen Rolle und Auf-

---

[389] Nach wohl ganz überwiegender Auffassung kommt der EU-Kommission im Rahmen von Art. 107 Abs. 3 AEUV im Gegensatz zu Abs. 2 ein Ermessensspielraum hinsichtlich der Vereinbarkeit mit dem Binnenmarkt zu; Vgl. im Einzelnen *Cremer* in: Calliess/Ruffert, Art. 107 AEUV, Rn. 31, 38 ff.

[390] Art. 106 Abs. 2 AEUV ist nach Auffassung der Kommission als Ausnahmetatbestand konzipiert; vgl. Mitteilung über die Anwendung der Vorschriften über staatliche Beihilfen auf den öffentlich-rechtlichen Rundfunk, ABl. der EU C 257, C 257, 27.10.2009, S. 1–14, Rn. 37.

[391] Vgl. hierzu zu Medienförderungsmöglichkeiten vor dem Hintergrund der Pandemie *Ukrow*, Schutz der Medienvielfalt und medienbezogene Solidaritätspflichten in Corona-Zeiten.
Bereits zahlreiche Mitgliedstaaten haben vor dem pandemischen Hintergrund Unterstützungsmaßnahmen für den Mediensektor getroffen. Dänemarks „COVID-19-Entschädigungsplan", der für den Mediensektor (Print, elektronische Medien, Rundfunk, etc.) eine Beihilfe in Höhe von umgerechnet etwa 32 Mio. EUR vorsieht, hat das Notifizierungsverfahren bereits durchlaufen, in dem die Kommission eine Rettungsbeihilfe nach 107 Abs. 2 Buchst. b) AEUV angenommen hat. Während die Kommission dabei maßgeblich auf wirtschaftliche Faktoren abgestellt hat, hob die dänische Regierung im Verfahren insbesondere die Notwendigkeit der staatlichen Förderung vor dem Hintergrund der Bedeutung kultureller Vielfalt als wesentlicher Wert in einer demokratischen Gesellschaft hervor, die neben öffentlich finanzierten Medien auch die Existenz privater Medien als Ausgleich fordere.

gabe zu beachten sind.³⁹² Diese wurden über Jahre hinweg in der Fallpraxis der Kommission fortgeschrieben – auch in Verfahren gegenüber Deutschland³⁹³ – und sind mittlerweile in einer Mitteilung der Kommission konkretisiert.³⁹⁴

Auf Unionsebene wird davon ausgegangen, dass trotz der im Allgemeinwohlinteresse liegenden Funktion des öffentlich-rechtlichen Rundfunks, eine staatliche Finanzierung nicht schrankenlos möglich sein kann. Obwohl die Bedeutung des öffentlich-rechtlichen Rundfunks für die Förderung der kulturellen Vielfalt sowie die Möglichkeit der Mitgliedstaaten, vielfaltserhöhende Maßnahmen zu treffen, betont wird³⁹⁵, verlangt die Kommission in Bezug auf die Etablierung von Finanzierungssystemen vor allem eine unabhängige Kontrolle, Transparenz und Maßnahmen gegen Überkompensation. Demgegenüber wird der Finanzierungsgrund, also im Falle des öffentlich-rechtlichen Rundfunks die Definition des öffentlichen Auftrags nur beschränkt überprüft, sodass den Mitgliedstaaten ein Spielraum für die kulturelle Schwerpunktsetzung verbleibt, die durch nationale Besonderheiten geprägt sein kann. Sie verlangt bei der Ausgestaltung der Modelle eine Berücksichtigung des Konkurrenzverhältnisses zu kommerziellen Rundfunkanbietern und Printmedien, welche potentiell negativ von einer staatlichen Finanzierung des öffentlich-rechtlichen Rundfunks hinsichtlich der Entwicklung neuer Geschäftsmodelle betroffen sein können. Weil diese Anbieter ebenfalls die kulturelle und politische Debatte bereichern und die Inhalteauswahl vergrößern, muss ihr Schutz mit bedacht werden.³⁹⁶ Daran lässt sich erkennen, dass – anders als im Rahmen der im vorangegangenen Kapitel angesprochenen Marktaufsicht – im Rahmen des Beihilferechts nicht nur die Mitgliedstaaten frei sind, ihrer kulturpolitischen Regelungskompetenz nachzukommen, sondern dass auch die Kommission gewisse vielfaltssichernde Aspekte in ihre beihilferechtliche Bewertung miteinfließen lässt.

---

392 EuGH, Rs. C-280/00, *Altmark Trans GmbH und Regierungspräsidium Magdeburg / Nahverkehrsgesellschaft Altmark GmbH*.
393 Mitteilung der Europäischen Kommission vom 24. April 2007, K(2007) 1761, abrufbar unter https://www.ard.de/download/74354/index.pdf.
394 Insbesondere durch die Mitteilung der Kommission über die Anwendung der Vorschriften über staatliche Beihilfen auf den öffentlich-rechtlichen Rundfunk, EU ABl. C 257 vom 27.10.2009, S. 1–14, https://eur-lex.europa.eu/legal-content/DE/TXT/?uri=celex:52009XC1027(01), sowie durch Einzelfallentscheidungen – eine Liste ist abrufbar unter http://ec.europa.eu/competition/sectors/media/decisions_psb.pdf.
395 Mitteilung der Kommission (wie vor), Rz. 13.
396 Mitteilung der Kommission (wie vor), Rz. 16.

C. Zur Bedeutung und rechtlichen Verankerung der Medienvielfalt auf EU-Ebene

Auch im Bereich kommerzieller Medien bestehen Fördermöglichkeiten[397] vor dem Hintergrund der Vielfaltssicherung für die Mitgliedstaaten insbesondere nach Art. 107 Abs. 3 Buchst. d) AEUV, welcher Beihilfen zur Förderung der Kultur und der Erhaltung des kulturellen Erbes erlaubt, soweit sie die Handels- und Wettbewerbsbedingungen in der Union nicht in einem Maß beeinträchtigen, das dem gemeinsamen Interesse zuwiderläuft. Die Bestimmung des Kulturbegriffs erfolgt parallel zu Art. 167 AEUV und erfasst damit insbesondere auch die Förderung des künstlerischen und literarischen Schaffens, einschließlich journalistisch-redaktioneller Betätigung, insbesondere im audiovisuellen Bereich.[398] In vergangenen Prüfungsverfahren hat die Kommission Medienförderungen teilweise unter Art. 107 Abs. 3 Buchst. d) AEUV geprüft, wobei eine restriktive Auslegung dazu führt, dass es bei der Prüfung auf den Inhalt und die Art des „Produkts" ankommt, nicht jedoch auf das Medium oder seine Verbreitungsweise per se.[399] Die Fördermaßnahme muss einen kulturellen Schwerpunkt haben. Bedingungen und Grenzen (insbesondere Transparenzvorgaben und Deckelungsgrenzen) speziell für den Bereich der Filmindustrie und anderer audiovisueller Werke ergeben sich aus einer entsprechenden Mitteilung der Kommission.[400] Die Förderung der audiovisuellen Produktion wird in diesem Rahmen auch und gerade als geeignetes Mittel zur Förderung der Vielfalt und des Reichtums der europäischen Kultur begriffen.[401] Betont wird dabei sogar, dass das Ziel der kulturellen Vielfalt die Besonderheit nationaler Beihilfen für Film und Fernsehen rechtfertigt und dass diese gerade entscheidend zur Ausformung des europäischen audiovisuellen Marktes beitragen.

---

[397] Zum Bereich der Fördermöglichkeiten für den privaten Rundfunk und insbesondere zur Prüfung der Vereinbarkeit staatlich veranlasster Finanzierung mit den europäischen Beihilfevorschriften vgl. *Cole/Oster*, Zur Frage der Beteiligung privater Rundfunkveranstalter in Deutschland an einer staatlich veranlassten Finanzierung, S. 26 ff.
[398] Hierzu eingehend und weiterführend: *Ress/Ukrow* in: Grabitz/Hilf/Nettesheim, Art. 167 AEUV, Rn. 128 f.
[399] Entscheidung vom 1. August 2016, C(2016) 4865 final, State aid SA.45512 (2016/N). Der Fall betraf die Förderung von Print- und Digitalmedien in Minderheitensprache.
[400] Mitteilung der Kommission über staatliche Beihilfen für Filme und andere audiovisuelle Werke, EU ABl. C 332 vom 15.11.2013, S. 1–11, https://eur-lex.europa.eu/legal-content/DE/LSU/?uri=CELEX:52013XC1115(01), in der Fassung der Mitteilung der Kommission 2014/C 198/02, https://eur-lex.europa.eu/legal-content/DE/TXT/?uri=CELEX:52014XC0627(02).
[401] Mitteilung der Kommission (wie vor), Rz. 4.

V. Verankerung des Ziels in Sekundärrechtsakten und weiteren Texten

Aufgrund mangelnder Rechtsetzungskompetenzen kann es im Bereich der Vielfaltssicherung kein Sekundärrecht geben, das unmittelbar diese Zielsetzung verfolgt.[402] Allerdings gibt es dennoch einen gewissen medienrechtlichen Rahmen auf EU-Ebene, innerhalb dessen sich Anknüpfungspunkte bezüglich einer Pluralismussicherung finden. Diese unterschiedlichen Rechtsakte und drüber hinausgehend rechtlich unverbindlichen, aber dennoch relevanten Maßnahmen sowie aktuelle Initiativen der EU werden umfassend im nachfolgenden Abschnitt D. dargestellt.

---

402 Vgl. bereits Kapitel B.

D. Sekundärrechtlicher Rahmen zum „Medienrecht" und Medienpluralismus

Mark D. Cole / Christina Etteldorf

I. Überblick

Im Jahr 1996 gab es von der Europäischen Kommission einen internen Entwurf für eine Richtlinie zur Medienvielfalt[403], der allerdings nach Widerständen noch vor einer Einführung in das Legislativverfahren auf Kommissionsebene zurückgezogen wurde. Dies war vor allem auf kompetenzrechtliche Zweifel zurückzuführen, da bereits der Titel der Richtlinie eine Berufung auf die Binnenmarktkompetenz nicht begründbar gemacht hätte und der Inhalt sich auf keine existierende Rechtsgrundlage hätte stützen können.[404] Ein nachfolgender Entwurf für eine Richtlinie zum Medieneigentum im Binnenmarkt[405] war zwar nicht primär auf die Sicherung von Medienvielfalt ausgerichtet, sondern sollte dieses Ziel mittelbar über eine Verwirklichung des Binnenmarktes erreichen, allerdings wurde die Berufung auf binnenmarktbezogene Kompetenzen ebenfalls stark angezweifelt.[406] Der Entwurf wurde schließlich aufgrund der Widerstände der Mitgliedstaaten ebenfalls zurückgezogen.[407] Im Übrigen blieben auch zahlreiche Versuche des Europäischen Parlaments insbesondere in den neunziger Jahren und dem ersten Jahrzehnt des 21. Jahrhunderts, die Europäische Kommission zu konkreten Maßnahmen der Medienvielfaltssicherung zu

---

403 Unveröffentlicht. Vgl. hierzu und zum Folgenden eingehend *Ress/Bröhmer*, Europäische Gemeinschaft und Medienvielfalt; *Cole*, Europarechtliche Rahmenbedingungen für die Pluralismussicherung im Rundfunk, S. 93, 94 ff.
404 *Paal*, Medienvielfalt und Wettbewerbsrecht, S. 178.
405 Unveröffentlicht. Vgl. hierzu und zum Folgenden eingehend *Ress/Bröhmer*, Europäische Gemeinschaft und Medienvielfalt. Weitere Hinweise zum Inhalt des Entwurfs *van Loon* in: Media Law & Policy 2001, 11, 17 f.; *Westphal* in: European Business Law Review 2002, 459, S, 465 ff.
406 Wie vor; siehe ebenfalls *Paal*, Medienvielfalt und Wettbewerbsrecht, S. 179, m.w.N.
407 *Frey* in: ZUM 1998, 985, 985.

bewegen, ohne Erfolg.[408] Bis heute gibt es unter Berücksichtigung der diesbezüglichen Zuständigkeit der Mitgliedstaaten kein sekundärrechtliches Regelungswerk der Europäischen Union, welches die Medienvielfalt unmittelbar zum Regelungsgegenstand hat.[409] Das Medienrecht insgesamt – auch im Sinne eines weiten Begriffsverständnisses einer Querschnittsmaterie – ist nicht und könnte auch nicht im Rahmen der Kompetenzverteilung auf europäischer Ebene voll harmonisiert (sein).

Allerdings gibt es eine Reihe sekundärrechtlicher Regelungen, die die Medien entweder unmittelbar adressieren oder sich zumindest in relevanter Weise auf die Medien selbst oder ihre Verbreitungswege auswirken und damit als Bestandteile eines „europäischen Medienrechts", das aber im Wesentlichen nur Vorgaben zur Umsetzung macht, nicht aber eine Vollharmonisierung anstrebt. Allen voran zu nennen ist dabei die Richtlinie über audiovisuelle Mediendienste (AVMD-Richtlinie), bei der – als einziges der nachfolgend noch darzustellenden Regelungswerke – die Regulierung von (in diesem Fall audiovisuellen) Medien im Sinne einer Inhalteregulierung im Vordergrund steht und die daher als Herzstück des „Europäischen Medienrechts" begriffen werden kann. Vor dem Hintergrund der modernen Medienlandschaft, in denen die Grenzen zwischen Inhalteanbietern und Plattformen mehr und mehr verschwimmen, Intermediäre einerseits als Gatekeeper für die Informationsgewinnung aus Nutzerperspektive und die Sichtbarkeit aus Medienanbieterperspektive agieren, andererseits aber auch in Konkurrenz mit klassischen Medienunternehmen treten, erlangt aber auch die E-Commerce-Richtlinie (ECRL) immer größere Bedeutung. Als horizontales Rechtsinstrument, das insbesondere Haftungsprivilegierungen für Dienste der Informationsgesellschaft bereithält, nimmt sie eine zentrale Rolle auch in Bezug auf die Verbreitung von medialen Inhalten ein. Da diese seit ihrem Erlass im Jahr 2000 nicht mehr geändert wurde, wird insoweit am stärksten auf Ebene der EU ein Handlungsbedarf erkannt, nachdem auf Initiative der letzten Kommission zahlreiche relevante

---

408 Hierzu: *Valcke*, Challenges of Regulating Media Pluralism in the European Union, S. 26.
409 Vgl. zum Für und Wider einer Verlagerung der Pluralismussicherung auf die Ebene der EU auch *Gounalakis/Zagouras* in: ZUM 2006, 716, 716 ff. die sich aus nachvollziehbaren Gründen für eine europäische Pluralismussicherung aussprechen ohne dabei allerdings auf das das kompetenzielle Problem näher einzugehen, sondern es zugunsten der EG aus Unterschieden in nationalen Regelungen begründen (724 f.); dagegen wiederum mit den überzeugenden Argumenten *Hain* in: AfP 2007, 527, 532 ff; insges. im Überblick *Cole*, Europarechtliche Rahmenbedingungen für die Pluralismussicherung im Rundfunk, S. 93 ff.

D. Sekundärrechtlicher Rahmen zum „Medienrecht" und Medienpluralismus

Sekundärrechtsakte geändert oder neu beschlossen worden sind.[410] Dazu zählen auch Regeln des Urheberrechts, Telekommunikationsrechts und des Verbraucherschutzrechts, insbesondere soweit sie Sonderbestimmungen oder Ausnahmetatbestände für die Medien enthalten. Daneben spielen auch die sekundärrechtlichen Konkretisierungen des Wettbewerbsrechts eine wichtige Rolle, wobei hier aufgrund des Zusammenhangs mit Vielfaltssicherung vornehmlich auf die Fusionskontroll-Verordnung einzugehen ist.

Diese sekundärrechtlichen Rechtsgrundlagen sollen im vorliegenden Kapitel betrachtet und im Hinblick auf den Zusammenhang mit der mitgliedstaatlichen Kompetenz für die Medienvielfaltssicherung untersucht werden. Ergänzt wird dieser Abschnitt durch einen Blick auf geplante Rechtsakte auf EU-Ebene, die Aufschluss über sich abzeichnende Tendenzen und eventuell auch Konflikte geben. Das Kapitel schließt mit einem Überblick zu aktuellen Maßnahmen der EU in Form von Koordinierungs- und Unterstützungsmaßnahmen, deren Betrachtung vor allem vor dem Hintergrund lohnt, dass diese Vorläufer von legislativen Maßnahmen sein können oder in Bereichen als Instrumente gewählt werden, in denen die EU über keine originäre Regelungskompetenz verfügt. Das Kapitel betrachtet also und fasst in den Schlussfolgerungen zusammen, welche Folgerungen aus den sekundärrechtlichen Grundlagen für die (Kompetenz zur) Sicherung von Medienvielfalt und den Erlass entsprechender Regulierung zu ziehen sind.

II. Anknüpfungspunkte im bestehenden Sekundärrecht

1. E-Commerce-Richtlinie

Die Richtlinie über den elektronischen Geschäftsverkehr (E-Commerce-Richtlinie, ECRL)[411] sollte einen kohärenten Rahmen für den Internethandel schaffen. Kern der Richtlinie ist daher auch die Beseitigung von

---

410 Vgl. hierzu im Überblick *Cole/Etteldorf/Ullrich*, Cross-border Dissemination of Online Content, S. 91 ff.
411 Richtlinie 2000/31/EG des Europäischen Parlaments und des Rates vom 8. Juni 2000 über bestimmte rechtliche Aspekte der Dienste der Informationsgesellschaft, insbesondere des elektronischen Geschäftsverkehrs, im Binnenmarkt ("Richtlinie über den elektronischen Geschäftsverkehr"), EU ABl. L 178, 17.7.2000, p. 1–16, https://eur-lex.europa.eu/legal-content/DE/ALL/?uri=celex%3A32000L0031.

Rechtsunsicherheiten für grenzüberschreitende Online-Dienste und die Gewährleistung des freien Verkehrs von Diensten der Informationsgesellschaft zwischen den Mitgliedstaaten.[412] Das deckt sich mit der Zielsetzung wie sie in Art. 1 ECRL niedergelegt ist: Die Richtlinie soll einen Beitrag zum einwandfreien Funktionieren des Binnenmarktes leisten, indem sie den freien Verkehr von Diensten der Informationsgesellschaft zwischen den Mitgliedstaaten sicherstellt und hierzu bestimmte innerstaatliche Regeln für Dienste der Informationsgesellschaft angleicht. Um dies zu gewährleisten, legt die ECRL das Herkunftslandprinzip sowie die Zulassungsfreiheit für Dienste der Informationsgesellschaft verbindlich fest und stellt Vorgaben auf, denen solche Dienste entsprechen müssen.[413] Dazu zählen Informationspflichten (auch in Bezug auf die kommerzielle Kommunikation), Bestimmungen zur Abwicklung von elektronischen Verträgen, zur außergerichtlichen Streitbeilegung, Klagemöglichkeiten und zur Zusammenarbeit. Konkrete Vorgaben zur Aufsicht über die erfassten Dienste enthält die ECRL dagegen nicht, sondern überlässt die Sicherstellung der Durchsetzung der ECRL vollständig den Mitgliedstaaten (Art. 20 ECRL). Den im Rahmen der ECRL verfolgten Mindestharmonisierungsansatz dokumentiert dabei bereits Erwgr. 10, der statuiert, dass gemäß dem Grundsatz der Verhältnismäßigkeit in dieser Richtlinie nur diejenigen Maßnahmen vorgesehen sind, die zur Gewährleistung des reibungslosen Funktionierens des Binnenmarktes für Dienste der Informationsgesellschaft – aus damaliger Sicht – unerlässlich sind.[414]

Kern der ECRL ist das horizontal anwendbare abgestufte Haftungssystem, das in den Art. 12 bis 15 niedergelegt ist. In Form einer Kategorisierung verschiedener Anbieter in Caching-, Access-, und Hosting-Anbieter, privilegiert es die Anbieter (ohne an dieser Stelle im Detail auf die einzelnen Bestimmungen und deren Auslegung durch den EuGH eingehen zu müssen[415]). Bedingung für die Haftungsfreistellung für über den Dienst verfügbare illegale Inhalte ist aber, dass es sich um lediglich passive Anbie-

---

412 Im Detail zur ECRL sowie zur Frage, ob sie den Gegebenheiten des Digitalzeitalters in Bezug auf den Mediensektor noch gerecht wird vgl. *Cole/Etteldorf/Ullrich*, Cross-border Dissemination of Online Content. Zur historischen Entwicklung vgl. *Valcke/Dommering* in: Castendyk/Dommering/Scheuer (Hrsg.), S. 1083.
413 Zu den Unterschieden beim Herkunftslandprinzip in der ECRL im Vergleich zur AVMD-Richtlinie (bzw. TwF-Richtlinie) *Cole*, The Country of Origin Principle, 113, 113 ff.
414 Vgl. zur ECRL eingehend etwa *Büllesbach u.a.*, Concise European IT Law, Part II; *Valcke/Dommering* in: Castendyk/Dommering/Scheuer, S. 1083 ff.
415 Im Detail *Cole/Etteldorf/Ullrich*, Cross-border Dissemination of Online Content, S. 169 ff.

D. Sekundärrechtlicher Rahmen zum „Medienrecht" und Medienpluralismus

ter von Diensten zur Verteilung von Fremdinhalten handelt und sie keine Kenntnisnahme von der Illegalität des jeweiligen Inhalts haben. Es dürfen diesen Anbietern zudem keine aktiven Überwachungspflichten auferlegt werden. Für die Medienregulierung relevant sind diese Bestimmungen einerseits, weil Medienunternehmen regelmäßig selbst auf solchen Plattformen eine Präsenz haben, die Dienste der Informationsgesellschaft also als Distributoren agieren, und andererseits, weil Medienunternehmen in bestimmten Fällen mit den Plattformen um den gleichen oder ähnlichen Rezipienten- und Werbemarkt konkurrieren (wenngleich und insoweit die Plattformen fremde, zum Beispiel nutzergenerierte Inhalte zur Verfügung stellen und nicht selbst Inhalteersteller sind, weil sie dann ohnehin unter eine andere Kategorie der Verantwortlichkeit fallen) oder auf den Plattformen mit anderen Inhalteanbietern im Wettbewerb stehen.

Während bei der Umsetzung der Regulierungen, die sich auf die Frage der Verantwortlichkeit von über Plattformen abrufbare Inhalte auswirkt, etwa die Haftungsprivilegien aus den Art. 12 bis 15 ECRL von den Mitgliedstaaten zu beachten sind, gilt dies nicht, wenn eine Regelung – etwa im Rahmen der mitgliedstaatlichen Medienregulierung – sich auch auf Anbieter auswirkt, die in den Anwendungsbereich der ECRL fallen. Die weite Definition von Diensten der Informationsgesellschaft aus der Informationsverfahren-Richtlinie[416] führt dazu, dass viele Angebote, die zum Zeitpunkt des Erlasses der ECRL noch nicht existierten, von dieser mit erfasst werden. Dies gilt auch, und gerade vor dem Hintergrund des digitalen Wandels und dem Verschwimmen der Grenzen zwischen Medienanbietern und Intermediären, für Angebotsformen die als Dienste der Informationsgesellschaft eine wichtige Rolle bei der Verbreitung von Informationen spielen wie z.B. VSP oder Suchmaschinen. Forderungen zur Schaffung einer neuen Kategorie von Plattformanbietern für die Inhalte(verbreitung) in der ECRL oder einem anderen Rechtsakt, die bereits bei der letzten Re-

---

[416] Richtlinie 98/34/EG des Europäischen Parlaments und des Rates vom 22. Juni 1998 über ein Informationsverfahren auf dem Gebiet der Normen und technischen Vorschriften, EU Abl. L 204, 21.7.1998, S. 37–48, aufgehoben durch Richtlinie (EU) 2015/1535 des Europäischen Parlaments und des Rates vom 9. September 2015 über ein Informationsverfahren auf dem Gebiet der technischen Vorschriften und der Vorschriften für die Dienste der Informationsgesellschaft, EU ABl. L 241, 17.9.2015, S. 1–15. Vgl. auch den konsolidierten Text der Richtlinie 98/34/EG abrufbar unter https://eur-lex.europa.eu/legal-content/DE/TXT/?uri=CELEX%3A01998L0034-20151007.

vision der AVMD-Richtlinie[417] und dann wieder bei den Diskussionen um die Reform der ECRL bzw. im Vorlauf des Gesetzgebungsvorschlags zum *Digital Services Act*[418] gefordert wurden, sind bislang noch nicht aufgegriffen worden. Einstweilen gilt damit die herkömmliche binnenmarktbezogene Ausrichtung der ECRL, die nicht nach der Art der Intermediäre – von der Unterscheidung im Rahmen der Kategorien bei den Haftungsprivilegien abgesehen – unterscheidet.

Im Blick auf die kompetenzielle Zuordnung der Sicherung des Medienpluralismus auf die mitgliedstaatliche Ebene, verweist die ECRL deshalb auf den Medienpluralismus als Ziel von allgemeinem öffentlichem Interesse in der Weise, dass trotz des weiten Anwendungsbereichs der Richtlinie, bestehende oder zu schaffende Regelungen der Mitgliedstaaten – und der Union – mit diesem Ziel unberührt bleiben.[419] Dazu heißt es in Art. 1 Abs. 6 ECRL:

> *Maßnahmen auf gemeinschaftlicher oder einzelstaatlicher Ebene, die unter Wahrung des Gemeinschaftsrechts der Förderung der kulturellen und sprachlichen Vielfalt und dem Schutz des Pluralismus dienen, bleiben von dieser Richtlinie unberührt.*

Das ist zunächst insoweit hervorzuheben, weil Art. 1 Abs. 6 ECRL auch von *gemeinschaftlichen* (aus damaliger Sicht; heute also „der Europäischen Union") Maßnahmen spricht, die der Förderung der kulturellen Vielfalt dienen. Dies darf aber nicht so missverstanden werden, dass es sich hierbei um eine Rechtsgrundlage für Regelungen zur Vielfaltssicherung handelt. Zum einen bedarf es für ein Handeln der Union einer Rechtsgrundlage im Primärrecht, wie oben ausführlich dargestellt worden ist. An einer solchen fehlt es gerade bezüglich Vielfaltssicherungsregelungen. Zum anderen begrenzt das Primärrecht ausdrücklich Unionshandeln im kulturellen Bereich auf Fördermöglichkeiten, wie sich aus der Kulturklausel des Art. 167 AEUV ergibt. Demnach bezieht sich die Vorschrift der ECRL auf Maßnah-

---

417 Vgl. *Bárd/Bayer/Carrera*, A comparative analysis of media freedom and pluralism in the EU Member States, S. 75, die solche Dienste separat adressieren wollen, die in der Übermittlung oder Verteilung von Informationen, die von einer anderen Person bereitgestellt wurden, bestehen.
418 Vgl. hierzu *ERGA*, Position Paper on the Digital Services Act, die die Einführung einer neuen Kategorie in Form von Online-Inhalte-Plattformen, befürwortet.
419 S.a. *Valcke*, Challenges of Regulating Media Pluralism in the EU, S. 27, mit Verweis auf die Art. 8 Abs. 1, 9 Abs. 4 und 18 Abs. 1 der Rahmenrichtlinie sowie deren Erwgr. 5, 6 und 31. Siehe dazu für den vergleichbaren Bereich der Netzregulierung vor allem unter D.II.5.

men, die etwa die Förderung der Zusammenarbeit zwischen Mitgliedstaaten und ggf. ergänzende Maßnahmen im Kultursegment zum Beispiel beim Erhalt des kulturellen Erbes zum Ziel haben. Dies wird durch den zugehörigen Erwgr. 63 bestätigt, der die Bereichsausnahme des Art. 1 Abs. 6 ECRL näher definiert und dabei lediglich Maßnahmen der Mitgliedstaaten adressiert sowie insbesondere die Unterschiedlichkeit der kulturellen Ziele anerkennt:

Die Annahme dieser Richtlinie hält die Mitgliedstaaten nicht davon ab, den verschiedenen sozialen, gesellschaftlichen und kulturellen Auswirkungen Rechnung zu tragen, zu denen das Entstehen der Informationsgesellschaft führt. Insbesondere darf sie nicht Maßnahmen verhindern, die die Mitgliedstaaten im Einklang mit dem Gemeinschaftsrecht erlassen könnten, um soziale, kulturelle und demokratische Ziele unter Berücksichtigung ihrer sprachlichen Vielfalt, der nationalen und regionalen Besonderheiten sowie ihres Kulturerbes zu erreichen und den Zugang der Öffentlichkeit zu der breitestmöglichen Palette von Diensten der Informationsgesellschaft zu gewährleisten und zu erhalten. Im Zuge der Entwicklung der Informationsgesellschaft muß auf jeden Fall sichergestellt werden, daß die Bürger der Gemeinschaft Zugang zu dem in einem digitalen Umfeld vermittelten europäischen Kulturerbe erhalten können.

Mitgliedstaatliche Regelungen zur Vielfaltssicherung bleiben damit von der ECRL bereits aus kompetenziell-systematischen Gründen unberührt.[420] Dies bezieht sich sowohl auf damals bereits bestehende Regeln ebenso wie jede zukünftig erlassene Regelung. Begrenzt werden die Mitgliedstaaten allerdings dadurch, dass die getroffenen Maßnahmen im Einklang mit dem Gemeinschafts-(heute: Unions-)recht stehen, insbesondere also mit den allgemeinen Rechtsgrundsätzen wie den Grundrechten vereinbar sein müssen.[421]

---

420 Vgl. hierzu *Paal*, Intermediäre: Regulierung und Vielfaltssicherung, S. 38, der sich dabei allerdings nicht im Sinne einer Ausnahme auf Art. 1 Abs. 6 stützt, sondern Maßgaben zur publizistischen Vielfaltssicherung bereits als nicht vom koordinierten Bereich der Richtlinie nach Art. 3 Abs. 2 i.V.m. Art. 2 Buchst. h) ECRL. Diese Vorschriften geben den Mitgliedstaaten auf, nicht aus Gründen, die in den koordinierten Bereich der Richtlinie fallen, den grenzüberschreitenden Zugang zu Diensten zu behindern. Jedoch bezieht sich der koordinierte Bereich nicht auf jede Vorschrift zu Diensten der Informationsgesellschaft, sondern nur für bestimmte Aspekte ihrer Tätigkeit. Eine Rechtsetzungskompetenz für andere Bereiche besteht für die Union auch gar nicht.
421 Vgl. dazu eingehend unter D.II.2.c. *Liesching* (Das Herkunftslandprinzip nach E-Commerce- und AVMD-Richtlinie, S. 78 f.) geht vor dem Hintergrund der dort

Neben dieser Bereichsausnahme gibt es – wiederum vergleichbar mit einem auch bei der AVMD-Richtlinie bekannten Verfahren – zudem noch eine im Zusammenhang mit der Regulierung von Medien relevante Abweichungsbefugnis von dem in der Richtlinie verankerten Herkunftslandprinzip. Während dieses im Regelfall die Mitgliedstaaten wie eben erwähnt daran hindert, den freien Verkehr von Diensten der Informationsgesellschaft aus einem anderen Mitgliedstaat aus Gründen einzuschränken, die in den koordinierten Bereich fallen, gibt es zum Schutz überragend wichtiger Rechtsgüter eine Möglichkeit davon abzuweichen: Nach Art. 3 Abs. 4 ECRL können die Mitgliedstaaten von diesem Grundsatz im Einzelfall abweichen, wenn dies aus Gründen des Jugendschutzes oder der Bekämpfung der Hetze wegen Rasse, Geschlecht, Glauben oder Nationalität erforderlich ist. Die Abweichungsbefugnis steht ebenfalls unter dem Vorbehalt der Angemessenheit und des Vorliegens einer Beeinträchtigung oder schwerwiegenden Gefahr für die genannten Schutzgüter. Zudem muss ein in Art. 4 lit b), 5 und 6 erläutertes Verfahren eingehalten werden – sofern es nicht um dringliche Fälle geht –, das die Beteiligung der Mitgliedstaates der Niederlassung des jeweiligen Anbieters und der Europäischen Kommission vorsieht.

Beide Aspekte, sowohl die Bereichsausnahme als auch die Abweichungsbefugnis dokumentieren, dass auch mit der ECRL keine Vereinheitlichung in dem Sinne erfolgt ist, dass mitgliedstaatliches Handeln zum Schutz von Allgemeininteressen wie etwa dem Medienpluralismus oder der Bekämpfung bestimmter Straftaten ausgeschlossen wird. Damit wird der Tatsache Rechnung getragen – vom abstrakten Problem abgesehen, dass Aktivitäten der Union in vollem Umfang von der jeweiligen Rechtsgrundlage gedeckt sein müssen und nicht Handeln der Mitgliedstaaten in diesen vorbehaltenen Bereichen verunmöglichen darf – dass für die Beurteilung bestimmter Zusammenhänge, wie hier den notwendigen Maßnahmen zur Pluralismussicherung, die Mitgliedstaaten in der besseren Position sind.

---

begutachteten Fragestellung allein zum Herkunftslandprinzip (und damit nicht im Fokus stehender Aspekte der Vielfaltssicherung) nicht näher auf Art. 1 Abs. 6 ein und verweist im Zusammenhang mit dem Herkunftslandprinzip lediglich auf die Ausführungen der Kommission im Notifizierungsverfahren zum MStV.

2. AVMD-Richtlinie

a. Historische Betrachtung im Kontext von Vielfaltssicherung

Als Vorgänger der AVMD-Richtlinie wurde die Richtlinie „Fernsehen ohne Grenzen" (Television without Frontiers Directive, TwF-Richtlinie)[422] 1989 mit dem Ziel geschaffen, Regelungen für die grenzüberschreitende Übertragung von Fernsehsendungen zu schaffen, die den Übergang von den nationalen Märkten zu einem gemeinsamen Markt für die Herstellung und Verbreitung von Programmen sichern und die unbeschadet der Funktion des Fernsehens, das Allgemeininteresse zu wahren, faire Wettbewerbsbedingungen gewährleisten.[423] Verfolgt wurde diese Zielsetzung mit dem Ansatz der Mindestharmonisierung[424] auf Basis des tragenden Herkunftslandprinzips[425] als Kernelement der Regulierung.

In materieller Hinsicht waren Kernpunkte der TwF-Richtlinie Quotenregelungen zur Förderung europäischer Werke – Regelungen, die sich aus Sicht der deutschen Länder außerhalb des Kompetenzbereichs der EU bewegten[426] –, die Regulierung von Werbung und Sponsoring, Bestimmungen zu Jugendschutz und zu zu Hass aufstachelnden Inhalten sowie das Recht auf Gegendarstellung. Insgesamt und in Bezug auf die einzelnen Regelungsbereiche sollte die Richtlinie dabei nur das „notwendige Mindestmaß" regeln, um den freien Sendeverkehr zu ermöglichen, nicht aber in die Zuständigkeit der Mitgliedstaaten für die Organisation, Finanzierung oder Programminhalte eingreifen.[427] Insbesondere sollten eigenständige kulturelle Entwicklungen in den Mitgliedstaaten und die Bewahrung der kulturellen Vielfalt in der Gemeinschaft nicht von der Richtlinie berührt werden.[428] Vielfaltssicherung spielte dabei weniger als eigenständiges Re-

---

422 Richtlinie 89/552/EWG des Rates vom 3. Oktober 1989 zur Koordinierung bestimmter Rechts- und Verwaltungsvorschriften der Mitgliedstaaten über die Ausübung der Fernsehtätigkeit, EU ABl. L 298, 17.10.1989, S. 23–30, https://eur-lex.europa.eu/legal-content/DE/ALL/?uri=CELEX%3A31989L0552.
423 Erwgr. 3 TwF-Richtlinie.
424 Bereits in der Richtlinie 89/552/EWG ist die Formulierung zu finden, dass diese Richtlinie „das notwendige Mindestmaß, um den freien Sendeverkehr zu verwirklichen", regelt.
425 Vgl. Hierzu *Cole*, The Country of Origin Principle, 113, 113 ff.
426 Vgl. BVerfGE 92, 203 (205 ff.).
427 Vgl. Erwägungsgrund 13 der TwF-Richtlinie.
428 Wie vor. Vgl. zur Historie der TwF- und AVMD-Richtlinie vor dem Hintergrund eines wirtschaftlichen Ansatzes auch *Broughton Micova*, The Audiovisual Media Services Directive: Balancing liberalisation and protection (DRAFT).

gulierungsziel eine Rolle, sondern vielmehr als Nebeneffekt: Indem Handlungen verhindert werden, die den freien Fluss von Sendungen beeinträchtigen oder die Entstehung von beherrschenden Stellungen begünstigen können, könne auch potentiellen Gefahren für Pluralismus und Informationsfreiheit begegnet werden.[429] Dies sicherzustellen, blieb aber als Aufgabe bei den Mitgliedstaaten verortet. Dokumentiert wird das insbesondere von drei Faktoren, die in der damaligen TwF-Richtlinie auszumachen waren:

(1.) den bewusst gewählten und durch die Erwägungen zur Richtlinie dokumentierten Ansatz der Mindestharmonisierung,
(2.) durch teils weite Gestaltungsspielräume selbst innerhalb harmonisierter Vorschriften – etwa im Sinne der Zielfestlegung durch die Richtlinie, den Weg dazu aber den Mitgliedstaaten überlassend –[430], und
(3.) die Einführung einer generellen Abweichungsbefugnis in Art. 3 Abs. 1 TwF-Richtlinie.

Letztere erlaubt es den Mitgliedstaaten, für Fernsehveranstalter, die ihrer Rechtshoheit unterworfen sind, strengere oder ausführlichere Bestimmungen in den von in dieser Richtlinie erfassten Bereichen vorzusehen, um etwa eine aktive Politik zugunsten einer bestimmten Sprache zu ermöglichen oder für andere „bestimmte Fälle"[431], wozu auch die Verfolgung kultureller Ziele zu rechnen ist.[432]

Eine eigene kulturpolitische Schwerpunktsetzung lässt sich demgegenüber auch aus den einzelnen inhaltlichen Regelungsbereichen der TwF-Richtlinie nicht ablesen. Vielmehr dienten diese jeweils der Wahrung anderer rechtlich geschützter Interessen insbesondere verbraucherschutzrechtlicher (bspw. Werbekennzeichnung und Sponsoring), jugendschutzrechtlicher (bspw. entwicklungsbeeinträchtigende Werbung) und binnenmarktwirtschaftlicher (bspw. Herkunftslandprinzip) Natur. Das gilt auch für die Vorschriften zur Förderung (unabhängiger) europäischer Werke,

---

429 Vgl. hierzu Erwägungsgrund 16 der TwF-Richtlinie.
430 So formulierte bspw. Art. 5 S. 1 TwF-Richtlinie in Bezug auf die Förderung unabhängiger europäischer Werke – als eines der Kernanliegen bei der Etablierung der Fernsehrichtlinie – dass die Mitgliedstaaten „im Rahmen des praktisch Durchführbaren" und mit „angemessenen Mitteln" dafür sorgen sollen, dass Fernsehveranstalter „mindestens" zehn Prozent ihrer Sendezeit unabhängigen Werken vorbehalten.
431 Erwägungsgründe 25, 26 TwF-Richtlinie.
432 Dazu später eingehend in Abschnitt D.II.2.c. Vgl. zur Fassung von Art. 3 in der TwF-Richtlinie auch *Dommering/Scheuer/Adler* in: Castendyk/Dommering/Scheuer (Hrsg.), S. 857 ff.

D. Sekundärrechtlicher Rahmen zum „Medienrecht" und Medienpluralismus

die sich zwar auf den ersten Blick als Maßnahmen zum Schutz der kulturellen Vielfalt und des Erhalts der europäischen Filmkultur darstellen, aber tatsächlich – wie die Erwgr. (vor allem 20, 23) dokumentieren – insbesondere die Begünstigung der Bildung von Märkten für Fernsehproduktionen in den Mitgliedstaaten, die Förderung neuer Quellen für Fernsehproduktionen sowie von Klein- und Mittelbetrieben in der Fernsehindustrie und die Schaffung von Beschäftigungsmöglichkeiten, mithin also die Industrie, Lauterkeit des Handelsverkehrs und des Wettbewerbs, in den Blick nahmen.[433] Diese Stärkung der europäischen Film- und Fernsehindustrie erfolgte nicht zuletzt auch aufgrund des Einflusses der starken US-Inhalteanbieter, deren Kanäle auf den europäischen Markt drängten.[434] Hintergrund für die besondere Betonung der wirtschaftlichen Beweggründe für die Regelung war dabei wohl auch die mangelnde kompetenzielle Grundlage für das Schaffen einer schwerpunktmäßig kulturpolitischen Regelung. Entsprechend zurückhaltend war deshalb auch die Formulierung der Vorschrift, die den Mitgliedstaaten die Beurteilung der Ergreifung angemessener Maßnahmen überließ.

Diese Linie wurde auch im Rahmen der in der folgenden Zeit jeweils einmal pro Jahrzehnt stattfindenden Reform der Richtlinie beibehalten.[435] In der Bestrebung, die Bestimmungen der TwF-Richtlinie an ein neues Werbeumfeld und technologische Entwicklungen im Fernsehbereich anzupassen, führte die Richtlinie 97/36/EG[436] wichtige Neuerungen in den Bereichen Teleshopping und der Übertragung von Großereignissen ein und vertiefte die jugendmedienschutzrechtlichen Vorgaben. In prozeduraler Hinsicht wurden die Zuständigkeitsbestimmungen in Form der Kriterien für die Bestimmung der Rechtshoheit konkretisiert und der Kontaktausschuss eingerichtet. Das Grundkonzept der Mindestharmonisierung wurde dabei allerdings beibehalten, insbesondere auch unter der Bekräfti-

---

[433] Entsprechend betonte auch die Kommission in ihrem Richtlinienvorschlag von 1986 bereits, dass „[d]ie Schwächen der europäischen Kulturindustrien nicht auf einem Mangel an Schöpferkraft [beruhen], sondern auf den zersplitterten Produktions- und Verbreitungssystemen", EG ABl. C 179, 17.7.1986, S. 4–10.
[434] *Broughton Micova*, The Audiovisual Media Services Directive: Balancing liberalisation and protection (DRAFT), S. 4 f.
[435] Ausführlich zur Genese der TwF-Richtlinie *Weinand*, Implementing the Audiovisual Media Services Directive, S. 70 ff.
[436] Richtlinie 97/36/EG des Europäischen Parlaments und des Rates vom 30. Juni 1997 zur Änderung der Richtlinie 89/552/EWG des Rates zur Koordinierung bestimmter Rechts- und Verwaltungsvorschriften der Mitgliedstaaten über die Ausübung der Fernsehtätigkeit, EU ABl. L 202, 30.7.1997, S. 60–70, https://eur-lex.europa.eu/legal-content/DE/TXT/?uri=CELEX:31997L0036.

gung, dass das von der TwF-Richtlinie gewählte Konzept einer grundlegenden Harmonisierung, weiterhin notwendig, aber auch hinreichend ist, um den freien Empfang von Fernsehsendungen in der Gemeinschaft sicherzustellen.[437] Entsprechend standen auch hier die Ziele in Form des Schutzes des Rechts auf Information (bspw. Übertragung von Großereignissen), eine verbesserte Wettbewerbsfähigkeit der Programmindustrie (bspw. Überarbeitung der Bestimmungen und Ausnahmen zur Förderung europäischer Werke), Verbraucher- (bspw. Regulierung des Teleshopping) und Jugendschutz (bspw. Verbot ernsthaft entwicklungsbeeinträchtigender Inhalte) im Vordergrund der Reform. Kulturellen Aspekten wurde dabei lediglich bei der Tätigkeit aufgrund anderer Bestimmungen Rechnung getragen, wie es die Verpflichtung aus der kulturellen Querschnittsklausel bereits damals verlangte.[438]

Während die Abweichungsbefugnis nach Art. 3 Abs. 1 TwF-Richtlinie auch im Rahmen der Reform im Wesentlichen unangetastet blieb, wurden in den Erwgr. nunmehr die „bestimmten anderen Fälle", in denen der Erlass strengerer Bestimmungen durch die Mitgliedstaaten möglich sein soll, konkretisiert. Erwgr. 44 listete hierfür insbesondere und unter anderem den Schutz der Interessen der Allgemeinheit in Bezug auf den Informations-, Bildungs-, Kultur- und Unterhaltungsauftrag des Fernsehens, die Wahrung der Informations- und Medienvielfalt und den Schutz des Wettbewerbs im Hinblick auf die Verhinderung des Missbrauchs beherrschender Stellungen auf. Wenngleich derartige mitgliedstaatlichen Regelungen mit dem Gemeinschaftsrecht vereinbar sein müssen, wird die Pluralismussicherung in den (audiovisuellen) Medien hier also doch deutlich im Kompetenz- und Interessenbereich der Mitgliedstaaten gesehen und das sogar in den Bereichen, in denen der europäische Gesetzgesetzgeber seinen Regulierungswillen und seine Regulierungskompetenz für dienstleistungsrechtliche/-wirtschaftliche Aspekte bereits durch Harmonisierung eben jener Regeln in der Richtlinie dokumentiert hat.

Diese Linie wurde in der nächsten Reform weitergeführt. Mit der Richtlinie 2007/65/EG[439] sollte 10 Jahre nach der letzten Überarbeitung der Richtlinie erneut auf neue technische Umgebungsbedingungen insbeson-

---

437 Erwägungsgrund 44 der Richtlinie 97/36/EG.
438 So ausdrücklich Erwägungsgrund 25 mit Verweis auf Art. 128 Abs. 4 des Vertrages zur Gründung der Europäischen Gemeinschaft (Amsterdam konsolidierte Fassung), EG ABl. C 340 vom 10.11.1997, S. 173–306 (heute Art. 167 AEUV).
439 Richtlinie 2007/65/EG des Europäischen Parlaments und des Rates vom 11. Dezember 2007 zur Änderung der Richtlinie 89/552/EWG des Rates zur Koordinierung bestimmter Rechts- und Verwaltungsvorschriften der Mitgliedstaaten über

D. Sekundärrechtlicher Rahmen zum „Medienrecht" und Medienpluralismus

dere vor dem Hintergrund der wachsenden Bedeutung des Internets reagiert werden und der Rechtsrahmen an die Konvergenz der Medien angepasst werden. Zu diesem Zweck wurden Bestimmungen für Abrufdienste im Rahmen eines abgestuften Regulierungsansatzes eingeführt, der zwar zwischen linearen und non-linearen Angeboten trennte, aber die Fernsehähnlichkeit von audiovisuellen on-Demand-Angeboten im Internet anerkannte und deshalb in bestimmten Bereichen ähnliche Pflichten einführte. Es gab eine erneute Konkretisierung der Zuständigkeitsbestimmungen, Informationspflichten für Anbieter wurden eingeführt oder überarbeitet, das Recht auf Kurzberichterstattung etabliert und Anpassungen im Bereich der kommerziellen Kommunikation, insbesondere bezüglich der Produktplatzierung, vorgenommen. Im Kontext von Art. 3 wurden zudem erstmals Ansätze der Selbst- und Koregulierung in die Richtlinie eingeführt, indem geregelt wurde, dass die Mitgliedstaaten solche Regelungen im koordinierten Bereich fördern – dies allerdings nur soweit nach nationalem Recht zulässig. Die Konkretisierung und der Umfang der Inanspruchnahme solcher Regulierungsinstrumente wurde allerdings – ganz im Sinne eines Mindestharmonisierungsansatzes – den Mitgliedstaaten überlassen.

Während Aspekte der medialen Vielfaltssicherung in den allgemeinen Erwägungen zur Richtlinie 2007/65/EG eine im Vergleich zu den Vorgängerrichtlinien höhere Rolle spielten[440], wird die Pluralismussicherung – entsprechend der fehlenden kompetenzrechtlichen Grundlage – nicht als unmittelbare Zielsetzung im Text der Richtlinie aufgegriffen. Ausdrücklich hatte die Kommission in ihrem Grünbuch zu Dienstleistungen von allgemeinem Interesse 2003 auch betont, dass „[d]erzeit […] das abgeleitete Gemeinschaftsrecht keine Bestimmungen zum unmittelbaren Schutz des Medienpluralismus [enthält]".[441] Allerdings wurden einzelne Neuerungen in den Kontext von Medienpluralismus gesetzt. So wurde die Klärung von Zuständigkeitsregeln unter den Gesichtspunkt gestellt, dass „zur Stärkung des Medienpluralismus in der gesamten Europäischen Union" jeweils nur ein Mitgliedstaat für einen Anbieter audiovisueller Mediendienste zuständig und der „Informationspluralismus ein grundlegendes Prinzip

---

die Ausübung der Fernsehtätigkeit, EU ABl. L 332, 18.12.2007, S. 27–45, https://eur-lex.europa.eu/legal-content/DE/TXT/?uri=celex%3A32007L0065.
440 Vgl. Erwägungsgründe 1, 3, 4, 5, 8, die sich auf die allgemeine Richtung der Regulierungspolitik der EU im audiovisuellen Bereich beziehen und dabei Meinungs- und Medienvielfalt als einen Eckpunkt begreifen.
441 Grünbuch zu Dienstleistungen von allgemeinem Interesse, KOM/2003/0270 endg, https://eur-lex.europa.eu/legal-content/DE/TXT/?uri=celex:52003DC0270, Rz. 74.

der Europäischen Union" sein sollte[442]; die Einführung des Rechts auf Kurzberichterstattung damit begründet, dass unbedingt der Pluralismus durch die Vielfalt der Nachrichten und Programme in der Europäischen Union gefördert werden muss[443]; die Förderpflicht für europäische Werke seitens audiovisuellen Mediendiensteanbietern auf Abruf zumindest damit unterlegt, dass die Anbieter damit (auch) einen aktiven Beitrag zur Förderung der kulturellen Vielfalt leisten[444].

Mit diesem höheren Stellenwert der Medienvielfalt, war allerdings keine Umorientierung der Richtlinie dahingehend verbunden, dass Vielfaltssicherung zu einer Zielsetzung der EU geworden wäre, die auf Sekundärrechtsebene mit konkreten Regeln verfolgt wird. Vielmehr war die stärkere Einbeziehung von Vielfaltsgesichtspunkten wohl auch entsprechenden Ausführungen in der Mitteilung der EU-Kommission zur Zukunft der europäischen Regulierungspolitik im audiovisuellen Bereich geschuldet, die der Reform unmittelbar vorangegangen war.[445] Hierin wird jedoch auch darauf verwiesen, dass der Schutz des Pluralismus in den Medien in erster Linie in den Zuständigkeitsbereich der Mitgliedstaaten fällt, aber gleichwohl einige gemeinschaftliche Rechtsakte mehr oder weniger indirekt zur Wahrung des Medienpluralismus beitragen, wie etwa das Wettbewerbsrecht und bestimmte Bestimmungen der TwF-Richtlinie (insb. Förderung von europäischen Werken). Entsprechend betont auch die 2007-Reform, dass es den Mitgliedstaaten freisteht, die geeigneten Instrumente entsprechend ihren Rechtstraditionen und etablierten Strukturen zur Richtlinienumsetzung zu wählen, wobei die gewählten Instrumente einen Beitrag zur Förderung des Medienpluralismus leisten sollten.[446]

2010 kam es zu einer Kodifizierung der Richtlinie, die alle bis dahin in den Änderungsrichtlinie niedergelegten Anpassungen in einem Text zusammenfasste und die Richtlinie als Richtlinie über audiovisuelle Mediendienste neu verkündete. Eine inhaltliche Veränderung ging damit nicht einher. Insbesondere wurden auch die Erwgr. der Richtlinie 2007/65/EG, die sich mit Gesichtspunkten der Vielfaltssicherung befassen, wortlautgetreu und vollständig in die Richtlinie 2010/13/EU übernommen, d.h. ihre

---

442 Erwägungsgrund 28 Richtlinie 2007/65/EG.
443 Erwägungsgrund 38 Richtlinie 2007/65/EG.
444 Erwägungsgrund 48 Richtlinie 2007/65/EG.
445 Mitteilung der Kommission vom 15. Dezember 2003 über die Zukunft der europäischen Regulierungspolitik im audiovisuellen Bereich COM(2003) 784 final, https://eur-lex.europa.eu/legal-content/DE/TXT/?uri=CELEX%3A52013DC0784&qid=1614597375820.
446 Erwägungsgrund 65 Richtlinie 2007/65/EG.

D. Sekundärrechtlicher Rahmen zum „Medienrecht" und Medienpluralismus

fortdauernde Geltung anerkannt.[447] Eine Änderung in der audiovisuellen Politik und der bisherigen Linie zur Verortung der Vielfaltssicherung auf mitgliedstaatlicher Ebene – wenngleich auch als wichtiges Prinzip auf EU-Ebene – hatte daher nicht stattgefunden.

b. AVMD-Reform 2018

Mit einer umfassenden Reform[448] wurde die AVMD-Richtlinie, eingeleitet durch einen Kommissionsvorschlag im Mai 2016[449], im Jahr 2018 überarbeitet und bezüglich des Anwendungsbereichs deutlich erweitert, um sie – erneut – an die Gegebenheiten einer sich rasch entwickelnden Medienlandschaft anzupassen. Die Vorgaben der Richtlinie waren durch die Mitgliedstaaten bis zum 19. September 2020 umzusetzen, wobei bis zum Ablauf der Umsetzungsfrist lediglich Deutschland und Dänemark eine finale Umsetzung sowie Österreich eine teilweise Umsetzung im nationalen Recht verabschiedet haben. In anderen Mitgliedstaaten wurden Gesetzesvorhaben allerdings bereits auf den Weg gebracht.[450]

---

447 Im Vergleich der Richtlinie 2007/65/EG mit der (Richtlinie 2010/13/EU): 1(4), 3(5), 4(6), 5(7), 8(12), 28(34), 38(48) und 65(94).
448 Für einen Überblick über die Entwicklungen im Trilogverfahren vgl. die Synopse des Instituts für Europäisches Medienrecht (EMR), abrufbar unter https://emr-sb.de/synopsis-avms/. Dort findet sich auch eine Gegenüberstellung der Versionen der Richtlinie vor und nach den Änderungen durch die 2018 verabschiedete Richtlinie sowie eine (nicht offizielle) konsolidierte Fassung der AVMD-Richtlinie.
449 Vorschlag für eine Richtlinie des europäischen Parlaments und des Rates zur Änderung der Richtlinie 2010/13/EU zur Koordinierung bestimmter Rechts- und Verwaltungsvorschriften der Mitgliedstaaten über die Bereitstellung audiovisueller Mediendienste im Hinblick auf sich verändernde Marktgegebenheiten, COM(2016) 287 final, 25.5.2016, https://eur-lex.europa.eu/legal-content/DE/TXT/?uri=celex:52016PC0287. Eine erste Bewertung des Änderungsvorschlags findet sich bei *Weinand*, Implementing the Audiovisual Media Services Directive, S. 719 ff; *Burggraf/Gerlach/Wiesner* in: Media Perspektiven 10/2018, 496, 496 ff.; sowie *Cole/Etteldorf*, Von Fernsehen ohne Grenzen zu Video-Sharing-Plattformen, Hate Speech und Overlays – die Anpassung der EU-Richtlinie über audiovisuelle Mediendienste an das digitale Zeitalter.
450 Vgl. hierzu die Übersichten in den Datenbank der Kommission (https://eur-lex.europa.eu/legal-content/DE/NIM/?uri=CELEX:32018L1808&qid=1599556794041) und der Europäischen Audiovisuellen Informationsstelle (https://www.obs.coe.int/en/web/observatoire/home/-/asset_publisher/9iKCxBYgiO6S/content/which-eu-countries-have-transposed-the-avmsd-into-national-legislation-?inheritRedirect=false&redirect=https%3A%2F%2Fwww.obs.coe.int%2Fen%2Fweb%2Fobservato

Angestoßen wurde die Reform 2013 durch das Grünbuch zur Medienkonvergenz, in dessen Rahmen die Kommission insbesondere die Frage nach der Zeitgemäßheit der bestehenden Regulierung und den Auswirkungen der Medienkonvergenz auf die Medienvielfalt gestellt hatte.[451] In Bezug auf Aspekte der Vielfaltssicherung vor dem Hintergrund der sich verändernden Medienlandschaft wurde darin unter anderem von der Kommission unterstrichen, dass die AVMD-Richtlinie und die Wettbewerbsvorschriften sowohl auf der Ebene der EU als auch auf mitgliedstaatlicher Ebene zum Erhalt des Medienpluralismus beitragen. Dabei erläuterte die Kommission in einer Fußnote, dass die AVMD-Richtlinie den Medienpluralismus (lediglich) unterstütze, indem sie auf der Grundlage des Herkunftslandprinzips und z. B. durch Artikel 14 den freien Verkehr audiovisueller Mediendienste im Binnenmarkt vorsehe, was wiederum zusammen mit den besonderen Bestimmungen über die Förderung europäischer Werke den Pluralismus der Medien fördere.[452] Auch in anderem Kontext, in dem es um die Werte geht, die der Regulierung audiovisueller Mediendienste zugrunde liegen, betont die Kommission im Grünbuch, dass die Förderung von Medienpluralismus und kultureller Vielfalt im Zusammenhang mit Art. 167 Abs. 4 AEUV zu sehen sei und diese Regulierungsziele nicht vorrangig seien für die Zwecke der AVMD-Richtlinie.[453] Potentielle Gefahren für die Meinungs- und Medienvielfalt wurden im Grünbuch insbesondere in Bezug auf die Filterung und Herausstellung von Inhalten durch Gate-Keeper wie Suchmaschinen und andere intermediäre Plattformen ausgemacht, da diese – obwohl sie die Handlungsfähigkeit des Bürgers zur Informationsgewinnung auch stärken können – ohne Wissen der Nutzer Einfluss auf das Spektrum von zugänglichen Medienangeboten nehmen können. Weitere Erwägungen wurden zum allgemeinen Rechtsrahmen, zur kommerziellen Kommunikation, zum Schutz von Minderjährigen, zur Barrierefreiheit von audiovisuellen Inhalten für Personen mit Behinderungen sowie weiteren ergänzenden Aspekten angestellt.

---

ire%2Fhome%3Fp_p_id%3D101_INSTANCE_9iKCxBYgiO6S%26p_p_lifecycle%3D0%26p_p_state%3Dnormal%26p_p_mode%3Dview%26p_p_col_id%3Dcolumn-1%26p_p_col_count%3D3).
451 Europäische Kommission, Grünbuch über die Vorbereitung auf die vollständige Konvergenz der audiovisuellen Welt: Wachstum, Schöpfung und Werte, COM(2013) 231 final, 24.4.2013, https://eur-lex.europa.eu/legal-content/DE/TXT/?uri=CELEX%3A52013DC0231&qid=1614597256678.
452 Wie vor, S. 15 Fn. 63.
453 Wie vor, S. 12, Rn. 50.

D. Sekundärrechtlicher Rahmen zum „Medienrecht" und Medienpluralismus

In der später verabschiedeten Änderungsrichtlinie (EU) 2018/1808 spiegeln sich diese Erwägungen wider.[454] Eine der maßgeblichen Änderungen ist die (erneute) Erweiterung des Anwendungsbereichs der AVMD-Richtlinie, und zwar auf die neu eingeführte Kategorie der Video-Sharing-Plattformen (VSP). Diese werden von der neuen Fassung der Richtlinie erstmals erfasst – vorausgesetzt sie waren zuvor nicht bei eigener redaktioneller Verantwortlichkeit bereits Anbieter non-linearer Dienste und unterfielen deshalb der AVMD-Richtlinie seit der Revision 2007 – und damit stärker in die Verantwortung genommen, insbesondere was den Schutz der Allgemeinheit vor bestimmten rechtswidrigen Inhalten, die kommerzielle Kommunikation sowie den Jugendmedienschutz betrifft. Auch die Regeln für non-lineare audiovisuelle Mediendienste wurden erneut angepasst und dabei noch weiter (aber nicht vollständig) an die Bestimmungen für Fernsehanbieter angenähert. Diese Änderungen erfolgten in der Erwägung, dass neuere Player auf dem audiovisuellen Markt, namentlich Streaming-Anbieter wie Netflix (im VoD-Bereich) und Videoverteil- bzw. -zugangsplattformen wie YouTube (im VSP-Bereich), mit Anbietern klassischer Dienste wie Fernsehen um die Aufmerksamkeit der gleichen Rezipienten und Werbekunden konkurrieren und daher zumindest einer angenähert ähnlichen Regulierung unterliegen sollten.

Weitere Neuerungen betreffen eine minimale Konkretisierung zur Klarstellung von Zuständigkeitskriterien bzgl. des Herkunftslandprinzips[455], die Vorgaben zum Jugendschutz[456] und zur „Hassrede",[457] die Modernisierung der Förderungsverpflichtung im Hinblick auf europäische Werke[458], die Verschärfung qualitativer und Liberalisierung quantitativer Werbebestimmungen[459], die sog. Signalintegrität[460] sowie die Verpflichtung der

---

[454] Für einen Überblick zur Reform vgl. auch *Cole/Etteldorf*, Von Fernsehen ohne Grenzen zu Video-Sharing-Plattformen, Hate Speech und Overlays – die Anpassung der EU-Richtlinie über audiovisuelle Mediendienste an das digitale Zeitalter.

[455] Vgl. eingehend *Cole*, The AVMSD Jurisdiction Criteria concerning Audiovisual Media Service Providers after the 2018 Reform.

[456] Hierzu: *Ukrow*, Por-No Go im audiovisuellen Binnenmarkt?.

[457] Hierzu: *Cole/Etteldorf* in: Medienhandbuch Österreich, 56, 60 f.

[458] Hierzu: *Cole*, Guiding Principles in establishing the Guidelines for Implementation of Article 13 (6) AVMSD; auch *Etteldorf* in: UFITA 2019, 498, 506 ff. in Bezug auf die Umsetzung von Förderpflichten im nationalen Recht.

[459] Hierzu: *Etteldorf*, Zwischen Fernsehen ohne Grenzen und Werbung ohne Grenzen.

[460] Hierzu: *Cole*, Die Neuregelung des Artikel 7 b Richtlinie 2010/13/EU (AVMD-RL).

Mitgliedstaaten zur Medienkompetenzförderung beizutragen. Zudem werden institutionelle und formelle Regelungen getroffen, die wiederum gewichtige Auswirkungen für das Gesamterscheinungsbild von Medienregulierung in der Zukunft haben können: es werden sog. Verhaltenskodizes (einschließlich europäischer Verhaltenskodizes) im Rahmen der insgesamt gestärkten Selbst- und Koregulierung als neue Regulierungsformen betont und es wird zu einer stärkeren Zusammenarbeit der Regulierer verpflichtet.[461]

In Bezug auf Aspekte der Vielfaltssicherung als Zielsetzung im Allgemeinen hat die Reform dabei keine wesentlichen Neuerungen gebracht. Obwohl Erwgr. 53 (im Kontext der Aufgabenerfüllung durch die nationalen Regulierungsbehörden) unter anderem von Medienpluralismus und kultureller Vielfalt als „Ziele dieser Richtlinie" spricht, wird die Umsetzung dieser Zielsetzung im Ergebnis auch von Erwgr. 61 derart bestätigt, dass diese auf Ebene der Mitgliedstaaten zu verorten ist: Diese sollen bei jeder Maßnahme gemäß der Richtlinie Meinungsfreiheit, Informationsfreiheit und Medienpluralismus sowie kulturelle und sprachliche Vielfalt im Sinne des UNESCO-Übereinkommens zum Schutz und zur Förderung der Vielfalt kultureller Ausdrucksformen[462] beachten.

In Bezug auf bestimme Regeln im Speziellen, spielt der Gedanke (auch) der Sicherung von medialer Vielfalt im Rahmen der jüngsten Reform der AVMD-Richtlinie jedoch eine größere Rolle. Teilbereiche, in deren Kontext die Sicherung von Pluralismus besonders betont wird, sind die (nun erstmals in der Form auf EU-Ebene im audiovisuellen Bereich verankerte) Pflicht zur Einrichtung unabhängiger Regulierungsstellen[463], die Möglichkeit zur Schaffung nationaler Vorschriften zur angemessenen Herausstel-

---

[461] Ein detaillierter Überblick zu den Änderungen findet sich bei *Weinand*, UFITA 2018, 260, 260 ff.; ferner *Jäger*, ZUM 62(2019)6, 477, 477 ff. Zu den institutionellen und formellen Neuregelungen vgl. eingehend *Cole/Etteldorf/Ullrich*, Cross-border Dissemination of Online Content, 101 ff., 152 ff.

[462] UNESCO, Übereinkommen über den Schutz und die Förderung der Vielfalt kultureller Ausdrucksformen, Generalkonferenz der Organisation der Vereinten Nationen für Bildung, Wissenschaft und Kultur, 3.-21.10.2005, https://www.unesco.de/sites/default/files/2018-03/2005_Schutz_und_die_F%C3%B6rderung_der_Vielfalt_kultureller_Ausdrucksformen_0.pdf.

[463] Vgl. Erwgr. 54 und 55 sowie die Ausführungen in der Ex-post REFIT Bewertung im Vorfeld der Reform, Commission staff working document SWD/2016/0170 final – 2016/0151 (COD), https://eur-lex.europa.eu/legal-content/EN/TXT/?qid=1596711526774&uri=CELEX:52016SC0170, in deren Rahmen das Vorhandensein unabhängiger regulierungsstellen auf nationaler Ebene als Voraussetzung für den Schutz der Medienvielfalt bewertet wurde.

D. *Sekundärrechtlicher Rahmen zum „Medienrecht" und Medienpluralismus*

lung von Inhalten von allgemeinem Interesse[464], Transparenzanforderungen bezüglich von Eigentümerstrukturen[465] sowie die (geänderte Verpflichtung zur) Förderung europäischer Werke, die in Abschnitt D.II.2.d. eingehend beschrieben werden.

Festzustellen bleibt allgemein und in Bezug auf die Sicherung von Medienvielfalt, dass trotz der Tatsache, dass der Anwendungs- und Harmonisierungsbereich der AVMD-Richtlinie im Laufe der Zeit ständig erweitert wurde, eine Vollharmonisierung auf dieser Ebene bei weitem noch nicht stattgefunden hat und der Ansatz der Mindestharmonisierung aus der TwF-Richtlinie in bestimmten Teilbereichen weiter fortgeführt wird. Das wird nicht nur generell und weiterhin durch den Charakter der AVMD-Richtlinie als Richtlinie[466] zum Ausdruck gebracht, sondern auch durch die explizit in Art. 4 Abs. 1 statuierte Befugnis zur Abweichung von den Vorschriften für die Mitgliedstaaten. Auch der EuGH hat erst kürzlich nochmal in seiner Vivendi-Entscheidung betont:

„[...] sowohl die Rahmenrichtlinie als auch die Richtlinie über audiovisuelle Mediendienste [harmonisieren] die nationalen Regelungen in ihren jeweiligen Bereichen nicht abschließend und [räumen] den Mitgliedstaaten für den Erlass von Entscheidungen auf nationaler Ebene ein Ermessen ein. Insbesondere bleiben die Mitgliedstaaten gemäß Art. 1 Abs. 3 der Rahmenrichtlinie unter Beachtung des Unionsrechts dafür zuständig, im Allgemeininteresse liegende Ziele insbesondere in Bezug auf die Regulierung von Inhalten und die audiovisuelle Politik zu verfolgen."[467]

c. Bedeutung von Art. 4 Abs. 1 AVMD-Richtlinie

Art. 4 Abs. 1 AVMD-Richtlinie regelt die Abweichungsbefugnis der Mitgliedstaaten, die sich auf die durch die Richtlinie koordinierten Regelungs-

---

464 Vgl. hierzu Erwgr. 25 Richtlinie (EU) 2018/1808.
465 Vgl. Erwgr. 16 Richtlinie (EU) 2018/1808.
466 Indem der Unionsgesetzgeber das Instrument der Richtlinie wählte, die nach Art. 288 Abs. 3 AEUV den innerstaatlichen Stellen die Wahl der Form und der Mittel zur Umsetzung überlässt, hat er zugleich auch der kulturpolitischen Querschnittsklausel in Art. 167 AEUV mit ihrer auch die medienpolitische Souveränität der Mitgliedstaaten schonenden Wirkung in einer auf den Rechtsaktstypus bezogenen Weise Rechnung getragen. Vgl. hierzu *Ukrow/Ress* in: Grabitz/Hilf/Nettesheim, Art. 167 AEUV, Rn. 148 ff.
467 EuGH, Rs. C-719/18, *Vivendi SA / Autorità per le Garanzie nelle Comunicazioni*, Rn. 47.

bereiche bezieht. Dies kann also auch bezüglich der harmonisierten Regelungen der AVMD-Richtlinie zu strengeren Regelungen im nationalen Recht führen, die aber dann nur auf unter eigener Rechtshoheit stehende Anbieter angewandt werden dürfen und – dem System des Herkunftslandprinzips folgend – nicht für aus dem EU-Ausland empfangene Dienste. Damit ist diese Regelung eines der Kernelemente des Gestaltungsspielraums, der den Mitgliedstaaten bei der Regulierung von audiovisuellen Mediendiensten verbleibt bzw. das Kernelement zur Bestimmung mitgliedstaatlicher Befugnisse, wenn es um Bereiche geht, die bereits von der Richtlinie (teil-)harmonisiert sind. Art. 4 Abs. 1 AVMD-Richtlinie ist allerdings nicht in den Fällen einschlägig, in denen Regelungen der Mitgliedstaaten sich zwar auf unter die Richtlinie fallende Dienste beziehen oder auswirken, nicht aber den von der AVMD-Richtlinie koordinierten Bereich betreffen, auch wenn sie grenzüberschreitende Auswirkungen[468] entfalten. Insoweit besteht ohnehin ein Handlungsspielraum für die Mitgliedstaaten.

Die Abweichungsbefugnis existierte bereits in der ursprünglichen TwF-Richtlinie. Während das Umgehungsverbot (Art. 4 Abs. 2 AVMD-RL) und das Verfahren der Inanspruchnahme von Anbietern unter anderer Rechtshoheit (Art. 4 Abs. 4 und 5 AVMD-RL) erst im Laufe der Zeit, nämlich mit den Richtlinien 1997/36/EG[469] und 2007/65/EG, etabliert und mit der Richtlinie (EU) 2018/1808 geändert wurden, hat sich Absatz 1 seit seiner Entstehung nur wenig verändert, wie sich aus der folgenden synoptischen Darstellung ersehen lässt.

89/552/EWG	97/36/EG	2007/65/EG	(EU) 2018/1808
Die Mitgliedstaaten können für Fernsehveran-	Die Mitgliedstaaten können Fernsehveran-	Die Mitgliedstaaten können **Mediendienstean-**	Die Mitgliedstaaten können Mediendienstean-

---

468 Hierzu insbesondere EuGH, C-244/10 und C-245/10, *Mesopotamia Broadcast A/S METV u. Roj TV A/S / Bundesrepublik Deutschland*, Rn. 37. Dazu ausführlich *Cole in:* R.D.T.I. 47/2012, 50, 50 ff.

469 Damit fand insbesondere bis dato bereits ständige Rechtsprechung des EuGH (etwa Rechtssachen 33/74, *Van Binsbergen / Bestuur van de Bedrijfsvereniging*, und C-23/93, *TV 10 SA / Commissariaat voor de Media*) Eingang in die Richtlinie, wonach ein Mitgliedstaat das Recht behält, gegen einen Fernsehveranstalter, der sich in einem anderen Mitgliedstaat niederlässt, dessen Tätigkeit aber ganz oder vorwiegend auf das Hoheitsgebiet des ersten Mitgliedstaats ausgerichtet ist, Maßnahmen zu ergreifen, wenn der Fernsehveranstalter sich in der Absicht niedergelassen hat, sich den Regelungen zu entziehen, die auf ihn anwendbar wären, wenn er im Gebiet des ersten Mitgliedstaats niedergelassen wäre.

stalter, die ihrer Rechtshoheit unterworfen sind, strengere oder ausführlichere Bestimmungen in den von in dieser Richtlinie erfassten Bereichen vorsehen.	stalter, die ihrer Rechtshoheit unterworfen sind, **verpflichten,** strengeren oder ausführlicheren Bestimmungen in den von dieser Richtlinie erfaßten Bereichen **nachzukommen.**	**bieter**, die ihrer Rechtshoheit unterworfen sind, verpflichten, strengeren oder ausführlicheren Bestimmungen in den von dieser Richtlinie **koordinierten** Bereichen nachzukommen, **sofern diese Vorschriften im Einklang mit dem Gemeinschaftsrecht stehen.**	bieter, die ihrer Rechtshoheit unterworfen sind, verpflichten, ausführlicheren oder strengeren Bestimmungen in den von dieser Richtlinie koordinierten Bereichen nachzukommen, sofern diese **Bestimmungen** mit dem **Unionsrecht** im Einklang stehen.

Die grundsätzliche Notwendigkeit dieser Regelung und ihr Kern in Form der Möglichkeit, überhaupt von dem harmonisierten Bereich der Richtlinie abweichende Regeln zu treffen, wurde dabei nie in Frage gestellt. So wurde zum Beispiel lediglich klargestellt, dass die von den Mitgliedstaaten erlassenen Vorschriften im Einklang mit dem Gemeinschafts- bzw. Unionsrecht stehen müssen – eine Vorgabe, die sich, wie in den vorangegangenen Abschnitten dargestellt, ohnehin bereits aus allgemeinen Grundsätzen des Unionsrechts ergibt und damit lediglich deklaratorische Wirkung hat. Im Rahmen der Auferlegung von strengeren Pflichten für audiovisuelle Mediendiensteanbieter ist dabei insbesondere an die Grundfreiheiten, Grundrechte und allgemeinen Grundsätze des Unionsrechts zu denken, namentlich die Dienstleistungsfreiheit (Art. 56 ff AEUV), die Medienfreiheit (Art. 11 GRC) und den allgemeinen Gleichbehandlungsgrundsatz.[470]

Die Definition des Ziels von „allgemeinem Interesse" ergibt sich dabei nicht aus der Richtlinie selbst. Allerdings lassen sich den Erwgr. bereits bestimmte Ziele entnehmen, die der EU-Gesetzgeber insbesondere unter diesen Begriff fasste und fasst. Hierzu zählen etwa Ziele, die an Sprachkriterien ausgerichtet sind[471] oder der Realisierung sprachpolitischer Ziele die-

---

[470] Vgl. dazu insbesondere EuGH, C-234/12, *Sky Italia srl / Autorità per le Garanzie nelle Comunicazioni*, Rn. 15 ff.
[471] Erwgr. 26 der Richtlinie 89/552/EWG.

nen⁴⁷² (die wiederum in einem inneren Zusammenhang zu kulturellen Maßnahmen stehen⁴⁷³), Verbraucherschutz, Jugendschutz und die Kulturpolitik.⁴⁷⁴ Die dortigen Aufzählungen sind aber keineswegs abschließend. Vielmehr knüpft der EU-Gesetzgeber mit Art. 4 Abs. 1 an die lange etablierte Rechtsprechung des EuGH an, die der Gerichtshof zur Definition des Allgemeininteresses über Jahrzehnte hinweg entwickelt hat.⁴⁷⁵ Entsprechend prüft auch der EuGH in seiner Rechtsprechung zu Art. 4 AVMD-Richtlinie (bzw. Art. 3 der TwF-Richtlinie)⁴⁷⁶ nicht zuerst das Vorliegen eines Ziels von allgemeinem Interesse, um die Anwendbarkeit des Art. 4 Abs. 1 AVMD-Richtlinie zu begründen, sondern verlagert diese Prüfung auf die Ebene der Prüfung der Verletzung von Unionsrecht, insbesondere von Grundfreiheiten, in deren Rahmen es ebenso um die Verfolgung von zwingenden Gründen des Allgemeininteresses geht.⁴⁷⁷ Daher kann an dieser Stelle auf die Ausführungen zur Bestimmung eines Ziels von Allgemeininteresse im Licht der Rechtfertigung von Grundrechts- und Grundfreiheitsbeschränkungen in Abschnitt C.II, C.III und C.IV.1 verwiesen werden, die insbesondere die Vielfaltssicherung als solches Ziel begreifen, was wie dort erläutert auf einen wiederum lange zurückreichenden Ansatz des EGMR zurückgeht. Daraus folgt, dass die Mitgliedstaaten unabhängig davon, ob eine Maßnahme eines Mitgliedstaats unter die von der Richtlinie erfassten Bereiche fällt, grundsätzlich zum Erlass solcher Maßnahme befugt bleiben, sofern sie dabei das Unionsrecht beachten.⁴⁷⁸

Was die Bestimmung des „von der Richtlinie koordinierten" Bereichs betrifft, für den Art. 4 Abs. 1 AVMD-Richtlinie allein gilt, während im übrigen Regelungen der Mitgliedstaaten in Bezug auf die von der Richtlinie erfassten Dienste „nur" an höherrangigem Recht wie den Grundrechten und Grundfreiheiten zu messen sind, ist ebenfalls auf die Rechtsprechung

---

472 Erwgr. 44 der Richtlinie 1997/36/EG.
473 So ausdrücklich EuGH, C-222/07, *Unión de Televisiones Comerciales Asociadas (UTECA) / Administración General del Estado*, Rn. 33.
474 Erwgr. 32 der Richtlinie 2007/65/EG.
475 So ausdrücklich unter Bezugnahme auf die Rechtsprechung zu Art. 43 und 49 EGV Erwgr. 32 der Richtlinie 2007/65/EG.
476 Insb. EuGH, C-6/98, aaO (Fn. 481); C-500/06, aaO (Fn. 481); C-222/07, aaO (Fn. 477); C-234/12, aaO (Fn. 474); C-314/14, *Sanoma Media Finland Oy – Nelonen Media gegen Viestintävirasto*.
477 Vgl. hierzu etwa EuGH, C-6/98, *Arbeitsgemeinschaft Deutscher Rundfunkanstalten (ARD) / Pro Sieben Media AG*; C-500/06, *Corporación Dermoestética SA / To Me Group Advertising Media*, Rn. 31 ff.
478 EuGH, C-222/07, aaO (Fn. 477), Rn. 19, 20; sowie C-244/10 und C-245/10, aaO (Fn. 472), Rn. 34.

D. Sekundärrechtlicher Rahmen zum „Medienrecht" und Medienpluralismus

des EuGH zu rekurrieren. In seiner *de Agostini* Entscheidung[479] hat der EuGH dabei zum einen klargestellt, dass der koordinierte Bereich allein diejenigen Dienste betreffen kann, die in den Anwendungsbereich der Richtlinie fallen (zum damaligen Zeitpunkt nur Fernsehprogramme) und zum anderen, dass die Koordinierung durch die Richtlinie auch einen bestimmten Grad erreicht haben muss, um die Reichweite des mitgliedstaatlichen Regelungsspielraums zu beeinflussen, insbesondere, eine Teilkoordinierung hierfür nicht ausreiche.[480] Dabei nahm der EuGH sogar für den Bereich der Werbung, zu dem die damalige Fassung der Richtlinie eine Reihe von Grundsätzen sowohl quantitativer als auch qualitativer Natur enthielt[481], lediglich eine solche Teilkoordinierung an. Die Entscheidung stammt aus dem Jahr 1997 und bezieht sich daher noch auf die TwF-Richtlinie in ihrer damaligen Fassung, sodass man die fortdauernde Geltung dieser Grundsätze in Frage stellen könnte. Allerdings bezog sich die Entscheidung auf den Bereich der Werbung, der damals wie heute ähnlich weitreichend geregelt ist. Außerdem nehmen auch neuere Entscheidungen, die zum Stand der Richtlinie 2010/13/EU ergangen sind, die *de Agostini*-Entscheidung und die dortigen Ausführungen zum koordinierten Bereich immer noch unter Betonung des nicht abschließenden Charakters der Richtlinie in Bezug.[482]

Darüber hinaus lässt sich im Übrigen aus der Regelung des Art. 4 Abs. 1 AVMD-Richtlinie folgender Schluss ziehen: Wenn bereits, das einzige Regelungswerk auf EU-Ebene, das den Mediensektor unmittelbar regulatorisch adressiert, den Mitgliedstaaten neben Gestaltungsspielräumen auch explizit den Erlass strengerer Bestimmungen in dem von der EU koordi-

---

[479] EuGH, C-34/95, C-35/95 und C-36/95, *Konsumentombudsmannen (KO) / De Agostini (Svenska) Förlag AB u.a.*

[480] Wie vor, Rn. 26 und 32. Dazu ausführlich die Urteilsanmerkungen von: *Novak* in: DB 1997, 2589, 2589 ff.; *Lange* in: EWS 1998, 189, 190; *Heermann* in: GRUR Int 1999, 579, 588 ff., *Stuyck* in: CML-Rev. 1997, 1445, 1466 f.

[481] Bestimmungen zur Art und Weise der Sendung, zum Einsatz bestimmter Werbetechniken und der Sendezeit, zu inhaltlichen Vorgaben (Menschenwürde, Diskriminierungen, Zigaretten und Tabakerzeugnisse, Arzneimittel und ärztliche Behandlungen, alkoholische Getränke) und zum Schutz Minderjähriger.

[482] Vgl. etwa EuGH, C-244/10 und C-245/10, *Mesopotamia Broadcast A/S METV und Roj TV A/S / Bundesrepublik Deutschland,* Rn. 32, 36 f. mit Verweis auf die Bereiche der öffentlichen Ordnung, guten Sitten und der öffentlichen Sicherheit; C-622/17, *Baltic Media Alliance Ltd / Lietuvos radijo ir televizijos komisija,* Rn. 73 f. allerdings vor dem Hintergrund von Art. 3 Abs. 1 AVMD-Richtlinie unter Berufung auf die Verfolgung von im Allgemeininteresse liegenden Zielen.

nierten Bereich für inländische Anbieter[483] erlaubt, insbesondere im kulturpolitischen Bereich der Sicherung von Medienvielfalt, so dürfen entsprechende Möglichkeiten auch in Bezug auf andere (koordinierte) Sektoren nicht prinzipiell versperrt werden, auf die sich vielfaltssichernde Maßnahmen auswirken. Insbesondere kann die durch Art. 4 Abs. 1 AVMD-Richtlinie vor dem Hintergrund kulturpolitischer und verfassungstradierter Erwägungen in den verschiedenen Mitgliedstaaten bewusst geschaffene Abweichungsbefugnis nicht durch andere sektorale Bestimmungen auf EU-Sekundärrechtsebene vollständig ausgehebelt werden. Das gilt insbesondere vor dem Hintergrund, dass die Inanspruchnahme der Abweichungsbefugnis durch den Erlass strengerer Regeln oftmals aus wettbewerbspolitischen und -rechtlichen Erwägungen heraus wenig attraktiv ist: Zum einen gilt es für die einzelnen Mitgliedstaaten aus wirtschaftlichen (Steuereinnahmen) und auch kulturpolitischen Interessen (vielfältige Medienlandschaft), ihre Attraktivität als Stand- bzw. Niederlassungsort für Medienunternehmen nicht zu verlieren oder zu verringern, und zum anderen, die inländischen Medienunternehmen nicht in ihrer Wettbewerbsfähigkeit im Konkurrenzverhältnis zu ausländischen Unternehmen zu beeinträchtigen.[484] Erst recht darf daher, wenn die Zielsetzung von Art. 4 Abs. 1 AVMD-Richtlinie, den Mitgliedstaaten die Möglichkeit zu geben, in bestimmten Bereichen ihre eigenen Rahmenbedingungen für die Medienpolitik zu schaffen, nicht mehr oder weniger sinnvoll erreicht werden kann, diese Zielsetzung nicht noch weiter dadurch behindert oder (noch) weiter eingeschränkt werden, dass in anderen Bereichen eine Harmonisierung stattfindet, die den Mediensektor regelmäßig nur reflexhaft betrifft.

---

483 *Liesching* (Das Herkunftslandprinzip nach E-Commerce- und AVMD-Richtlinie, S. 40) kommt in Bezug auf den Erlass von nationalen Bestimmungen auch für ausländische Anbieter in Bezug auf die allgemeine medienrechtliche Regulierung (außerhalb speziell vielfaltssichernder Regulierungsziele) zu dem Ergebnis, dass das Sendestaatprinzip nach Art. 3 AVMD-RL im koordinierten Bereich grundsätzlich keine nationalstaatlichen abstrakt-generellen Regelungen in Bezug auf Anbieter audiovisueller Mediendienste mit Niederlassung in einem anderen Mitgliedstaat erlaubt, soweit diese Regelungen in ihrer Anwendung Behinderungen der Weiterverbreitung ihrer Dienste bedeuten. Dies gilt dann nicht, wenn die Vorschriften zu einem anderen als den durch die Richtlinie harmonisierten Bereichen und Zielen dienen. Dazu zählen Maßnahmen zum Schutz des Medienpluralismus, die im Fokus der vorliegenden Studie stehen.
484 Vgl dazu etwa *Harrison/Woods*, Jurisdiction, forum shopping and the 'race to the bottom', 173, 174 ff.; *Vlassis* in: Politique européenne 2017/2, 102, 102 ff.

D. *Sekundärrechtlicher Rahmen zum „Medienrecht" und Medienpluralismus*

d. Einzelne Bestimmungen

Obwohl, wie zuvor eingehend dargestellt, die AVMD-Richtlinie nach wie vor nicht auf die Schaffung von Regeln mit kulturpolitischen Bezügen abzielt, sondern das Ermöglichen eines freien Verkehrs der Dienstleistung 'audiovisuelle Mediendienste' im europäischen Binnenmarkt sowie den Abbau von diesbezüglichen Hindernissen zum Gegenstand hat, finden sich Anknüpfungspunkte für die Vielfaltssicherung auch durch die Mitgliedstaaten, indem entweder aktiv bestimmte Medieninhalte durch diese bzw. deren Regulierungsrahmen gefördert werden sollen oder restriktiv auf bestimmte (auch im Lichte des Pluralismus) negative Entwicklungen oder Gefahren reagiert werden soll. Nachfolgend soll daher auf diejenigen Regeln eingegangen werden, die solche Bezüge zur medialen Vielfaltssicherung besitzen, um aus deren Ausgestaltung im Sinne einer Kompetenzwahrnehmung später Schlussfolgerungen für die Kompetenzbegrenzung zwischen Union und Mitgliedstaaten zu ziehen.

(1) Förderung europäischer Werke

Bereits unter Geltung der TwF-Richtlinie wurden Fernsehveranstalter verpflichtet, den Hauptanteil ihrer Sendezeit, die nicht aus Nachrichten, Sportberichten, Spielshows oder Werbe- und Teletextleistungen bestand, der Sendung von europäischen Werken vorzubehalten. 10 % der Sendezeit oder alternativ nach Wahl des Mitgliedsstaats 10 % der Haushaltsmittel sollten europäischen Werken von unabhängigen Produzenten vorbehalten bleiben. Über die Einhaltung dieser Quotenvorgabe müssen die Veranstalter Bericht erstatten. Die Vorschriften gelten – damals wie auch in der heutigen Ausprägung – jedoch nicht für Fernsehsendungen, die sich an ein lokales Publikum richten und die nicht an ein nationales Fernsehnetz angeschlossen sind, wodurch diese Anbieter insoweit durch eine Entpflichtung von Sende- und Berichtsauflagen privilegiert werden.[485] Zwar sind die Quotenregelungen sowohl aus kompetenzrechtlicher Perspektive als auch vor dem Hintergrund der unternehmerischen Freiheit von Medienanbietern und ihrer Ausgestaltung nicht nur im Urteil des BVerfG zur TwF-Richtlinie (dort zumindest im Zusammenhang mit der bundesseitigen Beachtung von Länderrechten im Rechtsetzungsverfahren im Rat als Aus-

---

[485] Eingehend auf die Ausnahme für lokale Anbieter: *Ukrow/Cole*, Förderung lokaler und regionaler Medienvielfalt, S. 91 ff.

druck der Pflicht zu länderfreundlichem Verhalten),[486] sondern auch im Schrifttum kritisch bewertet worden.[487] Ungeachtet der weder durch den EuGH noch durch das BVerfG bislang abschließend geklärten bzw. diskutierten Frage, ob der dienstleistungsbezogene Kompetenztitel der EU eine hinreichende Rechtsgrundlage für audiovisuelle Quotenregelungen schafft, stellen sich diese Quoten allerdings im Ergebnis als wichtiges Mittel zur Förderung kultureller Aspekte dar und sind von der Kommission in ihren regelmäßigen Berichten an das Europäische Parlament und den Rat basierend auf den Informationen aus den Mitgliedstaaten zumindest bezogen auf die Regelungen in der AVMD-Richtlinie und den jeweiligen nationalen Umsetzungen als sehr erfolgreich beschrieben worden.[488] Als mittelbare Adressaten einer verbindlichen europäischen Quotenregelung sind Medienanbieter dadurch zunächst belastet, sodass daraus abgeleitet werden könnte, das Hauptziel könne nicht die Sicherung von Medienvielfalt sein. Jedoch profitiert nicht nur die Filmproduktionslandschaft von der Quotenverpflichtung ebenso wie die aus Sicht der Zuschauer höhere Angebotsvielfalt. Vielmehr dient der damit verbundene Effekt einer Förderung auch der Produktion von nationalen Werken und europäischen Koproduktionen zu der auch für die Medienanbieter vorteilhaften Situation, dass ein größeres Angebot an Programmmaterial auf dem Markt zur Verfügung steht, von dem diese (für die Anbieter linearer und non-linearer Dienste gegebenenfalls auch wechselseitig[489]) profitieren können.

---

486 Vgl. BVerfGE 92, 203 (238 ff.). Vgl. hierzu *Bethge*, Deutsche Bundesstaatlichkeit und Europäische Union. Bemerkungen über die Entscheidung des Bundesverfassungsgerichts zur EG-Fernsehrichtlinie, S. 55 ff.; *Holtz-Bacha*, Medienpolitik für Europa, S. 127 ff.; *Deringer* in: ZUM 1995, 316, 316 ff.; *Gerkrath* in: RTDE 1995, 539, 539 ff.; *Kresse/Heinze* in: ZUM 1995, 394, 394 ff.; *Martín y Pérez de Nanclares* in: Revista de Instituciones Europeas 1995, 887, 887 ff.; *Müller-Terpitz*, Ein Karlsruher "Orakel" zum Bundesstaat im europäischen Staatenverbund, S. 568 ff.; *Trautwein* in: ZUM 1995, 614, 614 ff.; *Winkelmann* in: DöV 1996, 1, 1 ff.
487 Vgl. für den Bereich des Fernsehens: *Broughton Micova*, Content quotas: what and whom are the protecting; *Middleton* in: Denver Journal of International Law and Policy 31/2020, 607, 614 ff.
488 Vgl. etwa Bericht der Kommission an das Europäische Parlament, den Rat, den Europäischen Wirtschafts- und Sozialausschuss und den Ausschuss der Regionen, Erster Bericht über die Anwendung der Artikel 13, 16 und 17 der Richtlinie 2010/13/EU für den Zeitraum 2009–2010 Förderung europäischer Werke in nach Sendeplan und auf Abruf in der EU bereitgestellten audiovisuellen Mediendiensten, COM/2012/0522 final.
489 Vgl. etwa jüngst die Sicherung der US-Ausstrahlungsrechte für die unter anderem von der ARD mitproduzierte Serie „Babylon Berlin" durch Netflix. Vgl. hierzu im Übrigen auch *Etteldorf* in: UFITA 2019, 498, 506 ff.

D. Sekundärrechtlicher Rahmen zum „Medienrecht" und Medienpluralismus

Wie eingangs bei der historischen Betrachtung erwähnt, lag der Schwerpunkt der Einführung dieser Regel aber nicht in der Etablierung kulturpolitischer Vorgaben, sondern war vordergründig durch Gesichtspunkte wirtschaftlicher Natur begründet, was insbesondere auch Folge der mangelnden kompetenziellen Rechtsgrundlage für eine kulturpolitische Schwerpunktsetzung auf Unionsebene war (und weiterhin ist). Es sollten auf europäischer Ebene – durch eine schrittweise Herangehensweise – attraktive Märkte für Fernsehproduktionen begünstigt werden, sofern dies die Umgebungsbedingungen[490] in den jeweiligen Mitgliedstaaten erlauben. Diese schrittweise Einführung von Regeln, die allerdings die Wahl der angemessenen Mittel den Mitgliedstaaten überlassen sollte, insbesondere keine konkreten und streng vorgebenden Regelungen enthielt, dokumentiert dabei den – zumindest im Vergleich zu ursprünglichen Regelungsüberlegungen[491] – zurückhaltenden Ansatz. In der Reform 1997, die die einzelstaatlichen Rechtsvorschriften zur Förderung europäischer Werke weiter harmonisierte, wurde diese wirtschaftliche Schwerpunktsetzung beibehalten – Stärkung und verbesserte Wettbewerbsfähigkeit der Programmindustrie in Europa (Erwgr. 26, 28 Richtlinie 1997/36/EG).

Mit der Reform 2007, deren wesentlichste Neuerung die Aufnahme von non-linearen audiovisuellen Mediendiensten in den Anwendungsbereich der Richtlinie war, änderte sich auch teilweise die Herangehensweise in Bezug auf die Förderung europäischer Werke. Obwohl die Angleichung des Rechtsrahmens zwischen linearen und non-linearen Diensten für manche Regelungsbereiche auf der Erwägung basierte, dass wegen der Fernsehähnlichkeit dieser Dienste und einem ähnlichen Publikums- und Werbemarkt auch gleiche Wettbewerbsbedingungen gelten müssten (Erwgr. 7), und daher auch die ursprünglichen (im Schwerpunkt wirtschaftlichen) Bestrebungen zur Einführung bestehender Regeln fortgelten müssten, wurde die Einführung von Förderpflichten für europäische Werke von audiovisuellen Mediendienste auf Abruf (auch) mit der Erwägung begründet, dass diese Anbieter „im Rahmen des praktisch Durchführbaren die Produktion und Verbreitung europäischer Werke vorantreiben und damit einen aktiven Beitrag zur Förderung der kulturellen Vielfalt leisten"[492] sollen. Die konkrete Umsetzung dieser Zielsetzung wurde jedoch wie bei der Ursprungsvorschrift für lineare Anbieter im Wesentlichen den Mitgliedstaa-

---

490 So waren bereits damals Ausnahmen für Mitgliedstaaten vorgesehen, insbesondere abstellen auf Mitgliedstaaten mit niedriger Produktionskapazität oder begrenztem Sprachraum, vgl. Erwgr. 22.
491 Vgl. hierzu BVerfGE 92, 203 (243 f.).
492 Erwgr. 48 Richtlinie 2007/65/EG.

595

ten überlassen („sorgen im Rahmen des praktisch Durchführbaren und mit angemessenen Mitteln dafür"). Anders als die Quotenvorgabe bei den linearen Diensten („Hauptanteil der Sendezeit") war die Bestimmung hinsichtlich nicht-linearer Dienste offener gehalten, wobei die Richtlinie beispielhaft mögliche Vorgaben zur Erreichung dieser Förderung durch solche Anbieter aufzählte (Auferlegung von finanziellen Beitragspflichten oder Herausstellungspflichten).[493] Die auf dieser Basis erlassenen Regelungen in den einzelnen Mitgliedstaaten, sofern überhaupt vorhanden, sind daher sehr diffizil und unterscheiden regelmäßig zwischen Modellen von Quoten, Hervorhebung, Investitionspflichten und Indikatoren.[494]

Mit der letzten Änderungsrichtlinie 2018 wurden die Vorschriften für lineare und non-lineare Anbieter weiter angeglichen. Demnach trifft nun auch die Anbieter audiovisueller Mediendienste auf Abruf eine feste Quotenverpflichtung bereits aus den Vorschriften auf EU-Ebene (Art. 13 AVMD-Richtlinie). Im Gegensatz zu Fernsehveranstaltern (50 % – da „Hauptteil der Sendezeit") beträgt diese allerdings lediglich mindestens 30 % an europäischen Werken, die diese Anbieter in ihren Katalogen bereitstellen müssen. Zusätzlich sollen die Anbieter europäische Werke in ihren Katalogen angemessen herausstellen. Diese Verpflichtung – ebenso wie weitere finanzielle Beitragsverpflichtungen, die Mitgliedstaaten linearen wie nicht-linearen Diensteanbieter auferlegen können – gilt jedoch nicht für Mediendiensteanbieter mit geringen Umsätzen oder geringen Zuschauerzahlen. Auch können die Mitgliedstaaten von der Anwendung der Regel auf Anbieter bezüglich bestimmter Angebote absehen, wenn dies wegen der Art oder des Themas der audiovisuellen Mediendienste undurchführbar oder ungerechtfertigt wäre. Im Übrigen haben die Länder bei der Beratung dieser Richtlinie mittels einer entsprechenden Stellungnahme des Bundesrates daran festgehalten, dass über die Ausgestaltung der Förderung europäischer Werke allein die Mitgliedstaaten entscheiden.[495]

Für die konkrete Berechnung des Anteils europäischer Werke und für die Definition einer geringen Zuschauerzahl und eines geringen Umsatzes soll die Kommission nach Art. 13 Abs. 7 AVMD-Richtlinie Leitlinien her-

---

493 Zu damaligen Umsetzungsprozessen insgesamt: *Apa u.a.* in: Nikoltchev (Hrsg.), Videoabrufdienste und die Förderung europäischer Werke.
494 Vgl. hierzu umfassend *EAI*, Mapping of national rules for the promotion of European works in Europe; sowie *VVA* u.a., study on the Promotion of European Works in Audiovisual Media Services, SMART 2016/0061.
495 Vgl. https://www.bundesrat.de/SharedDocs/drucksachen/2016/0201-0300/288-2-16.pdf?__blob=publicationFile&v=5, Ziff. 20.

D. Sekundärrechtlicher Rahmen zum „Medienrecht" und Medienpluralismus

ausgeben.[496] Damit wird eine Praxis kodifiziert, wonach die Kommission bereits in der Vergangenheit durch die Zurverfügungstellung entsprechender Hinweise im Rahmen des Kontaktausschusses Vorgaben machen wollte, um eine weitgehend einheitliche Herangehensweise in den Mitgliedstaaten bei der Berechnung der Quoten zu erreichen.[497] Diese Leitlinien hat die Kommission im Juli 2020 veröffentlicht.[498] Die Leitlinien sind dabei zwar nicht rechtsverbindlich für die Mitgliedstaaten und stehen insoweit auch mitgliedstaatlichen Sonderregeln nicht entgegen, soweit diese dem Unionsrecht entsprechen. Allerdings sind sie Ausdruck der Interpretation der Vorgaben der AVMD-Richtlinie durch die Kommission und können – und es steht zu erwarten: werden auch – daher von ihr für künftige Bewertungsprozesse der mitgliedstaatlichen Umsetzung herangezogen.[499] Auch aufgrund dieser Wirkung wäre im Idealfalle davon auszugehen gewesen, dass die Leitlinien der Kommission bereits zu einem Zeitpunkt vorliegen, bei dem die Mitgliedstaaten diese in der Umsetzung noch berücksichtigen können. Dies gilt noch mehr für weitere Leitlinien, die die Kommission zur Festlegung des Kriteriums „wesentliche Funktion" für die Definition von Video-Sharing-Plattformen erlassen konnte und auch parallel im Juli 2020 veröffentlich hat (dazu unter Abschnitt D.II.2.d(5)). Da die Leitlinien bezüglich der Förderungsverpflichtung ebenfalls erst knapp vor dem Ende des Umsetzungszeitraums bekanntgegeben wurden, wird zu beobachten sein, welche Mitgliedstaaten diese überhaupt näher

---

496 Vgl. hierzu ausführlich *Cole*, Guiding Principles in establishing the Guidelines for Implementation of Article 13 (6) AVMSD.
497 Vgl. *Cole*, wie vor, m.w.N.; vgl. auch Bericht der Kommission an das Europäische Parlament, den Rat den Europäischen Wirtschafts- und Sozialausschuss und den Ausschuss der Regionen, Erster Bericht über die Anwendung der Artikel 13, 16 und 17 der Richtlinie 2010/13/EU für den Zeitraum 2009–2010 Förderung europäischer Werke in nach Sendeplan und auf Abruf in der EU bereitgestellten audiovisuellen Mediendiensten, COM/2012/0522 final, https://eur-lex.europa.eu/legal-content/DE/TXT/?uri=celex%3A52012DC0522. /.
498 Mitteilung der Kommission, Leitlinien gemäß Artikel 13 Absatz 7 der Richtlinie über audiovisuelle Mediendienste für die Berechnung des Anteils europäischer Werke an Abrufkatalogen und für die Definition einer geringen Zuschauerzahl und eines geringen Umsatzes, EU ABl. C 223, 7.7.2020, p. 10–16, https://eur-lex.europa.eu/legal-content/DE/TXT/?uri=uriserv:OJ.C_.2020.223.01.0010.01.ENG&toc=OJ:C:2020:223:TOC.
499 Vgl. hierzu Europäische Kommission – Questions and answers, Guidelines on the revised Audiovisual Media Services Directive, 2.7.2020, abrufbar unter https://ec.europa.eu/commission/presscorner/detail/en/QANDA_20_1208; Eingehend auch *Cole*, Guiding Principles in establishing the Guidelines for Implementation of Article 13 (6) AVMSD.

bei der Erarbeitung der gesetzlichen Grundlage berücksichtigt haben bzw. wie die Kommission dann damit umgeht, wenn die Leitlinien nicht zumindest in der Anwendungspraxis durch die Aufsichtsbehörden einbezogen werden. Der Ansatz im Medienstaatsvertrag, die Landesmedienanstalten in § 77 Satz 3 zu ermächtigen, Einzelheiten zur Durchführung der Quotenregelungen für Anbieter fernsehähnlicher Telemedien durch eine gemeinsame Satzung zu regeln, stellt insoweit eine europarechtlich nicht nur unbedenkliche, sondern willkommene Form dar, die Leitlinien in die Umsetzungs-Rechtsetzung einzubinden.

Neben der Quoten-Verpflichtung selbst besteht eine umfassende Evaluationspflicht zur Durchführung der unterschiedlichen in Art. 13 AVMD-Richtlinie vorgesehenen Fördermaßnahmen. Dazu müssen zunächst die Mitgliedstaaten der Kommission von der Anwendung der nationalen Vorschriften berichten, diese wiederum muss daraus und aus einer unabhängigen Evaluation über die Anwendung dieser Vorgaben durch die Mitgliedstaaten dem Europäischen Parlament und dem Rat berichten. Dabei soll sie der Marktlage und den technischen Entwicklungen sowie „dem Ziel der kulturellen Vielfalt" Rechnung tragen soll (Art. 13 Abs. 5 AVMD-Richtlinie). Durch diese Formulierung wird einerseits deutlich, dass unabhängig von der – auch aufgrund der ansonsten fraglichen Rechtsgrundlage – Betonung der wirtschaftlichen Zielsetzung bei Einführung der Förderungsverpflichtung, im Hintergrund immer schon das Ziel stand (europäische, d.h. der Mitgliedstaaten eigene) kulturelle Vielfalt sichern zu helfen. Dabei unterstreicht Art. 13 Abs. 5 AVMD-Richtlinie lediglich, dass dem Gesichtspunkt, inwiefern die Vorschrift und die auf dieser Basis ergriffenen Maßnahmen zur kulturellen Vielfalt und ihrer Sicherung (durch die Garantie der Produktion und des Vertriebs durch Ausstrahlung) beitragen, besondere Aufmerksamkeit zuzuwenden ist. Weder durch die Richtlinie noch durch die eher technisch orientierten Leitlinien, die sich auf Berechnungsparameter für den Kataloganteil von 30 % bzw. die von den Förderverpflichtungen auszunehmenden Dienste beziehen, wird die Ausgestaltungshoheit der Mitgliedstaaten für den kulturpolitischen Aspekt der Regelung in Frage gestellt. Insgesamt bewegt sich die Unionsvorschrift damit im kompetenzrechtlichen Rahmen und ist insbesondere von Art. 167 AEUV gedeckt, da es um die Unterstützung (Entfaltung) der Kulturen in der Union geht, die die Kulturpolitik der Mitgliedstaaten nicht beeinträchtigt und ihren Grund auch in der Wettbewerbsfähigkeit des europäischen audiovisuellen Marktes findet.[500]

---

500 So bereits *Harrison/Woods*, Television Quotas: protecting European Culture?.

D. Sekundärrechtlicher Rahmen zum „Medienrecht" und Medienpluralismus

Diese nur ergänzende Unterstützungsdimension wird auch deutlich in der Formulierung der Leitlinien durch die Kommission. Danach gehe es darum, „einen guten Ausgleich zu finden zwischen dem Ziel, kleineren Akteuren im audiovisuellen Bereich den notwendigen Innovationsspielraum zu erhalten, und dem Ziel, durch die angemessene Finanzierung europäischer Werke *im Rahmen der Kulturpolitik der Mitgliedstaaten* die kulturelle Vielfalt zu fördern".[501] Dennoch ist auch zukünftig darauf zu achten, dass nicht durch nur vage oder eng begrenzte Ermächtigungen zur näheren Ausgestaltung durch (nochmals: rechtlich nicht verbindliche) Leitlinien, die Kommission die Zuständigkeitsreserve der Mitgliedstaaten auch bei der Umsetzung von Richtlinien beschneiden kann. Tatsächlich – und im Zweifelsfall auch sinnvoller Weise – werden solche Leitlinien für Teilbereiche unabhängig von ihrer rechtlichen Unverbindlichkeit harmonisierend wirken, weil de facto Mitgliedstaaten nur bei einem aus ihrer Sicht notwendigen und begründbaren Abweichungsbedarf die Leitlinien unberücksichtigt lassen werden.

Ein weiterer Gestaltungsspielraum auf nationaler Ebene liegt bereits in der (auf EU-Ebene vorgegebenen) weiten Definition der europäischen Werke, worunter gemäß Art. 1 Abs. 1 Buchst. n) AVMD-RL Werke aus den Mitgliedstaaten und aus europäischen Drittländern[502], die Vertragsparteien des Europäischen Übereinkommens über grenzüberschreitendes Fernsehen des Europarates sind, sowie Werke, die im Rahmen der zwischen der Union und Drittländern im audiovisuellen Bereich geschlossenen Ab-

---

501 Leitlinien der Kommission, aaO (Fn. 502), Punkt III.1.
502 Insbesondere sind Absicherungen für die EWR-Staaten erforderlich, wenn sie von solchen Regeln profitieren wollen. Zu den Auswirkungen des Brexit auch in diesem Zusammenhang vgl. *Cole/Etteldorf/Ukrow*, Audiovisual Sector and Brexit: the Regulatory Environment. Als Unterzeichner des Abkommens über das grenzüberschreitende Fernsehen, zählen Produktionen aus dem Vereinigten Königreich zwar weiterhin als europäische Werke, eine Berichtspflicht gegenüber der Kommission wird aber entfallen. Die Regierung hatte nach einem Konsultationsverfahren angekündigt, die bestehenden Quotenregeln im britischen Recht überprüfen zu wollen, und sich (vorläufig) gegen die Einführung einer Abgabepflicht ausgesprochen. Vgl. hierzu Department for Digital, Culture, Media & Sport, Consultation outcome Audiovisual Media Services, Government response to public consultations on the government's implementation proposals, 30.5.2019, https://www.gov.uk/government/consultations/audiovisual-media-services/outcome/audiovisual-media-services-government-response-to-public-consultations-on-the-governments-implementation-proposals.

kommen in Koproduktion hergestellt werden⁵⁰³ und die den in den einzelnen Abkommen jeweils festgelegten Voraussetzungen entsprechen, zu verstehen sind. Dieses weite Begriffsverständnis erkennt die Möglichkeit der Mitgliedstaaten an, diese Definition unter Einhaltung des Unionsrechts und unter Berücksichtigung der Ziele der AVMD-Richtlinie für Mediendiensteanbieter, die ihrer Rechtshoheit unterworfen sind, zu präzisieren.⁵⁰⁴ Letzteres bedeutet insbesondere, dass die Mitgliedstaaten für nationale Anbieter eigene kulturelle Gesichtspunkte in diese Art der Förderung einfließen lassen können, insbesondere auf nationale Besonderheiten reagieren können, wenn sie den Begriff konkretisieren. So sind beispielsweise in Frankreich – einem Mitgliedstaat, der nicht nur über eine starke Filmwirtschaft verfügt, sondern in dessen Tradition der französische Film eine besondere Rolle spielt – Mediendiensteanbieter verpflichtet, einen Großteil ihrer Sende- und Bereitstellungspflichten mit französischsprachigen Werken zu bedienen, während in den Niederlanden das niederländisch- oder friesischsprachige Programm durch Quoten des öffentlich-rechtlichen Rundfunks geprägt wird.⁵⁰⁵

Entsprechend steht es den Mitgliedstaaten auch frei, etwa aus der Zielsetzung der Vielfaltssicherung heraus, Mediendiensteanbietern, die ihrer Rechtshoheit unterliegen, Investitionspflichten aufzuerlegen. Dies galt schon unter der Vorgängerregulierung, da es den Mitgliedstaaten vorbehalten blieb, wie die Förderverpflichtung im Einzelnen ausgestaltet wird.⁵⁰⁶ Durch die explizite Aufnahme in der AVMD-Richtlinie ist seit

---

503 Vgl. etwa das Übereinkommen des Europarats über die Gemeinschaftsproduktion von Kinofilmen (von 1992, 2017 überarbeitet), das einen umfassenden Rechtsrahmen und Standards für multilaterale Koproduktionen und bilaterale Koproduktionen zwischen Parteien bietet, die keinen bilateralen Vertrag geschlossen haben.
504 Vgl. Erwägungsgrund 32 der Richtlinie 2010/13/EU.
505 Hierzu rechtsvergleichend *Etteldorf*, UFITA 2019, 498, 507 f.
506 Vgl. hierzu etwa die deutsche Regelung im Filmfördergesetz (§ 152 FFG), die – bzw. deren Genehmigung durch die Europäische Kommission – sowohl von *Apple* als auch von *Netflix* vor dem Gericht der Europäischen Union (EuG) angegriffen wurde, da sie, so die Auffassung der klagenden Unternehmen, nicht mit dem in der AVMD-Richtlinie verankerten Herkunftslandprinzip und der Dienstleistungs- und Niederlassungsfreiheit sowie dem Diskriminierungsverbot vereinbar sei, da sie auch nicht in Deutschland ansässigen Unternehmen eine Abgabepflicht abhängig von in Deutschland erzielten Gewinnen auferlegt. Beide Klage von Apple (T-101/17, *Apple Distribution International / Europäische Kommission*) und Netflix (T-818/16, *Netflix International BV und Netflix, Inc. / Europäische Kommission*) wurden vom EuG bereits aufgrund eines mangelnden Beweises der "individuellen Betroffenheit" durch die klagenden Unternehmen als unzulässig ab-

2018 auch klargestellt, dass die Auferlegung solcher Investitions- oder Abgabeverpflichtungen auch gegenüber Anbietern möglich ist, die mit ihren Angeboten auf Zuschauer in einem Mitgliedsstaatgebiet abzielen, aber nicht unter dessen Rechtshoheit stehen, sondern in einem anderen Mitgliedstaat niedergelassen sind. Art. 13 Abs. 2 AVMD-Richtlinie verlangt insoweit lediglich, dass die entsprechenden Regeln verhältnismäßig und diskriminierungsfrei sind.

(2) Herausstellung von Inhalten im Allgemeininteresse

7 a AVMD-Richtlinie, der 2018 neu eingefügt wurde, greift ebenfalls Aspekte der Vielfaltssicherung, aber auf Basis eines anderen Ansatzes auf. Hiernach erfolgt eine Klarstellung, dass die Richtlinie die Möglichkeit der Mitgliedstaaten unberührt lässt, Diensteanbietern Verpflichtungen zur Gewährleistung der angemessenen Herausstellung von Inhalten aufzuerlegen, die nach festgelegten Zielen des Allgemeininteresses notwendig und verhältnismäßig sind. Dabei geht es also nicht um das Vorhandensein vielfältiger Inhalte wie im Rahmen der soeben dargestellten Quotenregelungen für europäische Werke oder um die Empfangsmöglichkeit von bestimmten Inhalte von Allgemeininteresse wie im Rahmen der noch darzustellenden Übertragungspflichten (must carry) aus dem Telekommunikationsrecht[507], sondern um die Sichtbarkeit derjenigen Inhalte, die für die Gesellschaft einen besonderen Wert haben. Im Vordergrund steht dabei also die Rezipientenperspektive, anders formuliert die dem Nutzer präsentierte Informationsqualität und -vielfalt.

Vor dem Hintergrund der Bedeutung von Informationsqualität und -vielfalt auch für den Prozess der freien demokratischen Willensbildung stehen diese allerdings auch in unmittelbarem Zusammenhang mit der Medienvielfalt bzw. der Vielfalt vorhandener Quellen, aus denen sich der Nutzer informieren kann. Eine plurale Medienlandschaft kann dort ihre

---

gewiesen. Unter anderem hätten die Unternehmen es versäumt darzulegen, dass ihre Dienste durch die Änderungen im FFG wesentlich beeinträchtigt worden und individuell betroffen seien. Dies hätte beispielsweise durch die Einreichung von nationalen Abgabebescheiden oder ähnlichem geschehen können. Eine unmittelbare Klage vor dem Gericht erfordere einen Rechtsakt mit Verordnungscharakter ohne weitere notwendige Durchführungsmaßnahmen, der hier nicht vorliege. Die zunächst von Apple hieraufhin eingerichtete Beschwerde beim EuGH (Rs. C-633/18 P) wurde in der Folge zurückgenommen.

507 Vgl. hierzu Abschnitt D.II.5.

Demokratiefunktion nicht erfüllen, wo die Inhalte überhaupt nicht wahrgenommen werden – eine Gefahr, die vor allem auf nutzerseitig (auch) zu Informationszwecken genutzten Plattformen, die Fremdinhalte gesammelt zur Verfügung stellen und daher als Gatekeeper für Medieninhalte fungieren, besteht und in Zusammenhang mit potentiell gefährdungssteigernden Phänomene wie Desinformation[508] – besonders illustrativ ist dies vor dem Hintergrund der Pandemie Covid19 geworden[509] – und Filterblasen und Echokammern[510] steht. Die Auswirkungen letzterer beider Phänomene, sofern sie algorithmisch gesteuert sind[511], auf den Informations-, Meinungs-, und Medienpluralismus werden gerade in jüngerer Zeit viel diskutiert.[512] Wenngleich eine Verbindung zwischen algorithmengesteuerter Personalisierung von Inhalten und dem Entstehen von Filterblasen oder Echokammern sowie deren Auswirkungen auf den Meinungspluralismus noch nicht abschließend empirisch untersucht und/oder belegt sind, insbesondere jüngere Untersuchungen die tatsächlichen Negativeffekte in der Praxis auf großen Plattformen relativieren, lassen sich Gefährdungspotentiale nicht von der Hand weisen.[513] Die algorithmische Steuerung und Personalisierung von Inhalten kann dazu führen, dass einerseits „sachfremde"

---

508 Der Zusammenhang zwischen Medienvielfalt einerseits und Desinformation andererseits ist noch nicht abschließend wissenschaftlich untersucht. Das Vorliegen eines Gefährdungspotentials bei fehlendem Pluralismus liegt aber nahe, da in diesen Fällen ein starker und lebhafter öffentlicher Diskurs fehlen könnte, der Desinformation mit rationaler Argumentation und gegensätzlichen Ansichten konfrontiert. Vgl. hierzu *Bayer* in: Was ist Desinformation?, S. 46.
509 Vgl. beispielhaft Gemeinsame Mitteilung der Kommission und des Hohen Vertreters, Bekämpfung von Desinformation im Zusammenhang mit COVID-19 – Fakten statt Fiktion, 10.6.2020, JOIN(2020) 8 final, https://eur-lex.europa.eu/legal-content/DE/TXT/HTML/?uri=CELEX:52020JC0008.
510 Zur begrifflichen und tatsächlichen Unterscheidung der beiden Phänomene vgl. *Stark/Magin/Jürgens*, Maßlos überschätzt. Ein Überblick über theoretische Annahmen und empirische Befunde zu Filterblasen und Echokammern (Preprint), m.w.N.
511 Hiervon zu unterscheiden ist die nutzergesteuerte Personalisierung von Inhalten (durch das gezielte Auswählen, Liken, Folgen oder Angeben von Interessen), die zwar auch dazu führen kann, dass sich Nutzer in einen „Informationskokon" (Vgl. hierzu bereits *Sunstein*, Infotopia: How Many Minds Produce Knowledge) einhüllen, die allerdings durch willensgesteuertes Handeln gerade Ausdruck demokratiebasierter Meinungs- und Informationsfreiheit ist und damit gleichermaßen Chance für den Pluralismus sein kann.
512 Vgl. hierzu auch *Cole/Etteldorf* in: Cappello (Hrsg.), Media pluralism and competition issues (erscheint in Kürze).
513 Vgl. für einen Überblick und eine Analyse des bisherigen Forschungsstandes statt vieler etwa *Stark/Magin/Jürgens*, Maßlos überschätzt. Ein Überblick über

D. Sekundärrechtlicher Rahmen zum „Medienrecht" und Medienpluralismus

Erwägungen in Form von wirtschaftlichen Interessen der Anbieter für die Auswahl der anzuzeigenden Inhalte relevant sind und diese Auswahlkriterien für die Nutzer häufig nicht oder nicht ausreichend transparent und steuerbar sind, diese also nicht wissen, warum sie was sehen und, vor allem, was sie nicht sehen. Andererseits birgt diese Art von Steuerung auch die Gefahr, dass Medien ihre Inhalte an dem Diktat der Algorithmen ausrichten, um (auch aus Refinanzierungsgründen) gesehen zu werden, also nicht mehr qualitativ hochwertige, plurale Inhalte von Allgemeininteresse im Vordergrund stehen.[514] Das BVerfG hat das etwa in einem anderen Urteils-Zusammenhang so formuliert, dass „[s]olche Angebote nicht auf Meinungsvielfalt gerichtet [sind], sondern durch einseitige Interessen oder die wirtschaftliche Rationalität eines Geschäftsmodells bestimmt [werden], nämlich die Verweildauer der Nutzer auf den Seiten möglichst zu maximieren und dadurch den Werbewert der Plattform für die Kunden zu erhöhen".[515] Faktoren, die den Umfang dieser Gefährdungspotentiale beeinflussen, sind neben der Transparenz algorithmischer Systeme sowie, in unmittelbarer Verbindung damit stehend, die Medienkompetenzen der Nutzer auch die Sichtbarkeit und Auffindbarkeit von Qualitätsinhalten.

Die neue Bestimmung des Art. 7a AVMD-Richtlinie ist im Zusammenhang mit der vorliegenden Studie auch deshalb interessant, weil sie die bestehende Kompetenzverteilung bei der Medienpluralismussicherung unterstreicht. Einerseits benennt der zur Vorschrift gehörige Erwgr. 25 als Ziele des Allgemeininteresses insbesondere den Medienpluralismus und

---

theoretische Annahmen und empirische Befunde zu Filterblasen und Echokammern (Preprint), die zwar zu dem Ergebnis gelangen, dass die tatsächliche Tragweite von Filterblasen und Echokammern weithin überschätzt wird, allerdings dennoch schlussfolgern, dass es außer Frage steht, dass algorithmische Personalisierung die individuelle und kollektive Meinungsbildung beeinflusst. Für einen englischsprachigen Überblick und eine Analyse des bisherigen Forschungsstandes siehe auch *Zuiderveen Borgesius* u.a. in: Internet Policy Review 1/2016, die zu einem ähnlichen Ergebnis kommen und in Bezug auf das Gefährdungspotential auf die Weiterentwicklungsmöglichkeiten algorithmischer Techniken verweisen. Weiterführend auch: *Helberger u.a.*, Implications of AI-driven tools in the media for freedom of expression, *Haim/Graefe/Brosius* in: Digital Journalism 3/2018, 330, 330 ff.; *Nechushtai/Lewis* in: Computers in Human Behavior 2019, 298, 298 ff.

514 Die EPRA weist auf diese Gefahr als „Rückkopplungseffekt" hin, vgl. Media plurality in the age of algorithms – New challenges to monitor pluralism and diversity, Background document 51st EPRA Meeting, https://www.epra.org/attachments/51st-epra-meeting-media-plurality-in-the-age-of-algorithms-new-challenges-to-monitor-pluralism-and-diversity-background-document.
515 BVerfG, 1 BvR 1675/16, u.a., Rn. 79.

die kulturelle Vielfalt. Dabei wird betont, dass „die Möglichkeit der Mitgliedstaaten unberührt" bleibt, Diensteanbietern Herausstellungsverpflichtungen aufzuerlegen. Weder sind Mitgliedstaaten verpflichtet, dies zu tun, noch gibt die Vorschrift vor, wie solche Herausstellungsverpflichtungen auszugestalten sind, falls sich der Mitgliedstaat dazu entschließt solche Verpflichtungen einzuführen – anders als die neue Bestimmung zur Signal- bzw. Inhaltsintegrität in Art. 7 b, die durch ihre bestimmende und konkretere Formulierung sowie die dazugehörigen Erläuterungen aus den Erwgr. den Mitgliedstaaten eine gewisse Prägung bei der Umsetzung auch aus verbraucherschutzrechtlicher Perspektive vorgibt[516]. Es wird lediglich deklaratorisch hingewiesen, dass die Verpflichtungen nur unter Berücksichtigung des Verhältnismäßigkeitsprinzips einzuführen sind und demzufolge mit Unionsrecht vereinbar sein müssen.

Obwohl es im Vorfeld des Reformvorschlags von Seiten einiger Mitgliedstaaten und vieler Regulierungsbehörden die Forderung nach einer Vorschrift zur Auffindbarkeit von Inhalten gab, wurde diese Option von der Kommission mit der Begründung abgelehnt, dass einerseits kein Konsens über Reichweite und Grenzen einer solchen Regel gefunden werden konnte und andererseits die AVMD-Richtlinie aufgrund ihres auf audiovisuelle Mediendienste (und nunmehr VSP) beschränkten Anwendungsbereichs, der gerade den Plattformbereich nicht erfasst, nicht das richtige Regelungswerk hierfür sei.[517] Im Vorschlag der Kommission war daher zunächst keine materielle Regelung zur angemessenen Herausstellung von public value Inhalten enthalten. Lediglich ein Erwgr.[518] sollte verdeutlichen, dass dies ein wichtiges Instrument sein kann, es aber in den Händen

---

516 Hierzu eingehend *Cole*, Die Neuregelung des Artikel 7 b Richtlinie 2010/13/EU (AVMD-RL).

517 Vgl. Commission staff working document SW(2016) 168 final, impact assessment accompanying the Proposal for a Directive of the European Parliament and of the Council amending Directive 2010/13/EU on the coordination of certain provisions laid down by law, regulation or administrative action in Member States concerning the provision of audiovisual media services in view of changing market realities, https://ec.europa.eu/digital-single-market/en/news/impact-assessment-accompanying-proposal-updated-audiovisual-media-services-directive.

518 Erwgr. 38 in der Fassung des Vorschlags der Kommission lautete: „Diese Richtlinie lässt die Möglichkeit der Mitgliedstaaten unberührt, Verpflichtungen zur Gewährleistung der Auffindbarkeit und Zugänglichkeit von Inhalten aufzuerlegen, die nach festgelegten Zielen des allgemeinen Interesses wie Medienpluralismus, Meinungsfreiheit und kulturelle Vielfalt von allgemeinem Interesse sind. Solche Verpflichtungen sollten nur auferlegt werden, wenn sie nötig sind, um von Mitgliedstaaten im Einklang mit dem Unionsrecht eindeutig festgelegte Ziele von allgemeinem Interesse zu erreichen. In dieser Hinsicht sollten die Mit-

D. Sekundärrechtlicher Rahmen zum „Medienrecht" und Medienpluralismus

der Mitgliedstaaten verbleibt, darüber zu befinden. Aufgrund der Bedeutung für die Nutzer, wurde Art. 7a im Entwurf auf Vorschlag des Parlaments – der im Unterschied zur finalen Fassung noch eine beispielhafte Aufzählung der Ziele von Allgemeininteresse im Normtext selbst und nicht lediglich in den Erwgr. enthielt – in die Trilogverhandlungen aufgenommen.[519] „Um Medienpluralismus und -vielfalt zu sichern, sollten die Mitgliedstaaten berechtigt sein, Maßnahmen für eine angemessene Herausstellung audiovisueller Mediendienste von allgemeinem Interesse zu ergreifen" – so die Begründung des Ausschusses für Kultur und Bildung des Europäischen Parlaments für den entsprechenden Vorstoß.[520] Auch wenn die endgültige Formulierung der Vorschrift sehr knapp ausgefallen ist und den Mitgliedstaaten ein umfassendes Ermessen bei der Frage schon des 'Ob' aber auch des 'Wie' einer Verpflichtungsregelung feststellt, ist sie interessant aus eben diesem Grunde: obwohl anerkannt wird, dass nicht nur die Angebotsvielfalt, sondern auch die Auswahlvielfalt beim Nutzer von hoher Relevanz ist, wird diese Frage eindeutig im Bereich der mitgliedstaatlichen Kompetenz verortet.

Art. 7a stellt sich daher als Regelung dar, die der Betrachtung von (Medien-)Pluralismus als Wert auch auf der Ebene der EU Rechnung trägt, ohne dabei in das Kompetenzgefüge im Kulturbereich einzugreifen. Es gilt das Gebot eines angemessenen Interessenabgleichs in der Umsetzung der jeweiligen Norm – das in verfassungsrechtlichen Kategorien als Gebot der Herstellung praktischer Konkordanz vertraut ist[521] – welches sich gegen eine ausschließlich vom Unionsgesetzgeber vorgegebene Auslegung der Umsetzungsspielräume bereits deshalb sperrt, weil der jeweilige unionsrechtlich vorgegebene Interessenab- und -ausgleich durch je unterschiedli-

---

gliedstaaten insbesondere die Notwendigkeit eines regulatorischen Eingreifens gegenüber den durch das Spiel der Marktkräfte erzielten Ergebnissen prüfen. Wenn Mitgliedstaaten beschließen, Auffindbarkeitsvorschriften zu erlassen, sollten sie den Unternehmen nur angemessene Verpflichtungen in Verfolgung legitimer öffentlicher Interessen auferlegen.

519 Vgl. Institut für Europäisches Medienrecht (EMR), AVMD-Synopse 2018, abrufbar unter https://emr-sb.de/synopsis-avms/.
520 Europäisches Parlament, Ausschuss für Kultur und Bildung, Entwurf eines Berichts über den Vorschlag für eine Richtlinie des Europäischen Parlaments und des Rates zur Änderung der Richtlinie 2010/13/EU zur Koordinierung bestimmter Rechts- und Verwaltungsvorschriften der Mitgliedstaaten über die Bereitstellung audiovisueller Mediendienste im Hinblick auf sich verändernde Marktgegebenheiten, 5.9.2016, https://www.europarl.europa.eu/RegData/commissions/cult/projet_rapport/2016/587655/CULT_PR(2016)587655_DE.pdf, S. 82.
521 Vgl. z.B. BVerfGE 41, 29 (51); 77, 240 (255); 81, 298 (308); 83, 130 (143).

che mitgliedstaatliche grundrechtliche Verfassungstraditionen vorgeprägt ist. Letztlich wäre auch ohne eine solche Regelung die mitgliedstaatliche Kompetenz zur Regelung von Herausstellungsverpflichtungen unberührt, für die Aufnahme einer solchen Vorschrift spricht aber aus Sicht der Gesetzgeber, dass damit erinnerlich gemacht wird, welche Bedeutung solche Maßnahmen zur effektiven Sicherung von Medienpluralismus und Angebotszugangsvielfalt haben können. Die Mitgliedstaaten werden damit sozusagen eingeladen, zur Verwirklichung dieses Ziels über die Einführung entsprechender Verpflichtungen intensiv nachzudenken. Diese stehen in engem Zusammenhang mit der eigentlichen Medienregulierung, so dass die Verortung außerhalb der infrastrukturbezogenen Regelungstexte, namentlich dem EEKK (dazu unten D.II.5), nachvollziehbar ist.

(3) Medienkompetenzförderung

Ein weiterer Bereich, der im Kontext zuvor beschriebener Erwägungen zur Auffindbarkeit von Inhalten, Desinformation, der algorithmisch gesteuerten Auswahl von Inhalten[522] und ähnlichen Phänomenen im Zusammenhang mit Medienpluralismus steht, ist auch die Medienkompetenzförderung. Diese hat mit der Novelle 2018 erstmals explizit Eingang in den Richtlinientext bei den materiellen Regelungen gefunden. Nach Art. 33 a AVMD-Richtlinie fördern die Mitgliedstaaten die Entwicklung von Medienkompetenz und ergreifen entsprechende Maßnahmen. Auch die ERGA soll Erfahrungen und bewährte Verfahren im Bereich der Medienkompetenz austauschen (Art. 30 b Abs. 3 Buchst. b)).

Medienkompetenz bezieht sich dabei auf die notwendigen Fähigkeiten und Kenntnisse sowie das nötige Verständnis für eine wirksame und sichere Nutzung der Medien durch die Verbraucher.[523] Eine Legaldefinition dieses Begriffs, der im EU-Kontext sehr weit verstanden wird[524] fehlt je-

---

522 Vgl. hierzu auch *Devaux* u.a., Studie über Medienkompetenz und Online-Empowerment-Themen, die aufgrund von algorithmisch gesteuerten Mediendiensten aufkommen, SMART 2017/0081, https://ec.europa.eu/digital-single-market/en/news/study-media-literacy-and-online-empowerment-issues-raised-algorithm-driven-media-services-smart.
523 Vgl. bereits Erwägungsgrund 47 der Richtlinie 2010/13/EU.
524 Der Rat der Europäischen Union fasst darunter etwa „sämtliche technischen, kognitiven, sozialen, staatsbürgerlichen und kreativen Fähigkeiten, die den Zugang zu den Medien und den kritischen Umgang und die Interaktion mit ihnen ermöglichen", Entwicklung der Medienkompetenz und des kritischen Denkens durch allgemeine und berufliche Bildung – Schlussfolgerungen des Rates

doch ebenso wie konkrete Regelungen, wie die Medienkompetenzförderung aussehen soll. Damit werden den Mitgliedstaaten keine Vorgaben zur Umsetzung gemacht. Lediglich Erwgr. 59 setzt die Regelung in den Zusammenhang, dass nur die notwendige Kompetenz im Umgang mit Medien die EU-Bürger in die Lage versetzt, auf verantwortungsvolle und sichere Weise auf Informationen zuzugreifen und Medieninhalte verwenden, kritisch beurteilen und erstellen zu können. Bürgern sollen Fähigkeiten des kritischen Denkens vermittelt werden, die notwendig sind, um Bewertungen vornehmen, komplexe Realitäten analysieren und zwischen Meinungen und Tatsachen unterscheiden zu können.

Während damit auch das Phänomen der Desinformation von dieser Erwägung erfasst wird, ist die Kompetenz im Umgang mit (vor allem digitalen) Medien generell erforderlich, um in der digitalen Informationsumgebung navigieren, insbesondere auf vielfältige Quellen zugreifen zu können. Medienkompetenz trägt damit mittelbar zum Medienpluralismus und zur Medienvielfalt bei, indem sie auf Nutzerseite die digitale Kluft verringern, eine fundierte Entscheidungsfindung erleichtern und die Erkennung und Bekämpfung falscher oder irreführender Informationen sowie schädlicher und illegaler Online-Inhalte ermöglichen und damit das Angebot zuverlässiger bzw. legaler und nicht schädlicher Inhalte fördern kann.[525] Wie bereits oben bei der Diskussion um Regelungen zur Herausstellung von bestimmten Inhalten ausgeführt, ist die bloße Existenz einer pluralistischen Medienlandschaft allein nicht zielführend, wenn sie nicht wahrgenommen wird bzw. aufgrund mangelnder Medienkompetenzen nicht (vollständig oder richtig) durch die Nutzer wahrgenommen werden kann.[526] Die Implementierung von Methoden aus der Verhaltenswissenschaft gegenüber Nutzern von beispielsweise sozialen Netzwerken, wird als möglicher Ansatz diskutiert, um kognitiver Voreingenommenheit entgegenzuwirken und pluralen Medienkonsum zu fördern.[527]

(30. Mai 2016), S. 6, http://data.consilium.europa.eu/doc/document/ST-9641-2016-INIT/de/pdf.
525 Recommendation CM/Rec(2018)1[1] of the Committee of Ministers to member States on media pluralism and transparency of media ownership, https://search.coe.int/cm/Pages/result_details.aspx?ObjectId=0900001680790e13, Rz. 10.
526 Vgl. auch *Cole/Etteldorf* in: Cappello (Hrsg.), Media pluralism and competition issues (erscheint in Kürze).
527 Vgl. hierzu und zu weiteren Vorschlägen etwa *Hoorens/ Lupiáñez-Villanueva (Hrsg.)*, Study on media literacy and online empowerment issues raised by algorithm-driven media services (SMART 2017/0081).

Die Zurückhaltung auf EU-Ebene bei der Regulierung dieser Materie („fördern", „ergreifen entsprechende Maßnahmen", jeweils bezogen auf die Mitgliedstaaten) ist einerseits der Tatsache geschuldet, dass die bisherigen Ansätze zur Medienkompetenzförderung in den Mitgliedstaaten sowohl im Hinblick auf den Umfang als auch hinsichtlich der Art und Grundlage stark voneinander abweichen. In vielen Mitgliedstaaten sind die relevanten Förderer Einrichtungen der Zivilgesellschaft, die nicht auf Basis eines gesetzlichen Auftrags agieren.[528] Daher tritt zur allgemeinen – jedoch vage formulierten – Förderpflicht des Art. 33 a der Mitgliedstaaten eine Berichtspflicht für diese hinzu. Die Kommission soll einen regelmäßigen Überblick darüber erhalten, welche Ansätze in den Mitgliedstaaten entwickelt werden und durch die – im dreijährigen Turnus erfolgende – Berichtspflicht besteht ein gewisser Druck zum Ergreifen entsprechender Maßnahmen, mit denen eine Umsetzung durch die Mitgliedstaaten belegt werden kann. Dies wird für so wichtig erachtet, dass die Kommission zur Sicherstellung einer vergleichbaren Art der Berichterstattung nach Art. 33 a Abs. 3 AVMD-Richtlinie ebenfalls Leitlinien veröffentlichen muss, die den „Umfang" solcher Berichte festlegen. Hinzu kommt eine entsprechende Aufgabe der ERGA nach Art. 30 b Abs. 3 Buchst. b) AVMD-Richtlinie, auf supranationaler Ebene eine gemeinsame Grundlage in Form von best practices zu finden.

Andererseits ist die (digitale) Bildung ein Bereich, der deutlich in der Kulturpolitik der Mitgliedstaaten verwurzelt ist, sodass diesen ein weitgehender Handlungs- und Gestaltungsspielraum verbleibt und verbleiben muss und die EU nicht über die AVMD-Richtlinie regulierend eingreifen darf. Erste Empfehlungen für die Mitgliedstaaten wurden in diesem Zusammenhang allerdings bereits auf EU-Ebene entwickelt. In den Schlussfolgerungen des Rates der EU zur Medienkompetenz in einer sich stetig wandelnden Welt vom Mai 2020[529] werden die Mitgliedstaaten, auch im Blick auf Erfahrungen mit der Corona-Krise, nicht nur um spezifisch medienkompetenzbezogene Aktivitäten gebeten, sondern u.a. auch ersucht, (1.) weiterhin Möglichkeiten für die Förderung und Stärkung des professionellen Journalismus als ein tragfähiges Element des globalen digitalen Medienumfelds auszuloten und (2.) bestehende Ausbildungsmodelle für die Entwicklung digitaler Kompetenzen in der europäischen Kultur- und

---

528 *EAI*, Mapping of media literacy practices and actions in EU-28.
529 Council conclusions on media literacy in an ever-changing world, 8274/20, v. 26.5.2020, https://www.consilium.europa.eu/media/44117/st08274-en20.pdf; vgl. hierzu *Ukrow*, MMR aktuell 11/2020.

D. *Sekundärrechtlicher Rahmen zum "Medienrecht" und Medienpluralismus*

Kreativwirtschaft zu verbessern – und erforderlichenfalls neue Modelle hierfür zu entwerfen –, um die wirksame Nutzung innovativer Technologien zu fördern und mit dem technologischen Fortschritt Schritt zu halten.[530]

(4) Einrichtung unabhängiger Regulierungsstellen

Auch bezüglich der Medienregulierung gilt die grundsätzliche Kompetenzverteilung bezüglich der Ausgestaltung der Verwaltung bzw. der Verwaltungsverfahren. Da (auch) die Anwendung von EU-Recht durch nationale Verwaltungen erfolgt, bleibt deren genauer Zuschnitt der Regelung durch mitgliedstaatliches Recht vorbehalten. Soweit eine Sachmaterie eine bestimmte Form der für die Durchführung zuständigen Einrichtung oder Behörde voraussetzt, kann dieser vom jeweiligen EU-Rechtsakt mit vorgegeben werden. Dies gilt etwa für die Garantie der Unabhängigkeit und Funktionsfähigkeit von Behörden zur Überwachung der Einhaltung der Datenschutzregeln schon unter Geltung der Datenschutzrichtlinie[531] und erst recht seit der Neufassung in Form einer Verordnung (EU) 2016/679[532].[533]

Soweit es um Aufsichtseinrichtungen oder Behörden geht, die die Einhaltung der Regelungen aus dem Medienrecht – einschließlich der nationalen Umsetzung der AVMD-Richtlinie – gegenüber Medienunternehmen

---

530 Eine ähnliche Form der Veranlassung zu Fördermaßnahmen mit dem Ziel der Stärkung des professionellen Journalismus und damit der Kreativlandschaft in der EU ist in der Absichtserklärung der Kommission zu sehen, mit einem *Media and Audiovisual Action Plan* den Medien- und audiovisuellen Sektor bei der digitalen Transformation durch den Einsatz von EU-Finanzierungsinstrumenten zu unterstützen. Dazu näher unter Abschnitt D.III.3.
531 Richtlinie 95/46/EG des Europäischen Parlaments und des Rates vom 24. Oktober 1995 zum Schutz natürlicher Personen bei der Verarbeitung personenbezogener Daten und zum freien Datenverkehr, EU ABl. L 281, 23.11.1995, S. 31–50.
532 Verordnung (EU) 2016/679 des Europäischen Parlaments und des Rates vom 27. April 2016 zum Schutz natürlicher Personen bei der Verarbeitung personenbezogener Daten, zum freien Datenverkehr und zur Aufhebung der Richtlinie 95/46/EG (Datenschutz-Grundverordnung), EU ABl. L 119, 4.5.2016, S. 1–88.
533 Art. 51 ff. DS-GVO, die insbesondere Vorgaben zur Gewährleistung der Unabhängigkeit der Aufsichtsbehörden auf mitgliedstaatlicher Ebene enthalten. Vgl. hierzu etwa EuGH, verbundene Rs. C-465/00, C-138/01 und C-139/01, Österreichischer Rundfunk u.a.; Rs. C-288/12, *Europäische Kommission / Ungarn*, Rn. 47; weiterführend auch *Cole/Etteldorf/Ullrich*, Cross-border dissemination of Online Content, S. 134 ff.

überwachen, fehlte es lange Zeit an Vorgaben in der Richtlinie, auch weil die Mitgliedstaaten aufgrund der eng mit tradierten Verständnissen der Medienfreiheit im nationalen Kontext verbundenen Vorgaben für die Form der Aufsicht – etwa in Deutschland durch eine Binnenkontrolle beim öffentlich-rechtlichen Rundfunk bzw. staatsfern eingerichtete Landesmedienanstalten beim privaten Rundfunk – eine Vereinheitlichung durch EU-Vorgaben ablehnten. Auch in der Neufassung der TwF-Richtlinie zur AVMD-Richtlinie 2007 wurde die Existenz unabhängiger Regulierungsbehörden auf nationaler Ebene lediglich durch Art. 23 b (durch Richtlinie 2010/13/EU zu Art. 30 umnummeriert) vorausgesetzt[534], ohne dass dazu Vorgaben gemacht wurden.[535] Im Gegenteil wurde der ursprüngliche Entwurf mit näheren Vorgaben ausdrücklich abgelehnt und in der letzten Fassung nur allgemein die Existenz dieser unabhängigen Re-

---

534 Art. 30 lautete: „Die Mitgliedstaaten ergreifen geeignete Maßnahmen, um sich gegenseitig und der Kommission, insbesondere über ihre zuständigen unabhängigen Regulierungsstellen, die Informationen zu übermitteln, die für die Anwendung dieser Richtlinie und insbesondere der Artikel 2, 3 und 4 notwendig sind".
Die dazugehörigen Erwgr. lauten: „(94) Im Einklang mit den Pflichten, die den Mitgliedstaaten durch den Vertrag über die Arbeitsweise der Europäischen Union auferlegt sind, sind sie verantwortlich für die wirksame Durchführung dieser Richtlinie. Es steht ihnen frei, die geeigneten Instrumente entsprechend ihren Rechtstraditionen und etablierten Strukturen und insbesondere die Form ihrer zuständigen unabhängigen Regulierungsstellen zu wählen, damit sie ihre Maßnahmen zur Umsetzung dieser Richtlinie unparteiisch und transparent durchführen können. Insbesondere sollten die von den Mitgliedstaaten gewählten Instrumente einen Beitrag zur Förderung des Medienpluralismus leisten.
(95) Eine enge Zusammenarbeit zwischen den zuständigen Regulierungsstellen der Mitgliedstaaten und der Kommission ist notwendig, um die ordnungsgemäße Anwendung dieser Richtlinie sicherzustellen. In gleichem Maße ist die enge Zusammenarbeit zwischen den Mitgliedstaaten und zwischen den Regulierungsstellen der Mitgliedstaaten von besonderer Bedeutung in Bezug auf die Wirkung, die die in einem Mitgliedstaat niedergelassenen Fernsehveranstalter möglicherweise auf einen anderen Mitgliedstaat haben. Sind im innerstaatlichen Recht Zulassungsverfahren vorgesehen und ist mehr als ein Mitgliedstaat betroffen, so ist es wünschenswert, dass die jeweiligen zuständigen Stellen vor der Erteilung der betreffenden Zulassungen Verbindung miteinander aufnehmen. Diese Zusammenarbeit sollte sich auf alle Bereiche erstrecken, die durch die vorliegende Richtlinie koordiniert werden".
535 Vgl. *ERGA* Report on the independence of NRAs; insgesamt auch Schulz/Valcke/Irion (Hrsg.), The Independence of the Media and Its Regulatory Agencies, darin insbesondere *Valcke/Voorhoof/Lievens*, Independent media regulators: Condition sine qua non for freedom of expression?.

D. Sekundärrechtlicher Rahmen zum „Medienrecht" und Medienpluralismus

gulierungsstellen genannt[536], während Erwgr. 94 (der kodifizierten Richtlinien 2010/13/EU) die Verantwortung für die wirksame Durchführung der Richtlinie als Pflicht der Mitgliedstaaten wiederholt und es diesen dabei freisteht, „die geeigneten Instrumente entsprechend ihren Rechtstraditionen und etablierten Strukturen und *insbesondere* die Form ihrer zuständigen unabhängigen Regulierungsstellen zu wählen" (Hervorhebung durch die Autoren).

Erst mit der Neufassung 2018 änderte sich dies.[537] In der Zwischenzeit hatte die Kommission mehrere Studien über die Unabhängigkeit und Effektivität der für die Medienaufsicht (bzw. die Einhaltung der Vorgaben aus der AVMD-Richtlinie) zuständigen nationalen Einrichtungen in Auftrag gegeben.[538] Wohl auch die Erkenntnis der sehr unterschiedlichen Herangehensweisen in den Mitgliedstaaten, die nicht immer eine ausreichende Garantie der Unabhängigkeit der Regulierungsstellen sicherzustellen vermochten, ermöglichte eine Kompromissfindung zwischen den Legislativorganen Parlament und Rat[539], die zu einer ausdrücklichen Vorgabe im materiellen Teil der Richtlinie führte. Seither schreibt Art. 33 Abs. 1 AVMD-Richtlinie die Benennung einer oder mehrerer nationaler Regulierungsbehörden oder -stellen durch die Mitgliedstaaten vor und dass diese dafür sorgen müssen, dass diese rechtlich von Regierungsstellen getrennt und funktionell unabhängig von ihren jeweiligen Regierungen und ande-

---

536 Dazu *Dörr* in: Dörr/Kreile/Cole, Rn. B 101; *Furnémont*, Independence of audiovisual media regulatory authorities and cooperation between them: time for the EU lawmaker to fill the gaps.
537 Hierzu *Dörr* in HK-MStV, B4 Rn. 101 ff.; *Gundel* in: ZUM 2019, 131, 136 ff.
538 *Cole u.a.*, AVMS-RADAR (SMART 2013/0083); INDIREG (SMART 2009/0001).
539 Der Vorschlag der Kommission, der die Etablierung des Merkmals der Unabhängigkeit vorsah, wurde vom Parlament so übernommen. Der Rat strich das Merkmal allerdings zunächst in seiner Allgemeinen Ausrichtung vom 10. Mai 2017 (abrufbar unter https://eur-lex.europa.eu/legalcontent/DE/TXT/PDF/?uri=CONSIL:ST_9691_2017_INIT) und nahm stattdessen in den Erwägungsgründen die folgende Formulierung auf: „Die Mitgliedstaaten sollten sicherstellen, dass ihre nationalen Regulierungsbehörden rechtlich von Regierungsstellen getrennt sind. Dies sollte die Mitgliedstaaten jedoch nicht daran hindern, die Aufsicht im Einklang mit ihrem nationalen Verfassungsrecht auszuüben. Es sollte davon ausgegangen werden, dass die Regulierungsbehörden oder -stellen der Mitgliedstaaten den geforderten Grad an Unabhängigkeit erreicht haben, wenn diese Regulierungsbehörden oder -stellen – einschließlich derjenigen, die als staatliche Behörden oder Stellen errichtet sind – funktionell und tatsächlich unabhängig von ihren jeweiligen Regierungen und von anderen öffentlichen oder privaten Einrichtungen sind [...]". Vgl. zur Entwicklung der Vorschrift im Trilog die Synopse des EMR, abrufbar unter https://emr-sb.de/synopsis-avms/.

ren öffentlichen oder privaten Einrichtungen sind, wobei damit nicht ausgeschlossen wird, dass „konvergente Regulierungsstellen" eingerichtet werden können, die für verschiedene Sektoren zuständig sind.[540] Weitere Details zu notwendigen Kompetenzen und Ressourcen, der Festlegung der auf die Regierungsstellen bezogenen Vorgaben in einer klaren gesetzlichen Grundlage sowie Vorgaben zur Schaffung von Regeln über die Besetzung bzw. Berufung und Abberufung von Funktionsträgern finden sich in den folgenden Absätzen.

Zwar ist damit eine klare Abkehr von der vorigen zurückhaltenden Formulierung von Vorgaben erfolgt und ein mit Regelungen aus dem Datenschutzrecht vergleichbarer Detailgrad erreicht. Jedoch wurde darauf geachtet, dass die grundsätzliche Ausgestaltungshoheit für die „behördliche" Aufsicht weiterhin im Kompetenzrahmen des mitgliedstaatlichen Verwaltungs(verfahrens)rechts verbleibt. Insbesondere sollten verfassungsrechtliche Besonderheiten hierfür von den Mitgliedstaaten einbezogen werden können, wie Erwgr. 53 ausdrücklich festhält. Eine Vereinheitlichung der „Behördenstruktur" wird durch die AVMD-Richtlinie auch in der Neufassung nicht angestrebt, vielmehr werden Mindestvorgaben gemacht, die erfüllt sein müssen, um den Unabhängigkeitsstatus einer solchen Regulierungsstelle ausreichend belegen zu können.

Die Unabhängigkeit der Aufsicht über den audiovisuellen Bereich wird dabei als zentral angesehen, um die Ziele der Richtlinie bei der Implementierung unter Wahrung der grundrechtlich vorgegebenen Staatsferne der Medien – und damit auch ihrer Aufsicht – zu erreichen. Art. 30 Abs. 2 nennt dabei als Ziele „insbesondere Medienpluralismus, kulturelle und sprachliche Vielfalt, Verbraucherschutz, Barrierefreiheit, Diskriminierungsfreiheit, das reibungslose Funktionieren des Binnenmarktes und Förderung eines fairen Wettbewerbs". In einer früheren Stellungnahme hat die ERGA die Regulierungsaufgaben der zuständigen Stellen etwas anders mit den Beispielen Zuschauerschutz, einschließlich des Schutzes von Minderjährigen, Meinungsfreiheit, Diversität, Pluralismus und Medieneigen-

---

540 Damit werden nunmehr auch Anforderungen an die Unabhängigkeit der Aufsicht von der Politik normiert, die bereits aus dem Bereich der Infrastruktur-Regulierungsbehörden für Telekommunikation (Vgl. dazu unter Abschnitt D.II.5.), Energie und Eisenbahnen sowie wie bereits eingangs erwähnt der Datenschutzbehörden bekannt sind. Vgl dazu auch *Gundel* in: ZUM 2019, 131, 136.

tum bezeichnet.⁵⁴¹ Bemerkenswert ist, dass seit der Neufassung des Art. 30 AVMD-Richtlinie zu den Zielen der Richtlinie ausdrücklich Medienpluralismus sowie kulturelle und sprachliche Vielfalt im Zusammenhang mit der Notwendigkeit der Unabhängigkeit der Regulierungsbehörden gezählt werden. Auch Erwgr. 54 betont, dass die von der Richtlinie erfassten Dienste als einen Zweck haben, „den Interessen von Einzelnen zu dienen und die öffentliche Meinung zu prägen" und um „Einzelpersonen und die Gesellschaft so vollständig wie möglich und mit dem größtmöglichen Grad an Vielfalt" zu informieren, eine Unabhängigkeit von staatlichen Eingriffen „und jeglichem Eingriff nationaler Regulierungsbehörden oder -stellen [...] über die bloße Rechtsumsetzung" hinaus gewährleistet sein muss.

In anderen Rechtsakten der EU finden sich solche Zielbestimmungen und Erläuterung, was zur Zielerreichung notwendigerweise dazu gehört, auch schon mit der ersten Fassung im materiellen Teil, häufig als einleitende Vorschrift. So soll die ECRL einen Beitrag zum einwandfreien Funktionieren des Binnenmarktes leisten und die Datenschutz-Grundverordnung die Grundrechte und Grundfreiheiten natürlicher Personen und insbesondere deren Recht auf Schutz personenbezogener Daten einerseits und den freien Fluss von Daten andererseits schützen. Im materiellen Teil der AVMD-Richtlinie fand sich vor 2018 eine derartige Deklarierung nicht. In Erwgr. 7 der Richtlinie 1997/36/EG wurde die „Schaffung eines rechtlichen Rahmens für den freien Dienstleistungsverkehr" als Ziel der Richtlinie genannt; in Erwgr. 67 der Richtlinie 2007/65/EG wurde dies mit dem Zusatz „bei gleichzeitiger Sicherstellung eines hohen Schutzniveaus für Ziele allgemeinen Interesses, insbesondere der Schutz von Minderjährigen und der menschlichen Würde sowie die Förderung der Rechte der Menschen mit Behinderungen" ergänzt. Mit der Erweiterung durch die Richtlinie (EU) 2018/1808 werden nunmehr weitere Ziele von allgemeinem Interesse explizit in Bezug genommen und nicht nur in den Erwgr. erwähnt. Dazu zählen auch Regulierungsziele, die für sich genommen ein (zumindest harmonisierendes) Handeln der EU nicht stützen könnten. Vielmehr geht es durch die Bezugnahme darum, ein Gesamtziel, das durch Umsetzung durch die Mitgliedstaaten realisiert wird, zu bezeichnen. Die Zielsetzung eines EU-Regelungswerkes kann auch nicht mit der Wahrnehmung einer entsprechenden Kompetenz gleichgesetzt werden, denn ähnlich wie im Primärrecht ist zwischen Zielen (dort: der Union) und Zuständigkeiten

---

541 ERGA statement on the independence of NRAs in the audiovisual sector, ERGA (2014)3, https://erga-online.eu/wp-content/uploads/2016/10/State_indep_nra_1014.pdf.

zu unterscheiden. Die Rechtsgrundlage zum Erlass des Rechtsakts findet sich jeweils im Einleitungsteil vor den Erwgr. und könnte auch für die AVMD-Richtlinie nicht auf einer Vorschrift des Primärrechts zur Pluralismussicherung gestützt werden, weil es an einer solchen mangelt. Art. 30 Abs. 2 bezieht sich wie erwähnt auf die Einrichtung unabhängiger Regulierungsstellen durch die Mitgliedstaaten und damit einen Bereich, der in seiner Ausgestaltung den Mitgliedstaaten obliegt und nur von allgemeinen Garantien bzw. Vorgaben aus dem EU-Recht geleitet wird.

(5) Regulierung von Video-Sharing-Plattformen

Wie bereits mehrfach erwähnt, ist eine der wesentlichen Neuerungen der Richtlinie (EU) 2018/1808, dass seither auch VSPs von der AVMD-Richtlinie mit erfasst werden. VSP-Dienste werden als Dienstleistungen definiert, deren Hauptzweck insgesamt oder in einem trennbaren Teil oder eine deren wesentlichen Funktionen hinsichtlich des Gesamtangebots darin besteht, Sendungen oder nutzergenerierte Videos, für die der Video-Sharing-Plattform-Anbieter keine unmittelbare (redaktionelle) Verantwortung trägt, der Allgemeinheit über elektronische Kommunikationsnetze zur Information, Unterhaltung oder Bildung bereitzustellen. Die Organisation der Sendungen oder Videos muss dabei vom VSP-Anbieter bestimmt werden, wozu auch der Einsatz von Algorithmen oder anderen automatischen Mitteln gehört. Die Definition ist demnach sehr weit gefasst.

Eine generelle Ausnahme, wie sie etwa Art. 17 Abs. 6 der neuen DSM-Urheberrechtsrichtlinie (dazu unter Abschnitt D.II.3.) für kleinere Anbieter in Bezug auf Verantwortlichkeiten bei der Nutzung geschützter Inhalte kennt, sieht die AVMD-Richtlinie nicht vor. Jedoch gibt es bei der Beurteilung der Angemessenheit zu treffender Maßnahmen Abstufungsmöglichkeiten. So werden nicht nur Angebote wie „YouTube" eindeutig von der Begriffsbestimmung VSP erfasst, sondern auch kleinere Plattformen sowie unter Umständen auch soziale Netzwerke[542] oder – sofern diese nicht sogar wegen redaktioneller Verantwortung unter die Definition eines nichtlinearen Dienstes fallen – eigenständige Bereiche von Online-Zeitungen mit audiovisuellen Sendungen oder nutzergenerierten Videos,[543] soweit diese „Bereiche als von ihrer Haupttätigkeit trennbar angesehen werden können". Für die zukünftige Beurteilung von nicht eindeutigen Fällen

---

542 Vgl. Erwägungsgrund 5 der Richtlinie (EU) 2018/1808.
543 Vgl. Erwägungsgrund 3 der Richtlinie (EU) 2018/1808.

D. Sekundärrechtlicher Rahmen zum „Medienrecht" und Medienpluralismus

wird die Auslegung des Kriteriums „wesentliche Funktion" des Dienstes maßgeblich sein.[544] Damit sollten Dienste, die nicht ohnehin klar als VSP zu erfassen sind, dann auch so kategorisiert werden können, wenn die wesentliche Funktion des Dienstes im Anbieten und Teilen von (auch nutzergenerierten) Videos besteht. Auch wenn soziale Netzwerke wie erwähnt nicht primäres Ziel der Regulierung waren, sollte durch diese Definition eine Entwicklungsoffenheit beibehalten werden, weil eine stärkere Nutzung von Videoverteilfunktionen auch auf bislang eher textgestützten Plattformen wahrscheinlich erschien.

Um bei der Umsetzung und Anwendung der Richtlinienbestimmungen eine gewisse Einheitlichkeit zu erzielen ermöglicht Erwgr. 5 der Richtlinie der Kommission, Leitlinien zur Bedeutung der wesentlichen Funktion zu erlassen. Anders als bei den oben dargestellten Leitlinien hinsichtlich der Vorschrift zur Förderung europäischer Werke, die eine Pflicht darstellen und im materiellen Teil als Auftrag an die Kommission formuliert sind, besteht bezüglich der VSP-bezogenen Leitlinien ein Ermessen der Kommission. Jedoch ist die Rechtsnatur, auch wenn hier die Möglichkeit nur in den Erwgr. genannt ist, ebenso wie bei den anderen Leitlinien gleich und der Text rechtlich nicht verbindlich. Die Kommission hat die Leitlinienbefugnis bereits wahrgenommen und im Juli 2020 Leitlinien für die praktische Anwendung des Kriteriums der wesentlichen Funktion[545] vorgestellt. Darin stellt die Kommission darauf ab, in welchem Verhältnis die audiovisuellen Inhalte zu anderen wirtschaftlichen Tätigkeiten des Dienstes stehen, welche qualitative und quantitative Bedeutung sie haben, wie und ob die audiovisuellen Inhalte monetarisiert werden und ob Instrumente vorhanden sind, die die Sichtbarkeit oder Attraktivität speziell audiovisueller Inhalte im Dienst erhöhen.

Neben der Begriffsbestimmung und einer gesonderten Regelung zur Rechtshoheit[546] in Art. 28a AVMD-Richtlinie findet sich die Anwendbarkeit bestimmter materieller Regelungen auf VSP in Art. 28b.

---

544 Eingehend hierzu *Kogler* in: K&R 2018, 537, 537 ff.
545 Mitteilung der Kommission, Leitlinien für die praktische Anwendung des Kriteriums der wesentlichen Funktion aus der Begriffsbestimmung für „Video-Sharing-Plattform-Dienst" der Richtlinie für audiovisuelle Mediendienste, 2020/C 223/02, EU ABl. C 223, 7.7.2020, p. 3–9, https://eur-lex.europa.eu/legal-content/de/TXT/?uri=uriserv:OJ.C_.2020.223.01.0003.01.ENG&toc=OJ:C:2020:223:TOC.
546 Nach Art. 28a Abs. 1 unterliegt ein VSP-Anbieter grundsätzlich der Rechtshoheit des Mitgliedstaats seiner Niederlassung. Allerdings gilt ein VSP-Anbieter nach Abs. 2 für die Zwecke dieser Richtlinie auch dann als im Hoheitsgebiet eines Mitgliedstaats niedergelassen, wenn entweder ein Mutter- oder ein Tochter-

Hinsichtlich der audiovisuellen kommerziellen Kommunikation sind VSP denselben Regelungen in Bezug auf insbesondere Schleichwerbung, unterschwellige Beeinflussung, Tabakwaren und alkoholische Getränke unterworfen wie bislang schon andere (audiovisuelle) Mediendiensteanbieter (Art. 28 b Abs. 2 i.V.m. Art. 9 Abs. 1 AVMD-Richtlinie). Lediglich die Konsequenz der Anwendbarkeit der Regelungen für den Anbieter sind anders als bei den bisher erfassten linearen und non-linearen Diensten, weil es auch auf die Frage des ökonomischen Vorteils für die Plattformanbieter ankommt, wenn über ihre Verantwortlichkeit entschieden wird. Gegenüber den Nutzern haben die Plattformen (lediglich) durch geeignete Maßnahmen auf eine Einhaltung der Bestimmungen zur kommerziellen Kommunikation zu drängen, wohingegen sie bei eigener Vermarktung, Verkauf oder Zusammenstellung der kommerziellen Kommunikation die Einhaltung der Vorgaben selbst sicherstellen müssen.

Darüber hinaus etabliert Art. 28 b einen Pflichtenkatalog, den die VSP-Anbieter zum Schutz Minderjähriger und der Allgemeinheit vor bestimmten (entwicklungsbeeinträchtigenden, strafbaren oder aufstachelnden) Inhalten einzuhalten haben, wobei die Richtlinie den Mitgliedstaaten aufträgt, entsprechende angemessene Maßnahmen zu treffen, die zu diesem Ergebnis führen. In der Richtlinie werden aber bereits konkrete Maßnahmen wie etwa die Anpassung von Allgemeinen Geschäftsbedingungen, die Einrichtung von Kategorisierungsmöglichkeiten für Uploader und von Altersverifikationsmechanismen sowie Melde- und Beschwerdesystemen erwähnt, die Mitgliedstaaten beispielhaft als Pflichten für die von der Vorschrift erfassten Anbieter unter ihrer Rechtshoheit vorsehen können, wobei die (gesetzliche) Festlegung von Maßnahmen durch die Mitgliedstaaten erfolgen muss, ihnen aber eine Auswahl der Maßnahmen vorbehalten wird („stellen sicher", „sorgen dafür", Art. 28 b Abs. 1 – 3 AVMD-Richtlinie). Zur Umsetzung der Vorgaben sollen die Mitgliedstaaten insbesondere Instrumente der Koregulierung gemäß Art. 4 a Abs. 1 AVMD-Richtlinie nutzen. Zudem können die Mitgliedstaaten und auch die Kommission die

---

unternehmen dieses Anbieters im Hoheitsgebiet eines Mitgliedstaats niedergelassen ist, oder der Anbieter Teil einer Gruppe ist und ein anderes Unternehmen dieser Gruppe im Hoheitsgebiet dieses Mitgliedstaats niedergelassen ist. Diese Regelung ist bemerkenswert, da sie eine Öffnung vom Herkunftslandprinzip darstellt, da für die Begründung der Zuständigkeit nicht mehr zwingend eine Niederlassung des Anbieters selbst notwendig ist, sondern eine Verbindung (auch über die für Mediendiensteanbieter subsidiär zur Niederlassung geltenden Jurisdiktionskriterien hinausgehend) ausreicht.

D. *Sekundärrechtlicher Rahmen zum „Medienrecht" und Medienpluralismus*

Selbstregulierung mithilfe von sog. Verhaltenskodizes der Union gemäß Artikel 4a Absatz 2 fördern.

Der Pflichtenkatalog für die VSP steht allerdings unter einem Zweckmäßigkeitsvorbehalt und der Vorgabe, die diesen von den Mitgliedstaaten auferlegten Pflichten an der Größe der Plattform auszurichten, was insoweit etwa kleinere oder nischenspezifische Angebote von übermäßigen Anforderungen schützen kann. Die AVMD-Richtlinie stellt klar, dass „angemessene" Maßnahmen zu treffen sind, was einerseits sowohl zugunsten als auch zulasten der Anbieter wirken kann, in dem Sinne dass die Anforderungen nicht unverhältnismäßig sein dürfen, aber im Blick auf die zu erreichenden Ziele auch effektive Auswirkungen haben müssen. Die Beurteilung der Angemessenheit der getroffenen Maßnahmen obliegt wiederum nach Art. 28b Abs. 5 AVMD-Richtlinie den mitgliedstaatlichen Regulierungsstellen, die entsprechend in ein System der Koregulierung mit entscheidender Wirkung einzubinden sind.

Damit wird also nicht nur eine neue Kategorie von Anbietern in die AVMD-Richtlinie aufgenommen, sondern auch eine neue Art des Umsetzungsauftrags an die Mitgliedstaaten und eine verstärkte Betonung des Instruments der Selbst- und Koregulierung. Grundsätzlich sind insbesondere für den Bereich der Medienregulierung in vielen Mitgliedstaaten Ko- und Selbstregulierungssysteme bereits etabliert.[547] Jedoch ist die spezifische Regulierung der VSP regelmäßig neu und wird daher neben den neu von der Regulierung erfassten Anbietern auch die Regulierungsstellen vor neue Herausforderungen in der Umsetzung stellen, gerade weil diesen die Aufgabe zukommt, die Angemessenheit der Maßnahmen auch innerhalb einer Koregulierungslösung regelmäßig zu bewerten.[548] Um eine konsistente Anwendung und Umsetzung dieser Regeln in der EU zu fördern, insbesondere auch weil die Anwendung der Vorschriften auf große VSP-Anbieter nur durch wenige Mitgliedstaaten erfolgen wird, da es nur eine sehr kleine Zahl den Markt in Europa (und auch global) insgesamt dominierender Anbieter gibt, hat die ERGA bereits eine entsprechende Arbeitsgruppe ins Leben gerufen. Diese konzentriert sich darauf, die Umsetzung der Bestimmungen des Art. 28b zu untersuchen und zu koordinieren.[549]

---

547 *Capello (Hrsg.)*, Selbst- und Ko-Regulierung in der neuen AVMD-Richtlinie.
548 Vgl. zu Herausforderungen und Möglichkeiten auch *Kukliš*, Video-Sharing platforms in AVMSD – a new kind of content regulation (draft); sowie *ders.* in: mediaLAWS 02/2020, 95, 95 ff.
549 Vgl. hierzu die Terms of Reference der Arbeitsgruppe „Implementation of the revised AVMS Directive", http://erga-online.eu/wp-content/uploads/2019/03/ERGA-2019-SG-3-ToR_adopted.pdf.

Zwar geben die Vorschriften für VSP in der Richtlinie den Mitgliedstaaten einen relativ detaillierten Handlungskatalog vor, jedoch bleiben diese zuständig für die konkrete Ausgestaltung. Zudem ist das Ziel der Regelung in Art. 28 b AVMD-Richtlinie insbesondere der Verbraucher- bzw. Jugendschutz, nicht aber vielfaltsfördernde Maßnahmen, bei denen im Blick auf die Zuständigkeit genauer geprüft werden müsste, ob der Handlungsspielraum nicht zu sehr eingeengt ist. Unabhängig davon ist aber auch die Regelung des Art. 28 b in einigen Kernelementen ausfüllungsbedürftig. Das betrifft neben der Definition von „redaktioneller Verantwortung" oder des „trennbaren" Teils eines Dienstes vor allem die Frage, wann ein Inhalt rechtswidrig im Sinne der AVMD-Richtlinie ist, also insbesondere zu Hass aufstachelt oder entwicklungsbeeinträchtigend ist und daher eine Reaktion durch den Anbieter erfordert. Auch wenn insoweit – ähnlich wie bei der konkreten Bewertung von jugendschutzrelevanten Inhalten[550] – mitgliedstaatliche Unterschiede unter Berücksichtigung nationaler Besonderheiten oder Verfassungstraditionen fortbestehen können, wird sich faktisch in der Praxis eine Konzentration der nennenswerten Anwendung dieser Vorschrift auf einen (oder wenige) Mitgliedstaaten ergeben.[551] Das ist der Tatsache geschuldet, dass sich die Niederlassungen der großen VSP-Anbieter[552] zu einem Großteil in einem Mitgliedstaat konzentrieren, da sich die Rechtshoheit für diese eindeutig nach Art. 28 a Abs. 1 AVMD-Richtlinie festlegen lässt.[553] Damit kommt der irischen Regulierungsbehörde als zuständige Aufsicht eine ganz entscheidende Rolle bei der Überwachung

---

550 Siehe hierzu EuGH, Rs. C-244/06, *Dynamic Medien Vertriebs GmbH / Avides Media AG*.
551 So auch *Barata*, Regulating content moderation in Europe beyond the AVMSD.
552 Vor dem Hintergrund des Brexit wird auch die Frage der Ausgestaltung von Kooperationsmechanismen von und mit mitgliedstaatlichen Regulierungsstellen außerhalb der EU interessant werden. Der Plum-Report (*Chan/Wood/Adshead*, Understanding video-sharing platforms under UK jurisdiction) identifiziert (mit Überschneidungen zu der irischen Bewertung durch die irische Regulierungsstelle, vgl. Fn. 557 sogleich) einige große Anbieter als „unter die Rechtshoheit des UK fallend", darunter Twitch.tv, Vimeo, Imgur, TikTok, Snapchat, LiveLeak und zwei größere Anbieter von Erwachseneninhalten.
553 In ihrem Beitrag zu einer Öffentlichen Konsultation der Regierung über die Regulierung schädlicher Inhalte und die Umsetzung der überarbeiteten Richtlinie über audiovisuelle Mediendienste (BAI, Submission to the Department of Communications, Climate Action & Environment Public Consultation on the Regulation of Harmful Content on Online Platforms and the Implementation of the Revised Audiovisual Media Service Directive, http://www.bai.ie/en/download/13 4036/) listete die irische Datenschutzbehörde dabei insbesondere YouTube, TikTok, Vimeo, DailyMotion und Twitch als ihrer Zuständigkeit unterliegende

D. Sekundärrechtlicher Rahmen zum „Medienrecht" und Medienpluralismus

der Maßnahmen der Anbieter und ggf. auch bei der Entwicklung von Leitlinien und best practices zu. Beispielsweise scheint der irische Gesetzgeber das von VSP zu etablierende Beschwerdesystem nach dem ersten Gesetzesentwurf in seiner konkreten Ausgestaltung, Funktionalität und dabei zu beachtenden Standards der zuständigen irischen Regulierungsstelle überlassen zu wollen.[554]

Um der beschriebenen Situation zu begegnen, dass die Mehrheit der Regulierungsstellen selbst nicht aktiv werden kann aufgrund der Rechtshoheit eines anderen Mitgliedstaates obwohl die über die VSP verbreiteten Inhalte in allen Mitgliedstaaten – in wesentlich größerem Umfang und einfacherem Zugriff – zugänglich sind, arbeiten die mitgliedstaatlichen Regulierungsstellen innerhalb der ERGA an Kooperationsformen, die zum Beispiele beschleunigte Mitteilungen über problematische Inhalte und Reaktionsverfahren vorsehen sollen.[555] Soweit die mitgliedstaatliche Regulierungshoheit für medienrechtliche Aspekte betroffen ist, kann ergänzen darauf verweisen werden, dass – in einer Art. 4 Abs. 1 AVMD-Richtlinie (der nur für audiovisuelle Mediendienste und damit nicht für VSP gilt) entsprechenden – Vorschrift des Art. 28 b Abs. 6 AVMD-Richtlinie es den Mitgliedstaaten freigestellt wird, ausführlichere oder strengere Maßnahmen für unter eigenen Rechtshoheit stehende Anbieter vorzusehen. Begrenzt werden sie bei dieser Form der „Inländerdiskriminierung" nur durch sonstige Vorgaben des Unionsrechts, namentlich der Artikel 12 bis 15 der ECRL oder des Artikels 25 der Richtlinie 2011/93/EU[556]. Weitergehende

---

VSPs auf sowie Facebook, Twitter, Instagram, Snapchat, LinkedIn und Reddit als (soziale Netzwerk-)Dienste, deren wesentliche Funktion im Angebot von audiovisuellen Inhalten besteht.

554 Vgl. General Scheme Online Safety Media Regulation Bill 2019 (https://www.dccae.gov.ie/en-ie/communications/legislation/Pages/General-Scheme-Online-Safety-Media-Regulation.aspx), erläuternd auch *Barata*, Regulating content moderation in Europe beyond the AVMSD.

555 Vgl. dazu den das angekündigte Arbeitsprogramm der ERGA für 2020 (https://erga-online.eu/wp-content/uploads/2020/01/ERGA_2019_WorkProgramme-2020.pdf) und 2021 (https://erga-online.eu/wp-content/uploads/2020/08/ERGA_WorkProgramme2021.pdf) sowie die Aufgabenbeschreibung für die ins Leben gerufene Subgroup 1 – Enforcement (Subgroup 1 – 2020 Terms of Reference, https://erga-online.eu/wp-content/uploads/2020/03/ERGA_SG1_2020_ToR_Adopted_2-03-2020.pdf).

556 Richtlinie 2011/93/EU des Europäischen Parlaments und des Rates vom 13. Dezember 2011 zur Bekämpfung des sexuellen Missbrauchs und der sexuellen Ausbeutung von Kindern sowie der Kinderpornografie sowie zur Ersetzung des Rahmenbeschlusses 2004/68/JI des Rates, EU ABl. L 335, 17.12.2011, S. 1–14, https://eur-lex.europa.eu/legal-content/DE/TXT/?uri=celex%3A32011L0093.

Maßnahmen bleiben – ähnlich wie es etwa für Dienste der Informationsgesellschaft nach Art. 1 Abs. 6 ECRL gilt – möglich. Es hat nur eine (begrenzte) Teilkoordinierung in Bezug auf VSP stattgefunden, die mitgliedstaatliche (strengere) Regeln für VSP vor dem Hintergrund der Vielfaltssicherung oder anderen Zielen im Allgemeininteresse nicht sperrt.

e. Zwischenfazit

Die Betrachtung der AVMD-Richtlinie insbesondere vor dem Hintergrund vielfaltssichernder Anknüpfungspunkte hat einen gewissen Wandel in der audiovisuellen Regulierungspolitik der EU dokumentiert. Während unter der TwF-Richtlinie noch ganz klar wirtschaftspolitische Ziele und die Gewährleistung eines freien Binnenmarkts im Vordergrund der Regulierung standen, hat sich der Charakter der AVMD-Richtlinie im Verlauf der Reformen teilweise gewandelt. Wenngleich die Dienstleistungsfreiheit weiterhin den Schwerpunkt bildet und die Kernprinzipien in Form des Ansatzes der Mindestharmonisierung, der Abweichungsbefugnis und des Herkunftslandprinzips beibehalten wurden, sind auch neue Anknüpfungspunkte hinzugetreten, die kulturpolitische Aspekte betreffen. Dies entspricht auch der Mitteilung der Europäischen Kommission über die Zukunft der europäischen Regulierungspolitik im audiovisuellen Bereich von 2003[557], in der sie betonte, dass die Regulierungspolitik in diesem Sektor auch in Zukunft bestimmte Interessen der Allgemeinheit wie kulturelle Vielfalt, Recht auf Information, Medienpluralismus, Jugendschutz und Verbraucherschutz wahren sowie Bewusstseinsbildung und Medienkompetenz der Allgemeinheit fördern muss.

In der erwähnten Mitteilung wurde allerdings gleichzeitig mit Verweis auf das Grünbuch der Kommission zu Dienstleistungen von allgemeinem Interesse[558] statuiert, dass der Schutz des Pluralismus in den Medien eindeutig in den Zuständigkeitsbereich der Mitgliedstaaten fällt.[559] Diese Position wird von der Kommission in allen relevanten Aktivitäten immer

---

557 Mitteilung der Kommission vom 15. Dezember 2003 über die Zukunft der europäischen Regulierungspolitik im audiovisuellen Bereich COM(2003) 784 final.
558 Grünbuch der Kommission vom 21. Mai 2003 zu Dienstleistungen von allgemeinem Interesse COM(2003) 270 final, EU ABl. C 76 vom 25.3.2004.
559 So auch die Erwägungsgründe 16, 25, 53, 61 der Richtlinie (EU) 2018/1808.

D. Sekundärrechtlicher Rahmen zum „Medienrecht" und Medienpluralismus

wieder betont.[560] Gleichwohl tragen aber einige gemeinschaftliche Rechtsakte zumindest indirekt zur Wahrung des Medienpluralismus bei. Eine so verstandene Regulierungspolitik[561] widerspricht nicht der Kompetenzverteilung, wenn eine Rechtsgrundlage bezüglich der primären Ziele zu finden ist und insbesondere darauf geachtet wird, dass die Möglichkeit mitgliedstaatlicher Regeln (die dann auf die Herstellung und Sicherung von Pluralismus gerichtet sind) nicht limitiert wird.

3. DSM-Urheberrechtsrichtlinie

Ein weiterer Schwerpunkt der Digitaler Binnenmarkt-Strategie der letzten Kommission war die Reform des Urheberrechts auf EU-Ebene. Eingeführt wurde zunächst die so genannte Online-SatCab-Richtlinie[562], die durch entsprechende Regeln die grenzüberschreitende Verfügbarkeit von Inhalten sicherstellt, ohne dass dabei aufgrund fehlender Lizenzabklärungen auf Instrumente wie Geo-Blocking zurückgegriffen werden muss, weil bei Empfang bzw. Weiterverbreitung in einem anderen als dem Mitgliedstaat ein eigener lizenzbenötigender Akt stattfindet. Vor allem aber wurden die Richtlinien 96/6/EG[563] und 2001/29/EG (Urheberrechtsrichtlinie)[564] durch

---

560 Vgl. etwa zuletzt im Hinblick auf die Vorbereitung des DSA im Rahmen der Digitalkonferenz anlässlich der deutschen Ratspräsidentschaft die Ausführungen von *Anthony Whelan*, Digital Policy Adviser, Kabinett von der Leyen, VoD abrufbar unter https://eu2020-medienkonferenz.de/en/session-1-en/.
561 Zudem gibt es immer wieder Ansätze namentlich des Europäischen Parlaments und der Kommission, der EU auch das Feld der Sicherung des Pluralismus als Bereich aktiver europarechtlicher Regulierung zu erschließen; vgl. hierzu und auf die verschiedenen (nicht rechtsverbindlichen) Initiativen von Europäischem Parlament und Europäischer Kommission eingehend *Komorek*, Media Pluralism and European Law, Kapitel 2.2.
562 Richtlinie (EU) 2019/789 des Europäischen Parlaments und des Rates vom 17. April 2019 mit Vorschriften für die Ausübung von Urheberrechten und verwandten Schutzrechten in Bezug auf bestimmte Online-Übertragungen von Sendeunternehmen und die Weiterverbreitung von Fernseh- und Hörfunkprogrammen und zur Änderung der Richtlinie 93/83/EWG des Rates. EU ABl. L 130, 17.5.2019, p. 82–91.
563 Richtlinie 96/9/EG des Europäischen Parlaments und des Rates vom 11. März 1996 über den rechtlichen Schutz von Datenbanken, EU ABl. L 77, 27.3.1996, S. 20–28, https://eur-lex.europa.eu/legal-content/DE/ALL/?uri=CELEX%3A31996L0009.
564 Richtlinie 2001/29/EG des Europäischen Parlaments und des Rates vom 22. Mai 2001 zur Harmonisierung bestimmter Aspekte des Urheberrechts und der ver-

die Verabschiedung einer gänzlich neuen Richtlinie mit Regelungen, die das Urheberrecht modernisieren sollen, angepasst: Mit der Richtlinie über das Urheberrecht im digitalen Binnenmarkt (DSM-Richtlinie)[565] sollte das Urheberrecht so aktualisiert werden, dass es auch im „digitalen Zeitalter" noch effektiv sein kann. Damit sollte wiederum die kulturelle Vielfalt in Europa und die Verfügbarkeit von Inhalten über das Internet gefördert werden, indem auch klarere Regeln für alle Internet-Akteure im Blick auf urheberrechtlich ausgelöste Pflichten festzulegen.[566]

Die DSM-Richtlinie enthält Regeln zum Urhebervertragsrecht, zum Text- und Data-Mining, zum Leistungsschutzrecht für Presseverlage, aber auch Regeln zur Nutzung geschützter Inhalte durch Online-Dienste. Neben den bestehenden Vorschriften zu urheberrechtlichen Schutzrechten, zur Verwertung von geschützten Werken und den Urheberrechtsschranken, die selbstverständlich im medialen Kontext sowohl in Bezug auf die Finanzierung von Angeboten als auch bei der Berichterstattung herausragende Bedeutung haben, sind dabei vor allem die beiden letztgenannten Neuerungen im Kontext dieser Studie von Interesse.

Dabei ist zunächst allgemein festzustellen, dass das europäische Urheberrecht den Mitgliedstaaten insbesondere dort einen Gestaltungsspielraum belässt, wo es um Aspekte der Sicherung der Medien- und Informationsfreiheit geht. So können die Mitgliedstaaten etwa von einem Katalog möglicher Grenzen und Ausnahmen vom ausschließlichen Vervielfältigungs- und Verbreitungsrecht des Urhebers (Art. 2 Urheberrechtsrichtlinie) auswählen, wenn es um Vervielfältigungen durch die Presse, die Berichterstattung über Tagesereignisse oder die Nutzung des Werkes im Wege des Zitats zum Zwecke der Kritik oder Rezension (Art. 5 Abs. 3 Buchst. c) und d) Urheberrechtsrichtlinie) ebenso wie andere Kontexte geht. Gleiches gilt für Ausnahmen und Begrenzungen der anderen ausschließlichen Rechte, die in der Urheberrechtsrichtlinie niedergelegt sind. Auch dabei wird deutlich, dass die Harmonisierung des Urheberrechts als

---

wandten Schutzrechte in der Informationsgesellschaft, EU ABl. L 167, 22.6.2001, S. 10–19, https://eur-lex.europa.eu/legal-content/DE/ALL/?uri=CELEX%3A32001L0029.

565 Richtlinie (EU) 2019/790 des Europäischen Parlaments und des Rates vom 17. April 2019 über das Urheberrecht und die verwandten Schutzrechte im digitalen Binnenmarkt und zur Änderung der Richtlinien 96/9/EG und 2001/29/EG, EU ABl. 130, 17.5.2019, S. 92–125, https://eur-lex.europa.eu/legal-content/DE/TXT/?uri=CELEX%3A32019L0790.

566 Vgl. hierzu die Pressemitteilung der EU-Kommission vom 14. September 2016, https://ec.europa.eu/commission/presscorner/detail/de/IP_16_3010.

D. Sekundärrechtlicher Rahmen zum „Medienrecht" und Medienpluralismus

Beitrag zum besseren Funktionieren des Binnenmarkts, namentlich des grenzüberschreitenden Handels mit uhreberrechtlich geschützten Werken, begrenzt bleibt, um mitgliedstaatliche Traditionen und Unterschiede bestehen lassen zu können. Obgleich allgemein Übereinstimmung darüber bestehen dürfte, dass das Urheberrecht die Berichterstattung über Tagesereignisse und damit den informierenden Beitrag zum Willensbildungsprozess der Gesellschaft nicht verunmöglichen darf, erfolgt insoweit keine Harmonisierung, es bleibt bei der Respektierung von Unterschieden in den Mitgliedstaaten, indem die Auswahl der Ausnahmebestimmungen den Mitgliedstaaten überlassen bleibt.[567]

Im Kontext vielfaltssichernder Maßnahmen sind allerdings die genannten neuen Regeln des Leistungsschutzrechts für Presseverlage sowie der neuen Regeln für Online-Dienste relevanter, da sie mit dem Ziel der Pluralismussicherung zusammenhängen.

Art. 15 DSM-Richtlinie sieht vor, dass die Mitgliedstaaten ein Leistungsschutzrecht für Presseverleger etablieren, das diesen einen angemessenen Anteil an den Einnahmen sichert, die durch die Online-Nutzung ihrer Presseveröffentlichungen von Anbietern von Diensten der Informationsgesellschaft generiert werden. Die Regelung geht ihrem Wortlaut nach sogar soweit, dass zukünftig nur noch das reine Setzen von Hyperlinks oder die "Nutzung einzelner Wörter oder sehr kurzer Auszüge aus einer Presseveröffentlichung" lizenzfrei möglich sein wird, gewährleistet also einen sehr weitreichenden Schutz dieser medialen Inhalte. Der Begriff des Dienstes der Informationsgesellschaft ist dabei deckungsgleich mit dem der ECRL, sodass hier ebenfalls eine Vielzahl von Anbietern erfasst sein kann. Grund für die Etablierung der Regelung waren aber vor allem Nachrichtenaggregatoren, Medienbeobachtungsdienste, allgemeine Newsdienste und -feeds, die Presseinhalte zusammenstellen und ausschnitthaft unter Nutzung der Originaltexte präsentieren. Die Regelung zielt dabei auf einen Investitionsschutz ab (und erkennt damit auch die Bedeutung von Investitionen in die journalistische Arbeit an), womit mittelbar auch die Finanzierung dieser Medienangebote gesichert wird, enthält also schließlich mittelbar auch eine Regelung mit vielfaltssicherndem Charakter in Bezug auf den Erhalt

---

[567] Der Auswahlkatalog der Ausnahmemöglichkeiten, von denen die Mitgliedstaaten diejenigen Ausnahmen umsetzen können, die sie für notwendig erachten, ist jedoch abschließend in der Urheberrechtsrichtlinie (nunmehr in der durch die DSM-Richtlinie geänderten Fassung) festgelegt. Dies hat der EuGH jüngst unterstrichen, vgl. EuGH, Rs. C-476/17, *Pelham GmbH u. a. / Ralf Hütter und Florian Schneider-Esleben*.

außenpluralistischer Strukturen.[568] Das ist nicht nur bemerkenswert, weil von EU-Ebene aus unmittelbar (und nicht wie bisher durch die Eröffnung mitgliedstaatlicher Gestaltungsspielräume) eine Regelung geschaffen wird, die sich explizit und ausschließlich auf den Schutz von Medienunternehmen bezieht[569], sondern auch, weil damit aktiv sichergestellt wird, dass solche Medienangebote weiterhin Aussicht auf Refinanzierung haben sollen. Erwgr. 54 stellt dabei sogar ausdrücklich auf eine vielfaltssichernde Zwecksetzung der neuen Regelung ab: Für Qualitätsjournalismus und den Zugang zu Informationen für die Bürger ist eine freie und pluralistische Presse unabdingbar. In Erwgr. 55 heißt es weiter „[u]m die Tragfähigkeit des Verlagswesens zu erhalten, gilt es, den organisatorischen und finanziellen Beitrag, den Verlage bei der Produktion von Presseveröffentlichungen leisten, zu würdigen und die Verlage auch künftig in dieser Tätigkeit zu bestärken, um so die Verfügbarkeit verlässlicher Informationen zu fördern".

Obwohl wirtschaftspolitische Ziele bei Schaffung der Regelung sicherlich auch eine Rolle gespielt haben – denn die Presse ist schließlich auch ein Dienstleistungs- und Arbeitsmarkt – spielten kulturpolitische Erwägungen zumindest auch eine Rolle, die die EU offenbar aufgrund der grenzüberschreitenden Tätigkeit der betreffenden Dienste der Informationsgesellschaft auf EU-Ebene harmonisiert sehen wollte. Der den Mitgliedstaaten verbleibende Umsetzungsspielraum ist dabei vergleichsweise klein. Trotz der vielfaltssichernden Zwecksetzung sei an dieser Stelle nicht unerwähnt, dass die Neuregelung gleichermaßen auch eine Gefahr für die mediale Vielfalt im Online-Bereich begründen könnte. Die Normadressaten, also etwa Newsaggregatoren, könnten aus Risikoerwägungsgründen auf die Verbreitung von Inhalten verzichten oder aus Kostenerwägungen heraus ihre Aggregation auf solche Dienste beschränken, die ihre Inhalte frei zur Verfügung stellen oder mit für die Vermittler günstigen Lizensierungsbedingungen einverstanden sind. In diesem Fall würde die Auswahl der Inhalte nicht von Faktoren wie Qualität, Aktualität oder Personalisierung durch Algorithmen abhängen, sondern von wirtschaftlichen Faktoren, was dem Bestreben nach Pluralismus insbesondere auf Rezipientenseite gerade zuwiderlaufen würde.

Auch die Regelung des Art. 17 liefert Anknüpfungspunkte im Bereich der Vielfaltssicherung. Sie bezieht sich auf Diensteanbieter, deren Tätigkeit

---

568 Vgl. hierzu auch *Cole/Etteldorf* in: Cappello (Hrsg.), Media pluralism and competition issues (erscheint in Kürze).
569 Erfasst werden sollen insbesondere nur journalistische Veröffentlichungen, vgl. Erwgr. 56.

D. Sekundärrechtlicher Rahmen zum „Medienrecht" und Medienpluralismus

„Dienste für das Teilen von Online-Inhalten" sind. Die DSM-Richtlinie definiert diese in Art. 2 Abs. 6 als Anbieter eines Dienstes der Informationsgesellschaft, bei dem der Hauptzweck bzw. einer der Hauptzwecke darin besteht, eine große Menge an von seinen Nutzern hochgeladenen, urheberrechtlich geschützten Werken oder sonstigen Schutzgegenständen zu speichern und der Öffentlichkeit Zugang hierzu zu verschaffen, wobei dieser Anbieter diese Inhalte organisiert und zum Zwecke der Gewinnerzielung bewirbt. Dabei erkennt Erwgr. 61 grundsätzlich an, dass solche Dienste „Vielfältigkeit und einen leichten Zugang zu Inhalten ermöglichen", aber dennoch Herausforderungen in Form der massenhaften unberechtigten Nutzung von urheberrechtlich geschützten Werken ohne entsprechende Vergütung der Urheber mit sich bringen. Art. 17 stellt daher zunächst klar, dass Diensteanbieter für das Teilen von Online-Inhalten eine Handlung der öffentlichen Wiedergabe im urheberrechtlichen Sinne vornehmen, wenn sie geschützte Werke einem Publikum zugänglich machen, und regelt sodann, dass die Anbieter auch für (von ihren Nutzern begangene) Urheberrechtsverletzungen verantwortlich sind, wenn sie nicht den gegenteiligen Nachweis erbringen, der an das Erfüllen bestimmter Kriterien geknüpft ist.

Diese Regelung, die unter dem Stichwort sog. „Upload-Filter" während und im Vorfeld der Reform intensiv diskutiert wurde[570], ist mit erhöhten Pflichten der adressierten Anbieter wie VSP verbunden, die beispielsweise die Lizensierung von Inhalten vor ihrer Freischaltung klären müssen und Systeme bereithalten müssen (deren konkrete Ausgestaltung der mitgliedstaatlichen Umsetzung überlassen ist, weshalb die Diskussionen um die Vorschrift und die adäquate Umsetzung sich fortsetzen[571]), die das Claimen, Melden und Erkennen von urheberrechtlich geschütztem Material im Zweifel ermöglichen müssen. Die DSM-Richtlinie weicht daher in dieser Hinsicht deutlich von den innerhalb der ECRL festgelegten Grundsätze zur begrenzten Verantwortung ab.[572] Zwar zielt auch diese Bestimmung

---

[570] Vgl. hierzu *Henrich*, Nach der Abstimmung ist (fast) vor der Umsetzung.

[571] Vgl. hierzu insbesondere die dem Diskussionsentwurf des BMJV zur DSM-Richtlinie gewidmete Ausgabe der Zeitschrift für Urheber- und Medienrecht (ZUM 2020, Heft 10), die mit Beiträgen verschiedener Autoren den Umsetzungsentwurf in Bezug auf insbesondere Art. 17 kommentiert.; auf den deutschen Umsetzungsvorschlag von Art. 17 eingehend auch *Husovec/Quintais* in: Kluwer Copyright Blog v. 26.8.2020.

[572] Vgl. *Kuczerawy*, EU Proposal for a Directive on Copyright in the Digital Single Market: Compatibility of Art. 13 with the EU Intermediary Liability Regime, 205, 205 ff.; s. außerdem: *Cole/Ettelddorf/Ullrich*, Cross-border Dissemination of Online Content, S. 139 ff.

vorrangig auf den Schutz der Urheber in ihren (auch wirtschaftlichen) Interessen auf Refinanzierbarkeit des Kreativschaffens, wobei im Unterschied zu Art. 15 hier nicht nur Medienunternehmen bzw. journalistische Veröffentlichungen zum geschützten Adressatenkreis gehören.

Obwohl es daher reflexhaft auch um den (finanziellen) Erhalt einer Vielzahl von vielfältigen Angeboten geht, wird die Zweiseitigkeit dieser Regelung vor dem Hintergrund der Pluralismussicherung durch die Formulierung in Erwgr. 61 deutlich, der darauf verweist, dass Online-Dienste Chance und Herausforderung für die Sicherung einer relevanten Vielfalt sind. Die Gefahren für die Vielfältigkeit von (auch medialen) Angeboten im Online-Bereich, die aufgrund der gesetzlichen Manifestation von Filterpflichten oder der praktischen Etablierung durch die Anbieter aus Risikoerwägungen heraus resultiert, wurde unter dem genannten Stichwort „Upload-Filter" bereits während der Reform diskutiert. Ohne dass auf diese Diskussion hier eingegangen werden muss, zeigt diese Neuregelung deutlich, dass nicht unmittelbar pluralismusbezogene Vorschriften im EU-Recht auch (stützende) Auswirkungen auf die Vielfalt von Angeboten aber durch die Sicherstellung eines ökonomischen Ausgleichs für die Investition in urheberrechtlich geschützte Werke – etwa durch Medienunternehmen, aber nicht nur – auch auf die Pluralität von Anbietern selbst haben können und sollen. Dadurch wird nicht in den Kompetenzbereich der Mitgliedstaaten für die Pluralismussicherung im Medienbereich eingegriffen, vielmehr ist einer der Gründe für die Aufnahme beider Regelungen in das harmonisierende EU-Recht die Erkenntnis, dass die faktische Situation bezüglich der relevantesten Onlineanbieter, die von beiden Vorschriften erfasst werden, für eine nicht nur mitgliedstaatliche, sondern aus Effektivitätsgründen supranationale Lösung sprach.

4. Fusionskontroll-Verordnung

Das EU-Wettbewerbsrecht wirkt – wie dies auch der Ansicht der Europäischen Kommission im medialen Kontext entspricht[573] – ebenfalls mindestens mittelbar vielfaltssichernd.[574] Es verbietet unter anderem Zusammenschlüsse (auch von Medienunternehmen), die zu einer Behinderung des

---

573 Mitteilung der Kommission über die Zukunft der europäischen Regulierungspolitik im audiovisuellen Bereich, aaO (Fn. 561).
574 Eingehend hierzu *Cole*, Europarechtliche Rahmenbedingungen für die Pluralismussicherung im Rundfunk, S. 93, 102 ff.

D. Sekundärrechtlicher Rahmen zum „Medienrecht" und Medienpluralismus

grenzüberschreitenden Wettbewerbs führen können, wenn marktbeherrschende Positionen erreicht werden.[575] Damit können Zusammenschlüsse schon im Blick auf die Marktmachtsituation untersagt werden, wodurch bei Unternehmen im Mediensektor bzw. mit Einfluss auf diesen bereits dadurch Vielfalt gesichert werden kann. Darüber hinaus anerkennt das ansonsten durch den Verordnungscharakter und die eindeutige Festlegung von Zuständigkeiten auf Ebene der EU vollständig harmonisierende Fusionskontrollrecht an, dass auch andere, nicht marktmachtbezogene Prüfungen und Untersagungsgründe bestehen können. Art. 21 Abs. 4 der Fusionskontrollverordnung (FKVO)[576] ermöglicht es den Mitgliedstaaten, auch eigentlich unter wettbewerbsrechtlicher Perspektive freizugebende Zusammenschlüsse zu untersagen, wenn diese aus anderen berechtigten Interessen der Mitgliedstaaten problematisch erscheinen. Als ein solche berechtigtes Interesse nennt die Vorschrift explizit die Medienvielfalt. Der Schutz dieser gibt den Mitgliedstaaten trotz der eigentlichen Zuständigkeit für Zusammenschlüsse von unionsweiter Bedeutung, die ausschließlich anhand des EU-Rechts und durch die Kommission entschieden werden, eine Abweichungsmöglichkeit. Damit haben die in den Mitgliedsstaaten zuständigen Behörden konkret die Möglichkeit, zum Schutz der Medienvielfalt Zusammenschlüsse selbst dann zu untersagen, wenn sie von der Kommission aus wettbewerbsrechtlicher Sicht als unbedenklich eingestuft wurden.[577] Sie können allerdings nicht solche Zusammenschlüsse, die von der Kommission untersagt wurden, im Nachhinein genehmigen, etwa mit dem Argument einer Erhöhung der Angebotsvielfalt.[578]

Die Regeln zum Medienkonzentrationsrecht sind in den Mitgliedstaaten sehr unterschiedlich und vor allem unterschiedlich stark ausgeprägt.[579]

---

575 Dazu bereits eingehend im primärrechtlichen Abschnitt C.IV.2.
576 Verordnung (EG) Nr. 139/2004 des Rates vom 20. Januar 2004 über die Kontrolle von Unternehmenszusammenschlüssen, EU ABl. L 24, 29.1.2004, S. 1–22.
577 Vgl. hierzu etwa den Fall Sky/Fox, der von der Kommission als wettbewerbsrechtlich unbedenklich eingestuft wurden, von der zuständigen Regulierungsbehörde des Vereinigten Königreichs allerdings als vor dem Hintergrund medienpluralistischer Bedenken dem öffentlichen Interesse widersprechend eingestuft wurde, Kommissionsentscheidung: M.8354 FOX / SKY, https://ec.europa.eu/com petition/elojade/isef/case_details.cfm?proc_code=2_M_8354, Ofcom: https://ww w.gov.uk/government/collections/proposed-merger-between-twenty-first-century -fox-inc-and-sky-plc.
578 Hierzu und zum Folgenden *Cole/Hans* in: Cappello (Hrsg.), Medieneigentum – Marktrealitäten und Regulierungsmaßnahmen, S. 27.
579 Vgl. bereits *European Institute for Media*, The Information of the Citizen in the EU.

Viele beschränken sich dabei weiterhin auf die Kontrolle der Konzentration im Rundfunkbereich; einige sehen auch die Überprüfung crossmedialer Verflechtungen vor.[580] Aber auch wenn die Medienkonzentration durch die Etablierung von Regeln zur Vielfaltsstellung limitiert wird, bedeutet das nicht automatisch die Herstellung von Medienpluralismus. Vielmehr bedarf es häufig der Implementierung weiterer Regeln über das Wettbewerbsrecht hinausgehend im Sinne etwa von Förderinstrumenten.[581]

Die FKVO und damit auch die ausschließliche Zuständigkeit der Kommission bezieht sich jedenfalls allein auf die Beurteilung der Auswirkungen von geplanten Zusammenschlüssen auf den Wettbewerb in den verschiedenen betroffenen Märkten innerhalb des Europäischen Wirtschaftsraums. Nicht in die Bewertung einbezogen werden solche Faktoren, die für die Beurteilung einer vorherrschenden Meinungsmacht relevant wären und damit Auskunft darüber geben, ob sich ein Zusammenschluss negativ auf eine pluralistische Medienlandschaft auswirken würde.[582] Der Zweck und die rechtlichen Rahmenbedingungen für die Beurteilung von Wettbewerb und Medienpluralität sind sehr unterschiedlich. Die Wettbewerbsregeln konzentrieren sich im Großen und Ganzen darauf, ob die Verbraucher infolge einer Transaktion mit höheren Preisen oder einer geringeren Innovationsfähigkeit konfrontiert wären. Eine Bewertung der Medienpluralität befasst sich in der Regel mit der Frage, ob Anzahl, Reichweite und Vielfalt der Personen oder Unternehmen, die Medienunternehmen kontrollieren, ausreichend plural sind. Diesen Unterschied und dass es dadurch zu unterschiedlichen Bewertungen von Zusammenschlüssen kommen kann, erkennt auch die Kommission an.[583]

Das Medienkonzentrationsrecht ist also ein Bereich, der bewusst aus dem Wirtschaftskonzentrationsrecht ausgeklammert ist. Art. 21 Abs. 4 FKVO ist eine bedeutsame Bestätigung, dass selbst in den ganz eindeutig im Kompetenzbereich der EU befindlichen Sachmaterien wie dem Wett-

---

580 *Cole/Hans* in: Cappello (Hrsg.), Medieneigentum – Marktrealitäten und Regulierungsmaßnahmen, S. 125 f.
581 *Cole/Hans* in: Cappello (Hrsg.), Medieneigentum – Marktrealitäten und Regulierungsmaßnahmen, S. 127.
582 Vgl. hierzu, aber auch zu möglicherweise nicht ausgeschöpften Potenzialen zur Berücksichtigung auch pluralismusrelevanter Aspekte im Rahmen der EU-Wettbewerbsordnung *Bania*, The Role of Media Pluralism in the Enforcement of EU Competition Law.
583 So auch die EU-Kommission im Zusammenhang mit dem Fall des Zusammenschluss von Sky und Fox, vgl. Pressmitteilung vom 7. April 2017, https://ec.europa.eu/commission/presscorner/detail/en/IP_17_902.

D. Sekundärrechtlicher Rahmen zum "Medienrecht" und Medienpluralismus

bewerbsrecht die mitgliedstaatliche Regelungshoheit – in diesem Fall durch die Anwendung in der Praxis auf Zusammenschlussvorhaben – respektiert und im einschlägigen Sekundärrechtsakt durch eine Sonderregelung operationabel gemacht wird.

5. Kodex für die elektronische Kommunikation

Der Europäische Kodex für die elektronische Kommunikation (EEKK)[584] ist am 21. Dezember 2018 in Kraft getreten und hat insbesondere die Richtlinien 2002/19/EG (Zugangsrichtlinie)[585], 2002/20/EG (Genehmigungsrichtlinie), 2002/21/EG (Rahmenrichtlinie) und 2002/22/EG (Universaldienstrichtlinie)[586] sowohl geändert als auch in einem umfassenden Regelungswerk für Telekommunikationsdienste zusammengefasst. Der EEKK regelt elektronische Kommunikationsnetze und -dienste, also Übertragungswege und technisch orientierte Dienste, enthält aber Bestimmungen, die im Zusammenhang mit der Sicherung von Pluralismus im Mediensektor hoch relevant sind.

Nach Art. 61 Abs. 2 Buchst. d) EEKK (ehemals Art. 5 Abs. 1 Buchst. b) Zugangsrichtlinie) können die Regulierungsbehörden der Mitgliedstaaten gegenüber Unternehmen mit beträchtlicher Marktmacht anordnen, digitalen Hörfunk- und Fernsehdiensten und damit verbundenen ergänzenden Diensten, Zugang zu Anwendungsprogramm-Schnittstellen (API) und elektronischen Programmführern (EPG) zu ausgewogenen und nichtdiskriminierenden Bedingungen zu gewähren. Zudem können die Mitgliedstaaten auch weiterhin nach Art. 114 Abs. 1 EEKK (ehemals Art. 31 Universaldienstrichtlinie) im nationalen Recht sog. Must-Carry-Pflichten vorse-

---

584 Richtlinie (EU) 2018/1972 des Europäischen Parlaments und des Rates vom 11. Dezember 2018 über den europäischen Kodex für die elektronische Kommunikation, EU ABl. L 321, 17.12.2018, S. 36–214, https://eur-lex.europa.eu/legal-content/DE/TXT/?uri=celex:32018L1972.
585 Richtlinie 2002/19/EG des Europäischen Parlaments und des Rates vom 7. März 2002 über den Zugang zu elektronischen Kommunikationsnetzen und zugehörigen Einrichtungen sowie deren Zusammenschaltung (Zugangsrichtlinie), EU ABl. L 108, 24.4.2002, S. 7–20, https://eur-lex.europa.eu/legal-content/DE/ALL/?uri=CELEX%3A32002L0019.
586 Richtlinie 2002/22/EG des Europäischen Parlaments und des Rates vom 7. März 2002 über den Universaldienst und Nutzerrechte bei elektronischen Kommunikationsnetzen und -diensten (Universaldienstrichtlinie), EU ABl. L 108, 24.4.2002, S. 51–77, https://eur-lex.europa.eu/legal-content/DE/TXT/?uri=celex:32002L0022.

hen, also Netzbetreiber zur Übertragung von bestimmten Hörfunk- und Fernsehkanälen und damit verbundenen ergänzenden Diensten verpflichten. Adressiert werden damit insbesondere Betreiber von Kabelfernsehnetzen, IP-TV, Satellitenrundfunknetzen und terrestrischen Rundfunknetzen sowie unter Umständen auch Betreiber anderer Netze, sofern diese (jetzt oder in Zukunft) von einer erheblichen Zahl von Endnutzern als Hauptmittel zum Empfang von Hörfunk- und Fernsehsendungen genutzt werden. Die Auferlegung der Pflichten steht dabei jeweils unter dem Vorbehalt, dass sie für ein (ausdrücklich festgelegtes) Ziel von allgemeinem Interesse erforderlich sowie verhältnismäßig und transparent sind. Zu solchen Zielen zählt insbesondere die Medienvielfaltssicherung. Entsprechend wurden die Vorschriften auch vor dem Hintergrund eingeführt, dass es den Mitgliedstaaten im Lichte ihrer Kulturhoheit möglich sein muss, zu gewährleisten, dass bestimmte Programme und vor allem die darin übermittelten Informationen einem breiten Publikum zugänglich sind.[587] Wichtig ist dabei, dass aufgrund des hohen Harmonisierungsgrades der Regelungen, die Autorisierung dafür bereits im EU-Recht angelegt sein muss, dieses aber den Mitgliedstaaten frei lässt, solche Übertragungspflichten einzuführen und auch bei deren Ausgestaltung nur Vorgaben zum Zweck und den zu erfüllenden Rahmenbedingungen aufgrund der Grundrechtsrelevanz des Eingriffs macht. Damit verbleibt, wie unten noch näher ausgeführt wird, der Gestaltungsspielraum auf der Seite der Mitgliedstaaten. Das Konzept der Sicherstellung eines Zugangs für das „breite Publikum" zu wichtigen Inhalten steht einerseits dem Konzept einer Grundversorgung nahe, wie es im deutschen Recht z.B. für Telekommunikationsdienste als Infrastruktureinrichtung in Art. 87 f Abs. 1 GG niedergelegt ist.[588] Andererseits kommt diese Idee auch aus der Einrichtung von public service-Anbietern bzw. Angeboten, deren staatlich veranlasste Finanzierung zu einem besonderen Status und einer Art „Zugangsanspruch" für die den Dienst finanzierenden Bürger führt. Dies ist in Deutschland, auch gestützt durch das Bundesverfassungsgericht, im Grundversorgungsauftrag niedergelegt, wonach nicht nur inhaltlich, sondern eben auch von der Erreichbarkeit her, der öffentlich-rechtliche Rundfunk einen umfas-

---

587 Vgl. hierzu bereits *Arino u.a.* in: EAI (Hrsg.), Haben oder nicht haben. Must-Carry-Regeln.
588 So auch *Assion*, Must Carry: Übertragungspflichten auf digitalen Rundfunkplattformen, S. 207.

D. Sekundärrechtlicher Rahmen zum „Medienrecht" und Medienpluralismus

senden Auftrag hat, der wiederum dessen Finanzierungsgrundlage rechtfertigt.[589]

Die Ziele des EEK sind (wie die der Vorgängerrichtlinien) nach Art. 1 Abs. 2 EEKK zum einen die Errichtung eines Binnenmarkts für elektronische Kommunikationsnetze und -dienste, der den Ausbau und die Nutzung von Netzen mit sehr hoher Kapazität bewirkt, einen nachhaltigen Wettbewerb und die Interoperabilität der elektronischen Kommunikationsdienste sowie die Zugänglichkeit und die Sicherheit von Netzen und Diensten gewährleistet und die Interessen der Endnutzer fördert. Zum anderen sollen die Bereitstellung unionsweiter hochwertiger, erschwinglicher, öffentlich zugänglicher Dienste durch wirksamen Wettbewerb und Angebotsvielfalt gewährleistet und die Fälle geregelt werden, in denen die Bedürfnisse von Endnutzern — einschließlich Nutzern mit Behinderungen im Hinblick darauf, dass sie in gleicher Weise wie andere Zugang zu den Diensten haben — durch den Markt nicht ausreichend befriedigt werden können, sowie die notwendigen Rechte der Endnutzer festgelegt werden. Es geht also um Binnenmarkt, Wettbewerb, Verbraucherschutz und auch um die Netzinfrastruktur innerhalb der EU. Die Nennung der „Angebotsvielfalt" in der Zielsetzung des EEKK (Art. 1 Abs. 2 lit b)) ist dabei nicht als kulturpolitische Ausrichtung im Blick auf über die Netze transportierte Inhaltsdienste zu verstehen, sondern meint das Vorhandensein einer Vielzahl (konkurrierender) Angebote der Kommunikationsnetze innerhalb der EU aus Sicht der Verbraucher. Dies stellt auch Erwgr. 7 klar, wonach der EEKK nicht die Inhalte von Diensten, die über elektronische Kommunikationsnetze und -dienste bereitgestellt werden, wie Rundfunkinhalte oder Finanzdienste und bestimmte Dienste der Informationsgesellschaft, betrifft. Darüber hinaus stellt aber Erwgr. 7 weiterhin unmissverständlich klar, dass durch den Kodex insbesondere Maßnahmen unberührt bleiben, die auf Unionsebene oder auf der Ebene der Mitgliedstaaten in Bezug auf diese Dienste getroffen werden, um die kulturelle und sprachliche Vielfalt zu fördern und die Wahrung des Pluralismus der Medien sicherzustellen. Im Hinblick auf die zunehmende technische Konvergenz der „Infrastruktur" anerkennt Erwgr. 7, dass die darüber transportierten Dienste aus regulatorischer Sicht weiterhin davon zu trennen sind, wenngleich dies „die Berücksichtigung von Verbindungen zwischen beiden, insbesondere zur Gewährleistung des Pluralismus der Medien, der kulturellen Vielfalt und des Verbraucherschutzes" nicht verhindere. Diese Mög-

---

589 Hierzu *Ukrow/Cole*, Aktive Sicherung lokaler und regionaler Medienvielfalt, S. 98.

lichkeit auch über die „technische" Regulierung kulturpolitische Ziele wie Pluralismus der Medien und Sicherung der kulturellen Vielfalt zu erreichen, wird allerdings vom EEKK wesentlich auf Ebene der Mitgliedstaaten[590] verortet. Ausdrücklich fordert Erwgr. 7 im Blick auf die nationalen Regulierungsbehörden, dass die „zuständigen Behörden [...] im Rahmen ihrer Zuständigkeiten dazu beitragen, dass für die Umsetzung der politischen Maßnahmen zur Förderung dieser Ziele gesorgt wird".

Dies gilt, wie bereits oben erwähnt, ausdrücklich auch für Zugangs- und die sog. Must-Carry-Regeln. Mit Art. 61 und 114 EEKK wird von der EU-Ebene aus grundsätzlich lediglich die Möglichkeit eröffnet diese durch die Mitgliedstaaten einzuführen. Dabei können diese insbesondere bezüglich letzterer entscheiden, ob Übertragungspflichten überhaupt eingeführt werden, und wenn ja, welche Anbieter oder welche Angebote (öffentlich-rechtlicher Rundfunk, privater Rundfunk, etc.) davon erfasst werden, ob, von wem und in welchem Umfang Entschädigungen und/oder Zahlungen für die Übertragung zu leisten sind, wie viele Anbieter oder Angebote von Übertragungspflichten profitieren sollten und weitere Rahmenbedingungen. Von dieser Möglichkeit haben die meisten Mitgliedstaaten[591] in unterschiedlicher Form Gebrauch gemacht, sich dabei aber in der Regel für die Grundregel an den Wortlaut der (bisher geltenden) Richtlinien angelehnt,[592] so dass die konkrete Anwendung durch die Regulierungsbehörden bzw. -stellen erfolgt.

Der EEKK, welcher bis zum 21. Dezember 2020 umzusetzen ist, ergänzt die bestehenden Regeln, an denen die bisherige mitgliedstaatliche Umsetzung noch orientiert ist, nicht unwesentlich wie sich aus nachfolgendem auszugsweisen synoptischen Überblick ablesen lässt.

---

590 Vgl. Erwgr. 115 „Zu solchen Zielen sollte auch die Förderung der kulturellen und sprachlichen Vielfalt sowie des Medienpluralismus gehören, wie sie von den Mitgliedstaaten im Einklang mit dem Unionsrecht festgelegt worden sind".
591 Lediglich in Zypern, Estland, Spanien, Italien (außer für lokale Angebote) und Luxembourg gibt es keine Übertragungspflichten; Regeln zur Auffindbarkeit in elektronischen Programmführern haben bislang etwa die Hälfte der EU-Mitgliedstaaten. Vgl. European Institute of Media, study to support Impact Assessment of AVMSD, S. 80.
592 *EAI (Hrsg.)*, Must-Carry: Renaissance oder Reformation?; hierzu umfassend in Bezug auf Art. 31 Universaldiensterichtlinie auch: EAI (Hrsg.), Access to TV platforms: must-carry rules, and access to free-DTT.

D. Sekundärrechtlicher Rahmen zum „Medienrecht" und Medienpluralismus

Zugangs-RL	EEKK
Erwgr. (10) Wettbewerbsregeln allein genügen möglicherweise nicht, um im Zeitalter des digitalen Fernsehens kulturelle Vielfalt und Medienpluralismus sicherzustellen. […]	Erwgr. (159) Wettbewerbsregeln allein genügen möglicherweise nicht **immer**, um im Zeitalter des digitalen Fernsehens kulturelle Vielfalt und Medienpluralismus sicherzustellen. […]
UDRL	**EEKK**
Art. 31 Abs. 1 Die Mitgliedstaaten können zur Übertragung bestimmter Hör- und Fernsehrundfunkkanäle und -dienste den unter ihre Gerichtsbarkeit fallenden Unternehmen, die für die öffentliche Verbreitung von Hör- und Fernsehrundfunkdiensten genutzte elektronische Kommunikationsnetze betreiben, zumutbare Übertragungspflichten auferlegen, wenn eine erhebliche Zahl von Endnutzern diese Netze als Hauptmittel zum Empfang von Hörfunk- und Fernsehsendungen nutzen.	**Art. 114** (1) Die Mitgliedstaaten können zur Übertragung bestimmter Hörfunk- und Fernsehkanäle **und damit verbundener, ergänzender, insbesondere zugangserleichternder Dienste, die Endnutzern mit Behinderungen einen angemessenen Zugang ermöglichen, sowie von Daten für Dienste des vernetzten Fernsehens und EPG den ihrer Rechtshoheit unterliegenden** Unternehmen, die für die öffentliche Verbreitung von Hörfunk- und Fernsehkanälen genutzte elektronische Kommunikationsnetze und -dienste betreiben, zumutbare Übertragungspflichten auferlegen, wenn eine erhebliche Zahl von Endnutzern diese Netze und Dienste als Hauptmittel zum Empfang von Hörfunk- und Fernseh**kanälen** nutzt.
Solche Verpflichtungen dürfen jedoch nur auferlegt werden, soweit sie zur Erreichung klar umrissener Ziele von allgemeinem Interesse erforderlich sind; sie müssen verhältnismäßig und transparent sein.	Solche **Pflichten** dürfen nur auferlegt werden, soweit sie zur Erreichung **der von den einzelnen Mitgliedstaaten ausdrücklich** festgelegten Ziele von allgemeinem Interesse erforderlich sind, und sie müs-

Sie werden regelmäßig überprüft.	sen verhältnismäßig und transparent sein.
	(2) Bis zum 21. Dezember 2019 und danach alle fünf Jahre überprüfen die Mitgliedstaaten die Pflichten nach Absatz 1, es sei denn der betreffende Mitgliedstaat hat eine solche Überprüfung innerhalb der vier vorangegangenen Jahre vorgenommen.
(2) Weder Absatz 1 dieses Artikels noch Artikel 3 Absatz 2 der Richtlinie 2002/19/EG (Zugangsrichtlinie) beeinträchtigt die Möglichkeit der Mitgliedstaaten, in Bezug auf die nach diesem Artikel auferlegten Verpflichtungen gegebenenfalls ein angemessenes Entgelt festzulegen; dabei ist zu gewährleisten, dass bei vergleichbaren Gegebenheiten keine Diskriminierung hinsichtlich der Behandlung der Unternehmen erfolgt, die elektronische Kommunikationsnetze betreiben. Sofern ein Entgelt vorgesehen ist, stellen die Mitgliedstaaten sicher, dass die Erhebung nach dem Grundsatz der Verhältnismäßigkeit und in transparenter Weise erfolgt.	(3) Weder Absatz 1 dieses Artikels noch **Artikel 59 Absatz 2** beeinträchtig**en** die Möglichkeit der Mitgliedstaaten, in Bezug auf die nach diesem Artikel auferlegten Verpflichtungen gegebenenfalls ein angemessenes Entgelt festzulegen; dabei ist zu gewährleisten, dass bei vergleichbaren Gegebenheiten keine Diskriminierung hinsichtlich der Behandlung der **Anbieter elektronischer Kommunikationsnetze und -dienste** erfolgt. Sofern ein Entgelt vorgesehen ist, stellen die Mitgliedstaaten sicher, dass die **Verpflichtung zur Entrichtung eines Entgelts — gegebenenfalls einschließlich der Kriterien zur Berechnung dieses Entgelts — im nationalen Recht eindeutig festgelegt ist.** Die Mitgliedstaaten stellen **ferner** sicher, dass die Entgelterhebung nach dem Grundsatz der Verhältnismäßigkeit und in transparenter Weise erfolgt.

Weitere ergänzende Klarstellungen finden sich auch in den Erwgr. der neuen Richtlinie, die ebenfalls über den Text der bisherigen Erwgr. zur Universaldienst-Richtlinie hinaus gehen. So stellt Erwgr. 308 klar, dass sich Übertragungspflichten auf bestimmte, spezifisch zu benennende Anbieter

D. Sekundärrechtlicher Rahmen zum „Medienrecht" und Medienpluralismus

von Hörfunk- oder Fernsehkanälen oder ergänzende Dienste hierzu beziehen müssen. Es wird noch stärker unterstrichen, dass die Regelungen dazu transparent, verhältnismäßig und „genau definiert" sein müssen und ausreichend Entwicklungsmöglichkeiten lassen, damit Netzbetreiber in ihre Infrastrukturen investieren. Der Überprüfungsturnus für solche Übertragungspflichten wird nach Erwgr. 309 jetzt konkret auf Fünfjahreszeiträume festgelegt, damit in vorgegebenem Umfang überprüft wird, ob die Marktentwicklung die Pflichten der Netzbetreiber, zu denen nach dem folgenden Erwgr. mittlerweile auch explizit „IP-TV" zählt, überflüssig gemacht hat. Wichtig ist ferner die Klarstellung, dass in „Anbetracht der zunehmenden Bereitstellung und Nutzung vernetzter Fernsehdienste und der nach wie vor bestehenden Bedeutung elektronischer Programmführer für die Auswahlmöglichkeiten der Endnutzer [...] die Übermittlung programmbezogener Daten, die für die Unterstützung von Funktionen des vernetzten Fernsehens und elektronischer Programmführer erforderlich sind, in die Übertragungspflichten aufgenommen werden" (Erwgr. 310) kann.

Während die Mitgliedstaaten (und damit auch die nationalen Regulierungsbehörden) auch unter Geltung des EEKK weiterhin hinsichtlich des „ob" der Einführung von Must-Carry-Regeln frei bleiben, nimmt der EEKK im Rahmen der Reform einige Konkretisierungen hinsichtlich des „wie" vor. Insbesondere muss die Zielsetzung von Allgemeininteressen, welche bei der Etablierung von Übertragungspflichten regelmäßig die Sicherung von Vielfalt ist, ausdrücklich gesetzlich verankert werden. Das gilt auch für das Entgelt, sofern die Mitgliedstaaten ein solches vorsehen. Wo vorher lediglich eine „regelmäßige" Überprüfung vorgesehen war, schreibt der EEKK nun eine Überprüfung alle fünf Jahre fest. Auch die Erweiterung der Must-Carry-Bestimmungen auf „ergänzende Dienste" ist neu. Solche ergänzenden Dienste können programmbezogene Dienste umfassen, die speziell konzipiert sind, um die Barrierefreiheit für Endnutzer mit Behinderungen zu verbessern (beispielsweise Videotext, Untertitel für gehörlose oder hörgeschädigte Endnutzer, Audiobeschreibung, gesprochene Untertitel und Gebärdensprachverdolmetschung) und können erforderlichenfalls auch den Zugang zu den diesbezüglichen Ursprungsdaten beinhalten, sowie programmbezogene Dienste des vernetzten Fernsehens.[593] Pro-

---

[593] Zum Begriff vgl. auch Entschließung des Europäischen Parlaments vom 4. Juli 2013 zu „Connected TV" (2012/2300(INI)), https://www.europarl.europa.eu/sides/getDoc.do?pubRef=-//EP//TEXT+TA+P7-TA-2013-0329+0+DOC+XML+V0//DE.

grammbezogene Daten meinen solche Daten, die für die Unterstützung von Funktionen des vernetzten Fernsehens und elektronischer Programmführer erforderlich sind und regelmäßig Informationen über den Programminhalt und die Art des Zugangs enthalten.[594] Jedoch lassen die Präzisierungen, die teilweise auch Urteile des EuGH aufgreifen[595], den Grundsatz unangetastet, dass trotz des hohen Harmonisierungsgrades im Bericht elektronischer Kommunikationsnetze und -dienste und auch trotz der technologischen Entwicklung, die dem Grundsatz nach mehr Angebotsvielfalt von den technischen Möglichkeiten her zulässt, weiterhin ergänzende Maßnahmen zur Vielfaltssicherung durch die Mitgliedstaaten und nur durch diese vorzunehmen sind. Damit wird anerkannt, dass die zur Entscheidung über die Notwendigkeit solcher Übertragungspflichten vorzunehmenden Bewertungen nur auf Ebene der und durch die Mitgliedstaaten bzw. nationalen Regulierungsbehörden erfolgen können.

Dies weitreichende Anerkennung des mitgliedstaatlichen Handlungsspielraums lässt auch das Ergebnis eines früheren EuGH-Urteils unberührt, wonach Übertragungspflichten ohne Verstoß gegen das unionsrechtliche Verhältnismäßigkeitsgebot dazu führen können, dass im (analogen) Kabelnetz sämtliche Programmplatzbelegungen vorgegeben sind.[596] Zwar ist die Frage der analogen Kabelbelegung kaum mehr relevant und der neue EEKK stellt klar, dass Übertragungsverpflichtungen insoweit nur noch ausnahmsweise vorzusehen sind. Es bleibt aber die Erkenntnis, dass trotz des Eingriffs in die Dienstleistungsfreiheit und Grundrechte der Netzbetreiber Mitgliedstaaten umfassende Steuerungsmöglichkeiten haben. Die übermäßige Inanspruchnahme der Netzbetreiber soll durch die genauen Vorgaben, welche Bedingungen bei Übertragungspflichten zu erfüllen sind, verhindert werden. Aber der vom EuGH unterstrichene Zweck, „den pluralistischen und kulturellen Charakter des Programmangebots in den Kabelfernsehnetzen [zu] wahren und den Zugang aller Fernsehzuschauer zu einem pluralistischen und vielfältigen Programmangebot [zu] gewährleisten"[597], ist auch weiterhin relevant, wenn es um andere Arten der Pflichten für Netzbetreiber geht, die diesen zum Zwecke der Pluralismussicherung aufgegeben werden. Der Mitgliedstaat muss aber in der Ausgestaltung die-

---

594 Vgl. hierzu Erwägungsgründe 153 und 310 des EEKK.
595 Vgl. EuGH, Rs. C-250/06, *United Pan-Europe Communications Belgium SA und andere / Belgischer Staat*, Rn. 31; Rs. C-353/89, *Kommission / Niederlande*, Rn. 25.
596 EuGH, Rs. C-336/07, *Kabel Deutschland / NLM*; vgl. dazu auch Cole in: HK-MStV, § 51 b Rn. 22 ff., zum Urteil insbes. 27 ff.
597 EuGH, Rs. C-250/06, *United Pan-Europe Communications Belgium SA und andere / Belgischer Staat*, Rn. 40.

D. Sekundärrechtlicher Rahmen zum „Medienrecht" und Medienpluralismus

ses Ziel konkret[598] in der gesetzlichen Regelung zum Ausdruck bringen. Zudem müssen die Regeln wie erwähnt verhältnismäßig und transparent sein, was wiederum wie in den vorigen Abschnitten eine Prüfung der nationalen Vorschriften am Unionsrecht und dort niedergelegten Grundprinzipien bedeutet, wie es konkret in Art. 61, 114 EEKK benannt ist. Auch insoweit überlässt aber der EuGH der mitgliedstaatlichen Ebene, in diesem Fall den zuständigen Gerichten, die Bewertung, ob im Einzelfall die Kriterien beachtet worden sind.[599] Den Mitgliedstaaten bleibt also auch im Rahmen der Infrastrukturregulierung im Lichte ihrer Kulturpolitik ein weiter Gestaltungsspielraum.

Von besonderer Relevanz ist aber Art. 1 Abs. 3 Buchst. b) EEKK. Dieser stellt schon eingangs der Richtlinie zum Anwendungsbereich klar, dass die von der Union oder den Mitgliedstaaten im Einklang mit dem Unionsrecht getroffenen Maßnahmen zur Verfolgung von Zielen des Allgemeininteresses vom EEKK unberührt bleiben. In der Beispielaufzählung wird neben dem Datenschutz als eines solchen Ziels auch „die Regulierung von Inhalten und die audiovisuelle Politik" explizit genannt. Wie bereits oben erwähnt stellt der zugehörige Erwgr. 7 klar, dass dies nicht eine strikte Trennung von Vorschriften über den technischen netzbezogenen Bereichen und denjenigen, die inhaltsbezogen sind, verlangt. Jedoch sind die beiden Bereiche voneinander zu unterscheiden und die Kompetenz für die Regelung ist bei der Inhalteregulierung insbesondere dann, wenn sie im Blick auf die Pluralismussicherung erfolgt, bei den Mitgliedstaaten zu verorten. Damit entspricht diese Regelung der Ausnahmeregelung wie sie in Art. 1 Abs. 6 ECRL festgeschrieben ist (vgl. Abschnitt D.II.1.) und belässt insoweit den Mitgliedstaaten auch vor dem telekommunikationsrechtlichen Hintergrund Raum für (zusätzliche) Regelungen zur Vielfaltssicherung, die sich auf vom EEKK erfasste Anbieter auswirken können. Jedoch gibt der EEKK insoweit den Mitgliedstaaten vor, dass er die beiden Bereiche auch unterschiedlich regelt und nicht etwa inhaltsbezogene Vorschriften durch das Umsetzungsrecht des EEKK mit erfasst.

---

598 Die bloße Formulierung von Grundsatzerklärungen und allgemeinpolitischen Zielen in der Begründung der nationalen Regelung kann insoweit nicht als ausreichend angesehen werden, vgl. EuGH, Rs. C-250/06, *United Pan-Europe Communications Belgium SA und andere / Belgischer Staat*, Rn. 46.

599 Wobei die Überprüfung hier allerdings im Zweifel von nationalen Gerichten zu erfolgen hat und nicht vom EuGH; vgl. EuGH, Rs. C-336/07, *Kabel Deutschland Vertrieb und Service GmbH & Co. KG / Niedersächsische Landesmedienanstalt für privaten Rundfunk*.

Im Blick auf die nationale Umsetzung auch in Deutschland bedeutet dies, dass eine ersatzlose Streichung vorhandener rundfunkbezogener Rücksichtnahmegebote im TKG mit der Umsetzungsverpflichtung in Bezug auf Art. 1 Abs. 3 EEKK nicht ohne Weiteres vereinbar erscheint. Zumindest würde eine auf eine solche ersatzlose Streichung gerichtete TKG-Novelle nicht nur aus verfassungsrechtlichen Gründen zumindest einen erheblichen Darlegungsaufwand zur Vereinbarkeit der Gesetzesnovelle mit höherrangigem Recht, d.h. auch EU-Recht, auslösen – zumal auch bei Umsetzungsakten für EU-Richtlinien die Bindung an das in Art. 11 Abs. 2 GRC verankerte Gebot besteht, die Pluralität der Medien zu achten.

6. Platform-to-Business-Verordnung

Wie bereits im Zusammenhang mit den neuen Regeln zur Herausstellung von Inhalten im Allgemeininteresse in der AVMD-Richtlinie angesprochen (Abschnitt D.II.2.d(2)), ist die Gewährleistung der Sichtbarkeit von medialen Inhalten ein bedeutendes Element der Vielfaltssicherung. Dieser Gedanke der „Sichtbarkeit" von Inhalten oder Informationen findet sich nicht nur im Sekundärrecht mit medienrechtlicher Ausrichtung, sondern ist auch angelegt in einem gerade erst anwendbar gewordenen Rechtsakt, der sich auf wettbewerbsorientierte Aspekte des Wirtschaftssektors (bestimmter) Online-Diensteanbieter bezieht. Die Platform-to-Business(P2B)-Verordnung[600] gilt seit dem 12. Juli 2020 in allen Mitgliedstaaten unmittelbar und ist im Gesamtkontext dieser Studie ebenfalls näher zu betrachten.

a. Geltungsbereich und Zielsetzung

Dieses Regelungswerk wurde mit dem Ziel geschaffen, mehr Transparenz, Fairness und wirksame Abhilfemöglichkeiten im Bereich von Online-Vermittlungsdiensten zu schaffen. Darunter versteht die Verordnung (Art. 2 Abs. 2) Dienste der Informationsgesellschaft, die es gewerblichen Nutzern auf Grundlage eines Vertragsverhältnisses ermöglichen, Verbrauchern Wa-

---

600 Verordnung (EU) 2019/1150 des Europäischen Parlaments und des Rates vom 20. Juni 2019 zur Förderung von Fairness und Transparenz für gewerbliche Nutzer von Online-Vermittlungsdiensten, ABl. L 186, 11.7.2019, S. 57–79, https://eur-lex.europa.eu/legal-content/DE/ALL/?uri=CELEX%3A32019R1150.

D. Sekundärrechtlicher Rahmen zum „Medienrecht" und Medienpluralismus

ren oder Dienstleistungen anzubieten, indem sie die Einleitung direkter Transaktionen zwischen diesen gewerblichen Nutzern und Verbrauchern vermitteln, unabhängig davon, wo diese Transaktionen letztlich abgeschlossen werden. Es geht also um Dienste, die als Vermittler und damit in vielen Fällen auch Gatekeeper (insbesondere in Bezug auf KMU) zwischen Waren- oder Dienstleistungsverkäufern und Konsumenten stehen. Da ein wesentlicher Teil des Online-Handels unter Beteiligung solcher Vermittler stattfindet, ist es aus Sicht der EU-Rechtsetzungsorgane wichtig, dass Unternehmen Vertrauen in diese Dienste haben und von diesen ihnen gegenüber Transparenz gewährleistet wird. Gesondert adressiert werden von der Richtlinie auch Online-Suchmaschinen, worunter ein digitaler Dienst verstanden wird, der es Nutzern ermöglicht, in Form eines Stichworts, einer Spracheingabe, einer Wortgruppe oder einer anderen Eingabe Anfragen einzugeben, um prinzipiell auf allen Webseiten oder allen in einer bestimmten Sprache, eine Suche zu einem beliebigen Thema vorzunehmen und Ergebnisse in einem beliebigen Format angezeigt zu bekommen, über die sie Informationen im Zusammenhang mit dem angeforderten Inhalt finden können. Auch Suchmaschinen agieren regelmäßig als Bindeglied und Gatekeeper zwischen Unternehmen und Konsumenten.

Die Verordnung reagiert mit der spezifischen Adressierung der Suchmaschinen auf die begründete Befürchtung, dass Suchmaschinen nicht neutral in der Anzeige ihrer Suchergebnisse und deren Anordnung sind.[601] Bei der Verordnung steht das reibungslose Funktionieren des Binnenmarktes im Vordergrund und sie reagiert auf ein (auch potentiell) ungleiches Machtgefüge in der digitalen Wirtschaft bzw. will negativen Auswirkungen dieses Machtgefüges vorbeugen. Damit bestehen Parallelen zur Situation bei den Beziehungen zwischen Rezipienten, Medienintermediären und Inhalteanbietern. Die P2B-Verordnung bezieht sich nicht auf das Allgemeininteresse Pluralismussicherung, das weder in ihrer Zielsetzung liegt, noch kompetenziell Anknüpfungspunkt sein könnte, aber die Parallelität der Anknüpfungspunkte führt dazu, dass sich die Verordnung in der praktischen Anwendung mindestens mittelbar vielfaltssichernd auswirken kann.

---

601 So bereits feststellend das EU-Projekt CHORUS in seiner Studie aus dem Jahr 2010: *Boujemaa u.a.*, Cross-disciplinary Challenges and Recommendations regarding the Future of Multimedia Search Engines. Vgl. im Übrigen auch *Meckel*, Vielfalt im digitalen Medienensemble, S. 12 f.

b. Die Transparenzvorgaben

Art. 5 P2B-Verordnung sieht vor, dass Anbieter von Online-Vermittlungsdiensten und Online-Suchmaschinen, die Hauptparameter, die bei ihren Diensten die Reihenfolge oder Gewichtung der Darstellung oder Auflistung („Ranking") durch klare und verständlich formulierte Erklärungen in den AGBs bzw. auf der Website des eigenen Dienstes nachvollziehbar machen müssen. Im Wesentlichen geht es hier also um die Beschreibung der Algorithmen, die die Anzeige und dadurch auch die Auffindbarkeit (mit)bestimmen. Online-Vermittlungsdienste werden unmittelbar von der Verordnung selbst verpflichtet, Beschwerdesysteme für gewerbliche Nutzer einzurichten, um die Umsetzung der Vorgaben der Verordnung auf Beschwerde gewerblicher Nutzer in der Praxis zu gewährleisten. Diese Verpflichtung gilt nicht unmittelbar für Online-Suchmaschinen. Allerdings werden die Mitgliedstaaten verpflichtet, eine angemessene und wirksame Durchsetzung der Verordnung bezogen auf alle von der Verordnung erfassten Anbieter sicherzustellen (Art. 15). Darüber hinaus ist eine konkrete Form der Überwachung der Auswirkungen der Verordnung durch die Kommission niedergelegt (Art. 16). Die Entwicklung von Verhaltenskodizes wird angemahnt (Art. 17), die die „ordnungsgemäße Anwendung" der Verordnung sicherstellen sollen, wobei die Formulierung „ordnungsgemäße Anwendung [...] unterstützen" verdeutlicht, dass sie als Instrument der konkretisierenden Koregulierung gemeint sind und es nicht zu einer reinen Selbstregulierung des Sektors kommen soll.

Da unter die Begriffsdefinition der „gewerblichen Nutzer"[602] bzw. „Nutzer mit Unternehmenswebsite"[603], die von der Verordnung und den festgelegten Transparenzverpflichtungen geschützt werden sollen, potentiell auch Medienunternehmen mit ihren Online-Angeboten fallen, wird (auch) diesen ein wichtiges Mittel an die Hand gegeben, um ihre Position gegenüber Gatekeepern wie Online-Suchmaschinen und sozialen Medi-

---

[602] Nach Art. 2 Abs. 1 P2B-VO jede im Rahmen einer geschäftlichen oder beruflichen Tätigkeit handelnde Privatperson oder jede juristische Person, die über Online-Vermittlungsdienste und für Zwecke im Zusammenhang mit ihrer gewerblichen, geschäftlichen, handwerklichen oder beruflichen Tätigkeit Verbrauchern Waren oder Dienstleistungen anbietet.

[603] Nach Art. 2 Abs. 7 P2B-VO eine natürliche oder juristische Person, die über eine Online-Schnittstelle, d. h. über eine Software (darunter Websites oder Teile davon und Anwendungen, einschließlich mobiler Anwendungen) und für Zwecke im Zusammenhang mit ihrer gewerblichen, geschäftlichen, handwerklichen oder beruflichen Tätigkeit Verbrauchern Waren oder Dienstleistungen anbietet.

en[604] zu stärken, die eine wichtige Rolle bei der Online-Verbreitung und Auffindbarkeit ihrer Inhalte spielen.[605] Insbesondere können (auch) diese davon profitieren, dass den Vermittlern und Suchmaschinen aufgegeben wird, genauere Informationen über die Funktionsweise ihrer Dienste offenzulegen. Zwar ist mit der Verpflichtung aus der Verordnung nicht die Offenlegung der detaillierten Funktionsweise oder der Algorithmen selbst verbunden, aber eine öffentlich verfügbare und stets aktuelle Erläuterung darüber, welche Bedeutung und Gewichtung einzelnen Parametern zukommt und ob das Ranking durch Leistung eines Entgelts (nicht nur in Form von Zahlungen) beeinflusst wird.

Zur Umsetzung dieser Vorgaben muss die EU-Kommission – ähnlich zu den neuen Bestimmungen der AVMD-Richtlinie – nach Art. 5 Abs. 7 auch bezüglich des wichtigsten Inhalts der Verordnung, die Anwendung der Vorschrift über das „Ranking", Leitlinien erlassen. Diese befinden sich derzeit noch in der Entwicklung.[606] Selbst wenn die konkreten Folgen der Verordnung, wie sie sich auch aus den Leitlinien ergeben werden, (auch) für den Mediensektor noch nicht im Detail absehbar sind, handelt es sich dennoch um eine Regelung, die im Zusammenhang mit der unverfälschten Wahrnehmbarkeit relevanter Dienstleistungen (auch: dem Angebot von Inhalten) steht und daher auch aus vielfaltssicherndem Blickwinkel in ihrer Auswirkung zu verfolgen ist. Durch die Transparenzgebote könnte auch die Überprüfung der Funktionsweise dieses Sektors im Allgemeinen verbessert werden, so dass in der Folge auf Basis so gefundener Forschungsergebnisse gegebenenfalls zukünftige Regulierungsvorschläge erarbeitet werden könnten.

c. Das Verhältnis zu weiteren mitgliedstaatlichen Regelungen

Vor dem Hintergrund des Schwerpunkts der vorliegenden Studie ist die P2B-Verordnung auch aus einem weiteren Grund zu betrachten, weil sie als Verordnung in allen Mitgliedstaaten unmittelbar geltendes Recht darstellt. Ihr Anwendungsbereich und die dargestellten Verpflichtungen für die Diensteanbieter, die wie gezeigt reflexhaft auch vielfaltsfördernde Ef-

---

604 Vgl. hierzu Erwägungsgrund 11 der P2B-Verordnung.
605 Zu den Möglichkeiten der Vielfaltssicherung durch Suchmaschinen vgl. *Nolte* in: ZUM 2017, 552, 552 ff.
606 Zum aktuellen Stand vgl. https://ec.europa.eu/digital-single-market/en/news/ranking-transparency-guidelines-framework-eu-regulation-platform-business-relations-explainer.

fekte im Mediensektor haben können, führt zur Frage, ob die Verordnung eine Sperrwirkung oder anderweitige Begrenzung gegenüber mitgliedstaatlichen Regelungsansätzen bezüglich bereits von der Verordnung erfasster Anbieter und Transparenzvorgaben für diese entfaltet. Dabei ist hervorzuheben, dass die Verordnung anders als etwa die AVMD-Richtlinie keine ausdrückliche Abweichungsbefugnis vom koordinierten Bereich der Richtlinie für strengere Regelungen oder wie die ECRL eine zusätzliche Einschränkungsbefugnis der Mitgliedstaaten aus Gründen beispielsweise des Jugendschutzes enthält. Art. 1 Abs. 4 P2B-Verordnung verweist lediglich auf bestimmte unberührt bleibende Regeln der Mitgliedstaaten aus dem jeweiligen nationalen Zivilrecht. Verordnungen sind in all ihren Teilen verbindlich und nicht wie Richtlinien lediglich hinsichtlich des zu erreichenden Ziels, sodass mitgliedstaatliche Ausführungsakte unnötig und sogar unzulässig sind, wenn sie die unmittelbare Geltung der Verordnung verbergen würden.[607] Das umfasst auch ein vom EuGH früh entwickeltes Wiederholungsverbot, wonach eine lediglich wiederholende Darstellung der Regelungsmaterie einer Verordnung im mitgliedstaatlichen Recht unzulässig ist, weil hierdurch Unsicherheiten über Urheber und Rechtsnatur eines Rechtsakts hervorgerufen und die gleichzeitige und einheitliche Anwendung des EU-Rechts gefährdet würden.[608] Anders ist dies bei Verordnungen, die an die Mitgliedstaaten gerichtete Durchführungsbestimmungen enthalten oder bewusst in ihrem räumlichen Anwendungsbereich beschränkt sind[609] oder durch häufig so genannte „Öffnungsklauseln" mitgliedstaatliche Handlungsspielräume für bestimmte Vorschriften der Verordnung trotz ihres Charakters als Verordnung eröffnen. Bei den hier relevanten Bestimmungen der P2B-Verordnung handelt es sich jedoch nicht um solche Arten von Vorschriften.

Das Verbot mitgliedstaatlicher Regelungen im Bereich einer Verordnung gilt allerdings nur soweit, wie ein Regelungsbereich – etwa die Vielfaltssicherung – von dieser erfasst wird. Die P2B-Verordnung befasst sich mit „potentiellen Reibungen in der Online-Plattformwirtschaft" aus der wettbewerbsrechtlichen und verbraucherschutzrechtlichen Perspektive (Erwgr. 2 und 3) und unterscheidet daher nicht zwischen bestimmten Unternehmen, die von der Transparenz profitieren sollen, ist also sektorneutral. Jedoch ist damit die Fragestellung nicht erfasst, dass möglicherweise für bestimmte Sektoren spezifische Faktoren eine Rolle spielen, die es für

---

607 Ruffert, in: Calliess/ders., Art. 288 AEUV, Rn. 19 m.w.N.
608 Vgl. etwa EuGH, Rs. 39–72, *Kommission / Italien*, Rn. 17.
609 Vgl. hierzu *Nettesheim* in Grabitz/Hilf/Nettesheim, Art. 288 AEUV, Rn. 99 ff.

D. Sekundärrechtlicher Rahmen zum „Medienrecht" und Medienpluralismus

die Unternehmen in diesem Sektor besonders relevant machen, mehr über die Funktionsweise des Dienstes durch eine transparente Darstellung von Rankingsystemen zu erfahren. Ebenso wenig adressiert die Verordnung das Allgemeininteresse an der Anzeige bestimmter Inhalte nach bestimmten Kriterien. Als Beispiel hierfür kann neben dem Mediensektor und der dort stattfindenden Informationsverbreitung, bei dem Aspekte der Vielfaltssicherung eine wichtige Rolle auch bei der Wahrnehmung durch den Endnutzer spielen, beispielsweise der Arzneimittelsektor beim Gesichtspunkt Gesundheitsschutz oder der Bereich der Politik bei der Chancengleichheit politischer Parteien vor dem Hintergrund des Demokratieprinzips genannt werden. Die in der Verordnung vorgenommene Unterscheidung von Anforderungen bezüglich der Darstellung der Ranking-Faktoren zwischen Online-Vermittlungsdiensten und Suchmaschinenbetreibern bedeutet dabei ebenfalls keine Berücksichtigung sektorspezifischer Besonderheiten, sondern hängt mit den unterschiedlichen Beziehungen zwischen den im Schutzbereich der Verordnung stehenden Unternehmen und den Diensteanbietern für diese beiden Kategorien zusammen, insbesondere dem Faktor, dass Suchmaschinen in keinem direkten vertraglichen Verhältnis zu den im Rahmen von Suchergebnissen angezeigten Unternehmen (bzw. deren Webseiten) stehen.

Allgemeininteressen, die einen besonderen Schutz bestimmter Unternehmen bzw. eine Einbeziehung der Öffentlichkeit bei der Offenlegung von Informationen erforderlich machen, werden von der Verordnung damit nicht abgedeckt. Diese bleibt im Rahmen der allgemeinen wettbewerbsbezogenen Erwägungen, wie sich auch aus den Erwägungsgründen wiederholt ergibt. Als horizontal anwendbares Rechtsinstrument, das den Wettbewerb vor unlauteren Praktiken, Verzerrungen und Ungleichbehandlungen in allen Wirtschaftssektoren schützen will, ist die Verordnung nicht darauf ausgelegt, andere sektorspezifische Interessen zu berücksichtigen.[610]

Im Online-Konsultationsverfahren zur Entwicklung der Leitlinien zur Transparenzverpflichtung weist die Kommission darauf hin, dass die Leitlinien unter anderem das Ziel haben sollen, wo nötig auch sektorspezifische Hinweise zur Anwendung der Transparenzverpflichtung zu geben.[611] Es gibt jedoch bislang keine Hinweise für welche Sektoren solche besonde-

---

610 Vgl. Erwgr. 51, der ausdrücklich nur das Wettbewerbsziel benennt: „…Gewährleistung eines fairen, vorhersehbaren, tragfähigen und vertrauenswürdigen Online-Geschäftsumfelds im Binnenmarkt".
611 "Provide sector specific guidance, if and where appropriate.", vgl. Targeted online survey on the ranking transparency guidelines in the framework of the EU

643

ren Hinweise gegeben werden bzw. welche Aspekte diese abdecken könnten. Welche Relevanz Transparenzvorgaben allerdings an solche Anbieter für Unternehmen aus dem Mediensektor haben, zeigt sich auch daran, dass sich vor allem Beteiligte aus dem Mediensektor mit der Darstellung der medienpolitischen Gesichtspunkte an der Online-Befragung beteiligt haben.[612] Die Leitlinien sollten nach Ankündigung der Kommission zum 12. Juli 2020 bereits veröffentlicht worden sein, sie fehlen jedoch bislang noch.

Die Kommission ist jedoch ohnehin in ihrer Leitlinienbefugnis an die Vorgaben aus der Verordnung gebunden und kann nicht über das hinausgehen, was von der Verordnung gedeckt ist. Befugnisse zum Erlass von Leitlinien werden dort erteilt, wenn allgemeinere Regeln näher auszufüllen und der zugrundeliegende Kontext sich dynamisch weiterentwickelt. Dies gilt auch für den stark technisierten und digitalen Bereich wie hier bei der Ermächtigung nach Art. 5 Abs. 7 P2B-Verordnung. Jedoch darf eine Ausgestaltung nicht einfach erfolgen, weil sie sinnvoll erscheint. Vielmehr muss die Kommission im Rahmen der Befugnis und damit der von der (in diesem Fall: Verordnung) erfassten Regelungszusammenhang bleiben, sonst würde dies indirekt zu einer faktischen Übertragung von Befugnissen auf die Kommission im Verwaltungsverbund führen, obwohl sie über diese Kompetenz nicht verfügt[613] oder verfügen soll.[614] Dies gilt auch für die Verfolgung kulturpolitischer Ziele in Bezug auf Transparenzvorgaben für Anbieter bestimmter Online-Vermittlungsdienste oder Suchmaschinen, die sich aufgrund der mitgliedstaatlichen Zuständigkeit und des limitierten Inhalts der Verordnung auch nicht aus den Leitlinien ergeben dürfen. Wenngleich die Kommission zum Ausdruck gebracht hat, dass sie „potenzielle rechtliche Überschneidungen" der P2B-Verordnung mit mit-

---

regulation on platform-to-business relations, https://ec.europa.eu/digital-single-market/en/news/targeted-online-survey-ranking-transparency-guidelines-framework-eu-regulation-platform.
612 Vgl. Die Stellungnahmen etwa der EBU oder ACT, abrufbar unter https://ec.europa.eu/digital-single-market/en/news/ranking-transparency-guidelines-framework-eu-regulation-platform-business-relations-explainer.
613 Zur Kritik in Bezug auf die Einräumung von Kompetenzen durch Leitlinienbefugnisse vgl. *Lecheler* in: DVBl. 2008, 873, 873 ff.; *Weiß* in: EWS 2010, 257, 257 ff.
614 Vgl. hierzu m.w.N. *Ruffert* in Calliess/ders., Art. 288 AEUV, Rn. 102, der auch auf die Gefahr einer Verschiebung verweist, die sich daraus ergibt, dass Leitlinien eine hohe Steuerwirkung entfalten können, demgegenüber aber nur eine schwache primärrechtliche Verankerung haben.

D. Sekundärrechtlicher Rahmen zum „Medienrecht" und Medienpluralismus

gliedstaatlicher Medienrechtssetzung erkennt[615], soweit letztere Transparenzvorgaben machen, findet diese Beobachtung keine Grundlage in der Verordnung, die gerade nicht die Zielsetzung der Medienvielfaltssicherung hat. Daher entfaltet weder die Verordnung und erst recht nicht die noch zu erlassenden rechtlich unverbindlichen Leitlinien eine Begrenzung mitgliedstaatlicher Handlungsmöglichkeiten zum Erreichen dieses Allgemeinwohlziels. Damit stehen die Regelungen der P2B-Verordnung beispielsweise auch nicht mitgliedstaatlichen Regelungen zur Förderung von Fairness und Transparenz bei neuen Medienakteuren wie Medienintermediären und Mediaagenturen[616] entgegen, solange diese nicht auf wirtschaftlichen Verbraucherschutz und grenzüberschreitende Verkehrsfähigkeit von Online-Dienstleistungen, sondern auf die Sicherung von Medienvielfalt unter den Bedingungen von Digitalisierung und Globalisierung und die Bewältigung neuer Gefährdungen für Vielfalt durch auf Aggregation, Selektion und Präsentation von Medieninhalten ausgerichtete Geschäftsmodelle zielen.

d. Das Verhältnis zur Richtlinie (EU) 2019/2161

Auch eine kurze Betrachtung der nur wenige Monate nach der P2B-Verordnung in Kraft getretenen Richtlinie (EU) 2019/2161[617] belegt die Offenhaltung mitgliedstaatlicher Spielräume zur Regelung des Allgemeinwohlziels Medienpluralismus. Die Richtlinie enthält verschiedene Vorgaben zur Durchsetzung und Modernisierung der Verbraucherschutzvorschriften der Union. Die Richtlinie bezieht sich im Gegensatz zur P2B-Verordnung nicht auf das Verhältnis zwischen Unternehmen und den von der Verordnung erfassten Plattformen (Online-Vermittlungsdienste und Suchmaschinen), sondern auf die Beziehung zwischen Endverbrauchern und den Plattformen. Auch in diesem Kontext spielen das Ranking oder eine hervorgehobene Platzierung von kommerziellen Angeboten in den Ergebnis-

---

615 Vgl. dazu die Bemerkungen der Kommission im Notifizierungsverfahren, aaO (Fn. 18), S. 9.
616 Vgl. *Ukrow/Cole*, Zur Transparenz von Mediaagenturen, S. 52 ff.
617 Richtlinie (EU) 2019/2161 (vom 27. November 2019 zur Änderung der Richtlinie 93/13/EWG des Rates und der Richtlinien 98/6/EG, 2005/29/EG und 2011/83/EU des Europäischen Parlaments und des Rates zur besseren Durchsetzung und Modernisierung der Verbraucherschutzvorschriften der Union, EU ABl. L 328 vom 18.12.2019), https://eur-lex.europa.eu/legal-content/DE/TXT/?uri=CELEX%3A32019L2161&qid=1614597549259.

sen einer Such-Anfrage durch Anbieter von Online-Suchfunktionen eine bedeutende Rolle, da diese erhebliche Auswirkungen auf die (Kaufentscheidung der) Verbraucher haben können.[618]

Durch eine Änderung der Verbraucherrechte-Richtlinie 2011/83/EU werden Anbieter von Online-Marktplätzen[619] zu weitreichenderen Informationspflichten im Verhältnis gegenüber Verbrauchern verpflichtet (Art. 6 a): Bevor ein Verbraucher durch einen Fernabsatzvertrag oder ein entsprechendes Vertragsangebot auf einem Online-Marktplatz gebunden ist, informiert der Anbieter des Online-Marktplatzes den Verbraucher in klarer, verständlicher und erkennbarer Weise unter anderem über allgemeine Informationen, die die Hauptparameter zur Festlegung des Rankings der Angebote, die dem Verbraucher als Ergebnis seiner Suchanfrage auf dem Online-Marktplatz präsentiert werden, sowie die relative Gewichtung dieser Parameter im Vergleich zu anderen Parametern. Diese Informationen müssen in einem bestimmten Bereich der Online-Benutzeroberfläche zur Verfügung gestellt werden, der von der Seite, auf der die Angebote angezeigt werden, unmittelbar und leicht zugänglich ist. Parallel wird in die Richtlinie über unlautere Geschäftspraktiken[620] ein entsprechender Tatbestand aufgenommen, der solche Angaben als wesentlich definiert und damit ihr Vorenthalten als irreführende Unterlassung klassifiziert. Letztere Bestimmung soll allerdings ausdrücklich nicht für Online-Suchmaschinen im Sinne der P2B-Verordnung gelten, auf die die Richtlinie über unlautere Geschäftspraktiken ansonsten aber Anwendung findet. Dies hat jedoch nicht zum Ziel eine Ausnahme für diese zu konstruieren, sondern eine Dopplung der bereits existierenden Pflichten zu vermeiden. Dies wird in Erwgr. 21 klargestellt, wonach die Transparenzanforderungen

---

618 Vgl. Erwägungsgrund 18 der Richtlinie (EU) 2019/2161.
619 Definiert als "einen Dienst, der es Verbrauchern durch die Verwendung von Software, einschließlich einer Website, eines Teils einer Website oder einer Anwendung, die vom Unternehmer oder im Namen des Unternehmers betrieben wird, ermöglicht, Fernabsatzverträge mit anderen Unternehmern oder Verbrauchern abzuschließen", Art. 2 Abs. 1 Nr. 17 der Richtlinie 2011/83/EU in der Fassung der Richtlinie (EU) 2019/2161.
620 Richtlinie 2005/29/EG des Europäischen Parlaments und des Rates vom 11. Mai 2005 über unlautere Geschäftspraktiken im binnenmarktinternen Geschäftsverkehr zwischen Unternehmen und Verbrauchern und zur Änderung der Richtlinie 84/450/EWG des Rates, der Richtlinien 97/7/EG, 98/27/EG und 2002/65/EG des Europäischen Parlaments und des Rates sowie der Verordnung (EG) Nr. 2006/2004 des Europäischen Parlaments und des Rates (Richtlinie über unlautere Geschäftspraktiken), EU ABl. L 149, 11.6.2005, S. 22–39, https://eur-lex.europa.eu/legal-content/DE/TXT/?uri=celex:32005L0029.

D. Sekundärrechtlicher Rahmen zum „Medienrecht" und Medienpluralismus

in vergleichbarer Weise wie bei der P2B-Verordnung durch die Richtlinie auch gegenüber den Verbrauchern gewährleistet werden soll. Da aber bezüglich der Suchmaschinen bereits aus der Verordnung eine umfassende Pflicht zur öffentlich zugänglichen Erläuterung über die Parameter besteht, ist insoweit eine Wiederholung unnötig.

Die Richtlinie sichert damit, dass die Verbraucher nicht nur reflexhaft von einer durch die P2B-Verordnung eingeführten höheren Transparenz von Rankingsystemen zwischen Unternehmern und Vermittlern profitieren, sondern explizite Garantien auch für den Verbraucher gelten. Dabei sind neben den Vorgaben in der Richtlinie die Mitgliedstaaten zudem nicht daran gehindert, zusätzliche Informationspflichten für Anbieter von Online-Marktplätzen aus Gründen des Verbraucherschutzes vorzusehen (Art. 6a Abs. 2). Damit wird zweierlei deutlich: Bereits aus Unionsrechtsperspektive sind Transparenzanforderungen an Online-Diensteanbieter aus unterschiedlicher Zielsetzung möglich, im EU-Recht bislang namentlich geregelt aus wettbewerbsrechtlicher (P2B-Verordnung) und verbraucherschutzrechtlicher Sicht (Richtlinie (EU) 2019/2161). Zudem wird anerkannt, dass auch bei Bestehen bestimmter Mindestanforderungen (hier: aus der Verordnung) darüber hinaus gehende oder konkretere Vorgaben zum Erreichen des anderen Ziels möglich sind. Wenn also etwa eine besondere Schutzbedürftigkeit für den Verbraucher besteht, kann eine besondere Ausgestaltung der Transparenzvorgaben erfolgen. Ebenso bleibt es für die Mitgliedstaaten möglich, aus einem wiederum anderen Blickwinkel, dessen Berücksichtigung in ihre Zuständigkeit fällt, weitergehende Transparenzvorgaben zu machen. Medienpluralismussicherung kann demnach solche Anforderungen an bestimmte Intermediäre, die (auch) bei der Verbreitung von medialen Inhalten eine bedeutende Rolle einnehmen, rechtfertigen und die entsprechende Handlungsmöglichkeit wird durch die P2B-Verordnung nicht versperrt.

III. Aktuelle Vorhaben zu Rechtsakten und Initiativen mit medienrechtlichem Kontext

1. Vorschlag für eine Verordnung zur Verhinderung der Verbreitung terroristischer Online-Inhalte

Im Herbst 2018 hat die Europäische Kommission den Entwurf einer Verordnung des Europäischen Parlaments und des Rates zur Verhinderung der Verbreitung terroristischer Inhalte im Internet (TERREG)[621] vorgelegt. Damit soll die Wirksamkeit der derzeitigen Maßnahmen zur Aufdeckung, Identifizierung und Entfernung terroristischer Inhalte auf Online-Plattformen verbessert werden. Der Vorschlag hatte im Trilogprozess allerdings bis zum Ablauf des Mandats der vergangenen Kommission noch keine Einigung gefunden.[622] Das Europäische Parlament hatte am 17. April 2019[623] den Vorschlag in erster Lesung behandelt, mit einer Reihe von Änderungsvorschlägen versehen und dadurch die erneute Befassung seit der Neuwahl des Parlaments und Konstitution einer neuen Kommission ermöglicht. Die Allgemeine Ausrichtung des Rates steht jedoch weiterhin aus, sodass nicht absehbar ist, ob in der kommenden Zeit tatsächlich eine solche Verordnung in Kraft treten wird und wie sich diese zu eventuell neu beschlossenen Rechtsakten mit Bezug zu den vom Verordnungsvorschlag erfassten Anbietern verhalten wird.

Die TERREG verfolgt nach dem Kommissionsvorschlag und – zu diesem Punkt grundsätzlich zustimmend auch durch das Parlament – dabei einen Ansatz, der sich auch im deutschen Netzwerkdurchsetzungsgesetz (NetzDG)[624] findet. Die vorgeschlagenen Regeln zielen in erster Linie auf Hostingdiensteanbieter im Sinne des Art. 14 ECRL ab, die ihre Dienste innerhalb der EU anbieten, unabhängig von ihrem Niederlassungsort oder ihrer Größe (insbesondere sind keine Schwellenwerte oder Ausnahmen für KMU vorgesehen).[625] Der Entwurf verweist dabei allerdings nicht auf die entsprechende Bestimmung der ECRL, sondern definiert in Art. 2 Abs. 1 Hosting-„Diensteanbieter" selbst als einen Anbieter von Diensten der Informationsgesellschaft, die darin bestehen, die durch einen Inhalteanbieter

---

[621] Vorschlag für eine Verordnung des Europäischen Parlaments und des Rates zur Verhinderung der Verbreitung terroristischer Online-Inhalte, Ein Beitrag der Europäischen Kommission zur Tagung der Staats- und Regierungschefs vom 19.-20. September 2018 in Salzburg COM/2018/640 final, https://eur-lex.europa.eu/legal-content/DE/TXT/?uri=COM%3A2018%3A640%3AFIN.

[622] Zum Verfahrensstand vgl. https://eur-lex.europa.eu/legal-content/DE/HIS/?uri=COM:2018:640:FIN.

[623] Legislative Entschließung des Europäischen Parlaments vom 17. April 2019 zu dem Vorschlag für eine Verordnung des Europäischen Parlaments und des Rates zur Verhinderung der Verbreitung terroristischer Online-Inhalte (COM(2018)0640 – C8- 0405/2018 – 2018/0331(COD)), https://eur-lex.europa.eu/legal-content/EN/TXT/?uri=EP:P8_TA(2019)0421.

[624] Netzwerkdurchsetzungsgesetz vom 1. September 2017 (BGBl. I S. 3352), das durch Artikel 274 der Verordnung vom 19. Juni 2020 (BGBl. I S. 1328) geändert worden ist.

[625] Punkt 3.2. der Folgenabschätzung des Entwurfs.

bereitgestellten Informationen im Auftrag des Inhalteanbieters zu speichern und die gespeicherten Informationen Dritten zur Verfügung zu stellen. Die Definition umschreibt den Hostinganbieter damit zwar in gewisser Weise als passiv, indem sie an die Funktion als Auftragserfüller anknüpft, setzt ausschließliche Passivität aber nicht (wie die ECRL) als zwingend voraus. Vielmehr könnten die so definierten Anbieter zumindest auch aktive Handlungen bei der Bereitstellung von Inhalten wahrnehmen. Im Rahmen der TERREG ist zwar auch der Inhalteanbieter der aktive Part, als der „Nutzer, der Informationen bereitgestellt hat, die in seinem Auftrag von einem Hostingdiensteanbieter gespeichert werden". Zu letzteren können dabei insbesondere auch Medienunternehmen gehören, die ihre Angebote (auch) über Hostingdienste verbreiten. Jedoch stehen im Fokus der Regulierung durch die geplante TERREG nicht unmittelbar die Inhalteanbieter, sondern die Hostingdiensteanbieter.

Bezüglich der Hostingdiensteanbieter enthält der TERREG-Entwurf Vorschriften über Sorgfaltspflichten, die von diesen anzuwenden sind, um die Verbreitung terroristischer Inhalte durch ihre Dienste zu verhindern und erforderlichenfalls die rasche Entfernung solcher Inhalte zu gewährleisten. Daneben sind eine Reihe von Maßnahmen genannt, die von den Mitgliedstaaten umzusetzen sind, um terroristische Inhalte zu ermitteln, deren rasche Entfernung durch die Hostingdiensteanbieter zu ermöglichen und die Zusammenarbeit mit den zuständigen Behörden der anderen Mitgliedstaaten, Hostingdiensteanbieter und gegebenenfalls den zuständigen Einrichtungen der Union zu erleichtern. Art. 4 des TERREG-Entwurfs sieht hierzu insbesondere vor, dass die zuständige nationale Behörde befugt ist, Entscheidungen zu erlassen, mit denen Hostingdiensteanbieter verpflichtet werden, terroristische Inhalte innerhalb einer Stunde zu entfernen oder zu sperren. Darüber hinaus müssen Anbieter unter Umständen oder auf Anweisung der Behörde auch proaktive Maßnahmen ergreifen, um terroristisches Material automatisch aufzuspüren und zu entfernen – obwohl Erwgr. 5 des Entwurfs betont, dass die Bestimmungen der ECRL, insbesondere Art. 14, unberührt bleiben sollen. Zudem sind die Etablierung von Beschwerdemechanismen, Transparenzpflichten und Kooperationsmechanismen vorgesehen.

Damit würde die TERREG nicht nur auf den Online-Sektor bezogene Detailregulierung schaffen, sondern den Mediensektor als Produzenten der verteilten Inhalte betreffen, weil bei der Entfernung von Inhalten auch die Meinungs- bzw. Medienfreiheit potentiell gefährdet ist. Diese Gefahr wird in Erwgr. 7 des Entwurfs aufgegriffen, wonach die zuständigen Behörden und Hostingdiensteanbieter nur streng zielgerichtete Maßnahmen ergreifen sollten, die innerhalb einer demokratischen Gesellschaft notwendig, angemessen und verhältnismäßig sind, wobei der besonderen Bedeutung der Meinungs- und Informationsfreiheit, die eine der wesentlichen Grundlagen einer pluralistischen, demokratischen Gesellschaft und einen der grundlegenden Werte der Union darstellt, Rechnung zu tragen ist. Hostingdiensteanbietern wird in diesem Geflecht eine zentrale Rolle beigemessen, weil sie öffentliche Debatten und Informationszugang erleichtern.[626] Meinungs-/Medienfreiheit und -pluralismus sind daher zwar nicht unmittelbarer Regelungsgegenstand des TERREG-Entwurfs, der vorrangig den Schutz der öffentlichen Sicherheit bezweckt, jedoch ist wegen der (potentiellen) Auswirkungen auf diese die begrenzende Funktion dieser grundrechtlich geschützten Güter auch bei einer möglichen Anwendung der TERREG, wie diese selbst in Form bestimmter Schutzmechanismen anerkennt, zu berücksichtigen. Hierzu gehören insbesondere Meldepflichten der Hostingdiensteanbieter gegenüber Behörden und Informationspflichten gegenüber den Inhalteanbietern, wenn Inhalte gesperrt oder entfernt werden, sowie die Etablierung von Beschwerdemechanismen für Inhalteanbieter und die Begrenzung von automatisierten Verfahren im Zusammenhang mit der Prüfung von Inhalten.

Ähnlich wie bei der P2B-Verordnung, ist der Gestaltungsspielraum, der den Mitgliedstaaten im Rahmen des Regelungsbereichs der TERREG verbleiben würde, allerdings gering – sowohl was die Pflichten der Anbieter als auch die Schutzmechanismen betrifft. Das wird nicht nur vom Charakter der TERREG als Verordnung bedingt, sondern auch von der Ausgestaltung und Formulierung der einzelnen Regeln selbst. Diese setzen bei der Zielerreichung auf angemessene und wirksame Maßnahmen der Hostinganbieter, so dass diese weitgehend vorgegeben sind und es weniger auf eine angemessene Sicherstellung der „Umsetzung" dieser Vorgaben durch die Mitgliedstaaten ankäme. Durch den Verordnungscharakter als Sekundärrecht der EU ergäbe sich eine Gleichrangigkeit der Ebene mit der ECRL, so dass proaktive Pflichten der Anbieter bei ihrer Einführung entweder mit den Haftungsprivilegien der ECRL abzustimmen wären oder die Verordnung würde – auch durch ihr der ECRL nachfolgende Verabschiedung – eine Abwendung von den dortigen Regeln bedeuten. Die Frage des Verhältnisses würde damit aber auf EU-Ebene geklärt, wobei sich dann die Frage stellen würde, ob eventuelle Haftungsprivilegien auf mitgliedstaatlicher Ebene in Umsetzung der ECRL weiterhin Bestand haben

---

[626] Vgl. zu der Frage inwiefern die Zielrichtung „Öffentlichkeit" eines Inhalts Anknüpfungspunkt einer dann greifenden Medienregulierung ist oder sein kann *Cole* in: UFITA 2018, 436, 436 ff., zur TERREG dort S. 452.

D. Sekundärrechtlicher Rahmen zum „Medienrecht" und Medienpluralismus

könnten oder nicht vom höherrangigen, dann wegen des Verordnungscharakters unmittelbar bindenden Recht verdrängt würden. Je nachdem, wie sich der Diskussionsprozess um den TERREG-Entwurf weiter entwickelt, ist jedoch zu beachten, dass mitgliedstaatliche Ausgestaltungsspielräume oder Ausnahmemöglichkeiten explizit vorzusehen sind, namentlich im Bereich von Schutzmechanismen zur Gewährleistung der Medienfreiheit bei der Entfernung oder Sperrung von Inhalten, um der Kompetenzverteilung auch insoweit zu entsprechen. Es wäre insbesondere wichtig klarzustellen, in welchem Verhältnis die TERREG zu Legislativakten auf nationaler Ebene[627] stehen würden, die zum Schutz der öffentlichen Sicherheit und Ordnung ebenfalls Verfahren zur Löschung von bestimmten illegalen Inhalten, aber nicht beschränkt auf terroristische Inhalte, vorsehen.

2. Überblick zum vorgeschlagenen Digital Services Act

In ihren politischen Leitlinien hatte die neue Kommissionspräsidenten *Ursula von der Leyen* schon zum Amtsantritt unter dem Titel „A Union that strives for more" angekündigt, Europa fit für das digitale Zeitalter machen zu wollen. Hierzu gehörte auch die Ankündigung eines neuen Gesetzes über digitale Dienste, das Haftung und Sicherheit auf digitalen Plattformen regeln soll. Diese Absicht wurde konkreter im Arbeitsprogramm der Kommission für 2020[628], das die Ankündigung eines Vorschlags für einen

---

627 Ähnliche Regelungswerke existieren bereits auf mitgliedstaatlicher Ebene wie zum Beispiel das NetzDG in Deutschland (aaO, Fn. 628) oder in Frankreich das Loi visant à lutter contre les contenus haineux sur internet (http://www.assemble e-nationale.fr/dyn/15/dossiers/lutte_contre_haine_internet), das allerdings jüngst vom französischen Verfassungsrat für teilweise verfassungswidrig erklärt wurde (Entscheidung Nummer 2020–801 DC vom 18. Juni 2020). Dennoch folgen viele Mitgliedstaaten dem Ansatz weiterhin wie zum Beispiel der österreichische Entwurf eines Bundesgesetzes über Maßnahmen zum Schutz der Nutzer auf Kommunikationsplattformen (https://ec.europa.eu/growth/tools-databases/tris/d e/search/?trisaction=search.detail&year=2020&num=544#:~:text=Das%20Bundes gesetz%20%C3%BCber%20Ma%C3%9Fnahmen%20zum,mit%20bestimmten% 20rechtswidrigen%20Inhalten%20vor.) dokumentiert.
628 Mitteilung der Kommission an das Europäische Parlament, den Rat, den Europäischen Wirtschafts- und Sozialausschuss und den Ausschuss der Regionen, Arbeitsprogramm der Kommission für 2020, COM(2020) 37 final, vom 28. Januar 2020, S. 5, mittlerweile vor dem Hintergrund der Corona-Pandemie angepasst durch Mitteilung der Kommission an das Europäische Parlament, den Rat, den Europäischen Wirtschafts- und Sozialausschuss und den Ausschuss der Regionen, angepasstes Arbeitsprogramm 2020 der Kommission, COM(2020)

Rechtsakt für das 4. Quartal 2020 enthielt, der dann am 15. Dezember vorgelegt wurde[629]. In ihrer Mitteilung „*Shaping Europe's Digital Future*" setzt die Kommission die geplanten Maßnahmen im Bereich der digitalen Dienste in einen Gesamtkontext, der auch die Inhaltsverbreitung und damit den Mediensektor betrifft: Es sei von wesentlicher Bedeutung, dass die für digitale Dienste in der gesamten EU geltenden Regeln gestärkt und modernisiert würden, indem die Rollen und Verantwortlichkeiten von Online-Plattformen geklärt werde, wobei insbesondere die Verbreitung von illegalen Inhalten online ebenso wirksam bekämpft werden müsse wie offline.[630] Das nunmehr als „*Digital Services Act package*" betitelte Paket an Reformmaßnahmen soll zwei Hauptpfeiler umfassen:

Erstens sollen klare Regeln vorgeschlagen werden, die die Verantwortlichkeiten der digitalen Dienste festlegen, um den Risiken, denen ihre Nutzer ausgesetzt sind, zu begegnen und ihre Rechte zu schützen. Dabei soll insbesondere auch ein modernes System der Zusammenarbeit bei der Überwachung von Plattformen gewährleistet und damit eine wirksame Durchsetzung der neuen Verpflichtungen garantiert werden. In der Folgenabschätzung[631] zu diesem Komplex identifiziert die Kommission insbesondere die Verbreitung illegaler Inhalte wie Kinderpornographie aber auch Hassrede und urheberrechtsverletzendes Material auf digitalen Plattformen sowie die Nutzung von Plattformen für gezielte Desinformationskampagnen und Propaganda und den mangelnden Schutz besonders verletzlicher Internetnutzer wie insbesondere Kinder als Gefährdungen im digitalen Umfeld, denen man sich im Rahmen des *Digital Services Act packa-*

---

440 final, vom 27. Mai 2020, abrufbar unter https://ec.europa.eu/info/publicatio ns/2020-commission-work-programme-key-documents_de. In Bezug auf das geplante Gesetz über digitale Dienste hat die Anpassung des Arbeitsprogramms allerdings keine Änderungen ergeben; vgl. S. 2 des angepassten Arbeitsprogramms.

629 https://eur-lex.europa.eu/legal-content/DE/TXT/?uri=CELEX%3A52020PC0825& qid=1614597643982.

630 Mitteilung der Kommission an das Europäische Parlament, den Rat, den Europäischen Wortschafts- und Sozialausschuss und den Ausschuss der Regionen, Gestaltung der digitalen Zukunft Europas, COM (2020) 67 final, 19. Februar 2020, https://ec.europa.eu/info/publications/communication-shaping-europes-digital-future_de, S. 13.

631 Kommission, Combined evaluation roadmap/inception impact assessment on Digital Services Act package: deepening the Internal Market and clarifying responsibilities for digital services, Ref. Ares(2020)2877686 – 04/06/2020, https:// ec.europa.eu/info/law/better-regulation/have-your-say/initiatives/12417-Digital-Services-Act-deepening-the-Internal-Market-and-clarifying-responsibilities-for-digital-services.

ges stellen will. Zudem weist die Kommission auf Informationsasymmetrien zwischen Plattformen, ihren Nutzern und Behörden hin sowie auf die nicht ausreichend effektive Aufsicht über Plattformen. Die für erforderlich gehaltenen Maßnahmen[632], insbesondere auch eine Überprüfung der Haftungsregeln der ECRL, will die Kommission auf die Rechtsgrundlage der Artikel 114 AEUV und möglicherweise die Artikel 49 und 56 AEUV stützen. Angesichts des grundsätzlich grenzüberschreitenden Charakters vieler digitaler Dienste und der damit verbundenen Risiken und Chancen, müsse die Anpassung des Regeln auf EU-Ebene erfolgen, da die Ziele von keinem Mitgliedstaat allein effektiv erreicht werden könnten.

Zweitens sollen Ex-ante-Regeln für große Online-Plattformen vorgeschlagen werden, die als Gatekeeper fungieren und daher Vorgaben machen können für ihre Nutzer ebenso wie im Blick auf Konkurrenten. Die Initiative solle sicherstellen, dass sich Plattformen im Wettbewerb fair verhalten, damit neue Marktteilnehmer und Konkurrenten sie in einem fairen Wettbewerb herausfordern können. Ziel solle es sein, dass Verbraucher größtmögliche Auswahl haben und der Binnenmarkt offen für Innovationen bleibt.[633] Gefährdungspotentiale werden in bestehenden marktbeherrschenden Positionen – auch auf Basis einer erheblichen Macht über eine Vielzahl von Daten – einiger weniger Plattformen gesehen, die durch geschlossene Plattformsysteme und Netzwerkeffekte den Zugang kleinerer Plattformen zum Markt erheblich erschweren.[634] Ex-ante Maßnahmen[635], die die Kommission in diesem Bereich ergreifen will, sollen sich voraussichtlich auf Art. 114 AEUV stützen, je nachdem, welche Maßnahmen letztlich vorgeschlagen werden. Auch in diesem Zusammenhang wird darauf hingewiesen, dass Einzelansätze in den Mitgliedstaaten vor dem Hintergrund des grenzüberschreitenden Charakters der Gatekeeper-Plattformen und deren Angeboten keinen Erfolg versprechen und sogar zu dem widersprüchlichen Ergebnis führen könnten, dass es für Startup-Plattformen und kleinere Unternehmen noch schwieriger würde, Zugang zum

---

632 Siehe hierzu unter F.I. im Detail.
633 Vgl. die Ankündigung der EU-Kommission, abrufbar unter https://ec.europa.eu/digital-single-market/en/digital-services-act-package.
634 Europäische Kommission, inception impact assessment, Digital Services Act package: Ex ante regulatory instrument for large online platforms with significant network effects acting as gate-keepers in the European Union's internal market, Ref. Ares(2020)2877647 – 04/06/2020, https://ec.europa.eu/info/law/better-regulation/have-your-say/initiatives/12418-Digital-Services-Act-package-ex-ante-regulatory-instrument-of-very-large-online-platforms-acting-as-gatekeepers.
635 Siehe hierzu unter Abschnitt F.I. im Detail.

Markt zu erhalten und in einen Wettbewerb mit bestehenden Anbietern zu treten.

In beiden Bereichen hatte die Kommission ein öffentliches Konsultationsverfahren gestartet, das bis zum 8. September 2020 lief und dessen Ergebnisse zwischenzeitlich vorgestellt wurden.[636] Die Auswirkungen der Bestandteile des *Digital Services Act* Pakets auf die Regulierung des Medienbereichs können weitreichend sein. Daher werden auf Basis der Zwischenergebnisse der Studie wichtige in der weiteren Diskussion des / der kommenden Rechtsaktsvorschlages/-vorschläge zu beachtende Eckpunkte unten bei Abschnitt F.II herausgearbeitet.

3. Media and Audiovisual Action Plan und European Democracy Action Plan

In ihrer Mitteilung *"Shaping Europe's Digital Future"*[637] hat die Kommission neben der oben erwähnten Konkretisierung des *Digital Services Acts* noch zwei weitere Maßnahmen für das 4. Quartal 2020 angekündigt, die am 3. Dezember 2020 vorgestellt wurden und im vorliegenden Zusammenhang relevant sind.

Zum einen soll ein Aktionsplan für Medien und audiovisuelle Medien (*Media and Audiovisual Action Plan*)[638] zur Unterstützung der digitalen Transformation und Wettbewerbsfähigkeit des audiovisuellen und Mediensektors, zur Förderung des Zugangs zu hochwertigen Inhalten und des Medienpluralismus beitragen. Darüber, welche Gestalt der Aktionsplan annehmen wird, ist noch wenig bekannt. Auf Anfrage aus dem Europäischen Parlament[639] teilte der zuständige Kommissar *Thierry Breton* mit, dass die Kommission vor dem Hintergrund der fortschreitenden Konvergenz die Notwendigkeit eines ganzheitlichen Ansatzes für den Mediensektor sehe, der den Rechtsrahmen und die finanziellen Unterstützungsinstrumente umfasse. In diesem Zusammenhang strebe die Kommission die

---

636 S. dazu https://ec.europa.eu/digital-single-market/en/news/summary-report-open-public-consultation-digital-services-act-package.
637 aaO (Fn. 634) S. 13 f.
638 Mitteilung der Kommission an das Europäische Parlament, den Rat, den Europäischen Wortschafts- und Sozialausschuss und den Ausschuss der Regionen, Europas Medien in der digitalen Dekade: Ein Aktionsplan zur Unterstützung der Erholung und des Wandels (*Media and Audiovisual Action Plan*), COM/2020/784 final.
639 Parlamentarische Anfrage von Petra Kammerevert vom 18. Dezember 2019, P-004472/2019, https://www.europarl.europa.eu/doceo/document/P-9-2019-004472_EN.html.

Vorlage eines Aktionsplans zur Wettbewerbsfähigkeit und zur pluralistischen Vielfalt des audiovisuellen Sektors und der Medien an. Insbesondere beabsichtige die Kommission, sich auf die Umsetzung der AVMD-Richtlinie und einen intelligenten Einsatz von EU-Finanzprogrammen und -Instrumenten zu konzentrieren, um den Medien- und audiovisuellen Sektor bei der digitalen Transformation zu unterstützen. Das werde ergänzt durch den vorgeschlagenen Digital Services Act in Bezug auf die Bekämpfung bestimmter Arten illegaler Inhalte.[640]

Zum anderen soll ein Europäischer Aktionsplan für Demokratie[641] die Widerstandsfähigkeit der demokratischen Gesellschaften in der EU verbessern, den Medienpluralismus unterstützen und den Gefahren einer externen Intervention bei den Europawahlen begegnen. Hierzu hat die Kommission bereits einen Fahrplan veröffentlicht, bevor sie im Dezember 2020 den Aktionsplan mitteilte. Mit ihrem Aktionsplan für Menschenrechte und Demokratie 2020–2024, der den Vorgängerplan für die Jahre 2015–2019 fortführt, bekräftigt die EU ihre Entschlossenheit, diese Werte weltweit zu fördern und zu schützen, wobei dem politischen Wandel und neuen Technologien Rechnung getragen werden soll. Als Kernziele betont die Kommission die Stärkung der Führungsrolle der EU im Bereich der Menschenrechte und Straffung ihrer Entscheidungsfindung, die Intensivierung der Partnerschaften mit Regierungen, Unternehmen und Sozialpartnern, die Beseitigung von Defiziten hinsichtlich der Rechenschaftspflicht und Verhinderung der Aushöhlung der Rechtsstaatlichkeit und die Ermittlung von Bereichen, in denen neue Technologien zur Stärkung der Menschenrechte beitragen können.[642] Als Rechtsgrundlage wird dabei die im EUV enthaltene Bekräftigung angegeben, dass sich die EU in ihrem auswärtigen Handeln von den Grundsätzen leiten lässt, die für ihre eigene Entstehung, Entwicklung und Erweiterung maßgebend waren und die sie in der Welt voranbringen will: die Universalität und Unteilbarkeit der Menschenrechte und Grundfreiheiten, die Achtung der Menschenwürde, die Demokra-

---

640 Antwort auf die parlamentarische Anfrage P-004472/2019, Thierry Breton, 14. Februar 2020, https://www.europarl.europa.eu/doceo/document/P-9-2019-004472-ASW_EN.html.
641 Mitteilung der Kommission an das Europäische Parlament, den Rat, den Europäischen Wortschafts- und Sozialausschuss und den Ausschuss der Regionen, Europäischer Aktionsplan für Demokratie, COM/2020/790 final, https://eur-lex.europa.eu/legal-content/DE/TXT/?uri=CELEX:52020DC0790.
642 Roadmap EU Action Plan on Human Rights and Democracy 2020–2024, Ref. Ares(2020)440026 – 23/01/2020, https://ec.europa.eu/info/law/better-regulation/have-your-say/initiatives/12122-EU-Action-Plan-on-Human-Rights-and-Democracy-2020-2024.

tie, die Rechtsstaatlichkeit, die Grundsätze der Gleichheit und die Achtung der Grundsätze der Charta der Vereinten Nationen und des Völkerrechts. Dabei soll der Aktionsplan aber nur komplementär zu den Politiken der Mitgliedstaaten treten.[643] In einem medienrechtlichen Kontext interessant ist dabei allerdings, dass die Führungsrolle der EU unter anderem auch dort gestärkt werden soll, wo es darum geht, die Grund- und Menschenrechte ins Bezug auf Desinformation und die Einschüchterung und Bedrohung von Journalisten und unabhängigen Medien zu schützen.[644] Konkret sollen hierzu Gesetzesinitiativen in den Bereichen Zugang zu Informationen, Recht auf Privatsphäre und Schutz personenbezogener Daten im Einklang mit europäischen und internationalen Standards und die wirksame Umsetzung dieser Vorschriften unterstützt, unabhängige Medien, Qualitätsjournalismus und investigativer Journalismus (auch auf lokaler Ebene) gefördert, sowie die Bemühungen zur Bekämpfung von Desinformation, Hetze, extremistischen und terroristischen Inhalten, einschließlich Online-Medienkompetenzen und digitaler Kompetenzen intensiviert werden.

Beide Initiativen bewegen sich dabei in einem Bereich, der grundsätzlich der Politik der Mitgliedstaaten vorbehalten ist. Entsprechend sind die Formulierungen auf EU-Ebene („fördern", „unterstützen", „Bemühungen intensivieren", etc.) zurückhaltend und in der Kompetenz für Unterstützungs-, Koordinierungs- und Ergänzungsmaßnahmen im Sinne von Art. 6 AEUV verortet. Bewusst geht die Kommission entsprechend auch in ihrem Rechtsstaatlichkeitsbericht 2020 lediglich beobachtend auf die Bereiche Medienfreiheit und Medienvielfalt ein.[645] Eine beschränkende Wirkung für Maßnahmen auf mitgliedstaatlicher Ebene insbesondere im Bereich der medialen Vielfaltssicherung lässt sich daraus nicht ableiten. Allerdings zeigen verwandte Maßnahmen der EU in hier adressierten Bereichen wie

---

643 Wie vor, S. 1.
644 Gemeinsame Mitteilung an das Europäische Parlament und den Rat, EU-Aktionsplan für Menschenrechte und Demokratie 2020–2024, JOIN(2020) 5 final, 25 März 2020, https://eur-lex.europa.eu/legal-content/DE/TXT/?uri=CELEX%3A520 20JC0005&qid=1614597685493.
645 Communication from the Commission to the European Parliament, the Council, the European Economic and Social Committee and the Committee of Regions, COM(2020) 580 final.
Dabei attestiert die Kommission den Mitgliedstaaten insbesondere das Vorhandensein hoher Standards im Bereich Medienfreiheit und -vielfalt, äußert allerdings Bedenken hinsichtlich der Unabhängigkeit und angemessenen Mittelausstattung (und damit auch effektiver Aufgabenwahrnehmung) der Medienbehörden in einigen Mitgliedstaaten sowie dem Vorhandensein von Bedrohungen für Journalisten.

D. Sekundärrechtlicher Rahmen zum „Medienrecht" und Medienpluralismus

Bekämpfung von Desinformation und Hassrede, dass die aus dem Aktionsplan folgenden konkreten Initiativen sich nicht nur in reinen Unterstützungsmaßnahmen erschöpfen, sondern etwa auch den Charakter einer Koordinierung der Selbstregulierung annehmen können, in deren Rahmen die Kommission mit Überprüfungsbefugnissen ausgestattet ist. Beispielsweise im Bereich der Bekämpfung von Desinformation, die zur Zeit maßgeblich durch die freiwillige Selbstverpflichtung von Plattformen zum Verhaltenskodex gegen Desinformation (dazu sogleich unter Abschnitt D.IV.3) geprägt ist, ist es erwartbar, dass die Kommission stärkere Regulierungsinstrumente etwa in Form der Hinzuziehung von Koregulierungsmechanismen ergreift – eine Forderung, die bereits von vielen Stellen ausgedrückt wurde.[646] Das gilt nicht zuletzt in Bereichen, in denen bestehende regulatorische Mittel als unzureichend bewertet werden.[647]

IV. Anknüpfungspunkte auf Ebene von EU-Unterstützungs- und Koordinierungsmaßnahmen

Der Bereich der Unterstützungs-, Koordinierungs- und Ergänzungsmaßnahmen auf EU-Ebene umfasst verschiedene Instrumente, die die Europäische Kommission entweder im Rahmen der Ausübung ihrer Befugnisse nach Art. 6 i.V.m. Art. 2 Abs. 5 AEUV, wenn die Europäische Union nicht über eine Kompetenz zum Erlass von bindenden Rechtsakten verfügt, oder zur Vorbereitung von (später dann in der Form von bindenden) Rechtsakten, für die sie etwa im Rahmen der geteilten Zuständigkeit (Art. 4 AEUV) zuständig ist, ergreift.[648] Zu diesen (koordinierenden oder vorbereitenden) Maßnahmen gehören u. a. die Ausarbeitung von „Fahrplänen", aus denen

---

646 Vgl. etwa die Stellungnahmen der ERGA oder der ACT: ERGA Position Paper on the Digital Services Act, https://erga-online.eu/wp-content/uploads/2020/06/ERGA_SG1_DSA_Position-Paper_adopted.pdf, S. 9; ACT, Feedback on Roadmap on European Democracy Action Plan, 10. August 2020, https://ec.europa.eu/info/law/better-regulation/have-your-say/initiatives/12506-European-Democracy-Action-Plan/F541816, S. 2.
647 Vgl. zum Verhaltenskodex zur Desinformation etwa die Studie von *VVA*, Assessment on the implementation of the code of practice on disinformation; sowie *ERGA*, Report on disinformation.
648 Die Union ist nach Art. 6 für die Durchführung von Maßnahmen zur Unterstützung, Koordinierung oder Ergänzung der Maßnahmen der Mitgliedstaaten zuständig, wovon auch der Bereich Kultur betroffen sein kann, ohne dass dabei eine Kompetenz der Union an die Stelle der Kompetenz der Mitgliedstaaten treten würde (Art. 2 Abs. 5 AEUV), vgl. hierzu bereits Abschnitt B.I.5.e.

hervorgeht, wie die Kommission eine Frage in Zukunft zu behandeln gedenkt, die Einsetzung von Arbeitsgruppen, die sich aus Experten und Interessengruppen zusammensetzen, und schließlich die Ausarbeitung und Abgabe von Empfehlungen, die von den rechtsaktsetzenden Organen als nicht verbindliche Instrumente angenommen werden.

In jüngerer Zeit ist die EU in diesem Bereich vor allem auch bezüglich des Mediensektors aktiv. Neben dem bereits parallel zu ersten Regulierungsansätzen für den Online-Sektor vor langem berücksichtigten Bereich des Jugendschutzes[649] bezieht sich dies nun auf die Bekämpfung von Desinformation sowie Hassrede und anderen illegalen Inhalten auf digitalen Plattformen. Diese beiden Bereiche sollen nachfolgend überblickhaft[650] dargestellt werden, da sie wichtige Anknüpfungspunkte auch mit Relevanz für vielfaltssichernde Instrumente bieten. Dies gilt sowohl in thematischer Hinsicht als auch in Bezug zu Vorgaben zu technischen Regulierungsinstrumenten zumindest für den Bereich Desinformation. Ferner bieten diese (Vor-)Arbeiten Hinweise, wie künftige regulatorische Ansätze der EU im Plattformbereich aussehen könnten. Schließlich lassen sich auch Erfahrungswerte im Zusammenhang mit Selbstregulierungsmechanismen daraus ableiten.

1. Verhaltenskodex zur Bekämpfung illegaler Hassreden im Internet

Im Mai 2016 einigte sich die Kommission mit Facebook, Microsoft, Twitter und Google (YouTube) auf einen „Verhaltenskodex zur Bekämpfung illegaler Hassreden im Internet", der darauf abzielt, die Verbreitung illegaler

---

649 Vgl. hierzu Empfehlung des Europäischen Parlaments und des Rates vom 20. Dezember 2006 über den Schutz Minderjähriger und den Schutz der Menschenwürde und über das Recht auf Gegendarstellung im Zusammenhang mit der Wettbewerbsfähigkeit des europäischen Industriezweiges der audiovisuellen Dienste und Online-Informationsdienste, EU ABl. L 378 vom 27.12.2006, S. 72–77; Empfehlung des Rates vom 24. September 1998 zur Steigerung der Wettbewerbsfähigkeit des europäischen Industriezweigs der audiovisuellen Dienste und Informationsdienste durch die Förderung nationaler Rahmenbedingungen für die Verwirklichung eines vergleichbaren Niveaus in Bezug auf den Jugendschutz und den Schutz der Menschenwürde, EU ABl. L 270 vom 7.10.1998, S. 48–55, eingehend und weiterführend dazu *Lievens*, Protecting Children in the Digital Era: The Use of Alternative Regulatory Instruments.

650 Eingehend hierzu auch vor dem Hintergrund der Ankündigung des *Digital Services Act*, *Cole/Etteldorf/Ullrich*, Cross-border Dissemination of Online Content, S. 152 ff.

D. Sekundärrechtlicher Rahmen zum „Medienrecht" und Medienpluralismus

Hassreden im Internet zu verhindern und zu bekämpfen, den Nutzern zu helfen, illegale Hassreden auf diesen Plattformen zu melden, sowie die Unterstützung durch die Zivilgesellschaft und die Koordinierung mit nationalen Behörden zu verbessern.[651] Mittlerweile sind auch Instagram, Snapchat, Dailymotion, Google+, Jeuxvideo.com und TikTok diesem Kodex beigetreten, so dass sich damit fast alle relevanten großen Marktbeteiligten in der EU dem Kodex angeschlossen haben.[652] Der Verhaltenskodex baut auf dem 2008 ergangenen Rahmenbeschluss des Rates zur strafrechtlichen Bekämpfung bestimmter Formen und Ausdrucksweisen von Rassismus und Fremdenfeindlichkeit auf[653] und überträgt die dort festgelegten Grundsätze in den neuen Zusammenhang digitaler Angebote. Dabei geht es jedoch weniger um an Staaten gerichtete Aufforderungen einer effektiven strafrechtlichen Absicherung der Bekämpfung solcher Inhalte, sondern um die Einbeziehung von Diensteanbietern, über deren Angebote Nutzer solche Inhalte verbreiten und konsumieren.

Die Verhaltenskodex befasst sich vor allem mit dem Problem, dass es zwar auf nationaler Ebene robuste Systeme zur Durchsetzung strafrechtlicher Sanktionen gegen einzelne Täter von Hassreden gibt, dass diese Systeme jedoch im Online-Bereich wirksam durch Maßnahmen der Vermittler wie Intermediären und sozialen Netzwerken ergänzt werden müssen. Die Unterzeichner verpflichten sich daher, klare und wirksame Verfahren zur Überprüfung von Meldungen über illegale Hassreden in ihren Diensten vorzusehen, damit sie solche Inhalte entfernen oder sperren können. Eine Überprüfung eines potentiell illegalen Inhalts soll – jedenfalls in einer Mehrheit der Fälle – nach dem Verhaltenskodex innerhalb von 24 Stunden

---

[651] Abrufbar unter https://ec.europa.eu/info/policies/justice-and-fundamental-rights/combatting-discrimination/racism-and-xenophobia/eu-code-conduct-countering-illegal-hate-speech-online_en.

[652] In ihrem Evaluierungsbericht (Assessment of the Code of Conduct on Hate Speech on line State of Play, Progress on combating hate speech online through the EU Code of conduct 2016–2019, https://ec.europa.eu/info/sites/info/files/aid_development_cooperation_fundamental_rights/assessment_of_the_code_of_conduct_on_hate_speech_on_line_-_state_of_play__0.pdf) gibt die Kommission an, dass damit 96 % des EU-Marktanteils von Online-Plattformen, die von den erfassten illegalen Inhalten betroffen sein können, dem Kodex unterworfen sind. Das berücksichtigte noch nicht den Beitritt von TikTok (2020) und damit einer Plattform, die gerade in jüngster Zeit erheblich an Marktanteilen gewonnen hat.

[653] Rahmenbeschluss 2008/913/JI des Rates vom 28. November 2008 zur strafrechtlichen Bekämpfung bestimmter Formen und Ausdrucksweisen von Rassismus und Fremdenfeindlichkeit, EU ABl. L 328 vom 6.12.2008, S. 55–58, https://eur-lex.europa.eu/legal-content/DE/TXT/?uri=CELEX%3A32008F0913.

ab einer entsprechenden Meldung über diesen Inhalt erfolgen. Darüber hinaus verpflichten sich die Unterzeichner, Regeln oder Gemeinschaftsrichtlinien aufzustellen, die klarstellen, dass die Förderung der Aufstachelung zu Gewalt und Hass auf diesen Plattformen verboten ist. Weitere wichtige Punkte betreffen die von den Unterzeichnern eingegangene Ankündigung, die bestehenden Informationspflichten in der praktischen Anwendung zu verbessern und gegenüber der Gesellschaft allgemein transparenter zu sein, unter anderem durch die bessere Bereitstellung von Hinweisen für Nutzer und die Kennzeichnung von Inhalten. Die Kommission evaluiert die Umsetzung der Kodex-„Regeln" bei den Unterzeichnern auf regelmäßiger Basis.

In ihrem zusammenfassenden Evaluierungsbericht für die Jahre 2016–2019[654], kommt die Kommission zu dem Ergebnis, dass der Verhaltenskodex dazu beigetragen hat, Fortschritte zu erzielen, insbesondere bei der raschen Überprüfung und Entfernung von Hassreden (im Durchschnitt wurden bei allen Anbietern gegenüber den 28 % Entfernung gemeldeter Inhalte 2016 im Jahr 2019 72 % entfernt; 2016 wurden 40 % der gemeldeten Inhalte innerhalb von 24 Stunden überprüft, 2019 waren es bereits 89 %). Der Verhaltenskodex habe das Vertrauen und die Zusammenarbeit zwischen IT-Unternehmen, zivilgesellschaftlichen Organisationen und Behörden der Mitgliedstaaten in Form eines strukturierten Prozesses des gegenseitigen Lernens und Wissensaustausches gestärkt. Nach Einschätzung der Kommission müssen die Plattformen jedoch ihr Feedback an die Nutzer, die Inhalte melden, weiter verbessern und insgesamt für mehr Transparenz sorgen.

Trotz dieser grundsätzlich positiven Bewertung der Auswirkungen des Verhaltenskodex durch die Kommission ist hervorzuheben, dass dieser nicht verbindlich ist und dass sich die Unterzeichner nur freiwillig verpflichtet haben. Ein Rücktritt von dieser Vereinbarung ist jederzeit einseitig möglich. Damit unterscheidet er sich trotz des inhaltlich in vielen Punkten dem deutschen Netzwerkdurchsetzungsgesetz (NetzDG) vergleichbaren Ansatzes[655] entscheidend von einer solchen rechtsverbindlichen Regulierung. Mechanismen zur Rechtsdurchsetzung oder Sanktionierungsmöglichkeiten[656] enthält der Verhaltenskodex ebenfalls nicht. Dies gilt auch für die von den beteiligten Anbietern zur Verfügung gestellten

---

654 aaO (Fn. 1594).
655 Vgl. hierzu eingehend Abschnitt E.V.1.a.
656 Die Veröffentlichung der Evaluierungsberichte durch die Kommission könnte man höchstens als eine Art „moralischer Sanktion" begreifen.

D. *Sekundärrechtlicher Rahmen zum „Medienrecht" und Medienpluralismus*

Daten, die die Grundlage für die Evaluierungsberichte der Kommission bilden. Dabei ist nicht klar, welche Daten zur Verfügung gestellt werden müssen, und der Zugang zu den Daten kann jederzeit einseitig eingeschränkt werden.

Der Verhaltenskodex setzt voraus, dass sich die Beteiligten zur Meinungsfreiheit bekennen und er betont die besondere Bedeutung des Schutzes dieses Grundrechts, jedoch finden sich abgesehen von Informationspflichten gegenüber den Nutzern keine expliziten Schutzmechanismen für die (ungerechtfertigte) Sperrung oder Löschung von Inhalten. Das kann vor allem wegen der sehr weiten Definition von illegaler Hassrede im Verhaltenskodex problematisch sein. Im Übrigen werden gegenüber dem Verhaltenskodex vergleichbare Bedenken, die zum NetzDG geäußert wurden[657], vorgebracht, wonach es insbesondere an prozessualen Garantien mangele, die Gefahr eines Overblockings verstärkt und die Bewertung der Illegalität von Inhalten in die Eigenverantwortung von Plattformen gelegt werde.[658] Eine Sperrwirkung oder Beschränkung für Maßnahmen der Mitgliedstaaten gegen illegale Inhalte, ob in Form bindender Gesetze oder vergleichbaren Ansätzen zur Selbstverpflichtung in Form von *soft law*, entfaltet der Kodex für sich genommen jedoch nicht. Die sich aus der Zusammenarbeit der Plattformen ergebenden Bewertungen und möglicherweise best practices,[659] können allerdings im politischen Prozess nutzbar gemacht werden.

2. Bekämpfung illegaler Online-Inhalte

Im Zusammenhang mit der Bekämpfung von illegalen Inhalten im Online-Bereich ist auch die von der Kommission im Jahr 2017 veröffentlichte Mitteilung zum Umgang mit illegalen Online-Inhalten[660] zu berücksichti-

---

657 Vgl. hierzu eingehend Abschnitt E.V.1.a.
658 Zur kritischen Bewertung vgl. insbesondere *Bukovská*, The European Commission's Code of Conduct for Countering Illegal Hate Speech Online.
659 Vgl. hierzu auch die Einbeziehung der und der Arbeit der High Level Group zur Bekämpfung von Rassismus, Fremdenfeindlichkeit und anderen Formen von Intoleranz, dazu https://ec.europa.eu/newsroom/just/item-detail.cfm?item_id=51025.
660 Mitteilung der Kommission an das Europäische Parlament, den Rat, den Europäischen Wirtschafts- und Sozialausschuss und den Ausschuss der Regionen, Umgang mit illegalen Online-Inhalten, Mehr Verantwortung für Plattformen, COM(2017) 555 final, vom 28. September 2017, https://ec.europa.eu/transparency/regdoc/rep/1/2017/DE/COM-2017-555-F1-DE-MAIN-PART-1.PDF.

gen, die dann zur Empfehlung (EU) 2018/334 der Kommission über Maßnahmen zur wirksamen Bekämpfung illegaler Online-Inhalte[661] führte.

Die ursprüngliche Mitteilung legte eine Reihe von Leitlinien und Grundsätzen für Online-Plattformen (insbesondere Hostingdienste im Sinne des Art. 14 ECRL) fest, die darauf abzielten, die Umsetzung bewährter Praktiken zur Verhinderung, Aufdeckung, Entfernung und Sperrung des Zugangs zu illegalen Inhalten zu erleichtern und zu intensivieren. Ziel ist es demnach, die wirksame Entfernung illegaler Inhalte, eine erhöhte Transparenz und den Schutz der Grundrechte auch im Online-Sektor zu gewährleisten. Ferner sollten die Plattformen mehr Rechtssicherheit über ihre Haftung erhalten, wenn sie proaktive Schritte unternehmen, um illegale Inhalte aufzudecken, zu entfernen oder den Zugang zu illegalen Inhalten zu sperren („Guter-Samariter-Maßnahmen").[662] Die Mitteilung fordert, dass Online-Plattformen ihre Zusammenarbeit mit den zuständigen Behörden in den Mitgliedstaaten systematisch verstärken, während letztere sicherstellen sollten, dass Gerichte in der Lage sind, wirksam auf illegale Online-Inhalte zu reagieren, und eine stärkere (grenzüberschreitende) Zusammenarbeit zwischen den Behörden erleichtert wird. In dieser Hinsicht sollten Online-Plattformen und Strafverfolgungsbehörden oder andere zuständige Behörden wirksame Kontaktstellen in der EU benennen und gegebenenfalls digitale Schnittstellen festlegen, um ihre Interaktion zu erleichtern. Darüber hinaus fördert die Kommission Transparenz, eine enge Zusammenarbeit zwischen Online-Plattformen und so genannten *trusted flaggers* sowie die Einrichtung leicht zugänglicher und benutzerfreundlicher Mechanismen, die es Nutzern ermöglichen, als illegal erachtete Inhalte zu melden. Ferner sollen die Anwendung automatischer Filter gegen das erneute Hochladen von Inhalten und Verfahren für Gegenbenachrichtigungen gefördert werden.

Die nachfolgende Empfehlung zur Bekämpfung illegaler Online-Inhalte, die den deskriptiven Ansatz aus der Mitteilung über die Bekämpfung

---

661 Empfehlung (EU) 2018/334 der Kommission vom 1. März 2018 für wirksame Maßnahmen im Umgang mit illegalen Online-Inhalten, C/2018/1177, EU ABl. L 63 vom 6.3.2018, S. 50–61, https://eur-lex.europa.eu/legal-content/DE/ALL/?uri=CELEX%3A32018H0334.

662 Die Kommission vertritt hier die Ansicht, dass proaktive Maßnahmen, die von diesen Online-Plattformen ergriffen werden, um illegale Inhalte, die sie hosten, aufzuspüren und zu entfernen – einschließlich des Einsatzes automatischer Werkzeuge und Hilfsmittel, die sicherstellen sollen, dass zuvor entfernte Inhalte nicht erneut hochgeladen werden – an sich nicht zu einem Verlust der Haftungsbefreiung führen.

illegaler Online-Inhalte in einer etwas gestrafften Form aufgreift, indem sie diese in die Form von konkret(er)en (aber rechtlich weiterhin nicht verbindlichen) Regeln überträgt, ist vor allem im Hinblick auf zwei Aspekte interessant: Zum einen enthält der erste Abschnitt eine Liste von Definitionen, die sich eng an bestehenden EU-Richtlinien orientieren – wie zum Beispiel die Definition von „Anbietern von Hosting-Diensten". Als „illegaler Inhalt" wird hier „jede Information, die nicht im Einklang mit dem Recht der Union oder dem Recht eines betroffenen Mitgliedstaates steht" definiert. Andererseits konzentriert sich die Empfehlung auf die Zusammenarbeit zwischen Hosting-Providern und Mitgliedstaaten (z.B. in Bezug auf benannte Kontaktstellen für Fragen im Zusammenhang mit illegalen Online-Inhalten und die Bereitstellung von Schnellverfahren zur Bearbeitung von Meldungen, die von zuständigen Behörden eingereicht werden), (andere) *trusted flagger* (z.B. die Bereitstellung von Schnellverfahren zur Bearbeitung von Meldungen, die von zertifizierten Experten eingereicht werden, die Veröffentlichung klarer und objektiver Bedingungen für die Bestimmung solcher besonders hervorgehobenen Meldestellen) und mit anderen Hosting-Providern (z.B. durch den Austausch von Erfahrungen, technologischen Lösungen und bewährten Verfahren).

Die beiden Dokumente enthalten – ohne dass sie verbindliche Wirkung entfalten würden – ein breites Spektrum an möglichen regulatorischen und technischen Maßnahmen für die Bekämpfung von illegalen Inhalten im Online-Bereich. Deshalb werden sie im Zusammenhang mit legislativen Vorhaben wie zum Beispiel den Vorschlägen für eine TERREG oder den *Digital Services Act* aufgegriffen.[663]

3. Desinformations-Verhaltenskodex

Auf EU-Ebene konkretisierten sich die Maßnahmen zur Bekämpfung von Online-Desinformation, auch als Reaktion auf eine Entschließung des Europäischen Parlaments, in der Einsetzung einer High Level Group zu Fake News und Online-Desinformation 2018. Diese gab nach einer Unter-

---

[663] Vgl. bspw. Deutscher Bundestag, Kurzinformation Follow-up zur Empfehlung der Europäischen Kommission für wirksame Maßnahmen im Umgang mit illegalen Online-Inhalten, https://www.bundestag.de/resource/blob/571506/df067279aaaa45b3e95efae57f5194f2/PE-6-125-18-pdf-data.pdf; *Hoffmann/Gasparotti*, Liability for illegal content online, S. 23 ff; *Chapuis-Doppler/Delhomme* in: European papers 5(2020)1, 411, 426.

suchung ihre Einschätzung in einem Bericht[664] ab, auf Basis dessen die Kommission wiederum ihre Mitteilung zur Bekämpfung von Desinformation[665] entwickelte und im April 2018 veröffentlichte.[666] Darin vertritt die Kommission die Auffassung, dass wirtschaftliche, technologische, politische und ideologische Umstände die Ursache für die Verbreitung von Desinformationen seien, wozu z.B. der Aufstieg von Plattformen im Mediensektor gehöre, der wiederum die „traditionelleren" Medien insofern beeinflusse, als sie neue Wege zur Monetarisierung ihrer Inhalte suchen (müssten), sowie die Schaffung neuer oder die Manipulation bestehender Technologien im Bereich der sozialen Netzwerke, die die Verbreitung von Desinformation ermöglichen oder zumindest erleichtern. Vor diesem Hintergrund kam die Kommission zu dem Schluss, dass der Kampf gegen Desinformation langfristig nur dann erfolgreich sein könne und werde, wenn er von einem klaren politischen Willen zur Stärkung der kollektiven Widerstandsfähigkeit und zur Unterstützung demokratischer Bemühungen und europäischer Werte begleitet werde. Zudem haben die Kommission und der Hohe Vertreter für Außen- und Sicherheitspolitik am 5. Dezember 2018 einen Aktionsplan gegen Desinformation[667] vorgelegt, in dessen Rahmen sie konkrete Maßnahmen zur Bekämpfung der Desinformation vorschlagen. Dazu gehören die Einrichtung eines Frühwarnsystems, die Erleichterung des Datenaustauschs zwischen den Mitgliedstaaten und die Bereitstellung zusätzlicher Mittel für Medienkompetenzprojekte.

Zu den im Rahmen des Aktionsplans vorgeschlagenen Maßnahmen gehört aber auch die genauere Überwachung der Umsetzung eines Selbstregulierungsinstruments, das nur wenige Wochen zuvor etabliert worden war, sowie eine Aufstockung der hierfür erforderlichen Mittel: Der Handlungsbedarf, der von der Kommission im Bereich Desinformation gesehen

---

664 *De Cock Buning* u.a., Report of the independent High level Group on fake news and online disinformation.
665 Mitteilung der Kommission an das Europäische Parlament, den Rat, den Europäischen Wirtschafts- und Sozialausschuss und den Ausschuss der Regionen, Bekämpfung von Desinformation im Internet: ein europäisches Konzept, COM/2018/236 final, https://eur-lex.europa.eu/legal-content/DE/TXT/?uri=CELEX%3A52018DC0236.
666 Zum gesamten Prozess vgl. eingehend *Ukrow/Etteldorf*, Fake News als Rechtsproblem.
667 Gemeinsame Mitteilung an das Europäische Parlament, den Europäischen Rat, den Rat, den Europäischen Wirtschafts- und Sozialausschuss und den Ausschuss der Regionen, Aktionsplan gegen Desinformation, JOIN(2018) 36 final, v. 5.12.2018, https://eeas.europa.eu/sites/eeas/files/aktionsplan_gegen_desinformation.pdf.

D. Sekundärrechtlicher Rahmen zum „Medienrecht" und Medienpluralismus

wurde, mündete im September 2018 in einen Verhaltenskodex zur Bekämpfung von Desinformation (Code of Practice on Disinformation, CPD)[668], auf den sich Vertreter von Online-Plattformen, führenden sozialen Netzwerken sowie aus der Werbe- und Plattformindustrie mit der Kommission einigten.[669] Der CPD legt – bei expliziter Bezugnahme auf die davon unberührt bleibenden Haftungsprivilegien aus der ECRL – eine breite Palette von (Selbst-)Verpflichtungen fest, die von der Transparenz in der politischen Werbung bis zur Sperrung gefälschter Konten/Accounts und der Demonetisierung der Verbreiter von Desinformation reichen. Er enthält Verpflichtungen hinsichtlich der Überprüfung von Anzeigenplatzierungen, politischer Werbung und themenbezogener Werbung, der Integrität von Diensten sowie der Stärkung der Verbraucher und der Forschungsgemeinschaft. Hinsichtlich der Überwachung der Wirksamkeit verpflichten sich die Unterzeichner, einen Jahresbericht über die von ihnen im Zusammenhang mit der Bekämpfung von Desinformation ergriffenen Maßnahmen zu veröffentlichen. Der Kodex enthält außerdem einen Anhang, in dem best practices aufgeführt sind, zu deren Anwendung sich die Unterzeichner zur Umsetzung der Bestimmungen des Kodex verpflichten. Im Bereich der Werbepolitik bekennen sich die Interessenvertreter zum Bemühen, der Desinformation entgegenzuwirken, indem sie „follow-the-money"-Ansätze[670] anwenden und verhindern, dass Verbreiter von Desinformation finanziell profitieren können. Im Bereich der politischen Werbung entwickeln Online-Plattformen Lösungen, um die Transparenz solcher Werbung zu erhöhen und es den Verbrauchern zu ermöglichen, nachvollziehen zu können, warum sie eine bestimmte Werbung sehen. Die Plattformen kündigen weiter an, Instrumente zu entwickeln, damit die Zivilgesellschaft in der Lage ist, das Ökosystem der politischen Online-Werbung besser zu verstehen. Plattformen wollen weiterhin versuchen, die Integrität der Dienste zu schützen, indem sie Richtlinien anwenden, die den Missbrauch ihres Dienstes durch nicht authentische Nutzer bzw.

---

[668] Code of Practice on Disinformation, abrufbar unter https://ec.europa.eu/digital-single-market/en/news/code-practice-disinformation.
[669] Darunter Facebook, Twitter, Mozilla, Google, Microsoft und TikTok, vgl. https://ec.europa.eu/digital-single-market/en/news/roadmaps-implement-code-practice-disinformation.
[670] Der „Follow the money"-Ansatz zielt im Allgemeinen darauf ab, die Einnahmen aus Rechtsverletzungen zu kürzen. Die Kommission hat sich in ihrer Mitteilung über eine Strategie für den digitalen Binnenmarkt zu einem "Follow-the-money"-Ansatz verpflichtet, der darauf abzielt, die Einnahmeströme zu verringern, die die Verletzung von gewerblichen Schutzrechten monetarisiert.

Konten einschränken, z.B. durch Richtlinien, die die Erstellung von Fake-Profilen einschränken.[671] Schließlich, um Verbraucher und Forscher in eine bessere Ausgangslage zu versetzen, kündigen Plattformen an, den Benutzern Informationen, Werkzeuge und Unterstützung zur Verfügung zu stellen, um die Verbraucher in ihrer Online-Kompetenz zu stärken. Dazu sollen auch Beschwerde- und Berichtssysteme zählen.

An den aufgelisteten best practices lässt sich erkennen, dass sich die Initiativen im Bereich Desinformation vor allem auf die Bereiche der (irreführenden) Werbung und der Wahlwerbung/politischen Werbung fokussieren. Dass Desinformation allerdings auch in anderen Bereichen erhebliche Gefahren bergen kann, haben die Entwicklungen im Rahmen der Corona-Pandemie gezeigt. Die Fülle an kursierenden Falschinformationen, die zu einer erheblichen Verunsicherung der Gesellschaft geführt hat, hat die Kommission (zusammen mit dem Hohen Vertreter der Union für Außen- und Sicherheitspolitik) dabei zum Anlass genommen, auch eine dezidierte Mitteilung zur Bekämpfung von Desinformation im Zusammenhang mit COVID-19 zu veröffentlichen.[672] In dieser werden Maßnahmen aus den bisherigen Initiativen aufgegriffen und nochmal spezifiziert, wobei vor allem Transparenz, Zusammenarbeit und Kommunikation als Mittel zur Bekämpfung von (Corona-)Desinformation im Vordergrund stehen. Dies könnte auch im Rahmen des vorgeschlagenen *Digital Services Act* eine Rolle spielen.[673] Auf der anderen Seite hat die Pandemie aber auch gezeigt, dass die Plattformen durchaus tatsächlich und technisch in der Lage sind, Maßnahmen zur Bekämpfung von Falschinformationen zu ergreifen.[674]

---

671 Bspw. YouTube Policy on impersonation, https://support.google.com/youtube/answer/2801947?hl=en-GB.
672 Gemeinsame Mitteilung an das Europäische Parlament, den Europäischen Rat, den Rat, den Europäischen Wirtschafts- und Sozialausschuss und den Ausschuss der Regionen, Bekämpfung von Desinformation im Zusammenhang mit COVID-19 – Fakten statt Fiktion, JOIN(2020) 8 final, v. 10.6.2020, https://ec.europa.eu/info/sites/info/files/communication-tackling-covid-19-disinformation-getting-facts-right_de.pdf.
673 Vgl. hierzu etwa den Draft report des Europäischen Parlaments zur DSA Initiative (Draft report with recommendations to the Commission on Digital Services Act: Improving the functioning of the Single Market (2020/2018(INL)) v. 24.4.2020), Nr. 11 ff., in dessen Rahmen insbesondere die Problematik der Desinformation zu Covid-19 im Bereich von Transparenzvorschriften angesprochen wird.
674 Bspw. listete der Suchmaschinendienst Google bei Suchanfragen in Zusammenhang mit Corona oder Krankheitssymptomen über allen anderen Suchergebnissen und optisch abgesetzt Informationen der Weltgesundheitsorganisation auf.

D. Sekundärrechtlicher Rahmen zum „Medienrecht" und Medienpluralismus

Daraus können bestimmte Rückschlüsse auf die Einflussmöglichkeiten dieser Anbieter gezogen werden.

Desinformation spielt auch eine Rolle vor dem Hintergrund der Vielfaltssicherung, wie die erwähnte Covid-Mitteilung der Kommission hervorhebt: freie und pluralistische Medien sind von zentraler Bedeutung für die Bekämpfung von Desinformation und für die faktenbasierte Information der Bürgerinnen und Bürger.[675] Auch wenn Desinformation auch in Staaten zu beobachten ist, die eine pluralistisch strukturierte Medienlandschaft kennen, wirkt Desinformation ohne eine solche Pluralität unter Umständen besonders gefährdend für die freie Information und Meinungsbildung und verstärkt damit dort die damit einhergehenden Gefahren. Solche Desinformation untergräbt das Vertrauen in die politischen Institutionen und in digitale und herkömmliche Medien. Sie schadet dem demokratischen Prozess, da die Bürger keine fundierten Entscheidungen mehr treffen können.[676]

Obwohl der CPD ebenso wie der Verhaltenskodex zur Hassrede nicht verbindlich ist, ist er detaillierter und enthält stärkere Formulierungen und konkretere Anforderungen. Allerdings gibt es auch hier keine Durchsetzungsmechanismen oder Sanktionen. Eine Überwachung erfolgt allerdings zumindest in gewissem Maß extern durch die Prüfberichte. Sowohl die Einhaltung der CPD-Regeln als auch die Bereitstellung der entsprechenden Daten durch die Unternehmen, damit Dritte die Maßnahmen überprüfen können, ist dennoch zurzeit lediglich freiwillig und kann nicht von einer Behörde gefordert oder im Falle der Nichtverfügbarkeit oder Nichteinhaltung sanktioniert werden. Die sich daraus ergebenden Bewertungsprobleme hat der Zusammenschluss der mitgliedstaatlichen Regulierungsstellen, die in der AVMD-Richtlinie vorgesehene ERGA, die von der Kommission gebeten wurde, als Beratungsgremium die Überwachung der Effektivität der Implementierung der Regeln aus dem CPD zu unterstützen, in ihrem Bericht über die Aktivitäten zur Unterstützung der Kommission bei der zwischenzeitlichen Überwachung des Verhaltenskodex zur Desinformation wie folgt dargestellt: „Die Plattformen waren nicht in der Lage, einem Ersuchen der ERGA nachzukommen, während des Überwachungszeitraums Zugang zur Werbedatenbank zu gewähren, und sei es auch nur in begrenztem Umfang. Dies stellte eine erhebliche Einschrän-

---

Auch auf YouTube wurden Videos von Fachinstitutionen sichtbar auf der Startseite gelistet.
675 aaO (Fn. 675), S. 13.
676 *Ukrow* in: Cappello (Hrsg.) Media pluralism and competition issues, S. 10 (erscheint demnächst).

kung des Überwachungsprozesses und der sich abzeichnenden Schlussfolgerungen dar"[677]. Auch in ihrem abschließenden Bericht für das Jahr 2019 kommt die ERGA zum Ergebnis, dass mehr Transparenz erforderlich sei, insbesondere für eine Bewertung der Effektivität von Maßnahmen detailliertere Daten zur Verfügung gestellt werden müssten, und schlägt daher vor, dass Plattformen Datensätze, Datenüberwachungsinstrumente und länderspezifische Informationen, die eine unabhängige Überwachung durch die nationalen Regulierungsstellen ermöglichen, zur Verfügung stellen sollten. Zudem wird in diesem Zusammenhang auch darauf verwiesen, dass viele Maßnahmen, die der CPD vorsieht, in ihrer Formulierung sehr allgemein gehalten sind, was zu einer sehr unterschiedlichen Umsetzung durch die Unterzeichner führe. Das derzeitige Selbstregulierungsmodell habe sich zwar als ein wichtiger und notwendiger erster Schritt erwiesen, aber es müsse wirksamer gegen die Desinformation im Internet vorgegangen werden etwa durch die Etablierung eines Koregulierungsansatzes.[678] Auch die Kommission griff diese Punkte in ihrer finalen Bewertung im September auf, ohne dabei allerdings auf konkrete zukünftige Maßnahmen einzugehen, um auf die vorgefundenen Mängel zu reagieren.[679]

Die Aktivitäten der Kommission in Bezug auf Desinformation fügen sich in die unter Abschnitt D.III.3. dargestellten Vorhaben im Bereich des *European Democracy Action Plan* ein.

V. Schlussfolgerungen und Ableitungen zur Medienpluralismus-Regelungskompetenz

Aus dem aktuellen und dem sich in der Entwicklung befindlichen EU-Sekundärrecht sowie aus den weiteren Maßnahmen und Initiativen der EU auf der Koordinierungs- und Unterstützungsebene folgt zweierlei:

Erstens findet sich auf dieser Ebene kein Regelungswerk und keine Initiative, die unmittelbar die Sicherung des Medienpluralismus als Regelungsgegenstand hat bzw. die Vorgaben mit (allein) dieser Zielrichtung

---

677 *ERGA*, Report of the activities carried out to assist the European Commission in the intermediate monitoring of the Code of practice on disinformation, 2019, S. 3, übersetzt aus dem Englischen.
678 *ERGA*, Report on Disinformation, 2020.
679 Assessment of the Code of Practice on Disinformation – Achievements and areas for further improvement, SWD(2020) 180 final, vom 10.9.2020, https://ec.europa.eu/digital-single-market/en/news/assessment-code-practice-disinformation-achievements-and-areas-further-improvement.

trifft, was schon aus kompetenzrechtlichen Gründen nicht möglich wäre. Vielmehr achtet das Sekundärrecht die Regelungsbefugnis der Mitgliedstaaten im Bereich des Medien- und Vielfaltssicherungsrechts, indem es kulturpolitische Ausnahmetatbestände enthält, die den Mitgliedstaaten einen weiten Gestaltungsspielraum für verfassungstradierte Erwägungen belassen, oder die kulturpolitischen Aspekte nicht zum jeweils koordinierten Bereich zählt. Das gilt sowohl für Rechtsakte, die die Medien unmittelbar adressieren, wie die Ausnahmetatbestände der AVMD-Richtlinie im Bereich von audiovisuellen Mediendiensten und VSP zeigen, als auch für solches Sekundärrecht, das eine wirtschaftsorientierte und damit nicht medien- und kulturbezogene Zielsetzung hat, wie etwa die Möglichkeit nach dem EEKK zum Erlass von Must-Carry-Bestimmungen oder die FKVO in Bezug auf medienkonzentrationsrechtliche Möglichkeiten zeigen. Dass stärker medienbezogene, weil insbesondere im Kontext der grundrechtlich geschützten Meinungsfreiheit relevante Vorhaben wie die Bekämpfung von Hassrede und Desinformation auf die Ebene von Koordinierungs- und Unterstützungsmaßnahmen auf Grundlage von Selbstregulierungsmechanismen verlagert werden, zeigt, dass die EU diesen mitgliedstaatlichen Hoheitsbereich respektiert. Dies entspricht der Begrenzung einer Unterstützungskompetenz der EU dahingehend, dass über Maßnahmen zur Unterstützung keine Vorprägung der mitgliedstaatlichen Wahrnehmung von Regulierungsspielräumen erfolgen darf.

Zweitens finden sich dennoch auch außerhalb von Gestaltungsspielräumen und Bereichsausnahmen für die Mitgliedstaaten Anknüpfungspunkte für die Vielfaltssicherung im sekundärrechtlichen Bereich. Das gilt namentlich für die AVMD-Richtlinie zum Beispiel im Rahmen der Vorschriften über die Förderung europäischer Werke oder die Medienkompetenzförderung, wenngleich diese zumindest auch mit wirtschaftsbezogenen Erwägungen begründet sind. Auch die P2B-Verordnung enthält Elemente, die für die Pluralismussicherung relevant sein dürften, wenn es um die Auffindbarkeit von Inhalten und Qualitätsjournalismus geht. Insbesondere deuten aber die Entwicklungen im Rahmen dieser Verordnung darauf hin, dass medienbezogene Aspekte auch bei einem wettbewerbsrechtlich basierten Regelungswerk eine Rolle spielen, so möglicherweise durch konkretisierende Vorgaben bei der Ausgestaltung in Leitlinien der Kommission. Dieser Ansatz, auch kulturpolitische Gesichtspunkte vermehrt in die Regulierung einfließen zu lassen, stellt sich als Tendenz dar, die sich in jüngerer Vergangenheit stärker als bislang auf Sekundärrechtsebene und untergesetzlichen Initiativen abzeichnet. Das begründet eine Gefahr, dass sich das Spannungsverhältnis zu nationalen Regelungen, die mit dem Ziel der Vielfaltssicherung erlassen werden, in Zukunft intensivieren könnte.

E. Völkerrechtliche Kernprobleme der Regulierung des „Mediensektors" im Hinblick auf mögliche Spannungsverhältnisse mit dem Recht der EU

Jörg Ukrow[680]

I. Einführung

Medienregulierung ist im Zeitalter von Digitalisierung und Globalisierung nicht ausschließlich ein Regulierungssystem im Spannungsfeld mitgliedstaatlicher und unionsrechtlicher Regulierungsmöglichkeiten und -vorgaben. Mitgliedstaatliche wie unionsrechtliche Regulierungsbemühungen müssen sich vielmehr auch an die (insbesondere menschenrechtlichen) Vorgaben halten, die den jeweiligen Akteuren durch Vorgaben völkervertragsrechtlicher Art gesetzt sind. Diese Vorgaben können in inhaltlicher Hinsicht ihren Ursprung in völkervertragsrechtlichen Rechtsquellen mit universellem Geltungsanspruch – wie den Internationalen Menschenrechtspakten[681] –, mit regionalem Geltungsanspruch – wie der Europäischen Menschenrechtskonvention – oder mit regionalem Ausgangspunkt, aber globaler Öffnung in der Teilhabemöglichkeit – wie bei der Cybercrime-Konvention des Europarates[682] – haben. Im Zusammenhang dieser Studie stellen sich aber in erster Linie Fragen kompetenzrechtlicher Art: Unter welchen Voraussetzungen dürfen die EU oder ihre Mitgliedstaaten Medienakteure in ihre Regulierung einbeziehen, die qua Angehörigkeit, wie sie z.B. durch die Staatsangehörigkeit oder den Sitz eines Akteurs begründet wird, nicht der Rechtssphäre der EU zugeordnet werden können.

---

680 Der nachfolgende Abschnitt E knüpft an Vorüberlegungen in einem unveröffentlichten Gutachten wie der Studie *Ukrow/Cole*, Aktive Sicherung lokaler und regionaler Medienvielfalt – Rechtliche Möglichkeiten und Grenzen der Förderung inhaltlicher Qualität in Presse-, Rundfunk- und Online-Angeboten an.
681 Vgl. Art. 19 und 20 des Internationalen Pakts über bürgerliche und politische Rechte vom 19. Dezember 1966 (BGBl. 1973 II 1553); Art. 15 des Internationalen Pakts über wirtschaftliche, soziale und kulturelle Rechte vom 19. Dezember 1966 (BGBl. 1973 II 1569).
682 Übereinkommen über Computerkriminalität vom 23.11.2011, SEV-Nr. 185, in Deutschland in Kraft getreten am 1.7.2009 (BGBl. 2008 II, 1242); hierzu *Fink* in: ZaöRV 2014, 505, 506 ff.

Die weltweite Ausbreitung von Übertragungs- und Verbreitungsmöglichkeiten für Medien begründet globale Wirkungsrisiken des Verhaltens von Medieninhalte-Anbietern wie von Infrastruktur-Akteuren, die auf die Aggregation, Auswahl, Präsentation und Wahrnehmbarkeit von Medieninhalten Einfluss nehmen. Solche Risiken stellen sich in besonderer Weise in einer Situation, in der sowohl bei Empfangsgeräten für audiovisuelle Medieninhalte wie auch bei Medienintermediären, seien es Suchmaschinen, seien es soziale Netzwerke, Konzentrationstendenzen feststellbar sind – im letzteren Falle insbesondere über die Netzwerkeffekte digitaler Plattformökonomie.[683] Indem der internationale Medienmarkt immer stärker von einem Oligopol von global operierenden, strukturell vernetzten, international operierenden Konzernen geprägt wird, stellt sich sowohl für die EU wie für deren Mitgliedstaaten die Frage nach einer völkerrechtskonformen Ausgestaltung einer Medienregulierung, die auch solche transnational agierenden Akteure mit global ausgerichteten Geschäftsmodellen in die Regulierung einbeziehen will.

II. Adressaten der Regulierung

1. Einleitung

Bei der Frage nach dem personellen Anwendungsbereich der Regulierung des „Mediensektors" sind neben den europarechtlichen Grenzen, die einem Zugriff auf Personen und Unternehmen, die nicht ihren Wohnsitz bzw. Sitz im regulierendem Mitgliedstaat der EU haben, auf der Grundlage des Prinzips der Herkunftslandskontrolle gesetzt sind, auch die völkerrechtlichen Grenzen zu beachten, die einer Regulierung *ratione personae* gesetzt sind.[684]

---

683 Vgl. hierzu z.B. *KEK*, Sicherung der Meinungsvielfalt im digitalen Zeitalter, S. 429 ff.; *Lobigs/Neuberger*, Meinungsmacht im Internet und die Digitalstrategien von Medienunternehmen, S. 34 ff.; *Neuberger/Lobigs*, Die Bedeutung des Internets im Rahmen der Vielfaltssicherung, S. 27 ff.
684 Soweit es dabei um die Klärung der Frage geht, ob die deutschen Regulierungsbehörden (rsp. das für die jeweils örtlich zuständige Landesmedienanstalt nach dem medienstaatsvertraglichen und jugendmedienschutzrechtlichen Organisationsrecht agierende Organ) befugt sind, wegen eines Verstoßes gegen materiellrechtliche Vorgaben des MStV und/oder des JMStV auch gegen ausländische Anbieter vorzugehen, bedarf es einer Auslegung des MStV wie des JMStV nach den klassischen Interpretationsmethoden semantischer, systematischer, teleologischer und historischer Auslegung (vgl. hierzu z.B. *Larenz/Canaris*, Methodenleh-

E. Völkerrechtliche Kernprobleme der Regulierung des „Mediensektors"

Im Zusammenhang mit der Frage, ob mitgliedstaatliche Medienregulierung oder Medienregulierung der EU auch auf (EU-) ausländische Anbieter Zugriff nehmen darf, stellt sich im Übrigen die Frage, inwieweit solche regulierenden Akte legislativer, exekutiver oder judikativer Art je nach Rechtspersönlichkeit des Anbieters auch an die Grundrechte – sei es des Grundgesetzes, namentlich die verfassungsrechtliche Rundfunkfreiheit des Art. 5 Abs. 1 Satz 2 GG, sei es der europäischen Grundrechtsordnung – gebunden sind.[685]

2. Völkerrechtliche Rahmenbedingungen einer Adressierung ausländischer Anbieter

a. Die Adressierung ausländischer Anbieter unter dem Blickwinkel des Gebots völkerrechtsfreundlicher Auslegung nationalen Rechts wie des Rechts der EU

Das Grundgesetz hat die deutsche öffentliche Gewalt programmatisch auf die internationale Zusammenarbeit (Art. 24 GG) und auf die europäische Integration (Art. 23 GG) festgelegt. Das Grundgesetz hat den allgemeinen Regeln des Völkerrechts Vorrang vor dem einfachen Gesetzesrecht eingeräumt (Art. 25 Satz 2 GG) und das Völkervertragsrecht durch Art. 59 Abs. 2 GG in das System der Gewaltenteilung eingeordnet. Es hat zudem die Möglichkeit der Einfügung in Systeme gegenseitiger kollektiver Sicherheit eröffnet (Art. 24 Abs. 2 GG), den Auftrag zur friedlichen Beilegung zwischenstaatlicher Streitigkeiten im Wege der Schiedsgerichtsbarkeit erteilt (Art. 24 Abs. 3 GG) und die Friedensstörung, insbesondere den Angriffskrieg, für verfassungswidrig erklärt (Art. 26 GG).

Mit diesem Normenkomplex zielt die deutsche Verfassung, auch ausweislich ihrer Präambel, darauf, die Bundesrepublik Deutschland als fried-

---

re der Rechtswissenschaft, S. 133 ff.; *Lodzig*, Grundriss einer verantwortlichen Interpretationstheorie des Rechts, S. 25 ff.; *Potacs*, Rechtstheorie, S. 153 ff.). Das hierbei gefundene Ergebnis muss sich sodann an den Maßstäben einer europa- und völkerrechtskonformen Auslegung messen lassen.

685 Die in diesem Abschnitt behandelte Frage nach der Befugnis zu Regulierungsmaßnahmen der EU und/oder ihrer Mitgliedstaaten ist im Übrigen deutlich zu unterscheiden von der Frage nach einer etwaigen Pflicht zum Tätigwerden, die nicht zuletzt aus staatlichen Schutzpflichten folgen könnte. Diese Pflichtendimension der Frage eines Vorgehens gegen ausländische Anbieter wird in Abschnitt E.IV erörtert.

liches und gleichberechtigtes Glied in eine dem Frieden dienende Völkerrechtsordnung der Staatengemeinschaft einzufügen. All dieses ist Ausdruck der Völkerrechtsfreundlichkeit des Grundgesetzes, das die Betätigung staatlicher Souveränität durch Völkervertragsrecht und internationale Zusammenarbeit sowie die Einbeziehung der allgemeinen Regeln des Völkerrechts fördert und deshalb nach Möglichkeit so auszulegen ist, dass ein Konflikt mit völkerrechtlichen Verpflichtungen der Bundesrepublik Deutschland nicht entsteht.[686]

Das Grundgesetz ist jedoch nicht die weitesten Schritte der Öffnung für völkerrechtliche Bindungen gegangen. Das Völkervertragsrecht ist innerstaatlich nicht unmittelbar, das heißt ohne Zustimmungsgesetz nach Art. 59 Abs. 2 GG, als geltendes Recht zu behandeln und – wie auch das Völkergewohnheitsrecht (vgl. Art. 25 GG) – nicht mit dem Rang des Verfassungsrechts ausgestattet. Dem Grundgesetz liegt deutlich die klassische Vorstellung zu Grunde, dass es sich bei dem Verhältnis des Völkerrechts zum nationalen Recht um ein Verhältnis zweier unterschiedlicher Rechtskreise handelt und dass die Natur dieses Verhältnisses aus der Sicht des nationalen Rechts nur durch das nationale Recht selbst bestimmt werden kann; dies zeigen die Existenz und der Wortlaut von Art. 25 und Art. 59 Abs. 2 GG. Die Völkerrechtsfreundlichkeit entfaltet ihre Wirkung nur im Rahmen des demokratischen und rechtsstaatlichen Systems des Grundgesetzes.[687]

Das Grundgesetz ordnet zwar weder die Unterwerfung der deutschen Rechtsordnung unter die Völkerrechtsordnung noch den unbedingten Geltungsvorrang von Völkerrecht vor dem Verfassungsrecht an. Es will aber „den Respekt vor friedens- und freiheitswahrenden internationalen Organisationen und dem Völkerrecht erhöhen, ohne die letzte Verantwortung für die Achtung der Würde des Menschen und die Beachtung der Grundrechte durch die deutsche öffentliche Gewalt aus der Hand zu geben". Dem entspricht eine „aus der Völkerrechtsfreundlichkeit des Grundgesetzes ergebende Pflicht, das Völkerrecht zu respektieren".[688]

Aber nicht nur die deutsche Verfassungsrechtsordnung, sondern auch die Rechtsordnung der EU als eines Gebildes *sui generis*[689] ist durch eine

---

686 BVerfGE 63, 343 (370); 111, 307 (317 f.).
687 BVerfGE 111, 307 (318).
688 BVerfGE 112, 1 (25 f.).
689 Vgl. hierzu BVerfGE 22, 293 (296).

Völkerrechtsfreundlichkeit geprägt.[690] Da dieser Integrationsverbund seinen Ausgangspunkt wie seine primärrechtliche Fortentwicklung in einer Reihe völkerrechtlicher Gründungsakten hat, ist eine gewisse Völkerrechtsfreundlichkeit der EU schon von ihrer Wurzel her inhärent. Im EU-Vertrag wird diese Völkerrechtsfreundlichkeit nicht zuletzt in Art. 3 Abs. 5 Satz 2 EUV und Art. 21 Abs. 1 EUV bestätigt. Im AEUV wird diese Völkerrechtsfreundlichkeit durch dessen Art. 216 Abs. 2 bekräftigt:

- Nach Art. 3 Abs. 5 Satz 2 EUV leistet die EU „einen Beitrag ... zur strikten Einhaltung und Weiterentwicklung des Völkerrechts, insbesondere zur Wahrung der Grundsätze der Charta der Vereinten Nationen".
- Nach Art. 21 Abs. 1 EUV lässt sich die EU bei ihrem Handeln auf internationaler Ebene „von den Grundsätzen leiten, die für ihre eigene Entstehung, Entwicklung und Erweiterung maßgebend waren und denen sie auch weltweit zu stärkerer Geltung verhelfen will", wozu u.a. auch „die Achtung der Grundsätze der Charta der Vereinten Nationen und des Völkerrechts" zählt.
- Nach Art. 216 Abs. 2 AEUV „(binden) die von der Union geschlossenen Übereinkünfte ... die Organe der Union und die Mitgliedstaaten".

Nicht zuletzt aus der Präambel sowie den Art. 23 bis 26 GG ist die „offene Staatlichkeit"[691] sowie die „Völkerrechtsfreundlichkeit" des Grundgesetzes, das heißt die Öffnung der deutschen Rechtsordnung für das Völkerrecht ableitbar. Besondere Bedeutung kommt dabei insbesondere Art. 25 GG zu, der lautet:

„Die allgemeinen Regeln des Völkerrechtes sind Bestandteil des Bundesrechtes. Sie gehen den Gesetzen vor und erzeugen Rechte und Pflichten unmittelbar für die Bewohner des Bundesgebietes."

Art. 25 Satz 1 GG erteilt einen generellen Rechtsanwendungsbefehl. Die Vorschrift hat zur Folge, dass „die allgemeinen Regeln des Völkerrechts

---

690 Vgl. hierzu auch *Schriewer*, Zur Theorie der internationalen Offenheit und der Völkerrechtsfreundlichkeit einer Rechtsordnung und ihrer Erprobung am Beispiel der EU-Rechtsordnung, S. 127 ff.
691 Vgl. hierzu z.B. *di Fabio*, Das Recht offener Staaten; *Fassbender*, Der offene Bundesstaat; *Giegerich* (Hrsg.), Der „offene Verfassungsstaat" des Grundgesetzes nach 60 Jahren,; *Häberle*, Der kooperative Verfassungsstaat, 141,-141 ff.; *Hobe*, Der offene Verfassungsstaat zwischen Souveränität und Interdependenz; *Schorkopf*, Grundgesetz und Überstaatlichkeit; *Sommermann*, Offene Staatlichkeit: Deutschland,3, 3 ff.; *Vogel*, Die Verfassungsentscheidung des Grundgesetzes für die internationale Zusammenarbeit, S. 42.

ohne ein Transformationsgesetz, also unmittelbar, Eingang in die deutsche Rechtsordnung finden und dem deutschen innerstaatlichen Recht [...] im Range vorgehen".[692] Zu den „allgemeinen Regeln des Völkerrechts" i.S. des Art. 25 GG zählen das Völkergewohnheitsrecht, einschließlich des völkerrechtlichen *ius cogens*, sowie die anerkannten allgemeinen Rechtsgrundsätze im Sinne von Art. 38 Abs. 1 Buchst. c) des IGH-Statuts.[693]

Zu diesen allgemeinen Regeln des Völkerrechts zählt auch der nachfolgend dargestellte Grundsatz der souveränen Gleichheit der Staaten, der heute insbesondere auch in Art. 2 Nr. 1 der UN-Charta eine völkervertragliche Verankerung (und in der *Friendly Relations Declaration*[694] eine Auslegung) gefunden hat.[695] Als Inhalte des Grundsatzes der souveränen Gleichheit werden traditionell angeführt, dass kein Staat ohne seinen Willen völkerrechtlichen Bindungen unterliegen soll und dass kein Staat sich durch die Gerichte anderer Staaten aburteilen lassen muss (*par in parem non habet iudicium*).[696] Die Gebietshoheit und die Personalhoheit der Staaten[697] sind unmittelbare Ausprägungen ihrer Souveränität; das Interventionsverbot dient dem Schutz der Souveränität, indem es anderen Staaten die Einmischung in die inneren Angelegenheiten untersagt.[698]

Auch die Pflicht zur strikten Einhaltung des Völkerrechts nach Art. 3 Abs. 5 Satz 2 EUV umfasst die Wahrung völkergewohnheitsrechtlicher Grenzen der Jurisdiktionsgewalt – in diesem Falle der EU. Dies folgt auch aus der Judikatur des EuGH, wonach die EU ihre regulatorischen Befugnisse, insbesondere auch ihre Rechtsetzungskompetenzen, unter Beachtung des Völkerrechts einschließlich der Regeln des Völkergewohnheitsrechts ausüben muss.[699] Diese Grenze gilt aber nicht nur für legislative, sondern auch für exekutive Tätigkeiten der EU, was z.B. auch im Hinblick auf völkerrechtliche Pflichten zum Schutz der kulturellen Vielfalt, wie sie

---

692 BVerfGE 6, 309 (363).
693 Vgl. z.B. *Talmon* in: JZ 2013, 12, 13.
694 UN Declaration on Principles of International Law concerning Friendly Relations and Cooperation among States vom 24.10.1970, International Legal Materials, 9 (1970), S. 1292 (auch abrufbar unter http://www.un-documents.net/a25r2625.htm).
695 Vgl. hierzu z.B. *Dombrowski*, Extraterritoriale Strafrechtsanwendung im Internet, S. 5; *Epping* in: Ipsen, § 5 Rn. 254 ff.; *Kau*, in: *Graf Vitzthum/Proelß* (Hrsg.), Dritter Abschnitt Rn. 87 ff.
696 Vgl. *Baker*, The Doctrine of Legal Equality of States, 1, 11 f.; *Kokott*, in: ZaöRV 2004, 517, 519.
697 Vgl. hierzu z.B. *Bertele*, Souveränität und Verfahrensrecht, S. 65 ff.
698 Vgl. z.B. *Stein/Buttlar/Kotzur*, Völkerrecht, S. 194 ff.
699 Vgl. EuGH, Rs. C-162/96, *Racke/ Hauptzollamt Mainz*, Rn. 45 f.

E. Völkerrechtliche Kernprobleme der Regulierung des „Mediensektors"

sich aus dem diesbezüglichen UNESCO-Abkommen ergeben, bedeutsam sein kann.[700]

Dass Vollzugsmaßnahmen einer Landesmedienanstalt auf der Grundlage des MStV und/oder des JMStV ebenso wie z.B. die Wettbewerbsaufsicht der EU-Kommission unter völkerrechtlichem Blickwinkel hoheitliches Handeln darstellen, ist unstreitig. Für die entsprechende Einordnung kommt es nicht darauf an, ob die betreffende Handlung Zwangscharakter aufweist.[701] Unabhängig von einem solchen Zwangscharakter ist auch die Einstufung der Maßnahme mit Blick auf die Frage eines Verstoßes gegen die Gebietshoheit eines Staates. Denn ein etwaiger Verstoß gegen diese Gebietshoheit durch Handlungen eines Staates oder der EU auf fremdem Staatsgebiet oder durch Maßnahmen mit extraterritorialer Wirkung kann nicht dadurch tatbestandlich entfallen, dass ein Zwangscharakter der Handlung rsp. Maßnahme durch Einwilligung des betroffenen Privaten entfällt. Völkerrechtliche Gebote wie das der Achtung der Gebietshoheit stehen nämlich nicht zur Disposition von Privaten.[702]

Allerdings ergeben sich immanente Grenzen der Reichweite des Art. 25 GG wie des Art. 3 Abs. 5 Satz 2 EUV auch mit Blick auf das Gebot der Achtung der Gebietshoheit eines Drittstaates aus dem Völkerrecht selbst.[703] Soweit das Völkerrecht der Geltung bzw. Anwendung des Völkergewohnheitsrechts Grenzen setzt, begrenzt dies auch dessen innerstaatliche Anwendung. Das BVerfG hat insoweit festgestellt, dass eine allgemeine Regel des Völkerrechts nur „mit ihrer jeweiligen völkerrechtlichen Tragweite" Bestandteil des Bundesrechts wird.[704] Wie nachfolgend im Einzelnen aufgezeigt wird, enthält das geltende Völkerrecht keinen Grundsatz (mehr),

---

700 Die EU hat am 18. Dezember 2006 das UNESCO-Übereinkommen über den Schutz und die Förderung der Vielfalt kultureller Ausdrucksformen ratifiziert, das auch in Deutschland ratifiziert wurde. Ein wesentlicher Grund für die Beteiligung der EU liegt darin, dass die vom Übereinkommen betroffenen Bereiche z.T. Kompetenzen der EU, z.T. Kompetenzen der Mitgliedstaaten betreffen. Vgl. hierzu *Klamert* in: ZöR 2009, 217, 217 ff.
701 Vgl. auch BVerfGE 63, 343 (372).
702 Vgl. *Dombrowski*, Extraterritoriale Strafrechtsanwendung im Internet, S. 10 f.; *Geck*, Hoheitsakte auf fremdem Staatsgebiet795, 795 f.; *Germann*, Gefahrenabwehr und Strafverfolgung im Internet, S. 642; *Okresek* in: ÖZöRV 1985, 325, 339 ff.; *Schmidt*, Die Rechtmäßigkeit staatlicher Gefahrenabwehrmaßnahmen im Internet, S. 264; *Valerius*, Ermittlungen der Strafverfolgungsbehörden in den Kommunikationsdiensten des Internet, S. 147.
703 Vgl. BVerfGE 15, 25 (34 f.); 23, 288 (317); 94, 315 (328); 95, 96 (129); 96, 68 (86); 112, 1 (25, 27 f.) sowie z.B. *Talmon* in: JZ 2013, 12, 12.
704 BVerfGE 46, 342 (403). Vgl. auch BVerfGE 18, 441 (448); 23, 288 (316 f.).

dass nationales oder unionales Verwaltungsrecht, sei es Medienrecht wie z.B. Jugendmedienschutz- oder Medienverbraucherschutzrecht von Mitgliedstaaten, sei es Wettbewerbsaufsichtsrecht der EU, nicht auch auf auslandsbezogene Inhalte angewendet werden darf.[705]

Insofern ist auch unter verfassungs- und europarechtlichem Blickwinkel bedeutsam, dass völkerrechtlich eine Jurisdiktionsgewalt auch desjenigen Staates oder derjenigen Staatengemeinschaft anerkannt ist, auf dessen Staatsgebiet oder deren territorialem Geltungsbereich sich Auswirkungen eines in einem Drittstaat getätigten Verhaltens zeitigen. Auch dieses objektive Territorialprinzip, das deutliche Parallelen zur Auswirkungstheorie im Kartellrecht aufweist,[706] wird nachfolgend in seiner Bedeutung für eine extraterritorial wirkende deutsche Medienregulierung beleuchtet.

b. Völkerrechtliche Schranken der Rechtssetzungsgewalt und Vollzugsgewalt eines Staates mit Bezug auf ausländische Anbieter

Ein wichtiger Bestandteil der staatlichen Souveränität i.S. des Völkerrechts[707] ist die als territoriale Souveränität verstandene Kontrolle über alle auf dem Staatsgebiet ausgeübte Hoheitsgewalt. Das eigene Territorium bleibt das im Wortsinne fundamentale Element eines Staates. Die Aufgliederung und rechtliche Ordnung der Welt erfolgt bis heute völkerrechtlich

---

705 Vgl. hierzu z.B. *Schmidt*, Die Rechtmäßigkeit staatlicher Gefahrenabwehrmaßnahmen, S. 257.
706 Vgl. *Fox* in: JILP 2009/2010, 159, 160, 167, 174; *Staker* in: Evans, International Law, S. 309 (316 ff.); *Oxman* in: MPEPIL, 546, 550; *Uerpmann-Wittzack* in: GLJ 2010, 1245, 1254.
707 Souveränität i.S.d. Völkerrechts ist die von niemandem abgeleitete oder abhängige, nur punktuell durch Schranken aus der Völkerrechtsgrundordnung (Mindestanforderungen an einen minimalen Menschenrechtsschutz, Verbot der Sklaverei etc.) begrenzte, ansonsten aber uneingeschränkte rechtliche Handlungsfähigkeit des Staates im Innern und nach außen. Die Souveränität umfasst insbesondere das Recht und die Rechtsmacht zur freien Wahl und Ausgestaltung der politischen, wirtschaftlichen und gesellschaftlichen Ordnung sowie die freie Wahl und Implementierung – und Verantwortung – eigener Lösungen zu allen auftretenden Sachproblemen für die politische Gemeinschaft und schließlich die freie Wahl und Ausübung – oder ggf. auch Einschränkung – der Kontakte zu anderen Staaten sowie internationalen und supranationalen Organisationen; vgl. zum völkerrechtlichen Begriff der Souveränität z.B. *von Arnauld*, Völkerrecht, Rn. 89 ff., 312 ff.

gebietsbezogen.[708] Allerdings geht mit dieser territorialen Souveränität auch eine völkergewohnheitsrechtlich anerkannte Verantwortlichkeit einher: Das Völkergewohnheitsrecht verbietet es einem Staat zu erlauben, dass sein Territorium genutzt wird, um Schaden auf dem Gebiet eines anderen Staates zu verursachen.[709] Hieraus wird in der Völkerrechtslehre zumindest schon vereinzelt eine Pflicht des Staates abgeleitet, Menschenrechte extraterritorial zu respektieren und zu schützen.[710] Es deutet sich damit völkerrechtlich ein sich wandelnder Souveränitätsbegriff an, der nicht auf eine negative Abwehrseite beschränkt ist, sondern Souveränität auch als Verantwortung begreift. So verstanden verlangt Souveränität die Übernahme von Pflichten für die Wahrung zentraler Gemeinschaftsgüter auch dort, wo es um die Abwehr von Verletzungen von Schutzgütern durch Private geht.[711]

Mit Blick auf Schutzgüter wie Menschenwürde und Jugendschutz in vergleichbarer Weise entwicklungsoffen bzw. von einer klassischen reinen staatenzentrierten Abwehr-Dogmatik zu einer Verantwortungsdogmatik in der Entwicklung befindlichen Betrachtungsweise zunehmend geprägt, erweist sich insoweit auch das völkerrechtliche Interventionsverbot. Dieses Verbot der Einmischung von Staaten in die inneren Angelegenheiten anderer Staaten zählt zu den die völkerrechtliche Ordnung konstituierenden

---

708 Die gebietsbezogenen Kompetenzen des Staates äußern sich in seiner Gebietshoheit, d.h. der (Ordnungs-)Gewalt in dem Gebiet, und in seiner territorialen Souveränität, d.h. der (Verfügungs-)Gewalt über das Gebiet. In der Staatenpraxis können beide auseinanderfallen, wenn es zur Ausübung von Hoheitsgewalt auf fremdem Staatsgebiet kommt. Souveränität i.S.d. Völkerrechts ist die von niemandem abgeleitete oder abhängige, nur punktuell durch Schranken aus der Völkerrechtsgrundordnung (Mindestanforderungen an einen minimalen Menschenrechtsschutz, Verbot der Sklaverei etc.) begrenzte, ansonsten aber uneingeschränkte rechtliche Handlungsfähigkeit des Staates im Innern und nach außen. Die Souveränität beinhaltet insbesondere das Recht und die Rechtsmacht zur freien Wahl und Ausgestaltung der politischen, wirtschaftlichen und gesellschaftlichen Ordnung sowie die freie Wahl und Implementierung – und Verantwortung – eigener Lösungen zu allen auftretenden Sachproblemen für die politische Gemeinschaft und schließlich die freie Wahl und Ausübung – oder ggf. auch Einschränkung – der Kontakte zu anderen Staaten sowie internationalen und supranationalen Organisationen; vgl. *Gornig/Horn* (Hrsg.), Territoriale Souveränität und Gebietshoheit, S. 21 ff., 35 ff.
709 Vgl. Trail Smelter Case (U.S. v. Canada), in: Reports of International Arbitral Awards, 16. April 1938 und 11. März 1941, 1905 (1941), https://legal.un.org/riaa/cases/vol_III/1905-1982.pdf.
710 Vgl. *de Schutter u.a.* in: Human Rights Quarterly 2012, 1084, 1169, 1095 f.
711 Vgl. *Seibert-Fohr* in: ZaöRV 2013, 37, 59 f.

Grundsätzen. Es ist zwar nicht ausdrücklich in der UN-Charta festgeschrieben,[712] aber – auch jenseits von regionalen Kodifikationen – als Norm des Völkergewohnheitsrechts unstrittig anerkannt.

Für das Verständnis dieser Norm ist die sog. *Friendly Relations Declaration* der UN von besonderer Bedeutung, die auf die *„Declaration on the Inadmissibility of Intervention in the Domestic Affairs of States and on their Independence and Sovereignty"* vom 21.12.1965 zurückgeht.[713] Demnach beinhaltet der Grundsatz die Pflicht, sich im Einklang mit der Charta nicht in Angelegenheiten einzumischen, die zur inneren Zuständigkeit eines Staates gehören:

> *„Kein Staat und keine Staatengruppe hat das Recht, sich aus irgendeinem Grund unmittelbar oder mittelbar in die inneren und äußeren Angelegenheiten eines anderen Staates einzumischen. Folglich sind die bewaffnete Intervention und alle anderen Formen von Einmischung oder Drohversuchen gegen die Rechtspersönlichkeit eines Staates oder gegen seine politischen, wirtschaftlichen und kulturellen Bestandteile völkerrechtswidrig. Kein Staat darf wirtschaftliche, politische oder irgendwelche anderen Maßnahmen anwenden oder zu deren Anwendung ermutigen, um gegen einen anderen Staat Zwang in der Absicht anzuwenden, von ihm einen Verzicht auf die Ausübung souveräner Rechte zu erreichen oder von ihm Vorteile irgendwelcher Art zu erlangen. [...] Jeder Staat hat ein unveräußerliches Recht, sein politisches, wirtschaftliches, soziales und kulturelles System ohne irgendeine Form der Einmischung von Seiten eines anderen Staates zu wählen. Die vorstehenden Absätze dürfen nicht so ausgelegt werden, als beeinträchtigen sie die einschlägigen Bestimmungen der Charta, die sich auf die Wahrung des Weltfriedens und der internationalen Sicherheit beziehen."*[714]

Das Schutzobjekt des Interventionsverbotes sind die inneren Angelegenheiten eines Staates. Dazu zählen alle die Angelegenheiten, die nicht durch völkerrechtliche Vereinbarungen aus der alleinigen staatlichen Zuständigkeit herausgehoben wurden. Grundsätzlich kann man davon ausgehen, dass die Verfassungsordnung, das politische, wirtschaftliche, soziale und kulturelle System eines Staates zu den inneren Angelegenheiten eines Staates zählen. Zu diesen inneren Angelegenheiten zählt aber auch der administrative Zugriff hoheitlicher Gewalt auf die Staatsangehörigen und

---

712 Diese regelt in Art. 2 Ziff. 7 lediglich das Verbot der Einmischung seitens der UNO in die Angelegenheiten der Vertragsstaaten.
713 Vgl. *Seibert-Fohr* in: ZaöRV 2013, 37, 59 f.
714 Annex 2625 (XXV), angenommen am 24. Oktober 1970, S. 123, https://treaties.un.org/doc/source/docs/A_RES_2625-Eng.pdf.

Staatszugehörigen eines Drittstaates. Allerdings nimmt der Umfang der inneren Angelegenheiten immer mehr ab, da durch die zunehmende Internationalisierung zahlreiche Fragen einer völkerrechtlichen Regelung unterzogen wurden. Das betrifft gerade auch das Gebiet der Menschenrechte, das auch in Bezug auf den Schutz der Menschenwürde und den Jugendmedienschutz zumindest in Teilbereichen zu einer internationalen Angelegenheit geworden ist.[715]

Das Interventionsverbot setzt indessen nicht nur der Rechtsetzungsgewalt und Vollzugsgewalt eines Staates oder einer Staatengemeinschaft mit Bezug auf ausländische Anbieter Grenzen. Es kann zugleich mit Blick auf den Schutz inländischer Bürger vor ausländischen Einflüssen durch Internetangebote aktiviert werden. Einen besonders markanten Ausdruck hat diese aus dem Interventionsverbot abgeleitete Pflicht zur Abstandnahme von schädigenden Einwirkungen in der Erklärung des Ministerrates des Europarates zu *Internet Governance*-Prinzipien aus 2011 gefunden.[716]

c. Die „genuine link" Doktrin und das Vorgehen gegen ausländische Anbieter auf der Grundlage von MStV und JMStV

Der völkerrechtliche Begriff der Hoheitsgewalt von Staaten (*„jurisdiction of states"*) beschreibt die Befugnis des Staates, die Rechts- und Lebensverhältnisse von natürlichen und juristischen Personen umfassend zu regeln. Gemäß dem in Art. 2 Abs. 1 der UN-Charta verankerten Grundsatz souveräner Gleichheit der Staaten und im Ergebnis des Interventionsverbots findet die Jurisdiktion eines Staates ihre Grenzen in der Jurisdiktion der anderen Staaten. Die wesentliche Ausprägung dieses Ansatzes ist, dass ein Staat (grundsätzlich nur) Gebietshoheit über sein Staatsgebiet und Personalhoheit über seine Staatsbürger ausüben darf. Eine Erweiterung dieser Jurisdiktionsgewalt bedarf einer völkervertragsrechtlichen Regelung oder einer Anerkennung im Völkergewohnheitsrecht. Dabei erfordert die Ausübung von solcher die Territorialhoheit und Personalhoheit übergreifender Juris-

---

715 Vgl. etwa *Ukrow* in: RdJB 2017, 278, 278 ff.
716 Das 3. Prinzip dieser Erklärung weist darauf hin, dass Staaten in Ausübung ihrer nationalen souveränen Rechte, "Abstand nehmen sollen von Handlungen, die direkt oder indirekt Personen oder Einrichtungen außerhalb ihres Territoriums negativ beeinflussen." Vgl. Europarat, Erklärung des Ministerkomitees des Europarates über Internet Governance-Prinzipien, angenommen bei der Sitzung der Stellvertreter der Minister am 21.9.2011, 1121.

diktion ein sog. *genuine link*.[717] Einem Staat sind danach völkerrechtlich nur Sachverhalte zur Regelung überantwortet, zu denen er nach einer Interessenabwägung mit den Souveränitätsinteressen anderer Staaten[718] einen hinreichend engen Bezug aufweist. Hierin findet nicht zuletzt das Willkürverbot seinen Ausdruck: Ein Staat darf Sachverhalte mit Auslandsbezug nur dann regeln, wenn dies nicht willkürlich erfolgt.[719]

Ausgehend vom Grundsatz der Gebietshoheit sind zunächst das Territorialitäts- sowie das damit verbundene Auswirkungsprinzip als Anknüpfungstatbestände i.S. des *genuine-link*-Kriteriums anerkannt. Darüber hinaus werden die Staatszugehörigkeit (aktives Personalitätsprinzip) und der Schutz bestimmter staatlicher Interessen (passives Personalitäts- und Schutzprinzip) als solche Anknüpfungspunkte völkerrechtlich akzeptiert.[720]

Nach dem Territorialitätsprinzip haben Staaten Jurisdiktionshoheit über die auf dem eigenen Staatsgebiet belegenen Sachen und Personen.[721] Umfasst von dieser territorialen Jurisdiktionsgewalt sind aber nicht nur Handlungen, die sich auf dem Staatsgebiet ereignen, sondern nach dem – in Fortentwicklung des Territorialitätsprinzips anerkannten – (Aus-) Wirkungsprinzip auch solche Handlungen, deren Erfolg sich auf dem Staatsgebiet realisiert. Das (Aus-) Wirkungsprinzip ergänzt insoweit das objektive Territorialitätsprinzip, als die Gebietshoheit der Staaten auch eine Regelungsmöglichkeit für alle Einflüsse auf das Staatsgebiet nahelegt.[722]

Eine uneingeschränkte Geltung des sog. Auswirkungsprinzips würde allerdings bei der Frage, ob ein Staat wegen Angeboten im Internet, die in seinem Staatsgebiet abrufbar sind, hoheitliche Maßnahmen gegen den Anbieter, der diese Angebote ins Netz gestellt hat, ergreifen darf, zu unter völkerrechtlichem Blickwinkel unerwünschten Ergebnissen führen. Denn im

---

717 Vgl. hierzu z.B. *Ziegenhain*, Exterritoriale Rechtsanwendung und die Bedeutung des Genuine link Erfordernisses, S. 47 m.w.N.
718 Vgl. *Ziegenhain*, Exterritoriale Rechtsanwendung und die Bedeutung des Genuine link Erfordernisses, S. 47 f.
719 Vgl. *Dombrowski*, Extraterritoriale Strafrechtsanwendung im Internet, S. 53.
720 Vgl. *Tietje/Bering/Zuber*, Völker- und europarechtliche Zulässigkeit extraterritorialer Anknüpfung einer Finanztransaktionssteuer, S. 9.
721 Vgl. *Hobe*, Einführung in das Völkerrecht, S. 99; *Stein/von Buttlar/Kotzur*, Völkerrecht, Rn. 611 f.
722 Vgl. *Burmester*, Grundlagen internationaler Regelungskumulation und -kollision unter besonderer Berücksichtigung des Steuerrechts, S. 95 ff., 104 ff.; *Hobe*, Einführung in das Völkerrecht, S. 99; *Stein/von Buttlar/Kotzur*, Völkerrecht, Rn. 613; *Tietje/Bering/Zuber*, Völker- und europarechtliche Zulässigkeit extraterritorialer Anknüpfung einer Finanztransaktionssteuer, S. 9.

Ergebnis eines solchen Ansatzes würde es zu potentiell universellen Kompetenzkonflikten kommen, da Inhalte im Internet regelmäßig von fast jedem Staat der Welt aus wahrnehmbar sind. Ohne Begrenzung des Auswirkungsprinzips müsste ein Angebot im Internet mit den Rechtsordnungen von über 200 Staaten übereinstimmen, um dem Anbieter Rechtssicherheit zu gewährleisten. Dies würde erkennbar die Möglichkeiten eines gewöhnlichen Online-Anbieters nachhaltig überschreiten. Solche nicht praktikablen und unangemessenen Ergebnisse sind erkennbar völkerrechtlich nicht gewollt.[723]

Eine Gestaltung des Angebots in deutscher Sprache kann zumindest dann als auf Deutschland ausgerichtet eingestuft werden, wenn keine Elemente hinzukommen, die dafür sprechen, dass durch das Angebot lediglich die Verkehrskreise in einem deutschsprachigen Drittstaat angesprochen werden sollten.[724]

Eine zielgerichtete Bestimmung auf eine Abrufbarkeit in oder eine Auswirkung auf Deutschland ist im Übrigen insbesondere gegeben, wenn sich ein Angebot konkret im Schwerpunkt oder ausschließlich mit der politischen, wirtschaftlichen, gesellschaftlichen, wissenschaftlichen oder kulturellen Situation Deutschlands in Gegenwart oder Vergangenheit befasst. Namentlich liegt ein *genuine link* mit Blick auf den Bezug zur Verfassungsidentität der Bundesrepublik Deutschland und die gegenbildlich identitätsprägende Bedeutung des Nationalsozialismus für die deutsche Rechtsordnung bei Verstößen gegen § 4 Abs. 1 Satz 1 Nrn. 1, 2, 3, 4 und 7 JMStV vor. Denn in diesen Normen findet die „gegenbildlich identitätsprägende Bedeutung des Nationalsozialismus für das Grundgesetz"[725] ihr jugendmedienschutzrechtliches Pendant. Die menschenverachtende Gewalt- und Willkürherrschaft des Nationalsozialismus war und ist für die Ausgestaltung der Verfassungsordnung von wesentlicher Bedeutung, so dass das Grundgesetz geradezu als Gegenentwurf zu dem Totalitarismus des nationalsozialistischen Regimes angesehen werden kann.[726] Diejenigen Rege-

---

723 Dies hat der IGH im Übrigen bereits in der vor digitalen Zeit im sogenannten *Barcelona Traction* Fall (ICJ Reports 1970, S. 3 Rn. 70, 101) (an-) erkannt und im Fall konkurrierender Anknüpfungspunkte zwischen diesen abgewogen und für die Kompetenzbegründung eines Staates auf den engeren Anknüpfungspunkt abgestellt. Vgl. hierzu z.B. auch *Dombrowski*, Extraterritoriale Strafrechtsanwendung im Internet, S. 60 f.
724 Eine entsprechende Ausrichtung auf einen Drittstaat stellt es z.B. dar, wenn die Preise für die Wahrnehmung eines Angebots ausschließlich in Schweizer Franken angegeben werden; vgl. OLG München, Urteil v. 8.10.2009, 29 U 2636/09.
725 BVerfGE 124, 300 (327 f.); BVerfG, Urteil v. 17.1.2017, 2 BvB 1/13, Rn. 591, 596.
726 BVerfGE 124, 300 (328); BVerfG, Urteil v. 17.1.2017, 2 BvB 1/13, Rn. 596.

lungen des JMStV, die Angebote zur Abgrenzung von der menschenverachtenden Gewalt- und Willkürherrschaft des Nationalsozialismus für unzulässig erklären, weisen mit Blick auf diese gegenbildlich identitätsprägende Bedeutung einen solch starken Bezug zur Verfassungsidentität Deutschlands auf, dass von einem *genuine link* ausgegangen werden kann.[727]

Auch wer als ausländischer Anbieter ein eigenes Angebot in eine Plattform eines Anbieters aufnehmen lässt, der seinerseits seinen Sitz in Deutschland hat und/oder sein Angebot ausschließlich oder zumindest auch in Deutschland zugänglich macht, zielt darauf, auch sein Angebot in Deutschland zugänglich zu machen. Er bemüht sich damit um eine Relevanz seines Angebots für den Prozess individueller und öffentlicher Meinungsbildung in Deutschland, was für die Begründung eines *genuine link* genügt. Gleiches gilt namentlich auch für einen ausländischen Anbieter, der auf eine vorrangige Berücksichtigung seines Angebots bei Suchanfragen in Deutschland hinwirkt. Wird in Deutschland generell oder über individualisierte Ansprache von in Deutschland Ansässigen für das Angebot eines ausländischen Anbieters geworben, so spricht dies unabhängig von der Sprache des Angebots selbst dafür, dass sich das beworbene Angebot bewusst und gewollt zumindest auch in Deutschland auswirken soll. Auch in Deutschland stattfindende kommerzielle Kommunikation für ein ausländisches Angebot begründet damit einen *genuine link* zu diesem Angebot. Schließlich begründet auch eine Mitgliedschaft in einer anerkannten Einrichtung der freiwilligen Selbstkontrolle einen *genuine link* zum deutschen System der regulierten Selbstkontrolle und hierüber zu der Bundesrepublik Deutschland.

Der Medienstaatsvertrag der Länder bewegt sich in diesem völkerrechtlichen Kontext, wenn er in § 1 Abs. 8 Satz 1 regelt, dass dieser Staatsvertrag

---

[727] Dieser Anknüpfungspunkt mag zwar mit Blick auf die Öffnung des Völkerstrafgesetzbuchs für eine Vielzahl der in § 4 Abs. 1 Satz 1 Nr. 4 JMStV angesprochenen Tatbestände auf Drittstaaten neben Deutschland zweifelhaft sein, da insoweit die mit dem genuine link verbundene Zielsetzung einer Einschränkung des Wirkungsprinzips gefährdet sein könnte. Allerdings zeigen nicht zuletzt die Genese des Völkerstrafrechts in Wurzeln des NS Unrechts wie die fortdauernde redaktionelle Sonderbehandlung Deutschlands über die Feindstaaten-Klausel der UN Charta die besondere Verantwortung Deutschlands auf, die in der völkerrechtlichen Befugnis zum wehrhaften Tätigwerden auch gegenüber ausländischen Gefährdern der freiheitlich demokratischen Grundordnung und des antinazistischen Erbes nach dem Grundsatz „keine Freiheit für die Feinde der Freiheit" ein zweckmäßiges Pendant findet. Vgl. hierzu auch *Ukrow*, Wehrhafte Demokratie 4.0.

E. Völkerrechtliche Kernprobleme der Regulierung des „Mediensektors"

„für Medienintermediäre, Medienplattformen und Benutzeroberflächen (gilt), soweit sie zur Nutzung in Deutschland bestimmt sind", und dabei in Satz 2 der Norm regelt, dass „Medienintermediäre, Medienplattformen oder Benutzeroberflächen ... dann als zur Nutzung in Deutschland bestimmt anzusehen (sind), wenn sie sich in der Gesamtschau, insbesondere durch die verwendete Sprache, die angebotenen Inhalte oder Marketingaktivitäten, an Nutzer in Deutschland richten oder in Deutschland einen nicht unwesentlichen Teil ihrer Refinanzierung erzielen." Gleiches gilt für den JMStV in der Fassung des Staatsvertrages zur Modernisierung der Medienordnung in Deutschland, wenn dieser in § 2 Abs. 1 Satz 2 nunmehr regelt, dass die Vorschriften dieses Staatsvertrages auch für Anbieter (gelten), die ihren Sitz nach den Vorschriften des Telemediengesetzes sowie des Medienstaatsvertrages nicht in Deutschland haben, soweit die Angebote zur Nutzung in Deutschland bestimmt sind und unter Beachtung der Vorgaben der Artikel 3 und 4 der AVMD-Richtlinie, sowie des Artikels 3 der ECRL. Wann von der Bestimmung zur Nutzung in Deutschland auszugehen ist, regelt § 2 Abs. 1 Satz 3 JMStV in seiner Fassung durch den Modernisierungsvertrag dabei textidentisch zu § 1 Abs. 8 Satz 2 MStV.

Das aktive Personalitätsprinzip, das an die Personalhoheit eines Staates anknüpft, gewährt einem Staat eine umfassende Herrschaftsgewalt über die Rechte und Pflichten seiner Staatsangehörigen. Dies gilt unabhängig davon, ob sich diese im In- oder Ausland aufhalten.[728] Vom aktiven Personalitätsprinzip umfasst sind auch kommerzielle audiovisuelle Aktivitäten jedweder Art – vom Veranstalten von Rundfunk über das Anbieten von Telemedien bis zum Selektieren, Aggregieren und Präsentieren von Inhalten. Mithin bietet das (aktive) Personalitätsprinzip auch einen Ansatz, Vollzugsmaßnahmen wegen einer Verletzung des MStV oder des JMStV gegenüber ausländischen Anbietern zu ergreifen, soweit es sich bei diesen Anbietern um im Ausland ansässige eigene Staatsangehörige handelt.

Im Unterschied zum aktiven Personalitätsprinzip hat das passive Personalitätsprinzip seinen Ausgangspunkt nicht in der Personalhoheit eines Staates, sondern ist in dessen Interesse begründet, Taten gegen eigene Staatsangehörige zu verhindern bzw. zu verfolgen. Obwohl (noch) nicht davon ausgegangen werden kann, dass dieses Prinzip völkergewohnheits-

---

728 Vgl. *Burmester*, Grundlagen internationaler Regelungskumulation und -kollision unter besonderer Berücksichtigung des Steuerrechts, S. 103 f.; *Crawford*, Brownlie's Principles of Public International Law, S. 459 f.; *Kment*, Grenzüberschreitendes Verwaltungshandeln, S. 114 ff.; *Stein/von Buttlar/Kotzur*, Völkerrecht, Rn. 617; *Tietje/Bering/Zuber*, Völker- und europarechtliche Zulässigkeit extraterritorialer Anknüpfung einer Finanztransaktionssteuer, S. 9.

rechtliche Anerkennung gefunden hat, lässt sich der Staatenpraxis zumindest eine Duldung bei bestimmten Delikten entnehmen.[729] Das dem passiven Personalitätsprinzip verwandte Schutzprinzip ermöglicht im Übrigen eine extraterritoriale Anknüpfung bei Sachverhalten, die staatliche Interessen von besonderer Bedeutung gefährden.[730]

d. Völkerrechtliche Anknüpfungspunkte und Schranken der Rechtsetzungsgewalt und Vollzugsgewalt eines Staates (jurisdiction to prescribe und jurisdiction to enforce)

Im Ergebnis der sog. *Lotus*-Judikatur hat sich in Bezug auf die Jurisdiktionsgewalt eines Staates oder sonstigen Völkerrechtssubjekts wie z.B. der EU im Völkerrecht die anerkannte und für eine präzise Erfassung von Jurisdiktionsproblemen unumgängliche Differenzierung zwischen der Rechtsetzungsgewalt, der Vollzugsgewalt und der Rechtsprechungsgewalt dieses Völkerrechtssubjekts *(jurisdiction to prescribe, jurisdiction to enforce und jurisdiction to adjudicate)* entwickelt.[731]

Für die völkerrechtliche Beurteilung der Zulässigkeit extraterritorialer Sachverhaltsanknüpfung ist zunächst zwischen dem *räumlichen Geltungsbereich* und dem *sachlichen Anwendungsbereich* einer Norm zu differenzieren.[732] Der räumliche Geltungsbereich bestimmt, in welchem territorialen Bereich eine Norm Geltung beansprucht. Im Falle einer verwaltungsrechtlichen Norm regelt der räumliche Geltungsbereich mithin den Bereich, in dem die Norm Behörden und Gerichte bei ihrer administrativen bzw. ju-

---

729 Vgl. *Burmester*, Grundlagen internationaler Regelungskumulation und -kollision unter besonderer Berücksichtigung des Steuerrechts, S. 107 ff.; *Stein/von Buttlar/Kotzur*, Völkerrecht, Rn. 620 f.; *Tietje/Bering/Zuber*, Völker- und europarechtliche Zulässigkeit extraterritorialer Anknüpfung einer Finanztransaktionssteuer, S. 9 f.
730 Vgl. *Burmester*, Grundlagen internationaler Regelungskumulation und -kollision unter besonderer Berücksichtigung des Steuerrechts, S. 98 ff.; Dahm/Delbrück/Wolfrum, Völkerrecht, Band I/1, S. 321; *Kment*, Grenzüberschreitendes Verwaltungshandeln, S. 123 f.; Stein/von Buttlar/Kotzur, Völkerrecht, Rn. 622; *Tietje/Bering/Zuber*, Völker- und europarechtliche Zulässigkeit extraterritorialer Anknüpfung einer Finanztransaktionssteuer, S. 10.
731 Vgl. hierzu z.B. *Crawford*, Brownlie's Principles of Public International Law, S. 456; *Epping/Gloria* in: Ipsen, Völkerrecht, § 23 Rn. 86; *Schweisfurth*, Völkerrecht, 9. Kapitel, Rn. 177.
732 Vgl. *Epping/Gloria*, in: Ipsen, Völkerrecht, § 23 Rn. 87; *Tietje/Bering/Zuber*, Völker- und europarechtliche Zulässigkeit extraterritorialer Anknüpfung einer Finanztransaktionssteuer, S. 6.

dikativen Tätigkeit bindet. Der sachliche Anwendungsbereich regelt demgegenüber, auf welche Sachverhalte eine Norm anwendbar ist. Dies können ggf. auch Sachverhalte außerhalb des territorialen Hoheitsgebietes des Staates sein, dessen Behörde auf der Grundlage einer verwaltungsrechtlichen Norm hoheitlich tätig geworden ist. Völkerrecht steht einer Unterscheidung zwischen Geltungs- und Anwendungsbereich nicht per se entgegen.[733]

Gemäß den fortdauernd den Stand der Völkerrechtsdogmatik wiedergebenden Ausführungen des Ständigen Internationalen Gerichtshofs (StIGH) des Völkerbundes in seiner *Lotus*-Entscheidung aus 1927[734] bleibt der räumliche Anwendungsbereich der Jurisdiktionsausübung im Regelfall zwar auf das eigene Territorium eines Staates beschränkt. Allerdings ergibt sich aus dem Urteil zugleich, dass Staaten frei sind, sachlich an Vorgänge im Ausland anzuknüpfen.[735] In das Gebot der Achtung fremder Hoheitsrechte greift die hoheitliche Regulierung eines Staates A deshalb nicht schon dann ein, wenn ein Staat B die Vornahme einer auf seinem Staatsge-

---

733 Vgl. hierzu z.B. *Koch*, Die grenzüberschreitende Wirkung von nationalen Genehmigungen für umweltbeeinträchtigende industrielle Anlagen, S. 32 f.; *Linke*, Europäisches Internationales Verwaltungsrecht, S. 28 f.; *Ohler* in: DVBl. 2007, 1083, 1088.

734 „Not the first and foremost restriction imposed by international law upon a State is that – failing the existence of a permissive rule to the contrary – it may not exercise its power in any form in the territory of another State. In this sense jurisdiction is certainly territorial; it cannot be exercised by a State outside its territory except by virtue of a permissive rule derived from international custom or convention. It does not, however, follow that international law prohibits a State from exercising jurisdiction in its own territory, in respect of any case which relates to acts which have taken place abroad, and in which it cannot rely on some permissive rule of international law. Such a view would only be tenable if international law contained a general prohibition to States to extend the application of their laws and the jurisdiction of their courts to persons, property and acts outside their territory, and if, as an exception to this general prohibition, it allowed States to do so in certain specific cases. But this is certainly not the case under international law as it stands at present. Far from laying down a general prohibition to the effect that States may not extend the application of their laws and the jurisdiction of their courts to persons, property and acts outside their territory, it leaves them in this respect a wide measure of discretion which is only limited in certain cases by prohibitive rules; as regards other cases, every State remains free to adopt the principles which it regards as best and most suitable". The Case of the S.S. Lotus, Judgment No. 9, P.C.I.J., Series A, No. 10 (1927), 18 f.

735 Vgl. *Tietje/Bering/Zuber*, Völker und europarechtliche Zulässigkeit extraterritorialer Anknüpfung einer Finanztransaktionssteuer, S. 7.

biet stattfindenden Handlung erlaubt, der Staat A indessen eine solche Handlung unabhängig davon, wo sie erfolgt, verwaltungsrechtlich verbietet und hoheitliche Gewalt des Staates A dieses Verwaltungsrecht auch bei Sachverhalten mit Drittstaatenbezug für anwendbar erklärt und eben dieses Verhalten wegen seiner Auswirkungen auf dem eigenen Staatsgebiet sanktioniert.[736]

Nach der *Lotus*-Entscheidung steht es Staaten weitgehend frei, wie weit sie den sachlichen Anwendungsbereich ihrer Rechtsordnung ausdehnen wollen. Rechtssetzungsgewalt ist völkerrechtlich insofern nicht exklusiv, sondern immer nur konkurrierend.[737] Demgegenüber ist die Vollzugsgewalt aufgrund der territorial beschränkten Gebietshoheit weitreichenden Beschränkungen unterworfen, sofern es um den Vollzug von Rechtsnormen außerhalb des Hoheitsgebietes der vollziehenden Staatsgewalt geht.[738] Allerdings steht die judikative Zurückhaltung in Bezug auf Fragestellungen eines extraterritorial wirkenden verwaltungsrechtlichen Verhaltens von Regulierungsbehörden sowie das bislang nur rudimentär vorhandene völkervertragsrechtliche Normenmaterial zu einem solchen über Grenzen hinausgreifenden Verhalten der völkerrechtlichen Zulässigkeit eines solchen Verhaltens nicht per se entgegen.

Das Völkerrecht verlangt nach alledem nicht, dass der räumliche Geltungsbereich nationaler Regelungen an der Staatsgrenze enden muss. Völkerrechtswidrig ist es demgegenüber grundsätzlich, wenn eine deutsche Behörde eigenständig Hoheitsgewalt auf fremdem Territorium ausübt, weil das Völkerrechtssubjekt Deutschland in diesem Fall regelmäßig in die Souveränität des betreffenden Drittstaates eingreift.[739]

Diese Abschichtung ist auch bedeutsam bei der Unterscheidung von *jurisdiction to prescribe* und *jurisdiction to enforce*. Während der sachliche Anwendungsbereich von MStV und JMStV, auf den hin die *jurisdiction to prescribe* ausgerichtet ist, auch jenseits der Bundesrepublik Deutschland eröffnet sein kann, ist der räumliche Geltungsbereich der beiden Staatsverträge,

---

736 So im Ansatz *Dombrowski*, Extraterritoriale Strafrechtsanwendung im Internet, S. 51.
737 *Dahm/Delbrück/Wolfrum*, Völkerrecht, Band I/1, S. 319.
738 Vgl. *Dahm/Delbrück/Wolfrum*, Völkerrecht, Band I/1, S. 318 f.; *Tietje/Bering/Zuber*, Völker und europarechtliche Zulässigkeit extraterritorialer Anknüpfung einer Finanztransaktionssteuer, S. 7.
739 Vgl. auch *Bertele*, Souveränität und Verfahrensrecht, S. 78 ff., 89.93; *Dombrowski*, Extraterritoriale Strafrechtsanwendung im Internet, S. 52; *Ziegenhain*, Exterritoriale Rechtsanwendung und die Bedeutung des Genuine-link-Erfordernisses, S. 2 ff.

auf den hin die *jurisdiction to enforce* ausgerichtet ist, auf das Gebiet der sechzehn Länder der Bundesrepublik Deutschland begrenzt. Eine *jurisdiction to enforce* außerhalb der Bundesrepublik würde nur dann eröffnet, wenn dies zum einen innerstaatlich vorgesehen würde und diese innerstaatliche Regelung zudem völkervertragsrechtlich abgesichert wäre.

3. *Die grenzüberschreitende Anwendung deutscher Medienregulierung – Staatsvertragliche Ausgangspunkte in MStV und JMStV und ihre Interpretation*

Der JMStV selbst enthält an keiner Stelle die Begriffe „Ausland", „Ausländer" oder vergleichbare Begrifflichkeiten. Insofern erweist er sich bei semantischer Auslegung in Bezug auf die Fragestellung, ob die Landesmedienanstalten oder das Organ KJM auf ausländische Anbieter Zugriff nehmen können, auf den ersten Blick als neutral. Allerdings bestimmt § 2 Abs. 1 Satz 2 JMStV in seiner durch Art. 3 Nr. 2 Buchst. a) des Staatsvertrags zur Modernisierung der Medienordnung in Deutschland geschaffenen Fassung ausdrücklich, dass die Vorschriften des JMStV „auch für Anbieter (gelten), die ihren Sitz nach den Vorschriften des Telemediengesetzes sowie des Medienstaatsvertrages nicht in Deutschland haben", soweit die Angebote zur Nutzung in Deutschland bestimmt sind und unter Beachtung der Vorgaben der Artikel 3 und 4 der novellierten AVMD-Richtlinie sowie des Artikels 3 der ECRL. Dies spricht semantisch für die grenzüberschreitende Offenheit des JMStV.

Für den MStV ergibt sich demgegenüber bereits vom Wortlaut des § 106 Abs. 1 Satz 2 MStV eine Öffnung in Richtung auf eine grenzüberschreitende Anwendung der staatsvertraglichen Normen: Für bundesweit ausgerichtete Angebote entscheidet danach aufsichtlich, sofern „der Veranstalter oder Anbieter seinen Sitz im Ausland (hat)", die Landesmedienanstalt, „die zuerst mit der Sache befasst worden ist". Von wem der Befassungsimpuls ausging, ist insoweit ohne Bedeutung; auch ein Agieren auf Eigeninitiative von Amts wegen ist danach möglich.

Dieses semantische Ergebnis, das auch nicht durch den Titel des MStV wie JMStV verklammernden Staatsvertrages zur Modernisierung der Medienordnung „in Deutschland" relativiert zu werden vermag, wird durch teleologische Erwägungen bestätigt: So ist z.B. Zweck des JMStV nach dessen § 1 „der einheitliche Schutz der Kinder und Jugendlichen vor Angeboten in elektronischen Informations- und Kommunikationsmedien, die deren Entwicklung oder Erziehung beeinträchtigen oder gefährden, sowie der Schutz vor solchen Angeboten in elektronischen Informations- und

Kommunikationsmedien, die die Menschenwürde oder sonstige durch das Strafgesetzbuch geschützte Rechtsgüter verletzen". Auch diese Zweckrichtung ist nicht ausdrücklich territorial eingehegt. § 1 nimmt nach seinem Wortlaut weder nur Kinder und Jugendliche, die in der Bundesrepublik Deutschland wohnhaft sind oder Staatsangehörige der Bundesrepublik Deutschland sind, in den Blick, noch bezieht er sich ausschließlich auf Angebote in elektronischen Informations- und Kommunikationsmedien, die über ein Kriterium wie z.B. den Sitz des Anbieters in der Bundesrepublik Deutschland zurechenbar sind. Vielmehr ist die Zweckrichtung des § 1 JMStV adressatenbezogen in doppelter Weise – sowohl mit Blick auf die Begünstigten rsp. Geschützten wie mit Blick auf die Gefährder – territorial offen formuliert.

Auch historische Aspekte bekräftigen das Ergebnis der Offenheit hin zu grenzüberschreitend wirkkräftiger Regulierung. Zwar finden sich in der amtlichen Begründung zum Jugendmedienschutz-Staatsvertrag[740] keine ausdrücklichen Ausführungen zur Frage, ob die KJM für die Befassung mit Angeboten zuständig ist, die vom Ausland aus verbreitet und in Deutschland rezipiert werden können. Allerdings findet sich in der amtlichen Begründung zu § 13 JMStV folgende Passage, die mit Blick auf die Beantwortung dieser Frage von erheblicher Bedeutung ist:

„§ 13 betrifft den Anwendungsbereich der Vorschriften über das Verfahren sowie den Vollzug für Anbieter mit Ausnahme des öffentlich-rechtlichen Rundfunks. Die §§ 14 bis 21 sowie § 24 Abs. 4 Satz 6 gelten danach nur für länderübergreifende Angebote. Länderübergreifende Angebote sind dabei sowohl bundesweit verbreitete oder zugänglich gemachte Angebote als auch Angebote, die nur in dem Gebiet von mehreren Ländern verbreitet oder zugänglich gemacht werden. Alle Angebote im Internet sind ohnehin länderübergreifend."

Der letzte Satz ist in mehrfacher Hinsicht für die die vorliegenden Zusammenhänge bedeutsam:

- Erstens nimmt der Gesetzgeber zur Kenntnis, dass „alle Angebote im Internet" länderübergreifend sind. „Alle" meint dabei erkennbar nicht nur diejenigen Angebote, die ihren Ursprung in der Bundesrepublik Deutschland haben.
- Für die Internet-Angebote geht der Gesetzgeber zweitens – wie die Kennzeichnung „ohnehin" belegt – von einer offenkundigen Zustän-

---

740 Abrufbar unter http://www.kjm-online.de/fileadmin/Download_KJM/Recht/Amtliche_Begruendung_zum_JMStV_korrigiert.pdf.

digkeit der KJM über das tatbestandliche Anknüpfungsmerkmal „länderübergreifend" aus.
- Drittens verzichtet der Gesetzgeber auf eine Differenzierung bei der Zuständigkeit der KJM je nachdem, ob ein Internet-Angebot seinen Ursprung in Deutschland oder einem Drittstaat hat. Eine solche Differenzierung hätte indessen mit Blick auf den vom Gesetzgeber erkannten potentiell globalen Problemhaushalt von jugendmedienschutzrechtlich bedenklichen Angeboten nahegelegen, wenn der Gesetzgeber die Zuständigkeit der KJM von vornherein ausschließlich auf Sachverhalte begrenzen wollte, die einzig inländische Anknüpfungspunkte aufweisen.

Einer solchen Differenzierung zur Begrenzung der Zuständigkeit der KJM mit Blick auf die Erkenntnis der internationalen Wirkungsmöglichkeiten im Internet hätte es nur dann nicht bedurft, wenn schon aus völkerrechtlichen Gründen heraus eine Zuständigkeit der KJM für Fälle, in denen die Verletzung der materiell-rechtlichen Bestimmungen des JMStV vom Ausland ausgeht, nicht in Frage kommt.

Für die Frage, ob der Gesetzgeber auch ausländische Angebote im Blick hat, ist zudem die amtliche Begründung von § 5 Abs. 3 JMStV bedeutsam. Diese lautet:

> „Als Alternative für Rundfunk und Telemedien sieht der Staatsvertrag vor, dass aufgrund der Zeit des Verbreitens oder Zugänglichmachens der Anbieter davon ausgehen kann, dass Kinder oder Jugendliche diese Angebote nicht wahrnehmen. Diese aus dem bisherigen Recht übernommene Regelung gilt auch für Telemedien. Auch hier hat sich gezeigt, dass mit entsprechender Software das zeitzonenübergreifende Angebot für einzelne Zeitzonen gesperrt und damit über den Zeitraum eines Tages unterschiedlich ausgestaltet werden kann. Dies ist jedoch nur eine Option für einen Anbieter, die ihm im Übrigen die Möglichkeit lässt, nach Nummer 1 durch technische oder sonstige Mittel andere Vorkehrungen zu treffen."

Eine solche Passage zur Behandlung eines zeitzonenübergreifenden Angebots wäre überflüssig, wäre der Gesetzgeber davon ausgegangen, dass überhaupt nur inländische Angebote Gegenstand eines etwaigen regulatorischen Zugriffs auf der Grundlage des JMStV sein können.

Die Landesmedienanstalten sind danach unter maßgeblicher Berücksichtigung einer semantischen, teleologischen und historischen Auslegung von MStV und JMStV zu Vollzugsmaßnahmen gegen ausländische Anbieter wegen Verletzung materiell-rechtlicher Vorgaben des MStV und/oder des JMStV befugt.

4. Die Zugriffsmöglichkeit auf ausländische Anbieter nach dem MStV und dem JMStV unter dem Blickwinkel des Rechts der EU – eine erste Betrachtung

a. Einleitung

Es geht bei der Frage des Verhältnisses von nationalem Medienrecht und EU-Recht nicht (mehr) um das Problem, ob Art. 5 Abs. 1 Satz 2 GG Sperrwirkung gegenüber Normen des sekundären EU-Rechts setzt.[741] Diese Frage ist spätestens seit der Entscheidung des BVerfG zur Fernsehrichtlinie der damaligen EWG[742] im Grundsatz in Richtung auf eine verfassungsgerichtliche Anerkennung der Regelungskompetenz der EU in Bezug auf audiovisuelle Medien unter Binnenmarkt-Blickwinkel geklärt. Es geht vielmehr um die Frage, ob das Recht der EU einem Ansatz, der Regulierungskompetenzen inländischer Behörden gegenüber (EU-) ausländischen Anbietern grundsätzlich anerkennt, von vornherein Schranken setzt.

Das in der Präambel sowie Art. 23 GG verankerte Ziel der Bundesrepublik, als gleichberechtigtes Glied in einem vereinten Europa dem Frieden der Welt zu dienen, ist zwar, wie nicht zuletzt das BVerfG in seiner Entscheidung zum Vertrag von Lissabon[743] betont hat, verfassungsgebunden; die Verfassung ist ihrerseits aber europaoffen und darüber hinausreichend auch auf internationale Zusammenarbeit ausgerichtet.[744] Daraus ergibt sich als Schlussfolgerung, dass das Grundgesetz nicht von einem Nebeneinander von nationaler, europäischer und Völkerrechtsordnung ausgeht,[745] sondern insbesondere auch eine Verschränkung und Einbeziehung des europäischen Gemeinwohls in die Auslegung und Anwendung der Grundrechte, also eine spezifische europarechtliche Grundrechtsinterpretation gebietet.[746]

Umgekehrt gebieten die dargestellten Kompetenzausübungsregelungen und -schranken ebenso wie die kultur- und medienpolitische Querschnitts-

---

741 Skeptisch insoweit schon frühzeitig z.B. *Ossenbühl*, Rundfunk zwischen nationalem Verfassungsrecht und europäischem Gemeinschaftsrecht, S. 58 ff.
742 BVerfGE 92, 203.
743 BVerfGE 123, 267 (345 ff.); kritisch zur Entscheidung im Hinblick auf die aufgezeigten Integrationsgrenzen z.B. *Ukrow* in: ZEuS 2009, 717, 720 ff.
744 Zur Entscheidung für eine offene Staatlichkeit vgl. *Vogel*, Die Verfassungsentscheidung des Grundgesetzes für eine internationale Zusammenarbeit; sowie z.B. *Kment*, Grenzüberschreitendes Verwaltungshandeln, S. 165 ff.
745 Vgl. im Ansatz bereits *Kirchhof*, in: JZ 1989, 453, 454.
746 Vgl. hierzu BVerfGE 73, 339 (386). Vgl. dazu bereits *Ress* in: VVDStRL 1990, 56, 81; *Streinz*, Bundesverfassungsgerichtlicher Grundrechtsschutz und Europäisches Gemeinschaftsrecht, S. 260 ff.

klausel des Art. 167 Abs. 4 AEUV und die Verpflichtung der EU auf die Achtung der Pluralität der Medien eine Anwendung und Auslegung europäischen Rechts, die auf eine Wahrung der Vielfaltssicherungsinstrumente der Mitgliedstaaten der EU hin ausgerichtet ist.

Dies erkennt zwar auch die Europäische Kommission in ihrer Mitteilung vom 27. April 2020 an die Bundesrepublik Deutschland im Rahmen des Notifizierungsverfahrens zum Staatsvertrag zur Modernisierung der Medienordnung in Deutschland[747] dem Grunde nach an.

In der Notifizierungsmitteilung begründeten die deutschen Behörden den Maßnahmenentwurf und die Anforderungen, die Online-Diensteanbietern von Medieninhalten (sog. „Gatekeeper") auferlegt wurden, mit der Notwendigkeit, den Medienpluralismus im Internet zu sichern.[748] Sie verweisen auf die grundlegenden Veränderungen in der Medienlandschaft, insbesondere auf die zunehmende Bedeutung bestimmter Online-Dienste (sog. „Gatekeeper") für die Auffindbarkeit medialer Angebote und den Zugang hierzu. Das Ziel des Vertragsentwurfs bestehe darin, den Pluralismus zu erhalten und die Vielfalt zu fördern. Hierauf reagierte die Europäische Kommission mit „(a)llgemeine(n) Bemerkungen" wie folgt:

„Der Medienpluralismus ist ein Grundwert der Europäischen Union, wie er in Artikel 11 (2) der Charta der Grundrechte der Europäischen Union verankert ist. In dieser Hinsicht anerkennt die Kommission das Ziel von Initiativen zur Förderung des Medienpluralismus und teilt es. Auf Unionsebene fördert die Kommission diesen Pluralismus unter anderem durch die Finanzierung des Monitors für Medienpluralismus, der derzeit die Auswirkungen der Digitalisierung auf den Medienpluralismus in der gesamten EU untersucht.

Die Kommission setzt sich auch dafür ein, die Medienvielfalt und den Medienpluralismus im Online-Umfeld zu wahren und zu fördern. In diesem Zusammenhang hat die Kommission angekündigt, auf EU-Ebene die Verantwortung von Online-Plattformen in Bezug auf Inhalte im angekündigten EU Rechtsakt zu Digitalen Diensten („Digital Services Act") zu regulieren.

---

747 Notifiziert wurden dabei gemäß der Richtlinie (EU) 2015/1535 Artikel 1 §§ 1, 2, 18, 19, 22, 74, 78 bis 96, 117 Abs. 1 Satz 2 Nrn. 2, 16, 21 bis 44 (als Regelungen des Medienstaatsvertrages) und Artikel 2 des Entwurfes eines Staatsvertrages zur Modernisierung der Medienordnung in Deutschland (als Aufhebung des Rundfunkstaatsvertrages).

748 Darüber hinaus beschreiben die deutschen Behörden den notifizierten Entwurf als teilweise Umsetzung der Richtlinie (EU) 2018/1808 vom 14. November 2018 zur Änderung der AVMD-Richtlinie.

> *Es soll ebenfalls geprüft werden, ob die Rolle von Online Plattformen als Online-„Gatekeeper" zu neuen ex ante Regeln auf EU-Ebene führen soll.*
> *Nach Prüfung des notifizierten Entwurfs und unter Berücksichtigung der Antworten der deutschen Behörden auf das Ersuchen der Dienststellen der Kommission um ergänzende Informationen hat die Kommission indessen gewisse Bedenken hinsichtlich der Frage, ob einige der in dem notifizierten Entwurf enthaltenen Maßnahmen den im Binnenmarkt geschützten freien Verkehr von Diensten der Informationsgesellschaft in unverhältnismäßiger Weise beschränken könnten."*

Wie im Folgenden aufgezeigt wird, erfolgt die Anerkennung mitgliedstaatlicher Initiativen zur Förderung des Medienpluralismus indessen in einer die zumindest vorrangige, wenn nicht ausschließliche Rechtsetzungskompetenz der Mitgliedstaaten zur Reaktion auf neue Gefährdungslagen für die Medienvielfalt nicht hinreichend berücksichtigenden Weise.

b. Die Zugriffsmöglichkeit auf ausländische Anbieter nach dem MStV und JMStV unter dem Blickwinkel des primären Unionsrechts

Aus dem Bekenntnis des GG zur europäischen Integration könnte mit Blick auf die Zuordnung von Verhalten der für die Wahrung des audiovisuellen Schutzes der Menschenwürde und des Jugendmedienschutzes zuständigen Behörden der Mitgliedstaaten ein Ansatz abgeleitet werden, dass deutsche Vollzugsbehörden gegenüber EU-ausländischen Anbietern i.S. einer umfassenden Verpflichtung zum Respekt des Verhaltens von Drittstaaten der EU per se gehindert sind, Vollzugsmaßnahmen zu ergreifen. Die europäische Integration hätte bei einer solchen Betrachtung eine Begrenzung der Handlungsoptionen von mitgliedstaatlichen Verwaltungsbehörden bei Sachverhalten, die Grenzen von EU-Mitgliedstaaten überschreiten, sich aber insgesamt noch im Raum der EU bewegen, zur Folge.

Eine solche Betrachtung würde zwar dem Ansatz der Herkunftslandkontrolle umfassend Rechnung tragen, der zu den grundlegenden, die Binnenmarkt-Konzeption des AEUV prägenden Grundsätzen zählt. Zugleich würde damit im Rechtsraum der EU die Gefahr konfligierender Verwaltungsentscheidungen nachhaltig eingedämmt – allerdings ggf. um den Preis einer unzureichenden Wahrung von Schutzgütern.

Eine solche einschränkende Betrachtung würde allerdings zugleich verkennen, dass das System der Herkunftslandkontrolle nur als Grundsatz gilt. So hat der EuGH u.a. für den Bereich der Glücksspielregulierung ausdrücklich entschieden, dass ein Mitgliedstaat die Geltung glücksspielrecht-

E. Völkerrechtliche Kernprobleme der Regulierung des „Mediensektors"

licher Erlaubnisse anderer Mitgliedstaaten nicht anerkennen muss, sondern das Anbieten von Glücksspielprodukten auf seinem Staatsgebiet vom Besitz einer von seinen eigenen Behörden erteilten Erlaubnis abhängig machen darf.[749] Was mit Blick auf eine Ausgangssituation aktiven staatlichen Tuns eines Drittstaates der EU – hier eine Lizenzerteilung – gilt, muss indessen erst recht für den Fall gelten, dass sich ein Drittstaat mit einem Verhalten einer ihm zurechenbaren Person noch überhaupt nicht befasst hat. Eine informelle Duldung eines bestimmten privaten Verhaltens durch einen EU-Drittstaat kann mithin erst recht keine generelle und umfassende Sperrwirkung in Bezug auf eigenes hoheitliches Handeln entfalten.[750] Ein Mitgliedstaat, auf dessen Territorium eine Dienstleistung, die namentlich gegen jugendschutzgerichtete, menschenwürdegewährleistende oder vielfaltssichernde Bestimmungen dieses Staates verstößt, genutzt wird, ist deshalb zu einer Kontrolle und Maßnahme gegen die Dienstleistung befugt – aber im Hinblick auf das Herkunftslandprinzip als Ausnahme hiervon nur dann, wenn ein Rechtfertigungsgrund zur Einschränkung der Dienstleistungsfreiheit vorliegt und dieser verhältnismäßig angewandt wurde.[751]

Dieser Ansatz ist im Bereich des Jugendmedienschutzes, Schutzes der Menschenwürde und Sicherung des Pluralismus z.B. auch durch Auffindbarkeitsregulierung mit Blick auf Vollzugsmaßnahmen gegenüber Anbietern außerhalb des Integrationsraumes der EU ohne Weiteres bereits deshalb übertragbar, weil die Dienstleistungsfreiheit des AEUV – anders als die Kapital- und Zahlungsverkehrsfreiheit[752] – keine *erga-omnes*-Wirkung aufweist, mithin Anbieter von außerhalb der EU sich nicht auf eine etwaige Verletzung der Dienstleistungsfreiheit durch jugendschutzrechtliche, menschenwürdegewährleistende oder vielfaltssichernde Aufsichtsmaßnahmen berufen können.

---

749 Vgl. z.B. EuGH, verb. Rs. C-316/07, C-358/07 bis C-360/07, C-409/07 und C-410/07, *Stoß u.a. / Land Baden-Württemberg*, Rn. 108 ff.
750 Zudem besteht jedenfalls die Möglichkeit der Beschwerde bei der Kommission, die ggf. ein Vertragsverletzungsverfahren gegen den anderen Mitgliedstaat einleiten kann; u.U. kann die Initiative für ein solches Verfahren sogar vom Mitgliedstaat, der von dieser Untätigkeit betroffen ist, selbst ausgehen.
751 Vgl. hierzu auch unten Abschnitt C.IV.1.
752 Zur *erga-omnes*-Wirkung der Kapital- und Zahlungsverkehrsfreiheit als Abweichung von der Dogmatik der übrigen Grundfreiheiten vgl. z.B. *Ukrow/Ress* in: Grabitz/Hilf/Nettesheim, Art. 63 AEUV (erscheint demnächst).

c. Die Zugriffsmöglichkeit auf ausländische Anbieter nach dem MStV und JMStV unter dem Blickwinkel der AVMD-Richtlinie

Dass auch EU-ausländische Anbieter Gegenstand von Rechtsetzungsakten der Mitgliedstaaten zur Umsetzung der AVMD-Richtlinie sein können, ergibt sich bereits unmittelbar aus der fortdauernden Offenheit dieser Richtlinie für Durchbrechungen des Prinzips der Herkunftslandkontrolle.

Auch die Europäische Kommission bestätigt dies dem Grunde nach in ihrer Mitteilung vom 27. April 2020 an die Bundesrepublik Deutschland im Rahmen des Notifizierungsverfahrens zum Staatsvertrag zur Modernisierung der Medienordnung in Deutschland. Ihre geäußerten Bedenken haben nicht das „ob" dieser legislativen regulatorischen Zugriffsmöglichkeit, sondern das „wie" der Ausformung namentlich in Bezug auf (a) das sog. Abweichungsverfahren nach Art. 3 Abs. 2 der novellierten AVMD-Richtlinie und (b) das sog. Anti-Umgehungsverfahren nach Art. 4 dieser Richtlinie zum Gegenstand. Die Kommission äußert dabei „insbesondere Zweifel an der Vereinbarkeit der §§ 104[753] und 52 des Medienstaatsvertragsentwurfs mit der geänderten AVMD-Richtlinie und damit den geltenden Binnenmarktregeln"[754].

Soweit die Kommission dabei moniert, dass der Grundsatz des freien Empfangs und der freien Weiterverbreitung nur teilweise umgesetzt werde, berührt dies zwar nicht die Frage der Zugriffsmöglichkeit auf ausländische Anbieter. Es kann allerdings dennoch bei Gelegenheit darauf hingewiesen werden, dass die Empfangsfreiheit – abweichend von der Sichtweise der Kommission – bereits deshalb keiner staatsvertraglichen oder sonstigen einfachgesetzlichen Regelung neben der Regelung der Zulässigkeit der Weiterverbreitung bedurfte, weil diese Freiheit unmittelbar in Art. 5 Abs. 1 GG als Jedermann-Grundrecht verankert ist. Sie findet sich zudem – diese verfassungsrechtliche Ausgangslage bestätigend, ohne insoweit originär konstitutive Wirkung in Bezug auf die Freiheit zu entfalten – in einer Reihe landesmedienrechtlicher Gesetzestexte. Es stellt einen weiteren Ausdruck fehlender Sensibilität für das medienrechtliche Mit- und Nebeneinander von Staatsvertragsnormen und Normen autonomen Landesmedienrechts dar, wenn die Kommission zudem moniert, dass „die nationalen Umsetzungsgesetze die Weiterverbreitung oder den Empfang nicht nur bundesweit, sondern auch in einem Teil des deutschen Hoheitsgebiets ermöglichen (müssen)". Denn solche Weiterverbreitungsregelungen in Be-

---

753 Nunmehr: § 103 MStV.
754 Notifizierung 2020/26/D, aaO (Fn. 18).

E. Völkerrechtliche Kernprobleme der Regulierung des „Mediensektors"

zug auf nicht bundesweit empfangbare Angebote finden sich im Medienrecht der einzelnen Länder, das in gleicher Weise wie MStV und JMStV zur Umsetzung der Vorgaben der AVMD-Richtlinie geeignet ist.

Dass die Länder durch die ausdrückliche Bezugnahme auf Art. 3 der AVMD-Richtlinie in § 104 Abs. 1 Satz 2 MStV und die Bezugnahme auf Art. 4 Abs. 3 der AVMD-Richtlinie in § 104 Abs. 4 MStV „nicht die notwendige Klarheit und Zugänglichkeit der auf nationaler Ebene geltenden Vorschriften gewährleisten, um die Rechtssicherheit bei der Anwendung der Richtlinie zu gewährleisten", ist ein Vorwurf der Kommission im Notifizierungsverfahren, der durch die bisherige Judikatur zu den Umsetzungserfordernissen in Bezug auf Richtlinien der EU nicht zweifelsfrei bestätigt wird.[755]

Auch soweit die Europäische Kommission in ihrer Mitteilung vom 27. April 2020 die Vereinbarkeit des in § 52 Abs. 2 MStV geregelten Verfahrens der Versagung einer Zulassung im Zusammenhang mit Umgehungstatbeständen mit Art. 4 der novellierten AVMD-Richtlinie in Zweifel zieht, berühren diese Zweifel nicht die Zugriffsmöglichkeit eines Mitgliedstaats auf ausländische Anbieter. Nach dem Regelungsmodell des § 52 Abs. 2 MStV würde das Niederlassungsland einem Anbieter, der sich in einem Hoheitsgebiet eines Mitgliedstaates niedergelassen hat, um die Bestimmungen des Ziellandes zu umgehen, die Zulassung versagen, ohne das Verfahren nach Art. 4 der novellierten AVMD-Richtlinie zu aktivieren. Ob dieser Mechanismus im Lichte der Anforderungen der Niederlassungsfreiheit und des freien Dienstleistungsverkehrs auch dann mit EU-Recht vereinbar wäre, wenn es sich nicht um den Anbieter eines Drittstaates außerhalb des Fernsehübereinkommens des Europarates handelt, wird von der Kommission zutreffend bezweifelt. Daher ist zwar im Ansatz nachvollziehbar, dass die Kommission Deutschland ersuchte, „klarzustellen, dass § 52 nicht für Anbieter gilt, die in Deutschland niedergelassen sind, wenn ihre Programme ganz oder teilweise auf die Bevölkerung eines anderen Mitgliedstaats ausgerichtet sind". Allerdings ist diese Aufforderung zumindest insoweit überschießend, als das in § 51 Abs. 1 MStV geregelte Zulassungserfordernis unionsrechtskonform auch für Anbieter gelten darf, die in Deutschland niedergelassen sind, wenn ihre Programme ganz oder teilweise auf die Bevölkerung eines anderen Mitgliedstaats ausgerichtet sind.

---

755 Dass eine wörtliche Übernahme der Vorgaben der AVMD-Richtlinie, wie sie z.B. in § 1 Abs. 3 Satz 2 MStV zu finden ist, das Umsetzungserfordernis zweifelsfrei erfüllt, ist unstrittig.

Von der Ebene legislativer Regulierung ist die Regulierung qua Vollzug zu trennen. Dass die Landesmedienanstalten durch Unionsrecht nicht generell gehindert sind, auch auf ausländische Anbieter wegen einer Verletzung von Vorgaben des MStV und JMStV Zugriff zu nehmen, ergibt sich aus dem in der AVMD-Richtlinie geregelten System von Ausnahmen von den Grundsätzen der Sendestaatskontrolle und der freien Weiterverbreitung. Diese Grundsätze gelten danach, wie bereits dargestellt, nicht uneingeschränkt. Vielmehr kann ein anderer Mitgliedstaat in bestimmten, wenn auch sehr eng begrenzten Ausnahmefällen (zum Beispiel aus Gründen des Jugend- und Menschenwürdeschutzes) unter Wahrung des in der AVMD-Richtlinie geregelten Verfahrens die (Weiter-) Verbreitung von audiovisuellen Mediendiensten auf seinem Hoheitsgebiet aussetzen.

Damit können ausländische Anbieter nach dem System der AVMD-Richtlinie zum Gegenstand von Vollzugsmaßnahmen gemacht werden, was die oben gefundene Interpretation einer Zugriffsmöglichkeit auf ausländische Anbieter im Interesse der Wahrung der Schutzzwecke des MStV und des JMStV im Kern unterstützt.

d. Die Zugriffsmöglichkeit auf ausländische Anbieter nach dem MStV und JMStV unter dem Blickwinkel der ECRL

In ihrer Mitteilung vom 27. April 2020 führt die Kommission zur Anwendbarkeit der ECRL zunächst aus, dass sie auf der Grundlage der der Kommission in dieser Notifizierung zur Verfügung gestellten Informationen der Auffassung sei,

„dass die Richtlinie 2000/31/EG („Richtlinie über den elektronischen Geschäftsverkehr"), die den horizontalen Rahmen für Dienste der Informationsgesellschaft bildet, auf die einschlägigen Bestimmungen des notifizierten Entwurfs anwendbar ist".

Die deutschen Behörden machten in dem Notifizierungsverfahren demgegenüber geltend, dass der notifizierte Entwurf unter Artikel 1 Absatz 6 der ECRL falle, wonach

„Maßnahmen auf gemeinschaftlicher oder einzelstaatlicher Ebene, die unter Wahrung des Gemeinschaftsrechts der Förderung der kulturellen und sprachlichen Vielfalt und dem Schutz des Pluralismus dienen, von dieser Richtlinie unberührt bleiben".

E. Völkerrechtliche Kernprobleme der Regulierung des „Mediensektors"

Hierzu führte die Kommission aus:

„Um sich auf eine solche Bestimmung zu berufen, müssen die Maßnahmen tatsächlich und objektiv dem Schutz des Medienpluralismus dienen und in einem angemessenen Verhältnis zu den Zielen der Maßnahme stehen. In ähnlichen, relevanten Rechtssachen hat der Gerichtshof der Europäischen Union (EuGH) an die Bedingungen erinnert, die die Mitgliedstaaten erfüllen müssen, wenn sie Maßnahmen zur Sicherung des Pluralismus ergreifen, welche eine Beschränkung des freien Dienstleistungsverkehrs darstellen könnte(n). Darüber hinaus müssen Mitgliedstaaten gemäß Artikel 1 Absatz 6, auch wenn die Richtlinie über den elektronischen Geschäftsverkehr die Maßnahmen der Mitgliedstaaten zur Förderung des Pluralismus nicht berührt, beim Erlass solcher Maßnahmen das weitere EU-Recht beachten, zu dem auch die Bestimmungen der Richtlinie über den elektronischen Geschäftsverkehr gehören.

Daher werden mit Artikel 1 Absatz 6 die Bestimmungen der Richtlinie (im Gegensatz zu Artikel 1 Absatz 5) nicht ausgeschlossen, sondern wird vielmehr die Bedeutung hervorgehoben, die die EU dem Schutz des Pluralismus als einem Faktor beimisst, den die Mitgliedstaaten bei der Regulierung der Erbringung von Diensten der Informationsgesellschaft berücksichtigen mögen (vgl. Erwägungsgrund 63 der Richtlinie)."

Diese Argumentationslinie der Kommission vermag nicht zu überzeugen: Dass mitgliedstaatliche, auf Art. 1 Abs. 6 der ECRL gestützte Maßnahmen tatsächlich und objektiv dem Schutz des Medienpluralismus dienen müssen, ist zwar zutreffend. Dass die von der Kommission kritisierten Regelungen des MStV nicht tatsächlich und objektiv dem Schutz des Medienpluralismus dienen, ist indessen von der Kommission in ihrer Mitteilung nicht dargelegt – und mit Blick auf die Gefährdungslagen für die Meinungsvielfalt, die länderseitig den Impuls für die entsprechende Regulierung gaben, auch nicht darlegbar.

In gleicher Weise seitens der Kommission nicht dargelegt ist, dass die im MStV ergriffenen Maßnahmen in keinem angemessenen Verhältnis zu den Zielen der Maßnahme stehen. Auch diese Unverhältnismäßigkeit ist im Übrigen nicht darlegbar. Namentlich sind die ergriffenen Maßnahmen zum Schutz des Medienpluralismus geeignet und zur rechtzeitigen Abwehr von Fehlentwicklungen, auf die das BVerfG in seiner Vielfaltsprophylaxe-Judikatur in ständiger Rechtsprechung verweist, erforderlich.

Die Kommission verkennt in ihrer Mitteilung grundlegend die Einschätzungs- und Beurteilungsprärogative, die der EuGH den Mitgliedstaaten bei Maßnahmen mit grundfreiheitenbeschränkender Wirkung, die durch zwingende Erwägungen des Gemeinwohls wie die Sicherung von

Medienpluralismus gerechtfertigt sind, einräumt.[756] Ihr Prüfprogramm überschreitet die Grenzen der in der Judikatur anerkannten Kontrollkompetenzen seitens der EU-Organe:

- Zwar ist es zutreffend, dass der EuGH eine Beschränkung einer Grundfreiheit nur dann als durch einen zwingenden Grund des Allgemeininteresses gerechtfertigt erachtet, wenn der Grundsatz der Verhältnismäßigkeit beachtet wird: Die mitgliedstaatlichen Maßnahmen müssen mithin dazu geeignet sein, die Verwirklichung des verfolgten Ziels zu gewährleisten,[757] und dürfen nicht über das hinausgehen, was zur Erreichung dieses Ziels erforderlich ist.
- Eine nationale Regelung ist dabei i. S. eines unionsrechtlichen Kohärenzkriteriums nur dann geeignet, die Verwirklichung des geltend gemachten Ziels zu gewährleisten, wenn sie tatsächlich dem Anliegen gerecht wird, es in kohärenter und systematischer Weise zu erreichen. Auch hinreichende Anhaltspunkte, dass die Regulierung des MStV diesem Kohärenzkriterium nicht genügt, sind nicht erkennbar.
- Ebenso wenig erkennbar ist, dass die mit der Regulierung durch den MStV verbundene Beschränkung von Grundfreiheiten in diskriminierender Weise angewandt wird.
- Ein Mitgliedstaat muss zwar neben den (geschriebenen oder ungeschriebenen) Rechtfertigungsgründen für eine Beschränkung einer Grundfreiheit, die er geltend machen kann, geeignete Beweise oder eine Untersuchung zur Geeignetheit und Verhältnismäßigkeit der von ihm erlassenen beschränkenden Maßnahme vorlegen sowie genaue Angaben zur Stützung seines Vorbringens machen. Mit dieser objektiven Nachprüfbarkeit wie der Rechtssicherheit der Grenzen der ungeschriebenen Ausnahmeklauseln kommt es auch in Bezug auf die zwingenden Erwägungen des Gemeinwohls zu einer verfahrensrechtlichen Effektuierung des Schutzes der Grundfreiheit.[758] Auch dieser Vorgabe können die Länder im Streitfall indessen problemlos mit Blick auf die Vielzahl von medien- und verfassungsrechtlichen Gutachten, die ihre Nachjus-

---

756 Vgl. hierzu und zum folgenden bereits oben, Abschnitt C.IV.1; eingehend auch *Cole*, Zum Gestaltungsspielraum der EU-Mitgliedstaaten bei Einschränkungen der Dienstleistungsfreiheit, S. 27 ff.
757 Hinsichtlich der Eignung beschränkt sich der EuGH auf eine Evidenzkontrolle, ob eine Maßnahme ex-ante offensichtlich ungeeignet ist, das angestrebte Ziel zu erreichen; vgl. *Cole*, Zum Gestaltungsspielraum der EU-Mitgliedstaaten bei Einschränkungen der Dienstleistungsfreiheit, S. 30 f.
758 Vgl. hierzu Ukrow/Ress in: Grabitz/Hilf/Nettesheim, Das Recht der EU, Art. 63 AEUV, Rn. 228 (erscheint demnächst).

tierungen im deutschen Medienrecht durch den MStV ausgelöst und fundiert haben, genügen.
- Zwar nimmt der EuGH insoweit im Streitfall eine eigene Kontrolle seitens eines Mitgliedstaates erfolgter Beschränkungen einer Grundfreiheit am Maßstab des Verhältnismäßigkeitsgrundsatzes vor – allerdings nur im Sinne einer Plausibilitätskontrolle hinsichtlich Eignung und Erforderlichkeit der Beschränkungen zur Zielverwirklichung.[759] Diesem Plausibilitätstest können die im Notifizierungsverfahren untersuchten Regelungen des MStV erkennbar unterworfen werden, ohne dass die fehlende Plausibilität darstellbar wäre.

Das Prüfprogramm der Kommission im Notifizierungsverfahren überschreitet dieses bereits ambitionierte Programm nach der Judikatur des EuGH, indem es eigene Einschätzungen zu Eignung und Erforderlichkeit an die Stelle der Beurteilung eines Mitgliedstaates treten lässt. Dies ist von der Kontrollkompetenz der Kommission in Bezug auf ungeschriebene Rechtfertigungsgründe nicht mehr gedeckt.

Zudem höhlt die Kommission die Bedeutung von Art. 1 Abs. 6 der ECRL aus, wenn sie zwar den Unberührtheitsgehalt dieser Regelung anerkennt, zugleich indessen die fortdauernde Bindung an ebendiese Richtlinie betont. Dass bestimmte Sachgegenstände in Art. 1 Abs. 5 der Regelung vom Anwendungsbereich der Richtlinie ausgenommen werden und Schutz des Pluralismus hiervon nicht erfasst ist, ist bei systematischer, teleologischer und historischer Interpretation nicht i.S. einer bewussten Einbeziehung von Maßnahmen des Schutzes des Pluralismus in den Anwendungsbereich der Richtlinie zu verstehen, sondern Ausdruck des Grundsatzes, dass es der EU zumindest im Zweifel an einer Kompetenz für Regelungen, deren Hauptzweck der Schutz des Pluralismus ist, fehlt. Dass der Schutz des Pluralismus in dem von der Kommission erwähnten Erwägungsgrund 63 der ECRL keine ausdrückliche Erwähnung findet, spricht für diese auf die Anerkennung und Wahrung mitgliedstaatlicher Regelungskompetenz für Pluralismussicherung gerichtete Interpretation.

Vieles spricht in diesem Zusammenhang dann auch dafür, dass die vom MStV neu erfassten Dienste, sofern die Anwendung der ECRL auf diese nicht bereits über Art 1 Abs. 6 der Richtlinie verneint wird, nicht ohne Weiteres den Regelungen der Richtlinie als „Dienste der Informationsge-

---

759 Vgl. hierzu *Ukrow/Ress* in: Grabitz/Hilf/Nettesheim, Das Recht der EU, Art. 63 AEUV, Rn. 229 (erscheint demnächst). Vgl. hierzu auch *Cole*, Zum Gestaltungsspielraum der EU-Mitgliedstaaten bei Einschränkungen der Dienstleistungsfreiheit, S. 30 ff.

sellschaft" unterworfen sind: Denn sie können zwar nicht wie die in Anhang I der Richtlinie (EU) 2015/1535 vom 9. September 2015 über ein Informationsverfahren auf dem Gebiet der technischen Vorschriften und der Vorschriften für die Dienste der Informationsgesellschaft[760] erfassten Rundfunkdienste ohne Weiteres qua Nutzungssituation aus der Kategorie der „auf individuellen Abruf eines Empfängers erbrachte(n) Dienstleistung", die von der ECRL erfasst ist, herausdefiniert werden. Von ihrer Bedeutung für den Prozess der individuellen und öffentlichen Meinungs- und Willensbildung her sind sie indessen mit diesen Rundfunkdiensten zunehmend funktional vergleichbar. Ihnen kommt im Übrigen erkennbar eine höhere Bedeutung für diesen der Regulierungskompetenz der Mitgliedstaaten unterliegenden Prozess zu als klassischen Telemedien, auf die die Kommission abstellt. Dies ergibt sich bereits aus den im MStV insoweit jeweils zur Definition der Dienste angeführten Qualifikationsmerkmale jenseits der bloßen Telemedien-Eigenschaft. Indessen spricht der generelle Ansatz einer engen Auslegung von Ausnahmebestimmungen zu primär- oder sekundärrechtlich begründeten Verpflichtungen dafür, dass ohne eine ausdrückliche Anpassung der Richtlinie (EU) 2015/1535 die Kommission im Rahmen ihrer Aufsichtstätigkeit davon ausgehen wird, dass die vom MStV neu erfassten Dienste von dieser Richtlinie erfasst sind.

Von der Ebene legislativer Regulierung ist auch im Zusammenhang der ECRL die Regulierung qua Vollzug zu trennen. Auch bei einem etwaigen Zugriff auf ausländische Anbieter sind die Beschränkungen der Verantwortlichkeit zu beachten, die durch die ECRL der EU ausgelöst und in der Bundesrepublik Deutschland durch das Telemediengesetz (TMG)[761] in nationales Recht umgesetzt sind. Namentlich haften auch ausländische Access- und Host-Provider[762] grundsätzlich nicht für von Nutzern übermittelte bzw. gespeicherte Daten, sondern können erst ab einem gewissen Grad an Beteiligung haftbar gemacht werden. Für Access-Provider ist dies etwa eine tatsächliche Veranlassung der Übermittlung oder ein verändernder Eingriff in die zu übermittelnde Information. Ein Host-Provider haftet erst dann für durch Nutzer gespeicherte Daten, wenn er Kenntnis von einer

---

760 ABl. EU 2015 Nr. L 241/1.
761 Telemediengesetz vom 26. Februar 2007 (BGBl. I S. 179), das zuletzt durch Artikel 11 des Gesetzes vom 11. Juli 2019 (BGBl. I S. 1066) geändert worden ist.
762 Dabei handelt es sich um jene Dienstleister, die den Nutzern entweder den Zugang zum Internet verschaffen (sogenannte Access-Provider) oder ihnen durch das Bereitstellen von Speicherplatz eine inhaltliche Nutzung des Internets ermöglichen (sogenannte Host-Provider); vgl. *die medienanstalten/Institut für Europäisches Medienrecht*, Europäische Medien- und Netzpolitik, S. 61.

rechtswidrigen Tätigkeit hat und nicht unverzüglich tätig wird, um die Daten zu entfernen oder den Zugang zu ihnen zu sperren.

Die Haftungsregeln erlauben es den EU-Mitgliedstaaten allerdings ausdrücklich, ihren Gerichten und Verwaltungsbehörden zu ermöglichen, vom Diensteanbieter zu verlangen, die Rechtsverletzung abzustellen oder zu verhindern. Von daher entfaltet auch die ECRL keine generelle Sperrwirkung gegenüber etwaigen Vollzugsmaßnahmen der Landesmedienanstalten gegen ausländische Anbieter auf der Grundlage des MStV oder JMStV.

III. Grundrechtsbindung bei Vollzugsmaßnahmen gegen ausländische Anbieter

1. Bindung an den europäischen Grundrechtsschutz

a. Einleitung

Die Grundrechtsbindung von Hoheitsträgern auf der Grundlage europäischen und internationalen Rechts ist bei Sachverhalten, in denen diese im deutschen Staatsgebiet handeln und die Hoheitsgewalt innerstaatlich wirkt, unzweifelhaft. Welche Geltung die europäischen und internationalen Grund- und Menschenrechte für das Handeln von deutschen Hoheitsträgern demgegenüber extraterritorial haben, bedarf einer vertieften Erörterung.

Nicht nur das BVerfG hat in seiner Judikatur Grundsätze einer exterritorialen Geltung der Grundrechte des GG entwickelt. Auch der EGMR hat in verschiedenen Entscheidungen die Extraterritorialgeltung der EMRK beleuchtet. Fragen der extraterritorialen Geltung können sich schließlich auch mit Blick auf die in der GRC der Europäischen Union und in dem Internationalen Pakt über bürgerliche und politische Rechte (IPBR)[763] verbrieften Grund und Menschenrechte stellen.

Dieser extraterritorialen Geltung kommt im vorliegenden Zusammenhang mit Blick auf Vollzugsmaßnahmen, die gegen ausländische Anbieter gerichtet sind, namentlich wegen des Schutzes der Rundfunk und Medienfreiheit in Art 10 EMRK, Art 11 Grundrechtecharta und (bei einem Verständnis der Norm, welches stärker als durch den Wortlaut, die Schranken

---

763 Vgl. für Deutschland Gesetz zu dem Internationalen Pakt vom 19. Dezember 1966 über bürgerliche und politische Rechte, BGBl. Nr. 60 vom 20.11.1973, S. 1533.

und das Kontrollsystem nahegelegt, deren praktische Relevanz unterstellt) Art. 19 Abs. 2 IPBR Bedeutung zu.

Von dieser extraterritorialen Geltung von europa- und völkerrechtlichen Grundrechtsnormen ist die Frage zu unterscheiden, in welchem Umfang die Medienregulierung eines Mitgliedstaates an die Grundrechte-Charta der EU gebunden ist.

b. Die extraterritoriale Geltung der EMRK und des Internationalen Pakts über bürgerliche und politische Rechte in ihrer Bedeutung für die Medienregulierung

Laut Art. 1 EMRK sichern die Vertragsstaaten allen ihrer Hoheitsgewalt unterstehenden Personen die in der Konvention niedergelegten Rechte und Freiheiten zu.[764] Hinsichtlich der Frage einer extraterritorialen Wirkung der EMRK knüpft die Judikatur des EGMR[765] an die Vorgaben des allgemeinen Völkerrechts zur *jurisdiction of states*[766] an: Der Gerichtshof betont, dass Art. 1 EMRK die Geltung der Konvention territorial begrenze. Ein extraterritoriales Handeln begründet nach dem EGMR in einer die Anwendbarkeit der EMRK eröffnenden Weise die Jurisdiktion eines Staates, wenn dieser (1.) aufgrund effektiver Gebietskontrolle als Folge einer kriegerischen Besetzung oder aufgrund der Einladung oder der ausdrücklichen oder stillschweigenden Zustimmung der Regierung des Territoriums alle oder einige der hoheitlichen Befugnisse ausübe, die normalerweise von dieser Regierung wahrgenommen würden oder (2.) auf der Grundlage anderer völkervertrags- oder völkergewohnheitsrechtlich anerkannter Anknüpfungspunkte extraterritorial Hoheitsgewalt ausübe – wie z.B. im Fall des Tätigwerdens des diplomatischen oder konsularischen Korps eines Staates. Eine weiterreichende Haftung sei von der EMRK nicht angestrebt. Es sei nicht Zweck des Art. 1 EMRK, jeden, der durch eine extraterritoriale Handlung der Vertragsstaaten in den durch die Konvention verbürgten

---

764 In der authentischen englischen und französischen Fassung der EMRK werden für Hoheitsgewalt die Begriffe „jurisdiction" bzw. „juridiction" benutzt. Diese Begriffe sind einem höchst unterschiedlichen deutschen semantischen Begriffsverständnis zugänglich.

765 Vgl. EGMR, Nr. 11755/85, *Stocké / Deutschland*, Rn. 166; Nr. 12747/87, *Drozd and Janousek / Frankreich und Spanien*, Rn. 91; Nr. 40/1993/435/514, *Loizidou / Türkei*, Rn. 62.; Nr. 25781/94, *Zypern / Türkei* Rn. 77; Nr. 20652/92, *Dijavit An / Zypern*, Rn. 18–23.

766 Vgl. hierzu oben, Abschnitt B.VI.

Rechten berührt werde, dem Schutz der Konvention zu unterstellen. Durch eine solche Interpretation würde die Frage, ob eine Person der Jurisdiktion der Staaten unterliege, der Frage gleichgestellt werden, ob eine Person in den durch die Konvention verbürgten Rechten verletzt worden sei.[767]

Dem EGMR zufolge muss das extraterritoriale Handeln demnach eine Situation begründen, in der die Staatsorgane Personen oder Sachen derart kontrollieren, dass die extraterritoriale Hoheitsausübung der innerstaatlichen vergleichbar ist. Dies kann durch effektive Gebietskontrolle oder die Zustimmung der Regierung des betreffenden Gebietes erreicht werden. Der Gerichtshof stellt demnach auf die Formen regelmäßiger Ausübung der staatlichen Hoheitsgewalt ab. Da der Vertragsstaat tatsächlich in der Lage sein muss, die Beachtung der Konventionsrechte zu gewährleisten, ist die Vollzugsgewalt, die *jurisdiction to enforce*, entscheidend. Normalerweise ist ein Staat nämlich nicht in der Lage, auch nur seinen eigenen, im Ausland weilenden Bürgern die Rechte und Freiheiten der Konvention zu gewährleisten, da ihm mangels Vollzugsgewalt nur die begrenzten Mittel des diplomatischen Schutzes zur Verfügung stehen.[768]

Der Schutz des IPBR erstreckt sich gemäß dessen Art. 2 Abs. 1 auf alle Personen, die sich im Gebiet eines Vertragsstaates und seiner Hoheitsgewalt befinden. Das vertraglich zuständige Kontrollorgan, der Ausschuss für Menschenrechte, geht in diesem Zusammenhang von einem extraterritorialen Schutz des Paktes aus.[769] Der Ausschuss hat bereits 1981 mit Blick auf den insoweit textidentischen Art. 2 Abs. 1 des UN-Sozialpaktes[770] festgestellt, dass es für die erforderliche Begründung von Herrschaftsgewalt nicht auf den Ort der staatlichen Handlung ankomme, sondern darauf, ob sich in der Beziehung zwischen Staat und Individuum eine Menschenrechtsverletzung ergebe.[771] Der Ausschuss bestätigte diesen Ansatz 2004 in seinem General Comment No. 31 und stellte unabhängig vom Ort des Ge-

---

767 Vgl. EGMR, Nr. 52207/99, *Bankovic u.a. / Belgien u.a.*, Rn. 66, 71, 73, abgedr. in: EuGRZ 2002, 133–142 sowie ILM 2002, 517–531.
768 Vgl. *Fischer-Lescano/Kreck*, Piraterie und Menschenrechte, S. 6 f.; *Krieger* in: ZaöRV 2002, 669, 672.
769 Hierzu und zum Folgenden *Fischer-Lescano/Kreck*, Piraterie und Menschenrechte, S. 12.
770 Internationaler Pakt über wirtschaftliche, soziale und kulturelle Rechte (UN-Sozialpakt). Zum Wortlaut des UN-Sozialpakts vgl. http://www.ohchr.org/EN/ProfessionalInterest/Pages/CESCR.aspx; eine deutsche Fassung ist zugänglich unter http://www.sozialpakt.info/.
771 Human Rights Committee, Delia Saldias de Lopez v. Uruguay, Communication No. 52/1979, U.N. Doc. CCPR/C/OP/1 (29.07.1981), §§ 12.1.-12.3.; ebenso Hu-

schehens allein darauf ab, ob sich die Person in der Gewalt oder unter effektiver Kontrolle des Staates befindet.[772]

Nach der aufgezeigten kategorialen Einordnung des EGMR kann sich ein ausländischer Anbieter, der durch die Ausübung deutscher Hoheitsgewalt dergestalt betroffen ist, dass auf ihn unter vielfalts- oder jugendmedienschutzrechtlichem Blickwinkel wegen einer Verletzung materiell rechtlicher Vorgaben des MStV oder des JMStV Zugriff genommen wird, zwar auf Konventionsrechte stützen, soweit es um die betreffenden Verwaltungsakte von zuständigen Landesmedienanstalten geht. Sofern es demgegenüber um etwaige Vollstreckungsmaßnahmen des Sitzstaates dieses Anbieters auf der Grundlage entsprechender völkerrechtlicher Abreden zwischen Bundesrepublik Deutschland und Sitzstaat des Anbieters gehen sollte, scheidet eine Berufung auf die EMRK vor Gerichten des Sitzstaates zumindest dann aus, wenn der Sitzstaat nicht seinerseits EU Mitgliedstaat und/oder Vertragspartei der EMRK ist.

c. Die Reichweite der Bindung der Mitgliedstaaten an die Grundrechtecharta der EU bei Maßnahmen der Medienregulierung

Die Mitgliedstaaten sind gemäß Art. 51 Abs. 1 Satz 1 2. Halbsatz GRC „ausschließlich bei der Durchführung des Rechts der Union" an die Charta gebunden. Recht der EU ist dabei Primär- wie Sekundärrecht, wie namentlich auch die AVMD-Richtlinie und die ECRL der EU. Zum Unionsrecht gehören zudem Rechtsvorschriften, die aufgrund sekundärrechtlicher Ermächtigung erlassen wurden, d.h. das sog. Tertiärrecht – wie z.B. die in der AVMD-Richtlinie angesprochenen Leitlinien der Kommission zur Anwendung einzelner Bestimmungen dieser Richtlinie.

Die „Durchführung" des Rechts der EU hat zum einen zweifelsfrei den administrativen Vollzug von Recht der EU, das – wie namentlich Teile des

---

man Rights Committee, Communication No. 106/1981: Uruguay, UN Doc. CCPR/C/18/D/ 106/1981 (31.03.1983), § 5.
772 Human Rights Committee, General Comment No. 31: Nature of the General Legal Obligation Imposed on States Parties to the Covenant, UN Doc. CCPR/C/21/Rev.1/ Add.13 (26.05.2004), § 10: „States Parties are required by article 2, paragraph 1, to respect and to ensure the Covenant rights to all persons who may be within their territory and to all persons subject to their jurisdiction. This means that a State Party must respect and ensure the rights laid down in the Covenant to anyone within the power or effective control of that State Party, even if not situated within the territory of the State Party.".

Primärrechts und das Sekundärrecht in Gestalt von Verordnungen – unmittelbar anwendbar ist, sowie die Auslegung und Anwendung des Unions- und Umsetzungsrechts durch nationale Gerichte zum Gegenstand.[773]

Umstritten bleibt, ob die Mitgliedstaaten auch in den Fällen an die Charta-Grundrechte gebunden sind, in denen sie europarechtlich gewährte Spielräume ausnutzen — zum Beispiel bei der Richtlinienumsetzung. Es geht dabei um die europarechtlich nicht zwingend vorgegebenen Teile des nationalen Umsetzungsrechts, die auch als nicht europarechtlich determiniert bezeichnet werden.[774] Gewichtiges spricht insoweit für eine Auslegung, dass die Bindung der Mitgliedstaaten zwar (auch) in diesem Bereich weitreichend, aber nicht grenzenlos ist: Eine Bindung besteht zumindest dann nicht, wenn die nationale Vorschrift keinen unional gewährten Spielraum nutzt und die Frage damit außerhalb des Unionsrechts liegt. Ein solcher unional gewährter Spielraum ist ein zur Umsetzung von Richtlinien gewährter Spielraum ebenso, wie der Spielraum zur Einschränkung der Grundfreiheiten. Dass die Union eine Zuständigkeit in einem Rechtsbereich besitzt, reicht mit Blick auf „Durchführung" nicht aus, wenn sie die Zuständigkeit noch nicht wahrgenommen hat.[775] An einer Einbindung an die Grundrechte-Charta der EU fehlt es mithin insbesondere auch in Bezug auf die Regelungen zu Benutzeroberflächen und Intermediären im MStV, selbst wenn diesbezüglich ggf. eine Kompetenz der EU zur rechtsharmonisierenden, auf den digitalen Binnenmarkt bezogenen Gestaltung besteht.

Allerdings weist die Judikatur des EuGH auf eine weitergehende Verdrängungswirkung des europäischen gegenüber dem nationalen Grundrechtsschutz, selbst wenn der Gerichtshof in seinem Urteil *Melloni* aus 2013 einen anderen Weg zu beschreiten scheint: Dort hatte der EuGH es nationalen Gerichten freigestellt, nationales Umsetzungsrecht auch an nationalen Grundrechten zu messen, „sofern weder das Schutzniveau der Charta, wie es vom Gerichtshof ausgelegt wird, noch der Vorrang, die Einheit und die Wirksamkeit des Unionsrechts beeinträchtigt werden".[776] Ob mit dieser Entscheidung eine Beschränkung des Anwendungsbefehls verbunden ist, wie er dem zeitlich vorgelagerten Urteil des EuGH im Fall

---

773 Vgl. *Jarass* in: NVwZ 2012, 457, 459 f.; *Tamblé*, Der Anwendungsbereich der EU-Grundrechtecharta (GRC) gem. Art. 51 I 1 GRC, S. 15.
774 Vgl. *Kingreen* in Calliess/Ruffert, Art. 51 GRC, Rn. 10; *Tamblé*, Der Anwendungsbereich der EU-Grundrechtecharta (GRC) gem. Art. 51 I 1 GRC, S. 16.
775 Vgl. *Jarass* in: NVwZ 2012, 457, 460; *Tamblé*, Der Anwendungsbereich der EU-Grundrechtecharta (GRC) gem. Art. 51 I 1 GRC, S. 20.
776 EuGH, Rs. C-399/11, *Melloni / Ministerio Fiscal*, Rn. 60.

Åkerberg Fransson 2013 zu entnehmen ist, muss bezweifelt werden. Dort hatte der EuGH entschieden, dass sich die mitgliedstaatliche Bindung an die Charta auf alle „unionsrechtlich geregelte(n) Fallgestaltungen" und damit auf alle Regelungen, die in den „Geltungsbereich des Unionsrechts" fielen, erstrecke.[777] Von einem echten grundrechtsschutzbezogenen Kooperationsverhältnis kann mit Blick auf die aufgezeigten Maßgaben nicht ohne Weiteres die Rede sein.[778] Das BVerfG ist der Ausdehnung des Anwendungsbereichs allerdings in seinem Urteil *Antiterrordatei* deutlich entgegengetreten.[779]

2. Bindung an den grundgesetzlichen Grundrechtsschutz – Extraterritoriale Geltung des Grundrechtsschutzes

a. Einleitung

Sofern Landesmedienanstalten gegen ausländische Anbieter tätig werden, stellt sich die Frage, in welchem Umfang sich diese Anbieter ggf. gegen entsprechende Vollzugsmaßnahmen auf grundrechtliche Rechtspositionen, namentlich die Rundfunkfreiheit nach Art. 5 Abs. 1 Satz 2 GG stützen können.

Der im Vorfeld von Globalisierung und Europäisierung herkömmliche Geltungsbereich der Grundrechte war das Inland in den Beziehungen der deutschen Staatsgewalt zu den Deutschen im Inland sowie zu den in Deutschland lebenden Ausländern, allerdings für letztere vom Anwendungsbereich her begrenzt auf die Jedermann-Grundrechte. Allerdings kann der Geltungsbereich der Grundrechte in der Bundesrepublik Deutschland, die in besonderer Weise auf Auslandsbeziehungen angewiesen ist, nicht mehr erschöpfend durch eine Inlandsbezogenheit definiert werden.[780]

Im „postnationalen Zeitalter" der „Zerfaserung" von Staatlichkeit[781] steht (auch deutsche) Staatsgewalt in einem komplexen politischen, öko-

---

[777] EuGH, Rs. C-617/10, *Åklagare / Åkerberg Fransson*, Rn. 19; vgl. dazu *Gstrein/Zeitzmann*, in: ZEuS 2013, 239, 239 ff.
[778] Kritisch z.B. *Tamblé*, Der Anwendungsbereich der EU-Grundrechtecharta (GRC) gem. Art. 51 I 1 GRC, S. 22 ff.
[779] BVerfG, 1 BvR 1215/07, NJW 2013, 1499, Rn. 88–91 – *Antiterrordatei*.
[780] Vgl. zur Einebnung der Statusunterschiede von In- und Ausländern durch Völker- und Europarecht *Gundel* in: Isensee/Kirchhof, Band IX, § 198 Rn. 11 ff.
[781] *Giegerich*, Internationale Standards – aus völkerrechtlicher Perspektive, 101, 176.

E. *Völkerrechtliche Kernprobleme der Regulierung des „Mediensektors"*

nomischen, kulturellen, zivilgesellschaftlichen wie individualbezogenen internationalen Beziehungsgeflecht, das auch rechtlich das nationale (Verfassungs-) Recht namentlich mit dem Völkerrecht, dem europäischen Recht (nicht zuletzt dem Recht der EU) sowie u.a. dem internationalen Verwaltungsrecht[782] und dem internationalen Strafrecht[783] und von diesen Rechtsgebieten aus mit dem ausländischen Recht verbindet. Inländische Staatsgewalt kommt mithin in vielfacher Weise mit ausländischen Rechtssubjekten und deren Rechtskreis in Berührung. Diese vielfache europäische und internationale Verbindung und Vernetzung hat zur Folge, dass Staatsgewalt der Bundesrepublik Deutschland nicht nur im Inland, sondern auch im Ausland, also extraterritorial, Wirkungen entfalten kann.[784]

Vor diesem Hintergrund binden die Grundrechte deutsche Staatsgewalt namentlich in der Ausübung von Hoheitsgewalt grundsätzlich auch dann, „soweit Wirkungen ihrer Betätigung im Ausland eintreten".[785]

Allerdings ergibt sich aus dem Umstand, dass Art. 1 Abs. 3 GG eine umfassende Bindung von Gesetzgebung, vollziehender Gewalt und Rechtsprechung an die Grundrechte vorsieht, noch keine abschließende Festlegung der räumlichen Geltungsreichweite der Grundrechte.

> *„Das Grundgesetz begnügt sich nicht damit, die innere Ordnung des deutschen Staates festzulegen, sondern bestimmt auch in Grundzügen sein Verhältnis zur Staatengemeinschaft. Insofern geht es von der Notwendigkeit einer Abgrenzung und Abstimmung mit anderen Staaten und Rechtsordnungen aus. Zum einen ist der Umfang der Verantwortlichkeit und Verantwortung deutscher Staatsorgane bei der Reichweite grundrechtlicher Bindungen zu berücksichtigen.[786] Zum anderen muss das Verfassungsrecht mit dem Völkerrecht abgestimmt werden. Dieses schließt freilich eine Geltung von Grundrechten bei Sachverhalten mit Auslandsbezügen nicht prinzipiell aus.*

---

782 Vgl. hierzu z.B. *Breining-Kaufmann* in: ZSR 2006, 5, 5 ff.; *Glaser*, Internationale Verwaltungsbeziehungen; *Kingsbury/Donaldson* in: MPEPIL, Rn. 4 ff.; *Kingsbury u.a.* in: Law & Contemporary Problems 2005/3-4, 1, 1 ff.; *Kment*, Grenzüberschreitendes Verwaltungshandeln; *Ohler*, Die Kollisionsordnung des Allgemeinen Verwaltungsrechts; *Tietje*, Internationalisiertes Verwaltungshandeln; *ders.*, Die Internationalität des Verwaltungsstaates; *ders.*, Die Exekutive. Verwaltungshandeln im Kontext von Globalisierung und Internationalisierung, 53, 53 ff.
783 Vgl. hierzu z.B. *Ambos/Rackow/Miller*, Internationales Strafrecht; *Gless*, Internationales Strafrecht; *Safferling*, Internationales Strafrecht.
784 Vgl. *Stern*, Das Staatsrecht der Bundesrepublik Deutschland. Band III/1, S. 1224 f.
785 BVerfGE 6, 290 (295); 57, 1 (23). Vgl. hierzu auch *Hofmann*, Grundrechte und grenzüberschreitende Sachverhalte, S. 31 ff.
786 Vgl. hierzu bereits BVerfGE 66, 39 (57 ff.); 92, 26 (47).

Ihre Reichweite ist vielmehr unter Berücksichtigung von Art. 25 GG aus dem Grundgesetz selbst zu ermitteln".[787]

Im Übrigen kann „ein Grundrecht wesensgemäß eine bestimmte Beziehung zur Lebensordnung im Geltungsbereich der Verfassung voraussetzen, so dass eine uneingeschränkte Durchsetzung in ganz oder überwiegend auslandsbezogenen Sachverhalten den Sinn des Grundrechtsschutzes verfehlen würde".[788]

Bei der Rundfunkfreiheit des Grundgesetzes ist spätestens im Zeitalter der (auch informationsbezogenen) Globalisierung nicht erkennbar, dass ein vollständiger Verzicht auf die Grundrechtsbindung bei Sachverhalten mit Auslandsbezug eine sachgerechte Abwägung zwischen Grundrechtsposition und Souveränitätsschutz darstellen würde.

Dass die Auswirkung von inländischen Hoheitsakten auf fremdes Staatsgebiet überwiegend völkerrechtliche Probleme aufwirft,[789] schließt nicht aus, dass die Thematik im Hinblick auf die Grundrechtsbindung auch von verfassungsrechtlicher Relevanz ist. Als ein erster entsprechender verfassungsrechtlicher Anknüpfungspunkt könnte dabei Art. 1 Abs. 2 GG gesehen werden. Dem dortigen Bekenntnis zu „unverletzlichen und unveräußerlichen Menschenrechten als Grundlage jeder menschlichen Gemeinschaft, des Friedens und der Gerechtigkeit in der Welt" ist indessen keine universelle Garantie der deutschen Grundrechte für alle natürlichen und juristischen Personen zu entnehmen, ohne dass ein Anknüpfungspunkt aus der Sicht des Grundgesetzes oder ein „genuine link" aus der Sicht des Völkerrechts vorläge. Ein universeller Geltungsanspruch der deutschen Grundrechte würde die völkerrechtliche Zuständigkeit Deutschlands erkennbar überdehnen. Ein solcher imperialer Grundrechtsanspruch[790] i.S. eines Grundrechtsoktroi stände mit der Völkerrechtsfreundlichkeit des Grundgesetzes wie der grundsätzlichen Achtung fremder Rechtsordnungen[791] erkennbar in Widerspruch.[792] Die völkerrechtlichen Grenzen qua

---

787 BVerfGE 100, 313 (362 f.).
788 BVerfGE 31, 58 (77).
789 Vgl. hierzu bereits *Beitzke* in: Strupp/Schlochauer S. 504 ff.; *Geck* in: Strupp/Schlochauer S. 55; *Schlochauer*, Die extraterritoriale Wirkung von Hoheitsakten nach dem öffentlichen Recht der Bundesrepublik Deutschland und nach internationalem Recht.
790 Vgl. hierzu *Isensee* in: VVDStRL 1974, 49, 63.
791 Vgl. hierzu bereits BVerfGE 18, 112 (120 f.).
792 Vgl. auch *Schröder*, Zur Wirkkraft der Grundrechte bei Sachverhalten mit grenzüberschreitenden Elementen, 137, 141; *Stern*, Das Staatsrecht der Bundesrepublik Deutschland. Band III/1, S. 1228.

Zuständigkeit zulässiger Ausübung von deutscher Hoheitsgewalt markieren deshalb zugleich die äußerste Grenze der möglichen Reichweite der Grundrechte.⁷⁹³

Unter Zugrundelegung dieser völkerrechtsfreundlichen und die souveräne Gleichheit der Rechtsordnungen beachtenden Abgrenzung sind grundsätzlich drei Ansätze zur Definition des Anwendungsbereichs der Grundrechte mit Blick auf Sachverhalte mit Auslandsbezug vorstellbar:

- Die im Hinblick auf die Grundrechtsgeltung außerhalb rein interner Sachverhalte restriktivste, zugleich aber auch die souveräne Gleichheit am stärksten betonende Abgrenzung würde es darstellen, wenn man die Grundrechtsgeltung i.S. des Territorialitätsprinzips grundsätzlich auf das deutsche Staatsgebiet beschränkt.⁷⁹⁴ In einem Zeitalter offener Staatlichkeit kann diese strikte Ausrichtung an der Gebietshoheit allerdings nicht mehr überzeugen.⁷⁹⁵
- Umgekehrt würde es die im Hinblick auf die Grundrechtsgeltung außerhalb rein interner Sachverhalte weitestgehende, zugleich aber auch die souveräne Gleichheit am stärksten belastende Abgrenzung darstellen, wenn man die Grundrechtsgeltung i.S. des Wirkungsprinzips überall annehmen würde, wo die Bundesrepublik Staatsgewalt ausübt oder wo diese Wirkungen zeitigt.⁷⁹⁶
- Eine zwischen diesen Polen vermittelnde Linie mit allerdings stärkeren Verknüpfungen zur Abgrenzung nach dem Wirkungsprinzip nimmt ein Ansatz ein, der i.S. eines Statusprinzips grundsätzlich an den *status passivus* des Grundrechtsprätendenten anknüpft, der entweder der Gebietshoheit oder der Personalhoheit Deutschlands unterstehen muss.⁷⁹⁷

Eine solche vermittelnde Linie i.S. einer moderat verstandenen Grundrechtsbindung verdient im Grundsatz Zustimmung. Denn „eine uneingeschränkte Durchsetzung [der Grundrechtsbindung] in ganz oder überwiegend auslandsbezogenen Sachverhalten (würde) den Sinn des Grund-

---

793 Vgl. *Isensee* in: ders./Kirchhof, § 190 Rn. 33 ff., 58.
794 Vgl. hierzu z.B. *Heintzen*, Auswärtige Beziehungen privater Verbände, S. 100 ff., 123 f.; *Oppermann*, Transnationale Ausstrahlungen deutscher Grundrechte?, 521, 523, 526.
795 Vgl. hierzu auch *Schröder*, Zur Wirkkraft der Grundrechte bei Sachverhalten mit grenzüberschreitenden Elementen, 137, 140 f.
796 Vgl. hierzu z.B. *Stern*, Das Staatsrecht der Bundesrepublik Deutschland. Band III/1, S. 1230.
797 Vgl. hierzu z.B. *Heintzen*, Auswärtige Beziehungen privater Verbände, S. 127 ff.; *Isensee* in: VVDStRL 1974, 49, 61 ff.

rechtsschutzes verfehlen". Es ist „jeweils durch Auslegung der entsprechenden Verfassungsnorm festzustellen, ob sie nach Wortlaut, Sinn und Zweck für jede denkbare Anwendung hoheitlicher Gewalt innerhalb der Bundesrepublik gelten will oder ob sie bei Sachverhalten mit mehr oder weniger intensiver Auslandsbeziehung eine Differenzierung zulässt oder verlangt".[798]

Folgt man dem letztgenannten Ansatz, so stellt dies sicher, dass die Grundrechtsbindung nach Art. 1 Abs. 3 GG auch räumlich hinreichend effektiv ist. Nicht nur ist alle Staatsgewalt gebunden, sondern auch die gesamte deutsche Staatsgewalt grundsätzlich überall dort, wo sie tätig wird oder sich auswirkt.[799] Dementsprechend genießt den Schutz der Grundrechte, wer der deutschen Staatsgewalt unterworfen ist. Wer ihr dagegen nicht ausgesetzt ist, kommt als Grundrechtsträger nicht in Betracht.[800] Dies bedeutet, dass sich vom Grundsatz her auch ausländische Anbieter, die sich Vollzugsmaßnahmen der Landesmedienanstalten auf der Grundlage des MStV oder des JMStV gegenübersehen, auf den Schutz der Grundrechte des Grundgesetzes berufen können.[801]

b. Die Entscheidung des BVerfG zur extraterritorialen Geltung von Grundrechten vom 19. Mai 2020

In seinem sog. BND-Urteil vom 19. Mai 2020 hat das BVerfG betont, dass die Bindung der deutschen Staatsgewalt an die Grundrechte nach Art. 1 Abs. 3 GG nicht auf das deutsche Staatsgebiet begrenzt sei. Allerdings könne sich der Schutz der einzelnen Grundrechte im Inland und Ausland unterscheiden. Jedenfalls der Schutz des Art. 10 Abs. 1 und des Art. 5 Abs. 1 Satz 2 GG als Abwehrrechte gegenüber einer Telekommunikationsüberwachung erstrecke sich auch auf Ausländer im Ausland. Art. 1 Abs. 3 GG begründet aus Sicht des BVerfG „eine umfassende Bindung der deutschen Staatsgewalt an die Grundrechte des Grundgesetzes. Einschränkende Anforderungen, die die Grundrechtsbindung von einem territorialen Bezug zum Bundesgebiet oder der Ausübung spezifischer Hoheitsbefugnisse ab-

---

798 BVerfGE 31, 58 (77).
799 Vgl. hierzu auch *Stern*, Das Staatsrecht der Bundesrepublik Deutschland. Band III/1, S. 1230.
800 Vgl. *Rüfner* in: *Isensee/Kirchhof*, Band IX, § 196 Rn. 34 f.
801 Zu den Besonderheiten der extraterritorialen Wirkung von Grundrechten bei grenzüberschreitender Veranstaltung von Rundfunk vgl. bereits *Stern*, Das Staatsrecht der Bundesrepublik Deutschland. Band III/1, S. 1233 m.w.N.

hängig machen, lassen sich der Vorschrift nicht entnehmen". Das gelte jedenfalls für die Grundrechte als Abwehrrechte gegenüber Überwachungsmaßnahmen, wie sie hier in Frage standen.[802]

Die Grundrechte binden aus Sicht des BVerfG die staatliche Gewalt „umfassend und ins- gesamt, unabhängig von bestimmten Funktionen, Handlungsformen oder Gegenständen staatlicher Aufgabenwahrnehmung. Das Verständnis der staatlichen Gewalt ist dabei weit zu fassen und erstreckt sich nicht nur auf imperative Maßnahmen oder solche, die durch Hoheitsbefugnisse unterlegt sind. Alle Entscheidungen, die auf den jeweiligen staatlichen Entscheidungsebenen den Anspruch erheben können, autorisiert im Namen aller Bürgerinnen und Bürger getroffen zu werden, sind von der Grundrechtsbindung erfasst. Eingeschlossen sind hiervon Maßnahmen, Äußerungen und Handlungen hoheitlicher wie nicht hoheitlicher Art. Grundrechtsgebundene staatliche Gewalt im Sinne des Art. 1 Abs. 3 GG ist danach jedes Handeln staatlicher Organe oder Organisationen, weil es in Wahrnehmung ihres dem Gemeinwohl verpflichteten Auftrags erfolgt". Dies umfasst ungeachtet der eigenen Grundrechtsträgerschaft von Landesmedienanstalten auch hoheitliche Maßnahmen der Landesmedienanstalten in Anwendung von MStV oder JMStV.[803]

Die Grundrechtsbindung der deutschen Staatsgewalt beschränkt sich dabei auch im Ausland nicht auf eine bloß objektivrechtliche Verpflichtung. Sie korrespondiert vielmehr mit einer Grundrechtsberechtigung derjenigen, die durch die jeweiligen Grundrechtsgarantien als geschützte Grundrechtsträger ausgewiesen sind: „Eine Grundrechtsbindung zugunsten individueller Grundrechtsträger, der dann aber keinerlei subjektivrechtliche Entsprechung gegenübersteht, sieht das Grundgesetz nicht vor. Der Charakter als Individualrecht gehört zum zentralen Gehalt des grundgesetzlichen Grundrechtsschutzes".[804]

Die Grundrechtsbindung der deutschen Staatsgewalt auch bei einem Handeln gegenüber Ausländern im Ausland entspricht, wie das BVerfG aufzeigt, zugleich der Einbindung der Bundesrepublik in die internationale Staatengemeinschaft.[805]

---

802 BVerfG, Urteil des Ersten Senats vom 19. Mai 2020, 1 BvR 2835/17, Rn. 88.
803 Wie vor, Rn. 91.
804 Wie vor, Rn. 92.
805 Wie vor, Rn. 93 ff.

c. Extraterritoriale Geltung auch der Rundfunkfreiheit für ausländische juristische Personen

Nicht beantwortet ist auch mit dem BND-Urteil allerdings die Frage, ob sich ausländische Anbieter, seien es Rundfunkveranstalter, Telemedienanbieter oder Intermediäre, *ratione personae* gegenüber auf den MStV oder den JMStV gestützten Vollzugsmaßnahmen auf den rundfunkfreiheitlichen Grundrechtsschutz stützen können. Insofern ist (auch) mit Blick auf die durch solche Vollzugsmaßnahmen ggf. beeinträchtigte Rundfunkfreiheit zwischen ausländischen Anbietern, bei denen es sich um natürliche Personen handelt, und Anbietern in Form juristischer Personen zu differenzieren.

Die Rundfunkfreiheit nach Art. 5 Abs. 1 Satz 2 GG ist als „Jedermann"-Grundrecht konzipiert. Mithin können sich nicht nur Deutsche, sondern auch Angehörige dritter Staatsangehörigkeit auf diese Freiheit berufen. Vor diesem Hintergrund ist zunächst klar, dass von Vollzugsmaßnahmen der Landesmedienanstalten auf der Grundlage des JMStV betroffene ausländische Anbieter in Gestalt von natürlichen Personen auf Art. 5 Abs. 1 Satz 2 GG wegen einer behaupteten Grundrechtsverletzung berufen können.

Schwieriger ist die Rechtslage dort, wo ausländische juristische Personen als Anbieter agieren. Insofern verdient im Ausgangspunkt Art. 19 Abs. 3 GG Beachtung. Danach „(gelten d)ie Grundrechte [...] auch für inländische juristische Personen, soweit sie ihrem Wesen nach auf diese anwendbar sind".

Dass die Rundfunkfreiheit des Art. 5 Abs. 1 Satz 2 GG ihrem Wesen nach allerdings auch auf juristische Personen – unabhängig davon, ob es sich um inländische oder ausländische Personen handelt – vom Ansatz her anwendbar ist, ist evident. Dies wird durch eine Vielzahl von Urteilen bestätigt, in denen sich inländische Unternehmen als juristische Personen des Privatrechts erfolgreich auf eine Verletzung dieses Grundrechts berufen konnten.[806]

Allerdings hat das BVerfG bis in die jüngere Vergangenheit entschieden, dass sich ausländische juristische Personen auf materielle Grundrechte wie die Rundfunkfreiheit – anders als auf prozessuale Grundrechte wie Art. 101 Abs. 1 Satz 2 und Art. 103 Abs. 1 GG[807] – nicht berufen können. Zur Begründung verwies das BVerfG hierbei auf Wortlaut und Sinn von

---

806 BVerfGE 95, 220 (234).
807 Vgl. BVerfGE 12, 6 (8); 18, 441 (447); 21, 362 (373); 64, 1 (11).

E. Völkerrechtliche Kernprobleme der Regulierung des „Mediensektors"

Art. 19 Abs. 3 GG, die eine entsprechende ausdehnende Auslegung verböten.[808]

In einer Entscheidung vom 19. Juli 2011 hatte sich das BVerfG erstmalig mit der spezielleren Frage zu befassen, ob ausländische juristische Personen, die ihren Sitz in der Europäischen Union haben, Träger materieller Grundrechte des Grundgesetzes sein können. Diese Frage war im Vorfeld in der Literatur umstritten.[809]

Nach dem Wortlaut von Art. 19 Abs. 3 GG gelten die Grundrechte zwar nur „für inländische juristische Personen". Wegen der Beschränkung auf inländische juristische Personen lässt sich eine Anwendungserweiterung nicht mit dem Wortlaut von Art. 19 Abs. 3 GG begründen. Es würde die Wortlautgrenze übersteigen, wollte man seine unionsrechtskonforme Auslegung auf eine Deutung des Merkmals „inländische" als „deutsche einschließlich europäische" juristische Personen stützen.[810] Auch handelt es sich bei EU-Drittstaaten zwar nicht mehr um „klassisches" Ausland, aber auch nicht um „Inland" im Sinne der territorialen Gebietshoheit.[811]

Allerdings lag Art. 19 Abs. 3 GG auch nicht der ausdrückliche Wille des Verfassungsgebers zugrunde, eine Berufung auf die Grundrechte auch seitens juristischer Personen aus Mitgliedstaaten der Europäischen Union dauerhaft auszuschließen. Die Europäische Union hat sich inzwischen zu einem hochintegrierten „Staatenverbund"[812] entwickelt, an dem die Bundesrepublik Deutschland gemäß Art. 23 Abs. 1 GG mitwirkt. Die Anwendungserweiterung von Art. 19 Abs. 3 GG nimmt diese Entwicklung auf.[813] Die Anwendungserweiterung des Grundrechtsschutzes auf juristische Personen aus der Europäischen Union entspricht den durch EUV und AEUV seitens der Bundesrepublik Deutschland übernommenen vertraglichen

---

808 Vgl. BVerfGE 21, 207 (208 f.); 23, 229 (236); 100, 313 (364).
 In anderen Entscheidungen hat das BVerfG die Grundrechtsberechtigung ausländischer juristischer Personen ausdrücklich dahingestellt (vgl. allgemein BVerfGE 12, 6 (8); 34, 338 (340); 64, 1 (11) sowie BVerfGE 18, 441 (447) hinsichtlich Art. 14 Abs. 1 GG.
809 Vgl. befürwortend *Drathen*, Deutschengrundrechte im Lichte des Gemeinschaftsrechts; *Dreier*, in: ders. (Hrsg.), Art. 19 Abs. 3 GG Rn. 20 f., 83 f.; *Kotzur* in: DÖV 2001, 192, 195 ff.; ablehnend *Bethge*, Die Grundrechtsberechtigung juristischer Personen nach Art. 19 Abs. 3 Grundgesetz, S. 46 ff.; *Quaritsch* in: Isensee/Kirchhof, Band V, § 120 Rn. 36 ff.; *Weinzierl*, Europäisierung des deutschen Grundrechtsschutzes?.
810 BVerfGE 129, 78 (96).
811 Vgl. BVerfGE 123, 267 (402 f.).
812 BVerfGE 123, 267 (348).
813 Vgl. BVerfGE 129, 78 (96 f.).

Verpflichtungen, wie sie insbesondere in den europäischen Grundfreiheiten und – subsidiär – dem allgemeinen Diskriminierungsverbot des Art. 18 AEUV zum Ausdruck kommen. „Die Grundfreiheiten und das allgemeine Diskriminierungsverbot stehen im Anwendungsbereich des Unionsrechts einer Ungleichbehandlung in- und ausländischer Unternehmen aus der Europäischen Union entgegen und drängen insoweit die in Art. 19 Abs. 3 GG vorgesehene Beschränkung der Grundrechtserstreckung auf inländische juristische Personen zurück".[814]

Durch die Anwendungserweiterung des Art. 19 Abs. 3 GG werden juristische Personen mit einem Sitz im EU-Ausland ebenso behandelt wie inländische juristische Personen. Damit geht allerdings umgekehrt auch einher, dass EU-Ausländern die gleichen Vorschriften der Verfassung (einschließlich der Schranken der Rundfunkfreiheit nach Art. 5 Abs. 2 GG) wie inländischen juristischen Personen entgegengehalten werden können.[815]

Zwar ließe sich im Ansatz daran denken, diese dogmatische Ableitung der Anwendungserweiterung des Art. 19 Abs. 3 GG, namentlich über das Diskriminierungsverbot des Art. 18 AEUV, nicht nur mit Blick auf Schutzbereich der Grundrechte und deren Schranken, sondern auch mit Blick auf grundrechtlich abgeleitete Schutzpflichten dergestalt fruchtbar zu machen, dass die entsprechende Schutzverpflichtung nicht nur gegenüber inländischen natürlichen und juristischen Personen, sondern auch gegenüber ausländischen natürlichen und juristischen Personen besteht. Ein solcher dogmatischer Ansatz würde allerdings verkennen, dass das Diskriminierungsverbot nur im Anwendungsbereich des AEUV gilt. Namentlich aus den Grundfreiheiten des AEUV sind indessen regelmäßig keine Schutzpflichten gegenüber privaten Dritten ableitbar.

---

814 BVerfGE 129, 78 (97).
815 Vgl. BVerfGE 129, 78 (97 f.).
 Die dem Bundesverfassungsgericht aufgegebene Kontrolle des europäischen Rechts auf Erhaltung der Identität der nationalen Verfassung, auf Einhaltung der nach dem System der begrenzten Einzelermächtigung überlassenen Kompetenzen und der Gewährleistung eines im Wesentlichen dem deutschen Grundrechtsschutz gleichkommenden Schutzniveaus bleibt erhalten. Die Identität der Verfassung (vgl. BVerfGE 123, 267 (354, 398 ff.); 126, 286 (302 f.) wird durch die Erweiterung der Anwendung des Art. 19 Abs. 3 GG offensichtlich nicht berührt; vgl. BVerfGE 129, 78 (100).

d. Zwischenfazit

Die Landesmedienanstalten sind unter Zugrundelegung einer teleologischen und historischen Auslegung des JMStV zu Vollzugsmaßnahmen gegen ausländische Anbieter wegen Verletzung materiell-rechtlicher Vorgaben des JMStV befugt. Diese Befugnis wird durch eine europarechtskonforme Auslegung des JMStV zumindest bei Sachverhalten, bei denen es sich um Anbieter handelt, die ihren Sitz in einem Mitgliedstaat der EU haben, im Ansatz bestätigt. Eine völkerrechtskonforme Auslegung des JMStV steht einer solchen Befugnis nicht per se entgegen: Denn das geltende Völkerrecht enthält keinen Grundsatz (mehr), dass nationales Verwaltungsrecht nicht auch auf auslandsbezogene Inhalte angewendet werden darf.

Soweit die Landesmedienanstalten gegen ausländische Anbieter vorgehen, sind diese an die grundrechtlichen Vorgaben des Grundgesetzes im Hinblick auf die Rundfunkfreiheit des Art. 5 Abs. 1 Satz 2 GG zumindest dann gebunden, wenn es sich bei dem Anbieter entweder um eine natürliche Person oder um eine juristische Person mit Sitz in der EU handelt.

IV. Pflicht zur Medienregulierung als Ausdruck hoheitlicher Schutzpflichten

1. Einleitung

Die Grundrechte des Grundgesetzes sind nach inzwischen herrschender verfassungsrechtlicher Dogmatik nicht nur Abwehrrechte gegen unverhältnismäßige staatliche Eingriffe in den von ihnen garantierten Freiheitsraum. Der Staat ist vielmehr grundsätzlich auch zu rechtlichen Regelungen verpflichtet, die die Grundrechte seiner Bürger schützen. Derartigen Schutzpflichten genügt der Präventionsstaat nicht allein durch Leistungen, sondern auch durch staatliche Maßnahmen, die von dritten Personen ausgehende Gefährdungen der grundrechtlichen Freiheit abwehren.[816]

Ausgangspunkt dieses verfassungsdogmatischen Ansatzes ist, dass Bedrohungen der grundrechtlich geschützten Rechtsgüter nicht nur vom Staat ausgehen, sondern auch durch die Natur (insbesondere in Form von Naturkatastrophen oder sonstigen außerordentliche Notlagen, insbesondere epidemische Lagen), aber auch von Dritten, seien es Menschen, seien es juristische Personen, ausgelöst werden können. Die verfassungsrechtliche

---

816 Vgl. *Würtenberger*, Schranken der Forschungsfreiheit und staatliche Schutzpflichten, S. 12.

Bewältigung solcher Bedrohungslagen bewegt sich zwischen der fehlenden Drittwirkung der Grundrechte einerseits, dem staatlichen Gewaltmonopol andererseits. Erstere führt mangels Grundrechtsverpflichtung Privater zum Risiko von Grundrechtsbeeinträchtigungen, letzteres setzt einem Selbstschutz des Grundrechtsberechtigten Grenzen.[817]

Die Schutzpflichten-Dogmatik knüpft vor diesem Hintergrund an das Verständnis der Grundrechte als objektive Wertordnung an, wobei der Staat vom Gegner zum Garanten der Grundrechte wird.[818]

2. Schutzpflichten in der Rechtsprechung des Bundesverfassungsgerichts

Die Doppelfunktion der Grundrechte als Abwehr- und Schutzrechte hat das BVerfG zwar insbesondere im Blick auf das Grundrecht auf Leben und körperliche Unversehrtheit entwickelt.[819] Ihr kommt aber auch mit Blick auf dritte Grundrechte dogmatische Bedeutung zu. In Bezug auf den Jugendmedienschutz ist im Übrigen allerdings bereits die staatliche Schutzpflicht in Bezug auf die körperliche Unversehrtheit ohne Weiteres erkennbar. In Bezug auf das Ziel der Vielfaltssicherung laufen im Übrigen verfassungsrechtlich die positive Ordnungs- und die Schutzpflicht des Staates in Gestalt der Länder parallel.

Die Schutzpflichten richten sich insbesondere, aber nicht ausschließlich an den Gesetzgeber. Von der Schutzpflicht der staatlichen Organe kann auch eine auf Grundrechtsgefährdungen bezogene Risikovorsorge umfasst sein.[820] Die verfassungsrechtliche Schutzpflicht kann eine solche Wahrnehmung hoheitlicher Gewalt gebieten, dass auch die Gefahr von Grundrechtsverletzungen eingedämmt bleibt; ob, wann und mit welchem Inhalt eine solche Wahrnehmung von Verfassungs wegen geboten ist, hängt von der Art, der Nähe und dem Ausmaß möglicher Gefahren, der Art und dem Rang des verfassungsrechtlich geschützten Rechtsguts sowie von den schon vorhandenen regulatorischen Absicherungen ab.[821] In Bezug auf die Wahrung von Medienpluralismus kommt diesem dynamischen Verständ-

---

817 Vgl. hierzu auch *Moritz,* Staatliche Schutzpflichten gegenüber pflegebedürftigen Menschen, S. 95 ff.
818 Vgl. BVerfGE 39, 1 (41 f.).
819 Vgl. BVerfGE 39, 1 (42); 46, 160 (164); 56, 54 (78); 90, 145 (195); 115, 320 (346); 121, 317 (356).
820 Vgl. BVerfGE 49, 89 (140 ff.); 52, 214 (220); 53, 30 (57).
821 Vgl. in Bezug auf die gesetzgeberische Dimension von Schutzpflichten BVerfGE 56, 54 (78).

E. Völkerrechtliche Kernprobleme der Regulierung des „Mediensektors"

nis von Schutzpflichten nicht zuletzt auch im Blick auf die Rolle der Medienintermediäre im digitalen Medienökosystem besondere Bedeutung zu.

Hat der Gesetzgeber eine Entscheidung getroffen, deren Grundlage durch neue, im Zeitpunkt des Gesetzeserlasses noch nicht abzusehende Entwicklungen entscheidend in Frage gestellt wird, dann kann er nach der Judikatur des BVerfG von Verfassungs wegen gehalten sein, zu überprüfen, ob die ursprüngliche Entscheidung auch unter den veränderten Umständen aufrechtzuerhalten ist.[822] Diese Evaluierungs-, Kontroll- und ggf. Nachbesserungspflicht, die auch im Blick auf verändertes Mediennutzungsverhalten mit Blick auf das bisherige fernsehzentrierte staatsvertragliche Recht der Sicherung von Vielfalt im Medienbereich durch Ziffer 5 der Protokollerklärung aller Länder zum Staatsvertrag zur Modernisierung der Medienordnung in Deutschland[823] dem Grunde nach anerkannt ist, gilt in gleicher Weise in den Fällen, in denen der Vollzug einer bestehenden, dem Schutz grundrechtlich fundierter Schutzgüter dienenden Gesetzgebung auf Grundlage einer Vollzugskonzeption erfolgt, deren Effektivität im Ergebnis neuer, im Zeitpunkt der Erarbeitung der Konzeption noch nicht abzusehender Entwicklungen entscheidend in Frage gestellt ist.

Das Bundesverfassungsgericht betont in ständiger Rechtsprechung,[824] dass über die Art und Weise, wie die aus dem jeweilgen Grundrecht hergeleitete Schutzpflicht zu erfüllen sei, in erster Linie die staatlichen Organe in eigener Verantwortung zu entscheiden hätten; sie befänden darüber, welche Maßnahmen zweckdienlich und geboten seien, um einen wirksamen Schutz zu gewährleisten. Dem entspricht eine Begrenzung der verfassungsrechtlichen Nachprüfung seitens des BVerfG darauf, ob den staatli-

---

822 Vgl. BVerfGE 49, 89 (143 f.); 56, 54 (79).
823 Unter einleitendem Hinweis darauf, dass sich die Länder einig sind, „dass die Anpassung des Rechtsrahmens an die digitale Transformation mit dem vorliegenden Staatsvertrag nicht abgeschlossen ist" erklären sie, dass sie u.a. zum Medienkonzentrationsrecht „weitergehende Reformvorschläge erarbeiten", wobei sie hierzu in der Protokollerklärung ausführen: „Die Länder setzen sich für ein zukunftsfähiges Medienkonzentrationsrecht ein. Dieses muss den real bestehenden Gefahren für die Meinungsvielfalt wirksam begegnen können. Die Medienmärkte haben in den letzten Jahren eine Öffnung erfahren, die neben dem Fernsehen auch andere Mediengattungen, die möglichen Folgen crossmedialer Zusammenschlüsse und auch solcher auf vor- und nachgelagerten Märkten verstärkt in den Fokus rückt. Ein reformiertes Medienkonzentrationsrecht muss daher alle medienrelevanten Märkte in den Blick nehmen."
824 BVerfGE 39, 1 (44); 46, 160 (164).

chen Organen eine evidente Verletzung der in den Grundrechten verkörperten Grundentscheidungen zur Last zu legen ist.[825]

> *„Diese erscheint deshalb geboten, weil es regelmäßig eine höchst komplexe Frage ist, w i e eine positive staatliche Schutz- und Handlungspflicht, die erst im Wege der Verfassungsinterpretation aus den in den Grundrechten verkörperten Grundentscheidungen hergeleitet wird, durch aktive gesetzgeberische Maßnahmen zu verwirklichen ist. Je nach der Beurteilung der tatsächlichen Verhältnisse, der konkreten Zielsetzungen und ihrer Priorität sowie der Eignung der denkbaren Mittel und Wege sind verschiedene Lösungen möglich. Die Entscheidung, die häufig Kompromisse erfordert, gehört nach dem Grundsatz der Gewaltenteilung und dem demokratischen Prinzip in die Verantwortung des vom Volk unmittelbar legitimierten Gesetzgebers und kann vom Bundesverfassungsgericht in der Regel nur begrenzt nachgeprüft werden, sofern nicht Rechtsgüter von höchster Bedeutung auf dem Spiele stehen. Diese Erwägungen fallen verstärkt ins Gewicht, wenn es nicht allein um die Frage geht, ob der Gesetzgeber eine aus den Grundrechten herleitbare Schutzpflicht verletzt hat, wenn vielmehr darüber hinaus die weitere Frage strittig ist, ob er diese Verletzung durch unterlassene Nachbesserung begangen hat. Einen Verfassungsverstoß dieser Art kann das Bundesverfassungsgericht erst dann feststellen, wenn evident ist, dass eine ursprünglich rechtmäßige Regelung wegen zwischenzeitlicher Änderung der Verhältnisse verfassungsrechtlich untragbar geworden ist, und wenn der Gesetzgeber gleichwohl weiterhin untätig geblieben ist oder offensichtlich fehlsame Nachbesserungsmaßnahmen getroffen hat".*[826]

Auch diese auf gesetzgeberische Ausprägungen grundrechtlicher Schutzpflichten abstellende Beschränkung gerichtlicher Kontrolle in der *Fluglärm-Entscheidung* des BVerfG gilt mit Blick auf die Wahrnehmung grundrechtlicher Schutzpflichten durch sonstige Träger hoheitlicher Gewalt entsprechend.

Grundrechtliche Schutzpflichten begründen dementsprechend für die hoheitliche Gewalt grundsätzlich keine konkreten Handlungspflichten. „Die Verfassung gibt den Schutz als Ziel vor, nicht aber seine Ausgestaltung im Einzelnen. Den Gerichten ist es verwehrt, ihre eigene Einschätzung, wie die Schutzpflicht zweckmäßig erfüllt werden sollte, an die Stelle des jeweils handelnden Organs zu setzen. Diese Zurücknahme der gerichtlichen Kontrolldichte folgt insbesondere aus dem Grundsatz der Gewal-

---

825 Vgl. BVerfGE 4, 7 (18); 27, 253 (283); 33, 303 (333); 36, 321 (330 f.).
826 BVerfGE 56, 54 (81).

E. Völkerrechtliche Kernprobleme der Regulierung des „Mediensektors"

tenteilung. Die Schutzpflichtenlehre bedeutet – als weitere Leistungsdimension der Grundrechte – ohnehin eine Erweiterung der gerichtlichen Kontrolle legislativen oder exekutiven Tuns und Unterlassen. Würden die Gerichte ihre Wertung über die Zweckmäßigkeit einer Schutzmaßnahme an die Stelle der jeweils handelnden Stelle setzen, würde aus der grundgesetzlich vorgesehenen Rechtmäßigkeitskontrolle durch die Gerichte eine mit dem Grundsatz der Gewaltenteilung nicht vereinbare umfassende Zweckmäßigkeitskontrolle und im Ergebnis Letztentscheidungskompetenz der Judikative".[827]

Bei der Erfüllung der grundrechtlichen Schutzpflichten hat nicht nur der Gesetzgeber,[828] sondern sämtliche staatliche Gewalt mithin einen weiten Einschätzungs-, Wertungs- und Gestaltungsspielraum. Dieser weite Entscheidungsspielraum besteht insbesondere bei Bezügen der Schutzpflichten zum außenpolitischen Bereich.[829]

Bei der Entscheidung, wie der Staat seiner Schutzpflicht innerhalb seines weiten Entscheidungsspielraums nachkommt, sind mehrere Faktoren zu berücksichtigen. Der objektive Schutzbedarf der Grundrechte, wie das subjektive Schutzbedürfnis des einzelnen Grundrechtsträgers hängen ab von der Sicherheitsempfindlichkeit des betroffenen Schutzgutes, von Art, Reichweite und Intensität des (potentiellen und aktuellen) Übergriffs, sowie von der Möglichkeit legitimer und zumutbarer Abhilfe durch den Grundrechtsträger selbst. Die Verpflichtung des Staates steht unter dem Vorbehalt des faktisch[830] und des verfassungsrechtlich Möglichen.

Der weite Einschätzungs-, Wertungs- und Gestaltungsspielraum wird allerdings dann unterschritten, wenn offensichtlich ist, dass die getroffenen Schutzmaßnahmen völlig unzulänglich oder ungeeignet sind. Insofern wird der Gestaltungsspielraum in eng begrenzten Ausnahmefällen durch das Untermaßverbot begrenzt.[831] Der Staat darf die Grundrechte seiner Bürger nicht unterhalb des gebotenen Maßes sichern.[832] Das Bundesverfassungsgericht kann die Verletzung einer solchen Schutzpflicht insoweit nur

---

827 VG Köln, Urteil v. 27.5.2015, 3 K 5625/14, Rn. 58, 60.
828 Vgl. hierzu BVerfGE 46, 160 (164).
829 VG Köln, Urteil v. 27.5.2015, 3 K 5625/14, Rn. 71, 73 unter Bezugnahme auf BVerfG, 2 BvR 1720/03, BVerfGK 14, 192; *von Arnauld*, Freiheit und Regulierung in der Cyberwelt: Transnationaler Schutz der Privatsphäre aus Sicht des Völkerrechts, 27, 28.
830 Vgl. hierzu auch *Moritz*, Staatliche Schutzpflichten gegenüber pflegebedürftigen Menschen, S. 120.
831 Vgl. BVerfGE 88, 203 (251 ff.); 98, 265 (356).
832 Vgl. hierzu auch *Moritz*, Staatliche Schutzpflichten gegenüber pflegebedürftigen Menschen, S. 115.

feststellen, wenn Schutzvorkehrungen entweder überhaupt nicht getroffen sind, wenn die getroffenen Regelungen und Maßnahmen offensichtlich ungeeignet oder völlig unzulänglich sind, das gebotene Schutzziel zu erreichen, oder wenn sie erheblich hinter dem Schutzziel zurückbleiben.[833]

Diese Vorgaben gelten auch in Bezug auf jugendmedienschutzrechtliche Schutzpflichten: Zwar ist nur in Art. 13 der Verfassung des Landes Baden-Württemberg, Art. 126 Abs. 3 der Verfassung des Freistaates Bayern, Art. 25 Abs. 1 und 2 der Verfassung der Freien Hansestadt Bremen, Art. 14 Abs. 3 der Verfassung des Landes Mecklenburg-Vorpommern, Art. 6 Abs. 2 der Verfassung für das Land Nordrhein-Westfalen, Art. 25 Abs. 2 Satz 1 der Verfassung für Rheinland-Pfalz, Art. 25 Satz 1 der Verfassung des Saarlandes, Art. 9 Abs. 2 der Verfassung des Freistaates Sachsen, Art. 24 Abs. 4 der Verfassung des Landes Sachsen-Anhalt und Art. 6 a der Verfassung des Landes Schleswig-Holstein der Schutz der Jugend ausdrücklich als staatliche Aufgabe definiert.[834] Indessen erschöpft sich die verfassungsrechtliche Dimension des Jugendschutzes auch außerhalb dieser landesverfassungsrechtlichen Besonderheiten nicht ausschließlich auf eine Qualität als Grundrechtsbeschränkungen rechtfertigender Schutzzweck. Vielmehr ist der Jugendschutz in der Bundesrepublik Deutschland insgesamt ein Rechtsgut mit Verfassungsrang.[835] Er ist dementsprechend den Grundrechten und den übrigen mit Verfassungsrang ausgestatteten Rechtsgütern – mit Ausnahme der allen übergeordneten Menschenwürde – gleichwertig.[836]

Das Recht von Kindern und Jugendlichen auf „Person-Werden"[837] wird durch das Recht auf freie Entfaltung der Persönlichkeit in Art. 2 Abs. 1 GG und die Menschenwürde-Garantie in Art. 1 Abs. 1 GG gewährleistet.[838] Dieses Recht auf „Person-Werden" hat über seine abwehrrechtliche Seite hinaus auch einen objektiv-rechtlichen Gehalt.[839] Dem Staat ist danach die Aufgabe zugewiesen, dieses Recht der Minderjährigen zu schützen bzw. Voraussetzungen dafür zu schaffen, dass es verwirklicht werden kann. Von

---

833 Vgl. BVerfGE 56, 54 (80); 77, 170 (215); 92, 26 (46); 125, 39 (78 f.) sowie hierzu z.B. *Würtenberger*, Schranken der Forschungsfreiheit und staatliche Schutzpflichten, S. 12 f.
834 Vgl. *Ukrow*, Jugendschutzrecht, Rn. 12.
835 Vgl. BVerfGE 30, 336 (347 f.); 47, 109 (117); 77, 345 (356); 83, 130 (139 ff.); BVerwGE 39, 197 (208); 77, 75 (82); 91, 223 (224 f.).
836 Vgl. *Ukrow*, Jugendschutzrecht, Rn. 12.
837 Vgl. *Ditzen* in: NJW 1989, 2519, 2519 („Recht auf Mensch-Werden"); *Engels* in: AöR 1997, 212, 219 ff., 226 ff.
838 Vgl. hierzu z.B. auch *Nikles* in: ders./Roll/Spürck/Erdemir/Gutknecht, Teil I Rn. 5.
839 Vgl. auch *Langenfeld* in: MMR 2003, 303, 305.

Minderjährigen sind staatlicherseits Einflüsse fernzuhalten, die zu erheblichen, schwer oder gar nicht korrigierbaren Fehlentwicklungen führen können.[840] Er hat „im Rahmen des Möglichen die äußeren Bedingungen für eine dem Menschenbild des Grundgesetzes entsprechende geistig-seelische Entwicklung der Kinder und Jugendlichen zu sichern".[841]

Die Frage, ob staatliche Schutzpflichten auch gegenüber Minderjährigen im Hinblick auf einen effektiven Jugendmedienschutz bestehen, war bislang noch nicht Gegenstand höchstrichterlicher Rechtsprechung. Eine entsprechende Ausdehnung der Schutzpflichten-Dogmatik auf Minderjährige bedarf einer gesonderten dogmatischen Begründung. Nur dort, wo ein Vergleich der Situation Minderjährigen in Situationen audiovisueller Konfrontation mit jugendgefährdenden oder entwicklungsbeeinträchtigenden Angebotsinhalten mit den Fallkonstellationen aus der bisherigen Schutzpflichten-Rechtsprechung eine vergleichbares Schutzerfordernis ergibt, scheint eine Ausdehnung verfassungsrechtlich geboten. Dass die Länder mit den Vorgaben des JMStV in ihrer Fassung durch Art. 3 des Staatsvertrages zur Modernisierung der Medienordnung in Deutschland einer solchen Schutzpflicht über legislative Maßnahmen, sofern sie angenommen wird, nicht entsprechen würden, ist nicht ersichtlich. Zudem ist spätestens nach dem Einstieg der Medienaufsicht in ein Einschreiten unmittelbar gegen ausländische Anbieter nicht erkennbar, dass auf Ebene des Vollzugs eine Schutzpflichtverletzung besteht, die unter Zugrundelegung des dogmatischen Ansatzes des Bundesverfassungsgerichts einer Grundrechtsverletzung gleichkommt.

3. Europäische Bezüge der grundrechtlich fundierten Schutzpflichtdogmatik

a. Schutzpflichten-Dogmatik und EMRK

In Bezug auf die EMRK lässt sich unter Auslegung einer Reihe von Urteilen das grundsätzliche Bestehen von Schutzpflichten („*positive obligations*" bzw. „*obligations positives*") – abgeleitet von Handlungspflichten – feststel-

---

840 Vgl. BVerfGE 30, 336 (347 f.); BVerwGE 77, 75 (82); *Dörr/Cole*, Jugendschutz in den elektronischen Medien, S. 20; *Engels* in: AöR 1997, 212, 219 ff., 226 ff.; *Isensee/Axer*, Jugendschutz im Fernsehen, S. 69.
841 *BVerwG* NJW 1987, 1429 (1430); *Schulz* in: MMR 1998, 182, 183; *Ukrow*, Jugendschutzrecht, Rn. 13.

len.⁸⁴² Zugleich besteht aber (auch) auf der Grundlage der EMRK ein Umsetzungsspielraum der Staaten bei der Ausübung der Schutzpflichten, sodass aus der Schutzpflicht nicht zwingend eine gesetzliche Regulierung folgen muss; in Betracht kommen stattdessen auch Untersuchungspflichten und Informationspflichten.⁸⁴³ Aus den Handlungspflichten können aber auch Pflichten zum Schutz im Verhältnis zwischen Privaten folgen.⁸⁴⁴

b. Schutzpflichten-Dogmatik im Lichte des EU-Rechts

Zwar findet sich im Rahmen des Unionsrechts noch keine der verfassungsrechtlichen Situation vergleichbare Schutzpflichten-Dogmatik auf der Grundlage der Grundrechte-Charta der EU.⁸⁴⁵ Ein solcher Schutzpflichten-Ansatz würde allerdings beim derzeitigen Stand der Integration ohnedies namentlich mit Art. 51 Abs. 2 der Charta kollidieren, wonach diese Charta „den Geltungsbereich des Unionsrechts nicht über die Zuständigkeiten der Union hinaus aus(dehnt) und ... weder neue Zuständigkeiten noch neue Aufgaben für die Union (begründet), noch ... die in den Verträgen festgelegten Zuständigkeiten und Aufgaben (ändert)".

Allerdings ist auch nicht ersichtlich, dass EUV oder AEUV der aufgezeigten grundgesetzlichen Schutzpflichten-Dogmatik europarechtliche Schranken setzen. Dagegen spricht nicht zuletzt, dass inzwischen anerkannt ist, dass die grundfreiheitlichen Beschränkungsverbote nicht nur in Bezug auf unmittelbar staatliches Verhalten gelten, sondern auch in Bezug auf einem Mitgliedstaat zurechenbares Verhalten Privater. Insoweit verdienen die auf die Reichweite der Warenverkehrsfreiheit bezogenen Überlegungen des EuGH in der Rs. *Kommission/Frankreich*⁸⁴⁶ aus 1997 *mutatis mutandis* auch für die Abgrenzung des Anwendungsbereichs der übrigen Grundfreiheiten Beachtung. Die grundfreiheitlichen Verbotsnormen verbieten damit nicht nur Maßnahmen, die auf einen Mitgliedstaat zurückzu-

---

842 Vgl. namentlich EGMR, Nr. 23144/93, *Özgür Gundem / Türkei*, Rn. 42 sowie z.B. *Dröge*, Positive Verpflichtungen der Staaten in der Europäischen Menschenrechtskonvention, S. 1 ff., 71 ff., 179 ff.; *Jaeckel*, Schutzpflichten im deutschen und europäischen Recht, S. 128 ff.; *Klatt* in: ZaöRV 2011, 691, 692 ff.; *Koenen*, Wirtschaft und Menschenrechte, S. 58; *Ress* in: ZaöRV 2004, 621, 628.
843 Vgl. *Koenen*, Wirtschaft und Menschenrechte, S. 59 ff.
844 Vgl. *Koenen*, Wirtschaft und Menschenrechte, S. 66 ff.
845 Vgl. *Jarass*, Charta der Grundrechte der Europäischen Union, Art. 51 Rn. 39; *Kingreen* in: Calliess/Ruffert Art. 51 GRC, Rn. 25 f.
846 EuGH, Rs. C-265/95, *Kommission/Frankreich*.

führen sind und selbst Beschränkungen für den Handel zwischen den Mitgliedstaaten schaffen, „sondern (können) auch dann Anwendung finden, wenn ein Mitgliedstaat keine Maßnahmen ergriffen hat, um gegen Beeinträchtigungen des freien Warenverkehrs (bzw. sonstiger Grundfreiheiten; Ergänzung der Verf.) einzuschreiten, deren Ursachen nicht auf den Staat zurückzuführen sind".[847] Die Grundfreiheiten können nämlich ebenso wie durch eine mitgliedstaatliche Handlung dadurch beeinträchtigt werden, dass ein Mitgliedstaat untätig bleibt oder es versäumt, ausreichende Maßnahmen zur Beseitigung von Hemmnissen für eine Grundfreiheit zu treffen, die insbesondere durch Handlungen von Privatpersonen in seinem Gebiet geschaffen wurden, die sich gegen die durch die Grundfreiheit geschützte Tätigkeit richten.[848] Art. 34 und 63 AEUV „verbiete(n) den MS somit nicht nur eigene Handlungen oder Verhaltensweisen, die zu einem Handelshemmnis (bzw. sonstigen Hemmnis für eine Grundfreiheit, Ergänzung d. Verf.) führen könnten, sondern verpflichte(n) sie in Verbindung mit Art. 5 EGV (nunmehr: Art. 4 Abs. 3 EUV) auch dazu, alle erforderlichen und geeigneten Maßnahmen zu ergreifen, um in ihrem Gebiet die Beachtung dieser Grundfreiheit(en) sicherzustellen".[849]

Die Maßnahmen, die ein Mitgliedstaat im Falle einer Beeinträchtigung einer Grundfreiheit des AEUV durch Private ergreift, müssen – unter Berücksichtigung der Häufigkeit und Schwere dieser Beeinträchtigung – ausreichen, um diese Grundfreiheit dadurch zu gewährleisten, „dass sie die Urheber der fraglichen Zuwiderhandlungen wirksam an deren Begehung und Wiederholung hinder(n) und sie davon abschrecken".[850] Der betreffende Mitgliedstaat hat „alle geeigneten Maßnahmen zu ergreifen, um die volle, wirksame und korrekte Anwendung des Gemeinschaftsrechts (nunmehr: Unionsrechts) im Interesse aller Wirtschaftsteilnehmer sicherzustellen, sofern er nicht nachweist, dass sein Tätigwerden Folgen für die öffentliche Ordnung hätte, die er mit seinen Mitteln nicht bewältigen könnte".[851]

Dabei kommt den Mitgliedstaaten zwar ein erheblicher Ermessensspielraum in Bezug auf die Frage zu, welche Maßnahmen in einer bestimmten Situation am geeignetsten sind, um Beeinträchtigungen der Grundfreihei-

---

847 Wie vor, Rn. 30; vgl. auch *Pache* in Schulze/Zuleeg/Kadelbach, § 10 Rn. 214.
848 Vgl. zum Ansatz des EuGH in seiner Warenverkehrs-Rechtsprechung EuGH, Rs. C-265/95, *Kommission / Frankreich*, Rn. 31.
849 Wie vor, Rn. 32.
850 Wie vor, Rn. 52; zur gebotenen Abschreckung vgl. im Übrigen *Meier*, Anmerkung, EuZW 1998, 87, 87.
851 Wie vor, Rn. 56.

ten von privater Seite zu beseitigen. Die EU-Organe sind dementsprechend nicht kompetent, sich an die Stelle der Mitgliedstaaten zu setzen und ihnen vorzuschreiben, welche Maßnahmen sie erlassen und tatsächlich anwenden müssen, um die Grundfreiheiten aus ihrem, in und durch ihr Gebiet zu gewährleisten.[852] Diese im Verhältnis der Mitgliedstaaten zur EU-Ebene anerkannte Einschätzungsprärogative weist erkennbare strukturelle Parallelitäten zur Einschätzungsprärogative staatlicher Organe im Verhältnis zu einer innerstaatlichen gerichtlichen Kontrollinstanz wie dem BVerfG in Bezug auf die Frage, wie einer Schutzpflicht genügt wird, auf.

Der EuGH ist allerdings zuständig, unter Berücksichtigung des vorbezeichneten Ermessens in den ihm unterbreiteten Fällen zu prüfen, ob der betreffende Mitgliedstaat zur Sicherstellung der Grundfreiheiten geeignete Maßnahmen ergriffen hat. Von einer Verletzung der grundfreiheiten-bezogenen Schutzpflicht kann mit Blick auf die Einschätzungsprärogative des Mitgliedstaates nur ausgegangen werden, wenn sich die Beeinträchtigung der Grundfreiheit als so gravierend erweist, dass das Verhalten des Mitgliedstaates auch unter Berücksichtigung der diesem zustehenden Einschätzungsprärogative nicht mehr tragbar erscheint.[853] Auch die Parallelitäten dieser Grenze der Einschätzungsprärogative mit dem Untermaßverbot in der Judikatur des BVerfG sind offenkundig.

c. Schutzpflichten im Verbund der Regulierungssysteme

In Anlehnung an die Solange-Judikatur des BVerfG[854] kann im Übrigen die These vertreten werden, dass die Schutzpflichten des Grundgesetzes solange und soweit nicht wahrgenommen werden müssen, solange eine im Ansatz vergleichbares Schutzniveau durch Tätigkeit von Drittstaaten besteht. Ein solcher auf Kooperation der Regulierungsbehörden im Interesse von Schutz der Menschenwürde und Jugendmedienschutz angelegter Ansatz trägt der Integrationsoffenheit und Völkerrechtsfreundlichkeit des Grundgesetzes Rechnung. Er erweitert den bisherigen justizorientierten Prozess wechselseitiger Rezeption von mitgliedstaatlichen, europäischen und internationalen Grundrechte-Gewährleistungen um eine die Schutzdimension in den Blick nehmende exekutive Facette und entlastet zugleich

---

852 Wie vor, Rn. 33 f.
853 Vgl. EuGH, Rs. C-112/00, *Schmidberger / Österreich*, Rn. 80 ff.; vgl. auch *Jeck/Langner*, Die Europäische Dimension des Sports, S. 25 f.; *Lengauer*, Drittwirkung von Grundfreiheiten, S. 218 ff. 227 ff.
854 Vgl. dazu bereits eingehend oben Abschnitt B.VI.2.

die Regulierungsbehörden von nicht gebotener Doppelarbeit. An einem solchen vergleichbaren Schutzniveau aufgrund völkerrechtlicher Verpflichtungen fehlt es indessen mit Blick auf den Schutz der Menschenwürde und in weiten Teilen auch den Jugendmedienschutz. Namentlich reichen die verfassungsrechtlichen Schutzpflichten über den reinen Schutz vor Kinderpornographie hinaus, der völkervertragsrechtlich inzwischen anerkannt ist.

V. *Materiell-rechtliche Aspekte*

Materiell-rechtlich weisen einige Regelungen in aktuellen innerstaatlichen Rechtsakte mit Bedeutung für den Mediensektor Ausformungen auf, bei denen sich nicht nur – im vorliegenden Zusammenhang nicht weiter erörterungsbedürftige – Fragen nach der innerstaatlichen Kohärenz der Regulierung stellen, sondern auch ein gewisses Konfliktpotential mit dem europäischen Rechtsrahmen zumindest nicht ausgeschlossen erscheint. Insbesondere das deutsche Netzwerkdurchsetzungsgesetz (NetzDG) hat seit seiner Entstehung kontroverse Debatten über seine Rechtskonformität ausgelöst – nicht nur im Hinblick auf Fragen seiner (vor allem formellen) Verfassungsmäßigkeit,[855] worauf im Folgenden nicht näher eingegangen

---

855 Kritisch zur Gesetzgebungskompetenz des Bundes z.B. *Feldmann* in: K&R 2017, 292, 294; *Gersdorf* in: MMR 2017, 439, 441; *Hain/Ferreau/Brings-Wiesen* in: K&R 2017, 433, 434; *Kalscheuer/Hornung* NVwZ 2017, 1721, 1721 ff.; *Müller-Franken* in: AfP 2018, 1, 2 f.; *Nolte* in: ZUM 2017, 552, 561; a.A. z.B. *Bautze* in: KJ 2019, 203, 208; *Peifer* in: AfP 2018, 14, 21 f.. Unmittelbar gegen Vorschriften des NetzDG gerichtete Verfassungsbeschwerden sind im Übrigen aus Sicht des BVerfG unzulässig (vgl. Beschluss v. 23.04.2019 – 1 BvR 2314/18, Rn. 6 f.),, da es an einer Erschöpfung des fachgerichtlichen Rechtswegs mangele, wenn nicht gegen den Vollzugsakt (etwa die Sperrung oder Löschung eines Inhalts durch die Netzanbieter) vorgegangen würde, wobei dann inzidenter auch die Verfassungsmäßigkeit der Vorschriften des NetzDG überprüft werden könne.

werden soll,[856] sondern auch im Hinblick auf seine Vereinbarkeit mit Unionsrecht, die in Teilen der Literatur bezweifelt wird.[857]

1. Anwendungsbereich bestimmter nationaler Rechtsakte

a. Herkunftslandprinzip und NetzDG

Gemäß Art. 3 Abs. 1 ECRL muss der Staat der Niederlassung eines Diensteanbieters dafür Sorge tragen, dass dieser mit seinem Angebot die innerstaatlichen Regelungen beachtet. Nach Art. 3 Abs. 2 der ECRL dürfen die Mitgliedstaaten den freien Verkehr von Diensten der Informationsgesellschaft aus einem anderen Mitgliedstaat nicht aus Gründen einschränken, die in den sog. „koordinierten Bereich" fallen. Dieses bereits oben beschriebene Herkunftslandprinzip soll den reibungslosen Dienstleistungsverkehr im Binnenmarkt für diesen Sektor gewährleisten. Andere Mitgliedstaaten dürfen damit grundsätzlich keine vom Herkunftsstaat abweichenden Regelungen auf Anbieter von anderen EU-Staaten festsetzen. Der neu eingeführte Art. 28 a Abs. 1, Abs. 5 AVMD-RL wiederholt dieses Prinzip für VSPs, zu denen auch soziale Netzwerke gehören können.[858]

Der Anwendungsbereich des 2017 in Deutschland in Kraft getretenen NetzDG gilt für Telemediendiensteanbieter, die mit Gewinnerzielungsabsicht Plattformen im Internet betreiben, die dazu bestimmt sind, dass Nutzer beliebige Inhalte mit anderen Nutzern teilen oder der Öffentlichkeit zugänglich machen (soziale Netzwerke) und erfasst damit grundsätzlich

---

856 Auch die Verfassungskonformität der Novelle des NetzDG durch das Gesetz zur Bekämpfung des Rechtsextremismus und der Hasskriminalität (BT-Drs. 19/17741 und 19/20163) ist strittig. Im Nachgang u.a. zu einem Gutachten des Wissenschaftlichen Dienstes des Deutschen Bundestages (abrufbar unter https://cdn.netzpolitik.org/wp-upload/2020/09/WD-10-030-20-Gesetz-Hasskriminalitaet.pdf) zögert nach Medienberichten (https://netzpolitik.org/2020/gutachten-zum-netzdg-gesetz-gegen-hasskriminalitaet-verfassungswidrig/#vorschaltbanner) der Bundespräsident wegen verfassungsrechtlicher Bedenken bei der Unterzeichnung der von Bundestag und Bundesrat beschlossenen Gesetzesnovelle. Vgl. auch tagesschau.de, „Verfassungsrechtliche Bedenken – Scheitert das Anti-Hass-Gesetz?" (17.09.2020), abrufbar unter: https://www.tagesschau.de/investigativ/ndr-wdr/hasskriminalitaet-gesetz-101.html.
857 So beispielsweise *Spindler* in: ZUM 2017, 473, 473 ff.; *Hoeren*, Netzwerkdurchsetzungsgesetz europarechtswidrig.
858 *Nölscher* in: ZUM 2020, 301, 306. Vgl. dazu bereits eingehend und m.w.N. oben in Abschnitt D.II.2.d(5).

E. Völkerrechtliche Kernprobleme der Regulierung des „Mediensektors"

auch Dienstanbieter mit Niederlassung im (EU-)Ausland. Die Regelungen definieren den Anwendungsbereich des Gesetzes entsprechend der Zielsetzung, Hasskriminalität sowie weitere im Gesetz benannte strafbare Inhalte auf den Plattformen sozialer Netzwerke wirksamer zu bekämpfen, um die damit verbundenen Gefahren für das friedliche Zusammenleben und für die freie, offene und demokratische Gesellschaft abzuwenden.[859] Das NetzDG steht damit in einem Spannungsverhältnis zum Herkunftslandprinzip, sofern es im Rahmen des Pflichtenkatalogs zur Löschung rechtswidriger Inhalte, den bußgeldbewerten Ordnungswidrigkeitstatbeständen oder dem Erfordernis inländischer Zustellungsbevollmächtigter, engere Regelungen festsetzt, als der jeweilige (EU-)Herkunftsstaat eines Netzwerks im Sinne des Gesetzes, das in Deutschland eine bestimmte Bedeutung hat.[860]

Art. 3 Abs. 4 ECRL bietet allerdings Ausnahmetatbestände zum Herkunftslandprinzip. So können gem. Art. 4 Abs. 4 Buchst. a) ECRL Mitgliedstaaten abweichend vom Herkunftslandprinzip Maßnahmen ergreifen, wenn sie zum Schutz der öffentlichen Ordnung, insbesondere Verhütung, Ermittlung, Aufklärung und Verfolgung von Straftaten, einschließlich des Jugendschutzes und der Bekämpfung der Hetze aus Gründen der Rasse, des Geschlechts, des Glaubens oder der Nationalität, sowie von Verletzungen der Menschenwürde einzelner Personen, erforderlich sind und einen bestimmten Dienst der Informationsgesellschaft betreffen, der eines dieser Ziele beeinträchtigt oder zumindest eine ernsthafte, schwerwiegende Gefahr für sie darstellt. Die Maßnahme muss dabei in einem angemessenen Verhältnis zum Schutzziel stehen.

Im Zusammenhang mit dem NetzDG werden dabei insbesondere die Merkmale der Betroffenheit eines „bestimmten Dienstes" der Informationsgesellschaft[861] sowie die Angemessenheit[862] als diskussionswürdig gesehen. Gemeint ist mit der Betroffenheit eines „bestimmten Dienstes", dass die in Art. 3 Abs. 3 ECRL festgelegte Ausnahme gerade keine Bereichsausnahme darstellt. Somit ist zumindest fraglich, ob die abstrakt-generellen Pflichten des NetzDG, beispielsweise im Hinblick auf die Berichtspflichten, die eine ganze Gruppe von Diensten der Informationsgesellschaft be-

---

859 Vgl. dazu die Begründung zum damaligen Gesetzesentwurf der Fraktionen der CDU/CSU und SPD des Deutschen Bundestages, BT-Drs. 18/12356 v. 16.5.2017, S. 18.
860 *Hoeren*, Netzwerkdurchsetzungsgesetz europarechtswidrig.
861 Näher hierzu *Nölscher* in: ZUM 2020, 301, 307.
862 Kritisch hierzu *Hoeren*, Netzwerkdurchsetzungsgesetz europarechtswidrig.

treffen, in diese Ausnahme fallen können.[863] Die Angemessenheit der Regelung wird zudem im Hinblick auf die pauschale Regelung zu den Reaktionszeiten und vermutete negative Auswirkungen auf die Meinungsäußerungsfreiheit im Internet von einzelnen Autoren sehr kritisch gesehen.[864]
Teilweise wird diese grundsätzliche Problematik der Vereinbarkeit mit dem Herkunftslandprinzip im aktuellen Entwurf eines Gesetzes zur Änderung des Netzwerkdurchsetzungsgesetzes (NetzDGÄndG-E)[865] bezüglich VSPs adressiert. Die Begründung zum NetzDGÄndG-E hebt dabei hervor, dass Artikel 28 a Abs. 5 AVMD-RL auf die Anwendung der ECRL für Anbieter von VSP-Diensten verweise. Für solche Dienste, die nicht in der Bundesrepublik Deutschland ansässig sind oder als dort ansässig gelten, soll das NetzDG daher grundsätzlich nicht gelten. Die nach § 4 NetzDG zuständige Behörde (das Bundesamt für Justiz) soll unter den Voraussetzungen des § 3 Abs. 5 TMG die grundsätzliche Anwendbarkeit des NetzDG und ihren Umfang im Hinblick auf die Pflichten nach §§ 2, 3 und 3 b (des dann geänderten) NetzDG allerdings im Einzelfall (für dann bestimmte Anbieter) festlegen können. Hierdurch soll dem in der ECRL verankerten Herkunftslandprinzip, auf dem auch die AVMD-Richtlinie basiert, Rechnung getragen werden.[866]
Obwohl die Unionsrechtmäßigkeit des Gesetzes nicht eindeutig ist in der aktuellen Fassung und insbesondere verfassungsrechtliche Bedenken gegen eine Aufsichtsfunktion einer nicht staatsunabhängigen Behörde wie des Bundesamts für Justiz im Anwendungsbereich der novellierten AVMD-Richtlinie[867] bestehen, stellt sich dennoch die Frage, wie bei einer sehr restriktiven Auslegung des Herkunftslandprinzips im Rahmen einer stark gewandelten Kommunikation ein angemessener Grundrechtsschutz überhaupt erreicht werden soll.[868] Gefahrenlagen werden in den Mitgliedstaaten unterschiedlich beantwortet und Regulierungsansätze folgen un-

---

863 *Nölscher* geht im Ergebnis davon aus, dass vieles für eine extensive Auslegung der Ausnahme spricht, ZUM 2020, 301, 310; kritisch bzgl. des Bezugs auf einen „bestimmten Dienst" *Spindler* in: ZUM 2017, 473, 476.
864 *Hoeren*, Netzwerkdurchsetzungsgesetz europarechtswidrig.
865 Deutscher Bundestag, Entwurf eines Gesetzes zur Änderung des Netzwerkdurchsetzungsgesetzes. BT-Drs. 19/18792 v. 27.4.2020.
866 So der Wissenschaftliche Dienst des Bundestags, WD 10 – 3000 – 023/20, abrufbar unter: https://www.bundestag.de/resource/blob/691846/cb11c99d9a39b6e73151549e22d76b73/WD-10-023-20-pdf-data.pdf.
867 Vgl. zum Erfordernis unabhängiger Regulierungsstellen nach der AVMD-Richtlinienreform 2018 bereits eingehend ob unter Abschnitt D.II.2.d(4).
868 Hierzu auch *Cole/Etteldorf/Ullrich*, Cross-border Dissemination of Online Content, S. 221 ff.

E. Völkerrechtliche Kernprobleme der Regulierung des „Mediensektors"

terschiedlichen Rahmenbedingungen und Interessenabwägungen. Mit der Festlegung bestimmter Standards für VSPs im Rahmen des Art. 28 b AVMD-RL hat sich der europäische Gesetzgeber in Teilen dieser Problematik gewidmet. Weitere Vorhaben sowohl auf Ebene der EU[869] als auch in anderen EU-Mitgliedstaaten[870] zeigen, dass digitalen Massenphänomenen wie sozialen Netzwerken, die ein Bestandteil der Kommunikation in demokratischen Gesellschaften geworden sind, eine besondere Verantwortung zukommt, für die auch regulatorisch ein Rahmen gefunden werden muss. Eine klarere Regelung, wie bei Aufrechterhaltung des Herkunftslandprinzips für bestimmte Fragen der Rechtsdurchsetzung auch ein Marktortprinzip oder Elemente eines solchen Anwendung finden können, ist auf EU-Ebene vorzunehmen.

b. Herkunftslandprinzip und MStV

Im Rahmen des Notifizierungsverfahrens[871] äußerte sich die EU-Kommission, wie bereits mehrfach dargestellt, zum Entwurf eines Staatsvertrags zur Modernisierung der Medienordnung in Deutschland. Darin kommt die Kommission zum Schluss, dass der Medienstaatsvertrag prinzipiell mit dem EU-Recht vereinbar ist, äußert aber Bedenken im Hinblick auf mögliche Konflikte mit der ECRL.

Das Notifizierungsverfahren nach der Richtlinie über ein Informationsverfahren auf dem Gebiet der technischen Vorschriften und der Vorschriften für die Dienste der Informationsgesellschaft (RL (EU) 2015/1535)[872] sieht verschiedene Reaktionsmöglichkeiten für die Kommission auf notifizierte Vorschriften vor, zu denen das Vorbringen von Bemerkungen (Art. 5 Abs. 2 RL (EU) 2015/1535) und die Abgabe einer ausführlichen Stellungnahme (Art. 6 Abs. 2 RL (EU) 2015/1535) zählen. Dabei kann die Abgabe einer ausführlichen Stellungnahme eine Verlängerung der sog. Stillhaltefrist auslösen. Die wie vorliegend geäußerten Bemerkungen hindern dem-

---

869 Vgl. eingehend bereits Abschnitt D.III.1.
870 Beispielsweise Frankreich mit dem *loi visant à lutter contre les contenus haineux sur internet*, aaO (Fn. 631).
871 Notifizierung 2020/26/D, aaO (Fn. 18).
872 Richtlinie (EU) 2015/1535 des Europäischen Parlaments und des Rates vom 9. September 2015 über ein Informationsverfahren auf dem Gebiet der technischen Vorschriften und der Vorschriften für die Dienste der Informationsgesellschaft, abrufbar unter: https://eur-lex.europa.eu/legal-content/DE/TXT/HTML/?uri=CELEX:32015L1535&from=DE.

gegenüber das nationale Gesetzgebungsverfahren nicht. Diese müssen allerdings nach Art. 5 Abs. 2 der RL (EU) 2015/1535 in der weiteren Handhabung so weit wie möglich beachtet werden.[873]

Aus materiell-rechtlicher Sicht sieht die Kommission dabei insbesondere die Regelung des § 1 Abs. 8 MStV zum räumlichen Anwendungsbereich für Medienintermediäre, Medienplattformen und Benutzeroberflächen in ihrer derzeitigen Form wegen eines möglichen Verstoßes gegen die ECRL kritisch. Grundsätzlich sieht § 1 Abs. 7 MStV vor, dass der Staatsvertrag nur für Anbieter von Telemedien gilt, wenn sie nach den Vorschriften des Telemediengesetzes in Deutschland niedergelassen sind. Abweichend hiervon bestimmte § 1 Abs. 8 MStV, dass für Medienintermediäre, Medienplattformen und Benutzeroberflächen der Staatsvertrag dennoch gilt, soweit sie zur Nutzung in Deutschland bestimmt sind. Dies wird angenommen für Dienste, „wenn sie sich in der Gesamtschau, insbesondere durch die verwendete Sprache, die angebotenen Inhalte oder Marketingaktivitäten, an Nutzer in Deutschland richten oder in Deutschland einen nicht unwesentlichen Teil ihrer Refinanzierung erzielen" (§ 1 Abs. 8 S. 3 MStV). Die genannten Dienstekategorien stellen dabei Dienste der Informationsgesellschaft dar; die materiell-rechtlichen Verpflichtungen betreffen zudem die Aufnahme oder Ausübung von Tätigkeiten im Anwendungsbereich der ECRL. Den Diensten werden beispielsweise im Rahmen der für diese Dienste geltenden Vorschriften zu Transparenz und Diskriminierungsfreiheit zusätzliche Verpflichtungen auferlegt.[874] Die Begründung zum Medienstaatsvertrag[875] führt hierzu aus:

„*Für diese besonderen Telemedien wird somit – abweichend von der grundsätzlichen Regelung des Absatzes 7 – das sog. Marktortprinzip verankert. Die Verankerung des Marktortprinzips ist auch in Ermangelung entsprechender europäischer Regelungen und aufgrund der fehlenden Regelungskompetenz der Europäischen Union notwendig, um Medienpluralismus sowie kommunikative Chancengleichheit in Deutschland sicherzustellen.*"

Die Länder berufen sich zudem auf Art. 1 Abs. 6 ECRL. Dieser regelt, dass Maßnahmen auf gemeinschaftlicher oder einzelstaatlicher Ebene, die un-

---

[873] Ausf. zur Bedeutung und zum Ablauf des Informationsverfahrens *Cole*, in: HK-MStV, § 61 Rn. 1 ff., v.a. 4 ff.

[874] Die Kommission nimmt dies insbesondere für die Anzeigepflicht gem. § 79 MStV sowie die Transparenz von Systemen für die Auswahl und Organisation von Inhalten gem. § 85 und § 93 MStV an.

[875] Begründung zum Staatsvertrag zur Modernisierung der Medienordnung in Deutschland, zu § 1, abrufbar unter: https://www.rlp.de/index.php?id=32764.

ter Wahrung des Gemeinschaftsrechts der Förderung der kulturellen und sprachlichen Vielfalt und dem Schutz des Pluralismus dienen, von der Richtlinie unberührt bleiben. Die Kommission führt hierzu aus, dass Maßnahmen tatsächlich und objektiv dem Schutz des Medienpluralismus dienen und in einem angemessenen Verhältnis zu den Zielen der Maßnahme stehen müssen. Darüber hinaus müssten Mitgliedstaaten beim Erlass solcher Maßnahmen das weitere EU-Recht beachten, zu dem auch die Bestimmungen der ECRL gehören.[876]

Diese Bedenken seitens der Kommission führten aber nicht zu einer ausführlichen Stellungnahme. Dieses Ergebnis des Notifizierungsverfahrens durch bloße Bemerkungen entfaltet zwar keine Sperr- oder Bindungswirkung in Hinblick auf eine etwaige spätere Prüfung der EU-Rechtskonformität durch die Kommission im Wege der Einleitung eines Vertragsverletzungsverfahrens vor dem EuGH.[877] Jedoch ist aus der Argumentation erkennbar, dass die Bedenken nicht als ausreichend angesehen wurden, um eine weitergehende Reaktion auf den Entwurf zu begründen. Dies entspricht dem oben ausführlich dargestellten Prüfungsergebnis, dass die Argumentationslinie der Kommission nicht überzeugt, soweit ein möglicher Verstoß gegen die ECRL angedeutet wird.[878]

2. Weitere materiell-rechtliche Erwägungen

a. NetzDG und Fragen der Verantwortlichkeit

Ein weiteres mögliches Spannungsverhältnis bei Fragen der Regulierung des Mediensektors besteht in Bezug zu den Verantwortlichkeitsregeln der ECRL. Auch insoweit wird teilweise argumentiert, dass das NetzDG zu einer unzulässigen Abweichung des Haftungsprivilegs der ECRL (Art. 14 Abs. 1 Buchst. b) für Hostingdienste) führe.[879]

---

[876] Vgl. zum Hintergrund von Abweichungsmöglichkeiten bereits die Ausführungen zur ECRL unter Abschnitt D.II.1. sowie zu den grundfreiheitlichen Anforderungen unter Abschnitt C.IV.1.

[877] Siehe auch *Holznagel*, Stellungnahme zur schriftlichen Anhörung des Ausschusses für Kultur und Medien des Landtags Nordrhein-Westfalen, 17/2858, abrufbar unter https://www.landtag.nrw.de/portal/WWW/dokumentenarchiv/Dokument/MMST17-2858.pdf.

[878] Siehe Abschnitt E.II.4.d.

[879] *Spindler* in. ZUM 2017, 473, 479ff.; *Wimmers/Heymann* AfP 2017, 93, 95.

Art. 14 ECRL regelt die Verantwortlichkeiten von Diensten der Informationsgesellschaft, die in der Speicherung von durch einen Nutzer eingegebenen Informationen bestehen. Hierunter fallen auch die von § 1 NetzDG genannten sozialen Netzwerke. Gem. Art. 14 ECRL sind solche Diensteanbieter nicht für die im Auftrag eines Nutzers gespeicherten Informationen verantwortlich, sofern sie keine tatsächliche Kenntnis von deren Rechtswidrigkeit haben, und, in Bezug auf Schadenersatzansprüche, sich auch keiner Tatsachen oder Umstände bewusst sind, aus denen die rechtswidrige Tätigkeit oder Information offensichtlich wird. Die Anbieter sind allerdings dazu verpflichtet unverzüglich nach Kenntnisnahme tätig zu werden, um die betreffende Information zu entfernen oder den Zugang zu ihr zu sperren.[880]

Die starren Fristen zur Entfernung oder Sperrung von rechtswidrigen Inhalten nach § 3 NetzDG könnten dabei im Widerspruch zum Merkmal der „Unverzüglichkeit" stehen.[881] Als Rechtsbegriff des Unionsrechts unterliegt dieses Kriterium der Auslegung durch den EuGH, der sich an den einschlägigen Erwägungsgründen orientiert.[882] Die Erwgr. 10 (in Bezug auf die generelle Zielsetzung der ECRL) und 46 (in Bezug auf die Haftungsprivilegien) erläutern, dass mit der abgestuften Verantwortlichkeit und der Notwendigkeit unverzüglicher Reaktion auf bekannt gewordene rechtswidrige Inhalte einerseits ein hoher Rechtsgüterschutz, andererseits die Meinungsfreiheit abgesichert werden sollen.

Die Organisationspflichten des § 3 NetzDG für Anbieter sozialer Netzwerke sehen ein Verfahren für den Umgang mit Beschwerden vor, wonach gewährleistet werden muss, dass unverzüglich von der Beschwerde Kenntnis genommen und geprüft wird, ob der in der Beschwerde gemeldete Inhalt rechtswidrig ist. Offensichtlich rechtswidrige Inhalte sollen demnach innerhalb von 24 Stunden nach Eingang der Beschwerde entfernt oder gesperrt werden, § 3 Abs. 2 Nr. 2 NetzDG. Sonstige rechtswidrige Inhalte sind gem. § 3 Abs. 2 Nr. 3 NetzDG unverzüglich, in der Regel innerhalb von sieben Tagen nach Eingang der Beschwerde zu entfernen bzw. zu sperren. Das NetzDG setzt damit für den Zeitablauf bereits beim Eingang der Beschwerde und demnach möglicherweise noch vor der nach der ECRL beschriebenen Kenntnis von der Rechtswidrigkeit an, die eine Auswertung der Beschwerde – falls nur auf diesem Wege die mögliche Rechts-

---

[880] Ausf. zur Bedeutung des Art. 14 ECRL und seiner Auslegung durch den EuGH *Cole/Etteldorf/Ullrich*, Cross-border Dissemination of Online Content, S. 183 ff.
[881] *Liesching* in Spindler/Schmitz, § 1 NetzDG, Rn. 20.
[882] *Cole/Etteldorf/Ullrich*, Cross-border Dissemination of Online Content, S. 188 ff.; *Nölscher* in: ZUM 2020, 301 (302).

widrigkeit angezeigt wurde – voraussetzt. Teilweise wird hierfür angenommen, dass Art. 14 ECRL die Mitgliedsstaaten zur Ausformung eines effektiven Verfahrens ermächtigt. Mitgliedstaatliche Regelungen zur Zeitspanne zwischen Beschwerdeeingang und Kenntnisnahme, wie explizit vom NetzDG aufgestellt, seien daher europarechtskonform.[883] Kritisiert wird jedoch teilweise die Bearbeitungsfrist ab Beschwerdeeingang. Diese könnte zu einer ordnungsrechtlichen Verantwortlichkeit des Diensteanbieters in Form von Bußgeldern nach § 4 Abs. 1 Nr. 3 NetzDG führen, wenn eine Beschwerde zwar eingegangen, aber noch keine konkrete Kenntnis von der Rechtswidrigkeit erreicht ist. Da Art. 14 ECRL an die Kenntnisnahme anknüpft, könnte darin eine Begrenzung einer ordnungsrechtlichen Verantwortlichkeit für den vorhergehenden Zeitraum liegen.

Zudem wird die kurz bemessene Frist zur Reaktion durch die Diensteanbieter im Falle der „offensichtlich rechtwidrigen Inhalte" als strenger als die europäische Vorgabe gesehen.[884] Dem wird jedoch entgegen gehalten, dass die 24-stündige Bearbeitungsfrist für solche Inhalte, bei denen sich die Rechtswidrigkeit unmittelbar aufdrängt, angemessen lang ist und somit die widerstreitenden Ziele der E-Commerce-RL dadurch in Einklang gebracht und ein Schutz der kollidierenden Rechtsgüter bei der Nutzung moderner Kommunikationswege möglich gemacht wird. Danach sei auch die Problematik des vorgezogenen Fristbeginns durch eine europarechtskonforme Auslegung im Rahmen der Sanktionsanordnung mit dem Unionsrecht in Einklang zu bringen. Es wird argumentiert, dass das NetzDG die Bearbeitung von Beschwerden beschleunige, nicht aber die in der ECRL festgelegte Verantwortlichkeit beseitige.[885]

Das Spannungsverhältnis zwischen solchen Regelungen, die die Verantwortung von Dienstanbietern wie soziale Netzwerke betreffen, wird in der Literatur somit zumindest als lösbar betrachtet.

---

883 *Nölscher* in: ZUM 2020, 301, 302. Zwar nicht auf die Fragen der Verfassungsmäßigkeit und Europarechtskonformität eingehend, aber das NetzDG auch vor einem europarechtlichen Hintergrund skizzierend und bewertend vgl. insbesondere *Eifert u.a.*, Evaluation des NetzDG.
884 *Spindler* in: ZUM 2017, 473, 479.
885 In diese Richtung argumentiert *Nölscher* in: ZUM 2020, 301, 304. Vgl. zum Diskussionsstand insbesondere *Eifert u.a.*, Evaluation des NetzDG, S. 9, m.w.N. *Eifert u.a.* verweisen insbesondere darauf, dass es bei der Frage nach einer möglichen Abweichung von Art. 14 ECRL auch stark darauf ankommt, welche Anforderungen nach dem NetzDG an die Beschwerde zu stellen sind.

b. Exkurs: Konfliktlagen bei ähnlichen Regelungen in anderen Staaten

Ein vergleichbares Konfliktpotenzial zwischen widerstreitenden Interessen zeigt sich nicht nur beim deutschen NetzDG, sondern auch bei Regelungsansätzen mit einer vergleichbaren Stoßrichtung in anderen Staaten.[886]

Der französische Verfassungsrat ordnete in einer Entscheidung vom 18. Juni 2020[887] bestimmte Passagen des dann verkündeten Gesetzes Nr. 2020-766 vom 24. Juni 2020 zur Bekämpfung von Hassinhalten im Internet[888] als verfassungswidrig ein. Der vorgesehene Art. 1 Abs. I des Gesetzes, das deutliche Parallelen zum deutschen NetzDG aufweist, gehörte dazu. Das Gesetz ermächtigt Verwaltungsbehörden, von Hosts oder Herausgebern eines Online-Kommunikationsdienstes zu verlangen, bestimmte terroristische oder kinderpornografische Inhalte zu entfernen. Im Falle der Nichteinhaltung dieser Verpflichtung ist die Anwendung einer Strafe von einem Jahr Freiheitsentzug und einer Geldstrafe von 250.000 Euro vorgesehen. Der Verfassungsrat begründete seine Entscheidung damit, dass die Feststellung der Rechtswidrigkeit des fraglichen Inhalts nicht auf seinem offenkundigen Charakter beruhe, sondern allein der Beurteilung durch die Verwaltung unterliege. Zudem gäbe es keine ausreichenden Rechtsschutzmöglichkeiten gegen Entfernungsanordnungen.[889]

Der Verfassungsrat erklärte weiterhin Art. 1 Abs. II des Gesetzes für verfassungswidrig, der bestimmte Betreiber von Online-Plattformen unter Androhung strafrechtlicher Sanktionen verpflichten sollte, innerhalb von 24 Stunden offensichtlich illegale Inhalte wegen ihres hasserfüllten oder sexuellen Charakters zu entfernen oder unzugänglich zu machen. Die Verpflichtung hätte weder einer vorherigen gerichtlichen Intervention noch anderen Bedingungen unterlegen. Es sei daher Sache des Betreibers, alle ihm gemeldeten Inhalte, auch wenn dies in großem Umfang geschehe, zu prüfen, um das Risiko strafrechtlicher Sanktionen zu vermeiden. Die Verpflichtung der Betreiber von Online-Plattformen, der Aufforderung zur Löschung oder Sperrung innerhalb von 24 Stunden nachzukommen, sei zudem angesichts der Schwierigkeiten bei der Beurteilung der offensichtli-

---

[886] Neben den hier kurz beleuchteten Staaten kann als weiteres Beispiel der Regelungsansatz Österreichs genannt werden, vgl. dazu bereits Abschnitt B.I.5.g und Fn. 93.
[887] Entscheidung n° 2020–801 DC vom 18.6.2020, abrufbar in französischer Sprache unter: https://www.conseil-constitutionnel.fr/decision/2020/2020801DC.htm.
[888] Loi n° 2020–766 aaO (Fn. 631).
[889] *Ukrow*, Frankreich: Verfassungsgericht zum „französischen NetzDG", MMR Aktuell, Ausgabe 14/2020 vom 25. August 2020.

chen Rechtswidrigkeit der gemeldeten Inhalte und der Gefahr zahlreicher, möglicherweise unbegründeter Meldungen besonders kurz.

In einer Gesamtschau kommt der Verfassungsrat zum Schluss, dass die angefochtenen Bestimmungen des Gesetzes angesichts der Schwierigkeiten bei der Beurteilung der offensichtlichen Rechtswidrigkeit der gemeldeten Inhalte, der ab dem ersten Verstoß verhängten Strafe und des Fehlens eines konkreten Grundes für eine Haftungsbefreiung die Betreiber von Online-Plattformen dazu ermutigen könnten, die ihnen gemeldeten Inhalte zu löschen oder zu sperren, unabhängig davon, ob sie tatsächlich offensichtlich rechtswidrig sind oder nicht.[890] Aus Sicht des Verfassungsrates beeinträchtige diese Bestimmung daher die Ausübung der Meinungs- und Kommunikationsfreiheit in einer Weise, die nicht angemessen, notwendig und verhältnismäßig im Hinblick auf das verfolgte Ziel war.

Auch außerhalb der EU sind ähnliche Gesetzesvorhaben zu betrachten, wobei im hier vorgestellten Beispiel durch die Ausgestaltung das Spannungsverhältnis und die schwierige Abwägung zwischen freier Meinungsäußerung und effektivem Rechtsgüterschutz noch deutlicher wird. In einem Eilverfahren ohne Anhörung von Interessengruppen verabschiedete das türkische Parlament am 29. Juli 2020 ein Gesetz zur Kontrolle sozialer Medien[891], dessen Regelungen am 1. Oktober 2020 in Kraft getreten sind. Das Gesetz bezweckt nach seiner Begründung die Bekämpfung von Hassrede und Belästigungen im Internet. Nach dem Gesetz, bei dessen Entstehung auf vermeintliche Bezüge zum NetzDG hingewiesen wurde, müssen alle sozialen Netzwerke mit mehr als zwei Millionen täglichen Nutzern einen lokalen Vertreter in der Türkei benennen. Diese lokalen Vertreter der Unternehmen werden verpflichtet auf Anfragen der Regierung zur Sperrung oder Entfernung von Inhalten zu reagieren.[892] Wenn ein Gerichtsbeschluss vorliegt und „Persönlichkeitsrechte" oder die „Privatsphäre" verletzt sind, müssen sie die Inhalte innerhalb von 48 Stunden entfernen. Netzwerken, die dagegen verstoßen, können Werbeverbote und Geldbußen auferlegt werden. Zukünftig können Richter zudem die Internet-

---

890 Zu einer Bewertung der Gefahren des NetzDG für das sog. Over-Blocking vgl. *Eifert u.a.*, Evaluation des NetzDG, S. 51 f.
891 İnternet Ortamında Yapılan Yayınların Düzenlenmesi ve Bu Yayınlar Yoluyla İşlenen Suçlarla Mücadele Edilmesi Hakkında Kanun, Kanun No. 7253, Kabul Tarihi: 29/7/2020, abrufbar in türkischer Sprache unter https://www.resmigazete.gov.tr/eskiler/2020/07/20200731-1.htm.
892 Vgl. zu bisherigen Regulierungsansätzen in der Türkei bezüglich online verfügbarer Inhalte *Keser* in: Cappello (Hrsg.), Medienrechtsdurchsetzung ohne Grenzen, S. 91, 100 f.

Provider anweisen, die Bandbreite von sozialen Netzwerken um bis zu 90 Prozent zu drosseln, wodurch der Zugang zu diesen Seiten praktisch blockiert wäre. Das Gesetz enthält darüber hinaus Bestimmungen, die die sozialen Netzwerke dazu verpflichten, die Daten der Nutzer lokal zu speichern. Anbieter können verpflichtet werden, diese Daten an türkische Behörden weiterzuleiten.[893]

Dieses Gesetz wird insbesondere wegen der Einleitung möglicher Sperrungen und die Überwachung durch staatliche Stellen kritisiert und es wird befürchtet, dass ein *chilling effect* auf die Wahrnehmung der Kommunikationsfreiheiten durch türkische Social-Media-Nutzer ausgehen könnte. In den vergangenen Jahren waren die traditionellen Print- und Rundfunk-Medien in der Türkei bereits zunehmend unter staatlichen Druck geraten.[894] Daher werden soziale Medien und kleinere Onlinenachrichtenportale häufiger für unabhängige Nachrichten genutzt.[895] Inwieweit das Gesetz einer gerichtlichen Überprüfung standhält, wird sich noch zeigen müssen.

c. Die urheberrechtliche freie Benutzung nach § 24 UrhG und die abschließende Harmonisierung

Ein weiteres Beispiel für mögliche Spannungsverhältnisse der Regulierung des Mediensektors mit EU-Recht hat sich im vergangenen Jahr im Bereich des Urheberrechts gezeigt. Dort stellte sich die Frage, wie weit bestimmte im nationalen Recht anerkannte Rechtsfiguren in abschließend harmonisierte Bereiche des europäischen Rechtsrahmens zum Urheberrecht fallen.

Mit Urteil vom 29. Juli 2019[896] hatte der EuGH in seinem „Sampling-Urteil" entschieden, dass § 24 des deutschen Urheberrechtsgesetzes (UrhG) europarechtswidrig ist. Die Vorschrift gestattete die Verwertung und Veröffentlichung eines anderen Werkes durch ein selbständiges Werk, das in

---

[893] *Ukrow*, Türkei: Gesetz zur Kontrolle sozialer Medien verabschiedet, MMR Aktuell, Ausgabe 15/2020 vom 9. September 2020.

[894] Vgl. *Keser* in: Cappello (Hrsg.), Medienrechtsdurchsetzung ohne Grenzen, S. 91 ff.

[895] Siehe auch netzpolitik.org, Türkisches Internet-Gesetz – Die bislang schlimmste Kopie des deutschen Netzwerkdurchsetzungsgesetzes (05.08.2020), abrufbar unter: https://netzpolitik.org/2020/tuerkisches-internet-gesetz-die-bislang-schlimmste-kopie-des-deutschen-netzwerkdurchsetzungsgesetzes/#vorschaltbanner.

[896] EuGH, Rs. C-476/17, *Pelham GmbH u. a. / Ralf Hütter und Florian Schneider-Esleben*.

freier Benutzung dieses Werkes eines anderen geschaffen worden ist.[897] Das Rechtsinstitut der freien Benutzung war im deutschen Urheberrecht verankert mit dem Ziel – gleichsam wie eine den Schutzgegenstand begrenzende Generalklausel –, die ausschließlichen Rechte und Interessen des Urhebers, nur selbst über die Nutzung seines Werkes entscheiden, mit den kulturellen Interessen der Allgemeinheit in Einklang zu bringen.[898] Der Gerichtshof nahm allerdings an, dass die Wirksamkeit der durch die Urheberrechtsrichtlinie bewirkten Harmonisierung des Urheberrechts und der verwandten Schutzrechte sowie das mit ihr verfolgte Ziel der Rechtssicherheit gefährdet sei, wenn jedem Mitgliedstaat ungeachtet des ausdrücklichen Willens des Unionsrechtsetzungsorgane gestattet würde, außerhalb der in Art. 5 Richtlinie 2001/29/EG vorgesehenen Ausnahmen und Beschränkungen Abweichungen von den ausschließlichen Rechten des Urhebers aus den Art. 2 bis 4 dieser Richtlinie vorzusehen.[899]

§ 24 UrhG, der in seiner praktischen Anwendung über die Nutzung von Werken zum Zwecke von Karikaturen, Parodien oder Pastiches, die zwar im europäischen Rechtsrahmen aufgeführt, nicht aber im deutschen Schrankensystem umgesetzt sind[900], hinaus geht, wurde damit aus Sicht des EuGH als gesetzliche Schranke aufgefasst, die nicht im abschließenden Katalog des Art. 5 Richtlinie 2001/29/EG vorgesehen ist. Aus deutscher Sicht wurde freie Benutzung zuvor hingegen an der Grenze zum Bearbeitungsrecht verortet (systematisch angelehnt an § 23 UrhG), welches im Gegensatz zum Schrankenkatalog des europäischen Urheberrechts noch keine umfassende Harmonisierung erfahren hat.[901] Eine allein auf mitgliedstaatlicher Ebene bestehende urheberrechtliche Rechtsfigur hätte somit in der Systematik zur Mindest- und Maximalharmonisierung des europä-

---

897 Vgl. zum Urteil *Frenz* in: DVBl. 2019, 1471, 1471 ff.; *Hieber* in: ZUM 2019, 738, 738 ff, insbesondere 747 f. in Bezug auf § 24 UrhG. Auf das Bearbeitungsrecht vor dem Hintergrund der Urteile des EuGH (Rs. C-476/17) und des BGH (Az. I ZR 115/16) eingehend auch *Döhl* in: UFITA 2020, 236, 236 ff.
898 *Schulze* in Dreier/Schulze, § 24 UrhG, Rn. 1.
899 EuGH, aaO (Fn. 899), Rn. 66.
900 Der Entwurf eines Zweiten Gesetzes zur Anpassung des Urheberrechts an die Erfordernisse des digitalen Binnenmarktes, Stand: 24. Juni 2020, sieht eine explizite Regelung der Schranken für Karikaturen, Parodien und Pastiches in § 51a UrhG-E vor, abrufbar unter: https://www.bmjv.de/SharedDocs/Gesetzgebungsverfahren/Dokumente/DiskE_II_Anpassung%20Urheberrecht_digitaler_Binnenmarkt.pdf?__blob=publicationFile&v=2.
901 *Schulze* in Dreier/Schulze, § 24 UrhG, Rn. 1.

ischen Rechtsrahmens bestehen können.[902] Der deutsche Gesetzgeber hat mittlerweile die Doppelfunktion des § 24 UrhG eingeräumt, wonach dieser zum einen den Schutzbereich für bestehende Werke begrenzt, zum anderen allerdings auch als Schranke des Urheberrechts fungiert. Mit der Einfügung der Schutzbereichsbegrenzung im Bereich des § 23 UrhG sowie der künftigen expliziten Aufnahme der in Art. 5 der Urheberrechtsrichtlinie genannten Ausnahmen in den deutschen Schrankenkatalog, soll diese Doppelfunktion gelöst werden.[903]

Interessant ist die vorgenannte Problematik insbesondere im Hinblick auf die geplanten deutschen Regelungen zur Verantwortlichkeit von Upload-Plattformen im Rahmen des Entwurfs eines Urheberrechts-Diensteanbieter-Gesetzes (UrhDaG-E)[904], die eine gesetzliche Erlaubnis für nichtkommerzielle Bagatellnutzungen vorsieht. Auch hiergegen wurde bereits Kritik vorgebracht, der vollharmonisierende Charakter des europäischen Urheberrechts würde einer solchen Lösung entgegenstehen.[905] Das Bundesjustizministerium ist hingegen der Auffassung, dass Artikel 17 DSM-Richtlinie ein neuartiges Haftungssystem etabliert, welches über das bestehende europäische Urheberrecht hinausgeht. Daher sei es zulässig, in diesem beschränkten Bereich der Nutzung von Werken auf Upload-Plattformen neue gesetzliche Erlaubnisse zu formulieren.[906]

---

902 Hierzu siehe auch Summaries of EU Legislation, Richtlinien der Europäischen Union, Art. 288 AEUV, abrufbar unter: https://eur-lex.europa.eu/legal-content/DE/TXT/HTML/?uri=LEGISSUM:l14527&from=DE.
903 Begründung des Entwurfs eines Zweiten Gesetzes zur Anpassung des Urheberrechts an die Erfordernisse des digitalen Binnenmarktes, Stand: 24. Juni 2020, S. 44.
904 Entwurf eines Zweiten Gesetzes zur Anpassung des Urheberrechts an die Erfordernisse des digitalen Binnenmarktes, aaO (Fn. 903).
905 So beispielsweise in der Stellungnahme von Bertelsmann im Rahmen der öffentlichen Konsultation zur Umsetzung der EU-Richtlinien im Urheberrecht (DSM-Richtlinie und Online-SatCab-Richtlinie) zu lesen, abrufbar unter: https://www.bmjv.de/SharedDocs/Gesetzgebungsverfahren/Stellungnahmen/2019/Downloads/090619_Stellungnahme_Bertelsmann_EU-Richtlinien_Urheberrecht.pdf?__blob=publicationFile&v=2.
906 FAQ zum Diskussionsentwurf zur Umsetzung der Urheberrechtsrichtlinien (EU) 789/2019 („Online-SatCab-Richtlinie") und (EU) 790/2019 („DSM-Richtlinie"), 24.6.2020, S. 3, abrufbar unter: https://www.bmjv.de/SharedDocs/Gesetzgebungsverfahren/Dokumente/DiskE_II_Anpassung%20Urheberrecht_digitaler_Binnenmarkt_FAQ.pdf?__blob=publicationFile&v=1.

F. Der vorgeschlagene Digital Services Act

Jörg Ukrow

I. Ausgangspunkt der Diskussion und Pläne

Kommissionspräsidentin *von der Leyen* hatte bereits in ihrer anlässlich des Berufungsverfahrens 2019 veröffentlichten „Agenda für Europa" unter dem Titel „Eine Union, die mehr erreichen will" die Einführung eines *„Digital Services Act"* angekündigt. Zu diesem hieß es in den von der designierten Kommissionspräsidentin vorgestellten „Politischen Leitlinien für die künftige Europäische Kommission 2019–2024":[907]

> *„Mit einem neuen Gesetz über digitale Dienste müssen bessere Haftungs- und Sicherheitsvorschriften für digitale Plattformen, Dienste und Produkte geschaffen und der digitale Binnenmarkt vollendet werden."*

Mit diesem Ansatz konnte *von der Leyen* an Vorarbeiten der DG Connect anknüpfen, die als Kern eines *„Digital Services Act"* – nicht zuletzt mit Blick auf den grundlegenden Wandel der Digitalwirtschaft und ihrer Produkte seit In-Kraft-Treten der ECRL im Jahr 2000 – bereits die Schließung regulatorischer Lücken, die Harmonisierung diverser Rechtsbereiche, Regelungen zu Hate Speech und politischer Desinformation auf EU-Ebene, größere Spielräume für innovative digitale Geschäftsmodelle sowie ein „Update" der Haftung von Plattformen, namentlich um Internet-Giganten wie Google, YouTube oder Amazon gezielter und umfassender regulieren zu können, ins Auge gefasst hatte.

In ihrer Mitteilung „Gestaltung der digitalen Zukunft Europas" vom 19. Februar 2020 kündigte die Kommission als „Schlüsselmaßnahmen" für das Ziel einer fairen und wettbewerbsfähigen Wirtschaft u.a. an:[908]

> *„im Rahmen des Pakets zum Rechtsakt über digitale Dienste wird die Kommission die Einführung von Ex-ante-Regulierungsmaßnahmen prüfen, um sicherzustellen, dass auf Märkten, die von großen Plattformen mit erhebli-*

---

[907] *Von der Leyen*, Eine Union, die mehr erreichen will. Meine Agenda für Europa, 2019, S. 16 (abrufbar unter https://ec.europa.eu/info/sites/info/files/political-guidelines-next-commission_de.pdf).

[908] COM(2020) 67 final, S. 11.

> chen Netzeffekten geprägt sind, die als Torwächter fungieren, Fairness und Wettbewerbsmöglichkeiten für Innovatoren, Unternehmen und neue Marktteilnehmer sichergestellt bleiben (4. Quartal 2020)."

Mit Blick auf das Ziel einer offenen, demokratischen und nachhaltigen Gesellschaft kündigte die Kommission in der Mitteilung als „Schlüsselmaßnahmen" u.a. an:[909]

> „Neue und überarbeitete Vorschriften zur Vertiefung des Binnenmarkts für digitale Dienste durch Ausweitung und Harmonisierung der Pflichten von Online-Plattformen und Informationsdienstleistern sowie Stärkung der Aufsicht über die Inhaltepolitik der Plattformen in der EU (4. Quartal 2020, als Teil des Pakets zum Rechtsakt über digitale Dienste);
> [...]
> Aktionsplan für die Medien und den audiovisuellen Sektor zur Unterstützung des digitalen Wandels und der Wettbewerbfähigkeit des audiovisuellen Sektors und der Medien, um den Zugang zu hochwertigen Inhalten und den Medienpluralismus zu fördern (4. Quartal 2020);
> Europäischer Aktionsplan für Demokratie zur Stärkung der Widerstandsfähigkeit unserer demokratischen Systeme, zur Unterstützung des Medienpluralismus und zur Bewältigung der Bedrohungen durch externe Eingriffe in europäische Wahlen (4. Quartal 2020)".

In einer Verbindung von Evaluierungsfahrplan und Wirkungsanalyse präsentierte die Kommission zunächst drei auf das „Update" der ECRL bezogene Optionen für die ex-post-Regulierung:[910]

- In Option 1 würde ein begrenztes Rechtsinstrument die Verfahrenspflichten von Online-Plattformen regeln und im Wesentlichen die horizontalen Bestimmungen der (nach Art. 288 Abs. 5 AEUV rechtlich unverbindlichen) „Empfehlung der Kommission vom 1.3.2018 für wirksame Maßnahmen im Umgang mit illegalen Online-Inhalten"[911] von 2018 verbindlich machen. Die Regulierung würde auf dem Anwendungsbereich der ECRL aufbauen und sich auf in der EU niedergelassene Dienste konzentrieren. Dabei würden die Verantwortlichkeiten von Online-Plattformen in Bezug auf den Verkauf illegaler Waren und

---

[909] COM(2020) 67 final, S. 14.
[910] Inception impact assessment – Ares(2020)2877686, abrufbar über https://ec.europa.eu/info/law/better-regulation/have-your-say/initiatives/12417-Digital-Services-Act-deepening-the-Internal-Market-and-clarifying-responsibilities-for-digital-services.
[911] C(2018) 1177 final.

F. Der vorgeschlagene Digital Services Act

Dienstleistungen sowie die Verbreitung illegaler Inhalte und anderer illegaler Aktivitäten ihrer Nutzer festgelegt werden. Bei dieser Option würden verhältnismäßige Verpflichtungen wie wirksame Benachrichtigungs- und Aktionsmechanismen zur Meldung illegaler Inhalte oder Waren sowie wirksame Abhilfeverpflichtungen in Verbindung mit Benachrichtigungsverfahren und Transparenzverpflichtungen eingeführt werden. Allerdings würden die Haftungsregeln der ECRL für Plattformen oder andere Online-Vermittler weder geklärt noch aktualisiert.

- Option 2 der Kommission sieht eine umfassendere Regulierung vor, bei der die Regeln der ECRL aktualisiert und modernisiert, ihre Hauptprinzipien allerdings erhalten blieben. Bei dieser Option würden die Haftungs- und Sicherheitsvorschriften für digitale Dienste klargestellt und aktualisiert und Hindernisse insbesondere für Online-Plattformdienste, die von freiwilligen Maßnahmen zur Bekämpfung illegaler Inhalte, Waren oder Dienstleistungen bislang zurückschrecken, beseitigt. Definitionen dessen, was online illegal ist, würden sich auf andere Rechtsakte auf EU- und nationaler Ebene stützen. Bei dieser Option sieht die Kommission vor, eine Reihe spezifischer, verbindlicher und verhältnismäßiger Verpflichtungen zu harmonisieren und die unterschiedlichen Verantwortlichkeiten insbesondere für Online-Plattformdienste festzulegen.[912] Zusätzlich zu einem Basissatz von allgemein anwendbaren Verpflichtungen könnten aus Sicht der Kommission bei dieser Option je nach Art, Größe und/oder Risikopotential eines digitalen Dienstes weitere asymmetrische Verpflichtungen erforderlich sein.

Zu den Verpflichtungen könnten gehören:
  o harmonisierte Verpflichtungen zur Aufrechterhaltung von „Notice-and-Action"-Systemen, die alle Arten illegaler Waren, Inhalte und Dienste abdecken, sowie „Know your customer"-Systeme für kommerzielle Nutzer von Online-Marktplätzen
  o Regeln, die eine wirksame Zusammenarbeit der Anbieter digitaler Dienste mit den zuständigen Behörden und trusted flaggern (z.B. die INHOPE-Hotlines für eine schnellere Entfernung von Material über sexuellen Kindesmissbrauch) und gegebenenfalls diesbezügliche Berichterstattungspflichten

---

912 Dabei wird insbesondere darauf hingewiesen, dass die Kohärenz mit den neuen Regeln der AVMD-Richtlinie insbesondere in Bezug auf VSP, gewährleistet werden soll. Vgl. Inception impact assessment – Ares(2020)2877686, aaO (Fn. 608), S. 5, Fn. 8.

- o Risikobewertungen könnten von Online-Plattformen für Fragen im Zusammenhang mit der Verwendung ihrer Dienste zur Verbreitung einiger Kategorien schädlicher, aber nicht illegaler Inhalte verlangt werden, wie z.B. im Bereich Desinformation
- o wirksamere Rechtsmittel und Schutz vor ungerechtfertigter Entfernung für legitime Online-Inhalte und -Güter
- o eine Reihe von Transparenz- und Berichterstattungspflichten im Zusammenhang mit diesen Prozessen
  Es würden bei dieser Option auch Transparenz-, Berichterstattungs- und unabhängige Prüfpflichten zur Gewährleistung der Rechenschaftspflicht in Bezug auf algorithmische Systeme für (automatisierte) Inhaltsmoderations- und Empfehlungssysteme sowie Online-Werbung und kommerzielle Kommunikation untersucht – einschließlich politischer Werbung und Micro-Targeting-Aspekten, und dies über die bestehenden Rechte und Pflichten im Zusammenhang mit dem Schutz personenbezogener Daten hinaus. Solche Maßnahmen würden aus Sicht der Kommission eine wirksame Aufsicht über Online-Plattformen ermöglichen und die Bemühungen zur Bekämpfung der Online-Desinformation unterstützen.
  Es würde bei dieser Option auch geprüft werden, ob solche Maßnahmen auf alle Dienste ausgeweitet werden können, die auf den europäischen Binnenmarkt ausgerichtet sind, auch wenn sie außerhalb der Union niedergelassen sind.
  Das bei dieser Option vorgesehene Regulierungsinstrument würde auch abschreckende und verhältnismäßige Sanktionen für systematische Verstöße gegen die harmonisierten Verantwortlichkeiten oder die Achtung der Grundrechte festlegen.
- Die Option 3 der Kommission, die in Ergänzung zu den vorgenannten Optionen darauf abzielt, das gemäß den Optionen 1 oder 2 aktualisierte Regelwerk zu stärken, sieht die Schaffung eines wirksamen Systems der Überwachung durch Regulierungsstellen, der Durchsetzung und Zusammenarbeit zwischen den Mitgliedstaaten vor, das auf EU-Ebene unterstützt wird. Auf der Grundlage des Herkunftslandprinzips würde es den Behörden der Mitgliedstaaten ermöglicht, mit illegalen Inhalten, Waren oder Dienstleistungen online umzugehen, einschließlich rascher und wirksamer Kooperationsverfahren für grenzüberschreitende Fragen bei der Regulierung und Aufsicht über digitale Dienste. Die Fähigkeiten der Behörden zur Überwachung digitaler Dienste würden gestärkt, u.a. durch angemessene Befugnisse für wirksame und abschreckende Sanktionen bei systemischem Versagen von Diensten, die entsprechenden Verpflichtungen zu erfüllen, was „möglicherweise auf EU-

Ebene unterstützt" würde. Es würden auch Optionen für wirksame Rechtsmittel geprüft.

Bei allen Optionen soll die Kohärenz mit sektorspezifischen Regelungen – z.B. der DSM-Richtlinie, der überarbeiteten AVMD-Richtlinie, dem TERREG-Vorschlag – sowie mit den internationalen Verpflichtungen der EU gewährleistet werden.[913]

Zugleich präsentierte die Kommission Überlegungen für einen ex ante-Rechtsrahmen für große Online-Plattformen mit erheblichen Netzwerkeffekten, die als „Torwächter" (Gatekeeper) im Binnenmarkt der EU fungieren, als zweiten Pfeiler der geplanten Regulierung.[914] Zu diesen Überlegungen zählen (mindestens) als Optionen:

- die Überarbeitung des in der P2B-Verordnung[915] festgelegten horizontalen Rahmens. Dabei könnten weitere horizontale Regeln für alle Online-Vermittlungsdienste festgelegt werden, die derzeit in den Anwendungsbereich dieser Verordnung fallen. Dies könnte präskriptive Regeln für verschiedene spezifische Praktiken, die derzeit durch Transparenzverpflichtungen in der Verordnung geregelt sind (z.B. über die Transparenz des Datenzugangs), sowie für neue Praktiken umfassen (z.B. über bestimmte Formen der "Selbstreferenzierung", den Zugang zu Daten und unlautere Vertragsbestimmungen). Eine überarbeitete P2B-Verordnung könnte auch die bestehenden Aufsichts-, Durchsetzungs- und Transparenzanforderungen verstärken. Diese Überarbeitung würde sich auf neue oder neu auftauchende Fragen stützen, die in laufenden Untersuchungen ermittelt wurden, sowie auf die Informationen, die – soweit bereits verfügbar – aus den Transparenzvorschriften der P2B-Verordnung gewonnen wurden. Diese Überarbeitung der P2B-Verordnung würde nicht darauf abzielen, die derzeitigen Bestimmungen der Verordnung insgesamt zu überprüfen, sondern sich auf bestimmte gezielte, horizontal anwendbare Zusatzbestimmungen im Hinblick auf die ermittelten spezifischen Fragen beziehen.
- die Verabschiedung eines horizontalen Rahmens, der die Regulierungsstellen ermächtigt, Informationen von großen Online-Plattformen, die als Gatekeeper fungieren, zu sammeln. Im Rahmen dieser Option könnten weitere horizontale Regeln ins Auge gefasst werden – mit dem Ziel, die Sammlung von Informationen von großen Online-Plattfor-

---

[913] Kommission, Ref. Ares(2020)2877686 – 04/06/2020, aaO (Fn. 635).
[914] Kommission, Ref. Ares(2020)2877647 – 04/06/2020, aaO (Fn. 638).
[915] Vgl. hierzu Abschnitt D.II.6.

men, die als Gatekeeper fungieren, durch eine spezielle Regulierungsstelle auf EU-Ebene zu ermöglichen, um z.B. weitere Einblicke in ihre Geschäftspraktiken und deren Auswirkungen auf die Nutzer dieser Plattformen zu gewinnen. Diese Regeln würden nicht nur (wie in der zuvor dargestellten Option) Transparenz vorsehen, sondern aus Sicht der Kommission auch die gezielte Sammlung von Informationen durch eine spezielle Regulierungsstelle auf EU-Ebene ermöglichen. Mit diesem horizontalen Ansatz würde zwar keine Befugnis impliziert werden, den großen Online-Plattformen, die in den Anwendungsbereich dieser Regeln fallen würden, materielle Verhaltens- und/oder strukturelle Abhilfemaßnahmen aufzuerlegen. Allerdings würden dadurch nach Ansicht der Kommission dennoch Durchsetzungsbefugnisse nicht ausgeschlossen, um dem Risiko einer Verweigerung der Bereitstellung der angeforderten Daten durch die Online-Plattformen zu begegnen.

- die Verabschiedung eines neuen und flexiblen Ex-ante-Regelungsrahmens für große Online-Plattformen, die als Gatekeeper fungieren. Diese Option würde einen neuen Ex-ante-Regelungsrahmen schaffen, der für große Online-Plattformen gelten würde, die von erheblichen Netzwerkeffekten profitieren und als Gatekeeper fungieren, der durch eine dazu ermächtigte Regulierungseinrichtung auf EU-Ebene überwacht und durchgesetzt werden. Der neue Rahmen würde die horizontal anwendbaren Bestimmungen der P2B-Verordnung ergänzen, die weiterhin für alle Online-Vermittlungsdienste gelten würden. Die begrenztere Untergruppe großer Online-Plattformen, die dem zusätzlichen Ex-ante-Rahmenwerk unterliegen, würde auf der Grundlage einer Reihe klarer, noch näher zu untersuchender Kriterien ermittelt, wie etwa erhebliche Netzwerkeffekte, die Größe der Nutzerbasis und/oder die Fähigkeit, Daten marktübergreifend zu nutzen. Diese Option würde zwei Unteroptionen umfassen:
  o Verbot oder Beschränkung bestimmter unlauterer Handelspraktiken durch große Online-Plattformen, die als Gatekeeper fungieren („schwarze Listen"). Ein solches Gefüge klar definierter und im Voraus festgelegter Verpflichtungen und verbotener Praktiken würde darauf abzielen, einen offenen und fairen Online-Handel zu gewährleisten, insbesondere wenn diese Praktiken potenziell marktverzerrend sind oder die wirtschaftliche Macht der großen Online-Plattformen stärken. Bei dieser Option werden sowohl prinzipienbasierte Verbote untersucht, die unabhängig von der Branche gelten, in der die betreffenden Online-Plattformen zwischengeschaltet sind (z.B. ein horizontales Verbot der plattforminternen Selbstpräferenzierung), als auch themenspezifischere inhalt-

liche Regelungen für neu auftretende Probleme, die nur mit bestimmten Akteuren zusammenhängen, z.B. in Bezug auf Betriebssysteme, algorithmische Transparenz oder Fragen im Zusammenhang mit Online-Werbeleistungen.
o Einzelfallorientierte Annahme weiterer Abhilfemaßnahmen, wo dies notwendig und gerechtfertigt ist. Beispiele für solche Abhilfemaßnahmen, die von einer zuständigen Regulierungsbehörde (die aus Sicht der Kommission prinzipiell auf EU-Ebene agieren würde) angenommen und durchgesetzt würden, könnten plattformspezifische Datenzugangsverpflichtungen außerhalb personenbezogener Daten, spezifische Anforderungen hinsichtlich der Übertragbarkeit personenbezogener Daten oder Interoperabilitätsanforderungen sein. Nach Auffassung der Kommission könnten dabei die Erfahrungen aus der gezielten Regulierung von Telekommunikationsdiensten (trotz bestehender Unterschiede) angesichts der Ähnlichkeiten, die sich aus der Netzwerkkontrolle und den Netzwerkeffekten ergeben, in dieser Hinsicht als Inspiration dienen Diese zweite Säule eines Ex-ante-Regulierungsrahmens würde sich mit der Vielfalt und schnellen Entwicklung spezifischer Phänomene in der Online-Plattformwirtschaft befassen.

Die verschiedenen politischen Optionen schließen sich aus Sicht der Kommission nicht gegenseitig aus, sodass diese nicht nur alternativ, sondern auch kumulativ als Regelungsoptionen in Betracht kommen könnten.[916]

II. Berücksichtigung der Untersuchungsergebnisse bei der Ausgestaltung des neuen Rechtsaktes

1. Transparenz

Die Digitalisierung der Medien und „insbesondere die Netz- und Plattformökonomie des Internet einschließlich der sozialen Netzwerke" be-

---

[916] Zwischenzeitlich hat die Europäische Kommission am 15. Dezember 2020 ihre Legislativvorschläge vorgelegt, https://eur-lex.europa.eu/legal-content/DE/TXT/?uri=CELEX%3A52020PC0825&qid=1614597643982, https://eur-lex.europa.eu/legal-content/DE/TXT/?uri=COM%3A2020%3A842%3AFIN. Für eine erste Diskussion s. *Ukrow*, Die Vorschläge der EU-Kommission für einen Digital Services Act und einen Digital Markets Act, und detailliert *Cole/Etteldorf/Ullrich*, Updating the Rules for Online Content Dissemination.

günstigen, wie das BVerfG in seinem *Rundfunkbeitrags-Urteil* betont hat, Konzentrations- und Monopolisierungstendenzen bei „Anbietern, Verbreitern und Vermittlern von Inhalten".[917] Damit erweitert das BVerfG selbst den Kreis der für eine positive Rundfunkordnung bedeutenden Medienakteure über die traditionellen Adressaten, die Rundfunkveranstalter, deutlich hinaus. Dieser Erweiterung kommt zwar keine unmittelbare unionsrechtliche Bedeutung zu. Mit Blick auf ein *level playing field* an der Schnittstelle von grundfreiheitlicher und wettbewerbsrechtlicher Regulierung seitens der EU, fortdauernder mitgliedstaatlicher Prärogative und Letztverantwortung für die Achtung des Pluralismusgebotes in den Medienordnungen ist diese Bestandsaufnahme allerdings auch nicht unionsrechtlich irrelevant. Dies gilt mit Blick auf die Doppelnatur von Medieninhalten als Kultur- wie Wirtschaftsgut auch für den Hinweis des BVerfG in dieser Entscheidung auf „die Gefahr, dass – auch mit Hilfe von Algorithmen – Inhalte gezielt auf Interessen und Neigungen der Nutzerinnen und Nutzer zugeschnitten werden, was wiederum zur Verstärkung gleichgerichteter Meinungen führt".[918] Solche Angebote seien nicht auf Meinungsvielfalt gerichtet, sondern würden durch einseitige Interessen oder die wirtschaftliche Rationalität eines Geschäftsmodells bestimmt, nämlich die Verweildauer der Nutzer auf den Seiten möglichst zu maximieren und dadurch den Werbewert der Plattform für die Kunden zu erhöhen. Insoweit seien auch Ergebnisse in Suchmaschinen vorgefiltert und teils werbefinanziert, teils von „Klickzahlen" abhängig. Algorithmischen Prozessen kommt insoweit erkennbar auch Bedeutung im medienwirtschaftlichen Ökosystem zu.

Die Rahmenbedingungen solcher algorithmengestützter Aggregations-, Auswahl- und Empfehlungsprozesse transparent zu machen ist ein in der Linie dieser Erweiterung des Anwendungsbereichs auf die wirtschaftliche Dimension von medienbezogenen Geschäftsmodellen zumindest naheliegende, wenn nicht im Interesse der Kohärenz von mit Transparenzpflichten verbundenen Grundfreiheitsbeschränkungen gebotene gesetzgeberische Reaktion.[919]

Unionsrechtlich unter ökonomischem Blickwinkel auferlegte Offenlegungspflichten in Bezug auf algorithmengestützte Aggregations-, Auswahl- und Empfehlungsprozesse können dabei einen wesentlichen Beitrag dazu liefern, neuen Unsicherheiten hinsichtlich Glaubwürdigkeit von Quellen

---

917 BVerfG, Urteil vom 18.07.2018, 1 BvR 1675/16, Rn. 79.
918 BVerfG, Urteil vom 18.07.2018, 1 BvR 1675/16, Rn. 79.
919 Vgl. zur Bedeutung von Transparenz auch *O'Neil*, Angriff der Algorithmen, S. 288 f.; *Schallbruch*, Schwacher Staat im Netz, S. 22; *Ukrow*, Algorithmen, APIs und Aufsicht, S. 8 f.

und Wertungen entgegenzuwirken. Sie entlasten den einzelnen Nutzer bei der Verarbeitung und massenmedialen Bewertung, die er aus Sicht des BVerfG[920] übernehmen muss, nachdem herkömmliche Filter professioneller Selektionen durch die Digitalisierung der Medien an Bedeutung eingebüßt haben.[921]

Schon das geltende unionale Medienrecht weist Anknüpfungspunkte auf, die mit Blick auf Gefährdungslagen durch unzureichende Transparenz des Handelns von neuen medien(verfassungs-)rechtlich relevanten Akteuren wie Anbieter von Medienplattformen, Benutzeroberflächen, Medienintermediären und Sprachassistenten ggf. aktiviert werden können. Denn im Rundfunkstaatsvertrag sind bereits Transparenzpflichten zumindest auch für private Medienakteure niedergelegt. Beachtung verdienen insoweit insbesondere Informationspflichten zur Identifizierung von Medienakteuren und Regelungen des Rechts kommerzieller Kommunikation. Die betreffenden Pflichten sind in der aktuellen Formulierung allerdings nicht geeignet, unmittelbar auf Herstellung von Transparenz ihres Handelns gerichtete Aufsichtshandlungen gegenüber den genannten neuen Medienakteuren auszulösen: Ein allgemeines, auch neue Akteure umfassendes Transparenzgebot für alle an der medialen Wertschöpfungskette Beteiligte lässt sich dem aktuellen medienrechtlichen Normenmaterial schon mit Blick auf die Grenzen, die einer erweiternden Auslegung sekundären Unionsrechts letztlich durch das Prinzip der begrenzten Ermächtigung gesetzt sind, nicht entnehmen. Auch aus verfassungsrechtlichen Erwägungen[922] lässt sich eine solche operationalisierbare Transparenzpflicht nicht ableiten: Auch aus dem unionalen Verfassungsrecht lässt sich allenfalls die Pflicht zur Transparenz, nicht deren Ausformung im Einzelnen ableiten. Eine sinngemäße Erweiterung der entsprechenden Tatbestände würde mit Blick auf das gleiche Regelungsziel jedoch möglich sein.[923]

Wenn einem digitalen Dienst seitens eines Nutzers eine Mitteilung gemacht wird, in der dieser um die Entfernung oder Sperrung des Zugangs zu illegalen Online-Inhalten illegale Online-Inhalte (z.B. illegale Aufstachelung zu Gewalt, Hass oder Diskriminierung aus irgendwelchen geschützten Gründen wie Rasse, ethnische Zugehörigkeit, Geschlecht oder sexuelle Orientierung; Material über sexuellen Kindesmissbrauch; terroristische Propaganda; Verleumdung; Inhalte, die geistige Eigentumsrechte

---

920 BVerfG, Urteil vom 18.07.2018, 1 BvR 1675/16, Rn. 80.
921 Vgl. *Ukrow*, Algorithmen, APIs und Aufsicht, S. 9.
922 Vgl. hierzu z.B. *Bröhmer*, Transparenz als Verfassungsprinzip.
923 Vgl. im Einzelnen bereits *Ukrow/Cole*, Zur Transparenz von Mediaagenturen, S. 46 ff.

verletzen, Verstöße gegen das Verbraucherrecht) gebeten wird, entspricht es dem Transparenzgedanken, dass der Nutzer über im Ergebnis dieser Mitteilung getätigte Maßnahme informiert wird.

Solche Transparenzerfordernisse sind im Binnenmarkt der EU ein vertrautes Phänomen; durchgreifende unionsrechtliche Bedenken dagegen, die Transparenzerfordernisse über die bisherigen Informationspflichten hinaus auch auf den Umgang mit Mitteilungen zu illegalen Online-Inhalten auszudehnen, sind dem Grunde nach nicht erkennbar. Sie können zwar bei oberflächlicher Betrachtung nur schwerlich als zur Verwirklichung des Binnenmarktes i.S. des Art. 26 Abs. 1 AEUV (und damit etwa durch Nutzung der Rechtsgrundlage aus Art. 114 AEUV) geboten eingestuft werden. Indessen würden die auf den Umgang mit Mitteilungen bezogenen Informationspflichten diese Einordnung mit den nach Art. 5 der novellierten AVMD-Richtlinie gebotenen Informationen teilen. Stärker noch als bei den Informationspflichten i.S. des Art. 5 AVMD-Richtlinie könnte bei Informationspflichten in Bezug auf den Umgang mit illegalen Online-Inhalten allerdings gelten, dass sie das System einer dezentralen Kontrolle der Anwendung des Unionsrechts stützen.

Zu den Informationspflichten nach Art. 5 der novellierten AVMD-Richtlinie wird im 15. Erwägungsgrund der Richtlinie (EU) 2018/1808 ausgeführt:

„Transparenz in Bezug auf die Eigentumsverhältnisse im Medienbereich steht in unmittelbarem Zusammenhang mit der Meinungsfreiheit, einem Eckpfeiler demokratischer Systeme. Informationen über die Eigentümerstruktur von Mediendiensteanbietern ermöglichen es Nutzern in Fällen, in denen die Eigentumsverhältnisse zu einer Kontrolle über die Inhalte der angebotenen Dienste oder zur Ausübung eines erheblichen Einflusses auf diese führen, sich ein fundiertes Urteil über die Inhalte zu bilden. Die Mitgliedstaaten sollten in der Lage sein zu bestimmen, ob und inwieweit Angaben zu den Eigentumsverhältnissen eines Mediendiensteanbieters für die Nutzer zugänglich sein sollten, sofern der Wesensgehalt der betreffenden Grundrechte und -freiheiten gewahrt wird und diese Maßnahmen notwendig und verhältnismäßig sind."

Auch auf den Umgang mit Mitteilungen zu illegalen Online-Inhalten bezogene Informationspflichten müssten selbstverständlich die Freiheit der Medien nach Art. 11 Abs. 2 GRC wahren und zudem in ihrer Ausformung verhältnismäßig sein.

Transparenzaspekte könnten zudem auch im Zusammenhang mit der Funktionsweise von Empfehlungssystemen über die bisherigen Vorgaben der P2B-Verordnung hinaus auch mit Blick auf sonstige Medienintermediäre rechtsharmonisierend fruchtbar gemacht werden. Denn die auffindbaren Informationen über die Funktionsweise der Empfehlungssysteme auf den unterschiedlichen Plattformen sind aktuell sehr unterschiedlich ausgestaltet. Teilweise finden sich diesbezüglich bereits Regelungen wie z.B. in § 93 MStV,[924] in der weit überwiegenden Mehrzahl der Mitgliedstaaten sind sie dagegen bislang nicht etabliert. Mit Blick auf die Doppelnatur von Rundfunk und vergleichbaren Telemedien als Kultur- wie als Wirtschaftsgut hat eine Möglichkeit zur Diskriminierung von Angeboten unmittelbare Binnenmarkt- und Wettbewerbsrelevanz. Insoweit sind Anknüpfungspunkte für eine Regulierung seitens der EU im Kern erkennbar. Allerdings ist derzeit nicht absehbar, dass eine Diskriminierung nach Kriterien erfolgt, die mit dem Integrationsprogramm der EU unvereinbar sind. Eine Gewichtung bei der Auffindbarkeit z.B. nach Sprache des Angebotes bleibt ungeachtet von Bemühungen um die Förderung einer europäischen Öffentlichkeit ein zulässiges Kriterium der Unterscheidung zumindest durch Intermediäre privater Provenienz.

Korrekturbedürftige Transparenzdefizite, die den *effet utile* der bisherigen Informationspflichten in Frage stellen, bestehen im Übrigen nicht zuletzt auch bei der Ermittlung von Verantwortlichen für illegale Online-Inhalte. Registrare verweisen insoweit oftmals auf tatsächliche oder vermeintliche Grenzen, die durch die Datenschutz-Grundverordnung gesetzt sind oder zu sein scheinen. Hinzu kommt, dass die Registrare bislang u.a. in Deutschland nicht verpflichtet sind, angegebene Daten zu verifizieren. Fantasienamen und -anschriften sind Ergebnis dieses sanktionslosen Fehlverhaltens, das die Schutzziele der Informationspflichten nach der AVMD-Richtlinie und ECRL leerlaufen lassen kann. Eine Nachsteuerung bei der Ausgestaltung des Regimes für Informationspflichten, in deren Ergebnis Regulierungsbehörden den Inhalteanbieter zuverlässig identifizieren können, könnte diese Lücke einer effektiven Aufsichtsmöglichkeit zur Einhaltung von EU-Recht durch die jeweils Verantwortlichen schließen.

---

924 Der Medienstaatsvertrag sieht in § 93 vor, dass Anbieter von Medienintermediären zur Sicherung der Meinungsvielfalt die nachfolgenden Informationen leicht wahrnehmbar, unmittelbar erreichbar und ständig verfügbar machen sollen: (1.) Die Kriterien, die über den Zugang eines Inhalts zu einem Medienintermediär und über den Verbleib entscheiden; (2.) die zentralen Kriterien einer Aggregation, Selektion und Präsentation von Inhalten und ihre Gewichtung einschließlich Informationen über die Funktionsweise der eingesetzten Algorithmen in verständlicher Sprache. Anbieter von Medienintermediären, die eine thematische Spezialisierung aufweisen, sind dazu verpflichtet, diese Spezialisierung durch die Gestaltung ihres Angebots wahrnehmbar zu machen.

2. Zum Kriterium der Illegalität des Inhaltes

Als problematisch erweist sich bei dem Bemühen, im Rahmen des *Digital Services Act* Minderjährige angemessen vor schädigenden Verhaltensweisen wie z.B. *Cybergrooming* oder *Bullying* oder entwicklungsbeeinträchtigenden Inhalten zu schützen, bereits die Unterscheidung zwischen illegalen (engl. *illegal*) Inhalten und schädlichen (engl. *harmful*) Inhalten, deren Definition sich teilweise auf europäischer und nationaler Ebene unterscheidet. Während die Europäische Kommission unter „illegalen Inhalten" augenscheinlich Inhalte versteht, die einen strafrechtlichen Bezug aufweisen, bezeichnet z.B. in Deutschland ein „illegaler Inhalt" einen Inhalt, der einer Verbotsnorm widerspricht – eine Verbotsnorm muss aber nicht unbedingt strafrechtlich sanktioniert sein, sondern kann auch in Form von Verwaltungsverfahren/Ordnungswidrigkeitsverfahren belangt werden.[925]

Der sehr wichtige Bereich des Schutzes vor entwicklungsbeeinträchtigenden Angeboten droht damit in eine europarechtliche Grauzone geringerer Schutzintensität zu fallen. Denn oftmals umfassen unional anerkannte Ausnahmevorschriften lediglich strafrechtliche Verfahren und damit nicht den für den effektiven Jugendmedienschutz notwendigen Bereich der Verwaltungsverfahren/Ordnungswidrigkeitsverfahren. Dies erschwert insbesondere im Online-Bereich die Durchsetzung der Regelungen erheblich. Eine zumindest klarstellende Anpassung des Verständnisses des Begriffes „illegal" i.S. einer Umfassung auch von verwaltungsrechtlichen Verboten wäre insoweit mit Blick auf die fortdauernd vorgesehene Schutzperspektive in Bezug auf (nicht zuletzt minderjährige) Nutzer von Diensten der Informationsgesellschaft bei der Gestaltung des vorgeschlagenen *Digital Services Act* hilfreich.

---

[925] So haben z.B. Anbieter von Angeboten, die geeignet sind, die Entwicklung von Kindern oder Jugendlichen zu einer eigenverantwortlichen und gemeinschaftsfähigen Persönlichkeit zu beeinträchtigen, nach § 5 JMStV über technische oder zeitliche Instrumente dafür Sorge zu tragen, dass Kinder oder Jugendliche diese üblicherweise nicht wahrnehmen. Ist ein solches Instrument nicht vorhanden, ist das Angebot nach deutschem Verständnis illegal, da es einer Verbotsnorm des JMStV widerspricht. Nach Verständnis des EU-Rechts hingegen wäre das Angebot lediglich schädlich, da der Verstoß nicht strafrechtlich sanktioniert ist.

3. Medienregulierung für Dienste der Informationsgesellschaft und neue Medienakteure mittels Selbst-, Ko- und kooperativer Regulierung

Nach Art. 4a Absatz 1 Satz 1 der novellierten AVMD-Richtlinie „unterstützen (die Mitgliedstaaten) die Nutzung der Koregulierung und die Förderung der Selbstregulierung mithilfe von Verhaltenskodizes, die auf nationaler Ebene in den von dieser Richtlinie koordinierten Bereichen angenommen werden, soweit das nach ihrem jeweiligen Rechtssystem zulässig ist."
Es liegt mit Blick auf einen möglichst großen Gleichklang grundlegender Strukturprinzipien von AVMD-Richtlinie und ECRL, zu denen bereits derzeit der Grundsatz der grenzüberschreitenden Angebotsfreiheit und das Prinzip der Herkunftslandkontrolle ebenso zählen wie Transparenzgebote in Bezug auf anbieterbezogene Informationspflichten, nahe, auch die Regulierungskonzeption der beiden Regelwerke zu parallelisieren. Damit würde auch den Grundsätzen der Subsidiarität und der Verhältnismäßigkeit regulierungstechnisch Rechnung getragen.[926] Zudem würden die Überlegungen in der Mitteilung der Kommission „Bessere Ergebnisse durch bessere Rechtsetzung – Eine Agenda der EU" fruchtbar gemacht. In dieser Mitteilung betonte die Kommission, dass sie bei der Prüfung von Lösungsansätzen für eine bessere Rechtsetzung gesetzgeberische wie auch nicht-gesetzgeberische Möglichkeiten, die den Grundsätzen für eine bessere Selbst- und Koregulierung entsprechen, in Betracht ziehen würde. Aufbauend auf diesen Überlegungen liegt es im Übrigen, der Konvergenz im Mediensektor entsprechend, nahe, über den vorgeschlagenen *Digital Services Act* das Ziel eines möglichst großen Gleichklangs grundlegender Strukturprinzipien nicht nur für Dienste der Informationsgesellschaft, sondern auch für neue Medienakteure wie z.B. Medienintermediäre vorzusehen.
In den Erwägungsgründen 12 bis 14 der novellierten AVMD-Richtlinie wurde im Blick auf die Regelung von Selbst- und Koregulierung in Art. 4a dieser Richtlinie ausgeführt:

„Mehrere Verhaltenskodizes, die in den von der Richtlinie 2010/13/EU koordinierten Bereichen aufgestellt wurden, haben sich nach den Grundsätzen für eine bessere Selbst- und Koregulierung als gut konzipiert bewährt. Das Bestehen eines gesetzgeberischen Auffangmechanismus wurde als wichtiger

---

[926] Vgl. zum Konnex zwischen Selbst- und Koregulierung zu diesen Grundsätzen als Kompetenzausübungsregelungen Art. 4a Abs. 2 Unterabs. 2 der AVMD-Richtlinie.

Erfolgsfaktor bei der Förderung der Einhaltung von Selbst- oder Koregulierungskodizes angesehen. Genauso wichtig ist, dass solche Kodizes konkrete Zielvorgaben und Zielsetzungen enthalten, die eine regelmäßige, transparente und unabhängige Überwachung und Bewertung ihrer Zielerfüllung ermöglichen. In den Verhaltenskodizes sollte auch die wirksame Durchsetzung geregelt werden. Die Selbst- und Koregulierungskodizes, die in den von der Richtlinie 2010/13/EU koordinierten Bereichen angenommen werden, sollten diesen Grundsätzen folgen.

Die Erfahrung hat gezeigt, dass sowohl Selbst- als auch Koregulierungsinstrumente, die im Einklang mit den unterschiedlichen Rechtstraditionen der Mitgliedstaaten angewandt werden, bei der Gewährleistung eines hohen Verbraucherschutzniveaus eine wichtige Rolle spielen können. Die Maßnahmen zur Verwirklichung der Ziele von öffentlichem Interesse im Bereich der neuen audiovisuellen Mediendienste sind wirksamer, wenn sie mit der aktiven Unterstützung der Diensteanbieter selbst ergriffen werden.

Die Selbstregulierung stellt eine Art freiwillige Initiative dar, die Wirtschaftsteilnehmern, Sozialpartnern, Nichtregierungsorganisationen und Vereinigungen die Möglichkeit gibt, untereinander und füreinander gemeinsame Leitlinien festzulegen. Sie sind für die Ausarbeitung, Überwachung und Durchsetzung der Einhaltung dieser Leitlinien selbst zuständig. Die Mitgliedstaaten sollten im Einklang mit ihren unterschiedlichen Rechtstraditionen die Rolle, die eine wirksame Selbstregulierung als Ergänzung zu den bestehenden Gesetzgebungs-, Gerichts- und Verwaltungsverfahren spielen kann, sowie ihren wertvollen Beitrag zur Verwirklichung der Ziele der Richtlinie 2010/13/EU anerkennen. Die Selbstregulierung sollte jedoch, obwohl sie eine ergänzende Methode zur Umsetzung bestimmter Vorschriften der Richtlinie 2010/13/EU sein kann, die Verpflichtung des nationalen Gesetzgebers nicht ersetzen. In ihrer Minimalform schafft Koregulierung im Einklang mit den Rechtstraditionen der Mitgliedstaaten eine rechtliche Verbindung zwischen Selbstregulierung und dem nationalen Gesetzgeber. Bei der Koregulierung teilen sich die Interessenträger und die Regierung oder die nationalen Regulierungsbehörden oder -stellen die Regulierungsfunktion. Zu den Aufgaben der einschlägigen öffentlichen Behörden zählen die Anerkennung des Koregulierungsprogramms, die Prüfung seiner Verfahren und die Finanzierung des Programms. Bei der Koregulierung sollten weiterhin staatliche Eingriffsmöglichkeiten für den Fall vorgesehen werden, dass ihre Ziele nicht erreicht werden. Unbeschadet der förmlichen Verpflichtungen der Mitgliedstaaten bezüglich der Umsetzung fördert die Richtlinie 2010/13/EU die Nutzung der Selbst-und Koregulierung. Dadurch werden weder die Mitgliedstaaten zur Festlegung von Regelungen zur Selbst-oder Koregulierung verpflichtet, noch werden gegenwärtige Koregulierungsinitiativen, die in den

F. Der vorgeschlagene Digital Services Act

Mitgliedstaaten bereits bestehen und effektiv funktionieren, beeinträchtigt oder gefährdet."

Diese Erwägungen, namentlich auch definitorischer Art sowie zu Chancen dieser Regulierungsinstrumente für eine effektive Erreichung von Schutzgütern wie den Verbraucherschutz und zu Vorgaben an die Ausgestaltung der Instrumente könnten *mutatis mutandis* auch bei einer Änderung und Ergänzung der ECRL im Rahmen des vorgeschlagenen *Digital Services Act* fruchtbar gemacht werden.[927]

Auch Maßnahmen zur Erreichung der im öffentlichen Interesse liegenden Ziele des vorgeschlagenen *Digital Services Act* namentlich im Bereich neuer Medienakteure dürften sich als wirksamer erweisen, wenn sie mit der aktiven Unterstützung der betroffenen Anbieter selbst ergriffen werden. Die Selbstregulierung sollte jedoch, obwohl sie eine ergänzende Methode zur Durchführung bestimmter Vorschriften einer novellierten und ergänzten ECRL sein könnte, die Verpflichtung der Mitgliedstaaten zur Umsetzung nicht zuletzt auch einer (zumindest mittelbar den Medienpluralismus sichernden) Regulierung zu Fragen der Auffindbarkeit durch diese EU-Regulierung nicht vollständig ersetzen. Dem entspricht es, den Mechanismen im MStV wie JMStV und NetzDG folgend, in einem System regulierter Selbstregulierung, das auch als System der Koregulierung bezeichnet wird, weiterhin staatliche Eingriffsmöglichkeiten für den Fall vorzusehen, dass die Ziele der Regulierung über Selbstregulierung allein nicht erreicht zu werden versprechen.

Bei der Koregulierung teilen sich, wie auch in der jüngsten Novelle der AVMD-Richtlinie betont wird,[928] die Interessenträger und die staatlichen Organe oder die nationalen Regulierungsstellen die Regulierungsfunktion. Zu den Aufgaben der einschlägigen öffentlichen Behörden zählen die An-

---

[927] Auch in Bezug auf Dienste der Informationsgesellschaft und Medienintermediäre müssten danach die Kodizes – in Entsprechung zu Art. 4a Abs. 1 Satz 2 der novellierten AVMD-Richtlinie – „a) derart gestaltet sein, dass sie von den Hauptbeteiligten in den betreffenden Mitgliedstaaten allgemein anerkannt werden, b) ihre Ziele klar und unmissverständlich darlegen, c) eine regelmäßige, transparente und unabhängige Überwachung und Bewertung ihrer Zielerfüllung vorsehen und d) eine wirksame Durchsetzung einschließlich wirksamer und verhältnismäßiger Sanktionen vorsehen".

[928] Vgl. den 14. Erwägungsgrund der Richtlinie (EU) 2018/1808 vom 14. November 2018 zur Änderung der Richtlinie 2010/13/EU zur Koordinierung bestimmter Rechts- und Verwaltungsvorschriften der Mitgliedstaaten über die Bereitstellung audiovisueller Mediendienste (Richtlinie über audiovisuelle Mediendienste) im Hinblick auf sich verändernde Marktgegebenheiten.

erkennung des Koregulierungsprogramms, die Prüfung seiner Verfahren und die Finanzierung des Programms. Bei der Koregulierung sollten weiterhin staatliche Eingriffsmöglichkeiten für den Fall vorgesehen werden, dass ihre Ziele nicht erreicht werden.

Für eine Einbeziehung des Ansatzes regulierter Selbstregulierung in das Gefüge des vorgeschlagenen *Digital Services Act*[929] sprechen neben den positiven Erfahrungen, die mit diesem Konzept bereits beim in gleicher Weise wie die Vielfaltssicherung als verfassungsrechtliches Schutzgut anerkannten Jugendschutzes in den Medien gewonnen wurden, ebenso die Grenzen, die generell ausschließlich traditionell hoheitlicher Regulierung unter den Bedingungen von Digitalisierung und Globalisierung gesetzt sind:[930]

- Ein solches traditionelles Regulierungskonzept kann die Interessen der Steuerungsobjekte nur sehr bedingt (namentlich durch die Lobbyarbeit während des Rechtsetzungsprozesses) aufnehmen und daher weniger Kooperations- als Widerstandswillen unter Ausschöpfung der Möglichkeiten des Rechts- und Rechtswegestaates befördern.
- Es zeigt sich ein zunehmendes Wissensdefizit (nicht nur) beim steuernden Hoheitsträger (ob EU oder Staat); selbst Forschungsergebnisse stehen nur begrenzt als Ressource für die Entwicklung einer hinreichend dem Prophylaxe-Gedanken zur Abwehr von Gefährdungslagen für die Vielfalt zur Verfügung; zudem ist solche Beforschung in besonderer Weise auf den Kooperationswillen beforschter Medienakteure angewiesen.
- In den modernen Informations- und Kommunikationsgesellschaften haben sich Meta-Daten über die Gewinnung, Verarbeitung und personalisierte Aufbereitung von Informationen zum wichtigen, oligopolistisch oder gar monopolistisch beherrschten „knappen Gut" entwickelt; diese Meta-Daten werden daher voraussichtlich immer stärker auch zu einer entscheidenden „Steuerungsressource" werden, über die EU wie Mitgliedstaaten nicht – auch wenn im konkreten Fall kein Wissensdefizit besteht – wie bei der Ressource „Macht" privilegiert verfügen, sondern bei der ihnen neue Machtträger gegenüberstehen.

---

929 Vgl. hierzu im Ansatz auch *Russ-Mohl*, Die informierte Gesellschaft und ihre Feinde: Warum die Digitalisierung unsere Demokratie gefährdet, S. 269 ff.
930 Vgl. zum Folgenden im Ansatz bereits *Schulz/Held*, Regulierte Selbstregulierung als Form modernen Regierens, S. A-8; *Ukrow*, Die Selbstkontrolle im Medienbereich in Europa, S. 10 ff.

- Globalisierung erhöht nicht mehr nur wie zu Beginn der rechtsdogmatischen Einordnungen neuer Regulierungssysteme die Möglichkeiten des so genannten „Forum-Shopping", um nationalen Regulierungen auszuweichen; inzwischen hat die Globalisierung vielmehr dazu geführt, dass der nationale Rechtsraum sämtlicher Staaten der EU als territorialer Anknüpfungspunkt demokratischer Souveränität im Blick auf das Angebot von Medienplattformen, Benutzeroberflächen, Sprachassistenten und Medienintermediäre durch Akteure beherrscht wird, deren Geschäftspolitik unternehmensrechtlich außerhalb der EU bestimmt wird.
- Eigeninitiative, Innovation und Verantwortungsbewusstsein kann nicht gesetzlich erzwungen werden.
- Zudem setzt traditionelle hoheitlich-imperative Steuerung typischerweise punktuell, nicht prozessorientiert an, wie es zur Steuerung bei komplexen regulatorischen Aufgaben, zu denen nicht zuletzt auch die Kontrolle des Einflusses algorithmengestützter Systeme auf die individuelle und öffentliche Meinungs- und Willensbildung zählt, sachangemessen wäre.[931]

Mit Blick auf etwaige auf den demokratischen Prozess bezogene Elemente des *Digital Services Act* verdient im Blick auf Selbstregulierungsansätze besondere Beachtung, dass sich – jenseits der strafrechtlichen Relevanz von Inhalten – unabhängige Überprüfungen von Fakten (sog. Fact Checking) weiterhin als effektiver Weg erweisen könnten, um Falschmeldungen zu identifizieren und darauf gestützte Desinformationskampagnen in ihrer Wirkung zu hemmen.[932] Darüber hinaus ist das Engagement einzelner Medienintermediäre, wie z. B. von Google und Facebook, zu erwähnen,

---

931 Vgl. *Ukrow*, Algorithmen, APIs und Aufsicht. Überlegungen zur organisations- und verfahrensrechtlichen Effektuierung einer positiven Ordnung der Vielfaltssicherung im digitalen Raum – und ein Regelungsvorschlag 2019, S. 16 f.
932 Bisher durchgeführte Studien zeichnen ein gemischtes Bild in Bezug auf die konkrete Wirksamkeit von Faktenprüfern (vor allem im Bereich politischer Informationen). Dabei ist auch und vor allem der Faktor relevant, dass die Rezipienten im digitalen Umfeld die von Faktencheckern korrigierenden Informationen aktiv auswählen oder vermeiden können. Der Beitrag des Fact Checking zur Bekämpfung von Desinformationskampagnen ist aber zumindest nicht insgesamt von der Hand zu weisen. Vgl. für einen Überblick zu Studien sowie für eine Einordnung insbesondere *Hameleers/van der Meer* in: Communication Research 2019–2, 227, 227 ff.; sowie *Barrera Rodriguez/Guriev/Henry/Zhuravskaya* in: Journal of Public Economics 2020, 104, 104 ff.

die gesicherte Informationen hervorheben und ständig verfügbar im News Feed z.B. zum Thema COVID-19 platzieren.

Während sich dies als Signal für eine Stärkung der Selbstregulierung erweist, gibt es anderseits auch gegenläufige Erfahrungswerte: So enthalten die Self-Assessment Reports (SAR) der Plattformen im Rahmen des Aktionsplans zur Bekämpfung von Desinformation der Europäischen Union Informationen zur Umsetzung der Verpflichtungen des Code of Practice against Disinformation.[933] Einer der größten Kritikpunkte an den SAR ist, dass sich die enthaltenen Daten und Informationen nur auf die europäische Ebene beziehen und nicht auf die einzelnen Mitgliedstaaten heruntergebrochen sind. Damit waren die SAR nicht ausreichend, um eine aussagekräftige und valide Analyse der Einhaltung der Verpflichtungen durchzuführen.

Im Übrigen können i.S. eines kooperativen Regulierungsansatzes auch Projekte, die – insbesondere bei der Meldung i.w.S. illegaler Online-Inhalte – auf eine verstärkte Zusammenarbeit zwischen Strafverfolgungsbehörden, Medienregulierern und Medienplayern setzen, dazu beitragen, die Verbreitung illegaler Inhalte im Online-Bereich konsequent zu bekämpfen[934], was einer der Zwecke des *Digital Services Act* werden könnte.

4. Regulierung nicht der EU zugehöriger Anbieter von Medieninhalten

Im Rahmen ihrer Aufsichtstätigkeit identifizieren Regulierungsbehörden der EU zunehmend illegale Inhalte, die aus Drittstaaten stammen, aber auf den jeweiligen mitgliedstaatlichen Markt der Regulierungsbehörde ausgerichtet sind. Dies gilt nicht zuletzt auch für die deutschen Landesmedienanstalten.

Bei Angeboten aus dem Nicht-EU-Ausland wenden die Medienanstalten derzeit ein ähnliches Verfahren wie bei EU-Angeboten nach Art. 3 AVMD-

---

933 Hierzu eingehend bereits oben, Abschnitt D.IV.3.
934 Beispielhaft kann insoweit – ohne chronologische Reihenfolge des Entstehens – auf die Projekte des Landesmedienzentrums Baden-Württemberg (https://www.lmz-bw.de/landesmedienzentrum/programme/respektbw/), der Bayerischen Landeszentrale für neue Medien (https://www.blm.de/konsequent-gegen-hass.cfm), der Landesanstalt für Medien NRW (https://www.medienanstalt-nrw.de/themen/hass/verfolgen-statt-nur-loeschen-rechtsdurchsetzung-im-netz.html) sowie der Landeszentrale für Medien und Kommunikation Rheinland-Pfalz (https://medienanstalt-rlp.de/medienregulierung/aufsicht/verfolgen-und-loeschen/) hingewiesen werden.

Richtlinie rsp. Art. 3 ECRL an. Auch wenn ein solches Verfahren nicht gesetzlich vorgeschrieben ist, wird im ersten Schritt die nationale Regulierungsbehörde des Herkunftslands zu dem Sachverhalt konsultiert.

Die zuständigen Behörden im Herkunftsstaat werden über das Angebot und die festgestellten Verstöße informiert und um Maßnahmen gebeten. Dies gilt sowohl für die Herkunftsländer von Inhalteanbietern als auch von Host-Providern. Schließt das Herkunftsland ein Eingreifen aus, erweist sich die Reaktion als unangemessen lang oder mit Blick auf das geschützte Rechtsgut als unzureichend, werden eigene Maßnahmen nach Anhörung des Anbieters ergriffen.[935]

Ziel des vorgeschlagenen *Digital Services Act* könnte es vor diesem Hintergrund auch sein mitgliedstaatliche Vorkehrungen einzufordern oder zu fördern, damit Unternehmen aus Drittstaaten nicht zu einfach durch Zuordnung zur Rechtshoheit eines Mitgliedstaates in den Genuss des Herkunftslandprinzips des EU-Binnenmarkts und des Haftungsprivilegs der ECRL gelangen, deren Geltung im EU-Binnenmarkt an die Einhaltung von gewissen Mindeststandards zum Schutz von Gemeinwohlinteressen gekoppelt ist. An solchen Mindeststandards fehlt es im Verhältnis zu Dienstleistern mit Sitz außerhalb der EU. Um ein unkoordiniertes regulatorisches Vorgehen gegen Unternehmen aus Drittstaaten zu vermeiden, erscheinen zudem unionale Vorgaben zu nachhaltigen und wirksamen Abreden zum Vorgehen gegen Unternehmen aus Nicht-EU-Drittstaaten zwischen den nationalen Regulierungsbehörden im Rahmen ihrer jeweiligen europäischen Gruppen (vor allem ERGA und GEREK) zielführend.

Da in Bezug auf Inhalte aus Nicht-EU-Drittstaaten derzeit keine eindeutigen unionsrechtlichen Regelungen bestehen, sind die mitgliedstaatlichen Regulierungsbehörden in diesen Verfahren auf die Kooperation des Herkunftslandes und des Providers angewiesen. Andernfalls bleibt nur der Zugriff auf inländische Dritte wie z. B. Telekommunikationsanbieter oder Zahlungsdienstleister zur Eindämmung des Risikos.

---

935 Im Falle eines Angebots aus Israel, das auf den deutschen Markt ausgerichtet war, hat das zuständige Ministerium ein eigenes Eingreifen abgelehnt und sein Einverständnis mit Maßnahmen seitens der deutschen Medienregulierer erklärt. Nach Anhörung und Erlass eines Bescheids konnte aufgrund der Kooperation des Anbieters eine Anpassung des Angebots erreicht werden (https://www.medienanstalt-nrw.de/presse/pressemitteilungen/pressemitteilungen-2020/2020/april/coin-master-an-deutschen-jugendschutz-angepasst.html).

Der geplante neue Glücksspielstaatsvertrag[936] trägt diesem Manko in Bezug auf die Erreichung der in § 1 GlüStV definierten Schutzziele in der Aufsichtspraxis durch ein entsprechendes Verantwortlichkeitsregime Rechnung. § 9 des demnächst zur Unterzeichnung anstehenden Staatsvertrages regelt:

„(1) Die Glücksspielaufsicht hat die Aufgabe, die Erfüllung der nach diesem Staatsvertrag bestehenden oder auf Grund dieses Staatsvertrages begründeten öffentlich-rechtlichen Verpflichtungen zu überwachen sowie darauf hinzuwirken, dass unerlaubtes Glücksspiel und die Werbung hierfür unterbleiben. Die für alle Länder oder in dem jeweiligen Land zuständige Behörde des jeweiligen Landes kann die erforderlichen Anordnungen im Einzelfall erlassen. Sie kann unbeschadet sonstiger in diesem Staatsvertrag und anderen gesetzlichen Bestimmungen vorgesehener Maßnahmen insbesondere
1. jederzeit Auskunft und Vorlage aller Unterlagen, Daten und Nachweise verlangen, die zur Prüfung im Rahmen des Satzes 1 erforderlich sind, sowie zum Zwecke dieser Prüfung während der üblichen Geschäfts- und Arbeitszeiten die Geschäftsräume und -grundstücke betreten, in denen öffentliches Glücksspiel veranstaltet oder vermittelt wird,
2. Anforderungen an die Veranstaltung, Durchführung und Vermittlung öffentlicher Glücksspiele und die Werbung hierfür sowie an die Entwicklung und Umsetzung des Sozialkonzepts stellen,
3. die Veranstaltung, Durchführung und Vermittlung unerlaubter Glücksspiele und die Werbung hierfür untersagen,
4. den am Zahlungsverkehr Beteiligten, insbesondere den Kredit- und Finanzdienstleistungsinstituten, nach vorheriger Bekanntgabe unerlaubter Glücksspielangebote die Mitwirkung an Zahlungen für unerlaubtes Glücksspiel und an Auszahlungen aus unerlaubtem Glücksspiel untersagen, ohne dass es einer vorherigen Inanspruchnahme des Veranstalters oder Vermittlers von öffentlichen Glücksspielen durch die Glücksspielaufsicht bedarf; ... und
5. nach vorheriger Bekanntgabe unerlaubter Glücksspielangebote Maßnahmen zur Sperrung dieser Angebote gegen im Sinne der §§ 8 bis 10 des Telemediengesetzes verantwortliche Diensteanbieter, insbesondere Zugangsvermittler und Registrare, ergreifen, sofern sich Maßnahmen gegenüber einem Veranstalter oder Vermittler dieses Glücksspiels als nicht durchführbar oder nicht erfolgversprechend erweisen; diese Maß- nahmen können auch erfol-

---

936 Die der Europäischen Kommission übermittelte Entwurfsfassung des Staatsvertrages ist abrufbar über https://ec.europa.eu/growth/tools-databases/tris/de/index.cfm/search/?trisaction=search.detail&year=2020&num=304&mLang=.

gen, wenn das unerlaubte Glücksspielangebot untrennbar mit weiteren Inhalten verbunden ist. [...]"

Überzeugende Gründe, die gegen eine Modellhaftigkeit nicht zuletzt der Regelungen zum IP- und Payment-Blocking bei einer Fortentwicklung der AVMD-Richtlinie wie der ECRL im Interesse einer menschenwürde-, jugend- und verbraucherschützerischen Zielsetzung des vorgeschlagenen *Digital Services Act* sprechen, sind bei Wahrung des unionalen Grundrechtsschutzes in seiner materiell- wie verfahrensrechtlichen Bedeutung nicht ersichtlich.

5. Reform der Verantwortlichkeitsregulierung in Bezug auf Service-Provider

Die in der ECRL getroffene Kategorisierung von Providertypen spiegelt den heutigen Stand der Digitalisierung nicht mehr wider.[937] Die Kategorisierung der Dienste entstand zu einer Zeit, in der die auf dem Markt agierenden Dienste viel überschaubarer und klarer abgrenzbar waren. In der Zwischenzeit sind viele Hybridformen entstanden, die je nach Geschäftszweig ihres Unternehmens unterschiedlich einzustufen sind. Ebenso sind Geschäftsmodelle der Diensteanbieter deutlich vielschichtiger geworden, was eine klare Einordung auch bei einer Schwerpunktbetrachtung schwierig macht.

Auch die Erfahrung aus der Praxis zeigt, dass viele Diensteanbieter bspw. als Host-Provider und als Content-Provider auftreten, d.h. sie verwalten Inhalte Dritter und stellen gleichzeitig eigene Inhalte auf ihrer Plattform zur Verfügung. Aus Sicht der Medienregulierer ist aber schwer einzuordnen, um welche Art von Inhalt es sich im spezifischen Fall handelt, da die Dienste entweder nicht klar gekennzeichnet werden oder nicht unbedingt eindeutig als bestimmte Dienste einzuordnen sind.

Dieser Mehrfachcharakter von Plattformen spiegelt sich auch in den über die letzten Jahre entstandenen europäischen Rechtsakten wider: Jeder dieser Rechtsakte entwickelt seine eigenen Dienste-Definitionen und teilt ihnen neue Verantwortlichkeiten zu (bspw. AVMD-RL – VSP; Urheberrechts-RL – Diensteanbieter für das Teilen von Online-Inhalten; P2B-VO – Online-Vermittlungsdienste und Online-Suchmaschinen; TERREG-Entwurf – darin werden zwar Hostingdiensteanbieter adressiert, jedoch in

---

[937] Eingehend *Cole/Etteldorf/Ullrich*, Cross-border Dissemination of Online-Content, S. 91 ff.

einer neuen Art und Weise, da aktive Pflichten an sie herangetragen werden)[938].

Neben der Dienstedefinition erscheint auch das Dienste-Haftungsregime zunehmend defizitär – wenn auch nicht in seinem Ausgangspunkt: Bei Vorliegen illegaler Online-Inhalte legt die ECRL bislang ein prioritäres Vorgehen gegen den Anbieter bzw. redaktionell Verantwortlichen des unzulässigen oder schädlichen Inhalts nahe. Dieser Grundgedanke scheint auch bei der Entwicklung des *Digital Services Act* aus Gründen des Verhältnismäßigkeitsgrundsatzes erhaltenswert. Deshalb sollten sich Verpflichtungen für traditionelle Service-Provider wie auch für neue Medienakteure wie Medienintermediäre, Medienplattformen und Benutzeroberflächen im Wesentlichen auf Mitwirkungspflichten beschränken. Diese Akteure sollten ihrer Gesamtverantwortung für ein freies und rechtskonformes Internet gerecht werden, indem sie unabhängigen Aufsichtsbehörden ermöglichen, bei Bedarf gegen Inhalteanbieter vorzugehen. Konkret erfordert dies die Einräumung von Auskunftsansprüchen für Medienaufsichtsbehörden.

Dies alleine reicht jedoch nach den seit In-Kraft-Treten der ECRL gewonnenen Erfahrungswerten vielfach nicht aus, um Gemeinwohlinteressen, die auch unter dem Schutz der Grundrechte und Grundwerte der EU stehen, zu wahren. Im Blick auf solche Fehlentwicklungen liegt es nahe, auch eine verbindliche Mitverantwortung der Plattformen bei fehlenden Durchsetzungsmöglichkeiten gegen den redaktionell Verantwortlichen eines Medieninhaltes vorzusehen.

Ein zukünftiges Haftungsregime sollte eine Inanspruchnahme des Diensteanbieters durch die Medienaufsicht immer dann ermöglichen, wenn dieser nicht willens oder nicht in der Lage ist, Auskunft über die Identität des rechtsverletzenden Nutzers zu erteilen. Dieses Prinzip ist dem europäischen Rechtsgefüge nicht unbekannt; insoweit könnte der *Digital Services Act* an regulatorische Vorbilder des EU-Rechts anknüpfen.

Dabei ist erwägenswert, den Umfang der Haftung eines Diensteanbieters grundsätzlich am Grad der Anonymisierung, die er für seine Nutzer zulässt, auszurichten: Je stärker ein Dienst auf die Anonymität seiner Nutzer setzt, desto früher scheint es verantwortbar, ihn für Inhalte haften zu lassen, die er nicht selber geschaffen oder sich inhaltlich zu eigen gemacht hat.

Ansatzpunkt einer möglichen Haftung könnte die letzte identifizierbare Person oder Organisation sein. Der Diensteanbieter profitiert in diesem Fall nur dann vom Haftungsprivileg, wenn er als reiner Hoster von Inhal-

---

938 Vgl. hierzu bereits eingehend in Kapitel D.

ten verifizierter Teilnehmer fungiert. Lässt er eine Anonymisierung auf seiner Plattform zu, kann er sich nicht auf das Haftungsprivileg berufen und haftet für mögliche Rechtsgutsverletzungen. Eine Anonymisierung auf Plattformen bliebe also unter der Voraussetzung möglich, dass der Diensteanbieter zur Bekämpfung von Rechtsverletzungen herangezogen werden kann.

6. Organisationsrechtliche Optionen für eine verbesserte Durchsetzung von medienbezogenen Gemeinwohlinteressen

Die Zusammenarbeit der mitgliedstaatlichen im Bereich und mit Bezug zur Medienregulierung tätigen Aufsichtsbehörden und -einrichtungen ist von grundlegender Bedeutung für eine nachhaltige Rechtsdurchsetzung im Netz. Zumindest wenn es gelingt, die Zusammenarbeit der verschiedenen zuständigen Einrichtungen im Bereich der Medienaufsicht, Telekommunikationsaufsicht, Datenschutzaufsicht und Wettbewerbsaufsicht in ihrem jeweiligen europäischen Organisationsverbund (namentlich ERGA, GEREK und EDSA) zu intensivieren und aufgabengerecht auszugestalten, erscheint der Aufbau einer EU-weit tätigen einheitlichen Regulierungsbehörde primärrechtlich problembehaftet – nicht zuletzt mit Blick auf die organisationsrechtliche Prägekraft des Subsidiaritätsprinzips. Die Erfahrungen mit der ERGA und der GEREK legen den Schluss nahe, dass eine dezentrale Struktur im Medienbereich bzw. in Bereichen mit Medienbezug am besten geeignet ist, europäische Grundwerte in ihren jeweiligen nationalen Ausprägungen zu schützen und gleichzeitig eine angemessene Sicherung der Meinungs- und Informationsfreiheit zu gewährleisten.

Dabei gilt es im Ausgangspunkt auch für neuere Medien im Online-Bereich wie auch für neue Medienakteure wie Mediaagenturen und Medienintermediäre, soweit nicht deren ökonomisches Handeln, sondern deren vielfaltsrelevante Aktivitäten in Rede stehen, das in Art. 30 der AVMD-Richtlinie festgeschriebene Prinzip der Staatsferne der Medienaufsicht zu wahren und so die Meinungsfreiheit zu schützen. Eine Aufsicht über vielfaltsrelevante Vorgänge, um die es sich auch bei der Aggregation, Selektion und Präsentation von medialen Inhalten in neuer digitaler Form handelt, durch eine Behörde, und sei es eine der Europäischen Union, die nicht in gesellschaftlicher Rückkopplung, sondern staatlich oder supranational geprägt agiert, ist mit dem demokratischen Verständnis einer von staatlichen und Einflüssen von EU-Organen unabhängigen Medienlandschaft, wie es für die EU durch deren Grundrechtsgebundenheit vorgegeben ist, nicht vereinbar.

Auch soweit Art. 30 der AVMD-Richtlinie eine finanzielle und personelle Ausstattung von Regulierungsstellen fordert, die diesen die Möglichkeit eröffnet, ein möglichst ganzheitliches Regulierungskonzept zu verfolgen, kommt dieser organisationsrechtlichen Konzeption Vorbildfunktion auch für die Regulierung neuer vielfaltsrelevanter Medienakteure zu. Dies setzt nicht zuletzt auch die Einbindung von Expertise in den Bereichen der Plattformökonomie und der künstlichen Intelligenz, insbesondere auch mit Blick auf algorithmische Aspekte der Auffindbarkeitsregulierung, voraus.

Es bedarf außerdem verbesserter rechtsverbindlicher Grundlagen für eine wirksame grenzüberschreitende Zustellung und Vollstreckung von Bescheiden und Entscheidungen der Medienregulierungsbehörden. Die zugrundeliegenden Verfahren müssen klarer und einfacher sein als diejenigen in europäischen und internationalen Abkommen, die sich auf Zivil- und Handelsstreitigkeiten beschränken (z. B. Verordnung (EG) Nr. 1393/2007 über die Zustellung von Schriftstücken; Haager Übereinkommen über die Zustellung gerichtlicher und außergerichtlicher Schriftstücke; Europäisches Gerichtsstands- und Vollstreckungsübereinkommen). Medienaufsichtsbehörden benötigen zudem Rechtshilfefähigkeit, um in bestimmten internationalen Sachverhalten zu einer effizienteren Rechtsdurchsetzung zu gelangen.

G. Gesamtergebnis und politische Handlungsoptionen

Mark D. Cole / Jörg Ukrow

I. Inhaltliche Aspekte

Das Bestehen eines Spannungsverhältnisses zwischen der Ebene der EU und derjenigen ihrer Mitgliedstaaten bei der Wahrnehmung von Handlungskompetenzen ist nicht neu. Es ist einem System inhärent, in dem die EU als supranationale Organisation gemäß dem Prinzip der begrenzten Einzelermächtigung bestimmte Regulierungskompetenzen von den Mitgliedstaaten übertragen bekommen hat, diese Kompetenzzuweisungen aber weder aus sich heraus klar verständlich sind, noch ohne Weiteres im Umkehrschluss Kompetenzbereiche erkennen lassen, in denen es bei einer uneingeschränkten Möglichkeit der Kompetenzausübung seitens der Mitgliedstaaten der EU verbleibt. Die Mitgliedstaaten als „Herren der Verträge" sind zwar allein zuständig für die Ermächtigung der EU aufgrund der völkerrechtlichen Verträge, mit der diese (ursprünglich als reine „Europäische Wirtschaftsgemeinschaft") geschaffen und ihre Funktionsmodalitäten geklärt wurden und werden. Diese Verträge wirken allerdings in ihrer Auslegung durch den EuGH als ein Fundament für ein dynamisches Verständnis der Kompetenzen der EU, das dem Prinzip der begrenzten Einzelermächtigung viel von seiner Kompetenzen der Mitgliedstaaten wahrenden Kraft nimmt. Gerade im Bereich der Medienregulierung, die aufgrund der Vielschichtigkeit der Regulierungselemente schon keiner Rechtsgrundlage allein zugeordnet werden kann, stellt sich das Spannungsverhältnis in besonders intensiver Weise dar. Denn Medienregulierung betrifft stets auch die kulturell-gesellschaftlichen Fundamente der Mitgliedstaaten ebenso wie die Funktionsfähigkeit demokratischer Gesellschaften und ist in besonderer Weise durch mitgliedstaatliche Traditionen und Unterschiede geprägt. Vor diesem Hintergrund klärt die vorliegende Studie grundlegende Fragen europa- und spezifisch medienrechtlicher Natur zur Handhabung der Kompetenzverteilung zwischen EU und Mitgliedstaaten insbesondere bei Maßnahmen, die medienvielfaltssichernde Wirkung erzielen sollen.

Die konkrete Aufteilung von Zuständigkeiten zwischen EU und Mitgliedstaaten erfolgt im EU-Recht anhand einer Zuordnung zu drei unterschiedlichen Kompetenztypen: ausschließlichen Kompetenzen der EU, zwischen der EU und ihren Mitgliedstaaten geteilten Zuständigkeiten und bloß unterstützenden bzw. ergänzenden Handlungsmöglichkeiten für die EU. Ein ausdrücklicher Negativkatalog von Bereichen, die vollständig vom EU-Recht unberührt bleiben, besteht nicht – weder existiert eine kulturelle noch eine medienbezogene Bereichsausnahme für die Kompetenzen der EU. Aber auch im Übrigen ist die Kompetenzaufteilung zwischen der EU und ihren Mitgliedstaaten von den europäischen Verträgen her in einer höchst komplexen und Streitigkeiten befördernden Weise geregelt: So dürfen z.B. bei geteilten Zuständigkeiten einerseits die Mitgliedstaaten nur handeln, soweit die EU noch nicht abschließend aktiv geworden ist, die EU muss dabei aber ihr Handeln mit der Notwendigkeit einer Wahrnehmung der Kompetenz auf ihrer Ebene begründen können. Das Subsidiaritätsprinzip verlangt die Beschränkung auf notwendiges Handeln aufgrund eines Mehrwerts auf EU-Ebene. Darüber hinaus muss die EU aber auch das Verhältnismäßigkeitsprinzip wahren und darf nur in dem Umfang tätig werden, wie es notwendig ist, um das angestrebte Ziel oberhalb mitgliedstaatlicher Herangehensweise zu erreichen. Andererseits stellt sich auch bei geteilter Zuständigkeit etwa für Regelungen zum besseren Funktionieren des Binnenmarktes hinsichtlich der Medienregulierung auch in konkreten Einzelaspekten die Frage, ob die jeweilige Regulierung tatsächlich auf wirtschaftsorientierter Basis steht und damit der Binnenmarktkompetenz unterfällt oder ob nicht auch oder sogar im Schwerpunkt medienvielfaltssichernde Aspekte – wobei Pluralismus das Leitziel des Medienrechts insgesamt ist – die Regulierung prägen, deren regulierende Einfassung den Mitgliedstaaten vorbehalten bleibt.

Dieses besondere Spannungsverhältnis kann auch in Konflikte münden. Die bislang in der Praxis noch immer wenig ausgeprägte Anwendung des Subsidiaritätsgrundsatzes, jedenfalls als Prüfungsgegenstand beim EuGH für die Kontrolle von Unionsrechtsakten, ist ein Grund für kritische Stellungnahmen auch von nationalen Verfassungsgerichten zum Umfang und zur Gestalt der Kompetenzwahrnehmung durch die Unionsorgane in manchen Bereichen. So verdeutlicht auch das Bundesverfassungsgericht in jüngster Zeit, dass ein Handeln der Union außerhalb des Kompetenzbereichs – also *ultra vires* – und die einhergehende Folge der Nichtbeachtung eines entsprechenden Rechtsakts im nationalen Kontext, keine rein theoretische Annahme ist. Die Berücksichtigung der nationalen Identität der Mitgliedstaaten ebenso wie des Grundsatzes der loyalen Zusammenarbeit, der nicht nur im Verhältnis der Staaten zur EU sondern auch umgekehrt gilt, verlangt, dass die EU ihre Kompetenzen insbesondere für die Errichtung eines Binnenmarktes und der Festlegung der für dessen Funktionieren erforderlichen Wettbewerbsregeln so wahrnimmt, dass mitgliedstaatliche Handlungsspielräume und Einschätzungsmöglichkeiten möglichst geschont werden.

Für die Medienregulierung bedeutet dies, dass auch die naheliegende Verlagerung von Regelungen auf den supranationalen Bereich insbesondere bezüglich Online-Angeboten, die aufgrund ihrer Natur grenzüberschreitend verteilt werden und empfangbar sind, nur möglich ist, soweit die unbestrittene primäre Zuständigkeit der Mitgliedstaaten zur Schaffung von medienvielfaltssichernden Regelungen unberührt bleibt. Ungeachtet der Anerkennung des Ziels Pluralismus in der Werteordnung der EU und der wichtigen unterstützenden Maßnahmen, die sie dazu trifft, bleibt die kultur- und vielfaltsbezogene Medienregulierung durch die Mitgliedstaaten vorrangig. Dies gilt nicht zuletzt auch mit Blick auf die Wahrung von lokaler und regionaler Vielfalt als Anknüpfungspunkt für fortdauernde Erfahrung demokratischer Teilhabemöglichkeiten in einer durch Digitalisierung und Globalisierung geprägten Welt. Gerade die besondere Bedeutung, die das Bundesverfassungsgericht einer positiven Medienordnung durch die Länder für die Wahrung der demokratischen und föderativen Fundamente der Verfassungsordnung des Grundgesetzes beimisst, verdeutlicht die fortdauernde Relevanz einer mitgliedstaatlichen Prärogative bei der Vielfaltssicherung und -förderung für den Mitgliedstaat Bundesrepublik Deutschland. Mediale Vielfaltssicherung in föderaler Verantwortung zählt zum Kern der seitens der EU nach Art. 4 Abs. 2 EUV zu achtenden nationalen Identität dieses Mitgliedstaates.

Zwar ist die Beantwortung der Frage, ob Rechtsakte und Handlungen der EU mit Auswirkung auf die Medienregulierung zulässig sind, nur im Einzelfall möglich, weil es an einer eindeutigen Bereichsausnahme für den Medienbereich als Adressat von EU-Regulierung fehlt und insbesondere die auf grenzüberschreitende Handelserleichterungen gerichtete Binnenmarktkompetenz der EU für das Handeln von Medienakteuren ebenso bedeutsam sein kann wie die Wettbewerbsaufsicht der EU. Im Zweifelsfall muss sich die EU aber dort bei harmonisierender oder gar rechtsvereinheitlichender Herangehensweise in der auf Marktöffnung und Wettbewerbssicherung gerichteten Regulierung zurückhalten, wo unverhältnismäßige negative Auswirkungen auf die an den Zielen des Pluralismus ausgerichteten Regulierungsmöglichkeiten der Mitgliedstaaten, insbesondere auch unter Berücksichtigung nationaler Besonderheiten, zu befürchten sind. Dies gilt nicht nur bei Rechtsetzung der EU, sondern auch, soweit die Kommission eine Kontrollaufgabe bezüglich der Einhaltung des Unionsrechts durch die Mitgliedstaaten und mitgliedstaatliche Medienunternehmen hat, da eine solche Kontrollaufgabe im Ausgangspunkt auch in Bezug auf medienvielfaltssichernde (und andere kompetenziell im mitgliedstaatlichen Bereich verbleibende) Regelungen der Mitgliedstaaten sowie in Bezug auf Vielfaltssicherung gerichtetes koordiniertes Verhalten von Unternehmen besteht. Dieses Rücksichtnahmegebot gilt es seitens der EU und ihrer Organe auch bei der Beantwortung der von Kommissionspräsidentin *von der Leyen* bezeichneten Herausforderungen zur Erreichung einer für das digitale Zeitalter fit gemachten EU bei damit einhergehenden zukünftigen Rechtsaktvorschlägen zu beachten.

Dieses Ergebnis zur Kompetenzverteilung wird weiter gestützt – und nicht etwa relativiert – durch die hervorgehobene Anerkennung des Ziels Medienpluralismus in der Rechtsordnung der EU. Auf die bezüglich der EMRK vom EGMR herausgearbeitete Bedeutung der Medienvielfalt als legitimes Ziel bei der Beschränkung von Freiheiten hinaus bezieht sich nicht nur der EuGH schon seit Jahrzehnten mit gleichem Verständnis in seiner Rechtsprechung. Diese Straßburger Rechtsprechung wird auch von den rechtsetzenden Organen der EU immer wieder in Bezug genommen. Über diesen EMRK-Ansatz hinaus ist Medienpluralismus sogar ausdrücklich als zu beachtender Parameter sowohl in der Werteordnung der EU nach Art. 2 EUV als auch in der Charta der Grundrechte der EU in deren Art. 11 Abs. 2 genannt.

Die Unionsorgane sind damit nicht etwa angehalten, selbst medienvielfaltssichernd im Sinne von Rechtsetzung tätig zu werden – denn weder Art. 2 EUV noch die Grundrechte-Charta begründen eigenständige Kompetenztitel der EU. In der Charta wird dies sogar ausdrücklich geregelt. Diese explizite Schranke, die das Prinzip der begrenzten Einzelermächtigung bekräftigt, unterstreicht die Pflicht zur Rücksichtnahme auf die Ausübung mitgliedstaatlicher Kompetenz zur Sicherung der – für den jeweiligen Mitgliedstaat relevanten – Aspekte der Meinungs- und Medienvielfalt, auch bei Vollzugsmaßnahmen der Unionsorgane. Da die Mitgliedstaaten der EU als Parteien der EMRK der vom EGMR entwickelten Garantenoder Schutzpflicht hinsichtlich der besonderen Rolle der Medien Rechnung tragen müssen und die EU ihrerseits die Vorgaben der EMRK möglichst zu berücksichtigen hat, auch wenn sie nicht selbst Vertragspartei ist, ist der Schutz von Meinungs- und Medienvielfalt von der EU als im Allgemeininteresse liegendes Ziel auch bei der Beschränkung von Grundfreiheiten durch die Mitgliedstaaten dergestalt anzunehmen, dass sie entsprechendes Handeln nicht beschneidet. Die Unterschiede bei Erwägungen demokratischer, ethischer, gesellschaftlicher, kommunikativer oder kultureller Natur zwischen den Mitgliedstaaten rechtfertigen es, dass diese über das angemessene Schutzniveau und die passenden Instrumente zur Erreichung ihrer diesbezüglichen Allgemeinwohlziele entscheiden und – soweit dabei Grenzen aus dem EU-Recht wie insbesondere das Verhältnismäßigkeitsprinzip beachtet werden – diese gegebenenfalls auch so ausüben, dass Unternehmen mit Sitz in anderen Mitgliedstaaten betroffen werden.

Unabhängig vom Befund, dass die EU nicht nur keine Rechtsetzungskompetenz bezüglich unmittelbar medienvielfaltssichernder Regelungen hat, sondern auch im Übrigen im anwendbaren Rechtsrahmen Rücksicht auf die diesbezügliche mitgliedstaatliche Zuständigkeit walten lassen muss, besteht eine Vielzahl relevanter, auf den Binnenmarkt bezogener harmonisierender Sekundärrechtsakte. Die wirtschaftliche Dimension von Medien und anderen für die Meinungsbildung bedeutsamen Angeboten, bei denen es sich im audiovisuellen Bereich meist um Dienstleistungen, ggf. aber auch (wie bei Benutzeroberflächen von Empfangsgeräten) um vielfaltsrelevante Ausformungen von Waren handeln kann, erlaubt Unionshandeln, soweit es die primärrechtlichen Grenzen einhält. Daher finden sich in unterschiedlicher Ausprägung in den einschlägigen Rechtsakten ausdrückliche Anwendungsausnahmen, in denen ausschließlich mitgliedstaatliches Recht eingreift, oder Verweise auf reservierte Zuständigkeiten der Mitgliedstaaten, die vom jeweiligen Rechtsakt unberührt bleiben. Dazu zählen etwa der EEKK und die ECRL, die ausdrücklich auf die weiterbestehende Kompetenz zur Vielfaltssicherung durch die Mitgliedstaaten verweisen. Auch bei der AVMD-RL, die in manchen Bereichen inhaltsbezogener Regulierung bereits eine weitgehende Harmonisierung erreicht, gelten weiterhin Umsetzungsspielräume und sogar Abweichungsmöglichkeiten der Mitgliedstaaten unabhängig vom Herkunftslandprinzip, so dass auch innerstaatliche Rechtsdurchsetzung gegenüber im EU-Ausland niedergelassenen Anbietern unter bestimmten Umständen möglich ist.

Es ist jedoch zu beachten, dass sich trotz der fehlenden Zuständigkeit für unmittelbare Regelungen zunehmend zumindest mittelbar für die Vielfaltssicherung bedeutsame Wirkungen aus nicht darauf gerichteten Rechtsakten ergeben. Dies gilt insbesondere für zwei jüngere Rechtsakte, die die Rolle und Pflichten von Online-Plattformen in neuer Weise adressieren (DSM-RL und P2B-VO). Auch diese Ansätze lösen aber – selbst wenn sie z.B. mit Transparenzvorgaben aus der Vielfaltssicherung vertraute Instrumente vorsehen – keine Sperrwirkung – auch in Bereichen ausschließlicher Zuständigkeit der Union – für darüber hinausgehende, aber mit anderer Zielrichtung getroffene Maßnahmen auf mitgliedstaatlicher Ebene aus, etwa Offenlegungspflichten zum Zwecke der Kontrolle der Pluralität der Medien.

Neben bindenden Rechtsakten sind auch ergänzende, rechtlich unverbindliche Maßnahmen der EU wie z.B. Empfehlungen oder Schlussfolgerungen zu beachten, insbesondere weil diese eine Vorstufe für spätere verbindliche Sekundärrechtsakte sein können. Solche unverbindlichen Rechtsakte finden sich zurzeit etwa für den Umgang mit illegalen Inhalten bzw. Desinformation. Aufgrund des nicht bindenden Charakters von Empfehlungen und anderen Mitteilungen besteht in der Praxis möglicherweise eine weniger ausgeprägte Berücksichtigung bestehender mitgliedstaatlicher Kompetenzreserven, weil Berührungspunkte als nicht so problematisch angesehen werden. Allerdings gilt die Kompetenzverteilung der EU-Rechtsordnung auch für solche unverbindlichen Rechtsakte. Wenn anknüpfend an solche Vorarbeiten später bindende Rechtsakte entwickelt werden, kann eine unterlassene frühzeitige Berücksichtigung mitgliedstaatlicher Kompetenzen problematisch werden, weshalb es sich – wie unten ebenfalls betont wird – für die Mitgliedstaaten, im Falle Deutschlands für den Bereich der Medienregulierung also die Länder, empfiehlt ein umfassendes regulatorisches Frühwarnsystem zu entwickeln und sich auch frühzeitig zu solchen Maßnahmen der Kommission in einer kompetenzwahrenden, zumindest aber -schonenden Weise zu positionieren. Aktuell gilt diese Monitoring- und Präsenzempfehlung etwa auch für den *Media and Audiovisual Action Plan* oder den *European Democracy Action Plan*. Bei diesen geht es um die Verteidigung oder Einigung auf gemeinsame Standards basierend auf zentralen europäischen Werten, was im Sinne der Stärkung der EU als einer Werteunion gerade auch im Zeichen neuer Bedrohungen dieses Wertefundaments innerhalb der EU wie von außen – etwa bezüglich des Rechtsstaatsprinzips – sinnvoll erscheint. Allerdings muss auch insoweit bei etwaigen Durchführungsmaßnahmen darauf geachtet werden, dass damit nicht nationale mediale Vielfaltssicherungsansätze bzw. Ausführungskompetenzen untergraben werden.

Auch eine berechtigte Schutzzwecke der Mitgliedstaaten sichernde Rechtsdurchsetzung, die auch mitgliedstaatliche Besonderheiten im konkreten Fall aufgreifen kann, erfolgt am besten auf mitgliedstaatlicher Ebene und entlang innerstaatlicher Verfahrensregeln, die ihrerseits allerdings dem Diskriminierungsverbot und Effektivitätsgebot genügen müssen. In Deutschland betrifft dies im Wesentlichen die Landesmedienanstalten, die unabhängig von der Festlegung gemeinsamer Standards und bestimmter Jurisdiktionsregeln auf EU-Ebene bei Beachtung völkergewohnheitsrechtlicher Grenzen der Jurisdiktionsgewalt grundsätzlich auch gegen ausländische Anbieter, die ihren Sitz nicht in einem der Mitgliedstaaten der EU haben, bei der Verletzung materiell-rechtlicher Vorgaben etwa aus dem MStV vorgehen können. Zwar ist es angemessen, die Rechtsdurchsetzung nach dem Grad der Zugriffsmöglichkeit zu differenzieren, aber ausländische Anbieter können nicht dauerhaft von der Rechtsdurchsetzung ausgeschlossen bleiben, wenn im Ausland keine Durchsetzungmaßnahmen er-

G. Gesamtergebnis und politische Handlungsoptionen

folgen, die ein vergleichbares Schutzniveau erreichen. Jedoch gilt die Bindung an Grundrechte im Vollzug auch dann und insbesondere bei einem Sitz des betroffenen Anbieters in einem anderen EU-Mitgliedstaat, dabei ist auf eine Gleichbehandlung bei der Anwendung von Grundrechtspositionen begrenzenden Maßnahmen wie auch auf die Einhaltung der EU-rechtlichen Vorgaben an die Durchbrechung des Prinzips der Herkunftslandkontrolle zu achten.

Völkerrechtliche Begrenzungen einer so verstandenen Jurisdiktionshoheit auch gegenüber „ausländischen" Anbietern ergeben sich zwar aus dem Gebot der Beachtung staatlicher Souveränität, aber bei Vorliegen eines *genuine link* eines Anbieters zum Inlandsterritorium – etwa durch im Schwerpunkt oder ausschließlich sich mit der politischen, wirtschaftlichen oder gesellschaftlichen Situation Deutschlands befassende Angebote – ist auch eine Durchsetzung gegenüber diesen Anbietern grundsätzlich möglich. Zwar steht bei Sekundärrechtsakten, die sich bezüglich der Jurisdiktionshoheit auf das Herkunftslandprinzip stützen, jede Rechtsdurchsetzung durch andere Staaten in einem Spannungsverhältnis mit diesem Prinzip, so dass sie nur unter bestimmten Umständen möglich ist, sie ist jedoch bereits heute in den hier relevanten Rechtakten nicht ausgeschlossen. Dennoch wäre es zu begrüßen, wenn – etwa in neuen horizontal anwendbaren Vorschriften im Unionsrecht – eine explizite Klarstellung erfolgt, dass sich die Rechtsdurchsetzung entlang gemeinsamer Maßstäbe unter bestimmten Umständen trotz der Weitergeltung des Herkunftslandprinzips am Marktortprinzip ausrichten darf.

II. Verfahrensaspekte

Die inhaltliche Analyse zeigt damit klar auf, dass die Kompetenzverteilung zwischen EU und Mitgliedstaaten nicht disponibel ist und vom Ansatz her eindeutigen Vorgaben folgt. Nicht zuletzt mit Blick auf Defizite einer rechtssicheren Abgrenzung der Zuständigkeiten zwischen der EU und ihren Mitgliedstaaten auf der materiell-rechtlichen Ebene kommt verfahrensrechtlichen Aspekten beim Auflösen von Spannungsfeldern in der Kompetenzverteilung besonderes Gewicht zu. Auch insoweit erweist sich das Auflösen des Spannungsverhältnisses im Bereich geteilter Zuständigkeiten wie auch mit Blick auf die Wahrung der vorrangigen Kompetenz der Mitgliedstaaten zur Regulierung von Vielfaltssicherung als nicht einfach.

Die im Vorfeld eines Rechtsaktbeschlusses bestehenden Mechanismen wie etwa die Subsidiaritätsrüge werden nur sehr zurückhaltend genutzt, weil sie als konfrontativ angelegt verstanden werden können. Dies gilt erst recht für mögliche Reaktionen auf in Kraft getretene Rechtsakte wie Nichtigkeitsklagen eines Mitgliedstaates vor dem EuGH, die in der Praxis – im Unterschied zu Vertragsverletzungsverfahren der EU-Kommission gegen Mitgliedstaaten – sehr selten sind. Inhaltlich stellt sich für Mitgliedstaaten zudem auch die Frage, ob sie sich bei einer eigentlich bestehenden Einigkeit über Notwendigkeit, Ziel und Sinnhaftigkeit einer legislativen Initiative der EU aus kompetenzrechtlichen Gründen gegen eine solche Initiative wenden, da sie diese als kompetenzüberschreitend einordnen. Bei einer solchen inhalte-fokussierten Betrachtung droht indessen eine Aushöhlung von Kompetenzschranken für die EU – und dies ohne Sicherheit, dass die Kompetenzwahrnehmung seitens der EU auch zukünftig dem medienregulatorischen Programm jedes Mitgliedstaates genügt.

Aus Sicht der Kommission stellt sich die Frage der Kompetenzrücksichtnahme anders: Sie ist nach den Verträgen verpflichtet als einzig dazu autorisiertes Organ der Union dort, wo sie Handlungsbedarf sieht, mit Vorschlägen einen Legislativprozess einzuleiten. Ferner muss sie als „Hüterin der Verträge" jedem von ihr als Rechtsverletzung eingeschätzten mitgliedstaatlichen Verhalten nachzugehen und ggf. sogar ein Vertragsverletzungsverfahren einzuleiten, wenn sie etwa ungerechtfertigte Behinderungen für den freien Verkehr von Dienstleistungen sieht.

Es liegt dabei in dem dynamischen, auf eine immer engere Union durch Rechtsvereinheitlichung ausgerichteten Integrationsansatz der EU-Kommission nahe, dass diese gerade angesichts der globalen Herausforderungen der Digitalisierung einen Handlungsbedarf für die EU zur Bewältigung dieser Herausforderungen betont, wobei dieser Bedarf nicht erst bejaht wird, wenn sich ein Handeln der Mitgliedstaaten zuvor als unzureichend erwiesen hat. Dementsprechend ist eine gewisse Tendenz zu beobachten, dass die EU Vorschläge für ein Handeln auf Unionsebene – orientiert am Vorsorgeprinzip – auch schon im Vorfeld mitgliedstaatlicher Regulierungsansätze unterbreitet. Das Bemühen um eine digitale Souveränität Europas kann dabei Überlegungen befördern, stärker als in der Vergangenheit auf das Instrument der Verordnung zu setzen – und damit einen Gewinn an Reaktionsschnelligkeit durch fehlendes Umsetzungserfordernis um den Preis eines Verlusts an Rücksichtnahmemöglichkeit auf Besonderheiten in den Mitgliedstaaten im Zuge der Umsetzung von EU-Richtlinien zu akzeptieren. Eine solche zunehmende Nutzung des Instruments der Verordnung könnte auch durch positive Erfahrungen angeregt werden, die mit der Wirkkraft der DS-GVO auch gegenüber nicht in der EU ansässigen Anbietern gemacht wurden.

Damit ist für die Zukunft gewichtiger noch als bereits bislang ein im Vergleich zur Sichtweise der Mitgliedstaaten unterschiedliches kompetenzbezogenes Grundverständnis der auf eine vertiefte Integration ausgerichteten EU-Organe Kommission und Parlament zu besorgen, das sowohl die Organisationsform als auch das institutionelle Setup betrifft und sogar in eindeutig zugeordneten Bereichen wie der Vielfaltssicherung zu verstärkten Spannungen führen kann.

Auch deshalb ist es besonders wichtig, dass sich Mitgliedstaaten – bei Föderalstaaten mit entsprechender Zuständigkeitsverteilung ggf. die Gliedstaaten – im politischen (Ver-)Handlungsprozess auf Unionsebene frühzeitig und umfassend einbringen. Dies gilt nicht nur bzw. erst bei konkreten Vorschlägen für Legislativakte, sondern auch für ergänzende Initiativen sowie generell im Vorfeld bei der Diskussion um mögliche Schwerpunktsetzungen. Dieses „Markieren von Präsenz" sollte durch Beteiligung in unterschiedlichen Foren dazu beitragen, Besonderheiten innerstaatlicher Herangehensweisen zu verdeutlichen und um entsprechende Berücksichtigung zu werben. Neben der formellen und informellen Beteiligung durch Austausch im Prozess der Rechtsetzung können dazu auch wissenschaftliche oder an die breitere Öffentlichkeit gerichtete Aktivitäten zählen. Im eigentlichen Rechtsetzungsprozess empfiehlt es sich dabei, im Zusammenwirken mit anderen EU-Mitgliedstaaten durch Regulierung(svorhaben) der EU ausgelöste Reibungspunkte bei der Wahrnehmung mitgliedstaatlicher Kompetenzen zu identifizieren und im Verbund mit anderen Mitgliedstaaten, die entweder vergleichbare Ausgangslagen namentlich beim Schutz von Medienvielfalt oder aus unterschiedlichen Gründen zu gleichen Punkten Bedenken im Hinblick auf eine zu weitgehende Harmonisierungstendenz haben, frühzeitig gemeinsam Stellung zu beziehen.

Konkret für den Medienregulierungsbereich bedeutet dies für die Länder, dass sie die bereits eingeschlagenen Wege zur Verdeutlichung ihrer Interessenlage „in Brüssel" eher noch ausbauen und verstärken sollten und die umfassende Berücksichtigung von sich auf Medien und den Online-Sektor auswirkenden Maßnahmen der EU durch eine entsprechend breit aufgestellte Reaktion widerspiegeln. Für die aktuelle Diskussion um den *Digital Services Act* bedeutet dies, dass nicht nur bezüglich des zu erwartenden inhaltebezogenen Rechtsaktsvorschlages, sondern auch – soweit es Berührungspunkte zur Medienregulierung gibt – für die aus EU-Sicht wichtige weitere Komponente der (auch neuen) wettbewerbsrechtlichen Instrumente zur Reaktion auf die Plattformökonomie eine Position herausgearbeitet werden sollte. Dabei kann es auch darum gehen aufzuzeigen, wie vergleichbare Instrumente dennoch nebeneinander in unterschiedlicher

Ausprägung bestehen können, weil sie unterschiedliche Zielrichtungen haben, wie dies etwa für Transparenzpflichten der Fall ist.

Einerseits geht es um die Beteiligung an Vorschlägen, wie bestimmte Regelungen auf Ebene des Unionsrechts am besten modernisiert werden können. Solche Fragen betreffen etwa die Klärung, was illegale Inhalte sind oder ob neben illegalen Inhalten schädliche Inhalte als gesonderte, ebenfalls zu klärende Kategorie einzuführen sind, oder die Klarstellung von Verantwortlichkeiten neben Haftungstatbeständen bei Diensteanbietern. Andererseits ist es aus Sicht der Mitgliedstaaten wichtig, auf ein funktionierendes Zusammenspiel von Unions- und eigener Ebene hinzuwirken. Dazu zählen etwa bei Beibehaltung der Vollzugszuständigkeit die Etablierung neuer oder konkreterer Kooperationsformen zwischen zuständigen Behörden oder Einrichtungen sowohl was deren Aufgabenbereich angeht, aber insbesondere auch in der grenzüberschreitenden Zusammenarbeit bei der Rechtsdurchsetzung.

Dazu gehört es aber auch, bestehende Regulierungsmodelle auf eine Übertragbarkeit in den hier relevanten Bereich zu prüfen und entsprechend auf Unionsebene vorzuschlagen: ein Beispiel dafür könnte es sein, dass auch bei Etablierung der DS-GVO als unmittelbar geltender Verordnung die Kompetenz der Mitgliedstaaten unter anderem dadurch beachtet wurde, dass z.B. Vorschriften über die Datenverarbeitung zu journalistischen Zwecken der Regulierung durch die Mitgliedstaaten vorbehalten bleiben (Art. 85 DS-GVO). Solche Öffnungsklauseln, die nicht nur bei Verordnungen, sondern auch mit Blick auf die Reichweite des Umsetzungserfordernisses einer Richtlinie in Betracht kommen, oder eine explizite Anerkennung von „reservierten" Zuständigkeiten der Mitgliedstaaten sind vielversprechende Scharnierfunktionen, die ein besseres Zusammenspiel im Mehrebenensystem versprechen. Eine solche Rücksichtnahme auf mitgliedstaatliche Besonderheiten nicht nur im Vollzug erlaubt selbst bei Verordnungen – im Einklang mit dem übrigen Wettbewerbsrecht der Union werden neue Instrumente in diesem Bereich voraussichtlich ebenfalls in dieser Rechtsaktform vorgeschlagen werden – erst recht aber bei der Rechtsaktform Richtlinie (wie z.B. wenn horizontale Vorschriften für Plattformen eingeführt werden, aber ergänzende mitgliedstaatliche Regelungen bzw. Regelungen zur Ausfüllung durch die Mitgliedstaaten etwa bezogen auf "Medienplattformen" ausdrücklich vorgesehen werden) die Berücksichtigung der den Mitgliedstaaten eigenen Verfassungstraditionen und Besonderheiten beim Erlass weiterführender Regeln.

Dieses Hinwirken auf die Berücksichtigung der mitgliedstaatlichen Zuständigkeit für die Medienvielfaltsregulierung bedarf auch einer institutionellen Absicherung. So ist es z.B. besonders wichtig, dass bei einer etwaigen, rechtlich unverbindlichen Verständigung auf Standards von Pluralismus und Demokratie dieser Grundbestand nicht zu einer Vereinheitlichung in der Durchsetzung oder – unbeschadet der Kontrolle über die Einhaltung der Werteordnung der EU nach Art. 7 EUV – einer Verlagerung der Aufsicht auf die Unionsebene führen muss. Solange die Mitgliedstaaten durch entsprechende Ermächtigung und Ausstattung effektive Rechtsdurchsetzung durch von ihnen – ggf. im Rahmen der Vorgaben aus dem EU-Sekundärrecht – eingerichtete Behörden oder Einrichtungen sicherstellen, können gemeinsame Standards durch unterschiedliche Beteiligte, die in festgelegter Weise kooperieren, durchgesetzt werden. Nicht zuletzt auch die organisationsrechtliche Dimension des Subsidiaritätsprinzips spricht im Bereich der Medienregulierung der EU für eine funktions- und bedarfsgerechte Ausstattung der mitgliedstaatlichen Regulierungsinstanzen. Denn ohne eine solche Ausstattung sinken mit Blick auf die unzureichende Wahrnehmbarkeit der positiven Ordnungsfunktion für die Medien in einem digitalen Umfeld die Schwellen, die EU-Aktivitäten durch das Subsidiaritätsprinzip gesetzt sind.

Im so verstandenen Sinne kann das Spannungsverhältnis zumindest abgefedert werden, indem die Zielerreichung durch Unionshandeln nicht dazu führen muss, dass mitgliedstaatliche Zuständigkeiten dauerhaft ausgehöhlt werden. Im Blick auf die weiterhin tendenziell integrationsfreundliche Rechtsprechung des EuGH, die in Einzelfällen eine Verengung der mitgliedstaatlichen Handlungsspielräume durch zu weitreichende inhaltliche Nachprüfung einer umstrittenen Maßnahme eines Mitgliedstaates bewirkt, ist es besonders wichtig, den Ausgleich bereits bei der Schaffung von Legislativakten und nicht erst bei ihrer Überprüfung bzw. der Kontrolle von Umsetzungsmaßnahmen zu versuchen herbeizuführen. In relevanten Verfahren, die teilweise reduziert werden auf die Grundfreiheits-Perspektive und dadurch die Auswirkung auf die mitgliedstaatliche Kompetenz zur Pluralismussicherung unberücksichtigt lassen, ist dennoch eine deutliche Positionsbestimmung der Länder anzustreben. Soweit eine solche Positionsbestimmung auch unter Wahrung der verfassungsrechtlichen Kompetenzverteilung zwischen Bund und Ländern nach Art. 23 GG auf europäischer Ebene vorgenommen werden kann, fördert dies die kompetenzrechtliche Absicherung des Vielfaltsziels zusätzlich.

Literaturverzeichnis

Albath, L.; Giesel, M.: Das Herkunftslandprinzip in der Dienstleistungsrichtlinie – eine Kodifizierung der Rechtsprechung, in: Europäische Zeitschrift für Wirtschaftsrecht, 2, 2006, S. 38–42.
Zitiert: *Albath/Giesel* in: EuZW 2006, 38, S.

Ambos, K.; Rackow, P.; Miller, D.: Internationales Strafrecht: Strafanwendungsrecht, Völkerstrafrecht, Europäisches Strafrecht, München 2006.
Zitiert: *Ambos/Rackow/Miller*, Internationales Strafrecht.

Assion, S.: Must Carry: Übertragungspflichten auf digitalen Rundfunkplattformen, Hamburg 2015.
Zitiert: *Assion*, Must Carry: Übertragungspflichten auf digitalen Rundfunkplattformen.

Barata, J.: New EU Proposal on the Prevention of Terrorist Content Online – An Important Mutation of the E-Commerce Intermediaries' Regime, white paper, http://cyberlaw.stanford.edu/publications/new-eu-proposal-prevention-terrorist-content-online-important-mutation-e-commerce.
Zitiert: *Barata*, New EU Proposal on the Prevention of Terrorist Content Online – An Important Mutation of the E-Commerce Intermediaries' Regime.

ders.: Regulating content moderation in Europe beyond the AVMSD, 25.2,2020, https://blogs.lse.ac.uk/medialse/2020/02/25/regulating-content-moderation-in-europe-beyond-the-avmsd/.
Zitiert: *Barata*, Regulating content moderation in Europe beyond the AVMSD.

Bárd, P.; Bayer, J.; Carrera, S: A comparative analysis of media freedom and pluralism in the EU Member States, study for the LIBE Committee, 2016, https://www.statewatch.org/media/documents/news/2016/oct/ep-study-media-freedom-in-EU.pdf.
Zitiert: *Bárd/Bayer/Carrera*, A comparative analysis of media freedom and pluralism in the EU Member States.

Barrera Rodriguez, O.; Guriev, S.; Henry, E.; Zhuravskaya, E.: Facts, Alternative Facts, and Fact Checking in Times of Post-Truth Politics, in: Journal of Public Economics 182(2020), S. 104–123, https://doi.org/10.1016/j.jpubeco.2019.104123.
Zitiert: *Barrera Rodriguez/Guriev/Henry/Zhuravskaya* in: Journal of Public Economics 2020, 104, S.

Baker, J.P.: The Doctrine of Legal. Equality of States, in: The British Year Book of International Law 1923–24, 4. Ausgabe, London 1923, S. 1–21.
Zitiert: *Baker*, The Doctrine of Legal Equality of States, 1, S.

Bania, K.: The Role of Media Pluralism in the Enforcement of EU Competition Law, Paris/New York 2019.
Zitiert: *Bania*, The Role of Media Pluralism in the Enforcement of EU Competition Law.

Literaturverzeichnis

Bauer, H.: Die Bundestreue, Tübingen 1992.
Zitiert: *Bauer*, Die Bundestreue.

Bautze, K.: Verantwortung im Netz – Anmerkungen zum Netzwerkdurchsetzungsgesetz, in: KJ 02/2019, S. 203–212.
Zitiert: *Bautze* in: KJ 2019, 203, S.

Becker, C.: Freiheitliche Ordnung, wehrhafte Demokratie und Staatsschutzstrafrecht, in: Bucerius Law Journal, 2013, S. 113–118.
Zitiert: *Becker* in: Bucerius Law Journal 2012, 113, S.

Becker, T.: Warum scheitert die Regulierung des Glücksspielmarktes?, in: ZfWG 06/2015, S. 410–419.
Zitiert: *Becker* in: ZfWG 2015, 410, S.

Benrath, D.: Die Konkretisierung von Loyalitätspflichten. Strukturen und Werkzeuge der Konkretisierung von Verfahrensregelungen in der EU durch den Grundsatz der loyalen Zusammenarbeit, Tübingen 2019.
Zitiert: *Benrath*, Die Konkretisierung von Loyalitätspflichten.

Bertele, J.: Souveränität und Verfahrensrecht. Eine Untersuchung der aus dem Völkerrecht ableitbaren Grenzen staatlicher extraterritorialer Jurisdiktion im Verfahrensrecht, Tübingen 1998.
Zitiert: *Bertele*, Souveränität und Verfahrensrecht.

Bethge, H.: Deutsche Bundesstaatlichkeit und Europäische Union. Bemerkungen über die Entscheidung des Bundesverfassungsgerichts zur EG-Fernsehrichtlinie, in: Wendt/Höfling/Kapern (Hrsg.) Staat – Wirtschaft – Steuern: Festschrift für Karl Heinrich Friauf zum 65. Geburtstag, Heidelberg 1996.
Zitiert: *Bethge*, Deutsche Bundesstaatlichkeit und Europäische Union. Bemerkungen über die Entscheidung des Bundesverfassungsgerichts zur EG-Fernsehrichtlinie.

ders.: Die Grundrechtsberechtigung juristischer Personen nach Art. 19 Abs. 3 Grundgesetz, Passau 1985.
Zitiert: *Bethge*, Die Grundrechtsberechtigung juristischer Personen nach Art. 19 Abs. 3 Grundgesetz.

Bickenbach, C.: Das Subsidiaritätsprinzip in Art. 5 EUV und seine Kontrolle, in: EuR, Jahrgang 48 (2013), Heft 5, S. 523–548.
Zitiert: *Bickenbach* in EuR 2013, 523, s.

Bieber, R.; Epiney, A.; Haag M.; Kotzur, M. (Hrsg.): Die Europäische Union. Europarecht und Politik, 13. Aufl., Baden-Baden 2019.
Zitiert: *Verfasser*, in: Bieber/Epiney/Haag/Kotzur.

Bilz, C.: Konfrontation statt Kooperation? „Solange III" und die Melloni-Entscheidung des EuGH, in: JuWissBlog, 15.03.2016 (verfügbar unter https://www.juwiss.de/26-2016/, letzter Abruf 08.01.2021).
Zitiert: *Bilz*, JuWissBlog, 15.03.2016.

Blanke, H.-J.; Mangiameli, S. (ed.): The Treaty on European Union (TEU). A Commentary, Heidelberg u.a. 2013.
Zitiert: *Verfasser* in: Blanke/Mangiameli.

Bleckmann, A.: Europarecht: das Recht der Europäischen Union und der Europäischen Gemeinschaften, 5. Aufl., Köln 1990.
Zitiert: *Bleckmann*, Europarecht.

Boujemaa, H. u.a.: Cross-disciplinary Challenges and Recommendations regarding the Future of Multimedia Search Engines, Publications Office of the European Union, Luxembourg 2009.
Zitiert: *Boujemaa u.a.*, Cross-disciplinary Challenges and Recommendations regarding the Future of Multimedia Search Engines.

Breier, S.: Der Streit um die richtige Rechtsgrundlage in der Rechtsprechung des Europäischen Gerichtshofes, in: EuR 1995, S. 47–53.
Zitiert: *Breier* in: EuR 1995, 47, S.

Breining-Kaufmann, C.: Internationales Verwaltungsrecht, in: ZSR 125 (2006), S. 5–73.
Zitiert: *Breining-Kaufmann* in: ZSR 2006, 5, S.

Bribosia, H.: Différenciation et avant-gardes au sein de l'Union Européenne, in: CDE 2000, p. 57–115.
Zitiert: *Bribosia* in: CDE 2000, 57, S.

Broadcasting Authority of Ireland: Submission to the Department of Communications, Climate Action & Environment Public Consultation on the Regulation of Harmful Content on Online Platforms and the Implementation of the Revised Audiovisual Media Service Directive, 2019, http://www.bai.ie/en/download/134036/.
Zitiert: *BAI*, Submission to the Department of Communications, Climate Action & Environment Public Consultation on the Regulation of Harmful Content on Online Platforms and the Implementation of the Revised Audiovisual Media Service Directive.*Bröhmer, J.*: Transparenz als Verfassungsprinzip: Grundgesetz und Europäische Union, Tübingen 2004.
Zitiert: *Bröhmer*, Transparenz als Verfassungprinzip.

Brogi, E.; Gori, P.: European Commission Soft and Hard Law Instruments for Media Pluralism and Media Freedom, in: European Union Competencies in Respect of Media Pluralism and Media Freedom, RSCAS Policy Papers No. 01. Robert Schuman Centre for Advanced Studies, Centre for Media Pluralism and Media Freedom, 2013.
Zitiert: *Brogi/Gori*, European Commission Soft and Hard Law Instruments for Media Pluralism and Media Freedom.

Broughton Micova, S.: The Audiovisual Media Services Directive: Balancing liberalisation and protection (DRAFT), in: Handbook on EU Media Law and Policy, Elda Brogi and Pier Luigi Parcu (Hrsg.) Cheltenham 2020 (noch nicht erschienen), https://papers.ssrn.com/sol3/papers.cfm?abstract_id=3586149.
Zitiert: *Broughton Micova*, The Audiovisual Media Services Directive: Balancing liberalisation and protection (DRAFT).

dies.: Content Quotas: What and Whom Are They Protecting?, in: Donders/Pauwels/Loisen (Hrsg.), Private Television in Western Europe, Brüssel u.a. 2013, S. 245–259.
Zitiert: *Broughton Micova*, The Audiovisual Media Services Directive: Balancing liberalisation and protection (DRAFT).

Büllesbach, A.; Gijrath, S.; Prins, C.; Poullet, Y. (Hrsg.): Concise European IT Law, 2. Aufl., Alphen aan den Rijn 2010.
Zitiert: Büllesbach u.a., Concise European IT Law.

Bukovská, B.: The European Commission's Code of Conduct for Countering Illegal Hate Speech Online – An analysis of freedom of expression implications, 2019, https://www.ivir.nl/publicaties/download/Bukovska.pdf.
Zitiert: *Bukovská*, The European Commission's Code of Conduct for Countering Illegal Hate Speech Online.

Bumke, U.: Die öffentliche Aufgabe der Landesmedienanstalten: Verfassungs- und organisationsrechtliche Überlegungen zur Rechtsstellung einer verselbständigten Verwaltungseinheit, München 1995.
Zitiert: *Bumke*, Die öffentliche Aufgabe der Landesmedienanstalten.

Burggraf, J.; Gerlach, C.; Wiesner, J.: Europäische Medienregulierung im Spannungsfeld zwischen EU- und mitgliedstaatlicher Kompetenz, in: Media Perspektiven 10/2018, S. 496–510.
Zitiert: *Burggraf/Gerlach/Wiesner* in: Media Perspektiven 10/2018, 496, S.

Burmester, G.: Grundlagen internationaler Regelungskumulation und -kollision unter besonderer Berücksichtigung des Steuerrechts, Baden-Baden 1993.
Zitiert: *Burmester*, Grundlagen internationaler Regelungskumulation und -kollision unter besonderer Berücksichtigung des Steuerrechts.

Calliess, C.: 70 Jahre Grundgesetz und europäische Integration: „Take back control" oder „Mehr Demokratie wagen"?, in: Neue Zeitschrift für Verwaltungsrecht (NVwZ) 2019, S. 684–692.
Zitiert: *Calliess* in: NVwZ 2019, 684, S.

ders.: Die Binnenmarktkompetenz der EG und das Subsidiaritätsprinzip, in: Berliner Online-Beiträge zum Europarecht, Nr. 25, 2005, https://www.jura.fu-berlin.de/forschung/europarecht/bob/berliner_online_beitraege/Paper25-Calliess/Paper25---Die-Binnenmarktkompetenz-der-EG-und-das-Subsidiaritaetsprinzip.pdf.
Zitiert: *Calliess* in: Berliner Online-Beiträge zum Europarecht 25(2005).

ders.: Die Werte in der Europäischen Union – Der europäische Staaten- und Verfassungsverbund als Werteverbund -, Berliner Online-Beiträge zum Europarecht, Nr. 1, 2004, https://www.jura.fu-berlin.de/forschung/europarecht/bob/berliner_online_beitraege/Paper01-Calliess/Paper01---Globalisierung-der-Wirtschaft-und-Internationalisierung-des-Staates.pdf.
Zitiert: *Calliess* in: Berliner Online-Beiträge zum Europarecht 1(2004).

Calliess, C.; Korte, S.: Dienstleistungsrecht in der EU, München 2011.
Zitiert: *Calliess/Korte*, Dienstleistungsrecht in der EU.

Calliess, C.; Ruffert, M.: EUV/AEUV, Das Verfassungsrecht der Europäischen Union mit Europäischer Grundrechtecharta, Kommentar, 5. Aufl., München 2016.
Zitiert: *Verfasser* in: Calliess/Ruffert.

Cannie, H.; Voorhoof, D.: The Abuse Clause and Freedom of Expression in the European Human Rights Convention: An Added Value for Democracy and Human Rights Protection? In: Netherlands Quarterly of Human Rights, Vol. 29, 2011, S. 54–83.
Zitiert: *Cannie/Voorhoof* in: Netherlands Quarterly of Human Rights, 2011-1, 54, S.

Cappello, M. (Hrsg.): Media pluralism and competition issues, IRIS Spezial 2020-1, Europäische Audiovisuelle informationsstelle, Straßburg, 2020.
Zitiert: *Verfasser* in: Cappello (Hrsg.), Media pluralism and competition issues.

dies. (Hrsg.): Medienrechtsdurchsetzung ohne Grenzen, IRIS Spezial, Europäische Audiovisuelle Informationsstelle, Straßburg, 2018, https://rm.coe.int/medienrechtsdurchsetzung-ohne-grenzen/1680907efd.
Zitiert: *Verfasser* in: Cappello (Hrsg.), Medienrechtsdurchsetzung ohne Grenzen.

dies. (Hrsg.) : Medieneigentum – Marktrealitäten und Regulierungsmaßnahmen, IRIS Spezial 2016-2, Europäische Audiovisuelle Informationsstelle, Straßburg 2016.
Zitiert: *Verfasser* in: Cappello (Hrsg.), Medieneigentum – Marktrealitäten und Regulierungsmaßnahmen.

Castendyk, O.; Dommering, E.; Scheuer, A. (Hrsg.): European Media Law, Berlin, Amsterdam und Saarbrücken 2008.
Zitiert: *Verfasser* in: Castendyk/Dommering/Scheuer.

Chan, Y. S.; Wood, S.; Adshead, S.: Understanding video-sharing platforms under UK jurisdiction, A report for the Department for Digital, Culture, Media & Sport December 2019, https://assets.publishing.service.gov.uk/government/uploads/system/uploads/attachment_data/file/865313/Understanding_VSPs_under_UK_jurisdiction.pdf.
Zitiert: *Chan/Wood/Adshead*, Understanding video-sharing platforms under UK jurisdiction.

Chapuis-Doppler, A.; Delhomme, V.: Regulating Composite Platform Economy Services: The State-of-play After Airbnb Ireland, in: European papers, Vol. 5, 2020, Nr. 1, S. 411–428, http://www.europeanpapers.eu/en/system/files/pdf_version/EP_EF_2020_I_018_Augustin_Chapuis_Doppler_Vincent_Delhomme_0.pdf.
Zitiert: *Chapuis-Doppler/Delhomme* in: European papers 5(2020)1, 411, S.

Classen, D.: Auf dem Weg zu einer einheitlichen Dogmatik der EG-Grundfreiheiten?, in: Europäisches Wirtschafts- und Steuerrecht, 1995, S. 97–106.
Zitiert: *Classen* in: EWS 1995, 97, S.

Cole, M.D.: Zum Gestaltungsspielraum der EU-Mitgliedstaaten bei Einschränkungen der Dienstleistungsfreiheit – Eine Untersuchung am Beispiel einer Regelung bezüglich der Medienvielfalt in Deutschland, in: AfP 2021, S. 1–7.
Zitiert: *Cole* in: AfP 2021, 1, S.

Literaturverzeichnis

ders.: Zum Gestaltungsspielraum der EU-Mitgliedstaaten bei Einschränkungen der Dienstleistungsfreiheit – Eine Untersuchung am Beispiel einer Regelung bezüglich der Medienvielfalt in Deutschland, 2020, https://emr-sb.de/wp-content/uplo ads/2020/06/Zum-Gestaltungsspielraum-der-EU-Mitgliedstaaten-bei-Einschr%c3 %a4nkungen-der-Dienstleistungsfreiheit.pdf.
Zitiert: *Cole*, Zum Gestaltungsspielraum der EU-Mitgliedstaaten bei Einschränkungen der Dienstleistungsfreiheit.

ders.: Guiding Principles in establishing the Guidelines for Implementation of Article 13 (6) AVMSD – Criteria for exempting certain providers from obligations concerning European Works, 2019, https://emr-sb.de/wp-content/uploads/ 2019/05/Study-AVMSD-guidelines-Art-13.pdf.
Zitiert: *Cole*, Guiding Principles in establishing the Guidelines for Implementation of Article 13 (6) AVMSD.

ders.: Das Zielpublikum „Öffentlichkeit" als Anknüpfungspunkt für (Medien-) Regulierung, in: UFITA 82(2018)2, S. 436–458.
Zitiert: *Cole* in: UFITA 2018, 436, S.

ders.: Note d'observations, "Roj TV" entre ordre public et principe du pays d'origine, in: Revue du Droit des Technologies de l'Information, Nr. 47, 2012, S. 50–61.
Zitiert: *Cole* in: R.D.T.I. 2012, 50, S.

ders.: The Country of Origin Principle. From State Sovereignty under Public International Law to Inclusion in the Audiovisual Media Services Directive of the European Union, in: Meng/Ress/Stein (Hrsg.), Europäische Integration und Globalisierung – Festschrift zum 60-jährigen Bestehen des Europa-Instituts, 2011, S. 113–130.
Zitiert: *Cole*, The Country of Origin Principle, 113, S.

ders.: Europarechtliche Rahmenbedingungen für die Pluralismussicherung im Rundfunk, in: BLM-Symposion Medienrecht, Freiheitssicherung durch Regulierung: Fördert oder gefährdet die Wettbewerbsaufsicht publizistische Vielfalt im Rundfunk?, München 2009, S. 93–129.
Zitiert: *Cole*, Europarechtliche Rahmenbedingungen für die Pluralismussicherung im Rundfunk.

Cole, M.D.; Etteldorf, C.: Von Fernsehen ohne Grenzen zu Video-Sharing-Plattformen, Hate Speech und Overlays – die Anpassung der EU-Richtlinie über audiovisuelle Mediendienste an das digitale Zeitalter, in: Medienhandbuch Österreich 2019, Wien 2019, S. 56–65.
Zitiert: *Cole/Etteldorf* in: Medienhandbuch Österreich 2019, 56, S.

Cole, M.D.; Etteldorf, C.; Ullrich, C.: Cross-Border Dissemination of Online Content – Current and Possible Future Regulation of the Online Environment with a Focus on the EU E-Commerce Directive, in: Schriftenreihe Medienforschung der Landesanstalt für Medien NRW, Bd. 81, 2020, https://doi.org/ 10.5771/9783748906438.
Zitiert: *Cole/Etteldorf/Ullrich*, Cross-Border Dissemination of Online Content.

Cole, M.D.; Etteldorf, C.; Ullrich, C.: Updating the Rules for Online Content Dissemination – Legislative Options of the European Union and the Digital Services Act Proposal, in: Schriftenreihe Medienforschung der Landesanstalt für Medien NRW, 2021 (im Erscheinen).
Zitiert: *Cole/Etteldorf/Ullrich*, Updating the Rules for Online Content Dissemination.

Cole, M.D.; Iacino, G.; Matzneller, P.; Metzdorf, J.; Schweda, S.: AVMS-RADAR: AudioVisual Media Services – Regulatory Authorities' Independence and Efficiency Review, Update on recent changes and developments in Member States and Candidate Countries that are relevant for the analysis of independence and efficient functioning of audiovisual media services regulatory bodies (SMART 2013/0083), study prepared for the Commission DG CNECT by the EMR and the University of Luxembourg, https://op.europa.eu/de/publication-detail/-/publication/b6e4a837-8775-11e5-b8b7-01aa75ed71a1/language-de.
Zitiert: *Cole u.a.*, AVMS-RADAR (SMART 2013/0083).

Cole, M.D.; Oster, J.: Zur Frage der Beteiligung privater Rundfunkveranstalter in Deutschland an einer staatlich veranlassten Finanzierung, Rechtsgutachten im Auftrag der ProSiebenSat1 Media S. E, 2016, https://www.prosiebensat1.com/uploads/2017/07/03/P7S1_RundfunkfinanzierungBeitrag_Gutachten.pdf.
Zitiert: *Cole/Oster*, Rundfunkfinanzierung und private Veranstalter.

Cole, M.D.; Ukrow, J.; Etteldorf, C.: Research for CULT Committee – Audiovisual Sector and Brexit: the Regulatory Environment, European Parliament, Policy Department for Structural and Cohesion Policies, Brüssel 2018.
Zitiert: *Cole/Ukrow/Etteldorf*, Research for CULT Committee – Audiovisual Sector and Brexit: the Regulatory Environment.

Cornils, M.: Der gemeinschaftsrechtliche Staatshaftungsanspruch: Rechtsnatur und Legitimität eines richterrechtlichen Haftungsinstituts, Baden-Baden 1995.
Zitiert: *Cornils*, Der gemeinschaftsrechtliche Staatshaftungsanspruch.

Costache, M.: De-regulation of european media policy (2000–2014) The debate on media governance and media pluralism in the EU, Barcelona 2014.
Zitiert: *Costache*, De-regulation of european media policy (2000–2014).

Craig, P.: Proportionality, Rationality and Review, in New Zealand Law Review 2010, S. 265 ff.
Zitiert: *Craig* in: New Zealand Law Review 2010, 265, S.

Craufurd Smith, R.: The Evolution of Cultural Policy in the European Union, in: Craig, P./de Búrca, G. (Hrsg.), The Evolution of EU Law, 2. Aufl., Oxford 2011, p. 869–895.
Zitiert: *Craufurd Smith*, in: Craig/de Búrca, 869, S.

dies.: Culture and European Union Law, in Yearbook of European Law, Volume 24, Issue 1, 2005, S. 626–633.
Zitiert: *Craufurd Smith*, Culture and European Law.

Crawford, J.: Brownlie's Principles of Public International Law, 8. Aufl., Oxford, 2012.
Zitiert: *Crawford*, Brownlie's Principles of Public International Law.

Literaturverzeichnis

Dänzer-Vanotti, W.: Der Europäische Gerichtshof zwischen Rechtsprechung und Rechtsetzung, in: Due/Lutter/Schwarze (Hrsg.), Festschrift für Ulrich Everling, Bd. I, Baden-Baden 1995, S. 205–221.
Zitiert: *Dänzer-Vanotti*, Der Europäische Gerichtshof zwischen Rechtsprechung und Rechtsetzung, 205, S.

Dahm, G.; Delbrück, J.; Wolfrum, R.: Völkerrecht, Band I/1, 2. Aufl., Berlin 1989.
Zitiert: *Dahm/Delbrück/Wolfrum*, Völkerrecht, Band I/1.

de Cock Buning, M. u.a.: Report of the independent High level Group on fake news and online disinformation, A multi-dimensional approach to disinformation, 30.4.2018, https://op.europa.eu/en/publication-detail/-/publication/6ef4df8b-4cea-11e8-be1d-01aa75ed71a1.
Zitiert: *de Cock Buning u.a.*, Report of the independent High Level Group on fake news and online disinformation.

de Schutter, O.; Eide, A.; Khalfan, A.; Orellana, M.; Salomon, M.; Seiderman, I.: Commentary to the Maastricht Principles on Extraterritorial Obligations of States in the Area of Economic, Social and Cultural Rights, in: Human Rights Quarterly, 34 (2012), S. 1084–1169.
Zitiert: *de Schutter u.a.* in: Human Rights Quarterly 2012, 1084, S.

de Vries, S.; Bernitz, U.; Weatherill, S. (Hrsg.): The EU Charter of Fundamental Rights as a Binding Instrument, Oxford 2015.
Zitiert: *Verfasser* in: de Vries/Bernitz/Weatherill.

Deringer, A.: Pyrrhussieg der Länder, in: ZUM 1995, S. 316–318.
Zitiert: *Deringer* in: ZUM 1995, 316, S.

Detjen, J.: Die Werteordnung des Grundgesetzes, Wiesbaden 2013.
Zitiert: *Detjen*, Die Werteordnung des Grundgesetzes.

di Fabio, U.: Das Recht offener Staaten, Tübingen 1998.
Zitiert: *di Fabio*, Das Recht offener Staaten.

ders.: Grundrechtsgeltung in digitalen Systemen, München 2016.
Zitiert: *di Fabio*, Grundrechtsgeltung in digitalen Systemen.

die medienanstalten; Institut für Europäisches Medienrecht (Hrsg.): Europäische Medien- und Netzpolitik, 2. Aufl., Leipzig 2016.
Zitiert: *die medienanstalten/Institut für Europäisches Medienrecht*, Europäische Medien- und Netzpolitik.

Ditzen, C.: Das Menschwerdungsgrundrecht des Kindes, in: NJW 1989, 2519–2520.
Zitiert: *Ditzen* in NJW 1989, 2519, S.

Döhl, F.: Systemwechsel – Vom Gebot des Verblassens zum Gebot der Interaktion. Kunstspezifische Betrachtung des Bearbeitungsrechts nach den Urteilen von EuGH (C-476/17) und BGH (I ZR 115/16) in Sachen Metall auf Metall, in: UFITA 84(2020)1), S. 236–283.
Zitiert: *Döhl* in: UFITA 2020, 236, S.

Dörr, D.: Das Zulassungsregime im Hörfunk: Spannungsverhältnis zwischen europarechtlicher Niederlassungsfreiheit und nationaler Pluralismussicherung, in: Becker/Gebrande (Hrsg.), Der Rundfunkstaatsvertrag als föderales Instrument der Regulierung und Gestaltung des Rundfunks, Symposion für Wolf-Dieter Ring zum 60. Geburtstag, UFITA-Schriftenreihe, Bd. 215, Baden-Baden 2004, S. 71–89.
  Zitiert: *Dörr*, Das Zulassungsregime im Hörfunk: Spannungsverhältnis zwischen europarechtlicher Niederlassungsfreiheit und nationaler Pluralismussicherung, 71, S.

Dörr, D.; Kreile, J.; Cole, M.D.: Medienrecht, 3., vollständig neu bearbeitete Aufl., Frankfurt 2021, erscheint demnächst.
  Zitiert: *Verfasser* in: Dörr/Kreile/Cole.

Dörr, D.; Cole, M.D.: Jugendschutz in den elektronischen Medien – Bestandsaufnahme und Reformabsichten, München 2001.
  Zitiert: *Dörr/Cole*, Jugendschutz in den elektronischen Medien.

Dombrowski, N.: Extraterritoriale Strafrechtsanwendung im Internet, Berlin 2014.
  Zitiert: *Dombrowski*, Extraterritoriale Strafrechtsanwendung im Internet.

Donders, K.; Pauwels, C.; Loisen, J (Hrsg.): The Palgrave Handbook of European Media Policy, London 2014.
  Zitiert: *Verfasser* in: Donders/Pauwels/Loisen.

Dony, M.: Droit de l'Union européenne, 5. Aufl., Brüssel 2014.
  Zitiert: *Dony*, Droit de l'Union européenne.

Drathen, K.: Deutschengrundrechte im Lichte des Gemeinschaftsrechts. Grundrechtsgewährleistungen für natürliche und juristische Personen der EU-Mitgliedstaaten im Bereich der Bürgerrechte und des Art. 19 Abs. 3 GG, Bonn 1994.
  Zitiert: *Drathen*, Deutschengrundrechte im Lichte des Gemeinschaftsrechts.

Dregger, S.: Die Verfassungsinterpretation am US-Supreme Court, Baden-Baden 2019.
  Zitiert: *Dregger*, Die Verfassungsinterpretation am US-Supreme Court.

Dreier, H. (Hrsg.): Grundgesetz Kommentar, Tübingen 2004.
  Zitiert: *Verfasser* in: Dreier (Hrsg.).

Dreier, T.; Schulze, G. (Hrsg.): Urheberrechtsgesetz: UrhG, Verwertungsgesellschaftengesetz, Kunsturhebergesetz, Kommentar, 6. Aufl., München 2018.
  Zitiert: *Verfasser* in: Dreier/Schulze.

Dröge, C.: Positive Verpflichtungen der Staaten in der Europäischen Menschenrechtskonvention, Berlin 2003.
  Zitiert: *Dröge*, Positive Verpflichtungen der Staaten in der Europäischen Menschenrechtskonvention.

Ehlers, D. (Hrsg.): Europäische Grundrechte und Grundfreiheiten, 4. Aufl., Berlin/Boston, 2014.
  Zitiert: *Verfasser* in: Ehlers.

Eifert, M. u.a.: Rechtsgutachten zur Evaluation des NetzDG im Auftrag des BMJV, 2020, https://www.bmjv.de/SharedDocs/Downloads/DE/News/PM/090920_Juristisches_Gutachten_Netz.pdf;jsessionid=F638B8E91234E5E5E9C7CCEBD48EF337.1_cid324?__blob=publicationFile&v=3.
Zitiert: *Eifert u.a.*, Evaluation des NetzDG.

Emilio, N.: The Principle of Proportionality in European Law: A Comparative Study, London 1997.
Zitiert: *Emilio*, The Principle of Proportionality in European Law.

Etteldorf, C.: Das Recht der Filmförderung im europäischen Vergleich, in: UFITA 83(2019)2, S. 498–519.
Zitiert: *Etteldorf* in: UFITA 2019, 498, S.

dies.: Zwischen Fernsehen ohne Grenzen und Werbung ohne Grenzen – Kommerzielle Kommunikation nun lieber liberal?, in: EMR Impuls, 2018, https://emr-sb.de/wp-content/uploads/2017/10/EMR-Impuls_AVMD-Trilog_Kommerzielle-Kommunikation.pdf.
Zitiert: *Etteldorf*, Zwischen Fernsehen ohne Grenzen und Werbung ohne Grenzen.

Engels, S.: Kinder- und Jugendschutz in der Verfassung, in: AöR 1997, S. 212–247.
Zitiert: *Engels* in: AöR 1997, 212, S.

ERGA: Position Paper on the Digital Services Act, 2020, https://erga-online.eu/wp-content/uploads/2020/06/ERGA_SG1_DSA_Position-Paper_adopted.pdf.
Zitiert: *ERGA*, Position Paper on the Digital Services Act.

dies.: Report on disinformation: Assessment of the implementation of the Code of Practice, 2020, https://erga-online.eu/wp-content/uploads/2020/05/ERGA-2019-report-published-2020-LQ.pdf.
Zitiert: *ERGA*, Report on disinformation, 2020.

dies.: Report of the activities carried out to assist the European Commission in the intermediate monitoring of the Code of practice on disinformation, 2019, https://erga-online.eu/wp-content/uploads/2019/06/ERGA-2019-06_Report-intermediate-monitoring-Code-of-Practice-on-disinformation.pdf.
Zitiert: *ERGA*, Report of the activities carried out to assist the European Commission in the intermediate monitoring of the Code of practice on disinformation, 2019.

EU network of independent experts on fundamental rights: Report on the situation of fundamental rights in the European Union in 2003, CFR-CDF.repSI.2003, Januar 2004.
Zitiert: *EU network of independent experts on fundamental rights*, Report on the situation of fundamental rights in the European Union in 2003.

Europäische Audiovisuelle Informationsstelle (Hrsg.): Mapping of national rules for the promotion of European works in Europe, Straßburg 2019, https://rm.coe.int/european-works-mapping/16809333a5.
Zitiert: *EAI*, Mapping of national rules for the promotion of European works in Europe.

dies. (Hrsg.): Mapping of media literacy practices and actions in EU-28, Bericht im Auftrag der Europäischen Kommission, SMART 2016/008, Straßburg 2016, https://ec.europa.eu/digital-single-market/en/news/reporting-media-literacy-europe.
Zitiert: *EAI*, Mapping of media literacy practices and actions in EU-28.

dies. (Hrsg.): Access to TV platforms: must-carry rules, and access to free-DTT European, Audiovisual Observatory for the European Commission – DG COMM, Straßburg 2015, https://rm.coe.int/16807835e4.
Zitiert: *Verfasser* in: EAI (Hrsg.), Access to TV platforms: must-carry rules, and access to free-DTT.

dies. (Hrsg.): Must-Carry: Renaissance oder Reformation?, IRIS plus 2012–5, Straßburg 2013, https://rm.coe.int/1680783db3.
Zitiert: *Verfasser* in: EAI (Hrsg.), Must-Carry: Renaissance oder Reformation?.

dies. (Hrsg.): Haben oder nicht haben. Must-Carry-Regeln, IRIS Spezial 2005–2, Straßburg 2005, https://rm.coe.int/168078349 a.
Zitiert: *Verfasser* in: EAI (Hrsg.), Haben oder nicht haben. Must-Carry-Regeln.

dies. (Hrsg.): Fernsehen und Medienkonzentration – Regulierungsmodelle auf nationaler und europäischer Ebene, IRIS Spezial 2001, Straßburg 2001.
Zitiert: *Verfasser* in: EAI (Hrsg.), Fernsehen und Medienkonzentration.

European Institute for the Media: The Information of the Citizen in the EU: Obligations for the Media and the Institutions Concerning the Citizen's Right to Be Fully and Objectively Informed, Studie im Auftrag des europäischen Parlaments, 2005, https://www.europarl.europa.eu/thinktank/ga/document.html?reference=IPOL-JOIN_ET%282004%29358896.
Zitiert: *European Institute for the Media*, The Information of the Citizen in the EU.

Evans, M.: International Law, 4. Aufl., Oxford 2014.
Zitiert: *Verfasser* in: Evans, International Law.

Everling, U.: Sind die Mitgliedstaaten der Europäischen Gemeinschaft noch Herren der Verträge? Zum Verhältnis von Europäischem Gemeinschaftsrecht und Völkerrecht, in: Bernhardt/Geck/Jaenicke (Hrsg.), Völkerrecht als Rechtsordnung – Internationale Gerichtsbarkeit – Menschenrechte, Festschrift für Hermann Mosler, Berlin 1983, S. 173 ff.
Zitiert: *Everling*, Sind die Mitgliedstaaten der Europäischen Gemeinschaft noch Herren der Verträge?

Fassbender, B.: Der offene Bundesstaat, Tübingen 2007.
Zitiert: *Fassbender*, Der offene Bundesstaat.

Feldmann, T.: Zum Referentenentwurf eines NetzDG: Eine kritische Betrachtung, in: K&R 5/2017, S. 292–297.
Zitiert: *Feldmann* in: K&R 2017, 292, S.

Fink, U.: Medienregulierung im Europarat, in: ZaöRV 74 (2014), S. 505–520.
Zitiert: *Fink* in: ZaöRV 2014, 505, S.

Fink, U.; Cole, M.D.; Keber, T.: Europäisches und Internationales Medienrecht, Heidelberg 2008.
Zitiert: *Verfasser* in: Fink/Cole/Keber, Europäisches Medienrecht.

Literaturverzeichnis

Fischer-Lescano, A.; Kreck, L.: Piraterie und Menschenrechte: Rechtsfragen der Bekämpfung der Piraterie im Rahmen der europäischen Operation Atalanta, Bremen 2009.
Zitiert: *Fischer-Lescano/Kreck*, Piraterie und Menschenrechte.

Foster, N.: Foster on EU Law, 7. Aufl., Oxford 2019.
Zitiert: *Foster*, EU Law.

Frantziou, E.: Further Developments in the Right to be Forgotten: The European Court of Justice's Judgment in Case C-131/12, Google Spain, SL, Google Inc v Agencia Espanola de Proteccion de Datos, in: HLRL 2014, Ausgabe 14, Heft 4, S. 761–777.
Zitiert: *Frantziou* in: HLRL 2014, 761, s.

Frenz, W.: Handbuch Europarecht Band 1: Europäische Grundfreiheiten, 2. Aufl., Heidelberg 2012.
Zitiert: *Frenz*, Handbuch Europarecht Bd. 1.

ders.: Anm. zu EuGH, Urt. v. 29.07.2019 — C-476/17 — Sampling, in: DVBL 22/2019, S. 1471–1473.
Zitiert: *Frenz* in: DVBl. 2019, 1471, S.

Frey, D.: Die europäische Fusionskontrolle und die Medienvielfalt, Zeitschrift für Urheber- und Medienrecht (ZUM) 1998, S. 985–1001.
Zitiert: *Frey* in: ZUM 1998, 985, S.

Furnémont, J.-F.: Independence of audiovisual media regulatory authorities and cooperation between them: time for the EU lawmaker to fill the gaps, Opinion on the EC proposal for amending the AVMS Directive and the EP CULT Committee draft report, 2016, https://www.die-medienanstalten.de/fileadmin/user_upload/die_medienanstalten/Ueber_uns/Positionen/Europa/Studie_zur_Unabhaengigkeit_der_Regulierungsbehoerden_im_Auftrag_des_Bueros_der_ERGA-Vorsitzenden_2.pdf.
Zitiert: *Furnémont*, Independence of audiovisual media regulatory authorities and cooperation between them: time for the EU lawmaker to fill the gaps.

Fox, E.M.: Modernization of Effects Doctrine: From Hands-Off to Hands-Linked, in: New York University Journal of Internal Law and Politics (JILP) 42(2009/2010), S. 159–174.
Zitiert: *Fox* in: JILP 2009/2010, 159, S.

Gamper, A. u.a. (Hrsg.): Föderale Kompetenzverteilung in Europa, Baden-Baden 2016.
Zitiert: *Verfasser* in: Gamper u.a. (Hrsg.).

Gerkrath, J.: L'arrêt du Bundesverfassungsgericht du 22 mars 1995 sur la directive « télévision sans frontières ». Les difficultés de la répartition des compétences entre trois niveaux de législation, in: RTDE 1995, S. 539–559.
Zitiert: *Gerkrath* in: RTDE 1995, 539, S.

Germann, M.: Gefahrenabwehr und Strafverfolgung im Internet, Berlin 2000.
Zitiert: *Germann*, Gefahrenabwehr und Strafverfolgung im Internet.

Gersdorf, H.: Hate Speech in sozialen Netzwerken, in: MMR 07/2017, S. 439–446.
Zitiert: Gersdorf in: MMR 2017, 439, S.

ders.: Funktionen der Gemeinschaftsgrundrechte im Lichte des Solange II-Beschlusses des Bundesverfassungsgerichts, in: AöR 1994, S. 400–426.
Zitiert: *Gersdorf* in: AöR 1994, 400, S.

Giegerich, T.: Mit der Axt an die Wurzel der Union des Rechts – Vier Fragen an das Bundesverfassungsgericht zum 70. Europa-Tag, 2020, http://jean-monnet-saar.eu/?page_id=2642.
Zitiert: *Giegerich*, Mit der Axt an die Wurzel der Union des Rechts.

ders.: Internationale Standards – aus völkerrechtlicher Perspektive, in: Paulus u.a. (Hrsg.), Internationales, nationales und privates Recht: Hybridisierung der Rechtsordnungen – Immunität, Heidelberg u.a. 2014, S. 101–186.
Zitiert: *Giegerich*, Internationale Standards – aus völkerrechtlicher Perspektive, 101, S.

ders.: Europäische Verfassung und deutsche Verfassung im transnationalen Konstitutionalisierungsprozeß: Wechselseitige Rezeption, konstitutionelle Evolution und föderale Verflechtung. Heidelberg 2012.
Zitiert: *Giegerich*, Europäische Verfassung und deutsche Verfassung im transnationalen Konstitutionalisierungsprozeß: Wechselseitige Rezeption, konstitutionelle Evolution und föderale Verflechtung.

ders. (Hrsg.): Der „offene Verfassungsstaat" des Grundgesetzes nach 60 Jahren, Berlin 2010.
Zitiert: *Giegerich (Hrsg.)*, Der „offene Verfassungsstaat" des Grundgesetzes nach 60 Jahren.

Glaser, M.A.: Internationale Verwaltungsbeziehungen, Tübingen 2010.
Zitiert: *Glaser*, Internationale Verwaltungsbeziehungen.

Gless, S.: Internationales Strafrecht. Grundriss für Studium und Praxis. 2. Aufl., München 2015.
Zitiert: *Gless*, Internationales Strafrecht.

Gornig, G.H.; Horn, H.-D.: Territoriale Souveränität und Gebietshoheit, Berlin 2016.
Zitiert: *Gornig/Horn (Hrsg.)*, Territoriale Souveränität und Gebietshoheit.

Gounalakis, G.; Zagouras, G.: Plädoyer für ein europäisches Medienkonzentrationsrecht, in: ZUM 2006, S. 716–725.
Zitiert: *Gounalakis/Zagouras* in: ZUM 2006, 716, S.

Grabitz, E.; Hilf, M.; Nettesheim, M.: Das Recht der Europäischen Union: EUV/AEUV, Kommentar, 70. Aufl., München 2020.
Zitiert: *Verfasser* in: Grabitz/Hilf/Nettesheim.

Graf Vitzthum, W.; Proelß, A. (Hrsg.): Völkerrecht, 7. Aufl., Berlin 2016.
Zitiert: *Verfasser* in: Graf Vitzthum/Proelß (Hrsg.).

Gstrein, O.; Zeitzmann, S.: Die „Åkerberg Fransson"-Entscheidung des EuGH – „Ne bis in idem" als Wegbereiter für einen effektiven Grundrechtsschutz in der EU?, in: ZEuS 2013, p. 239–260.
Zitiert: *Gstrein/Zeitzmann*, in: ZEuS 2013, 239, S.

Guber, T.: Discours de la méthode: Ist das PSPP-Urteil des BVerfG noch „nachvollziehbar"?, in: ZEuS 2020, S. 625–641.
Zitiert: *Guber* in: ZEuS 2020, 625, S.

Literaturverzeichnis

Gundel, J.: Die Fortentwicklung der europäischen Medienregulierung: Zur Neufassung der AVMD-Richtlinie, in: ZUM 2019, S. 131–139.
Zitiert: *Gundel* in: ZUM 2019, 131, S.

ders.: Die Kontrolle der europäischen Integration durch den französischen Verfassungsrat: zugleich Besprechung der Entscheidung des Conseil constitutionnel vom 31.12.1997 zur Verfassungsmäßigkeit des Vertrags von Amsterdam, in Europarecht (EuR) 1998, S. 371–385.
Zitiert: *Gundel* in: EuR 1998, 371, S.

Häberle, P.: Häberle, Nationalflaggen: Bürgerdemokratische Identitätselemente und Internationale Erkennungssymbole, Berlin 2008.
Zitiert: *Häberle*, Nationalflaggen: Bürgerdemokratische Identitätselemente und Internationale Erkennungssymbole.

ders.: Der kooperative Verfassungsstaat, in: Kaalbach/Krawietz (Hrsg.), Recht und Gesellschaft. Festschrift für Helmut Schelsky, Berlin 1978, S. 141–177.
Zitiert: *Häberle*, Der kooperative Verfassungsstaat, 141, S.

Hain, K.-E.: Sicherung des publizistischen Pluralismus auf europäischer Ebene?, in: AfP 2007, S. 527–534.
Zitiert: *Hain* in: AfP 2007, 527, S.

Hain, K.-E.; Ferreau, F.; Brings-Wiesen, T.: Regulierung sozialer Netzwerke revisited, in: K&R 07–08/2017, S. 433–438.
Zitiert: *Hain/Ferreau/Brings-Wiesen* in: K&R 07–08/2017, 433, S.

Haim, M.; Graefe, A.; Brosius, H.-B.: Burst of the Filter Bubble? Effects of personalization on the diversity of Google News, in: Digital Journalism, Ausgabe 6, Heft 3, 2018, S. 330–343, https://doi.org/10.1080/21670811.2017.1338145.
Zitiert: *Haim/Graefe/Brosius* in: Digital Journalism 3/2018, 330, S.

Hameleers, M.; van der Meer, T.G.: Misinformation and Polarization in a High-Choice Media Environment: How Effective Are Political Fact-Checkers?, in: Communication Research 47(2019)2, S. 227–250, https://doi.org/10.1177%2F0093650218819671.
Zitiert: *Hameleers/van der Meer* in: Communication Research 2019–2, 227, S.

Hans-Bredow-Institut für Medienforschung: Indicators for independence and efficient functioning of audiovisual media services regulatory bodies for the purpose of enforcing the rules in the AVMS Directive – INDIREG – study prepared for the European Commission, SMART 2009/0001, 2011, https://ec.europa.eu/digital-single-market/en/news/study-indicators-independence-and-efficient-functioning-audiovisual-media-services-regulatory-0.
Zitiert: INDIREG (SMART 2009/0001), Studie des HBI im Auftrag der Europäischen Kommission.

Harrison, J.; Woods, L.: Jurisdiction, forum shopping and the 'race to the bottom', in: Harrison/Woods, European Broadcasting Law and Policy, Cambridge 2007, S. 173–193.
Zitiert: *Harrison/Woods*, Jurisdiction, forum shopping and the 'race to the bottom', 173, S.

dies.: Television Quotas: Protecting European Culture?, in: Entertainment Law Review, 12(1), 5–14, 2001.
 Zitiert: *Harrison/Woods*, Television Quotas: Protecting European Culture?.
Harstein, R; Ring, W.-D.; Kreile, J.; Dörr, D.; Stettner, R.; Cole, M.D.; Wagner, E. (Hrsg.): Medienstaatsvertrag, Jugendmedienschutz-Staatsvertrag, Handkommentar (HK-MStV), München, Stand: August 2020.
 Zitiert: *Verfasser* in: HK-MStV.
Hatje, A.: Loyalität als Rechtsprinzip in der Europäischen Union, Baden-Baden 2001.
 Zitiert: *Hatje*, Loyalität als Rechtsprinzip in der Europäischen Union.
Heermann, P.W.: Artikel 30 EGV im Lichte der "Keck"-Rechtsprechung: Anerkennung sonstiger Verkaufsmodalitäten und Einführung eines einheitlichen Rechtfertigungstatbestands?, in: GRUR Int. 7/1998, S. 579–594.
 Zitiert: *Heermann* in: GRUR Int. 1998. 579, S.
Heintzen, M.: Auswärtige Beziehungen privater Verbände. Eine staatsrechtliche, insbesondere grundrechtskollisionsrechtliche Untersuchung, Berlin 1988.
 Zitiert: *Heintzen*, Auswärtige Beziehungen privater Verbände.
Helberger, N.; Eskens, S.; van Drunen, M.; Bastian, M.; Moeller, J.: Implications of AI-driven tools in the media for freedom of expression, in: Artificial Intelligence – Intelligent Politics Challenges and opportunities for media and democracy Background Paper, Ministerial Conference, Cyprus 2020, https://rm.coe.int/cyprus-2020-ai-and-freedom-of-expression/168097fa82.
 Zitiert: *Helberger u.a.*, Implications of AI-driven tools in the media for freedom of expression.
Hieber, T.: »Metall auf Metall« – doch ein Ende ohne Schrecken? – Anmerkung zu EuGH, Urteil vom 29.7.2019 – C-476/17 – Pelham u. a./Hütter u. a., in: ZUM 10/2019, S. 738–750.
 Zitiert: *Hieber* in: ZUM 2019, 738, S.
Hirsch, G.: Die aktuelle Rechtsprechung des EuGH zur Warenverkehrsfreiheit in: ZEuS 1999, S. 503–511.
 Zitiert: *Hirsch* in: ZEuS 1999, 503, S.
Hobe, S.: Einführung in das Völkerrecht, 10. Aufl., Tübingen 2014.
 Zitiert: *Hobe*, Einführung in das Völkerrecht.
ders.: Der offene Verfassungsstaat zwischen Souveränität und Interdependenz, Berlin 1998.
 Zitiert: *Hobe*, Der offene Verfassungsstaat zwischen Souveränität und Interdependenz.
Hochbaum, I.: Der Begriff der Kultur im Maastrichter und Amsterdamer Vertrag, in: BayVBl. 1997, S. 641–654.
 Zitiert: *Hochbaum* in: BayVBl. 1997, 641, S.
Hök, G.-S.: Vollstreckung öffentlicher-rechtlicher Forderungen im Ausland, in: Juristisches Internet Journal, http://www.eurojurislawjournal.net/RA/Hoek-Dr/Beitraege-d/Vollstr-Ausl-3-11-98.htm.
 Zitiert: *Hök*, Vollstreckung öffentlicher-rechtlicher Forderungen im Ausland.

Literaturverzeichnis

Hoeren, T.: Netzwerkdurchsetzungsgesetz europarechtswidrig, beck-blog v. 30.3.2017, abrufbar unter https://community.beck.de/2017/03/30/netzwerkdurchsetzungsgesetz-europarechtswidrig.
Zitiert: *Hoeren*, Netzwerkdurchsetzungsgesetz europarechtswidrig.

Hörnle, J.: International and Comparative Law Quarterly, Vol. 54, Issue 1, 2005, S. 89–126.
Zitiert: *Hörnle* in: International and Comparative Law Quarterly 1–2005, 89, S.

Hofmann, H.C.H.: General principles of EU law and EU administrative law, in: Barnard, C./Peers, S. 198 ff., European Union Law, 2. Aufl., Oxford 2017.
Zitiert: *Hofmann*, in: Barnard/Peers. S. 198, S.

Hofmann, R.: Grundrechte und grenzüberschreitende Sachverhalte, Berlin 1993.
Zitiert: *Hofmann*, Grundrechte und grenzüberschreitende Sachverhalte.

Hoffmann, A.; Gasparotti, A.: Liability for illegal content online Weaknesses of the EU legal framework and possible plans of the EU Commission to address them in a "Digital Services Act", März 2020, https://www.cep.eu/fileadmin/user_upload/cep.eu/Studien/cepStudie_Haftung_fuer_illegale_Online-Inhalte/cepStudy_Liability_for_illegal_content_online.pdf.
Zitiert: *Hoffmann/Gasparotti*, Liability for illegal content online.

Holtz-Bacha, C.: Medienpolitik für Europa, Berlin 2006.
Zitiert: *Holtz-Bacha*, Medienpolitik für Europa.

Holznagel, B.: Vielfaltskonzepte in Europa, in: Kohl (Hrsg.), Vielfalt im Rundfunk. Interdisziplinäre und internationale Annäherungen, Konstanz 1997, S. 94–104.
Zitiert: *Holznagel*, Vielfaltskonzepte in Europa.

Hoorens, S.; Lupiáñez-Villanueva, F. (Hrsg.): Study on media literacy and online empowerment issues raised by algorithm-driven media services, Studie im Auftrag der Europäischen Kommission (DG CNECT), SMART 2017/0081, Brüssel 2019.
Zitiert: Hoorens/Lupiáñez-Villanueva (Hrsg.), Study on media literacy and online empowerment issues raised by algorithm-driven media services (SMART 2017/0081).

Huber, P.: Europäisches und nationales Verfassungsrecht, in: VVDStRL 60 (2001), S. 194–245.
Zitiert: *Huber* in: VVDStRL 2001, 194, S.

Husovec, M.; Quintais, J.P.: Article 17 of the Copyright Directive: Why the German implementation proposal is compatible with EU law – Part 1, in: Kluwers Copyright Blog vom 26. August 2020, http://copyrightblog.kluweriplaw.com/2020/08/26/article-17-of-the-copyright-directive-why-the-german-implementation-proposal-is-compatible-with-eu-law-part-1/.
Zitiert: *Husovec/Quintais* in: Kluwer Copyright Blog v. 26.8.2020.

Institut für Europäisches Medienrecht (Hrsg.): Nizza, die Grundrechte-Charta und ihre Bedeutung für die Medien in Europa, Baden-Baden 2001.
Zitiert: *Institut für Europäisches Medienrecht (Hrsg.)*, Nizza, die Grundrechte-Charta und ihre Bedeutung für die Medien in Europa.

Ipsen, K. (Hrsg.): Völkerrecht, 6. Aufl., München 2014.
Zitiert: *Verfasser* in: Ipsen.

Isensee, J.: Die staatsrechtliche Stellung der Ausländer in der Bundesrepublik Deutschland, in: VVDStRL 32 (1974), S. 49–106.
Zitiert: *Isensee* in: VVDStRL 2001, 49, S.

Isensee, J.; Axer, P.: Jugendschutz im Fernsehen. Verfassungsrechtliche Vorgaben für staatsvertragliche Beschränkungen der Ausstrahlung indexbetroffener Sendungen, München 1998.
Zitiert: *Isensee/Axer*, Jugendschutz im Fernsehen.

Isensee, J.; Kirchhof, G. (Hrsg.) Handbuch des Staatsrechts der Bundesrepublik Deutschland, Band IV: Aufgaben des Staates, 3. Aufl., Heidelberg 2006.
Zitiert: *Verfasser*, in: Isensee/Kirchhof, Band IV.

dies.: Handbuch des Staatsrechts der Bundesrepublik Deutschland, Band V: Rechtsquellen, Organisation, Finanzen, 3. Aufl., Heidelberg 2007.
Zitiert: *Verfasser*, in: Isensee/Kirchhof, Band V.

dies.: Handbuch des Staatsrechts der Bundesrepublik Deutschland, Band IX: Allgemeine Grundrechtslehren, 3. Aufl., Heidelberg 2011.
Zitiert: *Verfasser*, in: Isensee/Kirchhof, Band IX.

dies.: Handbuch des Staatsrechts der Bundesrepublik Deutschland, Band XII: Normativität und Schutz der Verfassung, 3. Aufl., Heidelberg 2014.
Zitiert: Verfasser, in: Isensee/Kirchhof, Band XII.

Jarass, H.D.: Charta der Grundrechte der Europäischen Union, 3. Aufl., München 2016.
Zitiert: *Jarass*, Charta der Grundrechte der Europäischen Union.

ders.: Die Bindung der Mitgliedstaaten an die EU-Grundrechte, in: NVwZ 2012, S. 457–461.
Zitiert: *Jarass* in: NVwZ 2012, 457, S.

ders.: Die Kompetenzen der Europäischen Gemeinschaft und die Folgen für die Mitgliedstaaten, 1997.
Zitiert: *Jarass*, Die Kompetenzen der Europäischen Gemeinschaft und die Folgen für die Mitgliedstaaten.

Jaeckel, L.: Schutzpflichten im deutschen und europäischen Recht. Eine Untersuchung der deutschen Grundrechte, der Menschenrechte und Grundfreiheiten der EMRK sowie der Grundrechte und Grundfreiheiten der Europäischen Gemeinschaft, Baden-Baden 2001.
Zitiert: *Jaeckel*, Schutzpflichten im deutschen und europäischen Recht.

Jäger, M.: Die Novellierung der AVMD-RL – Anwendungsbereich und Werberegulierung – eine erneut vertane Chance?, in: ZUM 63 (2019) 6, S. 477–489.
Zitiert: *Jäger*, ZUM (2019)6, 477, S.

Jeck, T; Langner, B.: cepStudie. Die Europäische Dimension des Sports, Freiburg 2010.
Zitiert: *Jeck/Langner*, Die Europäische Dimension des Sports.

Jennert, C.: Die zukünftige Kompetenzabgrenzung zwischen der Europäischen Union und den Mitgliedstaaten, in: NVwZ 2003 Heft 8, S. 936–942.
Zitiert: *Jennert* in: NVwZ 2003, 936, S.

Literaturverzeichnis

Jungheim, S.: Medienordnung und Wettbewerbsrecht im Zeitalter der Digitalisierung und Globalisierung, Tübingen 2012.
Zitiert: *Jungheim*, Medienordnung und Wettbewerbsrecht im Zeitalter der Digitalisierung und Globalisierung.

Kalscheuer, F.; Hornung, C.: Das Netzwerkdurchsetzungsgesetz – Ein verfassungswidriger Schnellschuss, in: NVwZ 23/2017, S. 1721–1724.
Zitiert: *Kalscheuer/Hornung* in: NVwZ 2017, 1721, S.

Kaufmann, M.: Permanente Verfassungsgebung und verfassungsrechtliche Selbstbindung im europäischen Staatenverbund, in: Der Staat 1997, Ausgabe 36, Nr. 4, S. 521–546.
Zitiert: *Kaufmann*, Der Staat 1997, 521, S.

Keller, H.; Kühne, D.: Zur Verfassungsgerichtsbarkeit des Europäischen Gerichtshofs für Menschenrechte in: Zeitschrift für ausländisches öffentliches Recht und Völkerrecht, 2016, S. 246–305.
Zitiert: *Keller/Kühne* in: ZaöRV 2016, 246, S.

Kellerbauer, M.; Klamert, M.; Tomkin, J. (Hrsg.): EU Treaties and the Charter of Fundamental Rights: A Commentary, Oxford 2019.
Zitiert: *Verfasser* in Kellerbauer/Klamert/Tomkin.

Kiiver, P.: German Participation in EU Decision-Making after the Lisbon Case: A Comparative View on Domestic Parliamentary Clearance Procedures, in: German Law Journal, Ausgabe 10, Heft 8, 2009, S. 1287–1296.
Zitiert: *Kiiver* in: German Law Journal, 2009, 1287. S.

Kingreen, T.: Die Struktur der Grundfreiheiten des Europäischen Gemeinschaftsrechts, Berlin 1999.
Zitiert: *Kingreen*, Die Struktur der Grundfreiheiten des Europäischen Gemeinschaftsrechts.

Kingsbury, C.; Donaldson, M.: Global Administrative Law, in: Wolfrum (Hrsg.), The Max Planck Encyclopedia of Public International Law (MPEPIL), Oxford 2012, www.mpepil.com.
Zitiert: *Kingsbury/Donaldson* in: MPEPIL, Rn.

Kingsbury, B.; Krisch, N.; Stewart, R.B.; Wiener, J.B.: Global Governance as Administration — National and Transnational Approaches to Global Administrative Law, in: Law & Contemporary Problems 68(2005)3&4, S. 1–13.
Zitiert: *Kingsbury u.a.* in: Law & Contemporary Problems 2005/3–4, 1, S.

Kirchhof, P.: Die rechtliche Struktur der Europäischen Union als Staatenverbund, in: von Bogdandy (Hrsg.), Europäisches Verfassungsrecht, Dordrecht/Heidelberg u.a. 2003, S. 893–928.
Zitiert: *Kirchhof*, Die rechtliche Struktur der Europäischen Union als Staatenverbund.

ders.: Nach vierzig Jahren: Gegenwartsfragen an das Grundgesetz, in: JZ 10 (1989), S. 453–465.
Zitiert: *Kirchhof* in: JZ 1989, 453, S.

Klamert, M.: Rechtsprobleme gemischter Abkommen am Beispiel der UNESCO Konvention zum Schutz und der Förderung der Diversität kultureller Ausdrucksformen, in: ZöR 64 (2009), S. 217–235.
Zitiert: *Klamert* in: ZöR 2009, 217, S.

Klatt, M.: Positive Obligations under the European Convention on Human Rights, in: ZaöRV 71 (2011), S. 691–718.
Zitiert: *Klatt* in: ZaöRV 2011, 691, S.

Kment, M.: Grenzüberschreitendes Verwaltungshandeln, Tübingen 2010.
Zitiert: *Kment*, Grenzüberschreitendes Verwaltungshandeln.

Koch, S.: Die grenzüberschreitende Wirkung von nationalen Genehmigungen für umweltbeeinträchtigende industrielle Anlagen, Frankfurt/Main 2010.
Zitiert: *Koch*, Die grenzüberschreitende Wirkung von nationalen Genehmigungen für umweltbeeinträchtigende industrielle Anlagen.

Koenen, T.: Wirtschaft und Menschenrechte. Staatliche Schutzpflichten auf der Basis regionaler und internationaler Menschenrechtsverträge, Berlin 2012.
Zitiert: *Koenen*, Wirtschaft und Menschenrechte.

Kogler, M.R.: Hauptzweck und wesentliche Funktionalität der Bereitstellung audiovisueller Inhalte, in: K&R 2018, Heft 9, S. 537–543.
Zitiert: *Kogler* in: K&R 2018, 537, S.

Kokott, J.: Souveräne Gleichheit und Demokratie im Völkerrecht, ZaöRV 64 (2004), S. 517–533.
Zitiert: *Kokott* in: ZaöRV 2004, 517, S.

Kommission zur Ermittlung der Konzentration im Medienbereich: Sicherung der Meinungsvielfalt im digitalen Zeitalter, Bericht der Kommission zur Ermittlung der Konzentration im Medienbereich (KEK) über die Entwicklung der Konzentration und über Maßnahmen zur Sicherung der Meinungsvielfalt im privaten Rundfunk, in: Schriftenreihe der Landesmedienanstalten Band 52, 2018.
Zitiert: *KEK*, Sicherung der Meinungsvielfalt im digitalen Zeitalter.

Komorek, E. Media Pluralism and European Law, Alphen aan den Rijn 2013.
Zitiert: *Komorek*, Media Pluralism and European Law.

Kotzur, M.: Der Begriff der inländischen juristischen Personen nach Art. 19 Abs. 3 GG im Kontext der EU, in: DÖV 2001, Heft 5, S. 192–198.
Zitiert: *Kotzur* in DÖV 2001, 192, S.

Kresse, H.; Heinze, M.: Der Rundfunk: Das »jedenfalls auch kulturelle Phänomen«. Ein Pyrrhus-Sieg der Länder? – Eine Kurzanalyse des Urteils des BVerfG zur EU-Fernsehrichtlinie, in: ZUM 1995, S. 394–396.
Zitiert: *Kress/Heinze* in: ZUM 1995, 394, S.

Krieger, H.: Die Verantwortlichkeit Deutschlands nach der EMRK für seine Streitkräfte im Auslandseinsatz, in: ZaöRV 62 (2002), S. 669–703.
Zitiert: *Krieger* in: ZaöRV 2002, 669, S.

Literaturverzeichnis

Kuczerawy, A.: EU Proposal for a Directive on Copyright in the Digital Single Market: Compatibility of Article 13 with the EU Intermediary Liability Regime, in: Petkova/Ojanen (Hrsg.), Fundamental Rights Protection Online: The Future Regulation of Intermediaries, Cheltenham 2020, S. 205–219.
Zitiert: *Kuczerawy*, EU Proposal for a Directive on Copyright in the Digital Single Market: Compatibility of Art. 13 with the EU Intermediary Liability Regime, 205, S.

Kukliš, L.: Video-Sharing platforms in AVMSD – a new kind of content regulation (draft), in: Research Handbook on EU Media Law and Policy, Cheltenham 2020 (noch nicht erschienen).
Zitiert: *Kukliš*, Video-Sharing platforms in AVMSD – a new kind of content regulation (draft).

ders.: Media regulation at a distance: video-sharing platforms in AVMS Directive and the future of content regulation, in: mediaLAWS 02/2020, S. 95–110.
Zitiert: *Kukliš* in: mediaLAWS 02/2020, 95, S.

Landesanstalt für Medien NRW (Hrsg.): Was ist Desinformation? Betrachtungen aus sechs wissenschaftlichen Perspektiven, Düsseldorf, 2020, https://www.medienanstalt-nrw.de/fileadmin/user_upload/NeueWebsite_0120/Themen/Desinformation/WasIstDesinformation_Paper_LFMNRW.pdf.
Zitiert: *Autor* in: Was ist Desinformation?

Lange, W.K.: Sponsoring und Europarecht, in: EWS 6/1998, S. 189–195.
Zitiert: *Lange* in: EWS 1998, 189, S.

Langenfeld, C.: Die Neuordnung des Jugendschutzes im Internet, in: MMR 2003, Heft 5, S. 303–309.
Zitiert: *Langenfeld* in: MMR 2003, 303, S.

Larenz, K.; Canaris, C.-W.: Methodenlehre der Rechtswissenschaft, 3. Aufl., Berlin/Heidelberg 1995.
Zitiert: *Larenz/Canaris*, Methodenlehre der Rechtswissenschaft.

Lecheler, H.: Ungereimtheiten bei den Handlungsformen des Gemeinschaftsrechts – dargestellt anhand der Einordnung von „Leitlinien", in: DVBl. 2008, S. 873–880.
Zitiert: *Lecheler* in: DVBl. 2008, 873, S.

Lengauer, A.-M.: Drittwirkung von Grundfreiheiten: Ein Modell. Bausteine der Systematik, Berlin 2011.
Zitiert: *Lengauer*, Drittwirkung von Grundfreiheiten.

Lenski, S.C.: Öffentliches Kulturrecht, Tübingen 2013.
Zitiert: *Lenski*, Öffentliches Kulturrecht.

Lenz, C.: Immanente Grenzen des Gemeinschaftsrechts, in: Europäische Grundrechte-Zeitschrift, 1993, S. 57–65.
Zitiert: *Lenz* in: EuGRZ, 1993, 57, S.

Liehr, J.: Die Niederlassungsfreiheit zum Zwecke der Rundfunkveranstaltung und ihre Auswirkungen auf die deutsche Rundfunkordnung, München 1995.
Zitiert: *Liehr*, Die Niederlassungsfreiheit zum Zwecke der Rundfunkveranstaltung und ihre Auswirkungen auf die deutsche Rundfunkordnung.

Liesching, M.: Das Herkunftslandprinzip nach E-Commerce- und AVMD-Richtlinie. Anwendbarkeit von NetzDG, JuSchG, MStV und JMStV auf Soziale Netzwerke mit Sitz in anderen EU Mitgliedstaaten, München 2020.
Zitiert: *Liesching*, Das Herkunftslandprinzip nach E-Commerce- und AVMD-Richtlinie.

Lievens, E.: Protecting Children in the Digital Era: The Use of Alternative Regulatory Instruments, in: International Studies in Human Rights, Vol. 105, 2010.
Zitiert: *Lievens*, Protecting Children in the Digital Era: The Use of Alternative Regulatory Instruments.

Linke, C.E.: Europäisches Internationales Verwaltungsrecht, Frankfurt/Main 2001.
Zitiert: *Linke*, Europäisches Internationales Verwaltungsrecht.

Lodzig, B.: Grundriss einer verantwortlichen Interpretationstheorie des Rechts, Göttingen 2015.
Zitiert: *Lodzig*, Grundriss einer verantwortlichen Interpretationstheorie.

Mangold, A.: Der Widerspenstigen Zähmung, 13.05.2020, https://www.lto.de/recht/hintergruende/h/bverfg-ezb-urteil-provokation-eugh-eu-vertragsverletzungsverfahren/.
Zitiert: *Mangold*, Der Widerspenstigen Zähmung.

Martín y Pérez de Nanclares, J. Las competencias de los länder y el derecho derivado ante el Tribunal Constitucional Alemán (comentario a la sentencia del Tribunal Constitucional Alemán Bundesverfassungsgericht) de 22 de marzo de 1995, in: Revista de Instituciones Europeas, Ausgabe 22, Heft 3, 1995, S. 887–909.
Zitiert: *Martín y Pérez de Nanclares* in: Revista de Instituciones Europeas 1995, 887, S.

Martini, M.: Die Presseförderung im Fadenkreuz des Unionsrechts, in: EuZW 2015, S. 821–831.
Zitiert: *Martini* in: EuZW 2015, 821, S.

Maunz, T.; Dürig, G. (Begr.): Grundgesetz, Kommentar, 90. Aufl., München 2020.
Zitiert: *Verfasser* in Maunz/Dürig.

Mayer, H.; Stöger, K. (Hrsg.): Kommentar zu EUV und AEUV, Wien 2016.
Zitiert: *Verfasser*, in: Mayer/Stöger, Art. Rn.

Meckel, M. Vielfalt im digitalen Medienensemble. Gutachten im Auftrag von ICOMP, St. Gallen 2012.
Zitiert: *Meckel*, Vielfalt im digitalen Medienensemble.

Menasse, R.: Kurze Geschichte der Europäischen Zukunft, in: Hilpold/Steinmair/Perathoner (Hrsg.), Europa der Regionen, Berlin 2016, S. 27–37.
Zitiert: *Menasse* in: Hilpold/Steinmair/Perathoner, 27, S.

Merten, D.; Papier, H. J. (Hrsg.): Handbuch der Grundrechte in Deutschland und Europa, Band VI/1: europäische Grundrechte, München 2010.
Zitiert: *Verfasser* in: Merten/Papier, Band VI/1.

Meyer-Ladewig, J.; Nettesheim, M.; von Raumer, S. (Hrsg.): EMRK. Europäische Menschenrechtskonvention, Handkommentar, 4. Aufl., Baden-Baden 2017.
Zitiert: *Verfasser* in: Meyer-Ladewig/Nettesheim/von Raumer.

Literaturverzeichnis

Middleton, J.: The Effectiveness of Audiovisual Regulation Inside the European Union: The Television without Frontiers Directive and Cultural Protectionism Denver Journal of International Law and Policy 31/2020, S. 607–628.
Zitiert: *Middleton* in: Denver Journal of International Law and Policy 31/2020, 607, S.

Mojzesowicz, K.: Möglichkeiten und Grenzen einer einheitlichen Dogmatik der Grundfreiheit, Baden-Baden 2001.
Zitiert: *Mojzesowicz*, Möglichkeiten und Grenzen einer einheitlichen Dogmatik der Grundfreiheit.

Möllers, C.; Schneider, L.: Demokratiesicherung in der Europäischen Union, Studie zu einem Dilemma, Tübingen 2018.
Zitiert: *Möllers/Schneider*, Demokratiesicherung in der Europäischen Union.

Moritz, S.: Staatliche Schutzpflichten gegenüber pflegebedürftigen Menschen, Baden-Baden 2013.
Zitiert: *Moritz*, Staatliche Schutzpflichten gegenüber pflegebedürftigen Menschen.

Moussis, N.: Access to the European Union: Law, Economics, Policies, 22. Aufl., Cambridge 2016.
Zitiert: *Moussis*, Access to the European Union

Mühl, A.: Diskriminierung und Beschränkung. Grundansätze einer einheitlichen Dogmatik der wirtschaftlichen Grundfreiheiten des EG-Vertrages, Schriften zum Europäischen Recht, Band 104, Berlin 2004.
Zitiert: *Mühl*, Diskriminierung und Beschränkung. Grundansätze einer einheitlichen Dogmatik der wirtschaftlichen Grundfreiheiten des EG-Vertrages.

Müller-Franken, S.: Netzwerkdurchsetzungsgesetz: Selbstbehauptung des Rechts oder erster Schritt in die selbstregulierte Vorzensur? – Verfassungsrechtliche Fragen, in: AfP 01/2018, S. 1–14.
Zitiert: *Müller-Franken* in: AfP 2018, 1, S.

Müller-Terpitz, R. Ein Karlsruher "Orakel" zum Bundesstaat im europäischen Staatenverbund, in: Menzel (Hrsg.), Verfassungsrechtsprechung. Hundert Entscheidungen des Bundesverfassungsgerichts in Retrospektive, Tübingen 2000, S. 568–574.
Zitiert: *Müller-Terpitz*, Ein Karlsruher "Orakel" zum Bundesstaat im europäischen Staatenverbund.

Müssle, I.; Schmittmann, M.: Der Gemeinsame Markt und die Presse – Let's go Europe?, in: AfP 2002, S. 145–148.
Zitiert: *Müssle/Schmittmann* in: AfP 2002, 145, S.

Nechushtai, E.; Lewis, S. C.: What Kind of News Gatekeepers Do We Want Machines to Be? Filter Bubbles, Fragmentation, and the Normative Dimensions of Algorithmic Recommendations, in: Computers in Human Behavior, Januar 2019: S. 298–307, https://doi.org/10.1016/j.chb.2018.07.043.
Zitiert: *Nechushtai/Lewis* in: Computers in Human Behavior 2019, 298, S.

Neuberger, C.; Lobigs, F.: Meinungsmacht im Internet und die Digitalstrategien von Medienunternehmen: neue Machtverhältnisse trotz expandierender Internet-Geschäfte der traditionellen Massenmedien-Konzerne: Gutachten für die Kommission zur Ermittlung der Konzentration im Medienbereich (KEK), Leipzig 2018.
Zitiert: *Neuberger/Lobigs*, Meinungsmacht im Internet und die Digitalstrategien von Medienunternehmen.

dies.: Die Bedeutung des Internets im Rahmen der Vielfaltssicherung: Gutachten im Auftrag der Kommission zur Ermittlung der Konzentration im Medienbereich (KEK), Berlin 2010.
Zitiert: *Neuberger/Lobigs*, Die Bedeutung des Internets im Rahmen der Vielfaltssicherung.

Neumann, T.: Das Recht der Filmförderung in Deutschland, Konstanz 2016.
Zitiert: *Neumann*, Das Recht der Filmförderung in Deutschland.

Nettesheim, M.: Die Erteilung des mitgliedstaatlichen Einvernehmens nach Art. 4 Abs. 2 Uabs. 1 der FFH-Richtlinie – Vorgaben des Gemeinschaftsrechts und des Grundgesetzes, Tübingen 2007, http://www.fuesser.de/fileadmin/dateien/service/aktuelles/Einvernehmenserteilung/Gutachten_Einvernehmen_FFH.pdf.
Zitiert: *Nettesheim*, Die Erteilung des mitgliedstaatlichen Einvernehmens nach Art. 4 Abs. 2 Uabs. 1 der FFH-Richtlinie.

ders.: Horizontale Kompetenzkonflikte in der EG, in: EuR 1993, S. 243–260.
Zitiert: *Nettesheim* in: EuR 1993, 243, S.

Nielsen, J.: Die Medienvielfalt als Aspekt der Wertesicherung der EU, Berlin 2019.
Zitiert: *Nielsen*, Die Medienvielfalt als Aspekt der Wertesicherung der EU.

Nölscher, P.: Das Netzwerkdurchsetzungsgesetz und seine Vereinbarkeit mit dem Unionsrecht, in: ZUM 2020, S. 301 – 311.
Zitiert: *Nölscher* in: ZUM 2020, 301, S.

Nikles, B.W.; Roll, S.; Spürck, D.; Erdemir, M.; Gutknecht, S. (Hrsg.): Jugendschutzrecht. Kommentar zum Jugendschutzgesetz (JuSchG) und zum Jugendmedienschutz-Staatsvertrag (JMStV) mit auszugsweiser Kommentierung des Strafgesetzbuchs, 3. Aufl., München 2011.
Zitiert: *Verfasser* in Nikles/Roll/Spürck/Erdemir/Gutknecht.

Nikoltchev, S. (Hrsg.): Videoabrufdienste und die Förderung europäischer Werke, IRIS Spezial, Europäische Audiovisuelle Informationsstelle, Straßburg 2013.
Zitiert: *Verfasser* in: Nikoltchev (Hrsg.), Videoabrufdienste und die Förderung europäischer Werke.

Nolte, G.: Hate-Speech, Fake-News, das »Netzwerkdurchsetzungsgesetz« und Vielfaltsicherung durch Suchmaschinen, ZUM 07/2017, S. 552–564.
Zitiert: *Nolte* in: ZUM 2017, 552, S.

Novak, M.: Ungleichbehandlung von ausländischen Produkten oder Dienstleistungen – Einheitliche Rechtfertigungstatbestände im EG-Vertrag, in: DB 1997, 2589–2593.
Zitiert: *Novak* in: DB 1997, 2589, S.

Literaturverzeichnis

Nowrot, K.: Jenseits eines abwehrrechtlichen Ausnahmecharakters. Zur multidimensionalen Rechtswirkung des Widerstandsrechts nach Art. 20 Abs. 4 GG, in: Knops/Körner/Novrot (Hrsg.), Rechtswissenschaftliche Beiträge der Hamburger Sozialökonomie, Heft 5, 2016.
Zitiert: *Nowrot*, Jenseits eines abwehrrechtlichen Ausnahmecharakters – Zur multidimensionalen Rechtswirkung des Widerstandsrechts nach Art. 20 Abs. 4 GG.

Nußberger, A.: Das Verhältnismäßigkeitsprinzip als Strukturprinzip richterlichen Entscheidens in Europa, in: NVwZ 2013, Beilage 1, 60 Jahre BVerwG, Festheft, S. 36–44.
Zitiert: *Nußberger* in: NVwZ-Beilage 2013, 36, S.

O'Neil, C.: Angriff der Algorithmen: Wie sie Wahlen manipulieren, Berufschancen zerstören und unsere Gesundheit gefährden, München 2017.
Zitiert: *O'Neil*, Angriff der Algorithmen.

Obwexer, W.: EU-rechtliche Determinierung mitgliedstaatlicher Kompetenzen, in: ders. u.a. (Hrsg.), EU-Mitgliedschaft und Südtirols Autonomie. Die Auswirkungen der EU-Mitgliedschaft auf die Autonomie des Landes Südtirol am Beispiel ausgewählter Gesetzgebungs- und Verwaltungskompetenzen, Wien 2015.
Zitiert: *Obwexer*, EU-rechtliche Determinierung mitgliedstaatlicher Kompetenzen.

ders.: Der Beitritt der EU zur EMRK: Rechtsgrundlagen, Rechtsfragen und Rechtsfolgen, in: EuR, Jahrgang 47 (2012), Heft 2, S. 115–148.
Zitiert: *Obwexer* in: EuR 2012, 115, S.

Oesch, M.: Das Subsidiaritätsprinzip im EU-Recht und die nationalen Parlamente, in: Epiney/Diezig (Hrsg.), Schweizerisches Jahrbuch für Europarecht 2012/2013, S. 301–315.
Zitiert: *Oesch*, Das Subsidiaritätsprinzip im EU-Recht und die nationalen Parlamente, 301, S.

Ohler, C.: Die Entwicklung eines Internationalen Verwaltungsrechts als Aufgabe der Rechtswissenschaft, in: DVBl. 122 (2007), S. 1083–1090.
Zitiert: *Ohler* in: DVBl. 2007, 1083, S.

ders.: Die Kollisionsordnung des Allgemeinen Verwaltungsrechts – Strukturen des deutschen Internationalen Verwaltungsrechts, Tübingen 2005.
Zitiert: *Ohler*, Die Kollisionsordnung des Allgemeinen Verwaltungsrechts.

Okresek, W.: Hoheitsakte auf fremdem Staatsgebiet. Eine Betrachtung anhand praktischer Fälle, in: ÖZöRV 35 (1985), S. 325–344.
Zitiert: *Okresek* in: ÖZöRV 1985, 325, S.

Oppermann, T.: Transnationale Ausstrahlungen deutscher Grundrechte? Erörtert am Beispiel des transnationalen Umweltschutzes, in: Kroneck/Oppermann (Hrsg.), Im Dienste Deutschlands und des Rechtes : Festschrift für Wilhelm G. Grewe zum 70. Geburtstag am 16. Oktober 1981, Baden-Baden 1981, S. 521–538.
Zitiert: *Oppermann*, Transnationale Ausstrahlung deutscher Grundrechte?, 521, S.

Ory, S.: Medienpolitik mit prozessualen Mitteln: Regionale TV-Werbung in bundesweiten Programmen vor dem EuGH, in: NJW 2021, S. 736–740.
Zitiert: *Ory* in: NJW 2021, 736, S.

Ossenbühl, F: Rundfunk zwischen nationalem Verfassungsrecht und europäischem Gemeinschaftsrecht, Frankfurt/M. 1986.
Zitiert: *Ossenbühl*, Rundfunk zwischen nationalem Verfassungsrecht und europäischem Gemeinschaftsrecht.

Oxman, B.H.: Jurisdiction of States, in: Wolfrum (Hrsg.), The Max Planck Encyclopedia of Public International Law (MPEPIL), Oxford 2012, S. 546–557.
Zitiert: *Oxman* in: MPEPIL, 546, S.

Paal, B.: Intermediäre: Regulierung und Vielfaltssicherung, Rechtsgutachten im Auftrag der Landesanstalt für Medien Nordrhein-Westfalen, März 2018, https://www.medienanstalt-nrw.de/fileadmin/user_upload/lfm-nrw/Foerderung/Forschung/Dateien_Forschung/Paal_Intermediaere_Regulierung-und-Vielfaltssicherung_Gutachten-2018.pdf.
Zitiert: *Paal*, Intermediäre: Regulierung und Vielfaltssicherung.

ders.: Medienvielfalt und Wettbewerbsrecht, Tübingen 2010.
Zitiert: *Paal*, Medienvielfalt und Wettbewerbsrecht.

Pechstein, M.; Nowak, C.; Häde, U. (Hrsg.): Frankfurter Kommentar zu EUV, GRC und AEUV, Tübingen 2017.
Zitiert: *Verfasser* in: Pechstein u.a., Frankfurter Kommentar.

Peifer, K.-N.: Netzwerkdurchsetzungsgesetz: Selbstbehauptung des Rechts oder erster Schritt in die selbstregulierte Vorzensur? – Zivilrechtliche Aspekte, in: AfP 01/2018, S. 14–23.
Zitiert: *Peifer* in: AfP 01/2018, 14, S.

Pernice, I.: Europäisches und nationales Verfassungsrecht, in: VVDStRL 60 (2001), S. 148–193.
Zitiert: *Pernice* in: VVDStRL 2001, 148, S.

Plötscher, S.: Der Begriff der Diskriminierung im Europäischen Gemeinschaftsrecht, Berlin 2003.
Zitiert: *Plötscher*, Der Begriff der Diskriminierung im Europäischen Gemeinschaftsrecht.

Potacs, M.: Rechtstheorie, Wien 2015.
Zitiert: *Potacs*, Rechtstheorie.

Puttler, A.: Sind die Mitgliedstaaten noch "Herren" der EU? – Stellung und Einfluss der Mitgliedstaaten nach dem Entwurf des Verfassungsvertrages der Regierungskonferenz, in: Europarecht (EuR) 2004, S. 669–691.
Zitiert: *Puttler* in: EuR 2004, 669, S.

Reese, B.: Die Verfassung des Grundgesetzes. Rahmen- und Werteordnung im Lichte der Gefährdungen durch Macht und Moral, Berlin 2013.
Zitiert: *Reese*, Die Verfassung des Grundgesetzes. Rahmen- und Werteordnung im Lichte der Gefährdungen durch Macht und Moral.

Ress, G.: Supranationaler Menschenrechtsschutz und der Wandel der Staatlichkeit, in: ZaöRV 64 (2004), S. 621–639.
Zitiert: *Ress* in: ZaöRV 2004, 621, S.

Literaturverzeichnis

ders.: Staatszwecke im Verfassungsstaat — nach 40 Jahren Grundgesetz, in: VVDStRL 48 (1990), S. 56–118.
Zitiert: *Ress* in: VVDStRL 1990, 56, S.

ders.: Menschenrechte, europäisches Gemeinschaftsrecht und nationales Verfassungsrecht, in: Haller/Kopetzki/Novak/Paulson/Raschauer/Ress/Wiederin (Hrsg.), Staat und Recht: Festschrift für Günther Winkler, Vienna 1997, S. 897–932.
Zitiert: *Ress*, Menschenrechte, europäisches Gemeinschaftsrecht und nationales Verfassungsrecht, 897, S.

ders.: Die neue Kulturkompetenz der EG, in: DÖV 1992, S. 944–955.
Zitiert: *Ress* in: DÖV 1992, 944, S.

Ress, G.; Bröhmer, J.: Europäische Gemeinschaft und Medienvielfalt. Die Kompetenzen der Europäischen Gemeinschaft zur Sicherung des Pluralismus im Medienbereich, Saarbrücken 1998.
Zitiert: *Ress/Bröhmer*, Europäische Gemeinschaft und Medienvielfalt.

Ress, G.; Ukrow, J.: Die Niederlassungsfreiheit von Apothekern in Europa, Stuttgart 1991.
Zitiert: *Ress/Ukrow*, Die Niederlassungsfreiheit von Apothekern.

Rengeling, H.-W.; Middeke, A.; Gellermann, M. (Hrsg.): Handbuch des Rechtsschutzes in der Europäischen Union, 3. Aufl., München 2014.
Zitiert: *Verfasser* in: Rengeling/Middeke/Gellermann (Hrsg.).

Riecken, J.: Verfassungsgerichtsbarkeit in der Demokratie. Grenzen verfassungsgerichtlicher Kontrolle unter besonderer Berücksichtigung von John Hart Elys prozeduraler Theorie der Repräsentationsverstärkung, Berlin 2003.
Zitiert: *Riecken*, Verfassungsgerichtsbarkeit in der Demokratie.

Rodriguez Iglesias, G. C.: Zu den Grenzen der verfahrensrechtlichen Autonomie der Mitgliedstaaten bei der Anwendung des Gemeinschaftsrechts, EuGRZ 1997, S. 289–295.
Zitiert: *Rodriguez Iglesias* in: EuGRZ 1997, 289, S.

Roider, C.: Perspektiven einer Europäischen Rundfunkordnung, Berlin 2001.
Zitiert: *Roider*, Perspektiven einer Europäischen Rundfunkordnung.

Ruffert, M.: Die Globalisierung als Herausforderung an das Öffentliche Recht, Stuttgart u.a. 2004.
Zitiert: *Ruffert*, Die Globalisierung als Herausforderung an das Öffentliche Recht.

ders.: Kontinuität oder Kehrtwende im Streit um die gemeinschaftsrechtlichen Umweltschutzkompetenzen?, in: Jura 1994, S. 635–643.
Zitiert; *Ruffert* in: Jura 1994, 635, S.

Rupp, H.H.: Anmerkungen zu einer Europäischen Verfassung, in: JuristenZeitung 58. Jahrg., Nr. 1, S. 18–22.
Zitiert: *Rupp* in: JZ 2003, 18, S.

Russ-Mohl, S.: Die informierte Gesellschaft und ihre Feinde: Warum die Digitalisierung unsere Demokratie gefährdet, Köln 2017.
Zitiert: *Russ-Mohl*, Die informierte Gesellschaft und ihre Feinde: Warum die Digitalisierung unsere Demokratie gefährdet.

Safferling, C.: Internationales Strafrecht: Strafanwendungsrecht – Völkerstrafrecht – Europäisches Strafrecht, Berlin/Heidelberg 2011.
Zitiert: *Safferling*, Internationales Strafrecht.

Schallbruch, M.: Schwacher Staat im Netz: Wie die Digitalisierung den Staat in Frage stellt, Berlin 2018.
Zitiert: *Schallbruch*, Schwacher Staat im Netz.

Schmidt, S.: Die Rechtmäßigkeit staatlicher Gefahrenabwehrmaßnahmen im Internet unter besonderer Berücksichtigung des Europäischen Gemeinschaftsrechts, Frankfurt/M. u.a. 2006.
Zitiert: *Schmidt*, Die Rechtmäßigkeit staatlicher Gefahrenabwehrmaßnahmen im Internet unter besonderer Berücksichtigung des Europäischen Gemeinschaftsrechts.

Schmitt von Sydow, H.: Liberté, démocratie, droits fondamentaux et État de droit: analyse de l'article 7 du traité UE in: Revue du droit de l'union européenne, 2001, S. 285–328.
Zitiert: *Schmitt von Sydow* in: Revue du droit de l'union européenne 2001, 285, S.

Schmittmann, M.; Luedtke, A.: Die Medienfreiheiten in der Europäischen Grundrechtecharta, in: AfP 2000, S. 533–534.
Zitiert: *Schmittmann/Luedtke* in: AfP 2000, 533, S.

Stelkens, P.; Bonk, H.J.; Sachs, M. (Hrsg.): Verwaltungsverfahrensgesetz, 8. Aufl., München 2014.
Zitiert: *Verfasser* in: Stelkens/Bonk/Sachs.

Schnelle, E.: Freiheitsmissbrauch und Grundrechtsverwirkung, Versuch einer Neubestimmung von Artikel 18 GG, Berlin 2014.
Zitiert: *Schnelle*, Freiheitsmissbrauch und Grundrechtsverwirkung.

Schleper, N.: Auf dem Weg zu einer einheitlichen Dogmatik der Grundfreiheiten?, in: Institut für Völkerrecht der Universität Göttingen, Abteilung Europarecht – Göttinger Online-Beiträge zum Europarecht, Nr. 16 (2004), https://www.jura.fu-berlin.de/forschung/europarecht/bob/berliner_online_beitraege/Paper16-Schleper/Paper16---Auf-dem-Weg-zu-einer-einheitlichen-Dogmatik-der-Grundfreiheiten.pdf.
Zitiert: *Schleper* in: Göttinger Online-Beiträge zum Europarecht, Nr. 16 (2004)

Schlochauer, H.J.: Die extraterritoriale Wirkung von Hoheitsakten nach dem öffentlichen Recht der Bundesrepublik Deutschland und nach internationalem Recht, Frankfurt 1962.
Zitiert: *Schlochauer*, Die extraterritoriale Wirkung von Hoheitsakten nach dem öffentlichen Recht der Bundesrepublik Deutschland und nach internationalem Recht.

Schorkopf, F.: Grundgesetz und Überstaatlichkeit, Tübingen 2007.
Zitiert: *Schorkopf*, Grundgesetz und Überstaatlichkeit.

Literaturverzeichnis

Schriewert, B.: Zur Theorie der internationalen Offenheit und der Völkerrechtsfreundlichkeit einer Rechtsordnung und ihrer Erprobung am Beispiel der EU-Rechtsordnung, in: Veröffentlichungen des Walther-Schücking-Instituts für Internationales Recht an der Universität Kiel (VIIR), Band 197, Berlin 2017.
Zitiert: *Schriewert,* Zur Theorie der internationalen Offenheit und der Völkerrechtsfreundlichkeit einer Rechtsordnung und ihrer Erprobung am Beispiel der EU-Rechtsordnung.

Schröder, M.: Zur Wirkkraft der Grundrechte bei Sachverhalten mit grenzüberschreitenden Elementen, in: Münch (Hrsg.), Staatsrecht – Völkerrecht – Europarecht, Festschrift für Hans-Jürgen Schlochauer zum 75. Geburtstag am 28. März 1981, Frankfurt 1981, S. 137–150.
Zitiert: *Schröder,* Zur Wirkkraft der Grundrechte bei Sachverhalten mit grenzüberschreitenden Elementen, 137, S.

Schulz, W.: Jugendschutz bei Tele- und Mediendiensten, in: MMR 1998, Heft 4, S. 182–187.
Zitiert: *Schulz* in MMR 1998, 182, S.

Schulz, W.; Held, T.: Regulierte Selbstregulierung als Form modernen Regierens, Bericht im Auftrag des Bundesbeauftragten für Angelegenheiten der Kultur und der Medien, Mai 2002, https://www.hans-bredow-institut.de/uploads/media/Publikationen/cms/media/a80e5e6dbc2427639ca0f437fe76d3c4c95634ac.pdf.
Zitiert: *Schulz/Held,* Regulierte Selbstregulierung als Form modernen Regierens.

Schulz, W.; Valcke, P.; Irion, K.: The Independence of the Media and Its Regulatory Agencies – shedding new light on formal and actual independence against the national context, Chicago 2013.
Zitiert: *Verfasser* in: Schulz/Valcke/Irion (Hrsg.), The Independence of the Media and Its Regulatory Agencies.

Schulze, R.; Zuleeg, M.; Kadelbach, S. (Hrsg.): Europarecht. Handbuch für die deutsche Rechtspraxis, 3. Aufl., München 2015.
Zitiert: *Verfasser* in Schulze/Zuleeg/Kadelbach.

Schwartz, I.E.: Rundfunk, EG-Kompetenzen und ihre Ausübung, in: Stern (Hrsg.), Eine Rundfunkordnung für Europa – Chancen und Risiken; Vortragsveranstaltung vom 18. und 19. Mai 1990, München 1990.
Zitiert: *Schwartz,* Rundfunk, EG-Kompetenzen und ihre Ausübung.

Schwarz, T.: Subsidiarität und EG-Kompetenzen, in: Zeitschrift für Meiden- und Kommunikationsrecht, 1993, S. 409–417.
Zitiert: *Schwarz* in: AfP, 1993, 409, S.

Schwarze, J. (Hrsg.): Globalisierung und Entstaatlichung des Rechts, Tübingen 2008.
Zitiert: *Schwarze,* Globalisierung und Entstaatlichung des Rechts.

Schwarze, J.: Europäische Rahmenbedingungen für die Verwaltungsgerichtsbarkeit, in: NVwZ 2000 Heft 3, S. 241–251.
Zitiert: *Schwarze* in: NVwZ 2000, 241, S.

Schwarze, J. (Hrsg.): Die Entstehung einer europäischen Verfassungsordnung. Das Ineinandergreifen von nationalem und europäischem Verfassungsrecht, Baden-Baden 2000.
Zitiert: *Schwarze*, Die Entstehung einer europäischen Verfassungsordnung.

Schweisfurth, T.: Völkerrecht, Tübingen 2006.
Zitiert: *Schweisfurth*, Völkerrecht.

Sedelmeier, K.; Burkhardt, E. (Hrsg.): Löffler (Begründer), Kommentar zum Presserecht, 6. Aufl., München 2015.
Zitiert: *Verfasser* in: Sedelmeier/Burkhardt.

Seibert-Fohr, A.: Die völkerrechtliche Verantwortung des Staats für das Handeln von Privaten: Bedarf nach Neuorientierung?, in: ZaöRV 73 (2013), S. 37–60.
Zitiert: Seibert-Fohr in: ZaöRV 2013, 37, S.

Sommermann, K.-P.: Offene Staatlichkeit: Deutschland, in: von Bogdandy/Cruz Villalón/Huber (Hrsg.), Handbuch Ius Publicum Europaeum, Bd. II: Offene Staatlichkeit – Wissenschaft vom Verfassungsrecht, Heidelberg 2008, S. 3–35.
Zitiert: *Sommermann*, Offene Staatlichkeit: Deutschland, 3, S.

Spindler, G.: Der Regierungsentwurf zum Netzwerkdurchsetzungsgesetz – europarechtswidrig?, in: ZUM 2017, 473–506.
Zitiert: *Spindler* in: ZUM 2017, 473, S.

Spindler, G.; Schmitz, P. (Hrsg.): Telemediengesetz: TMG mit Netzwerkdurchsetzungsgesetz (NetzDG), Kommentar, 2. Aufl., München 2018.
Zitiert: *Verfasser* in: Spindler/Schmitz.

Stark, B.; Margin, M.; Jürgens, P.: Maßlos überschätzt. Ein Überblick über theoretische Annahmen und empirische Befunde zu Filterblasen und Echokammern (Preprint), erscheint in: Eisenegger/Blum/Ettinger/Prinzing (Hrsg.), Digitaler Strukturwandel der Öffentlichkeit: Historische Verortung, Modelle und Konsequenzen, 2020, auch abrufbar als Preprint unter http://melanie-magin.net/wp-content/uploads/2019/11/Stark_Magin_Juergens_2019_Preprint.pdf.
Zitiert: *Stark/Margin/Jürgens*, Maßlos überschätzt. Ein Überblick über theoretische Annahmen und empirische Befunde zu Filterblasen und Echokammern (Preprint).

Stein, T.; von Buttlar, C.; Kotzur, M.: Völkerrecht, 14. Aufl., München 2017.
Zitiert: *Stein/von Buttlar/Kotzur*, Völkerrecht.

Steinbeis, M.: Europarechtsbruch als Verfassungspflicht: Karlsruhe zündet die Identitätskontrollbombe, in: Verfassungsblog, 26.01.2016 (abrufbar unter https://verfassungsblog.de/europarechtsbruch-als-verfassungspflicht-karlsruhe-zuendet-die-identitaetskontroll-bombe/, zuletzt abgerufen 08.01.2021).
Zitiert: *Steinbeis*, Verfassungsblog, 26.01.2016.

Stern, K.: Das Staatsrecht der Bundesrepublik Deutschland. Band III/1, München 1988.
Zitiert: *Stern*, Das Staatsrecht der Bundesrepublik Deutschland, Band III/1.

Stern, K.; Sachs, M. (Hrsg.): Europäische Grundrechte-Charta: GRCh, München 2016.
Zitiert: *Verfasser* in: Stern/Sachs.

Literaturverzeichnis

Streinz, R.: Europarecht, 11. Aufl., Heidelberg 2019.
Zitiert: *Streinz*, Europarecht.

ders. (Hrsg.): EUV/AEUV, Vertrag über die Europäische Union, Vertrag über die Arbeitsweise der Europäischen Union, Charta der Grundrechte der Europäischen Union, Kommentar, 3. Aufl., München 2018.
Zitiert: *Verfasser* in: Streinz.

ders.: Die Interpretationsmethoden des Europäischen Gerichtshofs zum Vorantreiben der Integration, in: Rill (Hrsg.), Die Dynamik der europäischen Institutionen, München 2011, S. 27–40.
Zitiert: *Streinz*, Die Interpretationsmethoden des Europäischen Gerichtshofs zum Vorantreiben der Integration, 27, S.

ders.: Konvergenz der Grundfreiheiten. Aufgabe der Differenzierungen des EG-Vertrags und der Unterscheidung zwischen unterschiedlichen und unterschiedslosen Maßnahmen? Zu Tendenzen der Rechtsprechung des EuGH, in: Arndt/Knemeyer/Kugelmann (Hrsg.), Völkerrecht und deutsches Recht: Festschrift für Walter Rudolf zum 70. Geburtstag, München 2001, S. 199–221.
Zitiert: *Streinz*, Konvergenz der Grundfreiheiten, 199, S.

ders.: Bundesverfassungsgerichtlicher Grundrechtsschutz und Europäisches Gemeinschaftsrecht, Baden-Baden 1989.
Zitiert: *Streinz*, Bundesverfassungsgerichtlicher Grundrechtsschutz und Europäisches Gemeinschaftsrecht.

Streinz, R.; Michl, W.: Die Drittwirkung des europäischen Datenschutzgrundrechts (Art. 8 GRCh) im deutschen Privatrecht, in: EuZW 2011, S. 384–388.
Zitiert: *Streinz/Michl* in EuZW 2011, 384, S.

Strupp, K.; Schlochauer, H.-J. (Hrsg.): Wörterbuch des Völkerrechts, Bd. I, Berlin 1960.
Zitiert: *Verfasser* in: Strupp/Schlochauer, S.

Struth, A.: Hassrede und Freiheit der Meinungsäußerung: Der Schutzbereich der Meinungsäußerungsfreiheit in Fällen demokratiefeindlicher Äußerungen nach der Europäischen Menschenrechtskonvention, dem Grundgesetz und der Charta der Grundrechte der Europäischen Union, Berlin 2019.
Zitiert: *Struth*, Hassrede und Freiheit der Meinungsäußerung.

Stuyck, J.: Joined Cases C-34/95, C-35/95 and C-36/95, Konsumentombudsmannen (KO) v. De Agostini (Svenska) Förlag AB and Konsumentombudsmannen (KO) v. TV-Shop i Sverige AB, Judgment of 9 July 1997, in: CML-Rev. 6/1997, S. 1445–1468.
Zitiert: *Stuyck* in: CML-Rev. 1997, 1445, S.

Sunstein, C. R.: Infotopia: How Many Minds Produce Knowledge, Oxford 2006.
Zitiert: *Sunstein*, Infotopia: How Many Minds Produce Knowledge.

Talmon, S.: Die Grenzen der Anwendung des Völkerrechts im deutschen Recht, JZ 68 (2013), S. 12–21.
Zitiert: *Talmon* in: JZ 2013, 12, S.

Tamblé, P.: Der Anwendungsbereich der EU-Grundrechtecharta (GRC) gem. Art. 51 I 1 GRC – Grundlagen und aktuelle Entwicklungen, Halle 2014.
Zitiert: *Tamblé*, Der Anwendungsbereich der EU-Grundrechtecharta (GRC) gem. Art. 51 I 1 GRC.

Tichy, H.: Recommendations des Europarats, in: ZaöRV 76 (2016), S. 415–424.
Zitiert: *Tichy* in: ZaöRV 2016, 415, S.

Tietje, C.: Die Exekutive. Verwaltungshandeln im Kontext von Globalisierung und Internationalisierung, in: Delbrück/Einsele (Hrsg.), Wandel des Staates im Kontext europäischer und internationaler Integration, Baden-Baden 2006, S. 53–70.
Zitiert: *Tietje*, Die Exekutive. Verwaltungshandeln im Kontext von Globalisierung und Internationalisierung, 53, S.

ders.: Die Internationalität des Verwaltungsstaates – Vom internationalen Verwaltungsrecht des Lorenz von Stein zum heutigen internationalisierten Verwaltungshandeln, in: Quellen zur Verwaltungsgeschichte Nr. 16, Kiel 2001.
Zitiert: *Tietje*, Die Internationalität des Verwaltungsstaates.

ders.: Internationalisiertes Verwaltungshandeln, in: Veröffentlichungen des Walther-Schücking-Instituts für Internationales Recht an der Universität Kiel (VIIR), Band 136, Berlin 2001.
Zitiert: *Tietje*, Internationalisiertes Verwaltungshandeln.

Tietje, C.; Bering, J.; Zuber, T.: Völker- und europarechtliche Zulässigkeit extraterritorialer Anknüpfung einer Finanztransaktionssteuer, Halle 2014.
Zitiert : *Tietje/Bering/Zuber*, Völker- und europarechtliche Zulässigkeit extraterritorialer Anknüpfung einer Finanztransaktionssteuer.

Thiele, A.: Europarecht, 15. Aufl., Wien 2018.
Zitiert: *Thiele*, Europarecht

Trautwein, T.: Das BVerfG, der EuGH und das Fernsehen – Anmerkungen zum Urteil des BVerfG zur EG-Fernsehrichtlinie, in: ZUM 1995, S. 614–617.
Zitiert: *Trautwein* in: ZUM 1995, 614, S.

Trstenjak, V; Beysen, E.: Das Prinzip der Verhältnismäßigkeit in der Unionsrechtsordnung, in: in: EuR 2012, S. 265–284.
Zitiert: *Trstenjak/Beysen* in: EuR 2012, 265, S.

Uerpmann-Wittzack, R.: Principles of International Internet Law, in: German Law Journal (GLJ) 11(2010)11, S. 1245–1263.
Zitiert: *Uerpmann-Wittzack* in: GLJ 2010, 1245, S.

Ukrow, J.: Wehrhafte Demokratie 4.0 – Grundwerte, Grundrechte und Social Media-Exzesse, in: ZEuS 2021, S. 65–98.
Zitiert: *Ukrow* in: ZEuS 2021, S. 65, S.

ders.: Das aktuelle Stichwort: Sicherung regionaler Vielfalt – Außer Mode? Anmerkungen aus Anlass des Urteils des Europäischen Gerichtshofs vom 3. Februar 2021, Rs. C-555/19, Fussl Modestraße Mayr GmbH ./. SevenOne Media GmbH, ProSiebenSat.1 TV Deutschland GmbH, ProSiebenSat.1 Media SE, https://emr-sb.de/wp-content/uploads/2021/02/EMR_Aktuelles-Stichwort-zum-EuGH-Urteil-in-Sachen-Fussl-Modestrasse-Mayr.pdf.
Zitiert: *Ukrow*, Sicherung regionaler Vielfalt – Außer Mode?.

Literaturverzeichnis

ders.: Die Vorschläge der EU-Kommission für einen Digital Services Act und einen Digital Markets Act. Darstellung von und erste Überlegungen zu zentralen Bausteinen für eine digitale Grundordnung der EU, in: Impulse aus dem EMR, 2021, https://emr-sb.de/wp-content/uploads/2021/01/Impulse-aus-dem-EMR_DMA-und-DSA.pdf.
Zitiert: *Ukrow*, Die Vorschläge der EU-Kommission für einen Digital Services Act und einen Digital Markets Act.

ders.: Schutz der Medienvielfalt und medienbezogene Solidaritätspflichten in Corona-Zeiten. Eine europa- und verfassungsrechtliche Betrachtung, in: Impulse aus dem EMR, 2020, https://emr-sb.de/wp-content/uploads/2020/03/EMR-Impulse-Vielfalt-Corona-200330.pdf.
Zitiert: *Ukrow*, Schutz der Medienvielfalt und medienbezogene Solidaritätspflichten in Corona-Zeiten.

ders.: Élysée 2.0 im Lichte des Europarechts – Der Vertrag von Aachen und die „immer engere Union", in: Zeitschrift für Europarechtliche Studien 1/2019, S. 3 ff.
Zitiert: *Ukrow*, Élysée 2.0 im Lichte des Europarechts, ZEuS 2019, 3,

ders.: Online-Glücksspiel in der Regulierung – Kohärenz im Werden?, in: ZfWG 2019, S. 223–234.
Zitiert: *Ukrow* in: ZfWG 2019, 223, S.

ders.: Algorithmen, APIs und Aufsicht. Überlegungen zur organisations- und verfahrensrechtlichen Effektuierung einer positiven Ordnung der Vielfaltssicherung im digitalen Raum, in: Impulse aus dem EMR, 2019, https://emr-sb.de/impulse-aus-dem-emr-algorithmen-apis-und-aufsicht/.
Zitiert: *Ukrow*, Algorithmen, APIs und Aufsicht.

ders.: Indexierung des Rundfunkbeitrags und Stabilität der deutschen Rundfunkfinanzierung. Ansätze einer europarechtlichen Risikoanalyse, UFITA 83(2019)1, S. 279 ff.
Zitiert: *Ukrow* in: UFITA 2019, 279, S.

ders.: Wer ist gegen Europa? Analyse der Wahlen nach dem Brexit-Referendum, vorgänge 56 (2017) H. 220, 69.
Zitiert: *Ukrow*, Wer ist gegen Europa? vorgänge 56 (2017) H. 220, 69

ders.: Zum Anwendungsbereich einer novellierten AVMD-Richtlinie. Impulse für das anstehende AVMD-Trilog-Verfahren, 2017, https://emr-sb.de/wp-content/uploads/2017/09/EMR-AVMD-Impulse-1708-01-Anwendungsbereich.pdf.
Zitiert: *Ukrow*, Zum Anwendungsbereich einer novellierten AVMD-Richtlinie.

ders.: Por-No Go im audiovisuellen Binnenmarkt? Jugendmedienschutz im Level-Playing-Field und die geplante Abkehr vom absoluten Pornographieverbot im Fernsehen, in: EMR Impuls, 2017, https://emr-sb.de/wp-content/uploads/2017/10/EMR-AVMD-Impulse-1710-01-Jugendschutz.pdf.
Zitiert: *Ukrow*, Por-No Go im audiovisuellen Binnenmarkt?

ders.: Internationaler und europäischer Jugendmedienschutz – Bestandsaufnahme, Entwicklungstendenzen und Herausforderungen in: Recht der Jugend und des Bildungswesens (RdJB) 65(2017)3, S. 278–296.
Zitiert: *Ukrow* in: RdJB 2017, 278, S.

ders.: Wächst Europa an seinen rechtspopulistischen Feinden? Europäische wehrhafte Demokratie und Schutz der Grundwerte in der EU, in: vorgänge 55 (2016) H. 216, 47.
Zitiert: *Ukrow* in: vorgänge 55 (2016) 216, 47, S.

ders.: Ceterum censeo: CETA prohibendam esse? Audiovisuelle Medien im europäisch-kanadischen Freihandelssystem, in: EMR – Das aktuelle Stichwort, 2016, https://emr-sb.de/wp-content/uploads/2017/01/20170109_EMR_Das-aktuelle-Stichwort_CETA.pdf.
Zitiert: *Ukrow*, Ceterum censeo: CETA prohibendam esse? Audiovisuelle Medien im europäisch-kanadischen Freihandelssystem.

ders.: Deutschland auf dem Weg vom Motor zum Bremser der europäischen Integration? Kritische Anmerkungen zum „Lissabon"-Urteil des Bundesverfassungsgerichts vom 30. Juni 2009, in: ZEuS 2009, S. 717–729.
Zitiert: *Ukrow* in: ZEuS 2009, 717, S.

ders.: Jugendschutzrecht, München 2004.
Zitiert: *Ukrow*, Jugendschutzrecht.

ders.: Die Selbstkontrolle im Medienbereich in Europa, München, Berlin 2000.
Zitiert: *Ukrow*, Die Selbstkontrolle im Medienbereich in Europa.

ders.: Richterliche Rechtsfortbildung durch den EuGH. Dargestellt am Beispiel der Erweiterung des Rechtsschutzes des Marktbürgers im Bereich des vorläufigen Rechtsschutzes und der Staatshaftung, Baden-Baden 1995.
Zitiert: *Ukrow*, Richterliche Rechtsfortbildung durch den EuGH.

Ukrow, J.; Cole, M. D.: Aktive Sicherung lokaler und regionaler Medienvielfalt – Rechtliche Möglichkeiten und Grenzen der Förderung inhaltlicher Qualität in Presse-, Rundfunk- und Online-Angeboten, TLM Schriftenreihe Band 25, 2019.
Zitiert: *Ukrow/Cole*, Aktive Sicherung lokaler und regionaler Medienvielfalt.

dies.: Zur Transparenz von Mediaagenturen – Eine rechtswissenschaftliche Untersuchung, Gutachten im Auftrag der Friedrich-Ebert-Stiftung, 2017, abrufbar unter https://library.fes.de/pdf-files/akademie/13233.pdf.
Zitiert: *Ukrow/Cole*, Zur Transparenz von Mediaagenturen.

Ukrow, J.; Etteldorf, C.: Fake News" als Rechtsproblem, in Ory/Cole/Ukrow (Hrsg.), EMR/Script, Band 5, https://emr-sb.de/wp-content/uploads/2018/04/EMR-SCRIPT-Band-5_Fake-News-als-Rechtsproblem.pdf.
Zitiert: *Ukrow/Etteldorf*, Fake News als Rechtsproblem.

Ullrich, H.: Enhanced Cooperation in the Area of Unitary Patent Protection and European Integration, in: RdDI 2013, p. 325–351.
Zitiert: *Ullrich* in: RdDI 2013, 325, S.

Valcke, P.: Challenges of Regulating Media Pluralism in the European Union: the Potential of Risk-Based Regulation, Quaderns del CAC 38 Ausgabe XV (1), Juni 2012.
Zitiert: *Valcke*, Challenges of Regulating Media Pluralism in the European Union.

Literaturverzeichnis

Valdani, Vicari and Associates (VVA): Assessment on the implementation of the code of practice on disinformation, Studie im Auftrag der Europäischen Kommission, SMART 2019/0041, 2020, https://ec.europa.eu/digital-single-market/en/news/study-assessment-implementation-code-practice-disinformation.
Zitiert: *VVA*, Assessment on the implementation of the code of practice on disinformation.

VVA, KEA, attentional: Study on the Promotion of European Works in Audiovisual Media Services, SMART 2016/0061, study prepared for the European Commission DG Communications Networks, Content & Technology, 2020, https://ec.europa.eu/digital-single-market/en/news/study-promotion-european-works-1.
VVA u.a., study on the Promotion of European Works in Audiovisual Media Services, SMART 2016/0061.

Valerius, B.: Ermittlungen der Strafverfolgungsbehörden in den Kommunikationsdiensten des Internet. Hoheitliche Recherchen in einem grenzüberschreitenden Medium, Berlin 2004.
Zitiert: *Valerius*, Ermittlungen der Strafverfolgungsbehörden in den Kommunikationsdiensten des Internet. Hoheitliche Recherchen in einem grenzüberschreitenden Medium.

van Loon, A.: Freedom versus access rights in a European context, in: Media Law & Policy 2001–1, S. 12–31.
Zitiert: *van Loon* in: Media Law & Policy 2001, 12, S.

Vedder, C.; Heintschel von Heinegg, W. (Hrsg.): Europäisches Unionsrecht, EUV, AEUV, GRCh, EAGV, Kommentar, 2. Aufl., Baden-Baden 2018.
Zitiert: *Verfasser* in: Vedder/Heintschel von Heinegg.

Viķe-Freiberga, V.; Däubler-Gmelin, H.; Hammersley, B.; Maduro, L.: Hochrangige Gruppe zur Freiheit und Vielfalt der Medien, Bericht zu freien und pluralistischen Medien als Rückhalt der europäischen Demokratie, 2013, https://ec.europa.eu/newsroom/document.cfm?action=display&doc_id=4407.
Zitiert: *Viķe-Freiberga u.a.* (Hochrangige Gruppe zur Freiheit und Vielfalt der Medien), Bericht zu freien und pluralistischen Medien als Rückhalt der europäischen Demokratie, 2013.

Visionary Analytics, SQW Limited, Ramboll Management Consulting: Survey and data gathering to support the Impact Assessment of a possible new legislative proposal concerning Directive 2010/13/EU (AVMSD) and in particular the provisions on media freedom, public interest and access for disabled people, study prepared for the European Commission DG Communications Networks, Content & Technology, SMART 2015/0048, 2016, https://www.visionary.lt/wp-content/uploads/2016/05/AVMSD.pdf.
Zitiert: *Visionary Analytics et al.*, Study to support Impact Assessment of AVMSD.

Vlassis, A.: The review of the Audiovisual Media Services Directive. Many political voices for one digital Europe?, in: Politique européenne 2017/2 (Nr. 56), S. 102–123.
Zitiert: *Vlassis* in: Politique européenne 2017/2, 102, S.

Vogel, K.: Die Verfassungsentscheidung des Grundgesetzes für eine internationale Zusammenarbeit, Tübingen 1964.
Zitiert: *Vogel,* Die Verfassungsentscheidung des Grundgesetzes für eine internationale Zusammenarbeit.

von Arnauld, A.: Völkerrecht, 3. Aufl., Heidelberg 2016.
Zitiert: *von Arnauld,* Völkerrecht.

ders.: Freiheit und Regulierung in der Cyberwelt: Transnationaler Schutz der Privatsphäre aus Sicht des Völkerrechts, Heidelberg 2016, S. 27–30.
Zitiert: *von Arnauld,* Freiheit und Regulierung in der Cyberwelt: Transnationaler Schutz der Privatsphäre aus Sicht des Völkerrechts, 27, S.

von Bogdandy, A.: Rechtsfortbildung mit Artikel 5 EG-Vertrag. Zur Zulässigkeit gemeinschaftsrechtlicher Innovationen nach EG-Vertrag und Grundgesetz, in: Randelzhofer u.a. (Hrsg.), Gedächtnisschrift für Eberhard Grabitz, München 1995, S. 17–28.
Zitiert: *von Bogdandy,* Rechtsfortbildung mit Artikel 5 EG-Vertrag.

von Bogdandy, A.; Grabenwarter, C.; Huber, P.M. (Hrsg.): Ius Publicum Europaeum, Band VI: Verfassungsgerichtsbarkeit in Europa: Institutionen, München 2016.
Zitiert: *Verfasser* in: von Bogdandy/Grabenwarter/Huber, Band VI.

von Bogdandy, A.; Bast, J.: Die vertikale Kompetenzordnung der Europäischen Union, in: EuGRZ 2001, S. 441–458.
Auch verfügbar als englischsprachiger Beitrag: The European Union's vertical order of competences: The current law and proposals for its reform, in: 39 CMLRev. (2002), S. S. 227–268.
Zitiert: *von Bogdandy/Bast* in: EuGRZ 2001, 441, S / CMLRev. 2002, 227, S.

dies. (Hrsg.): Europäisches Verfassungsrecht, Berlin 2009.
Zitiert: *Verfasser* in: von Bogdandy/Bast.

von Bogdandy, A.; Schill, S.: Die Achtung der nationalen Identität unter dem reformierten Unionsvertrag Zur unionsrechtlichen Rolle nationalen Verfassungsrechts und zur Überwindung des absoluten Vorrangs, in: ZaöRV 70 (2010), S. 701–734.
Zitiert: *von Bogdandy/Schill* in: ZaöRV 2010, 701, S.

dies.: Overcoming Absolute Primacy: Respect for National identity under the Lisbon Law, in: CMLRev. 48 (2011), S.. 1417–1454.
Zitiert: *von Bogdandy/Schill* in: CMLRev. 2011, 1417, S.

von Danwitz, T.: Wert und Werte des Grundgesetzes, FAZ v. 22.01.2019, https://www.faz.net/aktuell/politik/die-gegenwart/thomas-von-danwitz-wert-und-werte-des-grundgesetzes-15998825.html?printPagedArticle=true#pageIndex_3.
Zitiert: *von Danwitz,* Wert und Werte des Grundgesetzes, FAZ v. 22.01.2019.

ders.: Die Kultur in der Verfassungsordnung der Europäischen Union, in: Neue Juristische Wochenschrift 2005, S. 529–536.
Zitiert: *von Danwitz* in: NJW 2005, 529, S.

ders.: Der Grundsatz der Verhältnismäßigkeit im Gemeinschaftsrecht, in: EWS 2003, S. 393–402.
Zitiert: *von Danwitz* in: EWS 2003, 393, S.

Literaturverzeichnis

Waldheim, S.J.: Dienstleistungsfreiheit und Herkunftslandprinzip: prinzipielle Möglichkeiten und primärrechtliche Grenzen der Liberalisierung eines integrierten europäischen Binnenmarktes für Dienstleistungen, Göttingen 2008.
Zitiert: *Waldheim*, Dienstleistungsfreiheit und Herkunftslandprinzip.

Weinand, J.: Implementing the EU Audiovisual Media Services Directive. Selected issues in the regulation of AVMS by national media authorities of France, Germany and the UK, Baden-Baden 2018.
Zitiert: *Weinand*, Implementing the EU Audiovisual Media Services Directive.

dies.: The revised Audiovisual Media Services Directive 2018 – has the EU learnt the right lessons from the past?, in: UFITA 82(2018)1, S. 260 – 293.
Zitiert: *Weinand*, UFITA 2018, 260, S.

Weinzierl, R.: Europäisierung des deutschen Grundrechtsschutzes? Der personelle Geltungsbereich des Art. 19 Abs. 3 GG und der Deutschengrundrechte im Lichte des europarechtlichen Diskriminierungsverbotes und Effektivitätsgebotes, Regensburg 2006.
Zitiert: *Weinzierl*, Europäisierung des deutschen Grundrechtsschutzes?

Weiß, W.: Das Leitlinien(und)wesen der Kommission verletzt den Vertrag von Lissabon, in: EWS 2010, Heft 7, S. 257–260.
Zitiert: *Weiß* in: EWS 2010, 257, S.

Westphal, D.: Media Pluralism and European Regulation, in: European Business Law Review, Volume 13, Heft 5 (2002), S. 459–487.
Zitiert: *Westphal* in: European Business Law Review, 2002, 459, S.

Winkelmann, I.: Die Bundesregierung als Sachwalter von Länderrechten – zugleich Anmerkung zum EG-Fernsehrichtlinienurteil des Bundesverfassungsgerichts, in: DöV 1996, S. 1–11.
Zitiert: *Winkelmann* in: DöV 1996, 1, S.

Würtenberger, T.: Schranken der Forschungsfreiheit und staatliche Schutzpflichten, 2013, https://www.ethikrat.org/fileadmin/PDF-Dateien/Veranstaltungen/anhoerung-25-04-2013-wuertenberger.pdf.
Zitiert: *Würtenberger*, Schranken der Forschungsfreiheit und staatliche Schutzpflichten.

Yamato, R.; Stephan J.: Eine Politik der Nichteinmischung – Die Folgen des zahnlosen Art. 7 EUV für das Wertefundament der EU am Beispiel Ungarns in: Die öffentliche Verwaltung 2014, S. 58–66.
Zitiert: *Yamato/Stephan* in: DöV 2014, 58, S.

Ziegenhain, H.-J.: Exterritoriale Rechtsanwendung und die Bedeutung des Genuinelink-Erfordernisses, München 1992.
Zitiert: *Ziegenhain*, Exterritoriale Rechtsanwendung und die Bedeutung des Genuine-link-Erfordernisses.

Zuiderveen Borgesius, F. J.; Trilling, D.; Möller, J.; Bodó, B.; de Vreese, C. H.: Should we worry about filter bubbles?, in: Internet Policy Review, Ausgabe 5, Heft 1, 2016, https://doi.org/10.14763/2016.1.401.
Zitiert: *Zuiderveen Borgesius u.a.* in: Internet Policy Review 1/2016.

Zuleeg, M.: Die föderativen Grundsätze der Europäischen Union, in: NJW 2000, S. 2846–2851.
Zitiert: *Zuleeg* in: NJW 2000, 2846, S.

Information on the contributors / Informationen zu den Mitwirkenden

The Institute of European Media Law (EMR) e.V.

The EMR was founded in 1990 as a non-profit association in Saarbrücken and has since made important contributions to the development of media law and media policy as well as related areas of law such as data protection, data security, telecommunications, copyright and competition law at both European and national level. Today, it is one of the renowned research and consulting institutions in Europe in this field, cooperating with numerous national and European institutions, bodies and market participants. It is also a partner institute of the European Audiovisual Observatory of the Council of Europe. The EMR is a service provider and considers itself a neutral platform for information, exchange and advice in the media sector. The focus of the Institute's activities is on the practice-oriented investigation of current issues in European, national and comparative media law. As part of and in order to introduce the results of this activity into professional dialogue, the EMR produces studies independently or at the request of public or private institutions, bodies and market participants, assumes editorial and authoring functions in professional journals, and designs and organizes conferences, workshops and seminars, also online as webinars, on media law.

More detailed information on the EMR and updates on recent developments can be found on our website at www.emr-sb.de.

Information on the contributors / Informationen zu den Mitwirkenden

Das Institut für Europäisches Medienrecht (EMR) e.V.

Das EMR wurde 1990 als gemeinnütziger Verein in Saarbrücken gegründet und hat seither mit wichtigen Beiträgen die Entwicklung von Medienrecht und Medienpolitik sowie angrenzender Rechtsgebiete wie des Datenschutz-, Datensicherheits-, Telekommunikations-, Urheber- und Wettbewerbsrechts europäisch wie national begleitet und mitgestaltet. Es zählt heute zu den renommierten Forschungs- und Beratungseinrichtungen in Europa auf diesem Gebiet, kooperiert mit zahlreichen nationalen und europäischen Institutionen, Einrichtungen und Marktteilnehmern und ist Partnerinstitut der Europäischen Audiovisuellen Informationsstelle des Europarats. Das EMR ist Dienstleister und versteht sich als neutrale Plattform für Information, Austausch und Beratung im Mediensektor. Der Schwerpunkt der Tätigkeit des Instituts konzentriert sich auf die praxisorientierte Untersuchung von aktuellen Fragen des europäischen, nationalen und vergleichenden Medienrechts. Im Rahmen von und zur Einführung der Ergebnisse dieser Tätigkeit in den fachlichen Dialog erstellt das EMR unabhängig oder auf Anfrage von öffentlichen oder privaten Institutionen, Einrichtungen und Marktteilnehmern Studien, nimmt Herausgeber- und Autorenfunktionen in Fachzeitschriften wahr und konzipiert und organisiert medienrechtliche Konferenzen, Workshops und Seminare, auch online als Webinare.

Ausführlichere Informationen zum EMR und Hinweise zu aktuellen Entwicklungen finden sich auf unserer Webseite unter www.emr-sb.de.

Institut für Europäisches Medienrecht (EMR) e.V.
Franz-Mai-Straße 6, 66121 Saarbrücken, Deutschland
Tel.: +49 / (0) 681 906 766 76
Fax.: +49 / (0) 681 968 638 90
E-Mail: emr@emr-sb.de

Information on the contributors / Informationen zu den Mitwirkenden

The German Broadcasting Commission

The German Basic Law provides the federal states ("German Länder") with the competence of regulating the media. In the Broadcasting Commission, the German Länder are in constant exchange on issues of media policy and legislation. The legal framework for the media in Germany is created in so-called "state treaties". The members of the Broadcasting Commission are the 16 Minister-Presidents of the German Länder, coordinated by the permanent chair of Rhineland-Palatinate. Commissioners of the Bundesrat represent the German Länder on EU level. These mandates are exercised by Minister-Presidents or Ministers of the Länder.

Additional information about current activities can be found on the Broadcasting Commission's website at https://www.rlp.de/de/regierung/staatskanzlei/medienpolitik/rundfunkkommission/.

Information on the contributors / Informationen zu den Mitwirkenden

Die Rundfunkkommission

Nach dem Grundgesetz ist die Medienregulierung Aufgabe der Länder. In der Rundfunkkommission stehen die Länder in ständigem Austausch zu Fragen der Medienpolitik und -gesetzgebung. In sogenannten „Staatsverträgen" wird der Rechtsrahmen für die Medien in Deutschland geschaffen. Die Rundfunkkommission setzt sich aus den 16 Ministerpräsidentinnen und Ministerpräsidenten der Länder zusammen und wird von dem ständigen Vorsitzland Rheinland-Pfalz koordiniert. Auf Ebene der Europäischen Union werden die Länder durch sogenannte Bundesratsbeauftragte vertreten. Die Vertretung wird durch einzelne Ministerpräsidentinnen und Ministerpräsidenten oder Ministerinnen und Minister wahrgenommen.
Weiterführende Informationen über gegenwärtige Aktivitäten finden sich auf den Webseiten der Rundfunkkommission unter https://www.rlp.de/de/regierung/staatskanzlei/medienpolitik/rundfunkkommission/.

Information on the contributors / Informationen zu den Mitwirkenden

Mainz Media Institute

The Mainzer Medieninstitut e.V. (Mainz Media Institute, MMI) was founded in 1999 as a non-profit association under private law whose purpose it is to promote science, research and education in the field of media law and media studies. Since its foundation, the MMI has been one of Germany's renowned media science institutions and is jointly supported by the state of Rhineland-Palatinate, the Zweites Deutsches Fernsehen, the Südwestrundfunk, the Medienanstalt Rheinland-Pfalz and the Westdeutscher Rundfunk. It organizes events on topics and issues of current media law and media policy in Mainz and in Brussels and accompanies the changes in the media landscape and media order on a national and European level. As an interdisciplinary forum, the MMI meets digital challenges with expertise in communications science and media law, promotes academic exchange and public discourse, and contributes to the further development of the media order. It prepares legal opinions and takes position on current topics of media law in the broadest sense through publications. In cooperation with the Johannes Gutenberg University in Mainz, the MMI has been organizing the master's degree course in media law since 2002, in which, among other things, the theoretical knowledge for the specialist lawyer in copyright and media law and the specialist lawyer in information technology law can be acquired.

Detailed information about the MMI and current information can be found at www.mainzer-medieninstitut.de.

Information on the contributors / Informationen zu den Mitwirkenden

Das Mainzer Medieninstitut

Das Mainzer Medieninstitut e.V. wurde 1999 als gemeinnütziger privatrechtlicher Verein gegründet, dessen Zweck es ist, die Wissenschaft, Forschung und Bildung auf dem Gebiet des Medienrechts und der Medienwissenschaften zu fördern. Das Mainzer Medieninstitut gehört seit seiner Gründung zu den renommierten medienwissenschaftlichen Einrichtungen Deutschlands und wird gemeinsam getragen vom Land Rheinland-Pfalz, dem Zweiten Deutschen Fernsehen, dem Südwestrundfunk, der Medienanstalt Rheinland-Pfalz und dem Westdeutschen Rundfunk. Das MMI führt Veranstaltungen zu aktuellen medienrechtlichen und medienpolitischen Themen und Fragestellungen in Mainz und in Brüssel durch und begleitet den Wandel der Medienlandschaft und -ordnung auf nationaler und europäischer Ebene. Als interdisziplinäres Forum beggnet es den digitalen Herausforderungen mit kommunikationswissenschaftlicher und medienrechtlicher Expertise, fördert den wissenschaftlichen Austausch sowie den öffentlichen Diskurs und wirkt an der Fortentwicklung der Medienordnung mit. Es erstellt Rechtsgutachten und nimmt durch Publikationen zu aktuellen Themen des Medienrechts im weitesten Sinne Stellung. In Kooperation mit der Johannes Gutenberg-Universität Mainz veranstaltet das Mainzer Medieninstitut seit 2002 den Masterstudiengang Medienrecht, in dem u.a. auch die theoretischen Kenntnisse für den Fachanwalt Urheber- und Medienrecht und den Fachanwalt Informationstechnologierecht erlangt werden können.

Ausführliche Informationen zum Mainzer Medieninstitut und aktuelle Hinweise finden sich unter www.mainzer-medieninstitut.de.

Mainzer Medieninstitut e.V.

Jakob-Welder-Weg 4, 55128 Mainz, Deutschland
Tel.: +49 / (0) 6131 39 37690
Fax.: +49 / (0) 6131 39 37695
E-Mail: info@mainzer-medieninstitut.de

Information on the contributors / Informationen zu den Mitwirkenden

The authors and translation coordination for the English language version

Mark D. Cole is Professor for Media and Telecommunication Law at the University of Luxembourg's Department of Law since March 2007. Since July 2014 he holds an additional position as Director for Academic Affairs at the Institute of European Media Law (EMR). In 2020, he was appointed to the Council auf Europe's Committee of Experts on Media Environment and Reform (MSI-REF) and acts as co-rapporteur for a Draft Recommendation on Principles for Media and Communication Governance. At the University of Luxembourg he is also Faculty Member of the Interdisciplinary Centre for Security, Reliability and Trust (SnT) and directs the Master in Space, Communication and Media Law (LL.M.). He is member of the Advisory Committee of the Luxembourg Independent Media Authority (Autorité luxembourgeoise indépendante de l'audiovisuel, ALIA). He is a regular speaker at international conferences and specializes on European and Comparative Media Law with a focus on the EU AVMSD and DSM regulatory framework, including ICT, data protection and intellectual property law. As co-editor of and contributor to various media law commentaries and a number of international journals he regularly publishes on these topics.

Jörg Ukrow is Assistant Director of the Media Regulatory Authority of Saarland (Landesmedienanstalt Saarland – LMS) and Executive Board Member of the EMR. He studied law, politics and history at the Saarland University from where he holds a law doctorate. He was research assistant from 1989 to 1992 at the Chair in Public Law, Public International Law and European Law and subsequently until 2003 head of the Media Division at the State Chancellery of Saarland. Jörg Ukrow belongs to the juridical Examination Office of the Saarland and was founding member of the editorial board of the Zeitschrift für Europarechtliche Studien (ZEuS). He is author of monographs on judge-made law of the ECJ and on youth protection law, co-author of monographs on digital audio broadcasting, investigative journalism and fake news, author of various articles on constitutional law, public international law and European law as well as co-author of various commentaries on EU law and media law. As Head of Legal of the LMS, Jörg Ukrow is closely involved in the implementation of the AVMSD (Medienstaatsvertrag as well as implementation acts by the competent national regulatory authorities) and coordination with his colleagues in Germany and other EU Member States.

Information on the contributors / Informationen zu den Mitwirkenden

Christina Etteldorf studied law at the University of Saarland with German and International Media and Information Law as her area of choice. Since 2017 she is research associate at the Institute of European Media Law (EMR). In this function she participated in numerous events and publications, including legal studies, country reports as well as the publication series edited by the EMR. Besides that, she is a self-employed consultant in the field of data protection law. Since 2020 she is lecturer at the University of Saarland and teaches in the field of intellectual property and media law. Recently, her research activities mainly focused on audiovisual media, funding of the media in the context of safeguarding media pluralism and data protection policy and law as well as issues of disinformation and the regulation of online platforms.

Sebastian Zeitzmann is a lawyer and research associate at the EMR and writes his doctoral thesis at Saarland University where he used to be a research associate at the European law chair. He also worked as director of studies and academic coordinator at the European Academy of Otzenhausen, as well as a freelance legal translator for the Court of Justice of the European Union. Sebastian Zeitzmann teaches European law, European integration and European politics at the Universities of Saarland and Würzburg and regularly presents and moderates events on the aforementioned topics for other universities, NGOs or think tanks. He is also a member of the editorial board of the Zeitschrift für Europarechtliche Studien (ZEuS).

Information on the contributors / Informationen zu den Mitwirkenden

Die Autoren und Koordination der Übersetzung für die englische Sprachfassung

Mark D. Cole ist seit März 2007 Professor für Medien- und Telekommunikationsrecht an der juristischen Fakultät der Universität Luxemburg. Seit Juli 2014 hat er eine zusätzliche Position als Direktor für akademische Angelegenheiten am Institut für Europäisches Medienrecht (EMR) inne. Im Jahr 2020 wurde er in den Expertenausschuss des Europarats für Medienumfeld und -reform (MSI-REF) berufen und fungiert als Mitberichterstatter für einen Empfehlungsentwurf zu Grundsätzen für die Medien- und Kommunikationssteuerung. An der Universität Luxemburg ist er außerdem Fakultätsmitglied des Interdiziplinären Zentrums für Sicherheit, Verlässlichkeit und Vertrauen (SnT) und leitet den Master in Raumfahrt-, Kommunikations- und Medienrecht (LL.M.). Er ist Mitglied des Beirats der unabhängigen Luxemburger Medienbehörde (Autorité luxembourgeoise indépendante de l'audiovisuel, ALIA). Er ist regelmäßiger Redner auf internationalen Konferenzen und spezialisiert auf europäisches und vergleichendes Medienrecht mit Schwerpunkt auf dem EU-Rechtsrahmen für AVMSD und DSM, einschließlich IKT, Datenschutz und Recht des geistigen Eigentums. Als Mitherausgeber und Mitwirkender verschiedener medienrechtlicher Kommentare und einer Reihe internationaler Fachzeitschriften veröffentlicht er regelmäßig zu diesen Themen.

Jörg Ukrow ist stellvertretender Direktor der Landesmedienanstalt Saarland (LMS) und geschäftsführendes Vorstandsmitglied des EMR. Er studierte Rechtswissenschaften, Politik und Geschichte an der Universität des Saarlandes, wo er zum Dr. jur. promoviert wurde. Von 1989 bis 1992 war er wissenschaftlicher Mitarbeiter am Lehrstuhl für Öffentliches Recht, Völkerrecht und Europarecht und anschließend bis 2003 Leiter des Referats Medien in der Staatskanzlei des Saarlandes. Jörg Ukrow gehört dem juristischen Prüfungsamt des Saarlandes an und war Gründungsmitglied der Redaktion der Zeitschrift für Europarechtliche Studien (ZEuS). Er ist Autor von Monographien zum Richterrecht des EuGH und zum Jugendschutzrecht, Mitautor von Monographien zu digitalem Hörfunk, investigativem Journalismus und Fake News, Autor verschiedener Aufsätze zum Verfassungsrecht, Völkerrecht und Europarecht sowie Mitautor verschiedener Kommentare zum EU-Recht und Medienrecht. Als Head of Legal der LMS ist Jörg Ukrow eng in die Umsetzung der AVMSD (Medienstaatsvertrag sowie Umsetzungsgesetze der zuständigen nationalen Regulierungsbehörden) und die Abstimmung mit seinen Kollegen in Deutschland und anderen EU-Mitgliedstaaten eingebunden.

Information on the contributors / Informationen zu den Mitwirkenden

Christina Etteldorf studierte Rechtswissenschaften an der Universität des Saarlandes mit dem Schwerpunktbereich Deutsches und Internationales Medien- und Informationsrecht. Seit 2017 ist sie wissenschaftliche Mitarbeiterin am Institut für Europäisches Medienrecht (EMR). In dieser Funktion hat sie an zahlreichen Veranstaltungen und Publikationen mitgewirkt, darunter Rechtsstudien, Länderberichte sowie der vom EMR herausgegebenen Schriftenreihe. Daneben ist sie als selbständige Beraterin im Bereich des Datenschutzrechts tätig. Seit 2020 ist sie Lehrbeauftragte an der Universität des Saarlandes und lehrt auf dem Gebiet Geistiges Eigentum und Medienrecht. Ihre Forschungsschwerpunkte lagen zuletzt vor allem im Bereich der audiovisuellen Medien, der Medienförderung im Kontext der Vielfaltssicherung, der Datenschutzpolitik und des Datenschutzrechts sowie Fragen der Desinformation und der Regulierung von Online-Plattformen.

Sebastian Zeitzmann ist Jurist und wissenschaftlicher Mitarbeiter am EMR und promoviert an der Universität des Saarlandes. Er war dort Mitarbeiter am europarechtlichen Lehrstuhl sowie als Studienleiter und wissenschaftlicher Koordinator an der Europäischen Akademie Otzenhausen tätig, zudem als freiberuflicher juristischer Übersetzer für den Gerichtshof der Europäischen Union. Sebastian Zeitzmann hält Lehraufträge für Europarecht, Europäische Integration und Europapolitik an den Universitäten des Saarlandes und Würzburg. Regelmäßig hält er zu diesen Themen zudem Vorträge für u.a. Universitäten, Nichtregierungsorganisationen und Think Tanks und ist zudem als Moderator aktiv. Daneben ist er Mitglied der Redaktion der Zeitschrift für Europarechtliche Studien (ZEuS).